STREI

Lincolnshire

First published in 2003 by

Philip's, a division of
Octopus Publishing Group Ltd
2-4 Heron Quays, London E14 4JP

First edition 2003
Third impression with revisions 2005

ISBN-10 0-540-08341-0 (pocket)
ISBN-13 978-0-540-08341-1 (pocket)

Printed and bound in Spain
by Cayfosa-Quebecor

Contents

III **Key to map symbols**

IV **Key to map pages**

VI **Route planning**

X **Administrative and Postcode boundaries**

1 **Street maps** at 1¼ inches to 1 mile

178 **Street maps** at 2½ inches to 1 mile

234 **Street map of Lincoln city centre** at 5 inches to 1 mile

235 **Index** of towns and villages

238 **Index** of streets, hospitals, industrial estates, railway stations, schools, shopping centres, universities and places of interest

Digital Data

The exceptionally high-quality mapping found in this atlas is available as digital data in TIFF format, which is easily convertible to other bitmapped (raster) image formats.

The index is also available in digital form as a standard database table. It contains all the details found in the printed index together with the National Grid reference for the map square in which each entry is named.

For further information and to discuss your requirements, please contact Philip's on 020 7644 6932 or james.mann@philips-maps.co.uk

Key to map symbols

22a	**Motorway** with junction number
	Primary route – dual/single carriageway
	A road – dual/single carriageway
	B road – dual/single carriageway
	Minor road – dual/single carriageway
	Other minor road – dual/single carriageway
	Road under construction
	Tunnel, covered road
	Rural track, private road or narrow road in urban area
	Gate or obstruction to traffic (restrictions may not apply at all times or to all vehicles)
	Path, bridleway, byway open to all traffic, road used as a public path
	Pedestrianised area
DY7	**Postcode boundaries**
	County and unitary authority boundaries
	Railway, tunnel, railway under construction
	Tramway, tramway under construction
	Miniature railway
Walsall	**Railway station**
	Private railway station
South Shields	**Metro station**
	Tram stop, tram stop under construction
	Bus, coach station

	Ambulance station
	Coastguard station
	Fire station
	Police station
	Accident and Emergency entrance to hospital
H	**Hospital**
	Place of worship
i	**Information Centre** (open all year)
P	**Parking**
P&R	**Park and Ride**
PO	**Post Office**
	Camping site
	Caravan site
	Golf course
	Picnic site
Prim Sch	**Important buildings, schools, colleges, universities and hospitals**
River Ouse	**Tidal water, water name**
	Non-tidal water – lake, river, canal or stream
	Lock, weir, tunnel
	Woods
	Built up area
Church	**Non-Roman antiquity**
ROMAN FORT	**Roman antiquity**
87 / 228	**Adjoining page indicators and overlap bands** The colour of the arrow and the band indicates the scale of the adjoining or overlapping page (see scales below)

Acad	**Academy**	Inst	**Institute**	Recn Gd	**Recreation Ground**
Allot Gdns	**Allotments**	Ct	**Law Court**	Resr	**Reservoir**
Cemy	**Cemetery**	L Ctr	**Leisure Centre**	Ret Pk	**Retail Park**
C Ctr	**Civic Centre**	LC	**Level Crossing**	Sch	**School**
CH	**Club House**	Liby	**Library**	Sh Ctr	**Shopping Centre**
Coll	**College**	Mkt	**Market**	TH	**Town Hall/House**
Crem	**Crematorium**	Meml	**Memorial**	Trad Est	**Trading Estate**
Ent	**Enterprise**	Mon	**Monument**	Univ	**University**
Ex H	**Exhibition Hall**	Mus	**Museum**	Wks	**Works**
Ind Est	**Industrial Estate**	Obsy	**Observatory**	YH	**Youth Hostel**
IRB Sta	**Inshore Rescue Boat Station**	Pal	**Royal Palace**		
		PH	**Public House**		

■ The small numbers around the edges of the maps identify the 1 kilometre National Grid lines

■ The dark grey border on the inside edge of some pages indicates that the mapping does not continue onto the adjacent page

Scale	Scale bar
The scale of the maps on the pages numbered in blue is 3.92 cm to 1 km • 2½ inches to 1 mile • 1: 25344	0 ¼ ½ ¾ 1 mile / 0 250 m 500 m 750 m 1 kilometre
The scale of the maps on pages numbered in green is 1.96 cm to 1 km • 1¼ inches to 1 mile • 1: 50688	0 ¼ ½ ¾ 1 mile / 0 250m 500m 750 m 1kilometre
The scale of the maps on pages numbered in red is 7.84 cm to 1 km • 5 inches to 1 mile • 1: 12672	0 220 yards 440 yards 660 yards ½ mile / 0 125 m 250 m 375 m ½ kilometre

Key to map pages

234	Map pages at 5 inches to 1 mile
180	Map pages at 2½ inches to 1 mile
138	Map pages at 1¼ inches to 1 mile

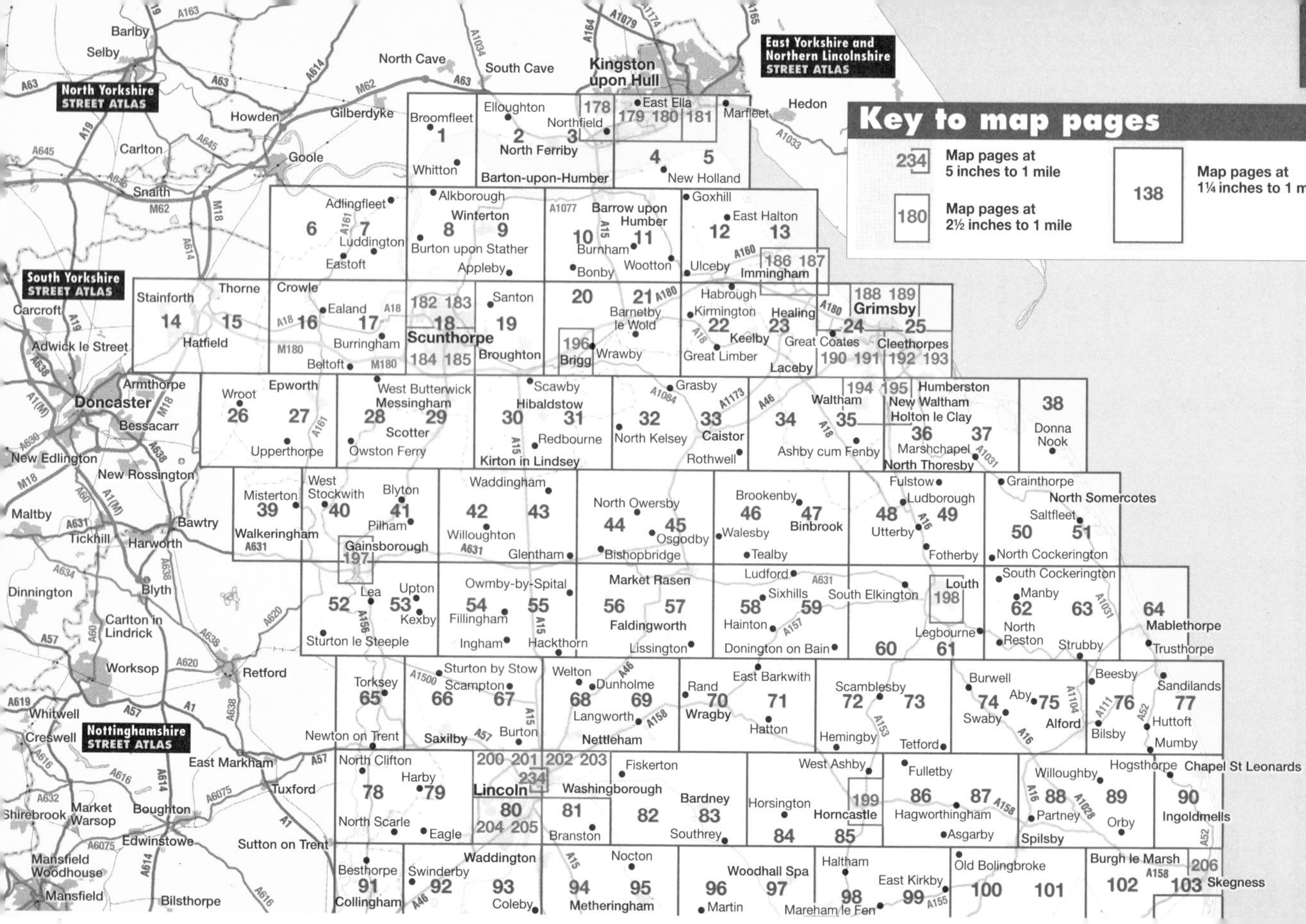

North Yorkshire STREET ATLAS

East Yorkshire and Northern Lincolnshire STREET ATLAS

South Yorkshire STREET ATLAS

Nottinghamshire STREET ATLAS

Bassingham
Boothby Graffoe
Timberland
207
Stickford
Wainfleet All Saints
116

Stapleford
104 105
Newark-on-Trent
Beckingham
Balderton
Fenton
Navenby
Wellingore
106 107
Leadenham
Fulbeck
Cranwell
Digby
108
Ruskington
Billinghay
109
Anwick
Coningsby
Tattershall Bridge
Chapel Hill
110 111
Gipsey Bridge
Stickney
112
Frithville
Midville
113
Sibsey
New Leake
114
Wainfleet St Mary
115
Wrangle

Claypole
117
Long Bennington
Stubton
Caythorpe
Hough-on-the-Hill
118 119
Marston
Honington
Leasingham
120
212
Sleaford
Ancaster
121
South Kyme
122 123
Heckington
Swineshead Bridge
Langrick
124 125
Cowbridge
Hubbert's Bridge
208 209
Boston
Hurn's End
Leverton
126 127
Butterwick
Fishtoft
Scrane End

128 129
Bottesford
Great Gonerby
Muston
Grantham
210 211
Barkston
Culverthorpe
130 131
Londonthorpe
Ropsley
Osbournby
132
Billingborough
Helpringham
133
Horbling
Swineshead
134 135
Bicker
Donington
Wyberton
Kirton
136 137
Sutterton

Denton
Harlaxton
Knipton
138 139
Croxton Kerrial
Saltby
140 141
Great Ponton
Ingoldsby
Irnham
Easton
Folkingham
Pointon
142 143
Dowsby
Rippingale
Gosberton
144 145
Gosberton Clough
Surfleet
Fosdyke
Holbeach St. Marks
146 147
Moulton Seas End
215
Holbeach St. Matthew
148 149
Gedney Drove End
Gedney Dyke

Sproxton
Colsterworth
150 151
South Witham
Wymondham
Corby Glen
Swinstead
Edenham
152 153
Castle Bytham
Morton
154 155
Bourne
213
Twenty
Pinchbeck
214
Moulton
Spalding
156 157
Moulton Chapel
Holbeach
Whaplode
Long Sutton
158 159
Whaplode St Catherine
216
160 161
Sutton Bridge
Terrington St Clement

Clipsham
162 163
Essendine
Ryhall
Thurlby
Baston
164 165
Market Deeping
217
Deeping St Nicholas
166 167
Shepeau Stow
Crowland
Tydd St Giles
168 169
Whaplode Drove
Gorefield
Foul Anchor
170
West Walton
Leverington

Stamford
218 219
Easton on the Hill
171
Maxey
Uffington
172 173
Barnack
Glinton
220 221
174 175
Newborough
Eye
Parson Drove
176 177
Thorney
Guyhirn
Wisbech

222 223
Castor
224 225
226 227
Newark
Peterborough
Water Newton
228 229
230 231
Farcet
Whittlesey
Haddon
Yaxley
232 233
Morborne

Rainworth
Blidworth
Southwell
Ravenshead
Hucknall
Calverton
Lowdham
Nottingham
Bingham
West Bridgford
Cotgrave
Keyworth
East Leake
Loughborough
Melton Mowbray
Sileby
Mountsorrel
Syston
Leicester
Oakham
Empingham
Market Harborough
Lutterworth
Desborough
Corby
Oundle
Sawtry
Ramsey
March
Littleport
Downham Market
King's Lynn
Hunstanton
Heacham
Snettisham
Dersingham

Leicestershire and Rutland STREET ATLAS
Northamptonshire STREET ATLAS
Cambridgeshire STREET ATLAS
Norfolk STREET ATLAS

Scale
0 5 10 15 20 km
0 5 10 15 miles

Route planning
Scale
0 5 10 km
0 1 2 3 4 5 6 miles
North Lincolnshire
HUMBER
Humber Bridge
Holme-on-Spalding-Moor
North Cave
South Cave
Cottingham
Kirk Ella
Anlaby
Hessle
North Ferriby
Barton-upon-Humber
Gilberdyke
Goole
Snaith
Carlton
Thorne
Stainforth
Hatfield
Crowle
Winterton
Scunthorpe
Broughton
Brigg
Messingham
Epworth
Hibaldstow
Kirton in Lindsey
Doncaster
Bessacarr
Armthorpe
Bentley
New Rossington
Bawtry
Tickhill
Harworth
Langold
Blyth
Carlton in Lindrick
Worksop
Retford
Gainsborough
Beckingham
Walkeringham
Laughton Forest
Saxilby
Lincoln
Nettleham
Washingborough
Boultham
North Hykeham
Waddington
Tuxford
East Markham
Ollerton
Boughton
Market Warsop
Edwinstowe
Clipstone
Bilsthorpe
Sutton on Trent
Collingham
Bassingham
Faldingworth
Metheringham
Read's Island
Redcliff Channel

Marton
West Newton
East Newton
Old Ellerby
Flinton
Swine
Coniston
Garton
Grimston
Bransholme
Sutton on Hull
Thirtleby
Sproatley
Humbleton
Fitling
Hilston
Ganstead
Lelley
Owstwick
Tunstall
Bilton
Elstronwick
Sutton Ings
Summergangs
Preston
Burton Pidsea
Roos
North End
Marfleet
West End
Waxholme
Salt End
Hedon
Owthorne
Withernsea
Haven Side
Burstwick
Rimswell
KINGSTON UPON HULL
Halsham
East End
Paull
Camerton
Thorngumbald
Keyingham
Ryehill
Hollym
Ottringham
Goxhill Haven
Winestead
Little Humber
Holmpton
Patrington
Thorney Crofts
Out Newton
Welwick
Weeton
Goxhill
South End
East Halton
Sunk Island
Skeffling
Easington
North Killingholme
Kilnsea
ROTTERDAM 12:30
ZEEBRUGGE 12:45
Ulceby Skitter
South Killingholme
Immingham
Habrough
Kirmington
Stallingborough
Brocklesby
Pyewipe
Grimsby
Healing
West Marsh
Keelby
Great Coates
CLEETHORPES
MOUTH OF THE HUMBER
Great Limber
Riby Cross Roads
Old Clee
Aylesby
Riby
Laceby
Nunsthorpe
Bradley
Scartho
North East Lincolnshire
Humberston
Irby upon Humber
Waltham
New Waltham
Barnoldby le Beck
Holton le Clay
Swallow
Tetney Lock
Caistor
Cabourne
Brigsley
Beelsby
Ashby cum Fenby
North Coates
Cuxwold
Hatcliffe
Waithe
Tetney
East Ravendale
Rothwell
Grainsby
Marshchapel
Eskham
Groxby
North Thoresby
Wragholme
Grainthorpe
Thorganby
Thoresway
Swinhope
Wold Newton
Fulstow
North Somercotes
Brookenby
Ludborough
Covenham St Bartholomew
Skidbrooke North End
Normanby le Wold
Conisholme
Covenham St Mary
Saltfleet
Stainton le Vale
Binbrook
South Somercotes
Utterby
Walesby
Kirmond le Mire
North Ormsby
Yarburgh
Skidbrooke
Fotherby
Saltfleetby St Clements
Little Grimsby
Alvingham
Tealby
Great Tows
North Elkington
North Cockerington
Market Rasen
North Willingham
Kelstern
Saltfleetby All Saints
Theddlethorpe St Helen
Ludford
South Elkington
South Cockerington
Keddington
Saltfleetby St Peter
Welton le Wold
Louth
Grimoldby
Theddlethorpe All Saints
Burgh on Bain
Stewton
Manby
Sixhills
Linwood
Legsby
Grimblethorpe
Gayton le Wold
Little Carlton
Meers Bridge
Mablethorpe
Great Carlton
Hallington
Legbourne
Bleasby
Hainton
Biscathorpe
Raithby
Trusthorpe
South Willingham
Donington on Bain
South Reston
East Torrington
Withcall
Little Cawthorpe
Gayton le Marsh
Lissington
West Torrington
Tathwell
North Reston
Strubby
Sutton on Sea
Benniworth
Thorpe
Haugham
Muckton
Tothill
Withern
Maltby le Marsh
Sandilands
Stenigot
East Barkwith
Authorpe
Beesby
West Barkwith
Cawkwell
Market Stainton
Maidenwell
Burwell
Woodthorpe
Hannah
Sotby
Saleby
Wragby
Panton
Goulceby
Ranby
Scamblesby
Farforth
Ruckland
Belleau
Markby
Aby
White Pit
Swaby
Oxcombe
Asserby
Hatton
Ketsby
Bilsby
Huttoft
South Thoresby
Langton by Wragby
Great Sturton
Rigsby
Alford
Belchford
South Ormsby
Calceby
Haugh
Anderby
Kingthorpe
Farlesthorpe
Hemingby
Tetford
Driby
Mumby
Authorpe Row
Baumber
Brinkhill
Well
Fulletby
Minting
Salmonby
Somersby
Cumberworth
Ulceby
Helsey
Chapel St Leonards
Gautby
Sutterby
Bonthorpe
Hogsthorpe
Wispington
West Ashby
Claxby
Bag Enderby
Harrington
Willoughby
Young Wood
Edlington
Ashby Puerorum
Langton
High Toynton
Sloothby
Greetham
Aswardby
Skendleby
Thimbleby
Bardney
Bucknall
Langton
Horncastle
Hagworthingham
Sausthorpe
Ingoldmells
Scrafield
Partney
Horsington
Thornton
Addlethorpe
Lusby
Scremby
Mareham on the Hill
Welton le Marsh
Raithby
Old Woodhall
Hameringham
Mavis Enderby
Candlesby
Orby
Southrey
Martin
Scrivelsby
Asgarby
Spilsby
Ashby by Partney
Burgh le Marsh
Winthorpe
Stixwould
Old Bolingbroke
Hundleby
Seathorne
Dalderby
Hareby
Bratoft
Reeds Beck
Great Steeping
Wood Enderby
Moorby
Toynton All Saints
Halton Holegate
Sots Hole
Roughton
Miningsby
West Keal
East Keal
Irby in the Marsh
Skegness
Roughton Moor
Haltham
Toynton St Peter
Woodhall Spa
Kirkstead
East Kirkby
Firsby
Toft Hill
Toynton Fen Side
Little Steeping
Kirkby on Bain
Mareham le Fen
Thorpe Culvert
Thorpe St Peter
Croft
Martin Dales
Revesby
Keal Cotes
Seacroft
Martin
Revesby Bridge
Thorpe Fendykes
Wainfleet All Saints
Tattershall Thorpe
Stickford
New Bolingbroke
Fen Side
Wainfleet Bank
L
I
N
C
O

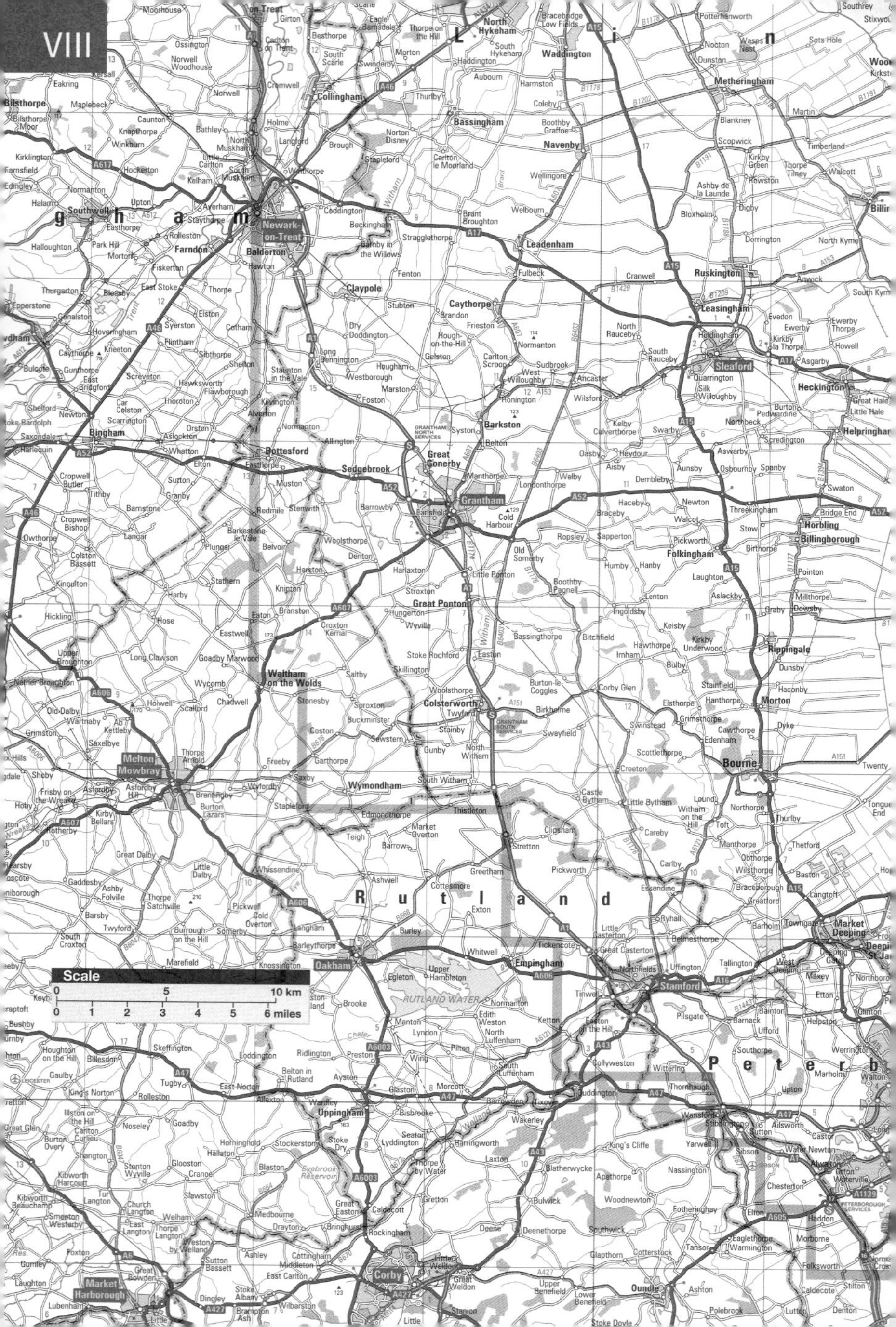

VIII
L i n
g h a m
Rutland
Peterb
Scale
0 5 10 km
0 1 2 3 4 5 6 miles
Newark-on-Trent
Grantham
Sleaford
Melton Mowbray
Oakham
Stamford
Corby
Market Harborough
North Hykeham
Waddington
Metheringham
Collingham
Bassingham
Navenby
Leadenham
Ruskington
Leasingham
Heckington
Helpringham
Southwell
Farndon
Balderton
Bingham
Bottesford
Sedgebrook
Great Gonerby
Claypole
Caythorpe
Barkston
Folkingham
Horbling
Billingborough
Rippingale
Morton
Bourne
Great Ponton
Colsterworth
Waltham on the Wolds
Wymondham
Empingham
Uppingham
Market Deeping
Oundle
Bilsthorpe
Moorhouse
Ossington
Norwell
Cromwell
Holme
North Muskham
South Muskham
Kelham
Averham
Staythorpe
Rolleston
Fiskerton
East Stoke
Thurgarton
Bleasby
Syerston
Flintham
Elston
Thorpe
Cotham
Kneeton
Car Colston
Scarrington
Aslockton
Whatton
Orston
Elton
Granby
Sutton
Barnstone
Langar
Plungar
Redmile
Barkestone-le-Vale
Belvoir
Harby
Stathern
Hose
Eastwell
Eaton
Branston
Knipton
Harston
Denton
Harlaxton
Stroxton
Little Ponton
Old Somerby
Ropsley
Boothby Pagnell
Lenton
Ingoldsby
Bitchfield
Irnham
Corby Glen
Swinstead
Swayfield
Burton-le-Coggles
Bassingthorpe
Skillington
Stoke Rochford
Easton
Woolsthorpe
Twyford
Stainby
Gunby
North Witham
South Witham
Buckminster
Sproxton
Sewstern
Coston
Saltby
Croxton Kerrial
Stonesby
Garthorpe
Saxby
Freeby
Thorpe Arnold
Brentingby
Burton Lazars
Stapleford
Edmondthorpe
Teigh
Market Overton
Thistleton
Barrow
Whissendine
Ashwell
Cottesmore
Greetham
Stretton
Clipsham
Pickworth
Castle Bytham
Little Bytham
Careby
Carlby
Witham on the Hill
Essendine
Ryhall
Exton
Burley
Whitwell
Tickencote
Great Casterton
Little Casterton
Belmesthorpe
Uffington
Tallington
Barholm
Greatford
Towngate
West Deeping
Deeping Gate
Maxey
Etton
Northborough
Helpston
Bainton
Barnack
Ufford
Southorpe
Pilsgate
Wittering
Thornhaugh
Wansford
Sibson
Stibbington
Sutton
Ailsworth
Castor
Water Newton
Alwalton
Orton Waterville
Chesterton
Haddon
Morborne
Elton
Yarwell
Nassington
Fotheringhay
Apethorpe
Woodnewton
King's Cliffe
Blatherwycke
Bulwick
Deenethorpe
Deene
Southwick
Glapthorn
Cotterstock
Tansor
Warmington
Eaglethorpe
Ashton
Polebrook
Lutton
Stoke Doyle
Upper Benefield
Lower Benefield
Great Weldon
Little Weldon
Stanion
Cottingham
Middleton
East Carlton
Rockingham
Gretton
Caldecott
Great Easton
Bringhurst
Drayton
Medbourne
Ashley
Sutton Bassett
Weston by Welland
Welham
Thorpe Langton
East Langton
Church Langton
Kibworth Harcourt
Kibworth Beauchamp
Smeeton Westerby
Foxton
Gumley
Laughton
Lubenham
Great Bowden
Dingley
Stoke Albany
Wilbarston
Brampton Ash
Rutland Water
Egleton
Upper Hambleton
Normanton
Edith Weston
North Luffenham
South Luffenham
Ketton
Tinwell
Easton on the Hill
Collyweston
Duddington
Tixover
Barrowden
Morcott
Glaston
Wing
Pilton
Lyndon
Manton
Preston
Ridlington
Ayston
Wardley
Belton in Rutland
Bisbrooke
Seaton
Harringworth
Wakerley
Laxton
Lyddington
Stoke Dry
Thorpe by Water
Eyebrook Reservoir
Stockerston
Blaston
Hallaton
Horninghold
Glooston
Cranoe
Slawston
Stonton Wyville
Noseley
Goadby
Rolleston
East Norton
Allexton
Tugby
Skeffington
Billesdon
Houghton on the Hill
Gaulby
King's Norton
Illston on the Hill
Carlton Curlieu
Burton Overy
Shangton
Great Glen
Loddington
Launde
Knossington
Marefield
Somerby
Burrough on the Hill
Pickwell
Cold Overton
Langham
Barleythorpe
Brooke
Little Dalby
Great Dalby
Thorpe Satchville
Twyford
Ashby Folville
Gaddesby
Barsby
South Croxton
Kirby Bellars
Asfordby
Asfordby Hill
Frisby on the Wreake
Hoby
Rotherby
Shoby
Grimston
Saxelbye
Ab Kettleby
Wartnaby
Old Dalby
Holwell
Scalford
Chadwell
Wycomb
Goadby Marwood
Long Clawson
Hickling
Upper Broughton
Nether Broughton
Kinoulton
Colston Bassett
Owthorpe
Cropwell Bishop
Cropwell Butler
Tithby
Harlequin
Saxondale
Newton
Shelford
East Bridgford
Gunthorpe
Caythorpe
Hoveringham
Gonalston
Epperstone
Halloughton
Park Hill
Morton
Easthorpe
Upton
Halam
Normanton
Edingley
Farnsfield
Kirklington
Hockerton
Winkburn
Knapthorpe
Caunton
Maplebeck
Bathley
Little Carlton
Eakring
Norwell Woodhouse
Carlton on Trent
Girton
Besthorpe
South Scarle
Eagle
Swinderby
Morton
Thorpe on the Hill
Thurlby
South Hykeham
Haddington
Aubourn
Harmston
Coleby
Boothby Graffoe
Wellingore
Welbourn
Brant Broughton
Carlton le Moorland
Stapleford
Norton Disney
Brough
Langford
Winthorpe
Coddington
Beckingham
Stragglethorpe
Barnby in the Willows
Fenton
Stubton
Dry Doddington
Long Bennington
Westborough
Hougham
Marston
Foston
Allington
Staunton in the Vale
Kilvington
Alverton
Normanton
Shelton
Sibthorpe
Hawksworth
Flawborough
Screveton
Thoroton
Muston
Easthorpe
Stenwith
Barrowby
Woolsthorpe
Earlsfield
Cold Harbour
Manthorpe
Londonthorpe
Belton
Syston
Honington
Carlton Scroop
Normanton
Gelston
Hough-on-the-Hill
Brandon
Frieston
Fulbeck
Sudbrook
West Willoughby
Ancaster
Wilsford
Kelby
Culverthorpe
Oasby
Heydour
Aisby
Welby
Dembleby
Haceby
Braceby
Sapperton
Newton
Walcot
Pickworth
Humby
Hanby
Laughton
Aslackby
Kirkby Underwood
Hawthorpe
Bulby
Keisby
Stainfield
Hanthorpe
Elsthorpe
Grimsthorpe
Edenham
Cawthorpe
Dyke
Scottlethorpe
Creeton
Lound
Toft
Manthorpe
Obthorpe
Wilsthorpe
Braceborough
Baston
Langtoft
Thetford
Thurlby
Northorpe
Tongue End
Twenty
Haconby
Dunsby
Millthorpe
Dowsby
Graby
Pointon
Birthorpe
Stow
Bridge End
Threekingham
Spanby
Swaton
Osbournby
Aunsby
Aswarby
Scredington
Swarby
Northbeck
Burton Pedwardine
Great Hale
Little Hale
Silk Willoughby
Quarrington
Holdingham
South Rauceby
North Rauceby
Cranwell
Evedon
Ewerby
Ewerby Thorpe
Kirkby la Thorpe
Asgarby
Howell
Anwick
South Kyme
North Kyme
Dorrington
Digby
Bloxholm
Ashby de la Launde
Rowston
Kirkby Green
Scopwick
Blankney
Thorpe Tilney
Walcott
Timberland
Martin
Dunston
Nocton
Wasps Nest
Potterhanworth
Sots Hole
Southrey
Bracebridge Low Fields

Martin
Scrivelsby
Asgarby
Spilsby
Ashby by Partney
Burgh le Marsh
Winthorpe
Seathorne
Reeds Beck
Dalderby
Hareby
Old Bolingbroke
Hundleby
Great Steeping
Bratoft
Skegness
Roughton
Wood Enderby
Moorby
Miningsby
West Keal
East Keal
Toynton All Saints
Halton Holegate
Irby in the Marsh
Boughton Moor
Haltham
Toynton St Peter
Firsby
Kirkby on Bain
Toft Hill
East Kirkby
Toynton Fen Side
Little Steeping
Mareham le Fen
Revesby
Keal Cotes
Thorpe Culvert
Thorpe St Peter
Croft
Seacroft
Tattershall Thorpe
Revesby Bridge
Stickford
Thorpe Fendykes
Wainfleet All Saints
Tattershall
Coningsby
New Bolingbroke
Fen Side
Wainfleet Bank
Tumby Woodside
Midville
New Leake
Wainfleet Tofts
Wainfleet St Mary
Medlam
Stickney
Eastville
Friskney Eaudike
Dogdyke
Hawthorn Hill
New York
Sandy Bank
Carrington
Friskney
Scrub Hill
Hundle Houses
Bunker's Hill
Lade Bank
Wrangle Bank
Friskney Tofts
Chapel Hill
Haven Bank
Northlands
Leake Commonside
Wrangle Lowgate
Frithville
Sibsey
Old Leake
Wrangle
Gipsey Bridge
Fishtoft Drove
Hurn's End
Holland Fen
Langrick
Anton's Gowt
Hilldyke
Boston Long Hedges
Leverton Outgate
Frith Bank
Leverton
Leverton Highgate
Amber Hill
Cowbridge
Benington
Leverton Lucasgate
Borthertoft
Boston West
Boston
Haltoft End
Butterwick
BOSTON DEEPS
LYNN DEEPS
East Heckington
Swineshead Bridge
Hubbert's Bridge
Chain Bridge
Skirbeck
Skirbeck Quarter
Freiston
Fishtoft
Scrane End
THE WASH
Old Hunstanton
Hunstanton
Ringstead
North End
Kirton Holme
Wyberton
Frampton West End
Fenhouses
Swineshead
Kirton End
Frampton
Drayton
Kirton
Bicker
Asperton
Sandholme
Skeldyke
Heacham
Seadyke
Donington
Wigtoft
Sutterton
Bucklegate
Algarkirk
Church End
Snettisham
Fosdyke
Quadring
Holbeach St Matthew
Shepherd's Port
Ingoldisthorpe
Gosberton
Westhorpe
Holbeach St Marks
Lynn Channel
Dersingham
Dawsmere
Risegate
Surfleet Seas End
Surfleet
Gedney Drove End
Moulton Seas End
Saracen's Head
Holbeach Hurn
Wolferton
Crossgate
Holbeach Bank
Pinchbeck
Halesgate
Holbeach Clough
Gedney Dyke
Lutton
Guy's Head
Castle Rising
Weston
Fleet Hargate
Chapelgate
Pinchbeck West
Moulton
Whaplode
Holbeach
Gedney
Little London
Ongar Hill
North Wootton
Spalding
Low Fulney
Fleet
Long Sutton
South Wootton
Roydon
Austendike
Gedney Broadgate
King's Lynn
Pode Hole
Little London
Clay Lake
Weston Hills
Sutton Bridge
Orange Row
Clenchwarton
Gaywood
Sutton Crosses
Whaplode St Catherine
Walpole Cross Keys
Terrington St Clement
West Lynn
Fairstead
Cowbit
Moulton Chapel
Tydd St Mary
Holbeach St Johns
Tydd Gote
Walpole St Andrew
Hay Green
Tilney High End
Tilney All Saints
Leziate
Sutton St James
Four Gotes
Walpole Marsh
Fair Green
Tower End
Deeping St Nicholas
Moulton Eaugate
Tydd St Giles
Walpole St Peter
Middleton
East Winch
West Winch
Brotherhouse Bar
Newton
Ingleborough
St John's Highway
Terrington St John
Saddle Bow
North Runcton
Tilney St Lawrence
Wiggenhall St Germans
Setchey
Blackborough End
Whaplode Drove
West Walton
Walpole Highway
Wiggenhall St Mary the Virgin
Tottenhill Row
Shepeau Stow
Holbeach Drove
Sutton St Edmund
Fitton End
West Walton Highway
Gedney Hill
Gorefield
Leverington
St John's Fen End
Wiggenhall St Mary Magdalen
Watlington
Tottenhill
Wormegay
Dowsdale
Walsoken
Norfolk
Crowland
Throckenholt
Church End
Marshland St James
Runcton Holme
Shouldham
Wisbech
New Walsoken
South Runcton
Shouldham Thorpe
Nene Terrace
Parson Drove
Wisbech St Mary
Emneth
Stowbridge
Newborough
Murrow
Tholomas Drove
Emneth Hungate
Stow Bardolph
Fincham
Rogue's Alley
Elm
Holly End
West Head
Wimbotsham
Thorney Toll
Friday Bridge
Outwell
Downham Market
Broomhill
Stradsett
Crimplesham
Eye Green
Thorney
Guyhirn Gull
Waldersey
Bexwell
Eye
Guyhirn
Ring's End
Coldham
Barroway Drove
Denver
Wereham
Dogsthorpe
Newark
Upwell
Nordelph
Stone Bridge Corner
Chainbridge
Three Holes
West Dereham
Fordham
Wretton
Peterborough
Eldernell
Westry
Norwoodside
Euximoor Drove
Nene (Old Course)
Hilgay
Wissey
Fengate
North Side
Coates
Ten Mile Bank
Old Fletton
March
Christchurch
Stanground
Eastrea
Whittlesey
Inham's End
Turves
Lakesend
Old Bedford River
Town End
Tipsend
Southery
Methwold Hythe
Farcet
Twenty Foot River
Welney
Flood's Ferry
Wimblington
Gold Hill
Brandon Creek
Pondersbridge
Doddington
Apes Hall
Yaxley
Nene
Benwick
Manea
Brandon Bank
Ramsey Mereside
Sixteen Foot Drain
Ramsey St Mary's
Forty Foot Drain
Vermuden's Drain
Purls Bridge
Ramsey Forty Foot
Horseway
Welches
Littleport
Little Ouse
A158
A52
A16
A155
A153
A1121
A17
A151
A1101
A47
A10
A149
A148
A134
A1122
A141
A605
A1139
A1078
A1101
B1192
B1183
B1184
B1195
B1391
B1181
B1397
B1357
B1356
B1180
B1165
B1168
B1359
B1166
B1167
B1169
B1187
B1040
B1443
B1093
B1096
B1098
B1099
B1101
B1160
B1094
B1411
B1440
B1439
B660

Administrative and Postcode boundaries

- County and unitary authority boundaries
- District boundaries
- Postcode boundaries
- Area covered by this atlas

Scale

0 10 20 30 km

0 5 10 15 20 miles

East Riding of Yorkshire

North Lincolnshire

NE Lincs

West Lindsey

East Lindsey

Lincolnshire

Lincoln

North Kesteven

Boston

South Holland

South Kesteven

Nottinghamshire

Leicestershire

Norfolk

Cambridgeshire

SE TA SK TF SP TL

HU1 HU2 HU3 HU4 HU9 HU10 HU13 HU14 HU15

DN3 DN7 DN8 DN9 DN10 DN14 DN15 DN16 DN17 DN18 DN19 DN20 DN21 DN22 DN31 DN32 DN33 DN34 DN35 DN36 DN37 DN38 DN39 DN40 DN41

LN1 LN2 LN3 LN4 LN5 LN6 LN7 LN8 LN9 LN10 LN11 LN12 LN13

NG23 NG24 NG31 NG32 NG33 NG34

LE14 LE15

PE1 PE2 PE3 PE4 PE5 PE6 PE7 PE8 PE9 PE10 PE11 PE12 PE13 PE14 PE20 PE21 PE22 PE23 PE24 PE25 PE34

Broomfleet, Brough, Anlaby, Kingston upon Hull, North Ferriby, Barrow-upon-Humber, Alkborough, Barton-upon-Humber, Winterton, Garthorpe, Appleby, Immingham, Ulceby, Stainforth, Thorne, Crowle, Healing, Grimsby, Hatfield, Edenthorpe, Scunthorpe, Broughton, Keelby, Cleethorpes, Barnetby le Wold, Laceby, Belton, Brigg, Grasby, Humberston, Wroot, Epworth, Messingham, Hibaldstow, Waltham, Holton le Clay, Caistor, Scotter, North Kelsey, Haxey, South Kelsey, Kirton in Lindsey, North Thoresby, Binbrook, North Somercotes, Walkeringham, Utterby, Hemswell, Osgodby, Tealby, Beckingham, Gainsborough, Market Rasen, Ludford, Louth, Manby, Mablethorpe, Faldingworth, Legbourne, Marton, Ingham, Lissington, Hainton, Welton, Burwell, Sutton on Sea, Wragby, Goulceby, Rampton, Saxilby, Nettleham, Alford, Belchford, Tetford, Chapel St Leonards, Cherry Willingham, Hogsthorpe, Harby, Lincoln, Washingborough, Bardney, Horncastle, Hagworthingham, Ingoldmells, North Scarle, Branston, Spilsby, Besthorpe, Waddington, Skegness, Swinderby, Woodhall Spa, Burgh le Marsh, Collingham, Ravesby, Bassingham, Metheringham, Navenby, Timberland, Coningsby, Wainfleet All Saints, Stickney, Newark-on-Trent, Billinghay, Leadenham, Ruskington, Sibsey, Wrangle, Balderton, South Kyme, Claypole, Caythorpe, Long Bennington, Sleaford, Heckington, Boston, Butterwick, Marston, Swineshead, Barkston, Helpringham, Kirton, Bottesford, Great Gonerby, Grantham, Sedgebrook, Horbling, Donington, Harlaxton, Ropsley, Folkingham, Billingborough, Fosdyke, Holbeach St Matthew, Knipton, Gosberton, Great Ponton, Rippingale, Pinchbeck, Whaplode, Holbeach, Corby Glen, Sutton Bridge, Sproxton, Colsterworth, Spalding, Moulton, Long Sutton, Bourne, Terrington St Clement, Wymondham, Thurlby, Tydd St Giles, Cowbit, Clipsham, Hop Pole, West Walton, Market Deeping, Gorefield, Ryhall, Gedney Hill, Crowland, Wisbech, Deeping St James, Church End, Stamford, Thorney, Helpston, Guyhirn, Eye, Wittering, Castor, Peterborough, Yaxley

Grid: 60 70 80 90 00 10 20 30 40 50 60

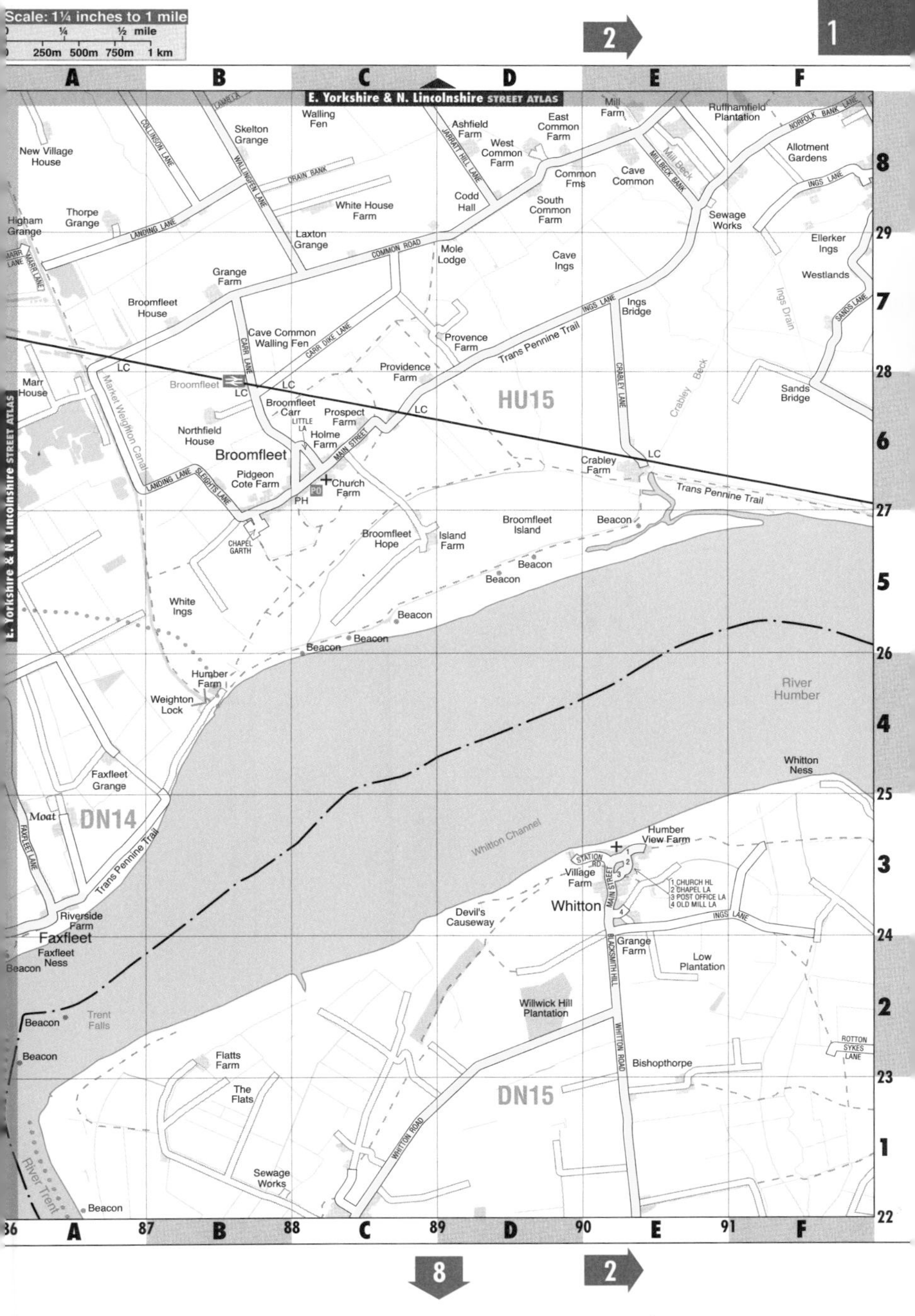

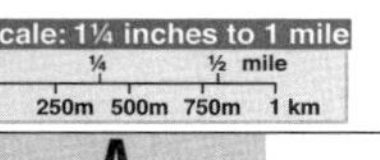

2

E. Yorkshire & N. Lincolnshire STREET ATLAS

Mill Farm
Ruffhamfield Plantation
Walling Fen
Skelton Grange
Ashfield Farm
East Common Farm
West Common Farm
NORFOLK BANK LANE
Allotment Gardens
New Village House
COLLINSON LANE
WALLINGFEN LANE
JARRATT HILL LANE
MILLBECK BANK
Mill Beck
DRAIN BANK
Common Fms
Cave Common
INGS LANE
Codd Hall
South Common Farm
Sewage Works
Higham Grange
Thorpe Grange
White House Farm
LANDING LANE
Laxton Grange
Ellerker Ings
MARR LANE
COMMON ROAD
Mole Lodge
Cave Ings
Grange Farm
Westlands
Broomfleet House
Ings Bridge
INGS LANE
Ings Drain
SANDS LANE
Cave Common Walling Fen
CARR DIKE LANE
Provence Farm
Trans Pennine Trail
CARR LANE
LC
Providence Farm
Marr House
Broomfleet
LC
LC
Market Weighton Canal
Broomfleet Carr
Prospect Farm
LC
HU15
CRABLEY LANE
Crabley Beck
Sands Bridge
LITTLE LA
Northfield House
Holme Farm
MAIN STREET
Broomfleet
LC
Crabley Farm
LANDING LANE
SLEIGHTS LANE
Pidgeon Cote Farm
Church Farm
PO
PH
Trans Pennine Trail
CHAPEL GARTH
Broomfleet Island
Beacon
Broomfleet Hope
Island Farm
Beacon
Beacon
White Ings
Beacon
Beacon
Beacon
Humber Farm
Weighton Lock
River Humber
Whitton Ness
Faxfleet Grange
Moat
DN14
Whitton Channel
Humber View Farm
FAXFLEET LANE
Trans Pennine Trail
STATION RD
MAIN STREET
Village Farm
1 CHURCH HL
2 CHAPEL LA
3 POST OFFICE LA
4 OLD MILL LA
Whitton
Devil's Causeway
INGS LANE
Riverside Farm
Faxfleet
Faxfleet Ness
Beacon
Grange Farm
BLACKSMITH HILL
Low Plantation
Willwick Hill Plantation
Beacon
Trent Falls
Beacon
ROTTON SYKES LANE
Flatts Farm
WHITTON ROAD
Bishopthorpe
The Flats
DN15
WHITTON ROAD
Sewage Works
River Trent
Beacon

8
2

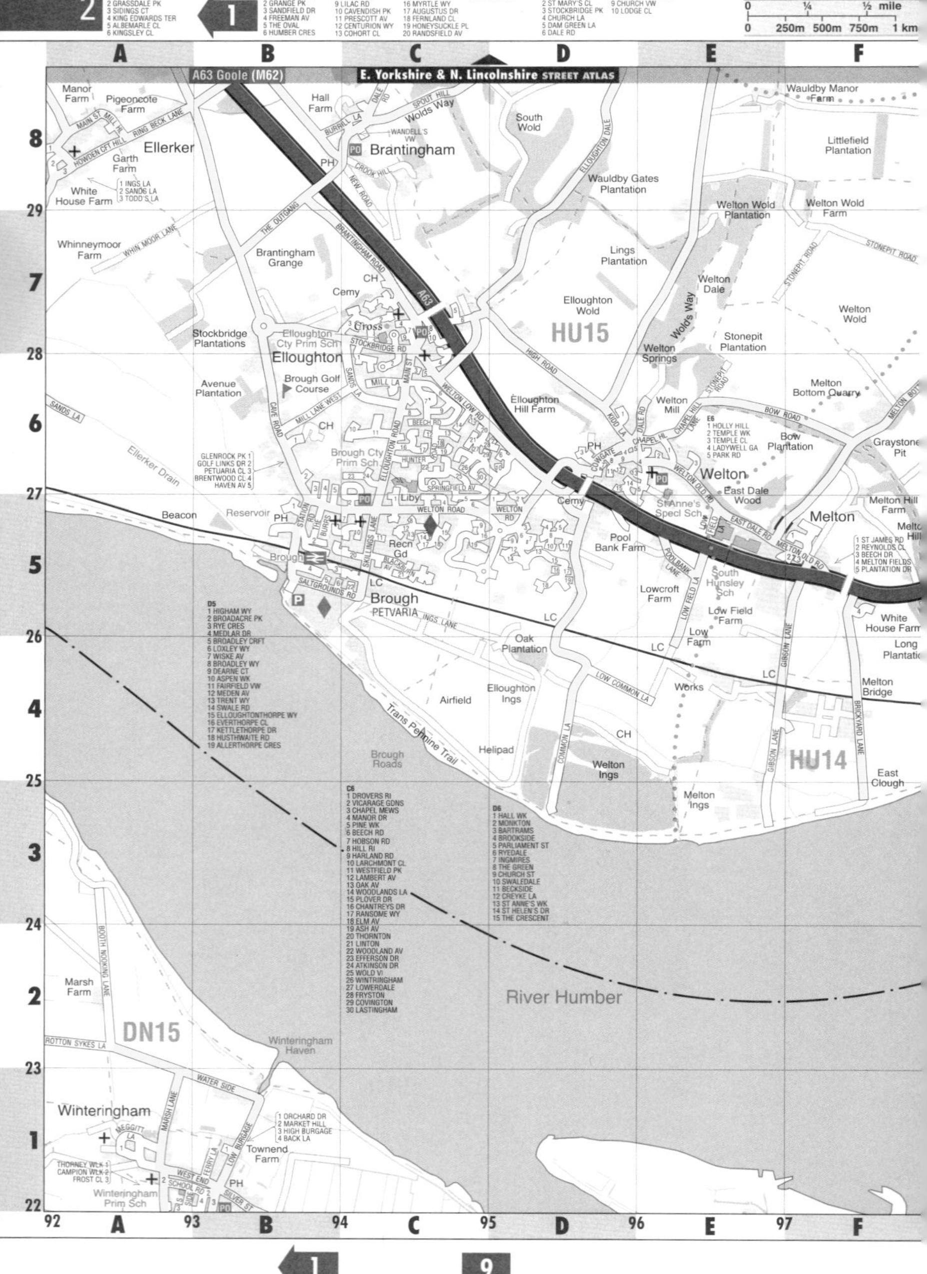

2
B5
1 HAVEN GARTH
2 GRASSDALE PK
3 SIDINGS CT
4 KING EDWARDS TER
5 ALBEMARLE CL
6 KINGSLEY CL
1
C5
1 TREMAYNE AV
2 GRANGE PK
3 SANDFIELD DR
4 FREEMAN AV
5 THE OVAL
6 HUMBER CRES
7 WRYGARTH AV
8 LEGION CL
9 LILAC RD
10 CAVENDISH PK
11 PRESCOTT AV
12 CENTURION WY
13 COHORT CL
14 FRESH FIELDS
15 NURSERY CT
16 MYRTLE WY
17 AUGUSTUS DR
18 FERNLAND CL
19 HONEYSUCKLE PL
20 RANDSFIELD AV
21 BUCCANEER WY
22 ARKLEY CL
C7
1 SPINDLEWOOD
2 ST MARY'S CL
3 STOCKBRIDGE PK
4 CHURCH LA
5 DAM GREEN LA
6 DALE RD
7 CHURCH ST
8 THORNHAM'S WY
9 CHURCH VW
10 LODGE CL
Scale: 1¼ inches to 1 mi
0 ¼ ½ mile
0 250m 500m 750m 1 km
A B C D E F
A63 Goole (M62)
E. Yorkshire & N. Lincolnshire STREET ATLAS
Manor Farm
Pigeoncote Farm
Hall Farm
Wolds Way
South Wold
Wauldby Manor Farm
Ellerker
Garth Farm
Brantingham
Littlefield Plantation
White House Farm
1 INGS LA
2 SANDS LA
3 TODD'S LA
Wauldby Gates Plantation
Welton Wold Plantation
Welton Wold Farm
Whinneymoor Farm
Brantingham Grange
Lings Plantation
Welton Dale
Welton Wold
Ellougthon Wold
HU15
Stockbridge Plantations
Elloughton Cty Prim Sch
Elloughton
Stonepit Plantation
Welton Springs
Avenue Plantation
Brough Golf Course
Melton Bottom Quarry
Elloughton Hill Farm
Welton Mill
E6
1 HOLLY HILL
2 TEMPLE WK
3 TEMPLE CL
4 LADYWELL GA
5 PARK RD
Bow Plantation
Graystone Pit
GLENROCK PK 1
GOLF LINKS DR 2
PETUARIA CL 3
BRENTWOOD CL 4
HAVEN AV 5
Brough Cty Prim Sch
Welton
East Dale Wood
Ellerker Drain
St Anne's Specl Sch
Melton Hill Farm
Beacon
Reservoir
Liby
Melton
Pool Bank Farm
1 ST JAMES RD
2 REYNOLDS CL
3 BEECH DR
4 MELTON FIELDS
5 PLANTATION DR
Recn Gd
Brough
Lowcroft Farm
South Hunsley Sch
White House Farm
Brough
PETVARIA
Low Field Farm
D5
1 HIGHAM WY
2 BROADACRE PK
3 RYE CRES
4 MEDLAR DR
5 BROADLEY CRFT
6 LOXLEY WY
7 WISKE AV
8 BROADLEY WY
9 DEARNE CT
10 ASPEN WK
11 FAIRFIELD VW
12 MEDEN AV
13 TRENT WY
14 SWALE RD
15 ELLOUGHTONTHORPE WY
16 EVERTHORPE CL
17 KETTLETHORPE DR
18 HUSTHWAITE RD
19 ALLERTHORPE CRES
Oak Plantation
Low Farm
Long Plantation
Elloughton Ings
Airfield
Works
Melton Bridge
Trans Pennine Trail
Helipad
Brough Roads
Welton Ings
HU14
East Clough
Melton Ings
C6
1 DROVERS RI
2 VICARAGE GDNS
3 CHAPEL MEWS
4 MANOR DR
5 PINE WK
6 BEECH RD
7 HOBSON RD
8 HILL RI
9 HARLAND RD
10 LARCHMONT CL
11 WESTFIELD PK
12 LAMBERT AV
13 OAK AV
14 WOODLANDS LA
15 PLOVER DR
16 CHANTREYS DR
17 RANSOME WY
18 ELM AV
19 ASH AV
20 THORNTON
21 LINTON
22 WOODLAND AV
23 EFFERSON DR
24 ATKINSON DR
25 WOLD VI
26 WINTRINGHAM
27 LOWERDALE
28 FRYSTON
29 COVINGTON
30 LASTINGHAM
D6
1 HALL WK
2 MONKTON
3 BARTRAMS
4 BROOKSIDE
5 PARLIAMENT ST
6 RYEDALE
7 INGMIRES
8 THE GREEN
9 CHURCH ST
10 SWALEDALE
11 BECKSIDE
12 CREYKE LA
13 ST ANNE'S WK
14 ST HELEN'S DR
15 THE CRESCENT
Marsh Farm
River Humber
DN15
Winteringham Haven
Winteringham
1 ORCHARD DR
2 MARKET HILL
3 HIGH BURGAGE
4 BACK LA
Townend Farm
THORNEY WLK 1
CAMPION WLK 2
FROST CL 3
Winteringham Prim Sch
8
29
7
28
6
27
5
26
4
25
3
24
2
23
1
22
92 A 93 B 94 C 95 D 96 E 97 F
1
9

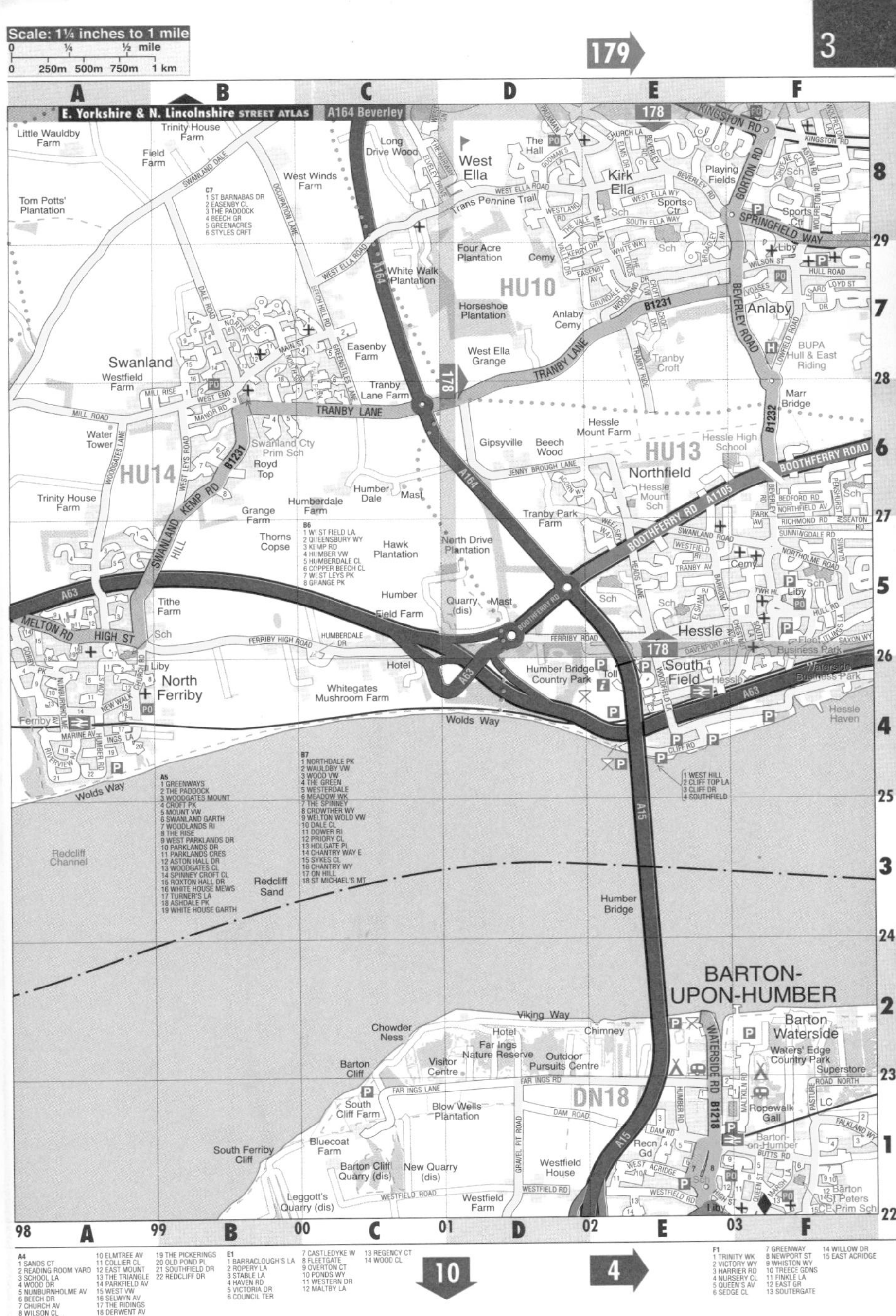

Scale: 1¼ inches to 1 mile
0 ¼ ½ mile
0 250m 500m 750m 1 km
179
3
E. Yorkshire & N. Lincolnshire STREET ATLAS
A164 Beverley
178
Little Wauldby Farm
Trinity House Farm
Field Farm
Tom Potts' Plantation
West Winds Farm
Long Drive Wood
West Ella
The Hall
Kirk Ella
Playing Fields
Sports Ctr
Four Acre Plantation
Cemy
HU10
White Walk Plantation
Horseshoe Plantation
Anlaby Cemy
Anlaby
Tranby Croft
BUPA Hull & East Riding
West Ella Grange
Easenby Farm
Swanland
Westfield Farm
Tranby Lane Farm
Marr Bridge
Water Tower
HU14
Swanland Cty Prim Sch
Royd Top
Gipsyville
Beech Wood
Hessle Mount Farm
Hessle High School
HU13
Northfield
Hessle Mount Sch
Trinity House Farm
Grange Farm
Humberdale Farm
Humber Dale
Mast
Tranby Park Farm
Thorns Copse
Hawk Plantation
North Drive Plantation
Tithe Farm
Humber Field Farm
Quarry (dis)
Hessle
North Ferriby
Hotel
Humber Bridge Country Park
Toll
South Field
Whitegates Mushroom Farm
Wolds Way
Hessle Haven
Fleet Business Park
Waterside Business Park
Redcliff Channel
Redcliff Sand
Humber Bridge
BARTON-UPON-HUMBER
Viking Way
Chowder Ness
Hotel
Far Ings Nature Reserve
Chimney
Barton Waterside
Waters' Edge Country Park
Barton Cliff
Visitor Centre
Outdoor Pursuits Centre
Superstore
South Cliff Farm
Blow Wells Plantation
DN18
Ropewalk Gall
Barton-on-Humber
South Ferriby Cliff
Bluecoat Farm
Barton Cliff Quarry (dis)
New Quarry (dis)
Westfield House
Recn Gd
Leggott's Quarry (dis)
Westfield Farm
Barton St Peters CE Prim Sch
C7
1 ST BARNABAS DR
2 EASENBY CL
3 THE PADDOCK
4 BEECH GR
5 GREENACRES
6 STYLES CRFT
B6
1 WEST FIELD LA
2 QUEENSBURY WY
3 KEMP RD
4 HUMBER VW
5 HUMBERDALE CL
6 COPPER BEECH CL
7 WEST LEYS PK
8 GRANGE PK
B7
1 NORTHDALE PK
2 WAULDBY VW
3 WOOD VW
4 THE GREEN
5 WESTERDALE
6 MEADOW WK
7 THE SPINNEY
8 CROWTHER WY
9 WELTON WOLD VW
10 DALE CL
11 DOWER RI
12 PRIORY CL
13 HOLGATE PL
14 CHANTRY WAY E
15 SYKES CL
16 CHANTRY WY
17 ON HILL
18 ST MICHAEL'S MT
A5
1 GREENWAYS
2 THE PADDOCK
3 WOODGATES MOUNT
4 CROFT PK
5 MOUNT VW
6 SWANLAND GARTH
7 WOODLANDS RI
8 THE RISE
9 WEST PARKLANDS DR
10 PARKLANDS DR
11 PARKLANDS CRES
12 ASTON HALL DR
13 WOODGATES CL
14 SPINNEY CROFT CL
15 ROXTON HALL DR
16 WHITE HOUSE MEWS
17 TURNER'S LA
18 ASHDALE PK
19 WHITE HOUSE GARTH
1 WEST HILL
2 CLIFF TOP LA
3 CLIFF DR
4 SOUTHFIELD
98 A 99 B 00 C 01 D 02 E 03 F
8 29 7 28 6 27 5 26 4 25 3 24 2 23 1 22
A4
1 SANDS CT
2 READING ROOM YARD
3 SCHOOL LA
4 WOOD DR
5 NUNBURNHOLME AV
6 BEECH DR
7 CHURCH AV
8 WILSON CL
9 TRIANGLE DR
10 ELMTREE AV
11 COLLIER CL
12 EAST MOUNT
13 THE TRIANGLE
14 PARKFIELD AV
15 WEST VW
16 SELWYN AV
17 THE RIDINGS
18 DERWENT AV
19 THE PICKERINGS
20 OLD POND PL
21 SOUTHFIELD DR
22 REDCLIFF DR
E1
1 BARRACLOUGH'S LA
2 ROPERY LA
3 STABLE LA
4 HAVEN RD
5 VICTORIA DR
6 COUNCIL TER
7 CASTLEDYKE W
8 FLEETGATE
9 OVERTON CT
10 PONDS WY
11 WESTERN DR
12 MALTBY LA
13 REGENCY CT
14 WOOD CL
10
4
F1
1 TRINITY WK
2 VICTORY WY
3 HARRIER RD
4 NURSERY CL
5 QUEEN'S AV
6 SEDGE CL
7 GREENWAY
8 NEWPORT ST
9 WHISTON WY
10 TREECE GDNS
11 FINKLE LA
12 EAST GR
13 SOUTERGATE
14 WILLOW DR
15 EAST ACRIDGE

4
3
Scale: 1¼ inches to 1 mile
0 ¼ ½ mile
0 250m 500m 750m 1 km
E. Yorkshire & N. Lincolnshire STREET ATLAS
179
180
A1174 Beverley
HU5
HU3
HU4
HU1
DN19
DN18
East Ella
Anlaby Park
West Park
Gipsyville
Pickering Park
New Holland
Barrow Haven
Barrow Hann
ANLABY ROAD
BOOTHFERRY ROAD
HESSLE ROAD
CLIVE SULLIVAN WAY
SPRING BANK WEST
St Andrews Quay
Trans Pennine Trail
New Holland Pier
Fairfield Pit Nature Reserve
Barrow Haven Reedbed Nature Reserve
Pasture Wharf Nature Reserve
Barrow Blow Wells Nature Reserve
The Castles (Motte & Baileys)
LINCOLN CASTLE WAY
WEST HANN LANE
EAST HANN LANE
MARSH LANE
OXMARSH LANE
Albert Dock
Victoria Pier
CASTLE ST
For full street detail of the highlighted area see pages 179 & 180.
11
E2
1 SCHOOL LA
2 WENTWORTH CR
3 FULFORD CR
4 WESTBURN AV
5 MORGAN WY
6 GLENEAGLES CR
7 ALBERT ST
8 MOUNT PL
9 PEPLOE LA
10 PEPLOE CR

D8
1 ENDEAVOUR CR
2 SPRINGDALE CL
3 BEWHOLME GR
4 MARFLEET AV
5 CYPRUS ST
6 LITTLEFAIR RD
7 DELHI ST
8 FRODSHAM ST
9 CEYLON ST
10 CORPORATION RD

E8
1 GREAT FIELD LA
2 ASHWELL AV
3 BOTHWELL GR
4 HEMSWELL AV
5 CHURCH LA
6 ELBA ST

F8
1 BAMFORD AV
2 SALTFORD AV
3 SOUTHWELL AV
4 FALKLAND RD
5 HALLIWELL CL
6 STOCKWELL GR
7 TOWER HOUSE LA

A1
1 WINDSOR GR
2 THE CLOSE
3 FARROWS POND
4 MILL LA
5 MEADOW CL
6 WILLOW LA

12

For full street detail of the highlighted area see page 181.

Scale: 1¼ inches to 1 mile
0 ¼ ½ mile
0 250m 500m 750m 1 km

16

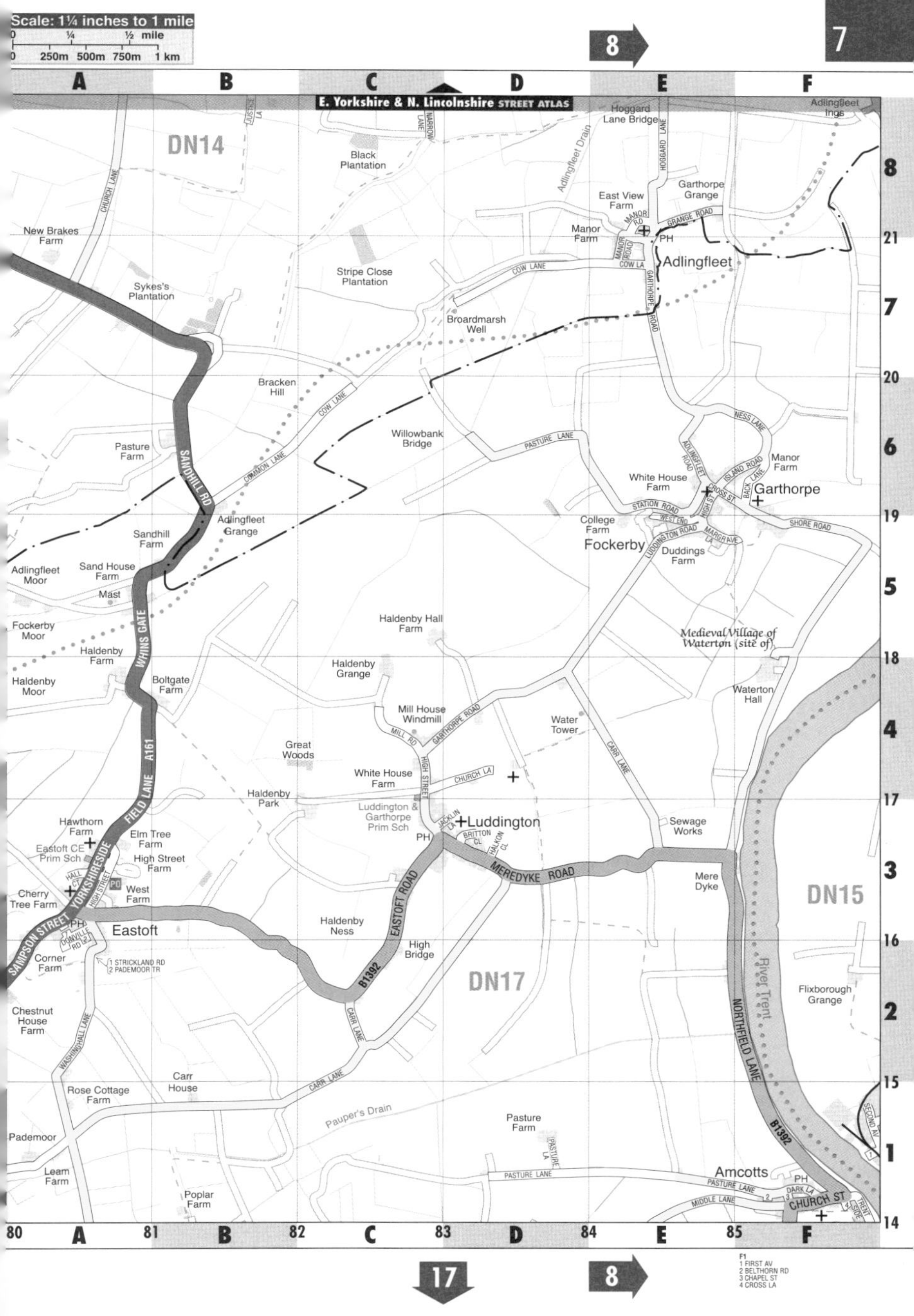
Scale: 1¼ inches to 1 mile
0 ¼ ½ mile
0 250m 500m 750m 1 km
8
A B C D E F
E. Yorkshire & N. Lincolnshire STREET ATLAS
DN14
JUSTICE LA
NARROW LANE
Black Plantation
Hoggard Lane Bridge
HOGGARD LANE
Adlingfleet Drain
Adlingfleet Ings
East View Farm
Garthorpe Grange
MANOR RD
GRANGE ROAD
Manor Farm
PH
MANOR ROAD
COW LA
Adlingfleet
CHURCH LANE
New Brakes Farm
Stripe Close Plantation
COW LANE
GARTHORPE ROAD
Sykes's Plantation
Broadmarsh Well
Bracken Hill
COW LANE
Willowbank Bridge
PASTURE LANE
NESS LANE
Pasture Farm
SANDHILL RD
COMMON LANE
ADLINGFLEET ROAD
ISLAND ROAD
Manor Farm
White House Farm
CROSS ST
BACK LANE
Garthorpe
STATION ROAD
HIGH ST
WEST END
Adlingfleet Grange
College Farm
SHORE ROAD
Sandhill Farm
LUDDINGTON ROAD
MARGRAVE LA
Fockerby
Duddings Farm
Adlingfleet Moor
Sand House Farm
Mast
Fockerby Moor
WHINS GATE
Haldenby Hall Farm
Medieval Village of Waterton (site of)
Haldenby Farm
Haldenby Moor
Boltgate Farm
Haldenby Grange
Waterton Hall
Mill House Windmill
GARTHORPE ROAD
MILL RD
Water Tower
Great Woods
CARR LANE
A161
White House Farm
CHURCH LA
HIGH STREET
FIELD LANE
Haldenby Park
Luddington & Garthorpe Prim Sch
JACKLIN LA
Luddington
Sewage Works
Hawthorn Farm
Elm Tree Farm
PH
BRITTON CL
HALKON CL
Eastoft CE Prim Sch
High Street Farm
MEREDYKE ROAD
Mere Dyke
HALL CT
YORKSHIRESIDE
HIGH STREET
PO
West Farm
Cherry Tree Farm
EASTOFT ROAD
DN15
SAMPSON STREET
PH
Eastoft
Haldenby Ness
DONVILLE RD
High Bridge
Corner Farm
1 STRICKLAND RD
2 PADEMOOR TR
B1392
DN17
River Trent
Flixborough Grange
Chestnut House Farm
CARR LANE
NORTHFIELD LANE
WASHINGHALL LANE
Carr House
Rose Cottage Farm
CARR LANE
SECOND AV
Pauper's Drain
Pasture Farm
B1392
Pademoor
PASTURE LA
Leam Farm
PASTURE LANE
Amcotts
PH
PASTURE LANE
DARK LA
MIDDLE LANE
CHURCH ST
TRENT SIDE
Poplar Farm
8 21 7 20 6 19 5 18 4 17 3 16 2 15 1 14
80 81 82 83 84 85
17
8
F1
1 FIRST AV
2 BELTHORN RD
3 CHAPEL ST
4 CROSS LA

Scale: 1¼ inches to 1 mile
0 ¼ ½ mile
0 250m 500m 750m 1 km

Scale: 1¼ inches to 1 mile
¼
½ mile
250m 500m 750m 1 km
A5
1 FARNDALE WY
2 WESLEY CL
3 NORTHLANDS AV
4 WALKER DR
5 NEVILLE CR
6 HILES AV
7 MARMION DR
8 TEANBY DR
9 BOYNTON CR
10 NORTHLANDS RD S
11 HIGH ST
12 MALKINSON CL
13 BLANKNEY CT
14 CHURCH SIDE
15 QUEEN ST
16 CHAPEL LA
17 SOUTH ST
18 LEEK HILL
19 WESTWINDS GD
20 HAWTHORNE CL
21 MALKINSON CL
22 WATERLOW DR
23 PLYMOUTH CL
24 LINCOLN DR
25 BOSTON CL
26 HILLSMERE GR
27 COATES AV
28 BENNETT DR
29 DRIFFIL WAY
30 BAKER DR
31 MARKET ST
2
10
9
A
B
C
D
E
F
HEWDE LA
CLIFF ROAD
Sports Gd
1 HARRISON CL
2 BACK LA
3 HIGH BURGAGE
ERMINE STREET
Read's Island
WINTERTON ROAD
Winteringham Grange
ROMANO-BRITISH SETTLEMENT (SITE OF)
South Channel
8
Eastfield Farm
Low Farm
SLUICE LANE
A1077
SLUICE RD
Lock
PH
21
Chalybeate Spring
COCKTHORNE LANE
Works
Chimney
Mere Farm
Spoil Heap
Ferriby Sluice
RED LANE
Winteringham Ings
MERE LANE
A1077
7
EARLSGATE RD
Northlands
WINTERINGHAM ROAD
Ferriby Sluice
East Drain
Mast
INGS LANE
20
A6
1 RYEDALE AV
2 DOVEDALE CL
East Field Farm
Winterton Ings
Booth House Farm
LEYS LANE
B5
1 MILL HOUSE LA
2 HAYTON CL
3 BURGON CR
4 HARTLA
5 WEST LA
6 ROSS LA
7 PARKHILL RI
8 HALL GD
9 CRAKEDALE RD
10 MOUNT AV
11 MARRIS DR
6
Huntingfield Farm
NORTHLANDS ROAD
Playing Field
Winterton Comp Sch
Chy
NORTH ST
CARR LANE
Winterton Carrs
DN18
NEWPORT DR
Horkstow Bridge
Winterton Cty Jun Sch
DALE PARK AV
B1207
CHURCH FIELDS
BRIDGE LANE
19
DE LACY WY
WEST ST
Lby
Cemy
Sedgeworth Farm
Swallows Low Wood
CEMETERY ROAD
Sandhall Farm
B1430
PO
KING ST
LOW ST
PARK STREET
Holme Hill Farm
Peadron Pig Farm
Maltby Farm
The Spinney
5
Winterton CE Inf Sch
MANLAKE AV
HENDERSON WY
Winterton
B1207
DN15
HOLMES LANE
18
Holy Well
CARR LANE
Cringlebeck Farm
ROXBY CAUSEWAY
Grange Farm
NORTH STREET
Walk House
Rat Abbey Farm
Roxby Carrs
4
New River Ancholme
Walk House Farm
Rat Abbey
EAST ST
Roxby
17
Scotney Farm
Highfield Farm
NORTH CARR LANE
Mickleholme Chicken Farm
Saxby All Saints Bridge
3
Gorse Covert
Mickleholme Farm
Youll Close
BRACKENHOLMES ROAD
16
Mickleholme Wood
DN20
Brackenholmes
Hall Plantation
West Drain
CARR LANE
Willow Plantation
2
Keb Farm
Ermine House
Medieval Village of Low Risby
KEB LA
CARR LANE
High Risby
Low Risby
CHURCH LANE
15
RISBY ROAD
SCHOOL LANE
BECK LA
ERMINE STREET
Rookery Plantation
Appleby
Old River Ancholme
1
D1
1 PAUL LA
2 HAYTONS LA
3 CHURCH SIDE
4 VICARAGE PK
Risby Warren Farm
Dudley Covert
Jeffrie's Covert
Maud's Covert
B1207
14
92
93
94
95
96
97
19
10

10
A7
1 ANDREWS RD
2 SANDS LA
3 QUEEN ELIZABETH AV
4 OLD POST OFFICE LA
5 LOW ST
6 SKINNERS LA
7 SCHOOL LA
8 BEAULAHLAND
9 BEAULAH VILLAS
10 MILL LA
11 OLD WARP LA
9
3
F8
1 CHAPEL LA
2 GEORGE ST
3 PRIESTGATE
4 ST MARY'S LA
5 BURGATE
6 BECK HL
7 SAXON CL
8 E ACRIDGE
9 NORMAN CL
10 GREEN LA
11 CHURCH VW
12 WHITECROSS ST
13 CASTLEDYKE ST
14 CASTLE CT
15 PRESTON LA
16 STEPHEN CR
17 HIGHFIELD CR
18 NICOLSON DR
19 DANSON CL
20 KINGSTON VW
21 RIVER VW
22 LODGE AV
23 ORCHARD CL
24 THE BRIDGES
25 PARK VW
26 HAWTHORN GATE
27 LINCOLN DR
28 BLYTH CT
29 FAIRFIELD DR
30 MILLBROOK WY
31 RAVENDALE
32 PRINCE CHARLES DR
33 QUEEN ELIZABETH WY
34 PRINCESS DR
Scale: 1¼ inches to 1 mile
0 ¼ ½ mile
0 250m 500m 750m 1 km
A B C D E F
Greengate Farm
Leggott's Quarry (dis)
Viking Way
Fox Covert
Green Gate
GRAVEL PIT ROAD
FERRIBY RD
HOLYDYKE
Recn Gd
St Peter's
A1077
Baysgarth House Mus
Baysgarth Sch
BOWMANDALE
BIRKDALE
TOFTS ROAD
Bowmandale Prim Sch
Swimming Pool
Baysgarth L Ctr
BAYSGARTH VW
MEADOW
PRINCE PHIL DR
EASTFIELD ROAD
Eastfield Farm
HORKSTOW ROAD
NORTH END
THE RISE
FARRISHES LA
Elm Farm
PO
SLUICE ROAD
HIGH ST
South Ferriby
FERRIBY ROAD
A1077
Grange Farm
E8
1 REGENCY CT
2 FURNISS CT
3 HUMBER VW
4 HESSLE VW
5 HILLSIDE DR
6 HARROWDYKE
7 BERETUN GN
8 RAMSDEN AV
9 CLIFF GR
10 TOFTS RD
11 SUNNYBANK
12 WARRENDALE
13 GRANGE AV
14 MOUNT AV
15 PARK AV
16 BEACON AV
17 PROVIDENCE CR
18 MILSON CL
19 BRADWELL CL
20 PELHAM CL
21 LUNN'S CR
22 MILLFIELDS
23 PITMAN AV
24 WARWICK DR
25 MASONS CT
26 NICHOLAS CT
27 GEORGINA CT
28 SUMMERDALE
29 ELMDALE
30 BOWMANDALE
31 BIRCHDALE
32 WELTON CL
33 STEVENSON'S WY
34 HARVEST AV
35 SHARPE CL
36 WEBB CL
37 GODDARD CL
38 APPLEYARD DR
39 VARAH CL
South Ferriby Prim Sch
HIGH STREET
The Grange
Chalk Pit
MIDDLEGATE LANE
BARTON-UPON-HUMBER
Beacon Hill
Barton Hill Farm
B1218
A15
HORKSTOW ROAD
Pit (disused)
North Wold Farm
Field House Farm
DN18
Barton Field Farm
Kingsforth
Kingsforth Farm
Chapel Farm
BRIGG ROAD
B1204
BRIDGE LANE
Manor Wold Farm
Horkstow Wolds
Turton's Covert
Pit (dis)
CHAPEL LA
OSTLER'S LA
Hall Top Farm
Viking Way
Horkstow
CARR LANE
MAIN STREET
Quarry (dis)
A15
The Oaks
Fox Covert Plantation
B1206
Old Belt Plantation
Beaumontcote Farm
Horkstow Grange
Field House Farm
Quarry (dis)
Bennett's New Covert
Pit (Dis)
SAXBY HILL
B1206
Saxby Wolds
NORTH CARR LANE
Hill Side Plantation
Pikendale Plantation
Grange Farm
Saxby All Saints
CHURCH LA
Bonby Lodge
Crow Wood Plantation
PARK LANE
PARK LA
DN20
MIDDLEGATE LANE
Forth Carr Plantation
SAXBY ROAD
CHURCH LANE
Tinsley Farm
Bonby Top Farm
South Plantation
North Wold Farm
Bonby
PO
Bonby Ings
Sports Ground
South Wold Farm
PH
MAIN STREET
Eleven Acre Plantation
CARR LANE
WOLD ROAD
FUSSEY GD
B1204
Land Drain
MIDDLE BARN HILL
Turnpike Top Farm
B1206
Bonby Carrs
BONBY ROAD
NEW RD
Worlaby
TOP RD
THE HILL
Bonby Ings
8 21 7 20 6 19 5 18 4 17 3 16 2 15 1 14
98 A 99 B 00 C 01 D 02 E 03 F
9
20
C2
1 HALL MD
2 CHURCH CL
3 MANOR DR
4 SHEEPDYKE LA
5 SCHOOL LA
6 FREEMANS LA

Scale: 1¼ inches to 1 mile
¼ ½ mile
250m 500m 750m 1 km

C7
1 HIGHFIELDS
2 BLACKSMITHS CL
3 OAK GR
4 ORCHARD CL
5 WOODLANDS CL
6 WOLSEY DR
7 PARK VIEW CL
8 FEATHER LA
9 BEECH GARTH

C8
1 CHESTNUT RI
2 HARVEST RI
3 THE BRAMBLES
4 HAWTHORN RI
5 HEDGEROW CL
6 ROWAN CL
7 SCHOFIELD CL
8 MILL LA
9 MILLFIELDS WY
10 GLEN HALL RI
11 PADDOCK RI
12 MIDDLEGATE CL

D8
1 NORTH ST
2 WILLOW GD
3 JOHN HARRISON'S CL
4 MANOR LA
5 MARTIN'S CL
6 PRIORY LA
7 NORTH ST
8 CROSS ST
9 THORNGARTH LA
10 BECK LA
11 OLD DAIRY
12 GLANFORD GR
13 THE SPINNEY
14 THE GR
15 PALMER LA
16 BARRICK CL
17 SIMPSONCL
18 GREEN LA
19 LORDS LA
20 ABBEY RI

4
12

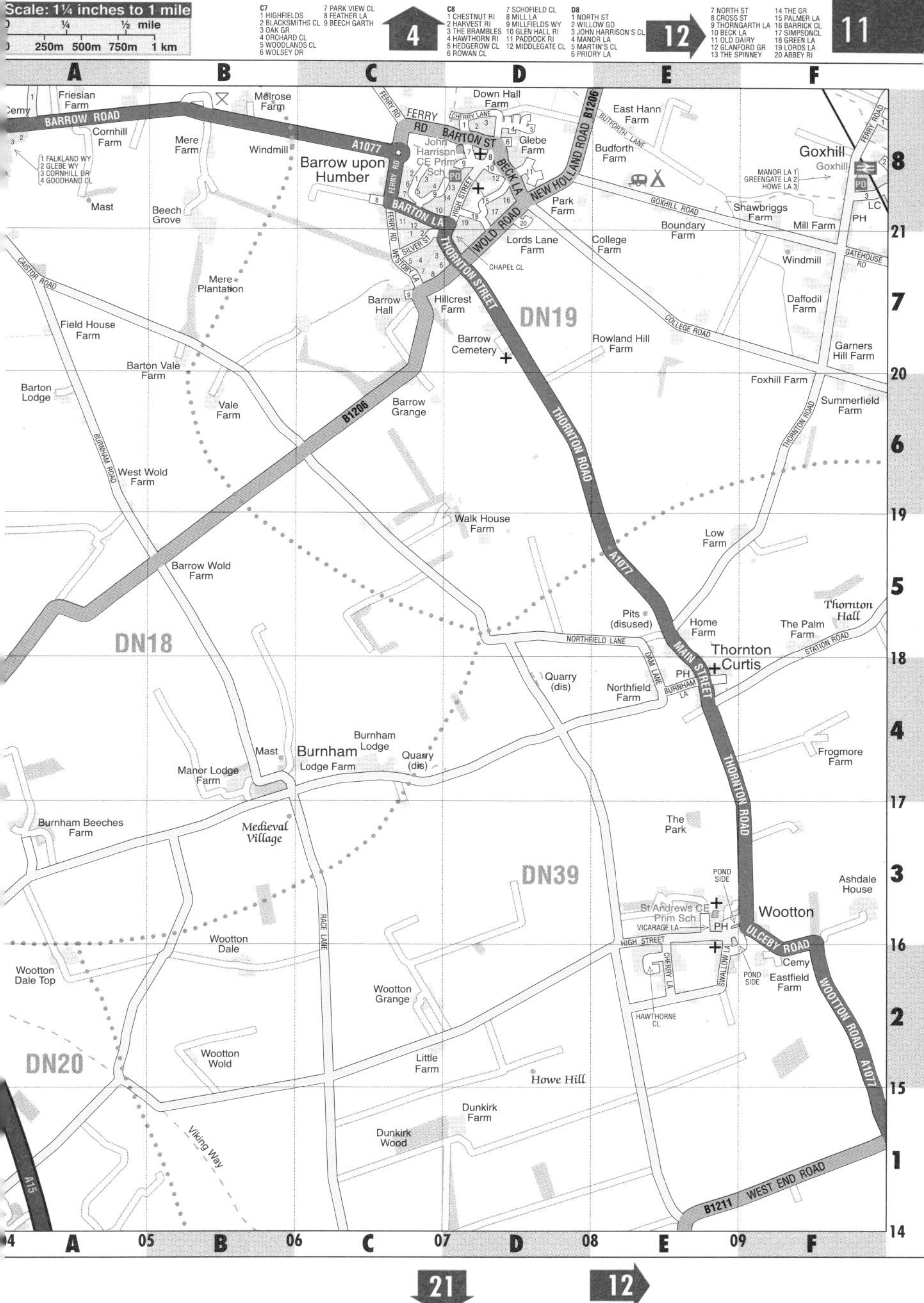

21
12

12
A8
1 WILLOW LA
2 JASMINE CT
3 ROWAN CT
4 CHESNUT WY
5 NORTH END
6 MANOR LA
7 STOTHARDS LA
8 HAWTHORNE GDNS
9 LIME GR
10 TRINITY CL
11 THE BRIDLES
12 THE SQUARE
13 WESTFIELD RD
14 GREENGATE LA
15 KING ST
16 CHURCH ST
17 ALL SAINTS' CL
18 SCHOOL LA
19 CHURCH SIDE
20 PIDGEON COTE LA
21 ST JOHNS CL
22 ST MICHAEL'S CT
11
5
Scale: 1¼ inches to 1 mile
0 ¼ ½ mile
0 250m 500m 750m 1 km
A B C D E F
8 21 7 20 6 19 5 18 4 17 3 16 2 15 1 14
10 11 12 13 14 15
Goxhill
Goxhill Prim Sch
Cemy
Airfield (disused)
Sandham Plantation
The Grange
Halton Marshes
Field House Farm
Chy
Pine Tree Farm
DN19
Littleworth Farm
Manor House Farm
JERICHO LA
Hallands Field Farm
Chapel
South End
Littlewick Farm
Ash Tree Farm
Moat
Manor Farm
Butters Wood
East Halton
Chase Hill Farm
Field Farm
East Halton Prim Sch
Kettlebridge Farm
KETTLEBRIDGE LA
College Farm
Wellclose Farm
PH
College Bridge
College Road Farm
West Field
Thornton Abbey
Grange Farm
Station Farm
Baysgarth Farm
Power Station
DN40
Priory Farm
Sewage Works
The Grange
South Cloister Covert
Westfield Farm
Abbey Farm
Church Farm
East Halton Beck
Earthworks
Sweet Briar Farm
Pit (dis)
Low Farm
Airfield (disused)
Manor Farm
Lindsey Oil Refinery
EAST MIDDLE MERE RD
Hillcrest
Northfield Farm
North Killingholme
Eastfield North Ind Est
DN39
Becklea Farm
Killingholme Prim Sch
North Field
Ashville Farm
Ulceby Carr
Skitter Beck
Pit (Dis)
South Killingholme
Eastfield South Ind Est
Glebe Farm
Ulceby Carr Farm
Mast
Sinks Covert
Manor Farm
PRIORY CRESCENT
MEADOW AV
WALKERS WY
Ulceby Grange
Ulceby Skitter
Beckhouse Farm
Ulceby
Coates Farm
Hill Farm
Glebe Farm
SPRUCE LANE
STATION ROAD
A1077
ULCEBY ROAD
A160
Hillgarth Farm
Rye Hill Farm
St Nicholas CE Prim Sch
B1211
BROCKLESBY RD
1 JAMES PL
2 MARTINS RD
3 WILLIAMS DR
4 SOUTHFIELD CL
A180
Pelham House Farm
Home Farm
STATION RD
FORGE CR
MOUNT ROYALE CL
Rye Hill Plantations
CHAPEL LA
A1
1 WEST END RD
2 CHURCH LA
3 STEPHEN CL
4 PARKS CL
5 CORONATION RD
6 HALLCROFT
7 FRONT ST
8 PITMOOR LA
9 NELTHORPE CL
11
22
E4
1 VICARAGE LA
2 ST CRISPINS CL
3 CLARKES RD
E3
1 CLARKES RD
2 ST DENY'S CL
3 MOAT LA
4 BRIAR CL
5 PILGRIM'S CL
6 MAYFLOWER CL
7 HAWKINS WY
8 SCHOOL RD
F2
1 PRIMITIVE CHAPEL LA
2 WOODS LA
3 MAYFIELD AV
4 BAPTIST CHAPEL LA

Scale: 1¼ inches to 1 mile

For full street detail of the highlighted area see pages 186 & 187.

186 23 187 187

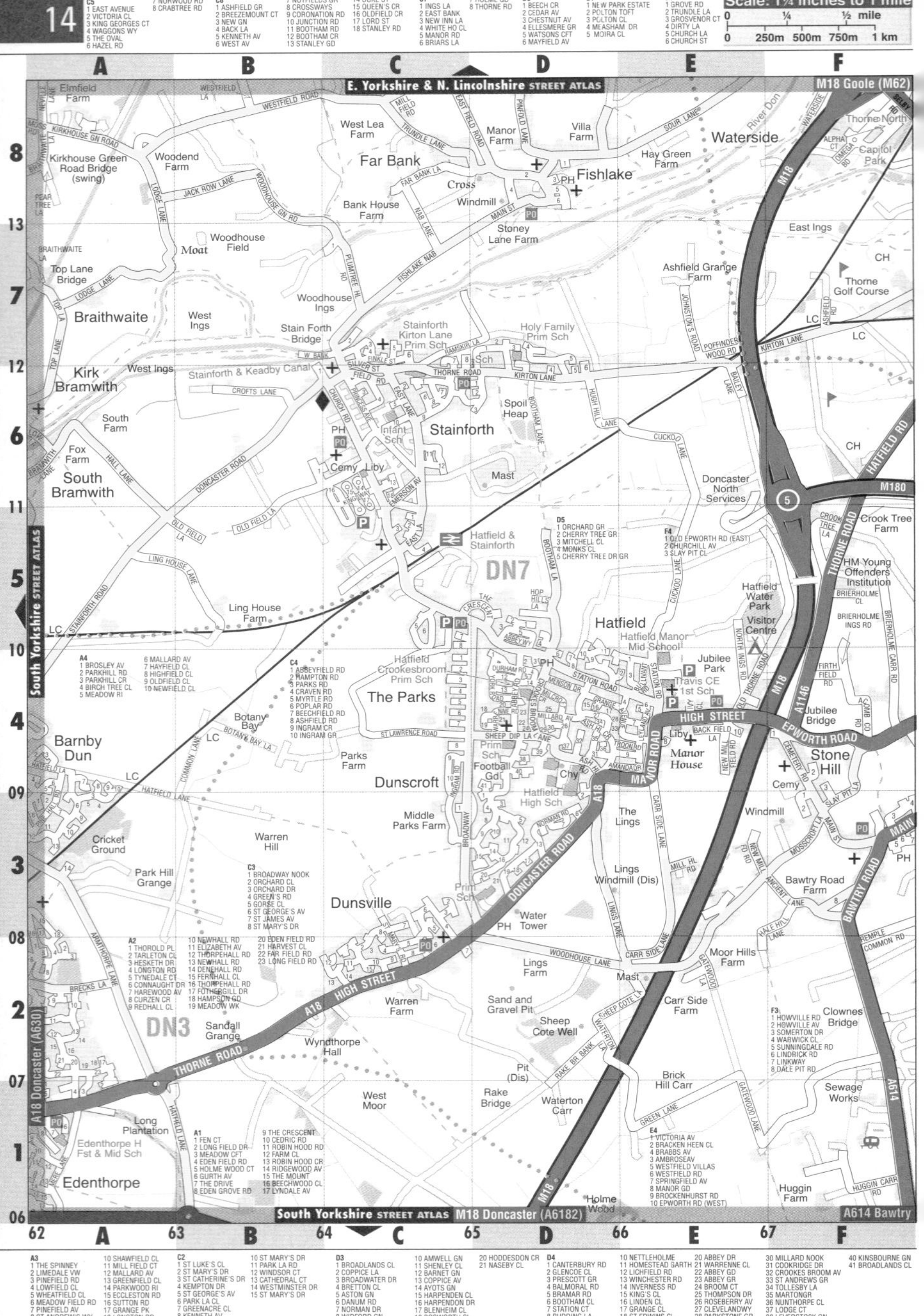
C5
1 EAST AVENUE
2 VICTORIA CL
3 KING GEORGES CT
4 WAGGONS WY
5 THE OVAL
6 HAZEL RD
7 NORWOOD RD
8 CRABTREE RD
C6
1 ASHFIELD GR
2 BREEZEMOUNT CT
3 NEW GN
4 BACK LA
5 KENNETH AV
6 WEST AV
7 NUTFIELDS GR
8 CROSSWAYS
9 CORONATION RD
10 JUNCTION RD
11 BOOTHAM RD
12 BOOTHAM CR
13 STANLEY GD
14 DUKE ST
15 QUEEN'S CR
16 OLDFIELD CR
17 LORD ST
18 STANLEY RD
C7
1 INGS LA
2 EAST BANK
3 NEW INN LA
4 WHITE HO CL
5 MANOR RD
6 BRIARS LA
7 HOLME GD
8 THORNE RD
D6
1 BEECH CR
2 CEDAR AV
3 CHESTNUT AV
4 ELLESMERE GR
5 WATSONS CFT
6 MAYFIELD AV
D7
1 NEW PARK ESTATE
2 POLTON TOFT
3 POLTON CL
4 MEASHAM DR
5 MOIRA CL
D8
1 GROVE RD
2 TRUNDLE LA
3 GROSVENOR CT
4 DIRTY LA
5 CHURCH LA
6 CHURCH ST
Scale: 1¼ inches to 1 mile
0 ¼ ½ mile
0 250m 500m 750m 1 km
A B C D E F
E. Yorkshire & N. Lincolnshire STREET ATLAS
M18 Goole (M62)
8
13
7
12
6
11
5
10
4
09
3
08
2
07
1
06
Elmfield Farm
West Lea Farm
Far Bank
Manor Farm
Villa Farm
Waterside
Thorne North
Kirkhouse Green Road Bridge (swing)
Woodend Farm
Fishlake
Hay Green Farm
Capitol Park
Cross
Windmill
Bank House Farm
Stoney Lane Farm
East Ings
Woodhouse Field
Moat
Top Lane Bridge
Ashfield Grange Farm
Thorne Golf Course
Braithwaite
West Ings
Woodhouse Ings
Stain Forth Bridge
Stainforth Kirton Lane Prim Sch
Holy Family Prim Sch
Kirk Bramwith
West Ings
Stainforth & Keadby Canal
Stainforth
Spoil Heap
South Farm
Fox Farm
South Bramwith
Infant Sch
Cemy
Liby
Mast
Doncaster North Services
M180
Hatfield & Stainforth
DN7
Crook Tree Farm
HM Young Offenders Institution
Ling House Farm
Hatfield
Hatfield Manor Mid School
Hatfield Water Park Visitor Centre
South Yorkshire STREET ATLAS
Hatfield Crookesbroom Prim Sch
The Parks
Jubilee Park
Travis CE 1st Sch
HIGH STREET
EPWORTH ROAD
Jubilee Bridge
Botany Bay
Barnby Dun
Parks Farm
Football Gd
Liby
Manor House
Stone Hill
Dunscroft
Hatfield High Sch
Cemy
Windmill
The Lings
Cricket Ground
Warren Hill
Middle Parks Farm
Park Hill Grange
Lings Windmill (Dis)
Bawtry Road Farm
Dunsville
Water Tower
DOncaster ROAD
Moor Hills Farm
Lings Farm
Mast
Warren Farm
Sand and Gravel Pit
Carr Side Farm
Clownes Bridge
DN3
Sandall Grange
Wyndthorpe Hall
Sheep Cote Well
Pit (Dis)
Brick Hill Carr
Sewage Works
THORNE ROAD
A18 Doncaster (A630)
West Moor
Rake Bridge
Waterton Carr
Long Plantation
Edenthorpe H Fst & Mid Sch
Edenthorpe
Holme Wood
Huggin Farm
D5
1 ORCHARD GR
2 CHERRY TREE GR
3 MITCHELL CL
4 MONKS CL
5 CHERRY TREE DR GR
F4
1 OLD EPWORTH RD (EAST)
2 CHURCHILL AV
3 SLAY PIT CL
A4
1 BROSLEY AV
2 PARKHILL RD
3 PARKHILL CR
4 BIRCH TREE CL
5 MEADOW RI
6 MALLARD AV
7 HAYFIELD CL
8 HIGHFIELD CL
9 OLDFIELD CL
10 NEWFIELD CL
C4
1 ABBEYFIELD RD
2 HAMPTON RD
3 PARKS RD
4 CRAVEN RD
5 MYRTLE RD
6 POPLAR RD
7 BEECHFIELD RD
8 ASHFIELD RD
9 INGRAM CR
10 INGRAM GR
C3
1 BROADWAY NOOK
2 ORCHARD CL
3 ORCHARD DR
4 GREEN'S RD
5 GORSE CL
6 ST GEORGE'S AV
7 ST JAMES AV
8 ST MARY'S DR
A2
1 THOROLD PL
2 TARLETON CL
3 HESKETH DR
4 LONGTON RD
5 TYNEDALE CT
6 CONNAUGHT DR
7 HAREWOOD AV
8 CURZEN CR
9 REDHALL CL
10 NEWHALL RD
11 ELIZABETH AV
12 THORPEHALL RD
13 NEWHALL RD
14 DENEHALL RD
15 FERNHALL CL
16 THORPEHALL RD
17 FOTHERGILL DR
18 HAMPSON GD
19 MEADOW WK
20 EDEN FIELD RD
21 HARVEST CL
22 FAR FIELD RD
23 LONG FIELD RD
F3
1 HOWVILLE RD
2 HOWVILLE AV
3 SOMERTON DR
4 WARWICK CL
5 SUNNINGDALE RD
6 LINDRICK RD
7 LINKWAY
8 DALE PIT RD
A1
1 FEN CT
2 LONG FIELD DR
3 MEADOW CFT
4 EDEN FIELD RD
5 HOLME WOOD CT
6 GURTH AV
7 THE DRIVE
8 EDEN GROVE RD
9 THE CRESCENT
10 CEDRIC RD
11 ROBIN HOOD RD
12 FARM CL
13 ROBIN HOOD CR
14 RIDGEWOOD AV
15 THE MOUNT
16 BEECHWOOD CL
17 LYNDALE AV
E4
1 VICTORIA AV
2 BRACKEN HEEN CL
4 BRABBS AV
3 AMBROSEAV
5 WESTFIELD VILLAS
6 WESTFIELD RD
7 SPRINGFIELD AV
8 MANOR GD
9 BROCKENHURST RD
10 EPWORTH RD (WEST)
South Yorkshire STREET ATLAS
M18 Doncaster (A6182)
A614 Bawtry
62 A 63 B 64 C 65 D 66 E 67 F
A3
1 THE SPINNEY
2 LIMEDALE VW
3 PINEFIELD RD
4 LOWFIELD CL
5 WHEATFIELD CL
6 MEADOW FIELD RD
7 PINEFIELD AV
8 ST ANDREW'S WY
9 HEATHFIELD CL
10 SHAWFIELD CL
11 MILL FIELD CT
12 MALLARD AV
13 GREENFIELD CL
14 PARKWOOD RI
15 ECCLESTON RD
16 SUTTON RD
17 GRANGE PK
18 LONGTON RD
C2
1 ST LUKE'S CL
2 ST MARY'S DR
3 ST CATHERINE'S DR
4 KEMPTON DR
5 ST GEORGE'S AV
6 PARK LA CL
7 GREENACRE CL
8 KENNETH AV
9 HAWTHORNE AV
10 ST MARY'S DR
11 PARK LA RD
12 WINDSOR CT
13 CATHEDRAL CT
14 WESTMINSTER DR
15 ST MARY'S DR
D3
1 BROADLANDS CL
2 COPPICE LA
3 BROADWATER DR
4 BRETTON CL
5 ASTON GN
6 DANUM RD
7 NORMAN DR
8 WIDFORD GN
9 BROADWATER DR
10 AMWELL GN
11 SHENLEY CL
12 BARNET GN
13 COPPICE AV
14 AYOTS GN
15 HARPENDEN CL
16 HARPENDON DR
17 BLENHEIM CL
18 BOSWORTH CL
19 MILE END AV
20 HODDESDON CR
21 NASEBY CL
D4
1 CANTERBURY RD
2 GLENCOE CL
3 PRESCOTT GR
4 BALMORAL RD
5 BRAMAR RD
6 BOOTHAM CL
7 STATION CT
8 PUDDING LA
9 HUND OAK DR
10 NETTLEHOLME
11 HOMESTEAD GARTH
12 LICHFIELD RD
13 WINCHESTER RD
14 INVERNESS RD
15 KING'S CL
16 LINDEN CL
17 GRANGE CL
18 ST EDWINS CL
19 ST EDWINS DR
20 ABBEY DR
21 WARRENNE CL
22 ABBEY GD
23 ABBEY GR
24 BROOM CT
25 THOMPSON DR
26 ROSEBERRY AV
27 CLEVELANDWY
28 PARKSTONE GR
29 WHITE HO CL
30 MILLARD NOOK
31 COOKRIDGE DR
32 CROOKES BROOM AV
33 ST ANDREWS GR
34 TOLLESBY LA
35 MARTONGR
36 NUNTHORPE CL
37 LODGE CT
38 LEVERSTOCK GN
39 OAKLAND AV
40 KINSBOURNE GN
41 BROADLANDS CL

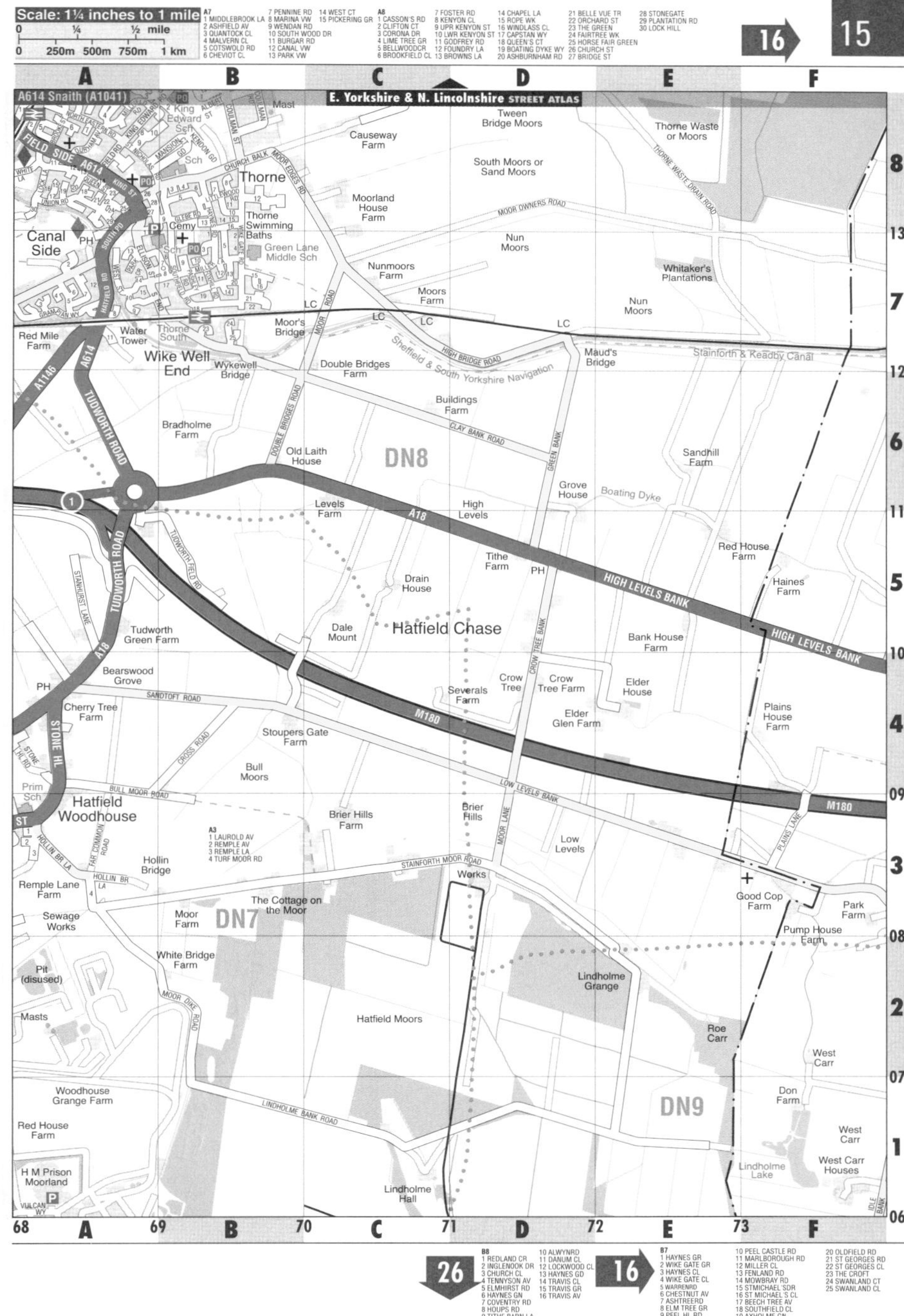

Scale: 1¼ inches to 1 mile
0 ¼ ½ mile
0 250m 500m 750m 1 km
A7
1 MIDDLEBROOK LA
2 ASHFIELD AV
3 QUANTOCK CL
4 MALVERN CL
5 COTSWOLD RD
6 CHEVIOT CL
7 PENNINE RD
8 MARINA VW
9 WENDAN RD
10 SOUTH WOOD DR
11 BURGAR RD
12 CANAL VW
13 PARK VW
14 WEST CT
15 PICKERING GR
A8
1 CASSON'S RD
2 CLIFTON CT
3 CORONA DR
4 LIME TREE GR
5 BELLWOODCR
6 BROOKFIELD CL
7 FOSTER RD
8 KENYON CL
9 UPR KENYON ST
10 LWR KENYON ST
11 GODFREY RD
12 FOUNDRY LA
13 BROWNS LA
14 CHAPEL LA
15 ROPE WK
16 WINDLASS CL
17 CAPSTAN WY
18 QUEEN'S CT
19 BOATING DYKE WY
20 ASHBURNHAM RD
21 BELLE VUE TR
22 ORCHARD ST
23 THE GREEN
24 FAIRTREE WK
25 HORSE FAIR GREEN
26 CHURCH ST
27 BRIDGE ST
28 STONEGATE
29 PLANTATION RD
30 LOCK HILL
16
15
A B C D E F
A614 Snaith (A1041)
E. Yorkshire & N. Lincolnshire STREET ATLAS
Mast
Tween Bridge Moors
Thorne Waste or Moors
Causeway Farm
South Moors or Sand Moors
King Edward Sch
Sch
Thorne
FIELD SIDE A614
KING ST
CHURCH BALK
MOOR EDGES RD
THORNE WASTE DRAIN ROAD
Moorland House Farm
MOOR OWNERS ROAD
8
Canal Side
PH
Cemy
Thorne Swimming Baths
Green Lane Middle Sch
Nun Moors
13
Nunmoors Farm
Whitaker's Plantations
Moors Farm
Nun Moors
7
LC
MOOR ROAD
Red Mile Farm
Water Tower
Thorne South
Moor's Bridge
LC
LC
LC
HIGH BRIDGE ROAD
Maud's Bridge
Stainforth & Keadby Canal
Wike Well End
Wykewell Bridge
Double Bridges Farm
Sheffield & South Yorkshire Navigation
12
A1146
A614
TUDWORTH ROAD
DOUBLE BRIDGES ROAD
Buildings Farm
Bradholme Farm
CLAY BANK ROAD
GREEN BANK
Sandhill Farm
Old Laith House
DN8
6
Grove House
Boating Dyke
1
Levels Farm
High Levels
A18
11
TUDWORTH FIELD RD
Tithe Farm
Red House Farm
STANHURST LANE
TUDWORTH ROAD
Drain House
PH
HIGH LEVELS BANK
Haines Farm
5
Tudworth Green Farm
Dale Mount
Hatfield Chase
Bank House Farm
HIGH LEVELS BANK
10
A18
CROW TREE BANK
Bearswood Grove
Crow Tree
Crow Tree Farm
Elder House
PH
SANDTOFT ROAD
Severals Farm
Cherry Tree Farm
M180
Elder Glen Farm
Plains House Farm
4
STONE HL
STONE HL RD
CROSS ROAD
Stoupers Gate Farm
Bull Moors
Prim Sch
BULL MOOR ROAD
LOW LEVELS BANK
Hatfield Woodhouse
Brier Hills Farm
Brier Hills
M180
09
ST
MOOR LANE
PLAINS LANE
A3
1 LAUROLD AV
2 REMPLE AV
3 REMPLE LA
4 TURF MOOR RD
Low Levels
FAR COMMON ROAD
HOLLIN BR LA
Hollin Bridge
STAINFORTH MOOR ROAD
3
Remple Lane Farm
HOLLIN BR LA
Works
Good Cop Farm
The Cottage on the Moor
Park Farm
Sewage Works
Moor Farm
DN7
Pump House Farm
08
Pit (disused)
White Bridge Farm
Lindholme Grange
MOOR DIKE ROAD
2
Masts
Hatfield Moors
Roe Carr
West Carr
07
Woodhouse Grange Farm
LINDHOLME BANK ROAD
Don Farm
DN9
Red House Farm
West Carr
1
Lindholme Lake
West Carr Houses
H M Prison Moorland
Lindholme Hall
VULCAN WY
IDLE BANK
06
68 A 69 B 70 C 71 D 72 E 73 F
26
B8
1 REDLAND CR
2 INGLENOOK DR
3 CHURCH CL
4 TENNYSON AV
5 ELMHIRST RD
6 HAYNES GN
7 COVENTRY RD
8 HOUPS RD
9 TITHE BARN LA
10 ALWYNRD
11 DANUM CL
12 LOCKWOOD CL
13 HAYNES GD
14 TRAVIS CL
15 TRAVIS GR
16 TRAVIS AV
16
B7
1 HAYNES GR
2 WIKE GATE GR
3 HAYNES CL
4 WIKE GATE CL
5 WARRENRD
6 CHESTNUT AV
7 ASHTREERD
8 ELM TREE GR
9 PEEL HL RD
10 PEEL CASTLE RD
11 MARLBOROUGH RD
12 MILLER CL
13 FENLAND RD
14 MOWBRAY RD
15 STMICHAEL'SDR
16 ST MICHAEL'S CL
17 BEECH TREE AV
18 SOUTHFIELD CL
19 AXHOLME GN
20 OLDFIELD RD
21 ST GEORGES RD
22 ST GEORGES CL
23 THE CROFT
24 SWANLAND CT
25 SWANLAND CL

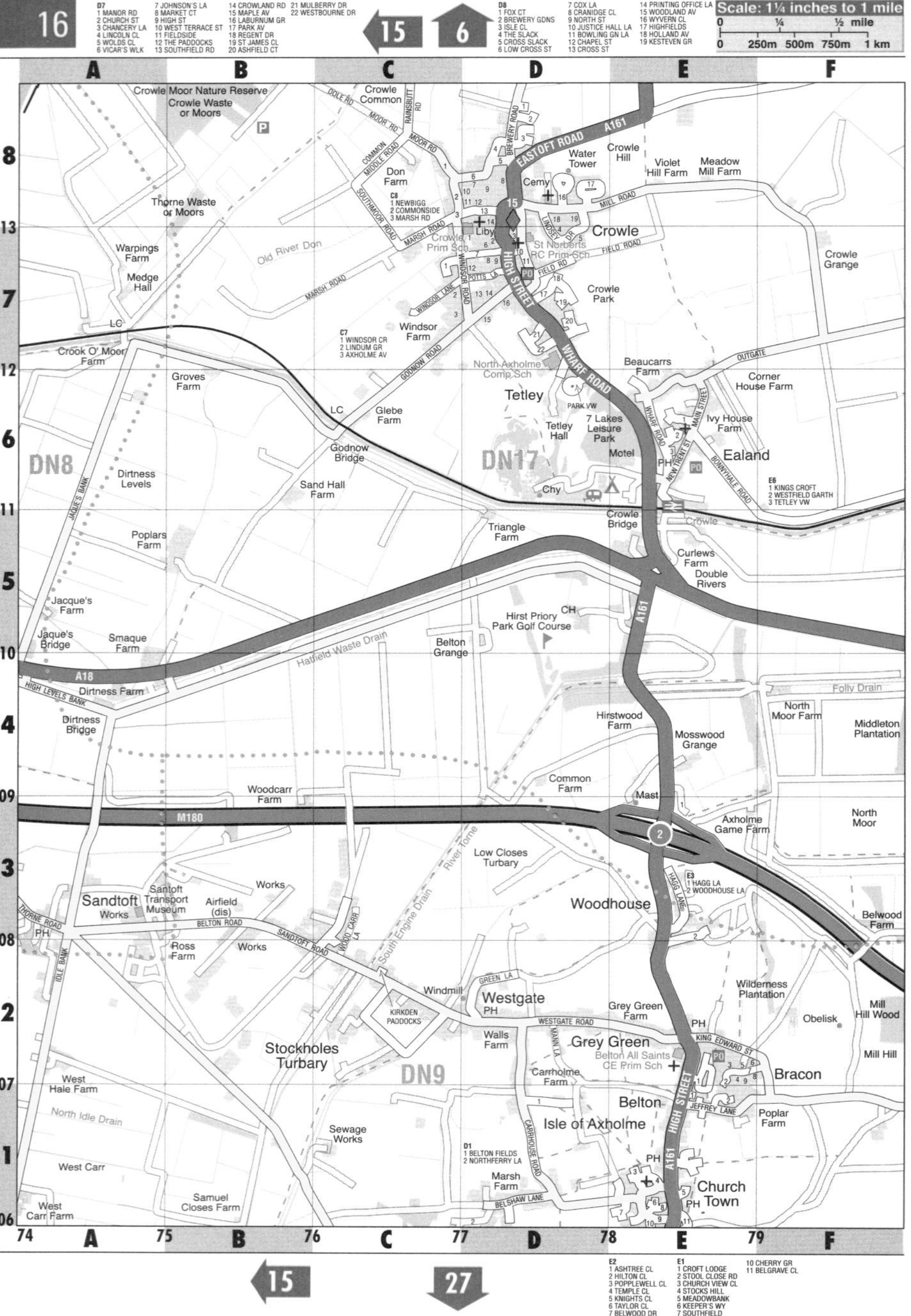
D7
1 MANOR RD
2 CHURCH ST
3 CHANCERY LA
4 LINCOLN CL
5 WOLDS CL
6 VICAR'S WLK
7 JOHNSON'S LA
8 MARKET CT
9 HIGH ST
10 WEST TERRACE ST
11 FIELDSIDE
12 THE PADDOCKS
13 SOUTHFIELD RD
14 CROWLAND RD
15 MAPLE AV
16 LABURNUM GR
17 PARK AV
18 REGENT DR
19 ST JAMES CL
20 ASHFIELD CT
21 MULBERRY DR
22 WESTBOURNE DR
15
6
D8
1 FOX CT
2 BREWERY GDNS
3 ISLE CL
4 THE SLACK
5 CROSS SLACK
6 LOW CROSS ST
7 COX LA
8 CRANIDGE CL
9 NORTH ST
10 JUSTICE HALL LA
11 BOWLING GN LA
12 CHAPEL ST
13 CROSS ST
14 PRINTING OFFICE LA
15 WOODLAND AV
16 WYVERN CL
17 HIGHFIELDS
18 HOLLAND AV
19 KESTEVEN GR
Scale: 1¼ inches to 1 mile
0 ¼ ½ mile
0 250m 500m 750m 1 km
A B C D E F
8 13 7 12 6 11 5 10 4 09 3 08 2 07 1 06
Crowle Moor Nature Reserve
Crowle Waste or Moors
Crowle Common
Thorne Waste or Moors
Warpings Farm
Medge Hall
Old River Don
Don Farm
C8
1 NEWBIGG
2 COMMONSIDE
3 MARSH RD
C7
1 WINDSOR CR
2 LINDUM GR
3 AXHOLME AV
Windsor Farm
Crook O' Moor Farm
Groves Farm
Glebe Farm
Godnow Bridge
DN8
Dirtness Levels
Sand Hall Farm
Poplars Farm
Jacque's Farm
Jaque's Bridge
Smaque Farm
Dirtness Farm
Dirtness Bridge
Hatfield Waste Drain
Belton Grange
Woodcarr Farm
M180
Low Closes Turbary
Sandtoft
Santoft Transport Museum
Airfield (dis)
Works
Ross Farm
Windmill
Westgate
Kirkden Paddocks
Stockholes Turbary
DN9
West Hale Farm
North Idle Drain
Sewage Works
West Carr
Samuel Closes Farm
West Carr Farm
D1
1 BELTON FIELDS
2 NORTHFERRY LA
Marsh Farm
Eastoft Road
A161
Water Tower
Crowle Hill
Violet Hill Farm
Meadow Mill Farm
Cemy
Mill Road
Crowle
Liby
Crowle Prim Sch
St Norberts RC Prim Sch
High Street
Crowle Park
Crowle Grange
North Axholme Comp Sch
Wharf Road
Tetley
Tetley Hall
7 Lakes Leisure Park
Motel
Park Vw
DN17
Beaucarrs Farm
Outgate
Corner House Farm
Ivy House Farm
Ealand
E6
1 KINGS CROFT
2 WESTFIELD GARTH
3 TETLEY VW
Chy
Crowle Bridge
Crowle
Triangle Farm
Curlews Farm
Double Rivers
A18
Hirst Priory Park Golf Course
Folly Drain
Hirstwood Farm
Mosswood Grange
North Moor Farm
Middleton Plantation
Common Farm
Mast
Axholme Game Farm
North Moor
E3
1 HAGG LA
2 WOODHOUSE LA
Woodhouse
Belwood Farm
Wilderness Plantation
Grey Green Farm
Grey Green
Belton All Saints CE Prim Sch
Westgate Road
Walls Farm
Carrholme Farm
Obelisk
Mill Hill Wood
Mill Hill
Bracon
Belton
Isle of Axholme
Poplar Farm
Church Town
74 75 76 77 78 79
15
27
E2
1 ASHTREE CL
2 HILTON CL
3 POPPLEWELL CL
4 TEMPLE CL
5 KNIGHTS CL
6 TAYLOR CL
7 BELWOOD DR
8 JOHNSON CL
9 BRACON CL
E1
1 CROFT LODGE
2 STOOL CLOSE RD
3 CHURCH VIEW CL
4 STOCKS HILL
5 MEADOWBANK
6 KEEPER'S WY
7 SOUTHFIELD
8 POACHER'S CRFT
9 CHURCHTOWN
10 CHERRY GR
11 BELGRAVE CL

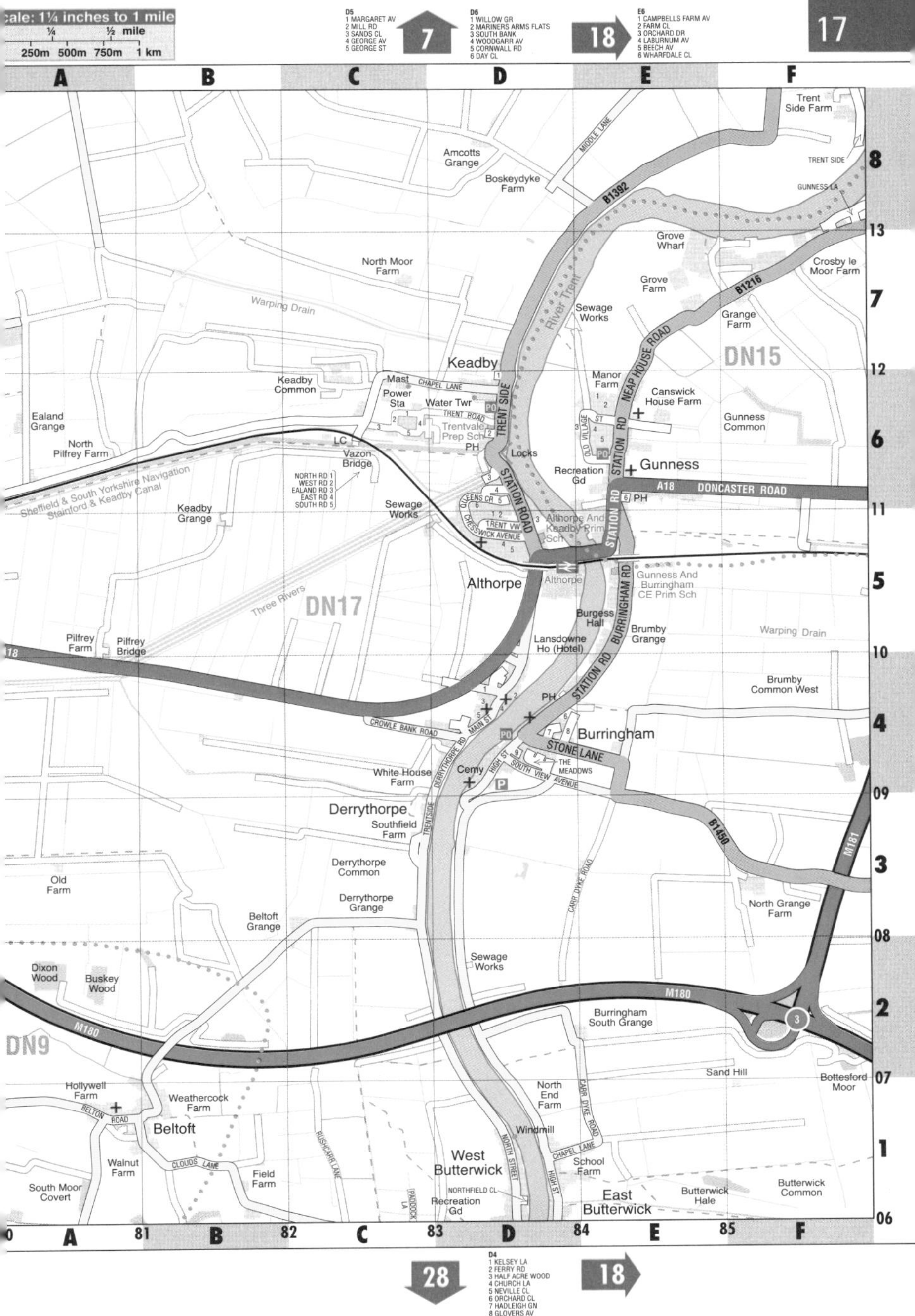

Scale: 1¼ inches to 1 mile
¼
½ mile
250m 500m 750m 1 km
D5
1 MARGARET AV
2 MILL RD
3 SANDS CL
4 GEORGE AV
5 GEORGE ST
7
D6
1 WILLOW GR
2 MARINERS ARMS FLATS
3 SOUTH BANK
4 WOODGARR AV
5 CORNWALL RD
6 DAY CL
18
E6
1 CAMPBELLS FARM AV
2 FARM CL
3 ORCHARD DR
4 LABURNUM AV
5 BEECH AV
6 WHARFDALE CL
A
B
C
D
E
F
8
13
7
12
6
11
5
10
4
09
3
08
2
07
1
06
Trent Side Farm
TRENT SIDE
GUNNESS LA
MIDDLE LANE
Amcotts Grange
Boskeydyke Farm
B1392
Grove Wharf
Crosby le Moor Farm
North Moor Farm
Grove Farm
B1216
River Trent
Sewage Works
Grange Farm
Warping Drain
NEAP HOUSE ROAD
DN15
Keadby
Keadby Common
Mast
CHAPEL LANE
Power Sta
Water Twr
TRENT ROAD
Trentvale Prep Sch
PH
TRENT SIDE
Manor Farm
Canswick House Farm
Gunness Common
Ealand Grange
North Pilfrey Farm
LC
Vazon Bridge
Locks
OLD VILLAGE ST
STATION RD
Gunness
Recreation Gd
NORTH RD 1
WEST RD 2
EALAND RD 3
EAST RD 4
SOUTH RD 5
Sheffield & South Yorkshire Navigation
Stainford & Keadby Canal
Keadby Grange
Sewage Works
QUEENS CR
STATION ROAD
A18
DOONCASTER ROAD
PH
TRENT VW
CHESSWICK AVENUE
Althorpe And Keadby Prim Sch
STATION RD
Althorpe
Gunness And Burringham CE Prim Sch
Althorpe
Three Rivers
DN17
Burgess Hall
BURRINGHAM RD
Brumby Grange
Warping Drain
Pilfrey Farm
Pilfrey Bridge
Lansdowne Ho (Hotel)
Brumby Common West
STATION RD
PH
CROWLE BANK ROAD
MAIN ST
Burringham
STONE LANE
THE MEADOWS
White House Farm
DERRYTHORPE RD
Cemy
HIGH ST
SOUTH VIEW AVENUE
Derrythorpe
Southfield Farm
TRENTSIDE
B1450
M181
Old Farm
Derrythorpe Common
CARR DYKE ROAD
Derrythorpe Grange
North Grange Farm
Beltoft Grange
Dixon Wood
Buskey Wood
Sewage Works
M180
Burringham South Grange
3
M180
DN9
Sand Hill
Bottesford Moor
Hollywell Farm
BELTON ROAD
Weathercock Farm
North End Farm
CARR DYKE ROAD
Beltoft
Windmill
NORTH STREET
CHAPEL LANE
Walnut Farm
CLOUDS LANE
RUSHCARR LANE
West Butterwick
School Farm
HIGH ST
South Moor Covert
Field Farm
NORTHFIELD CL
Recreation Gd
PADDOCK LA
East Butterwick
Butterwick Hale
Butterwick Common
80
81
82
83
84
85
28
18
D4
1 KELSEY LA
2 FERRY RD
3 HALF ACRE WOOD
4 CHURCH LA
5 NEVILLE CL
6 ORCHARD CL
7 HADLEIGH GN
8 GLOVERS AV
9 PASTURE AV

17
8

Scale: 1¼ inches to 1 mile

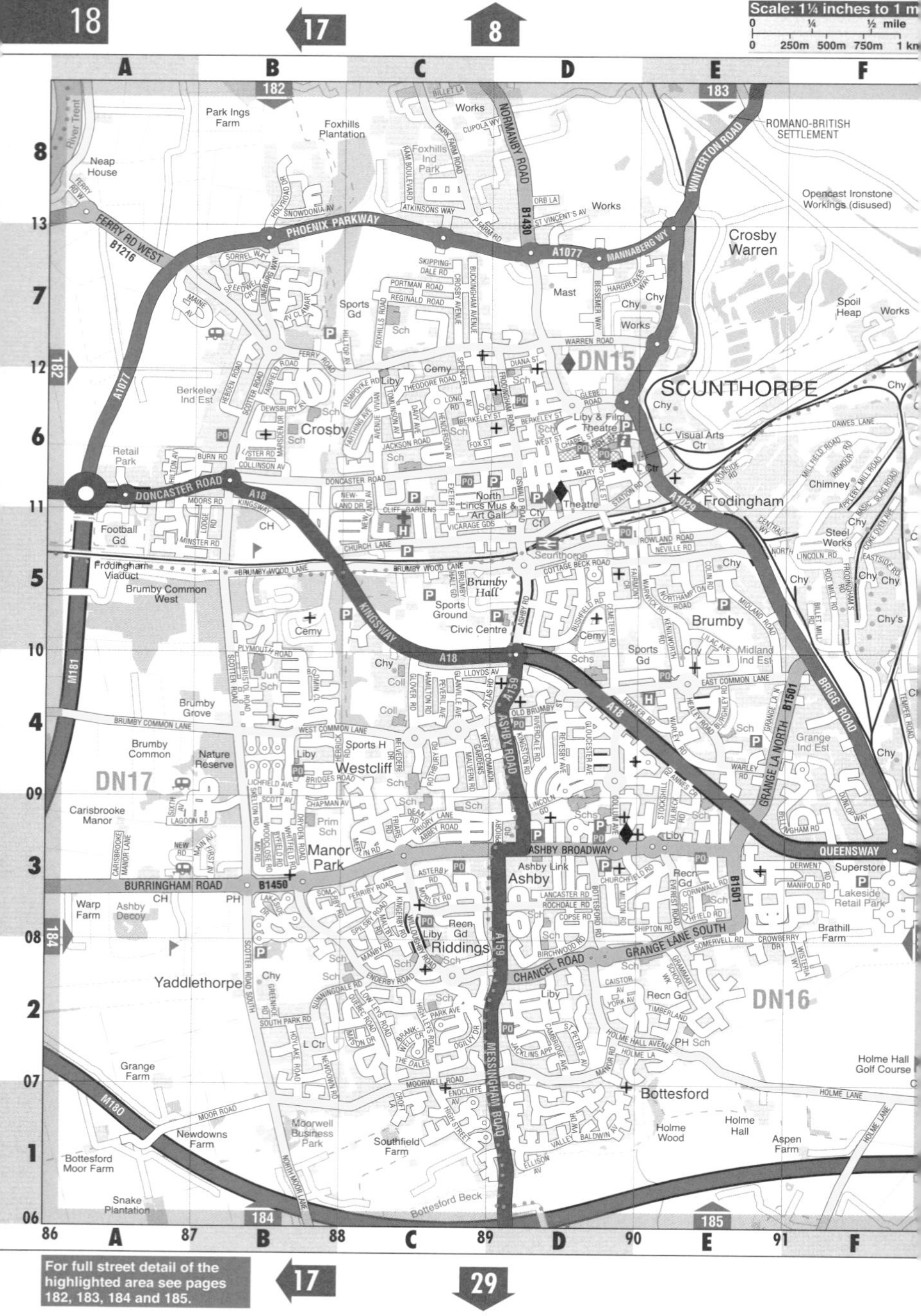

For full street detail of the highlighted area see pages 182, 183, 184 and 185.

17
29

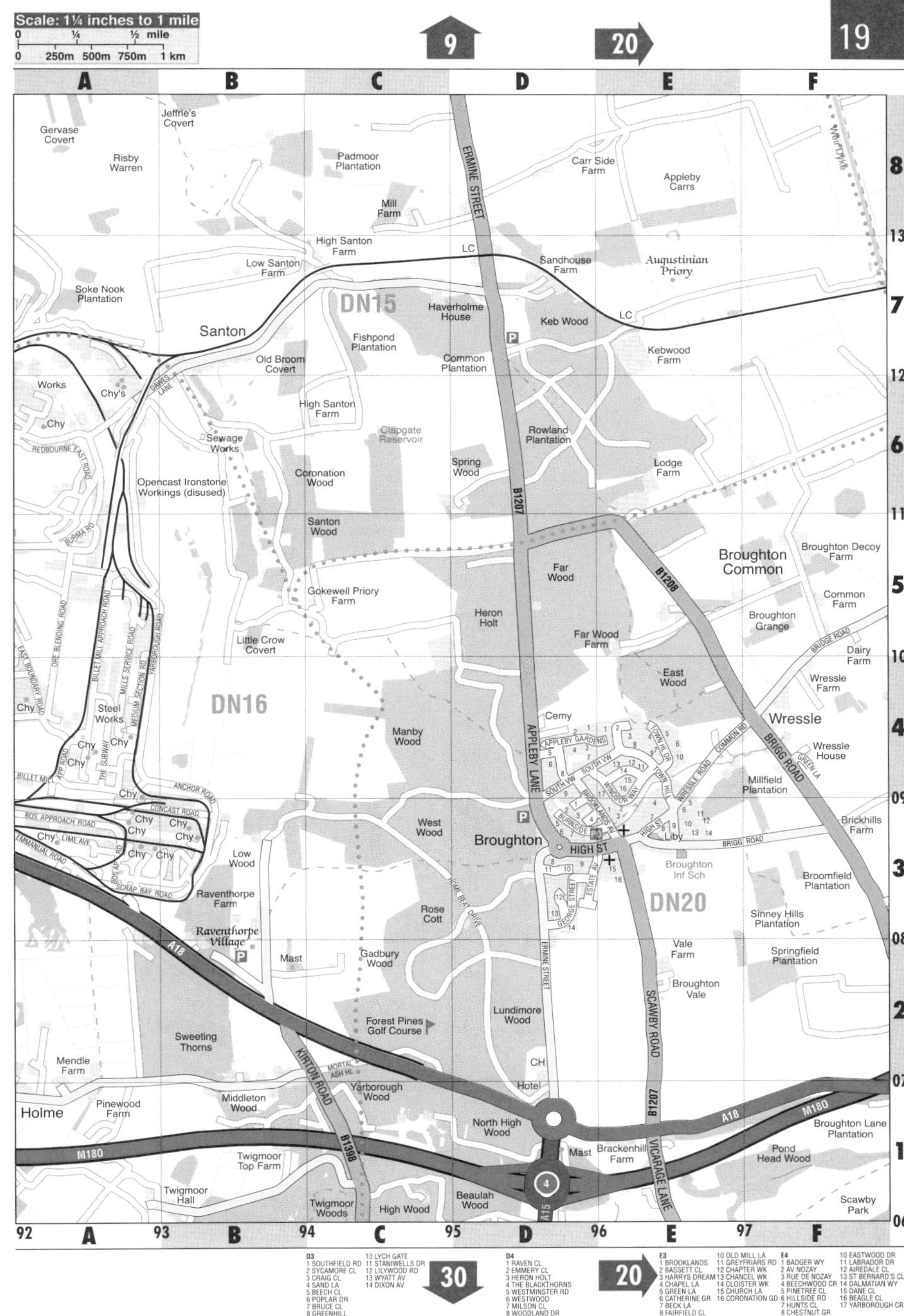

D3
1 SOUTHFIELD RD
2 SYCAMORE CL
3 CRAIG CL
4 SAND LA
5 BEECH CL
6 POPLAR DR
7 BRUCE CL
8 GREENHILL
9 STERNE AV
10 LYCH GATE
11 STANIWELLS DR
12 LILYWOOD RD
13 WYATT AV
14 DIXON AV

D4
1 RAVEN CL
2 EMMERY CL
3 HERON HOLT
4 THE BLACKTHORNS
5 WESTMINSTER RD
6 WESTWOOD
7 MILSON CL
8 WOODLAND DR
9 TRINITY CT

E3
1 BROOKLANDS
2 BASSETT CL
3 HARRYS DREAM
4 CHAPEL LA
5 GREEN LA
6 CATHERINE GR
7 BECK LA
8 FAIRFIELD CL
9 MILL LA
10 OLD MILL LA
11 GREYFRIARS RD
12 CHAPTER WK
13 CHANCEL WK
14 CLOISTER WK
15 CHURCH LA
16 CORONATION GD

E4
1 BADGER WY
2 AV NOZAY
3 RUE DE NOZAY
4 BEECHWOOD CR
5 PINETREE CL
6 HILLSIDE RD
7 HUNTS CL
8 CHESTNUT GR
9 SCHOOL HOUSES
10 EASTWOOD DR
11 LABRADOR DR
12 AIREDALE CL
13 ST BERNARD'S CL
14 DALMATIAN WY
15 DANE CL
16 BEAGLE CL
17 YARBOROUGH CR

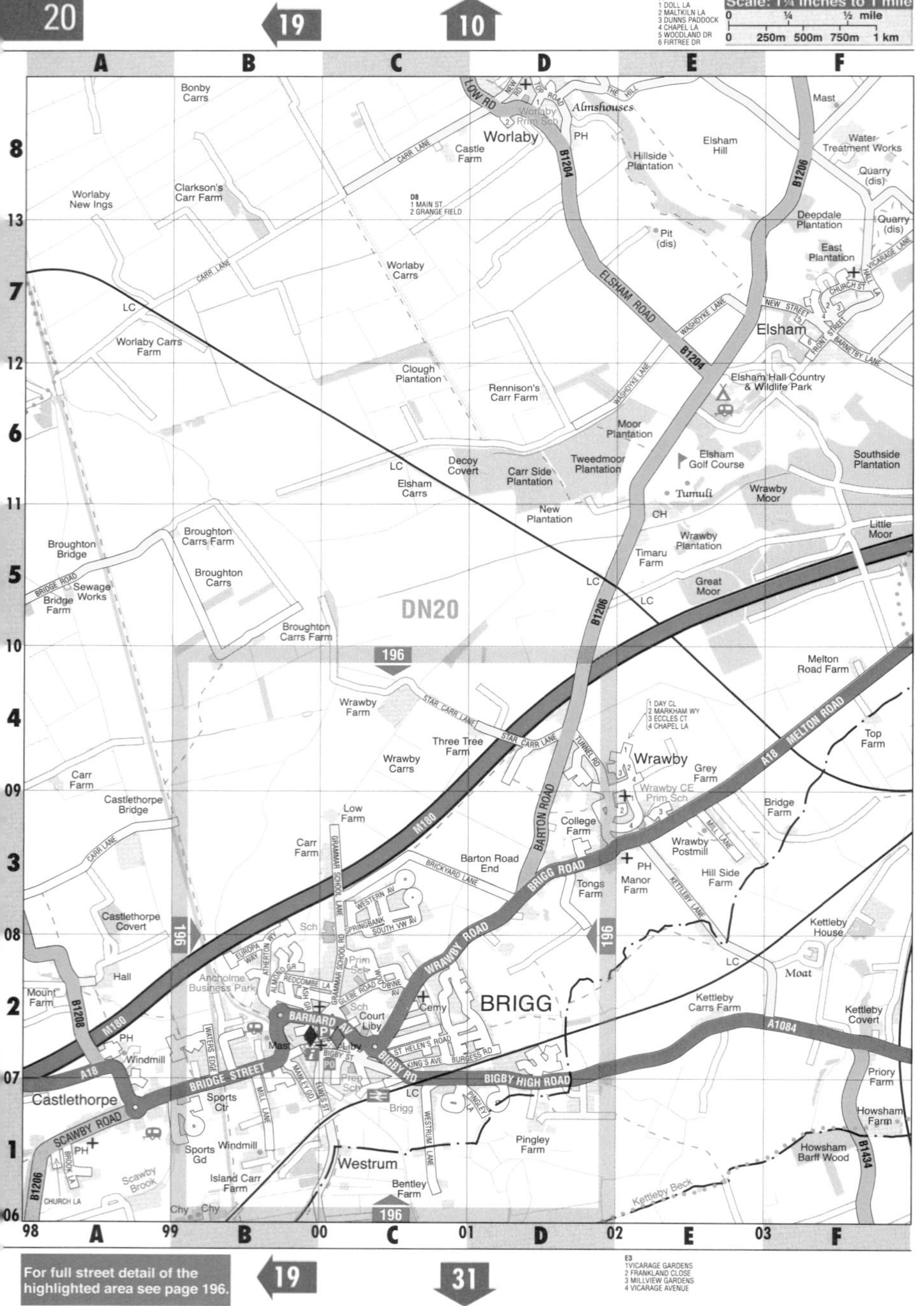

For full street detail of the highlighted area see page 196.

Scale: 1¼ inches to 1 mile
0 ¼ ½ mile
0 250m 500m 750m 1 km
11
22
A B C D E F
Elsham Wolds
Elsham Wold Ind Est
Viking Way
Long Close Plantations
DN39
Grange Farm
Marshall's Covert
A8
1 WELLINGTON WY
2 MERLIN DR
Quarry (dis)
Croxton Plantation
A15
A180
High Wood Farm
Croxton
DN20
Pit (dis)
Yarborough Camp
MIDDLEGATE LANE
Melton High Wood
Camp Covert
B1211
Quarry (dis)
CROXTON ROAD
Elsham Top
ROMAN SETTLEMENT (Site of)
FORTY FOOT LA
Moor Farm
Wrawby Moor
Melton Ross
Hall Farm
M180
A18
1 HILLSIDE CR
2 BAKERS CL
Melton Gallows
SCHIPHOL WY
Gallows Farm
Gallows Covert
Low Wood
WESTHOLME LA
Moat
LC
New Barnetby
Humberside International Airport
KING'S ROAD
WINDSOR WY
Stonecroft Farm
Coskills Farm
PH
BIRCH WY
RAILWAY STREET
Vale Farm
Hawthorn Farm
Thorntree Farm
PO
VICTORIA ROAD
Barnetby
SILVER ST
ST BARNABAS ROAD
DN38
St Barnabas CE Prim Sch
Windmill
Southfield Farm
WRAWBY JUNCTION
Sewage Works
Barnetby le Wold
MARSH LANE
WEST STREET
Gleadow Plantation
Glebe Farm
LC
Barnetby Wold Farm
Prospect Farm
Whitehall Farm
DN20
Bigby Top
Kettleby Thorpe Farm
Hendale Wood
Bigby
Low Farm
SMITHY LA
Somerby Top
SOMERBY WOLD LANE
Searby Top Farm
Bridge Farm
BIGBY HILL
Monument
SEARBY WOLD LANE
Somerby
LN7
Home Farm
Grange Farm
Viking Way
A1084
OWMBY WOLD LA
GRASBY WOLD LA
Dawson's Covert
8 13 7 12 6 11 5 10 4 09 3 08 2 07 1 06
04 A 05 B 06 C 07 D 08 E 09 F
B4
1 SYCAMORE CL
2 WOODLAND VW
3 FERNERIES LA
4 ST MARY'S AV
5 WALKER'S CL
6 CUTHBERT AV
7 SMITHY LA
8 OLD POST OFFICE LA
9 QUEEN'S RD
10 SOUTH ST
32
22

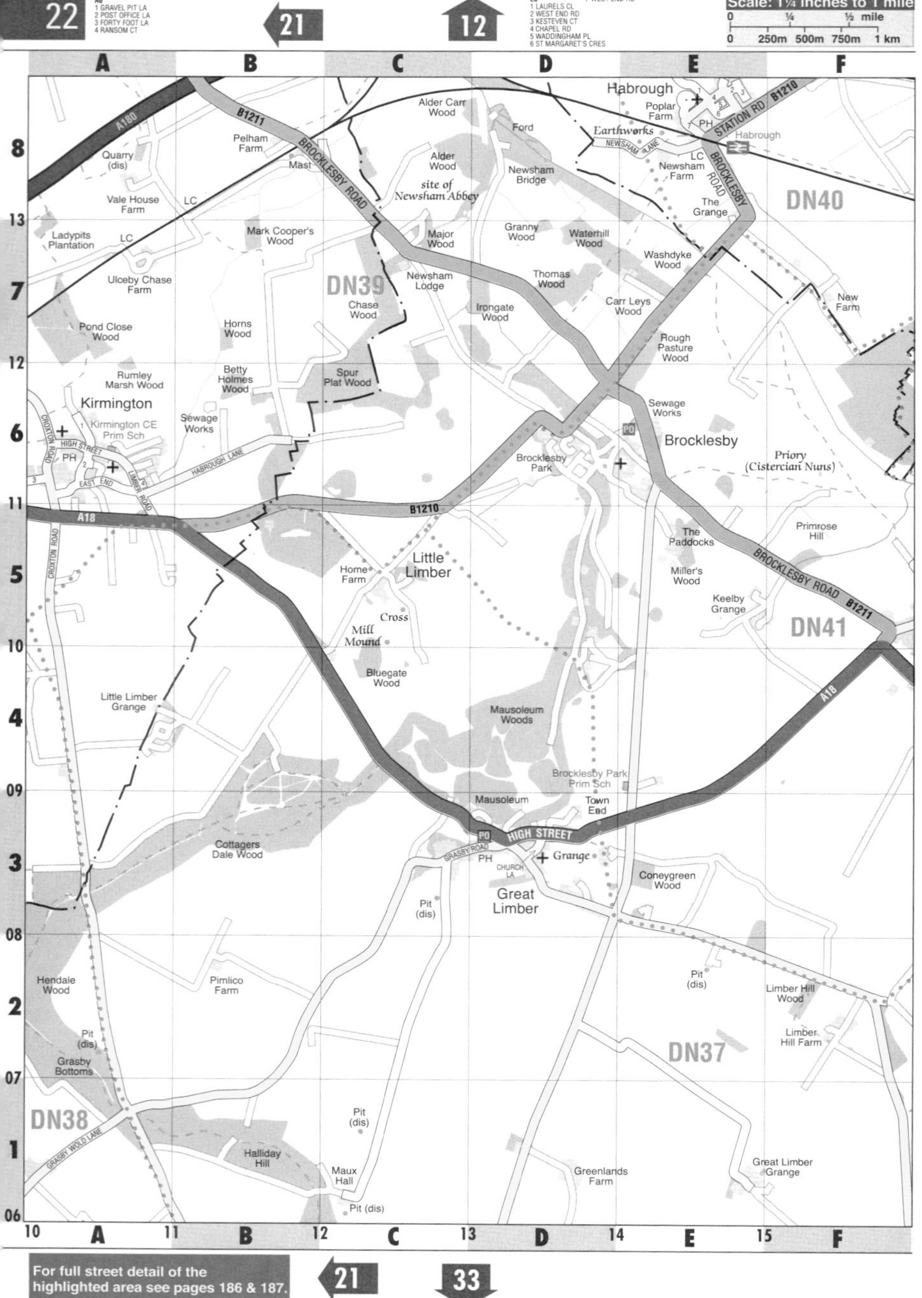
Habrough
Poplar Farm
Alder Carr Wood
Pelham Farm
Quarry (dis)
Mast
Alder Wood
site of Newsham Abbey
Ford
Earthworks
NEWSHAM LANE
Newsham Bridge
Newsham Farm
STATION RD
B1210
BROCKLESBY ROAD
B1211
A180
DN40
Vale House Farm
LC
The Grange
Ladypits Plantation
Mark Cooper's Wood
Major Wood
Granny Wood
Waterhill Wood
Washdyke Wood
Ulceby Chase Farm
DN39
Newsham Lodge
Thomas Wood
Carr Leys Wood
New Farm
Pond Close Wood
Horns Wood
Chase Wood
Irongate Wood
Rough Pasture Wood
Rumley Marsh Wood
Betty Holmes Wood
Spur Plat Wood
Kirmington
Kirmington CE Prim Sch
Sewage Works
Brocklesby
Priory (Cistercian Nuns)
HIGH STREET
CROXTON ROAD
LIMBER ROAD
EAST END
HABROUGH LANE
Brocklesby Park
A18
The Paddocks
Primrose Hill
Home Farm
Little Limber
Miller's Wood
Keelby Grange
Cross
Mill Mound
DN41
Bluegate Wood
Little Limber Grange
Mausoleum Woods
Brocklesby Park Prim Sch
Mausoleum
Town End
PO
PH
Cottagers Dale Wood
GRASBY ROAD
CHURCH LA
Grange
Coneygreen Wood
Great Limber
Pit (dis)
Hendale Wood
Pimlico Farm
Limber Hill Wood
Grasby Bottoms
Limber Hill Farm
DN37
DN38
GRASBY WOLD LANE
Halliday Hill
Maux Hall
Greenlands Farm
Great Limber Grange
A B C D E F
8 13 7 12 6 11 5 10 4 09 3 08 2 07 1 06
10 11 12 13 14 15

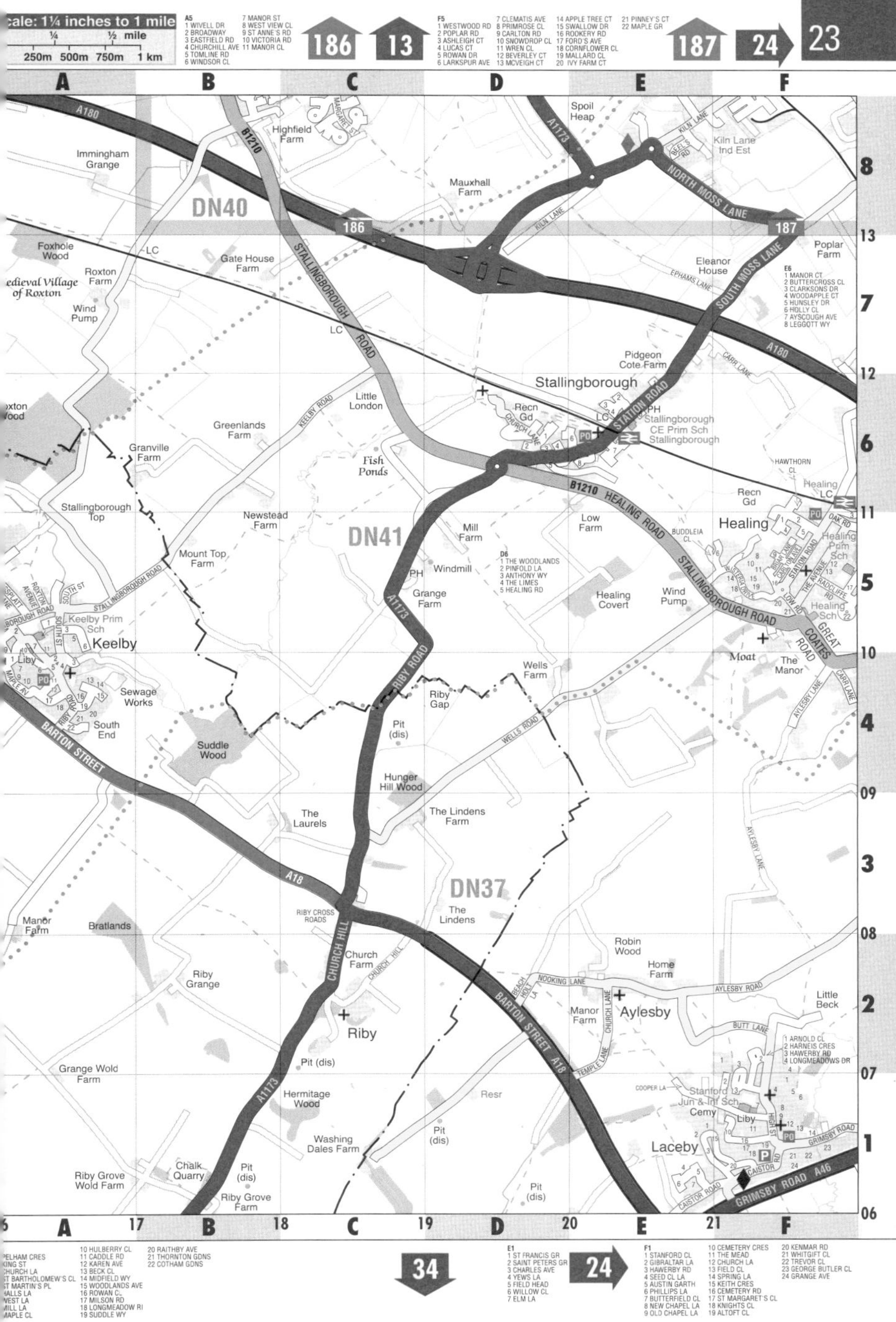
Scale: 1¼ inches to 1 mile
¼
½ mile
250m 500m 750m 1 km
A5
1 WIVELL DR
2 BROADWAY
3 EASTFIELD RD
4 CHURCHILL AVE
5 TOMLINE RD
6 WINDSOR CL
7 MANOR ST
8 WEST VIEW CL
9 ST ANNE'S RD
10 VICTORIA RD
11 MANOR CL
186
13
F5
1 WESTWOOD RD
2 POPLAR RD
3 ASHLEIGH CT
4 LUCAS CT
5 ROWAN DR
6 LARKSPUR AVE
7 CLEMATIS AVE
8 PRIMROSE CL
9 CARLTON RD
10 SNOWDROP CL
11 WREN CL
12 BEVERLEY CT
13 MCVEIGH CT
14 APPLE TREE CT
15 SWALLOW DR
16 ROOKERY RD
17 FORD'S AVE
18 CORNFLOWER CL
19 MALLARD CL
20 IVY FARM CT
21 PINNEY'S CT
22 MAPLE GR
187
24
A B C D E F
A180
B1210
Highfield Farm
Spoil Heap
A1173
KILN LANE
Kiln Lane Ind Est
Immingham Grange
NORTH MOSS LANE
Mauxhall Farm
DN40
186
187
13
Foxhole Wood
LC
Gate House Farm
Roxton Farm
Medieval Village of Roxton
Wind Pump
STALLINGBOROUGH ROAD
Eleanor House
EPHAMS LANE
Poplar Farm
SOUTH MOSS LANE
E6
1 MANOR CT
2 BUTTERCROSS CL
3 CLARKSONS DR
4 WOODAPPLE CT
5 HUNSLEY DR
6 HOLLY CL
7 AYSCOUGH AVE
8 LEGGOTT WY
7
Pidgeon Cote Farm
CARR LANE
A180
12
Stallingborough
Roxton Wood
Little London
KEELBY ROAD
Recn Gd
CHURCH LANE
STATION ROAD
PH
Stallingborough CE Prim Sch
Stallingborough
Greenlands Farm
Granville Farm
PO
6
Fish Ponds
HAWTHORN CL
B1210 HEALING ROAD
Healing
LC
Stallingborough Top
Newstead Farm
DN41
Mill Farm
Low Farm
Recn Gd
11
BUDDLEIA CL
Healing
OAK RD
Healing Prim Sch
Mount Top Farm
Windmill
PH
D6
1 THE WOODLANDS
2 PINFOLD LA
3 ANTHONY WY
4 THE LIMES
5 HEALING RD
STALLINGBOROUGH ROAD
STATION ROAD
THE AVENUE
RADCLIFFE RD
LOW RD
5
SOUTH ST
STALLINGBOROUGH ROAD
Grange Farm
A1173
Healing Covert
Wind Pump
Healing Sch
Keelby Prim Sch
Keelby
RIBY ROAD
GREAT COATES ROAD
10
Moat
The Manor
Wells Farm
CARR LANE
Sewage Works
Riby Gap
AYLESBY LANE
South End
Pit (dis)
WELLS ROAD
4
BARTON STREET
Suddle Wood
Hunger Hill Wood
09
The Laurels
The Lindens Farm
AYLESBY LANE
3
A18
DN37
RIBY CROSS ROADS
The Lindens
Manor Farm
Bratlands
08
Robin Wood
Home Farm
CHURCH HILL
Church Farm
Riby Grange
BEACH HOLT LA
NOOKING LANE
AYLESBY ROAD
Little Beck
2
Manor Farm
CHURCH LANE
Aylesby
BARTON STREET
Riby
BUTT LANE
1 ARNOLD CL
2 HARNEIS CRES
3 HAWERBY RD
4 LONGMEADOWS DR
Pit (dis)
Grange Wold Farm
TEMPLE LANE
07
A1173
Hermitage Wood
Resr
COOPER LA
Stanford Jun & Inf Sch
Cemy
Liby
HIGH ST
A18
Pit (dis)
Washing Dales Farm
1
PO
GRIMSBY ROAD
Laceby
P
CAISTOR RD
Chalk Quarry
Pit (dis)
Riby Grove Wold Farm
Riby Grove Farm
Pit (dis)
CAISTOR ROAD
GRIMSBY ROAD A46
06
16 A 17 B 18 C 19 D 20 E 21 F
PELHAM CRES
KING ST
CHURCH LA
ST BARTHOLOMEW'S CL
ST MARTIN'S PL
HALLS LA
WEST LA
MILL LA
MAPLE CL
10 HULBERRY CL
11 CADDLE RD
12 KAREN AVE
13 BECK CL
14 MIDFIELD WY
15 WOODLANDS AVE
16 ROWAN CL
17 MILSON RD
18 LONGMEADOW RI
19 SUDDLE WY
20 RAITHBY AVE
21 THORNTON GDNS
22 COTHAM GDNS
34
E1
1 ST FRANCIS GR
2 SAINT PETERS GR
3 CHARLES AVE
4 YEWS LA
5 FIELD HEAD
6 WILLOW CL
7 ELM LA
24
F1
1 STANFORD CL
2 GIBRALTAR LA
3 HAWERBY RD
4 SEED CL LA
5 AUSTIN GARTH
6 PHILLIPS LA
7 BUTTERFIELD CL
8 NEW CHAPEL LA
9 OLD CHAPEL LA
10 CEMETERY CRES
11 THE MEAD
12 CHURCH LA
13 FIELD CL
14 SPRING LA
15 KEITH CRES
16 CEMETERY RD
17 ST MARGARET'S CL
18 KNIGHTS CL
19 ALTOFT CL
20 KENMAR RD
21 WHITGIFT CL
22 TREVOR CL
23 GEORGE BUTLER CL
24 GRANGE AVE

A5
1 OAK RD
2 MEADOW DR
3 NICHOLSON RD
4 PINE WK
5 CHESTNUT WK
6 LINDSEY DR
7 RADCLIFFE RD
8 ELM GR

23

Scale: 1¼ inches to 1 mile

For full street detail of the highlighted areas see pages 187, 188, 190 & 191.

23 194 35

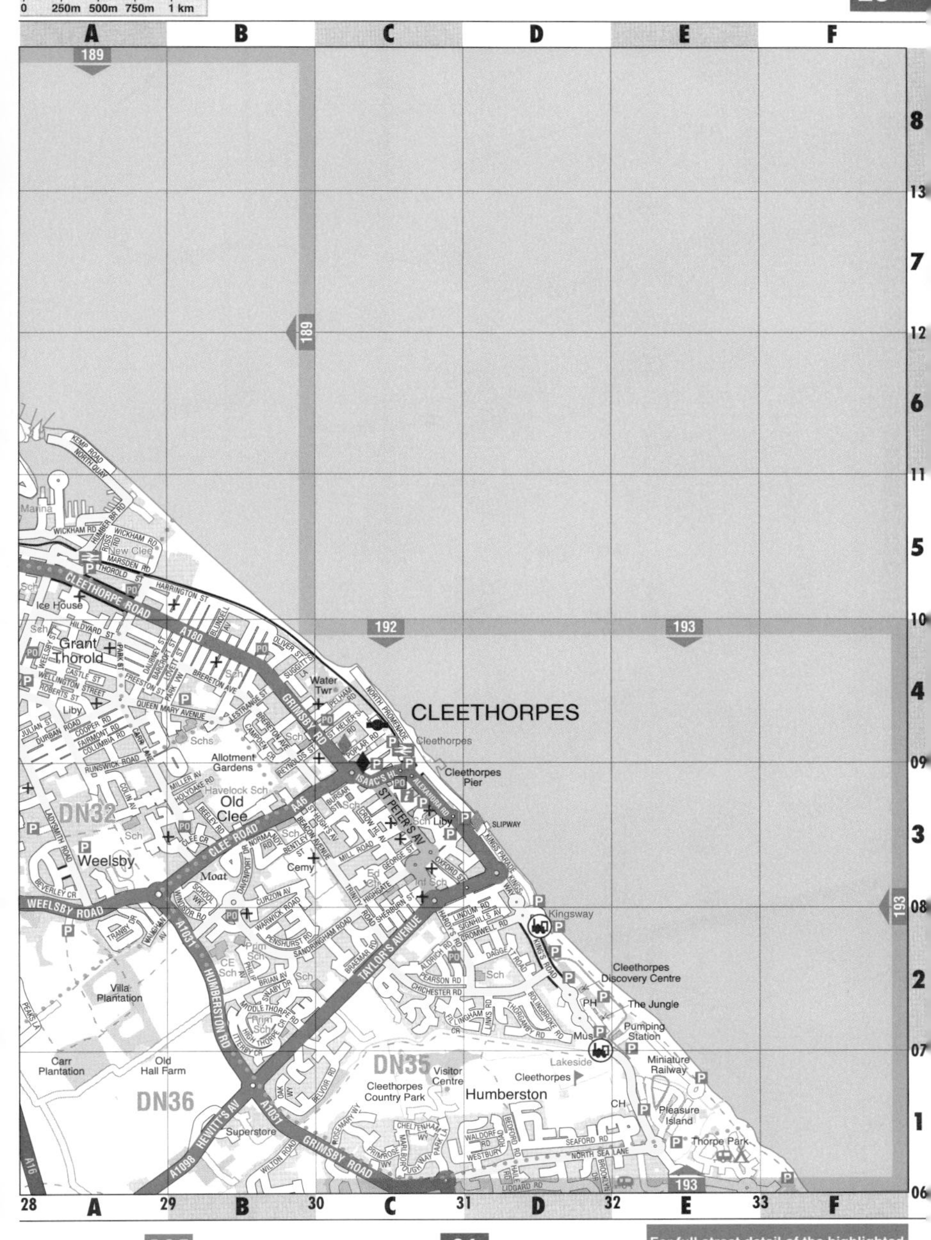

For full street detail of the highlighted areas see pages 189, 192 & 193.

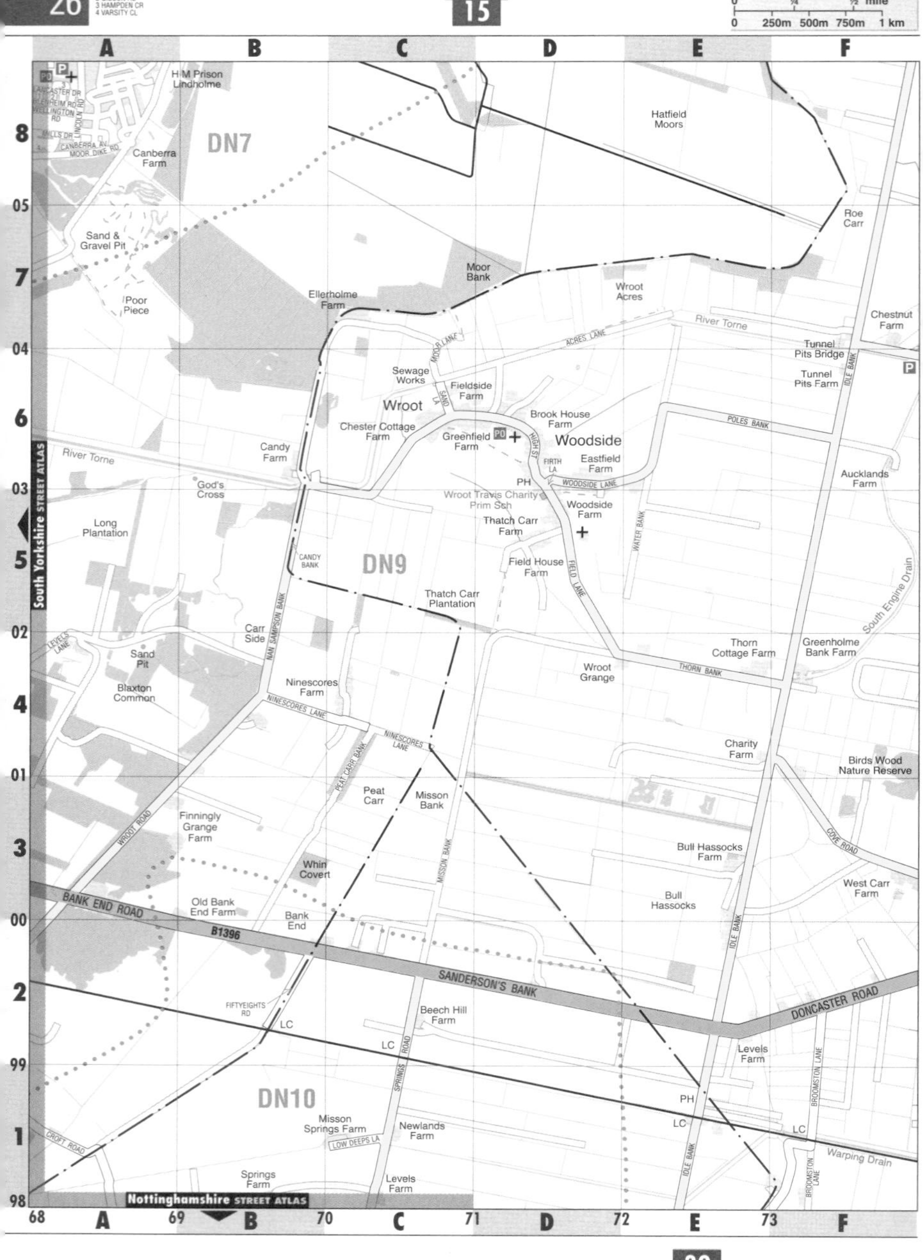
H M Prison Lindholme
DN7
Canberra Farm
Hatfield Moors
Roe Carr
Sand & Gravel Pit
Moor Bank
Ellerholme Farm
Poor Piece
Wroot Acres
River Torne
Chestnut Farm
ACRES LANE
Tunnel Pits Bridge
Sewage Works
Tunnel Pits Farm
Fieldside Farm
Wroot
Brook House Farm
POLES BANK
Chester Cottage Farm
Greenfield Farm
Woodside
Candy Farm
Eastfield Farm
River Torne
FIRTH LA
WOODSIDE LANE
Aucklands Farm
God's Cross
PH
Wroot Travis Charity Prim Sch
Long Plantation
Thatch Carr Farm
Woodside Farm
WATER BANK
CANDY BANK
DN9
Field House Farm
South Engine Drain
Thatch Carr Plantation
FIELD LANE
Carr Side
NAN SAMPSON BANK
Sand Pit
Thorn Cottage Farm
Greenholme Bank Farm
THORN BANK
Wroot Grange
Ninescores Farm
Blaxton Common
NINESCORES LANE
Charity Farm
Birds Wood Nature Reserve
PEAT CARR BANK
Peat Carr
Misson Bank
WROOT ROAD
Finningly Grange Farm
Bull Hassocks Farm
COVE ROAD
Whin Covert
MISSON BANK
West Carr Farm
BANK END ROAD
Old Bank End Farm
Bank End
Bull Hassocks
B1396
SANDERSON'S BANK
IDLE BANK
DONCASTER ROAD
FIFTYEIGHTS RD
LC
Beech Hill Farm
Levels Farm
SPRINGS ROAD
BROOMSTON LANE
DN10
PH
Misson Springs Farm
Newlands Farm
LC
CROFT ROAD
LOW DEEPS LA
Warping Drain
Springs Farm
Levels Farm
BROOMSTON LANE
South Yorkshire STREET ATLAS
Nottinghamshire STREET ATLAS

cale: 1¼ inches to 1 mile
¼
½ mile
250m 500m 750m 1 km
D7
1 SHEPHERD'S CFT
2 FERNBANK
3 FIELDS CL
4 ORCHARD CFT
5 TOTTERMIRE LA
6 SWALLOW CT
7 NICHOLSON WY
8 CORONATION CR
E6
1 CHURCH ST
2 MARKET PL
3 VINEGARTH
4 WESLEY CL
5 MOORLAND WY
6 CHAPEL ST
16
7 MANOR CT RD
8 ALBION HL
9 FAIRFIELD CFT
10 FERN CFT
11 GREEN GATE
12 LINDSEY CT
13 POPPLEWELL TR
28
14 ROOKERY CFT
15 PINFOLD
16 WOODLAND WY
17 NEWLAND VW
18 MELWOOD VW
19 HARVESTER CL
20 REAPER'S RI
21 CHERRY OR
22 SOUTH FURLONG CFT
23 MOWBRAY CT
A
B
C
D
E
F
8
05
7
04
6
03
5
02
4
01
3
00
2
99
1
98
Nature Reserve
Belton Brickworks
Belgraves Wood
Scawcett Farm
Folly Drain
Northcroft Farm
Ellers Cottage
Holly Tree Farm
A161
Lawns Farm
Bridge Farm
West End Farm
WEST END ROAD
Hill Top
Kelfield Catchwater
Ninevah Farm
Water Tower
Works
Windmill
BELTON ROAD
Sandhill Farm
Mill Farm
STATION ROAD
Windmill
D6
1 MANLEY CT
2 STANFIELD RD
3 CORONATION CR
4 PEAR TREE CL
5 MORFIELD GR
6 AXHOLME DR
7 THE LIDGETT
8 BIRCHFIELD RD
9 GUISEFIELD RD
10 SOUTHFIELD DR
11 MASSEY CL
ST ANDREW'S WY
Epworth
CASTLE DR
PH
BATTLE GN
FIELDSIDE
TUDCROSS
CARRSIDE
HIGH ST
Heritage Ctr
PO
HOLLINGSWORTH LA
LOCKWOOD BANK
WHEATFIELD CL
EASTFIELD RD
MELWOOD CL
QUEEN ST
Epworth Turbary Nature Reserve
Epworth Cty Prim Sch
South Axholme Com Sch
Liby
MOWBRAY ST
RECTORY ST
BLOW ROW
Dykedales Farm
Willow Farm
TURBARY ROAD
Holmes Farm
Turbary Farm
Epworth Turbary
Lone Oak Farm
Epworth L Ctr
Windmill
The Old Rectory
Skyers Farm
Cemy
White House Farm
MELWOOD HILL
BURNHAM ROAD
Harvester Farm
DN9
Walnut Farm
Kimber Farm
Low Burnham
High Melwood
Greenholme Bank
Tethers End
Holy Well
Field Side
Laburnham Farm
Cherry Fell
Starkey Farm
Haxey Turbary Nature Reserve
Haxey Carr
Axholme Line Nature Reserve
Poplar Farm
Skyers Farm
Star Carr
Summercroft Farm
Windmill
High Burnham
Field Farm
Haslams Farm
North Carr
Cliff Hill
Shawfield Farm
C2
1 HOLME DENE
2 NORTHSIDE
3 VINEHALL RD
EPWORTH ROAD
Park Farm
Nature Reserve
TURBARY ROAD
Rush Furlong Nature Reserve
Low Hall Farm
THE NOOKING
Mill House Farm
Upperthorpe
Westlake Farm
Poplar Farm
Haxey CE Prim Sch
Eastmoor Villas
Stonecrop Farm
Oaklands Farm
UPPERTHORPE HILL
CROSS HILL
Cross
BLACKMOOR RD
GOLLANDS LA
MILL LANE
Tower Hill
PARK LANE
THE MEADOWS
COMMON SIDE
PH
CHURCH
ST
HIGH ST
Wakefield Farm
FIELDS RD
BRACKENHILL ROAD
EAST LOUND ROAD
LOW ST
NEWBIGG
BRETHERGATE
TOWER HILL
CHURCH LA
Haxey
PO
Sedge Hole Close Nature Reserve
Westwoodside CE Prim Sch
Water Twr
Windmill
PH
Cross
East Lound
Lime Tree Farm
Carr House
B1396
Monkham Bridge Farm
Westwoodside
NETHERGATE
SANBEDS LA
GREENHILL RD
A161
GRAIZELOUND FIELDS ROAD
CARR LANE
HOLM RD
Close Farm
Sandbeds Farm
Croft House
THINHOLME LANE
Hound Farm
HAXEY LANE
LANGHOLME LANE
AKEFERRY ROAD
Chapel Farm
Langholme Farm
Graiselound
FERRY RD
Owston Grange
OWSTON FERRY ROAD
Pear Tree Farm
Sewage Works
STOCKWITH ROAD
STATION ROAD
PH
Pond Farm
Scotton Common Nature Reserve
Thurnholmes Farm
LC
4
A
75
B
76
C
77
D
78
E
79
F
A2
1 WESTMORELAND CL
2 AXHOLME RD
3 WEIR CL
4 THE ROWANS
5 COLLEYWELL CL
6 PK DR
7 PARK CL
8 THE BIRCHES
9 MOORLANDS
10 DREWRY LA
11 WEAVERS CFT
39
B2
1 TAVELLA CT
2 CHAPEL CL
3 CRAYCROFT RD
4 HIGHFIELD CR
5 WESTLAND RD
D2
1 HALLCROFT RD
2 MARLBOROUGH AV
3 LOWCROFT AV
4 LOWCROFT CL
5 ASH TREE DR
6 HAYFIELD CL
7 GRANARY CFT
8 REAPER'S WY
9 HAXEY GR
10 THE GOLDINGS
11 HOPGARTH
D3
1 HUNTER'S CFT
2 SADDLER'S WY
3 MOWBRAY CL
40
28

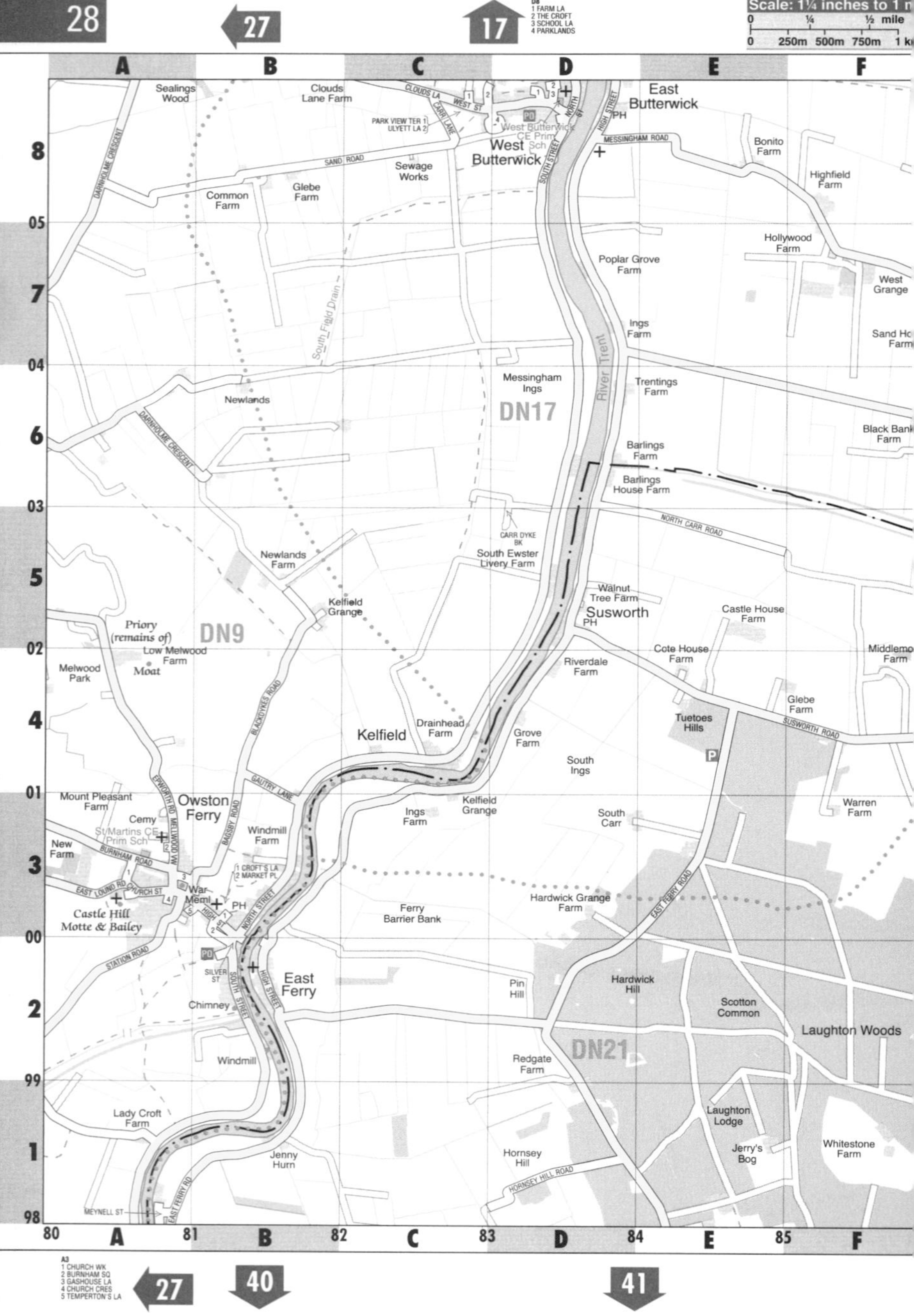
Scale: 1¼ inches to 1 mile
0 ¼ ½ mile
0 250m 500m 750m 1 km
A B C D E F
Sealings Wood
Clouds Lane Farm
CLOUDS LA
WEST ST
CARR LANE
PARK VIEW TER 1
ULYETT LA 2
West Butterwick CE Prim Sch
West Butterwick
East Butterwick
PH
HIGH STREET
NORTH ST
SOUTH STREET
MESSINGHAM ROAD
Bonito Farm
Highfield Farm
DARNHOLME CRESCENT
SAND ROAD
Sewage Works
Common Farm
Glebe Farm
Hollywood Farm
Poplar Grove Farm
West Grange
South Field Drain
Ings Farm
Sand Ho Farm
River Trent
Messingham Ings
Newlands
Trentings Farm
DN17
Black Bank Farm
Barlings Farm
Barlings House Farm
NORTH CARR ROAD
CARR DYKE BK
South Ewster Livery Farm
Newlands Farm
Kelfield Grange
Walnut Tree Farm
Susworth
Castle House Farm
Priory (remains of)
DN9
Low Melwood Farm
Moat
Melwood Park
Riverdale Farm
Cote House Farm
Middlemoor Farm
BLACKDYKES ROAD
Glebe Farm
Kelfield
Drainhead Farm
Grove Farm
Tuetoes Hills
SUSWORTH ROAD
South Ings
GAUTRY LANE
EPWORTH RD
MELWOOD VW
Mount Pleasant Farm
Owston Ferry
BAGSBY ROAD
Ings Farm
Kelfield Grange
South Carr
Warren Farm
Cemy
St Martins CE Prim Sch
Windmill Farm
New Farm
BURNHAM ROAD
1 CROFT'S LA
2 MARKET PL
EAST LOUND RD
CHURCH ST
War Meml
PH
HIGH ST
NORTH STREET
Hardwick Grange Farm
EAST FERRY ROAD
Castle Hill Motte & Bailey
Ferry Barrier Bank
STATION ROAD
SILVER ST
SOUTH STREET
HIGH STREET
East Ferry
Pin Hill
Hardwick Hill
Chimney
Scotton Common
Laughton Woods
Windmill
Redgate Farm
DN21
Lady Croft Farm
Laughton Lodge
Whitestone Farm
Jerry's Bog
Jenny Hurn
Hornsey Hill
HORNSEY HILL ROAD
EAST FERRY RD
MEYNELL ST
8
05
7
04
6
03
5
02
4
01
3
00
2
99
1
98
80
81
82
83
84
85

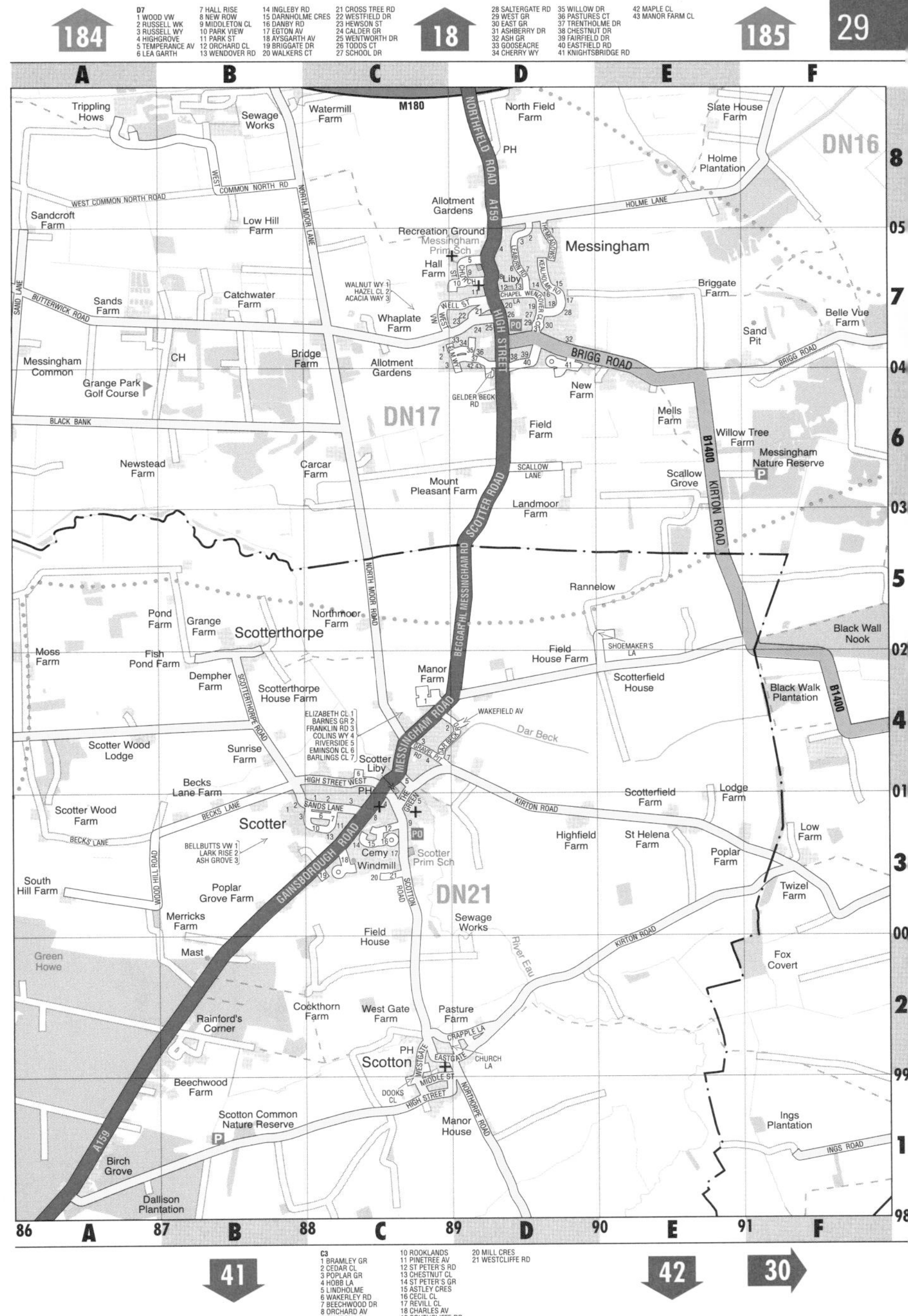

184
D7
1 WOOD VW
2 RUSSELL WK
3 RUSSELL WY
4 HIGHGROVE
5 TEMPERANCE AV
6 LEA GARTH
7 HALL RISE
8 NEW ROW
9 MIDDLETON CL
10 PARK VIEW
11 PARK ST
12 ORCHARD CL
13 WENDOVER RD
14 INGLEBY RD
15 DARNHOLME CRES
16 DANBY RD
17 EGTON AV
18 AYSGARTH AV
19 BRIGGATE DR
20 WALKERS CT
21 CROSS TREE RD
22 WESTFIELD DR
23 HEWSON ST
24 CALDER GR
25 WENTWORTH DR
26 TODDS CT
27 SCHOOL DR
18
28 SALTERGATE RD
29 WEST GR
30 EAST GR
31 ASHBERRY DR
32 ASH GR
33 GOOSEACRE
34 CHERRY WY
35 WILLOW DR
36 PASTURES CT
37 TRENTHOLME DR
38 CHESTNUT DR
39 FAIRFIELD DR
40 EASTFIELD RD
41 KNIGHTSBRIDGE RD
42 MAPLE CL
43 MANOR FARM CL
185
29
A B C D E F
Trippling Hows
Sewage Works
Watermill Farm
M180
North Field Farm
Slate House Farm
DN16
PH
Holme Plantation
8
WEST COMMON NORTH RD
NORTH MOOR LANE
NORTHFIELD ROAD
A159
Sandcroft Farm
Low Hill Farm
Allotment Gardens
HOLME LANE
Recreation Ground
Messingham Prim Sch
Messingham
05
Hall Farm
Liby
WALNUT WY 1
HAZEL CL 2
ACACIA WAY 3
Briggate Farm
Sand Lane
Butterwick Road
Sands Farm
Catchwater Farm
Whaplate Farm
WELL ST
CHAPEL LA
7
Belle Vue Farm
Sand Pit
HIGH STREET
PO
BRIGG ROAD
Messingham Common
CH
Bridge Farm
Allotment Gardens
04
Grange Park Golf Course
GELDER BECK RD
New Farm
Mells Farm
BLACK BANK
DN17
Field Farm
Willow Tree Farm
B1400
6
Messingham Nature Reserve
Newstead Farm
Carcar Farm
SCALLOW LANE
Mount Pleasant Farm
Scallow Grove
P
SCOTTER ROAD
KIRTON ROAD
Landmoor Farm
03
NORTH MOOR ROAD
BEGGAR HL MESSINGHAM RD
Rannelow
5
Pond Farm
Grange Farm
Scotterthorpe
Northmoor Farm
Black Wall Nook
Moss Farm
Fish Pond Farm
Field House Farm
SHOEMAKER'S LA
02
Dempher Farm
SCOTTERTHORPE ROAD
Manor Farm
Scotterfield House
Scotterthorpe House Farm
Black Walk Plantation
ELIZABETH CL 1
BARNES GR 2
FRANKLIN RD 3
COLINS WY 4
RIVERSIDE 5
EMINSON CL 6
BARLINGS CL 7
WAKEFIELD AV
MESSINGHAM ROAD
Dar Beck
4
Scotter Wood Lodge
Sunrise Farm
GRAVEL PIT RD
Scotter Liby
HIGH STREET WEST
Becks Lane Farm
PH
THE GREEN
Scotterfield Farm
Lodge Farm
01
SANDS LANE
KIRTON ROAD
Scotter Wood Farm
Scotter
BECKS LANE
BELLBUTTS VW 1
LARK RISE 2
ASH GROVE 3
PO
Highfield Farm
St Helena Farm
Low Farm
Cemy
Scotter Prim Sch
Poplar Farm
WOOD HILL ROAD
Windmill
3
South Hill Farm
GAINSBOROUGH ROAD
SCOTTON ROAD
DN21
Poplar Grove Farm
Twizel Farm
Merricks Farm
Sewage Works
Field House
00
KIRTON ROAD
River Eau
Green Howe
Mast
Fox Covert
2
Rainford's Corner
Cockthorn Farm
West Gate Farm
Pasture Farm
CRAPPLE LA
PH
Scotton
WESTGATE
EASTGATE
CHURCH LA
99
Beechwood Farm
MIDDLE ST
DOOKS CL
HIGH STREET
NORTHORPE ROAD
Scotton Common Nature Reserve
Manor House
Ings Plantation
P
1
INGS ROAD
Birch Grove
A159
Dallison Plantation
98
86 A 87 B 88 C 89 D 90 E 91 F
41
C3
1 BRAMLEY GR
2 CEDAR CL
3 POPLAR GR
4 HOBB LA
5 LINDHOLME
6 WAKERLEY RD
7 BEECHWOOD DR
8 ORCHARD AV
9 CHURCH LA
10 ROOKLANDS
11 PINETREE AV
12 ST PETER'S RD
13 CHESTNUT CL
14 ST PETER'S GR
15 ASTLEY CRES
16 CECIL CL
17 REVILL CL
18 CHARLES AV
19 SOUTHCLIFFE RD
20 MILL CRES
21 WESTCLIFFE RD
42
30

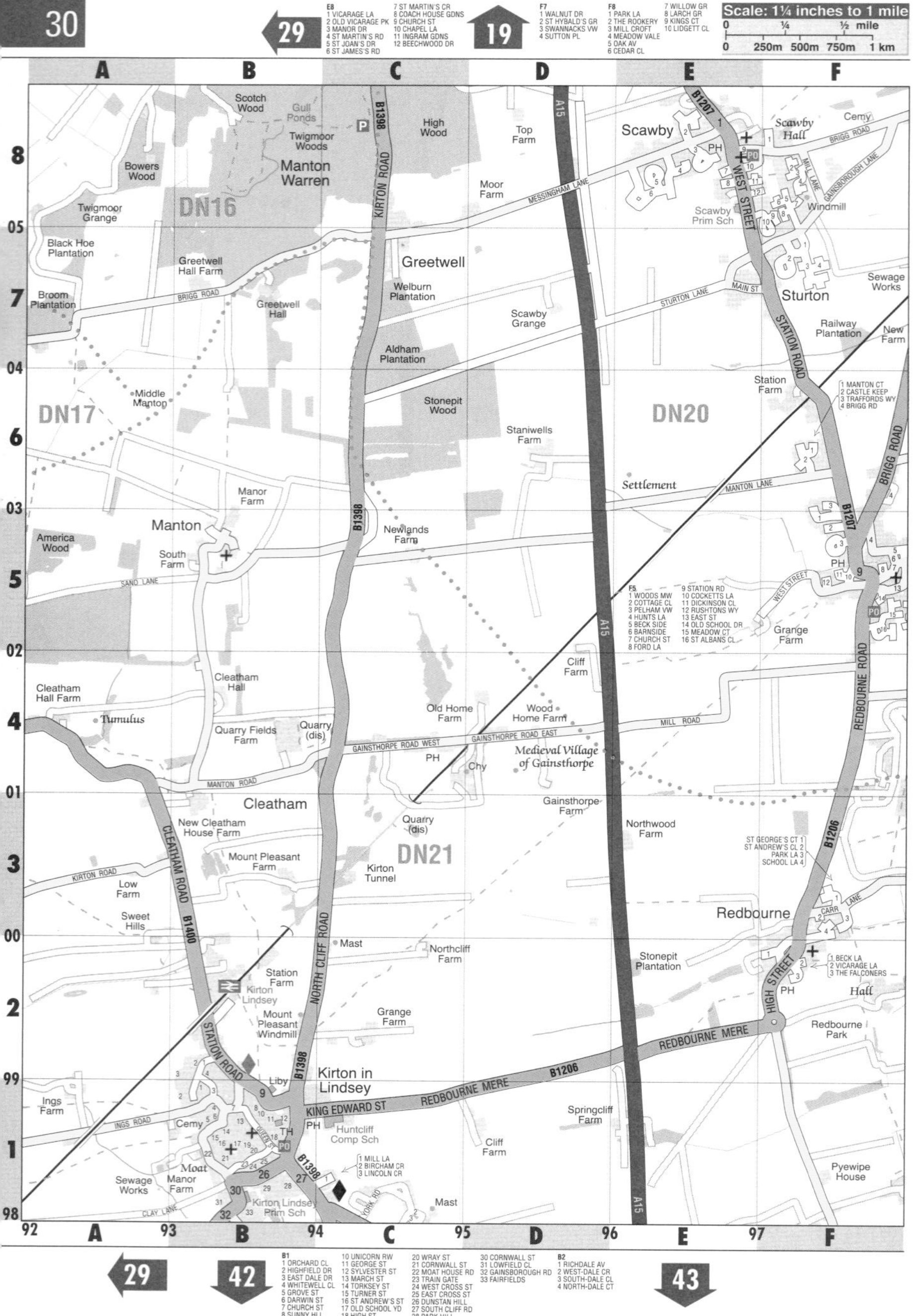
29
E8
1 VICARAGE LA
2 OLD VICARAGE PK
3 MANOR DR
4 ST MARTIN'S RD
5 ST JOAN'S DR
6 ST JAMES'S RD
7 ST MARTIN'S CR
8 COACH HOUSE GDNS
9 CHURCH ST
10 CHAPEL LA
11 INGRAM GDNS
12 BEECHWOOD DR
19
F7
1 WALNUT DR
2 ST HYBALD'S GR
3 SWANNACKS VW
4 SUTTON PL
F8
1 PARK LA
2 THE ROOKERY
3 MILL CROFT
4 MEADOW VALE
5 OAK AV
6 CEDAR CL
7 WILLOW GR
8 LARCH GR
9 KINGS CT
10 LIDGETT CL
Scale: 1¼ inches to 1 mile
0 ¼ ½ mile
0 250m 500m 750m 1 km
A B C D E F
8 05 7 04 6 03 5 02 4 01 3 00 2 99 1 98
92 93 94 95 96 97
Scotch Wood
Gull Ponds
Twigmoor Woods
Manton Warren
High Wood
Bowers Wood
DN16
Twigmoor Grange
Black Hoe Plantation
Top Farm
Moor Farm
Scawby
Scawby Hall
Cemy
PH
PO
WEST STREET
BRIGG ROAD
MILL LANE
GAINSBOROUGH LANE
MESSINGHAM LANE
KIRTON ROAD
B1398
A15
B1207
Scawby Prim Sch
Windmill
Greetwell
Greetwell Hall Farm
BRIGG ROAD
Broom Plantation
Greetwell Hall
Welburn Plantation
Scawby Grange
STURTON LANE
MAIN ST
Sturton
Sewage Works
STATION ROAD
Railway Plantation
New Farm
Aldham Plantation
Middle Manton
DN17
Stonepit Wood
Station Farm
1 MANTON CT
2 CASTLE KEEP
3 TRAFFORDS WY
4 BRIGG RD
DN20
Staniwells Farm
BRIGG ROAD
Settlement
MANTON LANE
Manor Farm
Manton
America Wood
South Farm
Newlands Farm
SAND LANE
WEST STREET
F5
1 WOODS MW
2 COTTAGE CL
3 PELHAM VW
4 HUNTS LA
5 BECK SIDE
6 BARNSIDE
7 CHURCH ST
8 FORD LA
9 STATION RD
10 COCKETTS LA
11 DICKINSON CL
12 RUSHTONS WY
13 EAST ST
14 OLD SCHOOL DR
15 MEADOW CT
16 ST ALBANS CL
Grange Farm
Cliff Farm
Cleatham Hall
Cleatham Hall Farm
Tumulus
Old Home Farm
Wood Home Farm
MILL ROAD
REDBOURNE ROAD
Quarry Fields Farm
Quarry (dis)
GAINSTHORPE ROAD WEST
GAINSTHORPE ROAD EAST
Medieval Village of Gainsthorpe
PH
Chy
MANTON ROAD
Cleatham
Gainsthorpe Farm
Northwood Farm
New Cleatham House Farm
Quarry (dis)
CLEATHAM ROAD
B1400
Mount Pleasant Farm
DN21
ST GEORGE'S CT 1
ST ANDREW'S CL 2
PARK LA 3
SCHOOL LA 4
B1206
KIRTON ROAD
Low Farm
Kirton Tunnel
CARR LANE
Redbourne
Sweet Hills
Mast
NORTH CLIFF ROAD
Northcliff Farm
Stonepit Plantation
1 BECK LA
2 VICARAGE LA
3 THE FALCONERS
Station Farm
Kirton Lindsey
HIGH STREET
PH
Hall
Mount Pleasant Windmill
Grange Farm
REDBOURNE MERE
Redbourne Park
STATION ROAD
Liby
Kirton in Lindsey
B1206
REDBOURNE MERE
KING EDWARD ST
Ings Farm
INGS ROAD
Cemy
TH
PH
Huntcliff Comp Sch
Springcliff Farm
QUEEN ST
Cliff Farm
Moat
Manor Farm
Sewage Works
1 MILL LA
2 BIRCHAM CR
3 LINCOLN CR
Pyewipe House
YORK RD
Mast
CLAY LANE
Kirton Lindsey Prim Sch
29
42
B1
1 ORCHARD CL
2 HIGHFIELD DR
3 EAST DALE DR
4 WHITEWELL CL
5 GROVE ST
6 DARWIN ST
7 CHURCH ST
8 SUNNY HLL
9 SPA HLL
10 UNICORN RW
11 GEORGE ST
12 SYLVESTER ST
13 MARCH ST
14 TORKSEY ST
15 TURNER ST
16 ST ANDREW'S ST
17 OLD SCHOOL YD
18 HIGH ST
19 WESLEY ST
20 WRAY ST
21 CORNWALL ST
22 MOAT HOUSE RD
23 TRAIN GATE
24 WEST CROSS ST
25 EAST CROSS ST
26 DUNSTAN HILL
27 SOUTH CLIFF RD
28 PARK HILL
29 DUNSTAN VILLAS
30 CORNWALL ST
31 LOWFIELD CL
32 GAINSBOROUGH RD
33 FAIRFIELDS
B2
1 RICHDALE AV
2 WEST-DALE CR
3 SOUTH-DALE CL
4 NORTH-DALE CT
43

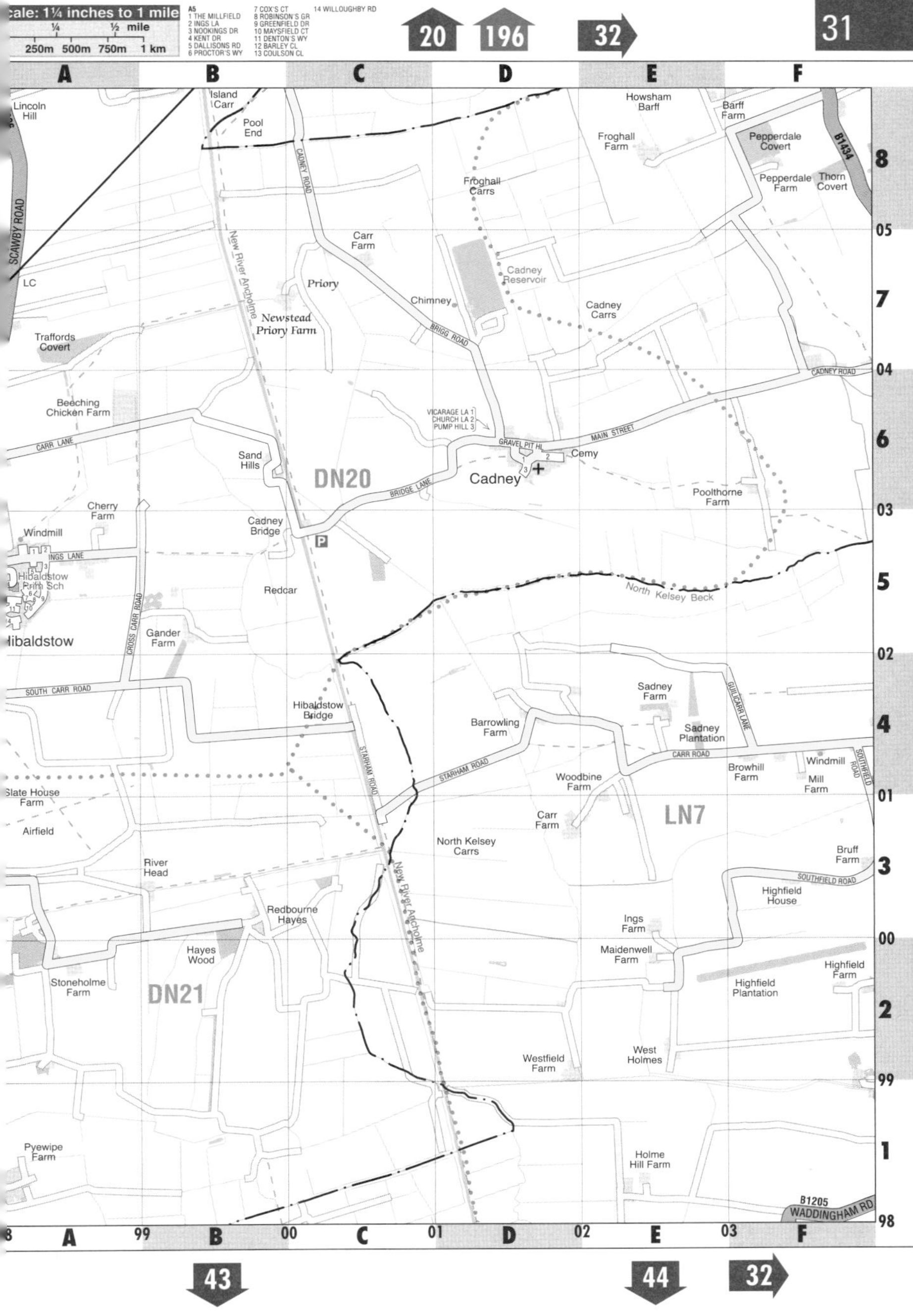

cale: 1¼ inches to 1 mile
¼
½ mile
250m 500m 750m 1 km
A5
1 THE MILLFIELD
2 INGS LA
3 NOOKINGS DR
4 KENT DR
5 DALLISONS RD
6 PROCTOR'S WY
7 COX'S CT
8 ROBINSON'S GR
9 GREENFIELD DR
10 MAYSFIELD CT
11 DENTON'S WY
12 BARLEY CL
13 COULSON CL
14 WILLOUGHBY RD
20
196
32
A
B
C
D
E
F
Lincoln Hill
Island Carr
Pool End
Howsham Barff
Barff Farm
Froghall Farm
Pepperdale Covert
B1434
8
Pepperdale Farm
Thorn Covert
Froghall Carrs
CADNEY ROAD
SCAWBY ROAD
05
New River Ancholme
Carr Farm
Cadney Reservoir
LC
Priory
Newstead Priory Farm
Chimney
Cadney Carrs
7
BRIGG ROAD
Traffords Covert
04
CADNEY ROAD
Beeching Chicken Farm
VICARAGE LA 1
CHURCH LA 2
PUMP HILL 3
MAIN STREET
GRAVEL PIT HL
6
CARR LANE
Sand Hills
Cemy
DN20
Cadney
BRIDGE LANE
Poolthorne Farm
Cherry Farm
03
Cadney Bridge
Windmill
INGS LANE
P
Hibaldstow Prim Sch
Redcar
5
North Kelsey Beck
CROSS CARR ROAD
Gander Farm
Hibaldstow
02
SOUTH CARR ROAD
Sadney Farm
GUILICARR LANE
Hibaldstow Bridge
Barrowling Farm
Sadney Plantation
4
STARHAM ROAD
CARR ROAD
Windmill
SOUTHFIELD ROAD
Brownhill Farm
Mill Farm
Woodbine Farm
Slate House Farm
01
Carr Farm
LN7
Airfield
North Kelsey Carrs
Bruff Farm
River Head
3
SOUTHFIELD ROAD
Highfield House
Redbourne Hayes
Ings Farm
00
Hayes Wood
Maidenwell Farm
Highfield Farm
Stoneholme Farm
DN21
Highfield Plantation
2
West Holmes
Westfield Farm
99
Pyewipe Farm
Holme Hill Farm
1
B1205
WADDINGHAM RD
98
8
A
99
B
00
C
01
D
02
E
03
F
43
44
32

31
21
D8
1 BACK LA
2 HOWSHAM LA
3 MAIN ST
4 OWMBY RD
E7
1 MAIN ST
2 CHURCH HL
3 CHURCH SIDE
4 FRONT ST
5 CANTY NOOK
6 BENTLEY LA
Scale: 1¼ inches to 1 m
0 ¼ ½ mile
0 250m 500m 750m 1 k
A B C D E F
8
05
7
04
6
03
5
02
4
01
3
00
2
99
1
98
Dawson's Covert
Oak Wood
Somerby Low Farm
Searby
SEARBY HILL
Viking Way
A1084
OWMBY WOLD LANE
GRASBY WOLD LANE
Owmby Mount
Quarry
Park Wood
Bull House Farm
OWMBY HILL
B1434
Hillside Farm
Manor Farm
Grasby All Saints CE Prim Sch
VICARAGE LANE
CLIXBY LANE
PH
DN38
Owmby
Grasby
MAIN ST
Roseholme Farm
Clixby Manor Farm
Fox Farm
LC
Low Farm
Pond Farm
Grasby House Farm
CADNEY ROAD
STATION LANE
STATION ROAD
Owmby Vale
Dale Farm
Brasted Farm
Howsham
Brandicar
Harding's Wood
Audleby Low Cove
Hill Farm
Stoneybridge Farm
BRIGG ROAD
Setcops Farm
White House Farm
OWMBY LANE
GRASBY ROAD
Twelve Month Hill Woods
CROSS LANE
Moor Farm
Folly Farm
Brook Farm
FOLLY LA
Landaum Farm
Caistor Moor
Cemy
CEMETERY LA
Fieldhouse Farm
Steingrave Farm
North Kelsey Moor
Wood Farm
WEST ST
Brickyard Farm
Highfield Farm
STATION ROAD
North Kelsey
PO
Kelsey Prim Sch
Smithfield Farm
CAISTOR ROAD
Pit (dis)
Far Farm
Moor Farm Nursery
PH
CARR RD
LANE
STREET
EASTHALL ROAD
Rochford Farm
Dairy Farm
Sheepcote Hill
Vicarage Farm
Drables Hill
Newlands Farm
SAND LANE
Drabble Hill Farm
Nettleton Lodge Game Farm
West Moor Farm
SOUTHFIELD RD
Ellmore Farm
Nettleton Lodge
Big Wood
Bruff Farm
South Barff Farm
GRANGE LANE
LN7
ELLMORE LANE
Moortown House Farm
Nettleton Manor
Watermill Farm
B1205
Manor Wood
Long Wood
Nettleton Moor
North End Farm
Moortown
Corner Farm
KELSEY RD
Black Wood
NORTH END LA
Mount Pleasant Farm
HOLTON ROAD
Holton Plantation
Nettleton Wood
South Kelsey
Riverhead Farm
Noble's Wood
1 FORGE CL
2 THORNTON RD
3 QUEENSFIELD
Sands Plantation
A46
Jervis Plantation
GIPSY LA
WADDINGHAM ROAD
Daisy Hill Farm
Stope Hill Farm
CAISTOR ROAD
04 A 05 B 06 C 07 D 08 E 09 F
31
44
45
A4
1 LINDUM WK
2 OLD SCHOOL LA
3 MILL LA
4 SCHOOL LA
5 PATRICKS CL
6 OCCUPATION LA
7 CHAPEL ST
8 HIGH ST
9 HALLS LA
10 CHURCH LA
11 MAIDENWELL LA
12 CHURCH ST
13 GREEN LA
14 MIDDLE ST
15 SOUTH ST

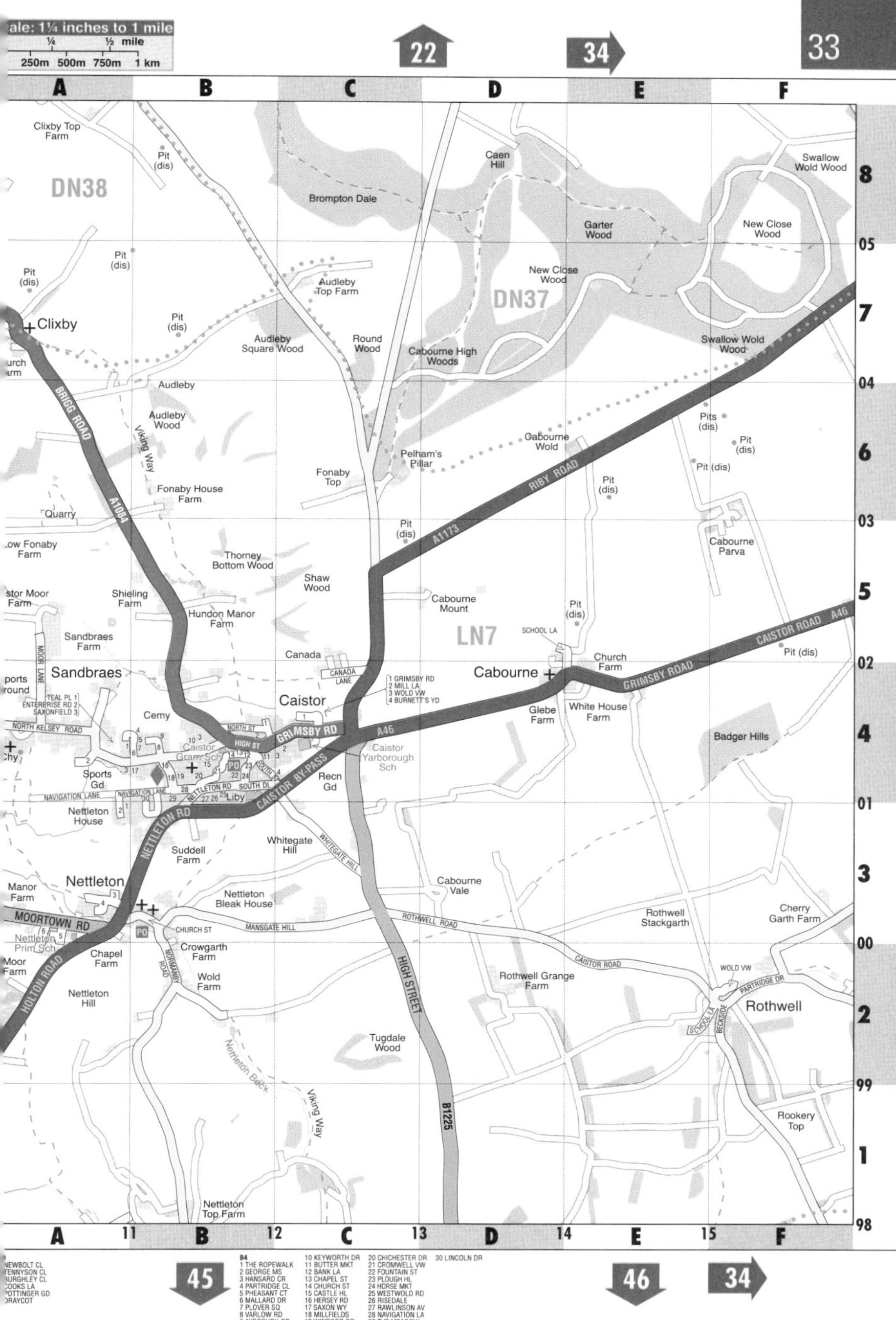

NEWBOLT CL
TENNYSON CL
BURGHLEY CL
COOKS LA
POTTINGER GD
DRAYCOT

B4
1 THE ROPEWALK
2 GEORGE MS
3 HANSARD CR
4 PARTRIDGE CL
5 PHEASANT CT
6 MALLARD DR
7 PLOVER SQ
8 VARLOW RD
9 AYSCOUGH GR
10 KEYWORTH DR
11 BUTTER MKT
12 BANK LA
13 CHAPEL ST
14 CHURCH ST
15 CASTLE HL
16 HERSEY RD
17 SAXON WY
18 MILLFIELDS
19 WINDSOR DR
20 CHICHESTER DR
21 CROMWELL VW
22 FOUNTAIN ST
23 PLOUGH HL
24 HORSE MKT
25 WESTWOLD RD
26 RISEDALE
27 RAWLINSON AV
28 NAVIGATION LA
29 THE MEADOW
30 LINCOLN DR

33
23

Scale: 1¼ inches to 1 mile

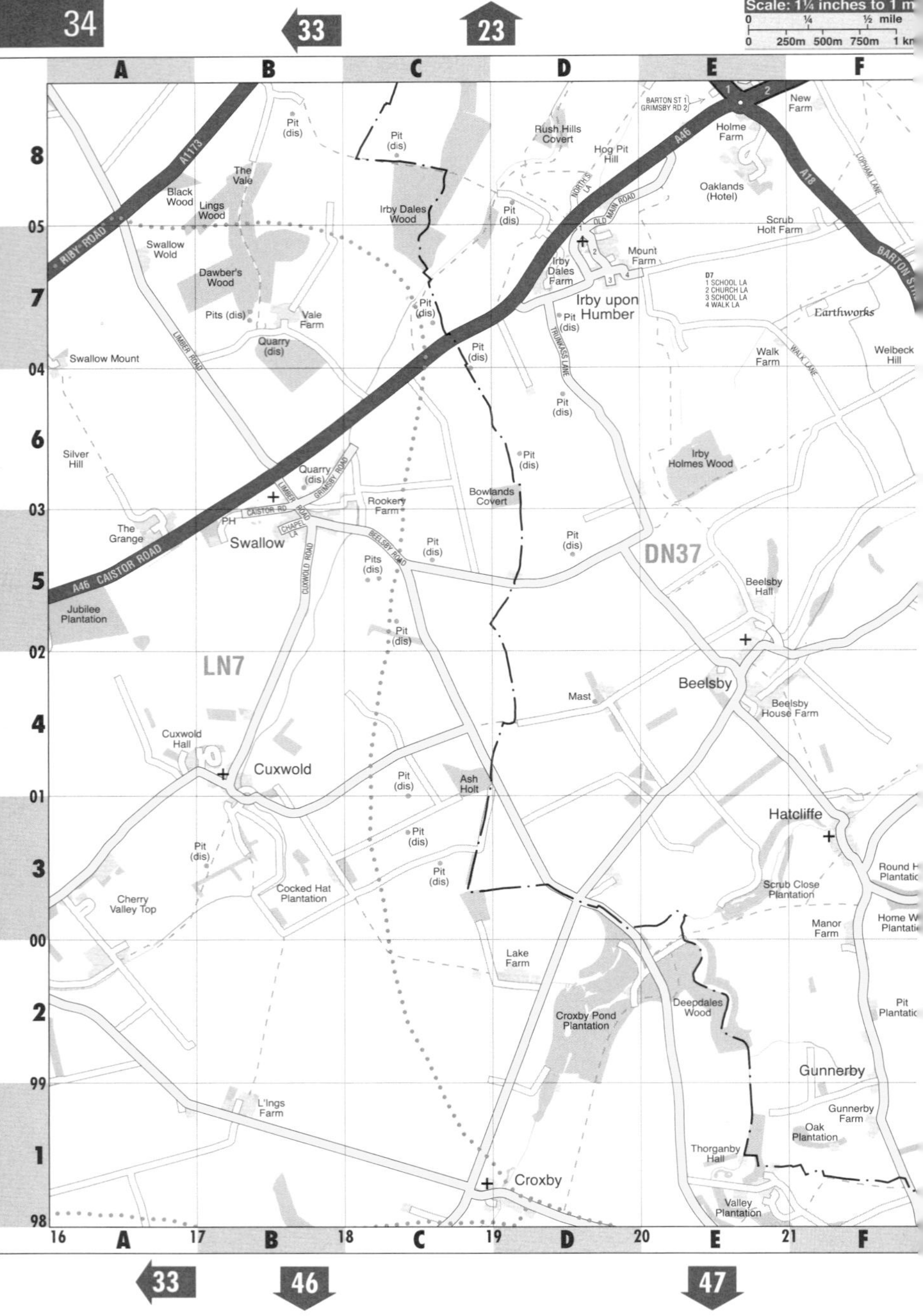

33
46
47

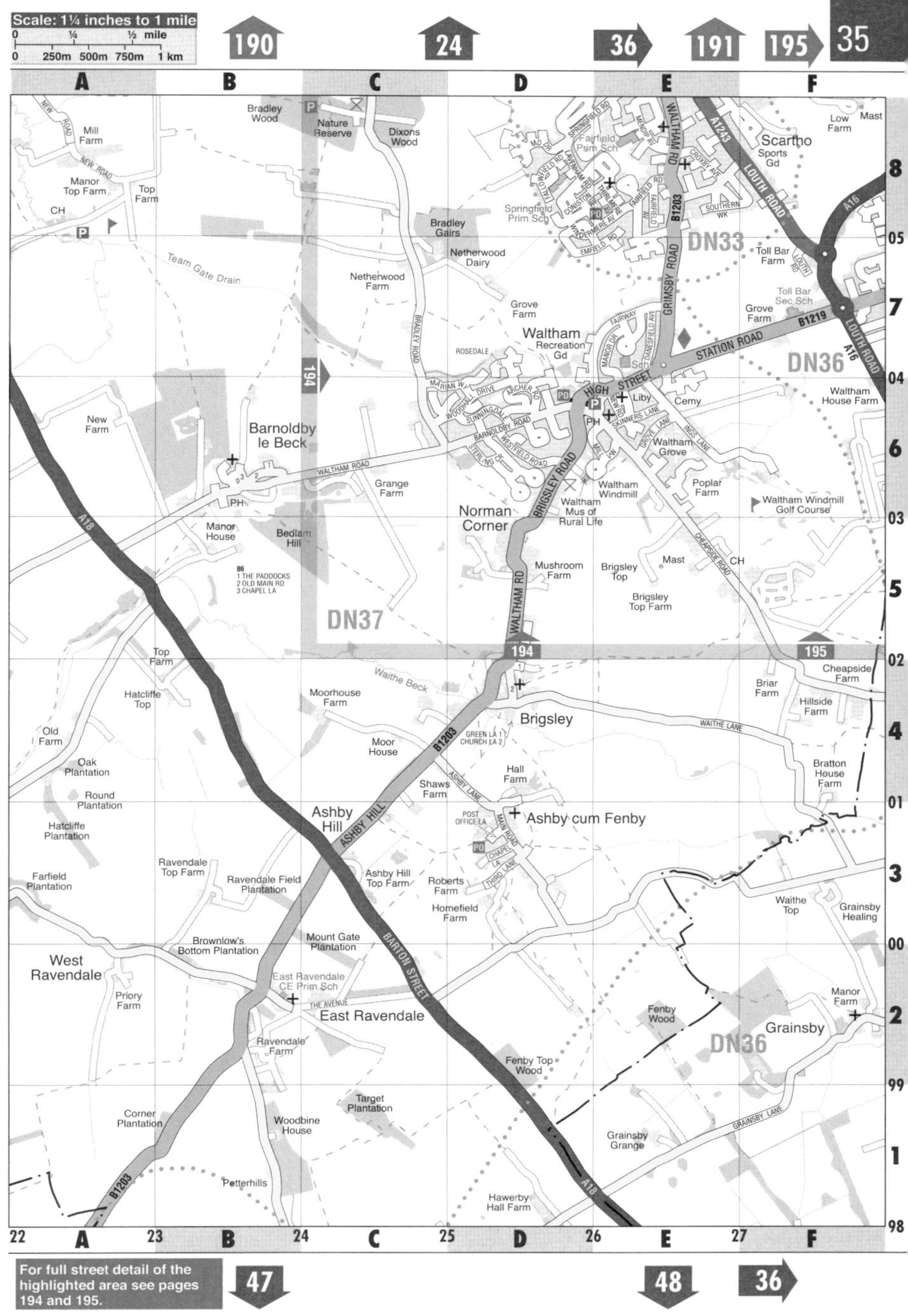

Scale: 1¼ inches to 1 mile
0 ¼ ½ mile
0 250m 500m 750m 1 km
190
24
36
191
195
35
A B C D E F
Bradley Wood
Nature Reserve
Dixons Wood
Mill Farm
New Road
Manor Top Farm
Top Farm
CH
Low Farm
Mast
Scartho
Sports Gd
Fairfield Prim Sch
Springfield Prim Sch
Waltham Rd
Louth Road
Bradley Gairs
Netherwood Dairy
Team Gate Drain
Netherwood Farm
DN33
Toll Bar Farm
Toll Bar Sec Sch
Grove Farm
Grove Farm
Bradley Road
Waltham
Recreation Gd
Rosedale
Station Road
B1219
DN36
Grimsby Road
B1203
A1243
A16
High Street
Liby
Cemy
Waltham House Farm
New Farm
Barnoldby le Beck
Waltham Road
Barnoldby Road
Brigsley Road
Grange Farm
Waltham Grove
Waltham Windmill
Waltham Mus of Rural Life
Poplar Farm
Waltham Windmill Golf Course
PH
Norman Corner
Manor House
Bedlam Hill
A18
B6
1 THE PADDOCKS
2 OLD MAIN RD
3 CHAPEL LA
Mushroom Farm
Brigsley Top
Mast
CH
Cheapside Road
Brigsley Top Farm
DN37
194
195
Top Farm
Waithe Beck
Hatcliffe Top
Moorhouse Farm
Briar Farm
Cheapside Farm
Hillside Farm
Brigsley
Waithe Lane
Old Farm
Green La 1
Church La 2
Moor House
Oak Plantation
Round Plantation
Hall Farm
Bratton House Farm
Shaws Farm
Ashby Lane
Hatcliffe Plantation
Ashby Hill
Post Office La
Main Road
Ashby cum Fenby
Chapel La
Third Lane
Farfield Plantation
Ravendale Top Farm
Ravendale Field Plantation
Ashby Hill Top Farm
Roberts Farm
Homefield Farm
Waithe Top
Grainsby Healing
Brownlow's Bottom Plantation
Mount Gate Plantation
Barton Street
West Ravendale
East Ravendale CE Prim Sch
The Avenue
East Ravendale
Priory Farm
Fenby Wood
Manor Farm
Grainsby
Ravendale Farm
DN36
Fenby Top Wood
Target Plantation
Corner Plantation
Woodbine House
Grainsby Grange
Grainsby Lane
Petterhills
Hawerby Hall Farm
8 05 7 04 6 03 5 02 4 01 3 00 2 99 1 98
22 23 24 25 26 27
For full street detail of the highlighted area see pages 194 and 195.
47
48
36

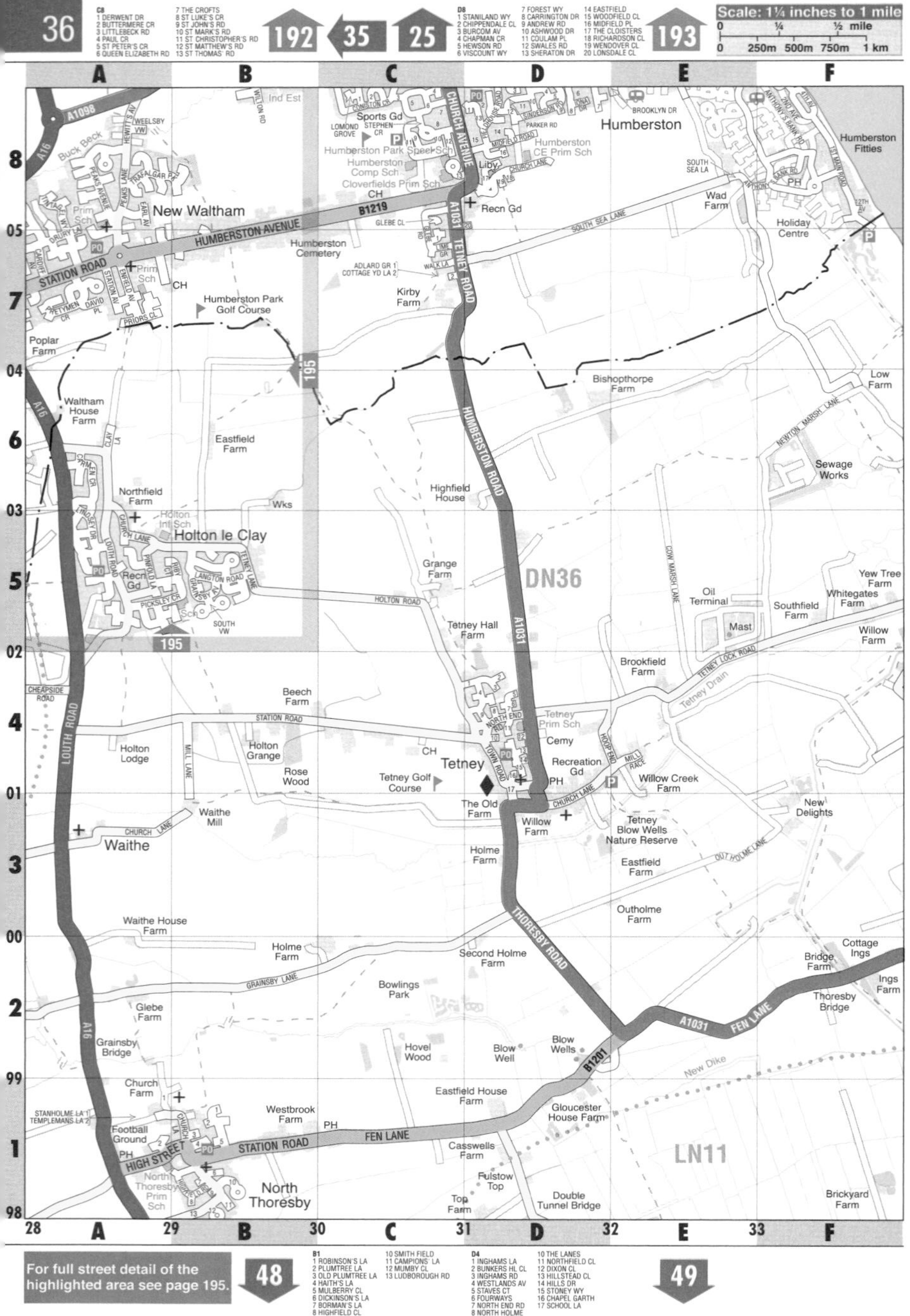
36
C8
1 DERWENT DR
2 BUTTERMERE CR
3 LITTLEBECK RD
4 PAUL CR
5 ST PETER'S CR
6 QUEEN ELIZABETH RD
7 THE CROFTS
8 ST LUKE'S CR
9 ST JOHN'S RD
10 ST MARK'S RD
11 ST CHRISTOPHER'S RD
12 ST MATTHEW'S RD
13 ST THOMAS' RD
192
35
25
D8
1 STANILAND WY
2 CHIPPENDALE CL
3 BURCOM AV
4 CHAPMAN CR
5 HEWSON RD
6 VISCOUNT WY
7 FOREST WY
8 CARRINGTON DR
9 ANDREW RD
10 ASHWOOD DR
11 COULAM PL
12 SWALES RD
13 SHERATON DR
14 EASTFIELD
15 WOODFIELD CL
16 MIDFIELD PL
17 THE CLOISTERS
18 RICHARDSON CL
19 WENDOVER CL
20 LONSDALE CL
193
Scale: 1¼ inches to 1 mile
0 ¼ ½ mile
0 250m 500m 750m 1 km
Humberston
New Waltham
HUMBERSTON AVENUE
STATION ROAD
CHURCH AVENUE
TETNEY ROAD
HUMBERSTON ROAD
Humberston Fitties
Holiday Centre
Wad Farm
SOUTH SEA LANE
Humberston Park Golf Course
Humberston Cemetery
Kirby Farm
Poplar Farm
Waltham House Farm
Bishopthorpe Farm
Low Farm
NEWTON MARSH LANE
Sewage Works
Eastfield Farm
Northfield Farm
Highfield House
Holton le Clay
Grange Farm
DN36
COW MARSH LANE
Oil Terminal
Mast
Southfield Farm
Whitegates Farm
Yew Tree Farm
Willow Farm
Tetney Hall Farm
HOLTON ROAD
195
Brookfield Farm
TETNEY LOCK ROAD
Tetney Drain
Beech Farm
STATION ROAD
Holton Lodge
Holton Grange
MILL LANE
Rose Wood
Tetney
Tetney Golf Course
The Old Farm
Recreation Gd
Willow Creek Farm
Cemy
Tetney Prim Sch
LOUTH ROAD
Waithe Mill
Waithe
CHURCH LANE
Willow Farm
Tetney Blow Wells Nature Reserve
New Delights
Holme Farm
Eastfield Farm
OUT HOLME LANE
Outholme Farm
Waithe House Farm
Holme Farm
Second Holme Farm
THORESBY ROAD
Cottage Ings
Bridge Farm
Ings Farm
Thoresby Bridge
GRAINSBY LANE
Bowlings Park
Glebe Farm
A1031 FEN LANE
Grainsby Bridge
Hovel Wood
Blow Well
Blow Wells
B1201
New Dike
Church Farm
Eastfield House Farm
Westbrook Farm
Gloucester House Farm
Football Ground
HIGH STREET
STATION ROAD
FEN LANE
Casswells Farm
LN11
North Thoresby
Fulstow Top
Top Farm
Double Tunnel Bridge
Brickyard Farm
28
29
30
31
32
33
For full street detail of the highlighted area see page 195.
48
B1
1 ROBINSON'S LA
2 PLUMTREE LA
3 OLD PLUMTREE LA
4 HAITH'S LA
5 MULBERRY CL
6 DICKINSON'S LA
7 BORMAN'S LA
8 HIGHFIELD CL
9 MARFLEET CR
10 SMITH FIELD
11 CAMPIONS' LA
12 MUMBY CL
13 LUDBOROUGH RD
D4
1 INGHAMS LA
2 BUNKERS HL CL
3 INGHAMS RD
4 WESTLANDS AV
5 STAVES CT
6 FOURWAYS
7 NORTH END RD
8 NORTH HOLME
9 NORTH END CR
10 THE LANES
11 NORTHFIELD CL
12 DIXON CL
13 HILLSTEAD CL
14 HILLS DR
15 STONEY WY
16 CHAPEL GARTH
17 SCHOOL LA
49

ale: 1¼ inches to 1 mile
¼
½ mile
250m 500m 750m 1 km
C5
1 SANDY CL
2 FITTIES LA
3 MARSH WY
4 KENNETH CAMPBELL RD
5 DYKE RD
6 SAMPHIRE CL
38
A
B
C
D
E
F
8
05
7
04
6
03
5
02
4
01
3
00
2
99
1
98
Tetney High Sands
Tetney Marshes Nature Reserve
Tetney Haven
Northcoates Point
Braybrook Farm
Stonebridge Farm
DYKE RD
Airfield (Dis)
PH
Tetney Lock
Horse Shoe Point
Tuttle Farm
SEA LANE
DN36
Low Farm
Grainthorpe Haven
PH
North Cotes
LOCK ROAD
FLEETWAY
North Cotes CE (Controlled) Prim Sch
Sewage Works
SHEEP MARSH LANE
Poplar Farm
The Fitties
INGS LA
MABLETHORPE ROAD
NORTH WAY
NORTH LANE
LN11
Seven Towns North Eau
Rookery Farm
Keyholme Farm
Marshchapel
HALLGARTH
PO
PH
Windmill
KEYHOLME LANE
Sea Bank Farm
Evergreen Farm
Sea Farm
Marshchapel Prim Sch
HARPHAM RD
DUCKTHORPE LANE
LOW ROAD
A1031
Willow Tree House
Holme Farm
New Farm
Eskham Farm
West End Farm
CHURCH LANE
Eskham
WEST END LANE
LOW GATE
Beacon Hill
SEA DYKE WAY
FIREBEACON LA
COAL SHORE LANE
Ivy House
Mast
GRAINS GATE
Beacon Hill Farm
LAND DIKE
Fulstow Bridge
Louth Canal
35
36
37
38
39
C2
1 SEA DYKE WY
2 VICTORIA CL
3 PLUM TREE DR
4 MILL LA
5 MILL CL
49
50
38

37
Scale: 1¼ inches to 1 m
0 ¼ ½ mile
0 250m 500m 750m 1 k
A B C D E F
8
05
7
04
6
North Sea
03
5
02
4
01
Somercotes Haven
3
DANGER AREA
Seven Towns South Eau
00
Stonebridge
Nature Reserve
Donna Nook
Porter's Sluice
2
Pye's Farm
LN11
Laramie
Sprakes Farm
Wells Farm
99
MARSH LANE
Fivehundred Acres
Marsh Grange
Porter's Marsh
1
Sewage Works
Holmes Farm
Poplar Farm
HOLMES LA
98
40 41 42 43 44 45
A B C D E F
37
50
51

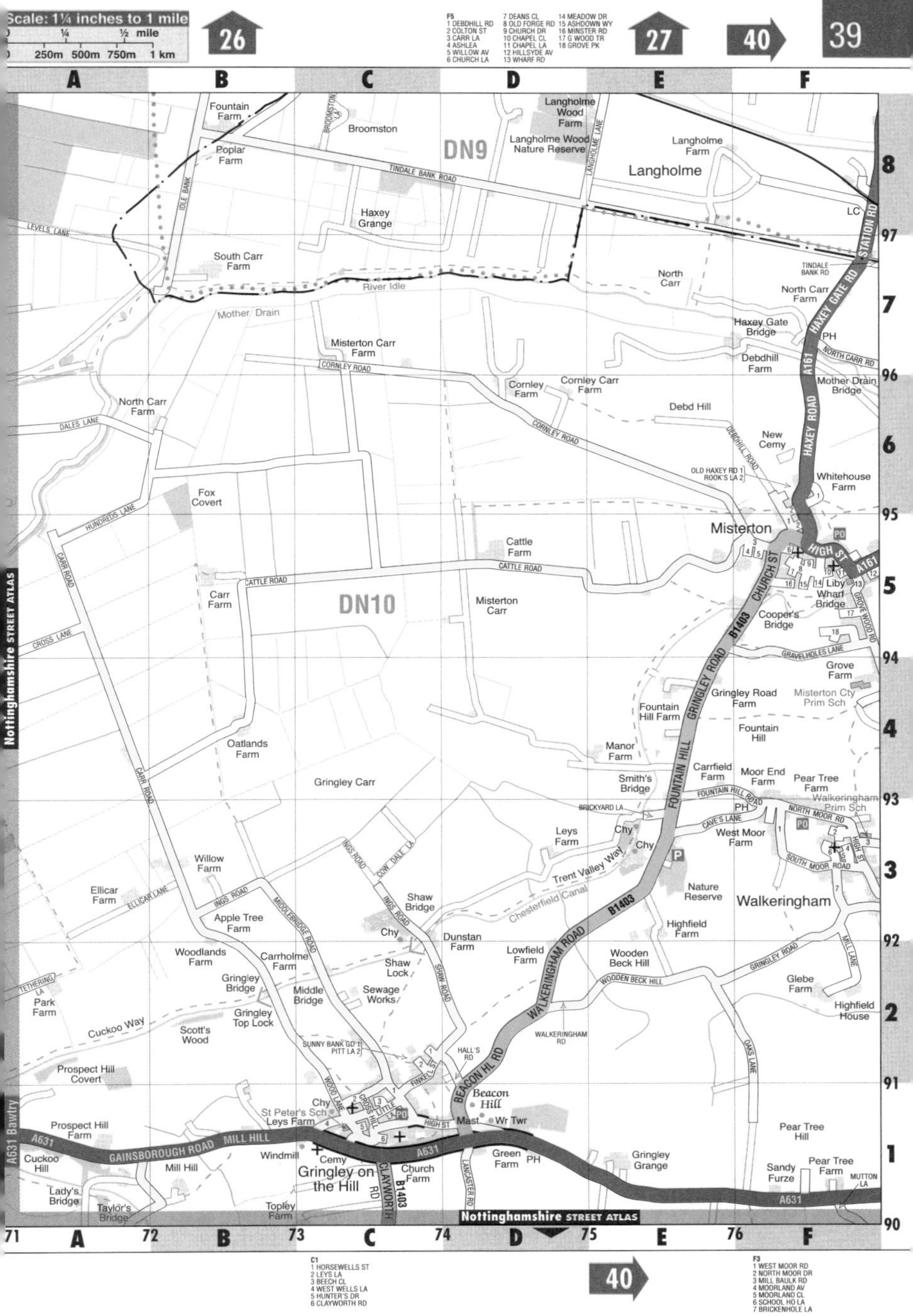
Scale: 1¼ inches to 1 mile
0 ¼ ½ mile
0 250m 500m 750m 1 km
26
27
40
F5
1 DEBDHILL RD
2 COLTON ST
3 CARR LA
4 ASHLEA
5 WILLOW AV
6 CHURCH LA
7 DEANS CL
8 OLD FORGE RD
9 CHURCH DR
10 CHAPEL CL
11 CHAPEL LA
12 HILLSYDE AV
13 WHARF RD
14 MEADOW DR
15 ASHDOWN WY
16 MINSTER RD
17 G WOOD TR
18 GROVE PK
A B C D E F
8 97 7 96 6 95 5 94 4 93 3 92 2 91 1 90
71 72 73 74 75 76
DN9
DN10
Fountain Farm
Broomston
BROOMSTON LA
Langholme Wood Farm
Langholme Wood Nature Reserve
LANGHOLME LANE
Langholme Farm
Langholme
Poplar Farm
TINDALE BANK ROAD
IDLE BANK
Haxey Grange
LEVELS LANE
LC
STATION RD
TINDALE BANK RD
South Carr Farm
North Carr
North Carr Farm
River Idle
Mother Drain
HAXEY GATE RD
Haxey Gate Bridge
PH
Misterton Carr Farm
CORNLEY ROAD
NORTH CARR RD
Debdhill Farm
A161
Cornley Farm
Cornley Carr Farm
Mother Drain Bridge
North Carr Farm
HAXEY ROAD
DALES LANE
Debd Hill
DEBDHILL ROAD
New Cemy
OLD HAXEY RD 1
ROOK'S LA 2
Whitehouse Farm
Fox Covert
HUNDREDS LANE
Misterton
PO
HIGH ST
Cattle Farm
CATTLE ROAD
CHURCH ST
Carr Farm
Misterton Carr
Liby
Wharf Bridge
GROVE WOOD RD
Cooper's Bridge
CARR ROAD
CROSS LANE
B1403
GRAVELHOLES LANE
Grove Farm
GRINGLEY ROAD
Gringley Road Farm
Misterton Cty Prim Sch
Fountain Hill Farm
Fountain Hill
Oatlands Farm
Manor Farm
FOUNTAIN HILL
Carrfield Farm
Moor End Farm
Pear Tree Farm
Gringley Carr
Smith's Bridge
FOUNTAIN HILL ROAD
Walkeringham Prim Sch
BRICKYARD LA
PH
NORTH MOOR RD
CAVE'S LANE
Leys Farm
Chy
West Moor Farm
Willow Farm
INGS ROAD
COW DALE LA
Trent Valley Way
P
SOUTH MOOR ROAD
Ellicar Farm
ELLICAR LANE
INGS ROAD
Shaw Bridge
Nature Reserve
Walkeringham
Chesterfield Canal
Apple Tree Farm
MIDDLEBRIDGE ROAD
Highfield Farm
Chy
Dunstan Farm
Woodlands Farm
Carrholme Farm
Lowfield Farm
WALKERINGHAM ROAD
Wooden Beck Hill
MILL LANE
GRINGLEY ROAD
TETHERING LA
Gringley Bridge
Shaw Lock
WOODEN BECK HILL
Glebe Farm
Park Farm
Middle Bridge
Sewage Works
SHAW ROAD
Highfield House
Cuckoo Way
Gringley Top Lock
Scott's Wood
WALKERINGHAM RD
OAKS LANE
SUNNY BANK GD 1
PITT LA 2
HALL'S RD
Prospect Hill Covert
FINKELL ST
BEACON HL RD
Beacon Hill
Chy
WOOD LANE
CROSS HILL
LITTLE LA
St Peter's Sch
Leys Farm
Mast
Wr Twr
Prospect Hill Farm
HIGH ST
Pear Tree Hill
A631 Bawtry
A631
MILL HILL
GAINSBOROUGH ROAD
Windmill
Cemy
Green Farm
PH
Gringley Grange
Cuckoo Hill
Mill Hill
Gringley on the Hill
CLAYWORTH RD
Church Farm
LANCASTER RD
Sandy Furze
Pear Tree Farm
MUTTON LA
Lady's Bridge
Taylor's Bridge
Topley Farm
Nottinghamshire STREET ATLAS
C1
1 HORSEWELLS ST
2 LEYS LA
3 BEECH CL
4 WEST WELLS LA
5 HUNTER'S DR
6 CLAYWORTH RD
F3
1 WEST MOOR RD
2 NORTH MOOR DR
3 MILL BAULK RD
4 MOORLAND AV
5 MOORLAND CL
6 SCHOOL HO LA
7 BRICKENHOLE LA

Scale: 1¼ inches to 1 mile

A1
1 CHURCH VW
2 RECTORY GDNS
3 OAKLANDS
4 THE GROVE
5 THE PADDOCKS
6 RAVENCROFT LA
7 THE LIMES

For full street detail of the highlighted area see page 197.

Scale: 1¼ inches to 1 mile
¼ ½ mile
250m 500m 750m 1 km
28
29
42
B5
1 HILL TOP LA
2 HICKMAN GR
C5
1 MARK RI
2 SAXON CT
3 CHURCH LA
4 ORCHARD CL
5 PADDOCK LA
6 FIELDSIDE
7 HAVEN CL
8 ST MARTIN'S CL
9 THE AVENUE
Laughton Wood
Park House Farm
Dallison Plantation
Northorpe Beck
Cemy
SCOTTER ROAD
EAST FERRY RD
Laughton
MORTON ROAD
Mount Pleasant Farm
Hall Farm
Holme Farm
MANTREE CROSS
PH
BLYTON ROAD
CHURCH ROAD
Laughton Endowed (Aided)
A159
DRING LANE
Grange Farm
Carmer Hole
Carmer Wood
Abbey Farm
Blyton Grange
B1205
Pyewipe Hall Farm
Sewage Works
LAUGHTON ROAD
Airfield (dis)
Sandbeck Farm
SANDBECK LANE
1 MEADOW RI
2 RUSTIC LA
Southorpe Farm
Blyton CE (Aided) Prim Sch
PH
B1205
KIRTON ROAD
Field Farm
Sunnyside Farm
Top Farm
LC
HIGH STREET A159
Old Hall Farm
PO
Cemy
Grange Farm
Windmill
Blyton
STATION ROAD
Ash Tree Farm
Catchwater Farm
GAINSBOROUGH ROAD
DN21
Glebe Farm
CARR LANE
Poplar Tree Farm
Lineside Farm
Bonsdale Farm
WHARTON ROAD
Mast
Station Farm
PILHAM LANE
Todd Lane Farm
Pilham
GREEN LANE
Oak Tree Farm
A159
Wharton Hall Farm
Firs Farm
Leverets Ley Farm
TODD LANE
Wharton
Manor Farm
Gilby Farm
Gilby Village
Aisby
Beck Farm
Moscar Farm
THONOCK ROAD
Netherdene Farm
PILHAM LANE
Northfield Farm
Duckles Wood
Wharton Wood
The Lake
Hall Farm
Mill Farm
Westfield Farm
Corringham Grange Farm
CHURCH LA
Windmill
MILLMERE ROAD
EAST LANE
MIDDLE STREET
Corringham CE Prim Sch
Birch Wood
POPLAR LA 1
EDMUND CL 2
Poplar Farm
PO
Corringham
PH
Corringham Windmill
HIGH STREET
PH
A631
Hornby Wood
Woodhouse Farm
1 CADMAN WY
2 LUSHER WY
CORRINGHAM ROAD
A631
CORRINGHAM ROAD
Sewage Works
SPRINGTHORPE ROAD
GRANGE RD
LONG WOOD RD
Industrial Estate
THORNDIKE WAY
Lodge Farm
Brickhill Wood
Staplegate Farm
HILL RD
New Church Farm
White's Wood Farm
A B C D E F
8 97 7 96 6 95 5 94 4 93 3 92 2 91 1 90
83 84 85 86 87 88
53
42

F8
1 YORK RD
2 LINCOLN CR
3 HENLOW CL
4 HALTON CL
5 BIRCHAM CR
6 CRANWELL CL

Scale: 1¼ inches to 1 mile

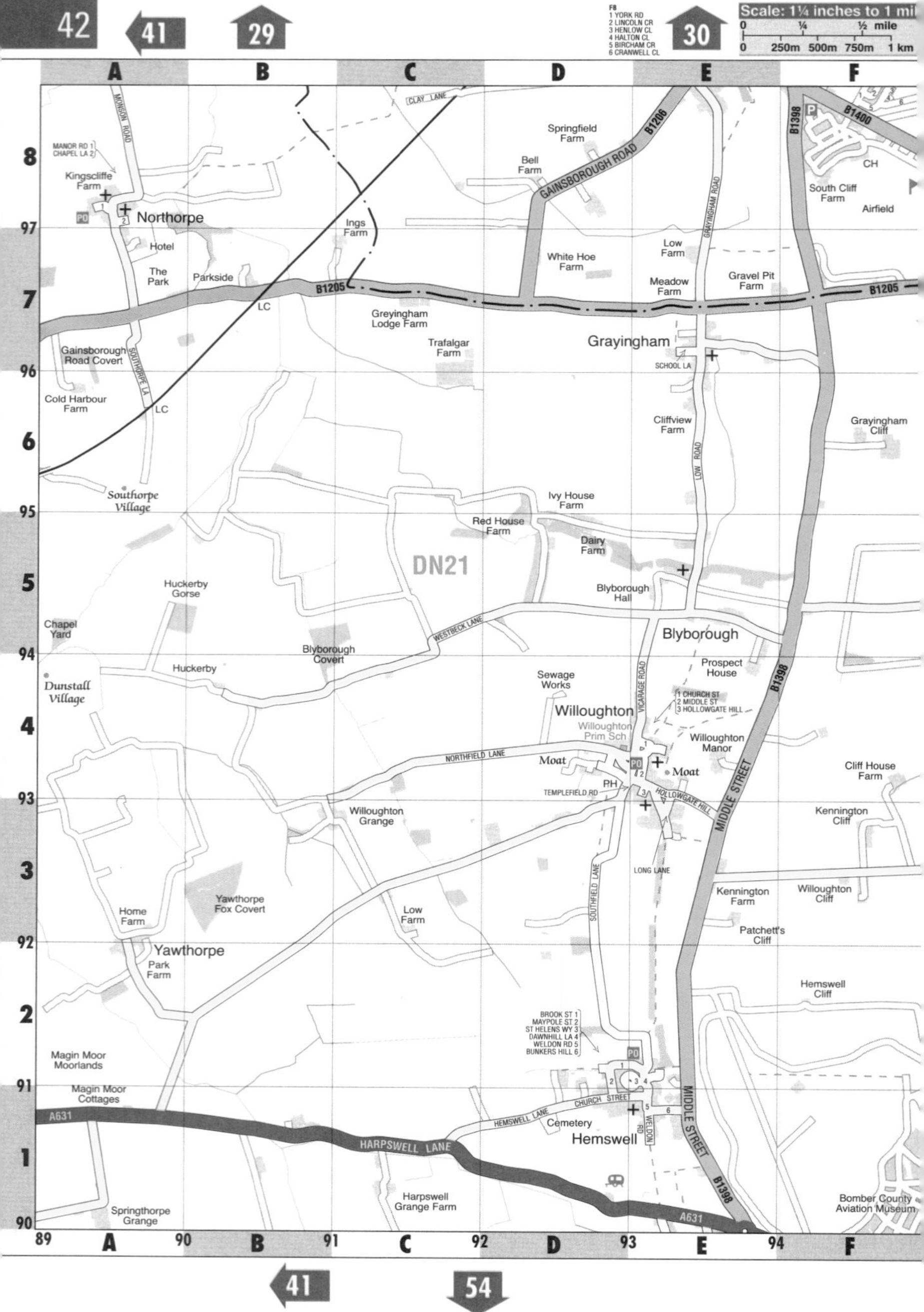

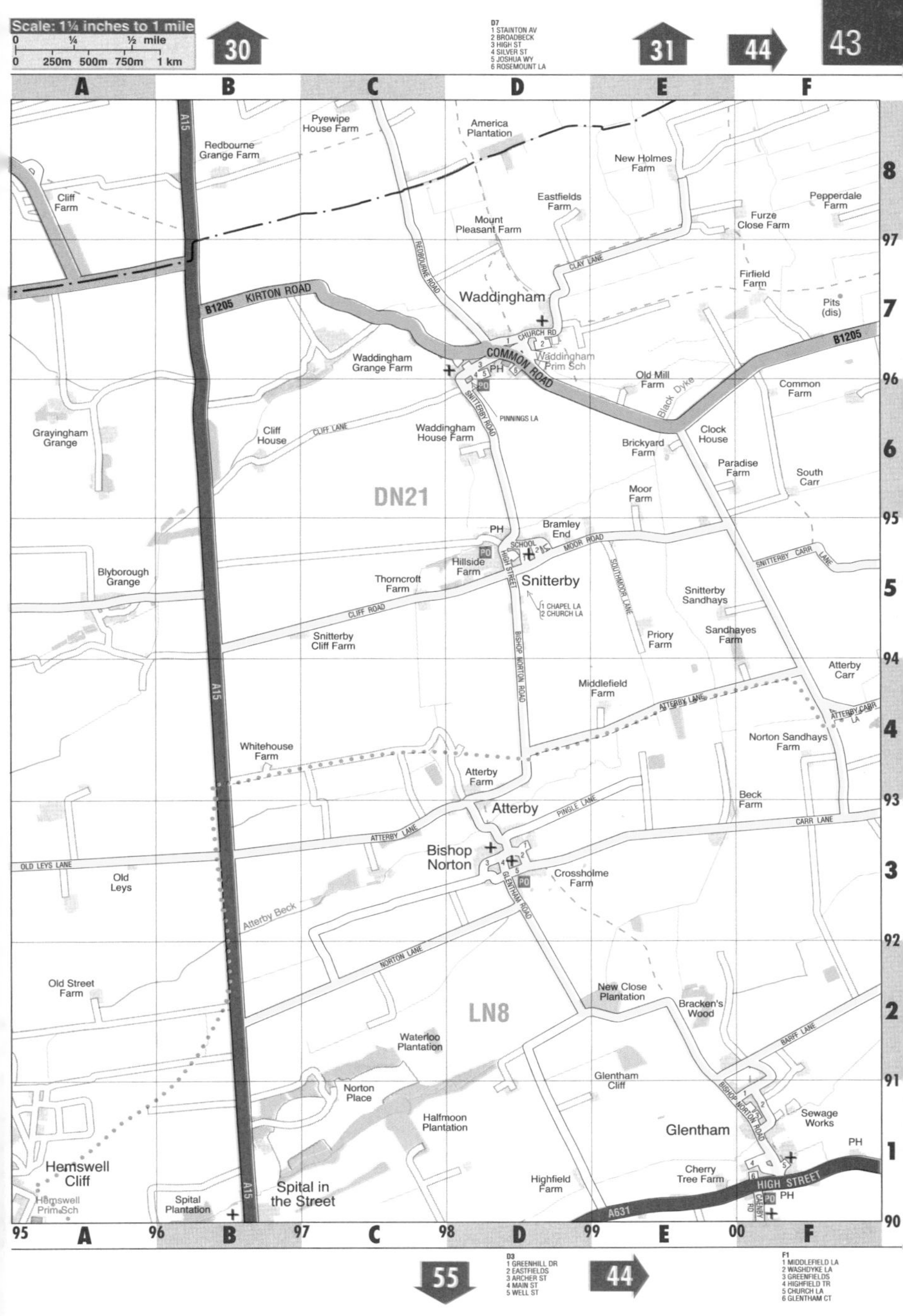
Scale: 1¼ inches to 1 mile
0 ¼ ½ mile
0 250m 500m 750m 1 km
30
31
44
D7
1 STAINTON AV
2 BROADBECK
3 HIGH ST
4 SILVER ST
5 JOSHUA WY
6 ROSEMOUNT LA
A B C D E F
Pyewipe House Farm
America Plantation
Redbourne Grange Farm
New Holmes Farm
Cliff Farm
Eastfields Farm
Pepperdale Farm
Mount Pleasant Farm
Furze Close Farm
CLAY LANE
Firfield Farm
REDBOURNE ROAD
B1205 KIRTON ROAD
Waddingham
Pits (dis)
CHURCH RD
COMMON ROAD
B1205
Waddingham Grange Farm
Waddingham Prim Sch
PH
PO
Old Mill Farm
Black Dyke
Common Farm
PINNINGS LA
SNITTERBY ROAD
Cliff House
CLIFF LANE
Waddingham House Farm
Clock House
Grayingham Grange
Brickyard Farm
Paradise Farm
South Carr
DN21
Moor Farm
PH
Bramley End
SCHOOL
MOOR ROAD
SNITTERBY CARR LANE
Blyborough Grange
Hillside Farm
HIGH STREET
SOUTHMOOR LANE
Thorncroft Farm
Snitterby
Snitterby Sandhays
1 CHAPEL LA
2 CHURCH LA
CLIFF ROAD
Snitterby Cliff Farm
BISHOP NORTON ROAD
Priory Farm
Sandhayes Farm
A15
Atterby Carr
Middlefield Farm
ATTERBY LANE
ATTERBY CARR LA
Whitehouse Farm
Norton Sandhays Farm
Atterby Farm
Atterby
PINGLE LANE
Beck Farm
CARR LANE
ATTERBY LANE
Bishop Norton
OLD LEYS LANE
Old Leys
Crossholme Farm
GLENTHAM ROAD
Atterby Beck
NORTON LANE
Old Street Farm
New Close Plantation
Bracken's Wood
LN8
Waterloo Plantation
BARFF LANE
Glentham Cliff
Norton Place
Halfmoon Plantation
Sewage Works
Glentham
BISHOP NORTON ROAD
PH
Hemswell Cliff
Cherry Tree Farm
Highfield Farm
HIGH STREET
Spital in the Street
Hemswell Prim Sch
Spital Plantation
A631
CAENBY RD
8
97
7
96
6
95
5
94
4
93
3
92
2
91
1
90
95 A 96 B 97 C 98 D 99 E 00 F
55
44
D3
1 GREENHILL DR
2 EASTFIELDS
3 ARCHER ST
4 MAIN ST
5 WELL ST
F1
1 MIDDLEFIELD LA
2 WASHDYKE LA
3 GREENFIELDS
4 HIGHFIELD TR
5 CHURCH LA
6 GLENTHAM CT

43 31 32

Scale: 1¼ inches to 1 mile

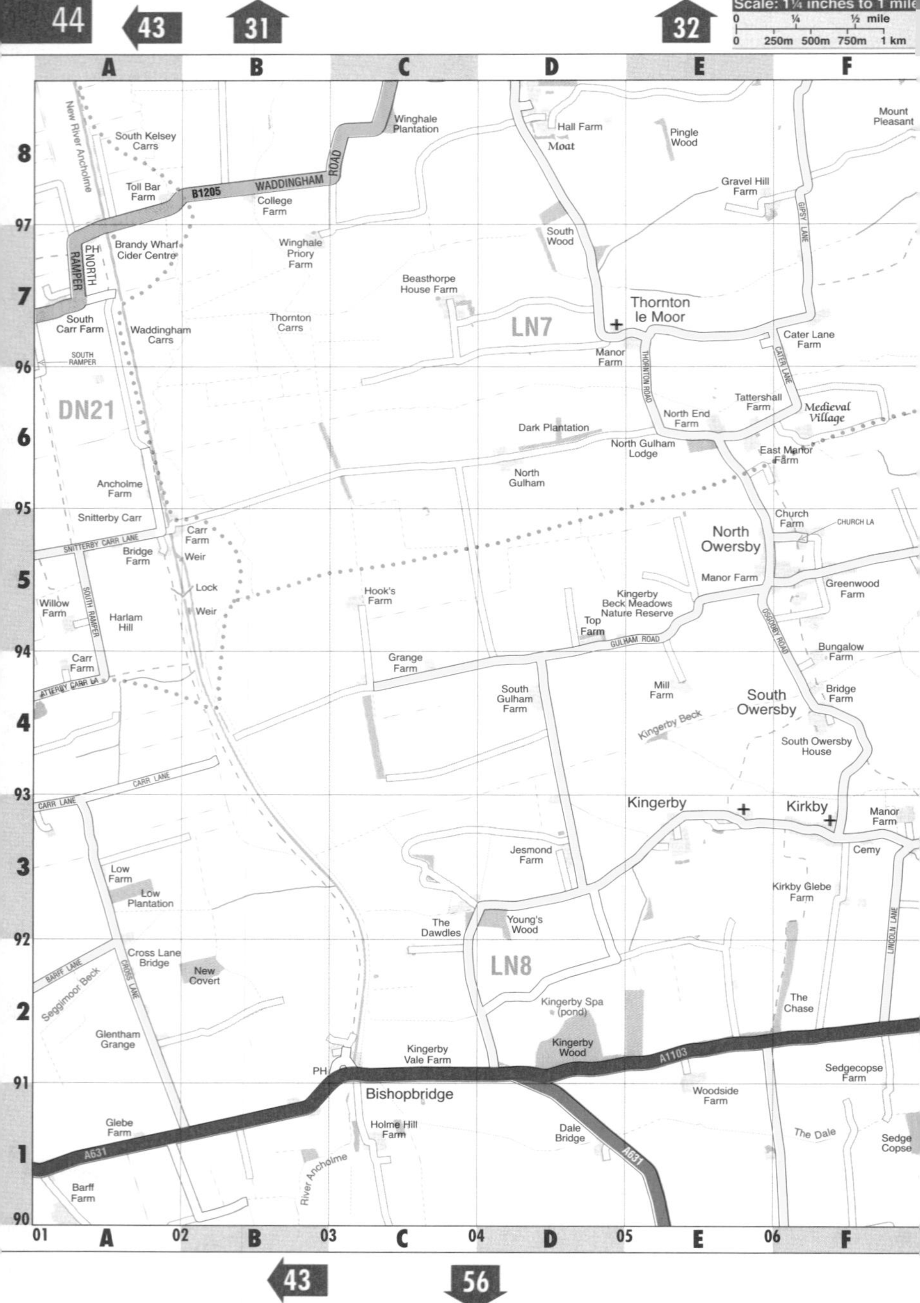

43 56

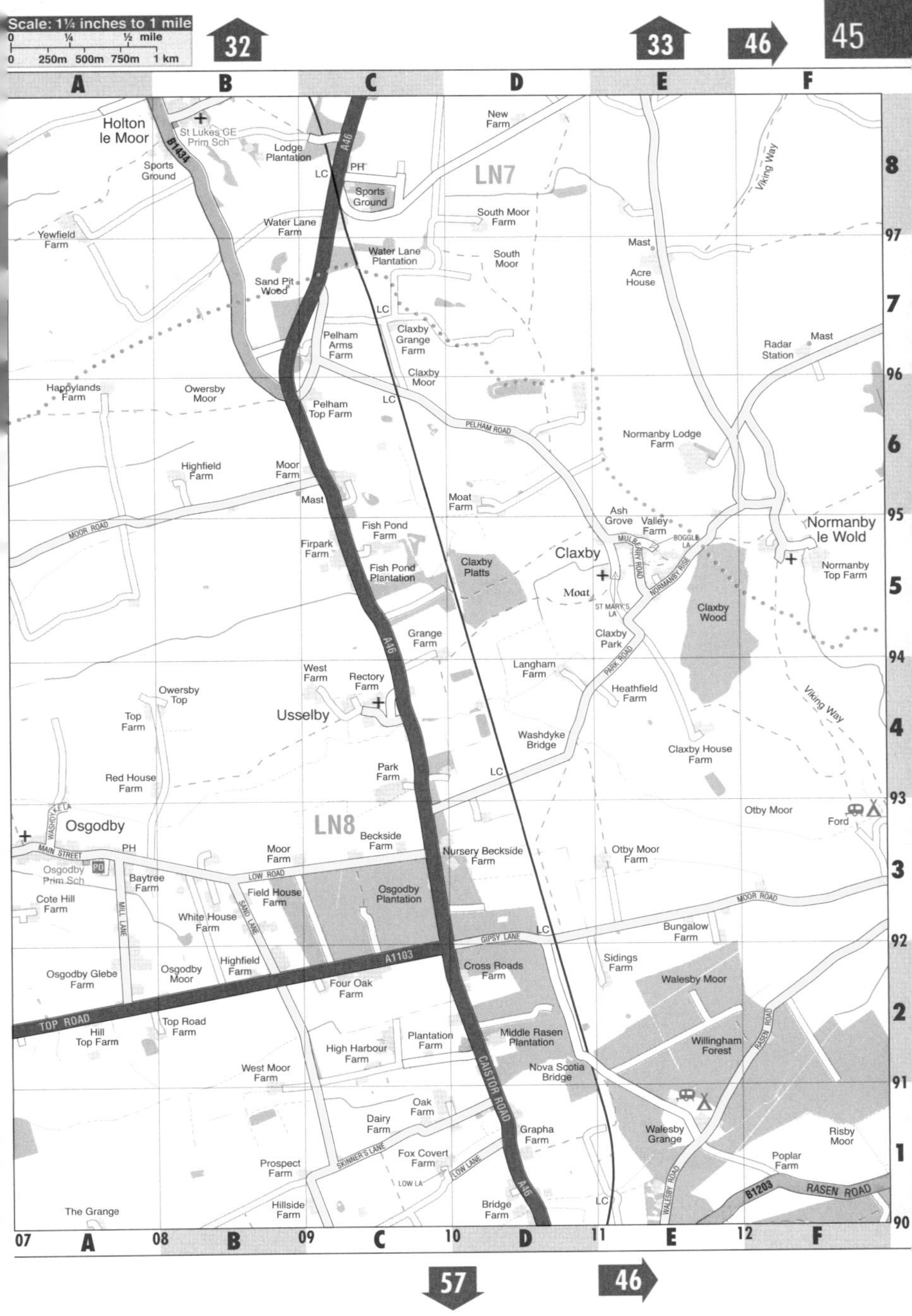
Scale: 1¼ inches to 1 mile
0 ¼ ½ mile
0 250m 500m 750m 1 km
32
33
46
A B C D E F
8
7
6
5
4
3
2
1
97
96
95
94
93
92
91
90
07 08 09 10 11 12
57
46
Holton le Moor
St Lukes CE Prim Sch
B1434
Sports Ground
Lodge Plantation
A46
LC
PH
Sports Ground
New Farm
LN7
Viking Way
South Moor Farm
Yewfield Farm
Water Lane Farm
Water Lane Plantation
South Moor
Mast
Acre House
Sand Pit Wood
Pelham Arms Farm
Claxby Grange Farm
Radar Station
Mast
Happylands Farm
Owersby Moor
Claxby Moor
Pelham Top Farm
PELHAM ROAD
Normanby Lodge Farm
Highfield Farm
Moor Farm
Mast
Moat Farm
MOOR ROAD
Fish Pond Farm
Ash Grove
Valley Farm
Normanby le Wold
Firpark Farm
Claxby
MULBERRY ROAD
BOGGLE LA
NORMANBY RISE
Fish Pond Plantation
Claxby Platts
Normanby Top Farm
Moat
ST MARY'S LA
Claxby Wood
Grange Farm
Claxby Park
PARK ROAD
Langham Farm
West Farm
Rectory Farm
Heathfield Farm
Owersby Top
Usselby
Top Farm
Washdyke Bridge
Claxby House Farm
Park Farm
Red House Farm
Otby Moor
Ford
Osgodby
WASHDYKE LA
LN8
Beckside Farm
MAIN STREET
PH
Moor Farm
Nursery Beckside Farm
Otby Moor Farm
Osgodby Prim Sch
PO
LOW ROAD
Baytree Farm
Field House Farm
Osgodby Plantation
Cote Hill Farm
MILL LANE
SAND LANE
White House Farm
MOOR ROAD
Bungalow Farm
GIPSY LANE
A1103
Highfield Farm
Cross Roads Farm
Sidings Farm
Osgodby Glebe Farm
Osgodby Moor
Four Oak Farm
Walesby Moor
TOP ROAD
Top Road Farm
Hill Top Farm
Plantation Farm
Middle Rasen Plantation
Willingham Forest
RASEN ROAD
High Harbour Farm
West Moor Farm
CAISTOR ROAD
Nova Scotia Bridge
Oak Farm
Dairy Farm
Grapha Farm
Walesby Grange
Risby Moor
SKINNER'S LANE
Fox Covert Farm
Poplar Farm
Prospect Farm
LOW LANE
LOW LA
WALESBY ROAD
B1203
RASEN ROAD
The Grange
Hillside Farm
Bridge Farm

45 33 34

Scale: 1¼ inches to 1 mile

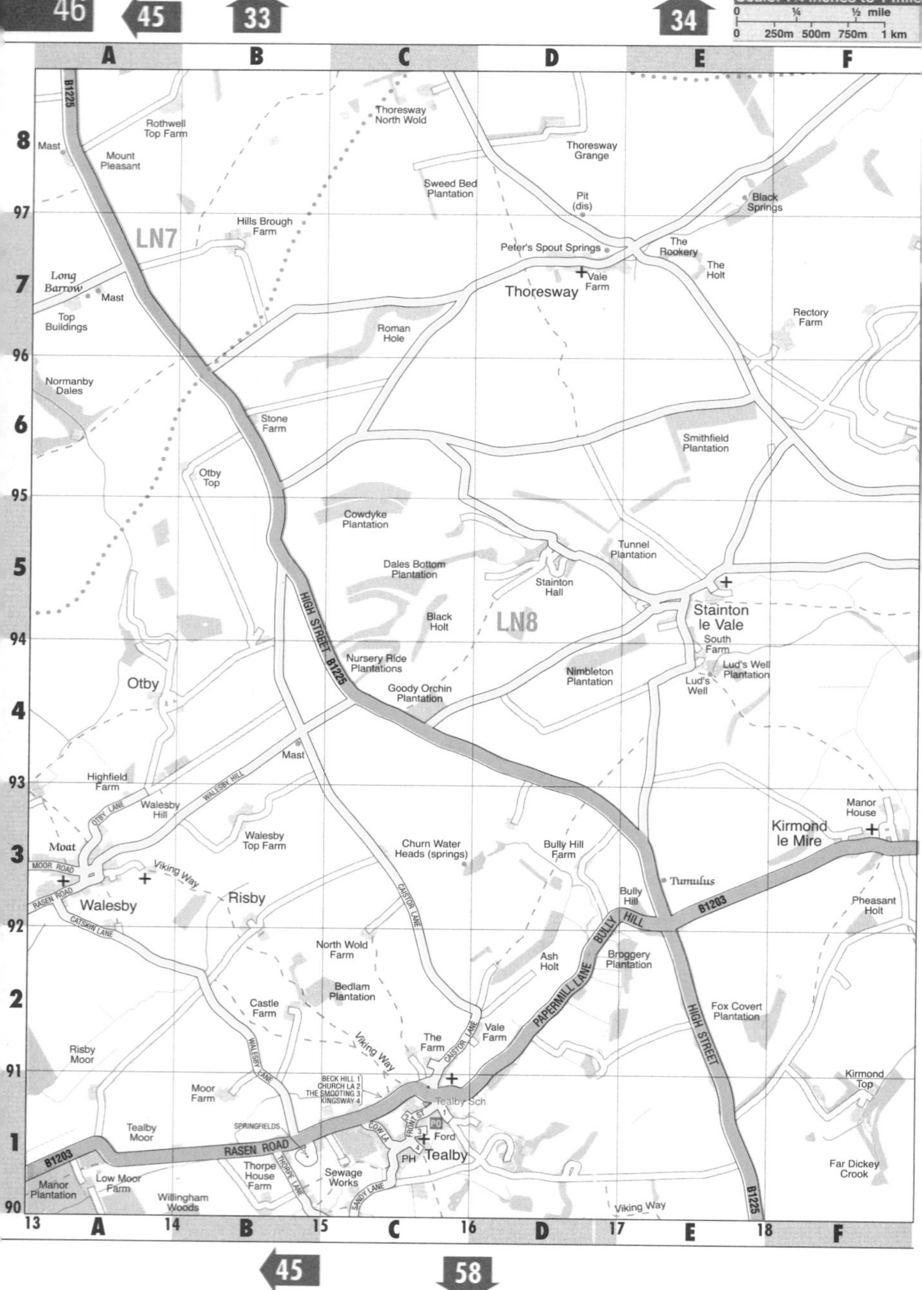

45 58

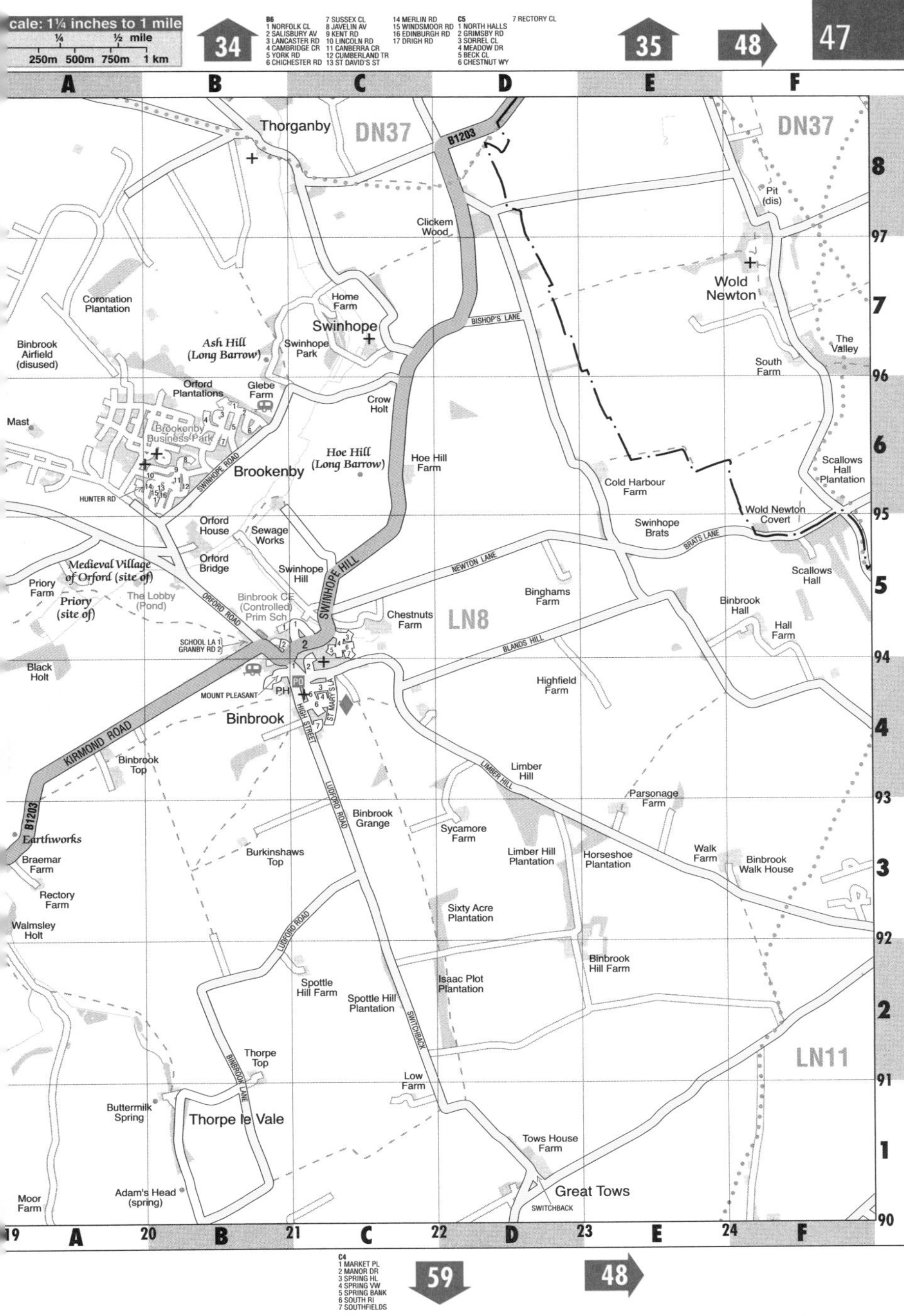
Scale: 1¼ inches to 1 mile
¼
½ mile
250m 500m 750m 1 km
34
B6
1 NORFOLK CL
2 SALISBURY AV
3 LANCASTER RD
4 CAMBRIDGE CR
5 YORK RD
6 CHICHESTER RD
7 SUSSEX CL
8 JAVELIN AV
9 KENT RD
10 LINCOLN RD
11 CANBERRA CR
12 CUMBERLAND TR
13 ST DAVID'S ST
14 MERLIN RD
15 WINDSMOOR RD
16 EDINBURGH RD
17 DRIGH RD
C5
1 NORTH HALLS
2 GRIMSBY RD
3 SORREL CL
4 MEADOW DR
5 BECK CL
6 CHESTNUT WY
7 RECTORY CL
35
48
A
B
C
D
E
F
Thorganby
DN37
B1203
Clickem Wood
Pit (dis)
Wold Newton
Home Farm
Coronation Plantation
Swinhope
BISHOP'S LANE
Binbrook Airfield (disused)
Ash Hill (Long Barrow)
Swinhope Park
The Valley
South Farm
Orford Plantations
Glebe Farm
Crow Holt
Mast
Brookenby Business Park
Hoe Hill (Long Barrow)
Hoe Hill Farm
Scallows Hall Plantation
Brookenby
SWINHOPE ROAD
Cold Harbour Farm
HUNTER RD
Wold Newton Covert
Orford House
Sewage Works
Swinhope Brats
BRATS LANE
Orford Bridge
Medieval Village of Orford (site of)
Swinhope Hill
SWINHOPE HILL
NEWTON LANE
Scallows Hall
Priory Farm
Priory (site of)
The Lobby (Pond)
ORFORD ROAD
Binbrook CE (Controlled) Prim Sch
Binghams Farm
Binbrook Hall
Chestnuts Farm
LN8
Hall Farm
SCHOOL LA 1
GRANBY RD 2
BLANDS HILL
Black Holt
MOUNT PLEASANT
PH
PO
Highfield Farm
HIGH STREET
ST MARY'S LA
Binbrook
KIRMOND ROAD
Binbrook Top
LIMBER HILL
Limber Hill
Parsonage Farm
B1203
Binbrook Grange
LUDFORD ROAD
Sycamore Farm
Earthworks
Burkinshaws Top
Limber Hill Plantation
Horseshoe Plantation
Walk Farm
Binbrook Walk House
Braemar Farm
Rectory Farm
Sixty Acre Plantation
Walmsley Holt
LUDFORD ROAD
Binbrook Hill Farm
Spottle Hill Farm
Isaac Plot Plantation
Spottle Hill Plantation
SWITCHBACK
LN11
Thorpe Top
BINBROOK LANE
Low Farm
Buttermilk Spring
Thorpe le Vale
Tows House Farm
Great Tows
SWITCHBACK
Adam's Head (spring)
Moor Farm
8
97
7
96
6
95
5
94
4
93
3
92
2
91
1
90
19
20
21
22
23
24
C4
1 MARKET PL
2 MANOR DR
3 SPRING HL
4 SPRING VW
5 SPRING BANK
6 SOUTH RI
7 SOUTHFIELDS
59
48

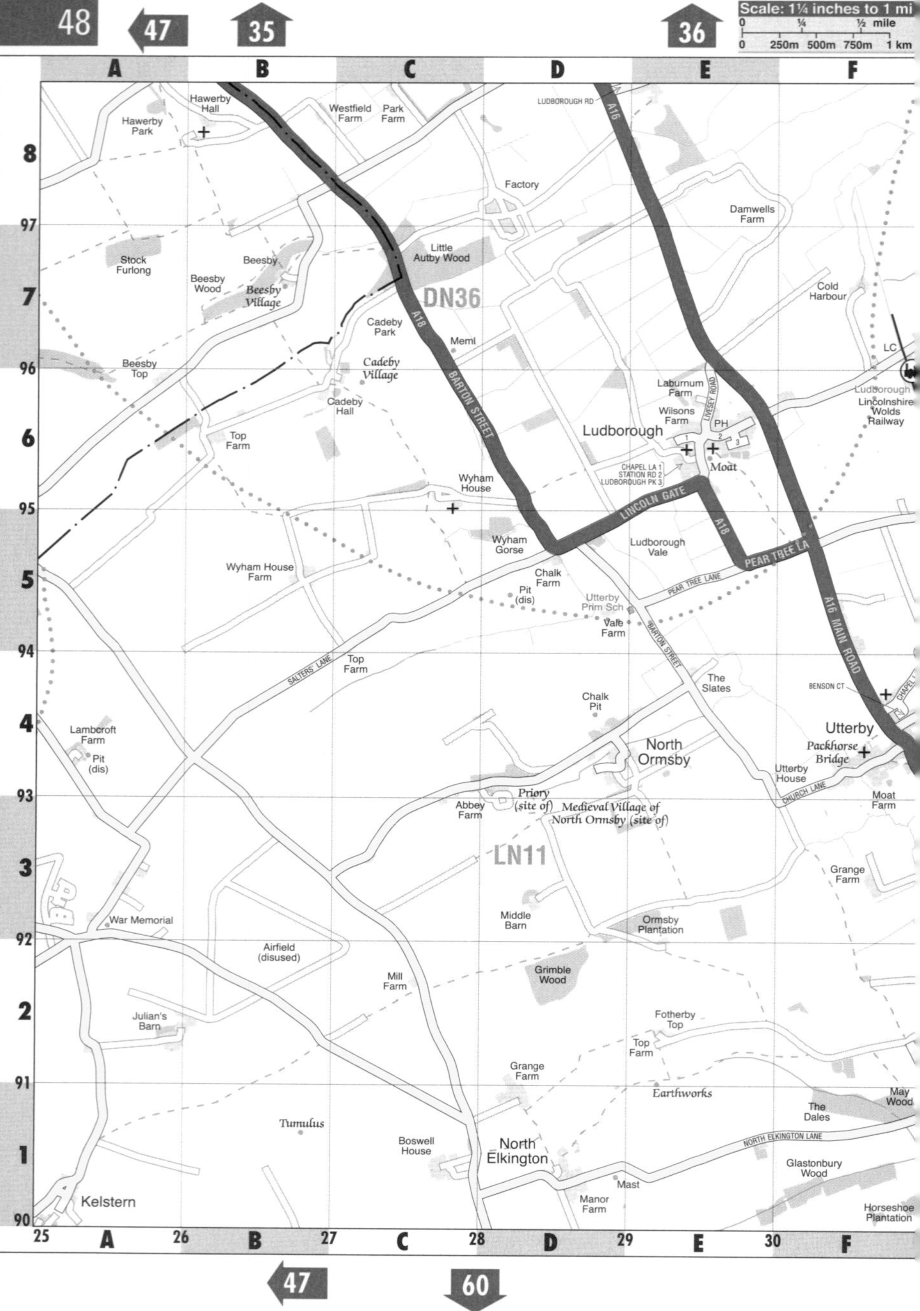
47
35
36
Scale: 1¼ inches to 1 mi
0 ¼ ½ mile
0 250m 500m 750m 1 km
A B C D E F
8 97 7 96 6 95 5 94 4 93 3 92 2 91 1 90
25 26 27 28 29 30
Hawerby Hall
Hawerby Park
Westfield Farm
Park Farm
LUDBOROUGH RD
A16
Factory
Damwells Farm
Stock Furlong
Beesby
Beesby Wood
Beesby Village
Little Autby Wood
DN36
A18
Cold Harbour
Cadeby Park
Meml
Beesby Top
Cadeby Village
Cadeby Hall
LC
Laburnum Farm
LIVESEY ROAD
Wilsons Farm
PH
Ludborough
Ludborough
Lincolnshire Wolds Railway
BARTON STREET
Top Farm
Moat
CHAPEL LA 1
STATION RD 2
LUDBOROUGH PK 3
Wyham House
LINCOLN GATE
Ludborough Vale
PEAR TREE LA
Wyham Gorse
Wyham House Farm
Chalk Farm
PEAR TREE LANE
Pit (dis)
Utterby Prim Sch
Vale Farm
A16 MAIN ROAD
SALTERS' LANE
Top Farm
The Slates
BENSON CT
CHAPEL
Chalk Pit
Lambcroft Farm
Utterby
Pit (dis)
North Ormsby
Packhorse Bridge
Utterby House
CHURCH LANE
Priory (site of)
Abbey Farm
Medieval Village of North Ormsby (site of)
Moat Farm
LN11
Grange Farm
B1
War Memorial
Middle Barn
Ormsby Plantation
Airfield (disused)
Mill Farm
Grimble Wood
Julian's Barn
Fotherby Top
Top Farm
Grange Farm
Earthworks
The Dales
May Wood
Tumulus
NORTH ELKINGTON LANE
Boswell House
North Elkington
Glastonbury Wood
Mast
Kelstern
Manor Farm
Horseshoe Plantation
A B C D E F
47
60

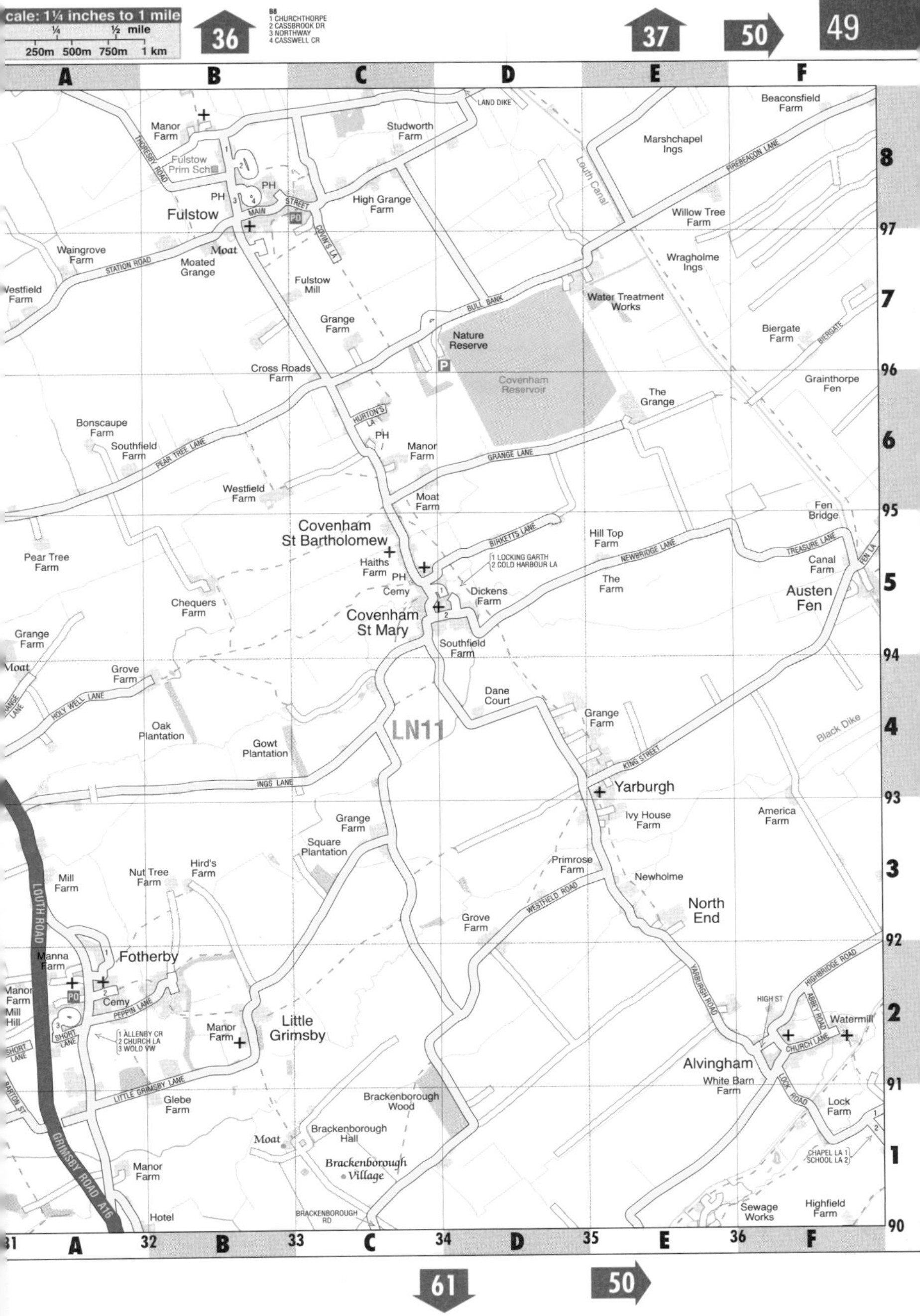
cale: 1¼ inches to 1 mile
¼
½ mile
250m 500m 750m 1 km
36
B8
1 CHURCHTHORPE
2 CASSBROOK DR
3 NORTHWAY
4 CASSWELL CR
37
50
49
A
B
C
D
E
F
8
97
7
96
6
95
5
94
4
93
3
92
2
91
1
90
Manor Farm
Fulstow Prim Sch
PH
Fulstow
MAIN STREET
PO
COVIN'S LA
Moat
THORESBY ROAD
Studworth Farm
LAND DIKE
High Grange Farm
Marshchapel Ings
Beaconsfield Farm
FIREBEACON LANE
Louth Canal
Willow Tree Farm
Wragholme Ings
Waingrove Farm
STATION ROAD
Moated Grange
Westfield Farm
Fulstow Mill
BULL BANK
Water Treatment Works
Grange Farm
Nature Reserve
P
Covenham Reservoir
Biergate Farm
BIERGATE
Cross Roads Farm
Grainthorpe Fen
The Grange
HURTON'S LA
Bonscaupe Farm
Southfield Farm
PEAR TREE LANE
Manor Farm
GRANGE LANE
Westfield Farm
Moat Farm
Fen Bridge
Covenham St Bartholomew
BIRKETTS LANE
Hill Top Farm
Haiths Farm
1 LOCKING GARTH
2 COLD HARBOUR LA
NEWBRIDGE LANE
TREASURE LANE
FEN LA
Canal Farm
Pear Tree Farm
Cemy
Dickens Farm
The Farm
Austen Fen
Chequers Farm
Covenham St Mary
Southfield Farm
Grange Farm
Moat
Grove Farm
HOLY WELL LANE
GRANGE LANE
Dane Court
Grange Farm
Black Dike
Oak Plantation
LN11
Gowt Plantation
KING STREET
INGS LANE
Yarburgh
Ivy House Farm
America Farm
Grange Farm
Square Plantation
Primrose Farm
Newholme
Mill Farm
Nut Tree Farm
Hird's Farm
LOUTH ROAD
WESTFIELD ROAD
North End
Grove Farm
Manna Farm
Fotherby
YARBURGH ROAD
HIGHBRIDGE ROAD
HIGH ST
ABBEY ROAD
Manor Farm
Mill Hill
PO
Cemy
PEPPIN LANE
Little Grimsby
Manor Farm
Watermill
SHORT LANE
1 ALLENBY CR
2 CHURCH LA
3 WOLD VW
CHURCH LANE
Alvingham
White Barn Farm
LITTLE GRIMSBY LANE
Glebe Farm
BARTON ST
LOCK ROAD
Lock Farm
Brackenborough Wood
Brackenborough Hall
Moat
CHAPEL LA 1
SCHOOL LA 2
GRIMSBY ROAD A16
Manor Farm
Brackenborough Village
Hotel
BRACKENBOROUGH RD
Sewage Works
Highfield Farm
31
32
33
34
35
36
61
50

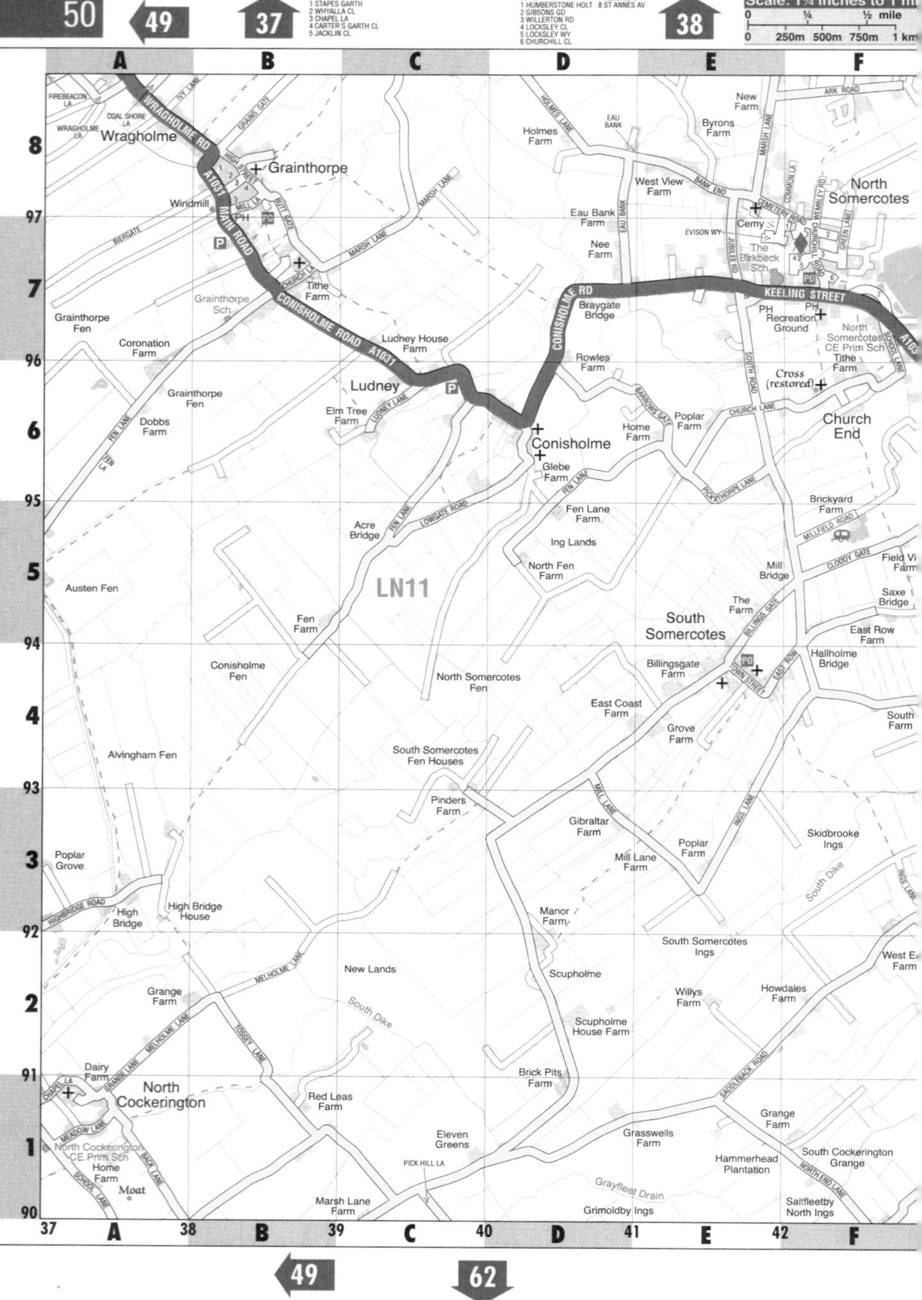
Scale: 1¼ inches to 1 mile
0 ¼ ½ mile
0 250m 500m 750m 1 km
Wragholme
Grainthorpe
Windmill
Grainthorpe Fen
Coronation Farm
Dobbs Farm
Austen Fen
Conisholme Fen
Alvingham Fen
Poplar Grove
High Bridge
High Bridge House
Grange Farm
Dairy Farm
North Cockerington
North Cockerington CE Prim Sch
Home Farm
Moat
Holmes Farm
West View Farm
Eau Bank Farm
Nee Farm
Braygate Bridge
Rowles Farm
Ludney House Farm
Ludney
Elm Tree Farm
Conisholme
Glebe Farm
Home Farm
Poplar Farm
Fen Lane Farm
Ing Lands
North Fen Farm
Acre Bridge
LN11
Fen Farm
North Somercotes Fen
South Somercotes Fen Houses
Pinders Farm
New Lands
South Dike
Red Leas Farm
Eleven Greens
Marsh Lane Farm
Brick Pits Farm
Scupholme
Scupholme House Farm
Manor Farm
Gibraltar Farm
Mill Lane Farm
Poplar Farm
East Coast Farm
Grove Farm
Billingsgate Farm
South Somercotes
The Farm
Mill Bridge
South Somercotes Ings
Willys Farm
Howdales Farm
Grasswells Farm
Grange Farm
Hammerhead Plantation
Grimoldby Ings
Grayfleet Drain
Saltfleetby North Ings
South Cockerington Grange
Skidbrooke Ings
West E. Farm
South Farm
Hallholme Bridge
East Row Farm
Saxe Bridge
Field Vi Farm
Brickyard Farm
Church End
Cross (restored)
Tithe Farm
North Somercotes CE Prim Sch
Recreation Ground
North Somercotes
The Birkbeck Sch
Cemy
New Farm
Byrons Farm
EAU BANK
Tithe Farm
Grainthorpe Sch
WRAGHOLME RD
A1031
MAIN ROAD
CONISHOLME ROAD
CONISHOLME RD
KEELING STREET
BANK END
HOLMES LANE
MARSH LANE
FEN LANE
LOWGATE ROAD
MELHOLME LANE
TOSSEY LANE
HIGHBRIDGE ROAD
SADDLEBACK ROAD
NORTH END LANE
MILL LANE
INGS LANE
BILLINGS GATE
TOWN STREET
EAST ROW
CLODDY GATE
MILLFIELD ROAD
PICKTHORPE LANE
CHURCH LANE
SOUTH ROAD
JUBILEE RD
CEMETERY ROAD
EVISON WY
ARK ROAD
PICK HILL LA
BARROWS GATE
LUDNEY LANE
GRANGE LANE
CHAPEL LA
MEADOW LANE
SCHOOL LANE
BACK LANE
FIREBEACON LA
COAL SHORE LA
WRAGHOLME LA
IVY LANE
GRAINS GATE
BIERGATE
CHURCH LA
BUTT GATE
HIGH STREET
MILL LA
SCHOOL LANE
A B C D E F
8 97 7 96 6 95 5 94 4 93 3 92 2 91 1 90
37 38 39 40 41 42

38

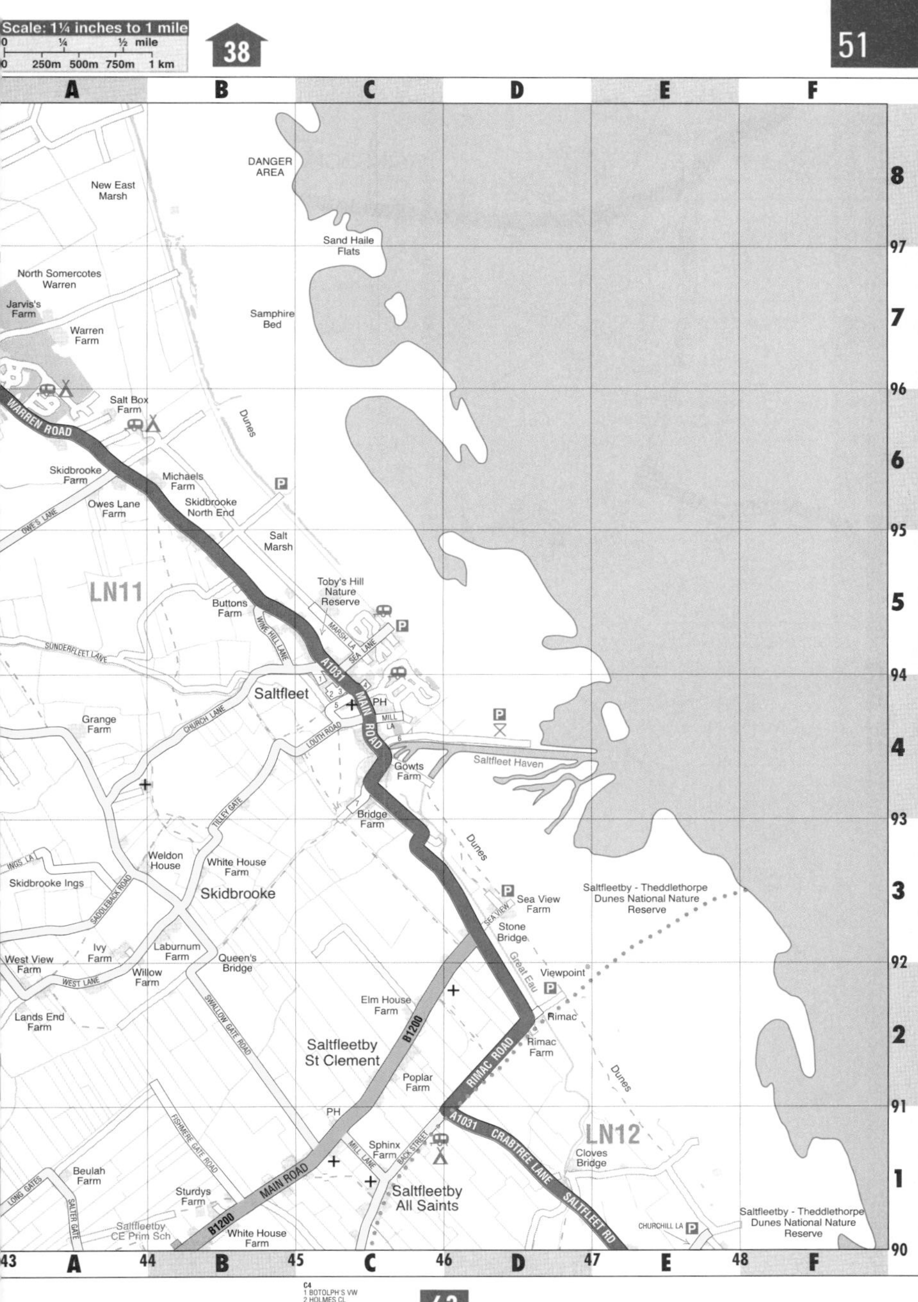

C4
1 BOTOLPH'S VW
2 HOLMES CL
3 JACKLIN DR
4 THE HILL
5 PUMP LA
6 HAVEN BANK
7 GREYFLEET BANK

63

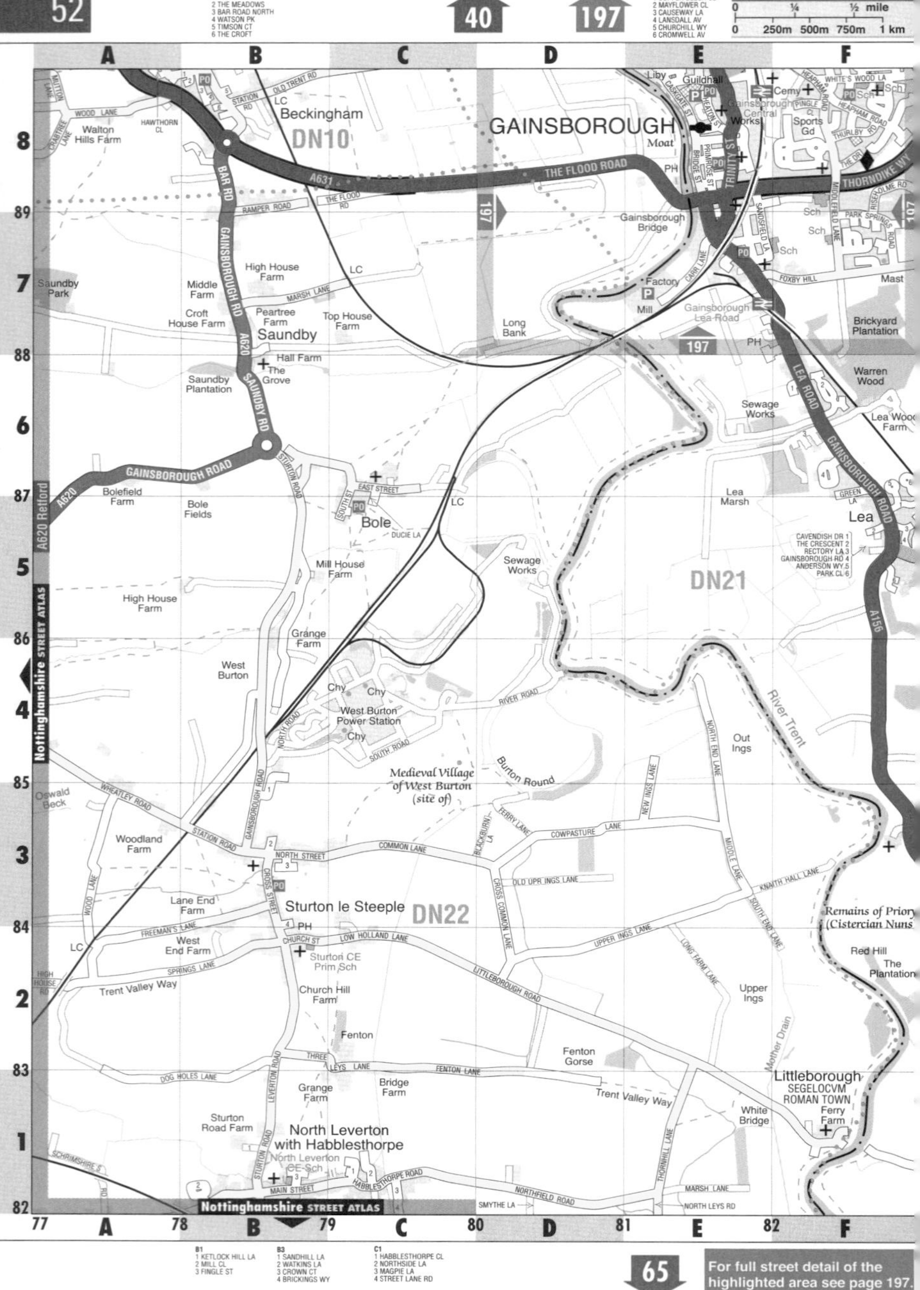
52
B8
1 HIGH ST
2 THE MEADOWS
3 BAR ROAD NORTH
4 WATSON PK
5 TIMSON CT
6 THE CROFT
7 BAR ROAD SOUTH
40
197
F6
1 COPPER BEECH CL
2 MAYFLOWER CL
3 CAUSEWAY LA
4 LANSDALL AV
5 CHURCHILL WY
6 CROMWELL AV
Scale: 1¼ inches to 1 mile
0 ¼ ½ mile
0 250m 500m 750m 1 km
A B C D E F
8 89 7 88 6 87 5 86 4 85 3 84 2 83 1 82
77 78 79 80 81 82
Beckingham
DN10
GAINSBOROUGH
Moat
Guildhall
Liby
Gainsborough Central
Works
Cemy
Sports Gd
THE FLOOD ROAD
A631
THORNDIKE WY
RAMPER ROAD
BAR RD
GAINSBOROUGH RD
A620
SAUNDBY RD
Walton Hills Farm
WOOD LANE
HAWTHORN CL
STATION RD
OLD TRENT RD
LC
Gainsborough Bridge
Saundby Park
Middle Farm
High House Farm
MARSH LANE
Croft House Farm
Peartree Farm
Top House Farm
Saundby
Hall Farm
The Grove
Saundby Plantation
Long Bank
Factory
Mill
Gainsborough Lea Road
197
PH
Brickyard Plantation
Warren Wood
LEA ROAD
Sewage Works
Lea Wood Farm
FOXBY HILL
Mast
Sch
GAINSBOROUGH ROAD
A620 Retford
Bolefield Farm
Bole Fields
EAST STREET
SOUTH ST
Bole
DUCIE LA
STURTON ROAD
Lea Marsh
Lea
GREEN LA
CAVENDISH DR 1
THE CRESCENT 2
RECTORY LA 3
GAINSBOROUGH RD 4
ANDERSON WY 5
PARK CL 6
DN21
A156
Mill House Farm
Sewage Works
High House Farm
Grange Farm
West Burton
Chy
West Burton Power Station
RIVER ROAD
NORTH ROAD
SOUTH ROAD
River Trent
Out Ings
Medieval Village of West Burton (site of)
Burton Round
NORTH END LANE
NEW INGS LANE
Oswald Beck
WHEATLEY ROAD
STATION ROAD
GAINSBOROUGH ROAD
Woodland Farm
NORTH STREET
COMMON LANE
BLACKBURN LA
FERRY LANE
COWPASTURE LANE
MIDDLE LANE
CROSS STREET
OLD UPR INGS LANE
CROSS COMMON LANE
KNAITH HALL LANE
Lane End Farm
Sturton le Steeple
DN22
Remains of Priory (Cistercian Nuns)
WOOD LANE
FREEMAN'S LANE
West End Farm
CHURCH ST
LOW HOLLAND LANE
UPPER INGS LANE
SOUTH END LANE
Sturton CE Prim Sch
Red Hill
The Plantation
SPRINGS LANE
HIGH HOUSE RD
Trent Valley Way
Church Hill Farm
LITTLEBOROUGH ROAD
LONG FARM LANE
Upper Ings
Fenton
Mother Drain
THREE LEYS LANE
FENTON LANE
Fenton Gorse
DOG HOLES LANE
LEVERTON ROAD
Grange Farm
Bridge Farm
Trent Valley Way
Littleborough
SEGELOCVM ROMAN TOWN
White Bridge
Ferry Farm
Sturton Road Farm
North Leverton with Habblesthorpe
North Leverton CE Sch
STURTON ROAD
THORNHILL LANE
SCHRIMSHIRE'S RD
MAIN STREET
HABBLESTHORPE ROAD
NORTHFIELD ROAD
MARSH LANE
SMYTHE LA
NORTH LEYS RD
Nottinghamshire STREET ATLAS
B1
1 KETLOCK HILL LA
2 MILL CL
3 FINGLE ST
B3
1 SANDHILL LA
2 WATKINS LA
3 CROWN CT
4 BRICKINGS WY
C1
1 HABBLESTHORPE CL
2 NORTHSIDE LA
3 MAGPIE LA
4 STREET LANE RD
65
For full street detail of the highlighted area see page 197.

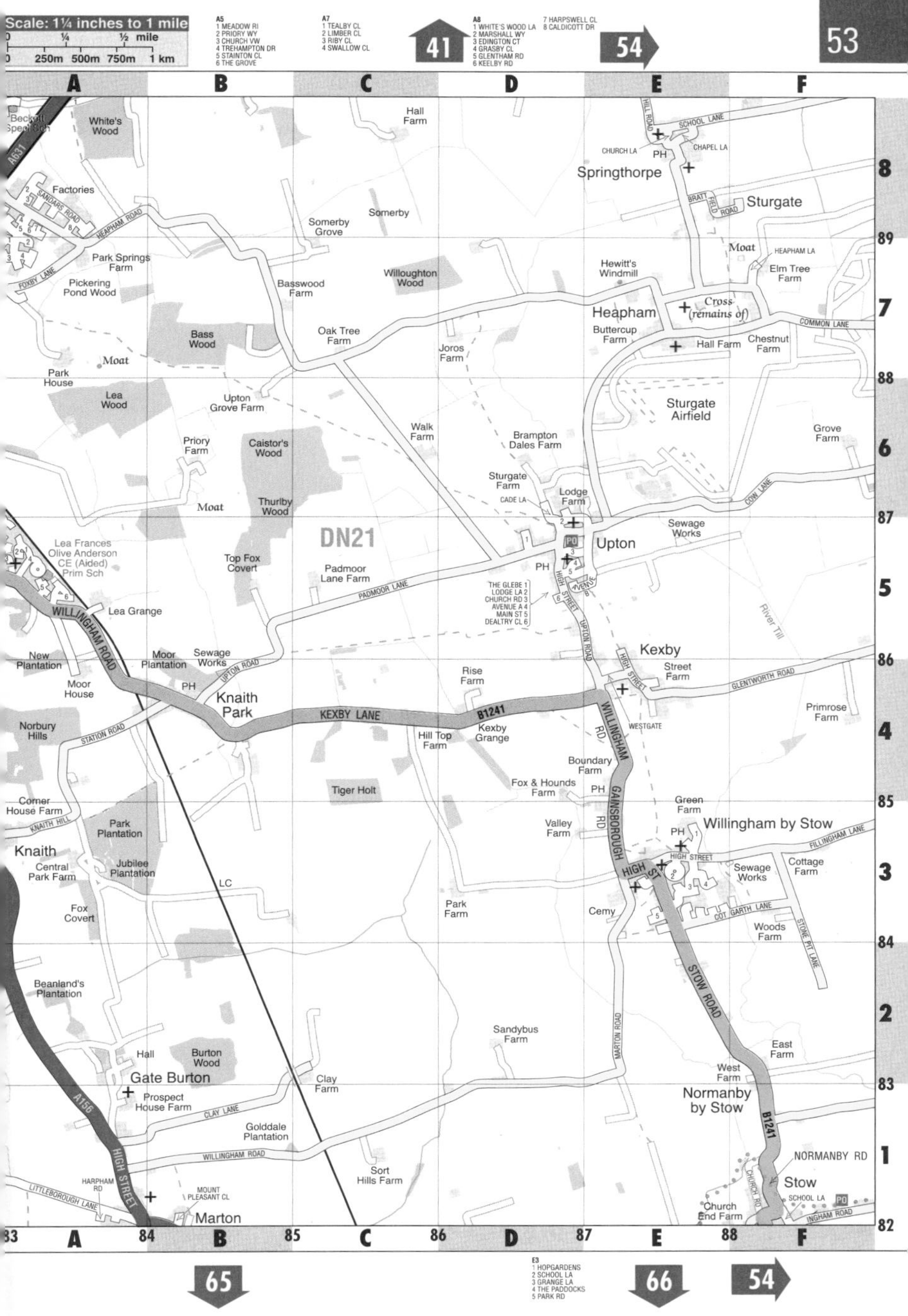

53
Scale: 1¼ inches to 1 mile
0 ¼ ½ mile
0 250m 500m 750m 1 km
A5
1 MEADOW RI
2 PRIORY WY
3 CHURCH VW
4 TREHAMPTON DR
5 STAINTON CL
6 THE GROVE
A7
1 TEALBY CL
2 LIMBER CL
3 RIBY CL
4 SWALLOW CL
41
A8
1 WHITE'S WOOD LA
2 MARSHALL WY
3 EDINGTON CT
4 GRASBY CL
5 GLENTHAM RD
6 KEELBY RD
7 HARPSWELL CL
8 CALDICOTT DR
54
A B C D E F
8 89 7 88 6 87 5 86 4 85 3 84 2 83 1 82
White's Wood
Hall Farm
SCHOOL LANE
HILL ROAD
CHURCH LA
PH
CHAPEL LA
Springthorpe
Sturgate
BRATT FIELD ROAD
A631
Factories
SANDARS ROAD
HEAPHAM ROAD
Somerby Grove
Somerby
Moat
HEAPHAM LA
Elm Tree Farm
Park Springs Farm
Pickering Pond Wood
FOXBY LANE
Basswood Farm
Willoughton Wood
Hewitt's Windmill
Heapham
Cross (remains of)
COMMON LANE
Bass Wood
Oak Tree Farm
Joros Farm
Buttercup Farm
Hall Farm
Chestnut Farm
Park House
Moat
Lea Wood
Upton Grove Farm
Sturgate Airfield
Walk Farm
Brampton Dales Farm
Grove Farm
Priory Farm
Caistor's Wood
Sturgate Farm
CADE LA
Lodge Farm
COW LANE
Moat
Thurlby Wood
DN21
Sewage Works
Upton
Lea Frances Olive Anderson CE (Aided) Prim Sch
Top Fox Covert
Padmoor Lane Farm
PH
PADMOOR LANE
THE GLEBE 1
LODGE LA 2
CHURCH RD 3
AVENUE A 4
MAIN ST 5
DEALTRY CL 6
HIGH STREET
AVENUE B
UPTON ROAD
River Till
WILLINGHAM ROAD
Lea Grange
Kexby
HIGH STREET
Street Farm
GLENTWORTH ROAD
New Plantation
Moor Plantation
Sewage Works
UPTON ROAD
Moor House
PH
Knaith Park
Rise Farm
KEXBY LANE
B1241
Kexby Grange
Hill Top Farm
WILLINGHAM RD
WESTGATE
Primrose Farm
Norbury Hills
STATION ROAD
Boundary Farm
Fox & Hounds Farm
PH
Tiger Holt
Corner House Farm
KNAITH HILL
Park Plantation
Valley Farm
GAINSBOROUGH RD
Green Farm
Willingham by Stow
PH
FILLINGHAM LANE
Knaith
Central Park Farm
Jubilee Plantation
LC
HIGH ST
HIGH STREET
Sewage Works
Cottage Farm
Fox Covert
Park Farm
Cemy
COT GARTH LANE
Woods Farm
STONE PIT LANE
Beanland's Plantation
STOW ROAD
MARTON ROAD
Sandybus Farm
East Farm
Hall
Burton Wood
Gate Burton
Clay Farm
West Farm
Prospect House Farm
CLAY LANE
Normanby by Stow
A156
Golddale Plantation
B1241
WILLINGHAM ROAD
NORMANBY RD
HIGH STREET
Sort Hills Farm
Stow
HARPHAM RD
LITTLEBOROUGH LANE
MOUNT PLEASANT CL
Marton
CHURCH RD
SCHOOL LA
Church End Farm
INGHAM ROAD
PO
83 A 84 B 85 C 86 D 87 E 88 F
65
E3
1 HOPGARDENS
2 SCHOOL LA
3 GRANGE LA
4 THE PADDOCKS
5 PARK RD
66
54

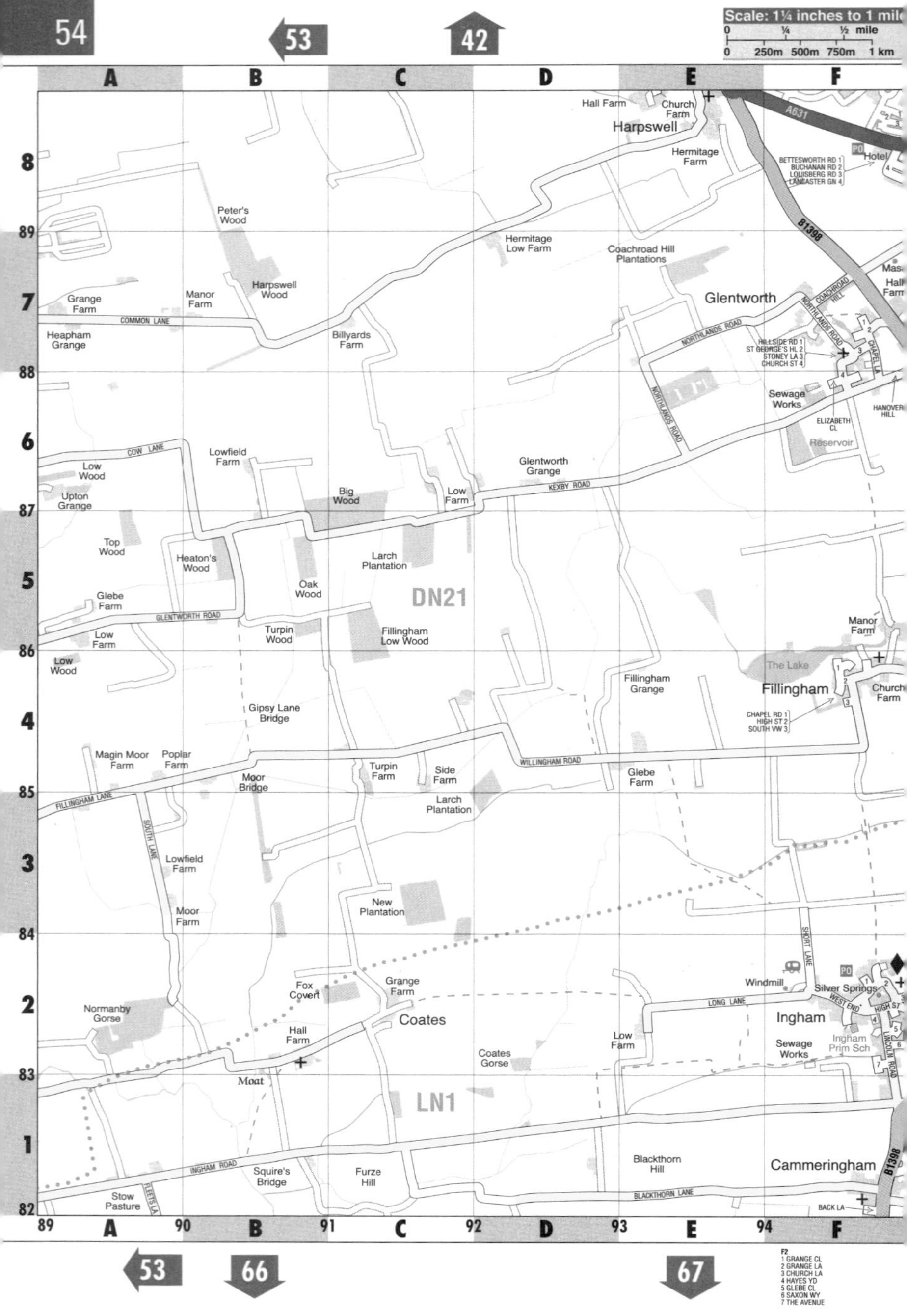
53
42
Scale: 1¼ inches to 1 mile
Harpswell
Hall Farm
Church Farm
Hermitage Farm
BETTESWORTH RD 1
BUCHANAN RD 2
LOUISBERG RD 3
LANCASTER GN 4
Hotel
A631
B1398
Peter's Wood
Hermitage Low Farm
Coachroad Hill Plantations
Harpswell Wood
Glentworth
Grange Farm
Manor Farm
COMMON LANE
Heapham Grange
Billyards Farm
NORTHLANDS ROAD
HILLSIDE RD 1
ST GEORGE'S HL 2
STONEY LA 3
CHURCH ST 4
Sewage Works
ELIZABETH CL
HANOVER HILL
Reservoir
Lowfield Farm
COW LANE
Low Wood
Glentworth Grange
KEXBY ROAD
Big Wood
Low Farm
Upton Grange
Top Wood
Heaton's Wood
Larch Plantation
DN21
Oak Wood
Glebe Farm
GLENTWORTH ROAD
Low Farm
Turpin Wood
Fillingham Low Wood
Low Wood
Manor Farm
The Lake
Fillingham
Church Farm
Fillingham Grange
CHAPEL RD 1
HIGH ST 2
SOUTH VW 3
Gipsy Lane Bridge
Magin Moor Farm
Poplar Farm
Turpin Farm
Side Farm
WILLINGHAM ROAD
Glebe Farm
Moor Bridge
FILLINGHAM LANE
Larch Plantation
SOUTH LANE
Lowfield Farm
New Plantation
Moor Farm
SHORT LANE
Windmill
Silver Springs
Fox Covert
Grange Farm
LONG LANE
WEST END
HIGH ST
Ingham
Normanby Gorse
Coates
Hall Farm
Low Farm
Sewage Works
Ingham Prim Sch
LINCOLN ROAD
Coates Gorse
Moat
LN1
Blackthorn Hill
Cammeringham
INGHAM ROAD
Squire's Bridge
Furze Hill
BLACKTHORN LANE
Stow Pasture
FLEETS LA
BACK LA
F2
1 GRANGE CL
2 GRANGE LA
3 CHURCH LA
4 HAYES YD
5 GLEBE CL
6 SAXON WY
7 THE AVENUE
53
66
67

Scale: 1¼ inches to 1 mile
¼ ½ mile
250m 500m 750m 1 km

A8
1 JAMES RD
2 ANDERSON RD
3 CAPPER AV
4 MINDEN PL
5 GIBRALTAR RD
6 PLASSEY RD
7 LANCASTER GN
8 CREAMPOKE CR

F6
1 MANOR CLIFF
2 FIELD LA
3 NORMANBY RD
4 RECTORY LA
5 CHURCH LA

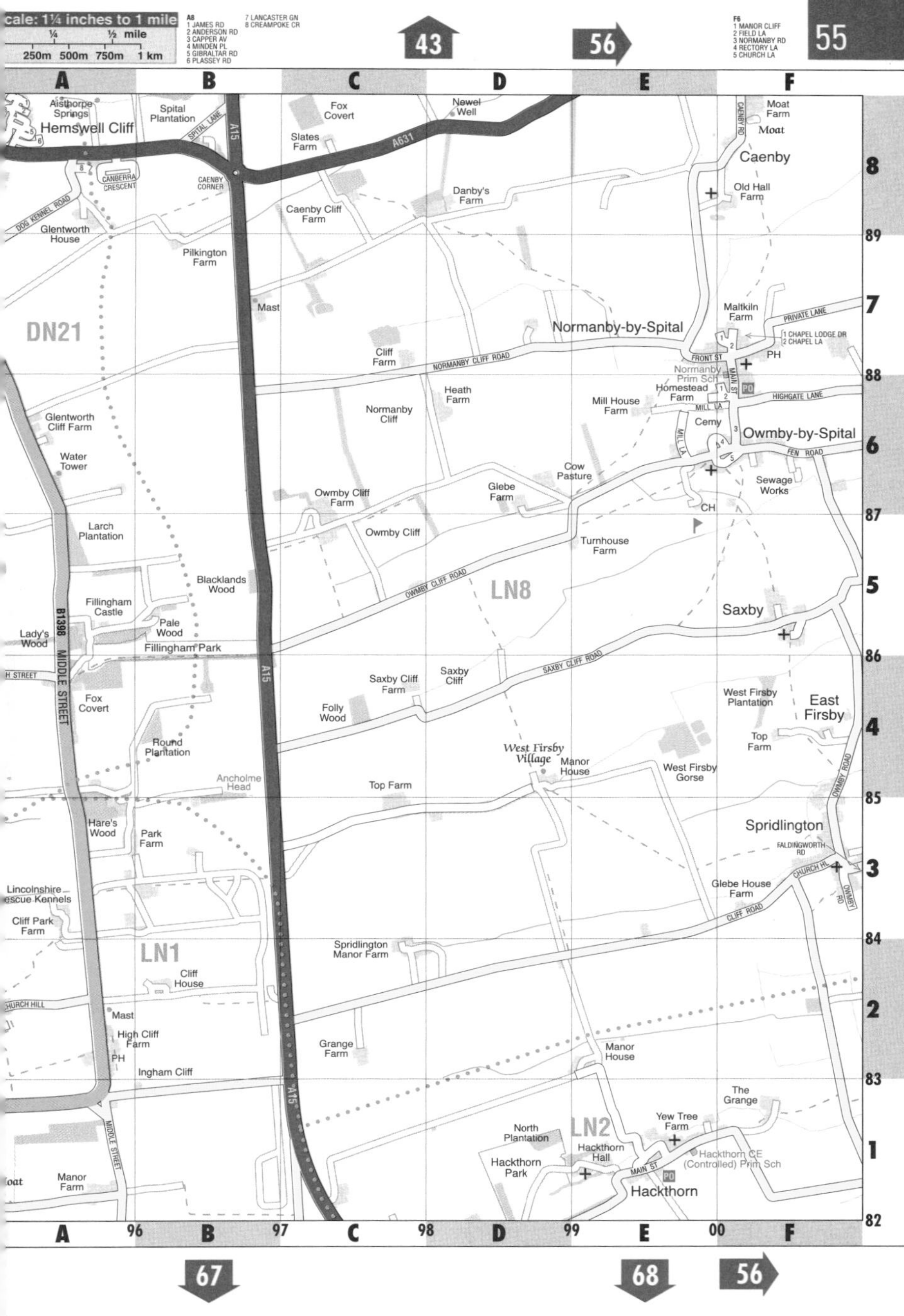

67
68
56

55
44

D5
1 TUDOR CL
2 FAIRFAX CL
3 PRINCE WILLIAM RD
4 ARLINGTON RD
5 WASHINGTON DR

Scale: 1¼ inches to 1 mi

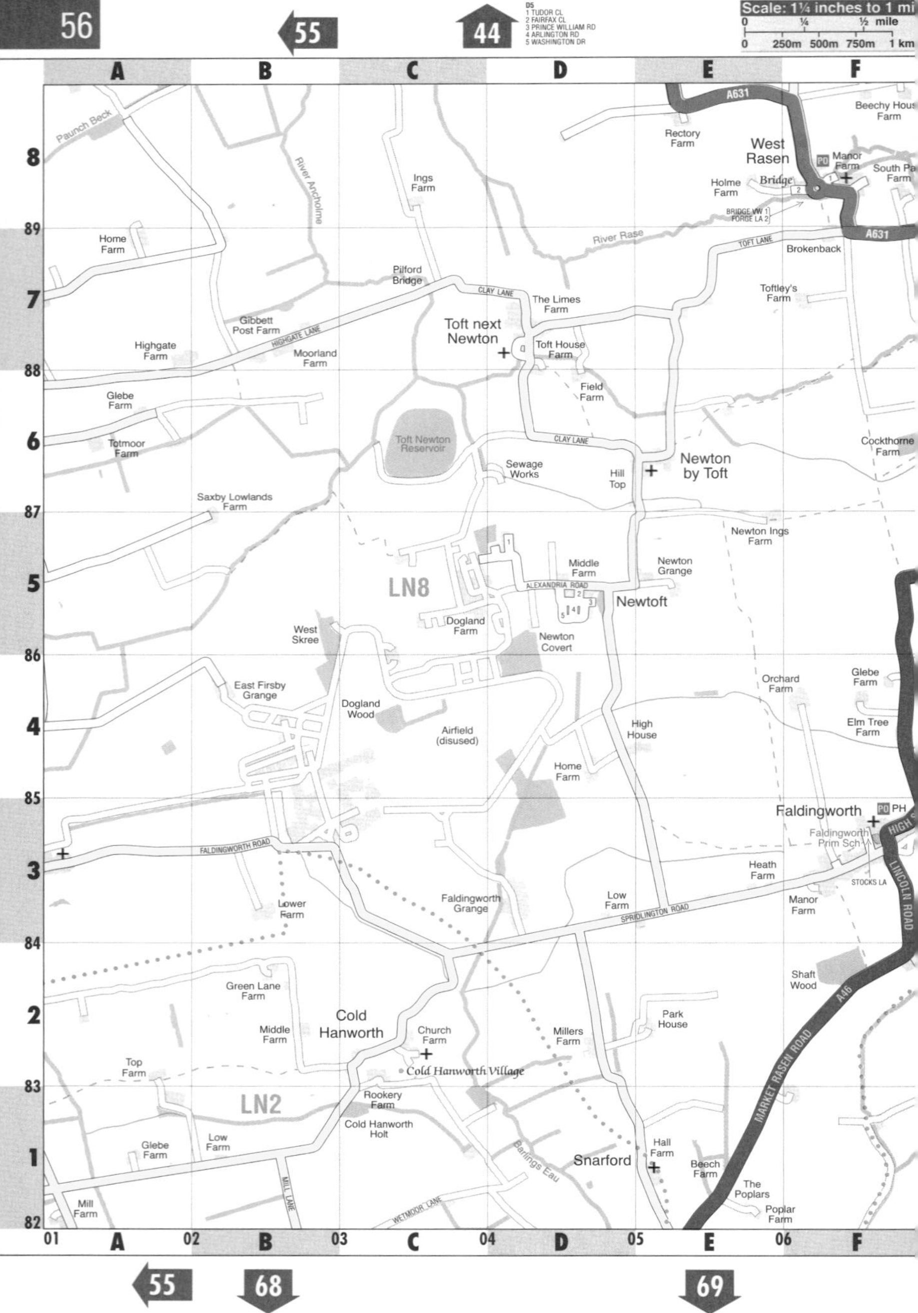

55
68
69

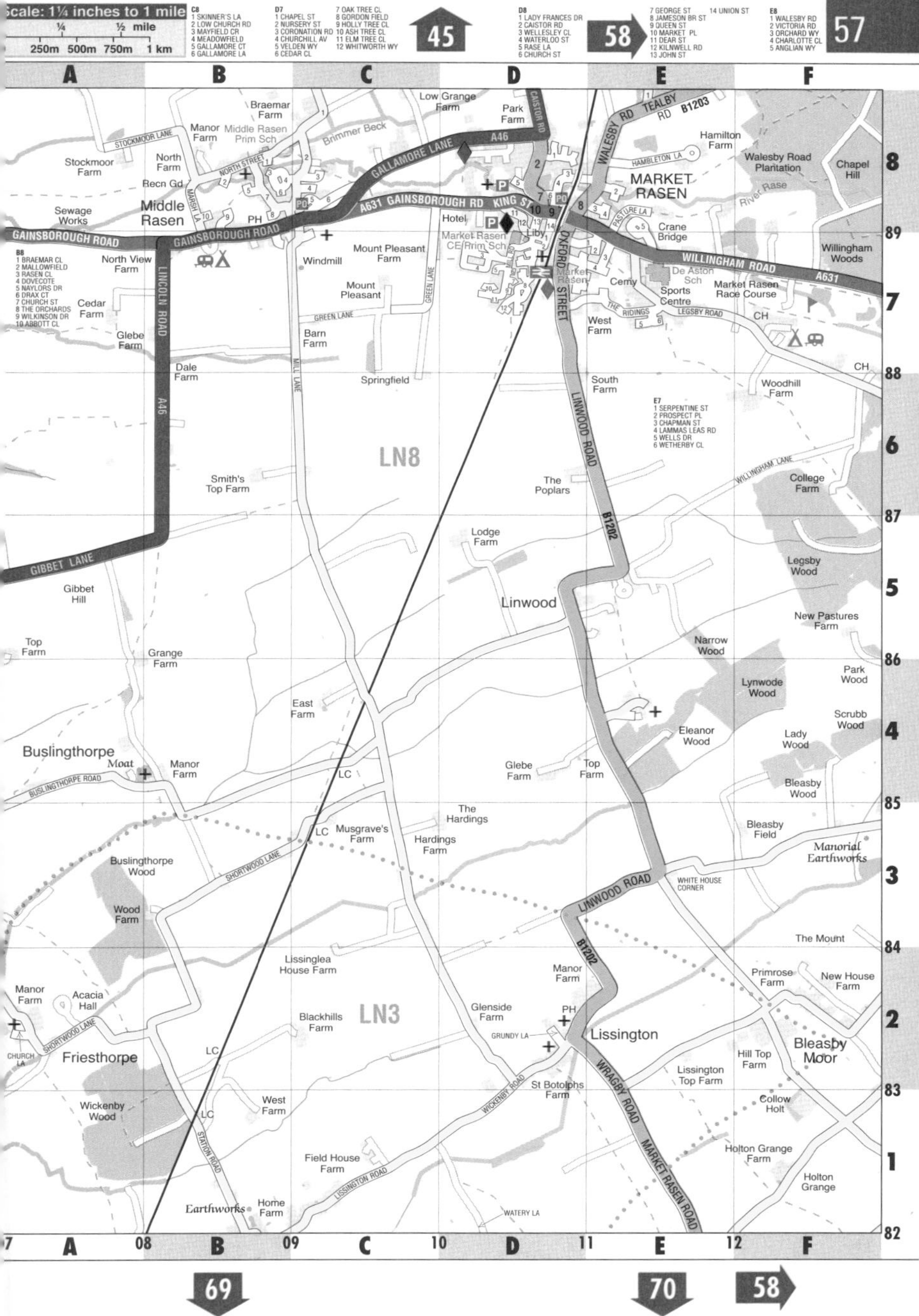
Scale: 1¼ inches to 1 mile
¼ ½ mile
250m 500m 750m 1 km
C8
1 SKINNER'S LA
2 LOW CHURCH RD
3 MAYFIELD CR
4 MEADOWFIELD
5 GALLAMORE CT
6 GALLAMORE LA
D7
1 CHAPEL ST
2 NURSERY ST
3 CORONATION RD
4 CHURCHILL AV
5 VELDEN WY
6 CEDAR CL
7 OAK TREE CL
8 GORDON FIELD
9 HOLLY TREE CL
10 ASH TREE CL
11 ELM TREE CL
12 WHITWORTH WY
45
D8
1 LADY FRANCES DR
2 CAISTOR RD
3 WELLESLEY CL
4 WATERLOO ST
5 RASE LA
6 CHURCH ST
58
7 GEORGE ST
8 JAMESON BR ST
9 QUEEN ST
10 MARKET PL
11 DEAR ST
12 KILNWELL RD
13 JOHN ST
14 UNION ST
E8
1 WALESBY RD
2 VICTORIA RD
3 ORCHARD WY
4 CHARLOTTE CL
5 ANGLIAN WY
57
B8
1 BRAEMAR CL
2 MALLOWFIELD
3 RASEN CL
4 DOVECOTE
5 NAYLORS DR
6 DRAX CT
7 CHURCH ST
8 THE ORCHARDS
9 WILKINSON DR
10 ABBOTT CL
E7
1 SERPENTINE ST
2 PROSPECT PL
3 CHAPMAN ST
4 LAMMAS LEAS RD
5 WELLS DR
6 WETHERBY CL
Braemar Farm
Low Grange Farm
Park Farm
Manor Farm
Middle Rasen Prim Sch
Brimmer Beck
Stockmoor Farm
North Farm
Recn Gd
Sewage Works
Middle Rasen
PH
GAINSBOROUGH ROAD
A631 GAINSBOROUGH RD KING ST
GALLAMORE LANE
A46
Hotel
Market Rasen CE Prim Sch
Liby
MARKET RASEN
Hamilton Farm
Walesby Road Plantation
Chapel Hill
River Rase
Crane Bridge
Willingham Woods
WILLINGHAM ROAD
De Aston Sch
Sports Centre
Market Rasen Race Course
Cemy
West Farm
North View Farm
Windmill
Mount Pleasant Farm
Mount Pleasant
Cedar Farm
Glebe Farm
Barn Farm
Dale Farm
Springfield
South Farm
Woodhill Farm
LN8
Smith's Top Farm
The Poplars
College Farm
Lodge Farm
Legsby Wood
Gibbet Hill
Linwood
New Pastures Farm
Top Farm
Grange Farm
Narrow Wood
Park Wood
Lynwode Wood
East Farm
Eleanor Wood
Scrubb Wood
Lady Wood
Buslingthorpe
Moat
Manor Farm
Glebe Farm
Top Farm
Bleasby Wood
The Hardings
Musgrave's Farm
Hardings Farm
Bleasby Field
Manorial Earthworks
Buslingthorpe Wood
WHITE HOUSE CORNER
Wood Farm
The Mount
Lissinglea House Farm
Manor Farm
Primrose Farm
New House Farm
Manor Farm
Acacia Hall
Blackhills Farm
LN3
Glenside Farm
Lissington
Bleasby Moor
Friesthorpe
CHURCH LA
Hill Top Farm
Lissington Top Farm
St Botolphs Farm
Wickenby Wood
West Farm
Collow Holt
Holton Grange Farm
Field House Farm
Holton Grange
Earthworks
Home Farm
LINCOLN ROAD
GIBBET LANE
MILL LANE
GREEN LANE
LINWOOD ROAD
OXFORD STREET
CAISTOR RD
WALESBY RD
TEALBY RD
B1203
B1202
WILLINGHAM LANE
LEGSBY ROAD
THE RIDINGS
STOCKMOOR LANE
NORTH STREET
MARSH LA
BUSLINGTHORPE ROAD
SHORTWOOD LANE
WICKENBY ROAD
GRUNDY LA
WRAGBY ROAD
MARKET RASEN ROAD
STATION ROAD
LISSINGTON ROAD
WATERY LA
A B C D E F
8 89 7 88 6 87 5 86 4 85 3 84 2 83 1 82
07 08 09 10 11 12
69
70
58

57
46

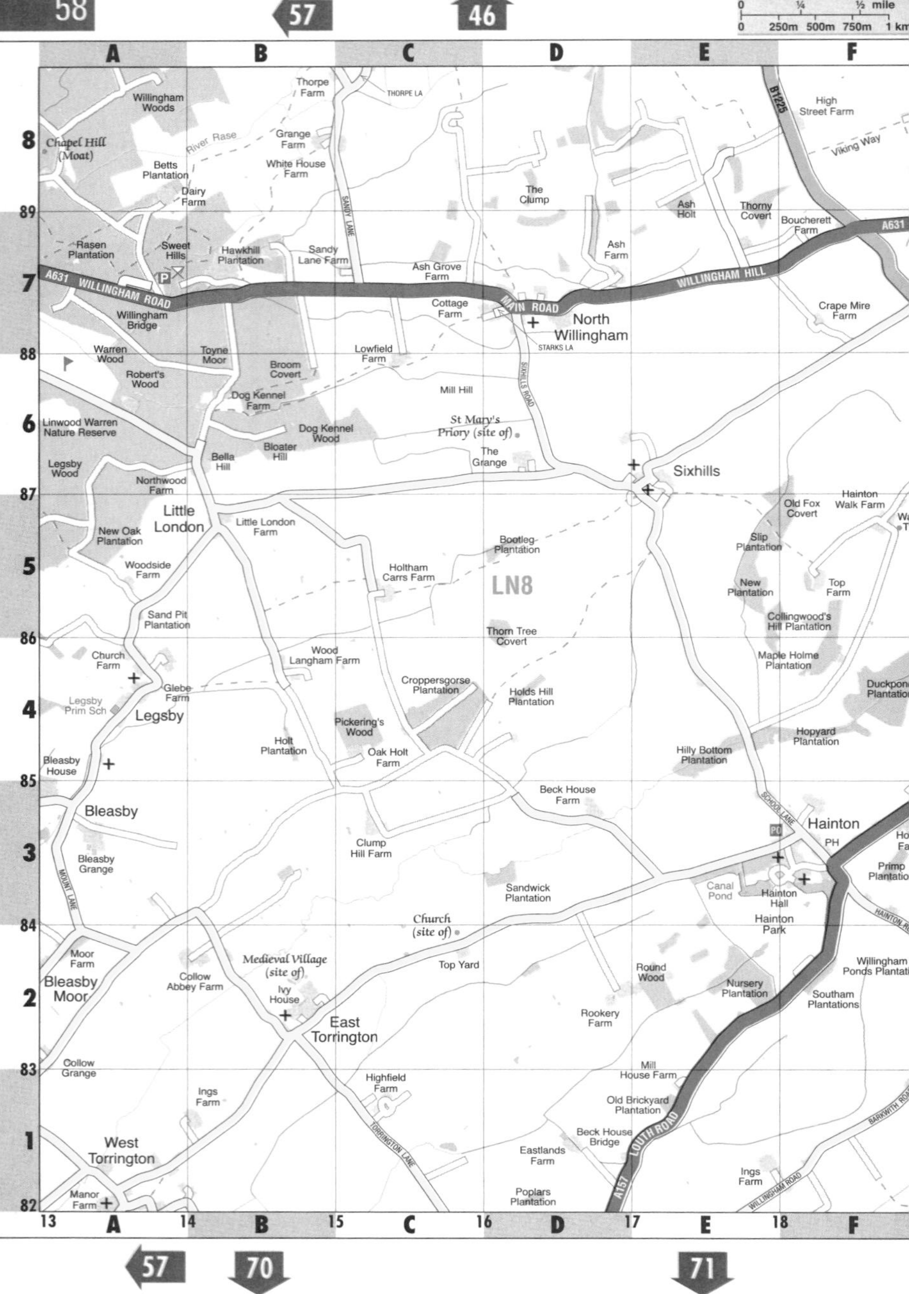
Scale: 1¼ inches to 1 mi
0 ¼ ½ mile
0 250m 500m 750m 1 km
A B C D E F
8
89
7
88
6
87
5
86
4
85
3
84
2
83
1
82
13 14 15 16 17 18
Willingham Woods
Thorpe Farm
THORPE LA
High Street Farm
B1225
Chapel Hill (Moat)
River Rase
Grange Farm
Viking Way
Betts Plantation
White House Farm
Dairy Farm
SANDY LANE
The Clump
Ash Holt
Thorny Covert
Boucherett Farm
A631
Rasen Plantation
Sweet Hills
Hawkhill Plantation
Sandy Lane Farm
Ash Grove Farm
Ash Farm
WILLINGHAM HILL
A631 WILLINGHAM ROAD
MAIN ROAD
Willingham Bridge
Cottage Farm
North Willingham
Crape Mire Farm
Warren Wood
Toyne Moor
Lowfield Farm
STARKS LA
Robert's Wood
Broom Covert
SIXHILLS ROAD
Mill Hill
Dog Kennel Farm
Linwood Warren Nature Reserve
Dog Kennel Wood
St Mary's Priory (site of)
Bloater Hill
Bella Hill
The Grange
Sixhills
Legsby Wood
Northwood Farm
Hainton Walk Farm
Old Fox Covert
Little London
Little London Farm
New Oak Plantation
Bootleg Plantation
Slip Plantation
Woodside Farm
Holtham Carrs Farm
LN8
New Plantation
Top Farm
Sand Pit Plantation
Collingwood's Hill Plantation
Thorn Tree Covert
Church Farm
Wood Langham Farm
Maple Holme Plantation
Glebe Farm
Croppersgorse Plantation
Duckpond Plantation
Legsby Prim Sch
Holds Hill Plantation
Legsby
Pickering's Wood
Hopyard Plantation
Holt Plantation
Oak Holt Farm
Hilly Bottom Plantation
Bleasby House
Beck House Farm
Bleasby
SCHOOL LANE
Hainton
PO
PH
Clump Hill Farm
Bleasby Grange
Primp Plantation
Canal Pond
Sandwick Plantation
Hainton Hall
MOUNT LANE
Church (site of)
Hainton Park
HAINTON RD
Moor Farm
Medieval Village (site of)
Top Yard
Willingham Ponds Plantation
Round Wood
Bleasby Moor
Collow Abbey Farm
Ivy House
Nursery Plantation
Southam Plantations
East Torrington
Rookery Farm
Collow Grange
Highfield Farm
Mill House Farm
Ings Farm
Old Brickyard Plantation
TORRINGTON LANE
BARKWITH ROAD
West Torrington
Beck House Bridge
LOUTH ROAD
Eastlands Farm
A157
Ings Farm
WILLINGHAM ROAD
Manor Farm
Poplars Plantation

57
70
71

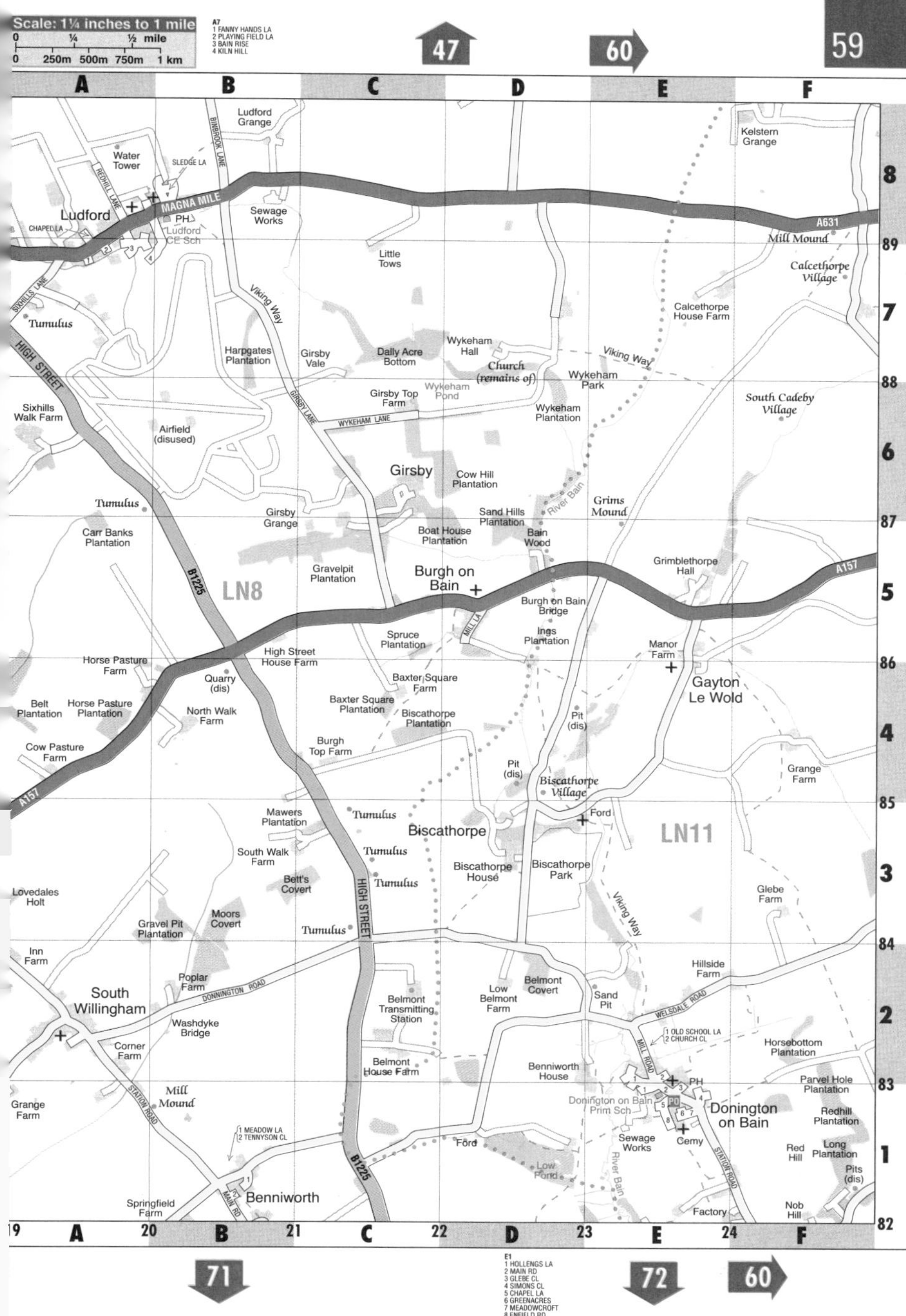

Scale: 1¼ inches to 1 mile
0 ¼ ½ mile
0 250m 500m 750m 1 km
A7
1 FANNY HANDS LA
2 PLAYING FIELD LA
3 BAIN RISE
4 KILN HILL
47
60
59
A B C D E F
8
89
7
88
6
87
5
86
4
85
3
84
2
83
1
82
19 20 21 22 23 24
Ludford Grange
BINBROOK LANE
Kelstern Grange
Water Tower
SLEDGE LA
REDHILL LANE
MAGNA MILE
Ludford
PH
Ludford CE Sch
CHAPEL LA
Sewage Works
A631
Mill Mound
Little Tows
Calcethorpe Village
SIXHILLS LANE
Tumulus
Viking Way
Calcethorpe House Farm
HIGH STREET
Harpgates Plantation
Girsby Vale
Dally Acre Bottom
Wykeham Hall
Church (remains of)
Viking Way
Wykeham Park
Sixhills Walk Farm
Airfield (disused)
GIRSBY LANE
Girsby Top Farm
Wykeham Pond
WYKEHAM LANE
Wykeham Plantation
South Cadeby Village
Girsby
Cow Hill Plantation
River Bain
Grims Mound
Tumulus
Girsby Grange
Sand Hills Plantation
Carr Banks Plantation
Boat House Plantation
Bain Wood
Gravelpit Plantation
Burgh on Bain
Grimblethorpe Hall
A157
B1225
LN8
Burgh on Bain Bridge
MILL LA
Spruce Plantation
Ings Plantation
Manor Farm
Horse Pasture Farm
High Street House Farm
Quarry (dis)
Baxter Square Farm
Gayton Le Wold
Belt Plantation
Horse Pasture Plantation
North Walk Farm
Baxter Square Plantation
Biscathorpe Plantation
Pit (dis)
Burgh Top Farm
Cow Pasture Farm
Pit (dis)
Grange Farm
A157
Biscathorpe Village
Mawers Plantation
Tumulus
Ford
Biscathorpe
LN11
South Walk Farm
Tumulus
Biscathorpe House
Biscathorpe Park
Bett's Covert
Tumulus
HIGH STREET
Glebe Farm
Lovedales Holt
Viking Way
Gravel Pit Plantation
Moors Covert
Tumulus
Inn Farm
Hillside Farm
Poplar Farm
Belmont Covert
South Willingham
DONINGTON ROAD
Belmont Transmitting Station
Low Belmont Farm
Sand Pit
WELSDALE ROAD
Washdyke Bridge
1 OLD SCHOOL LA
2 CHURCH CL
Horsebottom Plantation
Corner Farm
MILL ROAD
Belmont House Farm
Benniworth House
PH
Parvel Hole Plantation
Grange Farm
STATION ROAD
Mill Mound
Donington on Bain Prim Sch
PO
Donington on Bain
Redhill Plantation
1 MEADOW LA
2 TENNYSON CL
Ford
Sewage Works
Cemy
Red Hill
Long Plantation
B1225
Low Pond
River Bain
STATION ROAD
Pits (dis)
MAIN RD
Benniworth
Springfield Farm
Factory
Nob Hill
71
72
60
E1
1 HOLLENGS LA
2 MAIN RD
3 GLEBE CL
4 SIMONS CL
5 CHAPEL LA
6 GREENACRES
7 MEADOWCROFT
8 ENFIELD RD

59 48

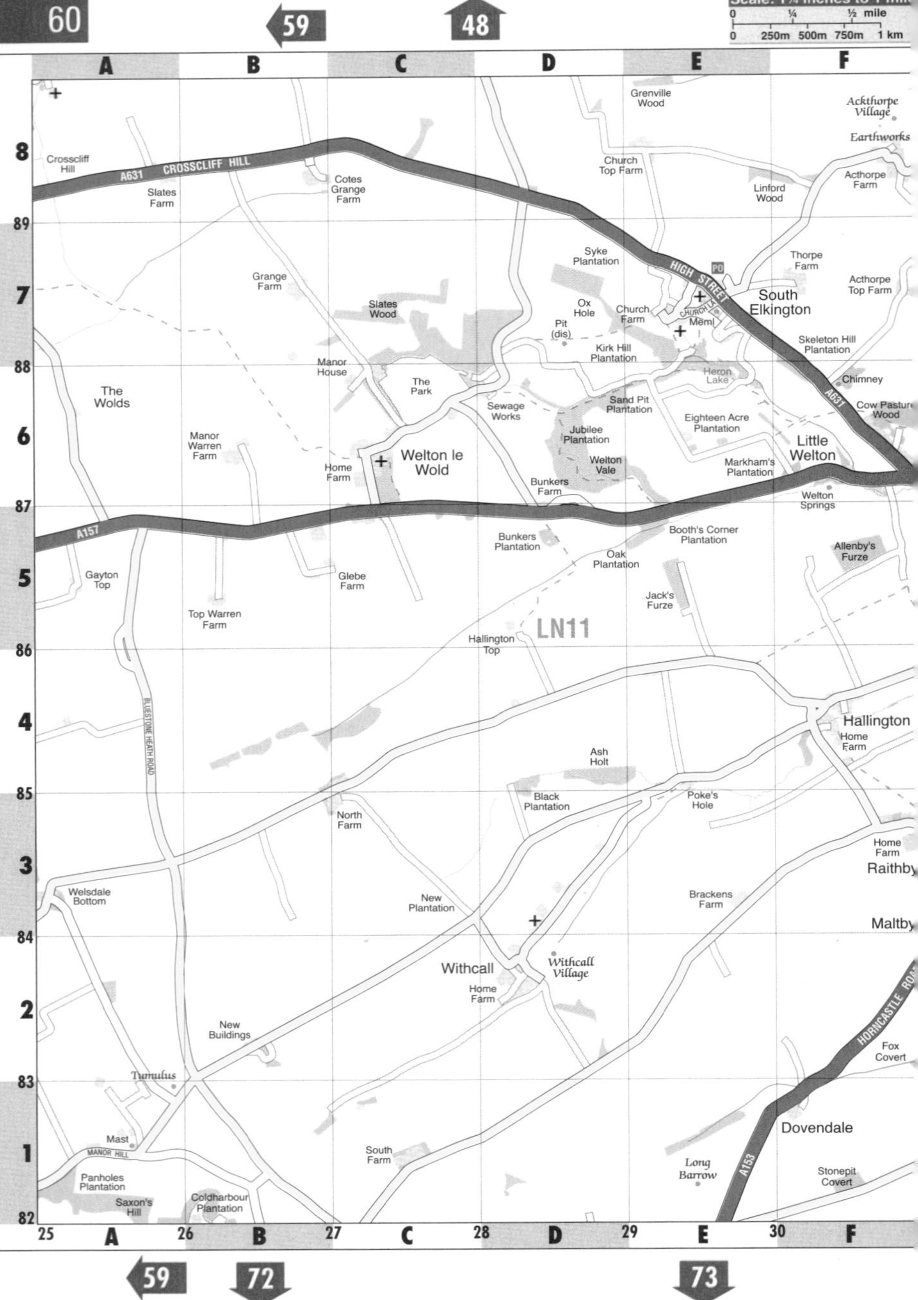

Scale: 1¼ inches to 1 mile
0 ¼ ½ mile
0 250m 500m 750m 1 km
A B C D E F
Crosscliff Hill
A631 CROSSCLIFF HILL
Slates Farm
Cotes Grange Farm
Grenville Wood
Church Top Farm
Linford Wood
Ackthorpe Village
Earthworks
Acthorpe Farm
Thorpe Farm
Acthorpe Top Farm
Grange Farm
Slates Wood
Syke Plantation
HIGH STREET
PO
South Elkington
Ox Hole
Church Farm
CHURCH LA
Meml
Pit (dis)
Kirk Hill Plantation
Skeleton Hill Plantation
Manor House
The Park
Heron Lake
Chimney
The Wolds
Sewage Works
Sand Pit Plantation
Eighteen Acre Plantation
A631
Cow Pasture Wood
Manor Warren Farm
Jubilee Plantation
Little Welton
Welton le Wold
Home Farm
Welton Vale
Markham's Plantation
Bunkers Farm
Welton Springs
A157
Bunkers Plantation
Booth's Corner Plantation
Allenby's Furze
Gayton Top
Glebe Farm
Oak Plantation
Jack's Furze
Top Warren Farm
LN11
Hallington Top
BLUESTONE HEATH ROAD
Hallington
Home Farm
Ash Holt
Black Plantation
Poke's Hole
North Farm
Home Farm
Raithby
Welsdale Bottom
New Plantation
Brackens Farm
Maltby
Withcall
Withcall Village
Home Farm
New Buildings
HORNCASTLE ROAD
Fox Covert
Tumulus
Dovendale
Mast
MANOR HILL
South Farm
Long Barrow
A153
Panholes Plantation
Stonepit Covert
Saxon's Hill
Coldharbour Plantation
8 89 7 88 6 87 5 86 4 85 3 84 2 83 1 82
25 26 27 28 29 30

59 72 73

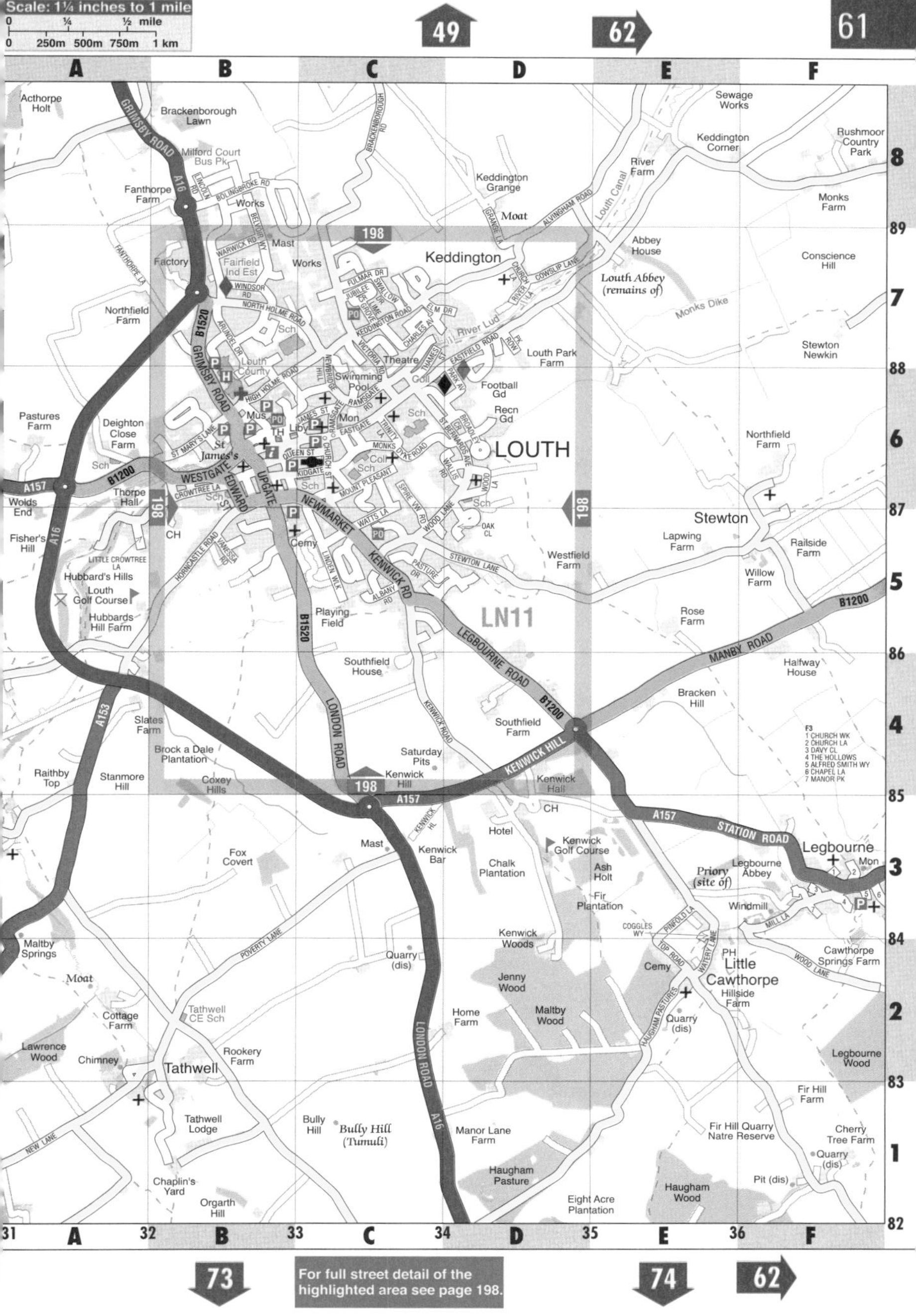

For full street detail of the highlighted area see page 198.

C6
1 CHURCH WK
2 MEADOW CL
3 CHRISTOPHER CL
4 ORCHARD PK
5 HAWTHORNE CL
6 ST EDITH GATE
7 SPINNEY CL
8 GRANGE LA
9 ST MARY'S CR
10 CANBERRA CR
11 PROVOST RD
12 JAVELIN RD

61 50

Scale: 1¼ inches to 1 mile

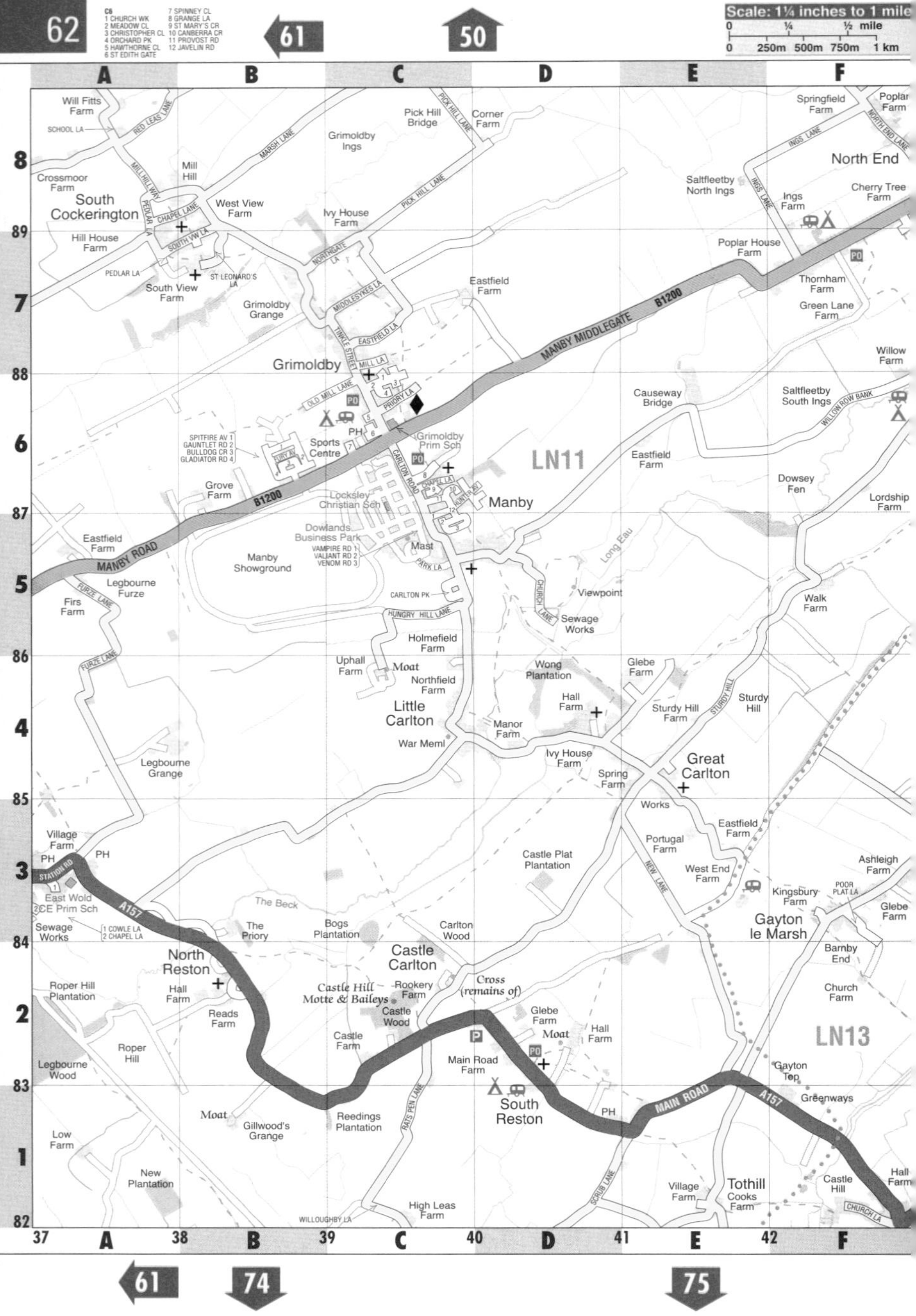

61 74 75

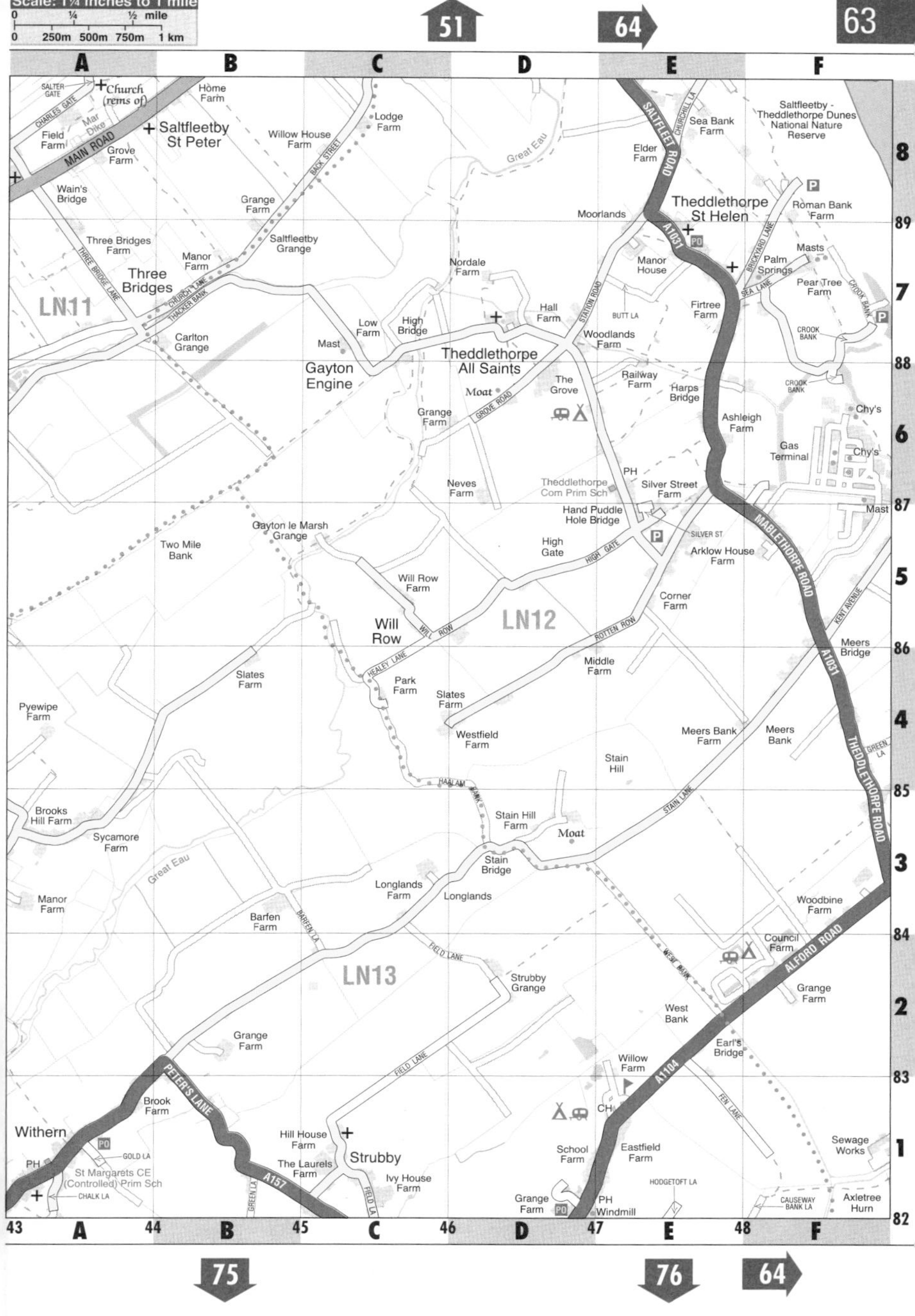
Scale: 1¼ inches to 1 mile
0 ¼ ½ mile
0 250m 500m 750m 1 km
51
64
A B C D E F
Saltfleetby St Peter
Three Bridges
LN11
Gayton Engine
Theddlethorpe All Saints
Theddlethorpe St Helen
Saltfleetby - Theddlethorpe Dunes National Nature Reserve
LN12
Will Row
LN13
Withern
Strubby
MAIN ROAD
SALTFLEET ROAD
A1031
MABLETHORPE ROAD
THEDDLETHORPE ROAD
ALFORD ROAD
A1104
PETER'S LANE
A157
Great Eau
75
76
64

B5
1 CAMBRIDGE RD N
2 LINKS AV
3 CAMBRIDGE RD S
4 IVEL GR
5 WHITEHEAD CL
6 IVEL CL
63
Scale: 1¼ inches to 1 mile
0 ¼ ½ mile
0 250m 500m 750m 1 km
A B C D E F
Saltfleetby - Theddlethorpe Dunes National Nature Reserve
North End Farm
MEERS BANK
PH
KENT AVE
The Seal Sanctuary & Nature Centre
POPLAR AV 1
CHALFONT AV 2
QUEBEC ROAD
GREEN LANE
GOLF ROAD
The Dunes Family Entertainment Centre
Fun Fair
Mablethorpe Community Prim Sch
Mon
Liby
Olde Curiosity Mus
MABLETHORPE
Mablethorpe Hall
Moat
A1104 ALFORD ROAD
HIGH STREET
VICTORIA RD
SEAHOLME ROAD
Art Gall
PH
LN12
CHURCH LANE
The Tennyson High Sch
Seahaven Springs
AQUA DR 1
MARIAN AV 2
MEDINA GD 3
CHAMPION WY 4
A4
1 THE FAIRWAY
2 THE DRIVE
3 ENTERPRISE RD
4 LYLE CL
5 THE GREEN
6 JACKLIN CR
7 EAGLE CL
Trusthorpe
Masts
Masts
SUTTON RD
Poplar Farm
Bourne Farm
MILE LANE
Bambers Farm
Bamber's Bridge
NORTH ROAD
Elder Farm
WHITE ROW LA
A52
TRUSTHORPE ROAD
Sewage Works
Bridge Farm
Crossing Farm
MAIN STREET
Thorpe Farm
Trusthorpe Hall
FEN LA
Thorpe
Boswell Farm
HIGH GATE
C3
1 QUEENS PK CL
2 NEWSTEAD RD
3 DYMOKE CL
4 BROOKE DR
5 DYMOKE RD
6 ARDEN CL
C2
1 MILL FIELD
2 PARKINSON'S WY
3 JAMES AV
4 ST PETER'S LA
5 BRAY AV
6 ETON RD
1 PARK RD E
2 CROMER AV
3 HIGH ST
4 PROMENADE
5 YORK RD
8 89 7 88 6 87 5 86 4 85 3 84 2 83 1 82
49 A 50 B 51 C 52 D 53 E 54 F 55
A3
1 ORCHARD WY
2 ORCHARD CL
3 CHURCH RD
4 MALBOROUGH DR
5 OAKHAM AV
6 WINCHESTER DR
7 CHELTENHAM WY
63
76
B3
1 MAXWELL DR
2 KNOWLE ST
3 KENSINGTON GD
4 STANLEY AV
5 NELSON RD
6 PARKLANDS
7 MAYFLOWER WY
8 TRENCHARD RD
9 THE STRAND
10 STRAND CL
11 HAMMOND CT
12 FOXE END
13 PARK AV
14 PARRY RD
15 VYNER CL
16 RIPON PL
17 ANCASTER RD
18 HARRIS BD
19 MARINA RD
20 KING ST
21 ELM AV
22 MARIAN AV
23 HARLEQUIN DR
24 TOWER CL
B4
1 LONG ACRE
2 ST ANDREWS RD
3 SHERWOOD RD
4 RUGBY RD
5 MALVERN RD
6 HARROW RD
7 REPTON RD
8 QUEENSWAY
9 SOMERSBY AV
10 FITZWILLIAM ST
11 WELLINGTON AV
12 CHAUCER AV
13 RUSKIN RD
14 KINGSLEY RD
15 CHARLES WRIGHT CL
16 TENNYSON AV
17 TENNYSON RD
18 HIGH ST
19 ADMIRALTY RD
20 STATION RD
21 ALEXANDRA RD
22 ALEXANDRA PK
77
C1
1 ASHLEY CL
2 HALL LEAS DR
3 TRUSTHORPE RD
4 HIGHGATE CL
5 HIGHFIELD AV
6 PARK VIEW
7 UPPINGHAM RD
8 OUNDLE RD
9 GROVE RD
10 PARK RD WEST
11 WILLOUGHBY RD
12 MARINE AV
13 HARDING CL

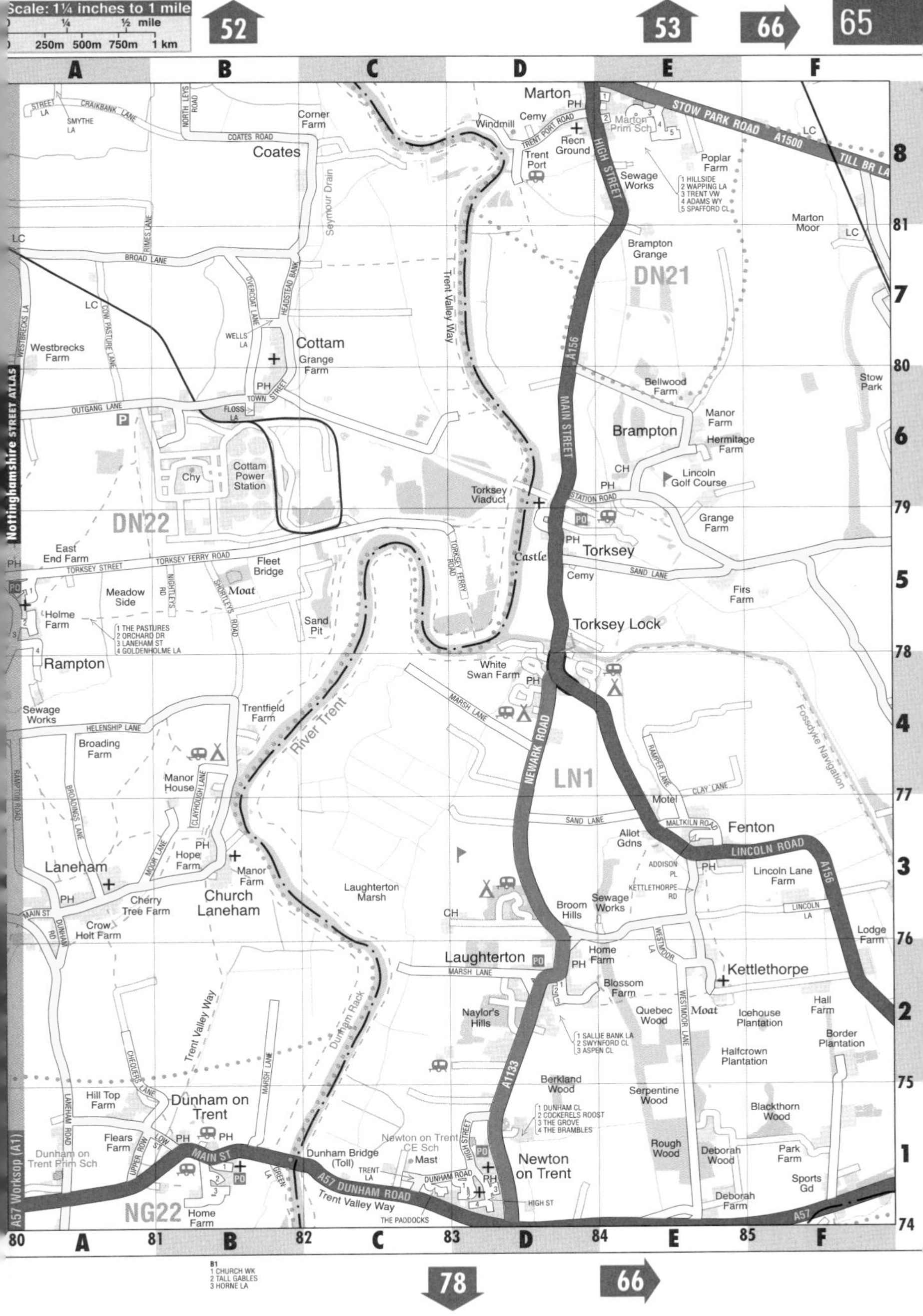

Scale: 1¼ inches to 1 mile
¼
½ mile
250m 500m 750m 1 km
52
53
66
65
A B C D E F
Nottinghamshire STREET ATLAS
Marton
Cemy
Windmill
TRENT PORT ROAD
Recn Ground
Trent Port
Marton Prim Sch
STOW PARK ROAD
A1500
TILL BR LA
LC
Poplar Farm
1 HILLSIDE
2 WAPPING LA
3 TRENT VW
4 ADAMS WY
5 SPAFFORD CL
Sewage Works
HIGH STREET
Marton Moor
Brampton Grange
DN21
STREET LA
CRAIKBANK LANE
SMYTHE LA
NORTH LEYS ROAD
COATES ROAD
Corner Farm
Coates
Seymour Drain
RIMES LANE
BROAD LANE
OVERCOAT LANE
HEADSTEAD BANK
Trent Valley Way
COW PASTURE LANE
WESTBRECKS LA
Westbrecks Farm
WELLS LA
Cottam
Grange Farm
TOWN STREET
FLOSS LA
OUTGANG LANE
A156
Bellwood Farm
Stow Park
Manor Farm
Brampton
Hermitage Farm
MAIN STREET
Cottam Power Station
Chy
CH
Lincoln Golf Course
Torksey Viaduct
STATION ROAD
DN22
Grange Farm
East End Farm
TORKSEY STREET
TORKSEY FERRY ROAD
Fleet Bridge
TORKSEY FERRY ROAD
Castle
Torksey
Cemy
SAND LANE
Meadow Side
NIGHTLEYS RD
Moat
SHORTLEYS ROAD
Firs Farm
Holme Farm
1 THE PASTURES
2 ORCHARD DR
3 LANEHAM ST
4 GOLDENHOLME LA
Sand Pit
Torksey Lock
Rampton
White Swan Farm
MARSH LANE
Sewage Works
Trentfield Farm
HELENSHIP LANE
River Trent
Fossdyke Navigation
Broading Farm
RAMPER LANE
NEWARK ROAD
LN1
RAMPTON ROAD
Manor House
CLAYHOUGH LANE
BROADINGS LANE
Motel
CLAY LANE
SAND LANE
MALTKILN RD
Fenton
Allot Gdns
LINCOLN ROAD
MOOR LANE
Hope Farm
Manor Farm
Laneham
ADDISON PL
Lincoln Lane Farm
KETTLETHORPE RD
Laughterton Marsh
Cherry Tree Farm
Church Laneham
Sewage Works
Broom Hills
LINCOLN LA
MAIN ST
DUNHAM RD
Crow Holt Farm
Lodge Farm
Home Farm
WESTMOOR LA
Laughterton
MARSH LANE
Kettlethorpe
Blossom Farm
Hall Farm
Naylor's Hills
Quebec Wood
Moat
Icehouse Plantation
WESTMOOR LANE
Dunham Rack
1 SALLIE BANK LA
2 SWYNFORD CL
3 ASPEN CL
Border Plantation
Trent Valley Way
MARSH LANE
CHEQUERS LANE
Halfcrown Plantation
A1133
Berkland Wood
Serpentine Wood
Hill Top Farm
LANEHAM ROAD
Dunham on Trent
1 DUNHAM CL
2 COCKERELS ROOST
3 THE GROVE
4 THE BRAMBLES
Blackthorn Wood
Flears Farm
LOW ST
UPPER ROW
Newton on Trent CE Sch
HIGH STREET
Mast
Rough Wood
Deborah Wood
Park Farm
Newton on Trent
Dunham on Trent Prim Sch
MAIN ST
Dunham Bridge (Toll)
TRENT LA
DUNHAM ROAD
Sports Gd
A57 Worksop (A1)
GREEN LA
A57 DUNHAM ROAD
HIGH ST
Deborah Farm
NG22
Home Farm
Trent Valley Way
THE PADDOCKS
A57
8 81 7 80 6 79 5 78 4 77 3 76 2 75 1 74
80 81 82 83 84 85
B1
1 CHURCH WK
2 TALL GABLES
3 HORNE LA
78
66

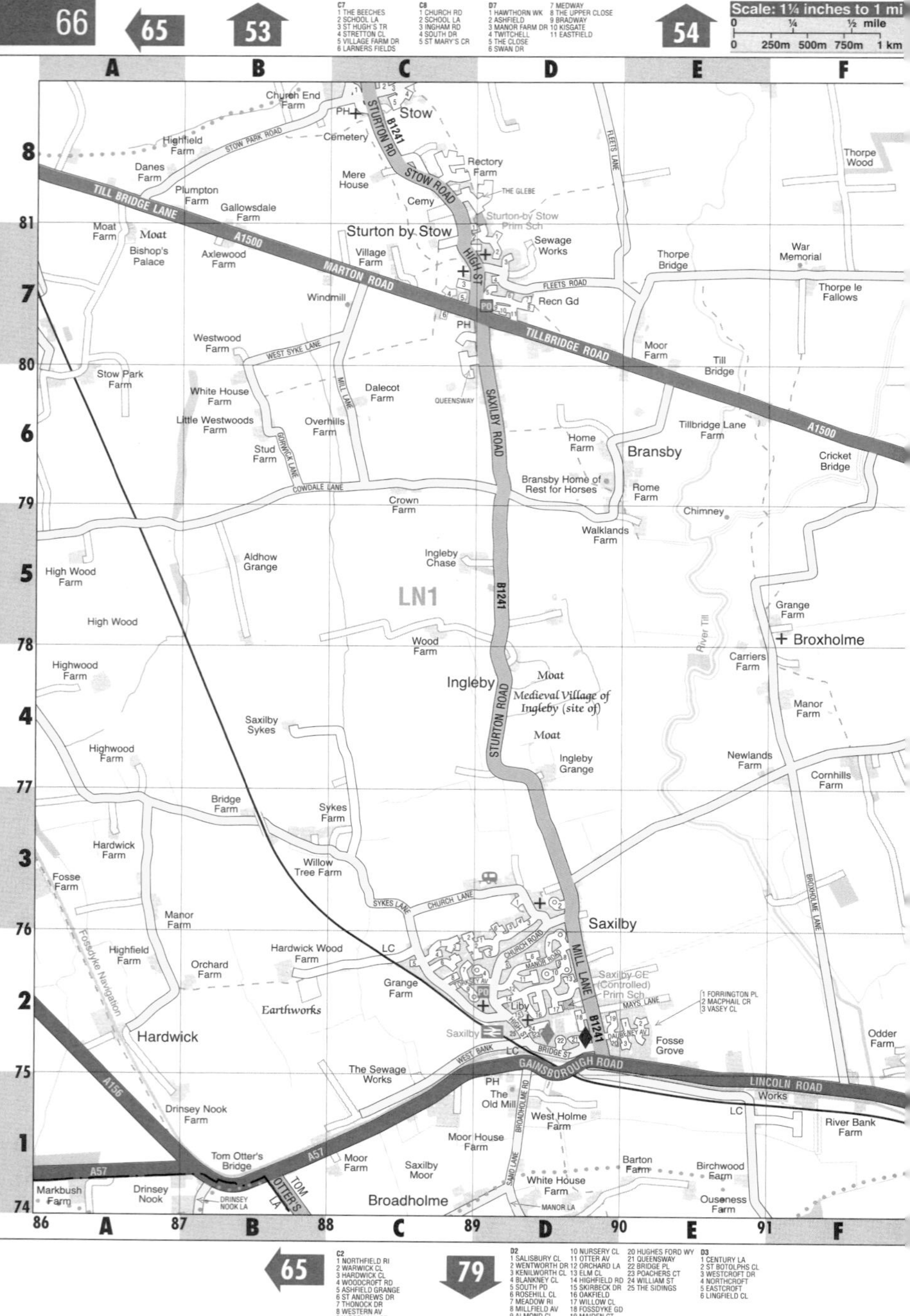
66
65
53
54
Scale: 1¼ inches to 1 mile
0 ¼ ½ mile
0 250m 500m 750m 1 km
C7
1 THE BEECHES
2 SCHOOL LA
3 ST HUGH'S TR
4 STRETTON CL
5 VILLAGE FARM DR
6 LARNERS FIELDS
C8
1 CHURCH RD
2 SCHOOL LA
3 INGHAM RD
4 SOUTH DR
5 ST MARY'S CR
D7
1 HAWTHORN WK
2 ASHFIELD
3 MANOR FARM DR
4 TWITCHELL
5 THE CLOSE
6 SWAN DR
7 MEDWAY
8 THE UPPER CLOSE
9 BRADWAY
10 KISGATE
11 EASTFIELD
Church End Farm
Stow
STURTON RD
B1241
Highfield Farm
STOW PARK ROAD
Cemetery
Danes Farm
Mere House
STOW ROAD
Rectory Farm
THE GLEBE
TILL BRIDGE LANE
Plumpton Farm
Cemy
Gallowsdale Farm
Sturton-by-Stow Prim Sch
Moat Farm
Moat
Bishop's Palace
A1500
Sturton by Stow
Axlewood Farm
MARTON ROAD
Village Farm
HIGH ST
Sewage Works
FLEETS LANE
Thorpe Bridge
War Memorial
Thorpe Wood
Windmill
FLEETS ROAD
Recn Gd
Thorpe le Fallows
PO
PH
TILLBRIDGE ROAD
Westwood Farm
WEST SYKE LANE
Moor Farm
Till Bridge
Stow Park Farm
MILL LANE
Dalecot Farm
White House Farm
QUEENSWAY
SAXILBY ROAD
Little Westwoods Farm
Overhills Farm
Home Farm
Tillbridge Lane Farm
Stud Farm
GORWICK LANE
Bransby
Cricket Bridge
Bransby Home of Rest for Horses
COWDALE LANE
Crown Farm
Rome Farm
Chimney
Walklands Farm
Aldhow Grange
Ingleby Chase
High Wood Farm
LN1
High Wood
Grange Farm
Broxholme
River Till
Wood Farm
Highwood Farm
Carriers Farm
Moat
Ingleby
Medieval Village of Ingleby (site of)
STURTON ROAD
Manor Farm
Saxilby Sykes
Moat
Highwood Farm
Ingleby Grange
Newlands Farm
Cornhills Farm
Bridge Farm
Sykes Farm
Hardwick Farm
Willow Tree Farm
Fosse Farm
BROXHOLME LANE
SYKES LANE
CHURCH LANE
Manor Farm
Saxilby
Fossdyke Navigation
Highfield Farm
Hardwick Wood Farm
LC
CHURCH ROAD
MANOR ROAD
Orchard Farm
TORKSEY AV
Grange Farm
MILL LANE
Saxilby CE (Controlled) Prim Sch
Earthworks
Liby
MAYS LANE
1 FORRINGTON PL
2 MACPHAIL CR
3 VASEY CL
Hardwick
Saxilby
DAUBENEY AV
Fosse Grove
Odder Farm
WEST BANK
BRIDGE ST
A156
The Sewage Works
GAINSBOROUGH ROAD
LINCOLN ROAD
PH
The Old Mill
Works
BROADHOLME RD
LC
Drinsey Nook Farm
West Holme Farm
River Bank Farm
Moor House Farm
Tom Otter's Bridge
A57
Moor Farm
Saxilby Moor
SAND LANE
Barton Farm
Birchwood Farm
White House Farm
Markbush Farm
Drinsey Nook
DRINSEY NOOK LA
TOM OTTER'S LA
Broadholme
MANOR LA
Ouseness Farm
A B C D E F
8 81 7 80 6 79 5 78 4 77 3 76 2 75 1 74
86 87 88 89 90 91
65
79
C2
1 NORTHFIELD RI
2 WARWICK CL
3 HARDWICK CL
4 WOODCROFT RD
5 ASHFIELD GRANGE
6 ST ANDREWS DR
7 THONOCK DR
8 WESTERN AV
9 WOODHALL CR
D2
1 SALISBURY CL
2 WENTWORTH DR
3 KENILWORTH CL
4 BLANKNEY CL
5 SOUTH PD
6 ROSEHILL CL
7 MEADOW RI
8 MILLFIELD AV
9 ALMOND CL
10 NURSERY CL
11 OTTER AV
12 ORCHARD LA
13 ELM CL
14 HIGHFIELD RD
15 SKIRBECK DR
16 OAKFIELD
17 WILLOW CL
18 FOSSDYKE GD
19 MAIDEN CT
20 HUGHES FORD WY
21 QUEENSWAY
22 BRIDGE PL
23 POACHERS CT
24 WILLIAM ST
25 THE SIDINGS
D3
1 CENTURY LA
2 ST BOTOLPHS CL
3 WESTCROFT DR
4 NORTHCROFT
5 EASTCROFT
6 LINGFIELD CL

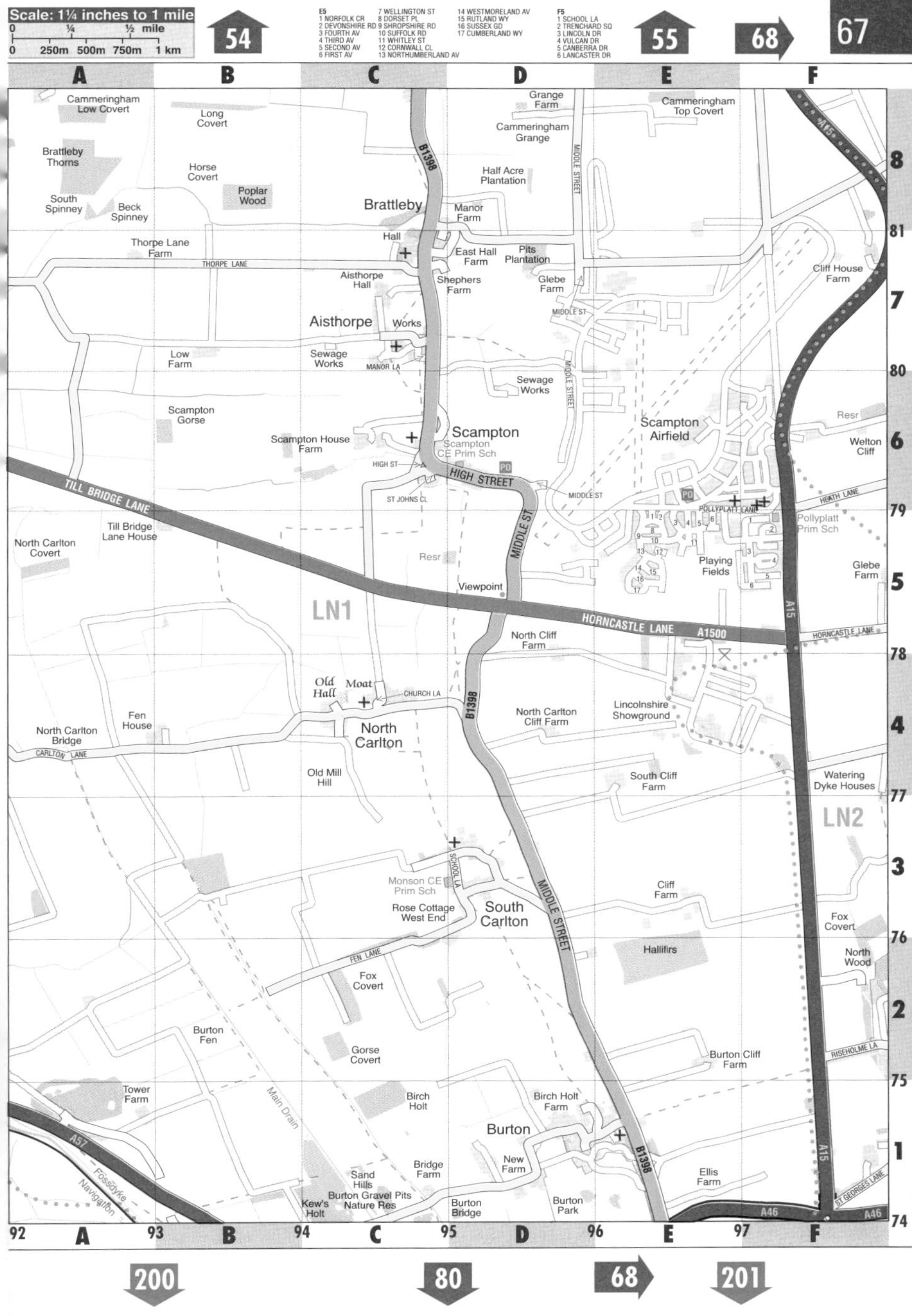

Scale: 1¼ inches to 1 mile
0 ¼ ½ mile
0 250m 500m 750m 1 km
54
E5
1 NORFOLK CR
2 DEVONSHIRE RD
3 FOURTH AV
4 THIRD AV
5 SECOND AV
6 FIRST AV
7 WELLINGTON ST
8 DORSET PL
9 SHROPSHIRE RD
10 SUFFOLK RD
11 WHITLEY ST
12 CORNWALL CL
13 NORTHUMBERLAND AV
14 WESTMORELAND AV
15 RUTLAND WY
16 SUSSEX GD
17 CUMBERLAND WY
F5
1 SCHOOL LA
2 TRENCHARD SQ
3 LINCOLN DR
4 VULCAN DR
5 CANBERRA DR
6 LANCASTER DR
55
68
67
A B C D E F
Cammeringham Low Covert
Long Covert
Brattleby Thorns
Horse Covert
Poplar Wood
South Spinney
Beck Spinney
Grange Farm
Cammeringham Grange
Cammeringham Top Covert
B1398
MIDDLE STREET
A15
Half Acre Plantation
Brattleby
Manor Farm
Hall
East Hall Farm
Pits Plantation
Thorpe Lane Farm
THORPE LANE
Aisthorpe Hall
Shephers Farm
Glebe Farm
Cliff House Farm
MIDDLE ST
Aisthorpe
Works
Low Farm
Sewage Works
MANOR LA
Sewage Works
Scampton Gorse
Scampton House Farm
Scampton
Scampton CE Prim Sch
PO
Scampton Airfield
Resr
Welton Cliff
HIGH ST
HIGH STREET
TILL BRIDGE LANE
ST JOHNS CL
MIDDLE ST
POLLYPLATT LANE
HEATH LANE
Pollyplatt Prim Sch
Till Bridge Lane House
North Carlton Covert
Resr
Playing Fields
Glebe Farm
Viewpoint
LN1
HORNCASTLE LANE
A1500
HORNCASTLE LANE
North Cliff Farm
Old Hall
Moat
CHURCH LA
North Carlton Cliff Farm
Lincolnshire Showground
Fen House
North Carlton Bridge
North Carlton
CARLTON LANE
Old Mill Hill
South Cliff Farm
Watering Dyke Houses
LN2
SCHOOL LA
Monson CE Prim Sch
Rose Cottage West End
South Carlton
Cliff Farm
Fox Covert
Hallifirs
North Wood
FEN LANE
Fox Covert
Burton Fen
Gorse Covert
Burton Cliff Farm
RISEHOLME LA
Tower Farm
Main Drain
Birch Holt
Birch Holt Farm
Burton
A57
Fossdyke Navigation
Sand Hills
Bridge Farm
New Farm
Ellis Farm
ST GEORGES LANE
Burton Gravel Pits Nature Res
Kew's Holt
Burton Bridge
Burton Park
A46
8 81 7 80 6 79 5 78 4 77 3 76 2 75 1 74
92 93 94 95 96 97
200
80
68
201

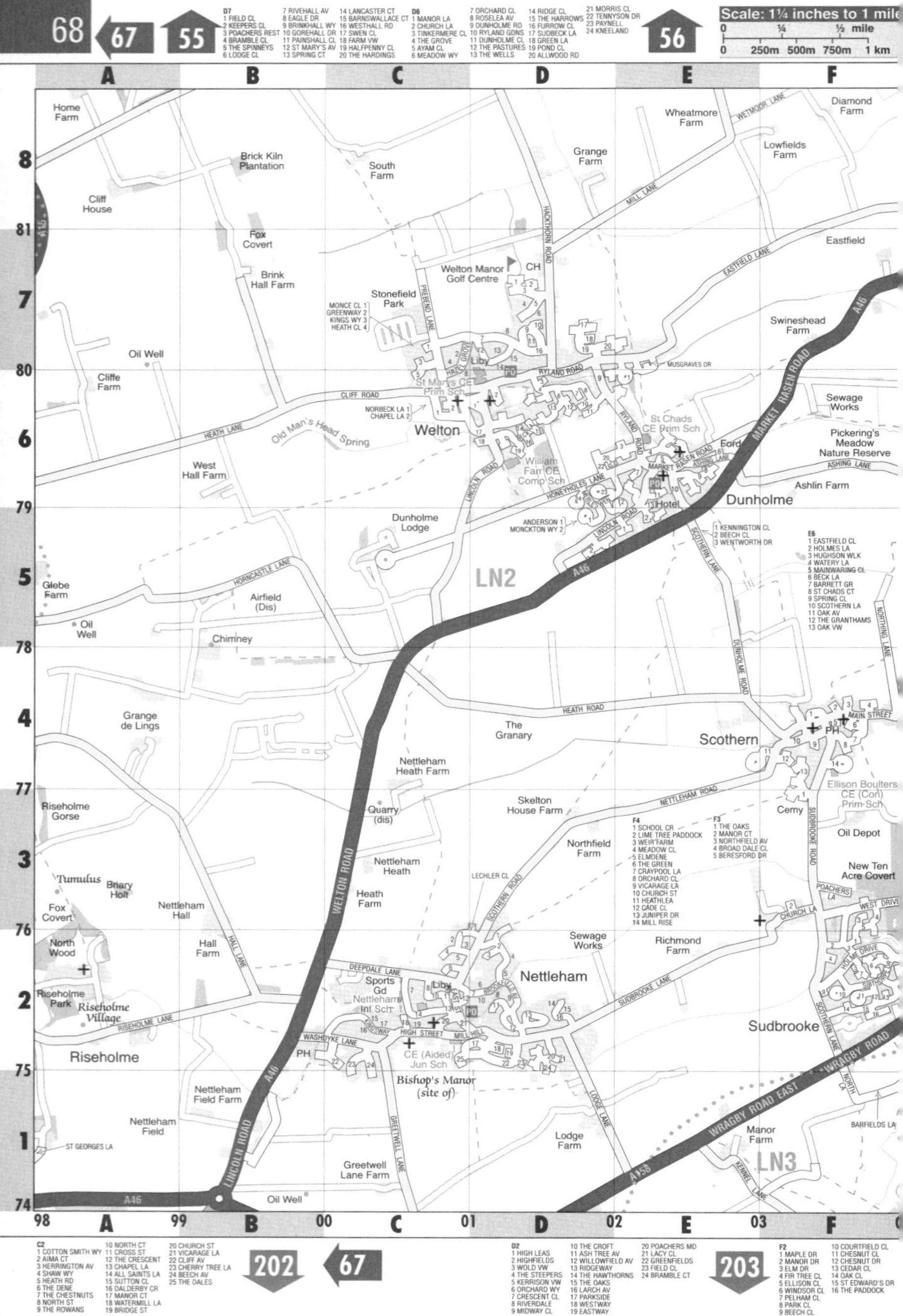
67
55
D7
1 FIELD CL
2 KEEPERS CL
3 POACHERS REST
4 BRAMBLE CL
5 THE SPINNEYS
6 LODGE CL
7 RIVEHALL AV
8 EAGLE DR
9 BRINKHALL WY
10 GOREHALL DR
11 PAINSHALL CL
12 ST MARY'S AV
13 SPRING CT
14 LANCASTER CT
15 BARNSWALLACE CT
16 WESTHALL RD
17 SWEN CL
18 FARM VW
19 HALFPENNY CL
20 THE HARDINGS
D6
1 MANOR LA
2 CHURCH LA
3 TINKERMERE CL
4 THE GROVE
5 AYAM CL
6 MEADOW WY
7 ORCHARD CL
8 ROSELEA AV
9 DUNHOLME RD
10 RYLAND GDNS
11 DUNHOLME CL
12 THE PASTURES
13 THE WELLS
14 RIDGE CL
15 THE HARROWS
16 FURROW CL
17 SUDBECK LA
18 GREEN LA
19 POND CL
20 ALLWOOD RD
21 MORRIS CL
22 TENNYSON DR
23 PAYNELL
24 KNEELAND
56
Scale: 1¼ inches to 1 mile
0 ¼ ½ mile
0 250m 500m 750m 1 km
A B C D E F
8
81
7
80
6
79
5
78
4
77
3
76
2
75
1
74
Home Farm
Brick Kiln Plantation
South Farm
Grange Farm
Wheatmore Farm
WETMOOR LANE
Diamond Farm
Lowfields Farm
Cliff House
A15
MILL LANE
HACKTHORN ROAD
Fox Covert
Brink Hall Farm
Welton Manor Golf Centre
CH
EASTFIELD LANE
Eastfield
Stonefield Park
PREBEND LANE
MONCE CL 1
GREENWAY 2
KINGS WY 3
HEATH CL 4
HAZEL GROVE
Liby
PO
RYLAND ROAD
MUSGRAVES DR
A46
Swineshead Farm
Oil Well
Cliffe Farm
St Marys CE Prim Sch
CLIFF ROAD
NORBECK LA 1
CHAPEL LA 2
HEATH LANE
Old Man's Head Spring
Welton
St Chads CE Prim Sch
MARKET RASEN ROAD
Sewage Works
Pickering's Meadow Nature Reserve
ASHING LANE
Ford
West Hall Farm
LINCOLN ROAD
William Farr CE Comp Sch
HONEYHOLES LANE
Hotel
Ashlin Farm
Dunholme
Dunholme Lodge
ANDERSON 1
MONCKTON WY 2
1 KENNINGTON CL
2 BEECH CL
3 WENTWORTH DR
SCOTHERN LANE
E6
1 EASTFIELD CL
2 HOLMES LA
3 HUGHSON WLK
4 WATERY LA
5 MAINWARING CL
6 BECK LA
7 BARRETT GR
8 ST CHADS CT
9 SPRING CL
10 SCOTHERN LA
11 OAK AV
12 THE GRANTHAMS
13 OAK VW
Glebe Farm
HORNCASTLE LANE
Airfield (Dis)
LN2
NORTHING LANE
Oil Well
Chimney
DUNHOLME ROAD
HEATH ROAD
MAIN STREET
Grange de Lings
The Granary
Scothern
PH
Nettleham Heath Farm
Ellison Boulters CE (Con) Prim Sch
Riseholme Gorse
Quarry (dis)
Skelton House Farm
NETTLEHAM ROAD
Cemy
F4
1 SCHOOL CR
2 LIME TREE PADDOCK
3 WEIR FARM
4 MEADOW CL
5 ELMDENE
6 THE GREEN
7 CRAYPOOL LA
8 ORCHARD CL
9 VICARAGE LA
10 CHURCH ST
11 HEATHLEA
12 CADE CL
13 JUNIPER DR
14 MILL RISE
F3
1 THE OAKS
2 MANOR CT
3 NORTHFIELD AV
4 BROAD DALE CL
5 BERESFORD DR
SUDBROOKE ROAD
Oil Depot
Northfield Farm
WELTON ROAD
Nettleham Heath
New Ten Acre Covert
Tumulus
Briary Holt
Heath Farm
LECHLER CL
SCOTHERN ROAD
POACHERS LA
WEST DRIVE
Fox Covert
Nettleham Hall
CHURCH LA
North Wood
Hall Farm
HALL LANE
Sewage Works
Richmond Farm
HOLME DRIVE
DEEPDALE LANE
Sports Gd
Liby
BROOKFIELD AV
Nettleham
SUDBROOKE LANE
SIBTHORPE DR
Riseholme Park
Riseholme Village
Nettleham Inf Sch
RISEHOLME LANE
KINGSWAY
HIGH STREET
MILL HILL
WASHDYKE LANE
SCOTHERN LANE
Sudbrooke
PH
CE (Aided) Jun Sch
WRAGBY ROAD
Riseholme
Bishop's Manor (site of)
WRAGBY ROAD EAST
NORTH LA
LODGE LANE
Nettleham Field Farm
Nettleham Field
GREETWELL LANE
BARFIELDS LA
Manor Farm
Lodge Farm
ST GEORGES LA
LINCOLN ROAD
Greetwell Lane Farm
LN3
A158
KENNEL LANE
A46
Oil Well
98 A 99 B 00 C 01 D 02 E 03 F
C2
1 COTTON SMITH WY
2 AIMA CT
3 HERRINGTON AV
4 SHAW WY
5 HEATH RD
6 THE DENE
7 THE CHESTNUTS
8 NORTH ST
9 THE ROWANS
10 NORTH CT
11 CROSS ST
12 THE CRESCENT
13 CHAPEL LA
14 ALL SAINTS LA
15 SUTTON CL
16 DALDERBY CR
17 MANOR CT
18 WATERMILL LA
19 BRIDGE ST
20 CHURCH ST
21 VICARAGE LA
22 CLIFF AV
23 CHERRY TREE LA
24 BEECH AV
25 THE DALES
202
67
D2
1 HIGH LEAS
2 HIGHFIELDS
3 WOLD VW
4 THE STEEPERS
5 KERRISON VW
6 ORCHARD WY
7 CRESCENT CL
8 RIVERDALE
9 MIDWAY CL
10 THE CROFT
11 ASH TREE AV
12 WILLOWFIELD AV
13 RIDGEWAY
14 THE HAWTHORNS
15 THE OAKS
16 LARCH AV
17 PARKSIDE
18 WESTWAY
19 EASTWAY
20 POACHERS MD
21 LACY CL
22 GREENFIELDS
23 FIELD CL
24 BRAMBLE CT
203
F2
1 MAPLE DR
2 MANOR DR
3 ELM DR
4 FIR TREE CL
5 ELLISON CL
6 WINDSOR CL
7 PELHAM CL
8 PARK CL
9 BEECH CL
10 COURTFIELD CL
11 CHESNUT CL
12 CHESNUT DR
13 CEDAR CL
14 OAK CL
15 ST EDWARD'S DR
16 THE PADDOCK

Scale: 1¼ inches to 1 mile
¼
½ mile
250m 500m 750m 1 km
56
57
70
A
B
C
D
E
F
Bridge Farm
Broadbent Theatre
Wickenby
LISSINGTON RD
SNARFORD ROAD
Manor Farm
Snarford Bridge
A46
Hill Farm
Willow Tree Farm
SNELLAND ROAD
WESTLABY LANE
Westlaby Farm
Wickenby Airport
PH
Welton Hill
Lindum Farm
Welton Hill Farm
Nook Farm
Fox Covert
Swinthorpe
Snelland
LC
Manor Farm
Airfield (disused)
White House Farm
Stone Road End
Home Farm
Wickenby Farm
The Grange
Reasby Grange
Grange Farm
Mickleholme Farm
Reasby
Top Farm
Fulnetby
Sunny Side
B1399
LN2
LN3
Fulnetby Wood
Stainton Wood
Claybridge Farm
Clay Bridge
Scothern Grange
LC
Oil Pumping Station
Rand Wood
Brown Cow Farm
STAINTON LANE
SCOTHERN LA
Stainton by Langworth
Woodlands Farm
A158
Bullington
White Bridge
SHORTWOOD LANE
Northfield Farm
STAINTON LANE
Far North End Wood
Short Wood
Red Barn Farm
Grove Farm
Newball Grange
LN8
LANGWORTH ROAD
LC
Shortwood Farm
Scothern Bridge
PH
Oil Depot
Langworth
MAIN STREET
MAIN ST
Langworth Bridge
Newball
West Drive Farm
Woodside Falconry & Conservation Centre
PO
STATION ROAD
Cemy
The Lake
LC
A158
The Spinney
Manor Farm
Newball Wood
Earthwork
Sudbrooke Park
South Moor
PH
Manor Farm
BARLINGS LANE
Coldstead Farm
Station Farm
Grange Farm
Barfield Farm
Reepham Moor
SPARROW LANE
Barfield Lane Farm
Gatecliff Wood
Chimney
Barlings Park
Gatecliffe Farm
Hardy Gang Wood
Barlings
Lodge Farm
Sewage Works
Oil Gathering Centre
BARLINGS LANE
Court House Farm
MEADOWS LA
Barlings Farm
Newball Common
MOOR LANE
Fiskerton Moor
Barlings Hall
Moor Farm
8
81
7
80
6
79
5
78
4
77
3
76
2
75
1
74
05
06
07
08
09
C3
1 BARLINGS CL
2 OXENEY DR
3 ST HUGH'S DR
82
70

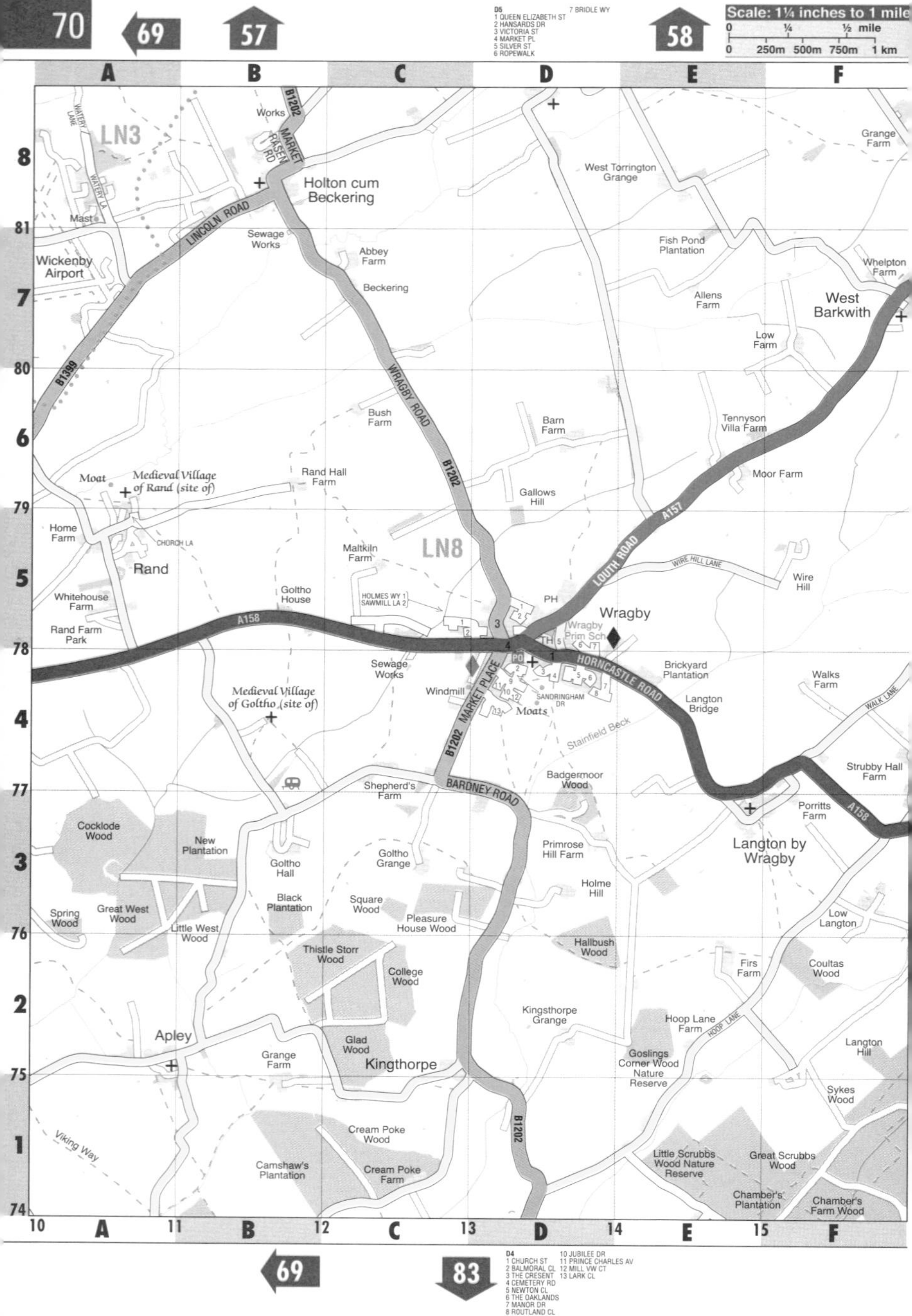
69
57
58
D5
1 QUEEN ELIZABETH ST
2 HANSARDS DR
3 VICTORIA ST
4 MARKET PL
5 SILVER ST
6 ROPEWALK
7 BRIDLE WY
Scale: 1¼ inches to 1 mile
0 ¼ ½ mile
0 250m 500m 750m 1 km
A B C D E F
8 81 7 80 6 79 5 78 4 77 3 76 2 75 1 74
10 11 12 13 14 15
LN3
LN8
Works
B1202
MARKET RASEN RD
Holton cum Beckering
LINCOLN ROAD
Mast
Wickenby Airport
WATERY LANE
WATERY LA
Sewage Works
Abbey Farm
Beckering
West Torrington Grange
Grange Farm
Fish Pond Plantation
Whelpton Farm
Allens Farm
West Barkwith
Low Farm
B1399
WRAGBY ROAD
Bush Farm
Barn Farm
Tennyson Villa Farm
Moat
Medieval Village of Rand (site of)
Rand Hall Farm
Gallows Hill
Moor Farm
A157
Home Farm
CHURCH LA
Rand
Maltkiln Farm
LOUTH ROAD
WIRE HILL LANE
Wire Hill
Whitehouse Farm
Goltho House
HOLMES WY 1
SAWMILL LA 2
PH
Wragby
Wragby Prim Sch
Rand Farm Park
A158
TH
PO
HORNCASTLE ROAD
Brickyard Plantation
Walks Farm
Sewage Works
Windmill
MARKET PLACE
SANDRINGHAM DR
Moats
Langton Bridge
Medieval Village of Goltho (site of)
Stainfield Beck
WALK LANE
Strubby Hall Farm
Shepherd's Farm
BARDNEY ROAD
Badgermoor Wood
Porritts Farm
Cocklode Wood
New Plantation
Goltho Grange
Primrose Hill Farm
Langton by Wragby
Goltho Hall
Holme Hill
Spring Wood
Great West Wood
Little West Wood
Black Plantation
Square Wood
Pleasure House Wood
Low Langton
Thistle Storr Wood
College Wood
Hallbush Wood
Firs Farm
Coultas Wood
Kingsthorpe Grange
Hoop Lane Farm
HOOP LANE
Langton Hill
Apley
Glad Wood
Grange Farm
Kingthorpe
Goslings Corner Wood Nature Reserve
Sykes Wood
Viking Way
Cream Poke Wood
Camshaw's Plantation
Cream Poke Farm
Little Scrubbs Wood Nature Reserve
Great Scrubbs Wood
Chamber's Plantation
Chamber's Farm Wood
69
83
D4
1 CHURCH ST
2 BALMORAL CL
3 THE CRESENT
4 CEMETERY RD
5 NEWTON CL
6 THE OAKLANDS
7 MANOR DR
8 ROUTLAND CL
9 MILL VW RD
10 JUBILEE DR
11 PRINCE CHARLES AV
12 MILL VW CT
13 LARK CL

Scale: 1¼ inches to 1 mile
¼
½ mile
250m 500m 750m 1 km
58
59
72
A
B
C
D
E
F
East Barkwith
Ivy House Farm
Manor Farm
East Barkwith CE Sch
Glebe Farm
Mast
Manor Farm
Lodge Farm
Back o' Frank's Hill
Cocked Hat Plantation
Goddard Hill
Skew Bridge
Panton
Valley Farm
Stonehills Plantation
Fox Covert Plantation
Ings Plantation
Grove Farm
Rattlesnake Plantation
Lodge Covert
Brick Pits Plantation
Carman Gorse
Whitepits Plantation
Panton Hall
Panton Park
Warren Farm
Warren Hill Plantation
Warren Hill
LN8
Whitegates Farm
Skirbeck Farm
Benniworth Moor
Barney's Covert
Benniworth Moor Farm
Benniworth Road Plantation
Priestmoor Plantation
Benniworth Moor
Mast
Sotby House Farm
Benniworth
Glebe Farm
Belmont House Farm
Cottage Farm
Top Farm
Mason's Covert
Wind Generator
Cottage Nags Head
Glebe Farm
Sotby
Dog Hill
Sycamore Farm
Sotby Meadows Nature Reserve
Brant Hills Wood
Gospel Hill Farm
Moor Farm
Dovecot Farm
Cop Hills Wood
Sotby Wood
Grange Farm
Hatton
Great Sturton
Park Farm
Corner Farm
Glebe Farm
Hatton Bridge
Cross Roads Farm
Oak Farm
Walkers Farm
The Beeches
PH
Moat
Baumber Top Yard
Chy
Big Wood
Hatton Meadows Nature Reserve
Hatton Wood
East Farm
White House Farm
Lodge Farm
Brickyard Farm
LN9
Stourton Wood
Black Plantation
Ash Holt Stourton Wood
West Farm
Hungram Farm
Greenfield Farm
Cherry Tree Farm
Hungram Gorse
New Farm
Minting House
Minting Wood
Hungram House
TORRINGTON LANE
PO
A157
LOUTH RD
LINCOLN ROAD
WILLINGHAM ROAD
PANTON ROAD
CHURCH LA
MAIN ROAD
SILVER ST
B1225
HIGH STREET
WASS LANE
BUTTERGATE HILL
MILL LANE
A158
COW LANE
MINTING LANE
PINFOLD LA
8
81
7
80
6
79
5
78
4
77
3
76
2
75
1
74
6
17
18
19
20
21
84
72

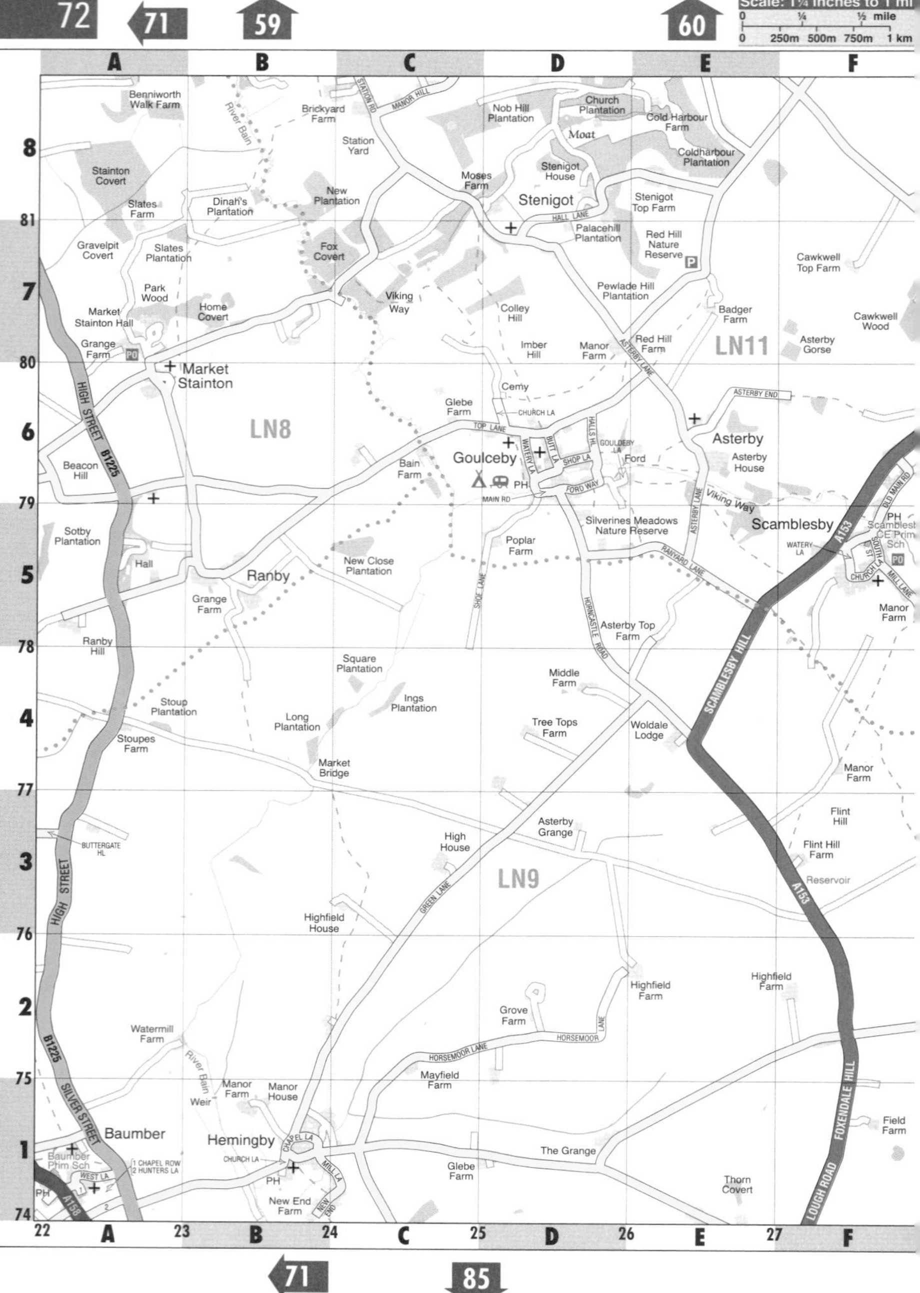
Scale: 1¼ inches to 1 mi
0 ¼ ½ mile
0 250m 500m 750m 1 km
A B C D E F
Benniworth Walk Farm
River Bain
Brickyard Farm
STATION RD
MANOR HILL
Nob Hill Plantation
Church Plantation
Cold Harbour Farm
Moat
Coldharbour Plantation
Station Yard
Stainton Covert
Stenigot House
Moses Farm
New Plantation
Dinah's Plantation
Slates Farm
Stenigot
Stenigot Top Farm
HALL LANE
Palacehill Plantation
Red Hill Nature Reserve
Gravelpit Covert
Slates Plantation
Fox Covert
Cawkwell Top Farm
Park Wood
Viking Way
Pewlade Hill Plantation
Market Stainton Hall
Home Covert
Colley Hill
Badger Farm
Cawkwell Wood
Grange Farm
Imber Hill
Manor Farm
Red Hill Farm
LN11
Asterby Gorse
Market Stainton
ASTERBY LANE
Cemy
ASTERBY END
Glebe Farm
CHURCH LA
LN8
TOP LANE
HALLS HL
Asterby
Asterby House
GOULDEBY LA
Goulceby
WATERY LA
BUTT LA
SHOP LA
Ford
Beacon Hill
Bain Farm
PH
FORD WAY
MAIN RD
Viking Way
OLD MAIN RD
HIGH STREET
B1225
Silverines Meadows Nature Reserve
ASTERBY LANE
Scamblesby
Scamblesby CE Prim Sch
Sotby Plantation
Poplar Farm
WATERY LA
A153
SOUTH ST
Hall
New Close Plantation
RANYARD LANE
CHURCH LA
MILL LANE
Ranby
SHOE LANE
HORNCASTLE ROAD
Grange Farm
Manor Farm
Asterby Top Farm
Ranby Hill
Square Plantation
Middle Farm
SCAMBLESBY HILL
Stoup Plantation
Ings Plantation
Long Plantation
Tree Tops Farm
Woldale Lodge
Stoupes Farm
Market Bridge
Manor Farm
Flint Hill
Asterby Grange
BUTTERGATE HL
High House
Flint Hill Farm
LN9
Reservoir
GREEN LANE
Highfield House
Highfield Farm
Highfield Farm
Grove Farm
HORSEMOOR LANE
Watermill Farm
HORSEMOOR
River Bain
Mayfield Farm
SILVER STREET
Manor Farm
Manor House
Weir
Field Farm
FOXENDALE HILL
Baumber
Hemingby
CHAPEL LA
Baumber Prim Sch
1 CHAPEL ROW
2 HUNTERS LA
CHURCH LA
The Grange
MILL LA
Glebe Farm
WEST LA
Thorn Covert
PH
A158
New End Farm
NEW END
LOUGH ROAD
22 23 24 25 26 27
8 81 7 80 6 79 5 78 4 77 3 76 2 75 1 74

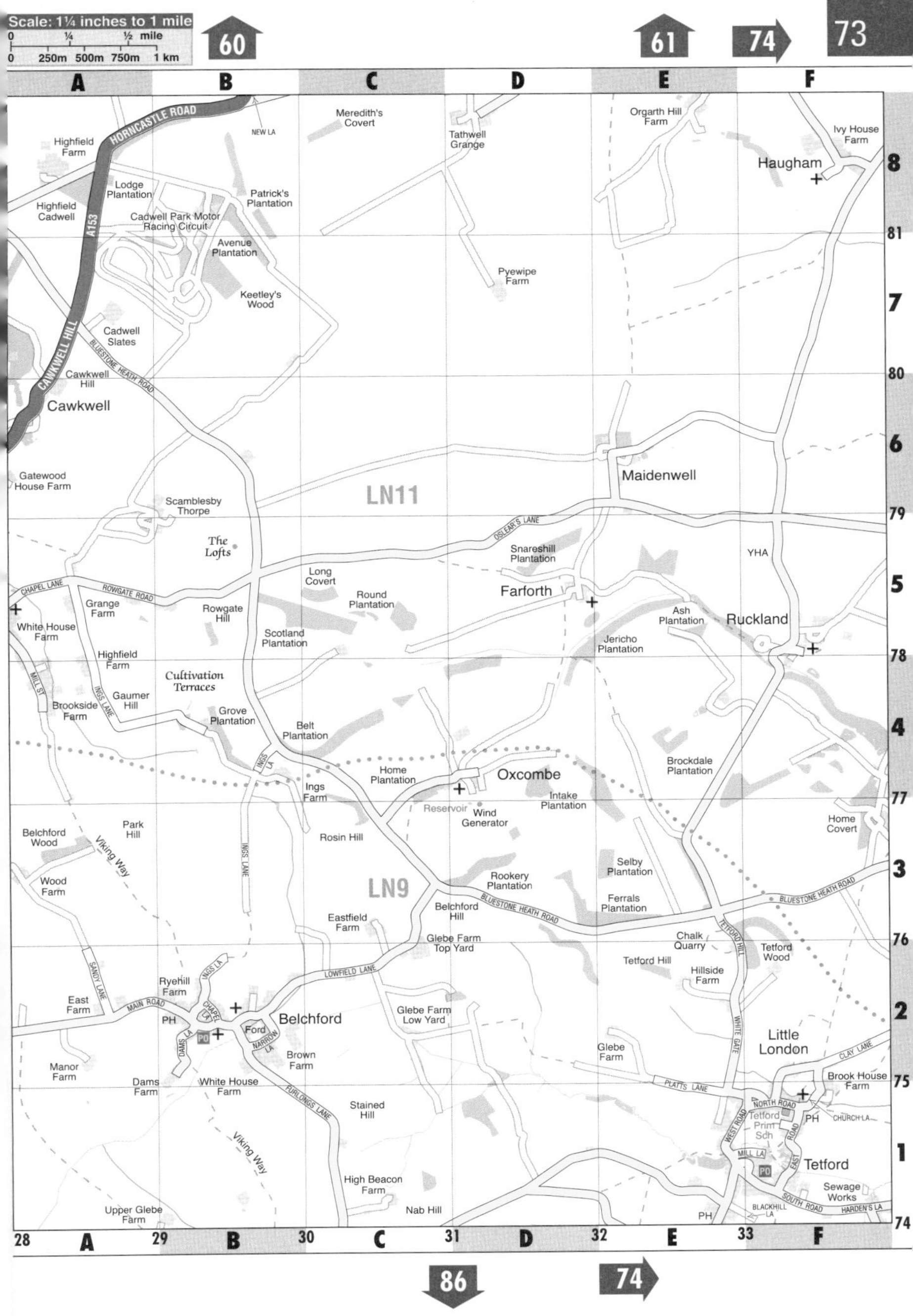
Scale: 1¼ inches to 1 mile
60
61
74
A
B
C
D
E
F
HORNCASTLE ROAD
NEW LA
Meredith's Covert
Tathwell Grange
Orgarth Hill Farm
Ivy House Farm
Haugham
Highfield Farm
Lodge Plantation
Patrick's Plantation
Highfield Cadwell
Cadwell Park Motor Racing Circuit
A153
Avenue Plantation
Pyewipe Farm
Keetley's Wood
Cadwell Slates
CAWKWELL HILL
BLUESTONE HEATH ROAD
Cawkwell Hill
Cawkwell
Maidenwell
Gatewood House Farm
LN11
Scamblesby Thorpe
OSLEAR'S LANE
The Lofts
Snareshill Plantation
YHA
CHAPEL LANE
ROWGATE ROAD
Long Covert
Farforth
Round Plantation
Grange Farm
Rowgate Hill
Ash Plantation
Ruckland
White House Farm
Scotland Plantation
Jericho Plantation
Highfield Farm
MILL ST
Cultivation Terraces
Gaumer Hill
INGS LANE
Brookside Farm
Grove Plantation
Belt Plantation
Brockdale Plantation
INGS LA
Home Plantation
Oxcombe
Ings Farm
Intake Plantation
Reservoir
Wind Generator
Home Covert
Belchford Wood
Park Hill
Viking Way
Rosin Hill
INGS LANE
Selby Plantation
Wood Farm
Rookery Plantation
LN9
Ferrals Plantation
Belchford Hill
BLUESTONE HEATH ROAD
Eastfield Farm
Chalk Quarry
Glebe Farm Top Yard
TETFORD HILL
Tetford Wood
SANDY LANE
Tetford Hill
Ryehill Farm
INGS LA
LOWFIELD LANE
Hillside Farm
East Farm
MAIN ROAD
CHAPEL LA
PH
Belchford
Glebe Farm Low Yard
WHITE GATE
Ford
DAMS LA
PO
NARROW LA
Little London
Manor Farm
Brown Farm
Glebe Farm
CLAY LANE
Brook House Farm
Dams Farm
White House Farm
PLATTS LANE
NORTH ROAD
FURLONGS LANE
Tetford Print Sch
PH
CHURCH LA
Stained Hill
Viking Way
WEST ROAD
ROAD
MILL LA
EAST
Tetford
PO
High Beacon Farm
Sewage Works
SOUTH ROAD
BLACKHILL LA
HARDEN'S LA
Upper Glebe Farm
Nab Hill
PH
8
81
7
80
6
79
5
78
4
77
3
76
2
75
1
74
28
29
30
31
32
33
86
74

73 61 62

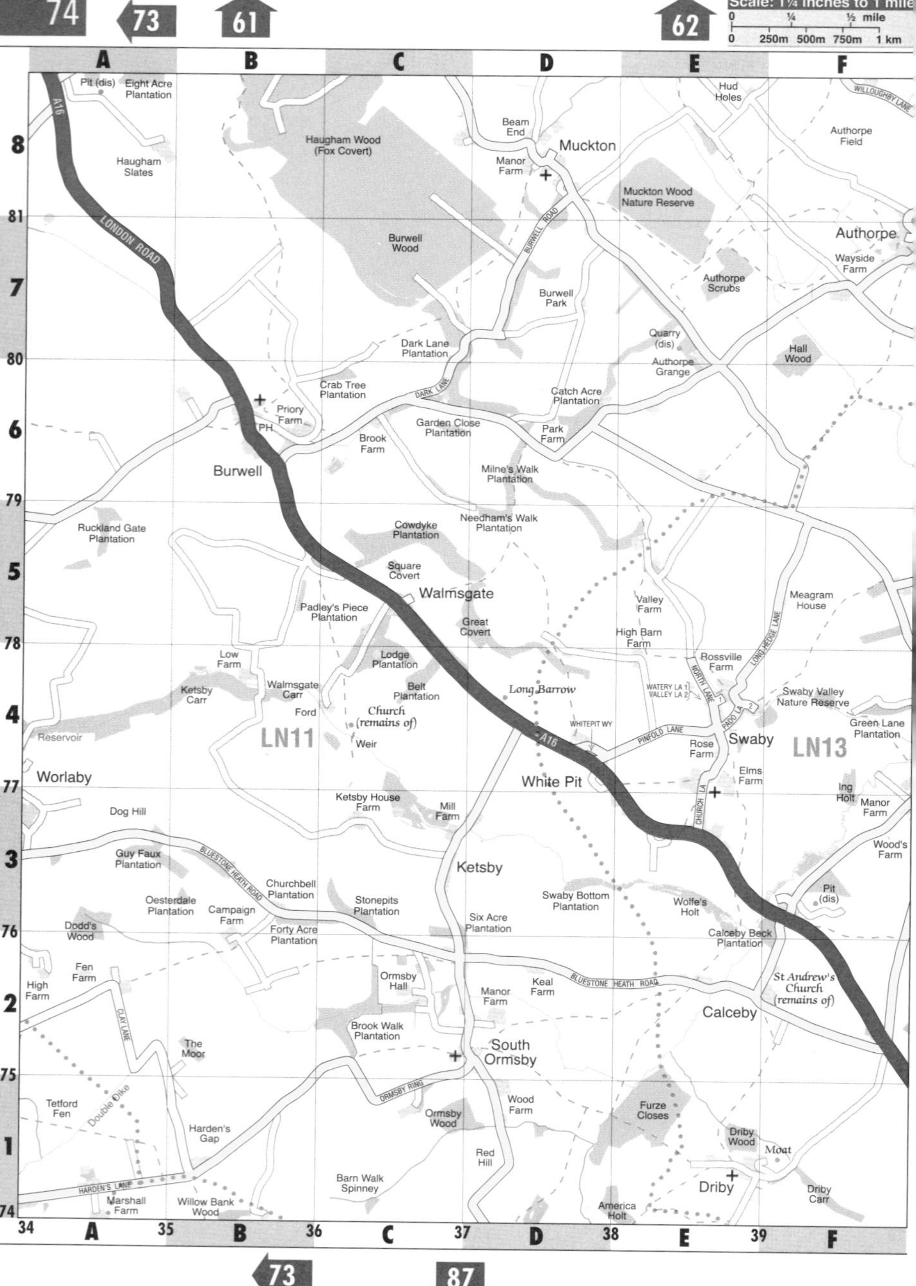

Scale: 1¼ inches to 1 mile
0 ¼ ½ mile
0 250m 500m 750m 1 km
A B C D E F
8 81 7 80 6 79 5 78 4 77 3 76 2 75 1 74
34 35 36 37 38 39
Pit (dis)
Eight Acre Plantation
Haugham Slates
Haugham Wood (Fox Covert)
Burwell Wood
Beam End
Muckton
Manor Farm
Hud Holes
WILLOUGHBY LANE
Authorpe Field
Muckton Wood Nature Reserve
Authorpe
Wayside Farm
Authorpe Scrubs
A16
LONDON ROAD
BURWELL ROAD
Burwell Park
Dark Lane Plantation
Quarry (dis)
Authorpe Grange
Hall Wood
Crab Tree Plantation
DARK LANE
Priory Farm
PH
Catch Acre Plantation
Garden Close Plantation
Brook Farm
Park Farm
Burwell
Milne's Walk Plantation
Ruckland Gate Plantation
Needham's Walk Plantation
Cowdyke Plantation
Square Covert
Walmsgate
Padley's Piece Plantation
Great Covert
Valley Farm
Meagram House
High Barn Farm
Low Farm
Lodge Plantation
Rossville Farm
LONG HEDGE LANE
NORTH LANE
Ketsby Carr
Walmsgate Carr
Belt Plantation
Long Barrow
WATERY LA 1
VALLEY LA 2
Swaby Valley Nature Reserve
Ford
Church (remains of)
WHITEPIT WY
PADDOCK LA
Green Lane Plantation
Reservoir
LN11
Weir
PINFOLD LANE
Rose Farm
Swaby
LN13
Worlaby
White Pit
Elms Farm
Ing Holt
CHURCH LA
Manor Farm
Dog Hill
Ketsby House Farm
Mill Farm
Wood's Farm
Guy Faux Plantation
BLUESTONE HEATH ROAD
Ketsby
Pit (dis)
Churchbell Plantation
Oesterdale Plantation
Swaby Bottom Plantation
Wolfe's Holt
Campaign Farm
Stonepits Plantation
Six Acre Plantation
Dodd's Wood
Forty Acre Plantation
Calceby Beck Plantation
Fen Farm
Ormsby Hall
Keal Farm
St Andrew's Church (remains of)
High Farm
Manor Farm
Calceby
CLAY LANE
Brook Walk Plantation
The Moor
South Ormsby
ORMSBY RING
Tetford Fen
Double Dike
Wood Farm
Furze Closes
Ormsby Wood
Driby Wood
Moat
Harden's Gap
Red Hill
Barn Walk Spinney
Driby
Driby Carr
HARDEN'S LANE
Marshall Farm
Willow Bank Wood
America Holt

73 87

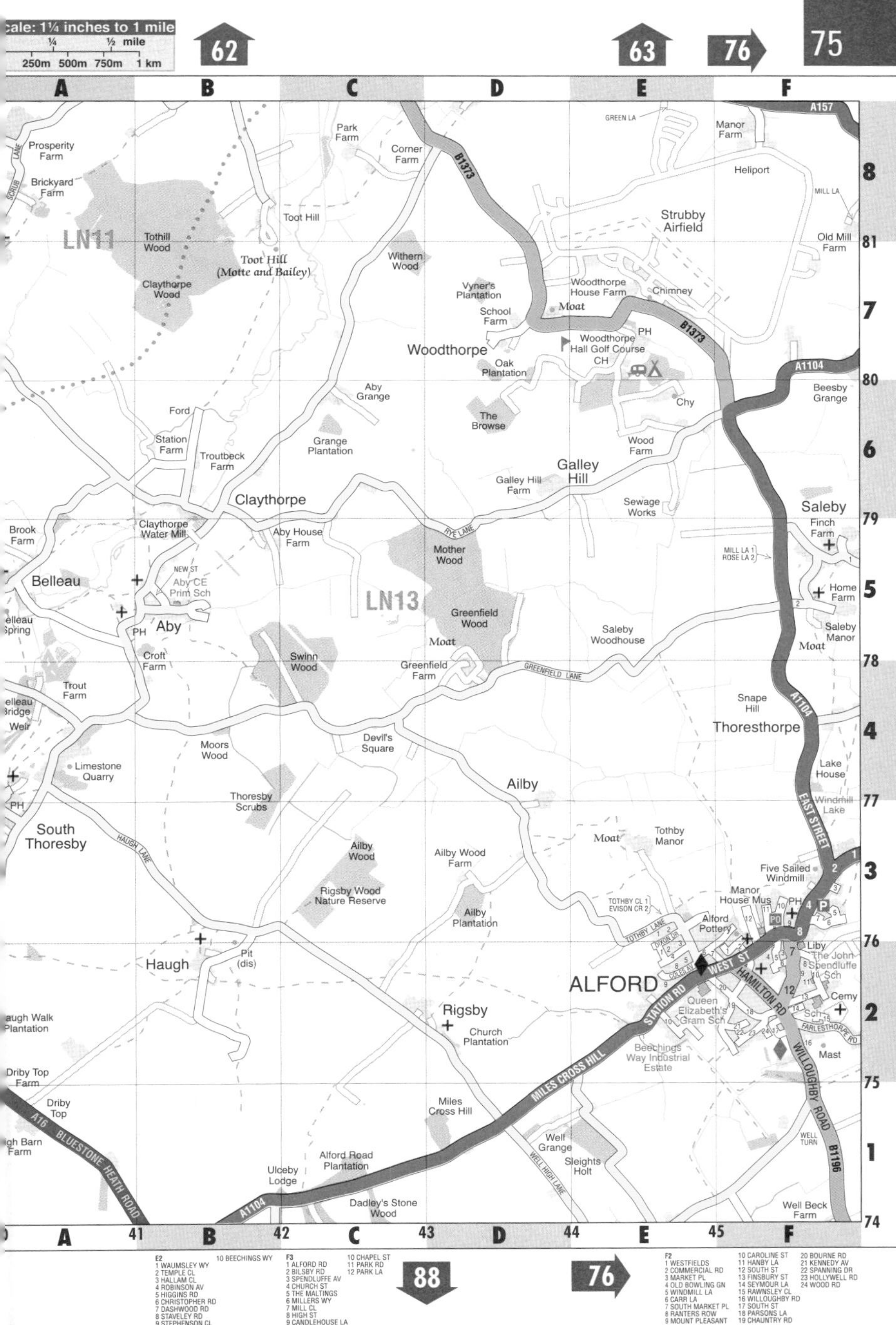

cale: 1¼ inches to 1 mile
¼
½ mile
250m 500m 750m 1 km
62
63
76
75
Prosperity Farm
Brickyard Farm
LN11
Tothill Wood
Claythorpe Wood
Toot Hill (Motte and Bailey)
Park Farm
Corner Farm
Toot Hill
Withern Wood
B1373
GREEN LA
Manor Farm
A157
Heliport
MILL LA
Strubby Airfield
Old Mill Farm
Vyner's Plantation
Woodthorpe House Farm
Chimney
School Farm
Moat
Woodthorpe
PH
Woodthorpe Hall Golf Course
CH
Oak Plantation
A1104
Beesby Grange
Aby Grange
The Browse
Chy
Ford
Station Farm
Troutbeck Farm
Grange Plantation
Wood Farm
Galley Hill
Galley Hill Farm
Claythorpe
Sewage Works
Saleby
Finch Farm
Brook Farm
Claythorpe Water Mill
Aby House Farm
RYE LANE
Mother Wood
MILL LA 1
ROSE LA 2
NEW ST
Belleau
Aby CE Prim Sch
LN13
Home Farm
Greenfield Wood
Aby
PH
Saleby Woodhouse
Saleby Manor
Moat
Croft Farm
Swinn Wood
Greenfield Farm
GREENFIELD LANE
Trout Farm
Snape Hill
Thoresthorpe
Devil's Square
Moors Wood
Limestone Quarry
Lake House
Ailby
Thoresby Scrubs
Windmill Lake
EAST STREET
South Thoresby
HAUGH LANE
Moat
Tothby Manor
Ailby Wood
Ailby Wood Farm
Five Sailed Windmill
Rigsby Wood Nature Reserve
Manor House Mus
TOTHBY CL 1
EVISON CR 2
Ailby Plantation
Alford Pottery
TOTHBY LANE
DIXON DR
Haugh
Pit (dis)
Liby
The John Spendluffe Sch
COLES AV
WEST ST
ALFORD
HAMILTON RD
STATION RD
Queen Elizabeth's Gram Sch
Cemy
Rigsby
Church Plantation
FARLESTHORPE RD
Beechings Way Industrial Estate
Mast
MILES CROSS HILL
WILLOUGHBY ROAD
Driby Top Farm
Driby Top
Miles Cross Hill
A16 BLUESTONE HEATH ROAD
Well Grange
WELL TURN
B1196
Sleights Holt
WELL HIGH LANE
Alford Road Plantation
Ulceby Lodge
A1104
Dadley's Stone Wood
Well Beck Farm
A
B
C
D
E
F
8
81
7
80
6
79
5
78
4
77
3
76
2
75
1
74
41
42
43
44
45
E2
1 WAUMSLEY WY
2 TEMPLE CL
3 HALLAM CL
4 ROBINSON AV
5 HIGGINS RD
6 CHRISTOPHER RD
7 DASHWOOD RD
8 STAVELEY RD
9 STEPHENSON CL
10 BEECHINGS WY
F3
1 ALFORD RD
2 BILSBY RD
3 SPENDLUFFE AV
4 CHURCH ST
5 THE MALTINGS
6 MILLERS WY
7 MILL CL
8 HIGH ST
9 CANDLEHOUSE LA
10 CHAPEL ST
11 PARK RD
12 PARK LA
88
76
F2
1 WESTFIELDS
2 COMMERCIAL RD
3 MARKET PL
4 OLD BOWLING GN
5 WINDMILL LA
6 CARR LA
7 SOUTH MARKET PL
8 RANTERS ROW
9 MOUNT PLEASANT
10 CAROLINE ST
11 HANBY LA
12 SOUTH ST
13 FINSBURY ST
14 SEYMOUR LA
15 RAWNSLEY CL
16 WILLOUGHBY RD
17 SOUTH ST
18 PARSONS LA
19 CHAUNTRY RD
20 BOURNE RD
21 KENNEDY AV
22 SPANNING DR
23 HOLLYWELL RD
24 WOOD RD

F8
1 HIGH GATE
2 HANSON DR
3 BRAEMAR RD
4 MARINE AV
5 BUCKNALL'S MD
6 HARDING CL
7 WILLIAM TOW CL
8 MARINE AV W
9 WILLIAM GN CL
10 MORRISON CL
11 CAMELOT GD
12 BALMORAL CL
13 SANDRINGHAM DR
14 HONEYSUCKLE CL
15 BUCKINGHAM CL
16 STATION RD
17 HUTTOFT RD

Scale: 1¼ inches to 1 mile

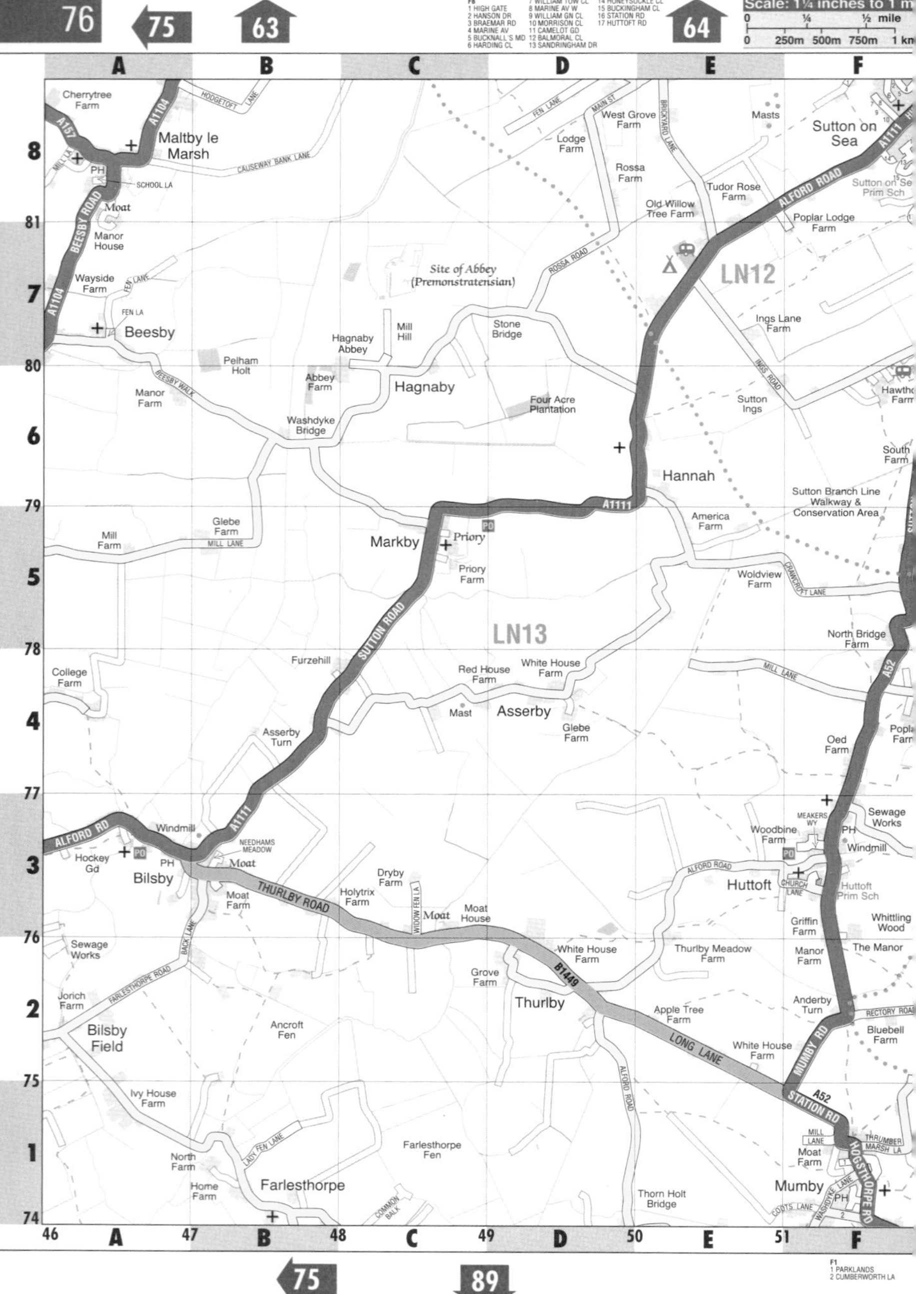

F1
1 PARKLANDS
2 CUMBERWORTH LA

Scale: 1¼ inches to 1 mile
¼
½ mile
250m 500m 750m 1 km
64
A7
1 COMPER SWIFT CL
2 HENSHAW AV
3 SHELLEY CL
4 KIPLING DR
5 SANDHURST RD
6 SANDHURST CT
7 RUDYARD CL
8 THE GLADE
9 ROSSALL CL
10 MASEFIELD DR
11 SHARMANS CL
12 TENNYSON CL
13 THE CRESCENT
14 GRANGE RD
15 SANDERS CL
16 THE COPSE
17 KEATS CL
18 WALKINGTON WY
19 DRAKES CL
20 HORNBY DR
21 WILYMAN CL
22 SANDILANDS CL
23 ST FRANCIS GD
24 BLUESTONE WY
25 CAWKWELL CL
A8
1 MORELAND AV
2 MARISCO CT
3 HODGSON WY
4 STANTON RD
5 SURFSIDE
6 YOULGRAVE AV
7 HILLSIDE AV
8 QUEENS RD
9 EDWALTON AV
10 BEACHSIDE
11 MARTINS WK
12 CISSBURY CL
13 LEWIS AV
14 CHURCH LA
15 DENNOR CL
16 CHURCH CL
17 CHURCH PK
18 WILMINGTON DR
19 CHANCTONBURY WY
20 CHANCTONBURY CL
21 LANSDOWNE DR
22 LANSDOWNE CL
23 THE SIDINGS
24 CADES FIELD RD
25 DE LA BERE AV
A B C D E F
8 81 7 80 6 79 5 78 4 77 3 76 2 75 1 74
52 53 54 55 56 57
Liby
FURLONGS RD
PROMENADE
CHURCH LANE
Sandilands
A52
SEA LA
PO
Hotel
Hotel
CRABTREE LA
HUTTOFT ROAD
PH
CH
Sandilands Pit Nature Reserve
Sandilands Golf Course
Fir Tree Farm
Boy Grift Bridge
Sea Bank Farm
Huttoft Bank Pit Nature Reserve
Yarlsgate Farm
NORTH INGS LANE
Stain Glebe Farm
Cob Hill
LN13
Greenacres Farm
SEA LANE
Ryluc Farm
Field Head Farm
Black House Farm
Huttoft Bank
Moggs Eye
Oakwell Farm
Bank Farm
ROMAN BANK
Eastfield Farm
Wold Sea Farm
JOLLY COMM LA
Anderby Creek
THE CUT
SANDY LA
OCCUPATION LA 1
GRACE CR 2
LAKESIDE 3
Manor Farm
Gowt Bridge
SEA ROAD
Seaton Farm
Anderby Drainage Mus
SEA ROAD
Priory Farm
Dairy Farm
Bank House
Church Farm
Main Drain
PE24
Sycamore Farm
Anderby
Wexham Farm
Wolla Bank Nature Reserves
Manor Farm
Langham Farm
EMBER LA
EMBER LANE
Chapel Six Marshes
ANDERBY ROAD
THRUMBER MARSH LANE
EMBER LANE
STONE'S LA
LN13
Field Farm

90

65

Scale: 1¼ inches to 1 mile

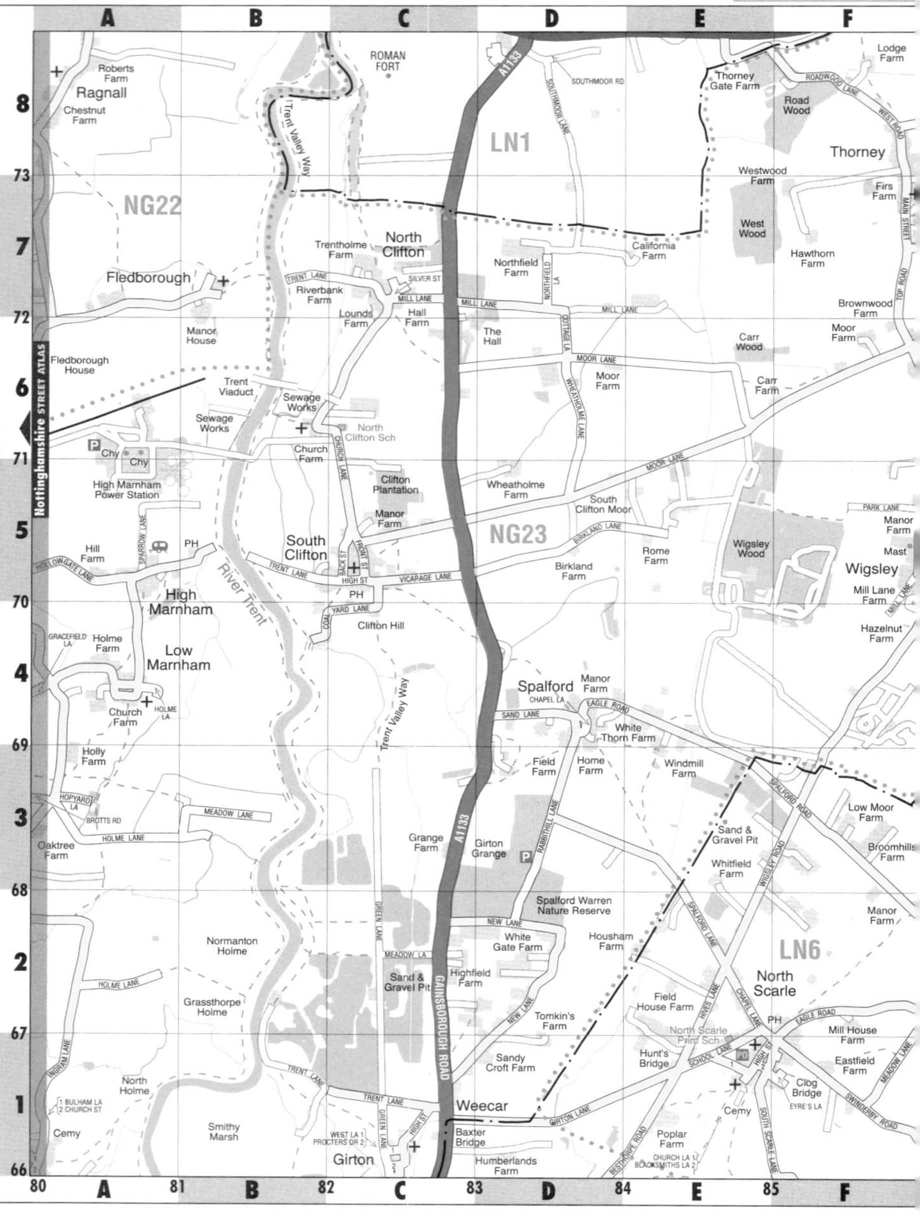

91

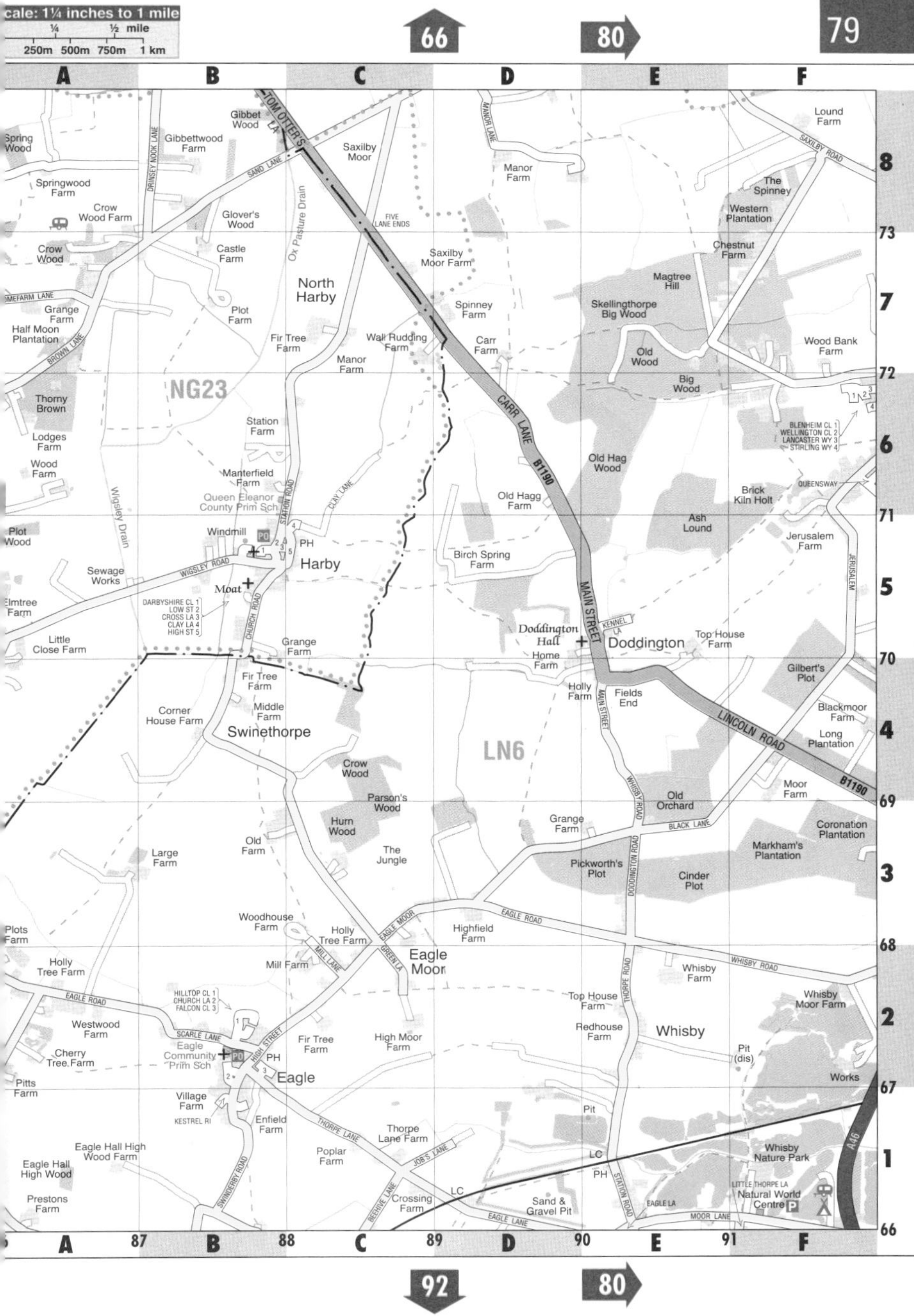
cale: 1¼ inches to 1 mile
¼ ½ mile
250m 500m 750m 1 km
66
80
A B C D E F
8 7 6 5 4 3 2 1
73 72 71 70 69 68 67 66
87 88 89 90 91
Spring Wood
Gibbet Wood
Gibbettwood Farm
DRINSEY NOOK LANE
TOM OTTER'S LA
SAND LANE
Saxilby Moor
MANOR LANE
Manor Farm
Lound Farm
SAXILBY ROAD
The Spinney
Western Plantation
Springwood Farm
Crow Wood Farm
Glover's Wood
Ox Pasture Drain
FIVE LANE ENDS
Crow Wood
Castle Farm
Saxilby Moor Farm
Chestnut Farm
Magtree Hill
North Harby
Skellingthorpe Big Wood
HOMEFARM LANE
Grange Farm
Plot Farm
Spinney Farm
Half Moon Plantation
BROWN LANE
Fir Tree Farm
Wall Rudding Farm
Carr Farm
Old Wood
Wood Bank Farm
Manor Farm
Big Wood
NG23
Thorny Brown
Station Farm
CARR LANE
BLENHEIM CL 1
WELLINGTON CL 2
LANCASTER WY 3
STIRLING WY 4
Lodges Farm
Old Hag Wood
Wood Farm
Manterfield Farm
B1190
Old Hagg Farm
Brick Kiln Holt
QUEENSWAY
Queen Eleanor County Prim Sch
CLAY LANE
STATION ROAD
Wigsley Drain
Ash Lound
Plot Wood
Windmill
PO
PH
Jerusalem Farm
Harby
Birch Spring Farm
Sewage Works
WIGSLEY ROAD
JERUSALEM
Moat
Elmtree Farm
MAIN STREET
DARBYSHIRE CL 1
LOW ST 2
CROSS LA 3
CLAY LA 4
HIGH ST 5
CHURCH ROAD
KENNEL LA
Doddington Hall
Doddington
Top House Farm
Little Close Farm
Grange Farm
Home Farm
Gilbert's Plot
Fir Tree Farm
Holly Farm
Fields End
Middle Farm
MAIN STREET
Blackmoor Farm
Corner House Farm
Swinethorpe
LINCOLN ROAD
Long Plantation
LN6
Crow Wood
Moor Farm
Parson's Wood
WHISBY ROAD
Old Orchard
B1190
Hurn Wood
Grange Farm
BLACK LANE
Coronation Plantation
Large Farm
Old Farm
The Jungle
Pickworth's Plot
Markham's Plantation
DODDINGTON ROAD
Cinder Plot
Woodhouse Farm
EAGLE ROAD
Plots Farm
Holly Tree Farm
EAGLE MOOR
Highfield Farm
Holly Tree Farm
MILL LANE
GREEN LA
Eagle Moor
WHISBY ROAD
Mill Farm
THORPE ROAD
Whisby Farm
EAGLE ROAD
HILLTOP CL 1
CHURCH LA 2
FALCON CL 3
Top House Farm
Whisby Moor Farm
Westwood Farm
SCARLE LANE
Redhouse Farm
Whisby
Eagle Community Prim Sch
HIGH STREET
Fir Tree Farm
High Moor Farm
Pit (dis)
Cherry Tree Farm
PH
Eagle
Works
Pitts Farm
Village Farm
Pit
KESTREL RI
Enfield Farm
THORPE LANE
Thorpe Lane Farm
A46
Eagle Hall High Wood Farm
Poplar Farm
JOB'S LANE
LC
Whisby Nature Park
Eagle Hall High Wood
SWINDERBY ROAD
PH
STATION ROAD
LITTLE THORPE LA
Prestons Farm
BEEHIVE LANE
Crossing Farm
LC
Sand & Gravel Pit
EAGLE LA
Natural World Centre
EAGLE LANE
MOOR LANE
92
80

79
67

For full street detail of the highlighted area see pages 200, 201, 204 and 205.
79
93

68
82

94
82 For full street detail of the highlighted area see pages 202 and 203.

A8
1 PLOUGH LA
2 LABURNUM CT
3 THE GREE
4 SMOOTING LA
5 MOOR LA
6 STATION RD
7 MEADOW CL

81
69

B1
1 FOSTER'S GDNS
2 QUEENSWAY
3 MAIN RD
4 CROSS ST
5 MIDDLE ST
6 CHURCH LA
7 NOCTON RD

81
95

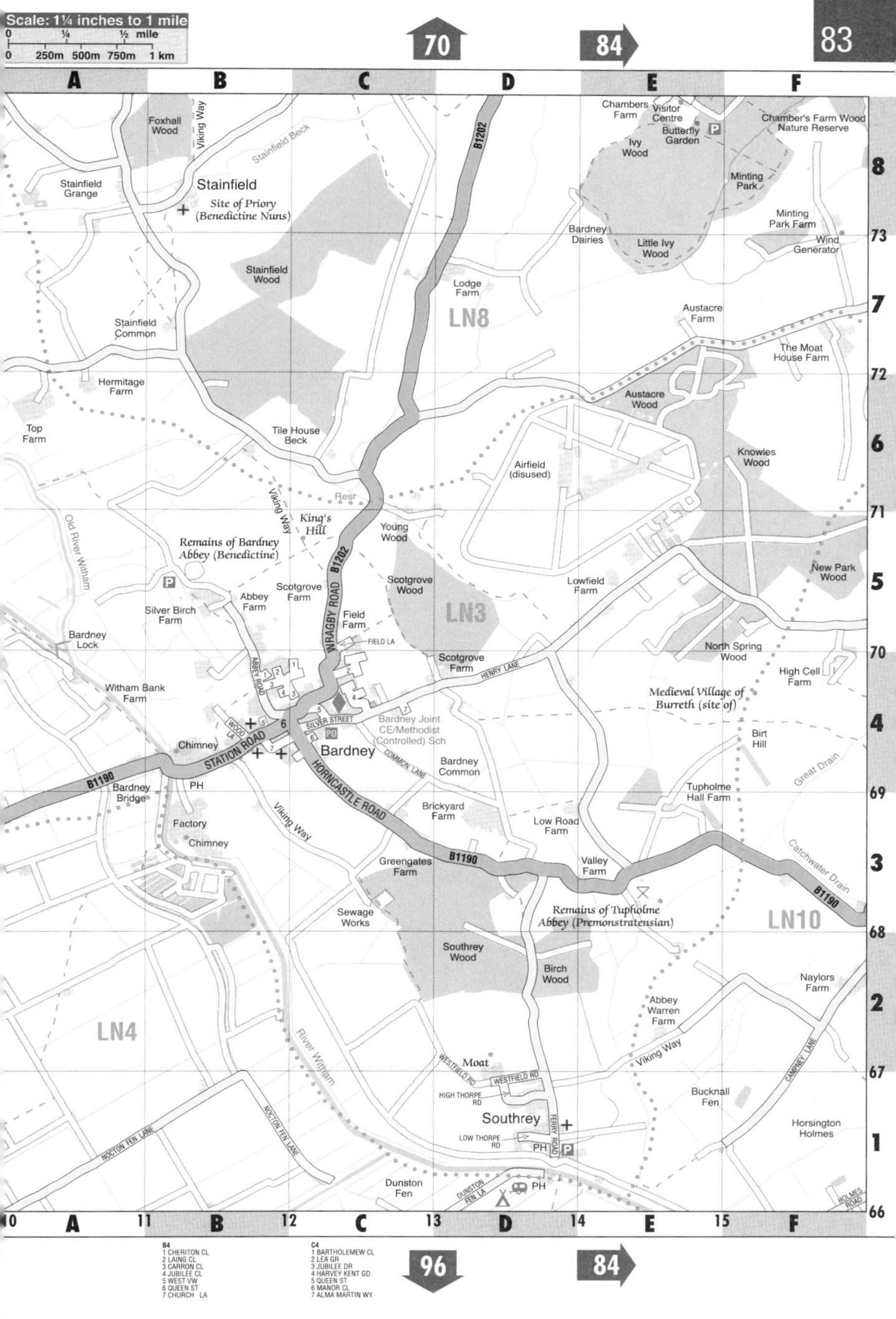

B4
1 CHERITON CL
2 LAING CL
3 CARRON CL
4 JUBILEE CL
5 WEST VW
6 QUEEN ST
7 CHURCH LA

C4
1 BARTHOLEMEW CL
2 LEA GR
3 JUBILEE DR
4 HARVEY KENT GD
5 QUEEN ST
6 MANOR CL
7 ALMA MARTIN WY

83
C8
1 COW LA
2 MINTING LA
3 THE GREEN
4 CHURCH LA
71

Scale: 1¼ inches to 1 mil
0 ¼ ½ mile
0 250m 500m 750m 1 km

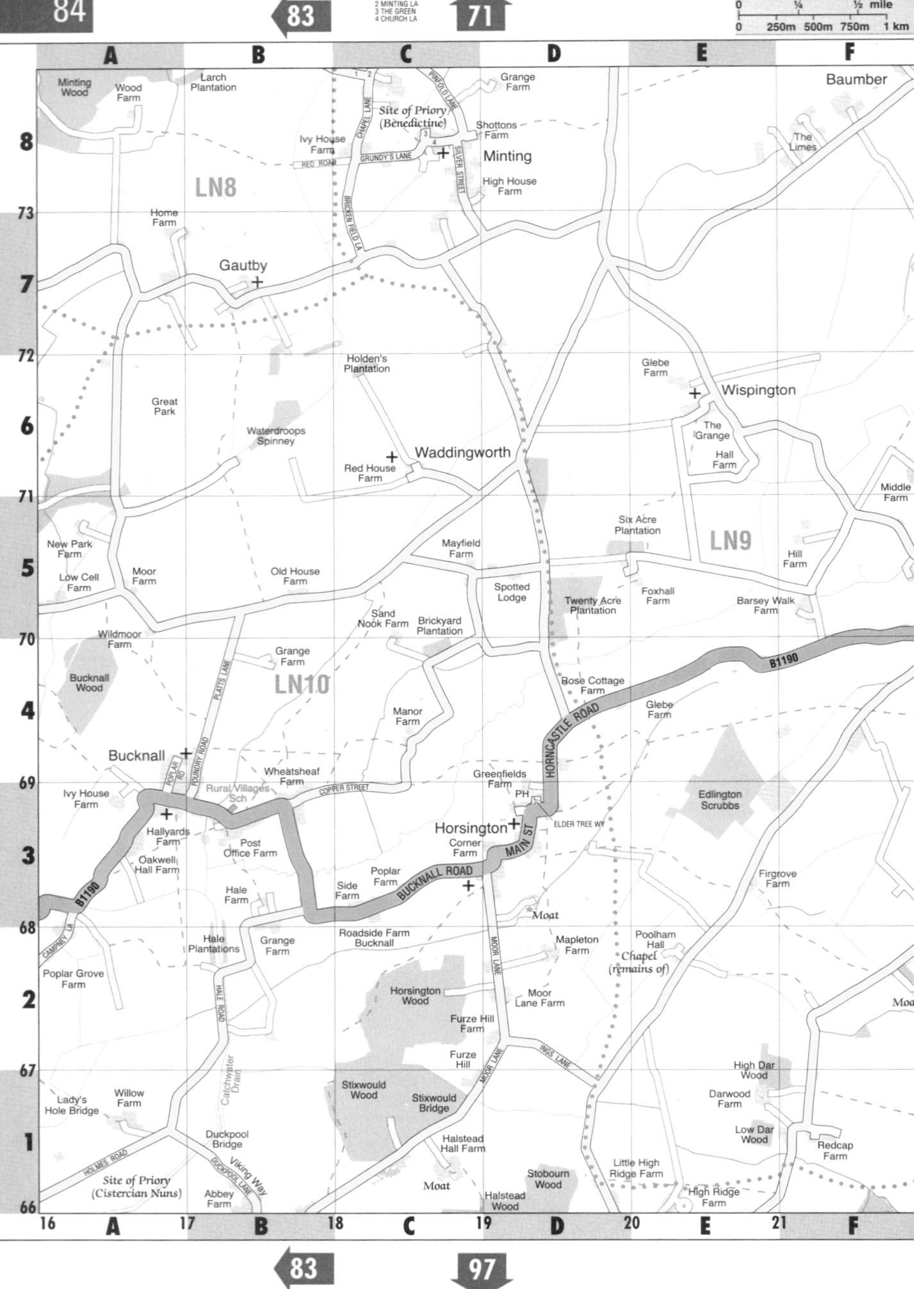

83
97

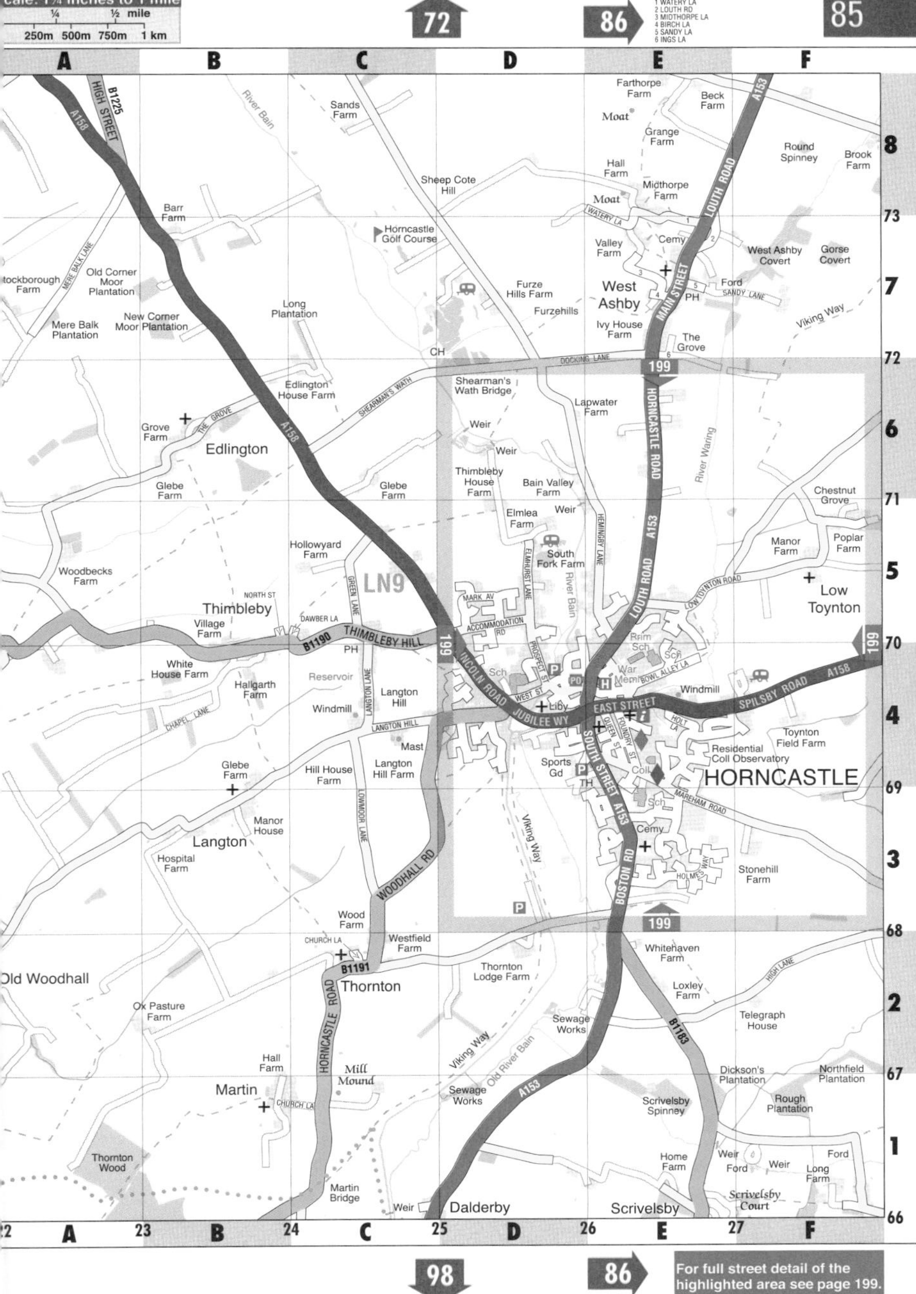

For full street detail of the highlighted area see page 199.

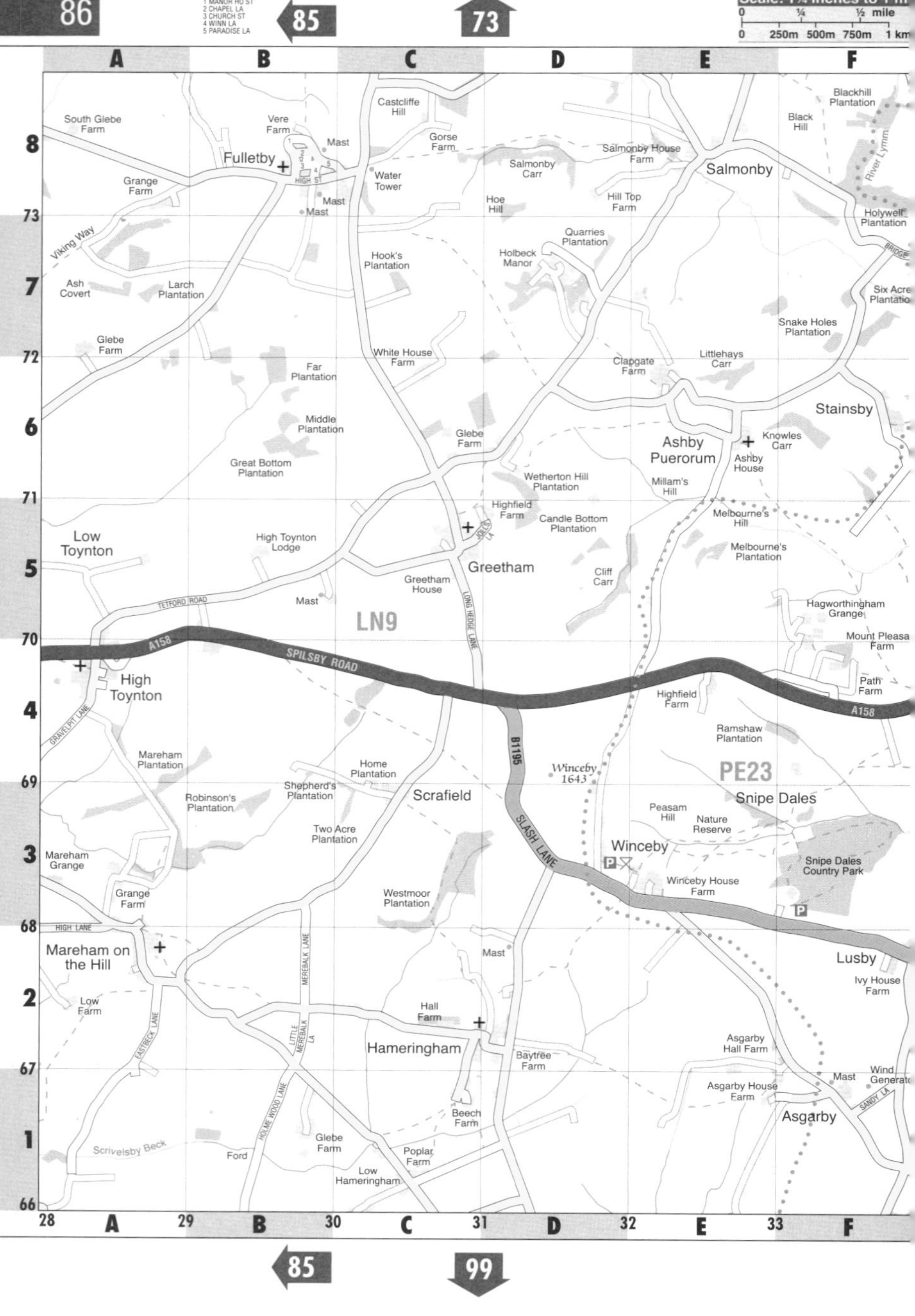
B8
1 MANOR HO ST
2 CHAPEL LA
3 CHURCH ST
4 WINN LA
5 PARADISE LA
85
73
Scale: 1¼ inches to 1 m
0 ¼ ½ mile
0 250m 500m 750m 1 km
A B C D E F
8
73
7
72
6
71
5
70
4
69
3
68
2
67
1
66
28 29 30 31 32 33
South Glebe Farm
Vere Farm
Mast
Fulletby
Grange Farm
HIGH ST
Mast
Mast
Castcliffe Hill
Gorse Farm
Water Tower
Salmonby Carr
Salmonby House Farm
Salmonby
Blackhill Plantation
Black Hill
River Lymn
Hoe Hill
Hill Top Farm
Holywell Plantation
BRIDGE
Viking Way
Ash Covert
Larch Plantation
Hook's Plantation
Holbeck Manor
Quarries Plantation
Six Acre Plantation
Glebe Farm
White House Farm
Snake Holes Plantation
Far Plantation
Clapgate Farm
Littlehays Carr
Middle Plantation
Stainsby
Glebe Farm
Ashby Puerorum
Knowles Carr
Ashby House
Great Bottom Plantation
Wetherton Hill Plantation
Millam's Hill
Highfield Farm
Candle Bottom Plantation
Melbourne's Hill
Low Toynton
High Toynton Lodge
JOLLS LA
Melbourne's Plantation
Greetham
Greetham House
Cliff Carr
TETFORD ROAD
Mast
LN9
LONG HEDGE LANE
Hagworthingham Grange
Mount Pleasa Farm
A158
SPILSBY ROAD
High Toynton
Path Farm
GRAVELPIT LANE
Highfield Farm
A158
Ramshaw Plantation
B1195
Mareham Plantation
Home Plantation
Winceby 1643
PE23
Shepherd's Plantation
Scrafield
Snipe Dales
Robinson's Plantation
Peasam Hill
Nature Reserve
Two Acre Plantation
SLASH LANE
Mareham Grange
Winceby
Snipe Dales Country Park
Winceby House Farm
Grange Farm
Westmoor Plantation
HIGH LANE
Mareham on the Hill
MEREBALK LANE
Mast
Lusby
Ivy House Farm
Low Farm
Hall Farm
EASTBECK LANE
LITTLE MEREBALK LA
Hameringham
Baytree Farm
Asgarby Hall Farm
Mast
Wind Generat
Asgarby House Farm
HOLME WOOD LANE
Beech Farm
SANDY LA
Asgarby
Scrivelsby Beck
Ford
Glebe Farm
Poplar Farm
Low Hameringham
85
99

A4
1 CHURCH LA
2 THORNWELL LA
3 BOND HAYS LA
4 MANOR RD
5 WATER LA

F1
1 BOWMANS RIDGE
2 MILNER'S LA
3 PARK AV
4 OLD MKT AV
5 MASONIC LA
6 WOODLANDS AV
7 WEST END
8 POOLE'S LA
9 WEST END CR
10 SPENCE ST
11 CHURCH ST
12 OLD MARKET AV
13 ERESBY AV

87
75

Scale: 1¼ inches to 1 mile

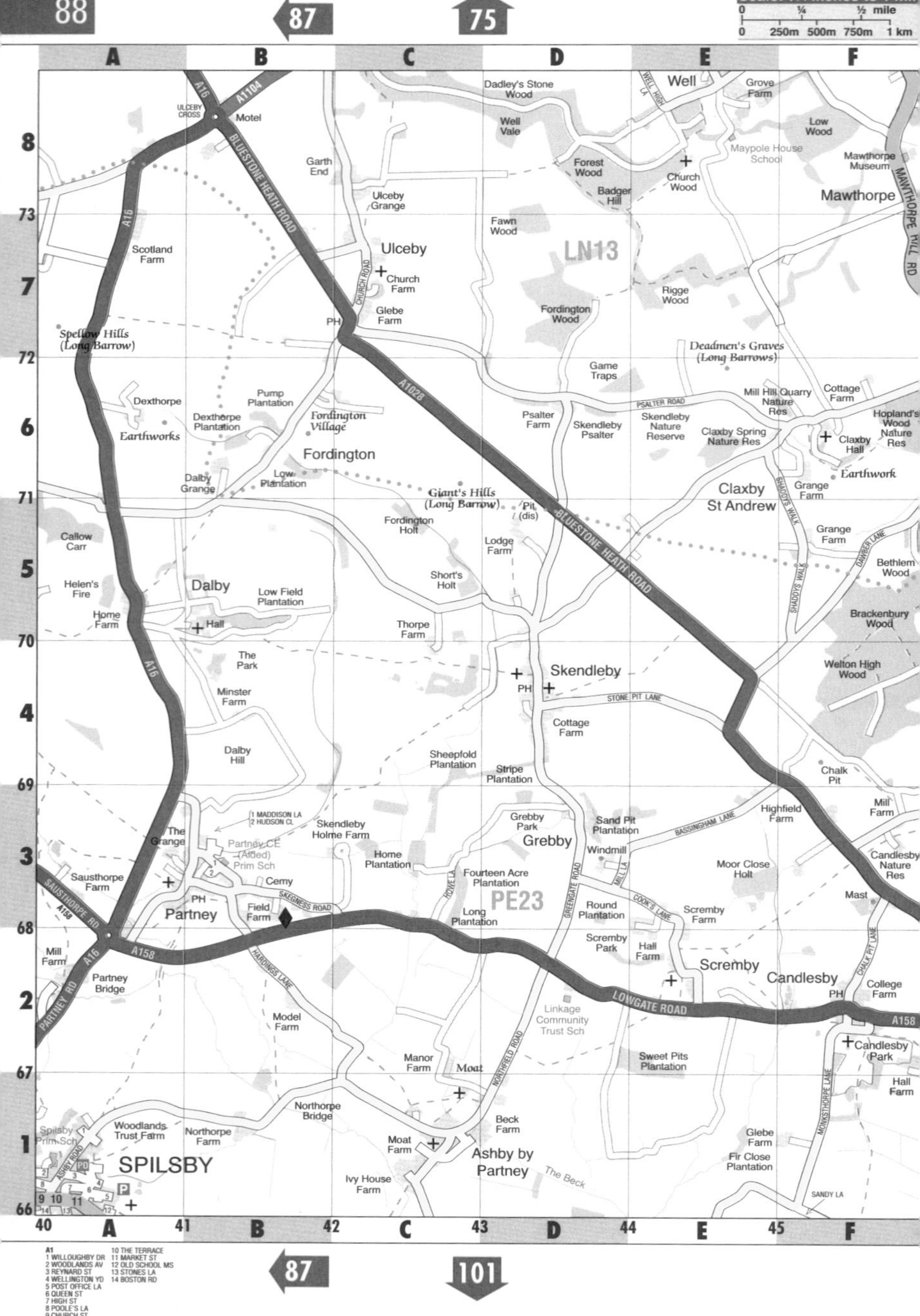

A1
1 WILLOUGHBY DR
2 WOODLANDS AV
3 REYNARD ST
4 WELLINGTON YD
5 POST OFFICE LA
6 QUEEN ST
7 HIGH ST
8 POOLE'S LA
9 CHURCH ST
10 THE TERRACE
11 MARKET ST
12 OLD SCHOOL MS
13 STONES LA
14 BOSTON RD

87
101

Scale: 1¼ inches to 1 mile
¼
½ mile
250m 500m 750m 1 km
76
90
A
B
C
D
E
F
Cornerways
School Farm
COMMON BALK
WESTFIELD LA
Woods Farm
ALFORD RD
WASHDYKE LANE
Cumberworth
A52
Farlesthorpe Fen
FARLESTHORPE ROAD
WESTFIELD LANE
WILLOUGHBY ROAD
MARSH LANE
Ings Lane Farm
Field Farm
Cherry Farm
Arborlow Farm
Elsom Farm
Buttercup Farm
Plains Holt
Bonthorpe
Butterbump Bridge
INGS LANE
Glebe Farm
Helsey
Willoughby Branch Line Nature Reserve
CUMBERWORTH ROAD
Slate Farm
Manor Farm
BONTHORPE ROAD
Tumuli
HELSEY LA
Glebe Farm
Listoft Farm
B1196
St Helenas CE Prim Sch
CHURCH LANE
LN13
Poplar Farm
Listoft
LISTOFT LA
STATION ROAD
Willoughby
CLOVER RD 1
TAVERN CL 2
JOHN SMITH CL 3
PH
Village Farm
Burlands Beck
Willoughby High Drain
Dam Close (Earthwork)
Cumberworth Ings
Wood Close Plantation
B1196
Willougby Meadow Nature Reserve
MILL LANE
SLOOTHBY HIGH LANE
Mabs Hole
Hogs Beck
Bethlehem Farm
Willoughby Wood
Gillwell Plantation
Hogsbeck House
GREEN LANE
Sloothby
Poplar Farm
Spring Farm
The Dairy Farm
Field Farm
Ings Farm
HASTHORPE ROAD
GREEN LANE
Jail Holt
Thwaite Hall
HANBY LANE
Castle Hill
Hasthorpe
Sloothby Ings
Moat
Welton Low Wood
Habertoft Farm
Ducky Plantation
Habertoft
Graves Farm
MILL LANE
PH
PO
Barn Farm
Holme Farm
Orby Beck
Rookery Farm
BECK LA
Low Farm
Bank Farm
Sycamore Farm
ORBY BANK
Beck Farm
Welton le Marsh
Boothby Hall
Boothby Grange
ORBY HOLME FIELD LANE
PE24
Pit (dis)
PE23
Turpits Plantation
Five Acre Plantation
Costard Hill
Ashington End
BAKER'S LANE
B1196
Yew Tree Farm
Bullock Plantation
Little Holme Farm
A1028
Beck Plantation
Church Farm
SAPPHIRE CL
Ivy House Farm
Orby
Marsh House Farm
Ashes Farm
MARSH LA
MARSH LANE
PH
Manor Farm
Moat
PH
MIDDLEGATE LA
Gunby Hall NT
BACK LA
Nursery Farm
Elmtree House
Orby Marsh
Icehouse Pond
GUNBY LANE
Gunby Park
Gunby
STATION ROAD
Station Road Farm
ORBY ROAD
FAULKERS LANE
Faulkers Fish Farm
Sycamores Farm
Lodge Farm
A158
Little Wood
Field Farm
CHALK LANE
COMMON LANE
INGOLDMELLS RD
8
73
7
72
6
71
5
70
4
69
3
68
2
67
1
66
46
47
48
49
50
51
102
90

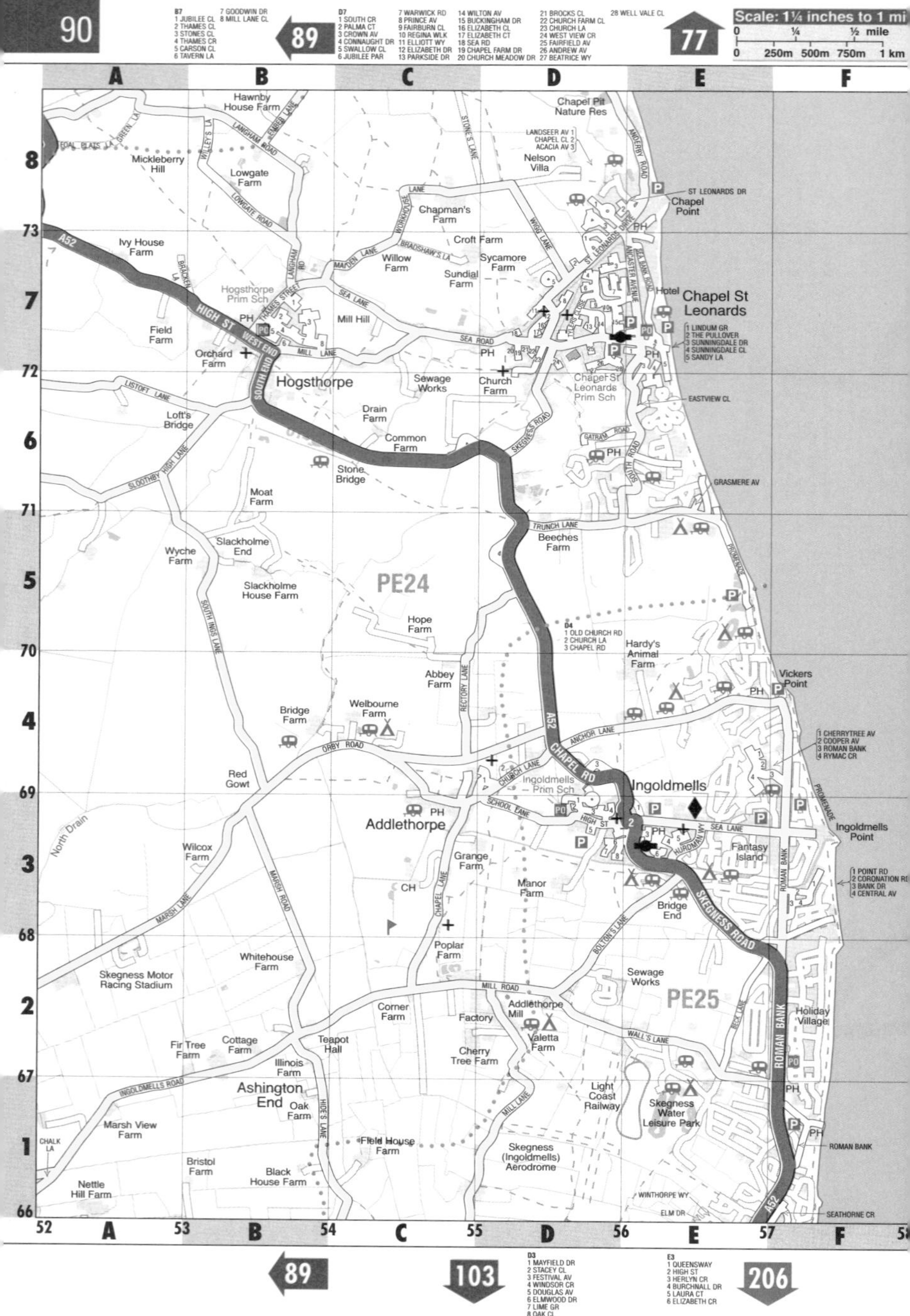
B7
1 JUBILEE CL
2 THAMES CL
3 STONES CL
4 THAMES CR
5 CARSON CL
6 TAVERN LA
7 GOODWIN DR
8 MILL LANE CL
89
D7
1 SOUTH CR
2 PALMA CT
3 CROWN AV
4 CONNAUGHT DR
5 SWALLOW CL
6 JUBILEE PAR
7 WARWICK RD
8 PRINCE AV
9 FAIRBURN CL
10 REGINA WLK
11 ELLIOTT WY
12 ELIZABETH DR
13 PARKSIDE DR
14 WILTON AV
15 BUCKINGHAM DR
16 ELIZABETH CL
17 ELIZABETH CT
18 SEA RD
19 CHAPEL FARM DR
20 CHURCH MEADOW DR
21 BROCKS CL
22 CHURCH FARM CL
23 CHURCH LA
24 WEST VIEW CR
25 FAIRFIELD AV
26 ANDREW AV
27 BEATRICE WY
28 WELL VALE CL
77
Scale: 1¼ inches to 1 mi
0 ¼ ½ mile
0 250m 500m 750m 1 km
A B C D E F
8 73 7 72 6 71 5 70 4 69 3 68 2 67 1 66
Hawnby House Farm
Chapel Pit Nature Res
Mickleberry Hill
Lowgate Farm
Nelson Villa
LANDSEER AV 1
CHAPEL CL 2
ACACIA AV 3
ST LEONARDS DR
Chapel Point
Chapman's Farm
Ivy House Farm
Croft Farm
Willow Farm
Sycamore Farm
Sundial Farm
Hogsthorpe Prim Sch
Chapel St Leonards
Hotel
1 LINDUM GR
2 THE PULLOVER
3 SUNNINGDALE DR
4 SUNNINGDALE CL
5 SANDY LA
Field Farm
Mill Hill
Orchard Farm
Hogsthorpe
Sewage Works
Church Farm
Chapel St Leonards Prim Sch
EASTVIEW CL
Loft's Bridge
Drain Farm
Common Farm
Stone Bridge
GRASMERE AV
Moat Farm
Beeches Farm
Wyche Farm
Slackholme End
Slackholme House Farm
PE24
Hope Farm
D4
1 OLD CHURCH RD
2 CHURCH LA
3 CHAPEL RD
Hardy's Animal Farm
Abbey Farm
Vickers Point
Bridge Farm
Welbourne Farm
1 CHERRYTREE AV
2 COOPER AV
3 ROMAN BANK
4 RYMAC CR
Red Gowt
Ingoldmells
Ingoldmells Prim Sch
Addlethorpe
Ingoldmells Point
North Drain
Wilcox Farm
Grange Farm
Fantasy Island
1 POINT RD
2 CORONATION RD
3 BANK DR
4 CENTRAL AV
Manor Farm
Bridge End
Poplar Farm
Whitehouse Farm
Skegness Motor Racing Stadium
Sewage Works
PE25
Corner Farm
Factory
Addlethorpe Mill
Holiday Village
Fir Tree Farm
Cottage Farm
Teapot Hall
Valetta Farm
Cherry Tree Farm
Illinois Farm
Ashington End
Oak Farm
Light Coast Railway
Skegness Water Leisure Park
Marsh View Farm
Field House Farm
Skegness (Ingoldmells) Aerodrome
ROMAN BANK
Bristol Farm
Black House Farm
Nettle Hill Farm
WINTHORPE WY
ELM DR
SEATHORNE CR
A52
HIGH ST
WEST END
SOUTH END
CHAPEL RD
SKEGNESS ROAD
ROMAN BANK
SEA LANE
SEA ROAD
MILL LANE
ORBY ROAD
MILL ROAD
MARSH LANE
INGOLDMELLS ROAD
TRUNCH LANE
ANCHOR LANE
CHURCH LANE
SCHOOL LANE
WALL'S LANE
52 53 54 55 56 57 58
89
103
D3
1 MAYFIELD DR
2 STACEY CL
3 FESTIVAL AV
4 WINDSOR CR
5 DOUGLAS AV
6 ELMWOOD DR
7 LIME GR
8 OAK CL
E3
1 QUEENSWAY
2 HIGH ST
3 HERLYN CR
4 BURCHNALL DR
5 LAURA CT
6 ELIZABETH CR
206

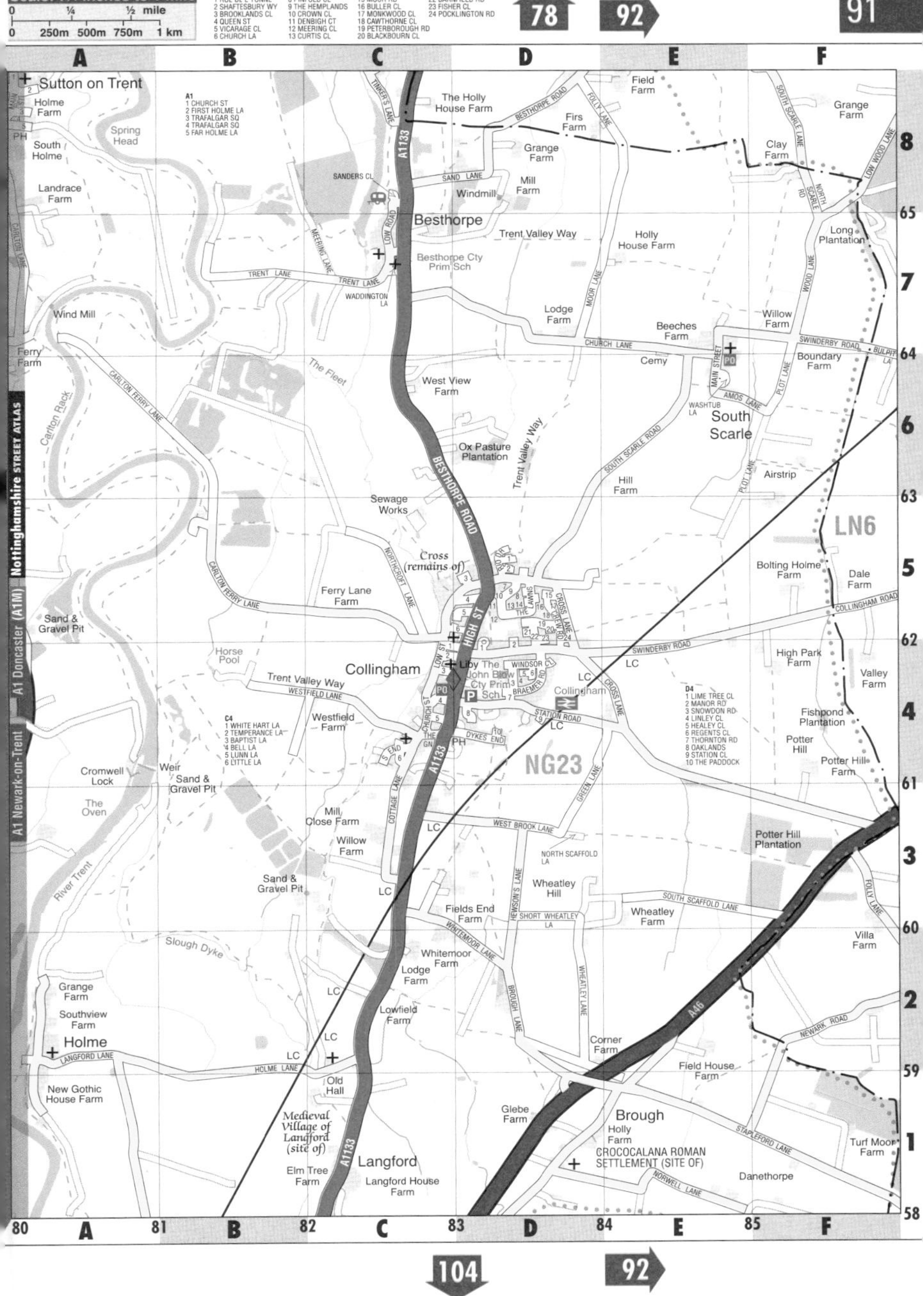
Scale: 1¼ inches to 1 mile
0 ¼ ½ mile
0 250m 500m 750m 1 km
D5
1 RUE DE L'YONNE
2 SHAFTESBURY WY
3 BROOKLANDS CL
4 QUEEN ST
5 VICARAGE CL
6 CHURCH LA
7 DEANE CL
8 PINFOLD CL
9 THE HEMPLANDS
10 CROWN CL
11 DENBIGH CT
12 MEERING CL
13 CURTIS CL
14 THE ROOKERY
15 MOOR RD
16 BULLER CL
17 MONKWOOD CL
18 CAWTHORNE CL
19 PETERBOROUGH RD
20 BLACKBOURN CL
21 FOSTER RD
22 BARNFIELD RD
23 FISHER CL
24 POCKLINGTON RD
78
92
A1
1 CHURCH ST
2 FIRST HOLME LA
3 TRAFALGAR SQ
4 TRAFALGAR SQ
5 FAR HOLME LA
C4
1 WHITE HART LA
2 TEMPERANCE LA
3 BAPTIST LA
4 BELL LA
5 LUNN LA
6 LITTLE LA
D4
1 LIME TREE CL
2 MANOR RD
3 SNOWDON RD
4 LINLEY CL
5 HEALEY CL
6 REGENTS CL
7 THORNTON RD
8 OAKLANDS
9 STATION CL
10 THE PADDOCK
Sutton on Trent
Holme Farm
South Holme
Spring Head
Landrace Farm
Wind Mill
Ferry Farm
Carlton Rack
CARLTON FERRY LANE
Sand & Gravel Pit
Cromwell Lock
Weir
The Oven
River Trent
Slough Dyke
Grange Farm
Southview Farm
Holme
LANGFORD LANE
HOLME LANE
New Gothic House Farm
The Holly House Farm
Besthorpe
SANDERS CL
SAND LANE
Windmill
Mill Farm
Grange Farm
Firs Farm
Field Farm
BESTHORPE ROAD
FOLLY LANE
TINKER'S LANE
LOW ROAD
MEERING LANE
TRENT LANE
WADDINGTON LA
Besthorpe Cty Prim Sch
Trent Valley Way
Holly House Farm
Lodge Farm
MOOR LANE
CHURCH LANE
Beeches Farm
Cemy
The Fleet
West View Farm
Ox Pasture Plantation
Sewage Works
BESTHORPE ROAD
Cross (remains of)
NORTHCROFT LANE
Ferry Lane Farm
Horse Pool
Collingham
HIGH ST
LOW ST
Liby
The John Blow Cty Prim Sch
WINDSOR CL
BRAEMER RD
CROSS LANE
SWINDERBY ROAD
STATION ROAD
DYKES END
Trent Valley Way
WESTFIELD LANE
Westfield Farm
CHURCH ST
THE GN
S END
COTTAGE LANE
Mill Close Farm
Willow Farm
LC
NG23
GREEN LANE
WEST BROOK LANE
NORTH SCAFFOLD LA
Wheatley Hill
HEWSON'S LANE
SHORT WHEATLEY LA
Fields End Farm
WHITEMOOR LANE
Whitemoor Farm
Lodge Farm
Lowfield Farm
BROUGH LANE
WHEATLEY LANE
Wheatley Farm
SOUTH SCAFFOLD LANE
Corner Farm
A46
A1133
Old Hall
Medieval Village of Langford (site of)
Elm Tree Farm
Langford
Langford House Farm
Glebe Farm
Brough
Holly Farm
CROCOCALANA ROMAN SETTLEMENT (SITE OF)
NORWELL LANE
STAPLEFORD LANE
Danethorpe
Field House Farm
NEWARK ROAD
Turf Moor Farm
Villa Farm
FOLLY LANE
Potter Hill Plantation
Potter Hill Farm
Potter Hill
Fishpond Plantation
Valley Farm
High Park Farm
COLLINGHAM ROAD
Dale Farm
Bolting Holme Farm
LN6
Airstrip
PLOT LANE
South Scarle
WASHTUB LA
AMOS LANE
MAIN STREET
SOUTH SCARLE ROAD
Hill Farm
Boundary Farm
SWINDERBY ROAD
BULPIT LA
Willow Farm
WOOD LANE
Long Plantation
Clay Farm
SOUTH SCARLE LANE
NORTH SCARLE RD
LOW WOOD LANE
Grange Farm
Nottinghamshire STREET ATLAS
A1 Doncaster (A1M)
A1 Newark-on-Trent
A B C D E F
80 81 82 83 84 85
58 59 60 61 62 63 64 65
1 2 3 4 5 6 7 8
104
92

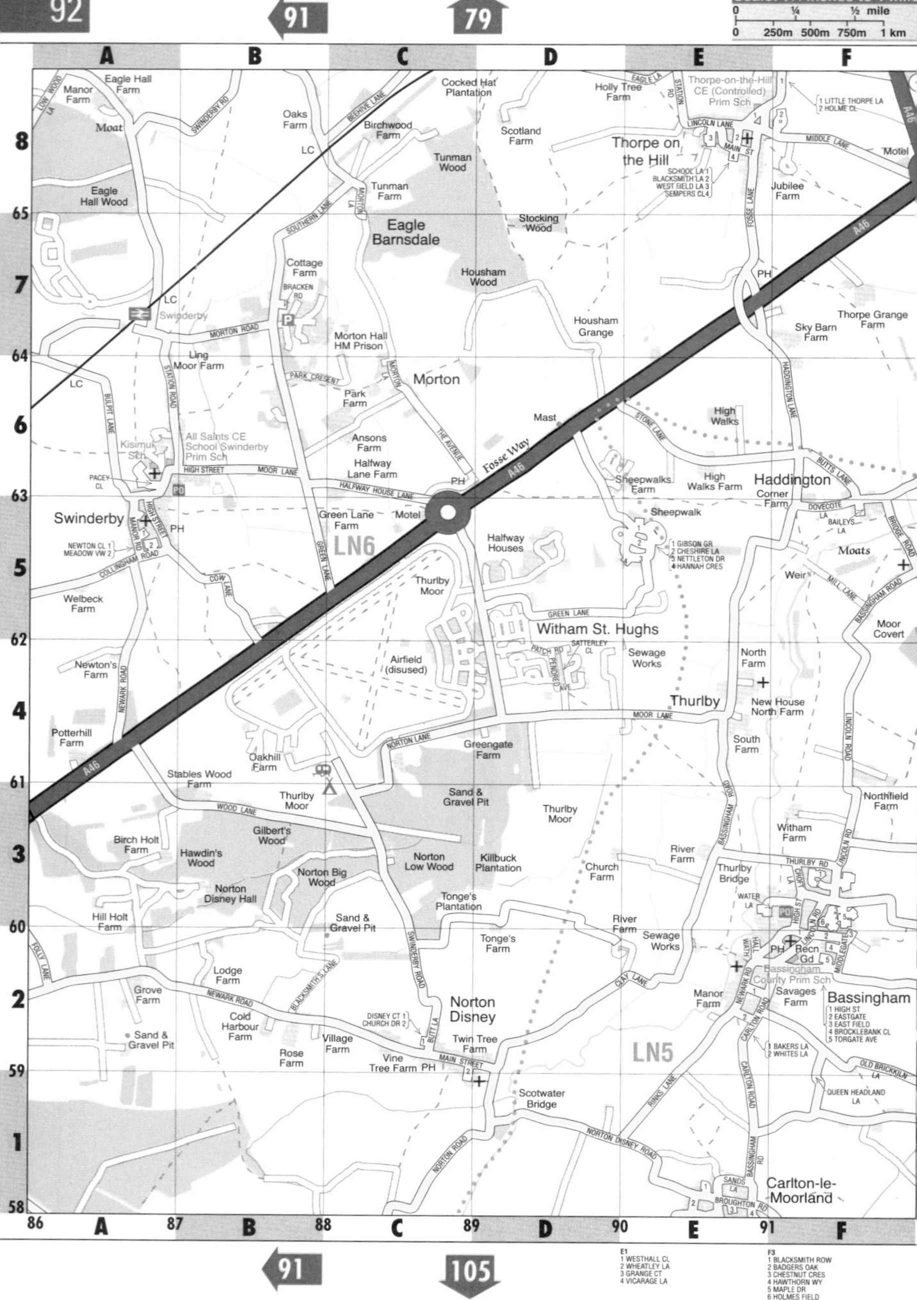
91
79
Scale: 1¼ inches to 1 mile
0 ¼ ½ mile
0 250m 500m 750m 1 km
A
B
C
D
E
F
Manor Farm
Eagle Hall Farm
LOW WOOD LA
SWINDERBY RD
Moat
Eagle Hall Wood
Oaks Farm
BEEHIVE LANE
Birchwood Farm
LC
Cocked Hat Plantation
Tunman Wood
Tunman Farm
MORTON LA
SOUTHERN LANE
Eagle Barnsdale
Scotland Farm
Stocking Wood
Housham Wood
Holly Tree Farm
EAGLE LA
STATION RD
Thorpe-on-the-Hill CE (Controlled) Prim Sch
1 LITTLE THORPE LA
2 HOLME CL
LINCOLN LANE
MAIN ST
MIDDLE LANE
Thorpe on the Hill
SCHOOL LA 1
BLACKSMITH LA 2
WEST FIELD LA 3
SEMPERS CL 4
Motel
Jubilee Farm
FOSSE LANE
A46
PH
Cottage Farm
BRACKEN RD
Swinderby
MORTON ROAD
Morton Hall HM Prison
Housham Grange
Thorpe Grange Farm
Sky Barn Farm
Ling Moor Farm
STATION ROAD
PARK CRESENT
Park Farm
MORTON LA
Morton
HADDINGTON LANE
LC
BULPIT LANE
Mast
STONE LANE
High Walks
Kisimul Sch
All Saints CE School Swinderby Prim Sch
Ansons Farm
THE AVENUE
Fosse Way
PACEY CL
HIGH STREET
MOOR LANE
Halfway Lane Farm
HALFWAY HOUSE LANE
PH
Sheepwalks Farm
High Walks Farm
Haddington
Corner Farm
BUTTS LANE
PO
Swinderby
HIGH STREET
MANOR RD
PH
Green Lane Farm
Motel
Sheepwalk
DOVECOTE LA
BAILEYS LA
BRIDGE ROAD
NEWTON CL 1
MEADOW VW 2
COLLINGHAM ROAD
LN6
GREEN LANE
Halfway Houses
1 GIBSON GR
2 CHESHIRE LA
3 NETTLETON DR
4 HANNAH CRES
Moats
COW LANE
Welbeck Farm
Thurlby Moor
Weir
MILL LANE
GREEN LANE
Witham St. Hughs
BASSINGHAM ROAD
Moor Covert
SATTERLEY CL
PATCH RD
PENDRED AVE
Sewage Works
North Farm
Newton's Farm
NEWARK ROAD
Airfield (disused)
Thurlby
New House North Farm
MOOR LANE
Potterhill Farm
NORTON LANE
Greengate Farm
South Farm
LINCOLN ROAD
Oakhill Farm
Stables Wood Farm
Thurlby Moor
Sand & Gravel Pit
Thurlby Moor
Northfield Farm
WOOD LANE
BASSINGHAM ROAD
Gilbert's Wood
Witham Farm
Birch Holt Farm
Hawdin's Wood
Norton Low Wood
Killbuck Plantation
Church Farm
River Farm
Thurlby Bridge
THURLBY RD
CROFT LA
LINCOLN RD
Norton Big Wood
Norton Disney Hall
Tonge's Plantation
WATER LA
PO
HIGH ST
Hill Holt Farm
Sand & Gravel Pit
River Farm
Sewage Works
LINCOLN RD
MIDDLEGATE
Tonge's Farm
HALL WATH
PH
Recn Gd
FOLLY LANE
Lodge Farm
BLACKSMITH'S LANE
SWINDERBY ROAD
CLAY LANE
NEWARK RD
Bassingham County Prim Sch
Grove Farm
NEWARK ROAD
Norton Disney
Manor Farm
Savages Farm
Bassingham
Cold Harbour Farm
DISNEY CT 1
CHURCH DR 2
BUTT LA
CARLTON ROAD
1 HIGH ST
2 EASTGATE
3 EAST FIELD
4 BROCKLEBANK CL
5 TORGATE AVE
Sand & Gravel Pit
Village Farm
Twin Tree Farm
1 BAKERS LA
2 WHITES LA
Rose Farm
Vine Tree Farm
PH
MAIN STREET
LN5
OLD BRICKKILN LA
RINKS LANE
Scotwater Bridge
QUEEN HEADLAND LA
CARLTON ROAD
NORTON DISNEY ROAD
NORTON ROAD
BASSINGHAM RD
SANDS LA
Carlton-le-Moorland
BROUGHTON RD
8
65
7
64
6
63
5
62
4
61
3
60
2
59
1
58
86
87
88
89
90
91
E1
1 WESTHALL CL
2 WHEATLEY LA
3 GRANGE CT
4 VICARAGE LA
F3
1 BLACKSMITH ROW
2 BADGERS OAK
3 CHESTNUT CRES
4 HAWTHORN WY
5 MAPLE DR
6 HOLMES FIELD
91
105

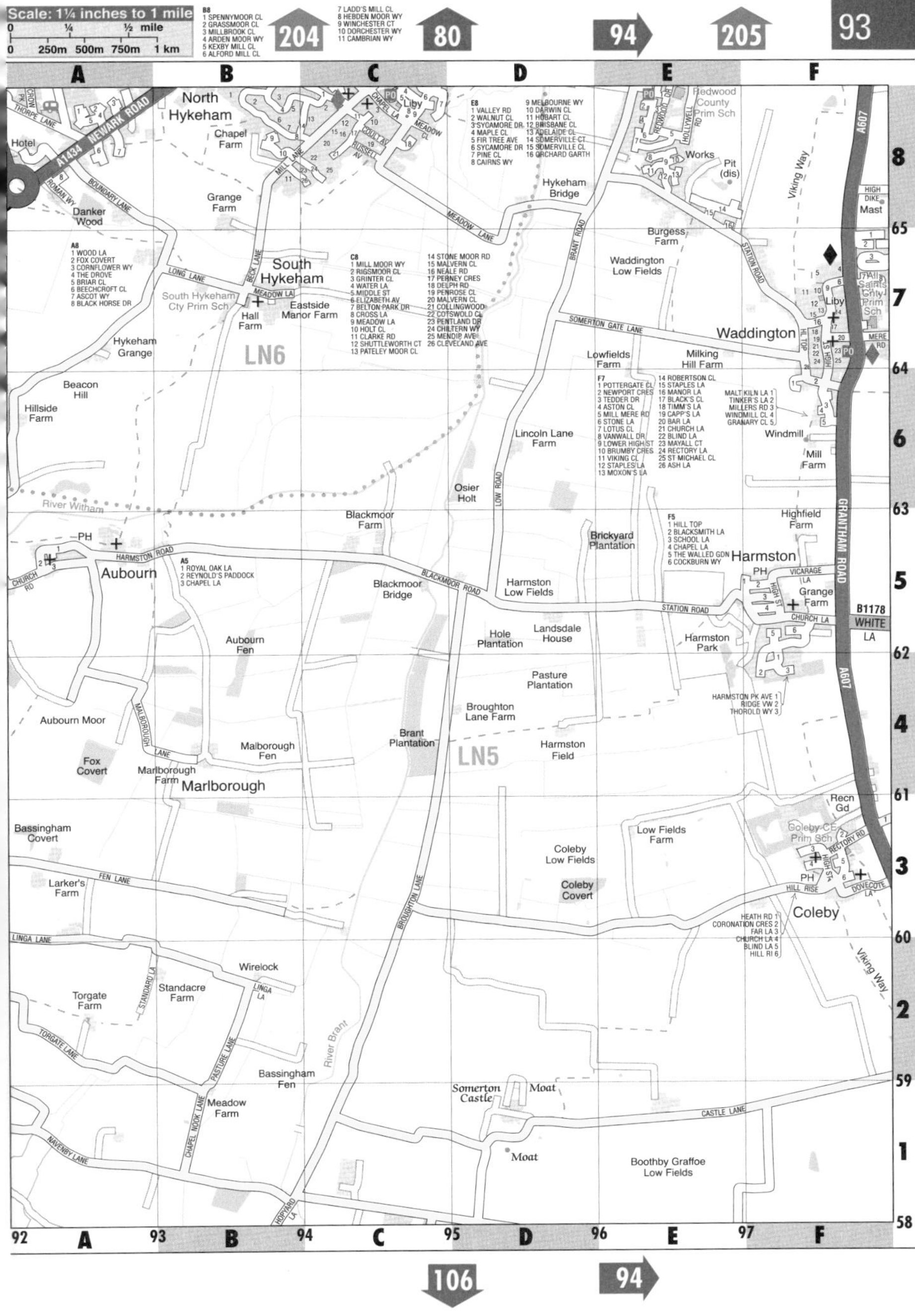
Scale: 1¼ inches to 1 mile
0 ¼ ½ mile
0 250m 500m 750m 1 km
B8
1 SPENNYMOOR CL
2 GRASSMOOR CL
3 MILLBROOK CL
4 ARDEN MOOR WY
5 KEXBY MILL CL
6 ALFORD MILL CL
7 LADD'S MILL CL
8 HEBDEN MOOR WY
9 WINCHESTER CT
10 DORCHESTER WY
11 CAMBRIAN WY
204
80
94
205
North Hykeham
Chapel Farm
Grange Farm
Danker Wood
Hotel
A1434 NEWARK ROAD
THORPE LANE
BOUNDARY LANE
ROMAN WY
MILL LANE
CHAPEL LA
MEADOW CL
RUSSELL AV
Liby
MEADOW LANE
E8
1 VALLEY RD
2 WALNUT CL
3 SYCAMORE DR
4 MAPLE CL
5 FIR TREE AVE
6 SYCAMORE DR
7 PINE CL
8 CAIRNS WY
9 MELBOURNE WY
10 DARWIN CL
11 HOBART CL
12 BRISBANE CL
13 ADELAIDE CL
14 SOMERVILLE CT
15 SOMERVILLE CL
16 ORCHARD GARTH
Hykeham Bridge
Redwood County Prim Sch
REDWOOD DR
HOLLYWELL RD
Works
Pit (dis)
Viking Way
A607
HIGH DIKE
Mast
Burgess Farm
BRANT ROAD
STATION ROAD
Waddington Low Fields
All Saints Cty Prim Sch
A8
1 WOOD LA
2 FOX COVERT
3 CORNFLOWER WY
4 THE DROVE
5 BRIAR CL
6 BEECHCROFT CL
7 ASCOT WY
8 BLACK HORSE DR
LONG LANE
BECK LANE
South Hykeham
MEADOW LA
South Hykeham Cty Prim Sch
Hall Farm
Eastside Manor Farm
C8
1 MILL MOOR WY
2 RIGSMOOR CL
3 GRINTER CL
4 WATER LA
5 MIDDLE ST
6 ELIZABETH AV
7 BELTON PARK DR
8 CROSS LA
9 MEADOW LA
10 HOLT CL
11 CLARKE RD
12 SHUTTLEWORTH CT
13 PATELEY MOOR CL
14 STONE MOOR RD
15 MALVERN CL
16 NEALE RD
17 PERNEY CRES
18 DELPH RD
19 PENROSE CL
20 MALVERN CL
21 COLLINGWOOD
22 COTSWOLD CL
23 PENTLAND DR
24 CHILTERN WY
25 MENDIP AVE
26 CLEVELAND AVE
SOMERTON GATE LANE
Waddington
HL TOP
HIGH ST
MERE RD
Hykeham Grange
LN6
Lowfields Farm
Milking Hill Farm
Beacon Hill
Hillside Farm
F7
1 POTTERGATE CL
2 NEWPORT CRES
3 TEDDER DR
4 ASTON CL
5 MILL MERE RD
6 STONE LA
7 LOTUS CL
8 VANWALL DR
9 LOWER HIGH ST
10 BRUMBY CRES
11 VIKING CL
12 STAPLES LA
13 MOXON'S LA
14 ROBERTSON CL
15 STAPLES LA
16 MANOR LA
17 BLACK'S CL
18 TIMM'S LA
19 CAPP'S LA
20 BAR LA
21 CHURCH LA
22 BLIND LA
23 MAYALL CT
24 RECTORY LA
25 ST MICHAEL CL
26 ASH LA
MALT KILN LA 1
TINKER'S LA 2
MILLERS RD 3
WINDMILL CL 4
GRANARY CL 5
Windmill
Lincoln Lane Farm
Mill Farm
LOW ROAD
Osier Holt
River Witham
GRANTHAM ROAD
Blackmoor Farm
Highfield Farm
Brickyard Plantation
F5
1 HILL TOP
2 BLACKSMITH LA
3 SCHOOL LA
4 CHAPEL LA
5 THE WALLED GDN
6 COCKBURN WY
Harmston
PH
VICARAGE LA
HIGH ST
Grange Farm
B1178
WHITE LA
CHURCH LA
HARMSTON ROAD
CHURCH RD
Aubourn
A5
1 ROYAL OAK LA
2 REYNOLD'S PADDOCK
3 CHAPEL LA
Blackmoor Bridge
BLACKMOOR ROAD
Harmston Low Fields
STATION ROAD
Hole Plantation
Landsdale House
Harmston Park
Aubourn Fen
Pasture Plantation
HARMSTON PK AVE 1
RIDGE VW 2
THOROLD WY 3
Aubourn Moor
MALBOROUGH LANE
Broughton Lane Farm
Brant Plantation
LN5
Harmston Field
Malborough Fen
Fox Covert
Marlborough Farm
Marlborough
Recn Gd
Bassingham Covert
Low Fields Farm
Coleby CE Prim Sch
RECTORY RD
Coleby Low Fields
Larker's Farm
FEN LANE
Coleby Covert
PH
HILL RISE
DOVECOTE LA
BROUGHTON LANE
Coleby
HEATH RD 1
CORONATION CRES 2
FAR LA 3
CHURCH LA 4
BLIND LA 5
HILL RI 6
LINGA LANE
Wirelock
Standacre Farm
LINGA LA
Torgate Farm
STANDARD LA
TORGATE LANE
PASTURE LANE
River Brant
Bassingham Fen
Somerton Castle
Moat
Meadow Farm
CASTLE LANE
CHAPEL NOOK LANE
NAVENBY LANE
Moat
Boothby Graffoe Low Fields
HOPYARD LA
A B C D E F
8 65 7 64 6 63 5 62 4 61 3 60 2 59 1 58
92 93 94 95 96 97
106
94

A7
1 TRENCHARD SQ
2 SLESSOR ST
3 TEDDER DR
4 EDINBURGH SQ
5 LINCOLN DR
6 LANCASTER CL
7 VALLIANT ST
8 HAMPDEN WY
9 VULCAN ST
10 VICTOR WY
11 MANCHESTER RD
12 WELLINGTON SQ

93
81

Scale: 1¼ inches to 1 mile
0 ¼ ½ mile
0 250m 500m 750m 1 km

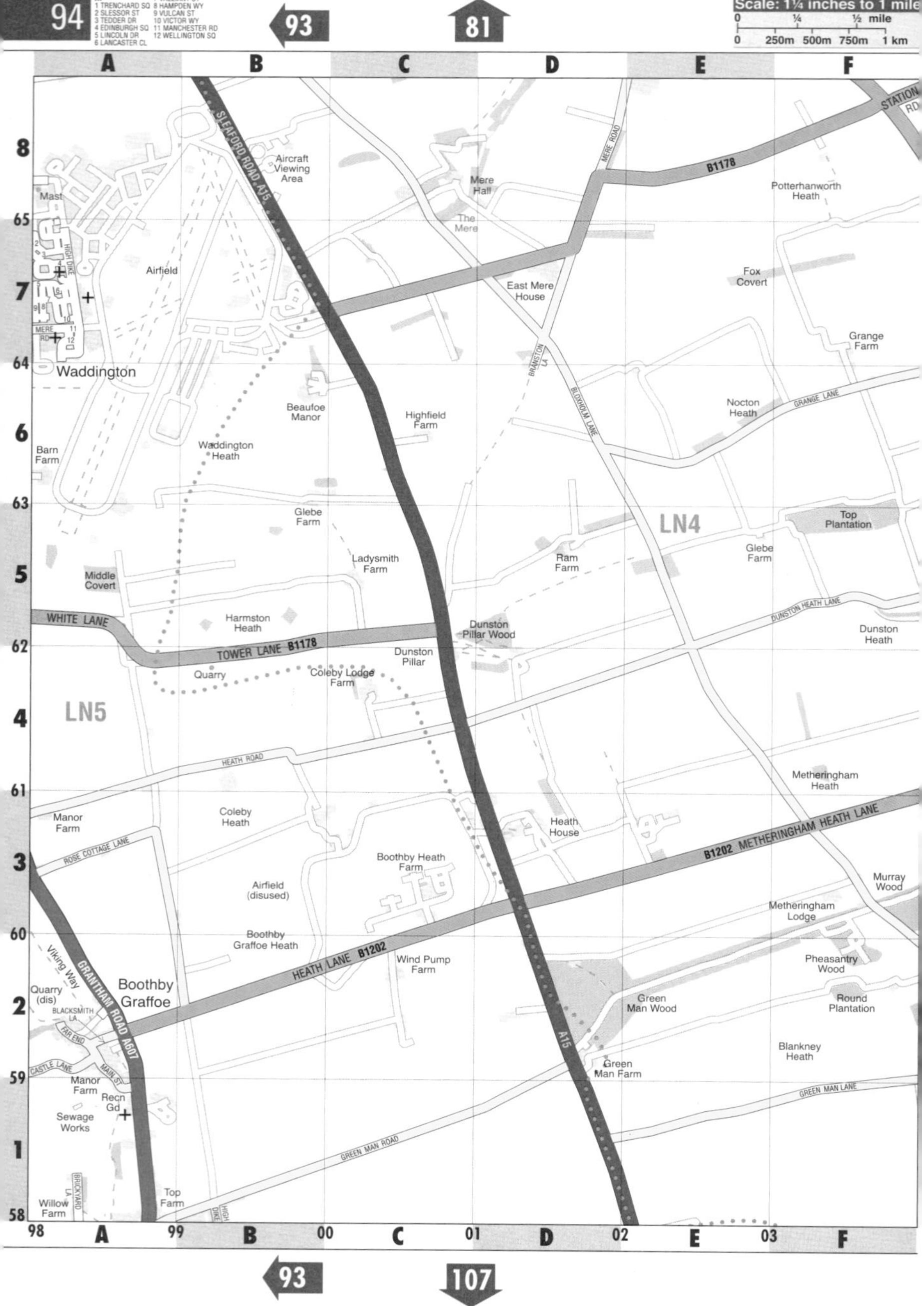

93
107

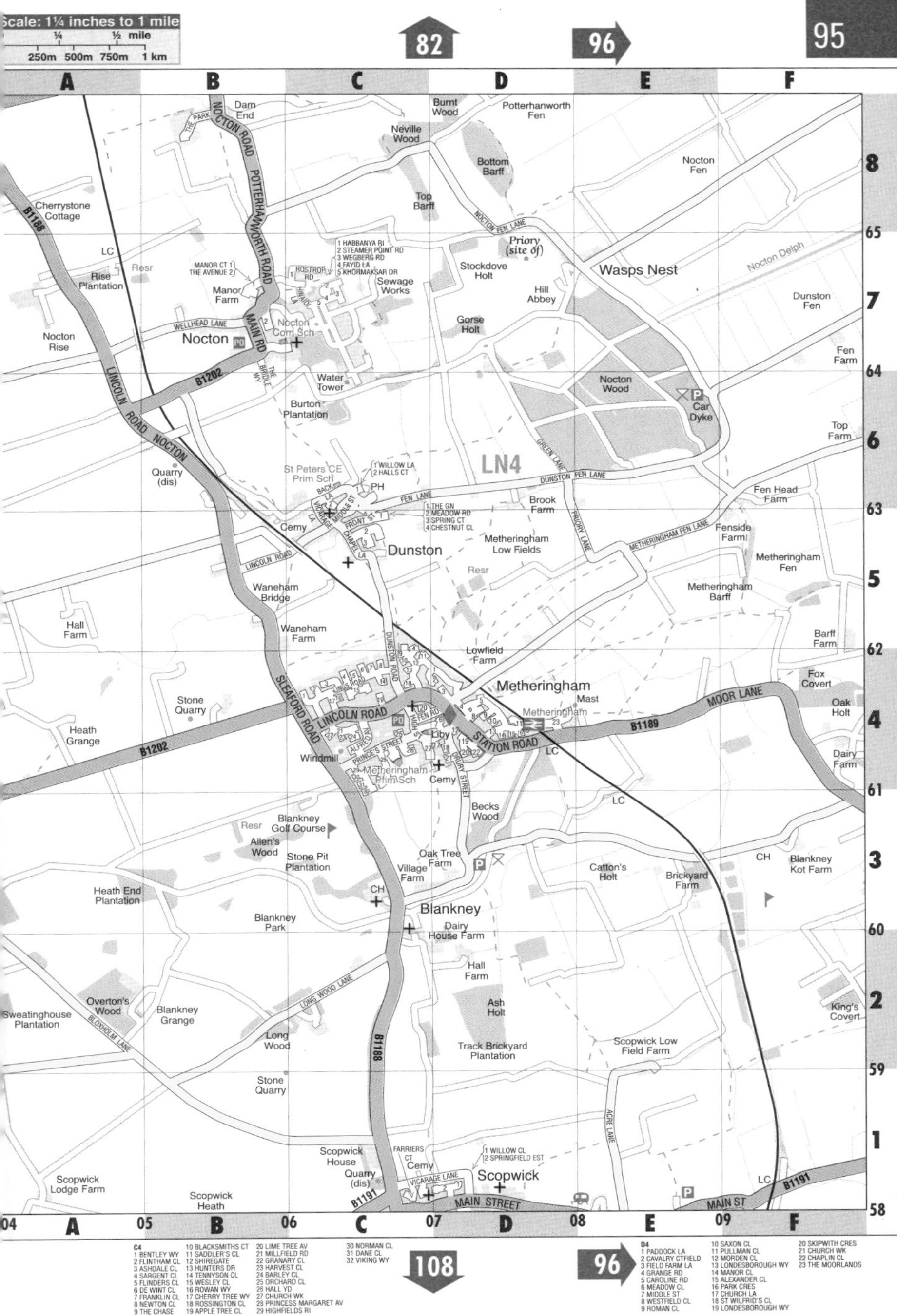
Scale: 1¼ inches to 1 mile
¼
½ mile
250m 500m 750m 1 km
82
96
A B C D E F
Dam End
THE PARK
NOCTON ROAD
POTTERHANWORTH ROAD
Burnt Wood
Potterhanworth Fen
Neville Wood
Bottom Barff
Nocton Fen
Top Barff
Cherrystone Cottage
B1188
NOCTON FEN LANE
Priory (site of)
Wasps Nest
Nocton Delph
LC
Resr
Rise Plantation
MANOR CT 1
THE AVENUE 2
1 HABBANYA RI
2 STEAMER POINT RD
3 WEGBERG RD
4 FAYID LA
5 KHORMAKSAR DR
ROSTROP RD
Sewage Works
Stockdove Holt
Hill Abbey
Manor Farm
Dunston Fen
WELLHEAD LANE
Nocton Com Sch
Gorse Holt
Nocton Rise
Nocton
MAIN RD
Fen Farm
LINCOLN ROAD
B1202
THE BRIDLE WY
Water Tower
Nocton Wood
Car Dyke
Burton Plantation
NOCTON
Top Farm
GREEN LANE
LN4
1 WILLOW LA
2 HALLS CT
St Peters CE Prim Sch
Quarry (dis)
PH
DUNSTON FEN LANE
Fen Head Farm
BACK LA
FEN LANE
1 THE GN
2 MEADOW RD
3 SPRING CT
4 CHESTNUT CL
Brook Farm
VICARAGE LA
MIDDLE ST
FRONT ST
Cemy
CHAPEL LA
PRIORY LANE
Fenside Farm
METHERINGHAM FEN LANE
Metheringham Low Fields
LINCOLN ROAD
Dunston
Metheringham Fen
Resr
Waneham Bridge
Metheringham Barff
Hall Farm
Waneham Farm
Barff Farm
DUNSTON ROAD
Lowfield Farm
SLEAFORD ROAD
Metheringham
Fox Covert
Stone Quarry
KINGS RD
Mast
MOOR LANE
LINCOLN ROAD
FEN RD
Metheringham
Oak Holt
HIGH ST
B1189
Heath Grange
STATION ROAD
B1202
ALFRED AV
Liby
LC
Dairy Farm
Windmill
PRINCE'S STREET
DRURY STREET
Metheringham Prim Sch
Cemy
LC
Becks Wood
Blankney Golf Course
Resr
Allen's Wood
Stone Pit Plantation
Oak Tree Farm
Catton's Holt
CH
Blankney Kot Farm
Village Farm
Brickyard Farm
Heath End Plantation
CH
Blankney
Blankney Park
Dairy House Farm
Hall Farm
LONG WOOD LANE
Overton's Wood
Ash Holt
King's Covert
Sweatinghouse Plantation
Blankney Grange
BLOXHOLM LANE
Long Wood
B1188
Track Brickyard Plantation
Scopwick Low Field Farm
Stone Quarry
ACRE LANE
Scopwick House
FARRIERS CT
1 WILLOW CL
2 SPRINGFIELD EST
Cemy
Quarry (dis)
Scopwick
VICARAGE LANE
Scopwick Lodge Farm
Scopwick Heath
B1191
MAIN STREET
LC
B1191
MAIN ST
8 65 7 64 6 63 5 62 4 61 3 60 2 59 1 58
04 05 06 07 08 09
108
96
C4
1 BENTLEY WY
2 FLINTHAM CL
3 ASHDALE CL
4 SARGENT CL
5 FLINDERS CL
6 DE WINT CL
7 FRANKLIN CL
8 NEWTON CL
9 THE CHASE
10 BLACKSMITHS CT
11 SADDLER'S CL
12 SHIREGATE
13 HUNTERS DR
14 TENNYSON CL
15 WESLEY CL
16 ROWAN WY
17 CHERRY TREE WY
18 ROSSINGTON CL
19 APPLE TREE CL
20 LIME TREE AV
21 MILLFIELD RD
22 GRANARY CL
23 HARVEST CL
24 BARLEY CL
25 ORCHARD CL
26 HALL YD
27 CHURCH WK
28 PRINCESS MARGARET AV
29 HIGHFIELDS RI
30 NORMAN CL
31 DANE CL
32 VIKING WY
D4
1 PADDOCK LA
2 CAVALRY CTFIELD
3 FIELD FARM LA
4 GRANGE RD
5 CAROLINE RD
6 MEADOW CL
7 MIDDLE ST
8 WESTFIELD CL
9 ROMAN CL
10 SAXON CL
11 PULLMAN CL
12 MORDEN CL
13 LONDESBOROUGH WY
14 MANOR CL
15 ALEXANDER CL
16 PARK CRES
17 CHURCH LA
18 ST WILFRID'S CL
19 LONDESBOROUGH WY
20 SKIPWITH CRES
21 CHURCH WK
22 CHAPLIN CL
23 THE MOORLANDS

95 83

Scale: 1¼ inches to 1 mile
0 ¼ ½ mile
0 250m 500m 750m 1 km

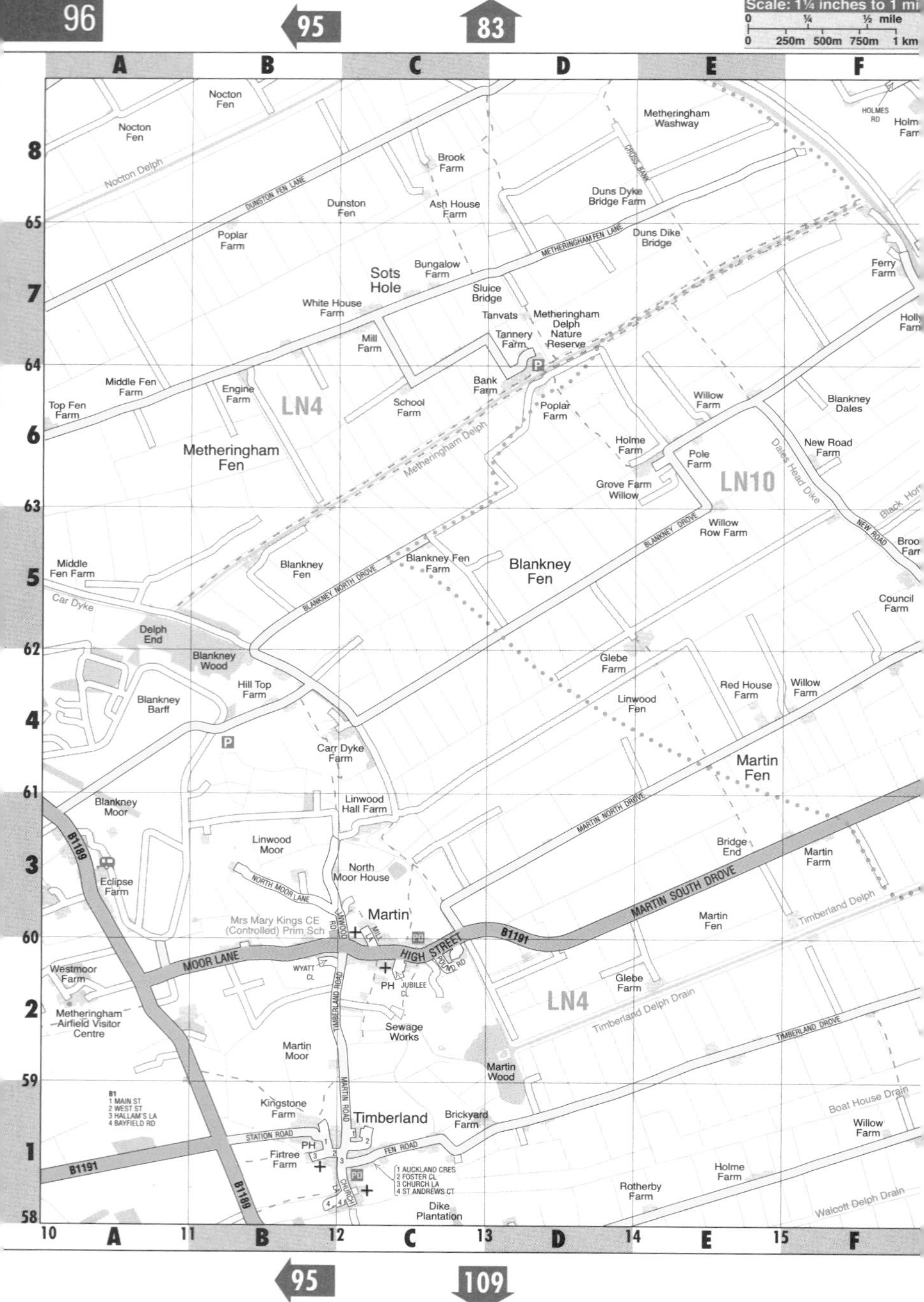

95 109

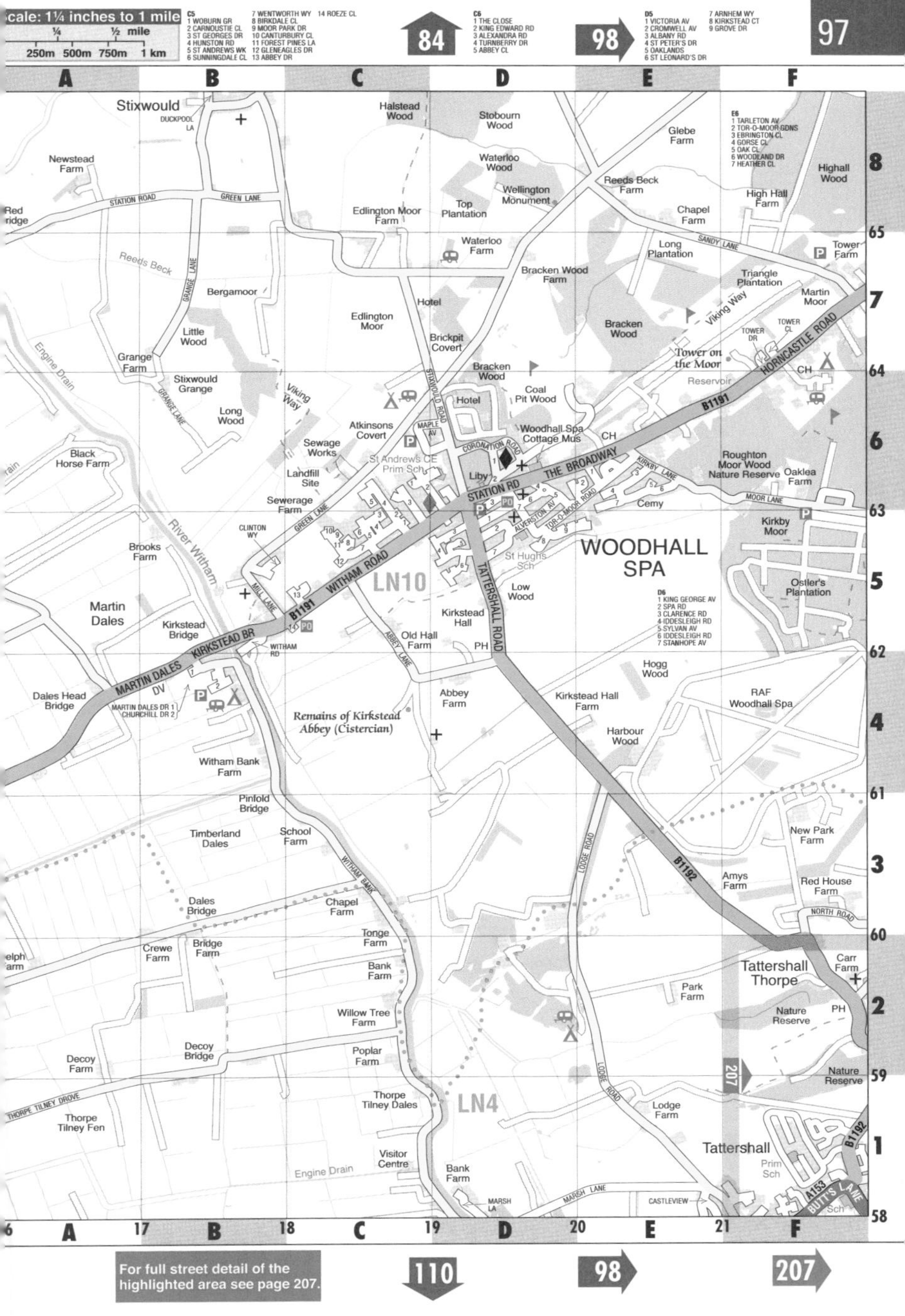

For full street detail of the highlighted area see page 207.

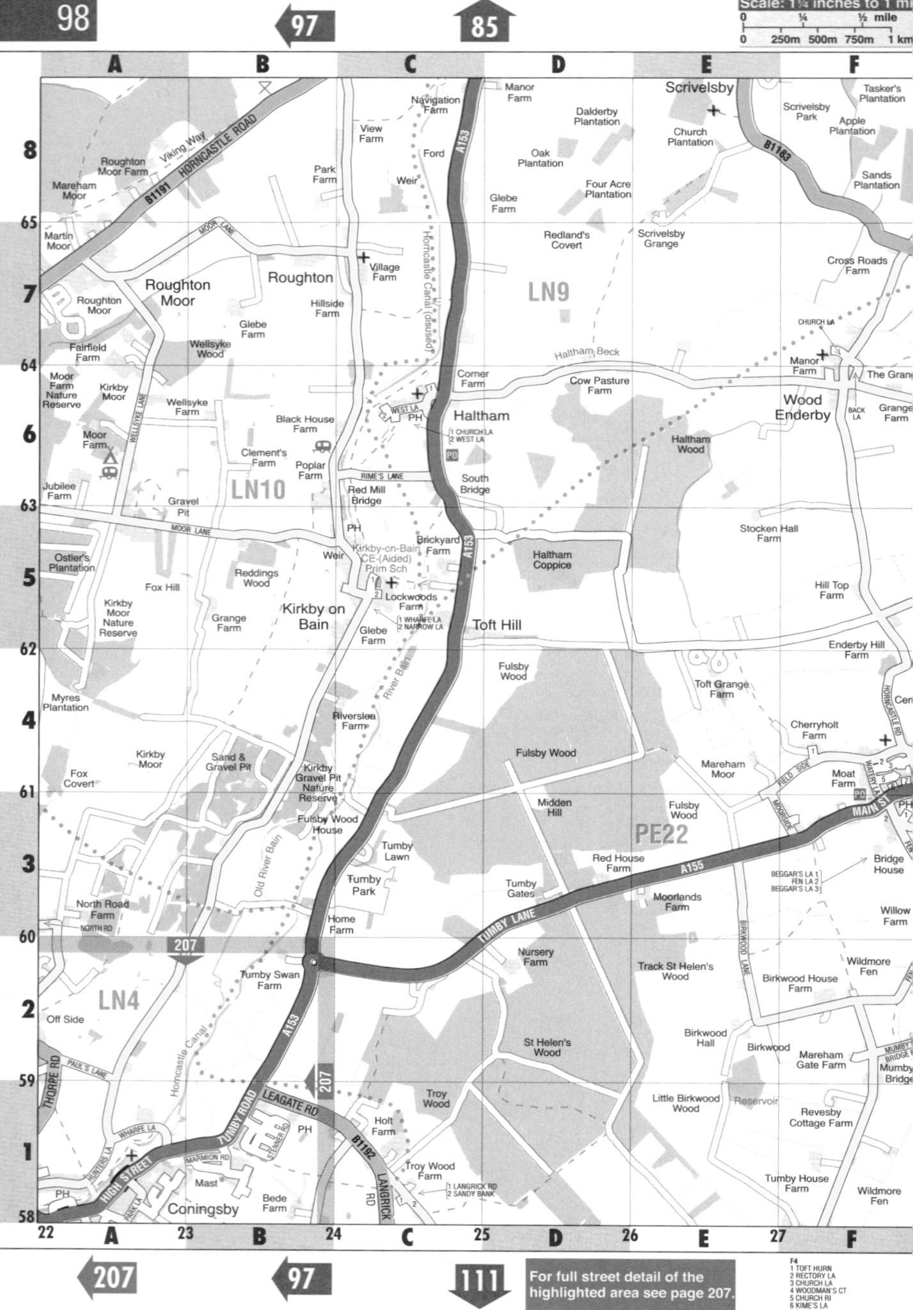

98
97
85
Scale: 1¼ inches to 1 mi
0 ¼ ½ mile
0 250m 500m 750m 1 km
A B C D E F
8 65 7 64 6 63 5 62 4 61 3 60 2 59 1 58
22 23 24 25 26 27
Navigation Farm
Manor Farm
Scrivelsby
Tasker's Plantation
Scrivelsby Park
Apple Plantation
View Farm
Dalderby Plantation
Church Plantation
Ford
Oak Plantation
B1183
Roughton Moor Farm
Viking Way
HORNCASTLE ROAD
B1191
Park Farm
Mareham Moor
Weir
Four Acre Plantation
Sands Plantation
Glebe Farm
Martin Moor
MOOR LANE
Redland's Covert
Scrivelsby Grange
Horncastle Canal (disused)
Village Farm
Cross Roads Farm
Roughton Moor
Roughton
LN9
Roughton Moor
Hillside Farm
Glebe Farm
CHURCH LA
Fairfield Farm
Wellsyke Wood
Haltham Beck
Manor Farm
Moor Farm Nature Reserve
Kirkby Moor
Corner Farm
Cow Pasture Farm
The Grange
WEST LA
Wood Enderby
Wellsyke Farm
Black House Farm
PH
Haltham
BACK LA
Grange Farm
WELLSYKE LANE
1 CHURCH LA
2 WEST LA
Moor Farm
Clement's Farm
Haltham Wood
PO
Poplar Farm
RIME'S LANE
South Bridge
Jubilee Farm
LN10
Red Mill Bridge
Gravel Pit
MOOR LANE
PH
Brickyard Farm
Stocken Hall Farm
A153
Ostler's Plantation
Weir
Kirkby-on-Bain CE (Aided) Prim Sch
Haltham Coppice
Reddings Wood
Fox Hill
Lockwoods Farm
Hill Top Farm
Kirkby Moor Nature Reserve
Grange Farm
Kirkby on Bain
1 WHARFE LA
2 NARROW LA
Toft Hill
Glebe Farm
Enderby Hill Farm
Fulsby Wood
River Bain
Toft Grange Farm
Myres Plantation
HORNCASTLE ROAD
Cem
Riverslea Farm
Cherryholt Farm
Kirkby Moor
Fulsby Wood
Sand & Gravel Pit
Kirkby Gravel Pit Nature Reserve
Mareham Moor
Fox Covert
FIELD SIDE
WATERY LA
Moat Farm
Midden Hill
Fulsby Wood
MOORSIDE
PO
PH
Fulsby Wood House
MAIN ST
PE22
Old River Bain
Tumby Lawn
Red House Farm
A155
Bridge House
BEGGAR'S LA 1
FEN LA 2
BEGGAR'S LA 3
Tumby Park
Tumby Gates
Moorlands Farm
North Road Farm
NORTH RD
Home Farm
TUMBY LANE
Willow Farm
207
Nursery Farm
Track St Helen's Wood
BIRKWOOD LANE
Wildmore Fen
Tumby Swan Farm
Birkwood House Farm
LN4
Off Side
Horncastle Canal
Birkwood Hall
Birkwood
St Helen's Wood
Mareham Gate Farm
MUMBY BRIDGE
Mumby Bridge
THORPE RD
PAUL'S LANE
207
Troy Wood
Little Birkwood Wood
Reservoir
Revesby Cottage Farm
LEAGATE RD
TUMBY ROAD
PH
Holt Farm
WHARFE LA
HUNTERS LA
STENNER RD
B1192
HIGH STREET
MARMION RD
Troy Wood Farm
LANGRICK RD
1 LANGRICK RD
2 SANDY BANK
Tumby House Farm
Wildmore Fen
PH
Mast
PARK LA
Coningsby
Bede Farm
A B C D E F
207
97
111
For full street detail of the highlighted area see page 207.
F4
1 TOFT HURN
2 RECTORY LA
3 CHURCH LA
4 WOODMAN'S CT
5 CHURCH RI
6 KIME'S LA
7 SHOP HL

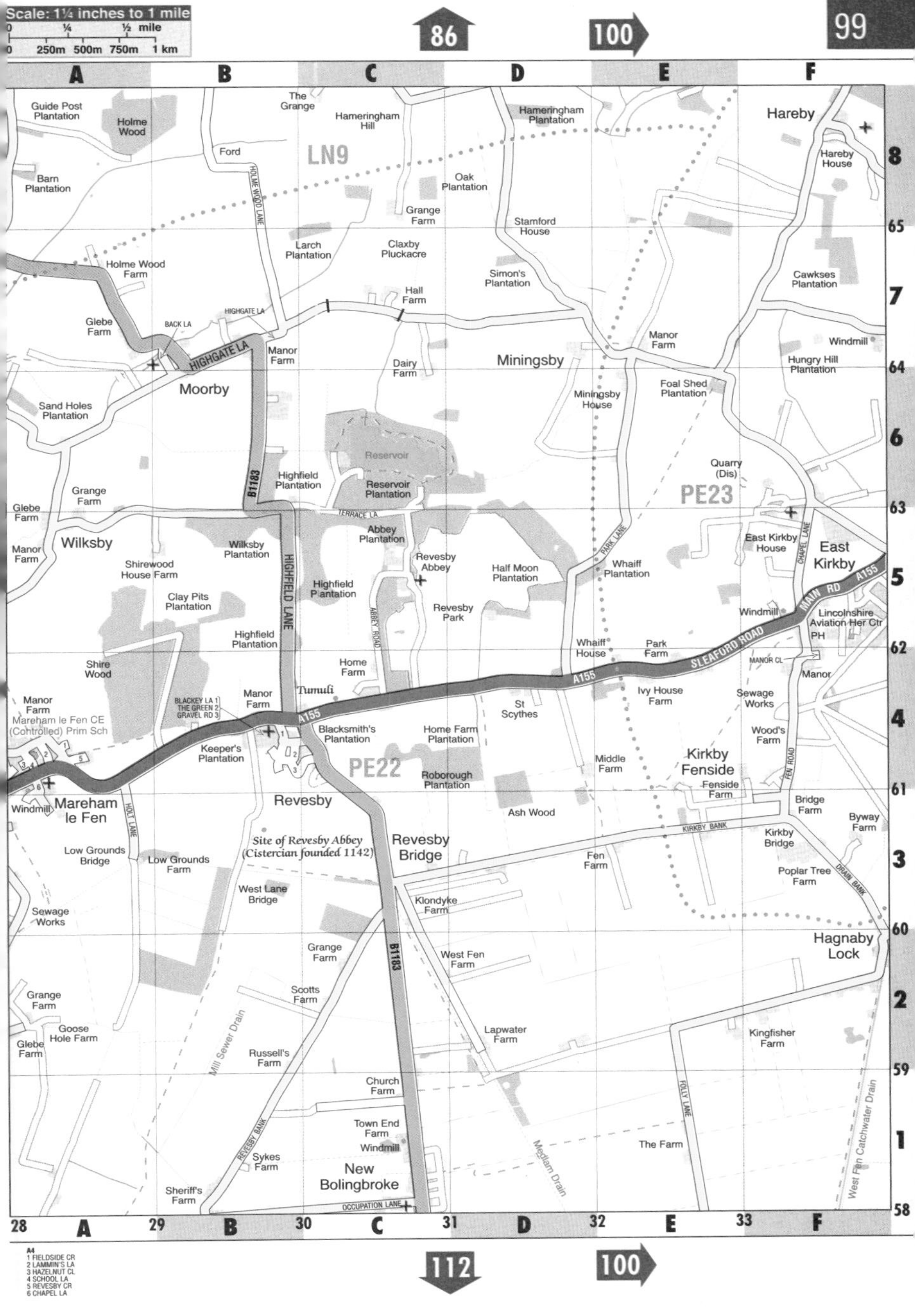

Scale: 1¼ inches to 1 mile
0 ¼ ½ mile
0 250m 500m 750m 1 km
86
100
99
A B C D E F
Guide Post Plantation
Holme Wood
The Grange
Hameringham Hill
Hameringham Plantation
Hareby
LN9
Ford
HOLME WOOD LANE
Barn Plantation
Oak Plantation
Hareby House
Grange Farm
Stamford House
Larch Plantation
Claxby Pluckacre
Holme Wood Farm
Simon's Plantation
Cawkses Plantation
Hall Farm
Glebe Farm
BACK LA
HIGHGATE LA
Manor Farm
Windmill
Dairy Farm
Miningsby
Hungry Hill Plantation
Moorby
Sand Holes Plantation
Foal Shed Plantation
Miningsby House
Reservoir
Quarry (Dis)
Highfield Plantation
Reservoir Plantation
PE23
Grange Farm
B1183
TERRACE LA
Glebe Farm
Abbey Plantation
East Kirkby House
Manor Farm
Wilksby
Wilksby Plantation
CHAPEL LANE
East Kirkby
Shirewood House Farm
Revesby Abbey
PARK LANE
Whaiff Plantation
Half Moon Plantation
HIGHFIELD LANE
Highfield Plantation
Clay Pits Plantation
ABBEY ROAD
Revesby Park
MAIN RD
A155
Windmill
Lincolnshire Aviation Her Ctr
PH
Highfield Plantation
Whaiff House
Park Farm
SLEAFORD ROAD
Shire Wood
Home Farm
MANOR CL
Manor
Manor Farm
Tumuli
A155
Ivy House Farm
Mareham le Fen CE (Controlled) Prim Sch
Manor Farm
BLACKEY LA 1
THE GREEN 2
GRAVEL RD 3
St Scythes
Sewage Works
Blacksmith's Plantation
Home Farm Plantation
Wood's Farm
Keeper's Plantation
PE22
Middle Farm
Kirkby Fenside
Roborough Plantation
FEN ROAD
Fenside Farm
Windmill
Mareham le Fen
Revesby
Ash Wood
Bridge Farm
Byway Farm
HOLT LANE
Site of Revesby Abbey (Cistercian founded 1142)
KIRKBY BANK
Revesby Bridge
Kirkby Bridge
Low Grounds Bridge
Low Grounds Farm
Fen Farm
Poplar Tree Farm
DRAIN BANK
West Lane Bridge
Klondyke Farm
Sewage Works
Hagnaby Lock
Grange Farm
West Fen Farm
Scotts Farm
Grange Farm
Goose Hole Farm
Mill Sewer Drain
Lapwater Farm
Kingfisher Farm
Glebe Farm
Russell's Farm
Church Farm
FOLLY LANE
Town End Farm
Windmill
Medlam Drain
West Fen Catchwater Drain
REVESBY BANK
Sykes Farm
The Farm
New Bolingbroke
Sheriff's Farm
OCCUPATION LANE
8
65
7
64
6
63
5
62
4
61
3
60
2
59
1
58
28 A 29 B 30 C 31 D 32 E 33 F
112
100
A4
1 FIELDSIDE CR
2 LAMMIN'S LA
3 HAZELNUT CL
4 SCHOOL LA
5 REVESBY CR
6 CHAPEL LA

99
87

Scale: 1¼ inches to 1 mile

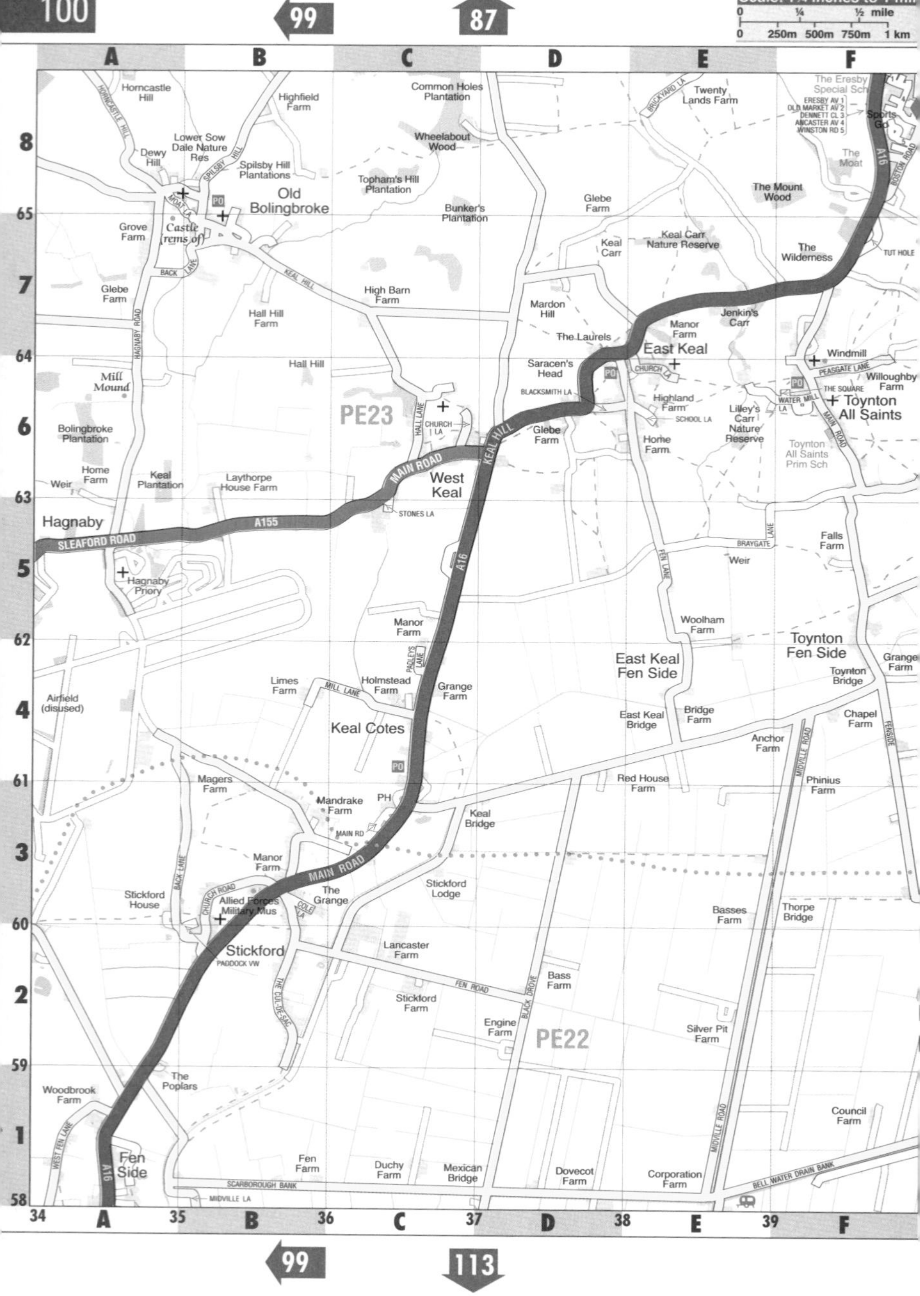

99
113

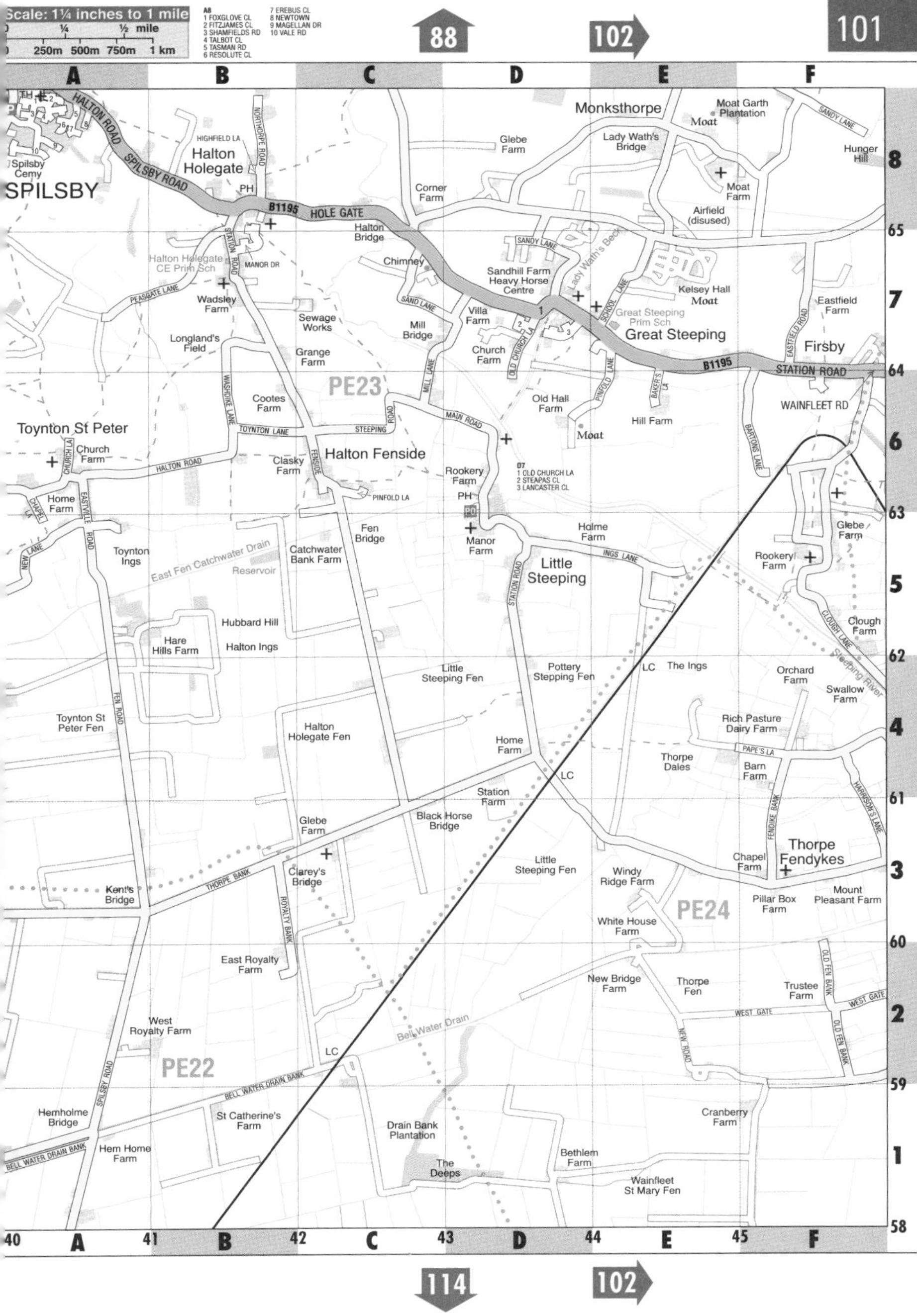
Scale: 1¼ inches to 1 mile
¼
½ mile
250m 500m 750m 1 km
A8
1 FOXGLOVE CL
2 FITZJAMES CL
3 SHAMFIELDS RD
4 TALBOT CL
5 TASMAN RD
6 RESOLUTE CL
7 EREBUS CL
8 NEWTOWN
9 MAGELLAN DR
10 VALE RD
88
102
101
A
B
C
D
E
F
HALTON ROAD
SPILSBY ROAD
HIGHFIELD LA
NORTHORPE ROAD
Halton Holegate
Spilsby Cemy
SPILSBY
PH
B1195
HOLE GATE
Monksthorpe
Moat Garth Plantation
Moat
SANDY LANE
Glebe Farm
Lady Wath's Bridge
Hunger Hill
Corner Farm
Moat Farm
Airfield (disused)
Halton Bridge
STATION ROAD
MANOR DR
Halton Holegate CE Prim Sch
Chimney
SANDY LANE
Lady Wath's Beck
Sandhill Farm Heavy Horse Centre
SCHOOL LANE
Kelsey Hall
Moat
Eastfield Farm
PEASGATE LANE
Wadsley Farm
SAND LANE
Villa Farm
Great Steeping Prim Sch
Great Steeping
EASTFIELD ROAD
Sewage Works
Mill Bridge
Longland's Field
Grange Farm
Church Farm
OLD CHURCH LA
Firsby
B1195
STATION ROAD
PE23
WASHDIKE LANE
MILL LANE
PINFOLD LANE
BAKER'S LA
Cootes Farm
Old Hall Farm
WAINFLEET RD
MAIN ROAD
STEEPING
Toynton St Peter
TOYNTON LANE
Hill Farm
Moat
BARTONS LANE
CHURCH LA
Church Farm
Halton Fenside
Clasky Farm
HALTON ROAD
FENSIDE
D7
1 OLD CHURCH LA
2 STEAPAS CL
3 LANCASTER CL
Rookery Farm
Home Farm
CHAPEL LA
EASTVILLE ROAD
PINFOLD LA
PH
PO
Fen Bridge
Holme Farm
Glebe Farm
NEW LANE
Toynton Ings
East Fen Catchwater Drain
Catchwater Bank Farm
Manor Farm
Little Steeping
INGS LANE
Rookery Farm
Reservoir
STATION ROAD
Hubbard Hill
Clough Farm
CLOUGH LANE
Hare Hills Farm
Halton Ings
Steeping River
Little Steeping Fen
Pottery Stepping Fen
LC
The Ings
Orchard Farm
Swallow Farm
Toynton St Peter Fen
FEN ROAD
Halton Holegate Fen
Rich Pasture Dairy Farm
Home Farm
PAPE'S LA
Thorpe Dales
Barn Farm
LC
Station Farm
HARRISON'S LANE
Black Horse Bridge
Glebe Farm
FENDIKE BANK
Thorpe Fendykes
Little Steeping Fen
Chapel Farm
Clarey's Bridge
Windy Ridge Farm
Kent's Bridge
THORPE BANK
Pillar Box Farm
Mount Pleasant Farm
ROYALTY BANK
PE24
White House Farm
East Royalty Farm
New Bridge Farm
Thorpe Fen
OLD FEN BANK
Trustee Farm
WEST GATE
West Royalty Farm
Bell Water Drain
NEW ROAD
WEST GATE
OLD FEN BANK
LC
PE22
SPILSBY ROAD
BELL WATER DRAIN BANK
Hemholme Bridge
St Catherine's Farm
Drain Bank Plantation
Cranberry Farm
Hem Home Farm
BELL WATER DRAIN BANK
Bethlem Farm
The Deeps
Wainfleet St Mary Fen
8
65
7
64
6
63
5
62
4
61
3
60
2
59
1
58
40
41
42
43
44
45
114
102

101
89

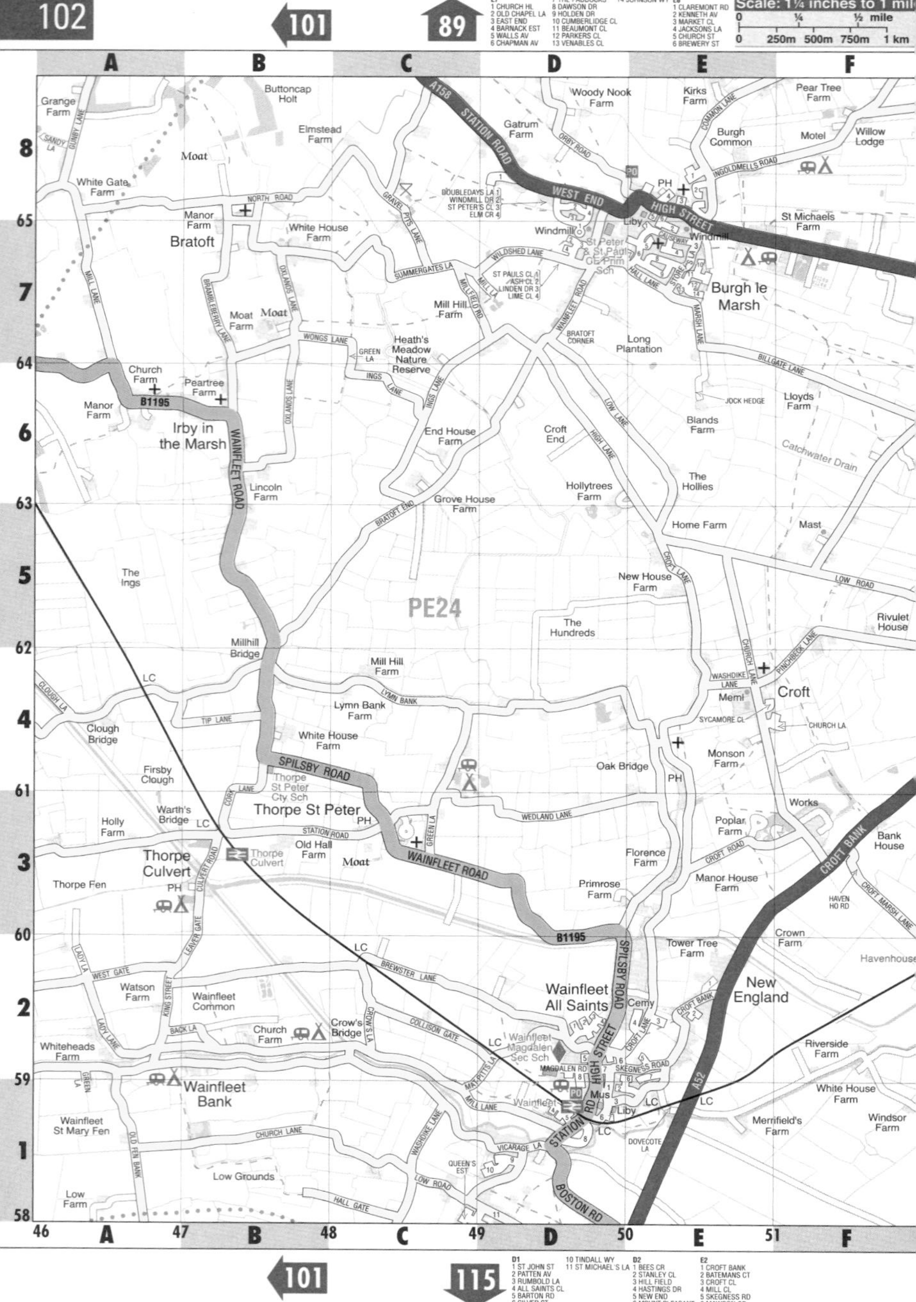

101
115

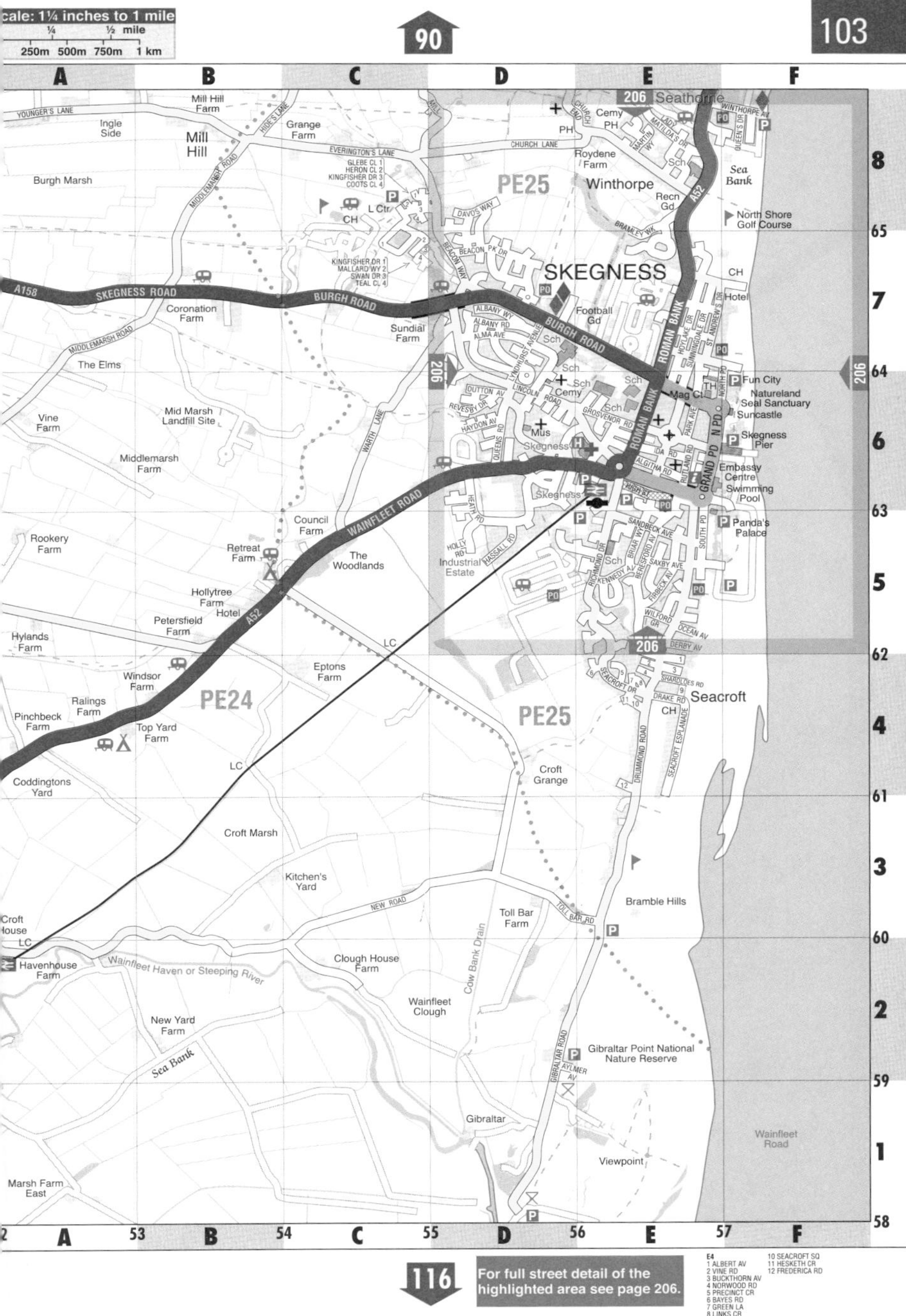

Scale: 1¼ inches to 1 mile
¼
½ mile
250m 500m 750m 1 km
90
103
A B C D E F
206 Seathorne
Mill Hill Farm
Younger's Lane
Ingle Side
Mill Hill
Hide's Lane
Grange Farm
Everington's Lane
Church Lane
Church End
Cemy
PH
Lady Matilda's Dr
Martin Wy
Winthorpe Av
Queen's Dr
Sea Bank
Roydene Farm
Winthorpe
Recn Gd
A52
Burgh Marsh
Middlemarsh Road
Glebe Cl 1
Heron Cl 2
Kingfisher Dr 3
Coots Cl 4
PE25
L Ctr
CH
Davos Way
Beacon Way
Beacon Pk Dr
Bramley Wk
North Shore Golf Course
Kingfisher Dr 1
Mallard Wy 2
Swan Dr 3
Teal Cl 4
SKEGNESS
Hotel
A158
Skegness Road
Burgh Road
Coronation Farm
Sundial Farm
Albany Wy
Albany Rd
Alma Ave
Football Gd
Roman Bank
Sch
Middlemarsh Road
The Elms
206
Lyndhurst Avenue
Lincoln Road
Dutton Av
Revesby Dr
Haydon Av
Cemy
Grosvenor Rd
Mag Ct
TH
Park Ave
North Pd
Hoylake Dr
Sunningdale Dr
St Andrew's Dr
Fun City
Natureland Seal Sanctuary
Suncastle
Vine Farm
Mid Marsh Landfill Site
Warth Lane
Mus
Skegness
Queens Rd
Grand Pd
N Pd
Skegness Pier
Middlemarsh Farm
Algitha Rd
Ida Rd
Rutland Rd
Embassy Centre
Swimming Pool
Wainfleet Road
Heath Rd
Skegness
High St
Rookery Farm
Council Farm
Sandbeck Ave
Briar Wy
Beresford Av
South Pd
Panda's Palace
Retreat Farm
The Woodlands
Holly Rd
Hassall Rd
Industrial Estate
Richmond Dr
Saxby Ave
Fireck Av
Kennedy Av
Hollytree Farm
Hotel
Petersfield Farm
Wilford Gr
Ocean Av
Derby Av
Hylands Farm
LC
206
Eptons Farm
Windsor Farm
Shardloes Rd
Seacroft Dr
Drake Rd
Seacroft
Ralings Farm
PE24
PE25
Pinchbeck Farm
Top Yard Farm
Drummond Road
Seacroft Esplanade
LC
Croft Grange
Coddingtons Yard
Croft Marsh
Kitchen's Yard
Bramble Hills
New Road
Toll Bar Farm
Toll Bar Rd
Croft House
LC
Havenhouse Farm
Clough House Farm
Cow Bank Drain
Wainfleet Haven or Steeping River
Wainfleet Clough
New Yard Farm
Sea Bank
Gibraltar Road
Gibraltar Point National Nature Reserve
Aylmer Av
Gibraltar
Wainfleet Road
Viewpoint
Marsh Farm East
8 65 7 64 6 63 5 62 4 61 3 60 2 59 1 58
52 53 54 55 56 57
116
For full street detail of the highlighted area see page 206.
E4
1 Albert Av
2 Vine Rd
3 Buckthorn Av
4 Norwood Rd
5 Precinct Cr
6 Bayes Rd
7 Green La
8 Links Cr
9 Sea Front Rd
10 Seacroft Sq
11 Hesketh Cr
12 Frederica Rd

91

Scale: 1¼ inches to 1 mile

For full street detail of Newark see Philip's STREET ATLAS of Nottinghamshire

117

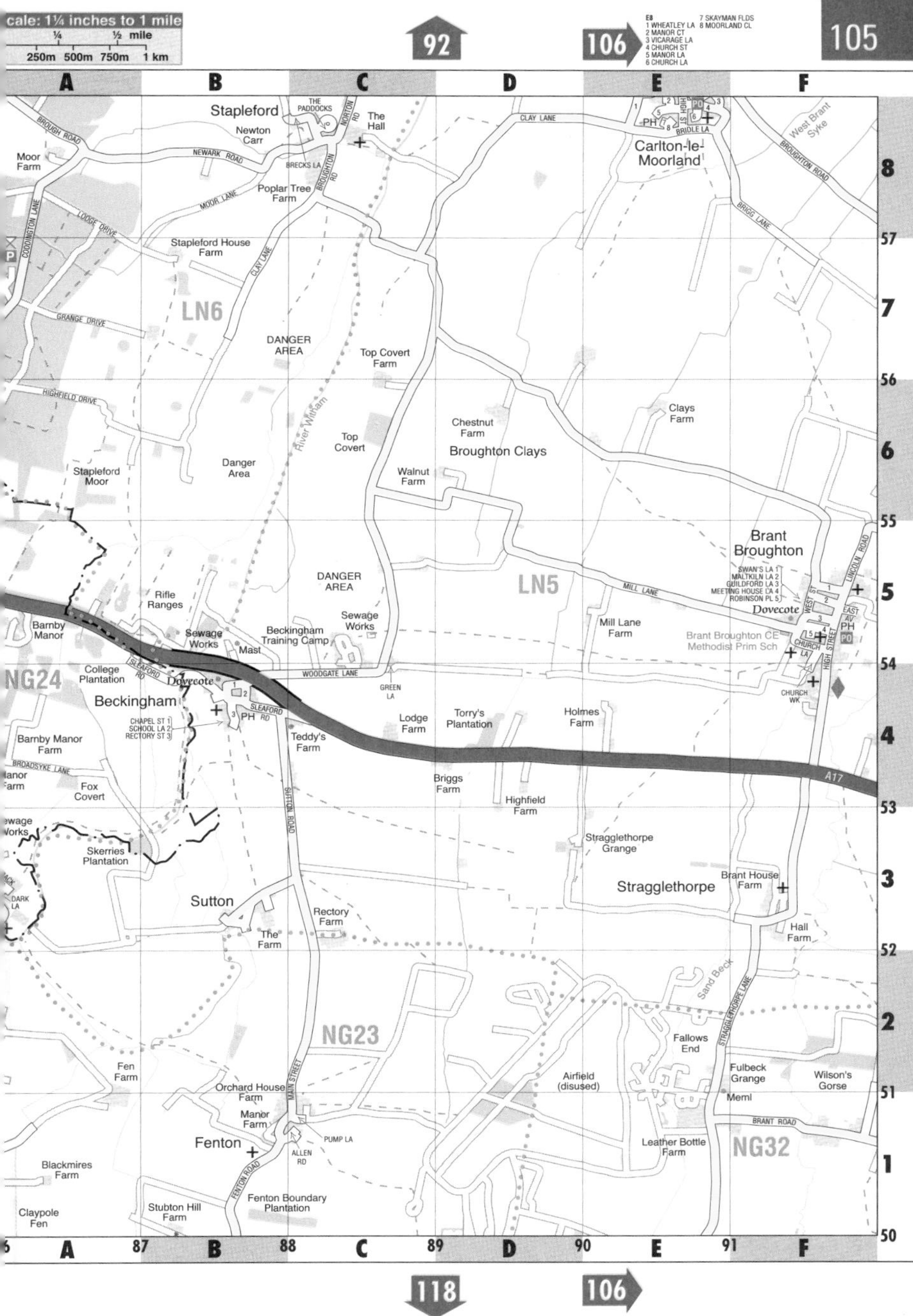
A B C D E F
Stapleford
THE PADDOCKS
The Hall
Newton Carr
NEWARK ROAD
BRECKS LA
BROUGHTON RD
NORTON RD
CLAY LANE
Carlton-le-Moorland
BRIDLE LA
HIGH ST
PH
PO
West Brant Syke
BROUGHTON ROAD
BRIGG LANE
Moor Farm
BROUGH ROAD
CODDINGTON LANE
LODGE DRIVE
MOOR LANE
Poplar Tree Farm
Stapleford House Farm
CLAY LANE
LN6
GRANGE DRIVE
DANGER AREA
Top Covert Farm
HIGHFIELD DRIVE
River Witham
Top Covert
Chestnut Farm
Broughton Clays
Clays Farm
Stapleford Moor
Danger Area
Walnut Farm
Brant Broughton
LINCOLN ROAD
SWAN'S LA 1
MALTKILN LA 2
GUILDFORD LA 3
MEETING HOUSE LA 4
ROBINSON PL 5
DANGER AREA
LN5
MILL LANE
WEST ST
Dovecote
EAST AV
PH
PO
Rifle Ranges
Sewage Works
Mill Lane Farm
Brant Broughton CE Methodist Prim Sch
CHURCH LA
HIGH STREET
Barnby Manor
Sewage Works
Beckingham Training Camp
Mast
WOODGATE LANE
GREEN LA
CHURCH WK
NG24
College Plantation
SLEAFORD RD
Dovecote
Beckingham
CHAPEL ST 1
SCHOOL LA 2
RECTORY ST 3
PH
SLEAFORD RD
Lodge Farm
Torry's Plantation
Holmes Farm
Teddy's Farm
Barnby Manor Farm
BROADSYKE LANE
Fox Covert
Briggs Farm
A17
SUTTON ROAD
Highfield Farm
Sewage Works
Skerries Plantation
Stragglethorpe Grange
DARK LA
Sutton
Stragglethorpe
Brant House Farm
Rectory Farm
The Farm
Hall Farm
Sand Beck
STRAGGLETHORPE LANE
NG23
Fallows End
Fen Farm
Airfield (disused)
Fulbeck Grange
Wilson's Gorse
Orchard House Farm
MAIN STREET
Meml
Manor Farm
BRANT ROAD
Fenton
PUMP LA
ALLEN RD
Leather Bottle Farm
NG32
Blackmires Farm
FENTON ROAD
Fenton Boundary Plantation
Stubton Hill Farm
Claypole Fen
8 57 7 56 6 55 5 54 4 53 3 52 2 51 1 50
86 87 88 89 90 91

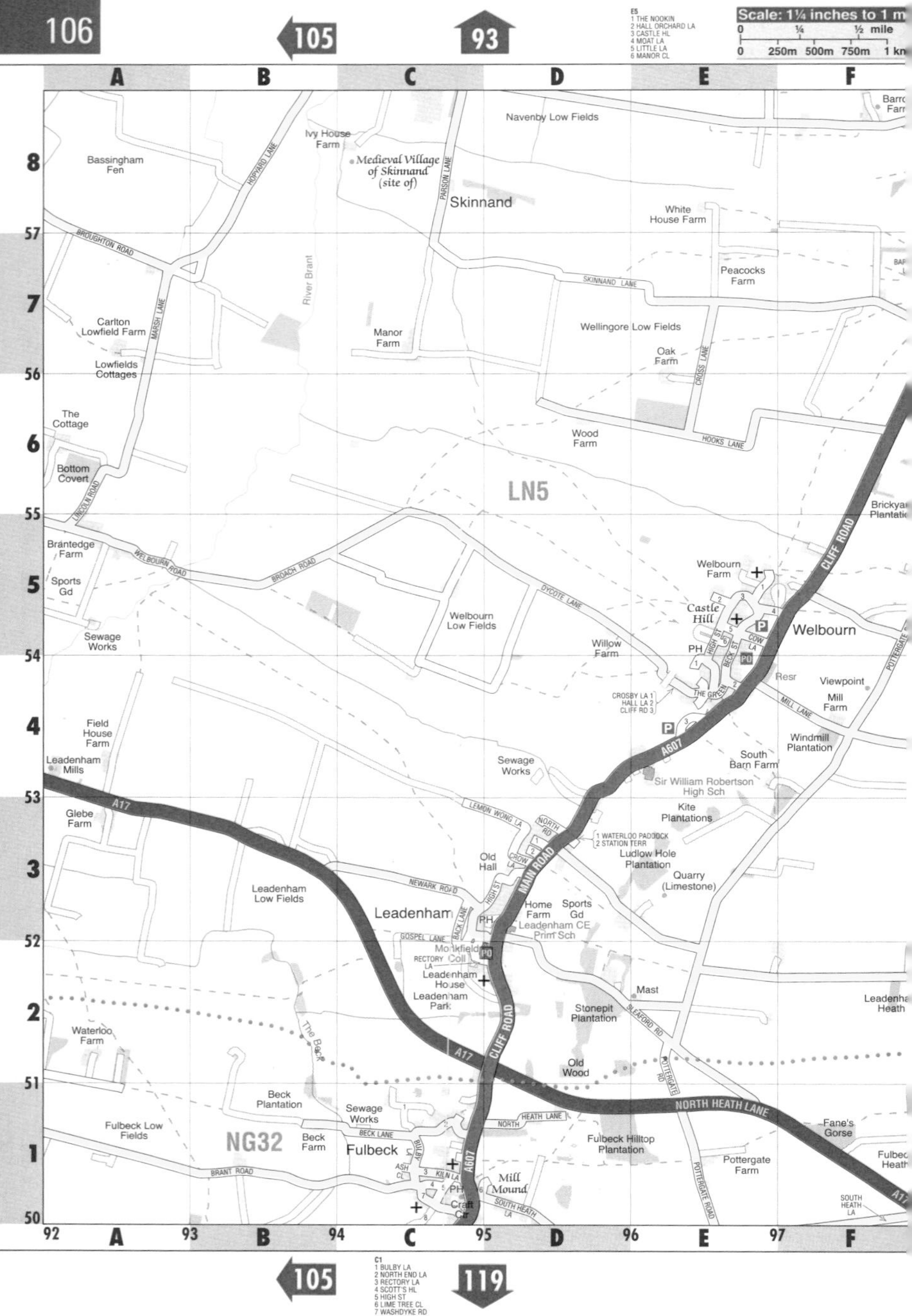

106
105
93
E5
1 THE NOOKIN
2 HALL ORCHARD LA
3 CASTLE HL
4 MOAT LA
5 LITTLE LA
6 MANOR CL
Scale: 1¼ inches to 1 mile
¼
½ mile
0
250m
500m
750m
1 km
A
B
C
D
E
F
Navenby Low Fields
Ivy House Farm
Bassingham Fen
HOPYARD LANE
Medieval Village of Skinnand (site of)
PARSON LANE
Skinnand
White House Farm
BROUGHTON ROAD
River Brant
Peacocks Farm
SKINNAND LANE
Carlton Lowfield Farm
MARSH LANE
Manor Farm
Wellingore Low Fields
Oak Farm
CROSS LANE
Lowfields Cottages
The Cottage
Wood Farm
HOOKS LANE
Bottom Covert
LINCOLN ROAD
LN5
Brantedge Farm
WELBOURN ROAD
BROACH ROAD
CLIFF ROAD
Welbourn Farm
Sports Gd
DYCOTE LANE
Castle Hill
Welbourn Low Fields
Welbourn
Sewage Works
PH
HIGH ST
BECK ST
COW LA
Willow Farm
Resr
Viewpoint
POTTERGATE
CROSBY LA 1
HALL LA 2
CLIFF RD 3
THE GREEN
Mill Farm
MILL LANE
Field House Farm
Windmill Plantation
A607
Leadenham Mills
Sewage Works
South Barn Farm
Sir William Robertson High Sch
A17
Glebe Farm
LEMON WONG LA
NORTH RD
Kite Plantations
1 WATERLOO PADDOCK
2 STATION TERR
Ludlow Hole Plantation
Old Hall
CROW LA
MAIN ROAD
Quarry (Limestone)
Leadenham Low Fields
NEWARK ROAD
HIGH ST
Leadenham
BACK LANE
Home Farm
Sports Gd
Leadenham CE Prim Sch
GOSPEL LANE
Monkfield Coll
RECTORY LA
Leadenham House
Mast
Leadenham Park
Stonepit Plantation
SLEAFORD RD
Leadenham Heath
Waterloo Farm
The Beck
CLIFF ROAD
Old Wood
POTTERGATE RD
Beck Plantation
Sewage Works
HEATH LANE
NORTH
NORTH HEATH LANE
Fulbeck Low Fields
BECK LANE
Fane's Gorse
NG32
Beck Farm
Fulbeck
BULBY LA
Fulbeck Hilltop Plantation
Pottergate Farm
POTTERGATE ROAD
BRANT ROAD
ASH CL
KILN LA
Mill Mound
Craft Ctr
SOUTH HEATH LA
SOUTH HEATH LA
92
93
94
95
96
97
50
51
52
53
54
55
56
57
C1
1 BULBY LA
2 NORTH END LA
3 RECTORY LA
4 SCOTT'S HL
5 HIGH ST
6 LIME TREE CL
7 WASHDYKE RD
8 SUDTHORPE HL
105
119

Scale: 1¼ inches to 1 mile
0 ¼ ½ mile
0 250m 500m 750m 1 km
A7
1 BOUNDARY PADDOCK
2 THE LINK
3 CLIFFSIDE
4 LARK DR
5 HIGHCLIFFE
6 MILL RI
7 THE SPURR
8 HOME CT
9 MEMORIAL HALL DR
10 MILLGATE
11 WEST ST
12 HIGH ST
13 BLACKSMITH'S LA
14 CUMBERLAND AVE
15 THE GREEN
16 HALL ST
17 GROSVENOR SQ
18 SLEAFORD RD
19 VICARAGE LA
20 PINGLE LA
94
108
B8
1 ERMINE DR
2 TURNER CL
3 ERMINE DR
4 OVERTON CL
5 THE GLEANINGS
6 HALES LA
7 HEADLAND WY
A
B
C
D
E
F
Navenby CE Prim Sch
Mrs Smith's Cottage
Navenby Heath
Factory
CHURCH LANE
HIGH ST
EAST RD
Navenby
CHAPEL LANE
GRANTHAM RD
A607
Temple High Grange Farm
Vine House Farm
Radio Masts
Windmill
Sports Gd
Heath Farm
POTTERGATE ROAD
A8
1 BRICKYARD LA
2 NORTH LA
3 FOSTERS CL
4 ADDISON CL
5 MAIDEN WELL LA
6 TENTER LA
7 GAS LA
8 LANSDOWNE RD
9 CLINT LA
10 MEGS LA
11 WINTON RD
12 CROSSFIELD RD
13 HENSON DR
14 DONCASTER GDNS
15 HEATH RD
16 THE RISE
Masts
Gorse Hill Covert
Highfield House Farm
Wellingore
CUCKOO LANE
Wellingore Park
GORSE HILL LANE
Cemy
Viking Way
A15
Pottergate Plantation
HIGH DIKE
Works
NAVENBY LANE
Wellingore Heath
Ashby Lodge
LN4
Heath Farm
Thompson's Bottom
Griffin's Covert
Griffin's Farm
LN5
Warren Houses
Slate House Farm
Overton Farm
Twr
Temple Farm
TEMPLE ROAD
Welbourn Heath
Cocked Hat Plantation
B1191
Cocked Hat Farm
High Dike
Moor Wood
Church Row Plantation
Little Plantation
High Dyke Farm
Grange Farm
Stone Quarry
Brauncewell
Dunsby Pit Plantation
LONG LANE
Hillside Plantation
New Homestead Farm
Dunsby Village
Stocks Heath Farm
Sandpit Plantation
LABURNUM RD
HILLCREST
Larch Plantation
Ryland Grange Farm
BRISTOL HOUSE RD
BEAGLE LA
1 LARCH GR
2 CHESTNUT AVE
3 BEECH CL
4 LIME CL
Sewage Works
NG32
Lord Bristol's Plantation
YORK RD
MALCOLM AV
PLANTATION ROAD
AIRSHIP ROAD
NG34
Pit (dis)
Viking Way
LIGHTER-THAN-AIR RD
Cranwell
Oxenford Farm
Reeve's Plantation
Playing Fields
NORTH DR
WESTSIDE RD
THOROLD AV
Mast
8
57
7
56
6
55
5
54
4
53
3
52
2
51
1
50
98
99
00
01
02
03
C1
1 LONGCROFT DR
2 HIGH DYKE RD
3 PRIMROSE LA
4 PRIMROSE LA
5 STRATTEN CL
6 BRAUNCEWELL RD
7 BEACON RD
120
108
F1
1 ST CHRISTOPHERS CL
2 ST MARTINS CL
3 EDMUNDS RD
4 ST GEORGES CL
5 DE GRAVEL DR
6 THE WILLOWS
7 NORTH RD
8 JOEL SQ
9 WILLOW LA

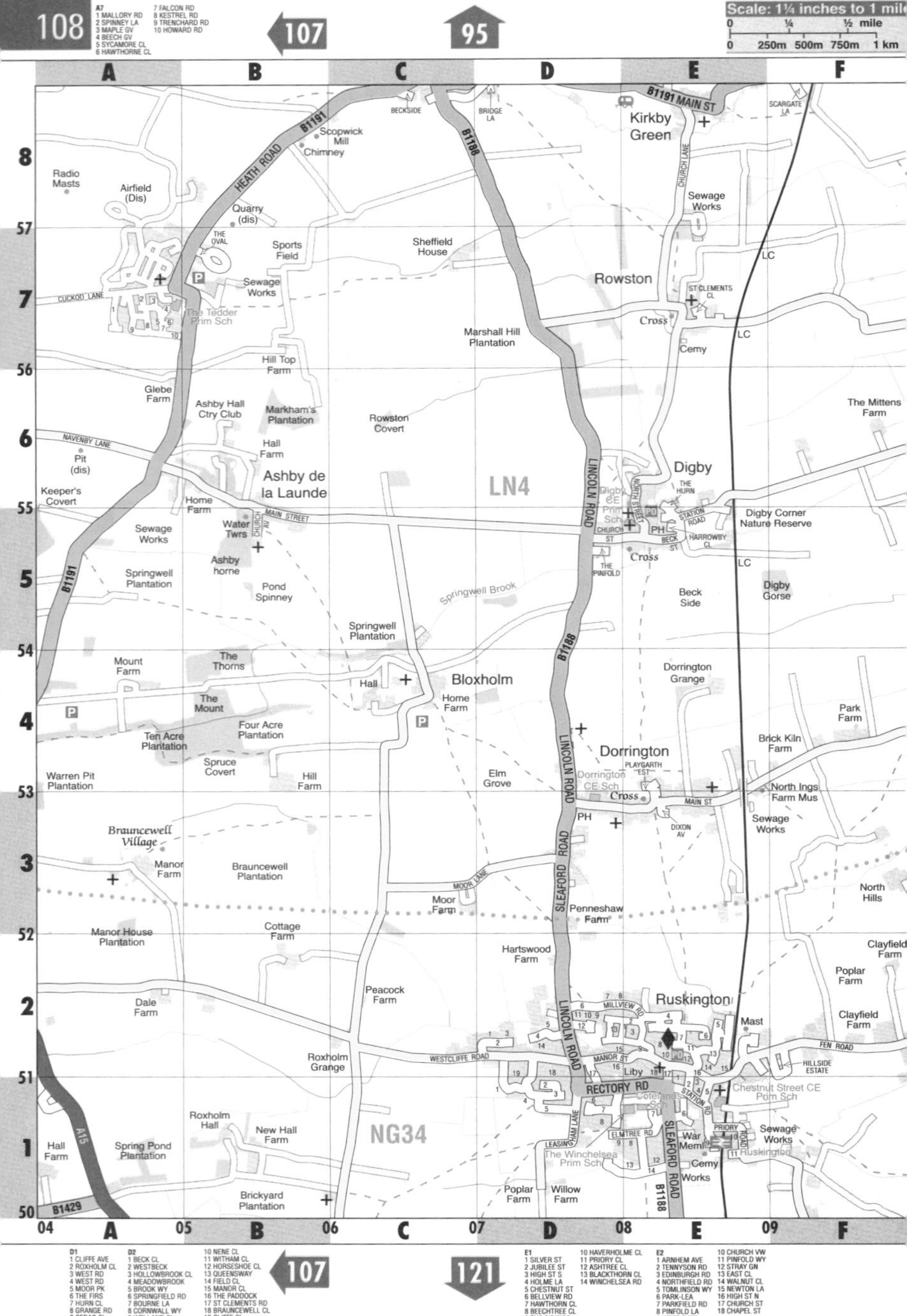
108
A7
1 MALLORY RD
2 SPINNEY LA
3 MAPLE GV
4 BEECH GV
5 SYCAMORE CL
6 HAWTHORNE CL
7 FALCON RD
8 KESTREL RD
9 TRENCHARD RD
10 HOWARD RD
107
95
Scale: 1¼ inches to 1 mile
0 ¼ ½ mile
0 250m 500m 750m 1 km
A B C D E F
B1191 MAIN ST
Kirkby Green
BECKSIDE
BRIDGE LA
SCARGATE LA
HEATH ROAD
B1191
B1188
Scopwick Mill
Chimney
Radio Masts
Airfield (Dis)
Quarry (dis)
THE OVAL
Sports Field
Sheffield House
CHURCH LANE
Sewage Works
CUCKOO LANE
The Tedder Prim Sch
Rowston
ST CLEMENTS CL
Cross
LC
Marshall Hill Plantation
Cemy
Hill Top Farm
Glebe Farm
Ashby Hall Ctry Club
Markham's Plantation
Rowston Covert
The Mittens Farm
NAVENBY LANE
Pit (dis)
Hall Farm
Ashby de la Launde
LN4
Digby
Keeper's Covert
Home Farm
LINCOLN ROAD
NORTH STREET
THE HURN
Digby CE Prim Sch
MAIN STREET
CHURCH AV
Water Twrs
STATION ROAD
Digby Corner Nature Reserve
Sewage Works
CHURCH ST
PH
BECK ST
HARROWBY CL
Ashby horne
THE PINFOLD
Springwell Plantation
Pond Spinney
Beck Side
Digby Gorse
Springwell Brook
Springwell Plantation
Dorrington Grange
Mount Farm
The Thorns
Hall
Bloxholm
Home Farm
The Mount
Park Farm
Four Acre Plantation
Ten Acre Plantation
Dorrington
Brick Kiln Farm
Spruce Covert
PLAYGARTH EST
Warren Pit Plantation
Hill Farm
Elm Grove
Dorrington CE Sch
North Ings Farm Mus
MAIN ST
PH
DIXON AV
Brauncewell Village
Manor Farm
Brauncewell Plantation
SLEAFORD ROAD
MOOR LANE
Moor Farm
Penneshaw Farm
North Hills
Manor House Plantation
Cottage Farm
Hartswood Farm
Clayfield Farm
Poplar Farm
Dale Farm
Peacock Farm
Ruskington
MILLVIEW RD
Mast
Clayfield Farm
FEN ROAD
Roxholm Grange
WESTCLIFFE ROAD
MANOR ST
Liby
HILLSIDE ESTATE
RECTORY RD
STATION RD
Chestnut Street CE Prim Sch
Cotelands Sch
A15
Roxholm Hall
New Hall Farm
NG34
PRIORY ROAD
Sewage Works
Hall Farm
Spring Pond Plantation
LEASINGHAM LANE
ELMTREE RD
War Meml
Ruskington
The Winchelsea Prim Sch
Cemy
Works
B1429
Brickyard Plantation
Poplar Farm
Willow Farm
B1188
SLEAFORD ROAD
04 A 05 B 06 C 07 D 08 E 09 F
D1
1 CLIFFE AVE
2 ROXHOLM CL
3 WEST RD
4 WEST RD
5 MOOR PK
6 THE FIRS
7 HURN CL
8 GRANGE RD
9 CEDAR CL
D2
1 BECK CL
2 WESTBECK
3 HOLLOWBROOK CL
4 MEADOWBROOK
5 BROOK WY
6 SPRINGFIELD RD
7 BOURNE LA
8 CORNWALL WY
9 WELLAND CL
10 NENE CL
11 WITHAM CL
12 HORSESHOE CL
13 QUEENSWAY
14 FIELD CL
15 MANOR CL
16 THE PADDOCK
17 ST CLEMENTS RD
18 BRAUNCEWELL CL
19 CLIFFE CL
107
121
E1
1 SILVER ST
2 JUBILEE ST
3 HIGH ST S
4 HOLME LA
5 CHESTNUT ST
6 BELLVIEW RD
7 HAWTHORN CL
8 BEECHTREE CL
9 THE SIDINGS
10 HAVERHOLME CL
11 PRIORY CL
12 ASHTREE CL
13 BLACKTHORN CL
14 WINCHELSEA RD
E2
1 ARNHEM AVE
2 TENNYSON RD
3 EDINBURGH RD
4 NORTHFIELD RD
5 TOMLINSON WY
6 PARK-LEA
7 PARKFIELD RD
8 PINFOLD LA
9 WEST GATE
10 CHURCH VW
11 PINFOLD WY
12 STRAY GN
13 EAST CL
14 WALNUT CL
15 NEWTON LA
16 HIGH ST N
17 CHURCH ST
18 CHAPEL ST

Scale: 1¼ inches to 1 mile
0 ¼ ½ mile
0 250m 500m 750m 1 km

96
110

F5
1 KING ST
2 CHURCH ST
3 BRIDGE ST
4 CHURCH LA
5 WATERSIDE
6 FITZWILLIAM PL
7 RING MOOR CL
8 ST MICHAELS CL

122
110

109
97

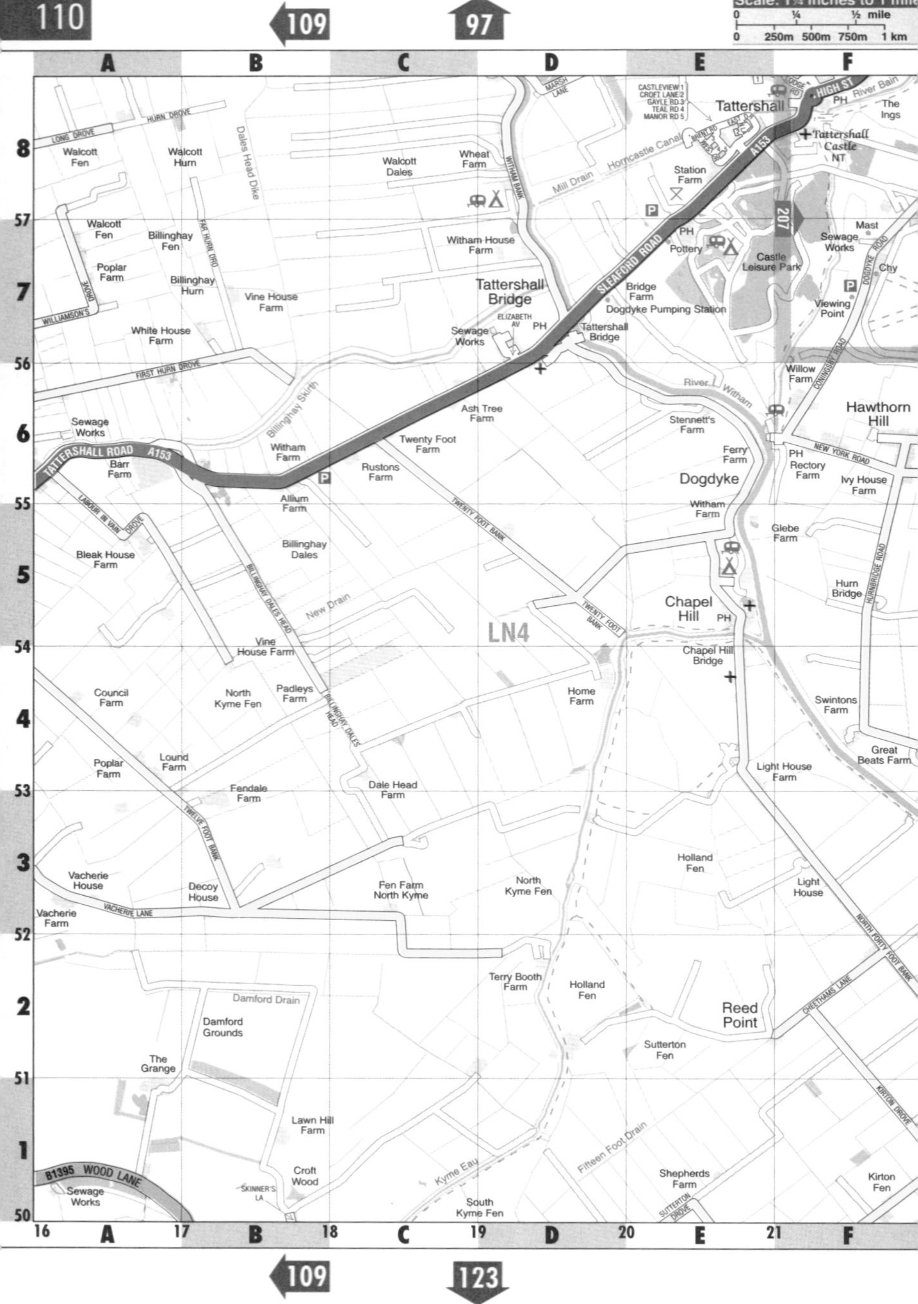

109
123

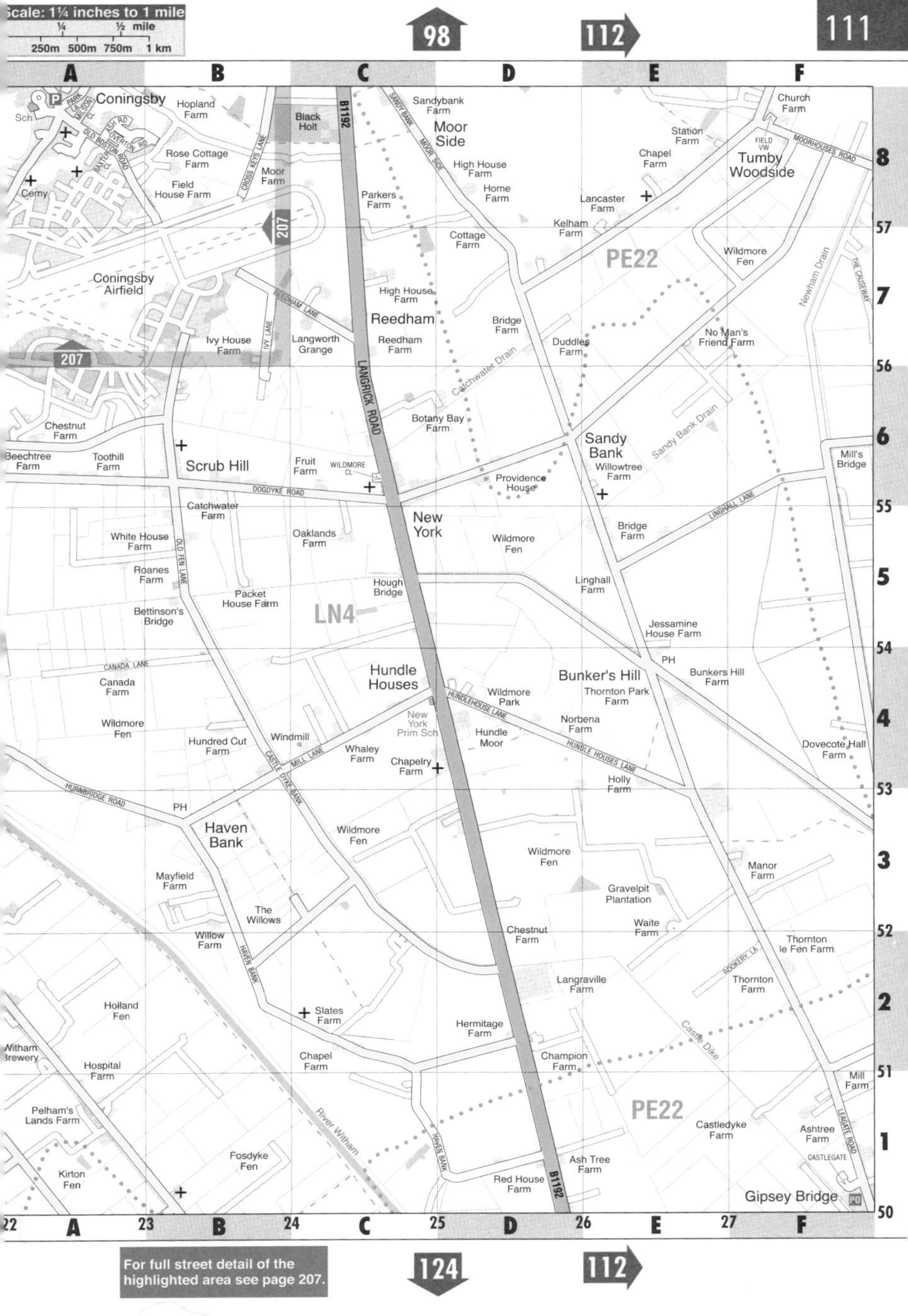

For full street detail of the highlighted area see page 207.

111
99
Scale: 1¼ inches to 1 mil
0 ¼ ½ mile
0 250m 500m 750m 1 km
A B C D E F
8 57 7 56 6 55 5 54 4 53 3 52 2 51 1 50
28 29 30 31 32 33
Wildmore Fen
Moorhouses Bridge
Moorhouses
MOORHOUSES ROAD
Church Farm
Mill Farm
REVESBY BANK
Watkinson's Bridge
Slate House Farm
Gaunt House
Glebe Farm
CHAPEL ROAD
Station Farm
Wheatsheaf Farm
PH
New Bolingbroke
PO
KINGS CL
B1183
Chapel Farm
Fen Farm
Medlam House
STICKNEY LANE
Musgrave Bridge
Musgrave's Farm
FOLLY LANE
Hill's Folly
WEST FEN LANE
Coronation Farm
Medlam Bridge
Bowsers Farm
HALL LAN
Boston Farm
Stickney Bridge
MEDLAM LANE
Medlam Manor
Sewage Works
MEDLAM CL
MAIN ROAD
Medlam
Medlam Farm
Whyte Acre
Glebe Farm
Stickney Grange
Rainbow End
West Fen Farm
COLD HARBOUR LANE
MEDLAM LANE
Royalty Farm
War Meml
Carrington Park
Chase House Farm
Carrington
Bramley Farm
Carrington House Farm
The Beeches
Skirbeck Farm
Carrington Grange
Chapel Farm
West Houses
Arkendale
WESTHOUSES
BEECHES LANE
Barkers Yard
PE22
Henley House
Sycamore Farm
War Memorial
Caudwell Farm
Tennant's Bridge
Mayfield Farm
Green Lane Farm
Westville Farm
SHORT'S CORNER
CARRINGTON ROAD
Harvestman Farm
Hakerley Bridge
Bishop's Farm
Bridge Farm
West Fen Drain
Wildmore Fen
Medlam Farm
White House Farm
Medlam Drain
WESTVILLE ROAD
Home Farm
Set Aside Farm
Bradleys Farm
STAUNT ROAD
Primrose Hill Farm
Riggalls Farm
THACKER'S ROAD
Home Farm
Grange Farm
Meml
Frithville
Works
Slate House Farm
Black House Farm
Newham Farm
Newham Drain
NEWHAM LANE
Newham
PEACOCK'S RD
CANISTER LANE
Black House Farm
Frithville Cty Sch
WESTVILLE ROAD
WEST FEN DRAIN BANK
HALE LANE
B1184
BOSTON ROAD
B1183
PH
Canister Bridge
B1184
111
125

B1
1 HARVESTER WY
2 MAIN RD
3 LITTLEPORT LA
4 VICARAGE LA
5 GLEBE CL
6 LITTLEPORT LA
7 MANOR CL
8 AMOS WY
9 SARGEANTS CL
10 BESANT CL
11 CHURCH CL
12 EVISON CT
13 LUCAN CL
14 CHAPEL LA

126 114

113
101

Scale: 1¼ inches to 1 mile
0 ¼ ½ mile
0 250m 500m 750m 1 km

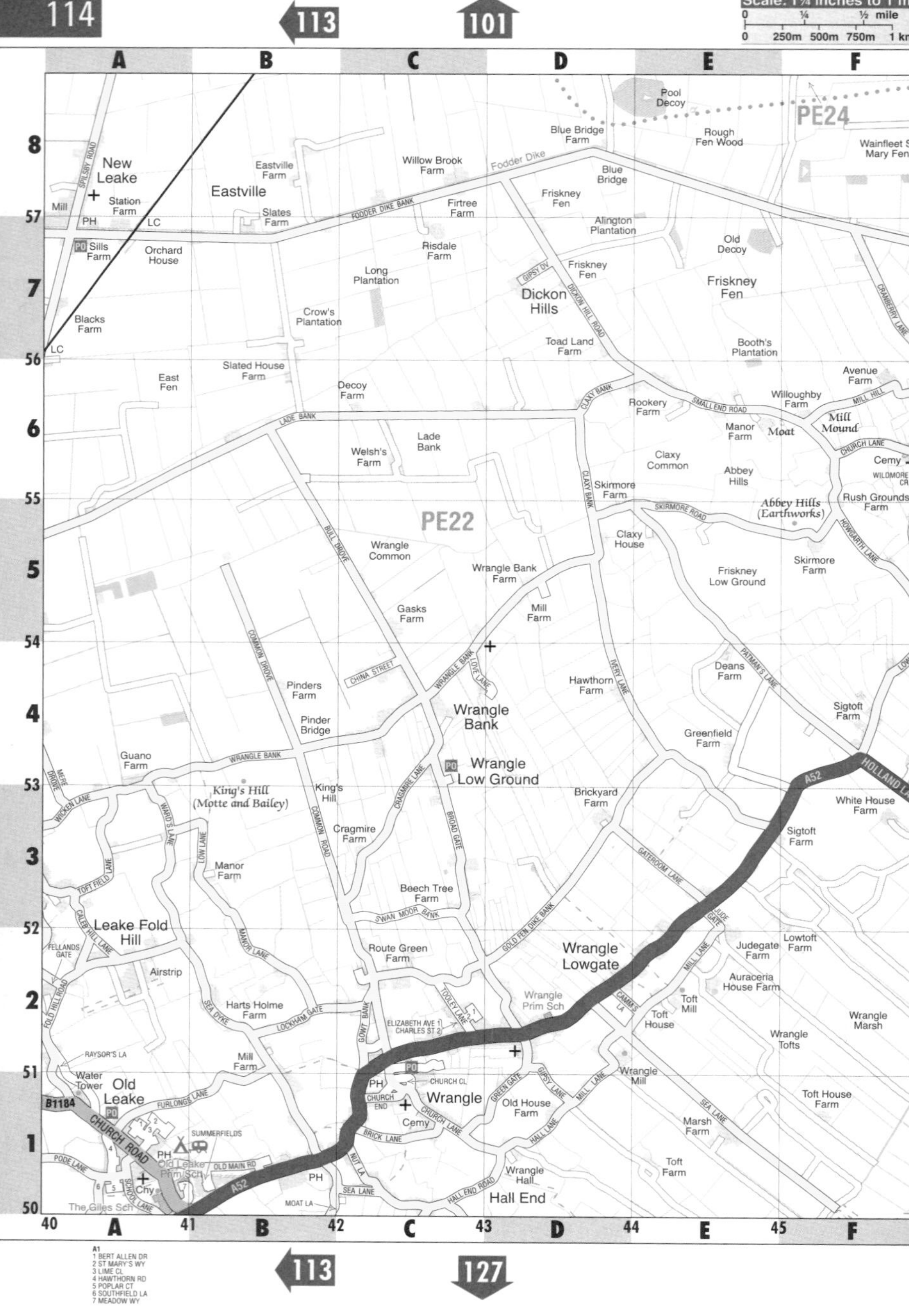

A1
1 BERT ALLEN DR
2 ST MARY'S WY
3 LIME CL
4 HAWTHORN RD
5 POPLAR CT
6 SOUTHFIELD LA
7 MEADOW WY

113
127

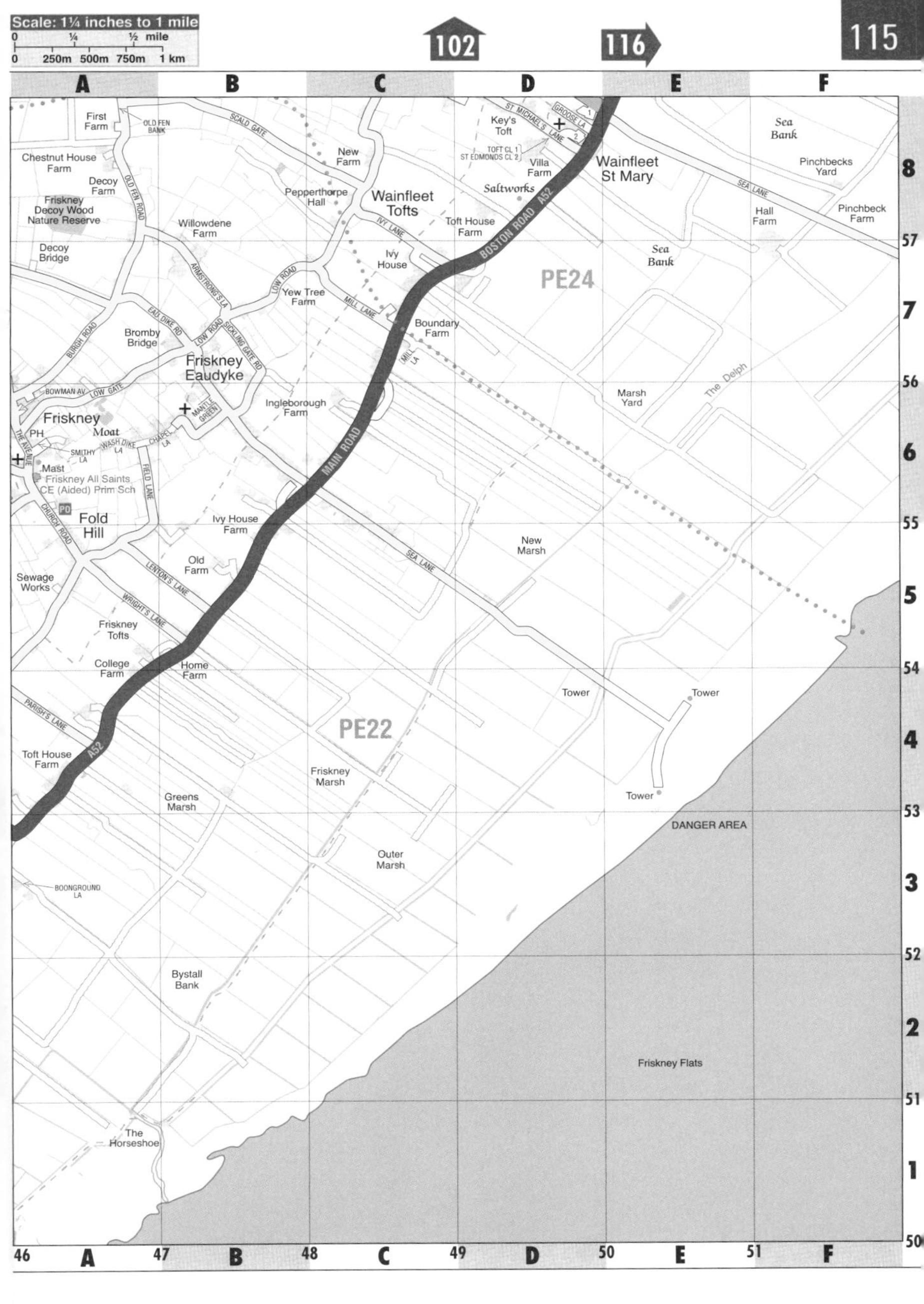
Scale: 1¼ inches to 1 mile
0 ¼ ½ mile
0 250m 500m 750m 1 km
102
116
A B C D E F
First Farm
OLD FEN BANK
SCALD GATE
Chestnut House Farm
Decoy Farm
OLD FEN ROAD
Friskney Decoy Wood Nature Reserve
Decoy Bridge
New Farm
Pepperthorpe Hall
Wainfleet Tofts
Key's Toft
ST MICHAEL'S LANE
GROOSE LA
TOFT CL 1
ST EDMONDS CL 2
Villa Farm
Saltworks
Wainfleet St Mary
Sea Bank
Pinchbecks Yard
SEA LANE
Hall Farm
Pinchbeck Farm
Willowdene Farm
IVY LANE
Toft House Farm
BOSTON ROAD A52
Ivy House
Sea Bank
ARMSTRONG'S LA
LOW ROAD
Yew Tree Farm
MILL LANE
PE24
EAU DIKE RD
BURGH ROAD
Bromby Bridge
LOW ROAD
SICKLING GATE RD
Boundary Farm
MILL LA
Friskney Eaudyke
BOWMAN AV
LOW GATE
MANTLE GREEN
Ingleborough Farm
The Delph
Marsh Yard
Friskney
Moat
THE AVENUE
PH
SMITHY LA
WASH DIKE LA
CHAPEL LA
FIELD LANE
MAIN ROAD
Mast
Friskney All Saints CE (Aided) Prim Sch
CHURCH ROAD
PO
Fold Hill
Ivy House Farm
New Marsh
Old Farm
SEA LANE
Sewage Works
LENTON'S LANE
WRIGHT'S LANE
Friskney Tofts
College Farm
Home Farm
Tower
Tower
PARISH'S LANE
PE22
A52
Toft House Farm
Friskney Marsh
Greens Marsh
Tower
DANGER AREA
Outer Marsh
BOONGROUND LA
Bystall Bank
Friskney Flats
The Horseshoe
8 57 7 56 6 55 5 54 4 53 3 52 2 51 1 50
46 47 48 49 50 51

102

103

206

E8
1 BAYES RD
2 PRECINCT CRES
3 GREEN LA
4 LINKS CRES
5 NORWOOD RD
6 VINE RD
7 ALBERT AVE
8 BUCKTHORN AVE
9 SHARDLOES RD
10 SEA FRONT RD
12 SEACROFT SQ
13 FREDERICA RD

Scale: 1¼ inches to 1 mile
0 ¼ ½ mile
0 250m 500m 750m 1 km

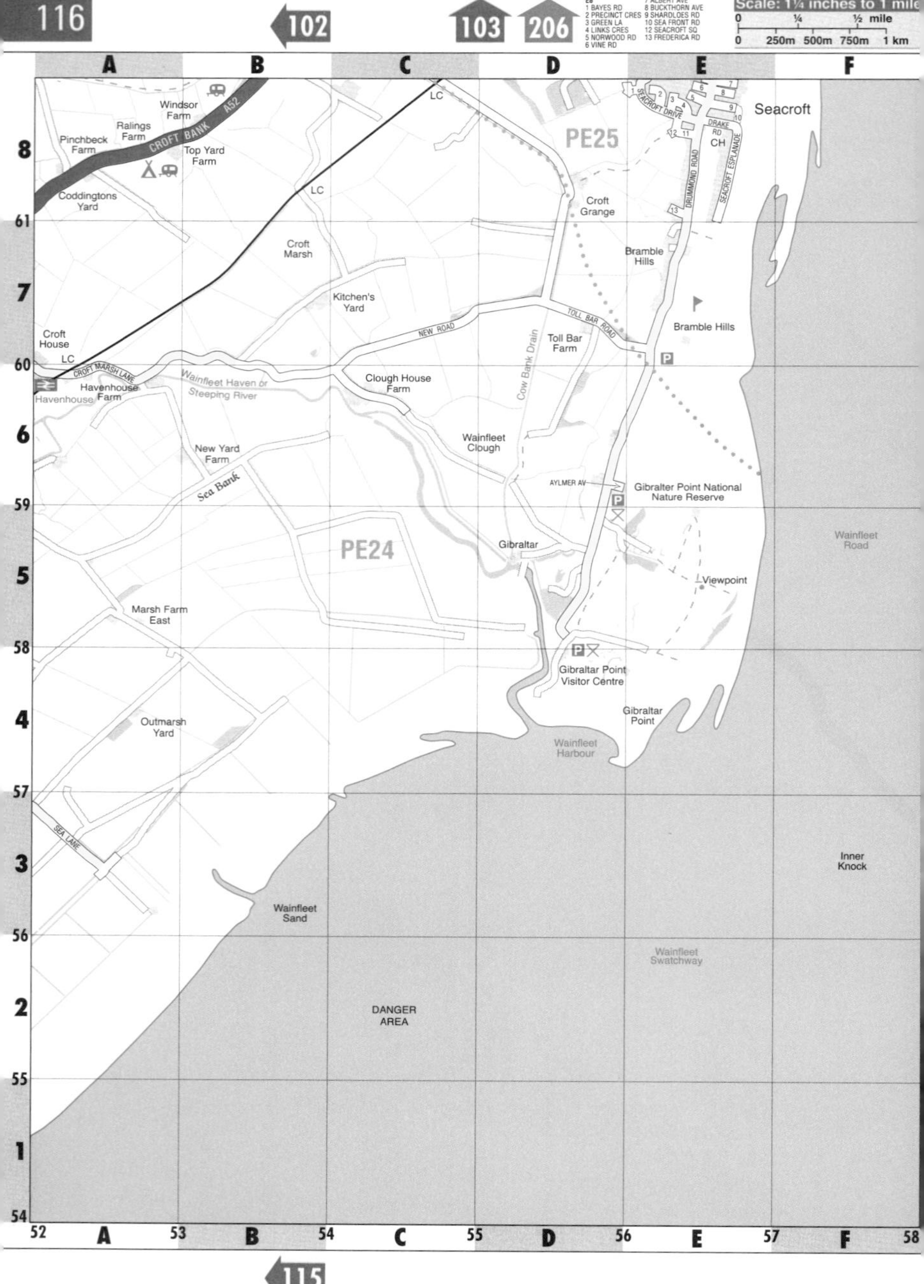

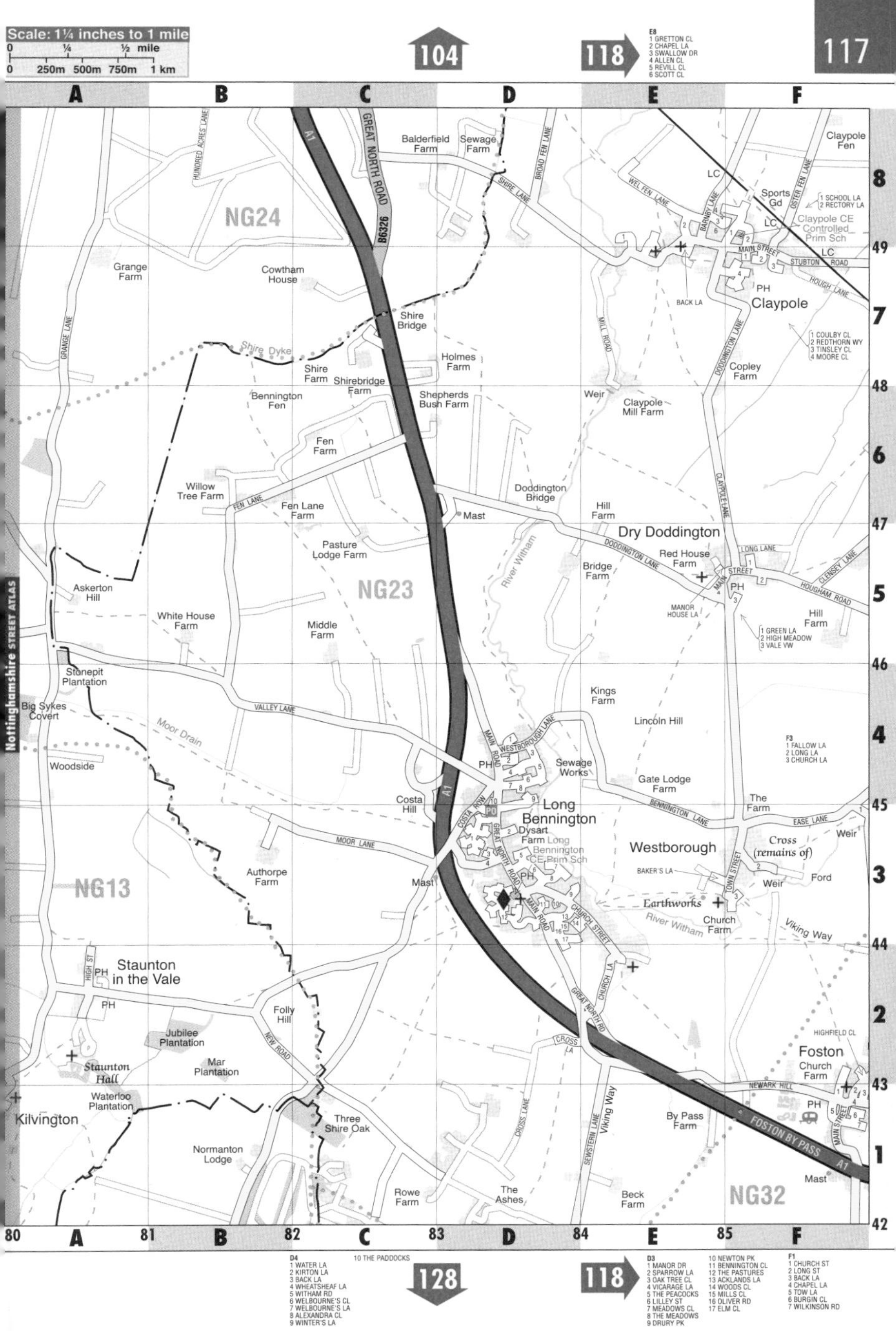

D4
1 WATER LA
2 KIRTON LA
3 BACK LA
4 WHEATSHEAF LA
5 WITHAM RD
6 WELBOURNE'S CL
7 WELBOURNE'S LA
8 ALEXANDRA CL
9 WINTER'S LA
10 THE PADDOCKS

128

118

D3
1 MANOR DR
2 SPARROW LA
3 OAK TREE CL
4 VICARAGE LA
5 THE PEACOCKS
6 LILLEY ST
7 MEADOWS CL
8 THE MEADOWS
9 DRURY PK
10 NEWTON PK
11 BENNINGTON CL
12 THE PASTURES
13 ACKLANDS LA
14 WOODS CL
15 MILLS CL
16 OLIVER RD
17 ELM CL

F1
1 CHURCH ST
2 LONG ST
3 BACK LA
4 CHAPEL LA
5 TOW LA
6 BURGIN CL
7 WILKINSON RD

117
105

Scale: 1¼ inches to 1 mile
0 ¼ ½ mile
0 250m 500m 750m 1 km

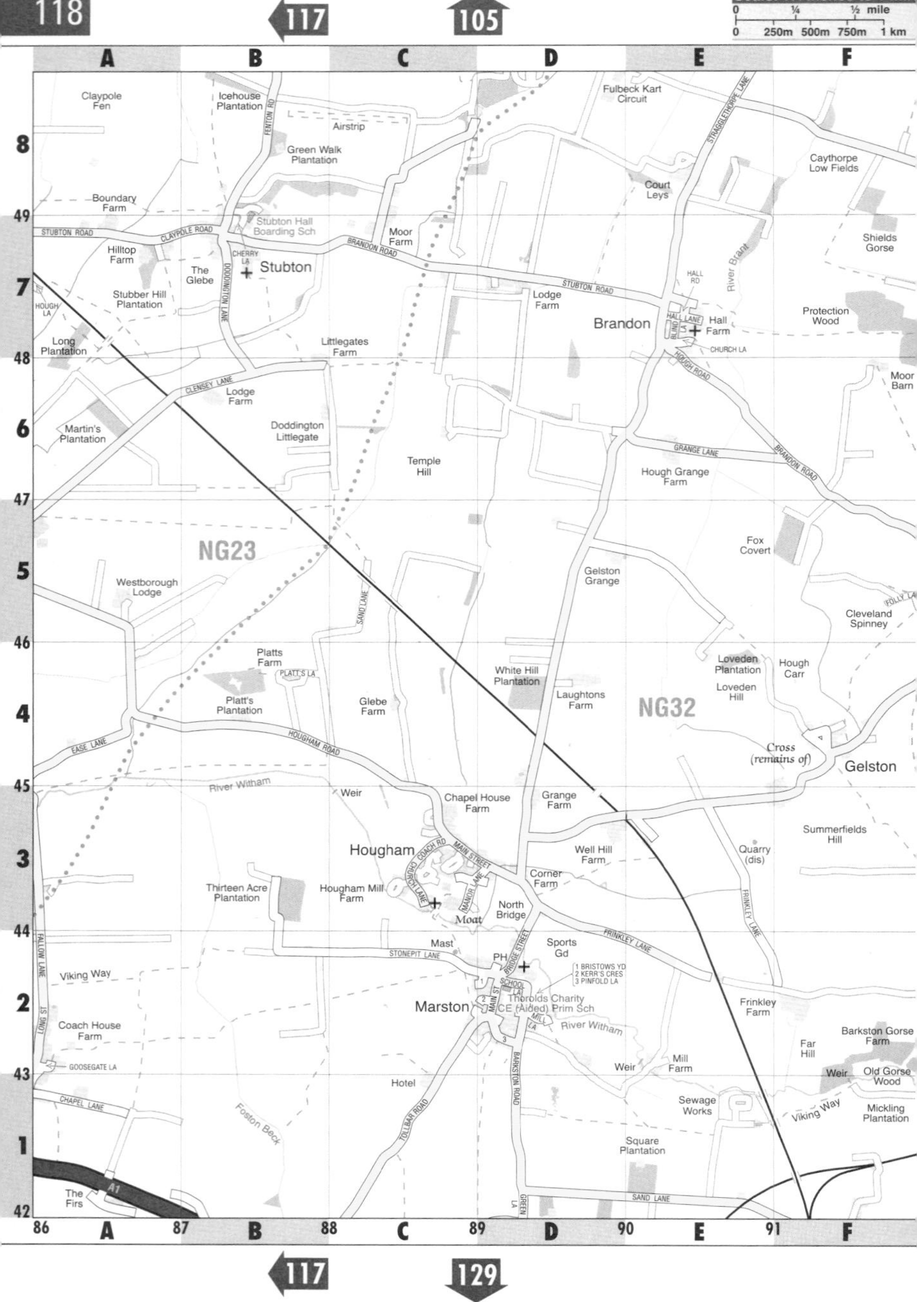

117
129

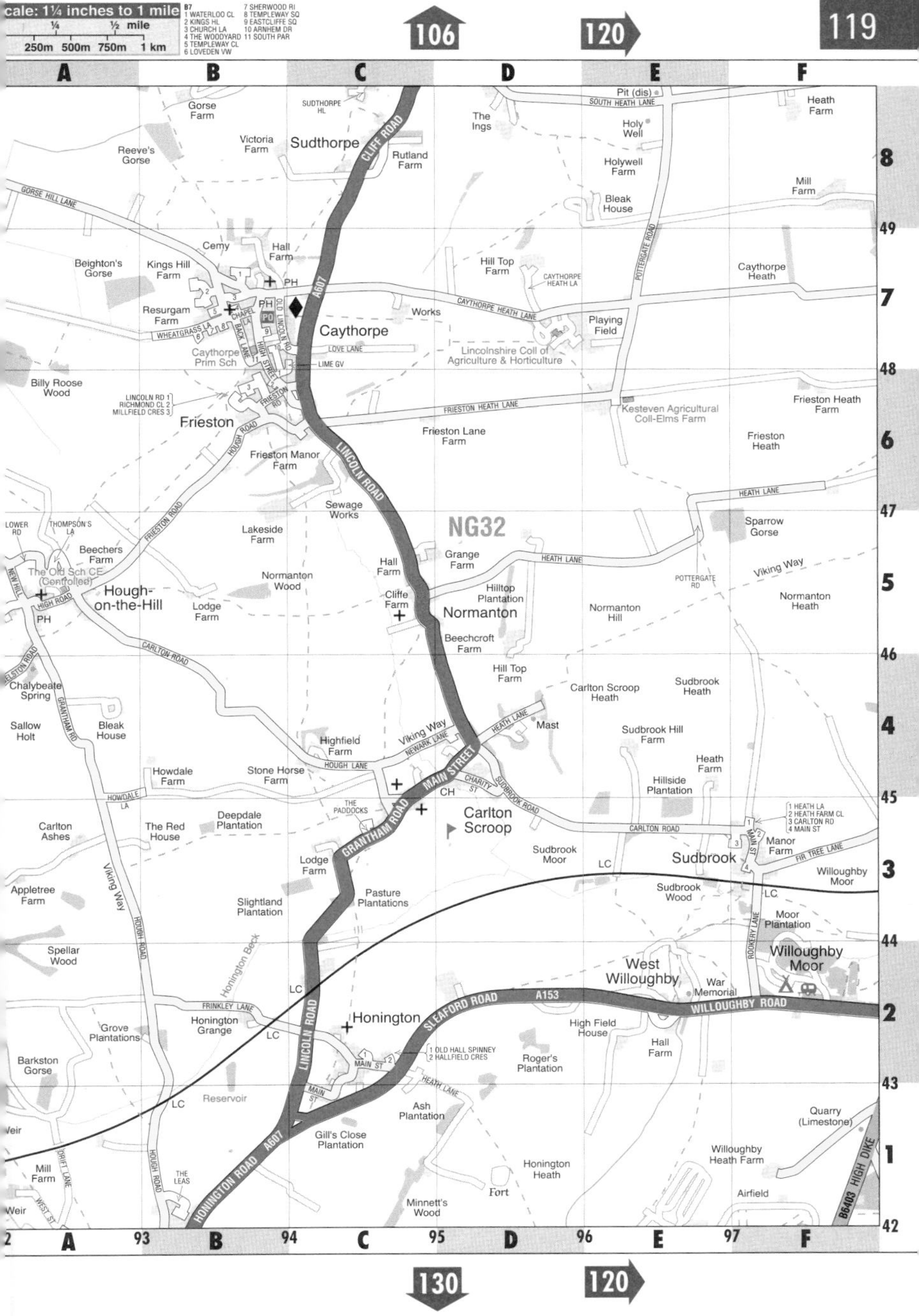
cale: 1¼ inches to 1 mile
¼
½ mile
250m 500m 750m 1 km
B7
1 WATERLOO CL
2 KINGS HL
3 CHURCH LA
4 THE WOODYARD
5 TEMPLEWAY CL
6 LOVEDEN VW
7 SHERWOOD RI
8 TEMPLEWAY SQ
9 EASTCLIFFE SQ
10 ARNHEM DR
11 SOUTH PAR
106
120
Gorse Farm
Sudthorpe
Victoria Farm
Reeve's Gorse
Rutland Farm
CLIFF ROAD
The Ings
Pit (dis)
SOUTH HEATH LANE
Holy Well
Heath Farm
Holywell Farm
Mill Farm
Bleak House
GORSE HILL LANE
POTTERGATE ROAD
Cemy
Hall Farm
Beighton's Gorse
Kings Hill Farm
PH
Hill Top Farm
CAYTHORPE HEATH LA
Caythorpe Heath
Resurgam Farm
CHAPEL LA
BACK LANE
OLD LINCOLN RD
A607
Works
CAYTHORPE HEATH LANE
Caythorpe
Playing Field
WHEATGRASS LA
LOVE LANE
Caythorpe Prim Sch
HIGH STREET
LIME GV
Lincolnshire Coll of Agriculture & Horticulture
Billy Roose Wood
LINCOLN RD 1
RICHMOND CL 2
MILLFIELD CRES 3
FRIESTON RD
FRIESTON HEATH LANE
Kesteven Agricultural Coll-Elms Farm
Frieston Heath Farm
Frieston
HOUGH ROAD
Frieston Lane Farm
Frieston Heath
Frieston Manor Farm
LINCOLN ROAD
HEATH LANE
Sewage Works
FRIESTON ROAD
NG32
LOWER RD
THOMPSON'S LA
Lakeside Farm
Sparrow Gorse
Beechers Farm
Grange Farm
HEATH LANE
Viking Way
The Old Sch CE (Controlled)
NEW HILL
Normanton Wood
Hall Farm
POTTERGATE RD
Hough-on-the-Hill
HIGH ROAD
Cliffe Farm
Hilltop Plantation
Normanton
Normanton Hill
Normanton Heath
PH
Lodge Farm
Beechcroft Farm
CARLTON ROAD
Hill Top Farm
BELSTON ROAD
Chalybeate Spring
Carlton Scroop Heath
Sudbrook Heath
GRANTHAM RD
Sallow Holt
Bleak House
HEATH LANE
Mast
Highfield Farm
Viking Way
NEWARK LANE
Sudbrook Hill Farm
Howdale Farm
HOUGH LANE
Stone Horse Farm
MAIN STREET
CHARITY ST
Heath Farm
HOWDALE LA
THE PADDOCKS
GRANTHAM ROAD
CH
SUDBROOK ROAD
Hillside Plantation
Carlton Ashes
The Red House
Deepdale Plantation
Carlton Scroop
CARLTON ROAD
1 HEATH LA
2 HEATH FARM CL
3 CARLTON RD
4 MAIN ST
Manor Farm
Sudbrook Moor
LC
Sudbrook
FIR TREE LANE
Willoughby Moor
Lodge Farm
Viking Way
Appletree Farm
Slightland Plantation
Pasture Plantations
Sudbrook Wood
LC
Moor Plantation
ROOKERY LANE
HOUGH ROAD
Spellar Wood
Honington Beck
West Willoughby
Willoughby Moor
War Memorial
LC
LINCOLN ROAD
FRINKLEY LANE
SLEAFORD ROAD
A153
WILLOUGHBY ROAD
Grove Plantations
Honington Grange
Honington
High Field House
LC
Hall Farm
1 OLD HALL SPINNEY
2 HALLFIELD CRES
MAIN ST
Roger's Plantation
Barkston Gorse
MAIN ST
HEATH LANE
Reservoir
LC
Ash Plantation
Quarry (Limestone)
Weir
A607
Gill's Close Plantation
Willoughby Heath Farm
DRIFT LANE
Mill Farm
HOUGH ROAD
THE LEAS
HONINGTON ROAD
Honington Heath
B6403 HIGH DIKE
Fort
Airfield
Minnett's Wood
WEST ST
Weir
A B C D E F
8 49 7 48 6 47 5 46 4 45 3 44 2 43 1 42
92 93 94 95 96 97
130
120

C8
1 ST MICHAEL'S WY
2 LIGHTER-THAN-AIR RD
3 LAWRENCE LA
4 ST ANDREW'S WY
5 HEADQUARTERS CR
6 YORK HOUSE RD
7 CENTRAL DR
8 EAST CAMP RD
9 WESTERN DR

119
107

D8
1 AMMAN SQ
2 BAGHDAD RD
3 DELHI SQ
4 EASTCHURCH RD
5 FLOWERDOWN AV

E8
1 FRANK WHITTLE CL
2 WESTSIDE RD
3 BRISTOW RD
4 ISON CL
5 THOROLD AV

F8
1 CRANE CL
2 OLD SCHOOL LA
3 WILLOW LA
4 HOME PK
5 WYLSON CL

Scale: 1¼ inches to 1 mile

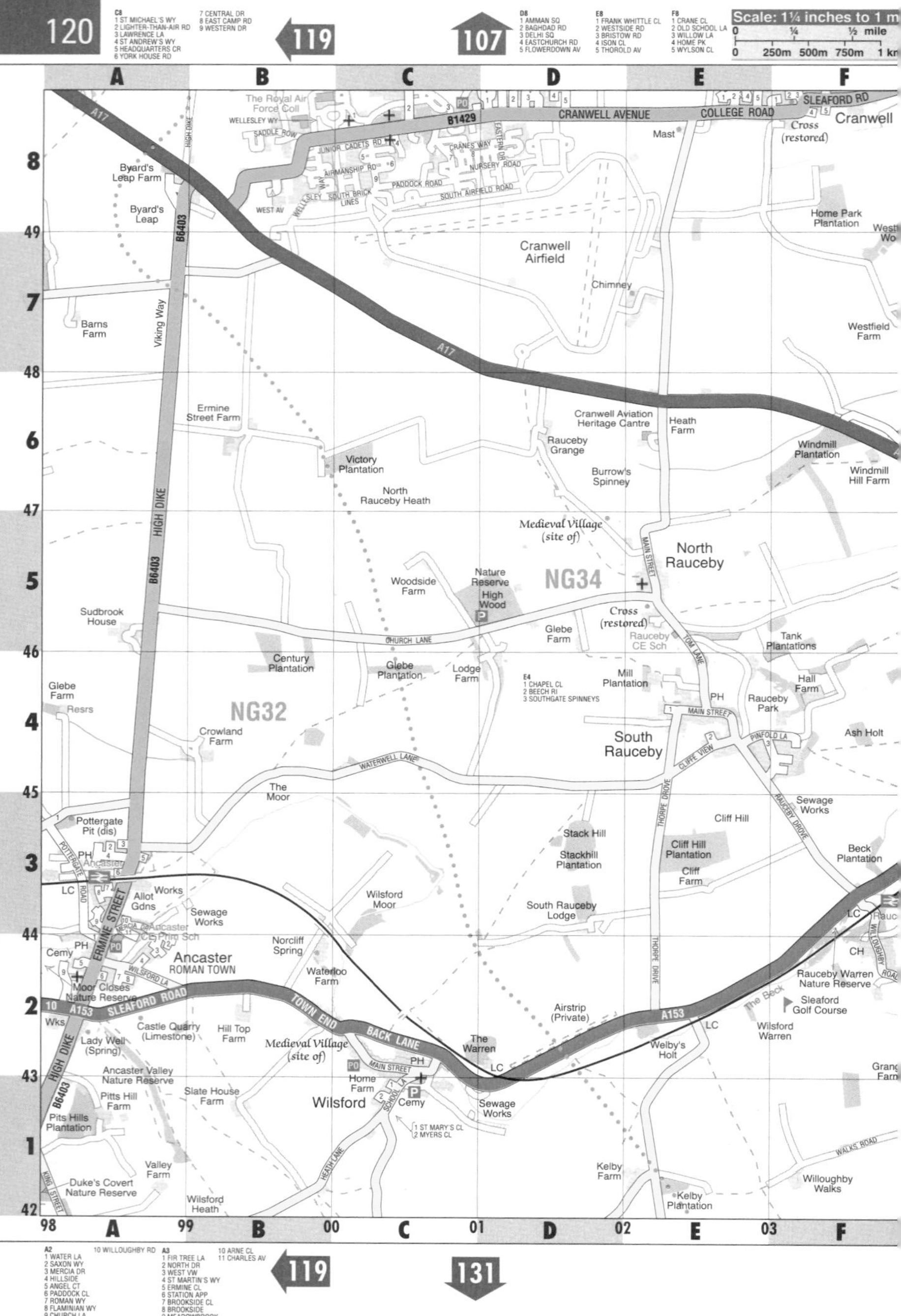

A2
1 WATER LA
2 SAXON WY
3 MERCIA DR
4 HILLSIDE
5 ANGEL CT
6 PADDOCK CL
7 ROMAN WY
8 FLAMINIAN WY
9 CHURCH LA
10 WILLOUGHBY RD

A3
1 FIR TREE LA
2 NORTH DR
3 WEST VW
4 ST MARTIN'S WY
5 ERMINE CL
6 STATION APP
7 BROOKSIDE CL
8 BROOKSIDE
9 MEADOWBROOK
10 ARNE CL
11 CHARLES AV

119
131

Scale: 1¼ inches to 1 mile
¼
½ mile
250m 500m 750m 1 km
B7
1 THE MALTINGS
2 CHAPEL LA
3 LINCOLN RD
4 THE SQUARE
5 SPRING LA
6 ST ANDREW'S CR
7 MANOR CL
8 WANSBECK RD
9 GORSE LA
10 JUNIPER CL
11 ST JOHN'S CL
12 FLAXWELL WY
13 ROOKERY LA
14 SLEAFORD RD
B8
1 LINCOLN RD
2 THE LINK
3 DEAN CL
4 KIRKDALE CL
5 LILBURN CL
6 ROBERTSON AV
7 RUSSELL RD
8 THE GREEN
9 JESSOP CL
108
122
A
B
C
D
E
F
Old Hall Farm
St John the Baptist's Church
SLEAFORD RD
B1188
A153
Moor Farm
Leasingham Moor
White House Farm
Leasingham
Kirkdale
Sewage Works
Rigg Farm
Deepdale Farm
LC
B1209
MOOR LANE
CHAPEL LA
PO
PH
St Andrews CE (Controlled) Prim Sch
1 MIDDLETON WY
2 DEEPDALE DR
3 HEATH LA
4 MAPLE CL
5 SEDGE CL
6 BRACKEN CL
PAPERMILL LANE
Washdike Bridge
Old River Slea
LINCOLN ROAD
Sleaford Moor
EAST ROAD
HOLDINGHAM LANE
212
New Wood
Moor Farm
A153
Evedon Plantation
Ford
Water Tower
Manor Farm
Motel
NG34
BONEMILL LA
Evedon
A17
Holdingham
Sewage Works
River Slea
Vine Farm
B1518
PH
WINCHESTER WY
Bonemill Bridge
Bone Mill Farm
Sleaford Wood
LC
EVEDON ROAD
Holdingham Plantation
A15
STOKES DR
YORK RD
RIPON DR
DURHAM AV
ALMOND WK
Sleaford Moor
HADLEY RD
Sumner's Plantation
SLEAFORD
NORTH GATE
Factory
WOODBRIDGE
EAST GATE
B1517
St Peter's Church
Padley Farm
Cemy
East Road Ind Est
DROVE LANE
THE DROVE
Sch
Kirkby la Thorpe
Field Farm
New Farm
Sleaford Fen
Coll
Kirkby la Thorpe CE Prim Sch
CHURCH LANE
Bouncing Hill
River Slea
WESTGATE
Liby
ST GILES AV
BOSTON ROAD
Bullywells Plantation South
Settlement
W BANKS
SOUTH GATE
RUSSELL CR
MARK AV
Quarry (dis)
Boiling Wells Farm
CASTLE CW
1 COLERIDGE GDNS
2 MILTON WY
3 KEATS DR
Mast
HAWKS WY
ROOKERY AV
Sleaford
Hotel
Bully Wells
CLAY HILL ROAD
GEORGE ST
MAREHAM LANE
MOUNT LANE
Greylees Pits (dis)
HERVEY RD
LONDON ROAD
HAWTHORN DR
BOUNDARY PASTURES
New Ballast Pit
Bone's Farm
GRANTHAM ROAD
ANCASTER DR
Allot Gdns
GRANTHAM RD
NORTHFIELD RD
AIDAN ROAD
OAK RD
Mareham Lane Farm
THE CRESCENT
MANOR RD
TOWN ROAD
OPIRA CL
Quarrington
STUMP CROSS HILL
Kirkby Mount
MOUNT LA
North Field
Mount Plantation
Lodge Farm
Mount Farm
LONDON ROAD
MAREHAM LANE
ROWAN DR
Butt Mound
Church Farm
Cross
Cliff Beck
SCHOOL LA
Sewage Works
Moat
Salt Box Farm
Burton Gorse Plantation
Folk Moot Moat
PH
Chapel (site of)
Silk Willoughby
Chy
WALKS ROAD
NEW RD
Bellhouse Farm
Willoughby Gorse
CHURCH LA 1
WILLOUGHBY CL 2
WHITECROSS LANE
Burton Plantation
GORSE LANE
Bellhouse Plantation
South View Farm
Cross
8
49
7
48
6
47
5
46
4
45
3
44
2
43
1
42
04
05
06
07
08
09
132
122
For full street detail of the highlighted area see page 212.

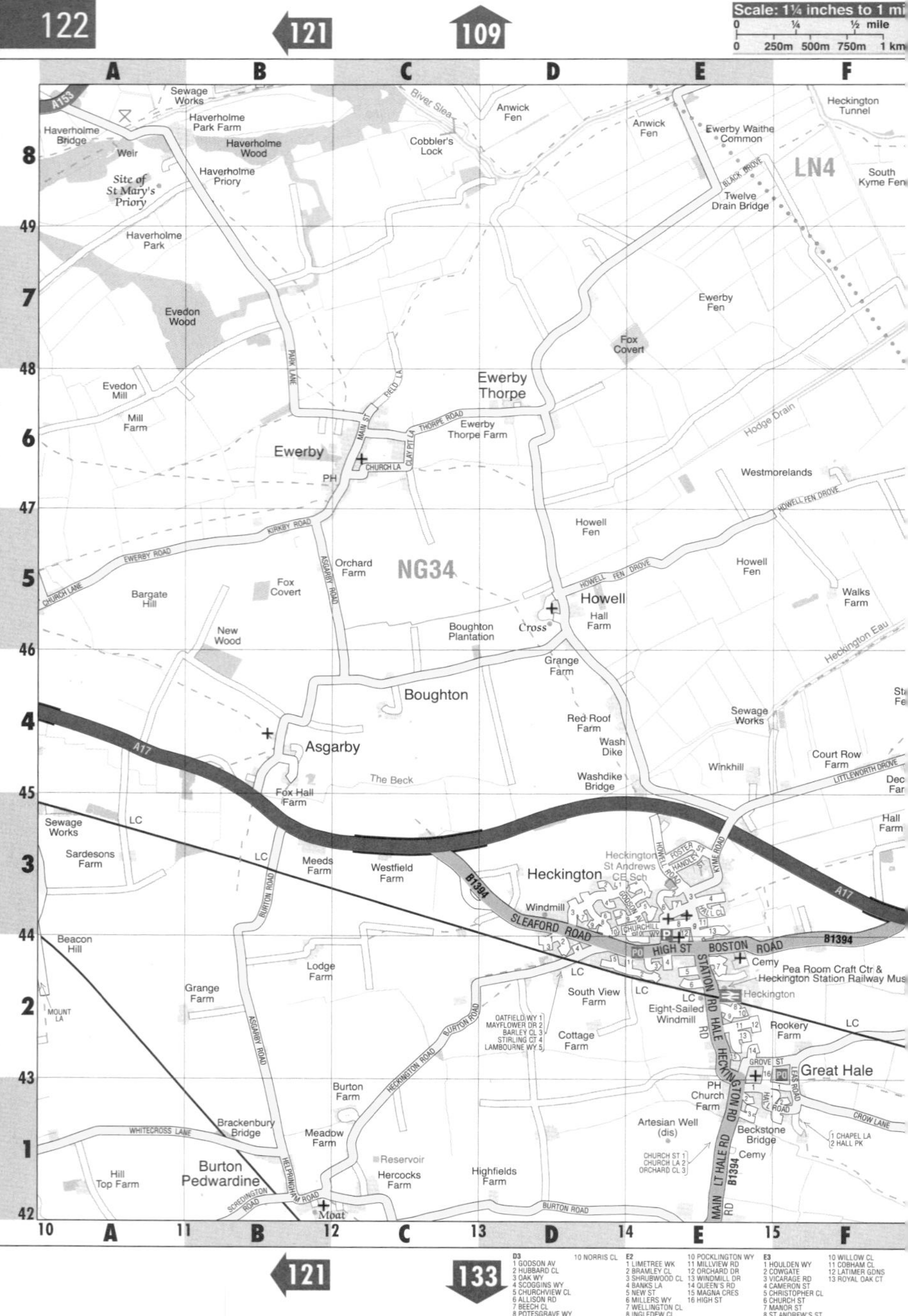
121
109
Scale: 1¼ inches to 1 mi
0 ¼ ½ mile
0 250m 500m 750m 1 km
Sewage Works
Haverholme Bridge
Weir
Haverholme Park Farm
Haverholme Wood
Site of St Mary's Priory
Haverholme Priory
Haverholme Park
Evedon Wood
River Slea
Cobbler's Lock
Anwick Fen
Ewerby Waithe Common
Heckington Tunnel
LN4
South Kyme Fen
Black Drove
Twelve Drain Bridge
Ewerby Fen
Fox Covert
Park Lane
Field La
Evedon Mill
Mill Farm
Ewerby Thorpe
Ewerby Thorpe Farm
Thorpe Road
Main St
Clay Pit La
Church La
Ewerby
PH
Hodge Drain
Westmorelands
Howell Fen Drove
Kirkby Road
Ewerby Road
Church Lane
Howell Fen
Orchard Farm
NG34
Asgarby Road
Fox Covert
Bargate Hill
New Wood
Howell
Hall Farm
Cross
Boughton Plantation
Walks Farm
Heckington Eau
Grange Farm
Boughton
Red Roof Farm
Sewage Works
A17
Asgarby
Wash Dike
Winkhill
Court Row Farm
The Beck
Fox Hall Farm
Washdike Bridge
Littleworth Drove
Sewage Works
LC
Sardesons Farm
Meeds Farm
Westfield Farm
B1394
Heckington
Heckington St Andrews CE Sch
Foster St
Handley St
Howell Road
Kyme Road
Godson Av
Windmill
Churchill Wy
Burton Road
Sleaford Road
High St
Boston Road
PO
Beacon Hill
Lodge Farm
Cemy
Pea Room Craft Ctr & Heckington Station Railway Mus
Grange Farm
South View Farm
Eight-Sailed Windmill
Station Rd
Hale Rd
Heckington
Mount La
Oatfield Wy 1
Mayflower Dr 2
Barley Cl 3
Stirling Ct 4
Lambourne Wy 5
Cottage Farm
Rookery Farm
Asgarby Road
Heckington Road
Heckington Rd
Grove St
Great Hale
Burton Farm
PH
Church Farm
Eastgate
Hall Road
Crow Lane
Artesian Well (dis)
Beckstone Bridge
1 Chapel La
2 Hall Pk
Brackenbury Bridge
Meadow Farm
Whitecross Lane
Church St 1
Church La 2
Orchard Cl 3
Cemy
Reservoir
Hill Top Farm
Burton Pedwardine
Hercocks Farm
Highfields Farm
Helpringham Road
Scredington Road
Moat
Burton Road
Main Rd
Lt Hale Rd
A B C D E F
8 49 7 48 6 47 5 46 4 45 3 44 2 43 1 42
10 11 12 13 14 15
121
133
D3
1 GODSON AV
2 HUBBARD CL
3 OAK WY
4 SCOGGINS WY
5 CHURCHVIEW CL
6 ALLISON RD
7 BEECH CL
8 POTESGRAVE WY
9 BECKETT CL
10 NORRIS CL
E2
1 LIMETREE WK
2 BRAMLEY CL
3 SHRUBWOOD CL
4 BANKS LA
5 NEW ST
6 MILLERS WY
7 WELLINGTON CL
8 INGLEDEW CL
9 HARE CL
10 POCKLINGTON WY
11 MILLVIEW RD
12 ORCHARD DR
13 WINDMILL DR
14 QUEEN'S RD
15 MAGNA CRES
16 HIGH ST
E3
1 HOULDEN WY
2 COWGATE
3 VICARAGE RD
4 CAMERON ST
5 CHRISTOPHER CL
6 CHURCH ST
7 MANOR ST
8 ST ANDREW'S ST
9 EASTGATE
10 WILLOW CL
11 COBHAM CL
12 LATIMER GDNS
13 ROYAL OAK CT

Scale: 1¼ inches to 1 mile
0 ¼ ½ mile
0 250m 500m 750m 1 km
110
124
A B C D E F
Remains of Priory
Kyme Eau
The Manor Farm
Kyme Tower
Manor Farm
South Kyme
Bottom Bridge
Sycamore House
Sutterton Fen
Maryland House
Dovecote Farm
Gooses Farm
Holland Fen
Chestnut House Farm
Mary Land
Sutterton Fen
Pattingden Farm
Fenmore Farm
LN4
Vicarage Farm
Fenmoor Farm
Bridge Farm
South Kyme Fen
Whitehouse Farm
White House Farm
Milt Green Farm
Holland Dike
Sadland Farm
Five Willow Wath Farm
Head Dike
Five Willow Wath Bridge
Holland Fen
Heckington Fen
Glebe Farm
Vine Farm
Whitehouse Farm
Fenside Farm
Star Fen Farm
Car Dyke Farm
Heckington Fen
Settlement (site of)
Holme House
Mast
Six Hundred Farm
Fen Farm
The Fen Prep Sch
PE20
Home Farm
The Rakes
NG34
Catlins Farm
Kane Farm
Poplars Farm
East Heckington
Garwick Farm
College Farm
East Heckington CE Sch
Mile House
Heckington Fen
Rakes Farm
Firths Farm
Parks Farm
Maze Farm
Poplar Farm
Last Farm
Great Hale Fen
Holland Fen
Bridge Farm
Hall Farm
Swineshead Bridge
Crow Lane Farm
White House Farm
Great Hale Eau
Royalty Farm
College Farm
Holland Fen
White House
16 17 18 19 20 21
42 43 44 45 46 47 48 49
1 2 3 4 5 6 7 8
134
124

123 111

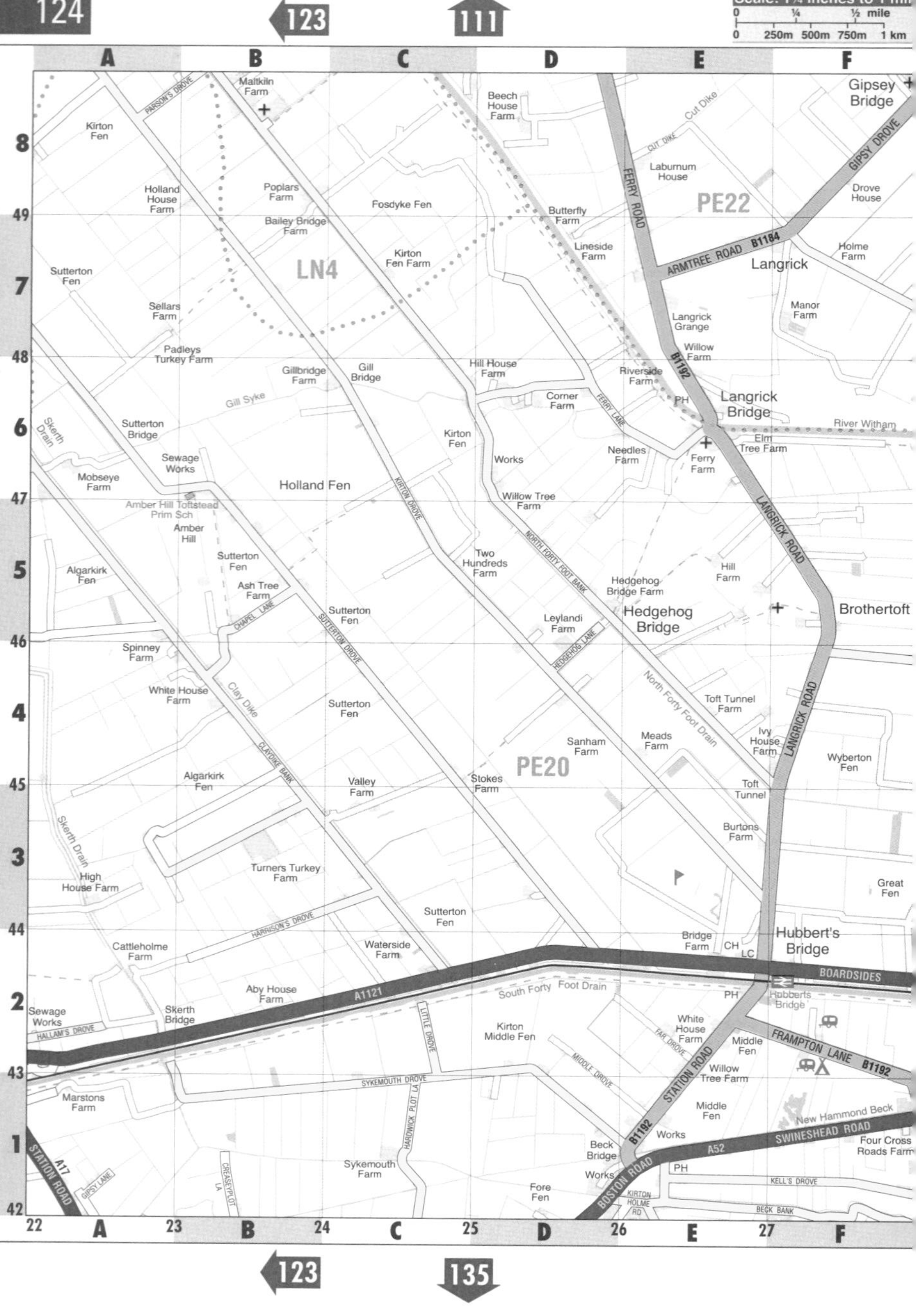

123 135

For full street detail of the highlighted area see pages 208 & 209.

125
113

Scale: 1¼ inches to 1 mile
0 ¼ ½ mile
0 250m 500m 750m 1 km

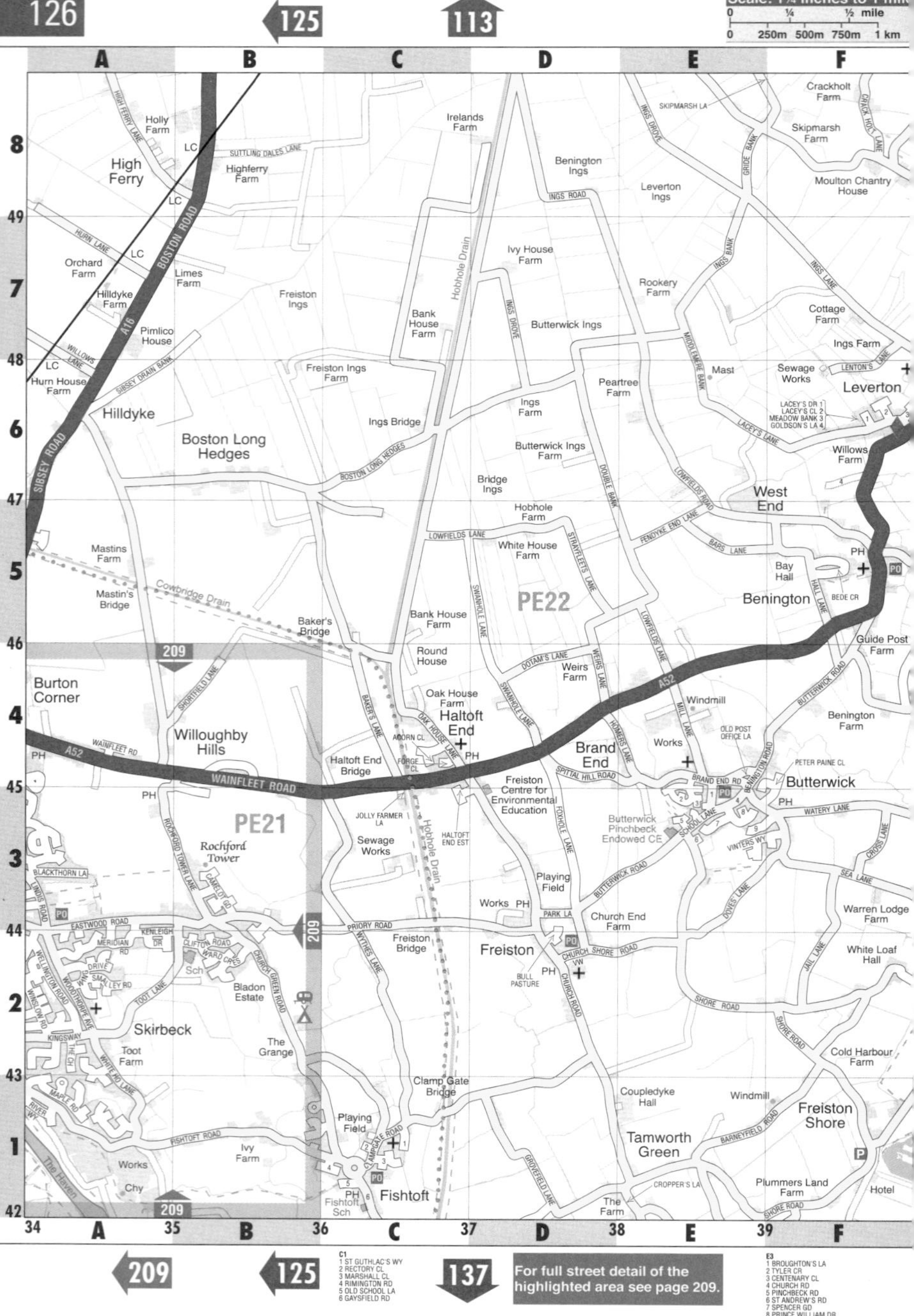

209
125
137

C1
1 ST GUTHLAC'S WY
2 RECTORY CL
3 MARSHALL CL
4 RIMINGTON RD
5 OLD SCHOOL LA
6 GAYSFIELD RD

For full street detail of the highlighted area see page 209.

E3
1 BROUGHTON'S LA
2 TYLER CR
3 CENTENARY CL
4 CHURCH RD
5 PINCHBECK RD
6 ST ANDREW'S RD
7 SPENCER GD
8 PRINCE WILLIAM DR
9 UPSALL RD

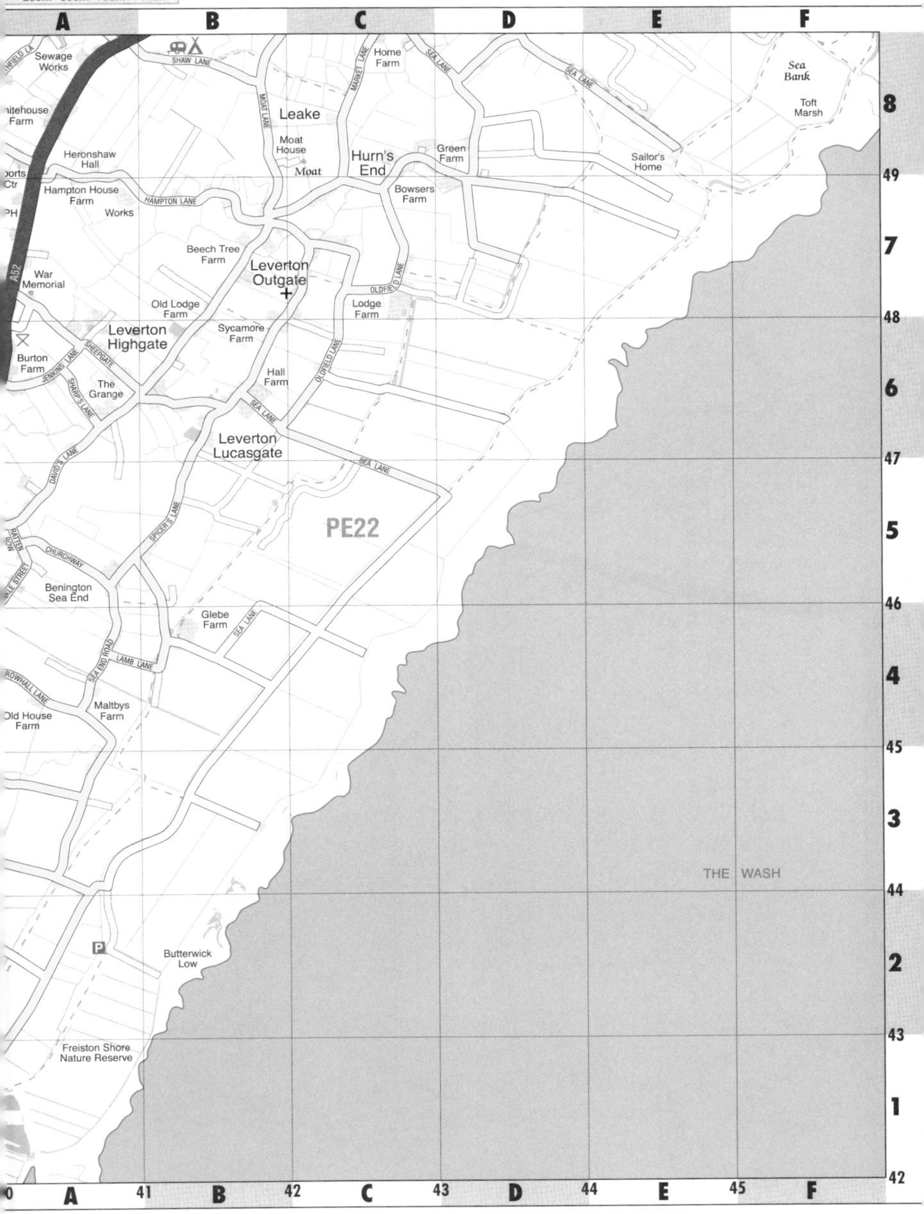
A
B
C
D
E
F
Sewage Works
SHAW LANE
Home Farm
MARKET LANE
SEA LANE
SEA LANE
Sea Bank
Toft Marsh
itehouse Farm
MOAT LANE
Leake
Moat House
Moat
Hurn's End
Green Farm
Heronshaw Hall
Sailor's Home
Hampton House Farm
HAMPTON LANE
Works
Bowsers Farm
Beech Tree Farm
Leverton Outgate
A52
War Memorial
OLDFIELD LANE
Old Lodge Farm
Lodge Farm
Leverton Highgate
Sycamore Farm
Burton Farm
SHEEPGATE
JENKINS LANE
OLDFIELD LANE
Hall Farm
The Grange
SHARP'S LANE
SEA LANE
Leverton Lucasgate
DAVID'S LANE
SEA LANE
PE22
SPICER'S LANE
RATTEN ROW
CHURCHWAY
Benington Sea End
Glebe Farm
SEA LANE
SEA END ROAD
LAMB LANE
ROWHALL LANE
Maltbys Farm
Old House Farm
THE WASH
P
Butterwick Low
Freiston Shore Nature Reserve
8
49
7
48
6
47
5
46
4
45
3
44
2
43
1
42
41
42
43
44
45

A5
1 NOTTINGHAM RD
2 LIME GR
3 WALNUT RD
4 HOOPERS CL
5 GRANBY DR
6 THE PADDOCKS
7 NORTH CR
8 SILVERWOOD RD
9 KEEL DR
10 SCHOOL VW
11 SOUTH CR
12 BELVOIR AV
13 VINE CL
14 HOWITTS RD
15 RUTLAND LA
16 BEECH DR
A6
1 SPIRE VW
2 BEACON VW
3 WIMBISHTHORPE CL
4 BOWBRIDGE GDNS
5 WINTERBECK CL
6 TOLL BAR AV
7 PINFOLD CL
8 RIVERSIDE WLK
9 WEST END CL
10 BOWBRIDGE LA
11 PINFOLD LA
12 FARMHOUSE CL
13 CHURCH VW
14 RIVERSIDE CL
15 ALBERT ST
16 CHAPEL ST
17 DEVON LA
18 ST MARY'S CL
19 BECKINGTHORPE DR
20 DAYBELL CL
21 WYGGESTON RD
22 WYGGESTON AV
117
F7
1 PARK RD
2 SIDE ST
3 THE GREEN
4 LAMBERT RD
5 BACK LA
6 MANOR PADDOCK
Scale: 1¼ inches to 1 m
0 ¼ ½ mile
0 250m 500m 750m 1 km
A B C D E F
8 41 7 40 6 39 5 38 4 37 3 36 2 35 1 34
80 81 82 83 84 85
SEWSTERN LA
Thackson Well Farm
Airfield (dis)
Ease Drain
Moss Plantation
LOWFIELDS LANE
Lowfields Farm
Earthworks
Normanton
Little Covert Farm
Allington
FOSTON LANE
SEWSTERN LANE
Elm Farm
Home Farm
Viking Way
West Wong Plantation
PK AV
PO
Endcliffe Farm
Sewage Works
Beacon Hill
BOTTESFORD ROAD
Dalestorth Farm
NORMANTON LANE
Mast
Glebe Farm
PEACH LA
Salt Well
SEDGEBROOK ROAD
LC
NG13
Bottesford
QUEEN ST
STATION ROAD
Bottesford
1 CHESTNUT CL
2 OLD STATION YD
3 FLEMING AV
4 VAUGHAN AV
The Debdale
Keeper's Plantation
Barn Farm
HIGH ST
RECTORY LA
SKERRY LANE
Manor Farm
Liby
Easthorpe
CHURCH ST
EASTHORPE RD
ALLINGTON ROAD
BARKESTONE LANE
BELVOIR ROAD
MARKET ST
MANOR ROAD
GRANTHAM ROAD
Coxs Walk Farm
WHATTON'S CL 1
CHURCH LA 2
Station Farm
GREEN LA
CASTLE VW RD
MUSTON LANE
GRANTHAM ROAD
LC
Belvoir High Sch
Castle View Farm
Muston
SKERRY LA
PH
Sedgebrook Manor
Winterbeck Bridge
EASTHORPE LANE
Hospital Farm
Sedgebrook
A52
A52 Nottingham
B5
1 EASTHORPE RD
2 EASTHORPE VW
3 CASTLE CL
4 WALKERS CL
MAIN ST
CHURCH LANE
A52
CASTLE VIEW ROAD
Peacock Farm
Toston Hill
Cross
Mill Farm
Willow Bridge
NG32
WOOLSTHORPE LANE
VILLAGE ST 1
BOWMANS WY 2
ABBEY LA 3
SCHOOL LA 4
BELVOIR ROAD
Shipman's Plantation
Muston Bridge
WOOLSTHORPE LANE
Weir
Hill Farm
Grantham Canal
Viking Way
Breeder Hills Farm
DENTON LANE
Longore Bridge
Moat
Weir
Nottinghamshire STREET ATLAS
Nature Reserve
Grantham Canal (dis)
Stenwith Bridge
Casthorpe Farm
Stenwith
Weir
Muston Gorse Covert
Muston Gorse
Muston Gorse Farm
Grange Farm
SEDGEBROOK ROAD
Woolsthorpe Bridge
BELVOIR ROAD
Mansells Barn Farm
PH
Locks
Longmoor Bridge
LONG LANE
Belvoir Farm
Saltbeck
HILLSIDE RD 1
WORTHINGTON LA 2
BELVOIR LA 3
Sewage Works
Cliff Wood
Glebe Farm
Viking Way
The Bushes
VILLAGE STREET
CLIFF ROAD
Woolsthorpe by Belvoir
PO
PH
Lane's Plantation

For full street detail of the highlighted area see pages 210 & 211.

139 130 211

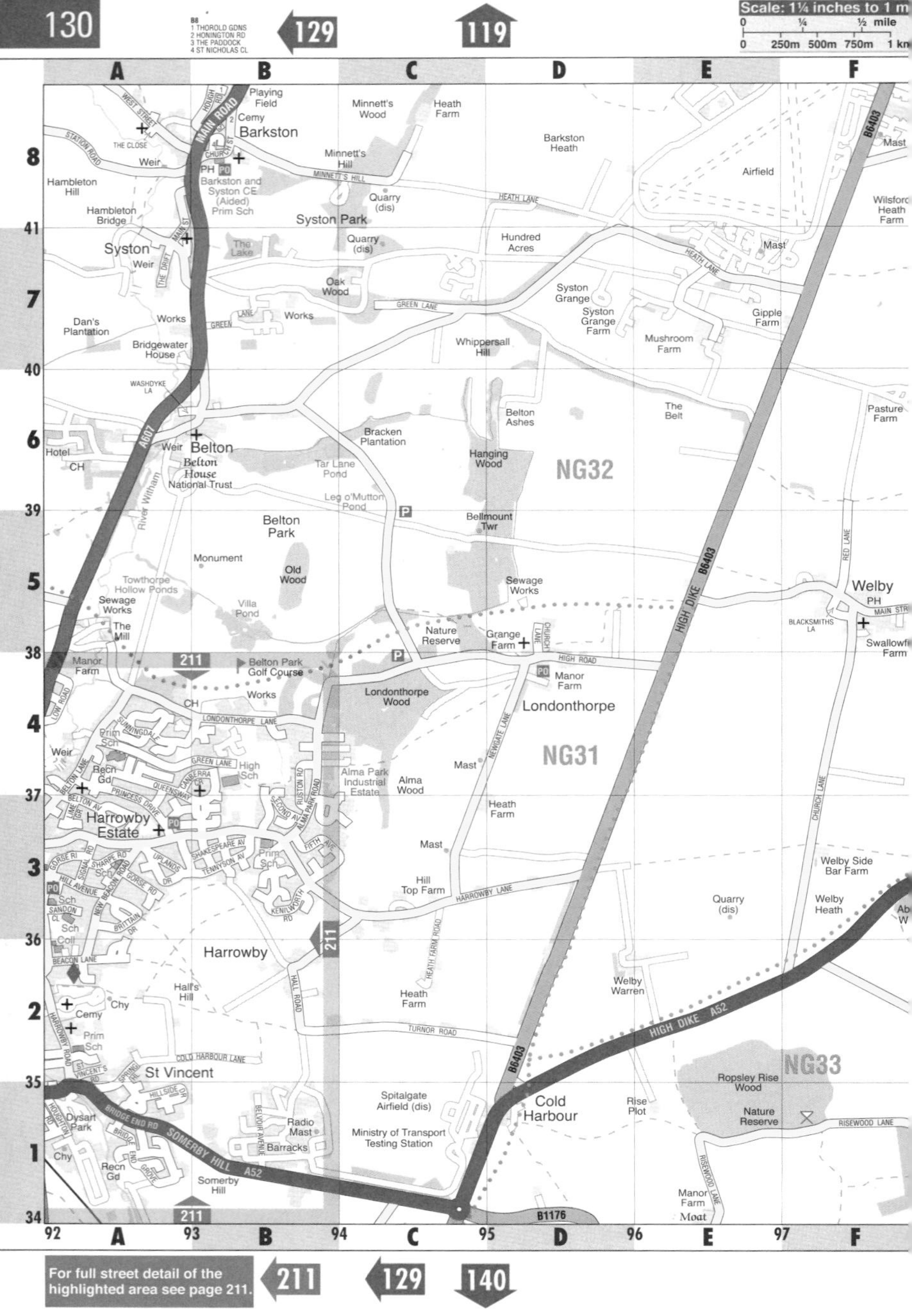
Barkston
Playing Field
Cemy
Minnett's Wood
Heath Farm
Barkston Heath
Airfield
Mast
Minnett's Hill
Hambleton Hill
Barkston and Syston CE (Aided) Prim Sch
Quarry (dis)
Hambleton Bridge
Syston Park
Wilsford Heath Farm
Syston
The Lake
Hundred Acres
Oak Wood
Syston Grange
Syston Grange Farm
Gipple Farm
Dan's Plantation
Works
Bridgewater House
Whippersall Hill
Mushroom Farm
Belton Ashes
The Belt
Pasture Farm
Belton
Belton House
National Trust
Bracken Plantation
Tar Lane Pond
Hanging Wood
NG32
Leg o'Mutton Pond
Belton Park
Bellmount Twr
Monument
Old Wood
Towthorpe Hollow Ponds
Sewage Works
Welby
Villa Pond
The Mill
Nature Reserve
Grange Farm
Swallowfield Farm
Manor Farm
Belton Park Golf Course
Londonthorpe Wood
Londonthorpe
NG31
Alma Park Industrial Estate
Alma Wood
Harrowby Estate
Hill Top Farm
Welby Side Bar Farm
Welby Heath
Harrowby
Hall's Hill
Welby Warren
St Vincent
NG33
Ropsley Rise Wood
Spitalgate Airfield (dis)
Cold Harbour
Rise Plot
Dysart Park
Radio Mast
Ministry of Transport Testing Station
Barracks
Somerby Hill
Moat
HIGH DIKE
A52
B6403
A607
B1176
211

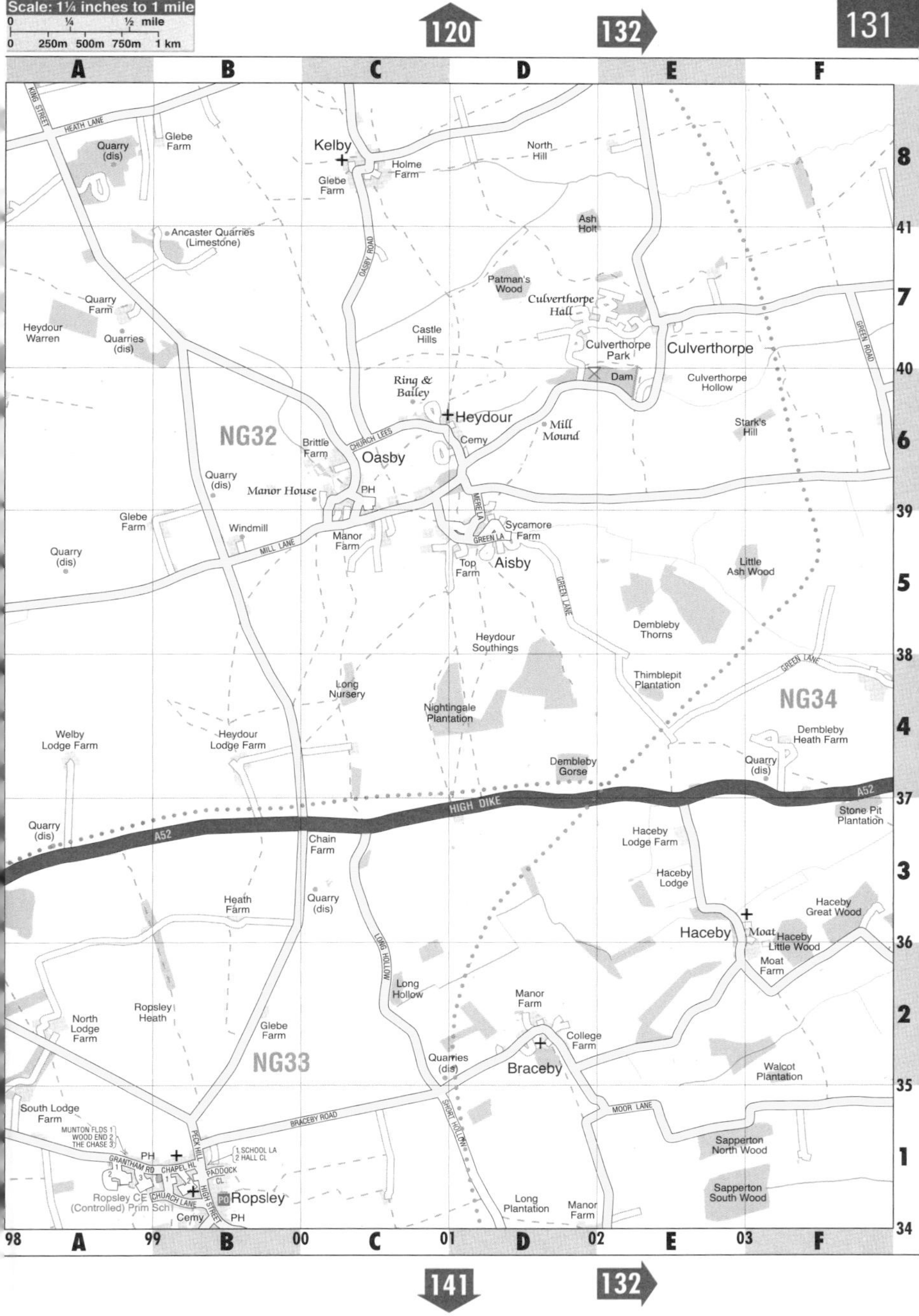
Scale: 1¼ inches to 1 mile
0 ¼ ½ mile
0 250m 500m 750m 1 km
120
132
A B C D E F
KING STREET
HEATH LANE
Quarry (dis)
Glebe Farm
Kelby
Holme Farm
Glebe Farm
North Hill
Ancaster Quarries (Limestone)
OASBY ROAD
Ash Holt
Patman's Wood
Culverthorpe Hall
Quarry Farm
Heydour Warren
Quarries (dis)
Castle Hills
Culverthorpe Park
Culverthorpe
GREEN ROAD
Dam
Culverthorpe Hollow
Ring & Bailey
Heydour
NG32
Brittle Farm
CHURCH LEES
Oasby
Cemy
Mill Mound
Stark's Hill
Quarry (dis)
Manor House
PH
Glebe Farm
Windmill
MERE LA
Sycamore Farm
GREEN LA
Manor Farm
MILL LANE
Quarry (dis)
Top Farm
Aisby
GREEN LANE
Little Ash Wood
Dembleby Thorns
Heydour Southings
Thimblepit Plantation
GREEN LANE
Long Nursery
NG34
Nightingale Plantation
Welby Lodge Farm
Heydour Lodge Farm
Dembleby Heath Farm
Dembleby Gorse
Quarry (dis)
HIGH DIKE
A52
Stone Pit Plantation
Quarry (dis)
A52
Chain Farm
Haceby Lodge Farm
Haceby Lodge
Heath Farm
Quarry (dis)
Haceby Great Wood
Haceby
Moat
Haceby Little Wood
LONG HOLLOW
Moat Farm
Long Hollow
Manor Farm
Ropsley Heath
North Lodge Farm
Glebe Farm
College Farm
NG33
Quarries (dis)
Braceby
Walcot Plantation
South Lodge Farm
BRACEBY ROAD
MOOR LANE
SHORT HOLLOW
MUNTON FLDS 1
WOOD END 2
THE CHASE 3
PH
PECK HILL
1 SCHOOL LA
2 HALL CL
Sapperton North Wood
GRANTHAM RD
CHAPEL HL
PADDOCK CL
Ropsley CE (Controlled) Prim Sch
CHURCH LANE
HIGH STREET
PO
Ropsley
Cemy
PH
Long Plantation
Manor Farm
Sapperton South Wood
8
41
7
40
6
39
5
38
4
37
3
36
2
35
1
34
98 99 00 01 02 03
141
132

131
121

Scale: 1¼ inches to 1 mile

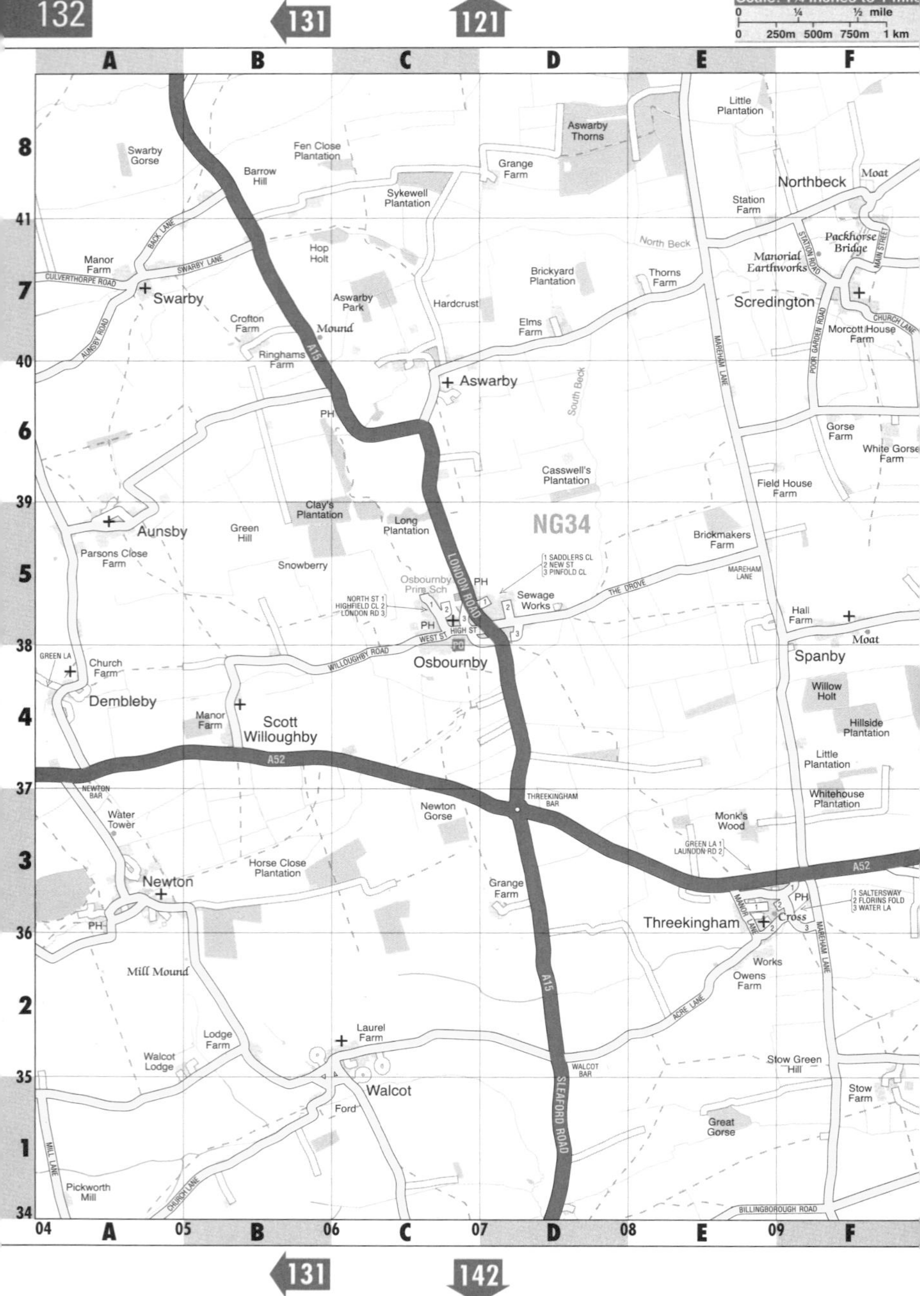

131
142

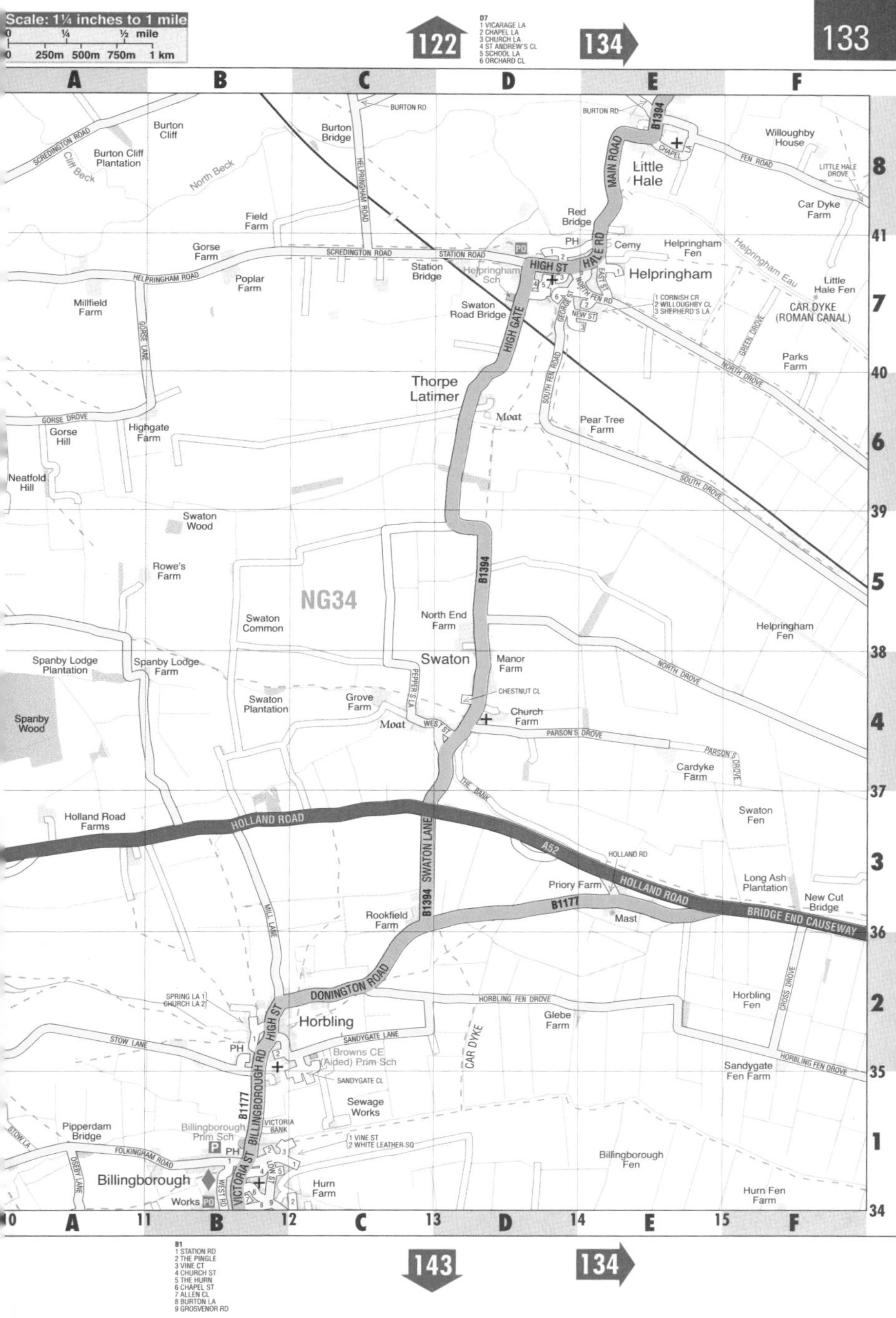
Scale: 1¼ inches to 1 mile
0 ¼ ½ mile
0 250m 500m 750m 1 km
122
D7
1 VICARAGE LA
2 CHAPEL LA
3 CHURCH LA
4 ST ANDREW'S CL
5 SCHOOL LA
6 ORCHARD CL
134
Burton Cliff
Burton Cliff Plantation
Cliff Beck
North Beck
Burton Bridge
BURTON RD
HELPRINGHAM ROAD
SCREDINGTON ROAD
B1394
Willoughby House
CHAPEL LA
FEN ROAD
LITTLE HALE DROVE
Little Hale
MAIN ROAD
Car Dyke Farm
Field Farm
Red Bridge
PH
Cemy
Helpringham Fen
Helpringham Eau
Gorse Farm
STATION ROAD
PO
HIGH ST
HALE RD
Helpringham
Station Bridge
Helpringham Sch
Poplar Farm
Little Hale Fen
Millfield Farm
Swaton Road Bridge
NORTH FEN RD
EAST ST
GEORGE ST
NEW ST
1 CORNISH CR
2 WILLOUGHBY CL
3 SHEPHERD'S LA
CAR DYKE (ROMAN CANAL)
GORSE LANE
HIGH GATE
GREEN DROVE
SOUTH FEN ROAD
Parks Farm
NORTH DROVE
Thorpe Latimer
GORSE DROVE
Gorse Hill
Highgate Farm
Moat
Pear Tree Farm
Neatfold Hill
SOUTH DROVE
Swaton Wood
Rowe's Farm
NG34
Swaton Common
North End Farm
Helpringham Fen
Spanby Lodge Plantation
Spanby Lodge Farm
Swaton
Manor Farm
NORTH DROVE
CHESTNUT CL
Spanby Wood
Swaton Plantation
Grove Farm
PEPPER'S LA
Church Farm
Moat
WEST ST
PARSON'S DROVE
Cardyke Farm
THE BANK
Holland Road Farms
HOLLAND ROAD
Swaton Fen
A52
HOLLAND RD
Priory Farm
Long Ash Plantation
New Cut Bridge
MILL LANE
B1394 SWATON LANE
B1177
Mast
BRIDGE END CAUSEWAY
Rookfield Farm
DONINGTON ROAD
CROSS DROVE
SPRING LA 1
CHURCH LA 2
HORBLING FEN DROVE
Glebe Farm
Horbling Fen
Horbling
STOW LANE
SANDYGATE LANE
CAR DYKE
PH
Browns CE (Aided) Prim Sch
Sandygate Fen Farm
SANDYGATE CL
Sewage Works
B1177
BILLINGBOROUGH RD
Pipperdam Bridge
Billingborough Prim Sch
VICTORIA BANK
1 VINE ST
2 WHITE LEATHER SQ
STOW LA
FOLKINGHAM ROAD
PH
Billingborough Fen
OSEBY LANE
Billingborough
WEST RD
VICTORIA ST
LOW ST
Hurn Farm
Hurn Fen Farm
Works
PO
A B C D E F
10 11 12 13 14 15
8 41 7 40 6 39 5 38 4 37 3 36 2 35 1 34
B1
1 STATION RD
2 THE PINGLE
3 VINE CT
4 CHURCH ST
5 THE HURN
6 CHAPEL ST
7 ALLEN CL
8 BURTON LA
9 GROSVENOR RD
143
134

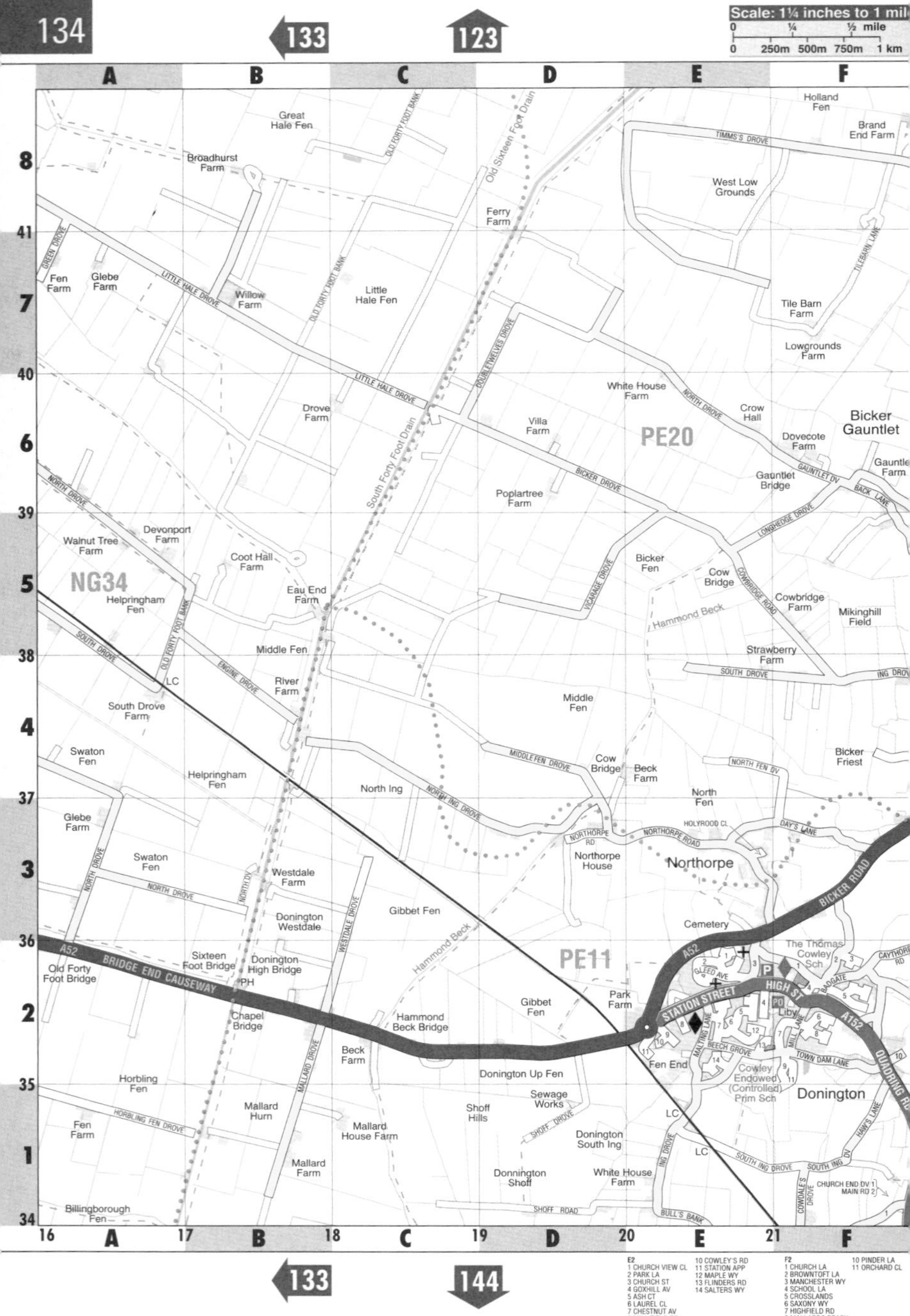
133
123
Scale: 1¼ inches to 1 mile
0 ¼ ½ mile
0 250m 500m 750m 1 km
Great Hale Fen
Broadhurst Farm
OLD FORTY FOOT BANK
Old Sixteen Foot Drain
Holland Fen
Brand End Farm
TIMMS'S DROVE
West Low Grounds
Ferry Farm
GREEN DROVE
Fen Farm
Glebe Farm
LITTLE HALE DROVE
Willow Farm
Little Hale Fen
TILEBARN LANE
Tile Barn Farm
Lowgrounds Farm
DOUBLETWELVES DROVE
White House Farm
NORTH DROVE
Crow Hall
Bicker Gauntlet
Drove Farm
Villa Farm
PE20
Dovecote Farm
Gauntlet Farm
Gauntlet Bridge
GAUNTLET DV
BACK LANE
BICKER DROVE
South Forty Foot Drain
Poplartree Farm
LONGHEDGE DROVE
Devonport Farm
Walnut Tree Farm
Coot Hall Farm
NG34
Bicker Fen
Cow Bridge
VICARAGE DROVE
COWBRIDGE ROAD
Cowbridge Farm
Mikinghill Field
Helpringham Fen
Eau End Farm
Hammond Beck
SOUTH DROVE
Middle Fen
Strawberry Farm
ENGINE DROVE
River Farm
LC
South Drove Farm
ING DROVE
Middle Fen
Swaton Fen
MIDDLE FEN DROVE
Cow Bridge
Beck Farm
NORTH FEN DV
Bicker Friest
Helpringham Fen
North Ing
NORTH ING DROVE
North Fen
Glebe Farm
HOLYROOD CL
DAY'S LANE
NORTHORPE RD
NORTHORPE ROAD
Swaton Fen
NORTH DROVE
Westdale Farm
NORTH DV
Northorpe House
Northorpe
BICKER ROAD
Donington Westdale
WESTDALE DROVE
Gibbet Fen
Cemetery
The Thomas Cowley Sch
CAYTHORPE RD
A52
BRIDGE END CAUSEWAY
Old Forty Foot Bridge
Sixteen Foot Bridge
Donington High Bridge
PH
Hammond Beck
PE11
GLEED AVE
HIGH ST
BADGATE
P
PO
Park Farm
STATION STREET
Gibbet Fen
Chapel Bridge
Hammond Beck Bridge
MALTING LANE
Liby
MILL LANE
A152
QUADRING RD
BEECH GROVE
TOWN DAM LANE
Beck Farm
Fen End
Cowley Endowed (Controlled) Prim Sch
Donington
Donington Up Fen
Horbling Fen
Sewage Works
MALLARD DROVE
Mallard Hurn
Shoff Hills
SHOFF DROVE
HAW'S LANE
HORBLING FEN DROVE
Fen Farm
Mallard House Farm
LC
Donington South Ing
ING DROVE
LC
SOUTH ING DROVE
SOUTH ING DV
Mallard Farm
Donnington Shoff
White House Farm
COWDALE'S DROVE
CHURCH END DV 1
MAIN RD 2
Billingborough Fen
SHOFF ROAD
BULL'S BANK
A B C D E F
8 41 7 40 6 39 5 38 4 37 3 36 2 35 1 34
16 17 18 19 20 21
133
144
E2
1 CHURCH VIEW CL
2 PARK LA
3 CHURCH ST
4 GOXHILL AV
5 ASH CT
6 LAUREL CL
7 CHESTNUT AV
8 MILL FIELD RD
9 BARNES RD
10 COWLEY'S RD
11 STATION APP
12 MAPLE WY
13 FLINDERS RD
14 SALTERS WY
F2
1 CHURCH LA
2 BROWNTOFT LA
3 MANCHESTER WY
4 SCHOOL LA
5 CROSSLANDS
6 SAXONY WY
7 HIGHFIELD RD
8 MALLARDS REACH
9 LINDUM WY
10 PINDER LA
11 ORCHARD CL

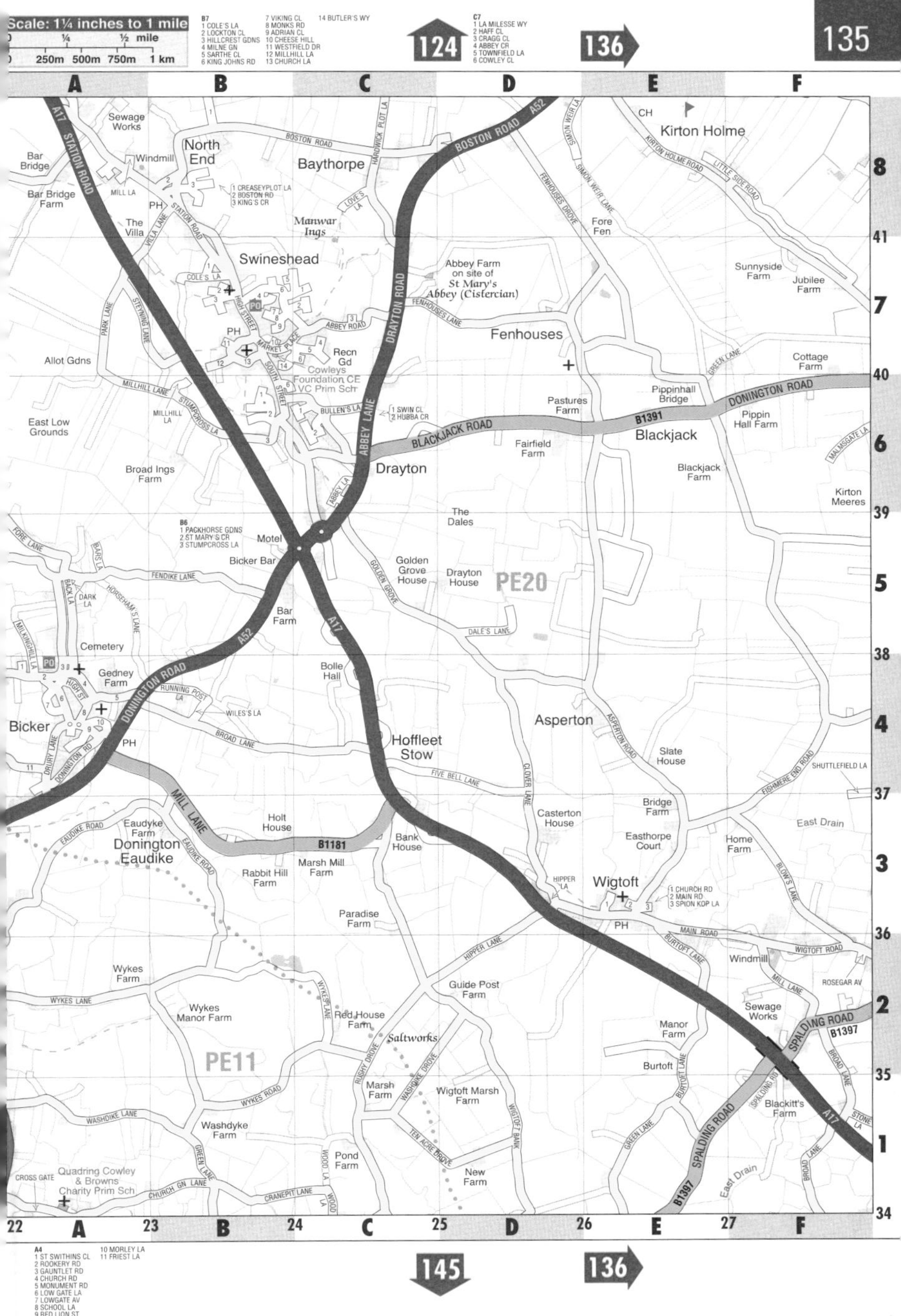

Scale: 1¼ inches to 1 mile
¼ ½ mile
250m 500m 750m 1 km
B7
1 COLE'S LA
2 LOCKTON CL
3 HILLCREST GDNS
4 MILNE GN
5 SARTHE CL
6 KING JOHNS RD
7 VIKING CL
8 MONKS RD
9 ADRIAN CL
10 CHEESE HILL
11 WESTFIELD DR
12 MILLHILL LA
13 CHURCH LA
14 BUTLER'S WY
124
136
C7
1 LA MILESSE WY
2 HAFF CL
3 CRAGG CL
4 ABBEY CR
5 TOWNFIELD LA
6 COWLEY CL
A
B
C
D
E
F
8
41
7
40
6
39
5
38
4
37
3
36
2
35
1
34
Sewage Works
Bar Bridge
Windmill
North End
Baythorpe
Bar Bridge Farm
MILL LA
PH
1 CREASEYPLOT LA
2 BOSTON RD
3 KING'S CR
The Villa
Manwar Ings
Swineshead
A17 STATION ROAD
STATION ROAD
VILLA LANE
BOSTON ROAD
HARDWICK PLOT LA
LOVE'S LA
A52 BOSTON ROAD
DRAYTON ROAD
CH
Kirton Holme
KIRTON HOLME ROAD
LITTLE SIDE ROAD
SIMON WEIR LA
SIMON WEIR LANE
FENHOUSES DROVE
Fore Fen
Abbey Farm on site of St Mary's Abbey (Cistercian)
Sunnyside Farm
Jubilee Farm
COLE'S LA
HIGH STREET
PO
PH
MARKET PLACE
ABBEY ROAD
FENHOUSES LANE
Fenhouses
Recn Gd
Allot Gdns
PARK LANE
STEYNING LANE
SOUTH STREET
Cowleys Foundation CE VC Prim Sch
GREEN LANE
Cottage Farm
MILLHILL LANE
STUMPCROSS LA
MILLHILL LA
BULLEN'S LA
1 SWIN CL
2 HUBBA CR
ABBEY LANE
Pastures Farm
Pippinhall Bridge
DONINGTON ROAD
B1391
Blackjack
Pippin Hall Farm
East Low Grounds
BLACKJACK ROAD
Fairfield Farm
MALMSGATE LA
Broad Ings Farm
Drayton
Blackjack Farm
ABBEY LA
Kirton Meeres
The Dales
B6
1 PACKHORSE GDNS
2 ST MARY'S CR
3 STUMPCROSS LA
Motel
FORE LANE
BARS LA
Bicker Bar
FENDIKE LANE
Golden Grove House
GOLDEN GROVE
Drayton House
PE20
BACK LA
DARK LA
HORSEHAM'S LANE
Bar Farm
A52
A17
DALE'S LANE
MILKINGHILL LA
Cemetery
PO
Gedney Farm
HIGH ST
Bolle Hall
DONINGTON ROAD
RUNNING POST LA
WILES'S LA
Bicker
PH
Asperton
DRURY LANE
DONINGTON RD
BROAD LANE
Hoffleet Stow
ASPERTON ROAD
Slate House
SHUTTLEFIELD LA
FIVE BELL LANE
CLOVER LANE
FISHMERE END ROAD
MILL LANE
Holt House
Casterton House
Bridge Farm
East Drain
Eaudyke Farm
EAUDIKE ROAD
Donington Eaudike
EAUDYKE ROAD
B1181
Bank House
Easthorpe Court
Home Farm
Rabbit Hill Farm
Marsh Mill Farm
HIPPER LA
Wigtoft
1 CHURCH RD
2 MAIN RD
3 SPION KOP LA
BLOW'S LANE
Paradise Farm
PH
MAIN ROAD
BURTOFT LANE
WIGTOFT ROAD
Windmill
HIPPER LANE
Wykes Farm
Guide Post Farm
MILL LANE
ROSEGAR AV
WYKES LANE
Wykes Manor Farm
WYKES LA
Red House Farm
Sewage Works
SPALDING ROAD
B1397
Saltworks
Manor Farm
PE11
Burtoft
BROAD LANE
RUSHY DROVE
Marsh Farm
WASHDIKE DROVE
Wigtoft Marsh Farm
WIGTOFT BANK
BURTOFT LANE
SPALDING RD
Blackitt's Farm
WYKES ROAD
WASHDIKE LANE
STONE LA
Washdyke Farm
GREEN LANE
TEN ACRE DROVE
GREEN LANE
SPALDING ROAD
A17
Pond Farm
WOOD LA
New Farm
BROAD LANE
Quadring Cowley & Browns Charity Prim Sch
CROSS GATE
CHURCH GN LANE
CRANEPIT LANE
WOOD LA
B1397
East Drain
22
23
24
25
26
27
A4
1 ST SWITHINS CL
2 ROOKERY RD
3 GAUNTLET RD
4 CHURCH RD
5 MONUMENT RD
6 LOW GATE LA
7 LOWGATE AV
8 SCHOOL LA
9 RED LION ST
10 MORLEY LA
11 FRIEST LA
145
136

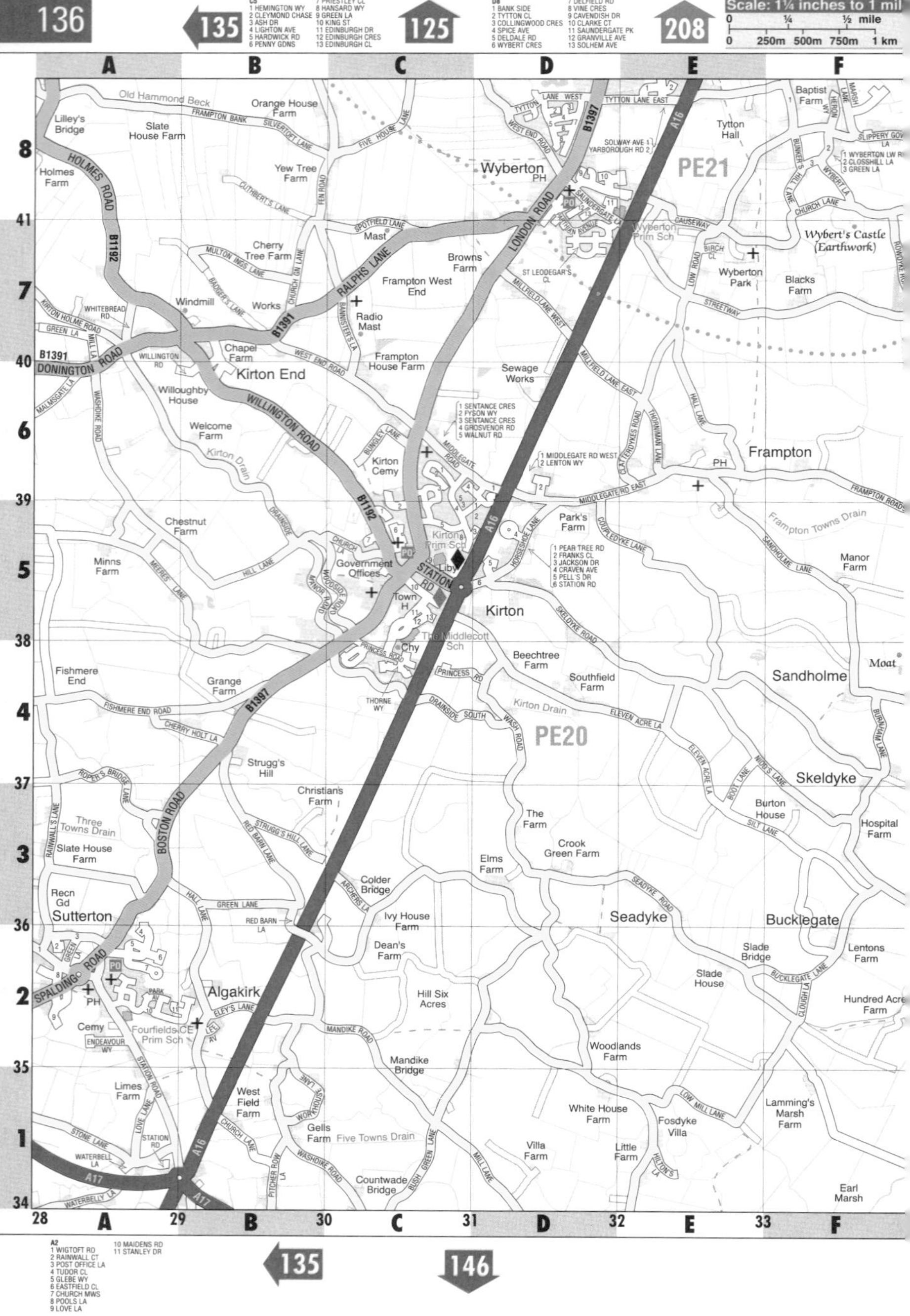
135
125
208
Scale: 1¼ inches to 1 mile
0 ¼ ½ mile
0 250m 500m 750m 1 km
C5
1 HEMINGTON WY
2 CLEYMOND CHASE
3 ASH DR
4 LIGHTON AVE
5 HARDWICK RD
6 PENNY GDNS
7 PRIESTLEY CL
8 HANSARD WY
9 GREEN LA
10 KING ST
11 EDINBURGH DR
12 EDINBURGH CRES
13 EDINBURGH CL
D8
1 BANK SIDE
2 TYTTON CL
3 COLLINGWOOD CRES
4 SPICE AVE
5 DELDALE RD
6 WYBERT CRES
7 DELFIELD RD
8 VINE CRES
9 CAVENDISH DR
10 CLARKE CT
11 SAUNDERGATE PK
12 GRANVILLE AVE
13 SOLHEM AVE
A B C D E F
8 41 7 40 6 39 5 38 4 37 3 36 2 35 1 34
28 29 30 31 32 33
Old Hammond Beck
Lilley's Bridge
Slate House Farm
Orange House Farm
Holmes Farm
HOLMES ROAD
Yew Tree Farm
Wyberton
PE21
Tytton Hall
Baptist Farm
Wybert's Castle (Earthwork)
Wyberton Park
Blacks Farm
Cherry Tree Farm
Mast
Browns Farm
Frampton West End
Radio Mast
Windmill
Works
RALPHS LANE
LONDON ROAD
Chapel Farm
Kirton End
DONINGTON ROAD
Willoughby House
Frampton House Farm
Sewage Works
WILLINGTON ROAD
Welcome Farm
Kirton Drain
Kirton Cemy
Frampton
Chestnut Farm
Park's Farm
Frampton Towns Drain
Minns Farm
Government Offices
STATION RD
Kirton
Manor Farm
Town H
The Middlecott Sch
Beechtree Farm
Fishmere End
Grange Farm
Southfield Farm
Sandholme
Moat
PE20
Strugg's Hill
Skeldyke
Christians Farm
Burton House
Hospital Farm
Three Towns Drain
The Farm
Slate House Farm
Crook Green Farm
BOSTON ROAD
Elms Farm
Colder Bridge
Recn Gd
Sutterton
Ivy House Farm
Seadyke
Bucklegate
Dean's Farm
Slade Bridge
Lentons Farm
Slade House
SPALDING ROAD
Algakirk
Hill Six Acres
Hundred Acre Farm
Cemy
Fourfields CE Prim Sch
Woodlands Farm
Mandike Bridge
Limes Farm
West Field Farm
White House Farm
Lamming's Marsh Farm
Fosdyke Villa
Gells Farm
Five Towns Drain
Villa Farm
Little Farm
Countwade Bridge
Earl Marsh
A16
A17
B1397
B1192
B1391
A2
1 WIGTOFT RD
2 RAINWALL CT
3 POST OFFICE LA
4 TUDOR CL
5 GLEBE WY
6 EASTFIELD CL
7 CHURCH MWS
8 POOLS LA
9 LOVE LA
10 MAIDENS RD
11 STANLEY DR
135
146

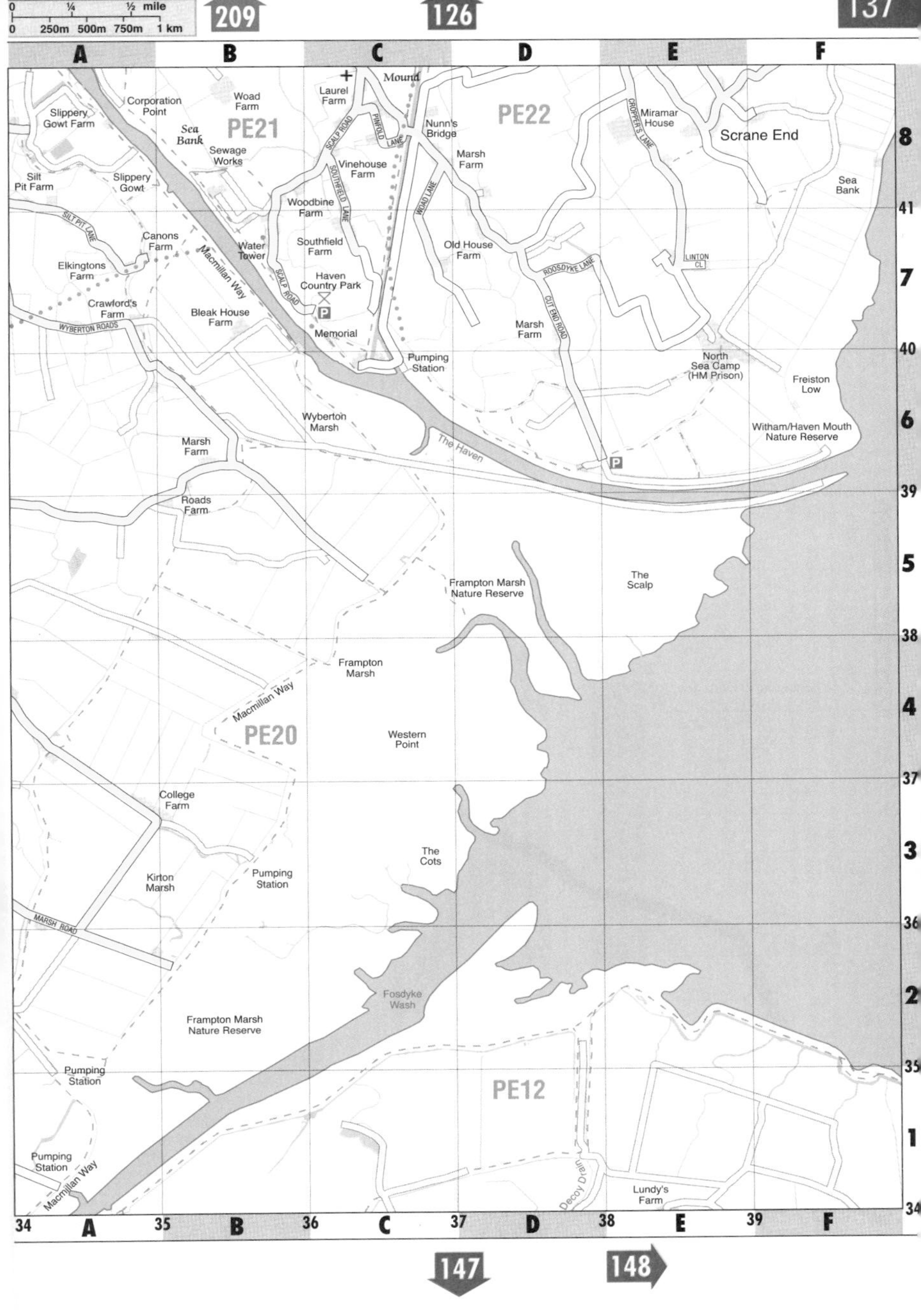

Scale: 1¼ inches to 1 mile
0 ¼ ½ mile
0 250m 500m 750m 1 km
209
126
A B C D E F
Slippery Gowt Farm
Corporation Point
Wood Farm
Laurel Farm
Mound
PE21
PE22
Sea Bank
Sewage Works
Nunn's Bridge
Miramar House
Scrane End
Silt Pit Farm
Slippery Gowt
Vinehouse Farm
Marsh Farm
Sea Bank
Woodbine Farm
Canons Farm
Water Tower
Southfield Farm
Old House Farm
Elkingtons Farm
Macmillan Way
Haven Country Park
Crawford's Farm
Bleak House Farm
Memorial
Marsh Farm
Pumping Station
North Sea Camp (HM Prison)
Freiston Low
Wyberton Marsh
Marsh Farm
The Haven
Witham/Haven Mouth Nature Reserve
Roads Farm
Frampton Marsh Nature Reserve
The Scalp
Frampton Marsh
Macmillan Way
PE20
Western Point
College Farm
The Cots
Kirton Marsh
Pumping Station
Fosdyke Wash
Frampton Marsh Nature Reserve
Pumping Station
PE12
Pumping Station
Macmillan Way
Decoy Drain
Lundy's Farm
SILT PIT LANE
WYBERTON ROADS
SCALP ROAD
PINFOLD LANE
SOUTHFIELD LANE
WOAD LANE
CROPPER'S LANE
LINTON CL
ROOSDYKE LANE
CUT END ROAD
MARSH ROAD
8 41 7 40 6 39 5 38 4 37 3 36 2 35 1 34
34 35 36 37 38 39
147
148

128

D4
1 CHAPEL LA
2 CHURCH LA
3 THORPES LA
4 TOP RD
5 SCHOOL LA
6 SHIRES DR
7 MILL LA

150

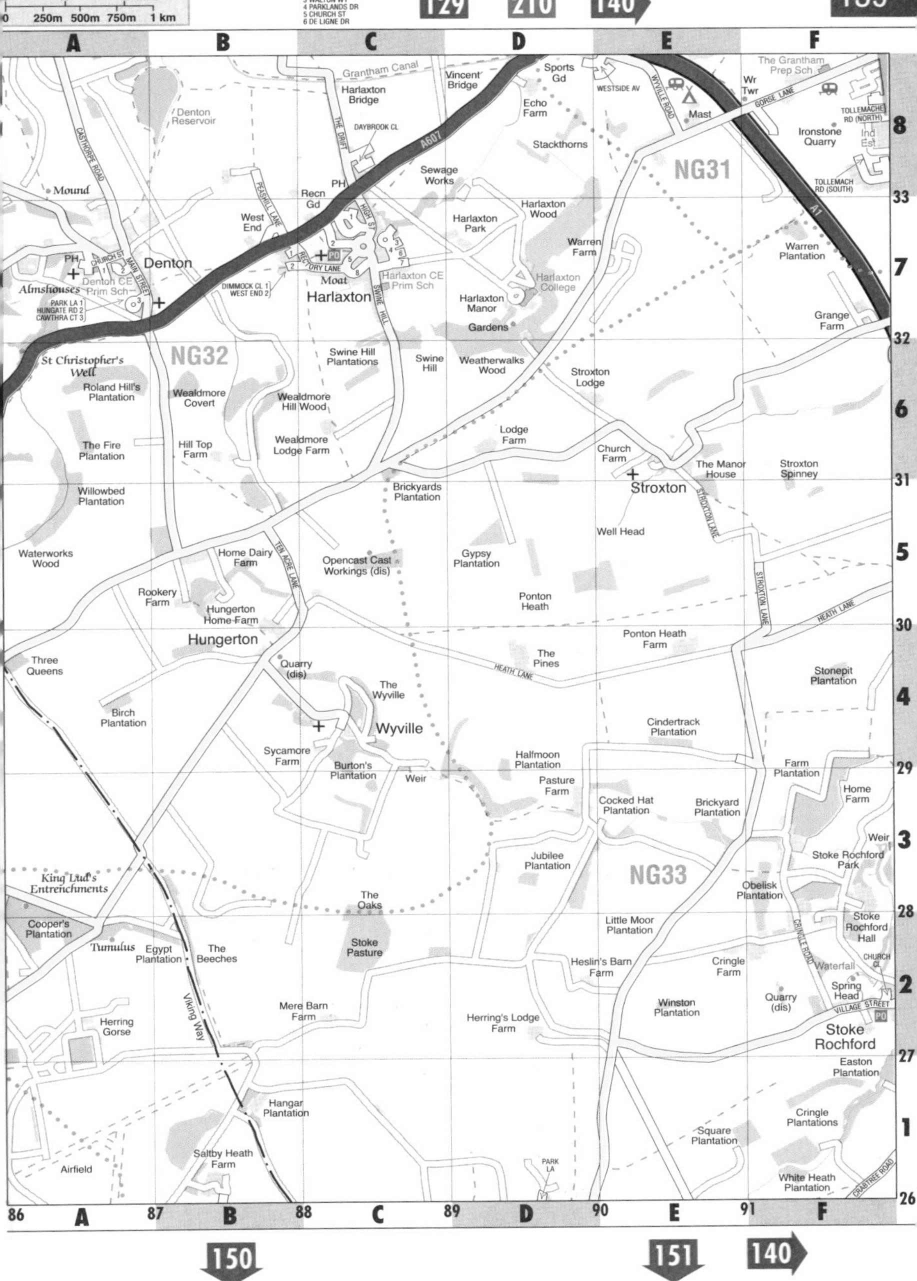

Scale: 1¼ inches to 1 mile
0 ¼ ½ mile
0 250m 500m 750m 1 km
C7
1 GREGORY CL
2 TROTTERS LA
3 WALTON WY
4 PARKLANDS DR
5 CHURCH ST
6 DE LIGNE DR
7 MANOR DR
8 POND ST
129
210
140
Grantham Canal
Harlaxton Bridge
Vincent Bridge
Sports Gd
WESTSIDE AV
WYVILLE ROAD
The Grantham Prep Sch
Wr Twr
GORSE LANE
Mast
Denton Reservoir
CASTHORPE ROAD
THE DRIFT
DAYBROOK CL
A607
Echo Farm
Stackthorns
TOLLEMACHE RD (NORTH)
Ironstone Quarry
Ind Est
NG31
TOLLEMACH RD (SOUTH)
Mound
PEASHILL LANE
Recn Gd
PH
HIGH ST
Sewage Works
Harlaxton Park
Harlaxton Wood
A1
West End
Warren Farm
Warren Plantation
PH
CHURCH ST
MAIN STREET
Denton
RECTORY LANE
PO
Harlaxton CE Prim Sch
Harlaxton College
Denton CE Prim Sch
Almshouses
DIMMOCK CL 1
WEST END 2
Moat
Harlaxton
SWINE HILL
Harlaxton Manor
Grange Farm
PARK LA 1
HUNGATE RD 2
CAWTHRA CT 3
Gardens
St Christopher's Well
NG32
Swine Hill Plantations
Swine Hill
Weatherwalks Wood
Stroxton Lodge
Roland Hill's Plantation
Wealdmore Covert
Wealdmore Hill Wood
The Fire Plantation
Hill Top Farm
Wealdmore Lodge Farm
Lodge Farm
Church Farm
The Manor House
Stroxton Spinney
Brickyards Plantation
Stroxton
STROXTON LANE
Willowbed Plantation
Well Head
Waterworks Wood
Home Dairy Farm
TEN ACRE LANE
Opencast Cast Workings (dis)
Gypsy Plantation
Rookery Farm
Hungerton Home Farm
Ponton Heath
Hungerton
Ponton Heath Farm
HEATH LANE
Three Queens
Quarry (dis)
The Pines
Stonepit Plantation
The Wyville
Birch Plantation
Wyville
Cindertrack Plantation
Sycamore Farm
Burton's Plantation
Weir
Halfmoon Plantation
Farm Plantation
Pasture Farm
Cocked Hat Plantation
Brickyard Plantation
Home Farm
Weir
Jubilee Plantation
Stoke Rochford Park
King Lud's Entrenchments
NG33
Obelisk Plantation
The Oaks
Cooper's Plantation
Little Moor Plantation
Stoke Rochford Hall
Tumulus
Egypt Plantation
The Beeches
Stoke Pasture
Heslin's Barn Farm
Cringle Farm
CRINGLE ROAD
CHURCH CL
Waterfall
Spring Head
Viking Way
Winston Plantation
Quarry (dis)
VILLAGE STREET
Herring Gorse
Mere Barn Farm
Herring's Lodge Farm
Stoke Rochford
Easton Plantation
Hangar Plantation
Cringle Plantations
Square Plantation
Saltby Heath Farm
PARK LA
Airfield
White Heath Plantation
CRABTREE ROAD
A B C D E F
8 33 7 32 6 31 5 30 4 29 3 28 2 27 1 26
86 87 88 89 90 91
150
151
140

211 139 130

139 151 152

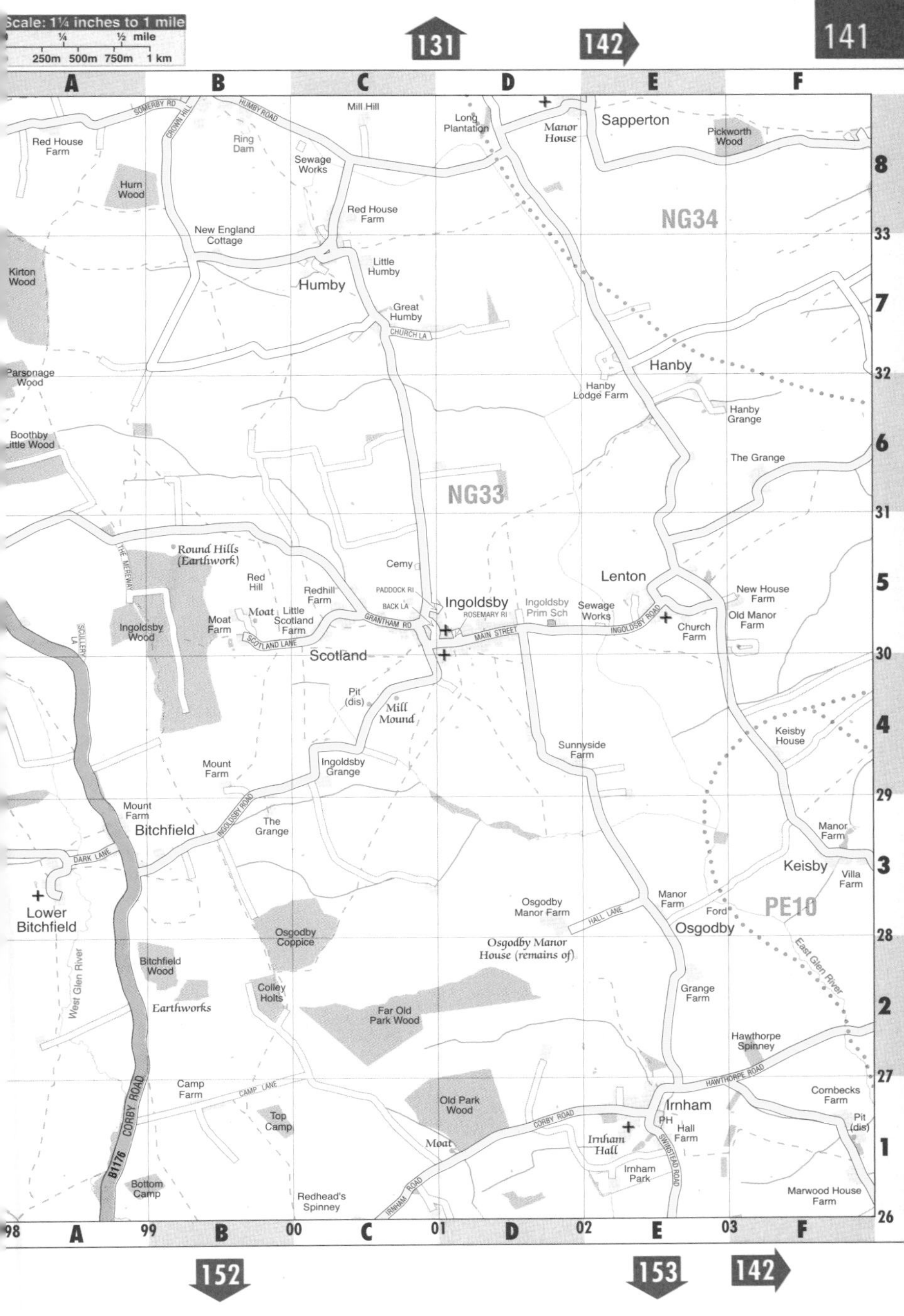
Scale: 1¼ inches to 1 mile
¼ ½ mile
250m 500m 750m 1 km
131
142
A B C D E F
Red House Farm
Hurn Wood
Ring Dam
Sewage Works
Mill Hill
Long Plantation
Manor House
Sapperton
Pickworth Wood
Red House Farm
New England Cottage
NG34
Kirton Wood
Little Humby
Humby
Great Humby
CHURCH LA
Parsonage Wood
Hanby
Hanby Lodge Farm
Hanby Grange
Boothby Little Wood
The Grange
NG33
Round Hills (Earthwork)
Cemy
Red Hill
Redhill Farm
Lenton
New House Farm
Old Manor Farm
Ingoldsby
Ingoldsby Prim Sch
Sewage Works
Moat
Little Scotland Farm
Moat Farm
Ingoldsby Wood
Church Farm
SCOTLAND LANE
GRANTHAM RD
MAIN STREET
INGOLDSBY ROAD
PADDOCK RI
BACK LA
ROSEMARY RI
Scotland
Pit (dis)
Mill Mound
Keisby House
Sunnyside Farm
Mount Farm
Ingoldsby Grange
Mount Farm
Bitchfield
The Grange
Manor Farm
Keisby
Villa Farm
DARK LANE
Lower Bitchfield
Osgodby Manor Farm
HALL LANE
Manor Farm
Ford
PE10
Osgodby
Osgodby Coppice
Osgodby Manor House (remains of)
East Glen River
Bitchfield Wood
Colley Holts
Earthworks
West Glen River
Far Old Park Wood
Grange Farm
Hawthorpe Spinney
HAWTHORPE ROAD
Camp Farm
CAMP LANE
Old Park Wood
Irnham
Cornbecks Farm
Top Camp
CORBY ROAD
PH
Hall Farm
Pit (dis)
Moat
Irnham Hall
SWINSTEAD ROAD
Irnham Park
B1176 CORBY ROAD
Bottom Camp
Redhead's Spinney
IRNHAM ROAD
Marwood House Farm
SOMERBY RD
CROWN HILL
HUMBY ROAD
THE MEREWAY
SCULLERY LA
8 33 7 32 6 31 5 30 4 29 3 28 2 27 1 26
98 99 00 01 02 03
152
153
142

141
132

D8
1 CHURCH LA
2 CHAPEL LA
3 TANNERY LA
4 SPRING LA
5 GREENFIELDS LA

Scale: 1¼ inches to 1 mile
0 ¼ ½ mile
0 250m 500m 750m 1 km

153
141
154

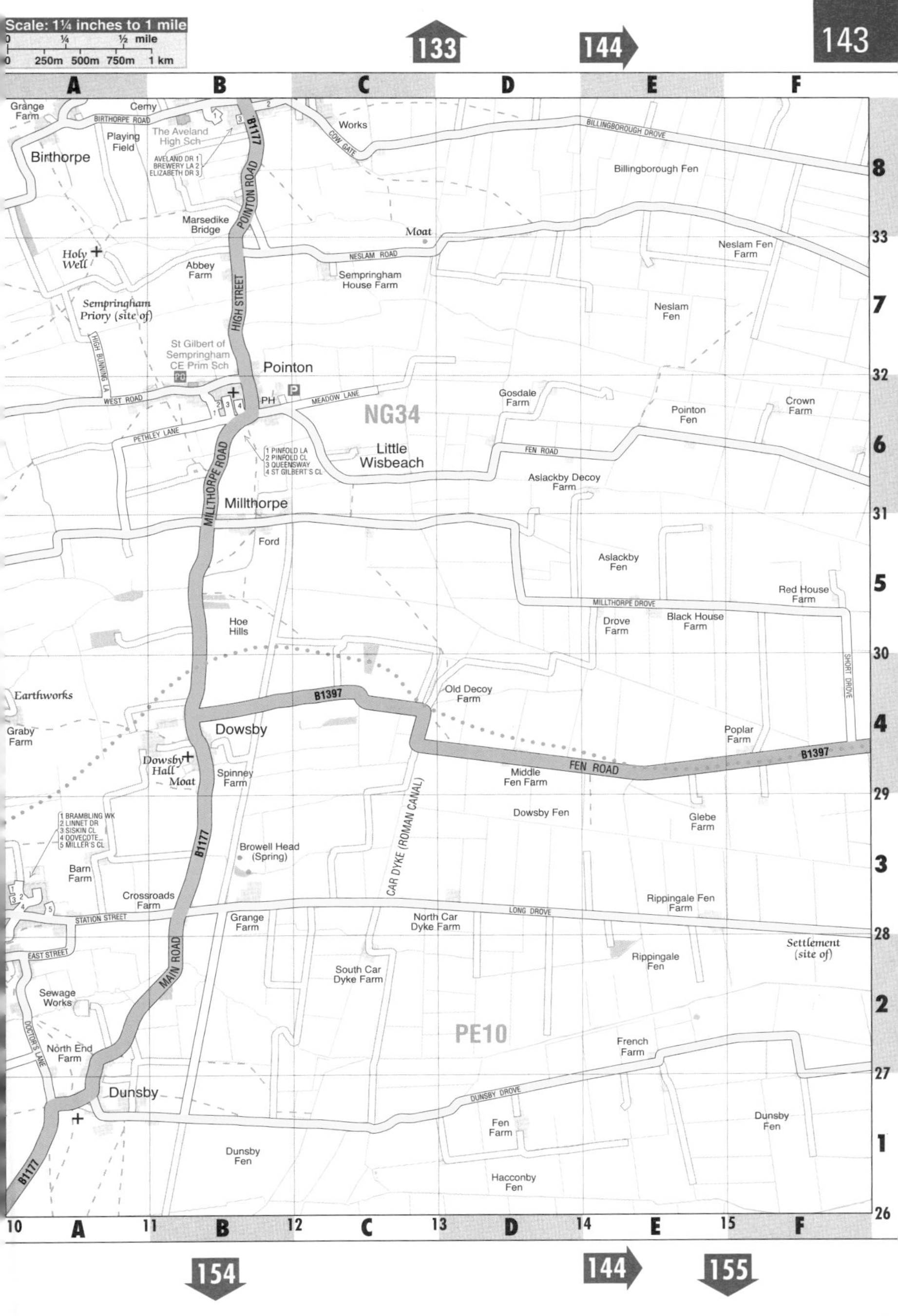
Scale: 1¼ inches to 1 mile
0 ¼ ½ mile
0 250m 500m 750m 1 km
133
144
A B C D E F
Grange Farm
Cemy
Birthorpe
BIRTHORPE ROAD
Playing Field
The Aveland High Sch
AVELAND DR 1
BREWERY LA 2
ELIZABETH DR 3
B1177
POINTON ROAD
Works
COW GATE
BILLINGBOROUGH DROVE
Billingborough Fen
Marsedike Bridge
Moat
Holy Well
Abbey Farm
NESLAM ROAD
Sempringham House Farm
Neslam Fen Farm
HIGH STREET
Sempringham Priory (site of)
Neslam Fen
HIGH BUNNING LA
St Gilbert of Sempringham CE Prim Sch
PO
Pointon
P
PH
WEST ROAD
MEADOW LANE
NG34
Gosdale Farm
Pointon Fen
Crown Farm
PETHLEY LANE
1 PINFOLD LA
2 PINFOLD CL
3 QUEENSWAY
4 ST GILBERT'S CL
Little Wisbeach
FEN ROAD
MILLTHORPE ROAD
Aslackby Decoy Farm
Millthorpe
Ford
Aslackby Fen
Red House Farm
MILLTHORPE DROVE
Hoe Hills
Drove Farm
Black House Farm
SHORT DROVE
Earthworks
B1397
Old Decoy Farm
Graby Farm
Dowsby
Poplar Farm
Dowsby Hall
Moat
Spinney Farm
FEN ROAD
Middle Fen Farm
Dowsby Fen
Glebe Farm
1 BRAMBLING WK
2 LINNET DR
3 SISKIN CL
4 DOVECOTE...
5 MILLER'S CL
Browell Head (Spring)
CAR DYKE (ROMAN CANAL)
Barn Farm
Crossroads Farm
Rippingale Fen Farm
STATION STREET
Grange Farm
LONG DROVE
North Car Dyke Farm
EAST STREET
MAIN ROAD
South Car Dyke Farm
Rippingale Fen
Settlement (site of)
Sewage Works
DOCTOR'S LANE
PE10
North End Farm
French Farm
Dunsby
DUNSBY DROVE
Fen Farm
Dunsby Fen
Dunsby Fen
Hacconby Fen
8 33 7 32 6 31 5 30 4 29 3 28 2 27 1 26
10 11 12 13 14 15
154
144
155

143
134

155
143
156

Scale: 1¼ inches to 1 mile
¼ ½ mile
250m 500m 750m 1 km
A8
1 BOYFIELDS
2 ASHWIN GATE
3 DOVECOTES
4 LUDLOW GD
5 CHARLOTTE WK
6 ST MARGARET'S
B6
1 PARK CL
2 YORK GD
3 WELBY DR
4 CHURCH ST
5 SALEM ST
6 FIELD CL
B7
1 LILA DR
2 POACHERS HIDE
3 OAKTREE CL
4 CAMBRIDGE GD
C6
1 DAIRY CL
2 POPLAR DR
3 MEDWAY CL
4 LOWBRIDGE LA
5 WHITEHALL
6 GODFREY AV
135
146
A B C D E F
Quadring
MAIN ROAD
Izzat Lane Farm
GREEN LA
WATER GATE
JUDY CROSS
SARAH GATE
Willow Farm
WOOD LA
RUSHY DV
NEW ROAD
Bedford Bridge
Eaudike Farm
Bresby House
PH
Quadring Eaudike
Lowgate Bridge
EAUDIKE ROAD
GREEN LANE
WIGTOFT BANK
SPALDING ROAD
Belton Farm
GREEN LA
Woodlands Farm
Bicker Haven
BOSTON ROAD
Bank House Farm
Rabbit Hill Farm
KIT CAT LANE
BROAD LA 1
WATERBELLY LA 2
DOWDYKE RD 3
Dowdyke Grange
PE20
Sutterton Marsh
COOK'S ROAD
Woodlands Farm
B1397
A152
PO
PH
AREHAMS LA
QUADRING ROAD
Monks Hall
Mast
Sewage Works
CHAINTOFT LA
CHURCHFLEET LANE
LOW GATE
Bridge Farm
Bank House
BOW GATE
NORTH GATE
HIGH STREET
Gosberton House Special Sch
Holly Bush Farm
Beech Tree Farm
MILL LANE
Boston Rd Pits Nature Reserve
White House Farm
Elm Tree Farm
GOSBERTON BANK
Bridge House Farm
Gosberton Marsh
Westhorpe Bridge
Gosberton
Gosberton Prim Sch
Cemy
HIGHBRIDGE LANE
PH
Hill House
Risegate Eau
FISH GROOM'S LA
Gosberton Fen
The Gables
Sandpit Farm
WARGATE WAY
Wargate Way Farm
BELCHMIRE LANE
Ball Hall Farm
Belnie Bridge
CUNSDIKE LANE
PETER SEADIKE LANE
CUNSDIKE LANE
SODS LA
SURFLEET BANK
Woad Farm
Cressy Hall
Moat
Cawood Hall
CAWOOD LANE
Wargate Bridge
STATION ROAD
BELNIE LANE
Belnie Farm
SPALDING ROAD
LC
B1397
Cressy Bridge
SWEETLANDS WAY
WARGATE FIELD LANE
Wargate
Wargate Field
Belnie
Burnt House Farm
CONEY GARTH LA
SURFLEET BANK
Windmill
Drummer's Bridge
Bird's Drove Farm
PE11
GOSBERTON ROAD
SCOLDALL LANE
BENDIKE LANE
Red House Farm
Coney Garth Farm
BIRDS DROVE
CLUBHURN LA
Willow Tree Farm
Sewage Works
COALBEACH LA
COALBEACH LA
Cheal Bridge
DOCKHOLME GATE
Cottage Fen
A152
A16
CLUBHURN LA
NEWLANDS RD
RESERVOIR ROAD
Gosberton Cheal
BAFFEN'S LA
Cheal House Farm
SALTFLEET LANE
GOSBERTON ROAD
THARY LA
COALBEACH LA
STATION ROAD
LC
Elm Farm
LITTLE LA
Surfleet Lows Nature Reserve
HUN GATE
Seas End Prim Sch
Cemy
PH
SEAS END ROAD
Surfleet Seas End
CH
STOCKHOUSE LANE
Marsh Farm
LC
GUBBOLE'S DROVE
BEACH BANK
LOW GATE
Surfleet
PO
Macmillan Way
PARK LANE
Spalding Golf Club
Beachbank Farm
PH
Newlands Farm
Blue Gowt Drain
River Welland
Hill Marsh
Daniels Cuckoo Farm
B1356
DUNNEGATE WAY
Hill Marsh Farm
Old Sea Drain
Pinchbeck Marsh
Crowtree Farm
Fenleigh Farm
BURTEY FEN LANE
LC
River Glen
CUCKOO LANE
HERDGATE LANE
PE12
SURFLEET ROAD
GREEN LA
Old Sea Drain
MARSH ROAD
STONE GATE
Burtey Fen Farm South
Manor Farm
TEN ACRE LANE
Spalding Bulb Museum
Spalding Marsh
LANGHOLE DROVE
MILESTONE LA
Crossgate
A16
Flints Farm
Vernatt's Drain
Wykeham
Wykeham Chapel (remains of)
LC
OLD FEN LANE
PH
Water Twr
CHURCH STREET
Pinchbeck Engine Mus
WEST MARSH RD
Captain's Drain
Pumping Station
THE CHASE
Moat
WYKEHAM LA
8
33
7
32
6
31
5
30
4
29
3
28
2
27
1
26
22 23 24 25 26 27
A B C D E F
B1
1 HERRING LA
2 KNIGHT ST
3 BROWNLOW CR
4 GLEN AV
156
C1
1 BACON'S LA
2 MEADOW CL
3 CROSSGATE LA
4 POACHERS GATE
5 CROSSGATE CR
6 FLAXMILL LA
7 THE MEADOWS
8 OLDHAM DR
9 CAPTAINS BECK
10 GROVE CL
11 RANVILLE CL
12 HORSEPIT LA
13 OAKLAND WY
14 BEAR LA
D2
1 SUNNYDALE CL
2 PARK LA
3 WOOD'S LA
4 WHITE CROSS LA
5 SURFLEET RD
6 OLD HALL LA
146
E3
1 COALBEACH LA
2 GLEN GD
3 HERON CL
4 KINGFISHER DR
5 SCHOOL CR
157

145
136

Scale: 1¼ inches to 1 mile

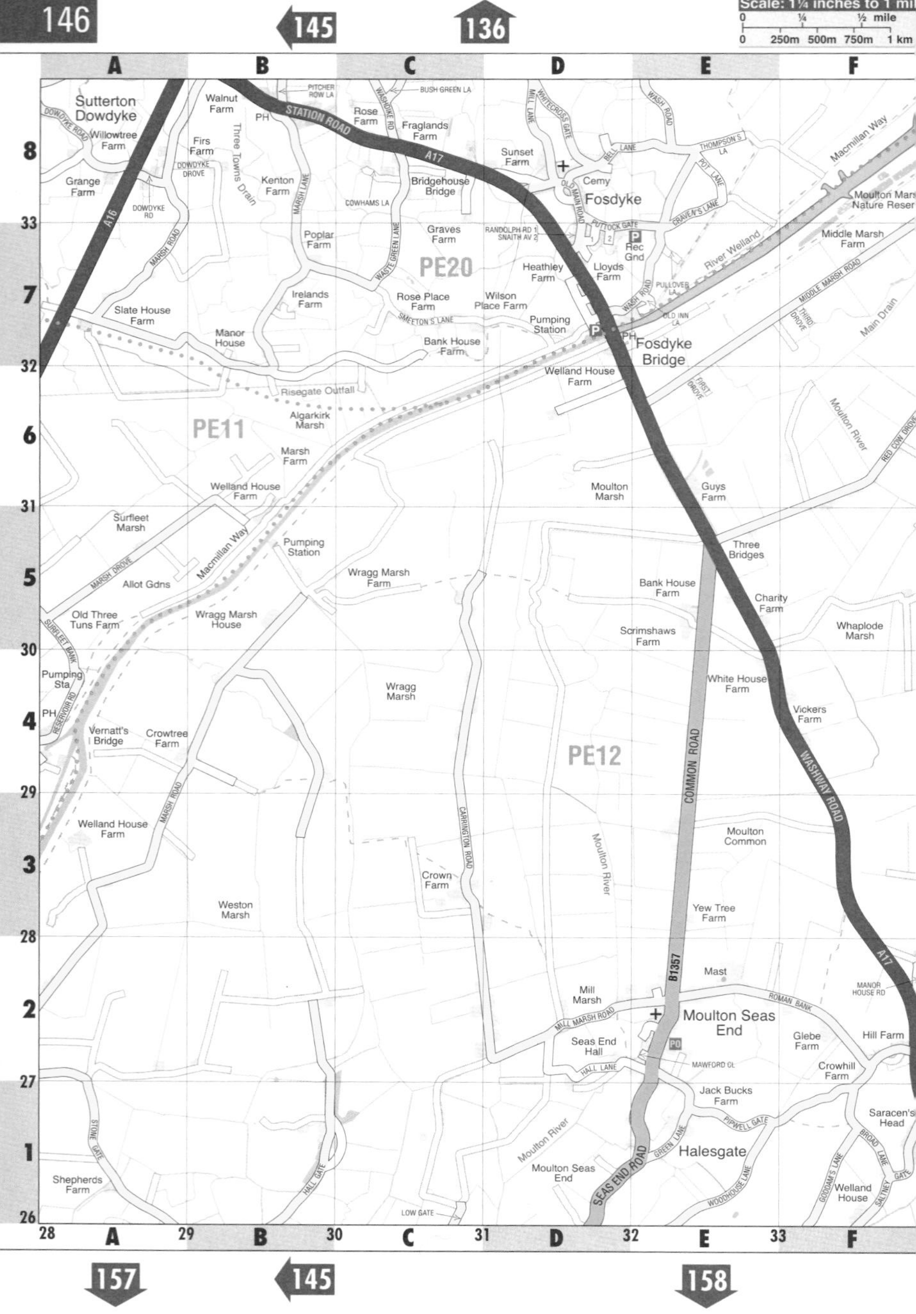

Scale: 1¼ inches to 1 mile
¼
½ mile
250m 500m 750m 1 km
137
148
147
A
B
C
D
E
F
8
33
7
32
6
31
5
30
4
29
3
28
2
27
1
26
Lundys Farm
LAPWATER LANE
Hospital Cottages
Hospital Farm
Leadenhall Farm
Decoy Drain
Reckerby Farm
Willow Tree House
Bingham Lodge
Trevethoe Farm
LAPWATER LANE
Leaden Hall
Holbeach St Marks CE Prim Sch
PH
CROWN AV 1
LAPWATER LA 2
ST MARK'S ROAD
Holbeach St Marks
Christie House
The Grange
Sluice Farm
THE CHASE
Caultons Farm
LINCOLN LANE
Major Farm
PE12
Holbeach River
Woodstoke House
MARSH ROAD
Petticoat Bridge
KEIGHTLEY RD
SLUICE ROAD
Keightley House Farm
MARSH ROAD
Holbeach Marsh
Home Farm
Middle Marsh House
Poplars Farm
EASTERN ROAD
Whaplode River
Bertie Lodge
FLINT HOUSE ROAD
Marsh Farm
Crowmarsh Farm
Whaplode Marsh Farm
Red House Farm
The Grove
215
Whaplode Manor
Hill House Farm
LITTLE COMMON
OLD SLUICE ROAD
Little Common
Allot Gdns
ROMAN BANK
Holbeach Bank
Bank Prim Sch
Clays Farm
Cowfield Gould
Grove Farm
MARSH ROAD
Coney Garth House
OAKLEY PL
BAILY'S LA
PH
LOW ROAD
Holbeach Clough
CLOUGH RD
Blank House Farm
STAR LANE
Old Brick Yard Farm
PEARTREE HOUSE ROAD
Sea Bank
HURN BANK
Holbeach Hurn
PH
Bulb Farm
WASHWAY ROAD
Osbourne House
DARK LA
Greenfield Farm
BOSTON ROAD
Cackle Hill Farm
CACKLE HILL LANE
Windmill
Star Cross Farm
Pennyhill Farm
Woodhouse Farm
Hurn Hall
ROMAN BANK
Holbeach & East Elloe
Cackle Hill
PENNY HILL ROAD
PH
TOLL'S LA
Mast
Porridge Pot Farm
HURN ROAD
ROMAN BANK
A17
MILL LANE
Old River
Penny Hill
Home Farm
Hovenden House
34
35
36
37
38
39
215
158
For full street detail of the highlighted area see page 215.
148
159

147

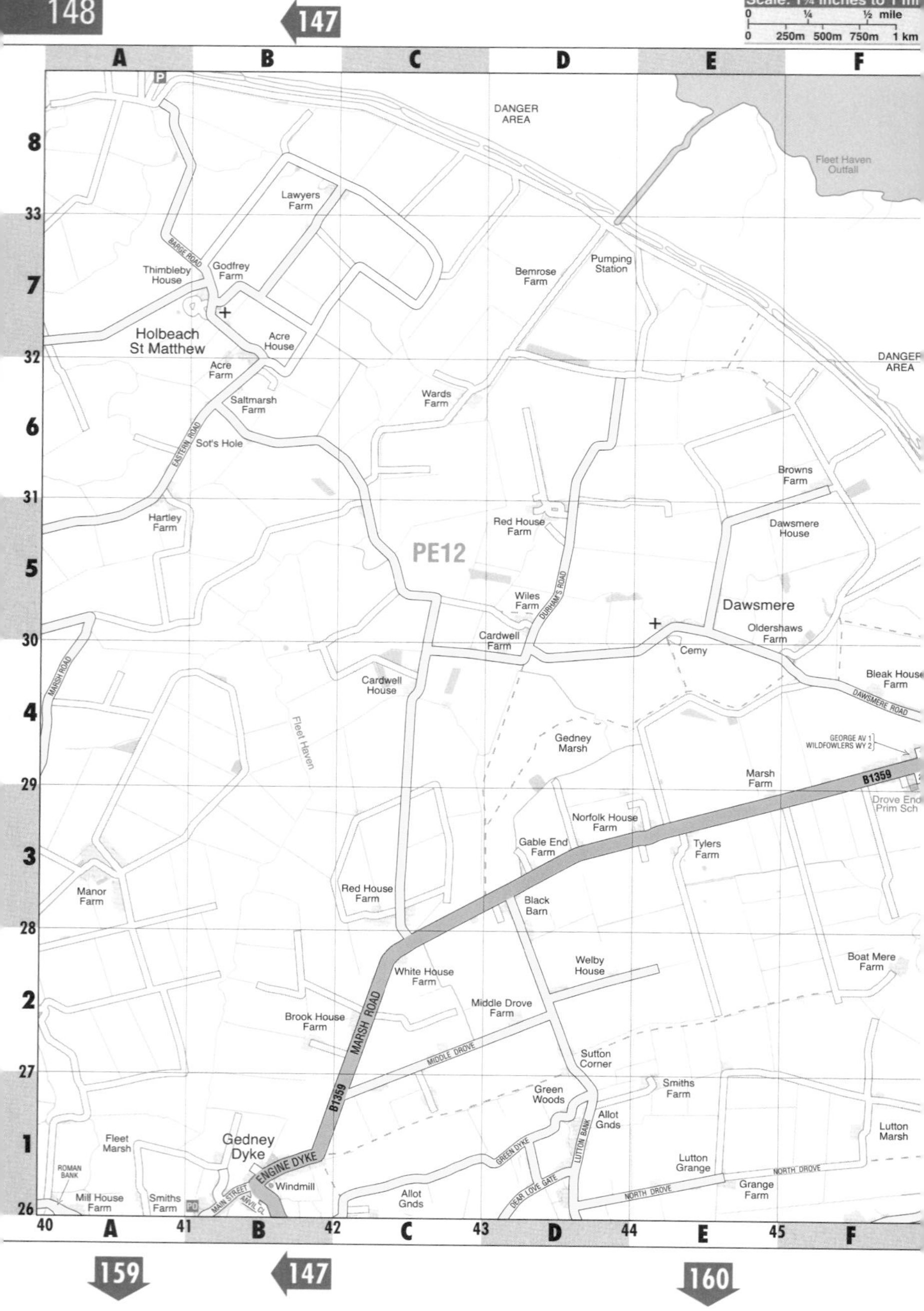

159
147
160

Scale: 1¼ inches to 1 mile
¼ ½ mile
250m 500m 750m 1 km

160
161

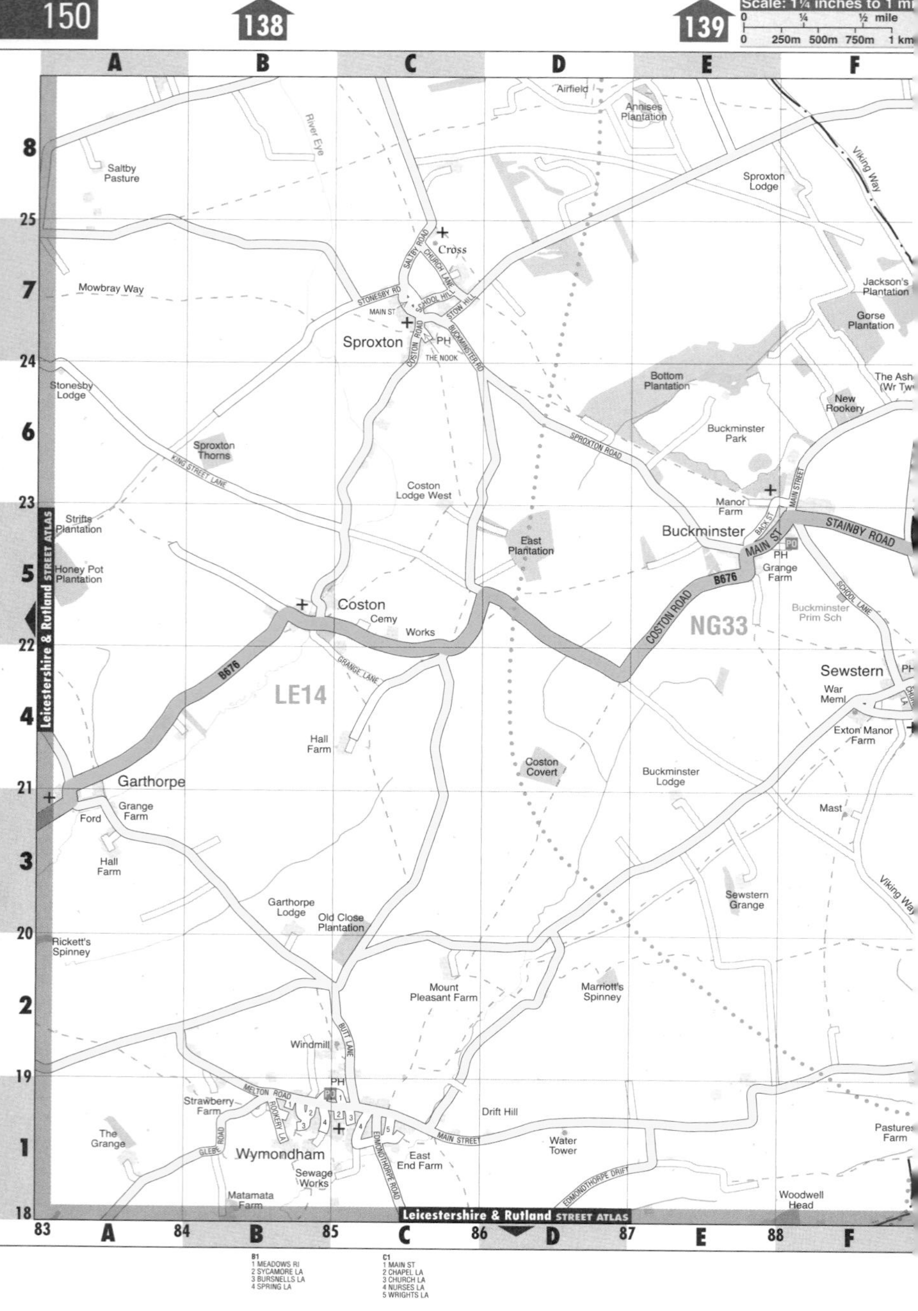

B1
1 MEADOWS RI
2 SYCAMORE LA
3 BURSNELLS LA
4 SPRING LA

C1
1 MAIN ST
2 CHAPEL LA
3 CHURCH LA
4 NURSES LA
5 WRIGHTS LA

cale: 1¼ inches to 1 mile
¼ ½ mile
250m 500m 750m 1 km
139
D7
1 THE CLOSE
2 INGLE CT
3 WOOLSTHORPE RD
4 READS LA
5 NEWTON WY
6 WATER LA
7 SCHOOL LA
8 SPRING LA
E6
1 MEADOW CL
2 TWYFORD CL
3 COLSTER WY
4 BELVOIR CL
5 TURNOR CL
6 BOURNE RD ESTATE
7 WEST GR
8 EAST GR
E7
1 WOODLANDS DR
2 BEECH CL
3 WALNUT GR
4 CHESTNUT GR
5 ASH CL
6 NEWTON CT
7 PASTURE CL
8 THE ROPEWALK
152
140
151
A
B
C
D
E
F
The Abbey
ROXTON ROAD
CHURCH STREET
Skillington
PH
Cemy
Fish Well
Sewage Works
Lower Farm
COLSTERWORTH ROAD
Tinkerhill Plantation
BUCKMINSTER LANE
A8
1 PARK LA
2 GRANTHAM RD
3 FISH WELL CL
4 BACK LA
5 MIDDLE ST
6 LORD'S LA
7 CHAPEL ROW
8 STONEPIT LA
CRABTREE ROAD
THE DRIFT
Aerodrome Farm
Quarry (Limestone)
Glebe Farm
Houghton's Plantation
Maddock's Plantation
Cotswold Farm
Bailey's Plantation
Lodge Farm
Ironstone Plantation
Wellspring Plantation
A1
B6403
HIGH DIKE
Cockle Holt
Ridd's Farm
Parson's Hole
Easton Wood
The Holt
Woolsthorpe-by-Colsterworth
Sewage Works
WOOLSTHORPE ROAD
BRIDGE END
Cemy
PH
Colsterworth CE Prim Sch
Colsterworth
Woolsthorpe Manor
National Trust
Cemy
HIGH STREET
BACK LA
War Memorial
Motel
Firs Farm
A151
STAINBY ROAD
PO
BOURNE ROAD
Motel
P
Mast
SKILLINGTON ROAD
Quarries (dis)
OLD POST LANE
Foxhole Spring
Allot Gdns
Quarry (dis)
Twyford Wood
Stainby Lodge
Sewage Works
Glebe Farm
COLSTERWORTH ROAD
B676
MAIN ROAD
BUCKMINSTER ROAD
Stainby
NG33
River Witham
STAMFORD ROAD
WATER LANE
Tower Hill
GUNBY ROAD
Park Farm
Motherford's Spring
B6403
HALL LA 1
POST OFFICE HILL 2
MIDDLE ST 3
Stainby Warren
NORTHERN'S CL
CHURCH STREET
Ford
Pig Farm
HONEY POT LANE
STAINBY ROAD
MAIN STREET
BACK LA
GUNBY ROAD
SEWSTERN ROAD
Mill Farm
GUNBY ROAD
North Witham
Allot Gdns
Mast
Factory
MAIN STREET
WITHAM ROAD
Grange Farm
RECTORY LA
Cross
Gunby
BULL LANE
Radio Mast
Bull Farm
WOOLLEY'S LANE
1 TIMBER HILL
2 STAMFORD RD
THE DRIFT
Mickley Wood
NORTH WITHAM ROAD
Preceptory of Knights Templars (site of)
Temple Hill
Gunby Gorse
The Forty Acre
Witham Common
Battlebourn Head
MOOR LANE
Cemy
Crown Point Farm
GREAT CL
Sewage Works
Woodbine Farm
PH
South Witham
South Witham Prim Sch
Motel
River Witham
Quarry (dis)
HIGH ST
PO
PH
BROADGATE ROAD
MORKERY LANE
South Witham Nature Reserve
Quarry (Limestone)
MILL LANE
THISTLETON LANE
Cribb's Lodge
Morkery Wood
Quarry (dis)
FOSSE LANE
Viking Way
SCHOOL LA
MAIN ST
WITHAM ROAD
NEW RD
LE15
Leicestershire & Rutland STREET ATLAS
A1 Stamford
8
25
7
24
6
23
5
22
4
21
3
20
2
19
1
18
89
90
91
92
93
94
D2
1 GREAT CL
2 TEMPLARS WY
3 WIMBERLEY WY
4 THE PARKSIDE
5 COVERLEY RD
6 WELLFIELD CL
7 HARRINGTON RD
8 HALFORD CL
9 TOLLEMACHE FIELDS
10 CHURCH ST
11 PRIORY CT
12 WATER LA
13 RUTLAND CL
14 HILL VIEW RD
15 CHURCH LA
16 STATION AV
17 RAILWAY CL
152

140 151 141

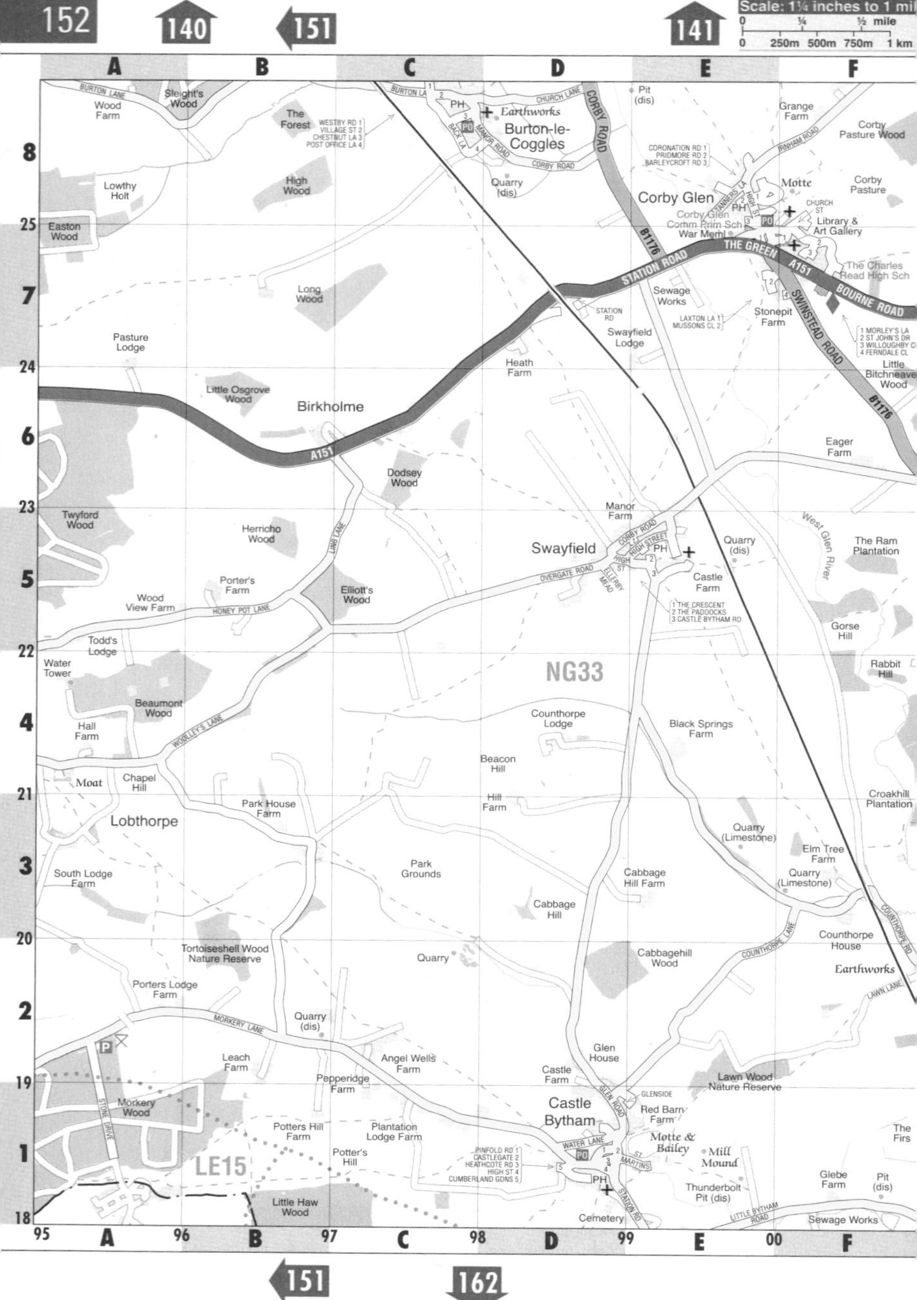
Scale: 1¼ inches to 1 mi
0 ¼ ½ mile
0 250m 500m 750m 1 km
A B C D E F
8 25 7 24 6 23 5 22 4 21 3 20 2 19 1 18
95 96 97 98 99 00
Burton Lane
Wood Farm
Sleight's Wood
The Forest
Westby Rd 1
Village St 2
Chestnut La 3
Post Office La 4
Burton La
Church Lane
PH
Earthworks
Burton-le-Coggles
Back La
Manor Road
Corby Road
Quarry (dis)
Pit (dis)
Grange Farm
Corby Pasture Wood
Irnham Road
Coronation Rd 1
Pridmore Rd 2
Barleycroft Rd 3
Motte
Corby Pasture
Corby Glen
Tanners La
High St
Church St
Corby Glen Comm Prim Sch
Library & Art Gallery
War Meml
The Green
The Charles Read High Sch
Bourne Road
B1176
Lowthy Holt
High Wood
Easton Wood
Long Wood
Station Road
A151
Station Rd
Sewage Works
Laxton La 1
Mussons Cl 2
Stonepit Farm
Swinstead Road
1 Morley's La
2 St John's Dr
3 Willoughby C
4 Ferndale Cl
Pasture Lodge
Swayfield Lodge
Heath Farm
Little Bitchneave Wood
Little Osgrove Wood
Birkholme
Eager Farm
Dodsey Wood
Twyford Wood
Manor Farm
Herricho Wood
Ling Lane
Corby Road
High Street
Swayfield
Quarry (dis)
West Glen River
The Ram Plantation
Porter's Farm
Elliott's Wood
Overgate Road
Ellerby Mead
Castle Farm
Wood View Farm
Honey Pot Lane
1 The Crescent
2 The Paddocks
3 Castle Bytham Rd
Gorse Hill
Todd's Lodge
Water Tower
Rabbit Hill
NG33
Beaumont Wood
Woolley's Lane
Countherpe Lodge
Black Springs Farm
Hall Farm
Beacon Hill
Moat
Chapel Hill
Hill Farm
Croakhill Plantation
Lobthorpe
Park House Farm
Quarry (Limestone)
Elm Tree Farm
South Lodge Farm
Park Grounds
Cabbage Hill Farm
Cabbage Hill
Countherpe Rd
Countherpe House
Tortoiseshell Wood Nature Reserve
Quarry
Cabbagehill Wood
Countherpe Lane
Earthworks
Porters Lodge Farm
Lawn Lane
Morkery Lane
Quarry (dis)
Glen House
Leach Farm
Angel Wells Farm
Castle Farm
Lawn Wood Nature Reserve
Pepperidge Farm
Glenside
Morkery Wood
Stone Drive
Castle Bytham
Glen Road
Red Barn Farm
Potters Hill Farm
Plantation Lodge Farm
Water Lane
Motte & Bailey
Mill Mound
The Firs
Potter's Hill
LE15
Pinfold Rd 1
Castlegate 2
Heathcote Rd 3
High St 4
Cumberland Gdns 5
St Martins
PO
PH
Thunderbolt Pit (dis)
Glebe Farm
Pit (dis)
Little Haw Wood
Station Rd
Cemetery
Little Bytham Road
Sewage Works

Scale: 1¼ inches to 1 mile
¼ ½ mile
250m 500m 750m 1 km
141
154
142
A B C D E F
8
25
7
24
6
23
5
22
4
21
3
20
2
19
1
18
02 03 04 05 06
South Wood
Cumberland Field
Southwood Farm
Irnham Pasture
SWINSTEAD ROAD
Catbury Wood
Great West Wood
Norwood
Little West Wood
Pit (dis)
Little Norwood
Home Farm
Bulby Hall
Ram Plantation
Breache's Wood
Hurn Wood
Pasture Wood
Thorny Wood
Scullar Wood
Elsthorpe Grange
HANGMAN'S LANE
Spring Wood
Brook Farm
Elsthorpe
Gunboro Farm
Cowslip Spinney
Woodlands Farm
Bitchneaves Wood
Park Dikes
Norwood Farm
BOURNE ROAD
The Blockings
Tower Farm
Limekiln Plantation
FORSTEDD HILL
The Oaks
Dairy Farm
A151
Featherwell Farm
ELSTHORPE ROAD
East Glen River
Gunboro Wood
PH
Featherwell Spring
NORTH AVE
LITTLE CL
Swinstead
HIGH STREET
BOURNE ROAD
Swinstead CE Prim Sch
Williamson's Plantation
Grimsthorpe Castle
Home Parks
Grimsthorpe
Galley Hill
PE10
NEW ESTATE 1
BERTIE CL 2
HIGH ST 3
CROAKE HL 4
Cross
PH
Bishopshall
Crow Wood
Red Bridge
Weir
The Groves
Edenham CE (Controlled) Prim Sch
Park Farm
Ford
Edenham Bridge
PH
SCHOOL LA
CHURCH LA
Earthworks
Edenham
Cross
CREETON ROAD
NG33
The Vaudey
Stew Pond
Maize Hill
PO
MAIN STREET
Long Plantation
Creeton Farm
B1176
Roots' Plantation
Mill Mound
Coronation Spinney
Randalls Farm
Scottlethorpe
Pillar Wood Farm
Black Burrows
Quarries (dis)
Jubilee Plantation
SCOTTLETHORPE ROAD
Tumble Row Farm
Gravel Bridge
Grimsthorpe Park
Spring Buildings Plantation
SWINSTEAD ROAD
Quarry Plantation
Round Plantation
No Mans Plantation
Quarry (dis)
Steel's Riding Plantation
CHESTNUT AVENUE
Millingtons Farm
Scottlethorpe Grange
Auster Wood
CHURCH LA
GLEN RD
Manor Farm
Creeton Corner Plantation
Elsea Wood
Elder Holt
Rough Hills Plantation
Creeton
LITTLE BYTHAM ROAD
Auster Lodge
Scutchback Plantation
HALE HOUSE ROAD
Kennel Plantation
Deer Park
Herring's Plantation
Home Wood
Stonepit Wood
Scottlethoprpe Lodge
The Bythams County Prim Sch
CREETON ROAD
Foxholes Corner Plantation
Red Deer Plantation
Lady Wood
Chy
B1176
Elderwood Farm
Bytham Park Plantation
Hale House Plantation
Pell's Wood
Dobbin's Wood
Hillside Farm
GLEN CL
HIGH ST
PH
West Lodge Plantation
Elder Wood
Lound
163
154

142
153
143

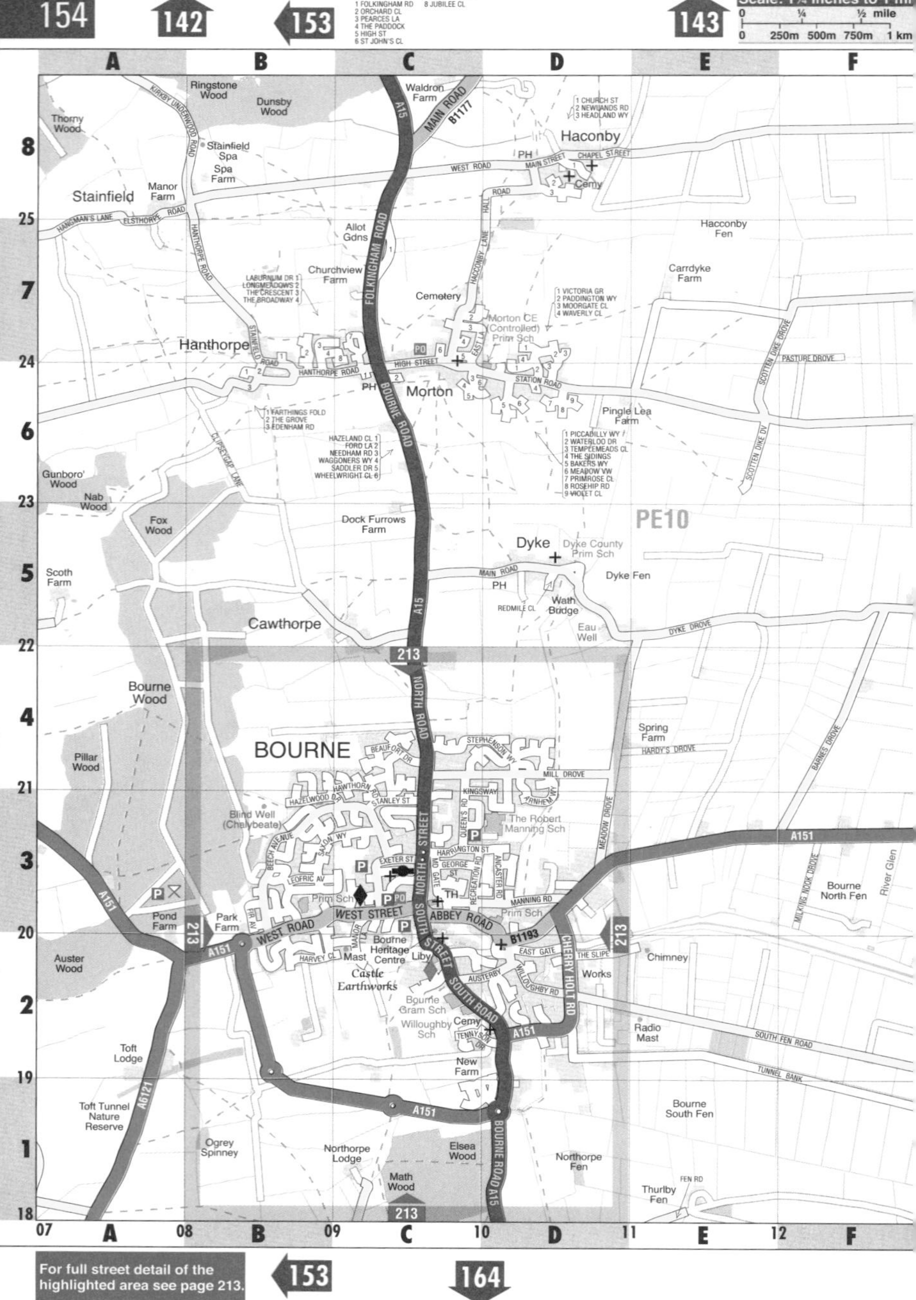

For full street detail of the highlighted area see page 213.
153
164

cale: 1¼ inches to 1 mile
¼ ½ mile
250m 500m 750m 1 km
143
156
144
A B C D E F
Middle Farm
Bakers Farm
Dunsby Fen
HACCONBY DROVE
Pinchbeck North Fen
BLACK HOLE DROVE
Royce Farm
Marriott Farm
Haconby Fen
New House Farm
MORTON NORTH DROVE
Engine Farm
Pinchbeck Fen
LEAVES LAKE DROVE
Nunnerley House Farm
Morton Fen
MORTON DROVE
Pointon Farm
Boardhouse Farm
Forty Foot Farm
BOURNE ROAD
A151
SLIPE DROVE
PE10
PE11
Dyke Fen
Guthram Gowt Bridge
Spinney Farm
Dyke Fen Farm
Pinchbeck South Fen
BOURNE DROVE
Bourne North Fen
Drainage Farm
Glen Farm
Guthram Gowt
TWENTY DROVE
Grange Farm
The Delph Drain
THE DELPH
IRON BAR DROVE
PICKWORTH'S DROVE
Bank House Farm
Sycamore Farm
Lodge Farm
Chestnut Farm
SPALDING ROAD
STATION RD
Twenty
FOSTER'S DV
The Earls Farm
River Glen
Home Grange Farm
Deeping Fen
COUNTER DRAIN DROVE
Macmillan Way
Pepper Hill Farm
Bourne Eau
Bourne North Fen
Sewage Works
Black House Farm
South Fen Farm
Works
Works
Grays Farm
Foundry
LONG DROVE
Carrington Farm
MILL DROVE
Sewage Works
EVERARD RD
NORTH DROVE
Northorpe Fen
13 14 15 16 17 18
8 25 7 24 6 23 5 22 4 21 3 20 2 19 1 18
165
156

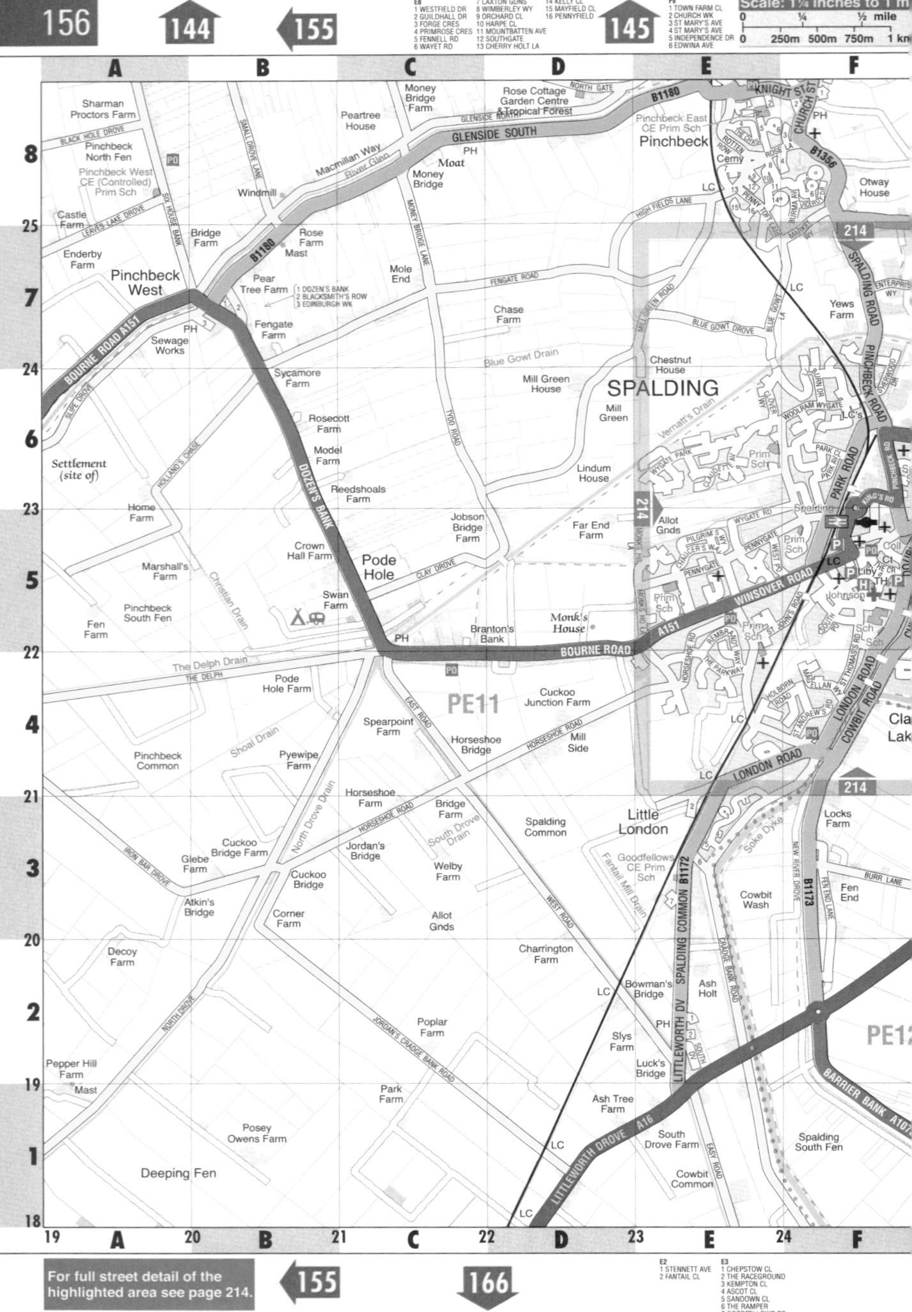

For full street detail of the highlighted area see page 214.

155

166

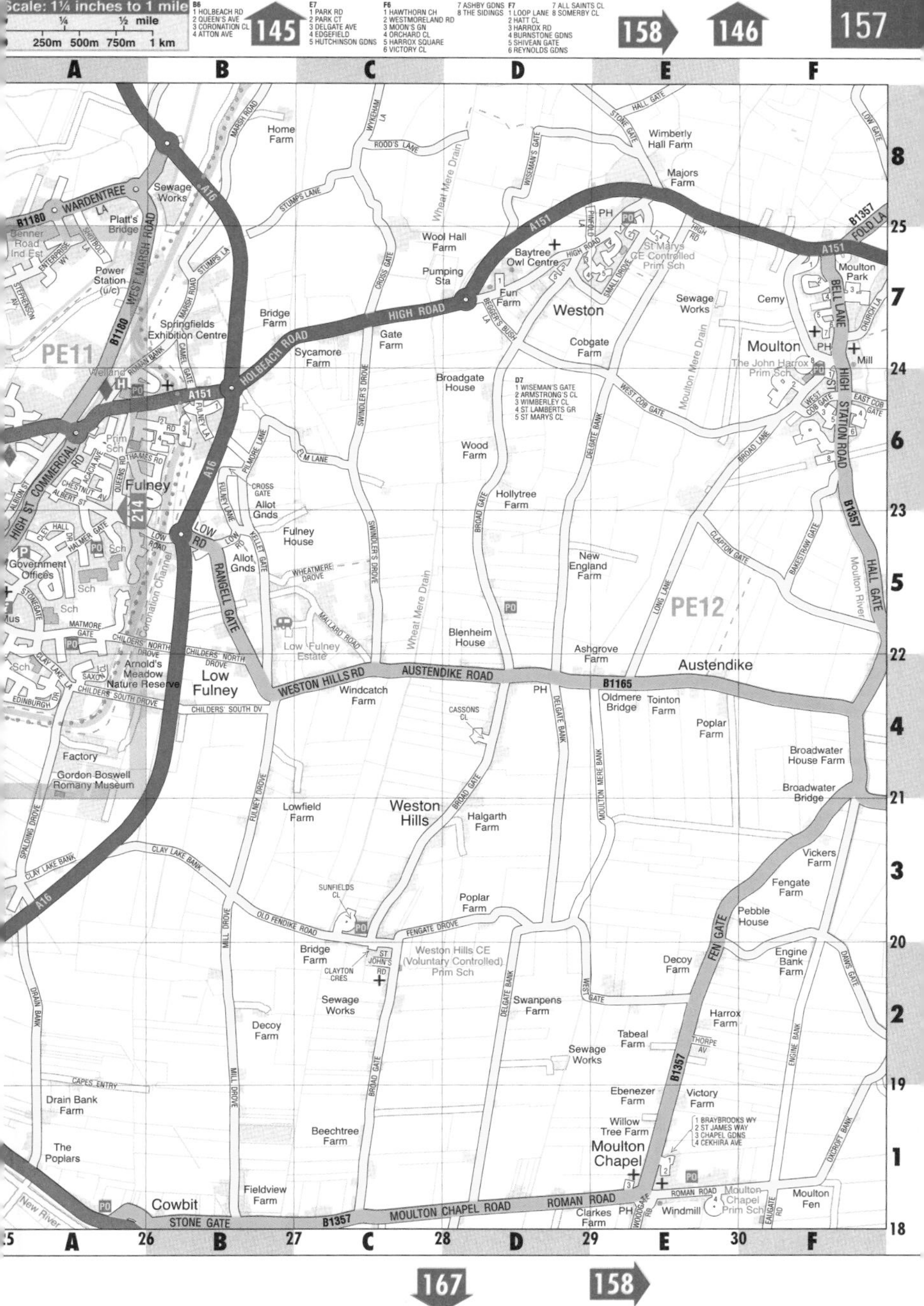
Scale: 1¼ inches to 1 mile
¼ ½ mile
250m 500m 750m 1 km
B6
1 HOLBEACH RD
2 QUEEN'S AVE
3 CORONATION CL
4 ATTON AVE
145
E7
1 PARK RD
2 PARK CT
3 DELGATE AVE
4 EDGEFIELD
5 HUTCHINSON GDNS
F6
1 HAWTHORN CH
2 WESTMORELAND RD
3 MOON'S GN
4 ORCHARD CL
5 HARROX SQUARE
6 VICTORY CL
7 ASHBY GDNS
8 THE SIDINGS
F7
1 LOOP LANE
2 HATT CL
3 HARROX RD
4 BURNSTONE GDNS
5 SHIVEAN GATE
6 REYNOLDS GDNS
7 ALL SAINTS CL
8 SOMERBY CL
158
146
A
B
C
D
E
F
8
7
6
5
4
3
2
1
25
24
23
22
21
20
19
18
26
27
28
29
30
PE11
PE12
Home Farm
Sewage Works
Platt's Bridge
Power Station (u/c)
Springfields Exhibition Centre
Bridge Farm
Sycamore Farm
Gate Farm
Wool Hall Farm
Pumping Sta
Fun Farm
Baytree Owl Centre
Weston
Cobgate Farm
Broadgate House
Wimberly Hall Farm
Majors Farm
St Marys CE Controlled Prim Sch
Sewage Works
Cemy
Moulton Park
Moulton
The John Harrox Prim Sch
Mill
D7
1 WISEMAN'S GATE
2 ARMSTRONG'S CL
3 WIMBERLEY CL
4 ST LAMBERTS GR
5 ST MARYS CL
Wood Farm
Hollytree Farm
Fulney
Allot Gnds
Fulney House
Government Offices
Sch
Prim Sch
New England Farm
Blenheim House
Low Fulney Estate
Arnold's Meadow Nature Reserve
Low Fulney
Windcatch Farm
Ashgrove Farm
Austendike
Oldmere Bridge
Tointon Farm
Poplar Farm
Broadwater House Farm
Broadwater Bridge
Factory
Gordon Boswell Romany Museum
Lowfield Farm
Weston Hills
Halgarth Farm
Vickers Farm
Fengate Farm
Pebble House
Poplar Farm
Bridge Farm
Weston Hills CE (Voluntary Controlled) Prim Sch
Sewage Works
Decoy Farm
Swanpens Farm
Decoy Farm
Engine Bank Farm
Harrox Farm
Tabeal Farm
Sewage Works
Drain Bank Farm
Ebenezer Farm
Victory Farm
Willow Tree Farm
1 BRAYBROOKS WY
2 ST JAMES WAY
3 CHAPEL GDNS
4 CEKHIRA AVE
The Poplars
Beechtree Farm
Moulton Chapel
Fieldview Farm
Cowbit
Clarkes Farm
Windmill
Moulton Chapel Prim Sch
Moulton Fen
A16
A151
B1180
B1357
B1165
HIGH ROAD
HOLBEACH ROAD
WEST MARSH ROAD
WARDENTREE LA
STUMPS LANE
ROOD'S LANE
WYKEHAM LA
CROSS GATE
SWINDLER'S DROVE
BROAD GATE
DELGATE BANK
WEST COB GATE
BROAD LANE
BELL LANE
HIGH STATION ROAD
HALL GATE
CLAPTON GATE
LONG LANE
BAKESTRAW GATE
ELM LANE
PILMORE LANE
FULNEY LANE
KELLET GATE
LOW RD
RANGELL GATE
WHEATMERE DROVE
MALLARD ROAD
WESTON HILLS RD
AUSTENDIKE ROAD
CHILDERS' NORTH DROVE
CHILDERS' SOUTH DROVE
CHILDERS' SOUTH DV
CLAY LAKE BANK
SPALDING DROVE
FULNEY DROVE
MOULTON MERE BANK
OLD FENDIKE ROAD
FENGATE DROVE
SUNFIELDS CL
CASSONS CL
ST JOHN'S RD
CLAYTON CRES
WEST GATE
FEN GATE
THORPE AV
ENGINE BANK
DAWS GATE
OXCROFT BANK
MILL DROVE
DRAIN BANK
CAPES ENTRY
MOULTON CHAPEL ROAD
ROMAN ROAD
STONE GATE
EAUGATE RD
New River
Wheat Mere Drain
Moulton Mere Drain
Moulton River
Coronation Channel
HIGH ST
COMMERCIAL RD
STONEGATE
EDINBURGH DR
MATMORE GATE
HALMER GATE
ALBERT ST
CHESTNUT AV
ACACIA AVE
QUEENS RD
THAMES RD
214
Welland
Mus
Benner Road Ind Est

B6
1 ABBOTS GD
2 COBGATE CL
3 SANDRINGHAM CL
4 BUTTERCUP PADDOCK
5 FRANCKLIN WK
6 GOLDEN HARVEST WY

B7
1 WHEATFIELDS
2 CHAPEL GD
3 ST MARY'S GD
4 GREEN PASTURES
5 CROSS ST
6 KIRK GATE
7 MIDDLE RD
8 MALTEN LA
9 IRBY CR
10 THE TILNEY

Scale: 1¼ inches to 1 mile
0 ¼ ½ mile
0 250m 500m 750m 1 km

For full street detail of the highlighted area see page 215.

147
160
148

Scale: 1¼ inches to 1 mile

C7
1 HARGATE CL
2 PARKLANDS
3 EASTGATE GD
4 BURGESS DR
5 CHARLES RD
6 PROCTORS CL
7 CHERRY LA
8 BRAMLEY CL
9 HAVEN CL
10 PINSTOCK LA

D7
1 PRIESTFIELD DV
2 ST MARY'S MS
3 BATEMAN'S CL
4 LEIGHTON WK
5 CHURCHGATE MS
6 RECTORY LA

169
160
For full street detail of the highlighted area see page 216.

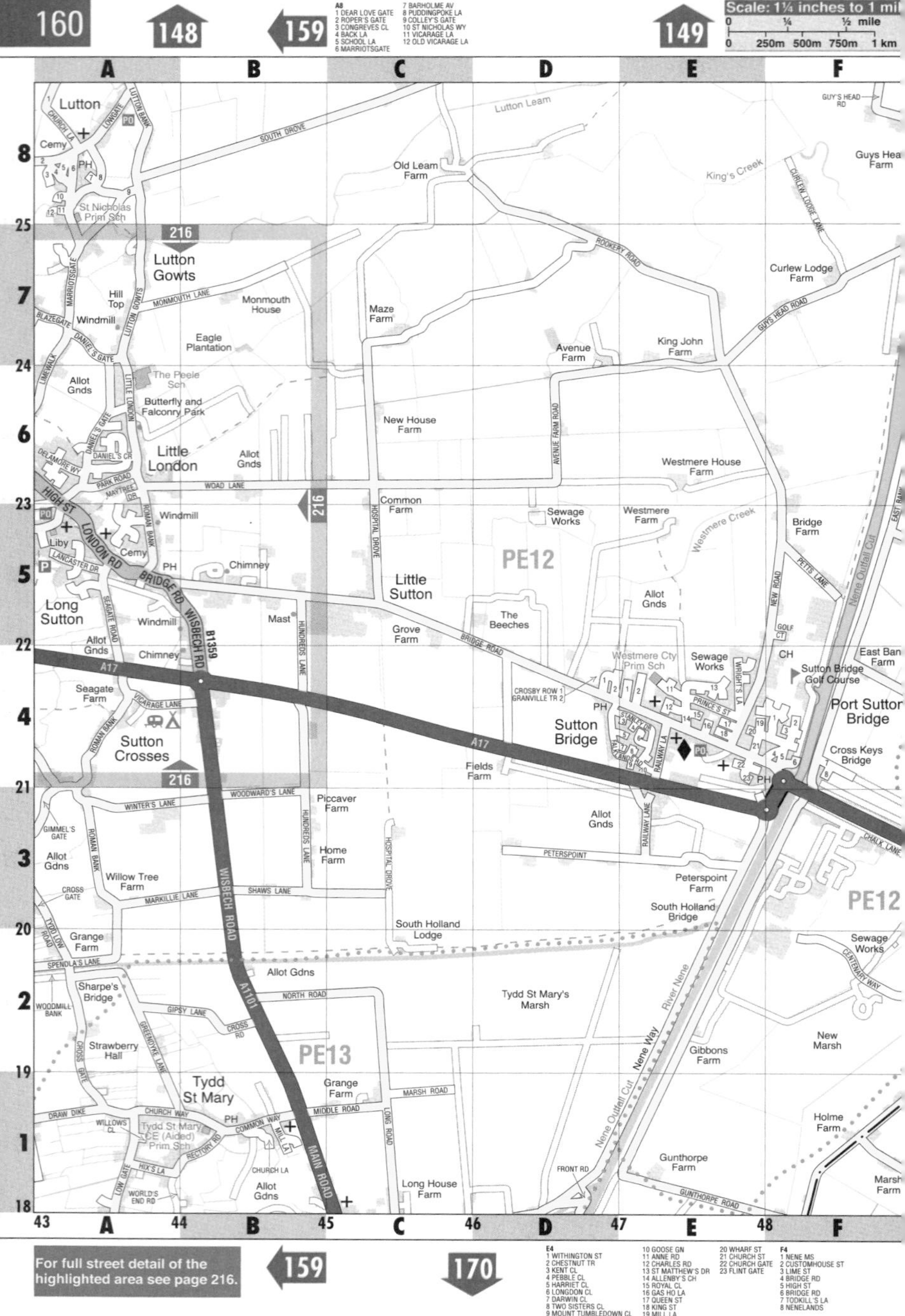
148
159
A8
1 DEAR LOVE GATE
2 ROPER'S GATE
3 CONGREVES CL
4 BACK LA
5 SCHOOL LA
6 MARRIOTSGATE
7 BARHOLME AV
8 PUDDINGPOKE LA
9 COLLEY'S GATE
10 ST NICHOLAS WY
11 VICARAGE LA
12 OLD VICARAGE LA
149
Scale: 1¼ inches to 1 mil
0 ¼ ½ mile
0 250m 500m 750m 1 km
Lutton
Cemy
PH
St Nicholas Prim Sch
SOUTH DROVE
Lutton Leam
Old Leam Farm
King's Creek
Guys Head Farm
GUY'S HEAD RD
CURLEW LODGE LANE
216
Lutton Gowts
MARRIOTSGATE
Hill Top
Windmill
MONMOUTH LANE
Monmouth House
Eagle Plantation
Maze Farm
ROOKERY ROAD
Curlew Lodge Farm
GUYS HEAD ROAD
Avenue Farm
King John Farm
BLAZEGATE
DANIEL'S GATE
LUTTON GOWTS
LIMEWALK
Allot Gnds
The Peele Sch
Butterfly and Falconry Park
LITTLE LONDON
New House Farm
AVENUE FARM ROAD
DANIEL'S CR
DELAMORE WY
PARK ROAD
MAYTREE DR
Little London
Allot Gnds
WOAD LANE
Westmere House Farm
HIGH ST
PO
Liby
LONDON RD
Cemy
ROMAN BANK
Windmill
Common Farm
HOSPITAL DROVE
Sewage Works
Westmere Farm
Westmere Creek
Bridge Farm
EAST BANK
LANCASTER DR
PH
Chimney
PE12
BRIDGE RD
Little Sutton
PETTS LANE
NEW ROAD
Nene Outfall Cut
Long Sutton
SEAGATE ROAD
Windmill
Mast
HUNDREDS LANE
Grove Farm
BRIDGE ROAD
The Beeches
Allot Gnds
GOLF CT
WISBECH RD
B1359
Allot Gnds
Chimney
A17
Westmere Cty Prim Sch
Sewage Works
WRIGHT'S LA
CH
East Bank Farm
Sutton Bridge Golf Course
Seagate Farm
VICARAGE LANE
CROSBY ROW 1
GRANVILLE TR 2
PRINCE'S ST
PH
Sutton Bridge
STANLEY DR
Port Sutton Bridge
ROMAN BANK
Sutton Crosses
Fields Farm
RAILWAY LA
Cross Keys Bridge
WINTER'S LANE
WOODWARD'S LANE
Piccaver Farm
Allot Gnds
RAILWAY LANE
CHALK LANE
GIMMEL'S GATE
Allot Gdns
Home Farm
PETERSPOINT
CROSS GATE
Willow Tree Farm
MARKILLIE LANE
SHAWS LANE
Peterspoint Farm
PE12
TYDD LOW ROAD
Grange Farm
South Holland Lodge
South Holland Bridge
Sewage Works
SPENDLA'S LANE
Allot Gdns
CENTENARY WAY
WOODMILL BANK
Sharpe's Bridge
NORTH ROAD
Tydd St Mary's Marsh
River Nene
GIPSY LANE
CROSS RD
A1101
Strawberry Hall
GREENDYKE LANE
PE13
Nene Way
New Marsh
CROSS GATE
Gibbons Farm
Tydd St Mary
Grange Farm
MARSH ROAD
Nene Outfall Cut
DRAW DIKE
CHURCH WAY
PH
MIDDLE ROAD
Holme Farm
WILLOWS CL
Tydd St Mary CE (Aided) Prim Sch
COMMON WAY
MILL LA
RECTORY RD
LONGS ROAD
MAIN ROAD
HIX'S LA
CHURCH LA
FRONT RD
Gunthorpe Farm
LOW GATE
Allot Gdns
Long House Farm
WORLD'S END RD
GUNTHORPE ROAD
Marsh Farm
A B C D E F
43 44 45 46 47 48
8 25 7 24 6 23 5 22 4 21 3 20 2 19 1 18
For full street detail of the highlighted area see page 216.
159
170
E4
1 WITHINGTON ST
2 CHESTNUT TR
3 KENT CL
4 PEBBLE CL
5 HARRIET CL
6 LONGDON CL
7 DARWIN CL
8 TWO SISTERS CL
9 MOUNT TUMBLEDOWN CL
10 GOOSE GN
11 ANNE RD
12 CHARLES RD
13 ST MATTHEW'S DR
14 ALLENBY'S CH
15 ROYAL CL
16 GAS HO LA
17 QUEEN ST
18 KING ST
19 MILL LA
20 WHARF ST
21 CHURCH ST
22 CHURCH GATE
23 FLINT GATE
F4
1 NENE MS
2 CUSTOMHOUSE ST
3 LIME ST
4 BRIDGE RD
5 HIGH ST
6 BRIDGE RD
7 TODKILL'S LA
8 NENELANDS

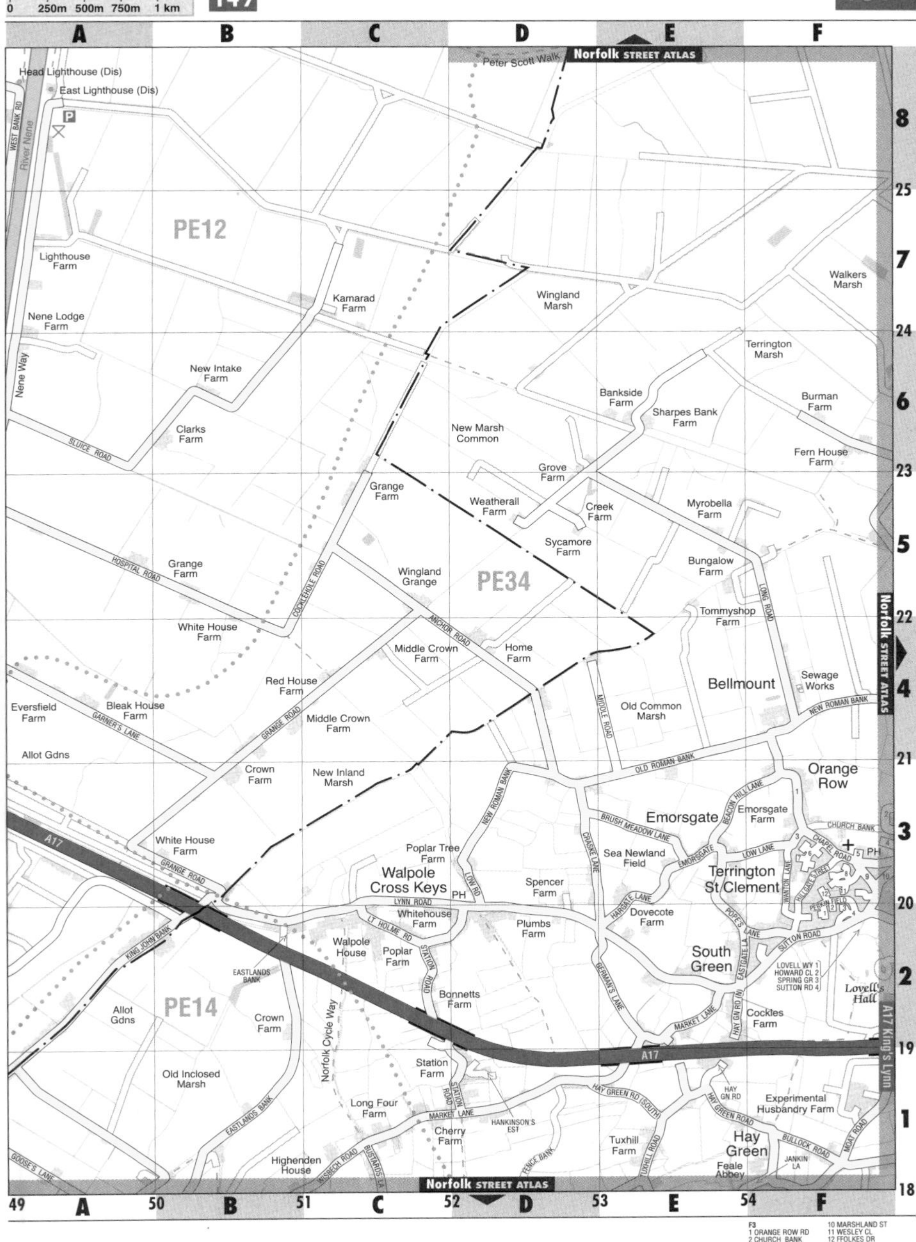

F3
1 ORANGE ROW RD
2 CHURCH BANK
3 ORANGE ROW
4 KING WILLIAM CL
5 WESLEY AV
6 THE SALTINGS
7 BRELLOWS HL
8 CAVE'S CL
9 WESLEY RD
10 MARSHLAND ST
11 WESLEY CL
12 FFOLKES DR

152

E8
1 LITTLE BYTHAM RD
2 REGAL GDNS
3 BYTHAM HEIGHTS
Scale: 1¼ inches to 1 mile
0 ¼ ½ mile
0 250m 500m 750m 1 km
A
B
C
D
E
F
NG33
Stocken Park
HM Prison
Lady Wood
Little Haw Wood
Addah Wood
Chimney
1 HESKETH CT
2 FLEETWOOD CT
3 WILSON CT
4 STOVE CT
Clipsham Park Wood
Quarry (dis)
STATION ROAD
Glebe Farm
Meadows End
CLIPSHAM ROAD
HOLYWELL ROAD
School Farm
Stretton Wood
BRADLEY LA 1
CHURCH LA 2
NEW RD 3
WEST ST 4
Moor Plantation
Clipsham Park
Clipsham
Belton Firs
Pillowsyke Holt
Lodge Farm
CASTLE BYTHAM ROAD
MAIN ST
New Wood
Stockton Lane Plantation
CLIPSHAM ROAD
STRETTON ROAD
BIDWELL LANE
Manor Farm
Hill Top Farm
The Quarries
Holywell Quarry
Holywell Hall
Holy Well
PH
MANOR RD
New Quarry House
New Quarry Plantation
HOLYWELL ROAD
Mill Farm
Bidwell Farm
White's Plantation
Quarries (dis)
Infield Holt
Clipsham Old Quarry (Limestone)
Holywell Wood
Pettywood Farm
Pattinson's Holt
Glebe Farm
Osbonall Wood
Quarry (dis)
Lincolnshire Gate
Robert's Field Nature Reserve
Big Pits Wood
Pickworth Great Wood
Newell Wood
Castle Dike
Greetham Wood Far
Quarry (dis)
LE15
The Grange
Clay Pit
PE9
A1 Grantham
A1
Quarry (dis)
Woolfox Wood
Church (remains of)
Pickworth
Airfield (dis)
The Coppice
Pit (dis)
Woolfox Depot
Turnpole Wood
Hardwick Wood
CH
Taylor's Farm
Pickworth Plain
Rutland County Golf Course
Leicestershire & Rutland STREET ATLAS
North Road Spinney
Exeter Gorse
Horn Farm
GREAT NORTH ROAD
Woodhead
East Wood
Medieval Village of Horn (site of)
Warren Plantation
Woodhead Castle (site of)
Little Oaks
North Brook
Bloody Oaks
PICKWORTH ROAD
Pug's Park Spinney
Tickencote Warren
Mounts Lodge
Quarry (dis)
Wing Plantations
Empingham Old Wood
Horn Mill Spinney
LOVES LA
Tickencote Laund
Quarry (dis)
A1
Leicestershire & Rutland STREET ATLAS
8
17
7
16
6
15
5
14
4
13
3
12
2
11
1
10
95
96
97
98
99
00

171

Scale: 1¼ inches to 1 mile
0 ¼ ½ mile
0 250m 500m 750m 1 km
A8
1 NEW ESTATE
2 HIGH ST
3 CHURCH LA
153
164
A B C D E F
Little Bytham
Ford
Quarry (dis)
Bytham Plantation
NG33
B1176
STATION ROAD
West Glen River
Warren Farm
Sand Pit
The Holt
Stanton's Pit Nature Reserve
West Farm
Bush Lees
Dog Kennel Wood
Woodyard Farm
Cowpasture Farm
Cow Pastures Wood
Nursery Plantation
Fountains Hill
The Sands
East Glen River
Hillside Farm
Toft
CH
A6121
Moxon's Hollow
Sewage Works
Marshalls Farm
MAIN STREET
Careby
Witham Hall Prep Sch
Witham on the Hill
Palace Farm
New Home Farm
PH
Hurd's Wood
Lings Farm
STAMFORD ROAD
PE10
Manthorpe Bridge
Docksight Wood
Careby Wood
Fort
Bowthorpe Park Farm
Wicker Holt
Racer Farm
Danes Hill
Weir
Monk's Wood
Carlby Hawes
Ford
Spur Bridge
The Heath
Medieval Village of Aunby (site of)
Aunby
1 FENTON DR
2 TEMPLEMAN DR
Barber's Hill
Lodge Farm
Barbers Hill Farm
Glebe Farm
Carlby
CHURCH ST
HIGH STREET
Little Warren
Heath Farm
Braceborough Great Wood
1 THE AVENUE
2 MANOR RD
Quarry (dis)
FARRIERS WY
Vale Farm
Dam
Braceborough Little Wood
Pit (dis)
LC
Grange Farm
Ryhall Heath Farm
Manorial Earthworks
BOURNE RD
Clay Hill
THE DRIFT
PE9
Essendine
Church Farm
The Bungalows
PO
Park Farm
Tolethorpe Oaks
Grange Farm
The Freewards
Walk Farm
1 TURNPIKE RD
2 CROWN ST
3 MILL ST
4 FOUNDRY RD
5 MANOR CL
ESSENDINE ROAD
Banthorpe Wood
West Glen River
Crow Spinney
Frith Farm
Bridge Farm
Pit (dis)
Pit (dis)
Gwash Valley Farm
Ford
Banthorpe Lodge
Rob Hall Farm
River Gwash
NEW ROAD
1 THE CRESCENT
2 FLINT CL
3 CASTLE RI
4 NEWSTEAD RD
North Lodge Farm
LC
RYHALL ROAD
BELMESTHORPE LANE
Sewage Works
Macmillan Way
Lby
Ryhall CE Prim Sch
RUTLAND WAY
Browne's Oaks
MAIN STREET
Tolethorpe Hall
Ryhall
Belmesthorpe
Seven Acre Wood
Uffington New Wood
Sewage Works
8 17 7 16 6 15 5 14 4 13 3 12 2 11 1 10
01 02 03 04 05 06
C1
1 HIGHLANDS
2 LEA VW
3 WATERSIDE
4 BRIDGE ST
5 THE SQUARE
6 ST JOHN'S CL
7 CHURCH ST
8 BALK RD
9 SPINNEY CL
10 SPINNEY LA
11 COPPICE RD
12 ST TIBBA WY
13 PARKFIELD RD
14 BURLEY RD
15 BEECH DR
16 MEADOW LA
D3
1 PLOVER RD
2 DUNLIN RD
3 MANOR FARM LA
4 AVOCET CL
5 MALLARD CL
6 STATION RD
7 GLEN CR
171
164
172

163 213 154

C8
1 WOODSIDE CL
2 CAPPITT DR
3 ELSEA DR
4 ELIZABETH WY
5 BECK WY
6 THE CAUSEWAY
7 VIKING WY
8 THE KIPPINGS
9 THE PINGLES
10 LAWRANCE WY
11 PINFOLD CL
12 PRIORY CL
13 MAPLE AVE
14 CROWN LA
15 PARK VW

E5
1 BRUDENELL CL
2 ST JOHNS CL
3 BEDE RD
4 MERCIA GV
5 THETFORD AVE
6 CHARIOTS WY
7 CAESAR CL
8 APPIAN WY
9 FOSSE CL
10 HADRIAN DR
11 MANOR CL
12 MANOR DR
13 CARDYKE DR

Scale: 1¼ inches to 1 mile
0 ¼ ½ mile
0 250m 500m 750m 1 km

172 163 173

E4
1 SCHOOL LA
2 CHURCH ST
3 AVELAND WY
4 CLARE CT
5 DENSHIRE CT
6 COLTON CL
7 CHESHAM DR

F3
1 BARN OWL CL
2 LIME CL
3 DEER PK RD
4 CLOVEN ENDS
5 REEDMANS CL
6 MANOR WY
7 THE RIDES

For full street detail of the highlighted area see page 217.

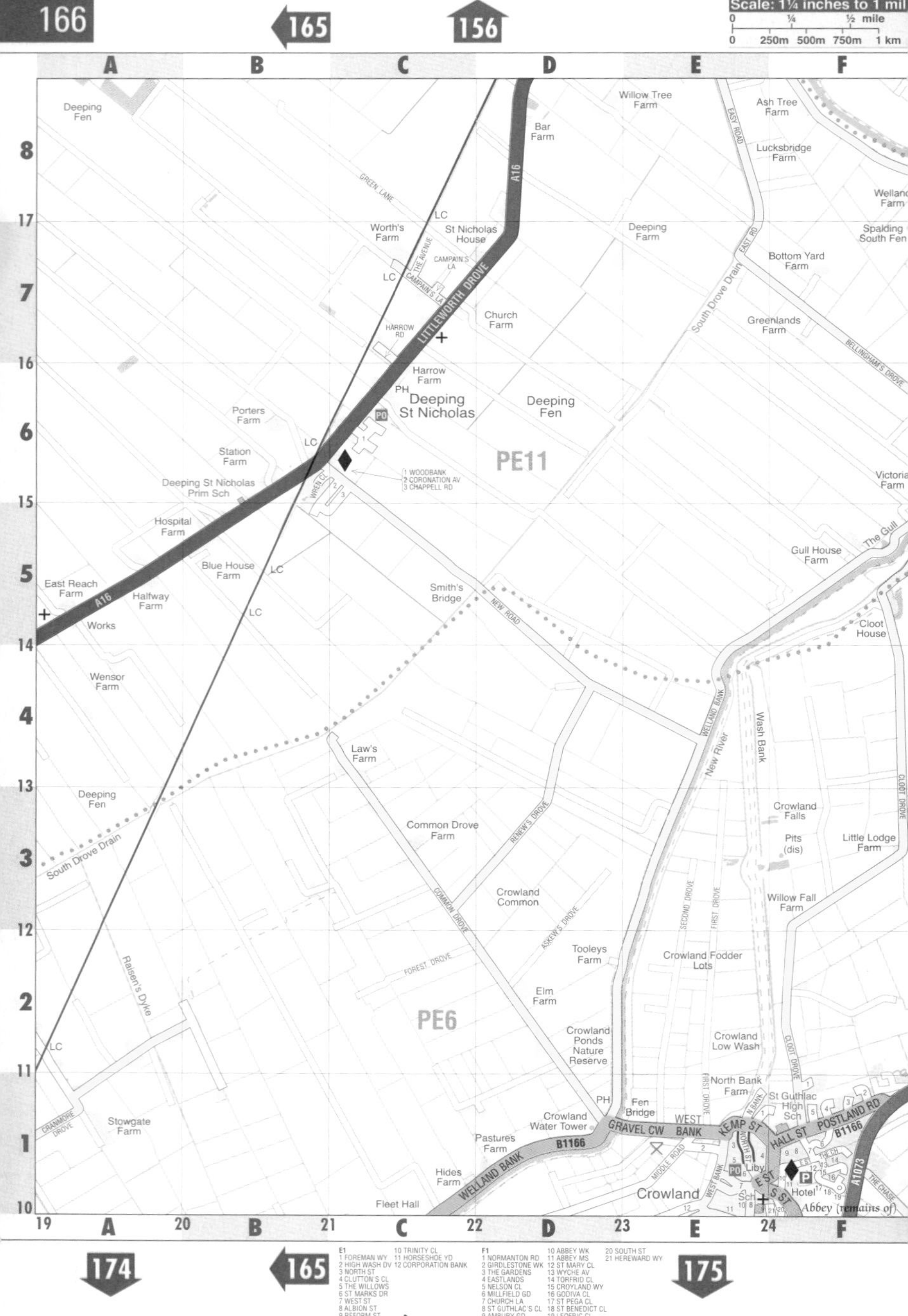
165
156
Scale: 1¼ inches to 1 mil
0 ¼ ½ mile
0 250m 500m 750m 1 km
Deeping Fen
Bar Farm
Willow Tree Farm
Ash Tree Farm
Lucksbridge Farm
Welland Farm
Spalding South Fen
GREEN LANE
A16
LC
Worth's Farm
St Nicholas House
THE AVENUE
CAMPAIN'S LA
Deeping Farm
EAST ROAD
EAST RD
Bottom Yard Farm
LITTLEWORTH DROVE
Church Farm
HARROW RD
South Drove Drain
Greenlands Farm
BELLINGHAM'S DROVE
Harrow Farm
PH
Deeping St Nicholas
PO
Deeping Fen
Porters Farm
Station Farm
PE11
1 WOODBANK
2 CORONATION AV
3 CHAPPELL RD
WREN CL
Deeping St Nicholas Prim Sch
Victoria Farm
Hospital Farm
Blue House Farm
The Gull
Gull House Farm
East Reach Farm
Halfway Farm
Smith's Bridge
NEW ROAD
Works
Cloot House
Wensor Farm
WELLAND BANK
Wash Bank
New River
Law's Farm
Deeping Fen
Crowland Falls
CLOOT DROVE
Common Drove Farm
RENEW'S DROVE
Pits (dis)
Little Lodge Farm
South Drove Drain
COMMON DROVE
Crowland Common
SECOND DROVE
FIRST DROVE
Willow Fall Farm
ASKEW'S DROVE
Raisen's Dyke
Tooleys Farm
Crowland Fodder Lots
FOREST DROVE
Elm Farm
PE6
Crowland Ponds Nature Reserve
Crowland Low Wash
North Bank Farm
St Guthlac High Sch
CRANMORE DROVE
Stowgate Farm
PH
Fen Bridge
Crowland Water Tower
GRAVEL CW
WEST BANK
KEMP ST
HALL ST
POSTLAND RD
B1166
Pastures Farm
MIDDLE ROAD
Liby
E ST
S ST
Hotel
A1073
THE CHASE
Hides Farm
WELLAND BANK
Crowland
Fleet Hall
Abbey (remains of)
A B C D E F
8 17 7 16 6 15 5 14 4 13 3 12 2 11 1 10
19 20 21 22 23 24
174
165
175
E1
1 FOREMAN WY
2 HIGH WASH DV
3 NORTH ST
4 CLUTTON'S CL
5 THE WILLOWS
6 ST MARKS DR
7 WEST ST
8 ALBION ST
9 REFORM ST
10 TRINITY CL
11 HORSESHOE YD
12 CORPORATION BANK
F1
1 NORMANTON RD
2 GIRDLESTONE WK
3 THE GARDENS
4 EASTLANDS
5 NELSON CL
6 MILLFIELD GD
7 CHURCH LA
8 ST GUTHLAC'S CL
9 AMBURY GD
10 ABBEY WK
11 ABBEY MS
12 ST MARY CL
13 WYCHE AV
14 TORFRID CL
15 CROYLAND WY
16 GODIVA CL
17 ST PEGA CL
18 ST BENEDICT CL
19 LEOFRIC CL
20 SOUTH ST
21 HEREWARD WY

Scale: 1¼ inches to 1 mile
B8
1 CLARKSON AV
2 RUSSELL DR
3 GLEBE WK
4 VICARAGE CL
5 ORCHARD WY
6 ST MARY'S GD
7 PARKIN RD
8 CURLEW DR
9 SEDGE PL
10 TEAL GR
11 MILFOIL LA
157
168
Cowbit
Moulton Fen
Moulton Eaugate
Cowbit Wash
Weston Fen
Cowbit Fen
Settlement (site of)
PE12
Moulton West Fen
Brotherhouse Bar
Queen's Bank Farm
St Guthlac's Cross
Crowland Airfield
Martins Farm
Moulton East Fen
Whipchicken Bridge
PE6
Thornbury Hall
Great Postland
Shepeau Stow
Caultons Farm
Patchett's Bridge
Dowsdale
Whaplode Drove Common
North Fen
175
168
176

167
158

Scale: 1¼ inches to 1 mile
0 ¼ ½ mile
0 250m 500m 750m 1 km
A B C D E F
8 17 7 16 6 15 5 14 4 13 3 12 2 11 1 10
31 32 33 34 35 36
Stennetts Farm
Fenland Airfield
Ashtree Farm
Holbeach Fen
Leedsgate Bridge
Fendike Farm
Puddle Down Farm
Peartree Hill Farm
Fen Farm
Griffins Farm
Decoy Farm
Whaplode Fen
Bank Farm
Shell Bridge
Coy Bridge
Glasshouse Farm
South Holland Main Drain
Settlement (site of)
Dowse Farm
Hallgate Farm
Turkey Farm
Water Tower
Ash Farm
Eastways
Fleet Fen
Langary Gate Farm
Works
Northolme
PE12
Aswick Grange
Hagbeach Farm
Coopers Farm
Red May Farm
Middlemoor Farm
Mole Drove Farm
North Barn Farm
North Farm
Little Postland
Gothic Farm
Sutton St Edmund
Northwood House Farm
Fleet Coy Farm
Holly Farm
Whaplode Drove
Willow Tree Farm
Waltons Farm
Ashtree Farm
Gedney Hill Golf Course
CH
Hollytree Farm
Hillbrook Farm
Langary Gate Farm
Holbeach Drove
Hillgate Farm
Eye Farm
The Mill
Gedney Hill CE (Controlled) Prim Sch
Sycamore Grange
Gedney Hill
Bliss Farm
PH
Mayfield
Holbeach Drove Common
PH
Lutton Gate Lodge
PH
White House Farm
Mackinder Farm
Ollards Farm
Fir Tree Farm
Peartree Cottage
The Limes
Hollard's Farm
Gatewood Farm
Manor Farm
North Fen
PO
PO
GELDER'S LANE
MILL GATE
JEKIL'S BANK
FOX HEADINGS
PEARTREE HILL ROAD
CRANE'S GATE
LITTLE DOG DROVE
B1168
NEW RIVER GATE
LAMBERT BANK
LANGARY GATE ROAD
QUICK LANE
FLAG LANE
GEDNEY HILL GATE
HAGBEACH DROVE
DOG DROVE
HOLBEACH DROVE GATE
LANGARY GATE ROAD
Fleet Drain
CHAPEL GATE
EUGATE ROAD
CHAPEL HILL
COOPERS CL
FARROW RD
PARSON'S LANE
BARR'S LANE
NORTH ROAD
LUTTON GATE ROAD
CHAPEL ROAD
BACK BANK
BROADGATE
DOG DROVE
ST POLYCARP'S DR
B1168
BROADGATE ROAD
MOLE DROVE
WEST DROVE NORTH
B1166
DROVE ROAD
LONG LANE
COMMON ROAD
CHAPEL DROVE
MILL LANE
CROSS DROVE
HALL GATE ROAD
WEST DV 1
LINCOLN'S AV 2
HILLGATE
OLD HUNDRED LA
NEW FEN DROVE
HIGHSTOCK LANE
WHALE DROVE
STATION ROAD
WEST DROVE SOUTH
HUBERT'S CL
OLD SOUTH EAU BANK
MOLE DROVE
B1166

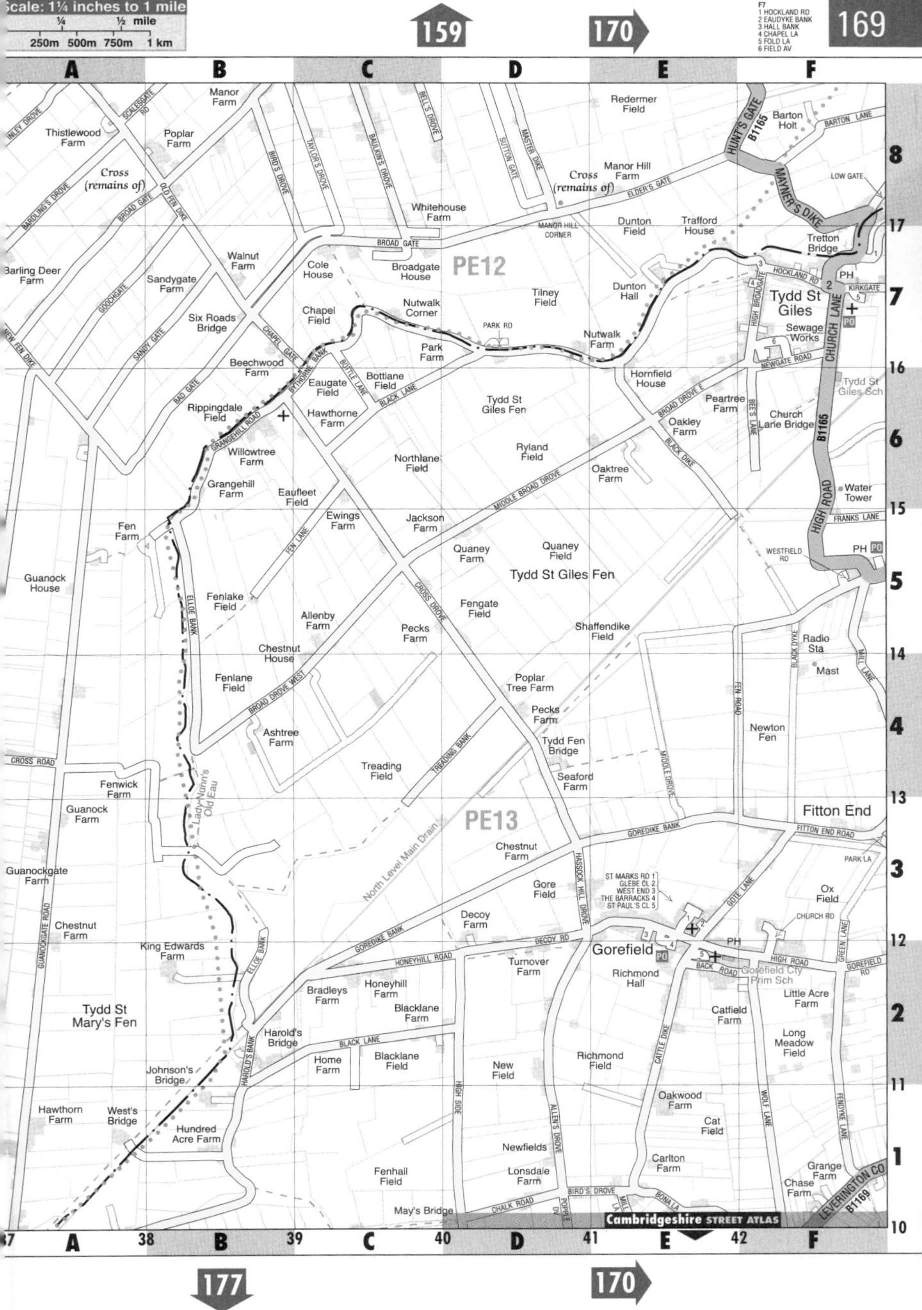
Scale: 1¼ inches to 1 mile
¼
½ mile
250m 500m 750m 1 km
159
170
F7
1 HOCKLAND RD
2 EAUDYKE BANK
3 HALL BANK
4 CHAPEL LA
5 FOLD LA
6 FIELD AV
169
A
B
C
D
E
F
8
17
7
16
6
15
5
14
4
13
3
12
2
11
1
10
Manor Farm
Thistlewood Farm
Poplar Farm
Cross (remains of)
Barling Deer Farm
Walnut Farm
Sandygate Farm
Six Roads Bridge
Beechwood Farm
Rippingdale Field
Willowtree Farm
Grangehill Farm
Eaufleet Field
Fen Farm
Guanock House
Fenlake Field
Allenby Farm
Chestnut House
Fenlane Field
Ashtree Farm
Fenwick Farm
Guanock Farm
Guanockgate Farm
Chestnut Farm
King Edwards Farm
Tydd St Mary's Fen
Johnson's Bridge
Hawthorn Farm
West's Bridge
Hundred Acre Farm
Harold's Bridge
Bradleys Farm
Honeyhill Farm
Blacklane Farm
Home Farm
Blacklane Field
Fenhall Field
May's Bridge
Whitehouse Farm
Cole House
Broadgate House
Chapel Field
Nutwalk Corner
Park Farm
Eaugate Field
Bottlane Field
Hawthorne Farm
Northlane Field
Ewings Farm
Jackson Farm
Quaney Farm
Pecks Farm
Fengate Field
Treading Field
PE12
PE13
Redermer Field
Manor Hill Farm
Cross (remains of)
Dunton Field
Trafford House
Dunton Hall
Tilney Field
Nutwalk Farm
Tydd St Giles Fen
Ryland Field
Oaktree Farm
Quaney Field
Shaffendike Field
Poplar Tree Farm
Pecks Farm
Tydd Fen Bridge
Seaford Farm
Chestnut Farm
Gore Field
Decoy Farm
Turnover Farm
Gorefield
Richmond Hall
New Field
Richmond Field
Newfields
Lonsdale Farm
Hornfield House
Oakley Farm
Peartree Farm
Barton Holt
Tretton Bridge
Tydd St Giles
Sewage Works
Church Lane Bridge
Tydd St Giles Sch
Water Tower
PH
PO
Radio Sta
Mast
Newton Fen
Fitton End
Ox Field
Gorefield Cty Prim Sch
Little Acre Farm
Catfield Farm
Long Meadow Field
Oakwood Farm
Cat Field
Carlton Farm
Grange Farm
Chase Farm
North Level Main Drain
Lady Nunn's Old Eau
ST MARKS RD 1
GLEBE CL 2
WEST END 3
THE BARRACKS 4
ST PAUL'S CL 5
BROAD GATE
ELDER'S GATE
HUNT'S GATE
MAYNER'S DIKE
HOCKLAND RD
CHURCH LANE
HIGH ROAD
B1165
GOREDIKE BANK
FITTON END ROAD
HONEYHILL ROAD
DECOY RD
BLACK LANE
HIGH ROAD
GOREFIELD RD
LEVERINGTON CO
B1169
CROSS ROAD
GUANOCKGATE ROAD
ELLOE BANK
MIDDLE BROAD DROVE
BROAD DROVE WEST
CROSS DROVE
Cambridgeshire STREET ATLAS
37
38
39
40
41
42
177
170

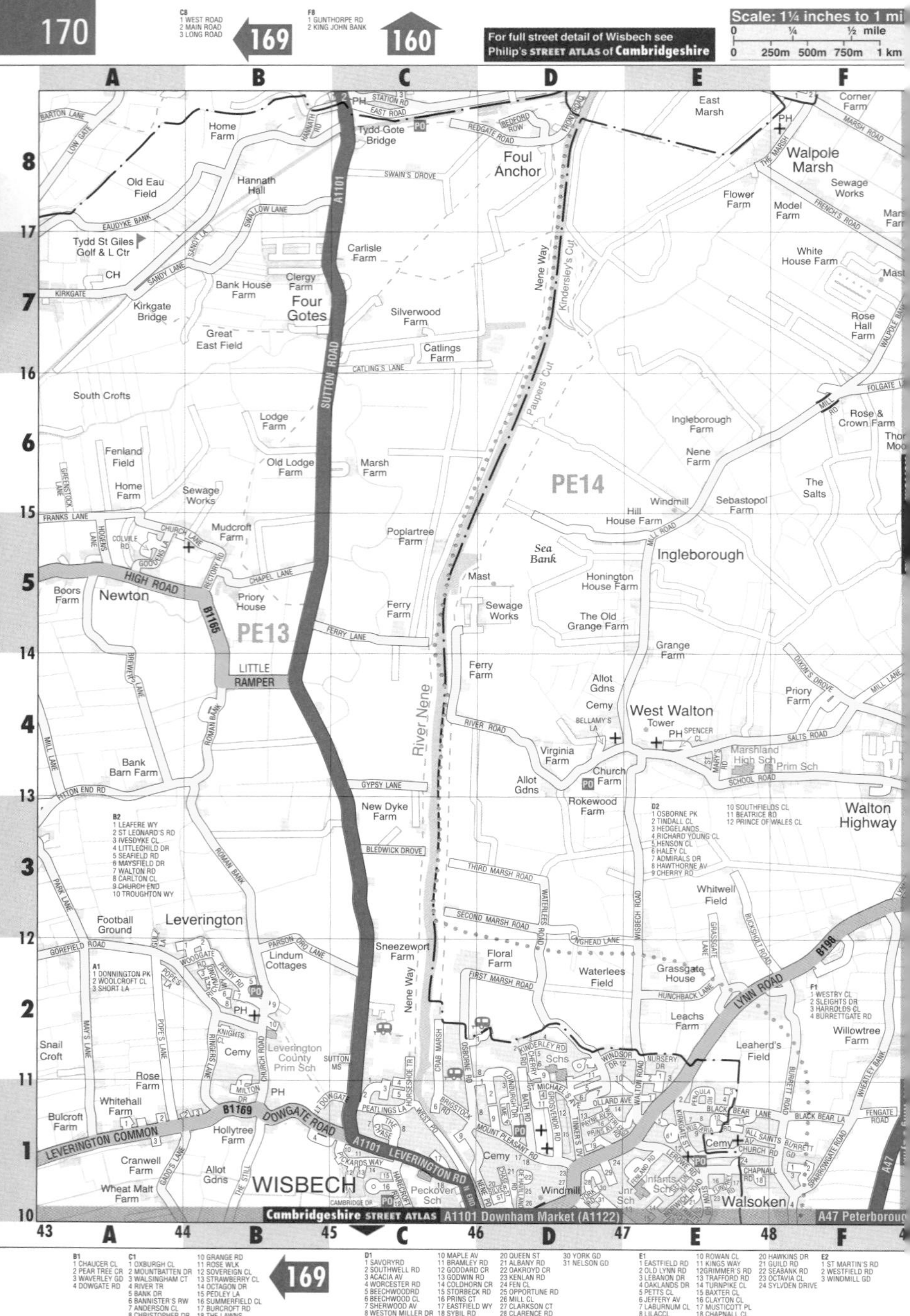

B1
1 CHAUCER CL
2 PEAR TREE CR
3 WAVERLEY GD
4 DOWGATE RD

C1
1 OXBURGH CL
2 MOUNTBATTEN DR
3 WALSINGHAM CT
4 RIVER TR
5 BANK DR
6 BANNISTER'S RW
7 ANDERSON CL
8 CHRISTOPHER DR
9 NENE PD
10 GRANGE RD
11 ROSE WLK
12 SOVEREIGN CL
13 STRAWBERRY CL
14 OCTAGON DR
15 PEDLEY LA
16 SUMMERFIELD CL
17 BURCROFT RD
18 THE LAWNS
19 CRICKETERS WY

169

D1
1 SAVORYRD
2 SOUTHWELL RD
3 ACACIA AV
4 WORCESTER RD
5 BEECHWOODRD
6 BEECHWOOD CL
7 SHERWOOD AV
8 WESTON MILLER DR
9 SOUTHWELL RD
10 MAPLE AV
11 BRAMLEY RD
12 GODDARD CR
13 GODWIN RD
14 COLDHORN CR
15 STORBECK RD
16 PRINS CT
17 EASTFIELD WY
18 SYBIL RD
19 KOOREMAN AV
20 QUEEN ST
21 ALBANY RD
22 OAKROYD CR
23 KENLAN RD
24 FEN CL
25 OPPORTUNE RD
26 MILL CL
27 CLARKSON CT
28 CLARENCE RD
29 SANDRINGHAM AV
30 YORK GD
31 NELSON GD

E1
1 EASTFIELD RD
2 OLD LYNN RD
3 LEBANON DR
4 OAKLANDS DR
5 PETTS CL
6 JEFFERY AV
7 LABURNUM CL
8 LILACCL
9 JASMIN CL
10 ROWAN CL
11 KINGS WAY
12GRIMMER'S RD
13 TRAFFORD RD
14 TURNPIKE CL
15 BAXTER CL
16 CLAYTON CL
17 MUSTICOTT PL
18 CHAPNALL CL
19 COUNCIL RD
20 HAWKINS DR
21 GUILD RD
22 SEABANK RD
23 OCTAVIA CL
24 SYLVDEN DRIVE

E2
1 ST MARTIN'S RD
2 WESTFIELD RD
3 WINDMILL GD

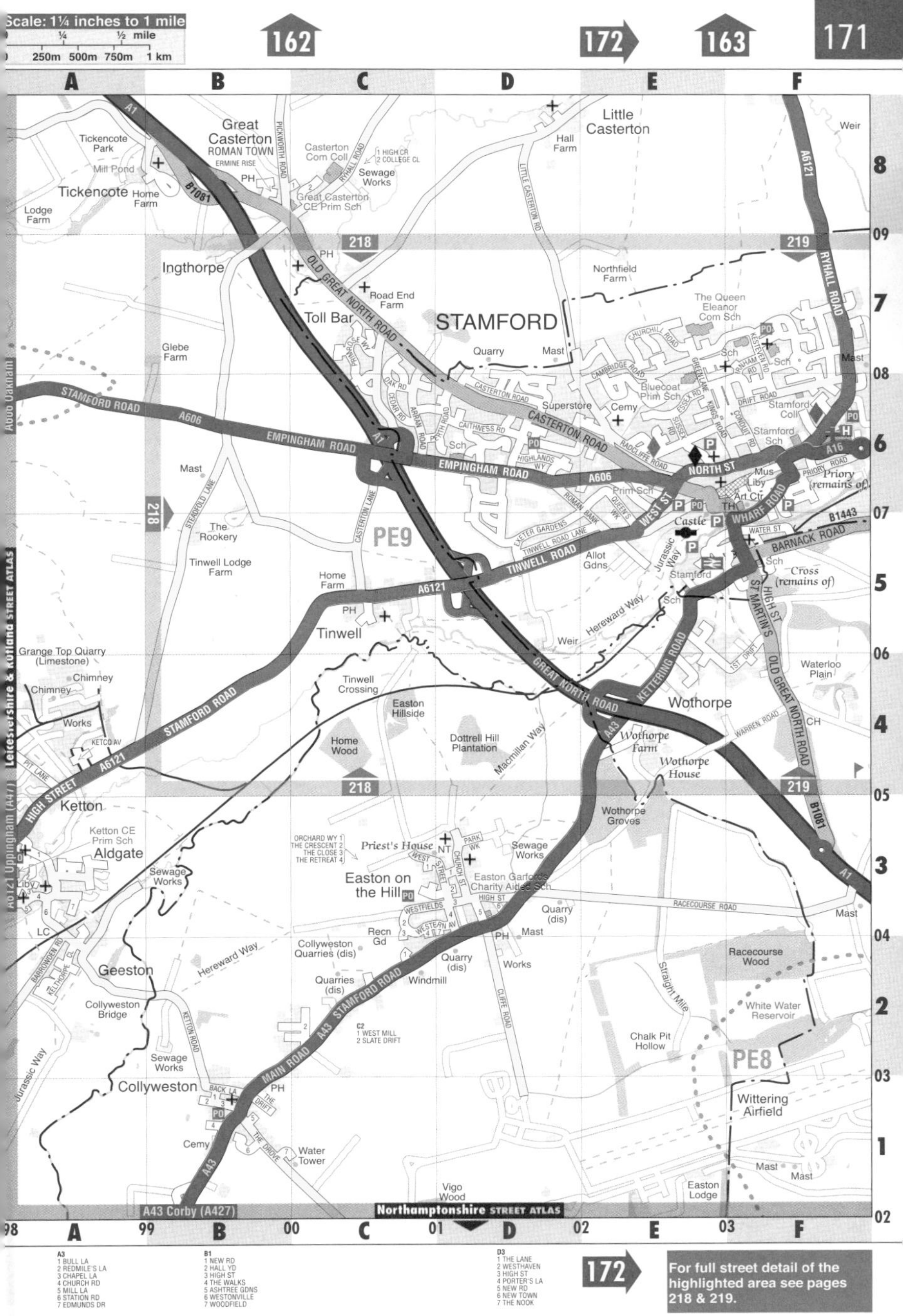
Scale: 1¼ inches to 1 mile
¼
½ mile
250m 500m 750m 1 km
162
172
163
A
B
C
D
E
F
8
7
6
5
4
3
2
1
09
08
07
06
05
04
03
02
98
99
00
01
Great Casterton
ROMAN TOWN
ERMINE RISE
Tickencote Park
Mill Pond
Tickencote
Home Farm
Lodge Farm
PICKWORTH ROAD
Casterton Com Coll
RYHALL ROAD
1 HIGH CR
2 COLLEGE CL
Sewage Works
Great Casterton CE Prim Sch
Little Casterton
Hall Farm
LITTLE CASTERTON RD
Weir
A6121
RYHALL ROAD
218
219
Ingthorpe
OLD GREAT NORTH ROAD
Road End Farm
Northfield Farm
The Queen Eleanor Com Sch
Toll Bar
STAMFORD
Quarry
Mast
Glebe Farm
STAMFORD ROAD
A606
EMPINGHAM ROAD
A1
CASTERTON ROAD
Superstore
Cemy
Bluecoat Prim Sch
Stamford Coll
Stamford Sch
NORTH ST
Mus
Liby
Art Ctr
Priory (remains of)
WHARF ROAD
Castle
Mast
STEADFOLD LANE
The Rookery
Tinwell Lodge Farm
CASTERTON LANE
PE9
Home Farm
A6121
TINWELL ROAD
Allot Gdns
Jurassic Way
Stamford
B1443
BARNACK ROAD
Cross (remains of)
ST MARTIN'S
HIGH ST
Hereward Way
Weir
Tinwell
Grange Top Quarry (Limestone)
Chimney
Works
KETCO AV
Tinwell Crossing
Easton Hillside
GREAT NORTH ROAD
KETTERING ROAD
Wothorpe
Waterloo Plain
OLD GREAT NORTH ROAD
CH
Home Wood
Dottrell Hill Plantation
Macmillan Way
A43
Wothorpe Farm
Wothorpe House
HIGH STREET
STAMFORD ROAD
Ketton
Ketton CE Prim Sch
Aldgate
Wothorpe Groves
B1081
ORCHARD WY 1
THE CRESCENT 2
THE CLOSE 3
THE RETREAT 4
Priest's House
NT
Sewage Works
Easton on the Hill
Easton Garfords Charity Aided Sch
RACECOURSE ROAD
Quarry (dis)
Mast
Sewage Works
LC
WESTFIELDS
WESTERN AV
Recn Gd
PH
Mast
Collyweston Quarries (dis)
Quarry (dis)
Works
Racecourse Wood
Geeston
Hereward Way
Quarries (dis)
Windmill
STAMFORD ROAD
CLIFFE ROAD
Straight Mile
White Water Reservoir
Collyweston Bridge
C2
1 WEST MILL
2 SLATE DRIFT
Chalk Pit Hollow
Jurassic Way
Sewage Works
KETTON ROAD
MAIN ROAD
PE8
Collyweston
BACK LA
THE DRIFT
Wittering Airfield
Cemy
THE DROVE
Water Tower
Mast
Mast
Vigo Wood
Easton Lodge
A43 Corby (A427)
Northamptonshire STREET ATLAS
Leicestershire & Rutland STREET ATLAS
A6121 Uppingham (A47)
A3
1 BULL LA
2 REDMILE'S LA
3 CHAPEL LA
4 CHURCH RD
5 MILL LA
6 STATION RD
7 EDMUNDS DR
B1
1 NEW RD
2 HALL YD
3 HIGH ST
4 THE WALKS
5 ASHTREE GDNS
6 WESTONVILLE
7 WOODFIELD
D3
1 THE LANE
2 WESTHAVEN
3 HIGH ST
4 PORTER'S LA
5 NEW RD
6 NEW TOWN
7 THE NOOK
172
For full street detail of the highlighted area see pages 218 & 219.

163
171
C6
1 SOMES CL
2 THE CHARTERS
3 MANNERS CL
4 LINDSEY RD
5 GREATFORD RD
6 SCHOOL LA
7 MAIN RD
8 BERTIE LA
F7
1 OLD RECTORY DR
2 WEST RD
3 ST LAWRENCE WY
4 CASEWICK LA
164
Scale: 1¼ inches to 1 mile
0 ¼ ½ mile
0 250m 500m 750m 1 km
Bungalow Grange Farm
Newstead Road
Wood Farm
New Wood
Grange Farm
Fox Covert
Belmesthorpe Grange
Weir
Macmillan Way
219
Casewick Park
Casewick Hall
Barholm Field
Pit (dis)
Morley Wood
Privet Plantation
Works
Dry Sk Centre
Carrs Lodge Farm
Casewick Road
LC
PH
River Gwash
Lower Home Farm
Folly Farm
Casewick Lane
Casewick Field
Works
Mast
Newstead
Tallington
Teesdales Farm
PO
Mill Lane
Mill Mound
1 HERONS CL
2 CHURCH LA
Works
Uffington Road
Uffington
PH
Main Road
West Marsh
Church Meadow
Allot Gdns
Weir
Ford
Uffington Park
A16
Copthill Farm
River Welland
Torpel Way
Spring Wood
Copthill Sch
Sewage Works
B1443
LC
Sewage Works
Torpel Way
LC
LC
The Dingle
PE9
MEADOWGATE 1
ST MARY'S CL 2
BADINTON LA 3
Deer Park
Burghley House
Bainton
Swimming Pool
Cross
Dog Kennel Bushes
The Butlands
Burghley Park
The Lake
Uffington Road
Pudding Bag La
Barnack Road
Pilsgate Farm
The Acres 1
Uffington RD 2
Jack Haws La 3
Little Northfields
Torpel Way
Dairy Farm
Box Hill
Station Road
Grossmith' Spinney
Pilsgate
Stamford Road
Bainton Road
Cross (remains of)
Quarry (dis)
The Synhams
Barnack CE Prim Sch
Barnack
Main St
Stamford Rd
River Welland
Hereward Way
Windmill
1 ORCHARD RD
2 ALLERTON CL
Down Halls
Barn End
Windmill Farm
Wittering Road
P
Rubbing House Spinney
Hills & Holes
Ufford Farm
Main Street
Quarry (dis)
Ufford Spinney
Wash Dyke Pond
Ufford Oaks
Ufford Hall
Ufford
Nature Reserve
Walcot Hall
Quarry (dis)
Barnack Drift
PH
Chy
Walcot Road
Marholm Rd
Allside
The Park
Flints Lodge Farm
Crow Spinney
Newport Farm
Main St (Southorpe)
Lambpits Spinney
Charles' Plantation
Quarry (dis)
Hall Farm
Middle Farm
Fox Covert
Sewage Works
Mill Farm
Airfield
A1
Southorpe
Little Wood
Pinewood Av
Merryshaws Spinney
Stud Farm
Main Street
Boar's Hill Planting
High Farm
Southey Wood
Recn Gd
PH
Liby
Grange Farm
Tom's Wood
1 ST MARY'S AVE
2 BALDWIN CL
3 HAMMOND CL
4 DARLEY CL
5 RADFORD CL
6 LAWRENCE RD
Wet Spinney
Southorpe Paddock Nature Reserve
PO
Prim Sch
Church Road
Boxer Rd
PE8
Wittering
Bushy Wood
Lady Wood
Cambridgeshire STREET ATLAS
A1 Peterborough (A47)
A B C D E F
04 05 06 07 08 09
8 09 7 08 6 07 5 06 4 05 3 04 2 03 1 02
B1
1 COLLYWESTON RD
2 WELLAND RD
3 GLEN RD
4 NENE CL
5 CHATER RD
6 TOWNSEND RD
7 BROWNES RD
8 EXETER RD
9 HOLT CL
10 FREEMAN CL
11 HARVEY CL
12 THE LIMES
13 MANOR CL
14 BURGHLEY AVE
15 ST JOHN'S RD
16 ST MICHAEL'S RD
17 ST GEORGE'S RD
18 BROADHURST RD
19 NEWMAN CL
20 MALTBY CL
21 CARNEGIE RD
22 EMBRY RD
23 PARKER RD
24 JEFFERSON CL
171
D3
1 SCHOOL RD
2 THE SQUARE
3 MILLSTONE LA
4 KINGSLEY CL
5 BISHOPS WK
6 CANON DR
7 OWEN CL
8 SAXON RD
9 WHITMAN CL
222
For full street detail of the highlighted area see page 219.

cale: 1¼ inches to 1 mile
¼
½ mile
250m 500m 750m 1 km
164
C7
1 SCHOOL CL
2 BARN CL
3 SCHOOL LA
4 BLIND LA
5 TORPEL WY
6 THE RETREAT
217
174
165
A
B
C
D
E
F
8
09
7
08
6
07
5
06
4
05
3
04
2
03
1
02
llington Lakes
Leisure Park
Middle
Field
STAMFORD ROAD A16
STAMFORD RD
KING STREET
West
Deeping
Cemy
PH
THE LANE
Manor
House
Horse
Marsh
Meadow
Farm
Church
Meadow
Mickle
Holmes
Little
Meadow
Weir
Lolham
Hall
Lyndon
Farm
Market
Deeping
Bridge
TH
LINCOLN ROAD
A15
Deeping
Gate
Fox Cover
Farm
Castle
Farm
Moat
MILL ROAD
CASTLE END ROAD
Maxey
WEST END ROAD
TUCKERS NOOK
HIGH STREET
MILL ROAD
PERKINS LA
QUARRY LANE
Works
Settlement
Woodgate
Farm
Sand &
Gravel Pit
Works
Maxey
Quarry
Nunton
Lodge
Farm
Weir
Maxey Cut
Cemy
Weir
Lolham
Bridges
MAXEY ROAD
WADE PK AV
SWIFT CL
HORSEGATE
Liby
PARK ROAD
BRIDGE ST
BELL LA
MILLFIELD RD
MANOR WAY
HEREWARD WAY
Sch
Ctr
Recn
Gd
BROADGATE LA
CHURCH ST
PO
SUTTON'S LANE
MAXEY VW
Market
Deeping
DEEPING ST JAMES RD
Deeping
St James
PEAKIRK ROAD
Newstead
Farm
LINCOLN ROAD
B1524
RIPPONS DROVE
Northborough
LINCOLN RD
B1162
MAXEY ROAD
CLAYPOLE DR
CLARE RD
CHURCH VW
Cemy
PINGLE LA
PASTURE LA
PARADIS
CHURCH STREET
Castle
Farm
PH
Manor
House
Northborough
County
Prim Sch
LINCOLN ROAD
Nine
Bridges
MILE DROVE
NORTH FEN ROAD
Pit
(dis)
PE9
LC
Weir
Church
Farm
MAIN ROAD
Etton
RECTORY LA
PE6
Rectory
Farm
PH
Glinton
Dovecote
OAK RD
HIGH ST
Sch
PEAKIRK ROAD
Cemy
WELMORE RD
B1443
LC
Cooks
Farm
arn
anor
arm
Ashton
River Welland
(Old Course)
LC
Cemy
Helpston
Quarry
Farm
PH
Works
LC
The
Elms
HELPSTON ROAD
House
Farm
Arthur Mellows
Village Coll
Torpel Way
Ring &
Bailey
WEST STREET
GLINTON ROAD
B1443
Manor
Farm
Lawn
Wood
Manor
House
The John Clare
County Prim Sch
PH
WOODGATE
Woodgate
Farm
A15
BROAD WHEEL ROAD
Rice
Wood
C4
1 CROMWELL MWS
2 GOLDEN DROP
3 CHURCH LA
4 THE NOOK
5 ARBORFIELD CL
6 MILL FIELD CL
College
Cott
LC
Works
WATERWORKS LANE
A15
WERRINGTON PARKWAY
LINCOLN ROAD
The
Jubilee
Hilly
Wood
Maxham
Farm
MAXHAM'S GN RD
Woodcroft
Castle
ROMAN
VILLA
HEATH ROAD
Cemy
Steeping
Wood
Pits
(dis)
Woodcroft
Lodge
LC
Windmill Hill
Plantation
New Close
Wood
Helpston
Quarry (dis)
Oxey
Wood
WOODCROFT ROAD
HURN ROAD
Gate House
Farm
PAPYRUS RD
The
Severals
Southey
Wood
Pit
(dis)
Simon's
Wood
Hayes
Wood
STAMFORD ROAD
Belham
Wood
Marholm
Peterborough
Crematorium
Blackthorn
Spinney
Pits
(dis)
Foster's
Coppice
Manor
Farm
WATER END
PH
WALTON ROAD
0
11
12
13
14
15
B4
1 CROSSBERRY WY
2 WOODLAND LEA
3 TEMPLES CT
223
224
174
For full street detail of the highlighted areas see pages 217 & 220.

For full street detail of the highlighted area see pages 220 & 221.

Scale: 1¼ inches to 1 mile
¼
½ mile
250m 500m 750m 1 km
166
B8
1 ABBOTS DR
2 GLEBE GD
3 CORONATION AV
4 CHAPEL ST
5 MONKS MEADOW
6 ALDERLANDS CL
7 PENWALD CL
8 TATWIN DR
9 BECCELM DR
C8
1 SNOWDEN CL
2 THORNEY RD
3 CRAWFORD GD
4 STRICKLANDS DR
5 KENNULPHS CL
6 HARRINGTON WY
7 HARRINGTON DR
176
167
175
A
B
C
D
E
F
Crowland High Wash
LOW ROAD
MILL DROVE
Mast
PLANK DROVE
CREASE DROVE
HARVESTER WY
BROADWAY
PETERBOROUGH ROAD
A1073
Allot Gdns
Crowland
B1040
Works
BARBERS DRO
THE CHASE
GREEN DROVE
SHEPPARD'S DROVE
Empsons Farm
Old South Eau
Fall's Bridge
North Fen
Greenbank Farm
South Eau Farm
Empsons Farm
FALL'S DROVE
CARRINGTON'S DV
Borough Fen
Kennulph's Farm
Eardley Grange Farm
WRIGHT'S DROVE
Poplar Farm
PETERBOROUGH ROAD
Vine House Farm
North Fen
Blue Bell Bridge
Falls Farm
FRENCH DROVE
Blue Bell Farm
FRENCH DROVE
Nene Terrace
Fens End
Hundreds Farm
HUNDREDS ROAD
Old Hall Farm
BELL DROVE
Old Farm
St Vincent's Cross
St Vincents Cross Farm
Ruff Fen
Bonnett's Pieces
Pepper Lake Farm
Horseshoe Bridge
Singlesole Farm
Cross (remains of)
GREEN DROVE
HANGMAN'S CORNER
Moor's Farm
Grays Farm
BLACK DROVE
Borough Fen
Hill Farm
Steam House Farm
Singlecote Farm
Morris Fen
Flood Farm
PE6
B1040
Mason's Bridge
B1443
Cat's Water Plantation
Slipe Farm
Little Tower's Fen
Lodge Farm
Hill Farm
Fletchers Farm
THORNEY ROAD
Powder Blue Farm
CROWLAND ROAD
Powder Blue Bridge
Hurn Farm
BUKEHORN ROAD
Buke Horn Farm
A1073
Cat's Water
Bedford Level (North Level)
B1443
Turves Farm
THE REACHES
Buke Horn Plantation
Rose Farm
Oakhurst Farm
Elm Tree Farm
Cat's Water Plantation
Middle West Farm
Thorney
Windmill
Northolm Farm
Great Tower's Fen
Hightrees Farm
Catwater Farm
A47
CROWLAND ROAD
NORTHAM CL
Eye Green
Northolme Coppice
THE CAUSEWAY
TURVES ROAD
NEWSTEAD CL
NIPCUT ROAD
Pode Hole Farm
Guy's Fen
Causeway Toll Farm
Tollhouse Farm
Pasture House Plantation
PH
Nature Reserve
Pastures House Farm
THORNEY ROAD
A47
Hayne's Farm
Chicell's Hurst
TONEHAM LANE
Cemy
THORNEY ROAD
Toneham Farm
EYE ROAD
Liby
PO
PH
HIGH ST
BACK LA
Mill Fen
Bar Pastures
WILLOW HALL LANE
Barlees Fen
Thorney River
Hill Farm
FOUNTAINS PL
Eye CE (Controlled) Sch
LINDISFARNE RD
Bar Pasture Farm
Hill Fen
WHITTLESEY RD
B1040
Eye
EYEBURY RD
Sand & Gravel Pit
Cambridgeshire STREET ATLAS
8
09
7
08
6
07
5
06
4
05
3
04
2
03
1
02
22
A
23
B
24
C
25
D
26
E
27
F
A1
1 MOORE'S LA
2 ST BENET'S GD
3 CLEVE PL
4 TINTERN RI
5 HODNEY RD
6 BEAULIEU CT
7 CHANCERY LA
8 BOXGROVE CL
9 NEW RD
10 THE CRESCENT
11 DELAPRE CT
12 BEECH LA
13 WALSINGHAM WY
14 CARTMEL WY
15 LITTLE CL
16 ST ALBAN'S DR
17 ST OLAVE'S DR
18 DEERHURST WY
19 ST BEE'S DR
20 GLASTONBURY CL
21 LEISTON CT
22 MONKS DR
23 PETERBOROUGH RD
24 WESTMINSTER GD
227
176
F3
1 ASH CL
2 BERBERIS CL
3 ORCHARD CT

167
175
168

Scale: 1¼ inches to 1 mile
0 ¼ ½ mile
0 250m 500m 750m 1 km

A3
1 KINGSLINE CL
2 ASH CL
3 CHESTNUT DR
4 BEECH CL
5 GAS LA
6 THE MALTINGS
7 LAUREL DR
8 THE CAUSEWAY
9 CHURCH ST
10 ABBEY PL
11 THE GREEN
12 RUSSELL CL
13 TOPHAM CR
14 SANDPIT RD
15 TAVISTOCK CL
16 BEDFORD CT

175

Scale: 1¼ inches to 1 mile
¼ ½ mile
250m 500m 750m 1 km
168
169
A B C D E F
Inkley's Farm
Hilton Hall Farm
LUTTON GATE ROAD
HALL GATE ROAD
BROADGATE ROAD
GUANOCKGATE RD
MARSHALL'S BANK
Throckenholt
B1166
Cloughs Cross
North Inham Field
SEALEY'S LANE
Sewage Works
Church Farm
PH
Warners Farm
ELBOW LA
Essex Farm
MAIN ROAD
CORONATION AVENUE
Cole's Bridge
Throckenholt Farm
THE BANK
Allens Bridge Farm
Rookery Farm
B1166
Woadmill Farm
Manor Farm
PE12
PO
Payne Sch
Henlow Farm
Parson Drove
BRIDGE DROVE
Poplar Tree Farm
RIVERSIDE GARDENS
PH
1 SPRINGFIELD RD
2 INGHAM HALL GDNS
3 NEWLANDS RD
SILVER'S LANE
South Inham Field
Old Eau Field Farm
Fen Farm
JOHNSON'S DROVE
Swanbridge Farm
Field End
B1187
SEADYKE ROAD
Drove Fen
MURROW BANK
Southfork Farm
Parson Drove Fen
Holly Farm
Apple Fen
Dearloves Farm
Sandlewood Farm
BACK ROAD
FRONT RD
Hiptoft Field
LONG DROVE
FRONT ROAD
Ivy Lodge Farm
Hiptoft Farm
Inkerson Fen
PH
Murrow
North Level Drain
MURROW LANE
MILL ROAD
1 MILL CL
2 INHAMS CL
3 PENTELOW CL
Murrow Field
Parson Drove Fen
STATION AV
Bank House Farm
Murrow County Prim Sch
Ravens Farm
Turf Fen Bridge
PE13
Willow Farm
Rose Cottage Golden Fen
Jubilee Farm
Rogues Alley
HOOK'S DROVE
LONG DROVE
PLASH DROVE
Alley Farm
Calves Field
Wisbech High Fen
Bishop Lands Farm
Plash Farm
White Lion Farm
CANT'S DROVE
The Homestead
FOLLY'S DROVE
BLACK DROVE
Bishop Lands
Poplar Farm
GULL BANK
Willow Farm
Hundreds Farm
Fort Farm
Guyhirn Field
Ivy Farm
Cooks Farm
GULL DROVE
B1187
GULL RD
LINDENS CL
PH
Wisbech High Fen
Guyhirn Gull
MAIN ROAD
Thorney Toll
WISBECH ROAD
Peartree Farm
High Fen
Poplars Farm
Towers Farm
GULL ROAD
Grange Farm
Halls Farm
THORNEY ROAD
Guyhirn
Redgate Farm
Bank House Farm
PH
HIGH ROAD
A47 Wisbech
New Wryde Drain
FEN ROAD
Chestnut Farm
Terrington Lands Farm
A47
Oaktree Farm
Bank Side Farm
A141
Elm Tree Farm
MARCH RD
Adventurers' Land
Ring's End Farm
MARCH ROAD
Guyhirn Wash
Nene Way
River Nene
Cambridgeshire STREET ATLAS
A141 March
8 09 7 08 6 07 5 06 4 05 3 04 2 03 1 02
34 35 36 37 38 39

3

E7
1 CROMWELL CT
2 WOODHILL CL
3 NORWOOD CL
4 WAULDBY CL
5 WEETON WY

E8
1 COLLYNSON CL
2 SETTERWOOD GARTH
3 OAKDALE AV

A B C D E F

8 7 29 6 5 28 4 3 27 2 1 26

West Ella
Kirk Ella
The Lunds
St Andrews Prim Sch
Wolfreton Sch
HU10
Playing Field
Haltemprice Leisure Centre
Springhead Prim Sch
Anlaby
Four Acre Plantation
Slight's Plantation
The Grove
White Walk Plantation
Horseshoe Plantation
Hut Plantation
West Ella Grange
Drydales
Hull High Sch for Girls
BUPA Hull & East Riding
Marr Bridge
Low Field
Howden Pit (dis)
HU13
Tranby Park
Tranby Park Farm
Stockdove Wood
Hessle Mount Sch
Hessle Mount
Hessle Lower Sch
Hessle Penshurst Prim Sch
Northfield
Cemetery
All Saints CE Jun Sch
North Drive Plantation
Hawk Plantation
Hessle High Sch
Bridgeview Sch
Quarry (dis)
Mast
Humber Field Farm
Hessle
Factory

F6
1 HILDYARD CL
2 DALEHOUSE DR
3 STATHERS WK
4 NANDIKE CL
5 GRIMSTON RD
6 SYKES CL
7 ANLAFGATE
8 JULIAN'S WK

E2
1 HALYCON AV
2 NORTHOLME CL
3 WESTBOURNE AV
4 THE CIRCLE
5 BRUNSWICK GR

01 A B 02 C D 03 E F

3 3

E1
1 SPIRE VW
2 TOWER HL MS
3 VICARAGE LA
4 CLOWES CT
5 FISHWICK AV

F1
1 MARGARET GR
2 BISHOP BLUNT CL
3 BISHOP KEMPTHORNE CLO
4 BISHOP GURDON CL

A3
1 BARNETBY RD
2 KELSTON DR
3 YARMOUTH AV
4 WINTHORPE RD
5 BROCKLESBY CL
6 CORRAN GARTH
B7
1 LANGFORD WK
2 HOLLYTREE AV
3 LABURNUM DR
4 ROSEWOOD CL
C8
1 PRIMROSE DR
2 COUNTY RD S
D8
1 LOCKTON GR
2 HACKNESS GR
3 BARGATE GR
4 SNAINTON GR
180
E6
1 AIRMYN AVE
2 ST MARTINS AVE
F6
1 HAWTHORN CT
E. Yorkshire & N. Lincolnshire STREET ATLAS
HU5
HU10
HU4
HU3
HU13
East Ella
Anlaby
Anlaby Common
Anlaby Park
Gipsyville
Recreation Ground
Costello Playing Fields
Pickering Park
Boating Lake
Boothferry Park (Hull City AFC)
Priory Park
Priory Bridge
Humberside Fire & Rescue Service HQ
Waterside Business Park
Trans Pennine Trail
Cemetery
Hull Coll
Playing Field
C7
1 LAVENDER WK
2 PINEWOOD GR
3 GARTON GR
4 SORBUS VW
5 MAPLE CL
6 CONIFER CL
B6
1 HARWOOD DR
2 GLENWOOD DR
3 WESTWOOD DR
4 INGLEWOOD DR
5 DERRINGHAM AV
6 ELSIEMERE WK
7 ANLABY AV
8 WORKINGTON AV
9 DITMAS AV
ASTLEY ST 1
BROUGHAM ST 2
COBDEN ST 3
CHATHAM ST 4
D2
1 KIPLING WK
2 WHEATFIELD CL
3 GEMSBOK CL
4 PRIORY FARM DR
BOOTHFERRY ROAD
ANLABY HIGH ROAD
ANLABY ROAD
ASKEW AVE
HESSLE ROAD
CLIVE SULLIVAN WAY
SPRING BANK W
A
B
C
D
E
F
8
7
6
5
4
3
2
1
29
28
27
26
05
06
A2
1 VALENTINE CL
2 BENEDICT CL
3 VINCENT CL
4 NEWLYN CL
5 CRISPIN CL
6 COTTESMORE RD
B2
1 AVONDALE
2 WOOLWICH DR
3 DATCHET GARTH
C6
1 THE GREENWAY
4
180

A5
1 CORDELLA CL
2 DORADO CL
3 SANDLEMERE CL
4 DARRISMERE VILLAS
5 BRIXHAM CT
6 OTTERBURN ST

A6
1 GRANVILLE ST
2 SANDRINGHAM ST
3 COULTAS CT
4 ACLAND ST
5 LONSDALE ST
6 CARNEGIE ST

179

B8
1 ROXBURGH ST
2 LANARK ST

C6
1 KINGS LEIGH
2 KING'S CROSS CL
3 THORN LEIGH

D6
1 BLOOMSBURY CT
2 ARLINGTON ST
3 ALMOND GR
4 BLACKTHORN CT
5 SORBUS CT

D8
1 BERKELEY ST
2 CROMWELL CL
3 BROWNING CL
4 LEONARD ST
5 TRAFALGAR ST
6 SHAKESPEARE CL

E7
1 COLLEGE ST
2 BLAKE CL
3 MARLBOROUGH TERR
4 PRYME ST
5 PEARSON ST
6 SPENCER ST
7 REED ST
8 PERCY ST
9 PORTLAND PL
10 ALBION ST
11 STORY ST

F7
1 CATHERINE ST
2 SYKES ST
3 CHARLES ST
4 EGGINTON ST
5 NEW GARDEN ST
6 WILBERFORCE DR

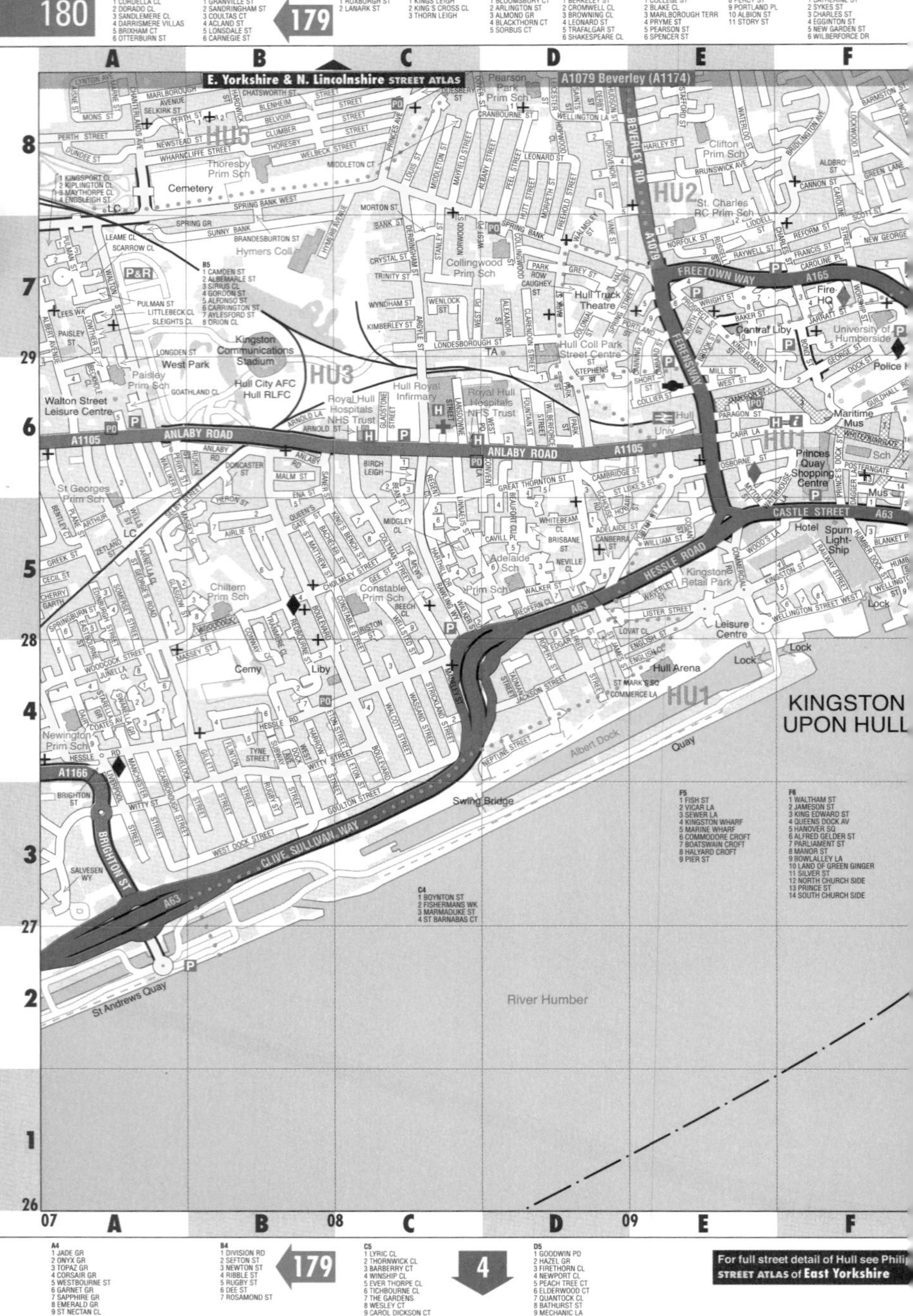

A4
1 JADE GR
2 ONYX GR
3 TOPAZ GR
4 CORSAIR GR
5 WESTBOURNE ST
6 GARNET GR
7 SAPPHIRE GR
8 EMERALD GR
9 ST NECTAN CL

B4
1 DIVISION RD
2 SEFTON ST
3 NEWTON ST
4 RIBBLE ST
5 RUGBY ST
6 DEE ST
7 ROSAMOND ST

179

C5
1 LYRIC CL
2 THORNWICK CL
3 BARBERRY CT
4 WINSHIP CL
5 EVER THORPE CL
6 TICHBOURNE CL
7 THE GARDENS
8 WESLEY CT
9 CAROL DICKSON CT

4

D5
1 GOODWIN PD
2 HAZEL GR
3 FIRETHORN CL
4 NEWPORT CL
5 PEACH TREE CT
6 ELDERWOOD CT
7 QUANTOCK CL
8 BATHURST ST
9 MECHANIC LA

For full street detail of Hull see Philip's STREET ATLAS of East Yorkshire

A6
1 BLAIDES STAITHE
2 GUILDHALL RD
3 HANOVER SQ
4 ALFRED GELDER ST
5 GEORGE YD
6 MARKET PL

A7
1 CHARTERHOUSE LE
2 APPLEGARTH RD
3 LITTLE MASON ST
4 CARROLL PL
5 CHARLOTTE ST
6 DOCK OFFICE ROW

B7
1 PEMBERTON ST
2 BLYTH ST
3 NAYLOR'S ROW
4 WILSON ST
5 EAST ST
6 ALMA ST

C7
1 PELHAM DR
2 EDWARD COLLINS SQ
3 HODGE CT
4 ROSEY ROW
5 ALDERSON MS
6 BROADLEY CL
7 DENMARK CT
8 EMILY ST

C8
1 NORNABELL ST
2 BALFOUR ST
3 ARUNDEL ST
4 HORNSEA PD
5 ST QUINTINS CL

D7
1 BUTTERCUP CL
2 PENISTONE CT
3 BEAUMONT CT
4 BRUMBY'S TR
5 EMPRINGHAM ST

E8
1 DOVEDALE GR
2 DEEPDALE GR
3 MIDDLEHAM CL
4 BYLAND CT

5
5

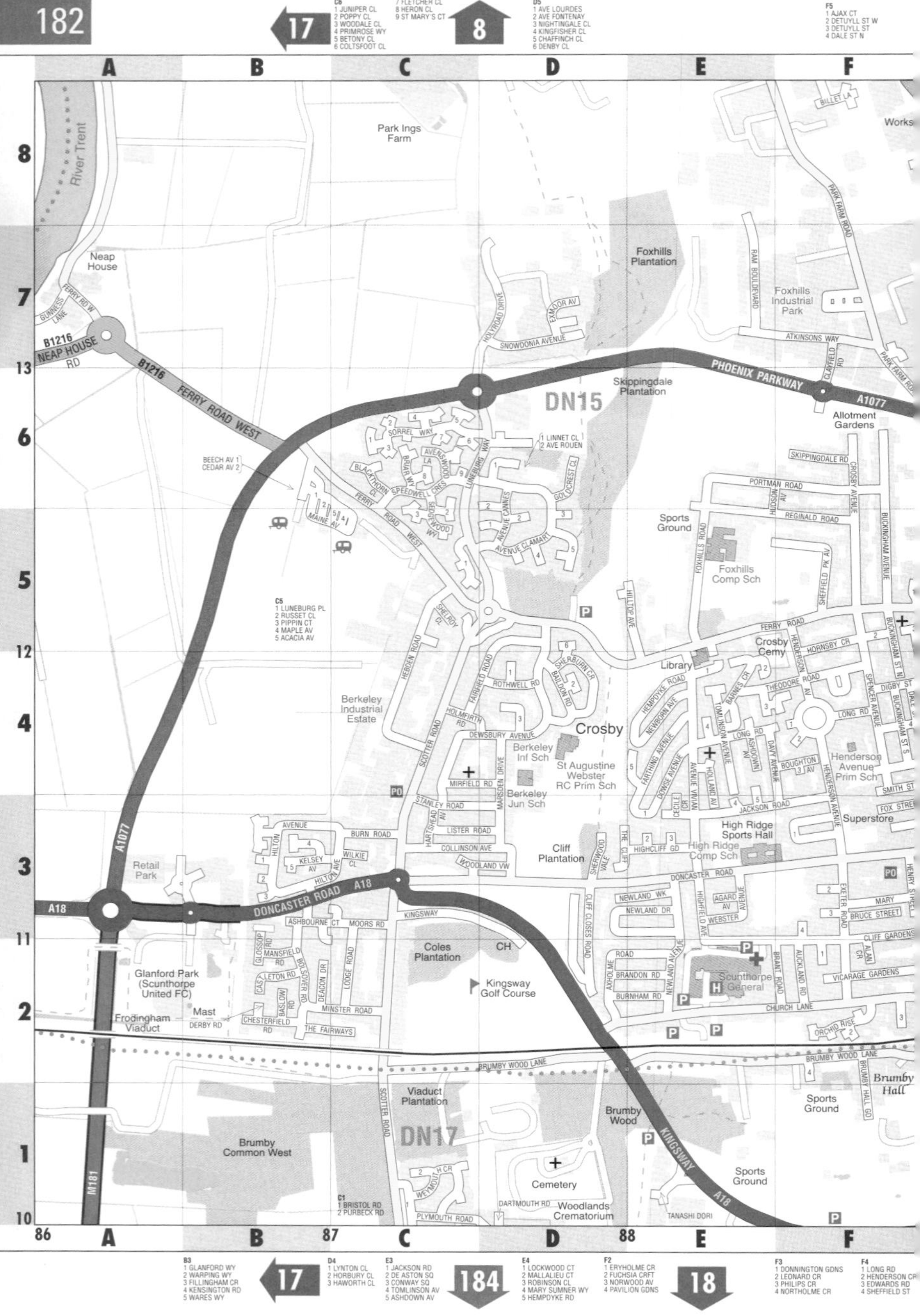
17
C6
1 JUNIPER CL
2 POPPY CL
3 WOODALE CL
4 PRIMROSE WY
5 BETONY CL
6 COLTSFOOT CL
7 FLETCHER CL
8 HERON CL
9 ST MARY'S CT
8
D5
1 AVE LOURDES
2 AVE FONTENAY
3 NIGHTINGALE CL
4 KINGFISHER CL
5 CHAFFINCH CL
6 DENBY CL
F5
1 AJAX CT
2 DETUYLL ST W
3 DETUYLL ST
4 DALE ST N
River Trent
Park Ings Farm
Works
Neap House
Foxhills Plantation
Foxhills Industrial Park
RAM BOULEVARD
PARK FARM ROAD
BILLET LA
ATKINSONS WAY
CLAYFIELD RD
FERRY RD W
GUINNESS LANE
B1216
NEAP HOUSE RD
FERRY ROAD WEST
HOLYROOD DRIVE
EXMOOR AV
SNOWDONIA AVENUE
PHOENIX PARKWAY
A1077
Skippingdale Plantation
DN15
Allotment Gardens
SORREL WAY
AVENSWOOD LA
BRIAR WY
BLACKTHORN CL
SPEEDWELL CRES
SEDGEWOOD WY
LUNEBURG WAY
1 LINNET CL
2 AVE ROUEN
GOLDCREST CL
BEECH AV 1
CEDAR AV 2
MAINE AV
AVENUE CANNES
AVENUE CLAMART
SKIPPINGDALE RD
PORTMAN ROAD
REGINALD ROAD
HODSON AV
CROSBY AVENUE
BUCKINGHAM AVENUE
Sports Ground
FOXHILLS ROAD
Foxhills Comp Sch
SHEFFIELD PK AV
C5
1 LUNEBURG PL
2 RUSSET CL
3 PIPPIN CT
4 MAPLE AV
5 ACACIA AV
SHELROY CL
HILLTOP AVE
FERRY ROAD
Crosby Cemy
HORNSBY CR
BUCKINGHAM ST N
HEBDEN ROAD
SHERBURN CR
BAILDON RD
ROTHWELL RD
FAIRFIELD ROAD
Library
HEMPDYKE ROAD
BARNES CR
THEODORE ROAD
SPENCER AVENUE
DIGBY ST
Berkeley Industrial Estate
HOLMFIRTH RD
NEWBORN AVE
TOMLINSON AVENUE
LONG RD
ASHDOWN AV
SCOTTER ROAD
DEWSBURY AVENUE
Crosby
Berkeley Inf Sch
St Augustine Webster RC Prim Sch
FARTHING AVENUE
DOWSE AVENUE
AVENUE VIVIAN
HOLLAND AV
DAVY AVENUE
BOUGHTON AV
HENDERSON AVENUE
Henderson Avenue Prim Sch
SMITH ST
MIRFIELD RD
MARSDEN DRIVE
Berkeley Jun Sch
STANLEY ROAD
HARTSHEAD AV
CECILE CR
JACKSON ROAD
FOX STREET
Superstore
High Ridge Sports Hall
AVENUE
BURN ROAD
HILTON AV
KELSEY AV
WILKIE CL
LISTER ROAD
COLLINSON AVE
WOODLAND VW
Cliff Plantation
SHERWOOD VALE
THE CLIFF
HIGHCLIFF GD
High Ridge Comp Sch
Retail Park
A18
DONCASTER ROAD
DONCASTER ROAD
NEWLAND WK
NEWLAND DR
AGARD AV
WEBSTER
HIGHFIELD AVE
EXETER ROAD
MARY
BRUCE STREET
HENRY STREET
ASHBOURNE CT
MOORS RD
KINGSWAY
CLIFF CLOSES ROAD
Coles Plantation
CH
CLIFF GARDENS
GLOSSOP RD
MANSFIELD RD
LODGE ROAD
ROAD
AXHOLME RD
NEWLAND AVENUE
BRANT ROAD
AUCKLAND RD
ALAN CR
Glanford Park (Scunthorpe United FC)
CASTLETON RD
BOLSOVER RD
DEACON DR
Kingsway Golf Course
BRANDON RD
Scunthorpe General
VICARAGE GARDENS
BASLOW RD
BURNHAM RD
CHURCH LANE
Mast
DERBY RD
MINSTER ROAD
Frodingham Viaduct
CHESTERFIELD RD
THE FAIRWAYS
ORCHID RISE
BRUMBY WOOD LANE
BRUMBY WOOD LANE
BRUMBY HALL GD
Brumby Hall
Viaduct Plantation
Brumby Wood
Sports Ground
M181
Brumby Common West
DN17
KINGSWAY
WEYMOUTH CR
Cemetery
Sports Ground
A18
C1
1 BRISTOL RD
2 PURBECK RD
PLYMOUTH ROAD
DARTMOUTH RD
Woodlands Crematorium
TANASHI DORI
86
87
88
A
B
C
D
E
F
8
7
13
6
5
12
4
3
11
2
1
10
B3
1 GLANFORD WY
2 WARPING WY
3 FILLINGHAM CR
4 KENSINGTON RD
5 WARES WY
17
D4
1 LYNTON CL
2 HORBURY CL
3 HAWORTH CL
E3
1 JACKSON RD
2 DE ASTON SQ
3 CONWAY SQ
4 TOMLINSON AV
5 ASHDOWN AV
184
E4
1 LOCKWOOD CT
2 MALLALIEU CT
3 ROBINSON CL
4 MARY SUMNER WY
5 HEMPDYKE RD
F2
1 ERYHOLME CR
2 FUCHSIA CRFT
3 NORWOOD AV
4 PAVILION GDNS
18
F3
1 DONNINGTON GDNS
2 LEONARD CR
3 PHILIPS CR
4 NORTHOLME CR
F4
1 LONG RD
2 HENDERSON CR
3 EDWARDS RD
4 SHEFFIELD ST

8
19
A
B
C
D
E
F
8
7
6
5
4
3
2
1
13
12
11
10
B1430
CUPOLA WAY
Conesby
Farm
NORMANBY ROAD
ROMANO-BRITISH
SETTLEMENT
A1077
WINTERTON ROAD
Millennium
Wood
Opencast Ironstone
Workings (disused)
ORB LANE
Works
ST VINCENT'S AVE
WYBECK RD
Crosby
Warren
MANNABERG WAY
PARK FARM RD
Mast
HARGREAVES WAY
BESSEMER WAY
DN15
A1029
Allotment
Gardens
Playing
Field
Chy
Chy
Works
Spoil
Heap
Works
A5
1 CHATTERTON CR
2 GRANGE AV
3 BURKE ST N
WARREN ROAD
OLD CROSBY
DIANA ST
GROSVENOR ST N
SCUNTHORPE
Lynton
Prep Sch
DIGBY ST
BURKE ST
MULGRAVE STREET
NORMANBY ROAD
KING ST 1
NORTH ST 2
CROSS ST 3
HIGH ST 4
CHURCH SQ 5
GLEBE ROAD
SHEFFIELD ST
GEORGE ST
Crosby
Prim
Sch
FRODINGHAM ROAD
BERKELEY STREET
Market
CROSBY RD
WINTERTON RD
HOME ST
TRAFFORD ST
Chimney
Council
Offices
Chy
Chy
Cemy
PERCIVAL ST
TEALE ST
GURNELL ST
WELLS ST
Scunthorpe
Shopping Ctr
Scunthorpe
CE Prim Sch
LC
DAWES LANE
PORTER ST
WEST STREET
CHAPEL ST
Central
Liby
CHURCH SQUARE
HIGH ST EAST
MILLFIELD ROAD
ALLANBY ST
FRANCES STREET
HIGH ST
JOHN STREET
Visual Arts
Ctr
OLD IRONSIDE ROAD
ARMOUR ROAD
HIGH STREET
ROBERT STREET
L Ctr
DEYNE AVE
GERVASE ST
OSWALD ROAD
DUNSTALL STREET
LANEHAM STREET
FENTON ST
MARY STREET
COLE STREET
LINDUM STREET
STATION ROAD
CASTELLA DR
COMMERCIAL RD
C3
1 TULIP RD
2 ALEXANDER RD
Chy
APPLEBY MILL ROAD
The
Parishes
Recreation
Ground
BLUEBELL CL
ROSE WK
MAIN APPROACH RD
Barton Magistrates Ct
Plowright Theatre
BASIC SLAG ROAD
Chy
North
Lincolnshire
Mus & Art Gall
COMFORTS AVE
Cty Ct
STATION ROAD
Frodingham
CENTRAL WAY
Chy
Chy
COKE OVEN AVENUE
REFINERY ROAD
Chy
CHURCH LA
BELL LA
Scunthorpe
Fordingham
Inf Sch
ROWLAND ROAD
NEVILLE ROAD
DN16
BRIGG ROAD
SERVICES ROAD
BASIC SLAG RD
NORTH LINCOLN RD
BURMA RD
Spoilheap
Hotel
HALLGARTH AV
TRENT ST
CLIFF ST
COTTAGE BECK ROAD
COTTAGE BECK ROAD
Chimney
EASTSIDE ROAD
Steel
Works
Chy
AVON ROAD
Territorial
Army
KETTERING RD
COLIN ROAD
BANBURY RD
Chy
EAST BOUNDARY ROAD
PLUM TREE WY
REDBOURN WY
HAIG AV
LYGON ST
EARL ST
FAIRMONT CRESCENT
NORTHAMPTON ROAD
NEATH RD
LYDBROOK RD
KING EDWARD STREET
ASHBY ROAD
MAPLE TREE WY
BUSHFIELD ROAD
CEMETERY ROAD
WARWICK ROAD
MIDLAND ROAD
NOSTELL RD
ROD MILL ROAD
FRODINGHAM SOUTH ROAD
BILLET MILL ROAD
Chy
Chy's
Brumby &
Fordingham
Cemetery
B1
1 SANDERSON CL
2 REDBOURN CL
3 BEAUCHAMP ST
C1
1 GLADSTONE DR
2 LEAMINGTON CL
3 SANDHOUSE CR
4 IVANHOE RD
A1029
SERAPHIM APPROACH RD
Civic
Centre
St Hughs
Sch
Bushfield Rd Inf Sch
Sports
Ground
KENILWORTH ROAD
LILAC AVENUE
WOODSTOCK RD
Chy's
SERAPHIM RD
89
90
91
A1
1 MAPLE TREE CL W
2 MAPLE TREE CL E
A2
1 ALBOURNE AV
2 WORTLEY ST
3 ABERCORN ST
A3
1 PARKINSON AV
2 CLARKE ST
3 ST JAMES CT
4 CORPORATION RD
18
A4
1 SHEFFIELD ST E
2 GROSVENOR ST S
3 ELIZABETH ST
B2
1 THE CROFTS
2 ALEXANDER RD
3 WILLIAM ST
4 WINN ST
5 PERCY ST
6 ROWLAND RD
7 MONTROSE ST
8 THE CLOSE
185
B3
1 BELGRAVE SQ
2 RAVENDALE ST N
3 FRODINGHAM FOOTPATH
4 MANLEY ST
5 CARLTON ST
6 LAVENDER WY
7 THOMPSON ST
8 RAVENDALE ST S
19
C2
1 REDBOURNE ST
2 LINDSEY ST
3 QUEEN ST
4 PINCHBECK AV
5 STRATFORD DR

17
C5
1 BETULA WY
2 CONIFER CL
3 ACER GR
C6
1 FOURTH AV
2 THIRD AV
3 SECOND AV
4 SHAKESPEARE AV
5 SIDNEY RD
C7
1 ROCHESTER CL
2 SALISBURY CL
3 ST ALBANS CL
182
D7
1 CANTERBURY CL
2 NEWBOLT AV
3 LANDOR AV
4 KIPLING AV
5 COVENTRY CL
D8
1 QUANTOCK CL
2 CLEVELAND CL
3 BARNSTAPLE RD
E6
1 BROWNING CL
2 MAVIS RD
3 MALLARD RD
4 KIPLING AV
5 PHEASANT CL
F8
1 NORMAN CR
2 GLANVILLE CR
3 HAWTHORNE CR
4 HAWTHORNE AV
A B C D E F
8 7 6 5 4 3 2 1
09 08 07 06
86 87 88
M181
M180
B1450
KINGSWAY
Cemy
Allotment Gardens
Brumby Grove
Parkwood Inf & Jun Sch
West Common Sports Hall
North Lindsey Coll
John Leggott Coll
Chy
BRUMBY COMMON LANE
WEST COMMON LANE
Nature Reserve
Brumby Common
Liby
Westcliff
Thomas Sumpter Sch
Priory Lane Jun Sch
Priory Lane Inf Sch
Westcliffe Prim Sch
Carisbrooke Manor
Manor Park
BURRINGHAM ROAD
Recreation Ground
Warp Farm
CH
PH
Ashby Decoy
Ashby Decoy Golf Course
Recn Gd
Riddings
Riddings Jun Sch
Riddings Inf Sch
South Leys Sch
Enderby Road Inf Sch
DN17
Leys Farm Cty Jun Sch
Yaddlethorpe
Bottesford Sports Ctr
West Glanford L Ctr
Grange Farm
Moorwell Business Park
Hillfoot Farm
Southfield Farm
Bottesford Moor Farm
Newdowns Farm
MOOR ROAD
F2
1 LEE FAIR GDNS
2 ST ANDREWS AV
Snake Plantation
Bottesford Beck
SCOTTER ROAD
SCOTTER ROAD SOUTH
SOUTH PARK ROAD
SUNNINGDALE ROAD
MOORWELL ROAD
PARK AVENUE
HIGH STREET
17
29
E3
1 WADDINGTON DR
2 THE OVAL
3 EDGBASTON AV
4 HEADINGLEY AV
5 JESMOND AV
6 LOW LEYS RD
F3
1 PRINCESS ALEXANDRA CT
2 SOUTHRIDGE CR
3 AUSTIN CR
4 THORNHILL CR
5 KIRMAN CR
F4
1 HARROW GD
2 KEDDINGTO RD

B6
1 MODDER ST
2 COLLUM GDS
3 ACACIA CT
4 ASHBERRY DR
5 ORCHARD CL
B8
1 MARLBOROUGH DR
2 TRAVISS CL
3 ALMOND GR
C6
1 NORTHFIELD CL
2 SPRINGFIELD CL
3 EMMANUEL CT
4 MACKENDER CT
5 ST MARGARET'S WK
C8
1 WARLEY AV
3 CUXWOLD RD
4 MARMION RD
5 ST MICHAEL'S CR
183
D5
1 AIREDALE RD
2 GLAISDALE RD
3 BEDALE RD
4 MALLORY RD
5 BRANSDALE RD
19
D7
1 MILL CFT
2 ST LAWRENCE'S PL
3 AMOS CR
4 TENNYSON RD
D8
1 IVANHOE RD
2 WOODSTOCK RD
Brumby
Brumby Jun Sch
Brumby Comp Sch
Midland Industrial Estate
Rowmills Plantation
Brumby Resource Centre
St Lukes Sch
Grange Industrial Estate
Lincoln Gardens Inf Sch
Lincoln Gdns Jun Sch
St Bede's RC Sch
Millbrook Sch
St Bernadettes RC Prim Sch
Library
ASHBY BROADWAY
ASHBY HIGH STREET
Ashby Market
Ashby
Sunshine Hall
Recreation Ground
Grange Lane Jun Sch
Lakeside Retail Park
Superstore
Brat Hill
Brathill Farm
Rochdale Road Jun Sch
Sunway Inf Sch
GRANGE LANE SOUTH
GRANGE LANE NORTH
QUEENSWAY
CHANCEL ROAD
ASHBY ROAD
MESSINGHAM ROAD
BRIGG ROAD
Recreation Gd
Frederick Gough Comp Sch
DN16
SCUNTHORPE
Recn Gd
Holme Valley Prim Sch
Holme Hall Golf Course
Bottesford
St John's Well
Templar's Bath
Botteford Jun & Inf Schs
Holme Wood
Holme Hall
Aspen Farm
HOLME LANE
M180
NORTHFIELD ROAD
E6
1 WHARFEDALE PL
2 SWALEDALE PL
C5
1 MARSHFIELD RD
2 IRVINE RD
B3
1 ROSEWOOD WY
2 REPTON DR
A1
1 LOBELIA DR
2 MONTBRETIA DR
3 AUBRETIA DR
4 ARMERIA DR
5 HALLBROOK CT
B2
1 STURMER CT
2 MARTIN CL
3 DUNNOCK CL
4 HAZEL GR
5 ACORN WY
6 CATKIN RD
7 MERRYWEATHER CT
B4
1 RINGWOOD CL
2 OAKWOOD RI
3 GIRTON CL
4 MAGDALEN CL
5 MOUNTBATTEN CL
6 NUFFIELD CL
29
D4
1 PLANTAIN CL
2 PIMPERNEL WY
3 HONEYSUCKLE CT
4 NUTWOOD VW
5 PEACH TREE CL
6 WEEPINGELM WY
19

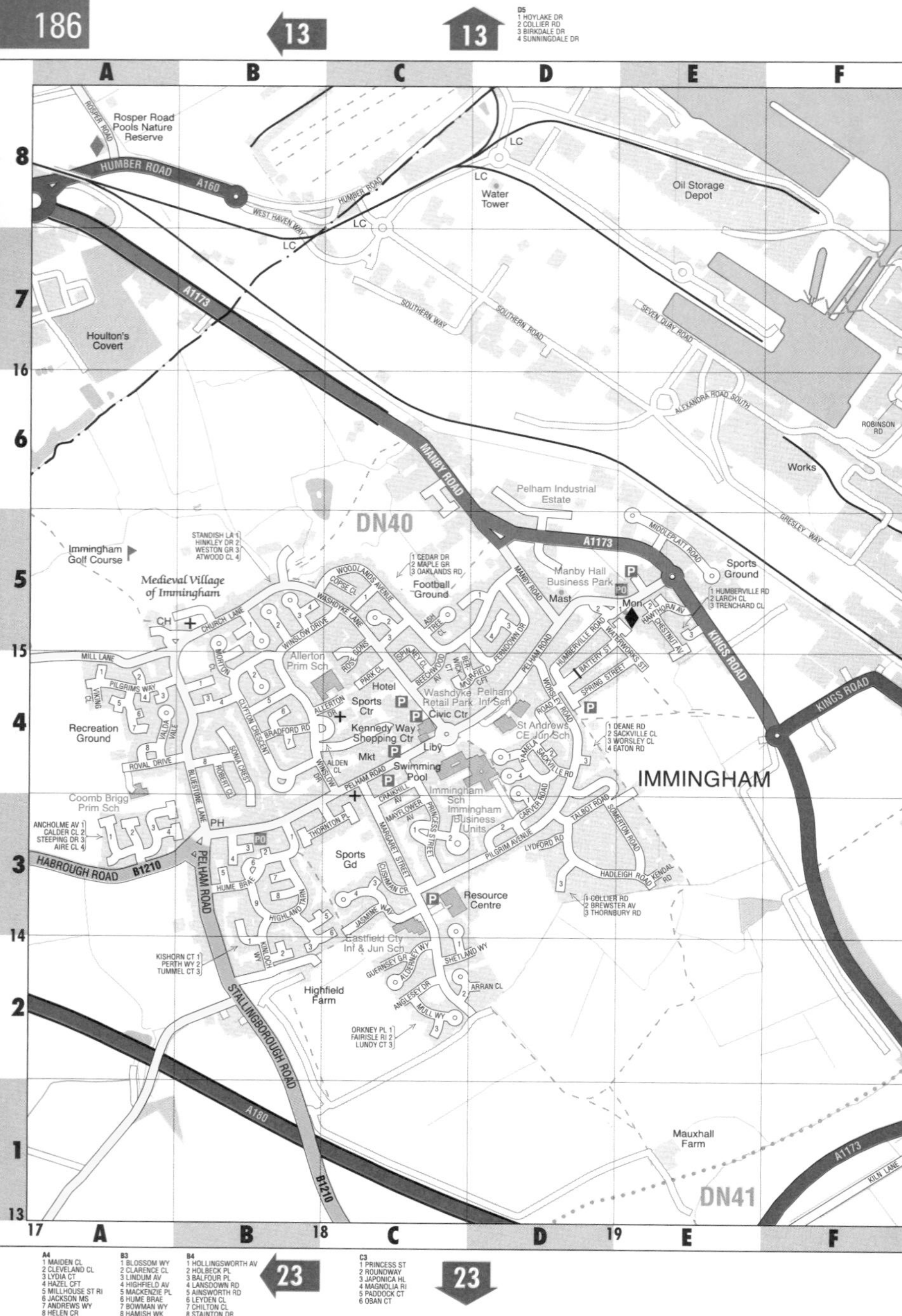

23
23

A4
1 MAIDEN CL
2 CLEVELAND CL
3 LYDIA CT
4 HAZEL CFT
5 MILLHOUSE ST RI
6 JACKSON MS
7 ANDREWS WY
8 HELEN CR

B3
1 BLOSSOM WY
2 CLARENCE CL
3 LINDUM AV
4 HIGHFIELD AV
5 MACKENZIE PL
6 HUME BRAE
7 BOWMAN WY
8 HAMISH WK
9 JAMES WY

B4
1 HOLLINGSWORTH AV
2 HOLBECK PL
3 BALFOUR PL
4 LANSDOWN RD
5 AINSWORTH RD
6 LEYDEN CL
7 CHILTON CL
8 STAINTON DR

C3
1 PRINCESS ST
2 ROUNDWAY
3 JAPONICA HL
4 MAGNOLIA RI
5 PADDOCK CT
6 OBAN CT

A
B
C
D
E
F
8
7
16
6
5
15
4
3
14
2
1
13
Immingham Dock
Oil Storage Depot
LC
Oil Storage Depot
LC
Chy
QUEENS RD
DN40
A1173
QUEENS ROAD
LAPORTE ROAD
Chimney
Works
Humber Bank Factories
Chimney
LC
EUROPA WAY
SCANDINAVIAN WAY
NETHERLANDS WAY
Kiln Lane Ind Est
Spoil Heap
KILN LANE
WORLDWIDE WAY
WORLDWIDE WY
Kiln Lane Ind Est
OSBORNE RD
BEEL'S RD
DN41
HOBSON WAY
South Marsh Road Ind Est
SOUTH MARSH ROAD
LC
NORTH MOSS LANE
SOUTH MARSH ROAD
Power Station
Chimney
Poplar Farm
20
21
22

24

A1
1 FERNDOWN
2 SERVICE RD 12
3 SERVICE RD 14
4 SERVICE RD 13
5 RAVENSCAR RD
6 SERVICE RD 10
7 SERVICE RD 9
8 SERVICE RD 8
9 SERVICE RD 26

A3
1 ATHENIAN WY
2 FISKERTON WY
3 SARGON WY

D1
1 BRIDGE GDNS
2 CLEVELAND GDNS
3 CLEVELAND ST
4 CLAYDEN ST
5 STANSTED ST
6 CLAVERING ST
7 STORTFORD ST
8 SANDFORD ST

E1
1 CORPORATION RD
2 ARMSTRONG PL W
3 ARMSTRONG PL E
4 AYSCOUGH ST

F1
1 ANNESLEY ST
2 WATKIN ST STH

190 24 24 191

A1
1 LOWER SPRING ST
2 ALBERT GDNS
3 CRESSEY ST
4 FOTHERBY ST

B1
1 TOMLINE ST
2 NACTON ST
3 BRIDGE ST NORTH
4 CHURCH ST
5 SERVICE RD NO 1
6 ALBERT ST W
7 SERVICE RD NO 2
8 GARIBALDI ST

B2
1 STUART WORTLEY ST
2 MURRAY ST
3 ROWLANDSON ST
4 RAILWAY PL

D1
1 CASSWELL CL
2 RUTLAND ST
3 MANSEL ST
4 SIDNEY ST

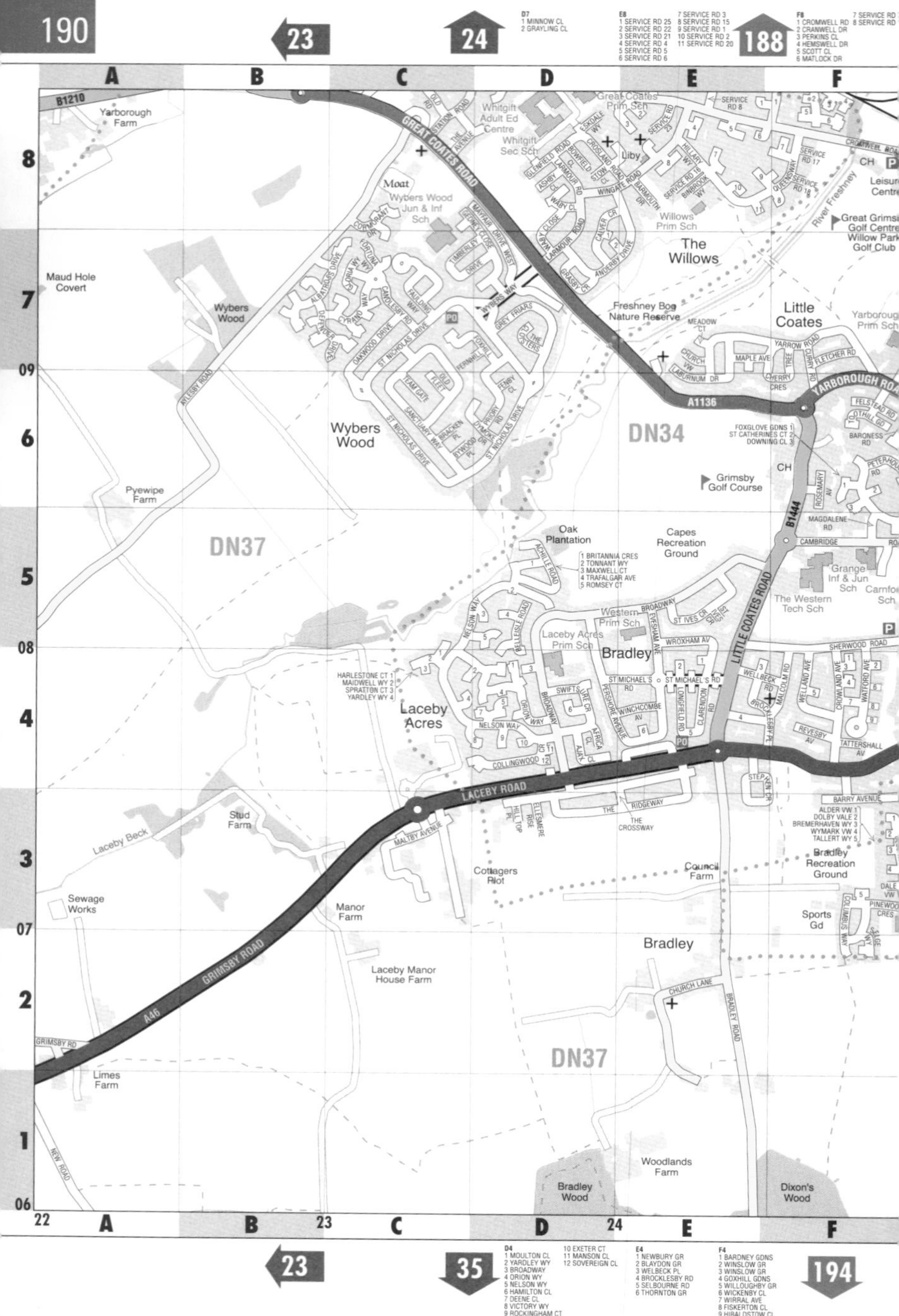
23
24
D7
1 MINNOW CL
2 GRAYLING CL
E8
1 SERVICE RD 25
2 SERVICE RD 22
3 SERVICE RD 21
4 SERVICE RD 4
5 SERVICE RD 5
6 SERVICE RD 6
7 SERVICE RD 3
8 SERVICE RD 15
9 SERVICE RD 1
10 SERVICE RD 2
11 SERVICE RD 20
188
F8
1 CROMWELL RD
2 CRANWELL DR
3 PERKINS CL
4 HEMSWELL DR
5 SCOTT CL
6 MATLOCK DR
7 SERVICE RD 3
8 SERVICE RD
A
B
C
D
E
F
8
7
09
6
5
08
4
3
07
2
1
06
22
23
24
B1210
Yarborough Farm
Maud Hole Covert
Wybers Wood
Pyewipe Farm
DN37
GREAT COATES ROAD
Whitgift Adult Ed Centre
Whitgift Sec Sch
Great Coates Prim Sch
Moat
Wybers Wood Jun & Inf Sch
Liby
Willows Prim Sch
The Willows
Freshney Bog Nature Reserve
Little Coates
Yarborough Prim Sch
Leisure Centre
Great Grimsby Golf Centre Willow Park Golf Club
River Freshney
A1136
YARBOROUGH RD
DN34
FOXGLOVE GDNS 1
ST CATHERINES CT 2
DOWNING CL 3
Grimsby Golf Course
B1444
Wybers Wood
AYLESBY ROAD
Oak Plantation
Capes Recreation Ground
1 BRITANNIA CRES
2 TONNANT WY
3 MAXWELL CT
4 TRAFALGAR AVE
5 ROMSEY CT
ACHILLE ROAD
Grange Inf & Jun Sch
The Western Tech Sch
LITTLE COATES ROAD
Western Prim Sch
Laceby Acres Prim Sch
Bradley
HARLESTONE CT 1
MAIDWELL WY 2
SPRATTON CT 3
YARDLEY WY 4
Laceby Acres
LACEBY ROAD
THE RIDGEWAY
THE CROSSWAY
Stud Farm
Laceby Beck
Sewage Works
Manor Farm
MALTBY AVENUE
Cottagers Plot
Council Farm
BARRY AVENUE
ALDER VW 1
DOLBY VALE 2
BREMERHAVEN WY 3
WYMARK VW 4
TALLERT WY 5
Bradley Recreation Ground
Sports Gd
Bradley
Laceby Manor House Farm
GRIMSBY ROAD
A46
CHURCH LANE
BRADLEY ROAD
DN37
Limes Farm
NEW ROAD
Woodlands Farm
Bradley Wood
Dixon's Wood
23
35
D4
1 MOULTON CL
2 YARDLEY WY
3 BROADWAY
4 ORION WY
5 NELSON WY
6 HAMILTON CL
7 DEENE CL
8 VICTORY WY
9 ROCKINGHAM CT
10 EXETER CT
11 MANSON CL
12 SOVEREIGN CL
E4
1 NEWBURY GR
2 BLAYDON GR
3 WELBECK PL
4 BROCKLESBY RD
5 SELBOURNE RD
6 THORNTON GR
F4
1 BARDNEY GDNS
2 WINSLOW GR
3 WINSLOW GR
4 GOXHILL GDNS
5 WILLOUGHBY GR
6 WICKENBY CL
7 WIRRAL AVE
8 FISKERTON CL
9 HIBALDSTOW CL
194

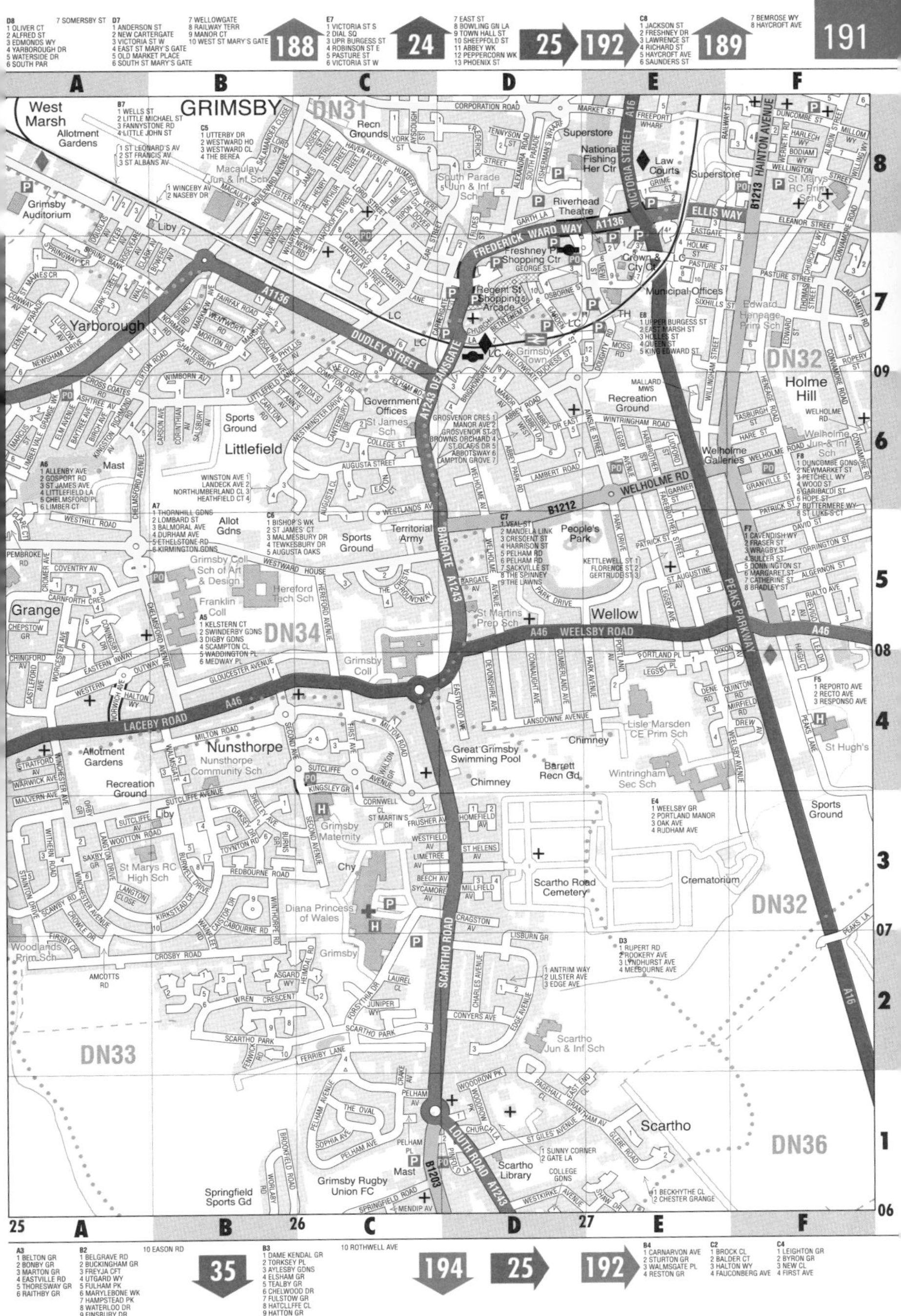

D8
1 OLIVER CT
2 ALFRED ST
3 EDMONDS WY
4 YARBOROUGH DR
5 WATERSIDE DR
6 SOUTH PAR
7 SOMERSBY ST
D7
1 ANDERSON ST
2 NEW CARTERGATE
3 VICTORIA ST W
4 EAST ST MARY'S GATE
5 OLD MARKET PLACE
6 SOUTH ST MARY'S GATE
7 WELLOWGATE
8 RAILWAY TERR
9 MANOR CT
10 WEST ST MARY'S GATE
188
E7
1 VICTORIA ST S
2 DIAL SQ
3 UPR BURGESS ST
4 ROBINSON ST E
5 PASTURE ST
6 VICTORIA ST W
24
7 EAST ST
8 BOWLING GN LA
9 TOWN HALL ST
10 SHEEPFOLD ST
11 ABBEY WK
12 PEPPERCORN WK
13 PHOENIX ST
25
192
C8
1 JACKSON ST
2 FRESHNEY DR
3 LAWRENCE ST
4 RICHARD ST
5 HAYCROFT AVE
6 SAUNDERS ST
189
7 BEMROSE WY
8 HAYCROFT AVE
191
A B C D E F
GRIMSBY
West Marsh
Allotment Gardens
DN31
Recn Grounds
Superstore
National Fishing Her Ctr
Law Courts
Riverhead Theatre
Freshney Pl Shopping Ctr
Crown & City Ct
Regent St Shopping Arcade
Municipal Offices
Grimsby Town
Grimsby Auditorium
Yarborough
Macaulay Jun & Inf Sch
South Parade Jun & Inf Sch
St Marys RC Prim Sch
Edward Heneage Prim Sch
DN32
Holme Hill
FREDERICK WARD WAY
ELLIS WAY
DUDLEY STREET
A1136
A1243 DEANSGATE
BARGATE A1243
VICTORIA STREET A16
B1213 HAINTON AVENUE
PEAKS PARKWAY
WELHOLME RD
B1212
WEELSBY ROAD
A46
LACEBY ROAD
SCARTHO ROAD
LOUTH ROAD A1243
B1203
Government Offices
St James Sch
Sports Ground
Littlefield
Mast
Recreation Ground
Welholme Galleries
Welholme Jun & Inf Sch
People's Park
Territorial Army
Allot Gdns
Grimsby Coll Sch of Art & Design
Hereford Tech Sch
Franklin Coll
Grange
DN34
St Martins Prep Sch
Wellow
Grimsby Coll
Lisle Marsden CE Prim Sch
St Hugh's
Nunsthorpe
Nunsthorpe Community Sch
Allotment Gardens
Recreation Ground
Great Grimsby Swimming Pool
Chimney
Barrett Recn Gd
Wintringham Sec Sch
Sports Ground
Grimsby Maternity
St Marys RC High Sch
Scartho Road Cemetery
Crematorium
Diana Princess of Wales
Grimsby
Woodlands Prim Sch
DN33
Scartho Jun & Inf Sch
Scartho
DN36
Scartho Library
Grimsby Rugby Union FC
Springfield Sports Gd
09 08 07 06
8 7 6 5 4 3 2 1
25 A B 26 C D 27 E F
A3
1 BELTON GR
2 BONBY GR
3 MARTON GR
4 EASTVILLE RD
5 THORESWAY GR
6 RAITHBY GR
B2
1 BELGRAVE RD
2 BUCKINGHAM GR
3 FREYJA CFT
4 UTGARD WY
5 FULHAM PK
6 MARYLEBONE WK
7 HAMPSTEAD PK
8 WATERLOO DR
9 FINSBURY DR
10 EASON RD
35
B3
1 DAME KENDAL GR
2 TORKSEY PL
3 AYLESBY GDNS
4 ELSHAM GR
5 TEALBY GR
6 CHELWOOD DR
7 FULSTOW GR
8 HATCLIFFE CL
9 HATTON GR
10 ROTHWELL AVE
194
25
192
B4
1 CARNARVON AVE
2 STURTON GR
3 WALMSGATE PL
4 RESTON GR
C2
1 BROCK CL
2 BALDER CT
3 HALTON WY
4 FAUCONBERG AVE
C4
1 LEIGHTON GR
2 BYRON GR
3 NEW CL
4 FIRST AVE

192
A5
1 SEAMER GR
2 CARNABY GR
3 GARTON GR
4 BEMPTON GR
5 SALTBURN GR
B6
1 EVELYN GR N
2 ROSINA GR N
3 EVELYN GR S
4 ROSINA GR S
191
24
189
D5
1 STEVENSON PL
2 APPLEGARTH CL
E7
1 PELHAM SQ
2 HUTCHINSON RD
3 CRAMPIN RD
4 BEACONTHORPE RD
5 POPLAR GR
F5
1 CHAPMAN GR
2 CHARLES ST
3 HUMBER ST
4 BARKHOUSE CL
5 BARKHOUSE LA
6 HIGHGATE
7 THRUNSCOE RD
8 NICHOLSON ST
25
F6
1 OSBORNE ST
2 SHORT ST
3 DE LACY LA
4 DOLPHIN ST
A
B
C
D
E
F
8
7
09
6
5
08
4
3
07
2
1
06
28
29
30
Grimsby Town Football Club
A180
Weelsby Prim Sch
Grant Thorold
Library
Sidney Park
Queen Mary Avenue Inf Sch
William Barcroft Jun Sch
Elliston Jun & Inf Schs
Water Tower
Poplar Rd Business Units
Cleethorpes
Leisureland
Cleethorpes Pier
DN32
Hardy Recn Gd
Sports Ground
Havelock Sch
Old Clee
Allotment Gardens
Reynolds Jun & Inf Sch
Recn Gd
Sussex Recn Gd
Bursar Prim Sch
Civic Offices
Factory
Old Clee Inf & Jun Sch
King George V Stadium
Weelsby
Mast
Clee Hall Farm
Lindsey Lower Sch
Cemy
St Peters CE Prim Sch
Thrunscoe Inf Sch
CLEETHORPES
Observatory
DN35
A46
CLEE ROAD
WEELSBY ROAD
ISAAC'S HILL
ALEXANDRA ROAD
A1098
B1374
QUEEN'S PDE
TAYLOR'S AVENUE
Haverstone Park
St Josephs RC Prim Sch
Matthew Humberstone CE Sch
Lindsey Upper Sch
Mast
Playing Field
Villa Plantation
Weelsby Woods
HUMBERSTON ROAD
A1031
Middlethorpe Prim Sch
Carr Plantation
Hall Farm
Peaks Tunnel Farm
HEWITT'S CIRCUS
DN36
Cleethorpes Country Park
Visitor Centre
Superstore
HEWITT'S AVENUE
Buck Beck
Sports Ground
Industrial Park
GRIMSBY ROAD
HUMBERSTON ROAD
Peaks Top Farm
Peaks Covert Farm
PEAKS PARKWAY A16
D2
1 HEWITTS MANOR
2 ELDERBERRY WY
3 PINE CT
4 CEDAR CL
5 HOLLINGSWORTH CL
191
24
195
E1
1 WOODLAND WK
2 BECK WK
3 MARIGOLD WK
4 VIOLET CL
5 GRASMERE GR
6 ENNERDALE CL
E3
1 LANSDOWN LINK
2 WESLEY CR
3 HEYTHROP RD
4 QUORN MS
F1
1 GOODWOOD LA
2 BLAKENEY LEA
3 BURNHAM REACH
4 HAYLING MERE
5 ARDEN VILLAGE
6 HAREWOOD GR
7 HAMPTON CL
8 LALRGATE PL
9 CRANBOURNE CL
F3
1 ESKHAM CL
2 MARSHCHAPEL CL
3 BEESBY DR
4 MANLEY GD
5 WALTHAM GR
6 LUDBOROUGH WY
36

A5
1 SOUTH ST
2 BRIGHTON ST
3 SEGMERE ST
4 HAIGH ST

25

A B C D E F

8
7
09
6
5
08
4
3
07
2
1
06

SLIPWAY
KINGS PARADE
KINGSWAY
CLIFF RD
A1098
Hotel
BRADFORD AVE
SEACROFT RD
LINDUM RD
SIGNHILLS AV
CROMWELL ROAD
HOWLETT RD
RYMER PL
GARBUTT PL
BASSETT RD
DAGGETT ROAD
LANGLEY PL
STRUBBY CL
Leisure Ctr
Kingsway
Visitor Centre
Paddling Pool
Fishing Lake
Signhills Inf & Jun Sch
Cleethorpes Coast Light Railway
Sand Pit
Cleethorpes Bowling Centre
Cleethorpes Discovery Centre
PH
Meridian Point
The Jungle
Pumping Station
Showground
KING'S ROAD
LINKS RD
RAVENDALE RD
BOLINGBROKE RD
THORGANBY RD
GAYTON RD
CLIXBY CL
SCRIVELSBY CT
Cleethorpes Coast Light Railway & Museum
Lakeside
Amusement Park
DN35
Miniature Railway
Cleethorpes
Humberston
CH
Pleasure Island Theme Park
CUMBERLAND RD
RUSSELL CT
BERKELEY RD
BEDFORD ROAD
ROCHESTER CT
WALDORF RD
MAYFAIR
WESTBURY RD
N SEA LA
CAVENDISH CL
CARLTON CL
HILTON CT
ROYAL CT
RIVERSIDE DR
FAIRWAY CT
KING'S MS
SEAFORD ROAD
BERNERS RD
NORTH SEA LANE
NORTH SEA LA
TOWNSEND CL
BROOKLYN DR
NEWLANDS PK
POPLAR DR
CARRINGTON DR
HURSTLEA DR
CLEE NESS DR
HALE RD
FIELDHOUSE RD
SOUTH VIEW
LIDGARD RD
FOREST DR
DN36
Beachcomber Holiday Centre
Thorpe Park
ANTHONY'S BANK ROAD

1 A B 32 C D 33 E F

A1
1 WESTPORT RD
2 WESTBURY PK
3 FAIRFIELD CT
4 WEYFORD RD
5 GROVENOR CT
6 WHITEHALL RD
7 KINGSTON CL

36

190
35
C5
1 CORAL DR
2 PEACE HAVEN
3 CARDINAL CT
4 ALBERTINE CT
5 FOUNTAIN CL
6 SWEET BRIAR CL
7 WHEATFIELD DR
8 FRANCES CT
9 WRAY CL
D8
1 BAYSWATER PL
2 WELL VALE
3 MAYFIELD CL
4 CORNFIELD CL
5 SAGEFIELD CL
191
E7
1 CONISTON AV
2 FLEETWOOD CL
3 BARBARA CL
4 WINDERMERE AV
5 ORCHARD CFT
6 HEATHERDALE CL
E8
1 TONBRIDGE
2 GRAMPIAN WY
3 CHILTERN WY
4 LANCING WY
5 PURBECK RD
6 DOVEDALE DR
F8
1 GORDON GD
2 COLLEGE GD
3 LINDSEY RI
4 HAWTHORNE AV
5 LINWOOD AV
6 WESTBOURNE GR
Nature Reserve
Bradley Wood
Dixons Wood
Springfield Sports Gd
Fairfield Prim Sch
Scartho
DN33
Springfield Prim Sch
SPRINGWOOD CR
WINDLESHAM AV
KIDDIES AV
HURFORD PL
WALTHAM ROAD
A1243
WOOD CL
MARKHAMS OR
Netherwood Dairy
Bradley Gairs
Netherwood Farm
Grove Farm
BRADLEY ROAD
TOTNES RD 1
DAWLISH RD 2
BRIXHAM CT 3
PAIGNTON CT 4
GRIMSBY ROAD
DN36
MEADOW CFT 1
NORSEFIELD AV 2
SUMMERFIELD CL 3
DOUGHTY CL 4
DOROTHY AV 5
DN37
Waltham
COLTSFOOT DR
Corner Farm
B1219
MOUNT PLEASANT
The Leas Jun & Inf Sch
HIGH STREET
Recreation Ground
LONGHORN CL
SHEARS CT
MARKHAM MS
Cemetery
STRAWBERRY HILL
WALTHAM ROAD
B1203
MILL CL
GREENWAY
Poplar Farm
Grange Farm
Waltham Museum of Rural Life
Waltham Windmill
BRIGSLEY ROAD
Norman Corner
CHEAPSIDE
CH
Mast
Mushroom Farm
Brigsley Top Farm
WALTHAM ROAD
ST HELEN'S CR
Brigsley
B1203
24
25
26
35
C4
1 DRURY CL
2 HARVEST CR
3 BARKWORTH CT
4 OLD FARM CT
5 LINDRICK WK
6 ASHBOURNE
7 CARNOUSTIE
8 SUNNINGDALE
9 BIRKDALE
10 GLENEAGLES
11 MUIRFIELD
12 MAYFAIR CR
13 CHESTNUT CL
35
D4
1 NEVILLE TURNER WY
2 LUDGATE CL
3 ORCHARD CT
4 PEAR TREE CL
5 ASCOT RD
6 KIRKSIDE
7 LABURNHAM CL
8 SALISBURY DR
9 COTSWOLD DR
E4
1 HIGH ST
2 CHURCH VW
3 CROSS ST
4 CHEESEMANS CL
5 MILL VW
6 ATKINSON LA

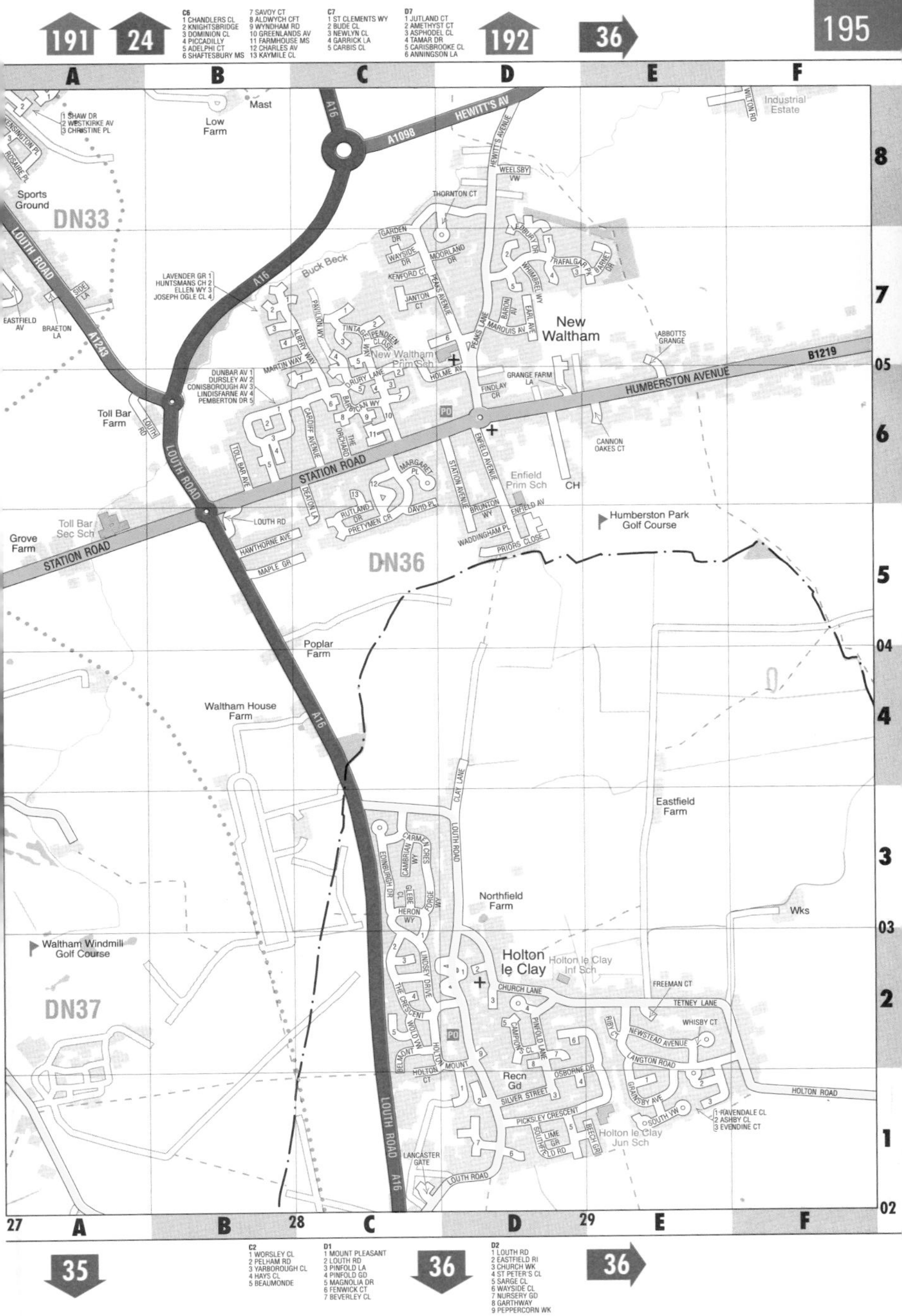

191
24
C6
1 CHANDLERS CL
2 KNIGHTSBRIDGE
3 DOMINION CL
4 PICCADILLY
5 ADELPHI CT
6 SHAFTESBURY MS
7 SAVOY CT
8 ALDWYCH CFT
9 WYNDHAM RD
10 GREENLANDS AV
11 FARMHOUSE MS
12 CHARLES AV
13 KAYMILE CL
C7
1 ST CLEMENTS WY
2 BUDE CL
3 NEWLYN CL
4 GARRICK LA
5 CARBIS CL
D7
1 JUTLAND CT
2 AMETHYST CT
3 ASPHODEL CL
4 TAMAR DR
5 CARISBROOKE CL
6 ANNINGSON LA
192
36
A
B
C
D
E
F
8
7
05
6
5
04
4
3
03
2
1
02
27
28
29
1 SHAW DR
2 WESTKIRKE AV
3 CHRISTINE PL
Low Farm
Mast
A16
HEWITT'S AV
A1098
Industrial Estate
WILTON RD
HEWITT'S AVENUE
WEELSBY VW
Sports Ground
DN33
THORNTON CT
LOUTH ROAD
GARDEN DR
WAYSIDE DR
MOORLAND DR
Buck Beck
KENFORD CT
JANTON CT
PEAKS AVENUE
LAVENDER GR 1
HUNTSMANS CH 2
ELLEN WY 3
JOSEPH OGLE CL 4
TRAFALGAR PK
BARNET DR
WHIMBREL WY
BARONI AV
EARL AVE
MARQUIS AV
PEAKS LANE
New Waltham
EASTFIELD AV
BRAETON LA
A1243
PAVILION WY
TINTAGEL WAY
PENDEEN CLOSE
ALBERY WAY
MARTIN WAY
New Waltham Prim Sch
ABBOTTS GRANGE
B1219
DUNBAR AV 1
DURSLEY AV 2
CONISBOROUGH AV 3
LINDISFARNE AV 4
PEMBERTON DR 5
DRURY LANE
BARBICAN WY
HOLME AV
GRANGE FARM LA
FINDLAY CR
HUMBERSTON AVENUE
Toll Bar Farm
LOUTH RD
PO
CARDIFF AVENUE
ORCHARD
THE
CANNON OAKES CT
TOLL BAR AVE
STATION ROAD
MARGARET PL
STATION AVENUE
ENFIELD AVENUE
Enfield Prim Sch
CH
DEATON LA
RUTLAND DR
PRETYMEN CR
DAVID PL
BRUNTON WY
ENFIELD AV
Toll Bar Sec Sch
Humberston Park Golf Course
Grove Farm
HAWTHORNE AVE
WADDINGHAM PL
PRIORS CLOSE
STATION ROAD
MAPLE GR
DN36
Poplar Farm
Waltham House Farm
A16
CLAY LANE
Eastfield Farm
LOUTH ROAD
EDINBURGH DR
CAMBRIAN WY
CARMEN CRES
GLEBE CL
HERON WY
FORGE WY
Northfield Farm
Wks
Waltham Windmill Golf Course
LINDSEY DRIVE
Holton le Clay
Holton le Clay Inf Sch
CHURCH LANE
FREEMAN CT
DN37
THE CRESCENT
WOLD VW
TETNEY LANE
CAMPIONS CL
PINFOLD LANE
RIBY CT
WHISBY CT
NEWSTEAD AVENUE
PO
HOLTON MOUNT
BELMONT
HOLTON CT
LANGTON ROAD
OSBORNE DR
Recn Gd
SILVER STREET
GRAINSBY AVE
HOLTON ROAD
PICKSLEY CRESCENT
SOUTH VW
1 RAVENDALE CL
2 ASHBY CL
3 EVENDINE CT
LOUTH ROAD
LIME GR
SOUTHFIELD RD
BEECH GR
Holton le Clay Jun Sch
LANCASTER GATE
LOUTH ROAD
A16
35
C2
1 WORSLEY CL
2 PELHAM RD
3 YARBOROUGH CL
4 HAYS CL
5 BEAUMONDE
D1
1 MOUNT PLEASANT
2 LOUTH RD
3 PINFOLD LA
4 PINFOLD GD
5 MAGNOLIA DR
6 FENWICK CT
7 BEVERLEY CL
36
D2
1 LOUTH RD
2 EASTFIELD RI
3 CHURCH WK
4 ST PETER'S CL
5 SARGE CL
6 WAYSIDE CL
7 NURSERY GD
8 GARTHWAY
9 PEPPERCORN WK
36

20
20
20
F6
1 FRANKLAND CL
2 VICARAGE AV
3 DOVECOTE MS
F7
1 GILLATTS CL
2 MARKHAM WY
3 ECCLES CT
4 CHAPEL LA
A
B
C
D
E
F
8
7
09
6
5
08
4
3
07
2
1
06
99
00
01
M180
B1206
STAR CARR LANE
Wrawby Farm
Three Tree Farm
Wrawby Carrs
BARTON ROAD
BAKERSFIELD
TUNNEL ROAD
OLD MILL LA
VICARAGE ROAD
Wrawby
LITTLE LA
College Farm
Ashdale Farm
Ivy House Farm
Low Farm
Carr Farm
GRAMMAR SCHOOL LANE
BRICKYARD LANE
DN20
A18
BRIGG ROAD
Manor Farm
Tongs Farm
Barton Road End
HIGH FIELD RD
WESTERN AVE
SUNNINGDALE AVE
NORTHERN AVE
DAVY CR
ATKINSON AVE
POPLAR DR
HIGHFIELD GROVE
HORSTEAD AVE
SPRINGBANK
SOUTH VIEW AVE
St Marys RC Prim Sch
Recn Gd Playing Field
Vale of Ancholme Sch
Recreation Ground
Football Gd
St Helens
EUROPA WAY
ATHERTON WAY
POPPYFIELD WY
FOXGLOVE
PRESTON DR
HAWTHORN AVE
Brigg Prim Sch
EAST PARADE
WOODBINE AV
WRAWBY ROAD
CHURCHILL AVENUE
HOLME CL
BRIGG
Ancholme Business Park
Sewage Works
REDCOMBE LANE
DIXON CL
ALMOND GR
ELM WY
ASH GROVE
GLEBE ROAD
Swimming Pool
BIRCH AVE
COLTON ST
WESLEY RD
Sir John Nelthorpe Sch
NICOLGATE LA
Cemy
YORK ROAD
BARNARD AVENUE
ANCHOLME WAY
CARY LA
DUDLEY RD
Clerk to the Justices
EASTFIELD RD
ST JAMES RD
Mast
SPRINGS WY
Liby
GLANFORD ROAD
O'HANLON AVE
YARBOROUGH RD
KENNEDY CL
WATERS EDGE
ISLAND CARR RD
KILN LA
BRIDGE ST
WRAWBY ST
BIGBY STREET
ST HELEN'S ROAD
BURGESS RD
PRINCES ST
ALBERT STREET
BIGBY ROAD
KING'S AVENUE
MAPLE CL
WILLOWBROOK DR
SCAWBY ROAD
BRIDGE STREET
WEST TR
ENGINE ST
JAMES ST
MANLEY GARDENS
ELWES ST
ST CLARES WY
WRAWBY ST
Brigg Pre Sch
TENNYSON CL
LC
BIGBY HIGH RD
BIGBY HIGH ROAD
A1084
PINGLEY MD
PINGLEY LANE
THE COPSE
Garden Centre
Ancholme L Ctr
SILVERSIDES LA
Sports Gd
RIVER MEADOW
MILL LANE
Brigg
ELWES STREET
Island Carr
Pingley Farm
New River Ancholme
Windmill
Westrum
WESTRUM LANE
Island Carr Farm
CADNEY ROAD
Bentley Farm
Chy
Chy
Chy
A3
1 THEMOORINGS
2 RIVERSIDE
3 THE NARROW BOATS
4 TEAL CL
5 MILL CL
6 MILLERS QUAY
7 ANCHORS WY
B3
1 FORRESTER ST
2 MARKET PL
3 CARY LA
4 ANCHORAGE ST
5 EXCHANGE PL
6 PARADISE PL
B4
1 BRAMBLE WY
2 KINGSWAY
3 CHERRY TREE AV
20
C3
1 MAGRATH CT
2 OLD COURTS RD
3 GRAMMAR SCHOOL RD
4 CROSS ST
5 GD ST
6 QUEEN ST
7 BIGBY RD
8 NEW ST
9 THE BOTTLINGS
10 ANCHOLME GD
31
D3
1 HEDGEROW LA
2 SPRINGFIELD RD
20
D4
1 WOLD VW
2 RIDGE VW
3 KETTLEBY VW
4 WELLBECK CL
5 WINSTON WY
6 CHAPEL WY
E3
1 SPRINGFIELD RI
2 OAKFIELD CL
3 ASHDOWN CL

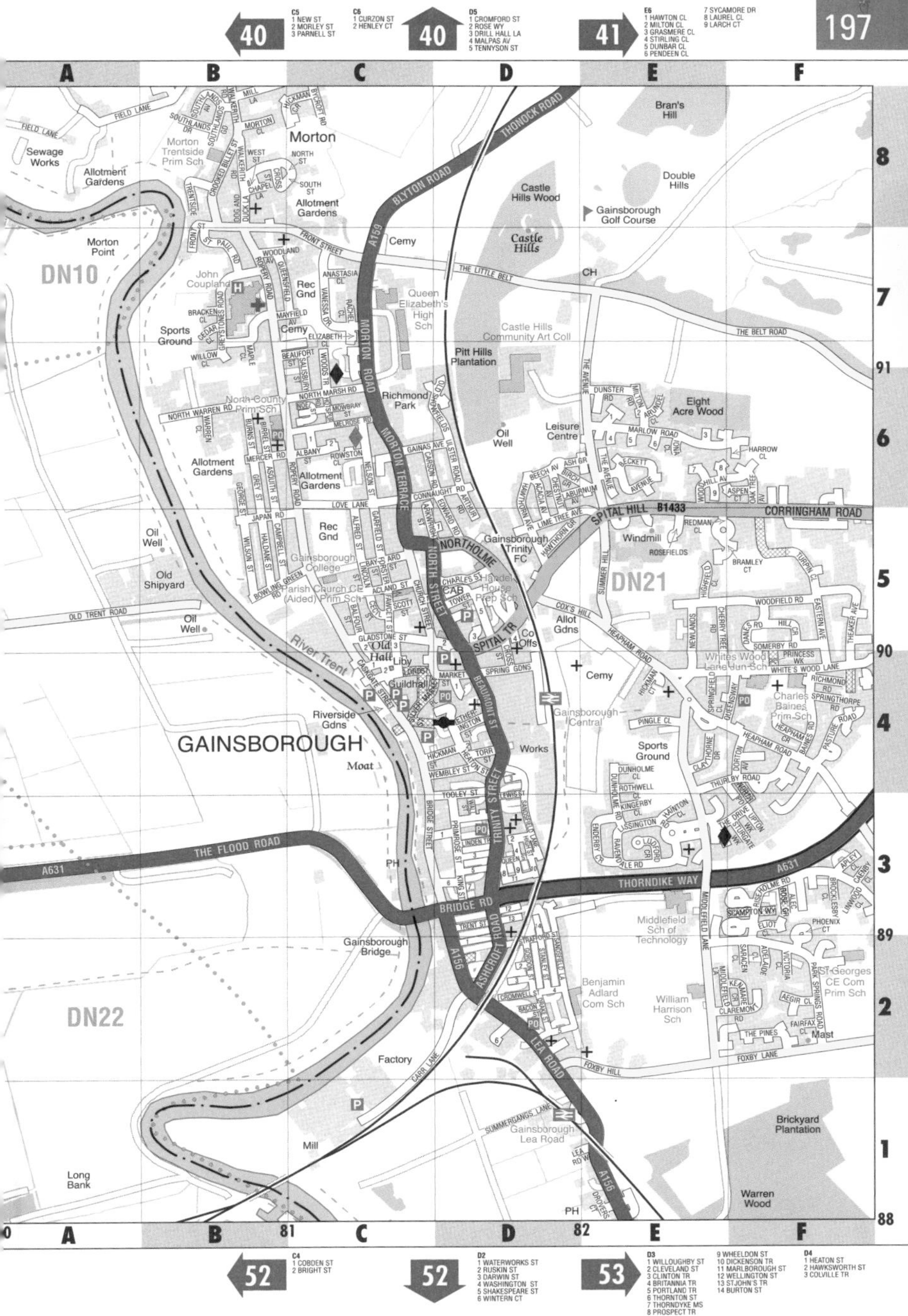
40
C5
1 NEW ST
2 MORLEY ST
3 PARNELL ST
C6
1 CURZON ST
2 HENLEY CT
40
D5
1 CROMFORD ST
2 ROSE WY
3 DRILL HALL LA
4 MALPAS AV
5 TENNYSON ST
41
E6
1 HAWTON CL
2 MILTON CL
3 GRASMERE CL
4 STIRLING CL
5 DUNBAR CL
6 PENDEEN CL
7 SYCAMORE DR
8 LAUREL CL
9 LARCH CT
A
B
C
D
E
F
8
7
91
6
5
90
4
3
89
2
1
88
Morton
Sewage Works
Allotment Gardens
Morton Trentside Prim Sch
Morton Point
DN10
John Coupland
Sports Ground
Rec Gnd
Cemy
Queen Elizabeth's High Sch
Bran's Hill
Double Hills
Castle Hills Wood
Gainsborough Golf Course
Castle Hills
THE LITTLE BELT
CH
THE BELT ROAD
Castle Hills Community Art Coll
Pitt Hills Plantation
Richmond Park
North County Prim Sch
Eight Acre Wood
Leisure Centre
Oil Well
Allotment Gardens
THONOCK ROAD
BLYTON ROAD
A159
MORTON ROAD
MORTON TERRACE
FRONT STREET
FIELD LANE
NORTH WARREN RD
NORTH MARSH RD
LOVE LANE
SPITAL HILL
B1433
CORRINGHAM ROAD
Windmill
ROSEFIELDS
Gainsborough Trinity FC
DN21
Rec Gnd
Gainsborough College
Parish Church CE (Aided) Prim Sch
Handel House Prep Sch
Old Shipyard
OLD TRENT ROAD
River Trent
Old Hall
Liby
Guildhall
Riverside Gdns
GAINSBOROUGH
Moat
NORTHOLME
NORTH STREET
SPITAL TR
Allot Gdns
Cemy
Gainsborough Central
Works
Whites Wood Lane Jun Sch
Charles Baines Prim Sch
Sports Ground
HEAPHAM ROAD
WHITE'S WOOD LANE
THE FLOOD ROAD
A631
THORNDIKE WAY
BRIDGE RD
TRINITY STREET
ASHCROFT ROAD
A156
PH
Gainsborough Bridge
Middlefield Sch of Technology
MIDDLEFIELD LANE
Benjamin Adlard Com Sch
William Harrison Sch
St Georges CE Com Prim Sch
DN22
Factory
LEA ROAD
FOXBY HILL
FOXBY LANE
Mast
CARR LANE
SUMMERGANGS LANE
Gainsborough Lea Road
Mill
Brickyard Plantation
Long Bank
Warren Wood
PH
81
82
52
C4
1 COBDEN ST
2 BRIGHT ST
52
D2
1 WATERWORKS ST
2 RUSKIN ST
3 DARWIN ST
4 WASHINGTON ST
5 SHAKESPEARE ST
6 WINTERN CT
53
D3
1 WILLOUGHBY ST
2 CLEVELAND ST
3 CLINTON TR
4 BRITANNIA TR
5 PORTLAND TR
6 THORNTON ST
7 THORNDYKE MS
8 PROSPECT TR
9 WHEELDON ST
10 DICKENSON TR
11 MARLBOROUGH ST
12 WELLINGTON ST
13 ST JOHN'S TR
14 BURTON ST
D4
1 HEATON ST
2 HAWKSWORTH ST
3 COLVILLE TR

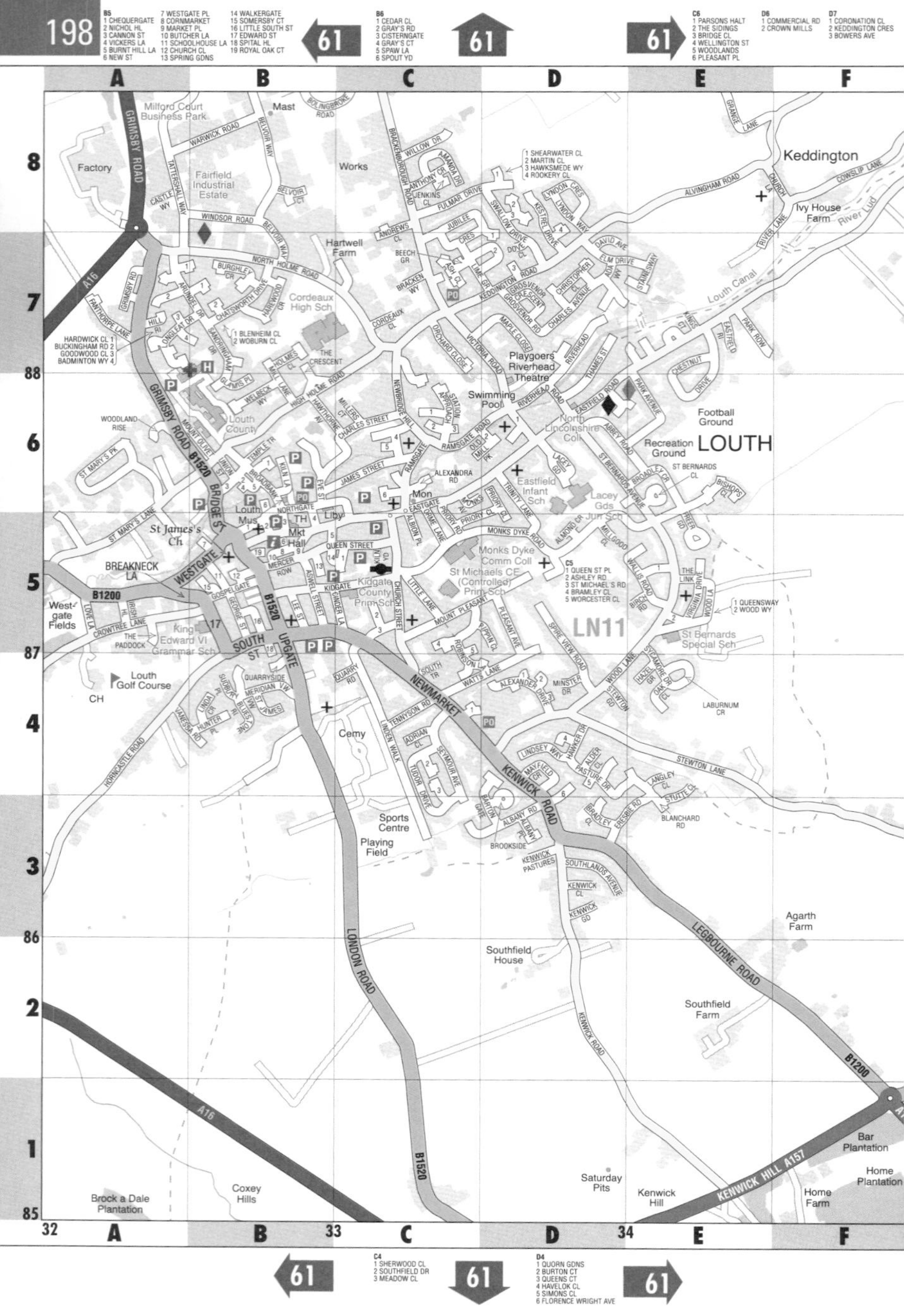
B5
1 CHEQUERGATE
2 NICHOL HL
3 CANNON ST
4 VICKERS LA
5 BURNT HILL LA
6 NEW ST
7 WESTGATE PL
8 CORNMARKET
9 MARKET PL
10 BUTCHER LA
11 SCHOOLHOUSE LA
12 CHURCH CL
13 SPRING GDNS
14 WALKERGATE
15 SOMERSBY CT
16 LITTLE SOUTH ST
17 EDWARD ST
18 SPITAL HL
19 ROYAL OAK CT
61
61
B6
1 CEDAR CL
2 GRAY'S RD
3 CISTERNGATE
4 GRAY'S CT
5 SPAW LA
6 SPOUT YD
61
C6
1 PARSONS HALT
2 THE SIDINGS
3 BRIDGE CL
4 WELLINGTON ST
5 WOODLANDS
6 PLEASANT PL
D6
1 COMMERCIAL RD
2 CROWN MILLS
D7
1 CORONATION CL
2 KEDDINGTON CRES
3 BOWERS AVE
A
B
C
D
E
F
8
7
88
6
5
87
4
3
86
2
1
85
32
33
34
Milford Court Business Park
Mast
Factory
Works
Fairfield Industrial Estate
GRIMSBY ROAD
WARWICK ROAD
BELVOIR WAY
BOLINGBROKE ROAD
BRACKENBOROUGH ROAD
WILLOW DR
AMANDA DR
ANTHONY CR
JENKINS CL
FULMAR DRIVE
1 SHEARWATER CL
2 MARTIN CL
3 HAWKSMEDE WY
4 ROOKERY CL
Keddington
ALVINGHAM ROAD
COWSLIP LANE
CHURCH LA
Ivy House Farm
River Lud
RIVER LANE
CASTLE WY
TATTERSHALL WAY
BELVOIR CT
WINDSOR ROAD
ANDREWS CL
Hartwell Farm
JUBILEE CRES
SWALLOW DRIVE
KESTREL DRIVE
LYNDON CRES
LYNDON WAY
DAVID AVE
ELM DRIVE
STAINESWAY
NORTH HOLME ROAD
BEECH GR
ASH CL
LIME GR
DOVE CL
A16
GRIMSBY RD
BURGHLEY CR
ARUNDEL DR
CHATSWORTH DRIVE
HARDWOOD CR
Cordeaux High Sch
BRACKEN WY
KEDDINGTON ROAD
GROSVENOR CRESCENT
CHRISTOPHER CL
CHARLES AVENUE
Louth Canal
FANTHORPE LANE
HILL RI
ONGLEAT DR
SANDRINGHAM DR
1 BLENHEIM CL
2 WOBURN CL
CORDEAUX CL
ORCHARD CLOSE
VICTORIA ROAD
MAPLE CLOSE
GROSVENOR RD
RIVERHEAD
THAMES ST
KINGS CL
EASTFIELD RI
PARK ROW
HARDWICK CL 1
BUCKINGHAM RD 2
GOODWOOD CL 3
BADMINTON WY 4
HOLMES CL
THE CRESCENT
CHESTNUT DRIVE
Playgoers Riverhead Theatre
GLAMIS PL
MILL LANE
HIGH HOLME ROAD
WELBECK WY
NEWBRIDGE HILL
STATION APPROACH
Swimming Pool
RIVERHEAD ROAD
EASTFIELD ROAD
PARK AVENUE
Football Ground
WOODLAND RISE
GRIMSBY ROAD
Louth County
MOUNT OLIVET
HAWTHORNE AV
MILLERS CT
CHARLES STREET
RAMSGATE ROAD
North Lincolnshire Coll
ABBEY ROAD
Recreation Ground
LOUTH
ST MARY'S PK
B1520
TEMPLE TR
KILN LA
JAMES STREET
RAMSGATE
ALEXANDRA RD
OLD MILL PK
LACEY GD
ST BERNARDS AVENUE
BROADLEY CR
ST BERNARDS CL
BISHOPS CL
UNION ST
BROADBANK
EVE ST
Mon
EASTGATE
PRIORY RD
MONKS AV
PRIORY CL
TRINITY LANE
Eastfield Infant Sch
Lacey Gds Jun Sch
BRIDGE ST
ST MARY'S LANE
Louth Mus
NORTHGATE
TH
Liby
St James's Ch
Mkt Hall
ALBION PL
ORME LANE
MONKS DYKE ROAD
ALMOND CR
MILLGOOD CL
FREER GD
QUEEN STREET
Monks Dyke Comm Coll
C5
1 QUEEN ST PL
2 ASHLEY RD
3 ST MICHAEL'S RD
4 BRAMLEY CL
5 WORCESTER CL
BREAKNECK LA
WESTGATE
MERCER ROW
St Michaels CE (Controlled) Prim Sch
WALLIS ROAD
THE LINK
VIRGINIA DRIVE
WOOD LA
1 QUEENSWAY
2 WOOD WY
B1200
GOSPELGATE
KIDGATE
Kidgate County Prim Sch
LITTLE LANE
BIRCH RD
West-gate Fields
LOVE LA
IRISH HL
GEORGE ST
LEE ST
ASWELL STREET
CINDER LA
CHURCH STREET
MOUNT PLEASANT
PLEASANT AVE
SPIRE VIEW ROAD
LN11
CROWTREE LANE
King Edward VI Grammar Sch
THE PADDOCK
SOUTH ST
UPGATE
ROBINSON LA
PIPPIN CL
St Bernards Special Sch
SYCAMORE DR
HAZEL GR
OAK CL
Louth Golf Course
CH
SUDBURY RI
QUARRYSIDE
MERIDIAN VW
LINGA CR
HUNTER PL
ST JAMES
QUARRY RD
NEWMARKET
SOUTH TR
WATTS LANE
ALEXANDER DRIVE
MINSTER DR
WOOD LANE
STEWTON GD
LABURNUM CR
VANESSA RD
HORNCASTLE ROAD
Cemy
TENNYSON RD
ADRIAN CL
LINDEN WALK
SEYMOUR AVE
TUDOR DRIVE
LINDSEY WAY
HAWKER DR
ALDER CL
MAYFIELD CR
PASTURE DR
STEWTON LANE
LANGLEY CL
STUTTE CL
KENWICK ROAD
BARTON GATE
ALBANY RD
ALBANY PL
BRADLEY CL
ERESBIE RD
BLANCHARD RD
Sports Centre
Playing Field
BROOKSIDE
KENWICK PASTURES
SOUTHLANDS AVENUE
KENWICK CL
KENWICK GD
Agarth Farm
LEGBOURNE ROAD
Southfield House
LONDON ROAD
KENWICK ROAD
Southfield Farm
B1200
A16
B1520
Bar Plantation
Home Plantation
Saturday Pits
Kenwick Hill
KENWICK HILL A157
Home Farm
Brock a Dale Plantation
Coxey Hills
C4
1 SHERWOOD CL
2 SOUTHFIELD DR
3 MEADOW CL
D4
1 QUORN GDNS
2 BURTON CT
3 QUEENS CT
4 HAVELOK CL
5 SIMONS CL
6 FLORENCE WRIGHT AVE
61
61
61

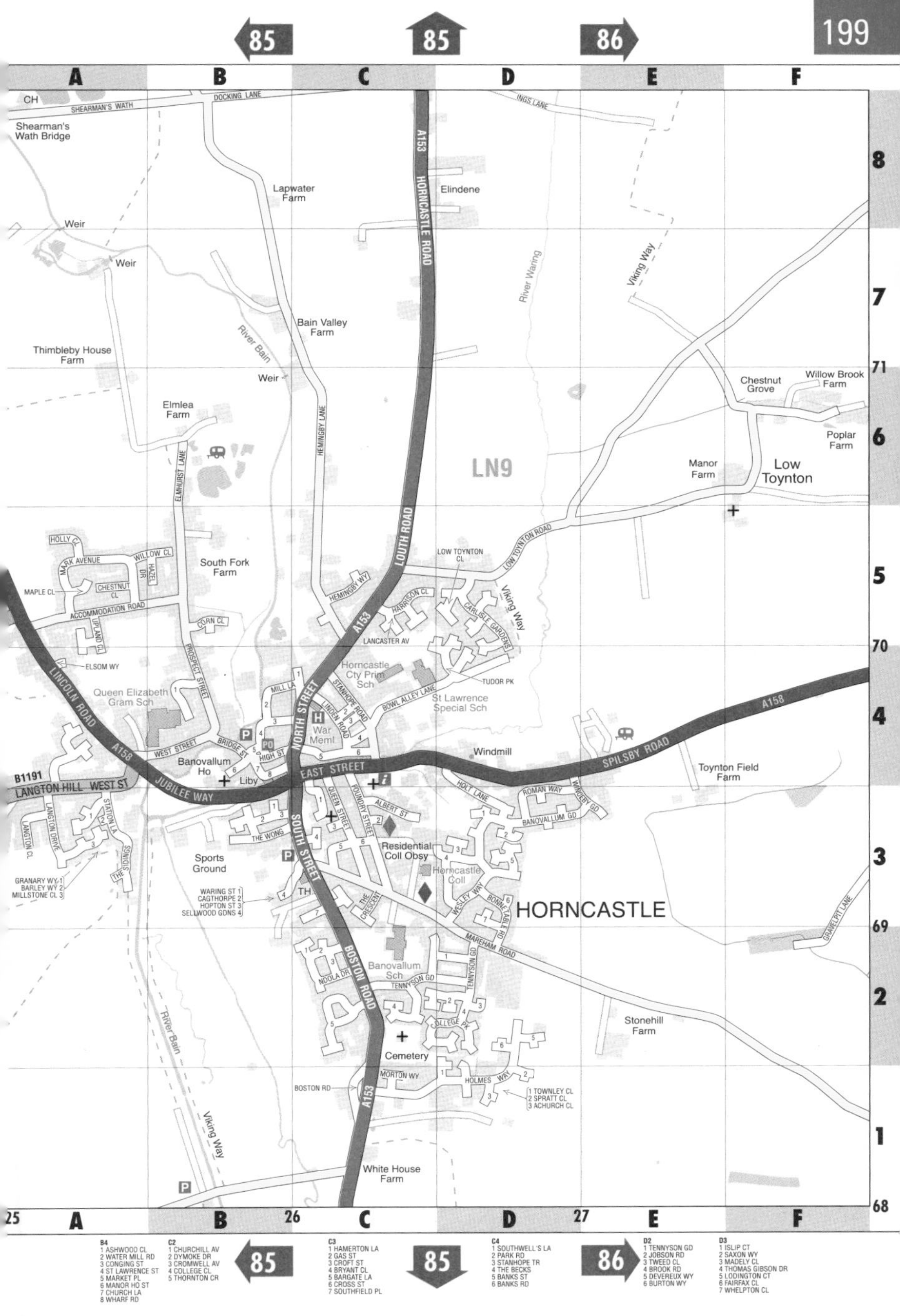

B4
1 ASHWOOD CL
2 WATER MILL RD
3 CONGING ST
4 ST LAWRENCE ST
5 MARKET PL
6 MANOR HO ST
7 CHURCH LA
8 WHARF RD

C2
1 CHURCHILL AV
2 DYMOKE DR
3 CROMWELL AV
4 COLLEGE CL
5 THORNTON CR

C3
1 HAMERTON LA
2 GAS ST
3 CROFT ST
4 BRYANT CL
5 BARGATE LA
6 CROSS ST
7 SOUTHFIELD PL

C4
1 SOUTHWELL'S LA
2 PARK RD
3 STANHOPE TR
4 THE BECKS
5 BANKS ST
6 BANKS RD

D2
1 TENNYSON GD
2 JOBSON RD
3 TWEED CL
4 BROOK RD
5 DEVEREUX WY
6 BURTON WY

D3
1 ISLIP CT
2 SAXON WY
3 MADELY CL
4 THOMAS GIBSON DR
5 LODINGTON CT
6 FAIRFAX CL
7 WHELPTON CL

A4
1 HAMPDEN CL
2 LANCASTER WY
3 HALIFAX CL
4 STIRLING WY
5 WHITLEY CL
6 SUNDERLAND CL
7 MITCHELL CL

B1
1 LUTON CL
2 PRESTWICK CL
3 CHIVENOR CL

79

C1
1 OLD WOOD
2 WASDALE CL
3 BURNMOOR CL
4 BAYWOOD CL
5 HICKORY RD RD
6 BRIAR CL
7 WHITETHORN GR
8 DELLFIELD CT
9 WOODFIELD CL
10 SATINWOOD CL
11 TULIPWOOD AV

204
80

D1
1 THIRLMERE WY
2 BUTTERMERE CL
3 ENNERDALE CL
4 RINGWOOD CL
5 PEARTREE CL
6 ELMWOOD CL
7 OLD POND CL

E1
1 STONES PL
2 GOLDCREST CL
3 SHEARWATER CL

D7
1 LEGBOURNE CL
2 BURTON RIDGE
3 OAKLAND CL
4 HIGSON RD
5 HONINGTON AP
E6
1 CLARENCE ST
2 CARISBROOKE CL
3 OSBORNE CL
4 BUCKFAST RD
E8
1 CLARENDON GD
2 TRELAWNEY CR
3 EDENDALE GD
4 PIETERMARITZ ST
5 GREYLING CL
6 TETNEY CL
7 AYLESBY CL
8 ERMINE CL
9 MINTING CL
10 MIDVILLE CL
67
F6
1 KENNETH ST
2 ANDERSON LA
3 ELVIN CL
4 BROADWAY CL
F7
1 STURTON CL
2 LISSINGTON CL
3 ROLLESTON CL
4 ROTHWELL RD
202
81
F8
1 SEDGEBROOK CL
2 BROXHOLME GD
3 SCOPWICK PL
4 HACKTHORN PL
5 WELLINGORE RD
6 EDLINGTON CL
201
Lowfields Farm
Waves Farm
LONG LEYS ROAD
SAXILBY ROAD
A46
Allot Gdns
LN1
St George's
West Common
Carholme Golf Course
Ballast Holes
Boultham Mere Nature Reserve
Swan Pool
LN6
Swanpool
LINCOLN
(LINDVM)
MIDDLE STREET
B1398
Playing Field
St Francis Sch
Yarborough Sch
Yarborough Leisure Centre
Ermine
RISEHOLME ROAD
B1226
LONGDALES RD
B1273
YARBOROUGH CRESCENT
LN2
Mount Street Inf Sch
Recn Gd
Newport Cemy
234
Windmill
Mus
Water Twr
Visitors Centre
Lincoln Crown Court
Castle
Lincoln City Assembly Rooms
Lincoln Cath
Bishop's Palace
Gallery
The Lincoln Nuffield
YARBOROUGH ROAD
CARHOLME ROAD
A57
Works
Police HQ
Council Offices
Cty Hall
CLASKETGATE
B1308
WEST PD
NEWLAND
BRAYFORD WAY
Hotel
University
Brayford Pool
SILVER ST
BROADGATE
New Boultham
Lincoln
Mag Ct
Cty Ct
LN5
HIGH STREET
B1262
TRITTON ROAD
CANWICK ROAD
A15
St Peter at Gowts CE Prim Sch
Sincil Bank (Lincoln City FC)
Bishop King CE Prim Sch
VALENTINE RD
B1360
DIXON STREET
B1003
SOUTH PK AV
A B C D E F
95 96 97
8 7 73 6 5 72 4 3 71 2 1 70
D1
1 RAILWAY PK CL
2 ST MATHEWS CL
3 PEPPERCORN CL
80
D3
1 ARTHUR TAYLOR ST
2 CHARLESWORTH ST
3 STAUNTON ST
4 WESTFIELD ST
5 HARVEY ST
6 WESTBOURNE GR
205
D4
1 TENNYSON ST
2 BEDFORD ST
3 COLENSO TR
4 WOODSTOCK ST
5 ALLISON PL
6 ST FAITH'S ST
7 SOUTH PD
F1
1 STANLEY PL
2 LUMLEY PL
3 LONSDALE PL
4 LANCASTER PL
5 LINTON ST
6 ARTHUR ST
7 BISHOP KING CT
8 HOOD ST
9 SAUSTHORPE ST
202
For full street detail of the highlighted area see page 234.

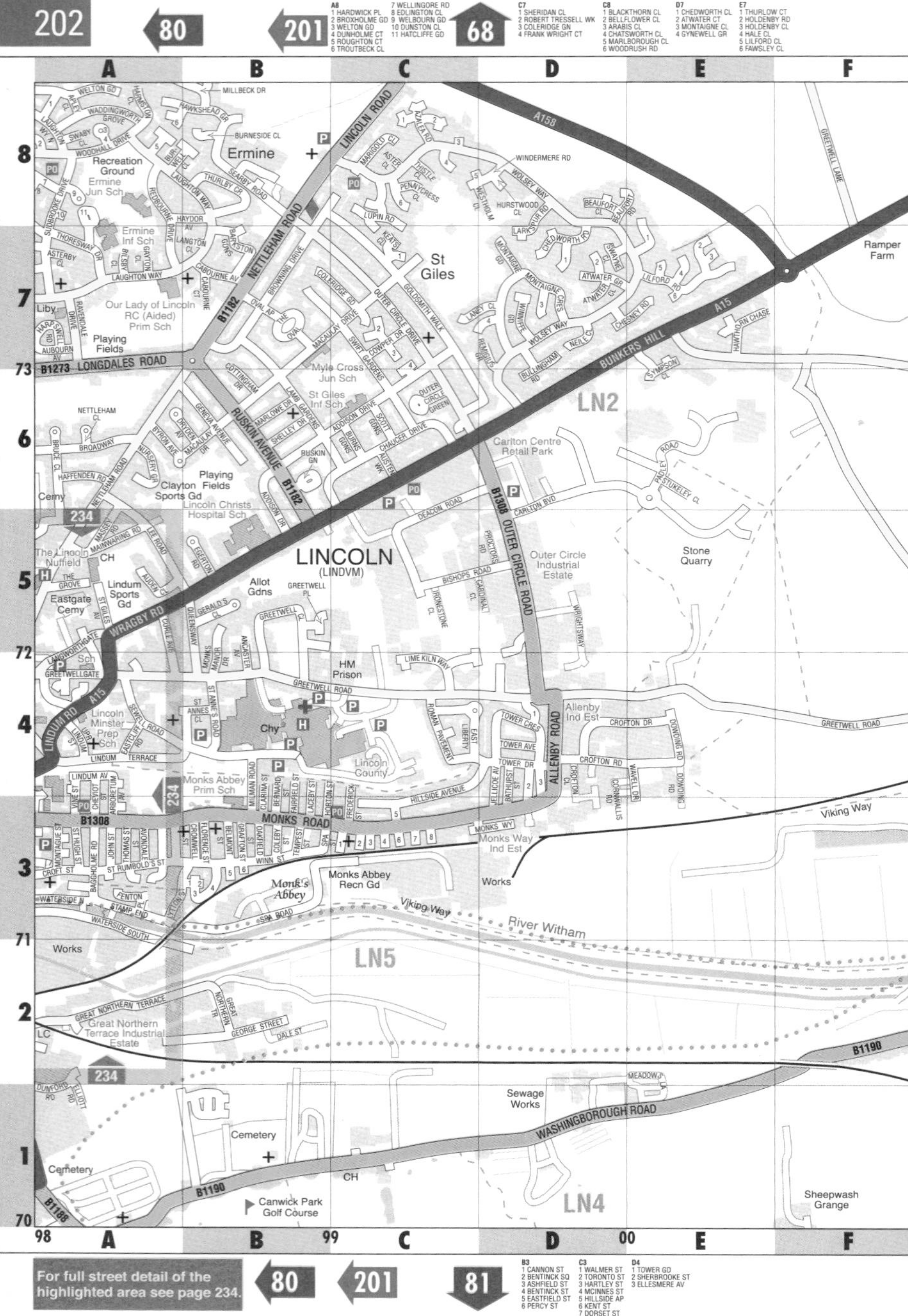
202
80
201
68
A8
1 HARDWICK PL
2 BROXHOLME GD
3 WELTON GD
4 DUNHOLME CT
5 ROUGHTON CT
6 TROUTBECK CL
7 WELLINGORE RD
8 EDLINGTON CL
9 WELBOURN GD
10 DUNSTON CL
11 HATCLIFFE GD
C7
1 SHERIDAN CL
2 ROBERT TRESSELL WK
3 COLERIDGE GN
4 FRANK WRIGHT CT
C8
1 BLACKTHORN CL
2 BELLFLOWER CL
3 ARABIS CL
4 CHATSWORTH CL
5 MARLBOROUGH CL
6 WOODRUSH RD
D7
1 CHEDWORTH CL
2 ATWATER CT
3 MONTAIGNE CL
4 GYNEWELL GR
E7
1 THURLOW CT
2 HOLDENBY RD
3 HOLDENBY CL
4 HALE CL
5 LILFORD CL
6 FAWSLEY CL
A B C D E F
8 7 73 6 5 72 4 3 71 2 1 70
98 99 00
Ermine
Recreation Ground
Ermine Jun Sch
Ermine Inf Sch
Our Lady of Lincoln RC (Aided) Prim Sch
Playing Fields
St Giles
Myle Cross Jun Sch
St Giles Inf Sch
Carlton Centre Retail Park
Clayton Sports Gd
Lincoln Christs Hospital Sch
LINCOLN
(LINDVM)
Outer Circle Industrial Estate
Stone Quarry
Ramper Farm
LN2
The Lincoln Nuffield
Lindum Sports Gd
Eastgate Cemy
Allot Gdns
HM Prison
Allenby Ind Est
Lincoln Minster Prep Sch
Chy
Lincoln County
Monks Abbey Prim Sch
Monks Way Ind Est
Works
Monks Abbey Recn Gd
Monk's Abbey
Viking Way
River Witham
LN5
Great Northern Terrace Industrial Estate
Sewage Works
Cemetery
Canwick Park Golf Course
LN4
Sheepwash Grange
A158
A15
BUNKERS HILL
LINCOLN ROAD
NETTLEHAM ROAD
B1182
B1273 LONGDALES ROAD
RUSKIN AVENUE
B1308 OUTER CIRCLE ROAD
WRAGBY RD
GREETWELL ROAD
ALLENBY ROAD
B1308 MONKS ROAD
LINDUM RD
WASHINGBOROUGH ROAD
B1190
B1188
GREETWELL LANE
234
For full street detail of the highlighted area see page 234.
80
201
81
B3
1 CANNON ST
2 BENTINCK SQ
3 ASHFIELD ST
4 BENTINCK ST
5 EASTFIELD ST
6 PERCY ST
C3
1 WALMER ST
2 TORONTO ST
3 HARTLEY ST
4 MCINNES ST
5 HILLSIDE AP
6 KENT ST
7 DORSET ST
8 DEVON ST
D4
1 TOWER GD
2 SHERBROOKE ST
3 ELLESMERE AV

E5
1 CHERRY HOLT
2 WESTHOLM
68
E6
1 BURTONFIELD CL
2 WEST MILL GA
3 EAST MILL GA
4 THE PADDOCK
82
E7
1 BELLWOOD GR
2 ST DAVID'S CL
3 ST MARK'S AV
4 ST PAUL'S AV
5 ST MATTHEW'S CL
6 ST JOHN'S AV
7 ST HUGH'S CL
8 ST PETER'S AV
9 ST SIMON'S DR
10 EAST CFT
A
B
C
D
E
F
North Greetwell
A158
WRAGBY ROAD EAST
WESTFIELD DRIVE
WESTFIELD AVE
LAWLEY CL
WESTFIELD AP
Westfield Farm
Reepham
THE GREEN
CHURCH LA
PLOUGH LA
KENNEL LANE
KENNEL WK
SPRING HL
CHAPEL CL
STATION RD
MELLOWS CL
DAWSONS LA
Reepham CE (Controlled) Prim Sch
HIGH ST
MANOR RI
Cemy
Stonefield Farm
ST LUKE'S CL
Cherry Willingham Community Sch
MINSTER DRIVE
CROFT LANE
JUBILEE CL
HAWTHORN ROAD
HAWTHORN AVE
THE PARADE
RUDGARD AVE
Liby
LC
LN3
LN2
ANCASTER CL
PO
THORNTON WY
DALE AVE
THE MEADWAY
LADY MEERS RD
THE LEYS
NEW CR
HIGH ST
JESSOP CL
PARK HL
MIDHOLM
Fox Covert
Walk Farm
GREEN LANE
Bleak Farm
BECKE CL
Sports Gd
WATERFORD LANE
ELM AVENUE
LIME GROVE
FERN GROVE
Cherry Willingham Prim Sch
CHURCH LANE
ORCHARD CL
LARKIN AV
OAK CR
NEWSTEAD AV
Cherry Willingham
LABURNUM DRIVE
GROVE
ASH
SYCAMORE CL
CEDAR AV
HOLLY CL
FISKERTON ROAD EAST
LINCOLN ROAD
FISKERTON ROAD
Fen Farm
Greetwell Hall
Willingham Fen
Viking Way
River Witham
LN4
FERRY LANE
THE ORCHARD
Whitehall Farm
WILLOW CT
Washingborough
The Longstongs
Washingborough Fen
LINCOLN ROAD
MAIN ROAD
PO
SCHOOL LA
Liby
Washingborough Prim Sch
ENDERBY CL
GRANSON WY
WITHAM VW
RAYTON CL
SUTTON CL
GRANSON WAY
NELSON DR
DRAKE AV
CHURCH HILL
HIGH STREET
OAK HL
PARK LA
PARK AVE
MALVERN AV
REPTON CL
BECKET CL
KEEBLE DRIVE
EXETER CL
FEN ROAD
B1190
Cottage Farm
Pear Tree Farm
GILDESBURGH RD
MANOR RD
HIGH MD
WINCHESTER DRIVE
PARK CRESCENT
ALABALA CL
HARROW CL
PARK LANE
CAMBRIDGE DR
BURTON MS
GERRARD MS
DURHAM CR
YORK CL
READING CL
CHESTER CL
WELLS CL
NORWICH CL
Manor Farm
PITTS ROAD
LEICESTER CL
MARLBOROUGH AVE
YALE CL
LEE AVE
JERMYN MS
EVE GARDENS
VICTORIA GR
SUNNINGDALE GR
BIRKDALE CL
CANTERBURY DRIVE
Washingborough Pits
OXFORD CL
SANDRA CR
JULIA RD
WENTWORTH CL
8
7
73
6
5
72
4
3
71
2
1
70
02
03
A2
1 HILLCROFT
2 CROMWELL CL
3 THORNTON CL
4 THURLBY CL
B2
1 FAVELL RD
2 TRAFALGAR CT
3 BURLAND CT
C2
1 PENFOLD LA
2 POLICEMANS LA
81
D1
1 HARVARD CL
2 GROSVENOR MS
3 CURZON MS
4 GLENEAGLES GR
5 CAVENDISH MS
6 CRANBOURNE MS
7 TROON CL
8 LYTHAM CL
9 CARLTON MS
10 DANIEL CR
11 ROWAN CT
82

B6
1 CHEDBURGH CL
2 WITCHFORD CL
3 WITCHFORD RD
4 GRAVELEY CL
5 LANGER CL
6 LISSETT CL
7 ELVINGTON CL
8 WYTON CL
9 SNAITH CL
B8
1 LUTON CL
2 HURN CL
3 STAVERTON CR
4 MARHAM CL
5 HALTON CL
6 HENLOW CL
79
C8
1 SALIX AP
2 ROSEWOOD CL
3 LANCEWOOD GD
4 OAKWOOD AV
5 SNOWBERRY GD
6 ST CLAIRE'S CT
200
80
D6
1 STENIGOT RD
2 CHIPPENDALE CL
3 CHIPPENDALE RD
4 JACOBEAN RD
5 WITTERING CL
6 WIGSLEY RD
7 WIGSLEY CL
8 LEEMING CL
9 FINNINGLEY CL
D8
1 REDWING GR
2 KINGFISHER CL
3 BITTERN WY
4 AVOCET CL
5 EGRET GR
6 KESTREL CL
7 ELSHAM CL
8 SPILSBY CL
9 STRUBBY CL
10 RIDGEWELL
11 FOLKINGHAM
12 BOTTESFORD
A B C D E F
8 7 69 6 5 68 4 3 67 2 1 66
Hospital Plantation
Lincoln City Council
Leisure Centre
Birchwood Jun Sch
Liby
Birchwood Shopping Centre
Chimney
St Hughs RC Prim Sch
Birchwood
Hartsholme Lake
Visitor Centre
Hartsholme Country Park
The Leslie Manser Prim Sch
Long Plantation
Football Ground
Hartsholme
Coronation Plantation
Swanholme Lakes
Motel
Works
Nature Reserve
Lincolnshire Road Transport Museum
Broomhill Farm
Lyndon Business Park
LN6
West Lodge Game Farm
Sand & Gravel Pit
Hykeham Station
Hykeham
Ling Moor Prim Sch
North Hykeham
Sand & Gravel Pits
Recreation Gd
Sailing Club
Pike Drain
Robert Pattinson Sch
Superstore
Sports Centre
Terry O'Toole Theatre
North Kesteven Sch
Low Moor Plantation
Caravan Park
Chy
All Saints CE Prim Sch
A46
B1190
LINCOLN ROAD
DODDINGTON ROAD
B1378
SKELLINGTHORPE ROAD
A1434
NEWARK ROAD
STATION ROAD
WHISBY ROAD
C7
1 SNETTERTON CL
2 ALDERGROVE CL
3 FALDINGWORTH CL
4 CADWELL CL
5 BROOKLANDS CL
6 MALLORY CL
7 CAISTOR CL
8 BROOKLANDS WY
9 DIGBY CL
10 HIBALDSTOW CL
11 BLYTON CL
12 BLYTON RD
13 BLYTON GR
14 BROUGH CL
15 STURGATE CL
16 LECONFIELD RD
17 SILVERSTONE RD
PETERSFIELD CL 1
WENTWORTH WAY 2
BROCKENHURST CL 3
GREENOCK WY 4
TURNBURY CL 5
D7
1 METHERINGHAM CL
2 ACER CT
3 BETULA GR
4 DOULTON CL
5 BESWICK CL
6 STAFFORDSHIRE CR
7 COALPORT CL
8 BINBROOK CL
9 WEDGEWOOD GR
10 WEDGEWOOD CL
11 WORCESTER CL
12 GOTHIC CL
13 GOXHILL GR
14 GOXHILL CL
15 SHERATON CL
16 WINTHORPE GR
17 WINTHORPE CL
18 ADAM CL
E8
1 NIGHTINGALE CR
2 SHEARWATER CL
3 HARRIER CT
4 SYCAMORE CL
5 SYCAMORE CR
6 LIME TREE CL
JARVIS CL 1
KEADBY CL 2
CROWLAND DR 3
NORTHORPE CL 4
WALCOT CL 1
CROXTON DR 2
DAWSON CL 3
ANDERBY CL 4
BARDNEY CL 5
1 COTTESMORE RD
2 LINDHOLME RD
3 FROME CL
4 PYKE RD
C6
1 KELSTERN CL
2 HARLAXTON CL
3 STENIGOT CL
4 HARLAXTON DR
5 BRIGG GR
6 BRIGG CL
7 LECONFIELD CL
8 KIRMINGTON CL
9 WALTHAM CL
10 SHAWBURY CL
11 KINLOSS CL
12 BOSCOMBE CL
13 ALCONBURY CL
14 WOODVALE CL
15 ABINGDON CL
16 SYWELL CL
17 LOCKING CL
F3
1 COLNE CL
2 WHARFEDALE DR
3 ALDER CL
4 ROSEDALE CL
92 93 94
C1
1 VICTOR DR
2 GREBE CL
3 LAKEVIEW CL
4 MALLARD CT
5 HAZE LA
6 NENE PK
7 AVONDALE
8 ASTRAL WY
79
D1
1 LINDEN DENE
2 HAWKSMOOR CL
3 MILL MOOR WY
93
D2
1 ST HILARY'S CL
2 ST BENEDICT'S CL
3 ST CRISPIN'S CL
4 HAMILTON RD
5 ST FRANCIS CT
6 NORTH WY
7 KESTEVEN CT
E1
1 MONTROSE CL
2 NASH LA
3 SEDGEMOOR CL
4 RAVENSMOOR CL
E2
1 ST JOHN'S AV
2 ST MARY'S RD
3 ST CLEMENT'S RD
4 CHATSWORTH DR
5 STAIDEN'S RD
6 BAMFORD CL
F1
1 CARLISLE CL
2 ALEXANDRE AV
3 EYAM WY
4 PHILIP CT
5 WINDSOR PK CL
6 HYDE PK CL
7 REGENTS PK CL
8 BURGHLEY PK CL
9 SCHOOL LA
F2
1 BIRCH CL
2 MILLERS DALE
3 MULBERRY AVE
4 CHERRY TREE CL
5 DOVE DL
6 BAKEWELL MS

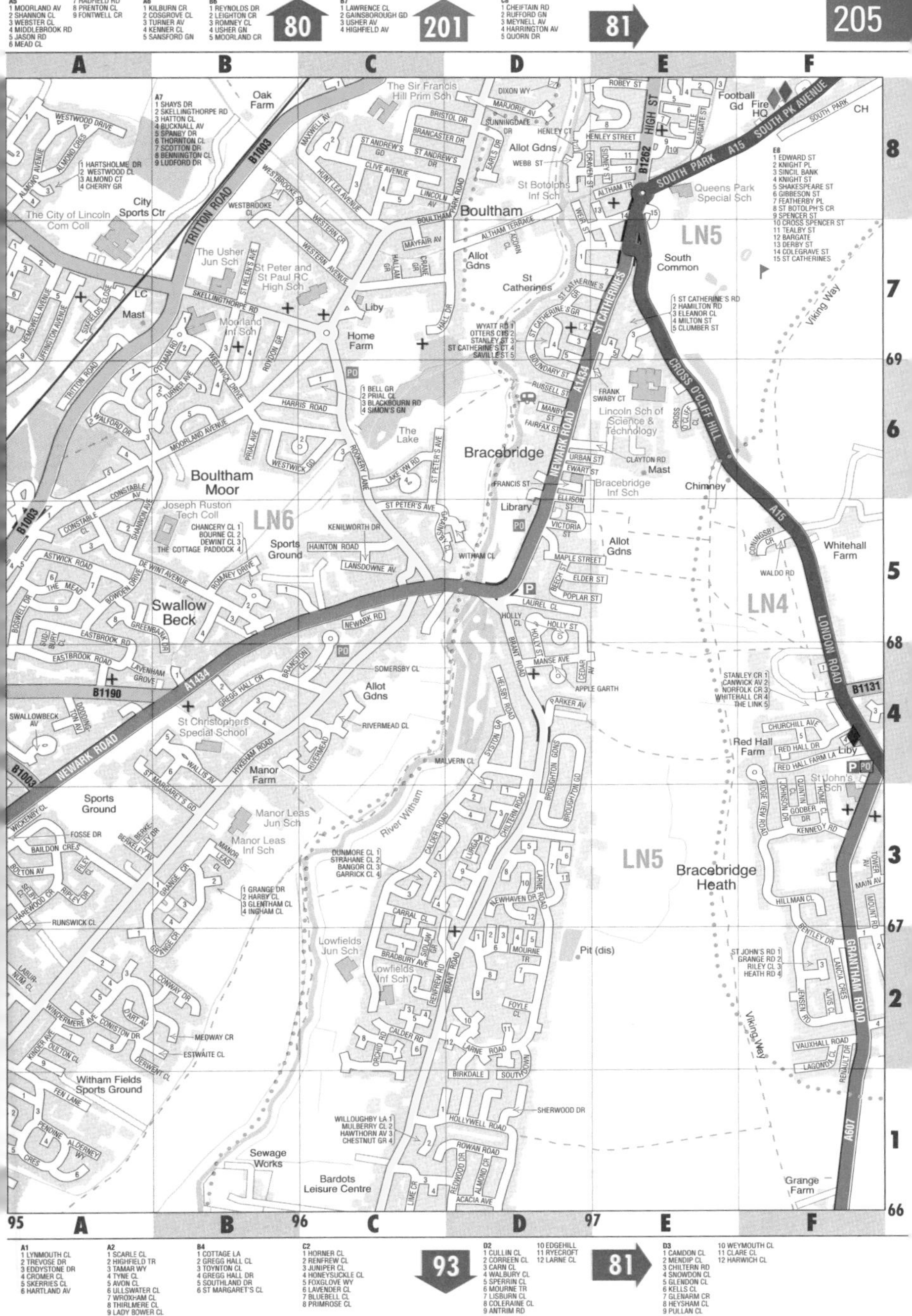

A5
1 MOORLAND AV
2 SHANNON CL
3 WEBSTER CL
4 MIDDLEBROOK RD
5 JASON RD
6 MEAD CL
7 HADFIELD RD
8 PRENTON CL
9 FONTWELL CR
A6
1 KILBURN CR
2 COSGROVE CL
3 TURNER AV
4 KENNER CL
5 SANSFORD GN
B6
1 REYNOLDS DR
2 LEIGHTON CR
3 ROMNEY CL
4 USHER GN
5 MOORLAND CR
80
B7
1 LAWRENCE CL
2 GAINSBOROUGH GD
3 USHER AV
4 HIGHFIELD AV
201
C8
1 CHEIFTAIN RD
2 RUFFORD GN
3 MEYNELL AV
4 HARRINGTON AV
5 QUORN DR
81
205
A7
1 SHAYS DR
2 SKELLINGTHORPE RD
3 HATTON CL
4 BUCKNALL AV
5 SPANBY DR
6 THORNTON CL
7 SCOTTON DR
8 BENNINGTON CL
9 LUDFORD DR
1 HARTSHOLME DR
2 WESTWOOD CL
3 ALMOND CT
4 CHERRY GR
E8
1 EDWARD ST
2 KNIGHT PL
3 SINCIL BANK
4 KNIGHT ST
5 SHAKESPEARE ST
6 GIBBESON ST
7 FEATHERBY PL
8 ST BOTOLPH'S CR
9 SPENCER ST
10 CROSS SPENCER ST
11 TEALBY ST
12 BARGATE
13 DERBY ST
14 COLEGRAVE ST
15 ST CATHERINES
1 ST CATHERINE'S RD
2 HAMILTON RD
3 ELEANOR CL
4 MILTON ST
5 CLUMBER ST
WYATT RD 1
OTTERS CTS 2
STANLEY ST 3
ST CATHERINE'S CT 4
SAVILLE ST 5
1 BELL GR
2 PRIAL CL
3 BLACKBOURN RD
4 SIMON'S GN
CHANCERY CL 1
BOURNE CL 2
DEWINT CL 3
THE COTTAGE PADDOCK 4
STANLEY CR 1
CANWICK AV 2
NORFOLK CR 3
WHITEHALL CR 4
THE LINK 5
DUNMORE CL 1
STRAHANE CL 2
BANGOR CL 3
GARRICK CL 4
1 GRANGE DR
2 HARBY CL
3 GLENTHAM CL
4 INGHAM CL
ST JOHN'S RD 1
GRANGE RD 2
RILEY CL 3
HEATH RD 4
WILLOUGHBY LA 1
MULBERRY CL 2
HAWTHORN AV 3
CHESTNUT GR 4
Oak Farm
The Sir Francis Hill Prim Sch
Boultham
Allot Gdns
St Botolphs Inf Sch
Football Gd
Fire HQ
CH
Queens Park Special Sch
LN5
South Common
The City of Lincoln Com Coll
City Sports Ctr
The Usher Jun Sch
St Peter and St Paul RC High Sch
Moorland Inf Sch
Liby
Home Farm
St Catherines
Mast
Frank Swaby Ct
Lincoln Sch of Science & Technology
The Lake
Bracebridge
Clayton Rd
Bracebridge Inf Sch
Chimney
Boultham Moor
Joseph Ruston Tech Coll
LN6
Sports Ground
Library
Whitehall Farm
LN4
Swallow Beck
Allot Gdns
St Christophers Special School
Manor Farm
Red Hall Farm
St John's Sch
Manor Leas Jun Sch
Manor Leas Inf Sch
River Witham
LN5
Bracebridge Heath
Lowfields Jun Sch
Lowfields Inf Sch
Pit (dis)
Viking Way
Witham Fields Sports Ground
Sewage Works
Bardots Leisure Centre
Grange Farm
TRITTON ROAD
NEWARK ROAD
SKELLINGTHORPE RD
MOORLAND AVENUE
HIGH ST
SOUTH PARK
SOUTH PK AVENUE
ST CATHERINES
CROSS O'CLIFF HILL
LONDON ROAD
GRANTHAM ROAD
BRANT ROAD
HYKEHAM ROAD
A1434
A15
A607
B1003
B1190
B1131
B1262
A B C D E F
8 7 69 6 5 68 4 3 67 2 1 66
95 96 97
A1
1 LYNMOUTH CL
2 TREVOSE DR
3 EDDYSTONE DR
4 CROMER CL
5 SKERRIES CL
6 HARTLAND AV
A2
1 SCARLE CL
2 HIGHFIELD TR
3 TAMAR WY
4 TYNE CL
5 AVON CL
6 ULLSWATER CL
7 WROXHAM CL
8 THIRLMERE CL
9 LADY BOWER CL
B4
1 COTTAGE LA
2 GREGG HALL CL
3 TOYNTON CL
4 GREGG HALL DR
5 SOUTHLAND DR
6 ST MARGARET'S CL
C2
1 HORNER CL
2 RENFREW CL
3 JUNIPER CL
4 HONEYSUCKLE CL
5 FOXGLOVE WY
6 LAVENDER CL
7 BLUEBELL CL
8 PRIMROSE CL
93
D2
1 CULLIN CL
2 CORREEN CL
3 CARN CL
4 WALBURY CL
5 SPERRIN CL
6 MOURNE TR
7 LISBURN CL
8 COLERAINE CL
9 ANTRIM RD
10 EDGEHILL
11 RYECROFT
12 LARNE CL
81
D3
1 CAMDON CL
2 MENDIP CL
3 CHILTERN RD
4 SNOWDON CL
5 GLENDON CL
6 KELLS CL
7 GLENARM CR
8 HEYSHAM CL
9 PULLAN CL
10 WEYMOUTH CL
11 CLARE CL
12 HARWICH CL

A5
1 WELLINGTON WY
2 CONINGSBY CL
3 BADER WY
4 CRANWELL CL
5 GIBSON PL
6 PERRIN AV
7 CHESHIRE GR
8 PORTAL GN
9 PRIMROSE CL
10 GRUNNILL CL
11 HARRIS CL
12 HUDSON WY

103

A6
1 BISCAY CL
2 ST VINCENT CL
3 TEAL CLOSE
4 BEACON PARK CL
5 THE HURST
6 FLAMBOROUGH CL
7 TAGGS DR
8 BURDETT CL
9 YARBOROUGH RD
10 BURGH RD

90

A7
1 GLEBE CL
2 KINGFISHER DR
3 JOHNSON CL
4 NELSON CL
5 JENKINS CL
6 PORTLAND DR
7 THE HORN
8 THE NEEDLES

D8
1 ROMAN BANK
2 FAINLIGHT CL
3 NORTH FORELAND DR
4 GILBERTS GR

B3
1 OLD WAINFLEET RD
2 GRANTHAM DR
3 CROSS ST
4 CHURCH RD SOUTH
5 MAYFIELD GR
6 MARIAN WY
7 BEVERLEY GR

B4
1 CHARLES CL
2 ST CLEMENT'S RD
3 WESTFIELD DR
4 SWABY CR

C2
1 RICHMOND CT
2 DENHAM CL
3 TENNYSON GN
4 BERESFORD CL
5 BERESFORD CR
6 FORSYTH CR

103

C3
1 DOROTHY CR
2 SUTTON CT
3 CORINNE CR
4 LINCOLN RD
5 BERRY WY
6 ROMAN BANK
7 WAINFLEET RD

103

C4
1 PELHAM RD
2 LANDSDOWNE RD
3 RONALD CL
4 THE CLOSE
5 GRANTHAM DR
6 SCHRIMSHAW CT
7 BRIAN AV
8 PEARL CL

D1
1 LETTWELL CR
2 SOMERSBY GR
3 CLIFTON GR
4 MERRIEMEADE DR
5 SYNE AV

D2
1 LAWN CR
2 ARCADIA CR
3 WILLOUGHTON RD
4 SOUTH VIEW CL
5 SERENA RD
6 BARBARA RD

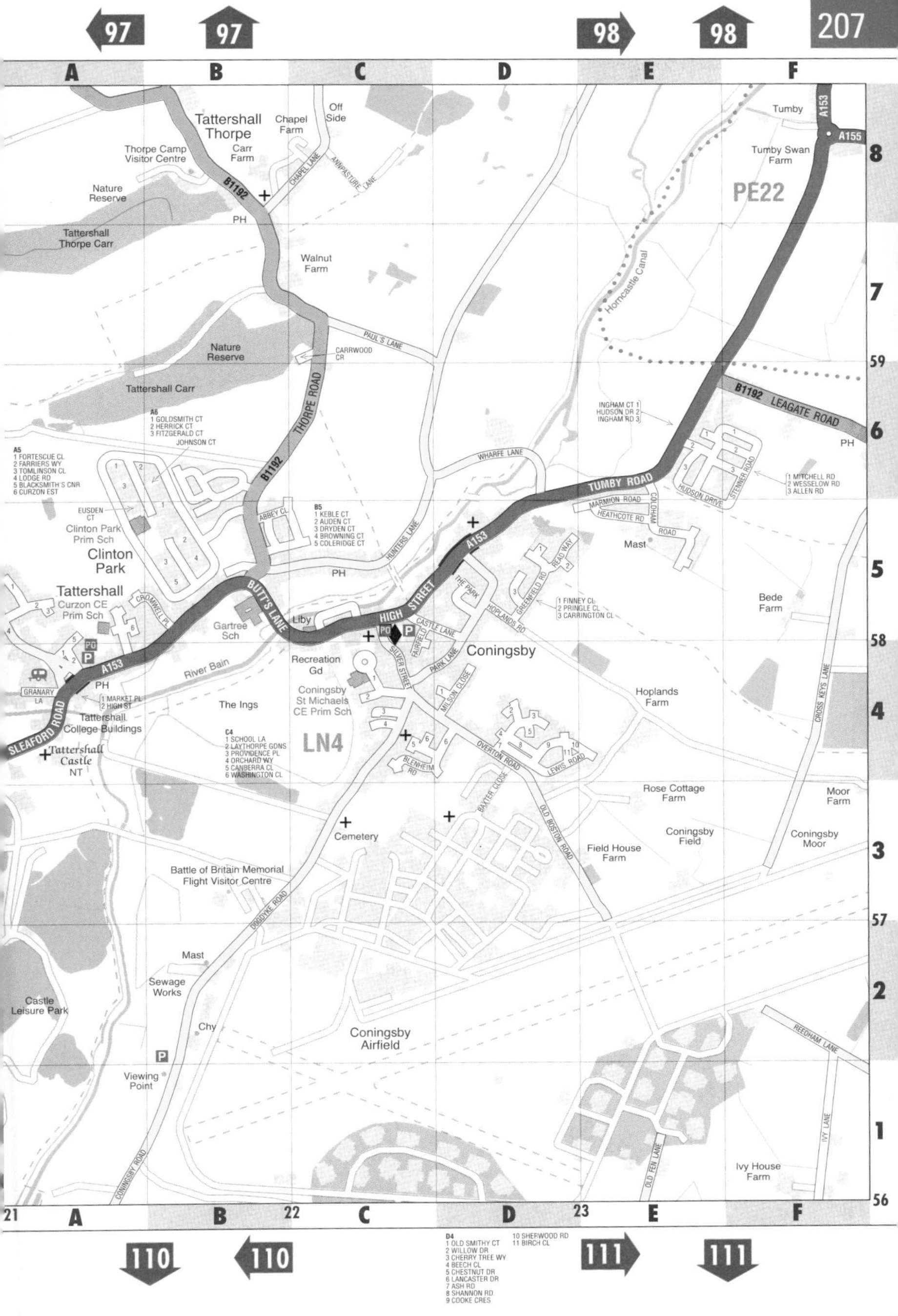
97
98
Tattershall Thorpe
Chapel Farm
Off Side
Thorpe Camp Visitor Centre
Carr Farm
Nature Reserve
Tattershall Thorpe Carr
Walnut Farm
Tumby
Tumby Swan Farm
PE22
Horncastle Canal
Tattershall Carr
Clinton Park Prim Sch
Clinton Park
Tattershall
Curzon CE Prim Sch
Gartree Sch
Liby
Coningsby
Mast
Bede Farm
Recreation Gd
Coningsby St Michaels CE Prim Sch
The Ings
River Bain
Tattershall College Buildings
Tattershall Castle NT
LN4
Hoplands Farm
Rose Cottage Farm
Moor Farm
Coningsby Field
Coningsby Moor
Field House Farm
Cemetery
Battle of Britain Memorial Flight Visitor Centre
Mast
Sewage Works
Castle Leisure Park
Chy
Coningsby Airfield
Viewing Point
Ivy House Farm
110
111

125
E6
1 BRADY ST
2 WITHAM CT
3 FRACKNAL'S ROW
4 WITHAM BANK EAST
125
E7
1 DAVEY CL
2 BURROWS CL
3 PARSONS DR
4 TUDOR DR
5 RAYBROOK CL
6 LOCKSLEY CL
F5
1 UNION PL
2 UNION ST
3 WITHAM ST
4 CHAPEL ST
5 NORMAN AV
6 RED LION ST
7 PARK GATE
8 WIDE BARGATE
9 THREADNEEDLE ST
10 FOUNTAIN PL
11 COLLEY ST
12 ARCHER LA
13 FOUNTAIN LA
14 TOWER ST
15 PETTICOAT LA
16 MITRE LA
17 MARKET SQ
18 PUMP SQ
19 CHURCH LA
20 CHURCH ST
21 MARKET PL
22 TOWN BRIDGE
23 CRAYTHORNE LA
F6
1 GRAND SLUICE LA
2 NORTH ST
3 STAFFORD ST
4 NORFOLK PL
5 PARK LA
A
B
C
D
E
F
8
7
45
6
5
44
4
3
43
2
1
42
30
31
32
High Hill Farm
White House Farm
1 BRACKENBURRY WY
2 SINCLAIR CL
3 MEDFORTH LA
Allot Gdns
RED CAP LANE
Memorial
B1183
River Witham
FENSIDE ROAD
Boundary Farm
WASHDYKE LANE
PUNCHBOWL LANE
CROMWELL CL 1
FAIRFAX CL 2
HAWORTH WY 3
LONGHURST GD 4
Crem
Boston Cemetery
FOREST DL
The Haven High Sch
MIDDLE DROVE
Boston Rowing Club
Boston Park Com Prim Sch
Norfolk Street Ind Est
WASHDYKE LA 1
LARKSPUR CFT 2
FOX CL 3
HURLE CR
CARLTON ROAD
COTTON ROAD
THE GRAYLINGS
FIELDFARE CT
JOY PAINE CLOSE
PORCHER WY
TILNEY AV
INGRAM ROAD
SUNNINGDALE DR
Recn Gd
Boston Marina
Boston Cty Ct
NORFOLK STREET
NORTH FORTY FOOT BANK
LANGRICK ROAD
LAUGHTON RD
ORCHARD ST
Central Park
Conway Prep Sch
Mayflower Sports Ground
CONINGSBY CL
ARGYLE ST
A1137
FYDELL ST
Lock
Shooting Range
GRANVILLE STREET
ALBERT ST
HORACE ST
Peter Paine Sports Centre
WOODHALL CL
ALMOND WK
BARTOL CRESCENT
Carlton Road Cty Prim Sch
St Botolphs Ch (The Stump)
Wyberton Fen
PE21
ROSEBERY AVE
ALMOND CL
Eurosure Tennis Centre
Boston Tennis Club
BROTHERTOFT RD
SYDNEY STREET
PORTLAND ST
Boston Station
City H & Lib
Mon
Boston West Prim Sch
ARCOTT DR
PRINCESS ST
LINCOLN LA
CAB
Ass Rms
SUSSEX AVENUE
Recn Gd
QUEEN ST
WEST STREET
Guildhall Mus
WESTFIELD AVENUE
Mast
Mun Bldg
FYDELL CRESCENT
SLEAFORD ROAD
CHERRY WALK
ARUNDEL CRESCENT
Endeavour Park Ind Est
JOHN ADAMS WAY
HESSLE AVENUE
Staniland County Prim Sch
BOARDSIDES
A1121
A52
LC
FRESHNEY WY
GLEN DRIVE
RYTON ROAD
BAIN ROAD
CHESTER WAY
SOUTH PARADE
MEDLAM RD
HESSLE DRIVE
STANILAND ROAD
NELSON WY
ST ANN'S LA
STELLS LA
WESTBRIDGE RD
WELLAND ROAD
Chain Bridge
Alban Retail Park
Superstore
COOKS LOCK
THORNTON AVE
Allot Gdns
BATH GD
NEW HAMMOND BECK RD
SWINESHEAD ROAD
CHAIN BRIDGE ROAD
MATTHEW FLINDERS WAY
Swing Bridge
SPALDING RD
A16
PH
Old Macdonalds Farm
Holland Park
Cherry Tree Farm
Windmill
Allot Gdns
Moat
WYBERTON WEST ROAD
OLD HAMMOND BECK ROAD
WEST END ROAD
WYBERTON WEST ROAD
GARDENERS WK 1
POPLAR CL 2
CATER WY 3
CARMEL GN 1
CORK TREE CR 2
GARFIT'S LA 3
Skirbeck Quarter
BAYSWOOD AVE
Water Tower
GARFIT'S LANE
LONDON ROAD
St Thomas CE (Controlled) Prim Sch
B1397
Abbey Dale
Hunter's Row
FIVE HOUSE LANE
Woodside
Allot Gdns
D3
1 HEATHER CL
2 WOODVILLE GD W
3 WOODVILLE GD E
4 FRANCIS BERNARD CL
125
136
E4
1 WALDEN GD
2 ALBERT TR
3 TRAFALGAR PL
4 WEST ROW
5 GEORGE ST
6 BRAMLEY LA
7 BLUE ST
8 BROADFIELD LA
9 NELSON WY
F1
1 FLEMING CT
2 WHITTLE CL
3 SIR ISAAC NEWTON DR
4 STEPHENSON CL
5 BELL CT
F2
1 WYBERTON LOW RD
2 MIDDLECOTT CL
3 WYBERTON LOW RD
4 ELMWOOD AV
F4
1 BOND ST
2 BRIDGE ST
3 SIBSEY LA
4 SHODFRIARS LA
5 SPAIN LA
6 PADDOCK GR
7 QUAKER LA
8 VICTORIA PL
9 GREYFRIARS LA
9 GREYFRIARS LA
10 WHITEHORSE LA
11 LIQUORPOND ST
12 PULVERTOFT LA
13 EDWIN ST
14 ROSEGARTH ST

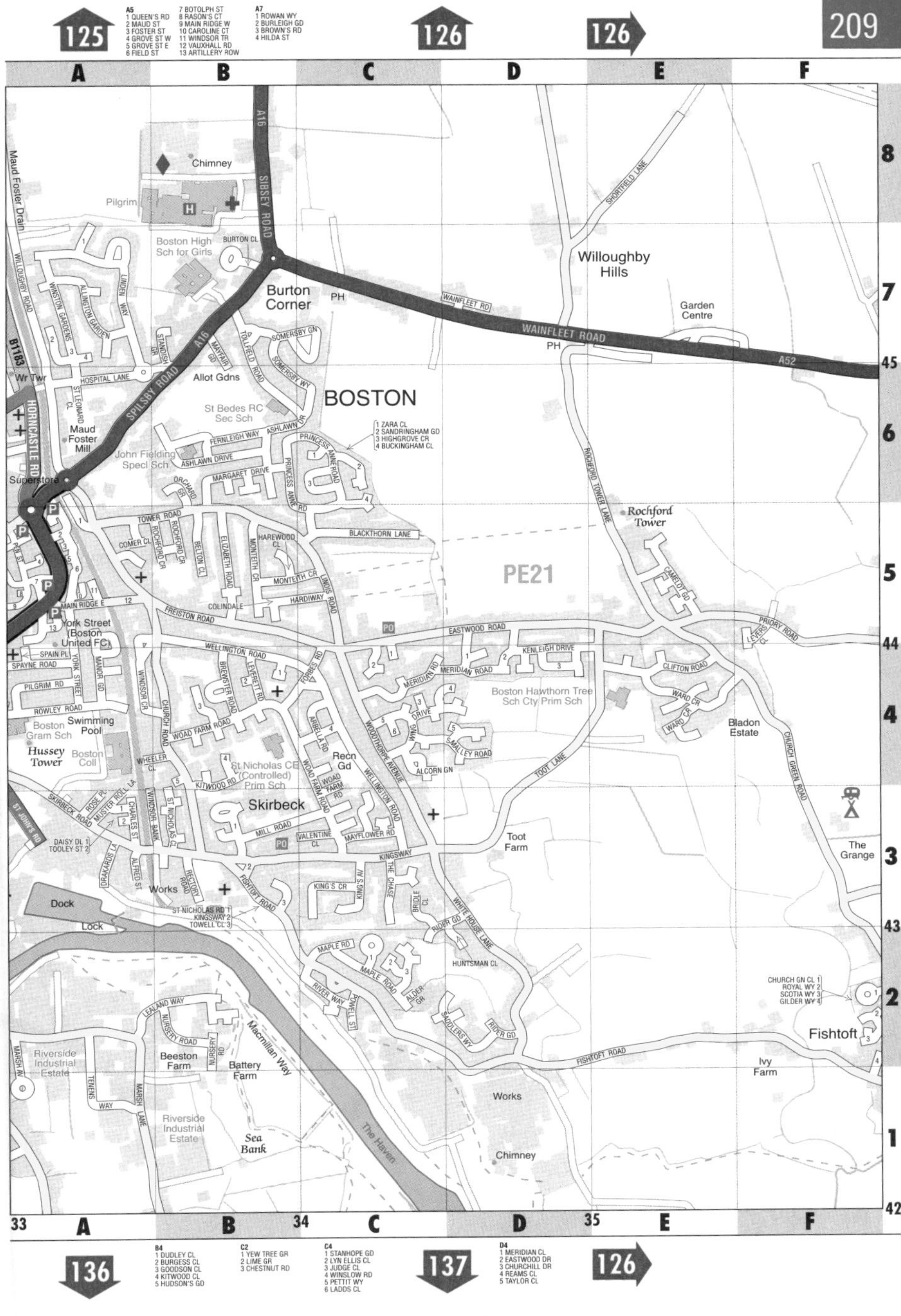
125
A5
1 QUEEN'S RD
2 MAUD ST
3 FOSTER ST
4 GROVE ST W
5 GROVE ST E
6 FIELD ST
7 BOTOLPH ST
8 RASON'S CT
9 MAIN RIDGE W
10 CAROLINE CT
11 WINDSOR TR
12 VAUXHALL RD
13 ARTILLERY ROW
A7
1 ROWAN WY
2 BURLEIGH GD
3 BROWN'S RD
4 HILDA ST
126
126
A
B
C
D
E
F
8
7
45
6
5
44
4
3
43
2
1
42
BOSTON
PE21
Chimney
Pilgrim
Maud Foster Drain
Boston High Sch for Girls
BURTON CL
SIBSEY ROAD
A16
Burton Corner
PH
WAINFLEET RD
WAINFLEET ROAD
A52
SHORTFIELD LANE
Willoughby Hills
Garden Centre
PH
WILLOUGHBY ROAD
WINSTON GARDENS
ALLINGTON GARDEN
LINDEN WAY
STANDISH GR
MAYFAIR GD
TOLLFIELD ROAD
SOMERSBY GN
SOMERSBY WY
B1183
Wr Twr
HOSPITAL LANE
SPILSBY ROAD
Allot Gdns
ST LEONARD CL
HORNCASTLE RD
Maud Foster Mill
St Bedes RC Sec Sch
ASHLAWN DR
FERNLEIGH WAY
ASHLAWN DRIVE
John Fielding Specl Sch
1 ZARA CL
2 SANDRINGHAM GD
3 HIGHGROVE CR
4 BUCKINGHAM CL
PRINCESS ANNE ROAD
PRINCESS ANNE RD
MARGARET DRIVE
ORCHARD GR
Superstore
ROCHFORD TOWER LANE
Rochford Tower
TOWER ROAD
ROCHFORD CR
BLACKTHORN LANE
COMER CL
BELTON CL
ELIZABETH ROAD
MONTEITH CR
HAREWOOD CL
LINDIS ROAD
CAMELOT GD
HARDIWAY
COLINDALE
MAIN RIDGE E
FREISTON ROAD
PO
EASTWOOD ROAD
PRIORY ROAD
LEVERS CL
York Street (Boston United FC)
SPAIN PL
SPAYNE ROAD
PILGRIM RD
ROWLEY ROAD
YORK STREET
MANOR GD
WELLINGTON ROAD
BREWSTER ROAD
LEVERETT RD
FORBES RD
MERIDIAN RD
MERIDIAN ROAD
KENLEIGH DRIVE
CLIFTON ROAD
Boston Hawthorn Tree Sch Cty Prim Sch
WARD CR
Bladon Estate
CHURCH GREEN ROAD
Boston Gram Sch
Swimming Pool
Hussey Tower
Boston Coll
WINDSOR CR
CHURCH ROAD
WOAD FARM ROAD
ARBELLA RD
WOODTHORPE AVENUE
WING DRIVE
MALLEY ROAD
ALCORN GN
TOOT LANE
WHEELER CL
KITWOOD RD
St Nicholas CE (Controlled) Prim Sch
Recn Gd
WELLINGTON ROAD
Skirbeck
SKIRBECK ROAD
ROSE PL
MUSTER ROLL LA
CHARLES ST
WINDSOR BANK
ST NICHOLAS CL
MILL ROAD
VALENTINE CL
MAYFLOWER RD
ST JOHN'S RD
Toot Farm
The Grange
DAISY DL 1
TOOLEY ST 2
DRAKARDS LA
ALFRED ST
Works
RECTORY ROAD
KINGSWAY
KING'S CR
KING'S AV
THE CHASE
BRIDLE CL
WHITE HOUSE LANE
FISHTOFT ROAD
Dock
Lock
ST NICHOLAS RD 1
KINGSWAY 2
TOWELL CL 3
RIDER GD
HUNTSMAN CL
MAPLE RD
MAPLE ROAD
ALDER GR
RIVER WAY
POWELL ST
CHURCH GN CL 1
ROYAL WY 2
SCOTIA WY 3
GILDER WY 4
Fishtoft
LEALAND WAY
NURSERY ROAD
NURSERY RD
Macmillan Way
SADDLERS WY
RIDER GD
FISHTOFT ROAD
Ivy Farm
Riverside Industrial Estate
Beeston Farm
Battery Farm
MARSH AV
TENENS WAY
MARSH LANE
Works
Riverside Industrial Estate
Sea Bank
The Haven
Chimney
33
34
35
A
B
C
D
E
F
136
B4
1 DUDLEY CL
2 BURGESS CL
3 GOODSON CL
4 KITWOOD CL
5 HUDSON'S GD
C2
1 YEW TREE GR
2 LIME GR
3 CHESTNUT RD
C4
1 STANHOPE GD
2 LYN ELLIS CL
3 JUDGE CL
4 WINSLOW RD
5 PETTIT WY
6 LADDS CL
137
D4
1 MERIDIAN CL
2 EASTWOOD DR
3 CHURCHILL DR
4 REAMS CL
5 TAYLOR CL
126

210
129
129
E8
1 EMMINSON WY
2 KELHAM RD
3 THE HAVERLANDS
4 ORCHARD CL
5 MALVERN DR
6 MENDIP CL
F5
1 PORTSMOUTH CL
2 WESTMINISTER WY
3 ROBERTSON RD
4 CAMPBELL CL
5 ELY WY
6 RURO CL
F7
1 CEDARWOOD CL
2 BROOMWOOD CL
3 PALMWOOD CL
4 BIRCHWOOD CL
5 LILACWOOD DR
6 BRIARWOOD CL
7 ROWANWOOD DR
8 HOLLYWOOD DR
F8
1 VIVIAN CL
2 BEAUMONT DR
3 MALIM WY
4 PEACHWOOD CL
5 APPLEWOOD DR
6 BRAMBLEWOOD CL
7 ORANGAWOOD CL
8 OSTLER CL
9 COCHRAN CL
A
B
C
D
E
F
8
7
37
6
5
36
4
3
35
2
1
34
Gonerby Hill Foot
Gonerby Tunnel
Stubbock Hill
Knowles Farm
Rectory Farm
THORNS LANE
CHURCH LANE
GRANTHAM RD
GONERBY HL
GONERBY ROAD
B1174
Gonerby Hill Foot CE Prim Sch
Royston Ford End
Recreation Gd
BRECON CL 1
GRAMPIAN WY 2
BRENDON CL 3
CHILTERN CL 1
CAMBRIAN CL 2
CHEVIOT CL 3
SWALLOW'S CL 4
NG31
Mill Hill
A52
A1
A5
1 RECTORY CLL
2 CHURCH ST
3 CASTHORPE RD
4 CHAPEL LA
5 LAWSON LEAS
6 HIGHFIELDS
7 BERRYFIELD END
8 GRANGE PADDOCK
Boundary Farm
D5
1 SALISBURY CL
2 BLACKBURN CL
3 ST EDMUNDS CL
4 NEWCASTLE RD
5 ST ALBANS CL
6 CARLISLE CL
7 COVENTRY CL
8 CHESTER GDNS
9 WARWICK CL
10 BRADFORD CL
1 GRIMSTHORPE CL
2 DOVER CL
3 OAKHAM CL
E5
1 CORFE CL
2 RIBER CL
3 TATTERSHALL CL
4 CAMARTHEN CL
5 BIRMINGHAM CL
6 CHICHESTER CL
7 NORWICH WY
8 HEREFORD WY
9 ROCHESTER DR
10 PETERBOROUGH CL
11 ROCHESTER DR
BALMORAL DRIVE
BARROWBY ROAD
PH
Poplar Farm
Green Hill
Barrowby
New Barn Farm
HIGH ROAD
MAIN STREET
OLD DR
DEBDALE RD
PASTURES ROAD
SOUTHWELL CL
MANCHESTER WAY
GLOUCESTER ROAD
WINCHESTER ROAD
CHELMSFORD DRIVE
WAKEFIELD CL
WORCESTER RD
BRISTOL CL
LINCOLN CL
Recreation Gd
HEDGE FIELD RD
1 THE NORTHINGS
2 ADAMSTILES
E4
1 DERBY CL
2 WESTBOURNE P
3 SHORWELL CL
Autumn Park Ind Est
WROXALL DRIVE
ST HELEN'S CL
HIGH MEADOW
Beeden Park Estate
VALLEY RD
DYSART ROAD
Fun Farm & Grantham Bowl
WESTRY CORNER
LOW ROAD
NG32
Barrowby Lodge
Ambergate Special Sch
Earl of Dysart Prim Sch
Meres Leisure Centre & Swimming Pool
St Hughs CE High Sch
The Isaac Newton Prim Sch
South Kesteven Works
F3
1 HODDER CL
2 BARNWELL TR
3 HARLAXTON RD
Earlesfield
Recreation Ground
BEECHCROFT RD
OAKLEIGH RD
HEATHFIELD RD
MERES RD
1 WALKERS WY
2 THE DRIFT
Grantham Town Football Club
Sports Stadium
Spitalgate CE (Controlled) Prim Sch
EARLESFIELD LANE
HARLAXTON ROAD
A607
Mag Ct
TRENT ROAD
KESTREL CT
BUCKMINSTER GD
Ellesmere Business Park
HORNSBY ROAD
SWINGBRIDGE ROAD
DENTON CL
Harlaxton Lower Lodge Farm
Grantham Canal Nature Reserve
The Walton Girls High Sch
ROSEMARY CRESCENT
DENTON AV
88
89
90
129
139
D2
1 CHESTNUT GR
2 LARCH CL
3 SYCAMORE CT
4 HAWTHORNE CT
E2
1 CLYDE CT
2 LYMN CT
3 WELLAND CT
4 NENE CT
5 TAMAR CT
6 COLNE CT
7 STOUR CT
8 GANNET CT
9 FALCON CT
10 MALLARD CT
11 GRESLEY CT
12 STURROCK CT
13 IVATT CT
14 STIRLING CL
15 HICKLING CL
16 KINOULTON CT

129
A5
1 PROSPECT PL
2 ALBION RD
3 GLADSTONE TR
4 BROWNDONS ST
5 BROAD ST
6 PREMIER CT
7 NORTH ST
8 BARROWBY RD
9 MOUNT ST
10 WONG ROW
11 WATERGATE
12 VINE ST
A7
1 DARLEY DALE CR
2 WESTERDALE RD
3 HAWKSDALE CL
A8
1 WENSLEYDALE CL
2 HATCLIFFE CL
3 MEADOWDALE CR
4 OAKDALE CL
5 FARNDALE CR
130
D6
1 PURCELL CL
2 BELMONT GR
130
E6
1 QUEENSWAY
2 EDINBURGH RD
3 WORDSWORTH CL
4 KIPLING CL
F6
1 ALMA PARK CL
2 SIXTH AV
3 SEVENTH AV
211
A
B
C
D
E
F
Manthorpe
1 BAYSDALE GR
2 BORROWDALE WY
3 RYEDALE CL
4 GLAISDALE GDNS
5 DOVEDALE CL
Manor Farm
D7
1 TURNBERRY CL
2 WALTON HEATH CL
3 BIRKDALE CL
4 LINDRICK CL
5 THE BELFRY
6 MOORTOWN CL
7 ASCOT DR
8 MONTROSE CL
9 JOHN FOSTER CL
10 CHRISTCHURCH RD
1 MUIRFIELD
2 GLENEAGLES
3 FULFORD CL
4 TROON CL
Belton Park Golf Course
Belton Park
8
HIGH ROAD
LOW ROAD
River Witham
CH
Works
LONDONTHORPE LANE
Cliffedale Prim Sch
MANTHORPE ROAD A607
FORMBY CL 1
BRAEMAR CL 2
ACORN CL 3
CORNWALL CL 4
ELSIE DAVIES CL 5
Weir
1 KILLARNEY CL
2 LYTHAM CL
3 PRESTWICK CL
4 CANTERBURY CL
WITHAMBROOK PK
WOODLAND DR
WARREN WY
7
Belton Lane Prim Sch
GREEN LANE
The Grantham Church VA High Sch
Alma Park Industrial Estate
The Central Tech Coll
Chimney
Grantham District
Liby
RIVERSIDE PARK
Queen Elizabeth Park
COTTESMORE CL
Recn Gd
Harrowby Estate
Recn Gd
37
6
1 MANNERS ST
2 LODGE WY
Weir
Harrowby CE (Aided) Inf Sch
Belmont Prim Sch
Wyndham Park
SLATE MILL PL
Orchard End
Cherry Orchard
ROSSETTI CT
NORTH PARADE
BROOK STREET
Little Gonerby CE (Aided) Infs Sch
Sedgewick Meadow (NT)
St Marys Catholic Prim Sch
5
The King's Sch
Grantham House National Trust
Kesteven & Grantham Girls Sch
1 LABURNUM CL
2 REGENCY GDNS
3 CENTRAL PL
SANDRINGHAM DR
1 WARDOUR DR
2 CROSSGILL CL
3 BURLEIGH CL
4 BEDFORD CL
5 CHATSWORTH AV
The National CE (Aided) Jun Sch
Sandon Sch
NG31
Superstore
Weir
Grantham Coll
Brickwork Annexe (Grantham Coll)
36
Harrowby
SAINT AUGUSTIN WAY
B1174 HIGH STREET
The George Shopping Ctr
Cty Ct
The Old Barracks
WOODLANDS DR
4
CAB
Co Off & Arts Ctr
Dudley House Sch
Newton's Mon
Grantham Mus & Liby
Mon
Hall's Hill
Shop Ctr
Crem
Cemetery
WHARF ROAD
A52
GRANTHAM
Huntingtower Road County Prim Sch
St Annes CE Prim Sch
St Vincent
3
COLD HARBOUR LANE
Grantham
Spittlegate
BLENHEIM WY
Radio Mast
35
LONDON ROAD
SOUTH PARADE
BRIDGE END RD
SOMERBY HL
Weir
Dysart Park
2
SPRINGFIELD ROAD A607
WULFRAM DR
River Witham
BRIDGE END ROAD
SOMERBY HILL
Radio Mast
Barracks
Chimney
Somerby Hill
Recreation Ground
HARROWBY CR
SOMERBY PL
A52
1
South Lincs Conference Centre
B1174
Grantham Cricket Ground
Paper Mill Farm
34
91
A
B
92
C
D
93
E
F
A3
1 ELTON ST
2 WILLIAM ST
3 RAILWAY TR
4 QUEEN ST
139
A4
1 THE GRANGE
2 MARKET PL
3 ELMER ST N
4 ST PETER'S HILL
5 GREENWOOD'S ROW
6 WELBY ST
7 STANTON ST
8 BATH ST
9 OLD WHARF RD
B4
1 MIDDLEMORE YD
2 AGNES ST
3 GROVE END RD
4 STONEMASONS CT
5 NEWTON ST
6 ST PETER'S HILL
140
D2
1 WELLINGTON DR
2 LANCASTER GDNS
3 HILLSIDE CR
4 EASTWOOD DR
5 HOLLY CL
6 PRIMROSE WY
130

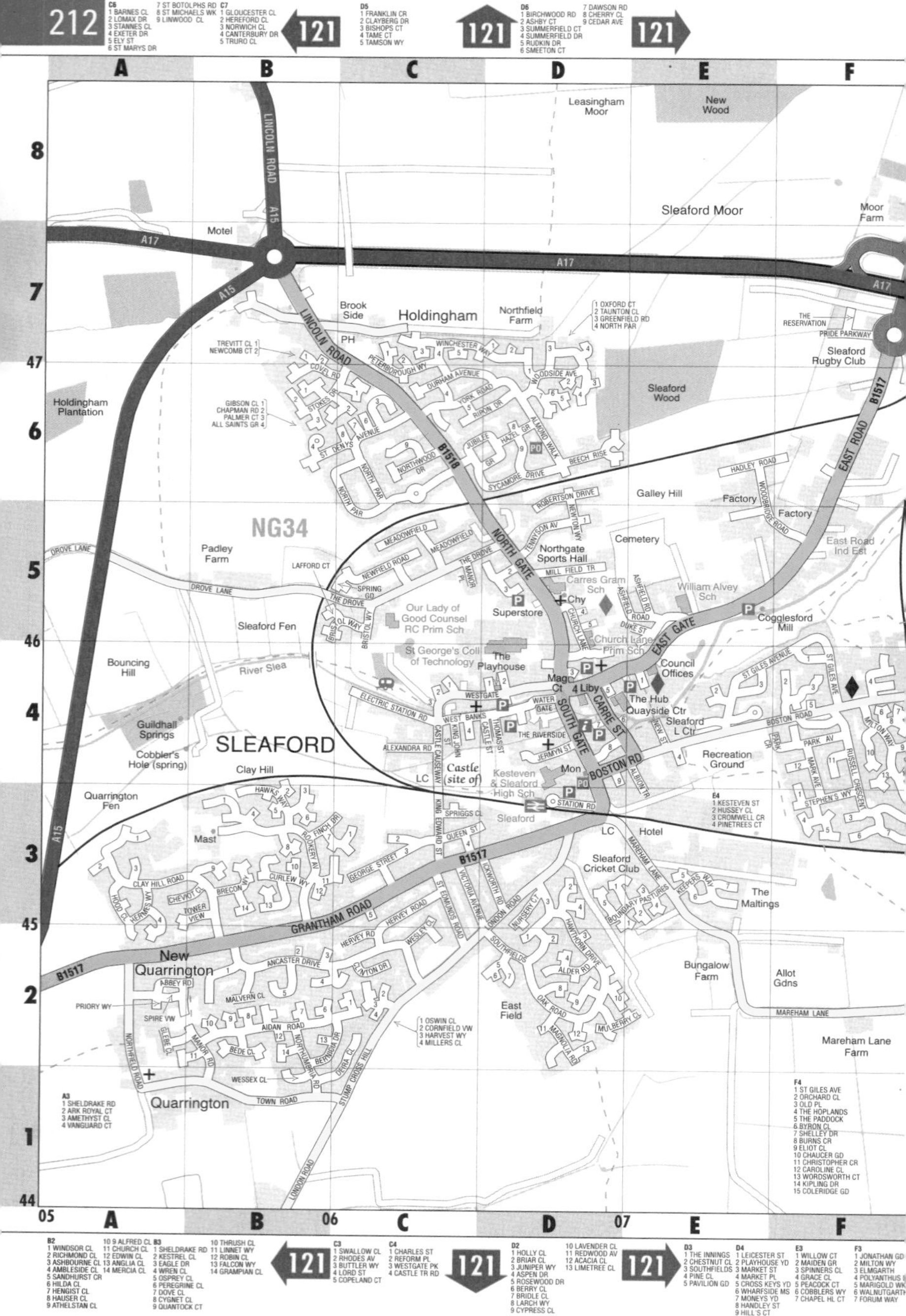
C6
1 BARNES CL
2 LOMAX DR
3 STANNES CL
4 EXETER DR
5 ELY ST
6 ST MARYS DR
7 ST BOTOLPHS RD
8 ST MICHAELS WK
9 LINWOOD CL
C7
1 GLOUCESTER CL
2 HEREFORD CL
3 NORWICH CL
4 CANTERBURY DR
5 TRURO CL
121
D5
1 FRANKLIN CR
2 CLAYBERG DR
3 BISHOPS CT
4 TAME CT
5 TAMSON WY
121
D6
1 BIRCHWOOD RD
2 ASHBY CT
3 SUMMERFIELD CT
4 SUMMERFIELD DR
5 RUDKIN DR
6 SMEETON CT
7 DAWSON RD
8 CHERRY CL
9 CEDAR AVE
121
A
B
C
D
E
F
8
7
47
6
5
46
4
3
45
2
1
44
Leasingham Moor
New Wood
LINCOLN ROAD
A15
A17
Motel
Sleaford Moor
Moor Farm
Brook Side
Holdingham
Northfield Farm
PH
1 OXFORD CT
2 TAUNTON CL
3 GREENFIELD RD
4 NORTH PAR
THE RESERVATION
PRIDE PARKWAY
Sleaford Rugby Club
TREVITT CL 1
NEWCOMB CT 2
COVEL RD
PETERBOROUGH WY
WINCHESTER WAY
DURHAM AVENUE
WOODSIDE AVE
YORK ROAD
RIPON DR
Sleaford Wood
Holdingham Plantation
GIBSON CL 1
CHAPMAN RD 2
PALMER CT 3
ALL SAINTS GR 4
STOKES DR
ST DENYS AVENUE
NORTHWOOD DR
NORTH PAR
B1518
JUBILEE GR
HAZEL GR
ALMOND WALK
PO
BEECH RISE
SYCAMORE DRIVE
HADLEY ROAD
EAST ROAD
B1517
ROBERTSON DRIVE
NEWTON WY
Galley Hill
Factory
WOODBRIDGE ROAD
NG34
MEADOWFIELD
TENNYSON AV
NORTH GATE
Cemetery
East Road Ind Est
DROVE LANE
Padley Farm
LAFFORD CT
NEWFIELD ROAD
THE DROVE
MANOR PL
Northgate Sports Hall
MILL FIELD TR
Carres Gram Sch
William Alvey Sch
SPRING GD
Our Lady of Good Counsel RC Prim Sch
Superstore
Chy
ASHFIELD ROAD
Cogglesford Mill
Sleaford Fen
BRISTOL WAY
CHURCH LANE
DUKE ST
EAST GATE
Church Lane Prim Sch
Bouncing Hill
River Slea
St George's Coll of Technology
The Playhouse
Council Offices
ST GILES AVENUE
ST GILES AVE
ELECTRIC STATION RD
WESTGATE
Magt Ct
Liby
CARRE ST
The Hub
Quayside Ctr
Sleaford L Ctr
Guildhall Springs
WEST BANKS
KING JOHN ST
THOMAS ST
CASTLE ST
WATER GATE
SOUTH GATE
THE RIVERSIDE
NEW ST
BOSTON ROAD
MILTON WAY
SLEAFORD
ALEXANDRA RD
CASTLE CAUSEWAY
JERMYN ST
PARK CR
PARK AV
Recreation Ground
Cobbler's Hole (spring)
Clay Hill
Castle (site of)
LC
Mon
BOSTON RD
ALBION TR
MARK AVE
RUSSELL CRESCENT
Quarrington Fen
HAWKS WAY
Kesteven & Sleaford High Sch
STATION RD
Sleaford
E4
1 KESTEVEN ST
2 HUSSEY CL
3 CROMWELL CR
4 PINETREES CT
STEPHEN'S WY
SPRIGGS CL
QUEEN ST
FINCH DR
ROOKERY AV
Mast
Hotel
MAREHAM LANE
Sleaford Cricket Club
KING EDWARD ST
GEORGE STREET
CURLEW WY
CLAY HILL ROAD
CHEVIOT CL
BRECON WY
TOWER VIEW
HERMES WY
HOOD CL
ST EDMUNDS ROAD
VICTORIA AVENUE
LOCKWORTH RD
LONDON ROAD
NURSERY CT
KEEPERS WAY
BOUNDARY PASTURES
The Maltings
GRANTHAM ROAD
HERVEY ROAD
WESLEY CL
HAWTHORN DRIVE
SOUTHFIELDS
New Quarrington
ANCASTER DRIVE
LINTON DR
ALDER RD
Bungalow Farm
Allot Gdns
ABBEY RD
PRIORY WY
MALVERN CL
East Field
OAK ROAD
MAREHAM LANE
SPIRE VW
AIDAN ROAD
1 OSWIN CL
2 CORNFIELD VW
3 HARVEST WY
4 MILLERS CL
MULBERRY CL
NORTHUMBRIA RD
BERNICIA DR
MAGNOLIA RD
Mareham Lane Farm
GLEBE CL
MANOR RD
BEDE CL
NORTHFIELD ROAD
DEIRA CL
STUMP CROSS HILL
WESSEX CL
Quarrington
TOWN ROAD
A3
1 SHELDRAKE RD
2 ARK ROYAL CT
3 AMETHYST CL
4 VANGUARD CT
F4
1 ST GILES AVE
2 ORCHARD CL
3 OLD PL
4 THE HOPLANDS
5 THE PADDOCK
6 BYRON CL
7 SHELLEY DR
8 BURNS CR
9 ELIOT CL
10 CHAUCER GD
11 CHRISTOPHER CR
12 CAROLINE CL
13 WORDSWORTH CT
14 KIPLING DR
15 COLERIDGE GD
LONDON ROAD
05
06
07
B2
1 WINDSOR CL
2 RICHMOND CL
3 ASHBOURNE CL
4 AMBLESIDE CL
5 SANDHURST CR
6 HILDA CL
7 HENGIST CL
8 HAUSER CL
9 ATHELSTAN CL
10 9 ALFRED CL
11 CHURCH CL
12 EDWIN CL
13 ANGLIA CL
14 MERCIA CL
B3
1 SHELDRAKE RD
2 KESTREL CL
3 EAGLE DR
4 WREN CL
5 OSPREY CL
6 PEREGRINE CL
7 DOVE CL
8 CYGNET CL
9 QUANTOCK CT
10 THRUSH CL
11 LINNET WY
12 ROBIN CL
13 FALCON WY
14 GRAMPIAN CL
121
C3
1 SWALLOW CL
2 RHODES AV
3 BUTTLER WY
4 LORD ST
5 COPELAND CT
C4
1 CHARLES ST
2 REFORM PL
3 WESTGATE PK
4 CASTLE TR RD
121
D2
1 HOLLY CL
2 BRIAR CL
3 JUNIPER WY
4 ASPEN DR
5 ROSEWOOD DR
6 BERRY CL
7 BRIDLE CL
8 LARCH WY
9 CYPRESS CL
10 LAVENDER CL
11 REDWOOD AV
12 ACACIA CL
13 LIMETREE CL
121
D3
1 THE INNINGS
2 CHESTNUT CL
3 SOUTHFIELDS
4 PINE CL
5 PAVILION GD
D4
1 LEICESTER ST
2 PLAYHOUSE YD
3 MARKET ST
4 MARKET PL
5 CROSS KEYS YD
6 WHARFSIDE MS
7 MONEYS YD
8 HANDLEY ST
9 HILL'S CT
E3
1 WILLOW CT
2 MAIDEN GR
3 SPINNERS CL
4 GRACE CL
5 PEACOCK CT
6 COBBLERS WY
7 CHAPEL HL CT
F3
1 JONATHAN GD
2 MILTON WY
3 ELMGARTH
4 POLYANTHUS
5 MARIGOLD WK
6 WALNUTGARTH
7 FORUM WAY

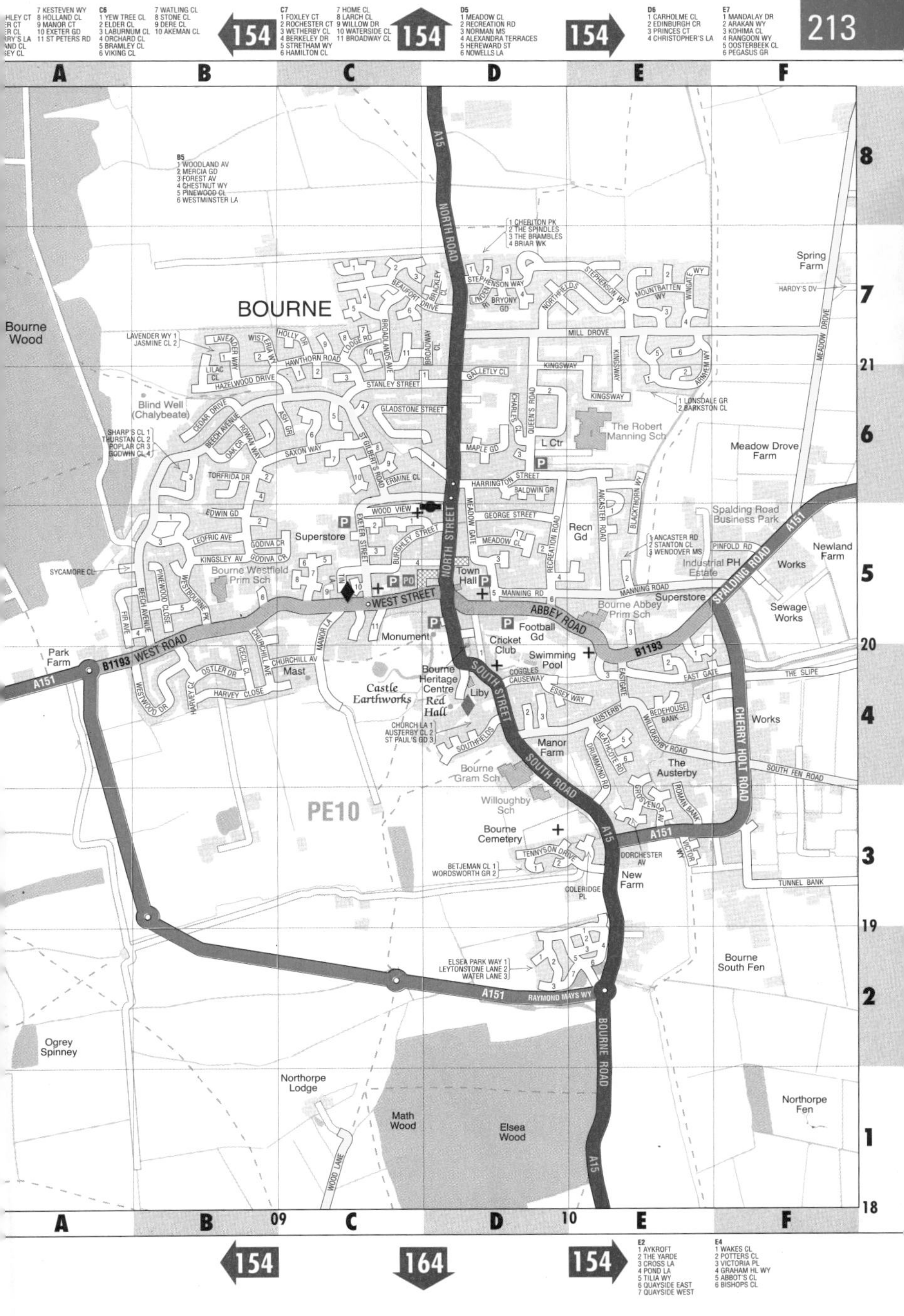
213
154
154
154
164
154
154
C6
1 YEW TREE CL
2 ELDER CL
3 LABURNUM CL
4 ORCHARD CL
5 BRAMLEY CL
6 VIKING CL
7 WATLING CL
8 STONE CL
9 DERE CL
10 AKEMAN CL
7 KESTEVEN WY
8 HOLLAND CL
9 MANOR CT
10 EXETER GD
11 ST PETERS RD
C7
1 FOXLEY CT
2 ROCHESTER CT
3 WETHERBY CL
4 BERKELEY DR
5 STRETHAM WY
6 HAMILTON CL
7 HOME CL
8 LARCH CL
9 WILLOW DR
10 WATERSIDE CL
11 BROADWAY CL
D5
1 MEADOW CL
2 RECREATION RD
3 NORMAN MS
4 ALEXANDRA TERRACES
5 HEREWARD ST
6 NOWELLS LA
D6
1 CARHOLME CL
2 EDINBURGH CR
3 PRINCES CT
4 CHRISTOPHER'S LA
E7
1 MANDALAY DR
2 ARAKAN WY
3 KOHIMA CL
4 RANGOON WY
5 OOSTERBEEK CL
6 PEGASUS GR
A
B
C
D
E
F
8
7
21
6
5
20
4
3
19
2
1
18
09
10
B5
1 WOODLAND AV
2 MERCIA GD
3 FOREST AV
4 CHESTNUT WY
5 PINEWOOD CL
6 WESTMINSTER LA
1 CHERITON PK
2 THE SPINDLES
3 THE BRAMBLES
4 BRIAR WK
BOURNE
Bourne Wood
Spring Farm
HARDY'S DV
LAVENDER WY 1
JASMINE CL 2
1 LONSDALE GR
2 BARKSTON CL
Blind Well (Chalybeate)
SHARP'S CL 1
THURSTAN CL 2
POPLAR CR 3
GODWIN CL 4
The Robert Manning Sch
L Ctr
Meadow Drove Farm
Spalding Road Business Park
1 ANCASTER RD
2 STANTON CL
3 WENDOVER MS
Superstore
Recn Gd
Industrial Estate
PH
Newland Farm
Works
SYCAMORE CL
Bourne Westfield Prim Sch
Town Hall
Bourne Abbey Prim Sch
Superstore
Sewage Works
Park Farm
Monument
Football Gd
Cricket Club
Swimming Pool
Mast
Castle Earthworks
Bourne Heritage Centre
Red Hall
Liby
Works
CHURCH LA 1
AUSTERBY CL 2
ST PAUL'S GD 3
Manor Farm
The Austerby
Bourne Gram Sch
Willoughby Sch
PE10
Bourne Cemetery
BETJEMAN CL 1
WORDSWORTH GR 2
New Farm
COLERIDGE PL
DORCHESTER AV
ELSEA PARK WAY 1
LEYTONSTONE LANE 2
WATER LANE 3
Bourne South Fen
Ogrey Spinney
Northorpe Lodge
Math Wood
Elsea Wood
Northorpe Fen
A15
NORTH ROAD
NORTH STREET
SOUTH STREET
SOUTH ROAD
BOURNE ROAD
WEST STREET
WEST ROAD
ABBEY ROAD
B1193
A151
SPALDING ROAD
CHERRY HOLT ROAD
RAYMOND MAYS WY
MEADOW DROVE
MILL DROVE
STEPHENSON WAY
STEPHENSON WY
MOUNTBATTEN WY
WINGATE WY
BEAUFORT DRIVE
BRACKLEY CL
LINDEN RI
BRYONY GD
NORTHFIELDS
KINGSWAY
ARNHEM WY
HAWTHORN ROAD
LODGE RD
BROADLANDS AVE
BROADWAY CL
HOLLY DR
WISTERIA WY
LAVENDER WY
LILAC CL
HAZELWOOD DRIVE
STANLEY STREET
GALLETLY CL
GLADSTONE STREET
CHARLES CL
QUEEN'S ROAD
CEDAR DRIVE
BEECH AVENUE
ROWAN WAY
OAK CR
ASH GR
SAXON WAY
ST GILBERT'S ROAD
MAPLE GD
HARRINGTON STREET
BALDWIN GR
ERMINE CL
TORFRIDA DR
EDWIN GD
WOOD VIEW
GEORGE STREET
ANCASTER ROAD
BLACKTHORN WY
LEOFRIC AVE
GODIVA CR
KINGSLEY AV
EXETER STREET
BURGHLEY STREET
MEADOW GATE
MEADOW CL
RECREATION ROAD
PINFOLD RD
MANNING RD
MANNING ROAD
PINEWOOD CLOSE
WESTBOURNE PK
FIR AVE
CHURCHILL AVE
CECIL CL
CHURCHILL AV
MANOR LA
OSTLER DR
HARVEY CL
HARVEY CLOSE
WESTWOOD DR
COGGLES CAUSEWAY
ESSEX WAY
EASTGATE
EAST GATE
THE SLIPE
AUSTERBY
BEDEHOUSE BANK
WILLOUGHBY ROAD
HEATHCOTE RD
DRUMMOND RD
SOUTHFIELDS
SOUTH FEN ROAD
GROSVENOR AV
ROMAN BANK
VICTOR WY
TENNYSON DRIVE
TUNNEL BANK
WOOD LANE
E2
1 AYKROFT
2 THE YARDE
3 CROSS LA
4 POND LA
5 TILIA WY
6 QUAYSIDE EAST
7 QUAYSIDE WEST
E4
1 WAKES CL
2 POTTERS CL
3 VICTORIA PL
4 GRAHAM HL WY
5 ABBOT'S CL
6 BISHOPS CL

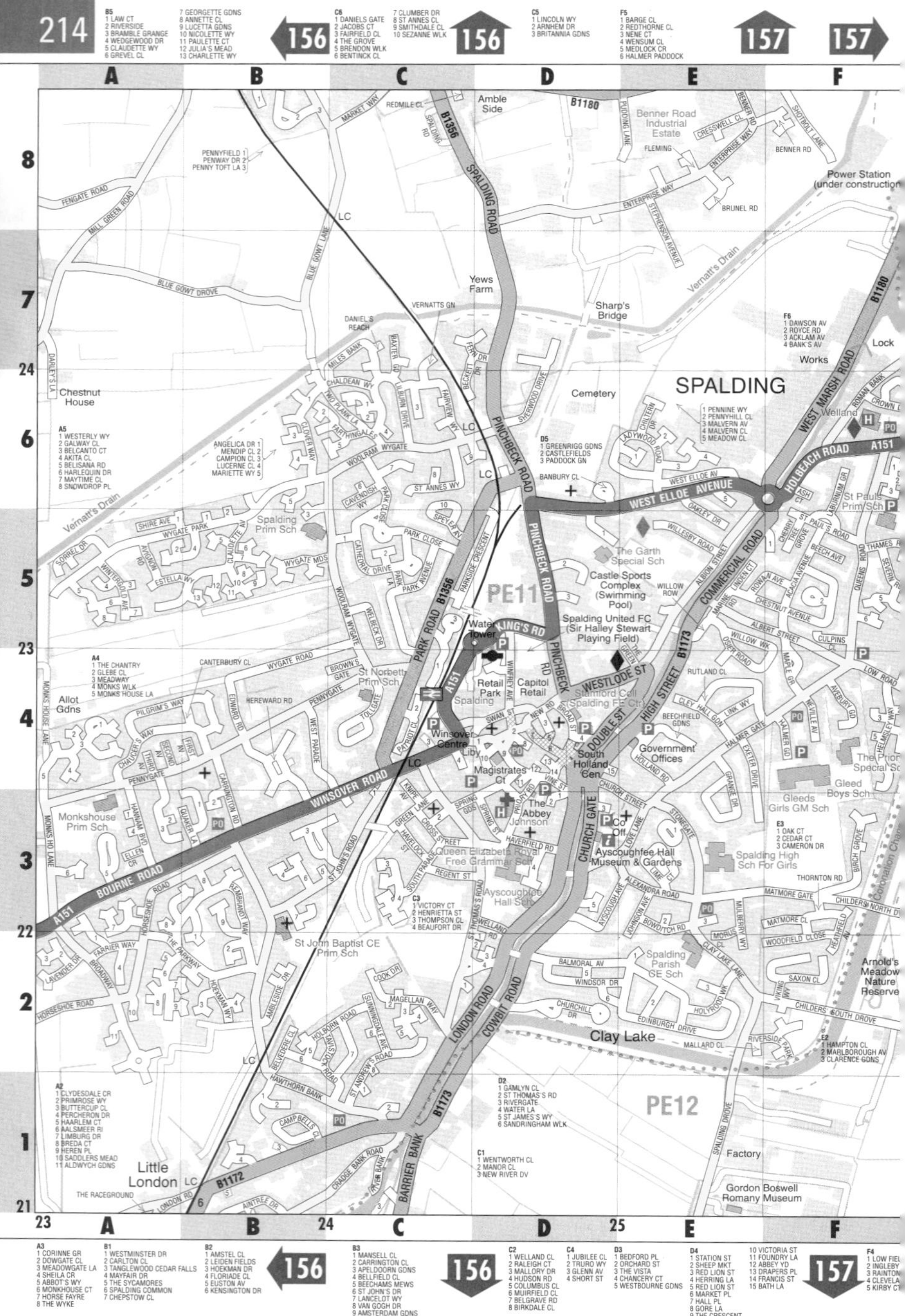
B5
1 LAW CT
2 RIVERSIDE
3 BRAMBLE GRANGE
4 WEDGEWOOD DR
5 CLAUDETTE WY
6 GREVEL CL
7 GEORGETTE GDNS
8 ANNETTE CL
9 LUCETTA GDNS
10 NICOLETTE WY
11 PAULETTE CT
12 JULIA'S MEAD
13 CHARLETTE WY
156
C6
1 DANIELS GATE
2 JACOBS CT
3 FAIRFIELD CL
4 THE GROVE
5 BRENDON WLK
6 BENTINCK CL
7 CLUMBER DR
8 ST ANNES CL
9 SMITHDALE CL
10 SEZANNE WLK
156
C5
1 LINCOLN WY
2 ARNHEM DR
3 BRITANNIA GDNS
F5
1 BARGE CL
2 REDTHORNE CL
3 NENE CT
4 WENSUM CL
5 MEDLOCK CR
6 HALMER PADDOCK
157
157
A
B
C
D
E
F
8
7
24
6
5
23
4
3
22
2
1
21
Amble Side
B1180
Benner Road Industrial Estate
REDMILE CL
MARKET WAY
B1356
SPALDING ROAD
PENNYFIELD 1
PENWAY DR 2
PENNY TOFT LA 3
FENGATE ROAD
MILL GREEN ROAD
BLUE GOWT LANE
BLUE GOWT DROVE
LC
CRESSWELL CL
BENNER RD
SHOTBOLT LANE
BENNER RD
FLEMING
ENTERPRISE WAY
STEPHENSON AVENUE
BRUNEL RD
Power Station (under construction)
Yews Farm
Vernatt's Drain
Sharp's Bridge
VERNATTS GN
DANIEL'S REACH
B1180
F6
1 DAWSON AV
2 ROYCE RD
3 ACKLAM AV
4 BANK'S AV
Lock
Works
WEST MARSH ROAD
DARLEY'S LA
Chestnut House
MILES BANK
BAXTER GD
CHALDEAN WY
TWO PLANK LA
LILBURN DRIVE
FAIRVIEW WY
BECKETT DR
FERN DR
SHERWOOD DRIVE
Cemetery
SPALDING
1 PENNINE WY
2 PENNYHILL CL
3 MALVERN AV
4 MALVERN CL
5 MEADOW CL
CHILTERN DR
LADYWOOD ROAD
Welland
ROMAN BANK
CROWN
A5
1 WESTERLY WY
2 GALWAY CL
3 BELCANTO CT
4 AKITA CL
5 BELISANA RD
6 HARLEQUIN DR
7 MAYTIME CL
8 SNOWDROP PL
ANGELICA DR 1
MENDIP CL 2
CAMPION CL 3
LUCERNE CL 4
MARIETTE WY 5
CLOVER WAY
FARTHINGALES
WOOLRAM WYGATE
PINCHBECK ROAD
D5
1 GREENRIGG GDNS
2 CASTLEFIELDS
3 PADDOCK GN
BANBURY CL
WEST ELLOE AV
HOLBEACH ROAD
A151
ST ANNES WY
CAVENDISH WY
SPEYER AV
WEST ELLOE AVENUE
OAKLEY DR
LABURNUM GR
ASH CT
St Pauls Prim Sch
Vernatt's Drain
SHIRE AVE
WYGATE PARK
Spalding Prim Sch
PARK CLOSE
WILLESBY ROAD
ST PAUL'S ROAD
CHERRY TREE GROVE
BEECH AVE
THAMES RD
SORREL DR
AVIGNON RD
CLAUDETTE AV
WYGATE MDS
CATHEDRAL DRIVE
PARK AVENUE
PARKSIDE CRESCENT
The Garth Special Sch
ALBION STREET
COMMERCIAL ROAD
QUEENS ROAD
SEVERN
WINTERGOLD AVE
ESTELLA WY
PE11
Castle Sports Complex (Swimming Pool)
WILLOW ROW
MARINE RD
LINDEN CT
ROWAN AVE
ACACIA AVENUE
CHESTNUT AVENUE
WOOLRAM WYGATE
WELBECK DR
PARK ROAD
Water Tower
KING'S RD
Spalding United FC (Sir Halley Stewart Playing Field)
ALBERT STREET
CULPINS CL
A4
1 THE CHANTRY
2 GLEBE CL
3 MEADWAY
4 MONKS WLK
5 MONKS HOUSE LA
CANTERBURY CL
WYGATE ROAD
BROWN'S GATE
St Norbett Prim Sch
WINFREY AVE
Retail Park
Capitol Retail
PINCHBECK RD
WESTLODE ST
THE GREEN
WILLOW WK
OSIER ROAD
MAPLE GR
LOW ROAD
RUTLAND CL
Allot Gdns
HEREWARD RD
PENNYGATE
TOLGATE
A151
Spalding
Stamford Coll (Spalding FE Ctr)
HIGH STREET
B1173
CLEY HALL GDN
LINK WY
AVEBURY GD
MONKS HOUSE LANE
PILGRIM'S WAY
CHAUCER'S WAY
EDWARD RD
WEST PARADE
PATRIOT CL
SWAN ST
NEW RD
BROAD ST
DOUBLE ST
BEECHFIELD GDNS
HALMER GATE
NEVILLE AV
HELMSLEY
Winsover Centre
Liby
Government Offices
HOLLAND RD
EXETER DRIVE
HALMER GD
The Priory Special Sch
THIRD AV
SECOND AV
FIRST AV
PENNYGATE
CARRINGTON RD
LC
Magistrates Ct
South Holland Cen
VINE ST
CHURCH STREET
GRANGE DR
Gleed Boys Sch
WINSOVER ROAD
KNIPE
GREEN LANE
SPRING GDS
SPRING ST
PRIORY RD
The Abbey
Johnson
Co Off
LOVE LANE
STONEGATE
Gleeds Girls GM Sch
Monkshouse Prim Sch
HANNAM BYD
QUAKER LA
ST JOHN'S ROAD
CROSS STREET
HAVELOCK ST
HAVERFIELD RD
CHURCH GATE
Ayscoughfee Hall Museum & Gardens
LIME CL
E3
1 OAK CT
2 CEDAR CT
3 CAMERON DR
BIRCH GROVE
MONKS HO LANE
ELLEN CR
REMBRANDT WAY
SOUTH PARADE
REGENT ST
Queen Elizabeth Royal Free Grammar Sch
Spalding High Sch For Girls
THORNTON RD
Coronation Chan
BOURNE ROAD
A151
HORSESHOE ROAD
C3
1 VICTORY CT
2 HENRIETTA ST
3 THOMPSON CL
4 BEAUFORT DR
ST THOMAS'S ROAD
Ayscoughfee Hall Sch
AYSCOUGH AVE
JOHNSON AVE
ALEXANDRA ROAD
BOWDITCH RD
MATMORE GATE
CHILDERS NORTH DR
MATMORE CL
HEATHFIELD AV
WELLAND
MORUS CL
MULBERRY WY
WOODFIELD CLOSE
FARRIER WAY
LAVENDER DR
BROADWAY
THE PARKWAY
St John Baptist CE Prim Sch
CLAY LAKE LANE
Arnold's Meadow Nature Reserve
HOEKMAN WY
AMBLESIDE DR
COOK DR
BALMORAL AV
WINDSOR DR
Spalding Parish CE Sch
SAXON CL
VIKING WAY
HORSESHOE ROAD
MAGELLAN WAY
LONDON ROAD
COWBIT ROAD
CHURCHILL DR
HOLYROOD WK
CHILDERS' SOUTH DROVE
HOLBORN ROAD
TAVISTOCK ROAD
SUNNINGDALE AVE
ST ANDREW'S ROAD
EDINBURGH DRIVE
Clay Lake
MALLARD CL
RIVERSIDE PARK
E2
1 HAMPTON CL
2 MARLBOROUGH AV
3 CLARENCE GDNS
LC
BELVEDERE CL
HAWTHORN BANK
A2
1 CLYDESDALE CR
2 PRIMROSE WY
3 BUTTERCUP CL
4 PERCHERON DR
5 HAARLEM CT
6 AALSMEER RI
7 LIMBURG DR
8 BREDA CT
9 HEREN PL
10 SADDLERS MEAD
11 ALDWYCH GDNS
CAMPBELLS CL
B1173
D2
1 GAMLYN CL
2 ST THOMAS'S RD
3 RIVERGATE
4 WATER LA
5 ST JAMES'S WY
6 SANDRINGHAM WLK
PE12
SPALDING DROVE
Factory
C1
1 WENTWORTH CL
2 MANOR CL
3 NEW RIVER DV
BARRIER BANK
RIVER BANK
CRADGE BANK ROAD
Little London
LC
B1172
THE RACEGROUND
LONDON RD
AINTREE DR
Gordon Boswell Romany Museum
23
A
B
24
C
D
25
E
F
A3
1 CORINNE GR
2 DOWGATE CL
3 MEADOWGATE LA
4 SHEILA CR
5 ABBOT'S WY
6 MONKHOUSE CT
7 HORSE FAYRE
8 THE WYKE
B1
1 WESTMINSTER DR
2 CARLTON CL
3 TANGLEWOOD CEDAR FALLS
4 MAYFAIR DR
5 THE SYCAMORES
6 SPALDING COMMON
7 CHEPSTOW CL
B2
1 AMSTEL CL
2 LEIDEN FIELDS
3 HOEKMAN DR
4 FLORIADE CL
5 EUSTON AV
6 KENSINGTON DR
156
B3
1 MANSELL CL
2 CARRINGTON CL
3 APELDOORN GDNS
4 BELLFIELD CL
5 BEECHAMS MEWS
6 ST JOHN'S DR
7 LANCELOT WY
8 VAN GOGH DR
9 AMSTERDAM GDNS
156
C2
1 WELLAND CL
2 RALEIGH CT
3 MALLORY DR
4 HUDSON RD
5 COLUMBUS CL
6 MUIRFIELD CL
7 BELGRAVE RD
8 BIRKDALE CL
C4
1 JUBILEE CL
2 TRURO WY
3 GLENN AV
4 SHORT ST
D3
1 BEDFORD PL
2 ORCHARD ST
3 THE VISTA
4 CHANCERY CT
5 WESTBOURNE GDNS
D4
1 STATION ST
2 SHEEP MKT
3 RED LION ST
4 HERRING LA
5 RED LION ST
6 MARKET PL
7 HALL PL
8 GORE LA
9 THE CRESCENT
10 VICTORIA ST
11 FOUNDRY LA
12 ABBEY YD
13 DRAPERS PL
14 FRANCIS ST
15 BATH LA
157
F4
1 LOW FIEL
2 INGLEBY
3 RAINTON
4 CLEVELA
5 KIRBY CT

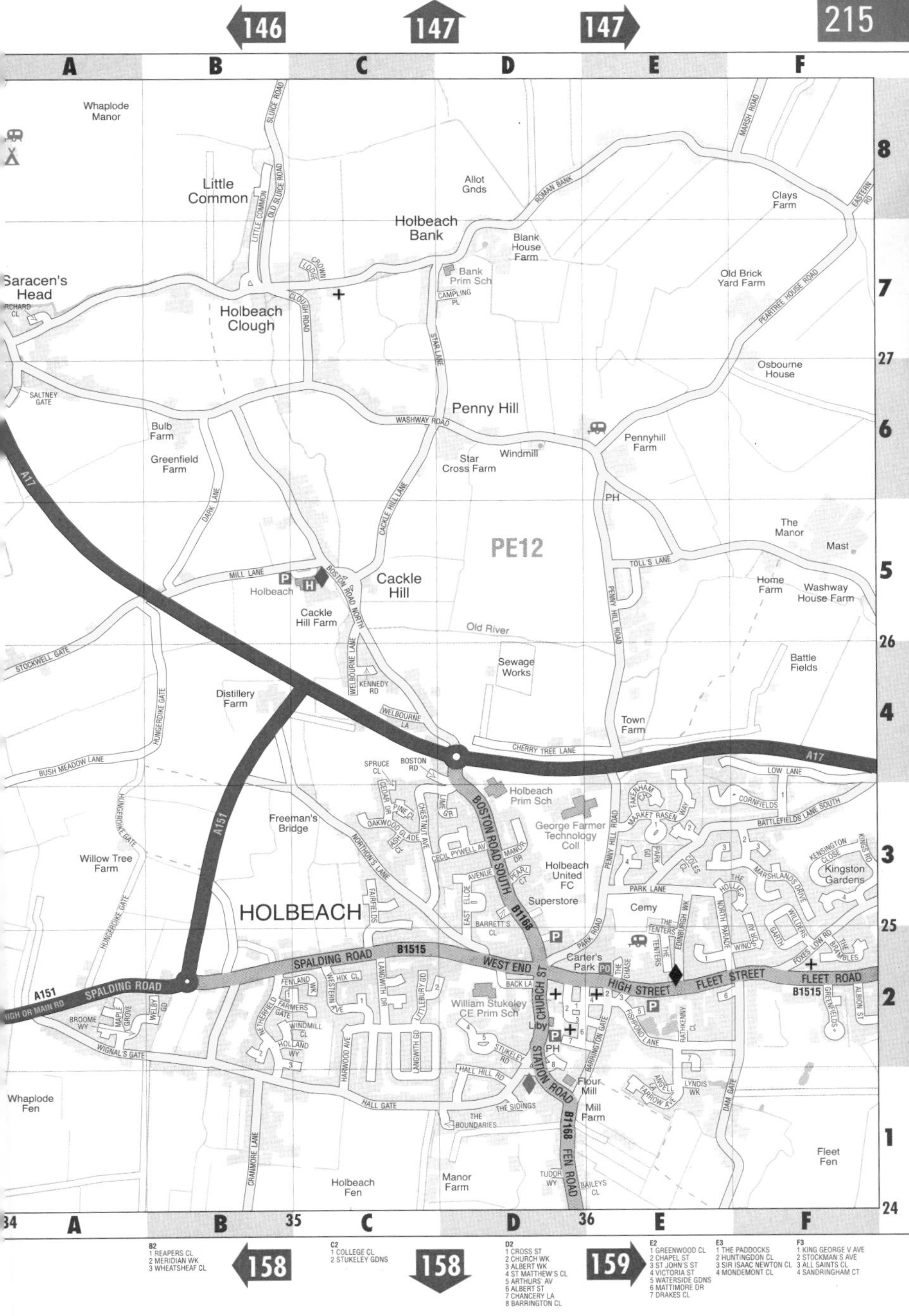
146
147
147
A
B
C
D
E
F
8
7
27
6
5
26
4
3
25
2
1
24
34
35
36
Whaplode Manor
Little Common
Holbeach Bank
Allot Gnds
Blank House Farm
Bank Prim Sch
Clays Farm
Old Brick Yard Farm
Saracen's Head
Holbeach Clough
Osbourne House
Penny Hill
Bulb Farm
Greenfield Farm
Star Cross Farm
Windmill
Pennyhill Farm
PH
PE12
The Manor
Mast
Cackle Hill
Holbeach
Cackle Hill Farm
Home Farm
Washway House Farm
Old River
Sewage Works
Battle Fields
Distillery Farm
Town Farm
Freeman's Bridge
Willow Tree Farm
Holbeach Prim Sch
George Farmer Technology Coll
Holbeach United FC
Superstore
Cemy
Kingston Gardens
HOLBEACH
Carter's Park
William Stukeley CE Prim Sch
Liby
Flour Mill
Mill Farm
Whaplode Fen
Holbeach Fen
Manor Farm
Fleet Fen
SLUICE ROAD
OLD SLUICE ROAD
LITTLE COMMON
CROWN LODGE
CLOUGH ROAD
CAMPLING PL
STAR LANE
ROMAN BANK
MARSH ROAD
EASTERN RD
PEARTREE HOUSE ROAD
SALTNEY GATE
WASHWAY ROAD
CACKLE HILL LANE
DARK LANE
MILL LANE
BOSTON ROAD NORTH
TOLL'S LANE
PENNY HILL ROAD
STOCKWELL GATE
WELBOURNE LANE
KENNEDY RD
WELBOURNE LA
HUNGERDIKE GATE
BUSH MEADOW LANE
CHERRY TREE LANE
A17
A151
B1168
B1515
SPRUCE CL
BOSTON RD
CEDAR DR
PINE CL
LIME GR
CHESTNUT AVE
OAKWOOD GLADE
ASH CL
NORTHON'S LANE
CECIL PYWELL AV
MANOR DR
AVENUE
PEARL CT
BOSTON ROAD SOUTH
FAKENHAM CH
MARKET RASEN WAY
LOW LANE
CORNFIELDS
BATTLEFIELDS LANE SOUTH
PARK GD
COLES CL
KENSINGTON CLOSE
KINGS RD
MARSHLANDS DRIVE
THE HOLLIES
PARK LANE
FAIRFIELDS
EAST ELLOE
BARRETT'S CL
PARK ROAD
THE TENTERS
EDINBURGH WK
NORTH PARADE
AV WINDS
GARTH
WILLDERS
FOXES LOW RD
THE BRAMBLES
THE CHASE
SPALDING ROAD
WEST END
HIGH STREET
FLEET STREET
FLEET ROAD
ALBION ST
GREENFIELDS
HIGH OR MAIN RD
BROOME WY
MAPLE GROVE
WELBY GD
FENLAND WK
HIX CL
WESTERN AVE
LANGWITH DR
LITTLEBURY GD
BACK LA
CHURCH ST
FARMERS GATE
WINDMILL CL
HOLLAND WY
NETHERFIELD
FISHPOND LANE
RATHKENNY CL
BARRINGTON GATE
STUKELEY RD
WIGNAL'S GATE
HARWOOD AVE
LANGWITH GD
HALL HILL RD
STATION ROAD
ANGELL LA
FARROW AVE
LYNDIS WK
DAM GATE
HALL GATE
THE SIDINGS
THE BOUNDARIES
CRANMORE LANE
FEN ROAD
TUDOR WY
BAILEYS CL
B2
1 REAPERS CL
2 MERIDIAN WK
3 WHEATSHEAF CL
158
C2
1 COLLEGE CL
2 STUKELEY GDNS
158
D2
1 CROSS ST
2 CHURCH WK
3 ALBERT WK
4 ST MATTHEW'S CL
5 ARTHURS' AV
6 ALBERT ST
7 CHANCERY LA
8 BARRINGTON CL
159
E2
1 GREENWOOD CL
2 CHAPEL ST
3 ST JOHN'S ST
4 VICTORIA ST
5 WATERSIDE GDNS
6 MATTIMORE DR
7 DRAKES CL
E3
1 THE PADDOCKS
2 HUNTINGDON CL
3 SIR ISAAC NEWTON CL
4 MONDEMONT CL
F3
1 KING GEORGE V AVE
2 STOCKMAN'S AVE
3 ALL SAINTS CL
4 SANDRINGHAM CT

159 159 160 160

B5
1 HIGHGROVE
2 CHURCHILL CT
3 SPENCER CL
4 YORK RIDE
5 SADDLERS WY

159 159 160 160

B4
1 SLEEPERS CL
2 FOLDS LA
3 WHITEACRES
4 CURLEW CL
5 STATION RD
6 WHIMBREL WY

A5
1 BELVOIR CL
2 PETWORTH CL
3 SANDRINGHAM WY
4 WOBURN CL
5 BURNSIDE AV
6 CHATSWORTH CL
7 OSBOURNE WY
8 DEENE CL
9 WOODCROFT CL
10 TATTERSHALL DR
11 MAXEY CL
12 GRIMSTHORPE CL
13 BELTON CL
14 CEDAR CL
15 ALTHORPE CL
164
A6
1 THE PADDOCK
2 LIME TREE AV
3 MILLFIELD RD
4 DOVECOTE RD
5 LINCOLN CL
6 CROMWELL WY
7 KESTEVEN DR
8 ROCKINGHAM CL
9 LAMPORT CL
10 HOLLAND CL
11 MEADWAY
12 FORGE CT
165
B5
1 ST GUTHLAC AV
2 THE SPINNEY
3 THE WOODLANDS
4 STAMFORD CL
5 THE PRECINCTS
B6
1 GLEBE VW
2 JOHN WAKE CL
3 CHESTNUT WY
4 HAWTHORN CL
5 HALL FARM
6 OAK GR
165
C5
1 BEAUFORT AV
2 WILLOUGHBY AV
3 EASTFIELD
4 FLORENCE WY
5 THE MEADOWS
6 LARK RI
7 LINNET CL
8 ROBIN CL
9 GODSEY CR
10 CHERRY GR
11 ROSEMARY AV
12 THYME AV
13 NIGHTINGALES
14 CURLEW WLK
15 WREN CL
A
B
C
D
E
F
8
7
11
6
5
10
4
3
09
2
1
08
14
15
NORTH FIELD ROAD
A16
A15
PETERBOROUGH RD
Swine's Meadow
SWINE'S MEADOW ROAD
CROSS ROAD
North Field
Mast
Sports Ground
Five House Farm
Swines Meadow Farm
STIRLING WAY
BLENHEIM WAY
WHITLEY WAY
TOWNGATE EAST
D6
1 SORREL CL
2 COWSLIP DR
3 BLACKTHORN CL
4 THE BRAMBLES
5 BRYONY WY
6 TEASLES
7 SPEEDWELL CT
8 BLUEBELLS
9 TOWNING CL
Sheepskin Hall
HALL MEADOW ROAD
WELLINGTON WY 1
SHACKLETON CL 2
LANCASTER WY
PETERBOROUGH ROAD
D5
1 PRIMROSES
2 SWEET CL
3 SWALLOW WLK
4 PENDLEBURY DR
5 ALLEN CL
6 PANTON CL
Motel
TOWNGATE WEST
PRESTLAND
JOHN EVE WAY
GODSEY LANE
Superstore
THE PASTURE
CAMPION DR
LINCHFIELD ROAD
Linch Field
MARKET DEEPING
LINDSEY AVE
HALFLEET
Market Deeping Community Prim Sch
LADY MARGARET'S AVENUE
BEECH CL
BLACK PRINCE AVENUE
FOXGLOVES
MARIGOLDS
Cemy
William Hildyard CE (Aided) Prim Sch
B1524
QUEEN'S AV
MEADOW ROAD
BURCHNALL CL
TOWNING CL
FRASER CL
THACKERS WAY
KNIGHT CL
TATTERSHALL DRIVE
MEADWAY
GREEN WK
CHURCH STREET
THE ORCHARD
GODSEY CR
1 THE LEES
2 SEWELL CL
3 LINCHFIELD CL
4 ERMINE WY
CROWFIELDS 1
THE PARSLINS 2
PARK DR
THE GROVE
BRAMLEY ROAD
FENELEY CL
PAWLETT CL
MILLFIELD ROAD
THE AVENUE
CLOVER RD
STILL CL
Linchfield Prim Sch
CROWSON WAY
Playing Field
SPALDING ROAD
B1525
TYGHES CL
RYCROFT AVENUE
ASCENDALE
B1162
BROADGATE LANE
TH
The Deepings Sch
MILLFIELD ROAD
WADE PK AVENUE
Liby
SWIFT CLOSE
SWIFT CL
L Ctr
STAMFORD ROAD
B1166
HIGH STREET
HORSEGATE
MANOR WAY
Market Deeping Bridge
PARK EST
PARK ROAD
Deeping St James Prim Sch
DIXONS RD 1
ELM CL 2
DOUGLAS RD 3
PARK ROAD
Deeping St James
BELL LA
WELLAND WAY
PRIORY CL
BRIDGE STREET
PE6
HEREWARD WAY
Recreation Gd
Cemy
SUTTON'S LANE
CHURCH STREET
EASTGATE
MAXEY VW
RIVERSIDE
Deeping Gate
LINCOLN ROAD
E4
1 EXETER CL
2 WATERTON CL
3 BURGHLEY CL
4 BROWNLOW DR
1 FAIRFAX WY
2 RIVERBANK CL
PEAKIRK ROAD
Fox Cover Farm
North Fen
Newstead Farm
DEEPING ST JAMES ROAD
D4
1 KESTEVEN CL
2 HOLLY WY
3 NEW ROW
4 ORCHARD CL
RIPPONS DROVE
ASHFIELDS
F4
1 RYCROFT CL
2 CHURCH GATE
3 BACK LA
4 STEPHENS WY
Northborough
CASTLE DRIVE
CLAYPOLE DRIVE
CLARE ROAD
CROWSON CR
1 CROMWELL CL
2 ST ANDREWS RD
3 EAST RD
4 CHURCH VW
1 WEST END RD
2 WOODGATE LA
WEST END ROAD
MAXEY ROAD
HIGH STREET
GRANVILLE AVENUE
CHURCH VIEW
PH
Maxey
Woodgate Farm
173
173
174

171
171
C7
1 FOXGLOVE RD
2 MEADOWSWEET
3 SWEETBRIAR
4 TOBIAS GR
5 BLACKTHORN
6 CLOVER GD
D6
1 FIR RD
2 BRAMBLE GR
3 ANGUS CL
4 SORREL CL
5 MORAY CL
6 ASH PL
D7
1 LAVENDER WY
2 BLUEBELL RD
3 BUTTERCUP CL
4 CAMPION GR
5 FOREST GD
6 BIRCH RD
E5
1 TENNYSON WY
2 KEATS GR
3 KIPLING CL
4 LUFFENHAM CL
5 COTTESMORE RD
6 EXTON CL
E6
1 BELVOIR CL
2 WALCOT WY
3 BARNWELL RD
4 ROCKINGHAM RD
5 GLENEAGLES CL
6 FALKIRK CL
7 OBAN CL
8 CROMARTY RD
9 MELROSE CL
10 MONTROSE CL
11 TROON CL
12 SHELLEY CL
F6
1 HARDWICK RD
2 ELTON CL
3 WAVERLEY PL
4 CALEDONIAN RD
5 BURNS RD
A B C D E F
8 7 08 6 5 07 4 3 06 2 1 05
Strawsons Farm
Great Casterton
Ingthorpe
Ingthorpe Farm
PH
Church Farm
OLD GREAT NORTH ROAD
Road End
Toll Bar
Road End Farm
B1081
A1
PRIMROSE WAY
Glebe Farm
Quarry
Mast
GAINSBOROUGH RD
LITTLE CASTERTON ROAD
OAK RD
WILLOW RD
CORNFLOWER CL 1
MARIGOLD CL 2
FIFE CLOSE
CHATSWORTH ROAD
HADDON RD
Works
CASTERTON ROAD
Superstore
WAVERLEY
PINE CL
BEECH GROVE
CEDAR RD
CHARLOCK DR
ABERDEEN CL
ARRAN ROAD
AYR CL
CASTERTON ROAD
B1081
STAMFORD ROAD
A606
EMPINGHAM ROAD
HAZEL GR
PERTH ROAD
BRAEMAR CL
CAITHNESS ROAD
ROXBURGH RD
FOX DALE
DUNDEE DRIVE
NAIRN RD
BYRON WY
DICKENS DR
SUTHERLAND WAY
PO
STIRLING ROAD
HIGHLANDS WAY
ERMINE WAY
Mast
CHESTNUT GD
ARRAN RD
Malcolm Sargent GM Sch
EMPINGHAM ROAD
PE9
The Rookery
Rugby Club
LONSDALE RD
ARGYLL WY 1
REFORM ST 2
ERMINE CL 3
SHERWOOD CL 4
LYNDON WY
BROOKE AV
HAMBLETON ROAD
Sports Gd
LAUNDE GD
GREAT NORTH ROAD
LONSDALE ROAD
EXETER GARDENS
TINWELL ROAD LANE
Tinwell Lodge Farm
CASTERTON LANE
A6121
Home Farm
TINWELL ROAD
PH
Tinwell
STEADFOLD LANE
South View Farm
GREAT NORTH ROAD
Weir
A1
STAMFORD ROAD
A6121
River Chater
Tinwell Crossing
Easton Hillside
Home Wood
Dottrell Hill Plantation
Macmillan Way
99 00 01

171
171

A5
1 VENCE CL
2 NEWBOULTS LA
3 RADCLIFFE RD
4 EMPINGHAM RD
5 THE PADDOCK
6 THE HERMITAGE
7 CLARE CL
8 WEST ST GD
9 ST CLEMENT'S
A7
1 AIREDALE RD
2 NEWHAM RD
3 GIRTON WY
4 KEBLE CL
5 DARWIN CL
6 OXFORD RD
7 ANCASTER RD
8 BURGHLEY RD
9 CHARLES RD
10 EDWARD RD
C5
1 STANLEY ST
2 CHAPEL YD
3 NEWGATES
4 STAR LA
5 IRONMONGER ST
6 ST GEORGE'S ST
7 CORNSTALL BG
8 ST LEONARD'S ST
9 BACK LA
10 WATERGATE
11 MAIDEN LA
12 ST MARY'S ST
13 ST GEORGE'S SQ
14 ST MARY'S PL
15 BLACKFRIARS ST
16 BELTON ST
17 ST MARY'S HL
18 CECIL CT
19 GAS ST
171
C6
1 PRINCES RD
2 EMLYNS ST
3 NEW CROSS RD
4 NEW ST
5 EMLYNS GD
6 BENTLEY ST
172
D7
1 LOSECOAT CL
2 TURNPOLE CL
3 ARMLEY GR
4 WOODHEAD CL
5 BERRYBUT WY
6 MASTERTON CL
172
A B C D E F
Northfields Farm
B5
1 CLIFF CR
2 FONTWELL GD
3 RADCLIFFE RD
4 ORCHARD RD
5 RADCLIFFE CL
6 ALL SAINTS' PL
7 CROWN ST
8 RED LION ST
9 TORKINGTON GD
10 ALL SAINTS' ST
11 SHEEP MKT
12 CASTLE ST
13 CASTLE DYKE
14 ST PETER'S HL
Bordeville
B7
1 PETERHOUSE CL
2 DOWNING CR
3 SOMERBY CL
4 WINDSOR CL
5 SANDRINGHAM CL
A6
1 SOMERVILLE RD
2 BLASHFIELD CL
3 LAMBETH WK
4 BEVERLEY GD
5 SARGENT'S CT
6 NORTHUMBERLAND AV
B6
1 ANDREW RD
2 ELIZABETH RD
3 ESSEX RD
4 WORCESTER CR
5 NORFOLK SQ
6 TOLETHORPE SQ
7 GLOUCESTER RD
8 CORNWALL RD
9 YORK RD
10 LANCASTER RD
River Gwash
Macmillan Way
A6121
Carrs Lodge Farm
RYHALL ROAD
The Queen Eleanor Com Sch
Markham Retail Park
Grindlepits Spinney
Works
Mast
Football Gd
St Augustines RC (Aided) Prim Sch
St Georges CE Prim Sch
D6
1 HILLARY CL
2 EDMONDS CL
3 ST GEORGES AV
4 MELBOURNE RD
Newstead
Mast
Northfields
Bluecoat Prim Sch
Teesdales Farm
UFFINGTON RD
Stamford Leisure Centre
Stamford Coll
Stamford Retail Park
Stamford Business Park
Cemetery
Playing Field
Works
Stamford & Rutland
UFFINGTON ROAD
A16
Allot Gdns
CASTERTON ROAD
Recn Gd
Stamford Sch
Priory (remains of)
Weir
Torpel Way
Ford
A606
SCOTGATE
NORTH STREET
A6121
Browne's Hosp
Gall
Mus
Liby
PE9
St Gilberts CE Prim Sch
WEST STREET
Castle
Art Ctr
Works
Newtown
ABBOTT'S CL
ST JOHN'S ST
WHARF RD
BARNACK ROAD
B1443
Lord Burghley's
WATER STREET
WELLAND MS
STAMFORD
Allot Gdns
The Meadows
Jurassic Way
Stamford High Sch
Stamford
Football Gd
Cross (remains of)
Stamford Jun Sch
PINFOLD LA
Chabonel Spinney
Jubilee Plantation
Hereward Way
River Welland
Burghley House
KETTERING ROAD
HIGH ST ST MARTIN'S
B1081
Waterloo Plain
Dog Kennel Bushes
Burghley Park
Deer Park
The Lake
THE MALTINGS
Wothorpe
Dairy Farm
CH
OLD GREAT NORTH ROAD
A43
WARREN ROAD
The Warren
Hereward Way
Wothorpe House
A1
STAMFORD ROAD
Cross (remains of)
George Farm
02 A B 03 C D 04 E F 05
B4
1 PETERGATE
2 AUSTIN FRIAR'S LA
3 WOTHORPE MS
4 GRESLEY DR
5 MALLARD CT
6 SEATON RD
C4
1 BROWNLOW QUAY
2 ALBERT RD
3 CHURCH CT
4 ST MARTIN'S CL
5 LAMBERT MS
6 PHILLIPS CT
7 DANIEL CT
8 CHURCH ST
9 CHURCH LA
171
172
172

173 173 174

F5
1 ROWLAND CT
2 FAR PASTURE
3 MIDDLE PASTURE
4 HOMEPASTURE
5 LONG PASTURE
6 CANDIDUS CT
7 DERWOOD GR
A
B
C
D
E
F
8
7
05
6
5
04
4
3
03
2
1
02
14
15
16
Glinton
HIGH ST
PH
Peakirk-cum-Glinton CE Sch
OAK RD
BEECH RD
ELM CR
CHESTNUT CL
HELPSTON ROAD
RECTORY LA
PO
Cemy
B1443
PEAKIRK ROAD
ST PEGA'S ROAD
HELPSTON ROAD
A15
House Farm
Arthur Mellows Village College
LINCOLN ROAD
SADDLERS CL
WEBSTERS CL
CLARENDON WAY
THE WILLOWS
WELMORE ROAD
SCOTTS RD
WALKER RD
VERGETTE RD
HOLMES RD
FOXCOVERT ROAD
D8
1 PEMBROKE GR
2 ST BENEDICTS CL
Werrington Lakes
C8
1 LINCOLN RD
2 THE GREEN
3 NORTH FEN RD
4 SCHOOL LA
5 RECTORY GD
6 WESTBOURNE DR
D7
1 ASHBURN CL
2 NEAVERSON RD
Fox Covert
Works
WATERWORKS LANE
LINCOLN RD
KILVERSTONE
HOLGATE LA
BARBERS HL
TANGLEWOOD
ASH PK
TEMPLE GRANGE
LIVERMORE GN
TARRANT
FOXCOVERT RD
SWEETBRIAR LA
WOODHALL RI
SAPPERTON
REDBRIDGE
HODGSON AVENUE
CHATSFIELD
ABBOTS GR
E5
1 KINGSBRIDGE CT
2 THE PADDOCKS
3 GASCOIGNE
4 MERELADE GR
SUNNYMEAD
DAVID'S LANE
WYCLIFFE GR
SOMERVILLE
LINCOLN ROAD
WERRINGTON PARKWAY
PE6
PE4
WOODCROFT ROAD
MONKS GR
PARTRIDGE GR
PHEASANT GR
TWELVETREE AVENUE
WAINWRIGHT
CARDINALS GATE
DAVID'S CL
DAVID'S LANE
CRANEMORE
SWALLOWFIELD
CANONSFIELD
Sports Ctr
Werrington Centre
Liby
Steeping Wood
OXLEY
SOUTHWELL AVE
HAZEL CROFT
RUSHTON AVE
GREENACRES
Werrington
FOXCOVERT ROAD
DANISH CT
LC
PRIORS GATE
Gate House Farm
HURN ROAD
PAPYRUS ROAD
STAVERTON ROAD
LINCOLN ROAD
SHARMA LEYS
COVENTRY CL
SALISBURY ROAD
BRISTOL AVE
WELLS CL
ELY CL
LICHFIELD AV
CANTERBURY RD
EDINBURGH AV
AINSDALE DR
BARRY CL
WOODCROFT ROAD
CARRON DRIVE
RIPON CL
CHURCH STREET
BARNES WY
DUKESMEAD
BENEDICT SQ
HELMSDALE
WERRINGTON GR
RIVENDALE
F1
1 WATERGALL
2 NORBURN
3 BRETTON WY
4 MARHOLM RD
5 MARHOLM RD
Belham Wood
BENEDICT SQUARE
Brookfields Industrial Park
WOODCROFT ROAD
CONINGSBY RD
Pocock's Wood
Cemetery
Crem
PE3
STIRLING WAY
Poplar Farm
Marholm Farm
Manor Farm
STAMFORD ROAD
WATER END
PH
Marholm
WALTON ROAD
STAXTON CL
MALLARD ROAD
GURNARD LEYS
BRETTON WAY
LINKSIDE
MEAD CL
CASTOR RD
Mucklands Wood
DUNSBERRY
MOWBRAY RD
MEWBURN
OLDBROOK
BRETTON WAY
OUTFIELD

174
174
A B C D E F
8
7
05
6
5
04
4
3
03
2
1
02
18
19
MILKING NOOK RD
GLINTON ROAD
Milking Nook
Twenty Foot Farm
ST MARTIN'S ROAD
Bungalow Farm
BAINTON ROAD
MIDDLE ROAD
MEADOW ROAD
DRAIN ROAD
Stone Bridge Farm
WERRINGTON BRIDGE ROAD
PE6
Newborough Fen
Lowlands Farm
BRIDGEHILL ROAD
The Firs
Fen Bridge
A5
1 CROWHURST
2 PLOVERLY
Werrington End Farm
CAR DYKE (ROMAN CANAL)
GUNTHORPE ROAD
PETERBOROUGH
PASTON PARKWAY
A15
D3
1 TROUTBECK CL
2 KESWICK CL
C3
1 ESKDALE CL
2 HAWKSHEAD WY
3 THIRLMERE GD
4 BUTTERMERE PL
Norwood Farm
Mast
Werrington Meadow
PE4
Gunthorpe Bridge
MANOR DRIVE
Works
Norwood County Prim Sch
Welbourne CE Prim Sch
Allot Gdns
E2
1 WASDALE GD
2 GUNTHORPE RIDINGS
3 PATTERDALE RD
NORWOOD LANE
Gunthorpe County Prim Sch
Rec Gd
Gunthorpe
Walton Comprehensive School
Walton
Walton Jun Sch
Walton Inf Sch
Recreation Ground
Paston
Honeyhill CP Comm Sch
Paston Ridings County J&I Sch
Rec Ground
Bagley End
SEYMOUR PL
SOKE PARKWAY
A47
LINCOLN RD
STANILAND WAY
GOODWIN WALK
SKATERS WAY
WELBOURNE
HALL LANE
THE GREEN
THE STEYNINGS
AMBERLEY SLOPE
STORRINGTON WAY
CISSBURY RING
ROCKINGHAM GR
ARUNDEL RD
CONWAY AV
DOVER RD
HASTINGS RD
RICHMOND AV
WARWICK ROAD
MOUNTSTEVEN AVE
MAGEE RD
CROYLAND RD
HOLLAND AVE
CAVERSTEDE RD
PASTON LA
FANE RD
HALLFIELDS LANE
FULBRIDGE ROAD
PASTON RIDINGS
CHURCHFIELD RD
ASTER DRIVE
AUBRETIA AVE
CAMELIA CL
GRASMERE GD
BLACKDOWN GARTH
LOWTHER GD
ULLSWATER AV
ENNERDALE RI
WINDERMERE WY
BEAUVALE GD
THORNTON CL
RUDYARD GR
LADYBOWER WY
CONISTON ROAD
BORROWDALE CL
AMBLESIDE GDNS
CAMPBELL DR
HYTHEGATE
LAKESIDE
BARON CT
BROOKSIDE
DONEGAL CL
PENNINE WAY
CHILTERN RI
CHEVIOT AV
MALVERN ROAD
MENDIP GR
TUDOR CL
WATT CL
LETHBRIDGE RD
HOLMES WY
DONALDSON DRIVE
PRATT AVENUE
ANDREWS CR
FRESTON
CALDBECK CL
ULDALE WY
MARDALE GD
SQUIRES GATE
MEALS GATE
GUNTHORPE RIDINGS
NIGHTINGALE CT
WHITWELL
CHADBURN
HONEYHILL
PASTON RIDINGS
SHEEPWALK
PAYNESHOLM
CATHWAITE
CRABTREE
WAVENEY GR
SWALE AVENUE
DERWENT DRIVE
SEVERN CL
AVON CT
PILTON CL
STOWEHILL
RINGSTEAD RD
TOPMOOR WAY
KENNET GD
WITHAM WY
WINDRUSH DR
ORWELL GR
HAREBELL CL

A3
1 BIRKDALE AV
2 WERRINGTON PARK AV
3 ADDINGTON WY
4 PIPISTRELLE CT
5 WERRINGTON MS
6 CHAPEL LA
7 LANCING CL

B1
1 LUDDINGTON RD
2 GALLIONS CL
3 CARLETON CREST
4 CARLETON CREST
5 GUTHLAC AV

C1
1 CAMBRIAN WY
2 BARTRAM GATE
3 COTSWOLD CL
4 BRENDON GARTH

C2
1 HAVESWATER CLOSE
2 THE PENTLANDS
3 CLEVELAND CT
4 DONALDSON DR
5 HAVESWATERCL

D1
1 DONALDSON DR
2 CHELMER GARTH

D2
1 BOWNESS WY
2 KENDAL CL
3 ILIFFE GATE
4 KENTMERE PL
5 WHISTON CL
6 RECTORS WY

225 174 226

172

Bushey Wood
Lady Wood
Gravel Pit
Dearden Wood
Wall Spinney
Beech Spinney
Crow Spinney
PE9
Mast
A1 Stamford
Sutton Wood
Hereward Way
Sacrewell Lodge Farm
OLD RECTORY DR
RUSSELL HILL
WINDGATE WAY
Sutton Heath
Sacrewell Farm and Country Centre
Top Field Spinney
OLD NORTH RD
THACKERS CL
Wansford
A47
A47 Leicester
ROBINS WOOD
BLACK SWAN SPINNEY
ROBINS FIELD
SWANHILL
Mast
PE5
OLD NORTH RD
A6118
OLD LEICESTER ROAD
NENE CL
PETERBOROUGH RD
River Nene
Nene Way
PE8
RIVERSIDE SPINNEY
BRIDGE END
WANSFORD ROAD
Old Hill Farm
Wansford Bridge
THE DRIFT
LONDON RD
PO
PH
CHAPEL CT
Nene Way
Stibbington
Stibbington Hall
OLD GREAT NORTH RD
ROMAN DR
CHURCH LA
CHURCH LANE
CHURCH LANE
CHURCH LA
NENE WAY
Manor Farm
NENE WY
LOVERS LA
GRAEME RD
MANOR ROAD
GRAEME RD
Sutton
Stibbington House
ELTON ROAD
Field Studies Centre
A1 GREAT NORTH ROAD
OLD GREAT NORTH ROAD
Hereward Way
Lock
Weir
NEW LANE
Toll Bar Spinney
B671
Nene Valley Railway
Northamptonshire STREET ATLAS
Cambridgeshire STREET ATLAS
A1 Huntington (A1(M), A14)
A B C D E F
8 7 6 5 4 3 2 1
01 00 99 98
07 08 09

173
224

228
224

173 223 220

223 229

220
221 226

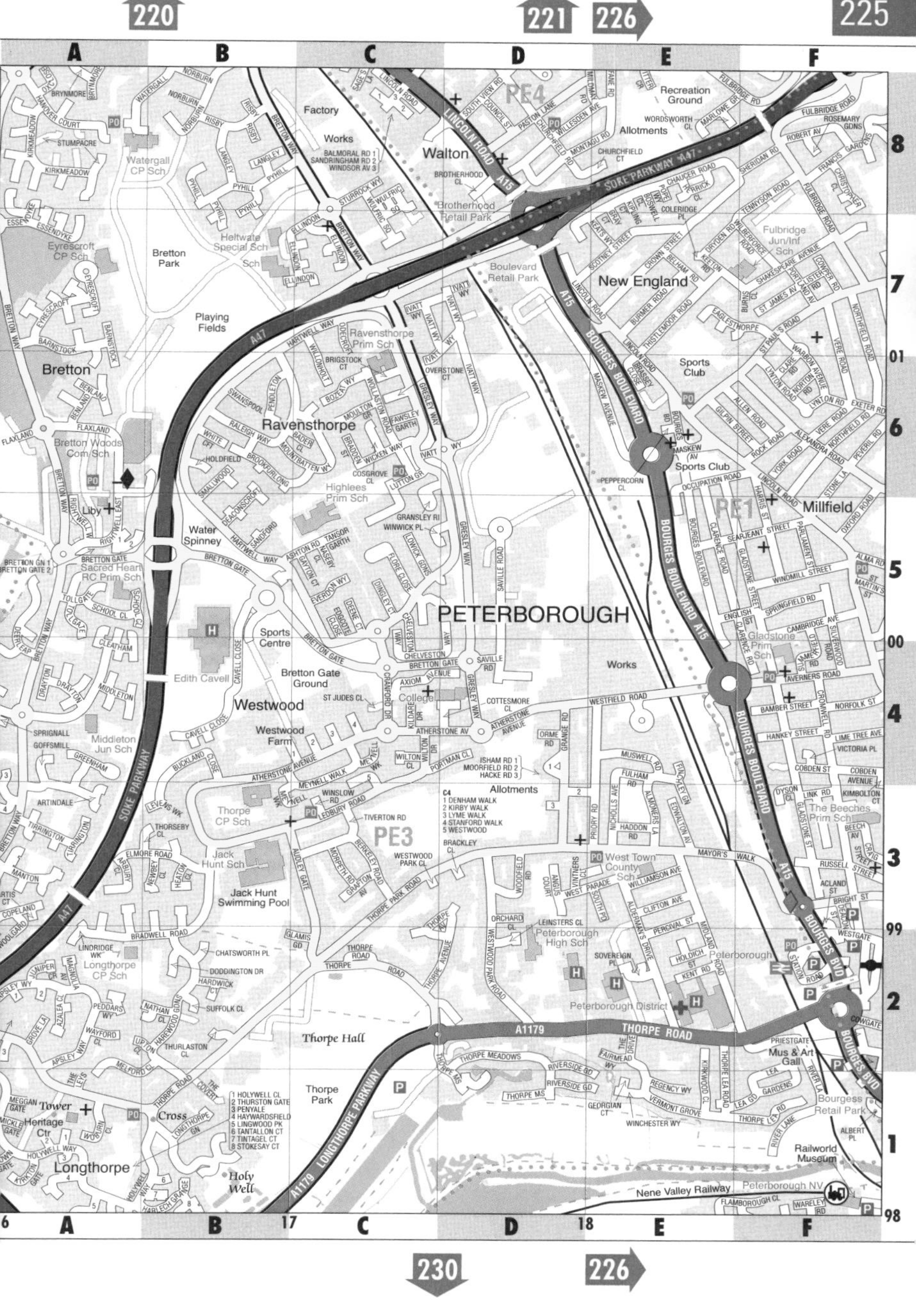

230 226

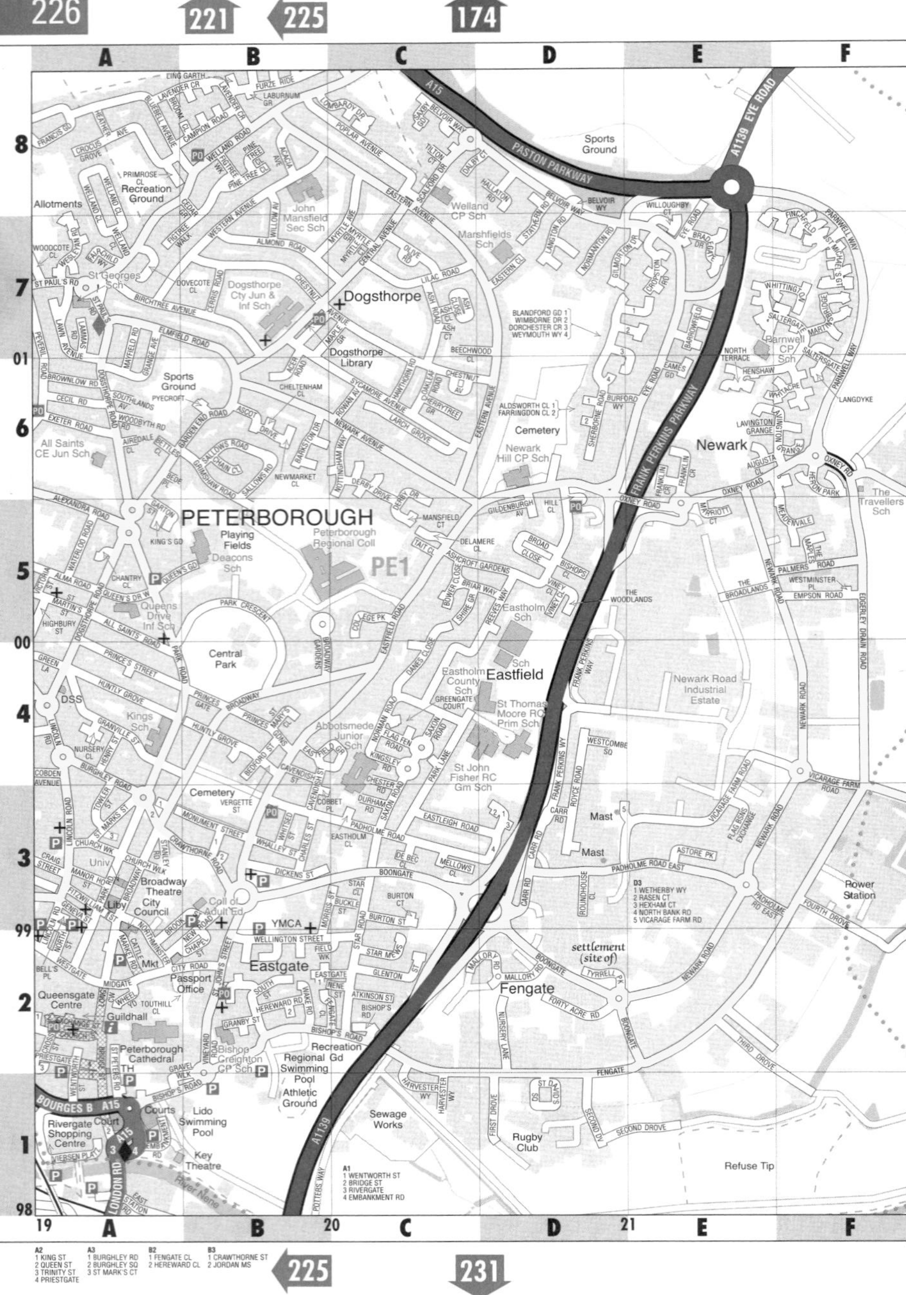

226
221
225
174
A
B
C
D
E
F
8
7
01
6
5
00
4
3
99
2
1
98
19
20
21
A15
A1139 EYE ROAD
PASTON PARKWAY
FRANK PERKINS PARKWAY
A1139
Sports Ground
Allotments
Recreation Ground
John Mansfield Sec Sch
Welland CP Sch
Marshfields Sch
St Georges Sch
Dogsthorpe Cty Jun & Inf Sch
Dogsthorpe
Dogsthorpe Library
Sports Ground
Cemetery
Newark Hill CP Sch
Newark
Parnwell CP Sch
All Saints CE Jun Sch
PETERBOROUGH
Playing Fields
Deacons Sch
Peterborough Regional Coll
PE1
Queens Drive Inf Sch
Central Park
Eastholm Sch
Eastfield
Eastholm County Sch
St Thomas Moore RC Prim Sch
Newark Road Industrial Estate
The Travellers Sch
DSS
Kings Sch
Abbotsmede Junior Sch
St John Fisher RC Gm Sch
Cemetery
Mast
Mast
Univ
Broadway Theatre
City Council
Liby
Coll of Adult Ed
YMCA
Eastgate
Mkt
Passport Office
Queensgate Centre
Guildhall
Peterborough Cathedral
TH
Bishop Creighton CP Sch
Recreation Regional Gd
Swimming Pool
Athletic Ground
Fengate
settlement (site of)
Power Station
Courts
Court
Lido Swimming Pool
Key Theatre
Rivergate Shopping Centre
Sewage Works
Rugby Club
Refuse Tip
River Nene
BOURGES B
LONDON RD
BOONGATE
PADHOLME ROAD
PADHOLME ROAD EAST
NEWARK ROAD
OXNEY ROAD
EASTFIELD ROAD
BROADWAY
PARK ROAD
LINCOLN ROAD
DOGSTHORPE ROAD
EASTERN AVENUE
CENTRAL AVENUE
WESTERN AVENUE
WELLAND ROAD
BIRCHTREE AVENUE
ELMFIELD ROAD
FENGATE
FOURTH DROVE
THIRD DROVE
SECOND DROVE
FIRST DROVE
VICARAGE FARM ROAD
EDGERLEY DRAIN ROAD
PARNWELL WAY
CITY ROAD
WESTGATE
WELLINGTON STREET
CRAWTHORNE ROAD
BISHOP'S ROAD
A1
1 WENTWORTH ST
2 BRIDGE ST
3 RIVERGATE
4 EMBANKMENT RD
D3
1 WETHERBY WY
2 RASEN CT
3 HEXHAM CT
4 NORTH BANK RD
5 VICARAGE FARM RD
BLANDFORD GD 1
WIMBORNE DR 2
DORCHESTER CR 3
WEYMOUTH WY 4
ALDSWORTH CL 1
FARRINGDON CL 2
A2
1 KING ST
2 QUEEN ST
3 TRINITY ST
4 PRIESTGATE
A3
1 BURGHLEY RD
2 BURGHLEY SQ
3 ST MARK'S CT
B2
1 FENGATE CL
2 HEREWARD CL
B3
1 CRAWTHORNE ST
2 JORDAN MS
225
231

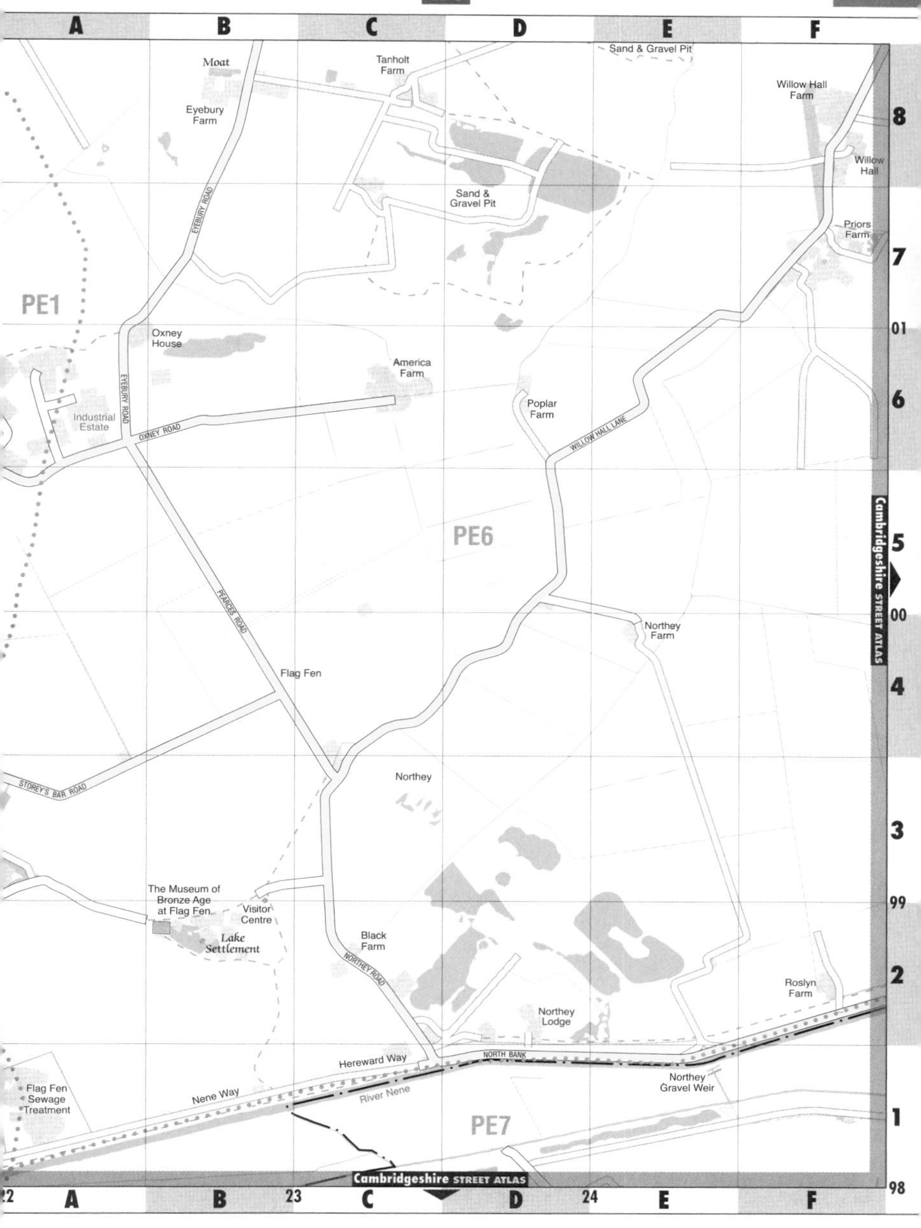
A
B
C
D
E
F
Moat
Tanholt Farm
Sand & Gravel Pit
Willow Hall Farm
Eyebury Farm
EYEBURY ROAD
Willow Hall
Sand & Gravel Pit
Priors Farm
PE1
Oxney House
America Farm
Industrial Estate
EYEBURY ROAD
OXNEY ROAD
Poplar Farm
WILLOW HALL LANE
PE6
PEARCES ROAD
Northey Farm
Flag Fen
STOREY'S BAR ROAD
Northey
The Museum of Bronze Age at Flag Fen
Visitor Centre
Lake Settlement
Black Farm
NORTHEY ROAD
Roslyn Farm
Northey Lodge
Hereward Way
NORTH BANK
Northey Gravel Weir
Nene Way
River Nene
Flag Fen Sewage Treatment
PE7
8
7
01
6
5
00
4
3
99
2
1
98
22
23
24
Cambridgeshire STREET ATLAS

223

A
B
C
D
E
F
Nene Valley Railway
STATION ROAD
PE5
SPLASH LA
Nene Way
River Nene
MILL LANE
Mill
A1 Stamford
Water
Newton
ELTON RD
OLD GREAT NORTH ROAD
A1
Hereward Way
The Castles
DVROBRIVAE
Roman Town
Water Newton
Bridge
ELTON ROAD
Brookfield
Spinney
PE8
Chesterton
Lodge
Crow
Spinney
Water
Newton Lodge
Manor
Farm
PRIORY GD
Chesterton
Hop
Spinney
OUNDLE ROAD
PE7
Sheepwalk
Farm
Road
Covert
Hill
Farm
Aylington
Close
BULLOCK RD
Cambridgeshire STREET ATLAS
8
7
97
6
5
96
4
3
95
2
1
94
10
11
12

224
230
A B C D E F
Gunwade Lake
Lynch Lake
Overton Lake
Ferry Meadows Country Park
Nene Park
Visitor Centre
Bluebell Bridge
ROMAN FORT
PE3
Ham Mere Bird Sanctuary
Hereward Way
Nene Valley Railway
Nene Way
River Nene
Lynch Bridge
PE5
Ferry Meadows
Nene Valley Railway
Orton Wistow
Orton Wistow Prim Sch
PETERBOROUGH
Back Dike
Lock
OUNDLE ROAD
A605
Business Park
Orton Brimbles
Orton Malley Prim Sch
PE2
Manor House
Alwalton
Alwalton Hall
ORTON PARKWAY
A1139
Orton Waterville
Bushfield Sports Centre
East of England Showground
Bushfield Com Coll
St Johns Church Sch CE Aided
Orton Goldhay
Clynebury Lodge
PE7
Orton Southgate
FLETTON PARKWAY
Bottom Lodge Farm
A1(M)
Upper Lodge Farm
Mast
Service Area
Hotel
13 14 15
94 95 96 97
1 2 3 4 5 6 7 8
232
230

229 225

PETERBOROUGH
PE3
PE2
PE7
Thorpe Meadows
Hotel
Nene Valley Railway
River Nene
Nene Way
Orton Mere
Orton Water
OUNDLE ROAD
NENE PARKWAY
A1260
LONGTHORPE PARKWAY A1179
St Botolphs Prim Sch
Lakeside Leisure Centre
Orton Longueville
Orton Longueville Sch
Clayton Sch
Orton Malbourne
Leighton CP Sch
Braybrook CP Sch
Winyates Prim Sch
FLETTON PARKWAY
A1139
THE SERPENTINE
Serpentine Green Shopping Centre
Hampton Hargate
Hampton Hargate Prim Sch
Cygnet Park
Reservoir
LONDON ROAD
A15
Woodston
Botolph Bridge
Regional Coll
Mast
Works
Factory
Cold Storage
Busway
St Augustines Jun Sch
Brewster Avenue Inf Sch
Liby
TA Ctr
Cemy
Fletton Prim Sch
NEW ROAD A1129
A605
DSS

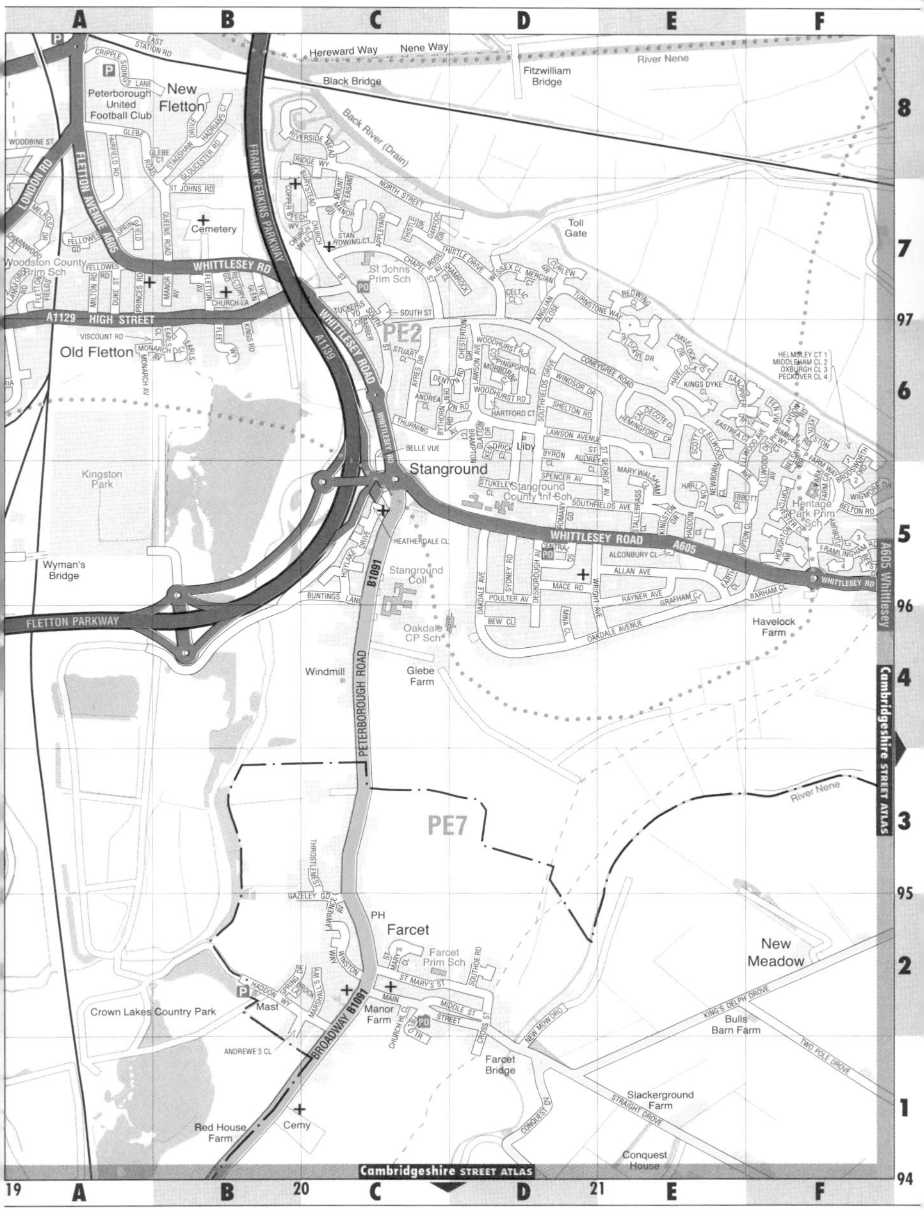
A
B
C
D
E
F
Hereward Way
Nene Way
River Nene
Black Bridge
Fitzwilliam Bridge
East Station Rd
Cripple Sidings Lane
New Fletton
Peterborough United Football Club
Back River (Drain)
Riverside Mead
Ridge Wy
North Street
London Rd
Fletton Avenue A605
Frank Perkins Parkway
Glebe Rd
Fairfield Rd
Stagshaw Drive
Hadrians Ct
Gloucester Rd
St Johns Rd
Queens Road
Cemetery
Toll Gate
Woodbine St
Woodston County Prim Sch
Whittlesey Rd
Thistle Drive
St Johns Prim Sch
Wessex Cl
Mercian Ct
Curlew Gr
Turnstone Way
Redwing Cl
A1129 High Street
South St
Viscount Rd
Old Fletton
Monarch Av
PE2
Whittlesey Road
A1139
Coneygree Road
Windsor Dr
Shelton Rd
Havelock Dr
Kings Dyke Cl
Helmsley Ct 1
Middleham Cl 2
Oxburgh Cl 3
Peckover Cl 4
Lawson Avenue
Hemingford Cr
Eastrea Ct
Belle Vue
Stanground
Stanground County Inf Sch
Mary Walsham Cl
Southfields Ave
Heritage Park Prim Sch
Kingston Park
Whittlesey Road A605
Heatherdale Cl
Stanground Coll
Alconbury Cl
Allan Ave
Mace Rd
Rayner Ave
Grafham Cl
Barham Cl
Oakdale Avenue
Wyman's Bridge
Fletton Parkway
Buntings Lane
B1091
Oakdale CP Sch
Havelock Farm
A605 Whittlesey
Windmill
Peterborough Road
Glebe Farm
Cambridgeshire STREET ATLAS
River Nene
PE7
Throstlenest
Gazeley Gd
PH
Farcet
Farcet Prim Sch
New Meadow
Winston Way
St Mary's St
Main Street
Middle St
Cross St
Haddon Wy
Mast
Crown Lakes Country Park
Broadway B1091
Manor Farm
Church Hl Cl
King's Delph Drove
Bulls Barn Farm
New Mdw Dro
Two Pole Drove
Andrewe's Cl
Farcet Bridge
Slackerground Farm
Straight Drove
Red House Farm
Cemy
Conquest Dv
Conquest House
Cambridgeshire STREET ATLAS
19
20
21
94
95
96
97
8
7
6
5
4
3
2
1

229

A
B
C
D
E
F
Haddon Lodge Farm
Service Area
A605
Alwalton Hill
NEW ROAD
Jones's Covert
A605 Oundle
Toon's Lodge
Two Pond Coppice
A1(M)
NEW ROAD
HADDON ROAD
Tollgate Farm
Manor Farm
Haddon
Grange Farm
PE7
Cambridgeshire STREET ATLAS
MORBORNE LANE
Morrison Farm
Morborne
Manor Farm
Earls Farm
Venetian Lodge
A1(M)
MORBORNE ROAD
Norman Cross
16
Rectory Farm
Sheep Lair Farm
FOLKSWORTH ROAD
B1043
Folksworth
MANOR RD
8
7
93
6
5
92
4
3
91
2
1
90
13
14
15
Cambridgeshire STREET ATLAS

A
B
C
D
E
F
Orton Brick Works
A15
Pit (dis)
LONDON ROAD
1 STEPHENSON CL
2 PARTRIDGE CL
3 NIGHTINGALE DR
Fourfields Prim Sch
Madam White's Covert
Yaxley
BROADWAY
B1091
Yaxley Jun Sch
Liby
PO
PE7
Spendelows Farm
Cemy
Manor Farm
PH
Yaxley Lodge Farm
WATERSLADE RD
CHURCH STREET
MAIN STREET
ASKEW'S LANE
MERE DROVE
LEADING DROVE
HOLME ROAD
Yards End Dyke
Heye's Farm
Hod Fen
HOD FEN DROVE
B1043
NORTH STREET
FEN DROVE
8
7
93
6
5
92
4
3
91
2
1
90
16
17
18

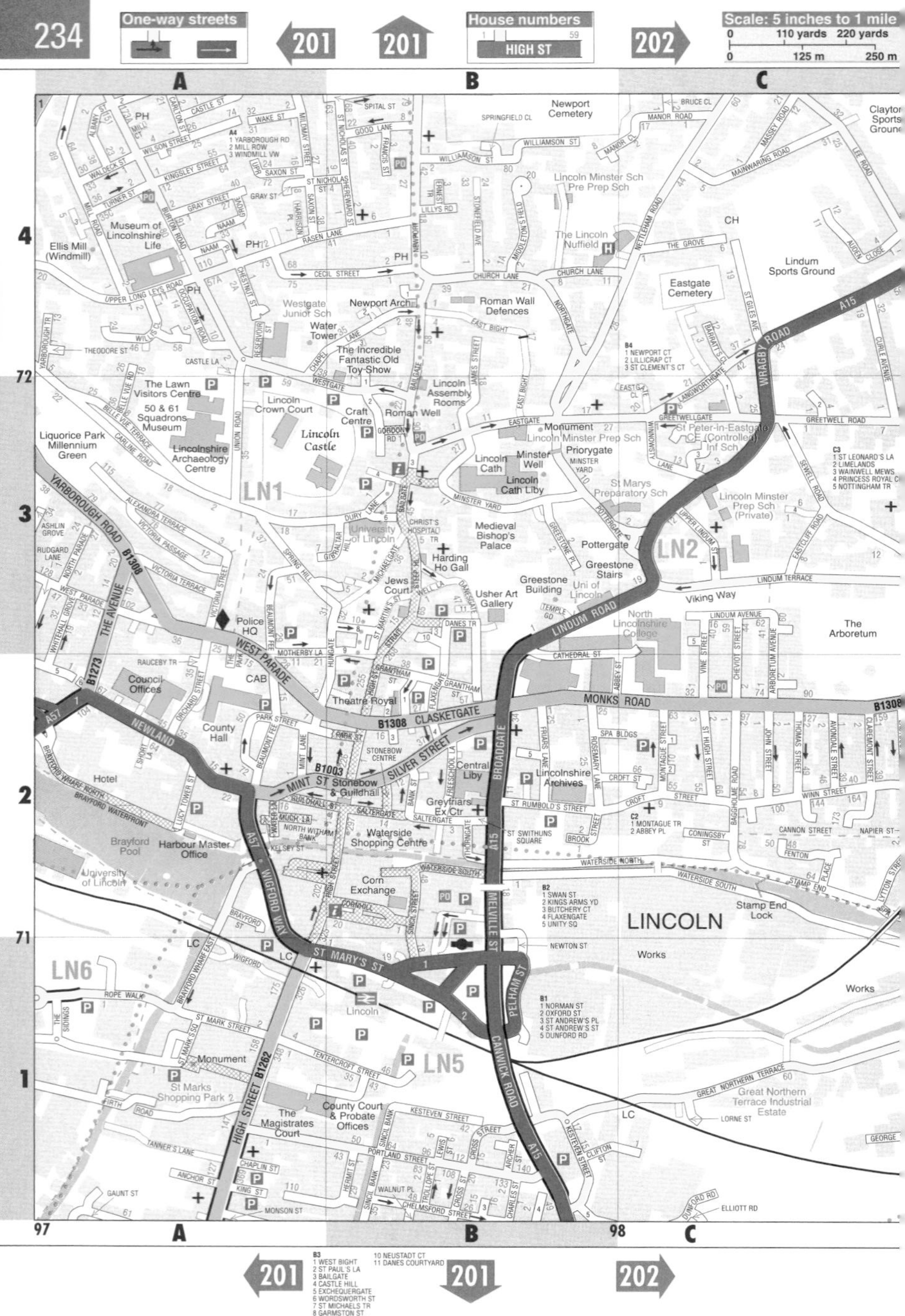

One-way streets
201
201
House numbers
1
59
HIGH ST
202
Scale: 5 inches to 1 mile
0
110 yards
220 yards
0
125 m
250 m
A
B
C
4
3
2
1
72
71
97
98
LINCOLN
LN1
LN2
LN5
LN6
Newport Cemetery
Museum of Lincolnshire Life
Ellis Mill (Windmill)
Lincoln Minster Sch Pre Prep Sch
The Lincoln Nuffield
Eastgate Cemetery
Lindum Sports Ground
Westgate Junior Sch
Newport Arch
Roman Wall Defences
Water Tower
The Incredible Fantastic Old Toy Show
The Lawn Visitors Centre
50 & 61 Squadrons Museum
Lincolnshire Archaeology Centre
Lincoln Crown Court
Lincoln Castle
Craft Centre
Roman Well
Lincoln Assembly Rooms
Monument
Lincoln Minster Prep Sch
Priorygate
St Peter-In-Eastgate CE (Controlled) Inf Sch
Liquorice Park Millennium Green
Lincoln Cath
Minster Well
Lincoln Cath Liby
St Marys Preparatory Sch
Lincoln Minster Prep Sch (Private)
University of Lincoln
Medieval Bishop's Palace
Pottergate
Harding Ho Gall
Greestone Stairs
Greestone Building
Uni of Lincoln
Usher Art Gallery
Jews Court
Viking Way
North Lincolnshire College
The Arboretum
Police HQ
Council Offices
CAB
Theatre Royal
County Hall
Stonebow & Guildhall
Central Liby
Lincolnshire Archives
Greyfriars Ex Ctr
Hotel
Waterside Shopping Centre
Brayford Pool
Harbour Master Office
University of Lincoln
Corn Exchange
Stamp End Lock
Works
Lincoln
Monument
St Marks Shopping Park
The Magistrates Court
County Court & Probate Offices
Great Northern Terrace Industrial Estate
YARBOROUGH ROAD
THE AVENUE
WEST PARADE
NEWLAND
CLASKETGATE
MONKS ROAD
SILVER STREET
MINT ST
BROADGATE
LINDUM ROAD
WRAGBY ROAD
WIGFORD WAY
ST MARY'S ST
MELVILLE ST
PELHAM ST
CANWICK ROAD
HIGH STREET
A57
A15
B1308
B1273
B1003
B1262
A4
1 YARBOROUGH RD
2 MILL ROW
3 WINDMILL VW
B4
1 NEWPORT CT
2 LILLICRAP CT
3 ST CLEMENT'S CT
C3
1 ST LEONARD'S LA
2 LIMELANDS
3 WAINWELL MEWS
4 PRINCESS ROYAL CL
5 NOTTINGHAM TR
C2
1 MONTAGUE TR
2 ABBEY PL
B2
1 SWAN ST
2 KINGS ARMS YD
3 BUTCHERY CT
4 FLAXENGATE
5 UNITY SQ
B1
1 NORMAN ST
2 OXFORD ST
3 ST ANDREW'S PL
4 ST ANDREW'S ST
5 DUNFORD RD
B3
1 WEST BIGHT
2 ST PAUL'S LA
3 BAILGATE
4 CASTLE HILL
5 EXCHEQUERGATE
6 WORDSWORTH ST
7 ST MICHAELS TR
8 GARMSTON ST
9 ST MARTIN'S LA
10 NEUSTADT CT
11 DANES COURTYARD
201
201
202

Index

Church Rd **6** Beckenham BR2..........**53** C6

Place name
May be abbreviated on the map

Location number
Present when a number indicates the place's position in a crowded area of mapping

Locality, town or village
Shown when more than one place has the same name

Postcode district
District for the indexed place

Page and grid square
Page number and grid reference for the standard mapping

Public and commercial buildings are highlighted in magenta . Places of interest are highlighted in blue with a star★

Abbreviations used in the index

Acad	**Academy**	Comm	**Common**	Gd	**Ground**	L	**Leisure**	Prom	**Prom**
App	**Approach**	Cott	**Cottage**	Gdn	**Garden**	La	**Lane**	Rd	**Road**
Arc	**Arcade**	Cres	**Crescent**	Gn	**Green**	Liby	**Library**	Recn	**Recreation**
Ave	**Avenue**	Cswy	**Causeway**	Gr	**Grove**	Mdw	**Meadow**	Ret	**Retail**
Bglw	**Bungalow**	Ct	**Court**	H	**Hall**	Meml	**Memorial**	Sh	**Shopping**
Bldg	**Building**	Ctr	**Centre**	Ho	**House**	Mkt	**Market**	Sq	**Square**
Bsns, Bus	**Business**	Ctry	**Country**	Hospl	**Hospital**	Mus	**Museum**	St	**Street**
Bvd	**Boulevard**	Cty	**County**	HQ	**Headquarters**	Orch	**Orchard**	Sta	**Station**
Cath	**Cathedral**	Dr	**Drive**	Hts	**Heights**	Pal	**Palace**	Terr	**Terrace**
Cir	**Circus**	Dro	**Drove**	Ind	**Industrial**	Par	**Parade**	TH	**Town Hall**
Cl	**Close**	Ed	**Education**	Inst	**Institute**	Pas	**Passage**	Univ	**University**
Cnr	**Corner**	Emb	**Embankment**	Int	**International**	Pk	**Park**	Wk, Wlk	**Walk**
Coll	**College**	Est	**Estate**	Intc	**Interchange**	Pl	**Place**	Wr	**Water**
Com	**Community**	Ex	**Exhibition**	Junc	**Junction**	Prec	**Precinct**	Yd	**Yard**

Index of localities, towns and villages

A

Aby 75 B5
Addlethorpe 90 C3
Adlingfleet 7 E7
Ailby 75 D4
Ailsworth 223 D3
Aisby Heydour 131 D5
Aisby Pilham 41 D4
Aisthorpe 67 C7
Aldgate 171 A3
Alford 75 E2
Algakirk 136 B2
Alkborough 8 C8
Allington 128 F7
Althorpe 17 D5
Alvingham 49 E2
Alwalton 229 B4
Amcotts 7 F1
Ancaster 120 B2
Anderby 77 A2
Anderby Creek 77 C3
Anlaby 179 A6
Anlaby Park 179 C5
Anton's Gowt 125 B6
Anwick 109 B1
Apley 70 A2
Appleby 9 D1
Asgarby Asgarby and Howell 122 B4
Asgarby Lusby with Winceby 86 F1
Ashby 185 B5
Ashby by Partney 88 D1
Ashby cum Fenby 35 D3
Ashby de la Launde 108 B6
Ashby Hill 35 C3
Ashby Puerorum 86 E6
Ashington End 90 B1
Ashton 173 A4
Aslackby 142 D5
Asperton 135 D4
Asserby 76 D4
Asterby 72 E6
Aswarby 132 D6
Aswardby 87 E5
Atterby 43 D3
Aubourn 93 A5
Aunby 163 B5
Aunsby 132 A5
Austendike 157 E4
Austen Fen 49 F5
Authorpe 74 F7
Aylesby 23 E2

B

Bag Enderby 87 B7
Bainton 172 F5
Balderton 104 C2
Bardney 83 C4
Barholm 164 C1
Barkston 130 B8
Barlings 69 D1
Barnack 172 E4
Barnby Dun 14 A4
Barnby in the Willows 104 F3
Barnetby le Wold 21 C4
Barnoldby le Beck 35 B6
Barrowby 210 A5
Barrow Hann 4 E1
Barrow Haven 4 B2
Barrow upon Humber 11 C8
Barton-Upon-Humber 10 F7
Barton Waterside 3 F2
Bassingham 92 F2
Bassingthorpe 140 E3
Baston 164 E4
Baumber 72 A1
Baythorpe 135 C8
Beacon Hill 104 B5
Beckingham Barnby in the Willows 105 A4
Beckingham 40 B1
Beelsby 34 E4
Beesby 76 A7
Belchford 73 B2
Belleau 75 A5
Bellmount 161 E4
Belmesthorpe 163 D1
Belnie 145 D5
Beltoft 17 B1
Belton Belton and Manthorpe 130 B6
Belton 16 E1
Belvoir 138 B8
Benington 126 F5
Benniworth 59 B1
Bescaby 138 B1
Besthorpe 91 C7
Bicker 135 A4
Bicker Gauntlet 134 F6
Bigby 21 C2
Billingborough 133 A1
Billinghay 109 F5
Bilsby 76 A3
Bilsby Field 76 A2
Binbrook 47 B4
Birchwood 204 D7
Birkholme 152 B6
Birthorpe 143 A8
Biscathorpe 59 D3
Bishopbridge 44 C1
Bishop Norton 43 D3
Bitchfield 141 B3
Blackjack 135 E6
Blankney 95 D3
Bleasby 58 A3
Bleasby Moor 57 F2
Bloxholm 108 C4
Blyborough 42 E5
Blyton 41 C5
Bole 52 C5
Bonby 10 C2
Bonthorpe 89 B7
Boothby Graffoe 94 A2
Boothby Pagnell 140 E5
Boston 209 C6
Boston Long Hedges 126 B6
Boston West 125 B4
Bottesford 128 A6
Bottesford Scunthorpe 185 B3
Boughton 122 C4
Boultham 205 D8
Boultham Moor 205 B6
Bourne 213 C7
Braceborough 164 B4
Bracebridge 205 D6
Bracebridge Heath 205 E3
Braceby 131 D2
Bracon 16 F2
Bradley 190 E2
Braithwaite 14 A7
Brampton 65 E6
Brand End 126 D4
Brandon 118 D7
Bransby 66 E6
Branston Branston and Mere 81 E2
Branston Croxton Kerrial 138 A4
Branston Booths 82 C4
Brant Broughton 105 F5
Brantingham 2 C8
Bratoft 102 B7
Brattleby 67 C8
Bretton 225 A6
Brigg 196 E4
Brigsley 35 D4
Brinkhill 87 C8
Broadholme 66 C1
Brocklesby 22 E6
Brookenby 47 B6
Broomfleet 1 B6
Brothertoft 124 F5
Brough 2 C5
Brough Collingham 91 E1
Broughton 19 D3
Broughton Common 19 F5
Broxholme 66 F5
Brumby 185 C8
Bucklegate 136 F3
Buckminster 150 E5
Bucknall 84 A4
Bulby 142 B1
Bullington 69 E4
Bunker's Hill 111 E4
Burgh le Marsh 102 E7
Burgh on Bain 59 D5
Burnham 11 C4
Burringham 17 E4
Burton 67 D1
Burton Corner 209 B7
Burton-le-Coggles 152 D8
Burton Pedwardine 122 B1
Burton Stather 8 B5
Burton upon Stather 8 B4
Burwell 74 B6
Buslingthorpe 57 A4
Butterwick 126 F4

C

Cabourne 33 D4
Cackle Hill 215 C5
Cadney 31 D6
Caenby 55 F8
Caistor 33 B4
Calceby 74 E2
Cammeringham 54 F1
Canal Side 15 A7
Candlesby 88 F2
Canwick 81 B4
Careby 163 B7
Carlby 163 D5
Carlton-le-Moorland 105 E8
Carlton Scroop 119 D3
Carrington 112 D6
Castle Bytham 152 D1
Castle Carlton 62 C2
Castlethorpe 20 A1
Castor 223 D1
Cawkwell 73 A6
Cawthorpe 154 B5
Caythorpe 119 C7
Chain Bridge 208 B3
Chapelgate 159 D7
Chapel Hill 110 E5
Chapel St Leonards 90 E7
Cherry Willingham 203 E5
Chesterton 228 F3
Church End 50 F6
Church Laneham 65 B3
Church Town 16 E1
Clark's Hill 159 B3
Claxby 45 D5
Claxby St Andrew 88 E6
Clay Lake 214 E2
Claypole 117 F7
Claythorpe 75 B6
Cleatham 30 B3
Cleethorpes 192 D5
Clinton Park 207 A5
Clipsham 162 B7
Clixby 33 A7
Coates North Leverton with Habblesthorpe 65 B8
Coates Stow 54 C2
Coddington 104 D5
Cold Hanworth 56 C2
Cold Harbour 130 D1
Coleby 93 F3
Coleby West Halton 8 E6
Collingham 91 C4
Collyweston 171 B1
Colsterworth 151 E7
Coningsby 207 D4
Conisholme 50 D6
Corby Glen 152 E8
Corringham 41 E2
Coston 150 C5
Cottam 65 C7
Covenham St Bartholomew 49 C5
Covenham St Mary 49 C5
Cowbit 157 B1
Cowbridge 125 E6
Cranwell 120 F8
Creeton 153 A2
Croft 102 F4
Crosby 182 D4
Crosby Warren 183 D6
Crossgate 145 C1
Crowland 166 E1
Crowle 16 D7
Croxby 34 D1
Croxton 21 F7
Croxton Kerrial 138 D4
Culverthorpe 131 E7

Cumberworth 89 F8
Cuxwold 34 B4

D

Dalby 88 B5
Dalderby 85 D1
Dawsmere 148 E5
Deeping Gate 217 C3
Deeping St James 217 D4
Deeping St Nicholas 166 C6
Dembleby 132 A4
Denton 139 B7
Derrythorpe 17 C3
Dickon Hills 114 D7
Digby 108 E6
Doddington 79 E5
Dogdyke 110 E6
Dogsthorpe 226 C7
Donington 134 F1
Donington Eaudike 135 A3
Donington on Bain 59 F1
Donna Nook 38 D2
Dorrington 108 E4
Dovendale 60 F1
Dowsby 143 B4
Dowsdale 167 D1
Dragonby 8 E1
Drayton 135 C6
Driby 74 E1
Dry Doddington 117 E5
Dunham on Trent 65 B1
Dunholme 68 E6
Dunsby 143 A1
Dunscroft 14 C4
Dunston 95 C5
Dunsville 14 C3
Dyke 154 D5

E

Eagle 79 C2
Eagle Barnsdale 92 C7
Eagle Moor 79 C2
Ealand 16 E6
Earlesfield 210 F3
East Barkwith 71 A8
East Butterwick 28 E8
East Ella 179 D7
East Ferry 28 B2
Eastfield 226 D4
East Firsby 55 F4
Eastgate 226 B2
East Halton 12 E6
East Heckington 123 D3
Easthorpe 128 B5
East Keal 100 E7
East Keal Fen Side 100 E4
East Kirkby 99 F5
East Lound 27 E2
East Marsh 189 B1
Eastoft 7 A3
Easton 140 B1
Easton on the Hill 171 C3
East Ravendale 35 C2
East Stockwith 40 C5
East Torrington 58 C2
Eastville 114 B8
Edenham 153 F4
Edenthorpe 14 A1
Edlington 85 B6
Ellerker 2 A8
Elloughton 2 B6
Elsham 20 F7
Emorsgate 161 E3
Epworth 27 E7
Epworth Turbary 27 C6
Ermine 202 B8
Eskham 37 C1
Essendine 163 D3
Etton 173 E5
Evedon 121 F6
Ewerby 122 B6
Ewerby Thorpe 122 D6
Eye 175 A1
Eye Green 175 B2

F

Faldingworth 56 F3
Far Bank 14 C8
Farcet 231 C2
Farforth 73 D5
Farlesthorpe 76 B1
Faxfleet 1 A2
Fengate 226 D2
Fenhouses 135 D7
Fen Side 100 A1
Fenton 65 E3
Fenton 105 B1
Ferriby Sluice 9 F7
Fillingham 54 F4
Firsby 101 F7
Fishlake 14 D8
Fishtoft 126 C1
Fishtoft Drove 125 D8
Fiskerton 82 A6
Fitton End 169 F3
Fledborough 78 A7
Fleet 159 C6
Fleet Hargate 159 C7
Flixborough 8 B1
Flixborough Stather 8 A1
Fockerby 7 E5
Fold Hill 115 A6
Folkingham 142 C8
Folksworth 232 D1
Fordington 88 C6
Fosdyke 146 D8
Fosdyke Bridge 146 E7
Foston 117 F2
Fotherby 49 A2
Foul Anchor 170 D8
Four Gotes 170 B7
Frampton 136 F6
Freiston 126 D2
Freiston Shore 126 F1
Friesthorpe 57 A2
Frieston 119 B6
Friskney 115 A6
Friskney Eaudyke 115 B7
Frith Bank 125 D5
Frithville 112 D1
Frodingham 183 C2
Frognall 165 D1
Fulbeck 106 C1
Fulletby 86 B8
Fulnetby 69 F6
Fulney 157 B6
Fulstow 49 B8

G

Gainsborough 197 B4
Galley Hill 75 E6
Garnsgate 159 E5
Garthorpe Garthorpe and Fockerby 7 F6
Garthorpe 150 A4
Gate Burton 53 B2
Gautby 84 B7
Gayton Engine 63 C6
Gayton le Marsh 62 F3
Gayton Le Wold 59 E4
Gedney 159 D7
Gedney Broadgate 159 D5
Gedney Drove End 149 A4
Gedney Dyke 148 B1
Gedney Hill 168 D2
Geeston 171 A2
Gelston 118 F4
Gipsey Bridge 124 F8
Gipsyville 179 E3
Girsby 59 C6
Girton 78 C1
Glentham 43 E1
Glentworth 54 E7
Glinton 220 D8
Gonerby Hill Foot 210 F8
Gorefield 169 E2
Gosberton 145 B6
Gosberton Cheal 145 A4
Gosberton Clough 144 D4
Goulceby 72 D6
Goxhill 12 A8
Graby 142 F4
Grainsby 35 F2
Grainthorpe 50 B8
Graiselound 27 C1
Grange 191 A5
Grantham 211 C3
Grant Thorold 192 A7
Grasby 32 F7
Grayingham 42 D7
Great Carlton 62 E4
Great Casterton 171 B8
Great Coates 24 B5
Greatford 164 B3
Great Gonerby 129 E5
Great Hale 122 F2
Great Limber 22 D3
Great Ponton 140 A5
Great Steeping 101 E7
Great Sturton 71 F3
Great Tows 47 D1
Grebby 88 D3
Green Hill 210 E5
Greetham 86 D5
Greetwell 30 C7
Grey Green 16 E2
Grimoldby 62 B7
Grimsby 191 B8
Grimsthorpe 153 E5
Gringley on the Hill 39 C1
Gunby Candlesby with Gunby 89 B1
Gunby Gunby and Stainby 151 C4
Gunnerby 34 F2
Gunness 17 E6
Gunthorpe Owston Ferry 40 D7
Gunthorpe Peterborough 221 B1
Guthram Gowt 155 E5
Guyhirn 177 F2

H

Habertoft 89 E4
Habrough 22 E8
Haceby 131 E3
Hackthorn 55 E1
Haconby 154 D8
Haddington 92 F6
Haddon 232 B6
Hagnaby East Kirkby 100 A5
Hagnaby Hannah cum Hagnaby 76 C6
Hagnaby Lock 99 F2
Hagworthingham 87 A4
Hainton 58 F3
Halesgate 146 E1
Hall End 114 D1
Hallington 60 F4
Haltham 98 C6
Haltoft End 126 C4
Halton Fenside 101 C6
Halton Holegate 101 B8
Hameringham 86 C2
Hampton Hargate 230 D2
Hanby 141 E7
Hannah 76 E6
Hanthorpe 154 B7
Harby 79 C5
Hardwick 66 A2
Hareby 99 F8
Harlaxton 139 C7
Harmston 93 F5
Harpswell 54 E8
Harrington 87 C7
Harrowby 211 F4
Harston 138 E6
Hartsholme 204 E6
Hasthorpe 89 C4
Hatcliffe 34 F3
Hatfield 14 D5
Hatfield Woodhouse 15 A3
Hatton 71 B3
Haugh 75 B2
Haugham 73 F8
Haven Bank 111 B3
Hawthorn Hill 110 F6
Hawthorpe 142 A2
Haxey 27 C2
Haxey Carr 27 B4
Hay Green 161 E1
Healing 23 F5
Heapham 53 E7
Heckdyke 40 C7
Heckington 122 D3
Hedgehog Bridge 124 E5
Heighington 81 F4
Helpringham 133 E7
Helpston 173 C4
Helsey 89 F7
Hemingby 72 B1
Hemswell 42 D1
Hemswell Cliff 55 A8
Hessle 178 D1
Heydour 131 D6
Hibaldstow 31 A5
High Ferry 126 A8
High Marnham 78 B5
High Risby 9 A1
High Toynton 86 A4
Hilldyke 126 A6
Hoffleet Stow 135 C4
Hogsthorpe 90 B6
Holbeach 215 C3
Holbeach Bank 215 C7
Holbeach Clough 215 B7
Holbeach Drove 168 B3
Holbeach Hurn 147 F2
Holbeach St Johns 158 E1
Holbeach St Marks 147 D6
Holbeach St Matthew 148 A7
Holdingham 212 C7
Holme 19 A1
Holme 91 A2
Holme Hill 191 F6
Holton cum Beckering 70 C8
Holton le Clay 195 D2
Holton le Moor 45 A8
Honington 119 C2
Hop Pole 165 F5
Horbling 133 C2
Horkstow 10 A5
Horncastle 199 D3
Horsington 84 C3
Hougham 118 C3
Hough-on-the-Hill 119 A5
Howell 122 D5
Howsham 32 A6
Hubbert's Bridge 124 F2
Humberston 193 A2
Humby 141 C7
Hundleby 87 F1
Hundle Houses 111 C4
Hungerton 139 B4
Hurn's End 127 C8
Huttoft 76 E3

I

Immingham 186 E4
Ingham 54 F2
Ingleborough 170 E5
Ingleby 66 C4
Ingoldmells 90 E4
Ingoldsby 141 D5
Ingthorpe 218 A8
Irby in the Marsh 102 B6
Irby upon Humber 34 D7
Irnham 141 E1
Island Carr 196 B2

K

Keadby 17 D7
Keal Cotes 100 C4
Keddington 198 F8
Keelby 23 A5
Keisby 141 F3
Kelby 131 C8
Kelfield 28 C4
Kelstern 48 A1
Ketsby 74 D3
Kettlethorpe 65 F2
Ketton 171 A3
Kexby 53 E5
Kilvington 117 A1
Kingerby 44 E3
Kingston upon Hull 180 F4
Kingthorpe 70 C2
Kirk Bramwith 14 A6
Kirkby 44 F3
Kirkby Fenside 99 E4
Kirkby Green 108 E8
Kirkby la Thorpe 121 F5
Kirkby on Bain 98 B5
Kirkby Underwood 142 D2
Kirk Ella 178 C8
Kirmington 22 A6
Kirmond le Mire 46 F3
Kirton 136 D5
Kirton End 136 B6
Kirton Holme 135 E8
Kirton in Lindsey 30 C2
Knaith 53 A3
Knaith Park 53 B4
Knipton 138 C6

L

Laceby 23 E1
Laceby Acres 190 C4
Lade Bank 113 F5
Laneham 65 A3
Langford 91 C1
Langholme 39 E8
Langrick 124 E7
Langrick Bridge 124 E6
Langtoft 164 F3
Langton Langton by Spilsby 87 F5
Langton 85 B3
Langton by Wragby 70 F3
Langworth 69 B3
Laughterton 65 D2
Laughton 41 C8
Lea 52 F5
Leadenham 106 C3
Leake 127 C8
Leake Commonside 113 F3
Leake Fold Hill 114 A2
Leasingham 121 B8
Legbourne 61 F3
Legsby 58 A4
Lenton 141 E5
Leverington 170 B3
Leverton 126 F6
Leverton Highgate 127 A6
Leverton Lucasgate 127 B6
Leverton Outgate 127 B7
Lincoln 234 C2
Linwood 57 D5
Lissington 57 E2
Listoft 89 F7
Littleborough 52 F1
Little Bytham 163 A8
Little Carlton 62 C4
Little Casterton 171 E8
Little Cawthorpe 61 E2
Little Coates 190 F7
Little Common 215 B8
Littlefield 191 B6
Little Grimsby 49 B2
Little Hale 133 E8
Little Limber 22 C5
Little London Legsby 58 A5
Little London Long Sutton 216 D5
Little London Spalding 156 E3
Little London Spalding 214 A1
Little London Tetford 73 F2
Little Ponton 140 A7
Little Steeping 101 D5
Little Sutton 160 C5
Little Welton 60 F6
Little Wisbeach 143 C6
Lobthorpe 152 A3
Londonthorpe 130 D4
Long Bennington 117 D3
Long Sutton 216 C4
Longthorpe 225 A1
Loosegate 158 A8
Louth 198 E6
Low Barlings 82 E8
Low Burnham 27 E5
Lower Bassingthorpe 140 E4
Lower Bitchfield 141 A3
Low Fulney 157 B4
Low Marnham 78 A4
Low Risby 9 A2
Low Toynton 199 F6
Ludborough 48 D6
Luddington 7 D3
Ludford 59 A8
Ludney 50 C6
Lusby 86 F2
Lutton 160 A8
Lutton Gowts 216 D8

M

Mablethorpe 64 C3
Maidenwell 73 E6
Maltby 60 F3
Maltby le Marsh 76 A8
Manby 62 D6
Manor Park 184 D6
Manthorpe Grantham 211 A8
Manthorpe Toft with Lound and Manthorpe 164 A7
Manton 30 B5
Manton Warren 30 B8
Mareham le Fen 99 A3
Mareham on the Hill 86 A2
Marfleet 5 E8
Marholm 220 C1
Markby 76 C5
Market Deeping 217 E6
Market Rasen 57 E8
Market Stainton 72 B6
Marlborough 93 B4
Marshchapel 37 B2
Marston 118 C2
Martin 96 C3
Martin Roughton 85 B1
Marton 65 D8
Mavis Enderby 87 C1
Mawthorpe 88 F8
Maxey 173 C7
Medlam 112 D7
Melton 2 F5
Melton Ross 21 D5
Messingham 29 D7
Metheringham 95 D4
Middle Rasen 57 B8
Midville 113 E8
Millfield 225 F5
Mill Hill 103 B8
Millthorpe 143 B6
Miningsby 99 D7
Minting 84 D8
Misterton 39 F5
Monksthorpe 101 E8
Moorby 99 B6
Moorhouses 112 A8
Moor Side 111 D8
Moortown 32 C2
Morborne 232 B3
Morton 197 C8
Morton 154 C6
Morton Thorpe on the Hill 92 C6
Moulton 157 F7
Moulton Chapel 157 E1
Moulton Eaugate 167 F8
Moulton Seas End 146 E2
Muckton 74 D8
Mumby 76 F1
Murrow 177 D5
Muston 128 C5

N

Navenby 107 A8
Nene Terrace 175 D6
Nettleham 68 D2
Nettleton 33 A3
Newark 226 E6
Newark-on-Trent 104 B4
New Balderton 104 A2
Newball 69 D3
New Barnetby 21 D5
New Bolingbroke 112 D8
Newborough 174 E4
New England Croft 102 E2
New England Peterborough 225 E7
New Fletton 231 B8
Newham 112 A1
New Holland 4 E2
New Leake 114 A8
New Meadow 231 F2
New Quarrington 212 A2
Newtoft 56 E5
Newton Newton and Haceby 132 A3
Newton 170 A5
Newton by Toft 56 E6
Newton on Trent 65 D1
New Waltham 195 D7
New York 111 C5

Nocton 95 B7
Normanby 8 C3
Normanby-by-Spital 55 E7
Normanby by Stow 53 E1
Normanby le Wold 45 F5
Norman Corner 194 C2
Norman Cross 232 F2
Normanton Bottesford 128 A7
Normanton 119 D5
Northbeck 132 F8
Northborough 217 E2
North Carlton 67 C4
North Carr 27 C3
North Clifton 78 C7
North Cockerington 50 A1
North Cotes 37 A3
North Elkington 48 D1
North End Alvingham 49 E3
North End Saltfleetby 62 F8
North End Swineshead 135 B8
North Ferriby 3 B4
Northfield 178 F2
Northgate 144 D1
North Greetwell 203 B8
North Harby 79 C7
North Hykeham 204 D2
North Kelsey 32 A4
North Kelsey Moor 32 D4
North Killingholme 12 D3
North Kyme 109 F4
Northlands 113 A4
North Leverton with Habblesthorpe 52 B1
North Ormsby 48 E4
Northorpe Donington 134 E3
Northorpe 42 A8
Northorpe Thurlby 164 C8
North Owersby 44 E5
North Rauceby 120 E5
North Reston 62 B2
North Scarle 78 F2
North Somercotes 50 F8
North Thoresby 36 B1
North Willingham 58 D7
North Witham 151 D4
Norton Disney 92 C2
Nunsthorpe 191 B4

O

Oasby 131 C6
Obthorpe 164 C6
Old Bolingbroke 100 B8
Old Clee 192 C6
Old Fletton 231 A6
Old Gate 159 F3
Old Leake 114 A1
Old Somerby 140 D8
Old Woodhall 85 A2
Orange Row 161 F3
Orby 89 C2
Orton Brimbles 229 D5
Orton Goldhay 229 F3
Orton Longueville 230 B5
Orton Malbourne 230 C4
Orton Southgate 229 C2
Orton Waterville 229 E4
Orton Wistow 229 C6
Osbournby 132 C4
Osgodby Lenton Keisby and Osgodby 141 E3
Osgodby 45 A3
Otby 46 A4
Owmby 32 D7
Owmby-by-Spital 55 F6
Owston Ferry 28 B3
Oxcombe 73 D4

P

Panton 71 B5
Parson Drove 177 D7
Partney 88 A3
Paston 221 D1
Peakirk 174 A5
Penny Hill 215 D6
Peterborough 225 D5
Pickworth 142 A8
Pickworth 162 E4
Pilham 41 D4
Pilsgate 172 C4
Pinchbeck 156 E8
Pinchbeck West 156 A7
Pode Hole 156 C5
Pointon 143 B7
Port Sutton Bridge 160 F4
Potterhanworth 82 B1
Potterhanworth Booths 82 C2
Pyewipe 188 C4

Q

Quadring 145 A8
Quadring Eaudike 145 C8
Quarrington 212 B1

R

Ragnall 78 A8
Raithby 60 F3
Raithby by Spilsby 87 D2
Rampton 65 A4
Ranby 72 B5
Rand 70 A5
Ravensthorpe 225 C6
Reasby 69 C6
Redbourne 30 F3
Reedham 111 C7
Reed Point 110 E2
Reepham 203 F8
Revesby 99 C3
Revesby Bridge 99 C3
Riby 23 C2
Riddings 184 F4
Rigsby 75 D2
Rippingale 142 F3
Risby 46 B3
Risegate 144 F4
Riseholme 68 A2
Ropsley 131 B1
Rothwell 33 F2
Roughton 98 B7
Roughton Moor 98 A7
Rowston 108 E7
Roxby 9 A3
Ruckland 73 F5
Ruskington 108 E2
Ryhall 163 C1

S

St Giles 202 C7
St Vincent 211 D3
Saleby 75 F6
Salmonby 86 E8
Saltby 138 F1
Saltfleet 51 B4
Saltfleetby All Saints 51 C1
Saltfleetby St Clement 51 C2
Saltfleetby St Peter 63 B8
Sandbraes 33 A4
Sandholme 136 F4
Sandilands 77 A8
Sandtoft 16 A3
Sandy Bank 111 E6
Santon 19 B7
Sapperton 141 E8
Saracen's Head 215 A7
Saundby 52 B7
Sausthorpe 87 E4
Saxby 55 F5
Saxby All Saints 10 A3
Saxilby 66 D3
Scamblesby 72 F5
Scampton 67 D6
Scartho 194 E8
Scawby 30 E8
Scopwick 95 D1
Scothern 68 E4
Scotland 141 C5
Scotter 29 B3
Scotterthorpe 29 B5
Scotton 29 C2
Scott Willoughby 132 B4
Scrafield 86 C3
Scrane End 137 F8
Scredington 132 E7
Scremby 88 E2
Scrivelsby 98 E8
Scrub Hill 111 B6
Scunthorpe 183 B5
Seacroft 103 E4
Seadyke 136 E3
Searby 32 C8
Seathorne 206 E8
Sedgebrook 128 F5
Sewstern 150 F4
Shepeau Stow 167 F3
Sibsey 113 B2
Silk Willoughby 121 C1
Sixhills 58 E6
Skegness 206 E4
Skeldyke 136 F4
Skellingthorpe 200 B4
Skendleby 88 D4
Skidbrooke 51 B3
Skillington 151 B8
Skinnand 106 C8
Skirbeck 209 B3
Skirbeck Quarter 208 D2
Sleaford 212 B4
Sloothby 89 D5
Snarford 56 D1
Snelland 69 D7
Snitterby 43 D5
Somerby 21 B1
Somersby 87 A7
Sotby 71 E5
Sots Hole 96 C7
South Bramwith 14 A6
South Carlton 67 D3
South Clifton 78 B5
South Cockerington 62 A8
South Elkington 60 E7
South End 12 B7
South Ferriby 10 B8
South Field 3 E4
South Green 161 E2
South Hykeham 93 B7
South Kelsey 32 A1
South Killingholme 12 E3
South Kyme 123 B8
South Ormsby 74 D2
Southorpe 172 E2
South Owersby 44 E4
South Rauceby 120 E4
South Reston 62 D1
Southrey 83 D1
South Scarle 91 E6
South Somercotes 50 E5
South Thoresby 75 A3
South Willingham 59 A2
South Witham 151 E2
Spalding 214 E6
Spalford 78 D4
Spanby 132 F4
Spilsby 101 A8
Spital in the Street 43 B1
Spittlegate 211 A3
Spridlington 55 F3
Springthorpe 53 E8
Sproxton 150 C7
Stainby 151 C5
Stainfield Haconby 154 A8
Stainfield 83 B8
Stainforth 14 C6
Stainsby 86 F6
Stainton by Langworth 69 C4
Stainton le Vale 46 E5
Stallingborough 23 E6
Stamford 219 D4
Stanground 231 C5
Stapleford 105 B8
Staunton in the Vale 117 A2
Stenigot 72 D8
Stenwith 128 D3
Stewton 61 E5
Stibbington 222 C2
Stickford 100 B2
Stickney 113 A8
Stixwould 97 B8
Stockholes Turbary 16 B2
Stoke Rochford 139 F2
Stone Hill 14 F4
Stow 66 C8
Stragglethorpe 105 E3
Stroxton 139 E5
Strubby 63 C1
Stubton 118 B7
Sturgate 53 F8
Sturton 30 F7
Sturton by Stow 66 C7
Sturton le Steeple 52 B3
Sudbrook 119 E3
Sudbrooke 68 F2
Sudthorpe 119 C8
Surfleet 145 C3
Surfleet Seas End 145 F3
Susworth 28 D5
Sutterby 87 E7
Sutterton 136 A3
Sutterton Dowdyke 146 A8
Sutton Beckingham 105 B3
Sutton 222 F2
Sutton Bridge 160 D4
Sutton Crosses 216 C1
Sutton on Sea 76 F8
Sutton on Trent 91 A8
Sutton St Edmund 168 F4
Sutton St James 159 D1
Swaby 74 E4
Swallow 34 B5
Swallow Beck 205 B5
Swanland 3 A7
Swarby 132 A7
Swaton 133 D4
Swayfield 152 D5
Swinderby 92 A5
Swineshead 135 B7
Swineshead Bridge 123 F1
Swinethorpe 79 B4
Swinhope 47 C7
Swinstead 153 A5
Syston 130 A7

T

Tallington 172 E7
Tamworth Green 126 E1
Tathwell 61 B2
Tattershall 207 A5
Tattershall Bridge 110 D7
Tattershall Thorpe 207 B8
Tealby 46 C1
Terrington St Clement 161 E3
Tetford 73 F1
Tetley 16 D6
Tetney 36 D4
Tetney Lock 37 A4
Thealby 8 D4
Theddlethorpe All Saints 63 D7
Theddlethorpe St Helen 63 E8
The Parks 14 C4
Thetford 164 E5
The Willows 190 E7
Thimbleby 85 B5
Thoresthorpe 75 F4
Thoresway 46 D7
Thorganby 47 B8
Thorne 15 B8
Thorney 78 F8
Thorney 176 A3
Thorney Toll 177 A2
Thornton 85 C2
Thornton Curtis 11 E4
Thornton le Moor 44 E7
Thorpe 64 A1
Thorpe Culvert 102 A3
Thorpe Fendykes 101 F3
Thorpe Latimer 133 C6
Thorpe le Vale 47 B1
Thorpe on the Hill 92 E8
Thorpe St Peter 102 B3
Thorpe Tilney 109 C8
Three Bridges 63 A7
Threekingham 132 E3
Throckenholt 177 B8
Thurlby Bilsby 76 D2
Thurlby 92 E4
Thurlby 164 C8
Tickencote 171 A8
Timberland 96 C1
Tinwell 218 D3
Toft 163 F8
Toft Hill 98 D5
Toft next Newton 56 C7
Toll Bar 218 C8
Torksey 65 E5
Torksey Lock 65 E5
Tothill 62 E1
Towngate 164 F1
Toynton All Saints 100 F6
Toynton Fen Side 100 F5
Toynton St Peter 101 A6
Trusthorpe 64 B2
Tumby Woodside 111 F8
Twenty 155 C3
Tydd St Giles 169 F7
Tydd St Mary 160 B1

U

Uffington 172 C6
Ufford 172 F3
Ulceby 12 B1
Ulceby Ulceby with Fordington 88 C7
Ulceby Skitter 12 C2
Upperthorpe 27 B3
Upton 53 E5
Upton 223 B6
Usselby 45 C4
Utterby 48 F4

V

Victoria Dock Village 181 C5

W

Waddingham 43 D7
Waddington 93 F7
Waddingworth 84 C6
Wainfleet All Saints 102 D2
Wainfleet Bank 102 B1
Wainfleet St Mary 115 E8
Wainfleet Tofts 115 C8
Waithe 36 A3
Walcot Alkborough 8 B8
Walcot Walcot Near Folkingham 132 C1
Walcott 109 D7
Walesby 46 A3
Walkeringham 39 F3
Walkerith 40 B4
Walmsgate 74 C5
Walpole Cross Keys 161 C3
Walpole Marsh 170 F8
Walsoken 170 E1
Waltham 194 D5
Walton 221 A1
Walton Highway 170 F3
Wansford 222 A4
Wargate 145 B5
Washingborough 203 D2
Wasps Nest 95 E7
Water Newton 228 C7
Waterside 14 E8
Weecar 78 D1
Weelsby 192 A5
Welbourn 106 F5
Welby 130 F5
Well 88 E8
Wellingore 107 A7
Wellow 191 E5
Welton 2 E6
Welton 68 C6
Welton Hill 69 A8
Welton le Marsh 89 B3
Welton le Wold 60 C6
Werrington 220 F4
West Ashby 85 E7
West Barkwith 70 F7
Westborough 117 E3
West Butterwick 28 D8
Westby 140 F3
Westcliff 184 E7
West Deeping 173 B8
West Ella 178 A8
West End 126 E6
West Field 12 C6
Westgate 16 D2
West Halton 8 E8
Westhorpe 144 F5
West Keal 100 C6
West Marsh 188 D1
Weston 157 D7
Weston Hills 157 C3
West Rasen 56 E8
West Ravendale 35 A2
Westrum 196 C1
West Stockwith 40 C6
West Torrington 58 A1
West Walton 170 E4
West Willoughby 119 E2
Westwood 225 B4
Westwoodside 27 A2
Whaplode 158 A7
Whaplode Drove 168 B4
Whaplode St Catherine 158 C2
Wharton 41 B4
Whisby 79 E2
White Pit 74 D4
Whitton 1 D3
Wickenby 69 F8
Wigsley 78 F5
Wigtoft 135 E3
Wike Well End 15 B7
Wildsworth 40 E8
Wilksby 99 A5
Willingham by Stow 53 F3
Willoughby 89 B7
Willoughby Hills 209 E7
Willoughby Moor 119 F2
Willoughton 42 D4
Will Row 63 C5
Wilsford 120 C1
Wilsthorpe 164 C4
Winceby 86 E3
Winteringham 2 A1
Winterton 9 A5
Winthorpe Langford 104 B8
Winthorpe Skegness 206 C8
Wisbech 170 B1
Wispington 84 E6
Witham on the Hill 163 D7
Witham St. Hughs 92 D5
Withcall 60 C2
Withern 63 A1
Wittering 172 B1
Wold Newton 47 F7
Wood Enderby 98 F6
Woodhall Spa 97 E5
Woodhouse 16 E3
Woodnook 140 C7
Woodside 26 D6
Woodston 230 E7
Woodthorpe 75 D7
Woolsthorpe by Belvoir 128 D1
Woolsthorpe-by-Colsterworth 151 D7
Wootton 11 F3
Worlaby Maidenwell 74 A4
Worlaby 20 D8
Wothorpe 219 B2
Wragby 70 E5
Wragholme 50 A8
Wrangle 114 C1
Wrangle Bank 114 C4
Wrangle Lowgate 114 D2
Wrangle Low Ground 114 D4
Wrawby 20 E4
Wressle 19 F4
Wroot 26 C6
Wybers Wood 190 C6
Wyberton 136 D8
Wykeham 145 F1
Wymondham 150 B1
Wyville 139 C4

Y

Yaddlethorpe 184 E3
Yarborough 191 A7
Yarburgh 49 E4
Yawthorpe 42 A2
Yaxley 233 E6

1

1st Drift PE9 219 B2
1st Main Rd DN36 36 F8

2

2nd Ave DN36 36 F8
2nd Drift PE9 219 B2

4

4th Ave DN36 36 F8

12

12th Ave DN36 36 F8

A

Aalsmeer Rise 6 PE11 214 A2
Abbey Cl
Coningsby LN4 207 B5
6 Skegness PE25 206 A4
5 Woodhall Spa LN10 97 C6
Abbey Cres 4 PE20 135 C7
Abbey Dr 20 Hatfield DN7 14 D4
13 Woodhall Spa LN10 97 C5
Abbey Dr E DN32 191 D6
Abbey Dr W DN32 191 D6
Abbey Gdns 22 DN7 14 D4
Abbey Gr 23 DN7 14 D4
Abbey La
Sedgebrook NG32 128 F4
Swineshead PE20 135 C6
Woodhall Spa LN10 97 C5
Abbey Mews 11 PE6 166 F1
Abbey Pk Rd DN32 191 D6
Abbey Pl 2 Lincoln LN2 234 C2
10 Thorney PE6 176 A3
Abbey Rd
Alvingham LN11 49 F2
Bardney LN3 83 B4
Bourne PE10 213 D5
Grimsby DN32 191 D6
Hatfield DN7 14 D4
Louth LN11 198 D6
Peterborough PE4 221 A1
Revesby PE22 99 C5
Scunthorpe DN17 184 F6
Sleaford NG34 212 A2
Swineshead PE20 135 C7
Ulceby DN39 12 A1
Abbey Rise 20 DN19 11 D8
Abbey St
Kingston upon Hull HU9 181 C7
Lincoln LN2 234 C2
Abbey Way DN7 14 D5
Abbey Wlk
10 Crowland PE6 166 F1
11 Grimsby DN32 191 D7
Abbey Yd 12 PE11 214 D4
Abbeydale Cres NG31 211 A8
Abbeyfield Rd 1 DN7 14 C4
Abbot St LN5 201 E1
Abbot Way PE7 233 D4
Abbot's Cl 5 PE10 213 E4
Abbot's Way 5 PE11 214 A3
Abbots Dr 1 PE6 175 B8
Abbots Gdns 1 PE12 158 B6
Abbots Rd DN17 184 F6
Abbotsbury PE2 230 A3
Abbotsmede Jun Sch
PE1 226 C4
Abbotsway DN32 191 D6
Abbott Cl 10 LN8 57 B8
Abbott's Cl PE9 219 D4
Abbotts Gr PE4 220 F6
Abbotts Grange DN36 195 E7
Abercorn St 3 DN16 183 A2
Aberdeen Cl PE9 218 D6
Aberporth Dr LN6 204 B8
Abingdon Ave LN6 204 C6
Abingdon Cl 15 LN6 204 C6
Aboyne Ave PE2 229 F5
Abraham Cl 5 NG31 129 E5
Aby CE Prim Sch LN13 75 B5
Acacia Ave
Chapel St Leonard PE24 90 D8
Gainsborough DN21 197 D6
Peterborough PE1 226 B8
5 Scunthorpe DN15 182 C5
Spalding PE11 214 F5
Waddington LN5 205 D1
3 Wisbech PE13 170 D1
Acacia Cl 12 NG34 212 D2
Acacia Ct 3 DN16 185 B6
Acacia Way
Boston PE21 208 C4
Messingham DN17 29 C7
Acadia Gr HU13 178 F1
Accommodation Rd
LN9 199 A5
Acer Cl LN6 204 D7
Acer Ct 2 LN6 204 D7
Acer Gr 3 DN17 184 C5
Acer Rd PE1 226 B6
Achille Rd DN34 190 D5
Achurch Cl LN9 199 D1
Acklam Ave 3 PE11 214 F6
Acklam Gr DN32 192 B6
Acklands La 13 NG23 117 D3
Acland St
Gainsborough DN21 197 C5
4 Kingston upon Hull HU3 180 A6
Peterborough PE1 225 F3
Acomb Comm Rd DN7 14 F4
Acorn Cl Freiston PE21 126 C4
Grantham NG31 211 C7
Lincoln LN5 205 D7
Acorn Way
5 Bottesford DN16 185 B2
Hessle HU13 178 B3
Acre Dyke La LN4 82 B4
Acre La Scopwick LN4 95 E1
Threekingham NG34 132 E2
Acres La DN9 26 D7
Acres The 1 PE9 172 D4
Ada Way LN11 198 D7
Adam Cl 18 LN6 204 D7
Adam Smith St DN31 188 F1
Adams Way DN21 65 E8
Adamstiles 2 NG32 210 B4
Addington Way 3 PE4 221 A3
Addison Cl 4 LN5 107 A8
Addison Dr LN2 202 B6
Addison Pl LN1 65 E3
Adelaide Cl
Gainsborough DN21 197 F2
13 Waddington LN5 93 E8
Adelaide Prim Sch
HU3 180 D5
Adelaide Sch HU3 180 D5
Adelaide St
Kingston upon Hull HU3 180 D5
Stamford PE9 219 D5
Adelphi Ct 5 DN36 195 C6
Adelphi Dr DN33 194 E7
Adlard Gr DN36 36 C7
Adlingfleet Rd DN17 7 E6
Admirals Dr 7 PE13 170 D2
Admiralty Rd 19 LN12 64 B4
Adrian Cl Louth LN11 198 C4
9 Skegness PE25 206 A4
9 Swineshead PE20 135 B7
Advent Ct 2 DN39 12 A1
Aegir Cl DN21 197 F2
Africa Cl DN34 190 D4
Agard Ave DN15 182 E3
Agnes St 2 NG31 211 B4
Aidan Rd NG34 212 B2
Aima Ct 2 LN2 68 C2
Ainsdale Dr PE4 220 F3
Ainslie St DN32 191 E6
Ainsworth Rd 5 DN40 186 B4
Ainthorpe Gr HU5 179 C7
Ainthorpe Prim Sch
HU5 179 C8
Aintree Dr PE11 214 B1
Aire Cl DN40 186 A3
Aire Rd NG31 210 E3
Airedale Cl
12 Broughton DN20 19 E4
Peterborough PE1 226 A6
Airedale Rd
1 Scunthorpe DN16 185 D5
1 Stamford PE9 219 A7
Airlie St HU3 180 B5
Airmanship Rd NG34 120 B8
Airmyn Ave 1 HU3 179 E6
Airship Rd NG34 107 C1
Aisne Cl LN1 201 E7
Aisne St HU5 180 A8
Ajax Cl DN34 190 D4
Ajax Ct DN15 182 F5
Akeferry Rd DN9 27 C1
Akeman Cl 10 PE10 213 C6
Akita Cl 4 PE11 214 A5
Alabala Cl LN4 203 C1
Alabala La LN4 81 F4
Alan Cres DN15 182 F2
Alba Cl DN17 184 D5
Alban Ret Pk PE21 208 B3
Albany Cl PE25 206 A5
Albany Pl LN11 198 D3
Albany Rd Louth LN11 198 D3
Skegness PE25 206 A5
21 Wisbech PE13 170 D1
3 Woodhall Spa LN10 97 D5
Albany St
Gainsborough DN21 197 C6
Kingston upon Hull HU3 180 D8
Lincoln LN1 234 A4
Albany Way PE25 206 A5
Albany Wlk PE2 230 D7
Albatross Dr DN37 190 B7
Albemarle Cl 5 HU15 2 B5
Albemarle St 2 HU3 180 B5
Albert Ave
Kingston upon Hull HU3 180 A7
Long Sutton PE12 159 E7
1 Skegness PE25 103 E4
Albert Cres LN1 201 D4
Albert Pl PE3 225 F1
Albert Rd
Cleethorpes DN35 192 F6
Scunthorpe DN16 185 A5
Skegness PE25 206 B3
2 Stamford PE9 219 C4
Albert St Boston PE21 208 D5
15 Bottesford NG13 128 A6
Brigg DN20 196 C3
Grantham NG31 211 C2
6 Holbeach PE12 215 D2
Horncastle LN9 199 C3
7 New Holland DN19 4 E2
Albert St *continued*
Spalding PE11 214 E5
Thorne/Moorends DN8 15 B8
Albert St E DN32 189 B1
Albert St W 6 DN32 189 B1
Albert Terr 2 PE21 208 E4
Albert Wlk 3 PE12 215 D2
Alberta Cres DN17 184 E3
Albertine Ct 4 DN37 194 C5
Albery Way DN36 195 C7
Albion Cl LN1 201 C6
Albion Cres LN1 201 C6
Albion Hill 8 DN9 27 E6
Albion Pl LN11 198 C5
Albion Rd 2 NG31 211 A5
Albion St
8 Crowland PE6 166 E1
Grimsby DN32 189 B1
Holbeach PE12 215 F2
10 Kingston upon Hull HU1 180 E7
Spalding PE11 214 E5
Albion Terr
4 Misterton DN10 40 A5
Sleaford NG34 212 E4
Albourne Ave 1 DN15 183 A2
Alconbury Cl
13 Birchwood LN6 204 C6
Peterborough PE2 231 E5
Alcorn Gn PE21 209 C4
Aldbro' St HU2 180 F8
Alden Cl DN40 186 C4
Alder Cl 3 Lincoln LN6 204 F3
Louth LN11 198 D4
Alder Gr PE21 209 C2
Alder Rd
Peterborough PE7 230 C3
Sleaford NG34 212 D2
Alder View DN33 190 F3
Aldergrove Cl 2 LN6 204 C7
Aldergrove Cres LN6 204 C7
Alderlands Cl 6 PE6 175 B8
Alderley Edge DN37 194 C4
Alderman's Dr PE3 225 E3
Alderney Way
Immingham DN40 186 C2
Lincoln LN6 205 A1
Alderson Mews 5 HU9 181 C7
Aldrich Rd DN35 192 F4
Aldsworth Cl 1 PE1 226 D6
Aldwych Croft 8 DN36 195 C6
Aldwych Ct HU5 179 E8
Aldwych Gdns 11 PE11 214 A2
Alec Rose Gr DN21 197 F3
Alexander Ave NG24 104 A6
Alexander Cl 15 LN4 95 D4
Alexander Dr LN11 198 D4
Alexander Rd
2 Scunthorpe DN16 183 C3
2 Scunthorpe DN16 183 B2
Alexandra Cl 8 NG23 117 D4
Alexandra Pk 22 LN12 64 B4
Alexandra Rd
Cleethorpes DN35 192 F6
Grantham NG31 210 F3
Grimsby DN31 188 F1
Louth LN11 198 C6
21 Mablethorpe/Sutton on Sea LN12 64 B4
Peterborough PE1 225 F6
Scunthorpe DN16 185 B6
Skegness PE25 206 B3
Sleaford NG34 212 C4
Spalding PE11 214 E3
3 Woodhall Spa LN10 97 C6
Alexandra Rd S DN40 186 E6
Alexandra Ret Pk
DN31 188 F1
Alexandra St HU3 180 D7
Alexandra Terr LN1 234 A3
Alexandra Terraces 4
PE10 213 D5
Alexandre Ave 2 LN6 204 F1
Alexandria Rd LN8 56 D5
Alfonso St 5 HU3 180 B5
Alford Mill Cl 6 LN6 93 B8
Alford Pottery* LN13 75 E3
Alford Prim Sch LN13 75 F2
Alford Rd 1 Alford LN13 75 F3
Bilsby LN13 76 A3
Huttoft LN13 76 E3
Mablethorpe/Sutton on Sea LN12 64 A3
Alford St NG31 211 B5
Alfred Ave LN4 95 C4
Alfred Cl 10 NG34 212 B2
Alfred Gelder St 6 HU1 180 F6
Alfred Smith Way 5
LN11 61 F3
Alfred St Boston PE21 209 A3
Gainsborough DN21 197 C5
2 Grimsby DN31 191 D8
Kingston upon Hull HU3 180 D5
Lincoln LN5 201 E1
Alfric Sq PE2 230 D6
Algernon St DN32 191 F5
Algitha Rd PE25 206 C3
Alkborough La DN15 8 D7
Alkborough Prim Sch
DN15 8 C8
All Saints Ave PE13 170 E1
All Saints CE Jun Sch
Kingston upon Hull HU13 178 F2
Peterborough PE1 226 A6
All Saints CE Prim Sch
LN6 204 E1
All Saints CE Sch Swinderby Prim School LN6 92 B6
All Saints' Cl 17 DN19 12 A8
All Saints Cl
3 Holbeach PE12 215 F3
7 Moulton PE12 157 F7
4 Wainfleet All Saints PE24 102 D1
All Saints Cty Prim Sch
LN5 93 F7
All Saints Gr 4 NG34 212 B6
All Saints La 14 LN2 68 C2
All Saints' Pl 6 PE9 219 B5
All Saints' Rd PE1 226 A5
All Saints' St
Kingston upon Hull HU3 180 D8
10 Stamford PE9 219 B5
Allan Ave PE2 231 E5
Allanby St DN15 183 A3
Allandale Cl LN1 201 D8
Allanhall Way HU10 178 B8
Allard Cl PE7 233 D6
Allen Cl
7 Billingborough NG34 133 B1
4 Claypole NG23 117 E8
5 Market Deeping PE6 217 D5
Allen Rd Coningsby LN4 207 F6
Fenton NG23 105 C1
Peterborough PE1 225 E6
Allenby Ave 1 DN34 191 A6
Allenby Cres LN11 49 A2
Allenby Ind Est LN2 202 D4
Allenby Rd LN2 202 D4
Allenby Way PE25 206 D8
Allenby's Chase 14 PE12 160 E4
Allen's Dro PE13 169 D1
Allerthorpe Cres 19 HU15 2 D5
Allerton Cl PE9 172 D3
Allerton Dr DN40 186 B4
Allerton Garth PE7 229 A4
Allerton Prim Sch
DN40 186 B4
Allestree Dr DN33 194 E7
Alliance Ave HU3 179 F7
Alliance La HU3 179 F7
Allington Dr DN37 188 A2
Allington Gdn PE21 209 A7
Allington La NG32 129 B4
Allington Rd NG32 128 F5
Allington with Sedgebrook CE Prim Sch NG32 129 A7
Allison Cl 3 DN17 29 D7
Allison Pl 5 LN1 201 D4
Allison Rd 6 NG34 122 D3
Allison St LN1 201 D4
Allotment La PE5 223 E2
Allwood Rd 20 LN2 68 D6
Alma Ave PE25 206 B5
Alma Cl
Kingston upon Hull HU10 178 D7
4 Skegness PE25 206 B5
Alma Martin Way 7 LN3 83 C4
Alma Pk Cl 1 NG31 211 F6
Alma Pk Ind Est
Grantham NG31 211 F7
Londonthorpe & Harrowby without NG31 130 C4
Alma Pk Rd NG31 211 F6
Alma Rd PE1 225 F5
Alma St 6 HU9 181 B7
Almond Ave
Heighington LN4 81 F4
Lincoln LN6 205 A8
Almond Cl Boston PE21 208 C5
9 Saxilby LN1 66 D2
Almond Cres
Lincoln LN6 205 A8
Louth LN11 198 D5
Waddington LN5 205 D1
Almond Ct LN6 205 A8
Almond Gr Brigg DN20 196 B4
Grantham NG31 211 C6
3 Kingston upon Hull HU3 180 D6
3 Scunthorpe DN16 185 B8
Skellingthorpe LN6 200 A4
Almond Rd PE1 226 B7
Almond Wlk
Boston PE21 208 D5
Sleaford NG34 212 D6
Almoners La PE3 225 E3
Alness Cl LN6 204 B8
Altham Terr LN5 205 D7
Althorpe & Keadby Prim Sch
DN17 17 D5
Althorpe Cl 15 PE6 217 A5
Althorpe Sta DN17 17 D5
Altoft Cl 19 DN37 23 F1
Altyre Way DN36 192 C1
Alverston Ave LN10 97 D5
Alveston Rd DN17 184 D8
Alvingham Ave DN35 192 F3
Alvingham Rd
Keddington LN11 198 E8
Scunthorpe DN16 185 B7
Alvis Cl LN4 205 F2
Alvis Dr PE7 233 D6
Alwyn Rd 10 DN8 15 B8
Amanda Dr Hatfield DN7 14 D4
Louth LN11 198 C8
Amber Hill Toftstead Prim Sch PE20 124 A5
Ambergate Specl Sch
NG31 210 D3
Amberley Cres PE21 208 C4
Amberley Slope PE4 221 A3
Amble Cl LN1 201 E8
Ambleside Cl 4 NG34 212 B2
Ambleside Dr PE11 214 B2
Ambleside Gdns PE4 221 B3
Ambrose Ave 3 DN7 14 E4
Ambury Gdns 9 PE6 166 F1
Amcott Ave DN10 40 A4
Amcotts Rd DN33 191 A2
Amesbury Ave DN33 194 D7
Amethyst Cl 3 NG34 212 A3
Amethyst Ct 2 DN36 195 D7
Amman Sq 1 NG34 120 D8
Amos Cl DN33 194 D7
Amos Cres 3 DN16 185 D7
Amos La NG23 91 E6
Amos Way 8 PE22 113 B1
Ampleforth Gr HU5 179 D8
Amstel Cl 1 PE11 214 B2
Amsterdam Gdns 9
PE11 214 B3
Amwell Gn 10 DN7 14 D3
Amy Johnson Sch
HU3 179 F5
Anastasia Cl DN21 197 C7
Ancaster Ave
Chapel St Leonard PE24 90 D7
Grimsby DN33 194 D8
Lincoln LN2 202 B5
Spilsby PE23 100 F8
Ancaster CE Prim Sch
NG32 120 A3
Ancaster Cl LN3 203 E6
Ancaster Ct DN16 185 A5
Ancaster Dr NG34 212 B2
Ancaster Rd
Bourne PE10 213 E5
17 Mablethorpe/Sutton on Sea LN12 64 B3
7 Stamford PE9 219 A7
Ancaster Sta NG32 120 A3
Ancaster Valley Nature Reserve* NG32 120 A2
Ancholme Ave DN40 186 A3
Ancholme Bsns Pk
DN20 196 A4
Ancholme Gdns 10
DN20 196 C3
Ancholme Leisure Ctr
DN20 196 A2
Ancholme Rd DN16 185 D6
Ancholme Way DN20 196 B3
Anchor La PE25 90 D4
Anchor Rd
Scunthorpe DN16 19 B4
Sutton Bridge PE34 161 C4
Anchor St LN5 234 A1
Anchorage St 4 DN20 196 B3
Anchors Way 7 DN20 196 A3
Ancient La DN7 14 E3
Anderby Cl LN6 204 F6
Anderby Dr
Grimsby DN37 190 D7
Lincoln LN6 204 F6
Anderby Drainage Mus*
PE24 77 C2
Anderby Rd PE24 77 D1
Anderson LN2 68 D5
Anderson Cl 7 PE13 170 C1
Anderson La 2 LN1 201 F6
Anderson Rd
2 Hemswell Cliff DN21 55 A8
Scunthorpe DN16 185 C7
Anderson St 1 DN31 191 D7
Anderson Way DN21 52 F5
Andover Cl LN6 204 B8
Andrea Cl PE2 231 C6
Andrew Ave 26 PE24 90 D7
Andrew Cl PE5 223 D2
Andrew Rd
9 Humberston DN36 36 D8
1 Stamford PE9 219 B6
Andrewe's Cl PE7 231 B1
Andrews Cl LN11 198 C7
Andrews Cres PE4 221 D2
Andrews Rd 1 DN18 10 A7
Andrews Way 7 DN40 186 A4
Angel Ct 5 NG32 120 A2
Angelica Dr PE11 214 B6
Angell La PE12 215 E1
Angerstein Rd DN17 184 F5
Anglesey Dr DN40 186 C2
Anglia Cl 13 NG34 212 B2
Anglian Cl PE2 231 D6
Anglian Way 5 LN8 57 E8
Angus Cl 3 PE9 218 D6
Angus Ct PE3 225 D3
Anlaby Acre Head Cty Prim Sch HU4 179 B7
Anlaby Ave 7 HU4 179 B6
Anlaby High Rd HU4 179 C6
Anlaby Jun Sch HU4 179 A6
Anlaby Pk Rd N HU4 179 B5
Anlaby Pk Rd S HU4 179 B2
Anlaby Rd HU3 179 F6
Anlafgate 7 HU10 178 F6
Ann Gr DN35 192 D4
Annandale Rd HU10 178 C8
Anne Rd Stamford PE9 219 A6
11 Sutton Bridge PE12 160 E4
Annes Cres DN16 185 C7
Annesley St 1 DN31 188 F1
Annette Cl 8 PE11 214 B5
Anningson La 6 DN36 195 D7
Annpasture La LN4 207 C8
Anson Cl LN6 200 A4
Anthony Cres LN11 198 C8
Anthony Way 3 DN41 23 D6
Anthony's Bank Rd
DN36 193 D1

Antrim Rd 9 LN5 205 D2
Antrim Way DN33 191 D2
Anvil Cl PE12 148 B1
Anvil Wlk 2 DN15 8 F3
Anzio Cres LN1 201 E7
Anzio Terr LN1 201 E7
Apeldoorn Gdns 3 PE11 214 B3
Apley Cl
 Gainsborough DN21 197 F3
 Lincoln LN2 202 A8
Appian Way 8 PE6 164 E5
Apple Garth LN5 205 D4
Apple Tree Cl 19 LN4 95 C4
Apple Tree Ct 14 DN41 23 F5
Appleby Cl DN17 184 F5
Appleby Gdns DN20 19 D4
Appleby La DN20 19 D4
Appleby Mill Rd DN16 183 E3
Appledore Cl HU9 181 C6
Applegarth Cl 2 DN35 192 D5
Applegarth Rd 2 HU8 181 A7
Appleton Gate NG24 104 A5
Appleton Way DN16 185 C6
Applewood Dr 5 NG31 210 F8
Appleyard PE2 231 C7
Appleyard Dr 38 DN18 10 E8
Apsley Way PE3 225 A2
Aqua Dr LN12 64 B2
Aquila Way PE6 164 E2
Arabis Cl 3 LN2 202 C8
Arakan Way 2 PE10 213 E7
Arbella Rd PE21 209 C4
Arboretum Ave LN2 234 C2
Arboretum The* LN2 234 C3
Arborfield Cl 5 PE6 173 C4
Arbury Cl PE3 225 A3
Arcadia Cres 2 PE25 206 D2
Arcadia Rd PE25 206 D3
Archer La 12 PE21 208 F5
Archer Rd Branston LN4 81 E2
 Waltham DN37 194 D4
Archer St
 3 Bishop Norton LN8 43 D3
 Lincoln LN5 234 B1
Archers Dro PE6 176 D6
Archers La PE20 136 C3
Archers Way NG33 140 A5
Archers Wood PE7 230 C3
Arcon Dr HU4 179 D6
Arcott Dr PE21 208 C5
Arden Cl 6 LN12 64 C3
Arden Moor Way 4 LN6 93 B8
Arden Village 5 DN35 192 F1
Ardent Rd DN18 4 A1
Argyle St Boston PE21 208 D5
 Kingston upon Hull HU3 180 C7
Argyll Way PE9 218 F5
Ariston St DN32 192 B7
Ark Rd LN11 50 F8
Ark Royal Ct 2 NG34 212 A3
Arkley Cl 22 HU15 2 C5
Arkwright St DN21 197 C5
Arkwright Way DN16 185 F6
Arlington Rd 4 LN8 56 D5
Arlington St 2 HU3 180 D6
Armeria Dr 4 DN17 185 A1
Armley Gr 3 PE9 219 D7
Armour Rd DN16 183 E3
Armstrong Pl E 3 DN31 188 E1
Armstrong Pl W 2 DN31 188 E1
Armstrong St DN31 188 E1
Armstrong's Cl 2 PE12 157 D7
Armstrong's La PE22 115 B7
Armthorpe La DN3 14 A3
Armtree Rd PE22 124 E7
Arne Cl 10 NG32 120 A3
Arnhem Ave 1 NG34 108 D2
Arnhem Dr
 10 Caythorpe NG32 119 B7
 2 Spalding PE11 214 C5
Arnhem Way
 Bourne PE10 213 E6
 7 Woodhall Spa LN10 97 D5
Arnold Ave NG31 210 E8
Arnold Cl DN37 23 F2
Arnold La HU3 180 B6
Arnold St HU3 180 B6
Arnold's Mdw Nature Reserve* PE12 214 F2
Arran Cl DN40 186 D2
Arran Rd PE9 218 D5
Arras Cl LN1 201 E6
Arthur Mellows Village Coll PE6 220 B8
Arthur Rd DN21 197 D6
Arthur St
 Grimsby DN31 191 C8
 Kingston upon Hull HU3 180 A5
 6 Lincoln LN5 201 F1
Arthur Taylor St 1 LN1 201 D3
Arthurs' Ave 5 PE12 215 D2
Artillery Row 13 PE21 209 A5
Artindale PE3 225 A3
Artis Ct PE3 225 A3
Arundel Cl
 Gainsborough DN21 197 E6
 Kingston upon Hull HU9 181 C8
Arundel Cres PE21 208 B4
Arundel Dr LN11 198 A7
Arundel Pl DN35 192 E5
Arundel Rd PE4 221 A1
Arundel St 3 HU9 181 C8
Ascendale PE6 217 F5
Ascot Cl 4 PE11 156 E3
Ascot Dr
 7 Grantham NG31 211 D7
Ascot Dr *continued*
 Peterborough PE1 226 B6
Ascot Rd 5 DN37 194 D4
Ascot Way 7 LN6 93 A8
Ascott Cl HU4 179 D5
Asgarby Rd NG34 122 B2
Asgard Way DN33 191 B2
Ash Ave 19 HU15 2 C6
Ash Cl
 Burgh Le Marsh PE24 102 D7
 5 Colsterworth NG33 151 E7
 Fulbeck NG32 106 C1
 Hessle HU13 178 C3
 Holbeach PE12 215 C3
 Langtoft PE6 164 E2
 Lincoln LN6 204 E8
 Louth LN11 198 C4
 Peterborough PE1 226 C7
 1 Thorney PE6 175 F3
Ash Ct
 Cleethorpes DN35 192 D2
 5 Donington PE11 134 E2
 Peterborough PE1 226 C7
 Spalding PE11 214 F6
Ash Dr
 Kingston upon Hull HU10 178 F8
 3 Kirton PE20 136 C5
Ash Gr Bourne PE10 213 C6
 Brigg DN20 196 B4
 Cherry Willingham/Reepham LN3 203 D5
 Gainsborough DN21 197 D6
 Grantham NG31 211 D7
 Lincoln LN6 204 F2
 32 Messingham DN17 29 D7
 Scunthorpe DN16 185 B7
Ash Hill Cres DN7 14 D4
Ash Hill Rd DN7 14 D4
Ash La 26 LN5 93 F6
Ash Pk PE4 220 F6
Ash Pl 6 PE9 218 D6
Ash Rd 7 Coningsby LN4 207 D4
 Peterborough PE1 226 C7
Ash Tree Ave 11 LN2 68 D2
Ash Tree Cl
 Immingham DN40 186 C5
 10 Market Rasen LN8 57 D7
Ash Tree Dr 5 DN9 27 D2
Ash Tree Rd 7 DN8 15 B7
Ashberry Dr
 31 Messingham DN17 29 D7
 4 Scunthorpe DN16 185 B6
Ashbourne 6 DN37 194 C4
Ashbourne Cl 3 NG34 212 B2
Ashbourne Ct DN15 182 B3
Ashburn Cl 1 PE6 220 D7
Ashburnham Rd 20 DN8 15 A8
Ashby Ave LN6 204 F7
Ashby Broadway DN16 185 A6
Ashby Cl Grimsby DN37 190 D8
 Holton le Clay DN36 195 E1
 Kingston upon Hull HU4 179 B7
Ashby Ct 2 NG34 212 D6
Ashby Gdns 7 PE12 157 F6
Ashby High St DN16 185 B6
Ashby Hill DN37 35 C3
Ashby La DN37 35 D4
Ashby Rd
 Cleethorpes DN35 192 D3
 Kingston upon Hull HU4 179 B4
 Scunthorpe DN16 183 A1
 Spilsby PE23 88 A1
Ashcroft Gdns PE1 226 C5
Ashcroft Rd DN21 197 D2
Ashdale Cl 3 LN4 95 C4
Ashdale Pk 18 HU14 3 A5
Ashdene Cl HU10 178 E7
Ashdown Ave 5 DN15 182 E3
Ashdown Cl 3 DN20 196 E3
Ashdown Way 15 DN10 39 F5
Asheridge LN4 81 E2
Ashfield 2 LN1 66 D7
Ashfield Ave 2 DN8 15 A7
Ashfield Ct 20 DN17 16 D7
Ashfield Gr 1 DN7 14 C6
Ashfield Grange 5 LN1 66 C2
Ashfield Rd
 8 Hatfield DN7 14 C4
 Sleaford NG34 212 D5
 Thorne DN8 14 F7
Ashfield St 3 LN2 202 B3
Ashfields PE6 217 D2
Ashing La LN2 68 F6
Ashlawn Dr PE21 209 B6
Ashlea 4 DN10 39 F5
Ashleigh PE2 229 C6
Ashleigh Ct 3 DN41 23 F5
Ashley Cl 1 LN12 64 C1
Ashley Dr NG31 210 E8
Ashley Pool La 5 PE6 176 A2
Ashley Rd 2 LN11 198 C5
Ashlin Gr LN1 234 A3
Ashridge Dr DN32 192 C5
Ashton Rd PE3 225 B5
Ashtree Ave DN34 191 A6
Ashtree Cl 1 Belton DN9 16 E2
 12 Ruskington NG34 108 E1
Ashtree Gdns 5 PE9 171 B1
Ashwell Ave 2 HU9 5 E8
Ashwin Gate 2 PE11 145 A8
Ashwood Cl 1 LN9 199 B4
Ashwood Dr 10 DN36 36 D8
Ashworth Cl LN6 204 F5
Askew Ave HU4 179 E4
Askew's Dro PE6 166 D2
Askew's La PE7 233 E4
Aslackby Rd NG34 142 D3
Aspen Cl LN1 65 D2
Aspen Ct
 Cleethorpes DN35 192 D2
 Gainsborough DN21 197 F6
Aspen Dr 4 NG34 212 D2
Aspen Gr DN16 185 B8
Aspen Wlk 10 HU15 2 D5
Asperton Rd PE20 135 E4
Asphodel Cl 3 DN36 195 D7
Asquith St DN21 197 B6
Aster Cl LN2 202 C8
Aster Dr PE4 221 B3
Asterby Cl LN2 202 A7
Asterby End LN11 72 E6
Asterby La LN11 72 E5
Asterby Rd DN17 184 F5
Astley Cres 15 DN21 29 C3
Astley St HU3 179 F7
Aston Cl 4 LN5 93 F7
Aston Gn 5 DN7 14 D3
Aston Hall Dr 12 HU14 3 A5
Aston Rd HU10 178 F8
Astore Pk PE1 226 E3
Astral Cl HU13 178 F3
Astral Rd HU13 178 F3
Astral Way 8 LN6 204 C1
Astwick Rd LN6 205 A5
Aswell St LN11 198 B5
Athelstan Cl 9 NG34 212 B2
Athenian Way 1 DN31 188 A3
Atherstone Ave PE3 225 B4
Atherton Way DN20 196 B4
Athol St HU3 179 F4
Atholl Ave HU13 178 E3
Atkinson Ave DN20 196 C5
Atkinson Dr 24 HU15 2 C6
Atkinson La 6 DN37 194 E4
Atkinson St PE1 226 C2
Atkinsons Way DN15 182 F7
Atlas Rd DN17 184 F8
Atterby Carr La DN21 43 F4
Atterby La LN8 43 C3
Atton Ave 4 PE11 157 B6
Atwater Cl LN2 202 D7
Atwater Ct 2 LN2 202 D7
Atwater Gr LN2 202 D7
Atwood Cl DN40 186 B5
Aubourn Ave LN2 201 F7
Aubretia Ave PE4 221 B3
Aubretia Dr 3 DN17 185 A1
Auckland Cres 1 LN4 96 C1
Auckland Rd
 Grimsby DN31 189 B2
 Scunthorpe DN15 182 F2
Auden Cl LN2 234 C4
Auden Ct 2 LN4 207 B5
Audern Rd DN16 185 A4
Audley Gate PE3 225 C3
Augusta Cl
 Grimsby DN34 191 C5
 Peterborough PE1 226 E6
Augusta Oaks 5 DN34 191 C6
Augusta St DN34 191 C6
Augustus Dr 17 HU15 2 C5
Aunsby Rd NG34 132 A7
Austen Wlk LN2 202 C6
Austendike Rd PE12 157 C4
Austerby PE10 213 E4
Austerby Cl PE10 213 D4
Austerby The PE10 213 E4
Austin Cres 3 DN17 184 F3
Austin Ct PE7 233 D6
Austin Friar's La 2 PE9 219 B4
Austin Garth 5 DN37 23 F1
Austin St PE9 219 B4
Autumn Pk Ind Est NG31 210 F4
Avebury Gdns PE11 214 F4
Aveland Cl
 Aslackby & Laughton NG34 142 E5
 5 Bourne PE10 213 C5
Aveland Dr NG34 143 B8
Aveland High Sch The NG34 143 B8
Aveland Way
 Aslackby & Laughton NG34 142 D5
 3 Baston PE6 164 E4
Avenswood La DN15 182 C6
Avenue A DN21 53 D5
Avenue B DN21 53 D5
Avenue Cannes DN15 182 D5
Avenue Clamart DN15 182 D5
Avenue Farm Rd PE12 160 D6
Avenue Fontenay 2 DN15 182 D5
Avenue Lourdes 1 DN15 182 D5
Avenue Nozay 2 DN20 19 E4
Avenue Rd NG31 211 B4
Avenue Rouen DN15 182 D6
Avenue The
 9 Blyton DN21 41 C5
 Burton upon Stather DN15 8 B4
 Carlby PE9 163 E4
 Deeping St Nicholas PE11 166 C7
 East Ravendale DN37 35 C2
 Friskney PE22 115 A6
 Gainsborough DN21 197 E6
 Grantham NG31 210 E4
 6 Great Gonerby NG31 129 D5
 Grimsby DN37 190 C8
 Healing DN41 23 F5
 7 Ingham LN1 54 F2
Avenue The *continued*
 Kingston upon Hull HU10 178 C7
 Lincoln LN1 234 A3
 Market Deeping PE6 217 B5
 Newark-on-Trent NG24 104 A4
 Nocton LN4 95 B7
 Swinderby LN6 92 C6
Avenue Vivian DN15 182 E4
Aviary Cl NG31 211 C5
Avignon Rd PE11 214 A5
Avocet Cl
 4 Birchwood LN6 204 D8
 4 Essendine PE9 163 D3
Avon Cl Grantham NG31 210 E3
 5 Lincoln LN6 205 A2
Avon Ct PE4 221 C2
Avon Rd DN16 183 C2
Avondale
 1 Kingston upon Hull HU4 179 B2
 7 Lincoln LN6 204 C1
Avondale St LN2 234 C2
Axholme Ave 3 DN17 16 C7
Axholme Dr 6 DN9 27 D6
Axholme Gn 19 DN8 15 B7
Axholme Line Nature Reserve* DN9 27 C4
Axholme Rd
 Scunthorpe DN15 182 D2
 2 Westwoodside DN9 27 A2
Axiom Ave PE3 225 C4
Ayam Cl 5 LN2 68 D6
Aydon Rd PE7 231 F6
Aykroft 1 PE10 213 E2
Aylesbury Gr HU5 179 D8
Aylesby Cl 7 LN1 201 E8
Aylesby Gdns 3 DN33 191 B3
Aylesby La DN37 23 F3
Aylesby Rd
 Aylesby DN37 190 B6
 Scunthorpe DN17 184 F5
Aylesford St 7 HU3 180 B5
Aylmer Ave PE24 103 D2
Aynsley Rd LN6 204 B6
Ayots Gn 14 DN7 14 D3
Ayr Cl PE9 218 E6
Ayres Dr PE2 231 C6
Ayscough Ave
 Spalding PE11 214 D3
 7 Stallingborough DN41 23 E6
Ayscough Gr 9 LN7 33 B4
Ayscough St 4 DN31 188 E1
Ayscoughfee Hall Mus & Gdns* PE11 214 D3
Ayscoughfee Hall Sch PE11 214 D3
Aysgarth Ave 18 DN17 29 D7
Azalea Cl PE3 225 A2
Azalea Rd LN2 202 C8

B

Bacheler St HU3 180 B5
Back Bank
 Crowland PE12 167 F3
 Whaplode PE12 168 A3
Back Field La DN7 14 E4
Back La
 5 Allington NG32 128 F7
 Aswarby & Swarby NG34 132 A7
 Barnby in the Willows NG24 105 A3
 Belvoir NG32 138 D6
 Bicker PE20 134 F6
 Bilsby LN13 76 A2
 Bolingbroke PE23 100 A7
 Buckminster NG33 151 A4
 Burton Coggles NG33 152 C8
 Cammeringham LN1 54 F1
 Candlesby with Gunby PE23 89 B1
 Caythorpe NG32 119 B7
 Claxby with Moorby PE22 99 B7
 Claypole NG23 117 E7
 Collyweston PE9 171 B1
 Colsterworth NG33 151 E7
 3 Deeping St James PE6 217 F4
 Dunston LN4 95 C6
 Eye PE6 175 A1
 3 Foston NG32 117 F1
 Garthorpe & Fockerby DN17 7 F6
 Heighington/Washingborough LN4 81 F4
 Holbeach PE12 215 D2
 Ingoldsby NG33 141 C5
 Leadenham LN5 106 C3
 Long Bennington NG23 128 D8
 Long Sutton PE12 216 D6
 4 Lutton PE12 160 A8
 Market Deeping PE6 174 A8
 North Cockerington LN11 50 A1
 1 Searby cum Owmby DN38 32 D8
 4 Skillington NG33 151 A8
 4 Stainforth DN7 14 C6
 9 Stamford PE9 219 C5
 Stickford PE22 100 A3
 Wainfleet All Saints PE24 102 A2
 Wilsford NG32 120 C2
 Winteringham DN15 2 B1
 Wood Enderby PE22 98 F6
 Yaxley PE7 233 E5
Back Rd Gorefield PE13 169 E2
Back Rd *continued*
 Murrow PE13 177 E6
Back St Alkborough DN15 8 C8
 Buckminster NG33 150 E5
 East Stockwith DN21 40 B5
 Saltfleetby LN11 51 C1
 South Clifton NG23 78 C5
 Sproxton LE14 138 F1
Backgate PE12 167 B8
Bacon St DN21 197 D2
Bacon's La 1 PE11 145 C1
Bad Gate PE12 169 B6
Bader Cl PE3 225 B6
Bader Way 3 PE25 206 A5
Badgate PE11 134 F2
Badger Cl PE7 233 F5
Badger Way 1 DN20 19 E4
Badger's La PE20 136 B7
Badgers Oak 2 LN5 92 F3
Badinton La PE9 172 F5
Badminton Way LN11 198 A7
Baffen's La PE11 145 A4
Baggholme Rd LN2 234 C2
Baghdad Rd 2 NG34 120 D8
Bagsby Rd DN9 28 B3
Baildon Cres LN6 205 A3
Baildon Rd DN15 182 D4
Bailey La DN7 14 E6
Baileys Cl PE12 215 D1
Baileys La LN5 92 F5
Bailgate 3 LN2 234 B3
Baily's La PE12 147 F2
Bain Cl PE9 219 C7
Bain Rd PE21 208 C3
Bain Rise 3 LN8 59 A7
Bain St LN1 201 D8
Baines Ave NG24 104 B2
Baines Rd DN21 197 F4
Bainton Rd
 Barnack PE9 172 D4
 Newborough PE6 221 D8
Baird Cl PE7 233 D6
Baker Cres LN6 204 E7
Baker Dr 30 DN15 9 A5
Baker St HU2 180 E7
Baker's La
 Candlesby with Gunby PE23 89 A2
 Fishtoft PE21 126 C4
 Great Steeping PE23 101 E6
 Westborough & Dry Doddington NG23 117 E3
Bakers Cl DN38 21 B5
Bakers La
 Bassingham LN5 92 E2
 Peterborough PE2 230 E7
Bakers Way PE10 154 D6
Bakersfield DN20 196 F7
Bakestraw Gate PE12 157 F5
Bakewell Mews 6 LN6 204 F2
Bakewell Rd PE2 229 C2
Bala Ct PE4 221 B3
Balder Ct 2 DN33 191 C2
Balderton La NG24 104 D3
Baldwin Ave DN16 185 B2
Baldwin Cl PE8 172 C1
Baldwin Gr PE10 213 D6
Balfour Pl 3 DN40 186 B4
Balfour St
 Gainsborough DN21 197 C5
 2 Kingston upon Hull HU9 181 C8
Balintore Rise PE2 229 D4
Balk Rd 8 PE9 163 C1
Ball's La PE12 159 A6
Balliol Dr DN16 185 B4
Balmoral Ave
 3 Grimsby DN34 191 A7
 Spalding PE11 214 D2
Balmoral Cl
 12 Mablethorpe/Sutton on Sea LN12 76 F8
 2 Wragby LN8 70 D4
Balmoral Dr NG31 210 E6
Balmoral Rd
 Cleethorpes DN35 192 C4
 4 Hatfield DN7 14 D4
 1 Peterborough PE4 225 C8
Balmoral Way PE12 159 A8
Bamber St PE1 225 F4
Bamford Ave 1 HU9 5 F8
Bamford Cl 6 LN6 204 E2
Banbury Cl PE11 214 D6
Banbury Rd DN16 183 D2
Bancroft Rd NG24 104 A3
Bangor Cl LN5 205 C3
Bank Dr
 Ingoldmells PE25 90 F3
 5 Wisbech PE13 170 C1
Bank End LN11 50 E8
Bank End Rd DN9 26 A3
Bank La 12 LN7 33 B4
Bank Prim Sch PE12 215 D7
Bank Side 1 PE21 136 D8
Bank St Boston PE21 208 F5
 Kingston upon Hull HU3 180 C7
 Lincoln LN2 234 B2
Bank The
 Parson Drove PE13 177 C7
 Swaton NG34 133 D4
Bank's Ave 4 PE11 214 F6
Banks La 4 NG34 122 E2
Banks Rd 6 LN9 199 C4
Banks St 5 LN9 199 C4
Bannister Dr HU9 181 C7

Bannister's La PE20 ...136 C7
Bannister's Row 6 PE13 ...170 C1
Banovallum Gdns LN9 ...199 D3
Banovallum Sch LN9 ...199 C2
Baptist Chapel La 4 DN40 ...12 F2
Baptist La 3 NG23 ...91 C4
Bar La 20 LN5 ...93 F7
Bar Rd DN10 ...52 B8
Bar Rd N 3 DN10 ...52 B8
Bar Rd S 7 DN10 ...52 B8
Barbara Cl 3 DN33 ...194 E7
Barbara Rd 6 PE25 ...206 D2
Barber Cl PE2 ...231 C7
Barberry Ct 3 HU3 ...180 C5
Barbers Dro PE6 ...175 C8
Barbers Hill PE4 ...220 F7
Barbican Way DN36 ...195 C6
Barcroft St DN35 ...189 E1
Bardling's Dro PE12 ...169 A7
Bardney PE2 ...230 A4
Bardney Ave DN16 ...185 A7
Bardney Cl LN6 ...204 F6
Bardney Gdns 1 DN34 ...190 F4
Bardney Joint CE/Methodist (Controlled) Sch LN3 ...83 C4
Bardney Rd
Branston & Mere LN4 ...82 C3
Wragby LN8 ...70 C4
Bardots Leisure Ctr LN5 ...205 C1
Barehams La PE11 ...145 A7
Barfen La LN13 ...63 B3
Barff La LN8 ...43 F2
Barff Rd LN4 ...82 B1
Barfields La LN3 ...68 F1
Barford Cl PE2 ...230 C7
Bargate Grimsby DN34 ...191 C5
12 Lincoln LN5 ...205 E8
Bargate Ave DN32 ...191 D5
Bargate Gr 3 HU5 ...179 D8
Bargate La 5 LN9 ...199 C3
Barge Cl 1 PE11 ...214 F5
Barge Rd PE12 ...148 A7
Barham Cl PE2 ...231 F5
Barholme Ave 7 PE12 ...160 A8
Bark St DN35 ...192 F5
Barkestone La NG13 ...128 A5
Barkham St 7 PE24 ...102 D2
Barkhouse Cl 4 DN35 ...192 F5
Barkhouse La 5 DN35 ...192 F5
Barkston & Syston CE (Aided) Prim Sch NG32 ...130 B8
Barkston Cl PE10 ...213 E6
Barkston Dr PE1 ...226 B6
Barkston Gdns LN2 ...202 B7
Barkston Rd NG32 ...118 D2
Barkwith Rd LN8 ...58 F1
Barkworth Cl HU10 ...178 D6
Barkworth Ct 3 DN37 ...194 C4
Barley Cl
Heckington NG34 ...122 D2
12 Hibaldstow DN20 ...31 A5
24 Metheringham LN4 ...95 C4
Barley Way LN9 ...199 A3
Barleycroft Rd NG33 ...152 E8
Barleyfield PE6 ...164 E2
Barlings Ave DN16 ...185 A7
Barlings Cl
1 Barlings LN3 ...69 C3
Scotter DN21 ...29 C4
Barlings La LN3 ...69 C2
Barmouth Dr DN37 ...190 E8
Barmston St HU2 ...180 F8
Barn Cl 2 Maxey PE6 ...173 C7
Peterborough PE4 ...220 F3
Barn Hill PE9 ...219 B5
Barn Owl Cl 1 PE6 ...164 F3
Barnack CE Prim Sch PE9 ...172 D4
Barnack Drift PE9 ...172 B3
Barnack Est 4 PE24 ...102 E7
Barnack Rd
Bainton PE9 ...172 E4
St Martin's without PE9 ...219 D4
Barnard Ave DN20 ...196 B3
Barnard Way 9 PE3 ...224 F3
Barnberry Way PE10 ...142 D2
Barnby Gate NG24 ...104 A4
Barnby La NG23 ...104 F1
Barnby Rd NG24 ...104 B3
Barnby Rd Prim Sch NG24 ...104 A4
Barnes Cl 1 NG34 ...212 C6
Barnes Cres DN15 ...182 E4
Barnes Dro PE10 ...154 F4
Barnes Gn DN21 ...29 C4
Barnes La LN5 ...106 F7
Barnes Rd
9 Donington PE11 ...134 E2
Skegness PE25 ...206 A5
Barnes Way PE4 ...220 F3
Barnet Dr DN36 ...195 E7
Barnet Gn 12 DN7 ...14 D3
Barnetby La DN20 ...20 F7
Barnetby Rd
1 Kingston upon Hull HU13 ...179 A3
Scunthorpe DN17 ...184 F5
Barnetby Sta DN38 ...21 B4
Barnett Pl DN35 ...192 B7
Barneyfield Rd PE22 ...126 E1
Barnfield Rd 22 NG23 ...91 D5
Barnoldby Rd DN37 ...194 C4
Barnside 6 DN20 ...30 F5
Barnstaple Rd 3 DN17 ...184 D8
Barnstock PE3 ...225 A7
Barnston Way 12 DN15 ...8 B4
Barnswallace Ct 15 LN2 ...68 D7
Barnwell Rd 3 PE9 ...218 E6
Barnwell Terr 2 NG31 ...210 F3
Baron Ave DN36 ...195 D7
Baron Ct PE4 ...221 B4
Baroness Rd DN34 ...190 F6
Barracks The PE13 ...169 E2
Barraclough's La 1 DN18 ...3 E1
Barr's La PE12 ...168 B4
Barratt's Cl LN2 ...234 C4
Barrett Gr 7 LN2 ...68 E6
Barrett's Cl PE12 ...215 D3
Barrick Cl 16 DN19 ...11 D8
Barrier Bank
Cowbit PE12 ...156 F2
Spalding PE12 ...214 C1
Barrington Cl 8 PE12 ...215 D2
Barrington Gate PE12 ...215 E1
Barrow Haven Sta DN19 ...4 C2
Barrow La HU13 ...178 D2
Barrow Rd
Barton-upon-Humber DN18 ...11 A8
New Holland DN19 ...4 E1
Barrowby CE (Controlled) Prim Sch NG32 ...129 B3
Barrowby Gate NG31 ...210 D4
Barrowby Rd 8 NG31 ...211 A5
Barrowden Rd PE9 ...171 A2
Barrowfield PE1 ...226 E7
Barrows Gate LN11 ...50 D6
Barry Ave DN34 ...190 F3
Barry Wlk 3 PE2 ...230 F7
Bars La Benington PE22 ...126 E5
Bicker PE20 ...135 A5
Bartholemew Cl 1 LN3 ...83 C4
Bartol Cres PE21 ...208 D5
Barton Dr HU13 ...178 D1
Barton Gate LN11 ...198 D4
Barton La
Barrow upon Humber DN19 ...11 C8
Tydd St Mary PE13 ...169 F8
Barton Outdoor Pursuits Ctr* DN18 ...3 D2
Barton Rd
5 Wainfleet All Saints PE24 ...102 D1
Wrawby DN20 ...196 F6
Barton St Aylesby DN37 ...23 D2
Barrow upon Humber DN19 ...11 C8
Fotherby LN11 ...49 A2
Irby DN37 ...34 F7
Keelby DN41 ...23 A4
Ludborough DN36 ...48 C6
Barton St Peters CE Prim Sch DN18 ...3 F1
Barton-on-Humber Sta DN18 ...3 F1
Bartons La PE23 ...101 F6
Bartram Gate 2 PE4 ...221 C1
Bartrams 3 HU15 ...2 D6
Basic Slag Rd DN16 ...183 E2
Basil Gn PE2 ...230 D6
Baslow Rd DN15 ...182 B2
Bassett Cl 2 DN20 ...19 E3
Bassett Rd DN35 ...193 A4
Bassingham Cres LN2 ...201 F7
Bassingham Cty Prim Sch LN5 ...92 F2
Bassingham La PE23 ...88 E3
Bassingham Rd LN5 ...92 F5
Baston CE Prim Sch PE6 ...164 E5
Baston Edge Dro PE10 ...164 E7
Baston Fen Nature Reserve* PE6 ...165 A8
Baston Outgang Rd PE6 ...165 A6
Bateman's Cl 3 PE12 ...159 D7
Batemans Ct 2 PE24 ...102 E2
Bath Gdns PE21 ...208 F3
Bath La 15 PE11 ...214 D4
Bath Rd
Bracebridge Heath LN4 ...81 A2
Wisbech PE13 ...170 D1
Bath Row PE9 ...219 B4
Bath St
8 Grantham NG31 ...211 A4
Grimsby DN32 ...189 C1
Bathurst PE2 ...230 A4
Bathurst St
8 Kingston upon Hull HU3 ...180 D5
Lincoln LN2 ...202 D3
Battery St DN40 ...186 D4
Battle Gn DN9 ...27 D7
Battle of Britain Meml Flight Visitor Ctr* LN4 ...207 B3
Battlefields La N PE12 ...159 A8
Battlefields La S PE12 ...215 F3
Baulkin's Dro PE12 ...159 C1
Baumber Prim Sch LN9 ...72 A1
Bawtry Cl LN6 ...204 C8
Bawtry Rd DN7 ...14 F3
Baxter Cl
Coningsby LN4 ...207 D3
15 Wisbech PE13 ...170 E1
Baxter Gdns PE11 ...214 C7
Bayard St DN21 ...197 C5
Bayes Rd 6 PE25 ...103 E4
Bayfield Rd 4 LN4 ...96 B1
Bayons Ave DN33 ...194 D8
Baysdale Gr NG31 ...211 B8
Baysdale Rd DN16 ...185 D5
Baysgarth House Mus* DN18 ...10 F8
Baysgarth Leisure Ctr DN18 ...10 F8
Baysgarth Sch DN18 ...10 F8
Baysgarth View DN18 ...10 F7
Bayswater Pl 1 DN33 ...194 D8
Bayswood Ave PE21 ...208 F1
Baytree Ave DN34 ...191 A6
Baytree Owl Ctr* PE12 ...157 D7
Baywood Cl 4 LN6 ...200 C1
Beach Bank
Pinchbeck PE11 ...144 E3
Surfleet PE11 ...145 A3
Beach Holt La DN37 ...23 D2
Beach La PE11 ...144 F3
Beachcomber Holiday Ctr DN36 ...193 C1
Beachside 10 LN12 ...77 A8
Beacon Ave
16 Barton-upon-Humber DN18 ...10 E8
Cleethorpes DN35 ...192 D6
Beacon Ct DN35 ...192 D6
Beacon Hill La PE34 ...161 E3
Beacon Hill Rd
Gringley on the Hill DN10 ...39 D1
Newark-on-Trent NG24 ...104 B4
Beacon La NG31 ...211 C4
Beacon Pk Cl 4 PE25 ...206 A6
Beacon Pk Dr PE25 ...206 A6
Beacon Rd 7 NG34 ...107 C1
Beacon View 2 NG13 ...128 A6
Beacon Way PE25 ...206 A6
Beaconsfield Dr 3 NG24 ...104 C5
Beaconthorpe Rd 4 DN35 ...192 E7
Beagle Cl 16 DN20 ...19 E4
Beagle La NG34 ...107 C1
Bean St HU3 ...180 C6
Bear La 14 PE11 ...145 C1
Beatrice Rd 11 PE13 ...170 D2
Beatrice Way 27 PE24 ...90 D7
Beatty Ave DN33 ...194 F7
Beauchamp St 3 DN16 ...183 B1
Beauchief Gdns DN16 ...185 A8
Beaufort Ave 1 PE6 ...217 C5
Beaufort Cl
Kingston upon Hull HU3 ...180 D6
Lincoln LN2 ...202 D8
Beaufort Cres DN35 ...192 D2
Beaufort Dr
Bourne PE10 ...213 C7
4 Spalding PE11 ...214 C3
Beaufort Rd LN2 ...202 D8
Beaufort St DN21 ...197 B7
Beaulah Villas 9 DN18 ...10 A7
Beaulahland 8 DN18 ...10 A7
Beaulieu Ct 6 PE6 ...175 A1
Beaumonde 5 DN36 ...195 C2
Beaumont Cl 11 PE24 ...102 E7
Beaumont Ct 3 HU9 ...181 D7
Beaumont Dr 2 NG31 ...210 F8
Beaumont Fee LN1 ...234 A2
Beaumont St DN21 ...197 D4
Beauvale Gdns PE4 ...221 C3
Beauvoir Pl PE7 ...233 E5
Beaver Cl 1 LN6 ...200 A5
Beccelm Dr 9 PE6 ...175 B8
Beck Bank
Gosberton PE11 ...144 C3
Kirton PE20 ...124 E1
Beck Cl 5 Binbrook LN8 ...47 C5
13 Keelby DN41 ...23 A4
1 Ruskington NG34 ...108 D2
Beck Hill
6 Barton-upon-Humber DN18 ...10 F8
Tealby LN8 ...46 C1
Beck La Appleby DN15 ...9 D1
Aubourn Haddington & South Hykeham LN6 ...93 B7
10 Barrow upon Humber DN19 ...11 D8
7 Broughton DN20 ...19 E3
Fulbeck NG32 ...106 C1
Heighington/Washingborough LN4 ...81 F4
Ingoldmells PE25 ...90 E2
Redbourne DN21 ...30 F2
Scunthorpe DN16 ...185 B3
Welton Le Marsh PE23 ...89 A3
6 Welton/Dunholme LN2 ...68 E6
Beck Side 5 DN20 ...30 F5
Beck St Digby LN4 ...108 E5
Welbourn LN5 ...106 E4
Beck Way 5 PE10 ...164 C8
Beck Wlk 2 DN35 ...192 E1
Becke Cl LN3 ...203 E5
Becket Cl LN4 ...203 D1
Beckett Ave DN21 ...197 E6
Beckett Cl
9 Heckington NG34 ...122 D3
2 Skegness PE25 ...206 C1
Beckett Dr PE11 ...214 C6
Beckett Specl Sch DN21 ...53 A8
Beckhall LN2 ...68 D6
Beckhole Cl HU3 ...180 A6
Beckhythe Cl DN33 ...191 E1
Beckingham PE2 ...229 F3
Beckingham Rd
Coddington NG24 ...104 C5
Walkeringham DN10 ...40 A2
Beckingthorpe Dr 19 NG13 ...128 A6
Becks La DN21 ...29 A3
Becks The 4 LN9 ...199 C4
Beckside 11 Brough HU15 ...2 D6
Rothwell LN7 ...33 F2
Scopwick LN4 ...108 C8
Beckside Cl DN36 ...192 E1
Bedale Rd 3 DN16 ...185 D5
Bede Cl NG34 ...212 B2
Bede Cres PE22 ...126 F5
Bede Pl PE1 ...226 A6
Bede Rd 3 PE6 ...164 E5
Bedehouse Bank PE10 ...213 E4
Bedford Cl NG31 ...211 F5
Bedford Ct 16 PE6 ...176 A3
Bedford Pl 1 PE11 ...214 D3
Bedford Rd
Humberston DN35 ...193 A1
Kingston upon Hull HU13 ...178 F3
Bedford Row PE13 ...170 D8
Bedford St
Grimsby DN32 ...189 C1
2 Lincoln LN1 ...201 D4
Peterborough PE1 ...226 B4
Bee's La PE13 ...169 F6
Beech Ave
Bourne PE10 ...213 B5
Gainsborough DN21 ...197 D6
Grimsby DN33 ...191 C3
5 Gunness DN15 ...17 E6
Kingston upon Hull HU10 ...178 D8
24 Nettleham LN2 ...68 C2
Peterborough PE1 ...225 F3
Scunthorpe DN15 ...182 B6
Spalding PE11 ...214 F5
Beech Cl
5 Broughton DN20 ...19 D3
2 Colsterworth NG33 ...151 E7
4 Coningsby LN4 ...207 D4
Dunholme LN2 ...68 E5
3 Gringley on the Hill DN10 ...39 C1
7 Heckington NG34 ...122 D3
Kingston upon Hull HU3 ...180 C5
Market Deeping PE6 ...217 B6
RAF Cranwell NG34 ...107 D1
9 Sudbrooke LN2 ...68 F2
4 Thorney PE6 ...176 A3
Beech Cres 1 DN7 ...14 D6
Beech Dr
16 Bottesford NG13 ...128 A5
6 North Ferriby HU14 ...3 A4
15 Ryhall PE9 ...163 C1
Welton HU14 ...2 F5
Beech Garth 9 DN19 ...11 C7
Beech Gr
Anlaby with Anlaby Common HU13 ...178 C3
3 Burton-upon-Stather DN15 ...8 B5
Donington PE11 ...134 E2
Holton Le Clay DN36 ...195 E1
Louth LN11 ...198 C7
4 Scopwick Heath LN4 ...108 A7
Stamford PE9 ...218 D6
4 Swanland HU14 ...3 C7
Beech Hill Rd HU14 ...3 C7
Beech La 12 PE6 ...175 A1
Beech Lawn HU10 ...178 E6
Beech Rd Branston LN4 ...81 D2
6 Brough HU15 ...2 C6
Glinton PE6 ...220 B8
Beech Rise
Sleaford NG34 ...212 D6
2 South Rauceby NG34 ...120 E4
Beech St LN5 ...205 D5
Beech Tree Ave 17 DN8 ...15 B7
Beech Way DN35 ...192 D2
Beechams Mews 5 PE11 ...214 B3
Beechcroft Cl 6 LN6 ...93 A8
Beechcroft Rd NG31 ...210 C3
Beeches Ave DN16 ...185 B4
Beeches La PE22 ...112 C5
Beeches Prim Sch The PE1 ...225 F3
Beeches The 1 LN1 ...66 C7
Beechfield Rd 7 DN7 ...14 C4
Beechings Way 10 LN13 ...75 E2
Beechings Way Ind Est LN13 ...75 E2
Beechtree Cl 8 NG34 ...108 E1
Beechway DN16 ...185 B7
Beechwood Ave
Grimsby DN33 ...190 F3
Immingham DN40 ...186 C4
Beechwood Cl
16 Kirk Sandall DN3 ...14 A1
Peterborough PE1 ...226 C7
6 Wisbech PE13 ...170 D1
Beechwood Cres 4 DN20 ...19 E4
Beechwood Dr
12 Scawby DN20 ...30 F8
7 Scotter DN21 ...29 C3
Beechwood Rd 5 PE13 ...170 D1
Beeden Pk Est NG31 ...210 C4
Beehive La LN6 ...79 C1
Beel's Rd DN41 ...187 B2
Beeley Rd DN32 ...192 C6
Beelsby Rd LN7 ...34 C5
Bees Cnr 1 PE24 ...102 D2
Beesby Dr 3 DN35 ...192 F3
Beesby Rd
Maltby Le Marsh LN13 ...76 A7
Scunthorpe DN17 ...184 E5
Beesby Wlk LN13 ...76 A6
Beeson St DN31 ...188 E1
Beeston Dr PE7 ...231 F5
Beetons Cl PE7 ...233 E5
Beevor St LN6 ...201 C2
Beggar Hill Messingham Rd DN21 ...29 D4
Beggar's La PE22 ...98 F3
Begger's Bush La PE12 ...157 D7
Beilby St HU3 ...179 F4
Belcanto Ct 3 PE11 ...214 A5
Belchmire La PE11 ...145 B5
Belfry The 5 NG31 ...211 D7
Belgrave Cl 11 DN9 ...16 E1
Belgrave Dr HU4 ...179 D5
Belgrave Rd
1 Grimsby DN33 ...191 B2
7 Spalding PE11 ...214 C2
Belgrave Sq 1 DN15 ...183 B3
Belgravia Cl LN6 ...200 E1
Belham Rd PE1 ...225 E7
Belisana Rd 5 PE11 ...214 A5
Bell Cl NG31 ...210 E7
Bell Ct 5 PE21 ...208 F1
Bell Dro PE6 ...175 F6
Bell Gr LN6 ...205 C6
Bell La
4 Collingham NG23 ...91 C4
Fosdyke PE20 ...146 D8
Market Deeping PE6 ...217 E4
Moulton PE12 ...157 F7
Scunthorpe DN15 ...183 A2
Bell Wr Drain Bank
Eastville PE22 ...101 B1
New Leake PE22 ...100 E1
Bellamy Ct HU9 ...181 C7
Bellamy's La PE14 ...170 D4
Bell's Dro PE12 ...159 C1
Bell's Pl PE1 ...226 A2
Bellbutts View DN21 ...29 B3
Belle Vue PE2 ...231 C6
Belle Vue Rd LN1 ...234 A3
Belle Vue Terr
Lincoln LN1 ...234 A3
21 Thorne/Moorends DN8 ...15 A8
Belleisle Rd DN34 ...190 D4
Bellfield Cl 4 PE11 ...214 B3
Bellflower Cl 2 LN2 ...202 C8
Bellingham Rd DN16 ...185 D7
Bellingham's Dro PE11 ...166 F7
Bellview Rd 6 NG34 ...108 E1
Bellwin Dr DN15 ...8 A1
Bellwood Cres 5 DN8 ...15 A8
Bellwood Grange 1 LN3 ...203 E7
Belmesthorpe La PE9 ...163 D1
Belmont DN36 ...195 C1
Belmont Cl DN35 ...192 D3
Belmont Gr 2 NG31 ...211 D6
Belmont Prim Sch NG31 ...211 E6
Belmont St
Kingston upon Hull HU9 ...181 D8
Lincoln LN2 ...202 B3
Scunthorpe DN16 ...185 A6
Belnie La PE11 ...145 D5
Belsay Dr PE2 ...231 F5
Belshaw La DN9 ...16 D1
Belsize Ave PE2 ...230 E6
Belt Rd The DN21 ...197 F7
Belthorn Rd 2 DN17 ...7 F1
Belton All Saints CE Prim Sch DN9 ...16 E2
Belton Ave
Grantham NG31 ...211 C6
Lincoln LN6 ...204 F6
Belton Cl Boston PE21 ...209 B5
13 Market Deeping PE6 ...217 A5
Belton Fields 1 DN9 ...16 D1
Belton Gr
Grantham NG31 ...211 B7
1 Grimsby DN33 ...191 A3
Belton House (NT)* NG32 ...130 B6
Belton La
Grantham NG31 ...211 C6
Great Gonerby NG31 ...129 E5
Belton La Prim Sch NG31 ...211 D7
Belton Pk* NG32 ...211 F8
Belton Pk Dr 7 LN6 ...93 C8
Belton Rd Belton DN9 ...17 A1
Epworth DN9 ...27 E7
Peterborough PE7 ...231 F5
Sandtoft DN9 ...16 B3
Belton St 16 PE9 ...219 C5
Belvedere Cl PE11 ...214 B2
Belvedere Dr DN17 ...184 E7
Belvedere Rd HU13 ...178 F2
Belvoir Ave
12 Bottesford NG13 ...128 A5
Grantham NG31 ...210 F1
Spitalgate NG31 ...211 E2
Belvoir Castle* NG32 ...138 B8
Belvoir Cl
4 Colsterworth NG33 ...151 E6
1 Market Deeping PE6 ...217 A5
1 Stamford PE9 ...218 E6
Belvoir Ct LN11 ...198 B8
Belvoir Gdns NG31 ...129 D5
Belvoir High Sch NG13 ...128 A5

Belvoir La NG32 ....128 D1
Belvoir Rd
- Bottesford NG13 ....128 A4
- Cleethorpes DN35 ....192 D2
- Croxton Kerrial NG32 ......138 A6

Belvoir St HU5 ....180 C8
Belvoir Way Eye PE1 ....226 D8
- Louth LN11 ....198 B8
- Peterborough PE1 ....226 C8

Belwood Dr 7 DN9 ......16 E2
Bempton Gr
- 4 Grimsby DN32 ....192 A5
- Kingston upon Hull HU5 ...179 D8

Bemrose Way 7 DN31 ..191 C8
Benams Cl PE5 ....223 E2
Ben's Gate PE12 ....159 B5
Benbow Way LN1 ......201 C6
Benderslough Dro
PE12 ....159 C3
Bendike La PE11 ....145 D4
Benedict Cl 2 HU4 .....179 A2
Benedict Rd HU4 ....179 A2
Benedict Sq PE4 ....220 E2
Benington Rd PE22 .....126 E3
Benjamin Adlard Com Sch
DN21 ....197 E2
Benland PE3 ....225 A6
Benner Rd PE11 ....214 E8
Benner Rd Ind Est
PE11 ....214 E8
Bennett Dr 28 DN15 ....9 A5
Bennett Rd
- Cleethorpes DN35 ....192 D7
- Scunthorpe DN16 ....185 C7

Bennington Cl
- 8 Lincoln LN6 ....205 A7
- 11 Long Bennington NG23 .117 D3

Bennington La NG23 ...117 E4
Benson Cl LN6 ....204 C6
Benson Cres LN6 ....204 C6
Benson Ct LN11 ....48 F4
Bentinck Cl 6 PE11 .....214 C6
Bentinck Sq 2 LN2 .....202 B3
Bentinck St 4 LN2 .....202 B3
Bentley Ave PE7 ....233 E6
Bentley Ct HU3 ....180 A5
Bentley Dr LN4 ....205 F3
Bentley La 6 DN38 ......32 E7
Bentley St
- Cleethorpes DN35 ....192 E6
- 6 Stamford PE9 ....219 C6

Bentley Way 1 LN4 ......95 C4
Benyon Gr PE2 ....230 B4
Berberis Cl 2 PE6 ......175 F3
Berea The 4 DN34 ......191 C5
Beresford Ave PE25 .....206 C2
Beresford Cl 4 PE25 ....206 C2
Beresford Cres 5 PE25 .206 C2
Beresford Dr 5 LN2 ......68 F3
Beretun Gn 7 DN18 ......10 E8
Berilldon Dr LN1 ....201 C7
Berkeley Ave LN6 ......205 A3
Berkeley Dr
- 4 Bourne PE10 ....213 C7
- Lincoln LN6 ....205 A3

Berkeley Ind Est DN15 ..182 C4
Berkeley Inf Sch
DN15 ....182 D4
Berkeley Jun Sch
DN15 ....182 D3
Berkeley Rd
- Humberston DN35 ....193 A2
- Peterborough PE3 ....225 C3

Berkeley St
- 1 Kingston upon Hull HU3 .....180 D8
- Scunthorpe DN15 ....183 A4

Berkshire Dr NG31 .....211 D7
Bermondsey Dr HU5 ....179 E8
Bernadette Ave HU4 ....179 B5
Bernard St LN2 ....202 B4
Berners Rd DN35 ....193 B1
Bernicia Dr NG34 ....212 B2
Berry Cl 6 NG34 ....212 D2
Berry Way 5 PE25 ......206 C3
Berrybut Way 5 PE9 ....219 D7
Berryfield End 7 NG32 .210 A5
Berryman Way HU13 ...179 A3
Bert Allen Dr 1 PE22 ...114 A1
Bertie Cl
- Long Sutton PE12 ....216 C3
- Swinstead NG33 ....153 A5

Bertie La 8 PE9 ....172 C6
Berwick Ct DN40 ....186 C4
Besant Cl 10 PE22 ......113 B1
Bessemer Way DN15 ...183 B6
Bestall Rd DN32 ....192 C6
Besthorpe Cty Prim Sch
NG23 ....91 C7
Besthorpe Rd
- Besthorpe NG23 ....91 C6
- North Scarle NG23 ....78 D1

Beswick Cl 5 LN6 ......204 D7
Bethlehem St DN32 .....191 D7
Bethlem Cres 9 PE24 ...102 D1
Bethune Ave HU4 ....179 A3
Bethune Ave W HU13 ...179 A3
Bethune Pk Prim Sch
HU4 ....179 B3
Betjeman Cl PE10 ......213 D3
Betony Cl 5 DN15 ......182 C6
Bettesworth Rd DN21 ....54 F8
Bettles Cl PE1 ....226 A6
Betula Gr 3 LN6 ....204 D7
Betula Way 1 DN17 .....184 C5
Beverley Cl 7 DN36 .....195 D1
Beverley Cres DN32 ....192 A5
Beverley Ct 12 DN41 .....23 F5
Beverley Dr 5 NG24 ....104 C5
Beverley Gdns 4 PE9 ...219 A6
Beverley Gr
- Lincoln LN6 ....204 F3
- 7 Skegness PE25 ....206 B3

Beverley Rd HU3 ....180 D8
Beverstone PE2 ....229 D5
Bew Cl PE2 ....231 D4
Bewholme Gr 3 HU9 ......5 D8
Bicker Dro PE20 ....134 D6
Bicker Rd PE11 ....134 F3
Bidwell La LE15 ....162 B6
Biergate LN11 ....49 F7
Bifield PE2 ....229 F3
Bigby Gr DN17 ....184 F4
Bigby High Rd DN20 ....196 D2
Bigby Hill DN38 ....21 C1
Bigby Rd 7 DN20 ....196 C3
Bigby St DN20 ....196 C3
Billet La DN15 ....182 F8
Billet Mill App Rd
DN16 ....19 A4
Billet Mill Rd DN16 .....183 E1
Billgate La PE24 ....102 E7
Billingborough Dro
NG34 ....143 E8
Billingborough Prim Sch
NG34 ....133 B1
Billingborough Rd
- Billingborough NG34 .....133 B1
- Folkingham NG34 ....132 E1

Billinghay CE Prim Sch
LN4 ....109 F6
Billinghay Ct DN35 .....192 F3
Billinghay Dales Head
LN4 ....110 B4
Billings Gate LN11 ....50 E5
Bilsby Cl LN2 ....202 A7
Bilsby Rd 2 LN13 ....75 F3
Bilsdale Gr HU9 ....181 F8
Bilsdale Rd DN16 ....185 E5
Binbrook (Controlled) Prim
Sch LN8 ....47 B5
Binbrook Cl 8 LN6 ......204 D7
Binbrook La LN8 ....47 B2
Binbrook Way DN37 .....190 E8
Birch Ave Brigg DN20 ....196 B4
- Grimsby DN34 ....191 A6

Birch Cl
- 11 Coningsby LN4 ....207 D4
- Kingston upon Hull HU5 ..179 B7
- 1 Lincoln LN6 ....204 F2
- Wyberton PE21 ....136 E7

Birch Gr
- Gainsborough DN21 ......197 D6
- Spalding PE11 ....214 F3

Birch La 4 LN9 ....85 E7
Birch Leigh HU3 ....180 C6
Birch Rd Louth LN11 .....198 E5
- 6 Stamford PE9 ....218 D7

Birch Tree Cl 4 DN3 .....14 A4
Birch Way DN38 ....21 C5
Bircham Cres DN21 ....30 C1
Birchdale 31 DN18 ....10 E8
Birchen Cl PE7 ....230 C3
Birches The 8 DN9 ....27 A2
Birchfield Rd 8 DN9 ......27 D6
Birchin Way DN31 ....188 D1
Birchtree Ave PE1 ......226 A7
Birchwood PE2 ....230 A3
Birchwood Ave
- Birchwood LN6 ....200 D1
- Kingston upon Hull HU5 ..179 A7

Birchwood Cl 4 NG31 ...210 F7
Birchwood Jun Sch
LN6 ....204 C8
Birchwood Rd
- Scunthorpe DN16 ....185 A4
- 1 Sleaford NG34 ....212 D6

Bird's Dro
- Gorefield PE13 ....169 D1
- Sutton St James PE12 ....169 B8

Birdcroft La DN10 ....40 A3
Birds Dro PE11 ....145 C4
Birds Holt Cl LN6 ....200 A3
Birds Wood Nature Reserve*
DN9 ....26 F4
Birkbeck Sch The LN11 ..50 E7
Birkdale Lincoln LN5 .....205 D1
- 9 Waltham DN37 ....194 C4

Birkdale Ave 1 PE4 .....221 A3
Birkdale Cl
- 3 Grantham NG31 ....211 D7
- Heighington/Washingborough LN4 ....203 E1
- Kingston upon Hull HU10 ....178 B8
- 1 Skegness PE25 ....206 D6
- 8 Spalding PE11 ....214 C2
- 8 Woodhall Spa LN10 .....97 C5

Birkdale Dr 3 DN40 .....186 D5
Birkdale Rd DN17 ....184 D3
Birkdale Way HU9 ....181 D8
Birketts La LN11 ....49 D5
Birkland La NG23 ....78 D5
Birkwood PE22 ....98 E2
Birkwood La PE22 ....98 E3
Birmingham Cl 5 NG31 .210 E5
Birrel St DN21 ....197 B6
Birthorpe Rd NG34 ......143 A8
Biscay Cl 1 PE25 ....206 A6
Bishop Alexander Prim Sch
NG24 ....104 A6
Bishop Blunt Cl 2
HU13 ....178 F1
Bishop Creighton CP Sch
PE1 ....226 B2
Bishop Gurdon Cl 4
HU13 ....178 F1
Bishop Kempthorne Clo 3
HU13 ....178 F1
Bishop King CE (Aided) Prim
Sch LN5 ....201 F1
Bishop King Ct 7 LN5 ...201 F1
Bishop La HU1 ....181 A6
Bishop Norton Rd LN8 ...43 E1
Bishop Temple Ct
HU13 ....178 F3
Bishopdale Cl NG31 .....129 F5
Bishop's La LN8 ....47 D7
Bishop's Pl 5 LN2 ....68 C6
Bishop's Rd PE1 ....226 A1
Bishop's Wlk 1 DN34 ...191 C6
Bishops Cl
- 6 Bourne PE10 ....213 E4
- Louth LN11 ....198 E6
- Peterborough PE1 ....226 D5

Bishops Ct 3 NG34 ......212 D5
Bishop's Pal The*
LN2 ....234 B3
Bishops Rd
- Leasingham NG34 ....121 B7
- Lincoln LN2 ....202 C5

Bishops Wlk 5 PE9 .....172 D3
Bishopthorpe Rd
DN35 ....192 F3
Bittern Cl HU4 ....179 D2
Bittern Way 3 LN6 ......204 D8
Black Bank DN17 ....29 A6
Black Bear La PE13 .....170 F1
Black Dike PE13 ....169 E6
Black Dro Anwick LN4 ...109 D2
- Baston PE6 ....165 B8
- Ewerby & Evedon NG34 ...122 E8
- Midville PE22 ....100 D2
- Thorney PE6 ....175 F5
- Wisbech St Mary PE13 ....177 B4

Black Dyke PE13 ....169 F4
Black Fen La LN4 ....82 C4
Black Hole Dro PE11 ....155 F8
Black Horse Dr 8 LN6 ....93 A8
Black La
- Doddington & Whisby LN6 ...79 E3
- Gorefield PE13 ....169 C2

Black Prince Ave PE6 ...217 B6
Black Swan Spinney
PE8 ....222 A4
Blackbourn Cl 20 NG23 ...91 D5
Blackbourn Rd LN6 .....205 C6
Blackburn Ave HU15 ......2 C5
Blackburn Cl 2 NG31 ...210 D5
Blackburn La DN22 ....52 D3
Blackdown Garth PE4 ...221 B3
Blackdykes Rd DN9 ....28 B4
Blackey La PE22 ....99 B4
Blackfriargate HU1 .....181 A5
Blackfriars St 15 PE9 ...219 C5
Blackhill La LN9 ....73 F1
Blackjack Rd PE20 ......135 C6
Blackmead PE2 ....230 B4
Blackmoor Rd
- Aubourn Haddington & South Hykeham LN5 ....93 C5
- Haxey DN9 ....27 D2

Black's Cl 17 LN5 ....93 F7
Blacksmith Hill DN15 ......1 E3
Blacksmith La
- Boothby Graffoe LN5 ......94 A2
- East Keal PE23 ....100 D6
- 2 Harmston LN5 ....93 F5
- Thorpe on the Hill LN6 ....92 E8

Blacksmith Rd 4 LN3 .....82 A7
Blacksmith Row 1 LN5 ...92 F3
Blacksmith's Cnr 5
LN4 ....207 A5
Blacksmith's La
- 13 Navenby/Wellingore LN5 ....107 A7
- Norton Disney LN6 ....92 B2

Blacksmith's Row
PE11 ....156 B7
Blacksmiths Cl 2 DN19 ...11 C7
Blacksmiths Ct 10 LN4 ...95 C4
Blacksmiths La
- North Scarle LN6 ....78 E1
- Welby NG32 ....130 F5

Blackthorn 5 PE9 ....218 C7
Blackthorn Cl
- 1 Lincoln LN2 ....202 C8
- 3 Market Deeping PE6 ...217 D6
- 13 Ruskington NG34 ......108 E1
- Scunthorpe DN15 ....182 C6

Blackthorn Ct 4 HU3 ....180 D6
Blackthorn La
- Boston PE21 ....209 C5
- Cammeringham LN1 ....54 E1
- Kingston upon Hull HU10 ....178 F7

Blackthorn Way PE10 ...213 E5
Blackthorns The 4
DN20 ....19 D4
Blackwell Rd PE7 ....230 C2
Bladon Est PE21 ....209 F4
Bladons Wlk HU10 ....178 D8
Blaides Staithe 1 HU1 ..181 A6
Blake Ave DN17 ....184 E7
Blake Cl 2 HU2 ....180 E7
Blakeney Lea 2 DN35 ...192 F1
Blanchard Cl PE10 ......142 F2
Blanchard Rd LN11 ......198 E3
Blandford Gdns 1 PE1 ..226 E7
Blands Hill LN8 ....47 D5
Blanket Row HU1 ....180 F5
Blankney Cl 4 LN1 ....66 D2
Blankney Cres LN2 ......201 F8
Blankney Ct 13 DN15 ......9 A5
Blankney Dro LN10 ....96 E5
Blankney N Dro LN4 ......96 B5
Blashfield Cl 2 PE9 .....219 A6
Blatherwick Rd NG24 ...104 B4
Blaydon Gr 2 DN34 .....190 E4
Blazegate PE12 ....216 B8
Bledwick Dro PE13 ......170 C3
Blenheim Cl
- 17 Hatfield DN7 ....14 D3
- Louth LN11 ....198 B7
- Skellingthorpe LN6 ....79 F6

Blenheim Ct DN16 ......185 A2
Blenheim Pl DN35 ......192 E4
Blenheim Rd
- Coningsby LN4 ....207 C4
- Lincoln LN1 ....201 D4
- Moorland Prison DN7 ......26 A8

Blenheim St HU5 ....180 B8
Blenheim Way
- Londonthorpe & Harrowby without NG31 ...211 D3
- Market Deeping PE6 ......217 B7
- Yaxley PE7 ....233 E5

Blenkin St HU9 ....181 B7
Blind La Coleby LN5 ......93 F3
- Hough-on-the-Hill NG32 ...118 E7
- 4 Maxey PE6 ....173 C7
- 22 Waddington LN5 ....93 F7

Bloom La DN15 ....8 C1
Bloomfield Ave HU5 .....179 C8
Bloomsbury Ct 1 HU3 ...180 D6
Blossom Way 1 DN40 ...186 B3
Blow Row DN9 ....27 E6
Blow's La PE20 ....135 F3
Bloxholm La
- Blankney LN4 ....95 A2
- Bracebridge Heath LN4 .....81 B1
- Nocton LN4 ....94 D6

Blue Gowt Dro PE11 ....214 A7
Blue Gowt La PE11 ......214 B7
Blue St 7 PE21 ....208 E4
Bluebell Ave PE1 ....226 A8
Bluebell Cl
- 7 Lincoln LN5 ....205 C2
- Scunthorpe DN15 ....183 C3

Bluebell Rd 2 PE9 ....218 D7
Bluebells 8 PE6 ....217 D6
Blueberry Ct HU4 ......179 C4
Bluecoat Prim Sch
PE9 ....219 B6
Bluegate NG31 ....211 A5
Bluestone Heath Rd
- Scamblesby LN11 ....73 A7
- Skendleby PE23 ....88 D5
- South Ormsby cum Ketsby LN11 ....74 B3
- South Thoresby LN13 ......75 A1
- Tetford LN11 ....73 F3
- Ulceby with Fordington LN13 ....88 B8
- Welton Le Wold LN11 ......60 A4

Bluestone La DN40 ......186 B4
Bluestone Rise LN11 ....198 B4
Bluestone Way 24 LN12 ...77 A7
Blundell Ave DN35 ......189 E1
Blyth Ct 28 DN18 ....10 F8
Blyth St 2 HU9 ....181 B7
Blyton CE (Aided) Prim Sch
DN21 ....41 C6
Blyton Cl 11 LN6 ....204 C7
Blyton Gr 13 LN6 ....204 C7
Blyton Rd
- 12 Birchwood LN6 ....204 C7
- Laughton DN21 ....41 B8
- Thonock DN21 ....197 C8

Boardsides
- Frampton PE20 ....124 F2
- Wyberton PE21 ....208 A3

Boating Dyke Way 19
DN8 ....15 A8
Boatswain Croft 7 HU1 .180 F5
Bodiam Way DN32 ......191 F8
Bodmin Cl DN17 ....184 D8
Bodmin Moor Cl LN6 ...204 D1
Boggle La LN8 ....45 E5
Bolingbroke Castle (remains
of)* PE23 ....100 A7
Bolingbroke Rd
- Cleethorpes DN35 ....193 A3
- Louth LN11 ....198 B8
- Scunthorpe DN17 ....184 E4

Bolsover Rd DN15 ....182 B2
Bolton Ave LN6 ....205 A3
Bolton's La PE25 ....90 D2
Bomber Cty Aviation Mus*
DN21 ....42 F1
Bon Accord Rd HU13 ...178 E1
Bona La PE13 ....169 E1
Bonby Gr
- 2 Grimsby DN33 ....191 A3
- Scunthorpe DN17 ....184 F5

Bonby Rd DN20 ....10 C1
Bond Hays La 3 PE23 ....87 A4
Bond St 1 Boston PE21 ..208 F4
- Kingston upon Hull HU1 ...180 F7

Bonemill La NG34 ....121 E6
Bonnetable Rd LN9 ......199 D3
Bonnyhale Rd DN17 ......16 E6
Bonthorpe Rd LN13 ......89 B7
Boongate PE1 ....226 C3
Boonground La PE22 ....115 A3
Boot La PE20 ....136 E3
Booth Nooking La DN15 ...2 A2
Bootham Cl 6 DN7 ....14 D4
Bootham Cres 12 DN7 ....14 C6
Bootham La DN7 ....14 D5
Bootham Rd 11 DN7 ......14 C6
Boothferry Pk (Hull City AFC)
HU4 ....179 E5
Boothferry Rd HU13 ....178 B2
Borman's La 7 DN36 .....36 B1
Borrowdale Cl PE4 .....221 C3
Borrowdale Way
NG31 ....211 B8
Borthwick Pl PE2 ....229 D6
Bos App Rd DN16 ....185 F7
Boscombe Cl 12 LN6 ....204 C6
Boston Aerodrome
PE21 ....125 B2
Boston Coll PE21 ....209 A4
Boston Gram Sch
PE21 ....209 A4
Boston Hawthorn Tree Sch
Cty Prim School
PE21 ....209 D4
Boston High Sch for Girls
PE21 ....209 B7
Boston Ind Ctr PE21 ....208 F6
Boston Long Hedges
PE22 ....126 C6
Boston Pk Com Prim Sch
PE21 ....208 E7
Boston Rd
- Algarkirk PE20 ....136 A3
- Frithville PE22 ....125 E7
- Gosberton PE11 ....145 C6
- Heckington NG34 ....122 E2
- Holbeach PE12 ....215 C4
- Horncastle LN9 ....199 C1
- Sleaford NG34 ....212 D4
- 14 Spilsby PE23 ....88 A1
- Spilsby PE23 ....100 F8
- Swineshead PE20 ....124 D1
- Wainfleet St Mary PE24 ...102 D1

Boston Rd N PE12 ......215 C5
Boston Rd Pits Nature
Reserve* PE11 ....145 C6
Boston Rd S PE12 ....215 D3
Boston Sta PE21 ....208 E5
Boston Stump (St Botolph's
Ch)* PE21 ....208 F5
Boston W Prim Sch
PE21 ....208 B5
Boswell Cl PE1 ....225 E8
Boswell Dr LN6 ....205 A5
Bosworth Cl 18 DN7 ......14 D3
Botany Bay La DN3 ......14 B4
Bothwell Gr 3 HU9 ....5 E8
Botolph Gn PE2 ....230 C7
Botolph St 7 PE21 ....209 A5
Botolph's View 1 LN11 ...51 C4
Botteford Jun & Inf Schools
DN16 ....185 A2
Bottesford Ave DN16 ....185 B5
Bottesford Cl 12 LN6 ...204 D8
Bottesford La DN16 .....185 B4
Bottesford Rd
- Allington NG32 ....128 E6
- Scunthorpe DN16 ....185 B5

Bottesford Sports Ctr
DN17 ....184 C3
Bottesford Sta NG13 ....128 B6
Bottle La PE13 ....169 C7
Bottlings The 9 DN20 ...196 C3
Bottom St NG32 ....128 F7
Boughton Ave DN15 .....182 F4
Boulevard HU3 ....180 B5
Boulevard Ave DN31 ....188 E1
Boulevard Ret Pk PE1 ..225 D7
Boultham Ave LN5 ....201 D1
Boultham Pk Rd LN6 ....201 D1
Boundaries The PE12 ...215 D1
Boundary La LN6 ....93 A8
Boundary Paddock 1
LN5 ....107 A7
Boundary Pastures
NG34 ....212 D3
Boundary Rd DN33 ......194 E6
Boundary St LN5 ....205 D7
Bourges Bvd PE1 ....225 D7
Bourgess Ret Pk PE3 ...225 F1
Bourne Abbey Prim Sch
PE10 ....213 E5
Bourne Cl LN6 ....205 B5
Bourne Dro PE10 ....155 A5
Bourne Gram Sch
PE10 ....213 D4
Bourne Heritage Ctr*
PE10 ....213 D4
Bourne La 7 NG34 ....108 D2
Bourne Outdoor Swimming
Pool PE10 ....213 D4
Bourne Rd 20 Alford LN13 .75 F2
- Baston PE6 ....164 E3
- Bourne PE10 ....213 E2
- Colsterworth NG33 ....151 E6
- Essendine PE9 ....163 E3
- Folkingham NG34 ....142 D8
- Morton PE10 ....154 C6
- Old Somerby NG33 ....140 D8
- Pinchbeck PE11 ....155 F5
- Spalding PE11 ....214 A3
- Swinstead NG33 ....153 A5
- Thurlby PE10 ....164 D8

Bourne Rd Est 6 NG33 ..151 E6
Bourne Westfield Prim Sch
PE10 ....213 B5
Bow Gate PE11 ....145 B6
Bow Rd HU15 ....2 E6
Bowbridge Gdns 4
NG13 ....128 A6

Bowbridge La
10 Bottesford NG13 ......128 A6
Hawton NG24 ......104 A1
Bowbridge Rd NG24 ....104 A2
Bowden Dr LN6 ......205 A5
Bowditch Rd PE11 ......214 E3
Bower Cl PE1 ......226 C5
Bowers Ave
Grimsby DN31 ......191 B7
3 Louth LN11 ......198 D7
Bowfield Cl DN37 ......190 D8
Bowl Alley La LN9 ......199 C4
Bowlalley La 9 HU1 ....180 F6
Bowling Gn La
11 Crowle DN17 ......16 D8
Grantham NG31 ......211 B3
8 Grimsby DN32 ......191 E7
Bowling Gn Rd DN21 ......197 B5
Bowling La DN35 ......192 E6
Bowman Ave PE22 ......115 A6
Bowman Cl PE21 ......208 D6
Bowman Way 7 DN40 ....186 B3
Bowmandale 30 DN18 ....10 E8
Bowmandale Prim Sch
DN18 ......10 E8
Bowmans Ridge 1 PE23 ..87 F1
Bowmans Way NG32 ....128 F4
Bowness Way 1 PE4 ...221 D2
Boxer Rd PE8 ......172 B1
Boxgrove Cl 8 PE6 ......175 A1
Boyfields 1 PE11 ......145 A8
Boynton Cres 9 DN15 ......9 A5
Boynton St 1 HU3 ......180 C4
Bozeat Way PE3 ......225 C6
Brabbs Ave 4 DN7 ......14 E4
Bracebridge Inf Sch
LN5 ......205 E6
Braceby Rd NG33 ......131 B1
Bracken Cl
Gainsborough DN21 ......197 B7
Leasingham NG34 ......121 C7
Bracken Heen Cl 2 DN7 ..14 E4
Bracken La PE24 ......90 A7
Bracken Pk DN33 ......194 E8
Bracken Pl DN37 ......190 C6
Bracken Rd LN6 ......92 B7
Bracken Way LN11 ......198 C7
Brackenborough Rd
Brackenborough with
Little Grimsby LN11 ......49 C1
Keddington LN11 ......61 C8
Louth LN11 ......198 C8
Brackenburry Way
PE21 ......208 E8
Brackenbury Fields
NG33 ......140 F6
Brackenhill Rd DN9 ......27 E2
Brackenholmes Rd
DN15 ......9 A2
Brackley Cl
Bourne PE10 ......213 D7
Peterborough PE3 ......225 D3
Brackwood PE2 ......229 D6
Bracon Cl 9 DN9 ......16 E2
Bradbury Ave LN5 ......205 C2
Bradden St PE3 ......225 C6
Bradegate Dr PE1 ......226 E7
Bradford Ave DN35 ......193 A5
Bradford Cl 10 NG31 ......210 D5
Bradford Rd
Boston PE21 ......208 D3
Immingham DN40 ......186 B4
Brading Ave NG31 ......210 E4
Bradley Cl LN11 ......198 D3
Bradley La LE15 ......162 B7
Bradley Rd
Bradley DN37 ......194 B6
Grimsby DN37 ......190 E2
Bradley St 8 DN32 ......191 F7
Bradman Ct 6 DN32 ......189 C1
Bradshaw's La PE24 ......90 C7
Bradway 9 LN1 ......66 D7
Bradwell Cl 19 DN18 ......10 E8
Bradwell Rd PE3 ......225 A2
Brady St 1 PE21 ......208 E6
Braemar Cl
Grantham NG31 ......211 C7
1 Middle Rasen LN8 ......57 B8
Stamford PE9 ......218 E6
Braemar Rd
Cleethorpes DN35 ......192 E4
3 Mablethorpe/Sutton on Sea
LN12 ......76 F8
Braemer Rd NG23 ......91 D4
Braeton La DN33 ......195 A7
Braids Wlk HU10 ......178 B8
Brailsford Cl 3 PE3 ......225 A4
Braithwaite La DN7 ......14 A8
Bramar Rd 5 DN7 ......14 D4
Bramble Cl 4 LN2 ......68 D7
Bramble Ct 24 LN2 ......68 D2
Bramble Gr 2 PE9 ......218 D6
Bramble Grange 3
PE11 ......214 B5
Bramble Hills PE25 ......103 E3
Bramble Way
1 Brigg DN20 ......196 B4
Humberston DN36 ......192 E1
Brambleberry La PE24 ..102 B7
Brambles The
3 Barrow upon Humber
DN19 ......11 C8
Bourne PE10 ......213 D7
Holbeach PE12 ......215 F2
4 Market Deeping PE6 ...217 D6
Brambles The *continued*
Newton on Trent LN1 ......65 D1
Bramblewood Cl 6
NG31 ......210 F8
Brambling Wlk PE10 ...143 A3
Bramhall St DN35 ......192 C7
Bramley Cl
5 Bourne PE10 ......213 C6
8 Fleet PE12 ......159 C7
2 Heckington NG34 ......122 E2
4 Louth LN11 ......198 C5
Bramley Cres DN16 ......185 A3
Bramley Ct
Gainsborough DN21 ......197 F5
Lincoln LN6 ......204 F4
Bramley Gr 1 DN21 ......29 C3
Bramley La 6 PE21 ......208 E4
Bramley Rd
Market Deeping PE6 ......217 B5
11 Wisbech PE13 ......170 D1
Bramley Wlk PE25 ......206 C6
Brampton Ct PE2 ......231 D6
Brampton Way DN35 ...192 D3
Bramwith La DN7 ......14 A6
Brancaster Dr
Lincoln LN6 ......205 C8
Skegness PE25 ......206 D5
Brancepeth Pl PE2 ......230 E7
Branches La PE12 ......159 A7
Brand End Rd PE22 ......126 E4
Brandesburton St
HU3 ......180 B7
Brandon Rd
Hough-on-the-Hill NG32 ...118 E6
Scunthorpe DN15 ......182 D2
Stubton NG23 ......118 C7
Brandy Wharf Cider Ctr*
DN21 ......44 A7
Brankwell Cres DN17 ....184 E3
Bransby Home of Rest for
Horses* LN1 ......66 D6
Bransdale Gr HU9 ......181 F8
Bransdale Rd 5 DN16 ...185 D5
Branston CE (Controlled) Inf
Sch LN4 ......81 D2
Branston Cl
Lincoln LN6 ......205 B4
4 Winthorpe NG24 ......104 B7
Branston Com Coll LN4 ..81 E3
Branston Cswy LN3 ......82 F3
Branston Cty Jun Sch
LN4 ......81 E2
Branston La LN4 ......94 D7
Branston Rd LN4 ......81 E3
Brant Broughton CE
Methodist Prim Sch
LN5 ......105 F5
Brant Rd Fulbeck NG32 ...105 F1
Lincoln LN5 ......205 D2
Scunthorpe DN15 ......182 E2
Waddington LN5 ......93 D7
Brantingham Rd HU15 ....2 B7
Brassey Cl PE1 ......225 E6
Bratoft Cnr PE24 ......102 D7
Bratoft End PE24 ......102 C5
Brats La LN8 ......47 E5
Bratt Field Rd DN21 ......53 F8
Brattleby Cres LN2 ......201 F7
Brauncewell Cl 18
NG34 ......108 D2
Brauncewell Rd 6
NG34 ......107 C1
Bray Ave 5 LN12 ......64 C2
Braybrook PE2 ......230 A3
Braybrook CP Sch
PE2 ......230 B4
Braybrooks Way PE12 ....157 E1
Brayfields 3 PE11 ......156 F8
Brayford St LN5 ......234 A2
Brayford Waterfront
LN1 ......234 A2
Brayford Way 1 LN1 ....234 A2
Brayford Wharf E LN5 ..234 A1
Brayford Wharf N LN1 ..234 A2
Braygate La PE23 ......100 E5
Brazenose La PE9 ......219 C5
Brazil St HU9 ......181 C8
Breakneck La LN11 ......198 A5
Brecks La
Kirk Sandall DN3 ......14 A2
Stapleford LN6 ......105 C8
Brecon Cl NG31 ......210 D8
Brecon Way NG34 ......212 B3
Breda Ct 8 PE11 ......214 A2
Breedon Dr LN1 ......201 D7
Breezemount Ct 2 DN7 ..14 C6
Brellows Hill 7 PE34 ....161 F3
Bremerhaven Way
DN33 ......190 F3
Brendon Cl NG31 ......210 D8
Brendon Garth 4 PE4 ...221 C1
Brendon Wlk 5 PE11 ....214 C6
Brent Rd LN4 ......110 E8
Brentwood Cl HU15 ......2 B6
Brereton Ave DN35 ......192 C8
Brethergate DN9 ......27 B2
Bretton Cl 4 DN7 ......14 D3
Bretton Gate 2 PE3 ......225 A5
Bretton Gn 1 PE3 ......225 A5
Bretton Way
Bretton PE3 ......225 A7
3 Peterborough PE3 ......220 F1
Peterborough PE3 ......224 F2
Bretton Woods Com Sch
PE3 ......225 A6
Brewerne PE2 ......230 B4
Brewers La PE13 ......170 A5
Brewery Gdns 2 DN17 ....16 D8
Brewery Hill NG31 ......211 B3
Brewery La NG34 ......143 B8
Brewery Rd DN17 ......16 D8
Brewery St 6 PE24 ......102 E8
Brewster Ave
Immingham DN40 ......186 D3
Peterborough PE2 ......230 F8
Brewster Ave Inf Sch
PE2 ......230 F8
Brewster La PE24 ......102 C2
Brewster Rd PE21 ......209 B4
Breydon Ct 3 DN15 ......8 B4
Brian Ave
Cleethorpes DN35 ......192 D3
Scunthorpe DN16 ......185 C5
7 Skegness PE25 ......206 C4
Waltham DN37 ......194 D4
Briar Cl
6 Birchwood LN6 ......200 C1
5 Lincoln LN6 ......93 A8
Skegness PE25 ......206 C3
2 Sleaford NG34 ......212 D2
4 South Killingholme DN40 .12 E3
Briar La Grimsby DN33 ...194 D8
Healing DN41 ......23 F5
Briar Way
Peterborough PE1 ......226 C5
Scunthorpe DN15 ......182 C6
Skegness PE25 ......206 C2
Briar Wlk PE10 ......213 D7
Briars La 6 DN7 ......14 C7
Briars The HU13 ......178 E3
Briarwood Cl 6 NG31 ...210 F7
Brick La
North Killingholme DN40 ....12 E5
Wrangle PE22 ......114 C1
Brickberry Cl PE7 ......230 C2
Bricken Field La LN9 ......84 C8
Brickenhole La 7 DN10 ....39 F3
Brickings Way 4 DN22 ...52 B3
Brickwork Annexe (Grantham
College) NG31 ......211 C5
Brickyard La
Folkingham NG34 ......142 D8
Hundleby PE23 ......87 E1
Mablethorpe & Sutton
LN12 ......76 E8
Melton HU14 ......2 F4
Navenby LN5 ......94 A1
Theddlethorpe St Helen
LN12 ......63 F7
Walkeringham DN10 ......39 E3
Wrawby DN20 ......196 D6
Bridge Cl
Kingston upon Hull HU9 ...181 D6
3 Louth LN11 ......198 C6
Bridge Dro PE13 ......177 B7
Bridge End
Colsterworth NG33 ......151 D7
Wansford PE8 ......222 A3
Bridge End Cswy
NG34 ......133 F3
Bridge End Gr NG31 ......211 D2
Bridge End Rd NG31 ......211 C2
Bridge Gdns 1 DN31 ......188 D1
Bridge La Cadney DN20 ....31 C6
Horkstow DN18 ......9 F5
Scopwick LN4 ......108 D8
Bridge Pl 22 LN1 ......66 D2
Bridge Rd
Aubourn Haddington &
South Hykeham LN5 ......92 F5
Gainsborough DN21 ......197 D3
Greetham with Somersby
LN9 ......86 F7
Long Sutton PE12 ......216 D3
6 Sutton Bridge PE12 ......160 F4
4 Sutton Bridge PE12 ......160 F4
Sutton Bridge PE12 ......160 C5
Bridge St
3 Billinghay LN4 ......109 F5
2 Boston PE21 ......208 F4
Brigg DN20 ......196 A3
Gainsborough DN21 ......197 C3
Grantham NG31 ......211 C3
Horncastle LN9 ......199 B4
Louth LN11 ......198 B6
Market Deeping PE6 ......217 D4
Marston NG32 ......118 D2
19 Nettleham LN2 ......68 C2
2 Peterborough PE1 ......226 A1
4 Ryhall PE9 ......163 C1
Saxilby LN1 ......66 D2
27 Thorne/Moorends DN8 ..15 A8
Bridge St N 3 DN32 ......189 B1
Bridge View LN8 ......56 F8
Bridgegate Dr HU9 ......181 C6
Bridgehill Rd PE6 ......221 D6
Bridges Rd DN17 ......184 E7
Bridges The 24 DN18 ......10 F8
Bridgeview Sch HU13 ....178 D1
Bridgewater Rd DN17 ....184 D8
Bridle Cl Fishtoft PE21 ...209 C3
7 Sleaford NG34 ......212 D2
Bridle La LN5 ......105 E8
Bridle Way 7 LN8 ......70 D5
Bridle Way The LN4 ......95 B7
Bridles The 11 DN19 ......12 A8
Bridlington Ave HU2 ....180 F8
Brierholme Carr Rd
DN7 ......14 F5
Brierholme Cl DN7 ......14 F5
Brierholme Ings Rd
DN7 ......14 F5
Brigg Cl 6 LN6 ......204 C6
Brigg Dr HU13 ......178 F3
Brigg Gr 5 LN6 ......204 C6
Brigg La LN5 ......105 F8
Brigg Prep Sch DN20 ...196 C3
Brigg Prim Sch DN20 ...196 C4
Brigg Rd
Barton-upon-Humber
DN18 ......10 E5
Broughton DN20 ......19 E3
Cadney DN20 ......31 D7
Grasby LN7 ......33 A6
Hibaldstow DN20 ......30 F6
North Kelsey LN7 ......32 A5
Scawby DN20 ......30 F8
Scunthorpe DN16 ......183 D2
South Kelsey LN7 ......32 A1
Wrawby DN20 ......196 F5
Brigg Sta DN20 ......196 C2
Briggate Dr 19 DN17 ....29 D7
Brighowgate DN32 ......191 D6
Bright St
2 Gainsborough DN21 ...197 C4
Kingston upon Hull HU8 ...181 B8
Peterborough PE1 ......225 F3
Brighton St
2 Cleethorpes DN35 ......193 A5
Kingston upon Hull HU3 ...180 A3
Brigsley Rd DN37 ......194 D2
Brigstock Ct PE3 ......225 C6
Brigstock Rd PE13 ......170 C1
Brimbles Way PE2 ......229 E5
Bringhurst PE2 ......230 A4
Brinkhall Way 9 LN2 ....68 D7
Brinkhill Pottery*
LN11 ......87 D8
Brinkle Spring La LN4 ...82 A4
Brisbane Cl
5 Skegness PE25 ......206 A4
12 Waddington LN5 ......93 E8
Brisbane St HU3 ......180 D5
Bristol Ave PE4 ......220 F3
Bristol Cl NG31 ......210 E4
Bristol Dr LN6 ......205 C8
Bristol House Rd
NG34 ......107 C1
Bristol Rd
Kingston upon Hull HU5 ...179 C8
1 Scunthorpe DN17 ......182 C1
Scunthorpe DN17 ......184 C8
Bristol Way NG34 ......212 B5
Bristow Rd 3 NG34 ......120 E8
Bristows Yd NG32 ......118 D2
Britannia Cres DN34 ......190 D5
Britannia Gdns 3 PE11 ..214 C5
Britannia Terr 4 DN21 ..197 D3
Brittain Dr NG31 ......211 C5
Britton Cl DN17 ......7 D3
Brixham Ct
Grimsby DN33 ......194 E6
5 Kingston upon Hull
HU3 ......180 A5
Broach Rd LN5 ......106 B5
Broad Cl PE1 ......226 D5
Broad Dale Cl 4 LN2 ......68 F3
Broad Dro PE11 ......144 B5
Broad Dro E PE13 ......169 E6
Broad Dro W PE13 ......169 B4
Broad Fen La NG23 ......104 D1
Broad Gate
Sutton St James PE12 ....169 A8
Weston PE12 ......157 C1
Wrangle PE22 ......114 C3
Broad La Bicker PE20 ....135 B4
Moulton PE12 ......157 F6
South Leverton DN22 ......65 A7
Sutterton PE20 ......135 F1
Whaplode PE12 ......146 F1
Broad St
5 Grantham NG31 ......211 A5
Spalding PE11 ......214 D4
Stamford PE9 ......219 B5
Broad Wheel Rd PE6 ...173 B3
Broadacre Pk 2 HU15 ....2 D5
Broadbank LN11 ......198 B6
Broadbeck 2 DN21 ......43 D7
Broadbent Theatre*
LN3 ......69 E8
Broadfield La 8 PE21 ...208 E4
Broadfield St PE21 ......208 E4
Broadgate
Gedney PE12 ......159 D6
Lincoln LN2 ......234 B2
Whaplode PE12 ......168 A3
Broadgate Dro PE12 ....167 C8
Broadgate La PE6 ......217 F4
Broadgate Rd
South Witham NG33 ......151 E2
Sutton St Edmund PE12 ....168 F3
Broadholme Rd LN1 ......66 D1
Broadhurst Rd 18 PE8 ...172 B1
Broadings La DN22 ......65 A4
Broadlands Ave PE10 ...213 C7
Broadlands Cl
41 Hatfield DN7 ......14 D4
1 Hatfield DN7 ......14 D3
Broadlands The PE1 ....226 E5
Broadley Ave HU10 ......178 D6
Broadley Cl 6 HU9 ......181 C7
Broadley Cres LN11 ......198 E6
Broadley Croft 5 HU15 ....2 D5
Broadley Way 8 HU15 ....2 D5
Broadsyke La NG24 ......105 A4
Broadwater Dr
9 Hatfield DN7 ......14 D3
3 Hatfield DN7 ......14 D3
Broadwater La PE12 ....158 A4
Broadway
Crowland PE6 ......175 B8
Farcet PE7 ......231 C1
3 Grimsby DN34 ......190 D4
Hatfield DN7 ......14 C3
Broadway *continued*
2 Keelby DN41 ......23 A5
Lincoln LN2 ......201 F6
Mablethorpe/Sutton on Sea
LN12 ......77 A8
Peterborough PE1 ......226 A3
Spalding PE11 ......214 A2
Yaxley PE7 ......233 E5
Broadway Cl
11 Bourne PE10 ......213 C7
4 Lincoln LN2 ......201 F6
Broadway Gdns PE1 ....226 B5
Broadway Nook 1 DN7 ..14 C3
Broadway The
Morton PE10 ......154 B7
Woodhall Spa LN10 ......97 D6
Broadway Theatre*
PE1 ......226 A3
Brock Cl 1 DN33 ......191 C2
Brockenhurst Cl LN6 ...204 B7
Brockenhurst Rd 9 DN7 ..14 E4
Brocklebank Cl LN5 ......92 F2
Brocklesby Cl
Gainsborough DN21 ......197 F3
5 Kingston upon Hull
HU13 ......179 A3
Brocklesby Pk Prim Sch
DN37 ......22 D4
Brocklesby Pl DN34 ....190 E4
Brocklesby Rd
Brocklesby DN41 ......22 E5
4 Grimsby DN34 ......190 E4
Habrough DN40 ......22 E8
Scunthorpe DN17 ......184 F4
Ulceby DN39 ......12 A1
Brocks Cl 21 PE24 ......90 D7
Brockton Cl HU3 ......179 F5
Brodsworth Rd PE7 ......231 F5
Bromwich Rd HU10 ......178 F8
Bronzegarth DN32 ......192 B5
Brook Dr 4 LN12 ......64 C3
Brook La Farcet PE7 ....231 B2
Scawby DN20 ......20 A1
Brook Rd 4 LN9 ......199 D2
Brook St
Grantham NG31 ......211 A5
Hemswell DN21 ......42 D2
Kingston upon Hull HU2 ...180 E7
Lincoln LN2 ......234 B2
Peterborough PE1 ......226 A2
Brook Way 5 NG34 ......108 D2
Brookdale Rd DN17 ......184 D6
Brooke Ave PE9 ......218 E4
Brooke St DN8 ......15 A8
Brookenby Bsns Pk
LN8 ......47 B6
Brookfield Ave LN2 ......68 D2
Brookfield Cl
2 Skellingthorpe LN6 ....200 A5
6 Thorne/Moorends DN8 ..15 A8
Brookfield Rd DN33 ....191 B1
Brookfields Ind Pk
PE4 ......220 F2
Brookfurlong PE3 ......225 B6
Brooklands 1 DN20 ......19 E3
Brooklands Ave
Broughton DN20 ......19 D4
Cleethorpes DN35 ......193 A5
Brooklands Cl
5 Birchwood LN6 ......204 C7
3 Collingham NG23 ......91 D5
Brooklands Rd HU5 ....179 E8
Brooklands Way 8 LN6 .204 C7
Brooklyn Dr DN36 ......193 B1
Brookside
8 Ancaster NG32 ......120 A3
4 Brough HU15 ......2 D6
Louth LN11 ......198 D3
Peterborough PE4 ......221 B2
Brookside Cl 7 NG32 ...120 A3
Broom Cl PE1 ......226 A8
Broom Ct 24 DN7 ......14 D4
Broom Gr DN16 ......185 B8
Broome Way PE12 ......215 A2
Broomfleet Sta HU15 ......1 B6
Broomston La DN9 ......26 F1
Broomwood Cl 2 NG31 .210 F7
Brosley Ave 1 DN3 ......14 A4
Brotherhood Cl PE4 ....225 D8
Brotherhood Ret Pk
PE4 ......225 D8
Brothertoft Rd PE21 ....208 D5
Brotts Rd NG23 ......78 A3
Brough Cl 14 LN6 ......204 C7
Brough Cty Prim Sch
HU15 ......2 C6
Brough La NG23 ......91 D2
Brough Rd LN6 ......105 A8
Brough Sta HU15 ......2 B5
Brougham St HU3 ......179 F7
Broughton Gdns LN5 ...205 D3
Broughton Inf Sch
DN20 ......19 E3
Broughton La LN5 ......93 C3
Broughton Rd
Carlton-le-Moorland LN5 ....92 E1
Stapleford LN6 ......105 C8
Broughton's La 1 PE22 .126 E3
Brown La NG23 ......79 A7
Browndons St 4 NG31 ..211 A5
Browne's Hosp* PE9 ....219 B5
Brownes Rd 7 PE8 ......172 B1
Browning Cl
3 Kingston upon Hull
HU3 ......180 D8
1 Scunthorpe DN17 ......184 E6
Browning Ct 4 LN4 ......207 B5
Browning Dr LN2 ......202 B7

Brownlow Cres 3 PE11 .145 B1
Brownlow Dr 4 PE6 .217 E4
Brownlow Quay 1 PE9 .219 C4
Brownlow Rd PE1 .226 A6
Brownlow's Dro PE12 .167 A8
Brownlow's Hill NG24 .104 D5
Browns CE (Aided) Prim Sch
NG34 .133 C2
Brown's Dro PE20 .123 F2
Brown's Gate
Long Sutton PE12 .216 B1
Spalding PE11 .214 C4
Brown's Rd 3 PE21 .209 A7
Browns La 13 DN8 .15 A8
Browns Orch DN32 .191 D6
Browntoft La 2 PE11 .134 F2
Broxholme Gdns 2 LN2 .201 F8
Broxholme La LN1 .66 F3
Bruce Cl
7 Broughton DN20 .19 D3
Lincoln LN2 .234 C4
Bruce St DN15 .182 F3
Brudenell PE2 .229 E2
Brudenell Cl 1 PE6 .164 E5
Brumby Comm La
DN17 .184 B7
Brumby Comp Sch
DN16 .185 B8
Brumby Cres 10 LN5 .93 F7
Brumby Hall Gdns
DN17 .182 F2
Brumby House Dr
DN16 .185 A8
Brumby Jun Sch
DN16 .185 B8
Brumby Resource Ctr
DN16 .185 C8
Brumby Wood La
DN15 .182 C2
Brumby's Terr 4 HU9 .181 D7
Brunel Cl DN16 .185 B4
Brunel Dr
Newark NG24 .104 B5
Yaxley PE7 .233 D6
Brunel Rd PE11 .214 E8
Brunslow Cl HU3 .179 E5
Brunswick Ave HU2 .180 E8
Brunswick Dr PE25 .206 C4
Brunswick Gr 5 HU13 .178 E2
Brunswick Sq 1 LN4 .109 F6
Brunton Way DN36 .195 D5
Brush Mdw La PE34 .161 E3
Bryant Cl 4 LN9 .199 C3
Brynmore PE3 .225 A8
Bryony Gdns PE10 .213 D7
Bryony Way 5 PE6 .217 D6
Buccaneer Way 21 HU15 .2 C5
Buchanan Cl LN1 .201 D8
Buchanan Rd DN21 .54 F8
Buck Beck Way DN36 .192 D2
Buckfast Rd 4 LN1 .201 E6
Buckingham Ave
DN15 .182 F5
Buckingham Cl
Fishtoft PE21 .209 C6
15 Mablethorpe & Sutton
LN12 .76 F8
Buckingham Dr 15 PE24 .90 D7
Buckingham Gr 2
DN33 .191 B2
Buckingham Rd LN11 .198 A7
Buckingham St N
DN15 .182 F5
Buckingham St S
DN15 .182 F4
Buckland Cl PE3 .225 B4
Buckle St PE1 .226 C3
Bucklegate La PE20 .136 F2
Buckminster Gdns
NG31 .210 F2
Buckminster La NG33 .151 A7
Buckminster Prim Sch
NG33 .150 F5
Buckminster Rd
Gunby & Stainby NG33 .151 A5
Sproxton LE14 .150 C7
Bucknall Ave 4 LN6 .205 A7
Bucknall Rd LN10 .84 C3
Bucknall's Mdw 5 LN12 .76 F8
Bucksholt Rd PE14 .170 E3
Buckthorn Ave
8 Skegness PE25 .103 E4
3 Skegness PE25 .103 E4
Buddleia Cl DN41 .23 E5
Buddleia Dr LN4 .81 D3
Bude Cl 2 DN36 .195 C7
Bukehorn Rd PE6 .175 D4
Bulby La 1 NG32 .106 C1
Bulham La NG23 .78 A1
Bull Bank LN11 .49 D7
Bull Dro PE22 .114 B5
Bull La 1 Ketton PE9 .171 A3
Long Sutton PE12 .216 C4
North Witham NG33 .151 E4
4 Peakirk PE6 .174 A5
Bull Moor Rd DN7 .15 A4
Bull Pasture PE22 .126 D2
Bull's Bank PE11 .144 E8
Bulldog Cres LN11 .62 B6
Bullen's La PE20 .135 C6
Buller Cl 16 NG23 .91 D5
Buller St 4 DN32 .191 F7
Bullfinch La DN35 .192 E1
Bullingham Rd LN2 .202 D6
Bullivant Rd DN7 .14 E4
Bullock Rd
Terrington St Clement
PE34 .161 F1
Bullock Rd *continued*
Thorney PE8 .228 B1
Bullock's Short Gate
PE12 .159 C4
Bullpit Rd NG24 .104 C3
Bully Hill LN8 .46 D2
Bulpit La LN6 .91 F7
Bulwick Ave DN33 .194 E7
Bungley La PE20 .136 C6
Bunker's Hill La PE21 .136 F8
Bunkers Hill
Hemswell DN21 .42 E1
Lincoln LN2 .202 D6
Bunkers Hill Cl 2 DN36 .36 D4
BUPA Hull & E Riding Hospl
HU10 .178 E5
Burchnall Cl PE6 .217 D6
Burchnall Dr 4 PE25 .90 E3
Burcom Ave 3 DN36 .36 D8
Burcott Garth HU4 .179 B3
Burcroft Rd 17 PE13 .170 C1
Burdett Cl 8 PE25 .206 A6
Burdock Rd DN16 .185 C4
Bure Cl LN6 .204 F3
Burford Way PE1 .226 D6
Burgar Rd 11 DN8 .15 A7
Burgate 5 DN18 .10 F8
Burgess Cl 2 PE21 .209 B4
Burgess Dr 4 PE12 .159 C7
Burgess Rd DN20 .196 E3
Burgh Old Rd PE25 .206 A6
Burgh Rd
Friskney PE22 .115 A7
Skegness PE25 .103 C7
Burghley Ave 14 PE8 .172 B1
Burghley Cl
Birchwood LN6 .200 E1
3 Market Deeping PE6 .217 E4
3 Nettleton LN7 .33 A3
Burghley Cres LN11 .198 B7
Burghley Ct 1 PE10 .213 C5
Burghley House* PE9 .219 F3
Burghley La PE9 .219 C4
Burghley Pk Cl 8 LN6 .204 F1
Burghley Rd
Birchwood LN6 .200 E1
1 Peterborough PE1 .226 A3
Scunthorpe DN16 .185 D7
8 Skegness PE25 .206 C1
8 Stamford PE9 .219 A7
Burghley Sq 2 PE1 .226 A3
Burghley St PE10 .213 C5
Burgin Cl 6 NG32 .117 F1
Burgon Cres 3 DN15 .9 B5
Burke St (North)
DN15 .183 A5
Burke St DN15 .183 A4
Burland Ct 3 LN4 .203 B2
Burleigh Cl NG31 .211 F5
Burleigh Gdns 2 PE21 .209 A7
Burleigh St HU8 .181 C8
Burley Ave DN35 .192 F3
Burley Rd 14 PE9 .163 C1
Burlies' Gate PE12 .159 E4
Burlington Rd PE25 .206 B3
Burma Dr HU9 .5 D8
Burma Rd DN16 .183 F2
Burmer Rd PE1 .225 E7
Burn Rd DN15 .182 C3
Burneside Cl LN2 .202 B8
Burnet Dr DN16 .185 C4
Burnett's Yd LN7 .33 C4
Burnham La
Kirton PE20 .136 F4
Thornton Curtis DN39 .11 E4
Burnham Rd
Barton-upon-Humber
DN18 .11 A6
Epworth DN9 .27 E6
Kingston upon Hull HU4 .179 B3
Owston Ferry DN9 .28 A3
Scunthorpe DN15 .182 D2
Burnham Reach 3
DN35 .192 F1
Burnham Sq 2 DN9 .28 A3
Burnmoor Cl 3 LN6 .200 C1
Burns Cl
Grantham NG31 .211 E6
Peterborough PE1 .225 F7
Burns Cres 8 NG34 .212 F4
Burns Gdns LN2 .202 C6
Burns Gr DN33 .191 B3
Burns Rd 5 PE9 .218 F6
Burns St DN21 .197 B6
Burnside DN20 .19 D3
Burnside Ave 5 PE6 .217 A5
Burnstone Gdns 4
PE12 .157 F7
Burnt Hill La 5 LN11 .198 B5
Burr La PE12 .156 F3
Burrett Gdns PE13 .170 F1
Burrett Rd PE13 .170 F2
Burrettgate Rd 4 PE13 .170 F1
Burrill La HU15 .2 B8
Burringham Rd
Burringham DN17 .17 E5
Scunthorpe DN17 .184 D5
Burrows Cl 2 PE21 .208 E7
Burrs The HU15 .2 B5
Bursar Prim Sch
DN35 .192 E6
Bursar St DN35 .192 E6
Bursnells La 3 LE14 .150 B1
Burswood PE2 .229 F2
Burtey Fen La PE11 .145 B2
Burtoft La PE20 .135 E2
Burton Cl PE21 .209 B7
Burton Ct 2 Louth LN11 .198 D4
Burton Ct *continued*
Peterborough PE1 .226 C3
Burton La
8 Billingborough NG34 .133 B1
Burton Coggles NG33 .140 E1
Easton NG33 .140 B1
Burton La End LN1 .200 C8
Burton Mews LN4 .203 D1
Burton Rd
Burton upon Stather DN15 .8 C4
Heckington NG34 .122 C2
Lincoln LN1 .234 A4
Burton Ridge 2 LN1 .201 D7
Burton St
14 Gainsborough DN21 .197 D3
Peterborough PE1 .226 C3
Burton Stather Prim Sch
DN15 .8 B4
Burton Way 6 LN9 .199 D2
Burtonfield Cl 1 LN3 .203 E6
Burwell Cl LN2 .202 A8
Burwell Dr DN33 .191 B3
Burwell Rd LN11 .74 D7
Burwell Reach PE2 .230 C7
Burystead PE2 .231 B8
Bush Cl HU4 .179 D3
Bush Gn La
Algarkirk PE20 .146 C8
Fosdyke PE20 .136 C1
Bush Mdw La PE12 .215 A4
Bushfield Com Coll
PE2 .229 E3
Bushfield Rd DN16 .183 B1
Bushfield Rd Inf Sch
DN16 .183 A1
Bushfield Sports Ctr
PE2 .229 E4
Buslingthorpe Rd LN8 .57 A4
Bustards' La PE14 .161 C1
Butcher La 10 LN11 .198 B5
Butchery Ct 3 LN2 .234 B2
Butforth La DN19 .11 E8
Butler Pl DN35 .192 B7
Butler's Way 14 PE20 .135 B7
Butlin Cl 1 PE25 .206 A4
Butt Gate LN11 .50 B8
Butt La Barrowby NG32 .210 A6
Goulceby LN11 .72 D6
Laceby DN37 .23 F2
Norton Disney LN6 .92 C2
Theddlethorpe All Saints
LN12 .63 E7
Walcott LN4 .109 C7
Wymondham LE14 .150 C2
Butter Mkt 11 LN7 .33 B4
Buttercake La PE22 .113 F2
Buttercross Cl 2 DN41 .23 E6
Buttercup Cl
1 Kingston upon Hull
HU9 .181 D7
3 Spalding PE11 .214 A2
3 Stamford PE9 .218 D7
Buttercup Paddock 4
PE12 .158 B6
Butterfield Cl 7 DN37 .23 F1
Buttergate Hill LN9 .71 F3
Buttermere Cl 2 LN6 .200 D1
Buttermere Cres 2
DN36 .36 C8
Buttermere Pl 4 PE4 .221 C3
Buttermere Way 7
DN32 .191 F8
Butterwick Cl DN35 .192 F3
Butterwick Pinchbeck
Endowed CE Sch
PE22 .126 E3
Butterwick Rd
Benington PE22 .126 F4
Messingham DN17 .29 A7
Buttery Cl LN6 .204 F4
Buttfield Rd HU13 .178 E1
Buttler Way 3 NG34 .212 C3
Butts La LN5 .92 F6
Butt's La LN4 .207 B5
Butts Rd DN18 .3 F1
Butts The LE14 .138 F1
Bycroft Rd DN21 .197 C8
Byfield Rd DN17 .184 D6
Byland Ct 4 HU9 .181 E8
Byrd Rd DN16 .185 E6
Byron Ave
Grantham NG31 .211 E6
Lincoln LN2 .202 A6
Byron Cl
Peterborough PE2 .231 D6
Scunthorpe DN17 .184 E6
6 Sleaford NG34 .212 F4
Byron Gr 2 DN33 .191 C4
Byron Rd LN12 .64 B4
Byron Way PE9 .218 E5
Bytham Hts 3 NG33 .162 E8
Bythams Cty Prim Sch The
NG33 .153 A2
Bythorn Rd PE2 .231 C6
Bythorne Bank PE13 .169 B6
Bywood Pl DN37 .190 C6

C

Cabourne Ave LN2 .202 B7
Cabourne Ct LN2 .202 B7
Cabourne Rd DN33 .191 B3
Cackle Hill La PE12 .215 C5
Caddle Rd 11 DN41 .23 A4
Cade Cl 12 LN2 .68 F4
Cade Dro PE12 .159 D4
Cade La DN21 .53 D6
Cades Field Rd 24 LN12 .77 A8
Cadman Way DN21 .41 A1
Cadney Rd DN20 .196 C1
Cadwell Cl 4 LN6 .204 C7
Cadwell Pk Motor Racing
Circuit* LN11 .73 B8
Caenby Cl DN21 .197 F3
Caenby Cnr LN8 .55 B8
Caenby Rd Caenby LN8 .43 F1
Cleethorpes DN35 .192 E4
Scunthorpe DN17 .184 E5
Caesar Cl 7 PE6 .164 E5
Cagthorpe LN9 .199 B3
Cairns Way 8 LN5 .93 E8
Caistor Ave DN16 .185 B4
Caistor By-Pass LN7 .33 B3
Caistor Cl 7 LN6 .204 C7
Caistor Dr
Bracebridge Heath LN4 .81 A2
Grimsby DN33 .191 B3
Caistor Gram Sch LN7 .33 B4
Caistor La LN8 .46 C3
Caistor Rd
Barton-upon-Humber
DN18 .11 A7
Birchwood LN6 .204 C7
Cabourne LN7 .33 F5
Caistor LN7 .32 E4
Laceby DN37 .23 E1
2 Market Rasen LN8 .57 D8
Middle Rasen LN8 .45 D2
Rothwell LN7 .33 E2
South Kelsey LN7 .32 A1
Swallow LN7 .34 A5
Caistor Yarborough Sch
LN7 .33 C4
Caithness Rd PE9 .218 E6
Caldbeck Cl PE4 .221 D2
Caldecote Cl PE2 .231 E6
Calder Cl
Grantham NG31 .210 E3
Immingham DN40 .186 A3
Calder Gn 24 DN17 .29 D7
Calder Rd Lincoln LN5 .205 C2
Scunthorpe DN16 .185 D6
Caldervale PE2 .230 C6
Caldicott Dr 8 DN21 .53 A8
Caleb Hill La
Leake Commonside
PE22 .113 F3
Old Leake PE22 .114 A3
Caledonia Pk HU9 .181 B5
Caledonian Rd 4 PE9 .218 F6
Callan's La PE10 .142 C2
Calver Cres DN37 .190 D7
Calvert La HU4 .179 D7
Calvert Rd HU5 .179 D8
Camargue Ave DN37 .194 F4
Camarthen Cl 4 NG31 .210 E5
Cambrian Cl NG31 .210 E7
Cambrian Way
Holton le Clay DN36 .195 C3
11 North Hykeham LN6 .93 B8
1 Peterborough PE4 .221 C1
Cambridge Ave
Lincoln LN1 .201 D4
Peterborough PE1 .225 F5
Scunthorpe DN16 .185 A3
Cambridge Cres 4 LN8 .47 B6
Cambridge Dr
Heighington/Washingborough
LN4 .203 D1
Wisbech PE13 .170 C1
Cambridge Gdns 4
PE11 .145 B7
Cambridge Rd
Grimsby DN34 .190 F5
Kingston upon Hull
HU13 .178 F3
Scunthorpe DN16 .185 C6
Stamford PE9 .219 A6
Cambridge Rd N 1 LN12 .64 B5
Cambridge Rd S 3 LN12 .64 B5
Cambridge St
Cleethorpes DN35 .192 F6
Grantham NG31 .211 B3
Kingston upon Hull HU3 .180 D6
Camden St 1 HU3 .180 B5
Camdon Cl 1 LN5 .205 D3
Camel Gate PE12 .157 B7
Camelia Cl PE4 .221 B3
Camelot Gdns
Boston PE21 .209 E5
11 Mablethorpe/Sutton on Sea
LN12 .76 F8
Cameron Dr 3 PE11 .214 E3
Cameron St 4 NG34 .122 E3
Camilla Cl HU9 .181 A5
Camm's La PE22 .114 D2
Camp La NG33 .141 B1
Campain's La PE11 .166 C7
Campbell Ave DN16 .185 B4
Campbell Cl 4 NG31 .210 F5
Campbell Dr PE4 .221 C4
Campbell St DN21 .197 B5
Campbells Cl PE11 .214 B1
Campbells Farm Ave 1
DN15 .17 E6
Campden Cres DN35 .192 D7
Campion Ave HU4 .179 B2
Campion Cl PE11 .214 B6
Campion Dr PE6 .217 D6
Campion Gr 4 PE9 .218 D7
Campion Rd PE1 .226 B8
Campions Cl DN36 .195 D2
Campions' La 11 DN36 .36 B1
Campling Pl PE12 .215 D7
Campney La LN10 .83 F1
Camwood Cres LN6 .200 C1
Canada La Caistor LN7 .33 C4
Wildmore LN4 .111 A4
Canal La DN10 .40 B5
Canal View 12 DN8 .15 A7
Canberra Ave DN7 .26 A8
Canberra Cl 5 LN4 .207 C4
Canberra Cres
11 Binbrook Tech Pk LN8 .47 B6
Grantham NG31 .211 D7
10 Manby LN11 .62 C6
Canberra Dr 5 LN1 .67 F5
Canberra Rd 8 NG24 .104 C5
Canberra St HU3 .180 D5
Canberra Way LN6 .200 A4
Candidus Ct 6 PE4 .220 F5
Candlehouse La 9 LN13 .75 F3
Candlesby Rd DN37 .190 C7
Candy Bank DN9 .26 B5
Canister La
Frithville PE22 .112 C1
Langriville PE22 .124 F8
Canning St HU1 .180 E6
Cannon Cl NG24 .104 C5
Cannon Oakes Ct
DN36 .195 E6
Cannon St
Kingston upon Hull HU2 .180 F8
1 Lincoln LN2 .202 B3
Lincoln LN2 .234 C2
3 Louth LN11 .198 B5
Cannonhill Dro PE12 .167 A8
Canon Dr 6 PE9 .172 D3
Canonsfield PE4 .220 E4
Canterbury Cl
Grantham NG31 .211 E7
1 Scunthorpe DN17 .184 D7
Spalding PE11 .214 B4
Canterbury Dr
Grimsby DN34 .191 C6
Heighington/Washingborough
LN4 .203 D1
4 Sleaford NG34 .212 C7
Canterbury Rd
1 Hatfield DN7 .14 D4
Peterborough PE4 .220 F3
Cant's Dro PE13 .177 C4
Canturbury Cl 10 LN10 .97 C5
Canty Nook 5 DN38 .32 E7
Canwell PE4 .221 A4
Canwick Ave LN4 .205 F4
Canwick Hill LN4 .81 A4
Canwick Rd
Canwick LN5 .81 A4
Lincoln LN5 .234 B1
Washingborough LN4 .81 D4
Capes Entry PE12 .157 A2
Capitol Pk DN8 .14 F8
Capper Ave 3 DN21 .55 A8
Cappitt Dr 2 PE10 .164 C8
Capp's La 19 LN5 .93 F7
Capstan Way 17 DN8 .15 A8
Captain's Hill NG34 .121 B7
Captains Beck 9 PE11 .145 C1
Capthorne Cl PE7 .230 C2
Caravan Pk LN6 .204 C1
Carbis Cl 5 DN36 .195 C7
Cardiff Ave DN36 .195 C6
Cardigan Rd HU3 .179 E6
Cardinal Cl LN2 .202 D5
Cardinal Ct 3 DN37 .194 C5
Cardinals Gate PE4 .220 E4
Cardyke Dr 13 PE6 .164 E5
Carew St HU3 .179 F7
Carholme Cl 1 PE10 .213 D6
Carholme Rd LN1 .201 C4
Carisbrooke Cl
2 Lincoln LN1 .201 E6
5 New Waltham DN36 .195 D7
Carisbrooke Manor La
DN17 .184 A5
Carleton Crest 3 PE4 .221 B1
Carline Rd LN1 .234 A3
Carlisle Cl
6 Grantham NG31 .210 D5
1 Lincoln LN6 .204 F1
Carlisle Gdns LN9 .199 D5
Carlisle Way LN4 .81 A2
Carlton Ave DN41 .23 F5
Carlton Bvd LN2 .202 D5
Carlton Cl
Humberston DN35 .193 B1
8 Leverington PE13 .170 B2
2 Spalding PE11 .214 B1
Carlton Ferry La NG23 .91 A6
Carlton Gr LN2 .201 F7
Carlton La
Broxholme LN1 .67 A4
Sutton-on-Trent NG23 .91 A7
Carlton Mews 9 LN4 .203 D1
Carlton Pk LN11 .62 C5
Carlton Rd
Ancaster NG32 .119 E3
Bassingham LN5 .92 E2
Boston PE21 .208 D5
Grimsby DN34 .191 B6
9 Healing DN41 .23 F5
Hough-on-the-Hill NG32 .119 B5
Manby LN11 .62 C6
Carlton Rd Cty Prim Sch
PE21 .208 E5
Carlton St
Kingston upon Hull HU3 .179 F4
Lincoln LN1 .234 A4
5 Scunthorpe DN15 .183 B3

Carmel Gn PE21 208 E2
Carmen Cres DN36 195 C3
Carn Cl 3 LN5 205 D2
Carnaby Gr 2 DN32 192 A5
Carnarvon Ave 1 DN34 191 B4
Carnegie Rd 21 PE8 172 B1
Carnegie St 6 HU3 180 A6
Carnforth Cres DN34 191 A5
Carnforth Sch DN34 190 F5
Carnoustie 7 DN37 194 C4
Carnoustie Cl 2 LN10 97 C5
Carol Dickson Ct 9 HU3 180 C5
Caroline Cl 12 NG34 212 F4
Caroline Ct 10 PE21 209 A5
Caroline Pl HU2 180 F7
Caroline Rd 5 LN4 95 D4
Caroline St 10 Alford LN13 75 F2
Kingston upon Hull HU2 180 F8
Carr Dike La HU15 1 C7
Carr Dyke Bank DN17 28 D5
Carr Dyke Rd DN17 17 D3
Carr La 6 Alford LN13 75 F2
Appleby DN15 9 D2
Bishop Norton LN8 43 F3
Blyton DN21 41 B5
Bonby DN20 10 B1
Broomfleet HU15 1 B7
Broughton DN20 196 A6
Burton upon Stather DN15 8 D4
Doddington & Whisby LN6 79 D6
Gainsborough DN21 197 C1
Garthorpe & Fockerby DN17 7 E4
Grimsby DN32 192 B7
Haxey DN9 27 E2
Healing DN41 23 F4
Hibaldstow DN20 31 A6
Horkstow DN18 9 F4
Kingston upon Hull HU1 180 E6
Luddington & Haldenby DN17 7 C1
3 Misterton DN10 39 F5
Redbourne DN21 30 F3
Stallingborough DN41 23 F7
Ulceby DN39 12 B3
West Butterwick DN17 28 C8
Wildsworth DN21 40 F8
Winterton DN15 9 D6
Worlaby DN20 20 B7
Carr Rd
Gringley on the Hill DN10 39 A4
North Kelsey LN7 31 E4
Peterborough PE1 226 D3
Carr Side La DN7 14 E2
Carr St LN1 201 D4
Carradale PE2 229 D5
Carral Cl LN5 205 C3
Carram Way LN1 201 C7
Carre St NG34 212 D4
Carres Gram Sch NG34 212 D5
Carre's Sq LN4 109 E6
Carrhouse Rd DN9 16 D1
Carrington Cl
Coningsby LN4 207 D5
2 Spalding PE11 214 B3
Carrington Dr
Deeping St Nicholas PE11 165 F5
8 Humberston DN36 36 D8
Humberston DN36 193 B1
Lincoln LN6 204 F7
Carrington Rd
Carrington PE22 112 D3
Moulton PE12 146 C3
Spalding PE11 214 B4
Carrington St 6 HU3 180 B5
Carrington's Dro PE6 175 C7
Carroll Pl 4 HU1 181 A7
Carron Cl 3 LN3 83 B4
Carron Dr PE4 220 E3
Carrside DN9 27 D6
Carrwood Cres LN4 207 C7
Carson Ave DN34 191 B6
Carson Cl 5 PE24 90 B7
Carson Rd DN21 197 C6
Carter's Garth Cl 4 LN11 50 B8
Cartergate DN32 191 C7
Carterplot Rd NG34 123 A2
Carters Cl 6 PE3 224 F3
Cartledge Ave DN32 192 B6
Cartmel Gr DN32 192 B6
Cartmel Way 14 PE6 175 A1
Carver Rd Boston PE21 208 D3
Immingham DN40 186 D3
Cary La 3 DN20 196 B3
Caryer Cl PE2 230 D6
Casewick La 4 PE9 172 F7
Casewick Rd PE9 172 E7
Caskgate St DN21 197 C4
Cassbrook Dr 2 LN11 49 B8
Cassons Cl PE12 157 D4
Casson's Rd 1 DN8 15 A8
Casswell Cl 1 DN32 189 D1
Casswell Cres 4 LN11 49 B8
Castella Dr DN16 183 D3
Casterton Com Coll PE9 171 C8
Casterton La PE9 218 C4
Casterton Rd PE9 218 E6
Casthorpe Rd
3 Barrowby NG32 210 A5
Denton NG32 139 A8
Castle Bytham Rd
Clipsham LE15 162 C7
Swayfield NG33 152 E5
Castle Cl 3 NG13 128 B5
Castle Cswy NG34 212 C4
Castle Ct 14 DN18 10 F8
Castle Dr Epworth DN9 27 E7
Northborough PE6 217 E2
Castle Dyke 10 PE9 219 B5
Castle Dyke Bank LN4 111 B4
Castle End Rd PE6 217 A1
Castle Hill 15 Caistor LN7 33 B4
4 Lincoln LN1 234 B3
3 Welbourn LN5 106 E5
Castle Hills Com Art Coll DN21 197 D7
Castle Keep DN20 30 F6
Castle La
Boothby Graffoe LN5 93 E1
Coningsby LN4 207 C5
Lincoln LN1 234 A4
Castle Rise PE9 163 D1
Castle Sports Complex PE11 214 E5
Castle St Boston PE21 208 D6
Grimsby DN32 192 A8
Kingston upon Hull HU1 180 E5
Lincoln LN1 234 A4
Sleaford NG34 212 D4
12 Stamford PE9 219 B5
Castle Terr Rd 4 NG34 212 C4
Castle View LN4 109 D7
Castle View Rd NG13 128 B4
Castle Way LN11 198 A8
Castledyke Bank PE22 125 A8
Castledyke Prim Sch DN18 3 E1
Castledyke S 13 DN18 10 F8
Castledyke W 7 DN18 3 E1
Castlefields 2 PE11 214 D5
Castleford Ave DN34 191 A4
Castlegate
Castle Bytham NG33 152 D1
Grantham NG31 211 B4
Thornton Le Fen PE22 111 F1
Castleton Bvd PE25 206 D4
Castleton Cres PE25 206 D4
Castleton Rd DN15 182 B2
Castleview
Coningsby LN4 110 E8
Tattershall LN4 97 E1
Castor CE Sch PE5 223 E2
Castor Hanglands Nature Reserve* PE6 223 D7
Castor Rd Marholm PE6 220 B1
Peterborough PE6 224 C6
Casworth Way PE5 223 D2
Cater La LN7 44 F7
Cater Way PE21 208 D2
Cates's Cove Cnr PE6 167 F4
Cathedral Ct
13 Hatfield DN7 14 C2
Scunthorpe DN17 185 A6
Cathedral Dr PE11 214 C5
Cathedral St LN2 234 B2
Catherine Cl PE2 230 B7
Catherine Gr 6 DN20 19 E3
Catherine St
7 Grimsby DN32 191 F7
1 Kingston upon Hull HU2 180 F7
Cathwaite PE4 221 E1
Catkin Rd 6 DN16 185 B2
Catling's La PE13 170 C7
Catskin La LN8 46 A3
Cattistock Rd DN35 192 E3
Cattle Dike PE13 169 E2
Cattle Mkt Rd PE1 226 A2
Cattle Rd DN10 39 B5
Caughey St HU3 180 D7
Causeway
Burgh le Marsh PE24 102 E7
Wyberton PE21 136 E7
Causeway Bank La LN13 63 F1
Causeway La 3 DN21 52 F6
Causeway Rd LN4 109 E5
Causeway The
6 Northorpe PE10 164 C8
Revesby PE22 111 F7
Thorney PE6 175 E2
Cavalry Ct 2 LN4 95 D4
Cave Rd HU15 2 B6
Cave's Cl 8 PE34 161 F3
Cave's La DN10 39 E3
Cavell Cl PE3 225 B4
Cavendish Cl DN35 193 B1
Cavendish Dr
9 Boston PE21 136 D8
Gainsborough DN21 52 F5
Cavendish Mews 5 LN4 203 D1
Cavendish Pk 10 HU15 2 C5
Cavendish Rd
Scunthorpe DN16 185 A4
Skegness PE25 206 C4
Cavendish St PE1 226 B3
Cavendish Way
1 Grimsby DN32 191 F7
Spalding PE11 214 C6
Caverstede Rd PE4 221 B1
Cavill Pl HU3 180 D5
Cawkwell Cl 25 LN12 77 A7
Cawkwell Hill LN11 73 A6
Cawood La PE11 145 B5
Cawthorne Cl 18 NG23 91 D5
Cawthorne Dr HU4 179 C3
Cawthra Ct NG32 139 A7
Caxton Theatre & Arts Ctr The* DN32 189 B1
Cayley Rd HU10 178 F6
Caythorpe Heath La NG32 119 D7
Caythorpe Prim Sch NG32 119 B7
Caythorpe Rd PE11 134 F2
Cecil Ave PE25 206 C4
Cecil Cl Bourne PE10 213 B4
16 Scotter DN21 29 C3
Cecil Ct 18 PE9 219 C5
Cecil Pywell Ave PE12 215 C3
Cecil Rd PE1 226 A6
Cecil St
Gainsborough DN21 197 C5
Grantham NG31 211 C3
Kingston upon Hull HU3 179 F5
Lincoln LN1 234 A4
Cecile Cres DN15 182 E3
Cedar Ave
Cherry Willingham/Reepham LN3 203 D5
Lincoln LN5 205 D4
Scunthorpe DN15 182 B6
9 Sleaford NG34 212 D6
2 Stainforth DN7 14 D6
Cedar Cl
4 Cleethorpes DN35 192 D2
Gainsborough DN21 197 B7
Kingston upon Hull HU10 178 D7
1 Louth LN11 198 B6
14 Market Deeping PE6 217 A5
6 Market Rasen LN8 57 D7
9 Ruskington NG34 108 D1
6 Scawby DN20 30 F8
2 Scotter DN21 29 C3
13 Sudbrooke LN2 68 F2
Cedar Ct 2 PE11 214 E3
Cedar Dr Bourne PE10 213 B6
Holbeach PE12 215 C4
Immingham DN40 186 C5
Cedar Gr PE1 226 B8
Cedar Rd PE9 218 D6
Cedarwood Cl 1 NG31 210 F7
Cedarwood Dr HU5 179 B7
Cedric Rd 10 DN3 14 A1
Cekhira Ave PE12 157 E1
Celta Rd PE2 230 F6
Celtic Cl PE2 231 D7
Cemetery Cres 10 DN37 23 F1
Cemetery La LN7 32 A5
Cemetery Rd
Hatfield DN7 14 F4
16 Laceby DN37 23 F1
North Somercotes LN11 50 E8
Scunthorpe DN16 185 B8
Winterton DN15 9 B5
4 Wragby LN8 70 D4
Centenary Cl 3 PE22 126 E3
Centenary Way PE12 160 F2
Central Ave
Ingoldmells PE25 90 F3
Peterborough PE1 226 C7
Central Dr 7 NG34 120 C8
Central Par DN34 191 A7
Central Pl NG31 211 D5
Central Prom DN35 192 F6
Central Sq PE2 231 D5
Central Tech Coll The NG31 211 A7
Central Way DN16 183 D2
Centurion Way 12 HU15 2 C5
Century La 1 LN1 66 D3
Cerris Rd PE1 226 B7
Ceylon St 9 HU9 5 D8
Chadburn PE4 221 E1
Chadwell Springs DN37 194 B4
Chaffinch Cl 5 DN15 182 D5
Chaffinch Dr DN35 192 E1
Chain Bridge Rd PE21 208 B3
Chain Cl PE1 226 B6
Chaintoft La PE11 145 A7
Chaldean Way PE11 214 B6
Chalfont Ave LN12 64 A5
Chalfont Cl HU13 178 D2
Chalfonts The LN4 81 E2
Chalgrove Way LN6 200 E2
Chalk La
Burgh Le Marsh PE24 89 F1
Sutton Bridge PE12 160 F3
Withern with Stain LN13 63 A1
Chalk Pit La PE23 88 F2
Chalk Rd PE13 169 D1
Chamber's Farm Wood Nature Reserve* LN8 83 F8
Chambers St NG31 211 A5
Chamomile Cl DN16 185 D5
Champion Way LN12 64 B2
Chancel Rd DN16 185 A4
Chancel Wlk 13 DN20 19 E3
Chancery Cl LN6 205 B5
Chancery Ct 4 PE11 214 D3
Chancery La
3 Crowle DN17 16 D7
7 Eye PE6 175 A1
7 Holbeach PE12 215 D2
Chanctonbury Cl 20 LN12 77 A8
Chanctonbury Way 19 LN12 77 A8
Chandlers PE2 229 E5
Chandlers Cl 1 DN36 195 C6
Chandos Rd DN17 184 F7
Chanterlands Ave HU5 180 A8
Chantreys Dr 16 HU15 2 C6
Chantry Cl
Grimsby DN31 191 C7
Peterborough PE1 226 A5
Chantry La DN31 191 C7
Chantry The 1 PE11 214 A4
Chantry Way 16 HU14 3 B7
Chantry Way E 14 HU14 3 B7
Chapel Cl
Barrow upon Humber DN19 11 D7
Chapel St Leonard PE24 90 D8
Cherry Willingham/Reepham LN3 203 F8
10 Misterton DN10 39 F5
1 South Rauceby NG34 120 E4
2 Westwoodside DN9 27 B2
Chapel Ct
5 Alkborough DN15 8 C8
Wansford PE8 222 B2
Chapel Dro PE12 168 B2
Chapel Farm Dr 19 PE24 90 D7
Chapel Field Rd DN19 5 C1
Chapel Garth
Broomfleet HU15 1 B5
18 Tetney DN36 36 D4
Chapel Gate
Sutton St James PE12 159 B1
Sutton St James PE12 169 B7
Whaplode PE12 168 B5
Chapel Gdns
Moulton PE12 157 E1
2 Whaplode PE12 158 B7
Chapel Hill Brough HU15 2 D6
Ropsley NG33 131 B1
Whaplode PE12 168 A4
Woolsthorpe By Belvoir NG32 138 D8
Chapel Hill Ct 7 NG34 212 E3
Chapel Hill La HU15 2 E6
Chapel La
Addlethorpe PE24 90 C3
Amber Hill PE20 124 B5
Anwick NG34 109 B1
Ashby cum Fenby DN37 35 D3
3 Aubourn Haddington & South Hykeham LN5 93 A5
3 Barnetby Le Beck DN37 35 B6
4 Barrowby NG32 210 A5
1 Barton-upon-Humber DN18 10 F8
Belchford LN9 73 B2
Branston & Mere LN4 81 E2
Caythorpe NG32 119 B7
2 Claypole NG23 117 E8
1 Croxton Kerrial NG32 138 D4
5 Donington on Bain LN11 59 E1
Dunston LN4 95 C5
East Kirkby PE23 99 F5
4 Elsham DN20 20 F7
2 Folkingham NG34 142 D8
4 Foston NG32 117 F1
Foston NG32 118 A1
Friskney Eaudike PE22 115 A6
2 Fulletby LN9 86 B8
Gainsborough DN21 197 B8
Glentworth DN21 54 F7
3 Grainthorpe LN11 50 B8
Habrough DN40 12 E1
4 Harmston LN5 93 F5
Heckington NG34 122 F1
Heighington/Washingborough LN4 81 E4
2 Helpringham NG34 133 D7
Hemingby LN9 72 B1
Horkstow DN18 10 A5
Keadby with Althorpe DN17 17 C6
3 Ketton PE9 171 A3
Kingston upon Hull HU1 181 A6
2 Leasingham NG34 121 B7
6 Legbourne LN11 61 F3
2 Legbourne LN11 62 A3
Lincoln LN1 234 A4
Little Hale NG34 133 E8
Ludborough DN36 48 E6
Ludford LN8 59 A8
Manby LN11 62 C6
6 Mareham Le Fen PE22 99 A4
Messingham DN17 29 D7
Minting LN9 84 C8
11 Misterton DN10 39 F5
Navenby/Wellingore LN5 107 A8
13 Nettleham LN2 68 C2
7 Newark-on-Trent NG24 104 D5
Newton PE13 170 B5
Normanby By Spital LN8 55 F7
North Cockerington LN11 49 F1
North Scarle LN6 78 E2
Northorpe PE10 164 C8
6 Peterborough PE4 221 A3
Peterborough PE2 229 F5
Scamblesby LN11 73 A5
10 Scawby DN20 30 E8
14 Sibsey PE22 113 B1
Snitterby DN21 43 D5
South Cockerington LN11 62 A8
Spalford NG23 78 D4
Springthorpe DN21 53 E8
Swallow LN7 34 B5
Tattershall Thorpe LN4 207 C8
Thimbleby LN9 85 B4
14 Thorne/Moorends DN8 15 A8
Toynton St Peter PE23 101 A6
4 Tydd St Giles PE13 169 F7
Utterby LN11 48 F4
Welton/Dunholme LN2 68 C6
Chapel La *continued*
West/East Butterwick DN17 17 D1
Whitton DN15 1 E3
16 Winterton DN15 9 A5
2 Winthorpe NG24 104 B7
Wrawby DN20 20 E4
2 Wymondham LE14 150 C1
Chapel Lodge Dr LN8 55 F7
Chapel Mews 3 HU15 2 C6
Chapel Nook La LN5 93 B1
Chapel Rd Branston LN4 81 E2
4 Broughton DN20 19 E3
Carrington PE22 112 B8
Fillingham DN21 54 F4
Fiskerton LN3 82 A7
4 Habrough DN40 22 E8
Ingoldmells PE25 90 D4
Leake Commonside PE22 113 F3
Sutton St Edmund PE12 168 E4
Terrington St Clement PE34 161 F3
Chapel Row
Baumber LN9 72 A1
7 Skillington NG33 151 A8
Chapel St 10 Alford LN13 75 F3
3 Amcotts DN17 7 F1
Beckingham LN5 105 B4
6 Billingborough NG34 133 B1
4 Boston PE21 208 F5
16 Bottesford NG13 128 A6
13 Caistor LN7 33 B4
4 Crowland PE6 175 B8
12 Crowle DN17 16 D8
6 Epworth DN9 27 E6
Goxhill DN19 12 A8
Haconby PE10 154 D8
2 Holbeach PE12 215 E2
1 Market Rasen LN8 57 D7
7 North Kelsey LN7 32 A4
Peterborough PE1 226 B2
18 Ruskington NG34 108 E2
Scunthorpe DN15 183 B3
Yaxley PE7 233 D5
Chapel St Leonards Prim Sch
Chapel St Leonards PE24 90 D6
Collingham NG23 91 D4
Chapel Way 6 DN20 196 D3
Chapel Yd 2 PE9 219 C5
Chapelgate PE12 159 D7
Chaplin Cl 22 LN4 95 D4
Chaplin St LN5 234 A1
Chapman Ave
6 Burgh le Marsh PE24 102 E7
Scunthorpe DN17 184 D6
Chapman Cres 4 DN36 36 D8
Chapman Gr 1 DN35 192 F5
Chapman Rd
Cleethorpes DN35 192 D7
2 Sleaford NG34 212 B6
Chapman St
Kingston upon Hull HU8 181 A8
3 Market Rasen LN8 57 E7
Chapnall Cl 18 PE13 170 E1
Chapnall Rd PE13 170 E1
Chappell Rd PE11 166 C6
Chapter Wk 12 DN20 19 E3
Chariots Way 6 PE6 164 E5
Charity St NG32 119 D4
Charles Ave
11 Ancaster NG32 120 A2
Grimsby DN33 191 D2
3 Laceby DN37 23 E1
Louth LN11 198 D7
12 New Waltham DN36 195 C6
18 Scotter DN21 29 C3
Charles Baines Prim Sch DN21 197 F4
Charles Cl
Bourne PE10 213 D6
1 Skegness PE25 206 B4
Charles Cope Rd PE2 229 F5
Charles Gate LN11 63 A8
Charles Lovell Way DN17 184 D8
Charles Rd
5 Fleet Hargate PE12 159 C7
9 Stamford PE9 219 A7
12 Sutton Bridge PE12 160 E4
Charles Read High Sch The NG33 152 F7
Charles St Boston PE21 209 A3
2 Cleethorpes DN35 192 F5
Gainsborough DN21 197 D5
3 Kingston upon Hull HU2 180 F7
Lincoln LN5 234 B1
Louth LN11 198 C6
Newark-on-Trent NG24 104 A4
Peterborough PE1 226 B3
1 Sleaford NG34 212 C4
Wrange PE22 114 C2
Charles St W LN1 201 D4
Charles Wright Cl 15 LN12 64 B4
Charlestown Way HU9 181 C6
Charlesworth St 2 LN1 201 D3
Charlette Way 13 PE11 214 B5
Charlock Dr PE9 218 D6
Charlotte Cl 4 LN8 57 E8
Charlotte St 5 HU1 181 A7
Charlotte Wlk 5 PE11 145 A8
Charlton St DN31 188 E1
Charnwood Cl PE2 231 A7
Charter Cl PE21 208 E7

Charterhouse Dr
DN16 185 C4
Charterhouse La 1
HU2 181 A7
Charter's La PE12 216 A5
Charters The 2 PE9 172 C6
Chase Hill Rd DN40 12 E5
Chase St PE13 170 D1
Chase The
Boston PE21 209 C3
Crowland PE6 166 F1
Holbeach PE12 215 E2
Long Sutton PE12 216 C4
9 Metheringham LN4 95 C4
Pinchbeck PE11 156 E8
Ropsley NG33 131 A1
Weston PE12 145 F1
Whaplode PE12 147 A6
Wisbech PE13 170 C1
Chasm & Northorpe Slipe Nature Reserve The*
PE10 165 B8
Chater Rd 5 PE8 172 B1
Chatham St HU3 179 F7
Chatsfield PE4 220 E6
Chatsworth Ave NG31 211 F5
Chatsworth Cl
4 Lincoln LN2 202 C8
6 Market Deeping PE6 217 A5
Chatsworth Dr
4 Lincoln LN6 204 E2
Louth LN11 198 B7
Chatsworth Pl
Cleethorpes DN35 192 C4
Peterborough PE3 225 B2
Chatsworth Rd PE9 218 E6
Chatsworth St HU5 180 B8
Chatterton Ave LN1 201 E8
Chatterton Cres DN15 183 A5
Chaucer Ave
12 Mablethorpe/Sutton on Sea
LN12 64 B4
Scunthorpe DN17 184 D7
Chaucer Cl 1 PE13 170 B1
Chaucer Dr LN2 202 C6
Chaucer Gdns 10 NG34 212 F4
Chaucer Rd PE1 225 E8
Chaucer's Way PE11 214 A4
Chauntry Rd 19 LN13 75 F2
Cheal La PE11 144 F2
Cheal Rd PE11 144 F4
Cheapside
Kingston upon Hull HU8 181 A8
Waltham DN37 194 F2
Cheapside Rd DN36 36 A4
Chedburgh Cl 1 LN6 204 B6
Chedworth Cl 1 LN2 202 D7
Chedworth Rd LN2 202 D7
Cheese Hill 10 PE20 135 B7
Cheesemans Cl 4
DN37 194 E4
Cheesemans La DN37 194 E4
Cheethams La LN4 110 F2
Chelmer Cl LN6 204 F4
Chelmer Garth 2 PE4 221 D1
Chelmsford Ave DN34 191 A5
Chelmsford Dr NG31 210 F4
Chelmsford Pl 5 DN34 191 A6
Chelmsford St LN5 234 B1
Chelsea Cl LN6 200 D2
Chelsea Wlk DN35 193 A1
Cheltenham Cl
Peterborough PE1 226 B6
Scunthorpe DN16 185 C4
Cheltenham Way
Humberston DN35 192 F1
7 Mablethorpe/Sutton on Sea
LN12 64 A3
Chelveston Way PE3 225 C4
Chelwood Dr 6 DN33 191 B3
Chelwood Rd DN17 184 F7
Chepstow Cl
1 Spalding PE11 156 E3
7 Spalding PE11 214 B1
Chepstow Gr DN34 191 A5
Chequergate 1 LN11 198 B5
Chequers La DN22 65 A2
Cheriton Cl 1 LN3 83 B4
Cheriton Pk PE10 213 D7
Cherry Ave LN4 81 D2
Cherry Cl 8 NG34 212 D6
Cherry Cnr PE22 113 A5
Cherry Cobb Sands Rd
HU12 13 F8
Cherry Dale DN35 192 D3
Cherry Garth HU3 180 A5
Cherry Gr 10 Belton DN9 16 E1
Lincoln LN6 205 A8
10 Market Deeping PE6 217 C5
Scunthorpe DN16 185 B6
Cherry Holt 1 LN3 203 E5
Cherry Holt La
13 Pinchbeck PE11 156 E8
Sutterton PE20 136 A4
Cherry Holt Rd PE10 213 F4
Cherry La
Barrow upon Humber
DN19 11 D8
7 Fleet PE12 159 C7
Stubton NG23 118 B7
Wootton DN39 11 E2
Cherry Mount DN16 185 C4
Cherry Orch
21 Epworth DN9 27 E6
Grantham NG31 211 D5
Cherry Orton Rd PE2 229 F5
Cherry Rd 9 PE13 170 D2
Cherry Tree Ave 3
DN20 196 B4
Cherry Tree Cl 4 LN6 204 F2
Cherry Tree Cres
DN34 190 F6
Cherry Tree Dr 5 DN7 14 D5
Cherry Tree Gr
2 Hatfield DN7 14 D5
Spalding PE11 214 F5
Cherry Tree La
Holbeach PE12 215 D4
23 Nettleham LN2 68 C2
Cherry Tree Rd DN21 197 E5
Cherry Tree Way
3 Coningsby LN4 207 D4
17 Metheringham LN4 95 C4
Cherry Way 34 DN17 29 D7
Cherry Willingham Com Sch
LN3 203 D7
Cherry Willingham Prim Sch
LN3 203 D5
Cherry Wlk PE21 208 D4
Cherryfields PE2 229 E6
Cherryholt La PE9 219 D5
Cherryholt Rd PE9 219 D5
Cherrytree Ave PE25 90 E4
Cherrytree Gr PE1 226 C6
Cherrywood Dr NG31 210 F8
Chesboule La PE11 144 E5
Chesham Dr 7 PE6 164 E4
Cheshire Gr 7 PE25 206 A5
Cheshire La LN6 92 E5
Cheshire Rd LN6 204 B5
Chesney Dr DN16 185 A3
Chesney Rd LN2 202 D7
Chesnut Cl 11 LN2 68 F2
Chesnut Dr 12 LN2 68 F2
Chesnut Way 4 DN19 12 A8
Chesswick Ave DN17 17 D5
Chester Cl LN4 203 D1
Chester Gdns 8 NG31 210 D5
Chester Grange DN33 191 E1
Chester Pl DN32 192 C5
Chester Rd PE1 226 C3
Chester Way PE21 208 C3
Chesterfield Rd DN15 182 B2
Chesterton Gr PE2 231 D6
Chestnut Ave
7 Donington PE11 134 E2
Edenham PE10 153 C2
Gainsborough DN21 197 D6
Holbeach PE12 215 C3
Immingham DN40 186 E5
Kingston upon Hull
HU13 178 E1
Peterborough PE1 226 B7
RAF Cranwell NG34 107 D1
Spalding PE11 214 E5
3 Stainforth DN7 14 D6
6 Thorne/Moorends DN8 15 B7
Chestnut Cl
Bottesford NG13 128 B6
Glinton PE6 220 B8
Horncastle LN9 199 A5
4 Metheringham LN4 95 C4
1 Peakirk PE6 174 A5
13 Scotter DN21 29 C3
2 Sleaford NG34 212 D3
Swaton NG34 133 D4
13 Waltham DN37 194 C4
Chestnut Cres 3 LN5 92 F3
Chestnut Dr
5 Coningsby LN4 207 D4
Louth LN11 198 E6
38 Messingham DN17 29 D7
3 Thorney PE6 176 A3
Chestnut Gdns PE9 218 D5
Chestnut Gr
8 Broughton DN20 19 E4
4 Colsterworth NG33 151 E7
1 Grantham NG31 210 D2
Waddington LN5 205 C1
Chestnut La NG33 152 C8
Chestnut Rd
3 Boston PE21 209 C2
Lincoln LN6 204 F2
Waltham DN37 194 C4
Chestnut Rise 1 DN19 11 C8
Chestnut St
Lincoln LN1 234 A4
5 Ruskington NG34 108 E1
Chestnut St CE Prim Sch
NG34 108 F1
Chestnut Terr 2 PE12 160 E4
Chestnut Way
6 Binbrook LN8 47 C5
4 Bourne PE10 213 B5
3 Market Deeping PE6 217 B6
Scunthorpe DN16 185 B8
Chestnut Wlk 5 DN41 24 A5
Chestnuts The 7 LN2 68 C2
Cheviot Ave PE4 221 C2
Cheviot Cl
Gonerby Hill Foot NG31 210 E7
Sleaford NG34 212 A3
6 Thorne/Moorends DN8 15 A7
Cheviot St LN2 234 C2
Chichester Cl 6 NG31 210 E5
Chichester Dr 20 LN7 33 B4
Chichester Rd
6 Binbrook Tech Pk LN8 47 B6
Cleethorpes DN35 192 F4
Chieftain Way 1 LN6 205 C8
Childers' N Dro
Cowbit PE12 157 B5
Spalding PE11 214 F3
Childers' S Dro
Cowbit PE12 157 B4
Childers' S Dro *continued*
Pinchbeck PE11 214 F2
Childersgate La PE12 159 D2
Childrens Highway 6
NG24 104 C1
Chiltern Cl NG31 210 E7
Chiltern Cres DN17 184 D8
Chiltern Dr
Spalding PE11 214 E6
Waltham DN37 194 D3
Chiltern Prim Sch
HU3 180 B5
Chiltern Rd 3 LN5 205 D3
Chiltern Rise PE4 221 B2
Chiltern Way
3 Grimsby DN33 194 E8
24 North Hykeham LN6 93 C8
Chilton Cl 7 DN40 186 B4
China St PE22 114 C4
Chingford Ave DN34 191 A4
Chippendale Cl
2 Birchwood LN6 204 D6
2 Humberston DN36 36 D8
Chippendale Rd 3 LN6 204 D6
Chippenham Mews 1
PE2 230 C7
Chisenhale PE2 229 E6
Chivenor Cl 3 LN6 200 B1
Cholmley St HU3 180 B5
Chopdike Dro PE11 144 D3
Christ's Hospl Terr
LN2 234 B3
Christchurch Rd 10
NG31 211 D7
Christine Pl DN33 195 A8
Christopher Cl
5 Heckington NG34 122 E3
Louth LN11 198 D7
3 Manby LN11 62 C6
Peterborough PE1 225 F8
Christopher Cres 11
NG34 212 F4
Christopher Dr 8 PE13 170 C1
Christopher Rd 6 LN13 75 E2
Christopher's La 4
PE10 213 D6
Church Ave
Ashby De La Launde & Bloxholm
LN4 108 B5
Humberston DN36 36 C8
7 North Ferriby HU14 3 A4
Church Balk DN8 15 B8
Church Bank 2 PE34 161 F3
Church Cl 2 Bonby DN20 10 C2
Donington on Bain LN11 59 E2
Grimsby DN32 192 B5
2 Louth LN11 198 B5
16 Mablethorpe/Sutton on Sea
LN12 77 A8
4 Newborough PE6 174 E4
11 Sibsey PE22 113 B1
11 Sleaford NG34 212 B2
Stoke Rochford NG33 139 F2
3 Thorne/Moorends DN8 15 B8
Wrangle PE22 114 C1
Church Cres 4 DN9 28 A3
Church Ct 3 PE9 219 C4
Church Dr Lincoln LN6 201 D1
9 Misterton DN10 39 F5
Norton Disney LN6 92 C1
Peterborough PE2 229 F4
Church End
Gedney PE12 159 D7
9 Leverington PE13 170 B2
Skegness PE25 206 B8
Wrangle PE22 114 C1
Church End Dro PE11 134 F1
Church Farm Cl 22 PE24 90 D7
Church Farm Mus*
PE25 206 B4
Church Fields
Pickworth NG34 142 A8
Winterton DN15 9 A5
Church Gate
Fleet PE12 159 B6
2 Market Deeping PE6 217 F4
Spalding PE11 214 D3
22 Sutton Bridge PE12 160 E4
Whaplode PE12 158 B6
Church Gn PE12 216 C4
Church Gn Cl PE21 209 F2
Church Gn La
Frampton PE20 136 B7
Quadring PE11 135 A1
Church Gn Rd PE21 209 F4
Church Hill
Belvoir NG32 138 C6
1 Burgh le Marsh PE24 102 E7
Castor PE5 223 E2
2 Grasby DN38 32 E7
Heighington/Washingborough
LN4 203 B2
Ingham LN1 55 A2
Riby DN37 23 C2
Spridlington LN8 55 F3
Whitton DN15 1 E3
Church Hill Cl PE7 231 C1
Church La
Addlethorpe PE24 90 D4
Algarkirk PE20 136 B1
Alvingham LN11 49 F2
9 Ancaster NG32 120 A2
Appleby DN15 9 D1
Aylesby DN37 23 E2
7 Bardney LN3 83 B4
Baumber LN9 72 B1
Benniworth LN8 71 E8
Besthorpe NG23 91 D7
Church La *continued*
4 Billinghay LN4 109 F5
Blyton DN21 41 C5
Bonby DN20 10 C2
19 Boston PE21 208 F5
Bottesford NG13 128 C4
Bourne PE10 213 D4
Brant Broughton LN5 105 F5
Brigsley DN37 35 D4
4 Brough HU15 2 C7
15 Broughton DN20 19 E3
Buckminster NG33 150 F4
Burton Coggles NG33 152 D8
Cadney DN20 31 D6
6 Carlton-le-Moorland
LN5 105 E8
3 Caythorpe NG32 119 B7
23 Chapel St Leonard PE24 90 D7
Cherry Willingham/Reepham
LN3 203 E5
Clipsham LE15 162 B7
Coleby LN5 93 F3
6 Collingham NG23 91 D5
Corringham DN21 41 E2
Counthorpe & Creeton
NG33 153 A2
Croft PE24 102 E5
7 Crowland PE6 166 F1
2 Croxton Kerrial NG32 138 D4
1 Donington PE11 134 F2
Eagle & Swinethorpe LN6 79 B2
East Keal PE23 100 E6
Edenham PE10 153 F4
Elkington LN11 60 E7
Ewerby & Evedon NG34 122 C6
5 Fishlake DN7 14 D8
1 Folkingham NG34 142 D8
Fotherby LN11 49 A2
Friesthorpe LN3 57 A2
Friskney PE22 114 F6
Frithville PE22 125 D8
5 Glentham LN8 43 F1
Goulceby LN11 72 D6
Grainthorpe LN11 50 B7
Great Gonerby NG31 210 C8
Great Limber DN37 22 D3
Grimsby DN37 190 E2
1 Hagworthingham PE23 87 A4
Harmston LN5 93 F5
Haxey DN9 27 C2
Heckington NG34 122 E1
3 Helpringham NG34 133 D7
3 Helpston PE6 173 C4
Holton le Clay DN36 195 D2
Horbling NG34 133 B2
7 Horncastle LN9 199 B4
Hougham NG32 118 C3
Humberston DN36 36 D8
Huttoft LN13 76 E3
Immingham DN40 186 B5
3 Ingham LN1 54 F2
Ingoldmells PE25 206 C8
2 Irby DN37 34 D7
4 Keadby with Althorpe
DN17 17 D4
Keddington LN11 198 E8
3 Keelby DN41 23 A4
Kingston upon Hull
HU10 178 C8
Kirkby La Thorpe NG34 121 F4
Kirton PE20 136 C5
12 Laceby DN37 23 F1
2 Legbourne LN11 61 F3
Lincoln LN2 234 B4
3 Little Bytham NG33 163 A8
Londonthorpe &
Harrowby without NG31 130 D5
Long Bennington NG23 117 E2
Luddington & Haldenby
DN17 7 D4
Lutton PE12 160 A8
14 Mablethorpe/Sutton on Sea
LN12 77 A8
3 Mareham Le Fen PE22 98 F4
Marshchapel DN36 37 B1
17 Metheringham LN4 95 D4
Minting LN9 84 C8
6 Misterton DN10 39 F5
Misterton LN13 89 B6
Moulton PE12 157 F7
Navenby LN5 107 A8
Newton PE13 170 A5
North Carlton LN1 67 C4
10 North Kelsey LN7 32 A4
North Kyme LN4 109 F3
North Rauceby NG32 120 C5
North Scarle LN6 78 E1
North Somercotes LN11 50 E6
Old Somerby NG33 140 E8
Owersby LN8 44 F5
5 Owmby LN8 55 F6
Peterborough PE2 229 F5
Pickworth NG34 132 A1
6 Potterhanworth LN4 82 B1
Rand LN8 70 A5
Ropsley & Humby NG33 131 B1
Roughton LN9 85 B1
Saltfleetby LN12 63 B7
Saxby All Saints DN20 10 B3
Saxilby with Ingleby LN1 66 C3
Scamblesby LN11 72 F5
Scawby DN20 20 A1
Scopwick LN4 108 E8
9 Scotter DN21 29 C3
Scotton DN21 29 D2
Scredington NG34 132 F7
Scunthorpe DN15 182 E2
Sedgebrook NG32 128 F4
Church La *continued*
Silk Willoughby NG34 121 B1
Skegness PE25 206 B8
Skidbrooke with Saltfleet Haven
LN11 51 B4
Sleaford NG34 212 D5
Snitterby DN21 43 D5
South Clifton NG23 78 C6
South Kyme LN4 123 A8
15 South Witham NG33 151 D2
Spilsby PE23 87 E1
Springthorpe DN21 53 E8
Sproxton LE14 150 C7
Stallingborough DN41 23 D6
9 Stamford PE9 219 C4
Sudbrooke LN2 68 F3
Swaby LN13 74 E3
13 Swineshead PE20 135 B7
Tallington PE9 172 F6
Tealby LN8 46 C1
Tetford LN9 73 F1
Tetney DN36 36 D3
3 Timberland LN4 96 C1
Toynton St Peter PE23 101 A6
Twin Rivers DN14 7 A8
Tydd St Giles PE13 169 F7
Tydd St Mary PE13 160 B1
2 Ulceby DN39 12 A1
Utterby LN11 48 F3
21 Waddington LN5 93 F7
Wainfleet St Mary PE24 102 B1
Waithe DN36 36 A3
Waltham DN37 194 E4
Wansford PE8 222 D2
Welby NG32 130 F3
2 Welton/Dunholme LN2 68 D6
West Keal PE23 100 C6
3 Westborough & Dry
Doddington NG23 117 F3
Withern with Stain LN13 62 F1
Wood Enderby LN9 98 F7
Wrangle PE22 114 C1
Wyberton PE21 136 F8
3 Wymondham LE14 150 C1
Church La Prim Sch
NG34 212 D5
Church Lees NG32 131 C6
Church Mdw Dr 20 PE24 90 D7
Church Mews 7 PE20 136 A2
Church Pk 17 LN12 77 A8
Church Rd
Aubourn Haddington &
South Hykeham LN5 93 A5
4 Bicker PE20 135 A4
Boston PE21 209 B4
4 Butterwick PE22 126 E3
Freiston PE22 126 D2
Friskney PE22 115 A6
Harby NG23 79 B5
4 Ketton PE9 171 A3
Laughton DN21 41 C8
Leverington PE13 170 E1
3 Mablethorpe/Sutton on Sea
LN12 64 A3
North Ferriby HU14 3 A4
Old Leake PE22 114 A1
Saxilby LN1 66 D2
Skellingthorpe LN6 200 A4
Stainforth DN7 14 C6
Stickford PE22 100 B3
1 Stow LN1 66 C8
Ulceby with Fordington
LN13 88 C7
Upton DN21 53 D5
Waddingham DN21 43 D7
Wigtoft PE20 135 E3
Wisbech PE13 170 B1
Wittering PE8 172 B1
Church Rd N PE25 206 B4
Church Rd S 4 PE25 206 B3
Church Rise 5 PE22 98 F4
Church Row HU8 181 A8
Church Side
3 Alkborough DN15 8 C8
3 Appleby DN15 9 D1
19 Goxhill DN19 12 A8
3 Grasby DN38 32 E7
3 West Halton DN15 8 E7
14 Winterton DN15 9 A5
Church Sq DN15 183 B3
Church St 4 Alford LN13 75 F3
Amcotts DN17 7 F1
Barkston NG32 130 B8
2 Barrowby NG32 210 A5
2 Baston PE6 164 E4
Beckingham DN10 40 A1
4 Billingborough NG34 133 B1
2 Billinghay LN4 109 F5
20 Boston PE21 208 F5
Bottesford NG13 128 A5
9 Brough HU15 2 D6
7 Brough HU15 2 C7
5 Burgh le Marsh PE24 102 E8
14 Caistor LN7 33 B4
Carlby PE9 163 D5
4 Carlton-le-Moorland
LN5 105 E8
Collingham NG23 91 C4
Corby Glen NG33 152 F8
2 Crowle DN17 16 D7
Denton NG32 139 A7
Digby LN4 108 D5
3 Donington PE11 134 E2
Easton on the Hill PE9 171 D3
Elsham DN20 20 F7

Church St *continued*
1 Epworth DN9 27 E6
6 Fishlake DN7 14 D8
1 Foston NG32 117 F1
3 Fulletby LN9 86 B8
Gainsborough DN21 197 C5
Glentworth DN21 54 F6
4 Gosberton PE11 145 B6
16 Goxhill DN19 12 A8
Grantham NG31 211 A5
4 Grimsby DN32 189 B1
1 Haconby PE10 154 D8
5 Harlaxton NG32 139 C7
Haxey DN9 27 C2
6 Heckington NG34 122 E3
Heckington NG34 122 E1
Hemswell DN21 42 D1
7 Hibaldstow DN20 30 F5
Holbeach PE12 215 D2
Kingston upon Hull HU10 178 E6
7 Kirton in Lindsey DN21 30 B1
Long Bennington NG23 117 D3
Louth LN11 198 C5
Market Deeping PE6 217 B5
6 Market Rasen LN8 57 D8
Messingham DN17 29 D7
7 Middle Rasen LN8 57 B8
Misterton DN10 39 F5
20 Nettleham LN2 68 C2
Nettleton LN7 33 B3
12 North Kelsey LN7 32 A4
North Witham NG33 151 D4
Northborough PE6 173 F6
Owston Ferry DN9 28 A3
Peterborough PE4 220 F3
Peterborough PE7 229 A4
Peterborough PE2 231 C7
Pinchbeck PE11 145 C1
17 Ruskington NG34 108 E2
7 Ryhall PE9 163 C1
9 Scawby DN20 30 E8
10 Scothern LN2 68 F4
Skillington NG33 151 A8
10 South Witham NG33 151 D2
Spalding PE11 214 D4
11 Spilsby PE23 87 F1
9 Spilsby PE23 88 A1
8 Stamford PE9 219 C4
Sturton Le Steeple DN22 52 B2
21 Sutton Bridge PE12 160 E4
1 Sutton on Trent NG23 91 A8
Sutton-on-Trent NG23 78 A1
26 Thorne/Moorends DN8 15 A8
9 Thorney PE6 176 A3
Thurlby PE10 164 D7
Willoughton DN21 42 E4
1 Wragby LN8 70 D4
Yaxley PE7 233 D4
Church View
2 Alkborough DN15 8 C8
11 Barton-upon-Humber DN18 10 F8
1 Beckingham DN10 40 A1
13 Bottesford NG13 128 A6
9 Brough HU15 2 C7
Freiston PE22 126 D2
3 Gainsborough DN21 53 A5
8 Great Gonerby NG31 129 D5
Great Gonerby NG31 210 D8
Grimsby DN34 190 E7
Northborough PE6 217 E1
10 Ruskington NG34 108 E2
2 Waltham DN37 194 E4
Church View Cl
3 Belton DN9 16 E1
1 Donington PE11 134 E2
Peterborough PE2 231 B7
Church View Cres LN3 82 B7
Church Way PE13 160 A1
Church Wlk
Brant Broughton & Stragglethorpe LN5 105 F4
1 Dunham-on-Trent NG22 65 B1
2 Holbeach PE12 215 D2
3 Holton le Clay DN36 195 D2
1 Legbourne LN11 61 F3
1 Manby LN11 62 C6
21 Metheringham LN4 95 D4
27 Metheringham LN4 95 C4
1 Owston Ferry DN9 28 A3
Peterborough PE1 226 A3
2 Pinchbeck PE11 156 F8
Sibsey PE22 113 B2
Upton PE6 223 B5
Churchfield Ct PE4 225 E8
Churchfield Rd
Peterborough PE4 221 B1
Scunthorpe DN16 185 B5
Churchfields Rd NG34 142 C8
Churchfleet La PE11 145 B7
Churchgate PE12 159 D7
Churchgate Mews 5 PE12 159 D7
Churchill Ave
Bourne PE10 213 B4
Bracebridge Heath LN4 205 F4
Brigg DN20 196 D4
2 Hatfield DN7 14 F4
1 Horncastle LN9 199 C2
4 Keelby DN41 23 A5
4 Market Rasen LN8 57 D7
2 Skegness PE25 206 D7
Churchill Cl 6 LN11 50 F7
Churchill Ct 2 PE12 216 B5
Churchill Dr
3 Boston PE21 209 D4
2 Martin LN10 97 B4
Spalding PE11 214 D2
Churchill La LN12 63 E8
Churchill Rd
Gorefield PE13 169 F3
North Somercotes LN11 50 F7
Stamford PE9 219 B7
Churchill St HU9 181 D7
Churchill Way
Grimsby DN32 191 F7
Heckington NG34 122 D3
5 Lea DN21 52 F6
Churchthorpe 1 LN11 49 B8
Churchtown 9 DN9 16 E1
Churchview Cl 5 NG34 122 D3
Churchway PE22 127 A5
Chuter Ede Prim Sch NG24 104 C2
Cinder La LN11 198 B5
Circle The 4 HU13 178 E2
Cissbury Cl 12 LN12 77 A8
Cissbury Ring PE4 221 A2
Cissplatt La DN41 23 A5
Cisterngate 3 LN11 198 B6
Citadel Way HU9 181 A6
City of Lincoln Com Coll The LN6 205 A8
City Rd PE1 226 A2
City Sports Ctr LN6 205 A8
Clampgate Rd PE21 126 C1
Clapton Gate PE12 157 E5
Clare Ave DN17 184 D7
Clare Cl 11 Lincoln LN5 205 D3
7 Stamford PE9 219 A5
Clare Ct 4 Baston PE6 164 E4
Grimsby DN34 191 A5
Clare Rd
Northborough PE6 217 E1
Peterborough PE1 225 F6
Claremont Rd
1 Burgh le Marsh PE24 102 E8
Gainsborough DN21 197 E2
Grimsby DN32 192 D6
Claremont St LN2 234 C2
Clarence Cl 2 DN40 186 B3
Clarence Gdns 3 PE11 214 E2
Clarence Rd
Peterborough PE1 225 E5
28 Wisbech PE13 170 D1
3 Woodhall Spa LN10 97 D6
Clarence St
Kingston upon Hull HU1 181 A6
1 Lincoln LN1 201 E6
Clarendon Gdns 1 LN1 201 E8
Clarendon Rd
Grimsby DN34 190 E4
Scunthorpe DN17 184 F7
Skegness PE25 206 A4
Clarendon St HU3 180 D7
Clarendon Way PE6 220 D8
Clarina St LN2 202 B4
Clark Ave DN31 191 A7
Clarke Ct 10 PE21 136 D8
Clarke Rd 11 Lincoln LN6 93 C8
Lincoln LN6 204 E4
Clarke St 2 DN15 183 A3
Clarkes Rd 3 DN40 12 E4
Clarkson Ave 1 PE12 167 B8
Clarkson Ct 27 PE13 170 D1
Clarkson Infants Sch The PE13 170 E1
Clarksons Dr 3 DN41 23 E6
Clasketgate LN2 234 B2
Clatterdykes Rd PE20 136 E6
Claudette Ave PE11 214 B5
Claudette Way 5 PE11 214 B5
Clavering St 6 DN31 188 D1
Claxby Rd DN17 184 F5
Claxy Bank PE22 114 D6
Clay Bank LN4 123 C7
Clay Bank Rd DN8 15 C6
Clay Dro PE11 156 C5
Clay Hill Rd NG34 212 A3
Clay La
Carlton-le-Moorland LN5 105 D8
Castor PE5 223 E2
Fenton LN1 65 E4
Gate Burton DN21 53 B1
Harby NG23 79 C5
Holton le Clay DN36 195 D3
Kirton in Lindsey DN21 30 A1
Newark NG24 104 B4
Norton Disney LN5 92 D2
Stapleford LN6 105 B7
Tetford LN9 73 F2
Toft Newton LN8 56 C7
Waddingham DN21 43 D7
Clay Lake Bank PE12 157 A3
Clay Lake La PE11 214 E2
Clay Pit La NG34 122 C6
Clayberg Dr 2 NG34 212 D5
Clayden St 4 DN31 188 D1
Claydike Bank PE20 124 B4
Clayfield Rd DN15 182 F6
Clayhough La DN22 65 B3
Claymore Cl DN35 192 E6
Claypole CE (Controlled) Prim Sch NG23 117 F8
Claypole Dr PE6 217 E1
Claypole La NG23 117 E6
Claypole Rd NG23 118 A7
Claythorne Dr DN21 197 E4
Claythorpe Water Mill* LN13 75 B5
Clayton Cl 16 PE13 170 E1
Clayton Cres PE12 157 C2
Clayton Rd LN5 205 E6
Clayton Sch PE2 230 B4
Clayworth Rd 6 DN10 39 C1
Cleatham PE3 225 A4
Cleatham Rd DN21 30 B3
Clee Cres DN32 192 C5
Clee Ness Dr DN36 193 A1
Clee Rd DN35 192 C5
Clee Village DN32 192 C6
Cleefields Cl DN32 192 B5
Cleethorpe Rd DN32 189 B1
Cleethorpes Coast Light Rly & Mus* DN35 193 B3
Cleethorpes Ctry Pk* DN35 192 F2
Cleethorpes Discovery Ctr* DN35 193 B3
Cleethorpes Showground* DN35 193 C3
Cleethorpes Sta DN35 192 F7
Clematis App LN6 204 C8
Clematis Ave 7 DN41 23 F5
Clematis Cl LN4 81 D2
Clematis Way DN16 185 C4
Clensey La NG23 117 F5
Clerke St DN35 192 B8
Cleve Pl 3 PE6 175 A1
Clevedon Rd DN17 184 D8
Cleveland Ave 26 LN6 93 C8
Cleveland Cl
2 Immingham DN40 186 A4
2 Scunthorpe DN17 184 D8
4 Spalding PE11 214 F4
Cleveland Ct 3 PE4 221 C2
Cleveland Gdns 2 DN31 188 D1
Cleveland St
2 Gainsborough DN21 197 D3
3 Grimsby DN31 188 D1
Kingston upon Hull HU8 181 A8
Cleveland Way 27 DN7 14 D4
Cley Hall Gdns PE11 214 E4
Cleymond Chase 2 PE20 136 C5
Cliff Ave 22 Nettleham LN2 68 C2
Winterton DN15 8 F5
Cliff Closes Rd DN15 182 D3
Cliff Cres 1 PE9 219 B5
Cliff Dr
Burton upon Stather DN15 8 B5
3 Kingston upon Hull HU13 3 E4
Cliff Gdns DN15 182 F2
Cliff Gr 9 DN18 10 E8
Cliff La Marston NG32 129 D8
Waddingham DN21 43 C6
Washingborough LN4 81 D4
Cliff Rd Fulbeck NG32 119 C8
Hessle HU13 3 E4
Leadenham LN5 106 D2
Snitterby DN21 43 C5
Spridlington LN8 55 F3
Stamford PE9 219 B5
Welbourn LN5 106 E4
Welton LN2 68 C6
Winteringham DN15 9 A8
Woolsthorpe By Belvoir NG32 128 D1
Cliff St DN16 183 C2
Cliff The DN15 182 D3
Cliff Top La 2 HU13 3 E4
Cliffe Ave 1 NG34 108 D1
Cliffe Cl 19 NG34 108 D2
Cliffe Rd
Easton on the Hill PE9 171 D2
Gonerby Hill Foot NG31 210 E7
Cliffe View NG34 120 E4
Cliffedale Prim Sch NG31 211 A8
Clifford Rd PE25 206 B4
Cliffside 1 LN5 107 A7
Clifton Ave PE3 225 E3
Clifton Ct 2 DN8 15 A8
Clifton Gr 3 PE25 206 D1
Clifton Prim Sch HU2 180 E8
Clifton Rd Boston PE21 209 E4
Grimsby DN34 191 A6
Clifton St LN5 234 B1
Clint La 9 LN5 107 A8
Clinton Dr NG34 212 C2
Clinton Pk Prim Sch LN4 207 A5
Clinton Terr 3 DN21 197 D3
Clinton Way LN10 97 B5
Clipseygap La PE10 154 B6
Clipsham Rd PE9 162 D8
Clive Ave LN6 205 C8
Clive Sullivan Way
Barton-upon-Humber DN19 4 A4
Kingston upon Hull HU4 179 C1
Clixby Cl DN35 193 A3
Clixby La DN38 32 E7
Cloddy Gate LN11 50 F5
Cloister Wk 14 DN20 19 E3
Cloisters The
Grimsby DN37 190 D7
17 Humberston DN36 36 D8
Cloot Dro PE6 166 F2
Close The
Barkston NG32 130 A8
1 Colsterworth NG33 151 D7
Easton on the Hill PE9 171 C3
2 Fiskerton LN3 82 A7
2 Goxhill DN19 5 A1
Grimsby DN34 191 C7
8 Scunthorpe DN16 183 B2
4 Skegness PE25 206 C4
5 Sturton by Stow LN1 66 D7
Close The *continued*
1 Woodhall Spa LN10 97 C6
Closshill La PE21 136 F8
Clouds La Belton DN9 17 B1
West Butterwick DN17 28 C8
Clough La Firsby PE23 101 F5
Kirton PE20 136 F2
Clough Rd
Gosberton PE11 144 D4
Holbeach PE12 215 B7
Cloven Ends 4 PE6 164 F3
Clover Gdns 6 PE9 218 C7
Clover La PE20 135 D4
Clover Rd
Market Deeping PE6 217 C5
Misterton LN13 89 A6
Clover Way PE11 214 B6
Cloverfields Prim Sch DN36 36 C8
Clowes Ct 4 HU13 178 E1
Clubhurn La PE11 145 D4
Clumber Ave NG24 104 A3
Clumber Dr 7 PE11 214 C6
Clumber Pl DN35 192 E5
Clumber St
Kingston upon Hull HU5 180 C8
Lincoln LN5 205 E7
Clutton's Cl 4 PE6 166 E1
Clyde Ct 1 NG31 210 E2
Clyde St HU3 179 F5
Clydesdale Cres 1 PE11 214 A2
Clyfton Cres DN40 186 B4
Coach House Gdns 8 DN20 30 E8
Coach Rd NG32 118 C3
Coachroad Hill DN21 54 F7
Coal Shore La LN11 37 D1
Coal Yd La NG23 78 C4
Coalbeach La 1 PE11 145 E3
Coalbeach La S PE11 145 E4
Coalport Cl 7 LN6 204 D7
Coates Ave 27 DN15 9 A5
Coates Rd DN22 65 B8
Cob Gate PE12 158 A6
Cobbet Pl PE1 226 B3
Cobblers Way 6 NG34 212 E3
Cobden Ave PE1 225 F4
Cobden St
1 Gainsborough DN21 197 C4
Kingston upon Hull HU3 179 F7
Peterborough PE1 225 F4
Cobgate Cl 2 PE12 158 B6
Cobham Cl 11 NG34 122 E3
Cobleas NG32 138 D8
Cochran Cl 9 NG31 210 F8
Cock Pit Cl HU10 178 C6
Cockbourn Fen Dike PE12 159 B2
Cockburn Way 6 LN5 93 F5
Cockerels Roost LN1 65 D1
Cocketts La 10 DN20 30 F5
Cocklehole Rd PE34 161 B5
Cockthorne La DN15 9 C7
Coddington CE Sch NG24 104 D5
Coddington La LN6 105 A7
Coddington Rd NG24 104 C3
Coelus St HU9 181 A7
Cogan St HU1 180 E5
Coggles Cswy PE10 213 D4
Coggles Way LN11 61 E3
Cogglesford Mill* NG34 212 F5
Cohort Cl 13 HU15 2 C5
Coke Oven Ave DN16 183 F2
Cold Harbour La
Carrington PE22 112 B6
Covenham St Mary LN11 49 D5
Grantham NG31 211 C2
Cold Hurn La PE11 144 F6
Coldham Rd LN4 207 E6
Coldhorn Cres 14 PE13 170 D1
Cole La PE22 100 B3
Cole St DN15 183 B3
Coleby CE Prim Sch LN5 93 F3
Coleby Rd DN15 8 E7
Coleby St LN2 202 B3
Colegrave St 14 LN5 205 E8
Colenso Terr 3 LN1 201 D4
Coleraine Cl 8 LN5 205 D2
Coleridge Ave DN17 184 D7
Coleridge Ct 5 LN4 207 B5
Coleridge Gdns
Lincoln LN2 202 B7
15 Sleaford NG34 212 F4
Coleridge Gn 3 LN2 202 C7
Coleridge Pl
Bourne PE10 213 E3
Peterborough PE1 225 E8
Coles Ave LN13 75 E2
Coles Cl PE12 215 E3
Cole's La 1 PE20 135 B7
Colin Ave DN32 192 B6
Colin Rd DN16 183 C2
Colindale PE21 209 B5
Colins Wlk DN21 29 C4
College Ave DN33 194 F8
College Cl
6 Alkborough DN15 8 C8
1 Holbeach PE12 215 C2
4 Horncastle LN9 199 C2
Lincoln LN1 201 F6
Stamford PE9 171 C8
7 Wainfleet All Saints PE24 102 D1
College Gdns 2 DN33 194 F8
College Pk
Horncastle LN9 199 C2
Peterborough PE1 226 C5
College Rd
Barrow upon Humber DN19 11 E7
Cranwell & Byard's Leap NG34 120 E8
Thornton Curtis DN39 12 B6
College St
Cleethorpes DN35 192 E6
Grantham NG31 211 B3
Grimsby DN34 191 C6
1 Kingston upon Hull HU2 180 E7
Colley St 11 PE21 208 F5
Colley's Gate PE12 216 C8
Colleywell Cl 5 DN9 27 A2
Collier Cl 11 HU14 3 A4
Collier Rd 2 DN40 186 D5
Collier St HU1 180 E6
Collingham PE2 229 F3
Collingham Rd LN6 91 F5
Collingham Sta NG23 91 D4
Collingwood 21 LN6 93 C8
Collingwood Cres
3 Boston PE21 136 D8
Grimsby DN34 190 D4
Collingwood Prim Sch HU3 180 C7
Collingwood St HU3 180 D7
Collinson Ave DN15 182 C3
Collinson La
11 Balderton NG24 104 C1
Newport HU15 1 A8
Collison Gate PE24 102 C2
Collum Ave DN16 185 B6
Collum Gdns 2 DN16 185 B6
Collum La DN16 185 B6
Collynson Cl 1 HU10 178 E8
Collyweston Rd 1 PE8 172 B1
Colne Cl 1 LN6 204 F3
Colne Ct 6 NG31 210 E2
Colne Valley Visitor Ctr* PE6 227 B2
Colonial St HU2 180 D7
Colson Pl DN35 192 B7
Colster Way 3 NG33 151 E6
Colsterworth CE Prim Sch NG33 151 E7
Colsterworth Rd NG33 151 C6
Colsuan Gdns PE12 216 C3
Coltman St HU3 180 C5
Colton Cl 6 PE6 164 E4
Colton St Brigg DN20 196 B4
2 Misterton DN10 39 F5
Coltsfoot Cl 6 DN15 182 C6
Coltsfoot Dr
Bradley DN37 194 B5
Peterborough PE2 230 E7
Columbia Rd DN32 192 A7
Columbus Cl 5 PE11 214 C2
Columbus Way DN33 190 F3
Colvile Rd PE13 170 A5
Colville Ave HU4 179 B6
Colville Terr 3 DN21 197 D4
Combe St DN35 192 C8
Comer Cl PE21 209 A5
Comforts Ave DN15 183 A2
Commerce La HU1 180 D4
Commercial Rd
2 Alford LN13 75 F2
Grantham NG31 211 A3
Kingston upon Hull HU1 180 E5
1 Louth LN11 198 D6
Scunthorpe DN16 183 D3
Spalding PE11 214 E5
Commodore Croft 6 HU1 180 F5
Common Balk LN13 76 C1
Common Dro
Crowland PE6 166 C3
Wrangle PE22 114 B5
Common La
7 Balderton NG24 104 C1
Bardney LN3 83 C4
Barnby Dun with Kirk Sandall DN3 14 B4
Burgh Le Marsh PE24 89 F1
Heapham DN21 53 F7
North Somercotes LN11 50 F8
Old Leake PE22 113 F4
Sturton Le Steeple DN22 52 C3
Twin Rivers DN14 7 B6
Welton HU15 2 D4
Common Mid Rd DN17 16 C8
Common Rd
Broughton DN20 19 E4
Gedney Hill PE12 176 F8
Moulton PE12 146 E3
Parson Drove PE12 176 F6
South Cave HU15 1 C7
Waddingham DN21 43 D7
Whaplode PE12 168 A2
Wrangle PE22 114 B3
Common Side Rd PE22 113 E4
Common Way PE13 160 B1
Commonside
2 Crowle DN17 16 C8
Westwoodside DN9 27 A2
Comper Swift Cl 1 LN12 77 A7
Compton Cl 1 PE25 206 C1
Compton Dr DN34 191 C7
Concast Rd DN16 19 A3
Conduit La NG31 211 A4
Conduit Rd PE9 219 C6

Coney Garth La PE11 145 F5
Coneygree Rd PE2 231 D6
Conference Ct DN16 185 A2
Conging St 3 LN9 199 B4
Congreves Cl 3 PE12 160 A8
Conifer Cl
6 Kingston upon Hull HU5 179 C7
2 Scunthorpe DN17 184 C5
Conifers The PE2 229 F6
Coningsby Airfield LN4 207 C2
Coningsby Cl
Boston PE21 208 D5
2 Skegness PE25 206 A5
Coningsby Cres LN4 205 F5
Coningsby Dr DN34 191 A5
Coningsby Rd
Coningsby LN4 207 A1
Peterborough PE3 220 E1
Scunthorpe DN17 184 D5
Coningsby St LN2 234 C2
Coningsby St Michaels CE Prim Sch LN4 207 C4
Conisborough Ave DN36 195 B6
Conisholme Rd LN11 50 B7
Coniston Ave 1 DN33 194 E7
Coniston Cres DN36 192 E1
Coniston Dr LN6 205 A2
Coniston Rd PE4 221 C3
Connaught Ave DN32 191 D4
Connaught Dr
4 Chapel St Leonard PE24 90 D7
6 Kirk Sandall DN3 14 A2
Connaught Rd DN21 197 C6
Conquest Dro PE7 231 D1
Consort Ct HU9 181 B5
Constable Ave LN6 205 A6
Constable Cl LN6 205 A5
Constable Prim Sch HU3 180 C5
Constable St HU3 180 C5
Constance Ave LN6 204 F4
Constitutional Ave DN35 192 C8
Convamore Rd DN32 191 F6
Convent La HU3 180 D6
Conway Ave
Grimsby DN34 191 A7
Peterborough PE4 221 A2
Conway Cl HU3 180 B5
Conway Dr LN6 205 B2
Conway Prep Sch PE21 208 F5
Conway Sq 3 DN15 182 E3
Conyard Rd DN35 192 E7
Conyers Ave DN33 191 D2
Cook Cl Rd PE7 233 D6
Cook Dr PE11 214 C2
Cooke Cres 9 LN4 207 D4
Cookridge Dr 31 DN7 14 D4
Cook's La PE23 88 E3
Cook's Rd PE11 145 E7
Cooks La Grimsby DN37 24 B5
4 Nettleton LN7 33 A3
Cooks Lock PE21 208 C3
Cookson Cl PE7 233 D4
Coomb Brigg Prim Sch DN40 186 A3
Cooper Ave PE25 90 E4
Cooper La DN37 23 E1
Cooper Rd DN32 192 A7
Coopers Cl PE12 168 B4
Coopers Holt Cl LN6 200 A3
Coots Cl PE25 103 C8
Coots La LN13 76 E1
Cope St DN32 192 A8
Copeland PE3 225 A3
Copeland Ct 5 NG34 212 C3
Copper Beech Cl
1 Gainsborough DN21 52 F6
6 Swanland HU14 3 B6
Copper Beech Way PE2 231 B7
Copper Beech Wlk DN16 185 B3
Copper St LN10 84 B3
Coppice Ave 13 DN7 14 D3
Coppice La 2 DN7 14 D3
Coppice Rd 11 PE9 163 C1
Coppice Side HU4 179 C6
Coppingford Cl PE2 231 D6
Copse Cl DN40 186 C5
Copse Rd DN16 185 B5
Copse The Brigg DN20 196 E2
Grimsby DN33 194 F8
16 Mablethorpe/Sutton on Sea LN12 77 A7
Copsewood PE4 221 A4
Copthill Sch PE9 172 C6
Coral Dr 1 DN37 194 C5
Corby Glen Com Prim Sch NG33 152 E8
Corby Pk HU14 3 A5
Corby Rd
Burton Coggles NG33 141 A1
Irnham NG33 141 D1
Swayfield NG33 152 D5
Cordeaux Cl LN11 198 C7
Cordeaux High Sch LN11 198 B7
Cordella Cl 1 HU3 180 A5
Corden Cl PE25 206 C1
Corfe Ave PE4 221 A2
Corfe Cl 1 NG31 210 E5
Corinne Cres 3 PE25 206 C3
Corinne Gr 1 PE11 214 A3
Corinthian Ave DN34 191 B6
Corinthian Way HU9 181 D6
Cork La PE24 102 B3
Cork Tree Cres PE21 208 E2
Cormorant Dr DN37 190 C8
Corn Cl Fiskerton LN3 82 B7
Horncastle LN9 199 B5
Cornfield Cl 4 DN33 194 D8
Cornfield View 2 NG34 212 C2
Cornfields PE12 215 F3
Cornflower Cl
18 Healing DN41 23 F5
Stamford PE9 218 C6
Cornflower Way 3 LN6 93 A8
Cornhill LN5 234 B2
Cornhill Dr DN18 11 A8
Cornish Cres NG34 133 E7
Cornley Rd DN10 39 C7
Cornmarket 8 LN11 198 B5
Cornstall Bldgs 7 PE9 219 C5
Cornwall Cl
Grantham NG31 211 C7
12 Scampton LN1 67 E5
Cornwall Rd
5 Keadby DN17 17 D6
Scunthorpe DN16 185 C5
8 Stamford PE9 219 B6
Cornwall St
30 Kirton in Lindsey DN21 30 B1
21 Kirton in Lindsey DN21 30 B1
Cornwall Way 8 NG34 108 D2
Cornwallis Rd LN2 202 D4
Cornwell Cl DN33 191 C3
Corona Dr 3 DN8 15 A8
Coronation Ave
3 Crowland PE6 175 B8
Deeping St Nicholas PE11 166 C6
Parson Drove PE12 177 A7
Coronation Cl
1 Louth LN11 198 D7
3 Spalding PE11 157 B6
Coronation Cres
Coleby LN5 93 F3
3 Epworth DN9 27 D7
3 Epworth DN9 27 D6
Coronation Gdns 16 DN20 19 E3
Coronation Rd
Cleethorpes DN35 192 F5
Corby Glen NG33 152 E8
Ingoldmells PE25 90 F3
3 Market Rasen LN8 57 D7
9 Stainforth DN7 14 C6
5 Ulceby DN39 12 A1
Woodhall Spa LN10 97 D6
Corporation Bank
12 Crowland PE6 166 E1
Crowland PE6 174 F8
Corporation Rd
1 Grimsby DN31 188 E1
Grimsby DN31 191 D8
10 Kingston upon Hull HU9 5 D8
4 Scunthorpe DN15 183 A3
Corran Garth 6 HU4 179 A3
Correen Cl 2 LN5 205 D2
Corringham CE Prim Sch DN21 41 E2
Corringham Rd DN21 197 F5
Corsair Gr 4 HU3 180 A4
Cosford Cl LN6 204 B8
Cosgrove Cl
2 Lincoln LN6 205 A6
Peterborough PE3 225 C6
Cosgrove St DN35 192 F6
Costa Row NG23 117 D3
Coston Rd NG33 150 E5
Cot Garth La DN21 53 E3
Cotelands Sch NG34 108 E1
Cotham Gdns 22 DN41 23 A4
Cotman Rd LN6 205 B6
Cotswold Cl
22 Lincoln LN6 93 C8
3 Peterborough PE4 221 C1
Cotswold Dr
Great Gonerby NG31 210 E7
9 Waltham DN37 194 D4
Cotswold Rd 5 DN8 15 A7
Cottage Beck Rd DN16 183 B2
Cottage Cl 2 DN20 30 F5
Cottage Dr HU10 178 B8
Cottage La
Collingham NG23 91 C3
1 Lincoln LN6 205 B4
North Clifton NG23 78 D7
Cottage Paddock The LN6 205 B5
Cottage Yd La DN36 36 C7
Cottesmore Cl
Grantham NG31 211 B6
Peterborough PE3 225 D4
Cottesmore Rd
Birchwood LN6 204 D5
Cleethorpes DN35 192 E2
Kingston upon Hull HU13 178 F2
5 Stamford PE9 218 E5
Cottingham Dr LN2 202 B7
Cotton Rd PE21 208 D6
Cotton Smith Way 1 LN2 68 C2
Coulam Pl 11 DN36 36 D8
Coulbeck Dr DN35 192 D5
Coulby Cl NG23 117 F7
Coulman Rd DN8 15 B8
Coulman St DN8 15 B8
Coulson Cl 13 DN20 31 A5
Coulson Dr HU13 178 F2
Coulson Rd LN6 201 D1
Coult Ave LN6 93 C8
Coultas Ct
3 Kingston upon Hull HU3 180 A6
3 Kingston upon Hull HU3 180 A6
Council Ave HU4 179 E3
Council Rd 19 PE13 170 E1
Council St PE4 225 D8
Council Terr 6 DN18 3 E1
Count Alan Rd PE25 206 D8
Counter Drain Dro PE11 155 E2
Counthorpe La NG33 152 E2
Counthorpe Rd NG33 152 F3
County Rd S 2 HU5 179 C8
Coupledyke La PE20 136 D5
Court The PE24 77 C3
Courtfield Cl 10 LN2 68 F2
Courtney St HU8 181 B8
Cove Rd DN9 26 F3
Covel Rd NG34 212 B6
Coventry Ave DN34 191 A5
Coventry Cl
7 Grantham NG31 210 D5
Peterborough PE4 220 F3
5 Scunthorpe DN17 184 D7
Coventry Rd 7 DN8 15 B8
Coverley Rd 5 NG33 151 D2
Covert Rd DN16 185 B5
Covert The PE3 225 B1
Covill Cl 2 NG31 129 D5
Covington 29 HU15 2 C6
Covin's La LN11 49 C8
Cow Dale La DN10 39 C3
Cow Dro LN4 123 B7
Cow Gate NG34 143 C8
Cow La Minting LN8 71 B1
Swinderby LN6 92 B5
Tealby LN8 46 C1
Twin Rivers DN17 7 C6
Upton DN21 53 F6
Welbourn LN5 106 E5
Cow Marsh La DN36 36 E5
Cow Pasture La DN22 65 A7
Coward's La PE11 144 F2
Cowbit Dro PE11 144 C1
Cowbit Rd PE12 214 D2
Cowbit St Mary's Endowed Prim Sch PE12 167 A8
Cowbridge Bsns Pk PE22 125 E7
Cowbridge Rd PE20 134 E5
Cowbroads La PE22 113 E2
Cowdale La LN1 66 B6
Cowdale's Dro PE11 134 F1
Cowes Rd NG31 210 E4
Cowgate Brough HU15 2 D6
2 Heckington NG34 122 E3
Peterborough PE1 225 F2
Cowhams La PE20 146 C8
Cowle La 1 LN11 62 A3
Cowley Cl 6 PE20 135 C7
Cowley Endowed (Controlled) Prim Sch PE11 134 E2
Cowley's Rd 10 PE11 134 E2
Cowpaddle La LN4 82 A5
Cowpasture La DN22 52 D3
Cowper Ave DN17 184 D7
Cowper Dr LN2 202 C7
Cowper Rd PE1 225 F7
Cowpers Gate PE12 216 A3
Cowslip Dr 2 PE6 217 D6
Cowslip La LN11 198 F8
Cox La 7 DN17 16 D8
Cox's Ct 7 DN20 31 A5
Cox's Dro PE6 167 C1
Cox's Hill DN21 197 D5
Cox's Wlk 8 NG31 129 E5
Coxwold Gr HU4 179 E5
Crab La PE20 123 C4
Crab Marsh PE13 170 C2
Crabley La HU15 1 E7
Crabtree PE4 221 F1
Crabtree La
Beckingham DN10 52 A8
Mablethorpe & Sutton LN12 77 A7
Saltfleetby LN12 51 D1
Crabtree Rd
Colsterworth NG33 151 B7
Easton NG33 140 A1
8 Hatfield DN7 14 C5
Skillington NG33 139 F1
Crack Holt La PE22 126 F8
Cradge Bank Rd
Deeping St Nicholas PE11 167 A7
Spalding PE11 214 C1
Cragg Cl 3 PE20 135 C7
Cragmire La PE22 114 C3
Cragston Ave DN33 191 D3
Craig Cl 3 DN20 19 D3
Craig St PE1 225 F3
Craikbank La DN22 65 A8
Craikhill Ave DN40 186 C4
Craithie Rd DN35 192 E4
Crake Ave DN33 191 C1
Crakedale Rd 9 DN15 9 B5
Crampin Rd 3 DN35 192 E7
Cranberry La PE22 114 F7
Cranberry Way HU4 179 C4
Cranbourne Cl 9 DN35 192 F1
Cranbourne Mews 6 LN4 203 D1
Cranbourne St HU3 180 C8
Crane Ave PE7 233 F6
Crane Cl 1 NG34 120 F8
Crane Gr LN6 205 C7
Crane Rd HU9 181 C6
Cranemore PE4 220 E4
Cranepit La PE11 135 B1
Crane's Gate PE12 158 C1
Cranford Dr PE3 225 C4
Cranidge Cl 8 DN17 16 D8
Cranmore Dro PE6 165 F1
Cranmore La PE12 215 B1
Cranwell Airfield NG34 120 D7
Cranwell Ave NG34 120 D8
Cranwell Aviation Heritage Cantre* NG34 120 D6
Cranwell Cl
6 Kirton in Lindsey DN21 42 F8
4 Skegness PE25 206 A5
Cranwell Dr 2 DN37 190 F8
Cranwell Prim Sch NG34 107 D1
Cranwell St LN5 201 E1
Crapple La DN21 29 C2
Craske La PE34 161 D3
Craven Ave 4 PE20 136 D5
Craven Prim Sch HU9 181 C8
Craven Rd
Cleethorpes DN35 192 B7
4 Hatfield DN7 14 C4
Craven St LN5 205 D8
Craven St N HU9 181 C8
Craven St S HU9 181 D7
Craven's La PE20 146 E7
Crawcroft La LN13 76 E5
Crawford Gdns 3 PE6 175 C8
Crawthorne Rd PE1 226 A3
Crawthorne St 1 PE1 226 B3
Craycroft Rd 3 DN9 27 B2
Craypool La 7 LN2 68 F4
Craythorne La 23 PE21 208 F5
Creampoke Cres 8 DN21 55 A8
Crease Dro PE6 175 B7
Creaseyplot La PE20 124 B1
Creeton Rd NG33 153 A1
Crescent Cl 7 LN2 68 D2
Crescent St 3 DN31 191 C7
Crescent The
Beckingham DN10 40 B1
Bracebridge Heath LN4 81 A2
15 Brough HU15 2 D6
Easton on the Hill PE9 171 C3
10 Eye PE6 175 A1
Fiskerton LN3 82 B7
Gainsborough DN21 52 F5
Hatfield DN7 14 C5
Holton le Clay DN36 195 C2
Horncastle LN9 199 C3
9 Kirk Sandall DN3 14 A1
Louth LN11 198 B7
13 Mablethorpe/Sutton on Sea LN12 77 A7
Morton PE10 154 B7
12 Nettleham LN2 68 C2
Peterborough PE2 230 C5
Ryhall PE9 163 D1
Sleaford NG34 121 A3
9 Spalding PE11 214 D4
Swayfield NG33 152 E5
Cresent The 3 LN8 70 D4
Cressey St 3 DN31 189 A1
Cresswell Cl PE11 214 E8
Cresta Cl LN6 204 D1
Cresta Dr DN17 184 E4
Cresta The DN34 191 C5
Crester Dr PE4 221 A3
Crew Rd NG23 91 D5
Creyke La 12 HU15 2 D6
Cricketers Way 19 PE13 170 C1
Cridling Pl DN35 192 D4
Cringle Rd NG33 139 F2
Cringleway NG33 140 A5
Cripple Sidings La PE2 231 A8
Crispin Cl 5 HU4 179 A2
Crispin Way DN16 185 B2
Croake Hill NG33 153 A5
Crocus Cl PE7 233 F6
Crocus Gr PE1 226 A8
Croft Bank Croft PE24 102 F3
1 Croft PE24 102 E2
Croft Cl 3 PE24 102 E2
Croft Dr
Grantham NG31 211 C3
Kingston upon Hull HU10 178 C6
Croft La Bassingham LN5 92 F3
Cherry Willingham LN3 203 E7
Coningsby LN4 110 E8
Croft PE24 102 E2
Scunthorpe DN17 184 E2
Croft Lodge 1 DN9 16 E1
Croft Marsh La PE24 102 F3
Croft Pk 4 HU14 3 A5
Croft Rd Croft PE24 102 E3
Finningley DN10 26 A1
Croft St
3 Horncastle LN9 199 C3
Lincoln LN2 234 B2
Croft The
6 Beckingham DN10 52 B8
10 Nettleham LN2 68 D2
28 Thorne/Moorends DN8 15 B7
2 West/East Butterwick DN17 28 D8
Croft View HU10 178 C6
Croft Way PE7 230 C2
Crofton Cl LN2 202 D4
Crofton Dr LN2 202 D4
Crofton Rd LN2 202 D4
Croft's La DN9 28 B3
Crofts La DN7 14 B6
Crofts The
7 Humberston DN36 36 C8
1 Scunthorpe DN16 183 B2
Cromarty Rd 8 PE9 218 E6
Cromer Ave
Grimsby DN34 191 A5
Mablethorpe/Sutton on Sea LN12 64 D1
Cromer Cl 4 LN6 205 A1
Cromford St 1 DN21 197 D5
Cromwell Ave
6 Gainsborough DN21 52 F6
3 Horncastle LN9 199 C2
2 Woodhall Spa LN10 97 D5
Cromwell Cl
Boston PE21 208 D7
2 Heighington/Washingborough LN4 203 A2
2 Kingston upon Hull HU3 180 D8
Northborough PE6 217 E1
Cromwell Cres 3 NG34 212 E4
Cromwell Ct 1 HU10 178 E7
Cromwell Mews 1 PE6 173 C4
Cromwell Pl LN4 207 A5
Cromwell Rd
Cleethorpes DN35 193 A4
Grimsby DN37 188 A1
Peterborough PE1 225 F4
Cromwell St
Gainsborough DN21 197 D2
Lincoln LN2 202 B3
Cromwell View 21 LN7 33 B4
Cromwell Way 6 PE6 217 A6
Crook Bank LN12 63 F6
Crook Hill HU15 2 C8
Crook Mill Rd DN40 12 C4
Crook Tree La DN7 14 F5
Crooked Billet St DN21 197 B8
Crookes Broom Ave 32 DN7 14 D4
Crookes Broom La DN7 14 D4
Cropper's La PE22 126 E1
Cropston Rd PE1 226 E7
Crosby Ave DN15 182 F6
Crosby La 1 LN5 106 E4
Crosby Prim Sch DN15 183 A4
Crosby Rd
Grimsby DN33 191 B2
Scunthorpe DN15 183 B4
Crosby Row PE12 160 D4
Crosland Rd DN37 190 D8
Cross Bank LN4 96 D8
Cross Carr Rd DN20 31 B5
Cross Coates Rd DN34 191 A6
Cross Comm La DN22 52 D3
Cross Dro Fleet PE12 168 B2
Holland Fen with Brothertoft PE20 125 B5
Horbling NG34 133 F2
Tydd St Giles PE13 169 C5
Cross Gate
Long Sutton PE12 159 F3
Quadring PE11 135 A1
Spalding PE12 157 B6
Tydd St Mary PE13 160 A2
Weston PE12 157 C7
Cross Hill
Gringley on the Hill DN10 39 C1
Haxey DN9 27 C3
Cross Keys La LN4 207 F4
Cross Keys Yd 5 NG34 212 D4
Cross La
4 Alkborough DN15 8 C8
4 Amcotts DN17 7 F1
Balderton NG24 104 B1
3 Bourne PE10 213 E2
Butterwick PE22 126 F3
Collingham NG23 91 D5
Flixborough DN15 8 B1
Glentham LN8 44 A2
Gringley on the Hill DN10 39 A5
Harby NG23 79 B5
8 Lincoln LN6 93 C8
Long Bennington NG23 117 D1
North Kelsey LN7 32 B5
Pinchbeck PE11 144 F1
Wellingore LN5 106 E6
Cross O'Cliff Cl LN5 205 E6
Cross O'Cliff Hill LN5 205 E6
Cross Rd Hatfield DN7 15 B4
Langtoft PE6 165 B4
Market Deeping PE6 217 F8
Sutton St Edmund PE12 169 A4
Tydd St Mary PE13 160 B2
Ulceby DN39 12 B3
Cross Slack 5 DN17 16 D8
Cross Spencer St 10 LN5 205 E8
Cross St
Barnby in the Willows NG24 104 F3
8 Barrow upon Humber DN19 11 D8
4 Brigg DN20 196 C3

Cross St *continued*
Cleethorpes DN35 192 E6
13 Crowle DN17 16 D8
Gainsborough DN21 197 B8
Garthorpe & Fockerby DN17 7 E6
Grimsby DN31 189 B2
1 Holbeach PE12 215 D2
6 Horncastle LN9 199 C3
Lincoln LN5 234 B1
11 Nettleham LN2 68 C2
Peterborough PE1 226 A2
4 Potter Hanworth LN4 82 B1
Scunthorpe DN15 183 B4
3 Skegness PE25 206 B3
Spalding PE11 214 C3
Sturton Le Steeple DN22 52 B3
3 Waltham DN37 194 E4
2 West Halton DN15 8 E8
5 Whaplode PE12 158 B7
Cross Tree Rd 21 DN17 29 D7
Crossbeck Rd DN16 185 A4
Crossberry Way 1 PE6 173 B4
Crosscliff Hill LN11 60 A8
Crossfield Rd
Kingston upon Hull HU13 178 E3
12 Navenby/Wellingore LN5 107 A8
Crossgate Cres 5 PE11 145 C1
Crossgate La 3 PE11 145 C1
Crossgill Cl NG31 211 F5
Crosslands 5 PE11 134 F2
Crossmoor Bank DN14 6 C5
Crossway The DN34 190 E3
Crossways 8 DN7 14 C6
Crow Hill Ave DN35 192 E6
Crow La Gedney PE12 159 D6
Great Hale NG34 122 F1
Leadenham LN5 106 D3
Crow Pk LN6 204 A1
Crow Tree Bank DN8 15 D4
Crowberry Dr DN16 185 D5
Crowdyke Gate PE12 158 B5
Crowfields PE6 217 F5
Crowhall La PE22 127 A4
Crowhurst 1 PE4 221 A5
Crowland Ave
Grimsby DN34 190 F4
Scunthorpe DN16 185 A7
Crowland Dr LN6 204 F7
Crowland Ponds Nature Reserve* PE6 166 D2
Crowland Rd
14 Crowle DN17 16 D7
Deeping St James PE6 174 D7
Eye PE6 175 A3
Crowle Bank Rd DN17 17 C4
Crowle Dr DN33 191 A3
Crowle Moor Nature Reserve* DN17 6 B1
Crowle Prim Sch DN17 16 C7
Crowle Rd DN17 6 F2
Crowle St HU9 181 D7
Crowle Sta DN17 16 E5
Crown Ave
3 Chapel St Leonard PE24 90 D7
Holbeach PE12 147 C6
Crown Cl 10 NG23 91 D5
Crown Ct 3 DN22 52 B3
Crown Dr PE11 214 F6
Crown Hill NG33 141 B8
Crown La 14 PE10 164 C8
Crown Lakes Ctry Pk* PE7 231 B2
Crown Lodge PE12 215 C7
Crown Mills 2 LN11 198 D6
Crown St
Peterborough PE1 225 E7
Ryhall PE9 163 C2
7 Stamford PE9 219 B5
Crow's La PE24 102 C2
Crowson Cres PE6 217 E1
Crowson Way PE6 217 D5
Crowther Way 8 HU14 3 B7
Crowtree La LN11 198 A5
Croxby Ave DN33 194 F8
Croxby Gr DN33 194 F7
Croxton Dr LN6 204 F6
Croxton Kerrial CE Prim Sch NG32 138 D4
Croxton La NG32 138 D5
Croxton Rd
Croxton DN39 21 F7
Kirmington DN39 22 A5
Sproxton LE14 138 E2
Croyland Rd PE4 221 B1
Croyland Way 15 PE6 166 F1
Crusader Rd LN6 201 C1
Crystal St HU3 180 C7
Cuckoo La
Ashby De La Launde & Bloxholm LN4 107 F7
Hatfield DN7 14 E6
Pinchbeck PE11 145 C2
Cul-de-sac The PE22 100 B2
Cullin Cl 1 LN5 205 D2
Culpins Cl PE11 214 F5
Culvert Rd PE24 102 B3
Culverthorpe Hall* NG32 131 D7
Culverthorpe Rd NG34 132 A7
Cumberland Ave
Grimsby DN32 191 D5
Cumberland Ave *continued*
14 Navenby/Wellingore LN5 107 A7
Cumberland Gdns NG33 152 D1
Cumberland Rd DN35 193 A2
Cumberland St HU2 181 A8
Cumberland Terr 12 LN8 47 B6
Cumberland Way 17 LN1 67 E5
Cumberlidge Cl 10 PE24 102 E7
Cumberworth La 2 LN13 76 F1
Cumberworth Rd LN13 89 C7
Cunningham Rd 1 DN7 26 A8
Cunsdike La PE11 145 D5
Cupola Way DN15 183 A8
Curle Ave LN2 234 C4
Curlew Cl 4 PE12 216 B4
Curlew Dr 8 PE12 167 B8
Curlew Gr PE2 231 D7
Curlew Lodge La PE12 160 F8
Curlew Way NG34 212 B3
Curlew Wlk 14 PE6 217 C5
Curry Rd DN34 190 F7
Curtis Cl 13 NG23 91 D5
Curtis Dr LN4 81 E1
Curzen Cres 8 DN3 14 A2
Curzon Ave DN35 192 D5
Curzon CE (Controlled) Prim Sch LN4 207 A5
Curzon Ct DN35 192 D5
Curzon Est 6 LN4 207 A5
Curzon Mews 3 LN4 203 D1
Curzon St
1 Gainsborough DN21 197 C6
Kingston upon Hull HU3 179 F7
Cushman Cres DN40 186 C3
Customhouse St 2 PE12 160 F4
Cut Dike PE22 124 D8
Cut End Rd PE22 137 D7
Cuthbert Ave 6 DN38 21 B4
Cuthbert's La PE20 136 B8
Cuxwold Rd
3 Scunthorpe DN16 185 C8
Swallow LN7 34 B5
Cydonia App LN6 204 C8
Cygnet Cl 8 NG34 212 B3
Cygnet Pk PE7 230 E3
Cynthia Rd DN32 192 C5
Cypress Cl
2 Peterborough PE3 225 A2
9 Sleaford NG34 212 D2
Cyprus St 5 HU9 5 D8
Cyrano Way DN37 190 C7

D

Daffodil Gr PE2 231 C7
Dagger La HU1 180 F6
Daggett Rd DN35 193 A4
Daimler Ave PE7 233 E6
D'aincourt Pk LN4 81 D2
Dairy Cl 1 PE11 145 C6
Dairy Dro PE6 176 E2
Dairycoates Ave HU3 180 A4
Dairycoates Rd HU4 179 E3
Daisy Dale PE21 209 A3
Dalby Ct PE1 226 C8
Dalderby Cres 16 LN2 68 C2
Dale Ave LN3 203 E6
Dale Cl
Peterborough PE2 229 F5
10 Swanland HU14 3 B7
Dale Cres 1 NG24 104 C1
Dale Pit Rd 8 DN7 14 F3
Dale Pk Ave DN15 9 A5
Dale Rd 6 Brough HU15 2 C7
Grantham NG31 211 A7
Swanland HU14 3 B7
Welton HU15 2 E6
Dale St Lincoln LN5 202 B2
Scunthorpe DN15 182 F4
Dale St N DN15 182 F5
Dale View DN33 190 F3
Dale Way 9 NG24 104 C1
Dalehouse Dr 2 HU10 178 F6
Dales La DN10 39 A6
Dale's La PE20 135 D5
Dales The
25 Nettleham LN2 68 C2
Scunthorpe DN17 184 E3
Dalesway HU10 178 B6
Dallisons Rd 5 DN20 31 A5
Dallygate NG33 140 A5
Dallygate La NG33 140 B5
Dalmatian Way 14 DN20 19 E4
Dam Gate PE12 215 E1
Dam Gn La 5 HU15 2 C7
Dam La DN39 11 E5
Dam Rd DN18 3 D1
Dame Kendal Gr 1 DN33 191 B3
Dams La LN9 73 B2
Danby Rd 16 DN17 29 D7
Dane Cl
15 Broughton DN20 19 E4
31 Metheringham LN4 95 C4
Danes Cl PE1 226 C4
Danes Ctyd 11 LN2 234 B3
Danes Rd DN21 197 F5
Danes Terr LN2 234 B3
Danesfield Ave DN37 194 E5
Danesgate LN2 234 B3
Danethorpe La NG24 104 D8
Danial Cl PE25 206 C8
Daniel Cres 10 LN4 203 D1
Daniel Ct 7 PE9 219 C4
Daniel's Cres PE12 216 C5
Daniel's Dro PE6 167 D1
Daniel's Gate PE12 216 C7
Daniel's Reach PE11 214 C7
Daniels Gate 1 PE11 214 C6
Danish Ct PE4 220 E4
Dansom La S HU8 181 B8
Danson Cl 19 DN18 10 F8
Danube Rd HU5 179 C8
Danum Cl 11 DN8 15 B8
Danum Rd
6 Hatfield DN7 14 D3
Scunthorpe DN17 184 F8
Dar Beck Rd DN21 29 C4
Darby Rd DN15 8 B4
Darbyshire Cl NG23 79 B5
Dark La Amcotts DN17 7 F1
Barnby in the Willows NG24 105 A3
Bicker PE20 135 A5
Bitchfield & Bassingthorpe NG33 141 A3
Burwell LN11 74 C6
Holbeach PE12 215 B5
Darley Cl PE8 172 C1
Darley Dale Cres 1 NG31 211 A7
Darley's La PE11 214 A6
Darnholme Cres
Epworth DN9 28 A8
15 Messingham DN17 29 D7
Darrismere Villas 4 HU3 180 A5
Dart Ave LN6 205 A2
Dartmouth Rd DN17 182 D1
Darwin Cl
5 Stamford PE9 219 A7
7 Sutton Bridge PE12 160 E4
10 Waddington LN5 93 E8
Darwin St
3 Gainsborough DN21 197 D2
6 Kirton in Lindsey DN21 30 B1
Dashwood Rd 7 LN13 75 E2
Datchet Garth 3 HU4 179 B2
Daubeney Ave LN1 66 D2
Daubney St DN35 189 E1
Davenport Ave HU13 178 D1
Davenport Dr DN35 192 C4
Davey Cl 1 PE21 208 E7
David Ave Lincoln LN1 201 D8
Louth LN11 198 D7
David Dr PE25 206 B6
David Pl DN36 195 C5
David St DN32 191 F5
David's Cl PE4 220 D4
David's La
Benington PE22 127 A5
Peterborough PE4 220 F5
Davie Pl DN35 192 B7
Davis's Cl HU10 178 C8
Davos Way PE25 206 A7
Davy Ave DN15 182 E4
Davy Cl 3 LN11 61 F3
Davy Cres DN20 196 C5
Dawber La
Claxby St Andrew LN13 88 F5
Thimbleby LN9 85 C5
Dawes La DN16 183 D4
Dawlish Rd DN33 194 E6
Dawnay Dr HU10 179 A6
Dawnhill La DN21 42 E2
Daws Gate
Moulton PE12 157 F2
Whaplode PE12 158 A2
Dawsmere Rd PE12 148 F4
Dawson Ave 1 PE11 214 F6
Dawson Cl Lincoln LN6 204 F6
6 Newborough PE6 174 E4
Dawson Dr 8 PE24 102 E7
Dawson Rd 7 NG34 212 D6
Dawsons La LN3 203 F8
Day Cl 6 Keadby DN17 17 D6
Wrawby DN20 20 E4
Daybell Cl 20 NG13 128 A6
Daybrook Cl NG32 139 C8
Day's La PE20 134 F3
De Aston Sch LN8 57 E7
De Aston Sq 2 DN15 182 E3
De Bec Cl PE1 226 C3
De Gravel Dr 5 NG34 107 F1
De Havilland Rd PE13 170 D1
De La Bere Ave 25 LN12 77 A8
De La Pole Ave HU3 179 F7
De Lacy Ave PE25 206 C8
De Lacy La 3 DN35 192 F6
De Lacy Way DN15 9 A5
De Ligne Dr 6 NG32 139 C7
De Wint Ave LN6 205 A5
De Wint Cl Lincoln LN6 205 B5
6 Metheringham LN4 95 C4
Deacon Dr DN15 182 B2
Deacon Rd LN2 202 C5
Deacon St PE1 225 F3
Deacons Sch PE1 226 B5
Deaconscroft PE3 225 B5
Dealtry Cl DN21 53 D5
Dean Cl 3 NG34 121 B8
Dean Rd DN17 184 E6
Deane Cl 7 NG23 91 D5
Deane Rd DN40 186 D4
Deans Cl 7 DN10 39 F5
Deansgate DN32 191 C6
Dear Love Gate
1 Gedney PE12 160 A8
Lutton PE12 148 D1
Dear St 11 LN8 57 D8
Dearne Ct 9 HU15 2 D5
Deaton La DN36 195 C6
Debdale Rd NG32 210 A5
Debdhill Rd 1 DN10 39 F5
Decoy Rd
Borough Fen PE6 174 D6
Gorefield PE13 169 D2
Dee St 6 HU3 180 B4
Deene Cl
7 Grimsby DN34 190 D4
8 Market Deeping PE6 217 A5
Deene Ct PE3 225 C5
Deep (Aquarium & Marine Research Centre) The* HU1 181 A5
Deep La PE23 87 A5
Deepdale Dr NG34 121 C7
Deepdale Gr 2 HU9 181 E8
Deepdale La LN2 68 C2
Deeping Rd PE6 164 E4
Deeping St James Prim Sch PE6 217 F4
Deeping St James Rd PE6 217 D2
Deeping St Nicholas Prim Sch PE11 166 B6
Deepings Leisure Ctr PE6 217 E4
Deepings Sch The PE6 217 E5
Deer Pk Rd 3 PE6 164 F3
Deerhurst Way 18 PE6 175 A1
Deerleap PE3 225 A5
Defender Dr DN37 190 B7
Deighton Cl Specl Sch LN11 61 A6
Deira Cl NG34 212 C1
Delamere Cl PE1 226 C5
Delamere Ct DN36 192 F1
Delamore Way PE12 216 C5
Delapre Ct 11 PE6 175 A1
Deldale Rd PE21 136 D8
Delfield Rd PE21 136 D8
Delgate Ave 3 PE12 157 E7
Delgate Bank PE12 157 D2
Delhi Sq 3 NG34 120 D8
Delhi St 7 HU9 5 D8
Delius Cl HU4 179 B4
Dell The
Peterborough PE2 230 E7
Scunthorpe DN17 184 D5
Dellfield Ave LN6 200 C1
Dellfield Cl LN6 200 C2
Dellfield Ct 8 LN6 200 C1
Delph Ct PE2 231 F6
Delph Fields PE12 216 A3
Delph Rd 18 Lincoln LN6 93 C8
Long Sutton PE12 216 A3
Delph The PE11 155 F4
Denbigh Ct 11 NG23 91 D5
Denby Cl 6 DN15 182 D5
Denby Dale Cl LN6 200 C2
Denby Dr DN35 192 C3
Dene Cl LN6 200 B3
Dene La LN4 109 C7
Dene Rd Grimsby DN32 191 E4
Skellingthorpe LN6 200 B3
Dene The
6 Nettleham LN2 68 C2
Skellingthorpe LN6 200 B3
Denefield LN6 200 B3
Denehall Rd 14 DN3 14 A2
Denesway HU13 178 D2
Denham Cl 2 PE25 206 C2
Denham Wlk 1 PE3 225 C4
Denis Dr PE2 230 A4
Denmark Ct 7 HU9 181 C7
Denmark Dr PE2 230 A4
Dennett Cl PE23 100 F8
Dennor Cl 15 LN12 77 A8
Denshire Ct 5 PE6 164 E4
Denton Ave NG31 210 F1
Denton CE Prim Sch NG32 139 A7
Denton Cl NG31 210 F1
Denton La
Barrowby NG32 128 F3
Belvoir NG32 138 E6
Denton Rd PE2 231 C6
Denton's Way 11 DN20 31 A5
Depot St LN1 201 D3
Derby Ave PE25 206 D1
Derby Cl
1 Grantham NG31 210 E4
9 Grimsby DN32 189 C1
Derby Dr PE1 226 C5
Derby Rd DN15 182 B2
Derby St
Kingston upon Hull HU3 180 D8
13 Lincoln LN5 205 E8
Dere Cl 9 PE10 213 C6
Derringham Ave 5 HU4 179 B6
Derringham St HU3 180 C7
Derry Way DN33 194 E8
Derrythorpe Rd DN17 17 D4
Derwent Ave 18 HU14 3 A4
Derwent Cl LN6 205 A2
Derwent Dr
1 Humberston DN36 36 C8
Humberston DN36 192 E1
Peterborough PE4 221 C2
Derwent Rd
Grantham NG31 210 F3
Scunthorpe DN16 185 E6
Derwent St LN1 201 C4
Derwood Gr 7 PE4 220 F5
Desborough Ave PE2 231 D5
Detuyll St DN15 182 F5
Detuyll St W DN15 182 F5
Devereux Way 5 LN9 199 D2
Devon La 17 NG13 128 A6
Devon St
Kingston upon Hull HU4 179 F3
8 Lincoln LN2 202 C3
Devonshire Ave DN32 191 D4
Devonshire Rd
2 Scampton Airfield LN1 67 E5
Scunthorpe DN17 184 F6
Dewberry Ct HU4 179 C4
Dewsbury Ave DN15 182 C4
Deyne Ave DN15 183 A3
Dial Sq 2 DN31 191 E7
Diana Princess of Wales Hospl DN33 191 C3
Diana St DN15 183 A5
Dick Turpin Way PE12 216 B5
Dickens Dr PE9 218 E5
Dickens Rd NG31 211 E6
Dickens St PE1 226 B3
Dickenson Terr 10 DN21 197 D3
Dickinson Cl 11 DN20 30 F5
Dickinson's La 6 DN36 36 B1
Dickon Hill Rd PE22 114 D7
Digby CE Prim Sch LN4 108 D6
Digby Cl 9 LN6 204 C7
Digby Cnr Nature Reserve* LN4 108 F5
Digby Gdns 3 DN34 191 A5
Digby Rd LN4 109 B6
Digby St DN15 182 F4
Dimmock Cl NG32 139 B7
Dingley Ct PE3 225 C5
Dirty La 4 DN7 14 D8
Disney Ct LN6 92 C2
Ditmas Ave 9 HU4 179 B6
Division Rd 1 HU3 180 B4
Dixon Ave
14 Broughton DN20 19 D3
Dorrington LN4 108 E3
Grimsby DN32 191 E4
Dixon Cl Brigg DN20 196 C4
Lincoln LN6 201 D1
12 Tetney DN36 36 D4
Dixon Dr LN13 75 E2
Dixon St LN5 201 D1
Dixon Way LN6 201 D1
Dixon's Dro PE14 170 F4
Dixons Rd PE6 217 C4
Dock Office Row 6 HU1 181 A7
Dock St HU1 180 F6
Dock Twr The* DN31 189 B3
Dockholme Gate PE11 145 A4
Docking La LN9 199 B8
Docking's Holt PE12 216 B6
Doctor's La PE10 143 A2
Doddington Ave LN6 205 A4
Doddington Dr PE3 225 B2
Doddington Hall* LN6 79 D5
Doddington La
Claypole NG23 117 E7
Stubton NG23 118 B7
Westborough & Dry Doddington NG23 117 E5
Doddington Rd
Birchwood LN6 204 C6
Doddington & Whisby LN6 79 E3
Lincoln LN6 204 F4
Dodswell Gr HU9 5 F8
Dog And Duck La DN21 197 B8
Dog Dro
Holbeach PE12 158 D2
Sutton St James PE12 159 A1
Dog Holes La DN22 52 A1
Dog Kennel Rd DN21 55 A8
Dogdyke Ppg Sta* LN4 110 D7
Dogdyke Rd
Coningsby LN4 207 B2
Wildmore LN4 111 B6
Dogsthorpe Cty Jun & Inf Sch PE1 226 B7
Dogsthorpe Rd PE1 226 A5
Dolby Vale DN33 190 F3
Dole Rd DN17 6 B1
Dole Wood Nature Reserve* PE10 164 C7
Doll La 1 DN20 20 F7
Doll's Bank PE12 159 A4
Dolman Cres DN17 184 F4
Dolphin St 4 DN35 192 F6
Dominion Cl 3 DN36 195 C6
Donaldson Dr 4 PE4 221 C2
Doncaster Gdns 14 LN5 107 A8
Doncaster Rd
Gunness DN15 17 E6
Hatfield DN7 14 D3
Haxey DN9 26 F2
Scunthorpe DN15 182 B3
Stainforth DN7 14 B6
Doncaster St HU3 180 B6
Donegal Cl PE4 221 B2
Donington on Bain Prim Sch LN11 59 E1
Donington Rd
Bicker PE20 135 A4
Horbling NG34 133 C2
Kirton PE20 135 F6
Donnington Gdns 1 DN15 182 F3
Donnington Pk 1 PE13 170 A1
Donnington Rd LN8 59 B2
Donnington St 5 DN32 191 F7
Donville Rd DN17 7 A2
Dooks Cl DN21 29 C1

Doon Garth HU4 ... 179 A3
Dorado Cl 2 HU3 ... 180 A5
Dorchester Ave PE10 ... 213 E3
Dorchester Cres 3 PE1 ... 226 D7
Dorchester Rd DN17 ... 184 C8
Dorchester Way 10 LN6 ... 93 B8
Dore Ave LN6 ... 204 E2
Dormy Ave PE25 ... 206 D8
Dorothy Ave
Skegness PE25 ... 206 C3
Waltham DN37 ... 194 E5
Dorothy Cl PE22 ... 113 A1
Dorothy Cres 1 PE25 ... 206 C3
Dorrington CE Sch
LN4 ... 108 D4
Dorset Cl E 6 DN15 ... 8 B4
Dorset Cl W 5 DN15 ... 8 B4
Dorset Pl 8 LN1 ... 67 E5
Dorset St
Kingston upon Hull HU4 ... 179 F3
7 Lincoln LN2 ... 202 C3
Dorton Ave DN21 ... 197 F4
Dotam's La PE22 ... 126 D4
Double Bank PE22 ... 126 D6
Double Bridges Rd
DN8 ... 15 B6
Double St PE11 ... 214 D4
Doubledays La PE24 ... 102 D8
Doubletwelves Dro
PE20 ... 134 D6
Doughty Cl DN37 ... 194 E5
Doughty Rd DN32 ... 191 E7
Doughty St PE9 ... 219 D6
Douglas Ave
Grimsby DN31 ... 191 A8
5 Ingoldmells PE25 ... 90 D3
Douglas Rd
Cleethorpes DN35 ... 192 D8
Market Deeping PE6 ... 217 C4
Doulton Cl 4 LN6 ... 204 D7
Dove Cl Louth LN11 ... 198 D7
7 Sleaford NG34 ... 212 B3
Dove Dale 5 LN6 ... 204 F2
Dovecote
4 Middle Rasen LN8 ... 57 B8
Rippingale PE10 ... 143 A3
Dovecote Cl PE1 ... 226 B7
Dovecote La
Aubourn Haddington & South Hykeham LN5 ... 92 F5
Coleby LN5 ... 93 F3
Wainfleet St Mary PE24 ... 102 E1
Yaxley PE7 ... 233 C5
Dovecote Mdws 3
DN20 ... 196 F6
Dovecote Rd 4 PE6 ... 217 A6
Dovecotes 3 PE11 ... 145 A8
Dovedale Cl
Grantham NG31 ... 211 B8
2 Winterton DN15 ... 9 A6
Dovedale Dr 6 DN33 ... 194 E8
Dovedale Gr 1 HU9 ... 181 E8
Dovedale Rd DN16 ... 185 D5
Dover Cl NG31 ... 210 E6
Dover Rd PE4 ... 221 A2
Dover St Grimsby DN31 ... 191 C8
Kingston upon Hull HU3 ... 180 C8
Doves' La PE22 ... 126 E3
Dowding Rd LN2 ... 202 E4
Dowdyke Dro PE20 ... 146 B8
Dowdyke Rd PE20 ... 145 F8
Dower Rise 11 HU14 ... 3 B7
Dowgate Cl 2 PE11 ... 214 A3
Dowgate Rd 4 PE13 ... 170 B1
Dowlands Bsns Pk
LN11 ... 62 C5
Down Gate PE3 ... 225 A1
Downing Cl DN34 ... 190 F6
Downing Cres
Scunthorpe DN16 ... 185 A3
2 Stamford PE9 ... 219 B7
Dowsdale Bank
Thorney PE6 ... 176 A8
Whaplode PE12 ... 167 E2
Dowse Ave DN15 ... 182 E3
Dowsing Way PE25 ... 206 A6
Dozen's Bank PE11 ... 156 B6
Dragonby Rd DN17 ... 184 E4
Drain Bank
Cowbit PE12 ... 157 A2
East Kirkby PE23 ... 99 F3
Newport HU15 ... 1 B8
Drain Rd PE6 ... 221 E7
Drainside PE20 ... 136 B5
Drainside S PE20 ... 136 C4
Drakards La PE21 ... 209 A3
Drake Ave
Grimsby DN32 ... 192 B6
Heighington/Washingborough LN4 ... 203 B1
Drake Rd PE25 ... 103 E4
Drake St
Gainsborough DN21 ... 197 D2
Lincoln LN1 ... 201 C4
Drakes Cl
7 Holbeach PE12 ... 215 E2
19 Mablethorpe & Sutton LN12 ... 77 A7
Drapers Pl 13 PE11 ... 214 D4
Draw Dike PE12 ... 159 D1
Drax Ct 6 LN8 ... 57 B8
Draycot 6 LN7 ... 33 A3
Drayton PE3 ... 225 A4
Drayton Rd PE20 ... 135 C7
Drew Ave DN32 ... 191 F4
Drewry La 10 DN9 ... 27 A2
Driffil Way 29 DN15 ... 9 A5
Drift Ave PE9 ... 219 C6
Drift Gdns PE9 ... 219 C6
Drift La NG32 ... 119 A1
Drift Rd PE9 ... 219 C6
Drift The
Barrowby NG32 ... 210 A3
Belvoir NG32 ... 138 F5
Buckminster NG33 ... 151 A4
Collyweston PE9 ... 171 B1
Croxton Kerrial NG32 ... 138 F5
Harlaxton NG32 ... 139 C8
Ryhall PE9 ... 163 B3
Skillington NG33 ... 151 A7
Syston NG32 ... 130 A7
Walcott LN4 ... 109 D7
Wansford PE5 ... 222 F3
Drigh Rd 17 LN8 ... 47 B6
Drill Hall La 3 DN21 ... 197 D5
Dring La DN21 ... 41 D7
Drinsey Nook La NG23 ... 66 B1
Drive The
Gainsborough DN21 ... 197 E3
Grantham NG31 ... 210 D3
Ingoldmells PE25 ... 206 E8
7 Kirk Sandall DN3 ... 14 A1
2 Mablethorpe/Sutton on Sea LN12 ... 64 A4
Peterborough PE3 ... 225 E2
Waltham DN37 ... 194 F3
1 Winthorpe NG24 ... 104 B7
Drove End Prim Sch
PE12 ... 148 F3
Drove La
Coddington NG24 ... 104 D7
Sleaford NG34 ... 212 A5
Drove Rd
Crowland PE12 ... 167 F3
Whaplode PE12 ... 168 A3
Drove The
4 Aubourn Haddington & South Hykeham LN6 ... 93 A8
Collyweston PE9 ... 171 B1
Osbournby NG34 ... 132 D5
Sleaford NG34 ... 212 B5
Drovers Ct DN21 ... 197 E1
Drovers Rise 1 HU15 ... 2 C6
Drummond Rd
Bourne PE10 ... 213 E4
Skegness PE25 ... 206 D1
Drury Cl 1 DN37 ... 194 C4
Drury La Bicker PE20 ... 135 A4
New Waltham DN36 ... 195 C6
Drury Pk 9 NG23 ... 117 D3
Drury St LN4 ... 95 D4
Dry Leys PE2 ... 230 C6
Drydales HU10 ... 178 C6
Dryden Ave LN2 ... 202 B6
Dryden Cl NG31 ... 211 D6
Dryden Ct 3 LN4 ... 207 B5
Dryden Rd
Peterborough PE1 ... 225 E7
Scunthorpe DN17 ... 184 D6
Drypool Way HU9 ... 181 B6
Duchess St DN32 ... 191 D6
Ducie La DN22 ... 52 C5
Duckpool La LN10 ... 84 B1
Duckthorpe La DN36 ... 37 B2
Dudley Cl 1 PE21 ... 209 B4
Dudley House Sch
NG31 ... 211 B4
Dudley Pl DN35 ... 192 D4
Dudley Rd Brigg DN20 ... 196 C3
Grantham NG31 ... 211 B4
Scunthorpe DN16 ... 185 E6
Dudley St DN31 ... 191 C7
Duesbery St HU3 ... 180 C8
Dugard Rd DN32 ... 192 B7
Duke of Bedford Sch
PE6 ... 176 A3
Duke Rd PE22 ... 113 F3
Duke St Boston PE21 ... 208 E4
8 Grimsby DN32 ... 189 C1
Grimsby DN32 ... 192 B8
Peterborough PE2 ... 231 A7
Sleaford NG34 ... 212 E5
14 Stainforth DN7 ... 14 C6
Duke's Covert Nature Reserve* NG32 ... 120 A1
Dukesmead PE4 ... 220 E2
Dunbar Ave DN36 ... 195 B6
Dunbar Cl 5 DN21 ... 197 E6
Dunblane Dr PE2 ... 229 D4
Duncombe Gdns 1
DN32 ... 191 F8
Duncombe St DN32 ... 191 F8
Dundee Dr PE9 ... 218 E6
Dundee St HU5 ... 180 A8
Dunes Family Entertainment Ctr The* LN12 ... 64 C4
Dunford Rd 5 LN5 ... 234 B1
Dunham Cl LN1 ... 65 D1
Dunham on Trent Prim Sch
NG22 ... 65 A1
Dunham Rd DN22 ... 65 A3
Dunholme Cl
Gainsborough DN21 ... 197 E4
11 Welton/Dunholme LN2 ... 68 D6
Dunholme Ct 4 LN2 ... 202 A8
Dunholme Rd
Gainsborough DN21 ... 197 E4
9 Welton/Dunholme LN2 ... 68 D6
Dunholme St Chads CE Prim Sch LN2 ... 68 E6
Dunkirk Rd LN1 ... 201 D6
Dunlin Dr PE12 ... 216 B4
Dunlin Rd 2 PE9 ... 163 D3
Dunlop St LN5 ... 201 F1
Dunlop Way DN16 ... 185 E7
Dunmires La DN14 ... 6 E8
Dunmore Cl LN5 ... 205 C3
Dunmow St DN31 ... 188 D1
Dunnegate Way PE11 ... 145 D2
Dunnock Cl 3 DN16 ... 185 B2
Dunns Paddock 3 DN20 ... 20 F7
Dunsberry
Marholm PE6 ... 220 D1
Peterborough PE3 ... 224 F8
Dunsby Dro PE10 ... 143 D1
Dunstall St DN15 ... 183 A3
Dunstan Hill 26 DN21 ... 30 B1
Dunstan Villas 29 DN21 ... 30 B1
Dunster Rd DN21 ... 197 E6
Dunston Cl 10 LN2 ... 202 A8
Dunston Dr HU13 ... 178 D1
Dunston Fen La LN4 ... 83 D1
Dunston Heath La LN4 ... 94 E5
Dunston Rd
Kingston upon Hull HU5 ... 179 D7
Metheringham LN4 ... 95 C5
Durban Rd DN32 ... 192 A7
Durham Ave
4 Grimsby DN34 ... 191 A7
Sleaford NG34 ... 212 C6
Thorne/Moorends DN8 ... 15 A8
Durham Cl
Birchwood LN6 ... 200 D2
Grantham NG31 ... 210 C4
Durham Cres LN4 ... 203 D1
Durham Rd
Cleethorpes DN35 ... 192 C4
Hatfield DN7 ... 14 D4
Peterborough PE1 ... 226 C3
Durham's Rd PE12 ... 148 D5
Dursley Ave DN36 ... 195 B6
Dury La LN1 ... 234 B3
Dutton Ave PE25 ... 206 A4
Dycote La LN5 ... 106 D5
Dyke Cty Prim Sch
PE10 ... 154 D5
Dyke Dro PE10 ... 154 E5
Dyke Rd 5 DN36 ... 37 C5
Dykes End NG23 ... 91 D4
Dymoke Cl 3 LN12 ... 64 C3
Dymoke Dr
Grimsby DN37 ... 190 C6
2 Horncastle LN9 ... 199 C2
Dymoke Rd 5 LN12 ... 64 C3
Dysart Rd NG31 ... 210 E4
Dyson Cl PE1 ... 225 F3

E

Eagle Cl 7 LN12 ... 64 A4
Eagle Com Prim Sch
LN6 ... 79 B2
Eagle Dr
3 Sleaford NG34 ... 212 B3
8 Welton/Dunholme LN2 ... 68 D7
Eagle La LN6 ... 79 D1
Eagle Moor LN6 ... 79 C3
Eagle Rd
Doddington & Whisby LN6 ... 79 D3
North Scarle LN6 ... 78 F2
Spalford NG23 ... 78 D4
Eaglesthorpe PE1 ... 225 E7
Ealand Rd 3 DN17 ... 17 C6
Eames Gdns PE1 ... 226 D7
Earl Ave DN36 ... 195 D7
Earl of Dysart Prim Sch
NG31 ... 210 D3
Earl of Scarbrough High Sch
The PE25 ... 206 C5
Earl of Scarbrough Sports Ctr PE25 ... 206 B5
Earl Spencer Ct PE2 ... 230 E8
Earl St Grimsby DN31 ... 191 C7
Scunthorpe DN16 ... 183 B1
Earle's Rd HU9 ... 181 D7
Earlesfield La NG31 ... 210 F3
Earls Cl PE2 ... 231 B6
Earls Dr LN5 ... 205 D8
Earlsfield Cl LN6 ... 204 B5
Earlsgate Gdns 3 DN15 ... 8 F5
Earlsgate Rd DN15 ... 8 F5
Earlswood PE2 ... 229 E5
Earth Cl PE2 ... 231 E5
Ease La NG23 ... 117 F3
Easenby Ave HU10 ... 178 C6
Easenby Cl 2 HU14 ... 3 C7
Eason Rd 10 DN33 ... 191 B2
East Acridge
15 Barton-upon-Humber DN18 ... 3 F1
8 Barton-upon-Humber DN18 ... 10 F8
East Ave
Brant Broughton LN5 ... 105 F5
Grantham NG31 ... 210 E3
1 Stainforth DN7 ... 14 C5
East Bank
2 Stainforth DN7 ... 14 C7
Sutton Bridge PE12 ... 160 F5
East Barkwith CE Sch
LN8 ... 71 A8
East Bight LN2 ... 234 B3
East Boundary Rd
DN16 ... 183 F2
East Camp Rd 8 NG34 ... 120 C8
East Cl 13 NG34 ... 108 E2
East Cob Gate PE12 ... 157 F6
East Comm La DN16 ... 185 B8
East Croft 10 LN3 ... 203 E7
East Cross St 25 DN21 ... 30 B1
East Dale Dr 3 DN21 ... 30 B2
East Dale Rd HU14 ... 2 E5
East Dr LN4 ... 110 E8
East Ella Dr HU4 ... 179 C6
East Elloe Ave PE12 ... 215 D3
East End
3 Burgh le Marsh PE24 ... 102 E7
Humberside Airport DN39 ... 22 A6
Langtoft PE6 ... 164 F3
East End Cl DN33 ... 191 D1
East Fen La PE22 ... 113 B7
East Ferry Rd
East Ferry DN21 ... 28 E3
Laughton DN21 ... 41 B8
Wildsworth DN21 ... 40 D8
East Field LN5 ... 92 F2
East Field Rd DN7 ... 14 C8
East Gate Bourne PE10 ... 213 E4
Fleet PE12 ... 159 C7
Moulton PE12 ... 158 A7
Sleaford NG34 ... 212 E4
Whaplode PE12 ... 158 C7
East Gn 30 DN17 ... 29 D7
East Gr
12 Barton-upon-Humber DN18 ... 3 F1
8 Colsterworth NG33 ... 151 E6
Kingston upon Hull HU4 ... 179 D4
East Halton Prim Sch
DN40 ... 12 D6
East Halton Rd DN40 ... 12 E3
East Hann La DN19 ... 4 E1
East Heckington CE Sch
PE20 ... 123 E3
East La Corringham DN21 ... 41 E2
Morton PE10 ... 154 C7
Stainforth DN7 ... 14 C6
East Liberty LN2 ... 202 C4
East Lound Rd
Haxey DN9 ... 27 D2
Owston Ferry DN9 ... 28 A3
East Marsh Rd DN19 ... 5 C3
East Marsh St 2 DN31 ... 191 E8
East Mid Mere Rd
Immingham DN40 ... 12 F4
South Killingholme DN40 ... 13 A4
East Mill Gate 3 LN3 ... 203 E6
East Mount 12 HU14 ... 3 A4
East of England Showground* PE2 ... 229 C4
East Par DN20 ... 196 C4
East Ravendale CE Prim Sch
DN37 ... 35 C2
East Rd
Deeping St Nicholas PE11 ... 156 C4
4 Keadby with Althorpe DN17 ... 17 C6
Navenby/Wellingore LN5 ... 107 B8
Northborough PE6 ... 217 E1
Sleaford NG34 ... 212 F6
Tetford LN9 ... 73 F1
Tydd St Mary PE13 ... 170 C8
East Rd Ind Est NG34 ... 212 F5
East Row LN11 ... 50 E4
East St Alford LN13 ... 75 F4
Bole DN22 ... 52 C6
Crowland PE6 ... 166 E1
Grantham NG31 ... 211 B4
7 Grimsby DN32 ... 191 E7
Helpringham NG34 ... 133 E7
13 Hibaldstow DN20 ... 30 F5
Horncastle LN9 ... 199 C4
5 Kingston upon Hull HU9 ... 181 B7
Nettleham LN2 ... 68 C2
Rippingale PE10 ... 143 A2
Roxby cum Risby DN15 ... 9 A3
Stamford PE9 ... 219 C5
East St Mary's Gate 4
DN31 ... 191 D7
East Sta Rd PE2 ... 231 B8
East View LN4 ... 109 D7
East Wold CE Prim Sch
LN11 ... 62 A3
Eastbeck La LN9 ... 86 A2
Eastbourne St
Kingston upon Hull HU3 ... 180 A5
Lincoln LN2 ... 234 C2
Eastbourne Way DN33 ... 194 F7
Eastbrook Rd LN6 ... 205 A5
Eastchurch Rd 4 NG34 ... 120 D8
Eastcliff Rd LN2 ... 234 C3
Eastcliffe Sq 9 NG32 ... 119 B7
Eastcroft 5 LN1 ... 66 D3
Eastern Ave
Gainsborough DN21 ... 197 F5
Peterborough PE1 ... 226 C8
Eastern Cl PE1 ... 226 D7
Eastern Dr
3 Balderton NG24 ... 104 C1
RAF Cranwell NG34 ... 120 D8
Eastern Inway DN34 ... 191 A4
Eastern Rd PE12 ... 215 F8
Eastfield
14 Humberston DN36 ... 36 D8
3 Market Deeping PE6 ... 217 C5
11 Sturton by Stow LN1 ... 66 D7
Eastfield Ave DN33 ... 195 A7
Eastfield Cl
1 Dunholme LN2 ... 68 E6
6 Sutterton PE20 ... 136 A2
Eastfield Cty Inf & Jun Sch
DN40 ... 186 C2
Eastfield Gr PE1 ... 226 B4
Eastfield Inf Sch LN11 ... 198 D6
Eastfield La Manby LN11 ... 62 C7
Welton LN2 ... 68 E7
Eastfield N Ind Est
DN40 ... 12 F3
Eastfield Prim Sch
HU4 ... 179 D6
Eastfield Rd
Barton-upon-Humber DN18 ... 10 F7
Brigg DN20 ... 196 D3
Epworth DN9 ... 27 E6
Firsby PE23 ... 101 F7
Immingham DN40 ... 12 F3
3 Keelby DN41 ... 23 A5
Kingston upon Hull HU4 ... 179 D6
Louth LN11 ... 198 D6
40 Messingham DN17 ... 29 D7
North Killingholme DN40 ... 12 E5
Peterborough PE1 ... 226 C4
Scunthorpe DN16 ... 185 C5
1 Wisbech PE13 ... 170 E1
Eastfield Rise
2 Holton le Clay DN36 ... 195 D2
Louth LN11 ... 198 E7
Eastfield S Ind Est
DN40 ... 12 F3
Eastfield St 5 LN2 ... 202 B3
Eastfield Way 17 PE13 ... 170 D1
Eastfields 2 LN8 ... 43 D3
Eastgate
Bassingham LN5 ... 92 F2
Bourne PE10 ... 213 E4
Grimsby DN32 ... 191 E8
Heckington NG34 ... 122 E3
Kingston upon Hull HU13 ... 178 E2
Lincoln LN2 ... 234 B3
Louth LN11 ... 198 C6
Market Deeping PE6 ... 217 F3
Peterborough PE1 ... 226 B2
Scotton DN21 ... 29 C2
Eastgate Cl LN2 ... 234 C3
Eastgate Gdns 3 PE12 ... 159 C7
Eastgate La PE34 ... 161 E2
Easthall Rd LN7 ... 32 B4
Eastholm Cl PE1 ... 226 C3
Eastholm Cty Sch PE1 ... 226 C4
Eastholm Sch PE1 ... 226 D5
Eastholme Gdns 10 DN15 ... 8 B4
Easthorpe La NG13 ... 128 C5
Easthorpe Rd
1 Bottesford NG13 ... 128 B5
2 Great Gonerby NG31 ... 129 E5
Easthorpe View 2
NG13 ... 128 B5
Eastlands 4 PE6 ... 166 F1
Eastlands Bank PE14 ... 161 B1
Eastleigh Cl LN6 ... 200 B1
Eastleigh Rd PE1 ... 226 C3
Eastmoor Villas DN9 ... 27 D3
Eastoft CE Prim Sch
DN17 ... 7 A3
Eastoft Rd Crowle DN17 ... 16 D8
Luddington & Haldenby DN17 ... 7 C3
Easton Garfords Charity Aided Sch PE9 ... 171 D3
Easton La NG33 ... 140 A2
Eastrea Ct PE2 ... 231 E6
Eastside Rd
Grimsby DN31 ... 189 B1
Scunthorpe DN16 ... 183 F2
Eastview Cl PE24 ... 90 E6
Eastville Rd
4 Grimsby DN33 ... 191 A3
Toynton St Peter PE23 ... 101 A6
Eastway 19 LN2 ... 68 D2
Eastwood Ave DN32 ... 191 D4
Eastwood Day Hospl
NG24 ... 104 A3
Eastwood Dr
2 Boston PE21 ... 209 D4
10 Broughton DN20 ... 19 E4
4 Grantham NG31 ... 211 D2
Eastwood Rd PE21 ... 209 D5
Easy Rd PE11 ... 156 E1
Eaton Ct DN34 ... 191 C6
Eaton Rd Boston PE21 ... 208 E3
Immingham DN40 ... 186 D4
Eau Bank LN11 ... 50 D7
Eau Dike Rd PE22 ... 115 A7
Eaudike Rd
Donington PE20 ... 135 A3
Quadring PE11 ... 145 C8
Eaudyke Bank 1 PE13 ... 169 F7
Eaugate Rd PE12 ... 157 F1
Ebony Gr LN6 ... 200 C1
Ebrington Cl 3 LN10 ... 97 E6
Eccles Ct 3 DN20 ... 196 F7
Eccleston Rd 15 DN3 ... 14 A3
Eddystone Dr 3 LN6 ... 205 A1
Eden Cl 6 PE25 ... 206 C1
Eden Dene DN16 ... 185 D5
Eden Field Rd
20 Kirk Sandall DN3 ... 14 A2
4 Kirk Sandall DN3 ... 14 A1
Eden Gr Rd 8 DN3 ... 14 A1
Edendale Gdns 3 LN1 ... 201 E8
Edenfield PE2 ... 230 C6
Edenham CE (Controlled) Prim Sch PE10 ... 153 F5
Edenham Rd PE10 ... 154 B6
Edenthorpe Hall Fst & Mid Sch DN3 ... 14 A1
Edgar St HU3 ... 180 D5
Edgbaston Ave 3 DN17 ... 184 E3
Edgcote Cl PE3 ... 225 C5

Edge Ave DN33 191 D2
Edgefield 4 PE12 157 E7
Edgehill 10 LN5 205 D2
Edgerley Drain Rd
PE1 226 F5
Edinburgh Ave
Peterborough PE4 220 F3
2 Skegness PE25 206 D3
Edinburgh Cl 13 PE20 136 C5
Edinburgh Cres
2 Bourne PE10 213 D6
12 Kirton PE20 136 C5
Edinburgh Dr
Holton le Clay DN36 195 C3
11 Kirton PE20 136 C5
Spalding PE11 214 E2
Wisbech PE13 170 D2
Edinburgh Rd
16 Binbrook Tech Pk LN8 47 B6
2 Grantham NG31 211 E6
3 Ruskington NG34 108 E2
Stamford PE9 219 B6
Edinburgh Sq 4 LN5 94 A7
Edinburgh St HU3 180 A5
Edinburgh Wlk
Holbeach PE12 215 E2
Pinchbeck PE11 156 B7
Edington Ct 3 DN21 53 A8
Edith Cavell PE3 225 B4
Edlington Cl 6 LN2 201 F8
Edmonds Cl 2 PE9 219 D6
Edmonds Way 3 DN31 191 D8
Edmondthorpe Drift
LE14 150 D1
Edmondthorpe Rd
LE14 150 C1
Edmund Cl DN21 41 D2
Edmunds Dr 7 PE9 171 A3
Edmunds Rd 3 NG34 107 F1
Edna St LN5 201 F1
Edwalton Ave
9 Mablethorpe/Sutton on Sea
LN12 77 A8
Peterborough PE3 225 E3
Edward Barker Rd LN4 81 F4
Edward Collins Sq 2
HU9 181 C7
Edward Cres PE25 206 B3
Edward Heneage Prim Sch
DN32 191 F7
Edward Rd
Gainsborough DN21 197 D6
Spalding PE11 214 B4
10 Stamford PE9 219 A7
Edward St
Cleethorpes DN35 192 E5
Grantham NG31 211 B2
Grimsby DN32 191 F7
Kingston upon Hull
HU13 178 F1
1 Lincoln LN5 205 E8
17 Louth LN11 198 B5
Edwards Rd 3 DN15 182 F4
Edwin Cl 12 NG34 212 B2
Edwin Gdns PE10 213 B5
Edwin St 13 PE21 208 F4
Edwina Ave 6 PE11 156 F8
Egar Way PE3 224 F2
Egerton Rd LN2 202 B5
Egginton Cl HU10 178 C7
Egginton St 4 HU2 180 F7
Egret Gr 5 LN6 204 D8
Egton Ave 17 DN17 29 D7
Egton St HU8 181 A8
Eighth Ave DN15 8 A1
Elan Cl PE21 208 E5
Elba St 6 HU9 5 E8
Elbow La PE13 177 F8
Elder Cl 2 Bourne PE10 213 C6
Skegness PE25 206 A5
Elder St LN5 205 D5
Elder Tree Way LN10 84 D3
Elderberry Dr HU4 179 C4
Elderberry Way 2
DN35 192 D2
Elder's Gate PE12 169 E8
Elderwood Ct 6 HU3 180 D5
Eleanor Cl Lincoln LN5 205 E7
Stamford PE9 219 A6
Eleanor St DN32 191 F8
Electric Sta Rd NG34 212 C4
Eleven Acre La PE20 136 D4
Eley's La PE20 136 B2
Elgar Rd HU4 179 B4
Eliot Cl
Gainsborough DN21 197 F3
9 Sleaford NG34 212 F4
Elizabeth Ave
Dogdyke LN4 110 D7
11 Kirk Sandall DN3 14 A2
6 Lincoln LN6 93 C8
Lincoln LN6 204 F1
Wrangle PE22 114 C2
Elizabeth Cl
16 Chapel St Leonard PE24 90 D7
Gainsborough DN21 197 C7
Glentworth DN21 54 F6
Grimsby DN33 194 D7
Scotter DN21 29 C4
Elizabeth Cres
6 Ingoldmells PE25 90 E3
Pinchbeck PE11 144 D1
Elizabeth Ct 17 PE24 90 D7
Elizabeth Dr
Billingborough NG34 143 B8
Elizabeth Dr *continued*
12 Chapel St Leonard PE24 90 D7
Elizabeth Rd
Boston PE21 209 B5
2 Stamford PE9 219 B6
Elizabeth St 3 DN15 183 A4
Elizabeth Way 4 PE10 164 C8
Ella Pk HU10 178 D7
Ellen Cres PE11 214 A3
Ellen Way DN36 195 B7
Ellerby Mead NG33 152 D5
Ellesmere Ave 3 LN2 202 D4
Ellesmere Bsns Pk
NG31 210 E2
Ellesmere Gr 4 DN7 14 D6
Ellesmere Rise DN34 190 D3
Ellicar La DN10 39 A3
Ellindon PE3 225 B7
Elliot Ave PE3 224 F2
Elliot Cl NG31 211 E6
Elliott Rd LN5 234 C1
Elliott Way 11 PE24 90 D7
Ellis St HU9 181 C8
Ellis Way DN32 191 E8
Ellison Ave DN16 185 A1
Ellison Boulters CE (Con)
Prim Sch LN2 68 F4
Ellison Cl 5 LN2 68 F2
Ellison St Lincoln LN5 205 D5
Thorne/Moorends DN8 15 A7
Elliston Jun & Inf Schs
DN35 192 C8
Elliston St DN35 192 C8
Ellmore La LN7 32 C3
Elloe Bank PE13 169 B2
Elloughton Cty Prim Sch
HU15 2 B7
Elloughton Dale HU15 2 D8
Elloughton Rd HU15 2 C6
Elloughtonthorpe Way 15
HU15 2 D5
Ellwood Ave PE2 231 E5
Elm Ave 18 Brough HU15 2 C6
Cherry Willingham/Reepham
LN3 203 D5
Cleethorpes DN35 192 E6
Grimsby DN34 191 A6
21 Mablethorpe/Sutton on Sea
LN12 64 B3
Newark-on-Trent NG24 104 A3
Elm Cl Lincoln LN6 204 F2
17 Long Bennington NG23 117 D3
Market Deeping PE6 217 C4
13 Saxilby LN1 66 D2
Yaxley PE7 233 F7
Elm Cres
Burgh le Marsh PE24 102 D8
Glinton PE6 220 B8
Elm Dr
Ingoldmells PE25 206 D8
Louth LN11 198 D7
Skegness PE25 90 E1
3 Sudbrooke LN2 68 F2
Elm Gdns DN35 192 E6
Elm Gr Grantham NG31 211 C6
8 Healing DN41 24 A5
Scunthorpe DN16 185 B8
Elm La Goxhill DN19 5 A1
7 Laceby DN37 23 E1
Low Fulney PE12 157 C6
Elm Rd
Cleethorpes DN35 192 E6
Waltham DN37 194 E3
Elm St
Peterborough PE2 230 F7
Stamford PE9 219 C5
Elm Tree Cl 11 LN8 57 D7
Elm Tree Gr 8 DN8 15 B7
Elm Way Brigg DN20 196 B4
Messingham DN17 29 C7
Elmdale 23 DN18 10 E8
Elmdene 5 LN2 68 F4
Elmer St N 3 NG31 211 A4
Elmer St S NG31 211 A4
Elmfield Rd PE1 226 A7
Elmgarth 3 NG34 212 F3
Elmhirst Ave PE25 206 D6
Elmhirst Rd 5 DN8 15 B8
Elmhurst La LN9 199 B6
Elmore Rd PE3 225 A3
Elms Dr HU10 178 C8
Elms View 4 NG31 129 D5
Elmswood HU13 178 C2
Elmtree Ave 10 HU14 3 A4
Elmtree Rd NG34 108 D1
Elmwood Ave 4 PE21 208 F2
Elmwood Cl 6 LN6 200 D1
Elmwood Dr 6 PE25 90 D3
Elsea Dr 3 PE10 164 C8
Elsea Pk Way PE10 213 D2
Elsenham Rd DN31 188 D1
Elsham Cl 7 LN6 204 D8
Elsham Cres LN6 204 D8
Elsham Dr DN37 194 C3
Elsham Gr 4 DN33 191 B3
Elsham Rd DN20 20 D7
Elsham Rise HU13 178 D1
Elsham Wold Ind Est
DN20 21 A8
Elsie Davies Cl NG31 211 C7
Elsiemere Wlk 6 HU4 179 B6
Elsom Way LN9 199 A4
Elsthorpe Rd
Edenham PE10 153 E6
Haconby PE10 154 A7
Elstone PE2 230 A4
Elton Cl 2 PE9 218 F6
Elton Rd Thorney PE8 228 B6
Elton Rd *continued*
Wansford PE8 222 B2
Elton St 1 NG31 211 A3
Elveley Dr HU10 178 A7
Elvin Cl 3 LN2 201 F6
Elvington Cl 7 LN6 204 B6
Elvington Rd LN6 204 B6
Elwes St DN20 196 C2
Elwyn Pl DN35 192 D2
Ely Cl PE4 220 F3
Ely St Lincoln LN1 201 D4
5 Sleaford NG34 212 C6
Ely Way 5 NG31 210 F5
Embankment Rd 4 PE1 226 A1
Ember La
Chapel St Leonards PE24 77 B1
Hogsthorpe PE24 90 B8
Embry Rd 22 PE8 172 B1
Emerald Gr 8 HU3 180 A4
Emerson Ave DN7 14 C5
Emfield Gr DN33 194 E7
Emfield Rd DN33 194 D6
Emily St 8 HU9 181 C7
Eminson Cl DN21 29 C4
Emlyns Gdns 5 PE9 219 C6
Emlyns St 2 PE9 219 C6
Emmanual Rd DN16 185 F6
Emmanuel Ct 3 DN16 185 C6
Emmanuel Dr DN16 185 A3
Emmanuel Rd PE9 219 B7
Emmery Cl 2 DN20 19 D4
Emminson Way 1
NG31 210 E8
Emorsgate PE34 161 E3
Empingham Rd
4 Stamford PE9 219 A5
Tinwell PE9 218 B6
Empringham St 5 HU9 181 D7
Empson Rd PE1 226 F5
Ena St HU3 180 B6
Endcliffe Ave DN17 184 F2
Endeavour Cres 1 HU9 5 D8
Endeavour Pk Ind Est
PE21 208 B4
Endeavour Way PE20 136 A2
Enderby Cl LN4 203 A2
Enderby Cres DN21 197 E3
Enderby Rd DN17 184 E4
Enderby Rd Inf Sch
DN17 184 D4
Endsleigh St HU3 180 A7
Enfield Ave DN36 195 D5
Enfield Prim Sch
DN36 195 D6
Enfield Rd 8 LN11 59 E1
Engaine PE2 230 B5
Engine Bank PE12 157 F2
Engine Dro NG34 134 B4
Engine Dyke PE12 148 B1
Engine St DN20 196 B3
English Cl HU3 180 E4
English Rd PE6 176 B5
English St
Kingston upon Hull HU3 180 E4
Peterborough PE1 225 E5
Ennerdale Cl
3 Birchwood LN6 200 D1
6 Humberston DN36 192 E1
Ennerdale Rise PE4 221 B2
Enterprise Rd
Caistor LN7 33 A4
3 Mablethorpe/Sutton on Sea
LN12 64 A4
Enterprise Way
Grimsby DN32 192 A6
Pinchbeck PE11 214 E8
4 Winterton DN15 8 F5
Ephams La DN41 23 E7
Epsom Cl LN6 204 B8
Epsom Rd LN6 204 B8
Epworth Cty Prim Sch
DN9 27 D6
Epworth Leisure Ctr
DN9 27 D6
Epworth Rd (West) 10
DN7 14 E4
Epworth Rd Hatfield DN7 14 F4
Haxey DN9 27 D3
Owston Ferry DN9 28 A4
Epworth Turbary Nature
Reserve* DN9 27 B6
Erebus Cl 7 PE23 101 A8
Eresbie Rd LN11 198 D3
Eresby Ave
13 Spilsby PE23 87 F1
Spilsby PE23 100 F8
Eresby Specl Sch The
PE23 100 F8
Ermine Cl
5 Ancaster NG32 120 A3
Bourne PE10 213 C6
Grantham NG31 211 D5
8 Lincoln LN1 201 E8
Stamford PE9 218 F5
Ermine Dr 3 LN5 107 B8
Ermine Inf Sch LN2 202 A7
Ermine Jun Sch LN2 202 A8
Ermine Rise PE9 171 B8
Ermine St
Ancaster NG32 120 A2
Appleby DN15 9 C1
Winteringham DN15 9 B8
Ermine Way
Market Deeping PE6 217 E5
Stamford PE9 218 F5
Ernest Terr LN2 234 B4
Eryholme Cres 1 DN15 182 F2
Escart Ave DN32 192 B6
Esk Cl LN6 204 F4
Eskdale Cl 1 PE4 221 C3
Eskdale Rd NG31 211 A7
Eskdale Way DN37 190 D8
Eskham Cl 1 DN35 192 F3
Essendine Rd PE9 163 C2
Essendyke PE3 225 A7
Essex Dr 9 DN15 8 B4
Essex Rd 3 PE9 219 B6
Essex St HU4 179 E3
Essex Way PE10 213 D4
Estate Ave DN20 19 D3
Estate Rd No 1 DN31 188 B2
Estate Rd No 2 DN31 188 B1
Estate Rd No 3 DN31 188 B3
Estate Rd No 4 DN31 188 B2
Estate Rd No 5 DN31 188 B2
Estate Rd No 6 DN31 188 B2
Estate Rd No 7 DN31 188 B1
Estate Rd No 8 DN31 188 B1
Estcourt Prim Sch
HU9 181 D8
Estcourt St HU9 181 D8
Estella Way PE11 214 A5
Estuary Way DN31 188 D2
Estwaite Cl LN6 205 B2
Ethelstone Rd 5 DN34 191 A7
Etherington St DN21 197 D4
Eton Cl LN6 200 D3
Eton Dr DN17 184 F3
Eton Rd
Heighington/Washingborough
LN4 203 C1
6 Mablethorpe/Sutton on Sea
LN12 64 C2
Eton St Grantham NG31 211 B4
Kingston upon Hull HU3 180 C4
Eudo Rd PE25 206 D7
Eugate Rd PE6 167 F4
Europa Bsns Pk DN31 188 C2
Europa Way
Brigg DN20 196 A4
Immingham DN41 187 B3
Eurosure Tennis Ctr
PE21 208 C5
Eusden Ct LN4 207 A5
Euston Ave 5 PE11 214 B2
Euston Cl LN6 200 D2
Eve Gdns LN4 203 D1
Eve St LN11 198 B6
Evedon Rd NG34 121 F5
Evelyn Gr N 1 DN32 192 B6
Evelyn Gr S 3 DN32 192 B6
Evendine Ct DN36 195 E1
Ever Thorpe Cl 5 HU3 180 C5
Everard Rd PE11 155 C1
Everdon Way PE3 225 C5
Everest Rd DN16 185 C5
Everingham PE2 229 D5
Everington's La PE25 103 C8
Everthorpe Cl 16 HU15 2 D5
Eves Cl 9 PE6 174 E5
Evesham Ave DN34 190 E5
Evison Cres 2 LN13 75 E3
Evison Ct 12 PE22 113 B1
Evison Way LN11 50 E7
Ewart St LN5 205 D6
Ewerby Rd NG34 122 A5
Exchange Cl LN6 204 E4
Exchange Pl 5 DN20 196 B3
Exchange Rd LN6 204 E4
Exchange St PE1 226 A2
Exchequergate 5 LN2 234 B3
Exeter Cl 3 Bourne PE10 213 C5
Grantham NG31 210 C5
Heighington/Washingborough
LN4 203 E2
1 Market Deeping PE6 217 E4
Exeter Ct
2 Bourne PE10 213 C5
10 Grimsby DN34 190 D4
Exeter Dr
4 Sleaford NG34 212 C6
Spalding PE11 214 E4
Exeter Gdns
10 Bourne PE10 213 C5
Stamford PE9 218 F4
Exeter Rd
Peterborough PE1 225 F6
Scunthorpe DN15 182 F3
8 Wittering PE8 172 B1
Exeter St PE10 213 C5
Exmoor Ave DN15 182 D7
Exmoor Cl LN6 204 D1
Exmoor Rd DN17 184 C8
Exton Cl 6 PE9 218 E5
Eyam Way 3 LN6 204 F1
Eye CE (Controlled) Sch
PE6 175 B1
Eye Rd PE1 174 F1
Eyebury Rd Eye PE6 175 A1
Peterborough PE6 227 A6
Eyre Ave DN16 185 B5
Eyre's La LN6 78 F1
Eyrescroft PE3 225 A7
Eyrescroft CP Sch
PE3 225 A7

F

Fagans Way 7 PE25 206 C1
Fainlight Cl 2 PE25 206 D8
Fair View Ave DN35 192 E6
Fairburn Cl 9 PE24 90 D7
Fairchild Way PE1 226 A7
Fairfax Cl Boston PE21 208 D7
Gainsborough DN21 197 F2
Fairfax Cl *continued*
6 Horncastle LN9 199 D3
2 Toft Newton LN8 56 D5
Fairfax Rd DN31 191 B7
Fairfax St LN5 205 D6
Fairfax Way PE6 217 E3
Fairfield LN4 207 C4
Fairfield Ave
25 Chapel St Leonard PE24 90 D7
Grimsby DN33 194 E7
Fairfield Cl
8 Broughton DN20 19 E3
3 Spalding PE11 214 C6
Fairfield Croft 9 DN9 27 E6
Fairfield Ct 3 DN35 193 A1
Fairfield Dr
29 Barton-upon-Humber
DN18 10 F8
39 Messingham DN17 29 D7
Fairfield Est LN11 198 B8
Fairfield Prim Sch
DN33 194 E8
Fairfield Rd
Grimsby DN33 194 E7
Peterborough PE2 231 A8
Scunthorpe DN15 182 C4
Fairfield St LN2 202 B4
Fairfield View 11 HU15 2 D5
Fairfields
Holbeach PE12 215 C3
33 Kirton in Lindsey DN21 30 B1
Fairisle Rise DN40 186 C2
Fairleas LN4 81 E2
Fairmead Way PE3 225 E2
Fairmont Cres DN16 183 B2
Fairmont Rd DN32 192 A7
Fairtree Wlk 24 DN8 15 A8
Fairview Way PE11 214 C6
Fairway DN37 194 D5
Fairway Ct DN35 193 C1
Fairway The
Kingston upon Hull
HU10 178 A8
1 Mablethorpe/Sutton on Sea
LN12 64 A4
Fairways PE10 164 A8
Fairways The DN15 182 B2
Fakenham Chase
PE12 215 E3
Falcon Cl LN6 79 B2
Falcon Ct
9 Grantham NG31 210 E2
Kingston upon Hull HU4 179 D2
Falcon Rd 7 LN4 108 A7
Falcon Way 13 NG34 212 B3
Falconers The DN21 30 F2
Faldingworth Cl 3 LN6 204 C7
Faldingworth Prim Sch
LN8 56 F3
Faldingworth Rd LN8 55 F3
Falkirk Cl 6 PE9 218 E6
Falkland Rd 4 HU9 5 F8
Falkland Way DN18 3 F1
Falklands Cl LN1 201 E8
Falklands Rd PE12 160 D4
Fallodan Rd PE2 229 C3
Fallow La Foston NG32 118 A2
1 Westborough & Dry
Doddington NG23 117 F3
Fallowfield PE2 229 D5
Fallowfield Rd DN33 194 D7
Fall's Dro PE6 175 F7
Falsgrave Gr HU5 179 D7
Fane Cl PE9 219 B7
Fane Rd PE4 221 C1
Fanny Hands La 1 LN8 59 A7
Fannystone Rd 3 DN34 191 B7
Fantail Cl 2 PE11 156 E2
Fantasy Island* PE25 90 E3
Fanthorpe La LN11 198 A7
Far Bank La DN7 14 C8
Far Comm Rd DN7 15 A3
Far Dro PE20 124 E2
Far End LN5 94 A2
Far Field Rd 22 DN3 14 A2
Far Holme La 5 NG23 91 A8
Far Hurn Dro LN4 110 B7
Far Ings La DN18 3 C1
Far Ings Nature Reserve*
DN18 3 D2
Far Ings Rd DN18 3 D1
Far La LN5 93 F3
Far Pasture 2 PE4 220 F5
Farcet Prim Sch PE7 231 C2
Fardell Rd DN16 185 D7
Farebrother St DN32 191 E6
Faringdon Rd DN31 189 C2
Farleigh Fields PE2 229 D6
Farlesthorpe Rd
Alford LN13 75 F2
Bilsby LN13 76 A2
Willoughby with Sloothby
LN13 89 B8
Farm Cl 2 Gunness DN15 17 E6
12 Kirk Sandall DN3 14 A1
Farm La 1 DN17 28 D8
Farm View Castor PE5 223 E2
18 Welton LN2 68 D7
Farmers Gate PE12 215 B2
Farmhouse Cl 12 NG13 128 A6
Farmhouse Mews 11
DN36 195 C6
Farndale Cres 5 NG31 211 A8
Farndale Way
26 Winterton DN15 9 A5
25 Winterton DN15 9 A5
1 Winterton DN15 9 A5
Farnella Cl HU3 180 A5

Farrier Rd LN6 204 B5
Farrier Way PE11 214 A2
Farriers Ct
Peterborough PE2 230 D7
Scopwick LN4 95 C1
Farriers Way
Carlby PE9 163 D4
2 Tattershall LN4 207 A5
Farringdon Cl 2 PE1 226 D6
Farrington Cres LN6 200 D2
Farrishes La DN18 10 A8
Farrow Ave PE12 215 E1
Farrow Rd PE12 168 A4
Farrows Pond 3 DN19 5 A1
Farthing Ave DN15 182 E4
Farthingales PE11 214 C6
Farthings Fold PE10 154 B6
Fauconberg Ave 4 DN33 191 C2
Faulding La DN40 12 F2
Faulding Way DN37 190 C7
Faulkers La PE24 89 E1
Favell Rd 1 LN4 203 B2
Faversham Ave HU4 179 B6
Fawcett St DN21 197 C5
Fawsley Cl 6 LN2 202 E7
Fawsley Garth PE3 225 C6
Faxfleet La DN14 1 A3
Fayid La LN4 95 C7
Feale Abbey PE34 161 E1
Feather La 8 DN19 11 C7
Featherby Pl 7 LN5 205 E8
Fellands Gate PE22 113 F3
Fellowes Gdns PE2 231 A7
Fellowes Rd PE2 231 A7
Felstead Rd DN34 190 F6
Fen Cl 24 PE13 170 D1
Fen Ct 1 DN3 14 A1
Fen Dike PE12 159 B3
Fen Dro PE7 233 D1
Fen End La PE12 156 F3
Fen Gate PE12 157 E2
Fen La Balderton NG24 104 D2
Bassingham LN5 93 A3
Beesby with Saleby LN13 76 A7
Conisholme LN11 50 C5
Dunston LN4 95 C6
East Keal PE23 100 E5
Grainthorpe LN11 49 F5
Lincoln LN6 205 A1
Long Bennington NG23 117 B6
Mablethorpe & Sutton LN12 64 A1
Maltby Le Marsh LN13 63 E1
Mareham Le Fen PE22 98 F2
North Somercotes LN11 50 D6
North Thoresby DN36 36 C1
South Carlton LN1 67 C2
Tydd St Giles PE13 169 B5
Fen Prep Sch The NG34 123 C3
Fen Rd Billinghay LN4 109 F6
Dowsby PE10 143 D4
East Kirkby PE23 99 F4
Frampton PE20 125 B1
Gosberton PE11 144 A4
Heighington LN4 82 A4
Heighington/Washingborough LN4 203 E2
Holbeach PE12 215 D1
Little Hale NG34 133 F8
Metheringham LN4 95 C4
Newton PE13 169 E4
Owmby LN8 55 F6
Pointon & Sempringham NG34 143 D6
Ruskington NG34 108 F2
Stickford PE22 100 C2
Thurlby PE10 154 E1
Timberland LN4 96 C1
Toynton St Peter PE23 101 A4
Wisbech St Mary PE13 177 E2
Fen View
Heighington LN4 81 F4
Peterborough PE2 231 F6
Fen Wlk DN36 37 C5
Fenbridge Rd PE4 221 A4
Fenby Cl DN37 190 D6
Fence Bank PE34 161 D1
Fendike Bank PE24 101 F3
Fendike La PE20 135 B5
Fendyke End La PE22 126 E5
Fendyke La PE13 169 F1
Feneley Cl PE6 217 D5
Fengate PE1 226 D1
Fengate Cl 1 PE1 226 B2
Fengate Dro PE12 157 C3
Fengate Rd
Pinchbeck PE11 214 A8
Walsoken PE14 170 F1
Fenhouses Dro PE20 135 D8
Fenhouses La PE20 135 C7
Fenland Airfield PE12 168 B8
Fenland Rd
13 Thorne/Moorends DN8 15 B7
Wisbech PE13 170 E1
Fenland Wlk PE12 215 B2
Fennell Rd 5 PE11 156 E8
Fenside
Halton Holegate PE23 101 C6
Toynton All Saints PE23 100 F4
Fenside Dr 5 PE6 174 E5
Fenside Rd
Boston PE21 208 C6
Holland Fen with Brothertoft PE21 125 C5
Fenton Dr PE9 163 E5
Fenton La DN22 52 C1
Fenton Pl LN2 234 C2
Fenton Rd
Fenton NG23 105 B1
Stubton NG23 118 B8
Fenton St DN15 183 B3
Fenwick Ct 6 DN36 195 D1
Fenwick Rd DN33 191 B2
Ferensway HU2 180 E7
Fern Croft 10 DN9 27 E6
Fern Ct HU13 179 A1
Fern Dr PE11 214 C7
Fern Gr LN3 203 D5
Fernbank 2 DN9 27 D7
Ferndale PE7 233 D6
Ferndale Cl NG33 152 F7
Ferndown 1 DN37 188 A1
Ferndown Dr DN40 186 D4
Ferneries La 3 DN38 21 B4
Fernhall Cl 15 DN3 14 A2
Fernhill DN37 190 C7
Fernie Cl 3 PE6 174 E4
Fernland Cl 18 HU15 2 C5
Fernleigh Way PE21 209 B6
Ferriby High Rd HU14 3 B5
Ferriby La DN33 191 C2
Ferriby Rd
Barton-upon-Humber DN18 10 E8
Hessle HU13 178 B1
Scunthorpe DN17 184 E5
Ferriby Sta HU14 3 A4
Ferries St HU9 181 D7
Ferry Dr PE6 224 D3
Ferry Hill PE5 224 B1
Ferry La
Holland Fen with Brothertoft PE20 124 D6
Newton PE13 170 B5
North Kyme LN4 109 F2
Skellingthorpe LN6 200 C5
South Kyme LN4 109 F1
Sturton Le Steeple DN22 52 D3
Washingborough LN4 203 B2
Winteringham DN15 2 B1
Ferry Mdws Ctry Pk* PE2 229 D8
Ferry Mdws Sta PE2 229 E7
Ferry Rd Bardney LN3 83 D1
Barrow upon Humber DN19 4 C1
Fiskerton LN3 82 D6
Haxey DN9 27 D1
2 Keadby with Althorpe DN17 17 D4
Kingston upon Hull HU13 178 E1
Langriville PE22 124 D8
Scunthorpe DN15 182 E5
Ferry Rd W DN15 182 A6
Ferryside 2 LN3 82 B6
Ferryside Gdns 3 LN3 82 B6
Ferryview PE2 229 E6
Festival Ave 3 PE25 90 D3
Ffolkes Dr 12 PE34 161 F3
Field Ave 6 PE13 169 F7
Field Cl
6 Gosberton PE11 145 B6
13 Laceby DN37 23 F1
23 Nettleham LN2 68 D2
14 Ruskington NG34 108 D2
1 Welton LN2 68 D7
Field Dr 2 NG24 104 C1
Field Farm La 3 LN4 95 D4
Field Head 5 DN37 23 E1
Field La Bardney LN3 83 C5
Eastoft DN17 7 A3
Ewerby & Evedon NG34 122 C6
Friskney PE22 115 A6
Morton DN21 197 A8
2 Normanby By Spital LN8 55 F6
Strubby with Woodthorpe LN13 63 C1
Wroot DN9 26 D5
Field Rd Billinghay LN4 109 E6
Crowle DN17 16 D7
Stainforth DN7 14 C6
Thorne/Moorends DN8 15 A8
Field Rise PE7 233 D5
Field Side
Mareham Le Fen PE22 98 F4
Thorne DN8 15 A8
Field St 6 Boston PE21 209 A5
Kingston upon Hull HU9 181 B7
Field Terr PE7 231 C2
Field View PE22 111 F8
Field Wlk PE1 226 B2
Fieldfare Croft PE21 208 C6
Fieldfare Dr PE2 231 E6
Fieldhouse Rd DN36 193 A1
Fields Cl 3 DN9 27 D7
Fields Rd DN9 27 E2
Fieldside 6 Blyton DN21 41 C5
11 Crowle DN17 16 D7
Epworth DN9 27 D6
Fieldside Cres 1 PE22 99 A4
Fife Cl PE9 218 D6
Fifth Ave
Fixborough Ind Est DN15 8 A1
Grantham NG31 211 F6
Scunthorpe DN17 184 B6
Fifth Dro PE11 144 A4
Fiftyeights Rd DN10 26 B2
Figtree Wlk PE1 226 A7
Fildes St DN31 191 D7
Filey Cl LN6 205 A3
Filey Rd DN32 192 A5
Fillingham Cres
Cleethorpes DN35 192 F3
3 Scunthorpe DN15 182 B3
Fillingham La DN21 53 F3
Finch Cl LN6 204 D8
Finch Dr NG34 212 B3
Finchfield PE1 226 F7
Finchley Gn PE3 225 E4
Findlay Cres DN36 195 D6
Fingle St 3 DN22 52 B1
Finisterre Ave PE25 206 A6
Finkell St DN10 39 C1
Finkin St NG31 211 A4
Finkle La 11 DN18 3 F1
Finkle St
Benington PE22 127 A5
Stainforth DN7 14 C7
Finney Cl LN4 207 D5
Finningley Cl 9 LN6 204 D6
Finningley Rd LN6 204 D6
Finns La NG32 138 C6
Finsbury Dr 9 DN33 191 B2
Finsbury St 13 LN13 75 F2
Fir Ave PE10 213 A5
Fir Cl DN16 185 A4
Fir Rd 1 PE9 218 D6
Fir Tree Ave 5 LN5 93 E8
Fir Tree Cl 4 LN2 68 F2
Fir Tree La NG32 119 F3
Fir Trees HU10 178 D6
Firbeck Ave PE25 206 D1
Fircroft NG31 211 C1
Firdale Cl 3 PE6 174 A5
Firebeacon La
Grainthorpe LN11 49 E8
Marshchapel LN11 37 D1
Firethorn Cl 3 HU3 180 D5
Firs The 6 NG34 108 D1
Firsby Cres DN33 191 A2
First Ave
1 Fixborough Ind Est DN15 7 F1
Grantham NG31 211 E6
4 Grimsby DN33 191 C4
6 Scampton Airfield LN1 67 E5
Scunthorpe DN17 184 C6
Spalding PE11 214 B4
First Dro Crowland PE6 166 E2
Gosberton PE11 144 C3
Moulton PE12 146 E6
Peterborough PE1 226 D1
First Holme La 2 NG23 91 A8
First Hurn Dro LN4 110 A6
First La HU10 179 A5
First Marsh Rd PE13 170 C2
Firth Field Rd DN7 14 F4
Firth La DN9 26 D6
Firth Rd LN6 234 A1
Firtree Ave LN6 200 C1
Firtree Dr 6 DN20 20 F7
Fish Dock Rd DN31 189 B2
Fish Groom's La PE11 145 E6
Fish St 1 HU1 180 F5
Fish Well Cl 3 NG33 151 A8
Fishemore Ave HU13 178 F2
Fisher Cl 23 NG23 91 D5
Fisher Pl DN35 192 D7
Fishergate PE12 159 B1
Fisherman's Wharf DN31 191 D8
Fishermans Wlk 2 HU3 180 C4
Fishlake Nab DN7 14 C7
Fishmere End Rd
Sutterton PE20 136 A4
Wigtoft PE20 135 F3
Fishmere Gate Rd LN11 51 B1
Fishpond La PE12 215 E2
Fishtoft Dro PE22 125 C7
Fishtoft Rd PE21 209 B3
Fishtoft Sch PE21 126 C1
Fishwick Ave 5 HU13 178 E1
Fiskerton CE (Controlled) Prim Sch LN3 82 B7
Fiskerton Cl 8 DN34 190 F4
Fiskerton Dr LN2 201 F8
Fiskerton Rd
Cherry Willingham LN3 203 C4
Cherry Willingham/Reepham LN3 82 A8
Fiskerton Rd E LN3 203 E4
Fiskerton Way 2 DN31 188 A3
Fitties La 2 DN36 37 C5
Fitton End Rd PE13 169 F3
Fitzgerald Ct 3 LN4 207 A6
Fitzjames Cl 2 PE23 101 A8
Fitzwilliam Hospl PE6 224 E2
Fitzwilliam Mews DN35 192 E2
Fitzwilliam Pl 6 LN4 109 F5
Fitzwilliam Rd PE9 219 A7
Fitzwilliam St
10 Mablethorpe/Sutton on Sea LN12 64 B4
Peterborough PE1 226 A3
Five Arches PE2 229 C6
Five Bell La PE20 135 C4
Five House La
Frampton PE20 136 C8
Wyberton PE21 208 B1
Five La Ends NG23 79 C8
Five Mile La LN4 82 B5
Flag Bsns Exchange PE1 226 E3
Flag Fen Bronze Age Mus* PE6 227 B3
Flag Fen Rd PE1 226 C4
Flag La PE12 168 B7
Flamborough Cl
Peterborough PE2 225 E1
6 Skegness PE25 206 A6
Flaminian Way 8 NG32 120 A2
Flarepath The DN20 21 A8
Flaxengate 4 LN2 234 B2
Flaxland PE3 225 A6
Flaxmill La 6 PE11 145 C1
Flaxwell Way 12 NG34 121 B7
Fleet Rd Fleet PE12 159 B7
Holbeach PE12 215 F2
Fleet St Holbeach PE12 215 E2
Lincoln LN1 201 C4
Fleet Way PE2 231 B6
Fleetgate 8 DN18 3 E1
Fleets La LN1 54 A1
Fleets Rd LN1 66 D7
Fleetway DN36 37 A3
Fleetwood Cl 2 DN33 194 E7
Fleetwood Ct LE15 162 A8
Fleming Ave NG13 128 B6
Fleming Ct 1 PE21 208 F1
Fleming Rd PE11 214 E8
Fleming Wlk HU4 179 D2
Fletcher Cl
Kingston upon Hull HU13 178 E2
7 Scunthorpe DN15 182 C6
Fletcher Rd DN34 190 F7
Fletcher St NG31 211 A3
Fletton Ave PE2 231 A8
Fletton Fields PE2 231 A7
Fletton Parkway PE2 229 F2
Fletton Prim Sch PE2 230 F6
Flinders Cl 5 LN4 95 C4
Flinders Rd 13 PE11 134 E2
Flint Cl PE9 163 D1
Flint Gate 23 PE12 160 E4
Flint House Rd PE12 147 C3
Flintham Cl 2 LN4 95 C4
Flinton St HU3 180 B3
Flixborough Rd DN15 8 B4
Flood Rd The DN21 197 B3
Flore Cl PE3 225 C5
Florence Ave HU13 178 F1
Florence St
Grimsby DN32 191 E5
Lincoln LN2 202 B3
Florence Way 4 PE6 217 C5
Florence Wright Ave 6 LN11 198 D4
Floriade Cl 4 PE11 214 B2
Florins Fold NG34 132 F3
Floss La DN22 65 B6
Flour Sq DN31 189 A1
Flowerdown Ave 5 NG34 120 D8
Foal Plats La LN13 90 A8
Fodder Dike Bank
Eastville PE22 114 C7
Midville PE22 113 E7
Fold Hill Rd PE22 114 A2
Fold La Moulton PE12 157 F7
5 Tydd St Giles PE13 169 F7
Folds La 2 PE12 216 B4
Folgate La PE14 170 F6
Folkingham Cl 11 LN6 204 D8
Folkingham Rd
Billingborough NG34 133 A1
1 Morton PE10 154 C7
Pickworth NG34 142 A8
Folksworth Rd PE7 232 E1
Folly Cl PE7 233 C5
Folly La
Branston & Mere LN4 81 C2
Hough-on-the-Hill NG32 118 F5
North Kelsey LN7 32 C5
North Scarle NG23 91 D8
West Fen PE22 99 E1
Folly's Dro PE13 177 F3
Fontwell Cres 9 LN6 205 A5
Fontwell Gdns 2 PE9 219 B5
Foote's Dro PE12 167 C8
Forbes Rd PE21 209 C4
Ford La
8 Hibaldstow DN20 30 F5
Morton PE10 154 C6
Ford Way LN11 72 D6
Fordham Dr LN1 201 C7
Fordingham Inf Sch DN16 183 B2
Ford's Ave 17 DN41 23 F5
Fore La PE20 135 A5
Foredyke Prim Sch HU9 5 D8
Foreman Way 1 PE6 166 E1
Forest Ave 3 PE10 213 B5
Forest Dale PE21 208 F7
Forest Dr DN36 193 B1
Forest Dro PE6 166 C2
Forest Gdns 5 PE9 218 D7
Forest Pines La 11 LN10 97 C5
Forest Way 7 DN36 36 D8
Forester Way HU4 179 D3
Forge Cl Freiston PE22 126 C4
South Kelsey LN7 32 A1
Forge Cres
3 Pinchbeck PE11 156 E8
Ulceby DN39 12 A1
Forge Ct 12 PE6 217 A6
Forge End PE7 229 A4
Forge La LN8 56 F8
Forge Way DN36 195 C3
Forkedale DN18 10 E8
Forman's La NG34 109 B1
Formby Cl NG31 211 C7
Forrester St 1 DN20 196 B3
Forrington Pl LN1 66 E2
Forstedd Hill NG33 153 B5
Forster St DN21 197 C5
Forsyth Cres 6 PE25 206 C2
Forsythia Dr DN33 191 C2
Fortescue Cl 1 LN4 207 A5
Fortuna Way DN37 190 C7
Forty Acre HU10 178 F7
Forty Acre Rd PE1 226 D2
Forty Foot La
Humberside Airport DN39 21 F6
Old Leake PE22 113 D3
Forty Stps HU10 178 F7
Forum Way 7 NG34 212 F3
Foss Bank LN1 201 D3
Foss St LN1 201 D3
Fossdyke Gdns 18 LN1 66 D2
Fosse Cl 9 PE6 164 E5
Fosse Dr LN6 205 A3
Fosse La
Thistleton LE15 151 B1
Thorpe on the Hill LN6 92 E7
Fosse Way Prim Sch LN6 204 F2
Foster Cl 2 LN4 96 C1
Foster Rd
21 Collingham NG23 91 D5
7 Thorne/Moorends DN8 15 A8
Foster St 3 Boston PE21 209 A5
Heckington NG34 122 E3
Lincoln LN5 201 E1
Foster's Dro PE10 155 A3
Foster's Gdns 1 LN4 82 B1
Fosters Cl 3 LN5 107 A8
Foston by Pass NG32 117 F1
Foston Cres LN6 204 F7
Foston La NG32 128 F7
Foston Rd NG31 210 E3
Fotherby Rd DN17 184 F4
Fotherby St 4 DN31 189 A1
Fothergill Dr 17 DN3 14 A2
Foundry La
11 Spalding PE11 214 D4
12 Thorne/Moorends DN8 15 A8
Foundry Rd
Bucknall LN10 84 B3
Ryhall PE9 163 C2
Stamford PE9 219 A5
Foundry St LN9 199 C4
Fountain Cl
Kingston upon Hull HU13 178 C3
5 Waltham DN37 194 C5
Fountain Hill DN10 39 E3
Fountain Hill Rd DN10 39 E4
Fountain La 13 PE21 208 F5
Fountain Pl 10 PE21 208 F5
Fountain St
22 Caistor LN7 33 B4
Kingston upon Hull HU3 180 D6
Fountains Pl PE6 175 B1
Four Acre Cl HU10 178 C6
Fourfields CE Prim Sch PE20 136 A2
Fourfields Prim Sch PE7 233 E6
Fourth Ave
2 Fixborough Ind Est DN15 8 A1
Grantham NG31 211 F6
3 Scampton Airfield LN1 67 E5
1 Scunthorpe DN17 184 C6
Fourth Dro
Gosberton PE11 144 B4
Peterborough PE1 226 F3
Fourways 6 DN36 36 D4
Fowler Rd DN16 185 B8
Fox Cl PE21 208 C6
Fox Covert 2 LN6 93 A8
Fox Covert La DN10 40 A4
Fox Ct 1 DN17 16 D8
Fox Dale PE9 218 F6
Fox Headings PE12 158 C1
Fox St DN15 182 F3
Foxby Hill DN21 197 E2
Foxby La DN21 197 F2
Foxcovert Rd PE6 220 E8
Foxe End 12 LN12 64 B3
Foxendale Hill LN9 72 F1
Foxes Low Rd PE12 215 F2
Foxfield Cl LN6 200 A5
Foxglove Cl
Brigg DN20 196 B4
1 Spilsby PE23 101 A8
Foxglove Gdns DN34 190 F6
Foxglove Rd 1 PE9 218 C7
Foxglove Way 5 LN5 205 C2
Foxgloves PE6 217 D6
Foxhill DN37 190 C7
Foxhill Rd DN8 15 B7
Foxhills Comp Sch DN15 182 E5
Foxhills Ind Pk DN15 182 F7
Foxhills Rd DN15 182 E5
Foxhole La PE22 126 D3
Foxley Cl PE4 221 A4
Foxley Ct 1 PE10 213 C7
Foyle Cl LN5 205 D2
Fracknal's Row 3 PE21 208 E6
Framlingham Rd PE7 231 F5
Frampton Bank PE20 136 B8
Frampton La PE20 124 E2
Frampton Marsh Nature Reserve* PE20 137 D5
Frampton Pl PE21 208 D4
Frampton Roads PE20 136 F6
Frances Askew Prim Sch HU4 179 F4
Frances Ct 8 DN37 194 C5
Frances St DN15 183 A3
Francis Bernard Cl 4 PE21 208 D3
Francis Gdns PE1 225 F8

Francis St
Kingston upon Hull HU2 180 F7
Lincoln LN1 234 B4
14 Spalding PE11 214 D4
Francklin Wlk 5 PE12 158 B6
Frank Perkins Parkway
PE1 226 E6
Frank Perkins Way
PE1 226 D3
Frank Swaby Ct LN5 205 E6
Frank Whittle Cl 1
NG34 120 E8
Frank Wright Ct 4 LN2 202 C7
Frankland Cl
2 Wrawby DN20 20 E3
1 Wrawby DN20 196 F6
Frankland Pl DN35 192 D7
Franklin Ave PE25 206 D1
Franklin Cl
Boston PE21 208 C6
7 Metheringham LN4 95 C4
Franklin Coll DN34 191 B5
Franklin Cres
Peterborough PE1 226 E6
Scunthorpe DN16 185 E6
1 Sleaford NG34 212 D5
Franklin Rd DN21 29 C4
Franklin St HU9 181 C8
Franklin Way DN38 21 F5
Franks Cl 2 PE20 136 D5
Franks La PE13 169 F5
Fraser Cl PE6 217 D5
Fraser St 2 DN32 191 F7
Fraserburgh Way 2
PE2 229 D4
Frederica Rd
13 Skegness PE25 103 E4
12 Skegness PE25 103 E4
Frederick Gough Comp Sch
DN16 185 C4
Frederick St
Cleethorpes DN35 192 E6
Grimsby DN31 191 D8
Lincoln LN2 202 C3
Frederick Ward Way
DN31 191 D7
Freehold St HU3 180 D7
Freeman Ave 4 HU15 2 C5
Freeman Cl 10 PE8 172 B1
Freeman Ct DN36 195 E2
Freeman Rd LN6 204 D3
Freeman St DN32 189 B1
Freeman's La DN22 52 A2
Freemans La 6 DN20 10 C2
Freeport Wharf DN31 191 E8
Freer Gdns LN11 198 E6
Freeschool La LN2 234 B2
Freesia Way PE7 233 F6
Freeston St DN35 192 B8
Freetown Way HU2 180 E7
Freightliner Rd HU3 179 F2
Freiston Rd PE21 209 B5
French Dro PE6 175 E7
French's Rd PE14 170 F8
Fresh Fields 14 HU15 2 C5
Freshney Bog Nature
Reserve* DN37 190 E7
Freshney Dr 2 DN31 191 C8
Freshney Way PE21 208 B3
Freston PE4 221 D2
Freyja Croft 3 DN33 191 B2
Friar Way PE21 208 F6
Friars La LN2 234 B2
Friars Rd DN17 184 E6
Friest La 11 PE20 135 A4
Frieston Heath La
NG32 119 D6
Frieston Rd NG32 119 B6
Frinkley La
Honington NG32 119 B2
Hougham NG32 118 D2
Frisby Cl PE6 164 D4
Friskney All Saints CE
(Aided) Prim Sch
PE22 115 A6
Friskney Decoy Wood Nature
Reserve* PE22 115 A8
Frith Bank PE22 125 D6
Friths La PE20 125 B1
Frithville Cty Sch
PE22 112 D1
Frithville Rd PE22 113 A1
Frobisher Ave DN32 192 B6
Frodingham Footpath 3
DN15 183 B3
Frodingham Rd DN15 183 A4
Frodingham S Rd
DN16 183 E2
Frodsham St 8 HU9 5 D8
Frognall PE6 165 D1
Frog's Abbey Gate
PE12 158 E4
Frome Cl LN6 204 D5
Front Rd
Tydd St Mary PE13 160 D1
Wisbech St Mary PE13 177 D6
Front St Alkborough DN15 8 C8
Barnby in the Willows
NG24 104 F3
Dunston LN4 95 C5
East Stockwith DN21 40 B5
Elsham DN20 20 F7
Gainsborough DN21 197 B7
4 Grasby DN38 32 E7
Normanby By Spital LN8 55 E7
Front St *continued*
South Clifton NG23 78 C5
Tealby LN8 46 C1
Ulceby DN39 12 A1
Frost Cl DN15 2 A1
Frostley Gate PE12 158 F3
Frusher Ave DN33 191 C3
Fryston 28 HU15 2 C6
Fuchsia Croft 2 DN15 182 F2
Fuchsia Dr HU4 179 B2
Fulbeck Rd DN16 185 C6
Fulbridge Jun/Inf Sch
PE1 225 F7
Fulbridge Rd PE4 221 A3
Fulford Cl NG31 211 D8
Fulford Cres
Kingston upon Hull
HU10 179 A8
3 New Holland DN19 4 E2
Fulford Way PE25 206 C6
Fulham Pk 5 DN33 191 B2
Fulham Rd PE3 225 E4
Fuller St DN35 192 D8
Fulmar Dr LN11 198 C8
Fulmar Rd LN6 204 D8
Fulney Dro PE12 157 B3
Fulney La PE12 157 B6
Fulstow Gr 7 DN33 191 B3
Fulstow Prim Sch LN11 49 B8
Fun Farm* PE12 157 D7
Fundrey Rd PE13 170 E1
Furlongs La
Belchford LN9 73 B1
Old Leake PE22 114 A1
Furlongs Rd LN12 77 A8
Furniss Ct 2 DN18 10 E8
Furrow Cl 16 LN2 68 D6
Further Old Gate
PE12 158 D5
Fury Ave LN11 62 B6
Furze La LN11 62 A5
Furze Ride PE1 226 B8
Fussey Gdns DN20 10 C1
Fydell Cres PE21 208 E4
Fydell Ct PE21 208 E6
Fydell St PE21 208 E5
Fyson Way PE20 136 C6

G

Gables Hospl The PE23 87 F1
Gadd's La PE13 170 A1
Gainas Ave DN21 197 C6
Gainsborough Central Sta
DN21 197 E4
Gainsborough Coll
DN21 197 C5
Gainsborough Gdns 2
LN6 205 B7
Gainsborough La DN20 30 F8
Gainsborough Lea Rd Sta
DN21 197 D1
Gainsborough Rd
Blyton DN21 41 B4
Bole DN22 52 A6
Girton NG23 78 C2
32 Kirton in Lindsey DN21 30 B1
Kirton in Lindsey DN21 42 D8
Little Casterton PE9 218 F7
Middle Rasen LN8 57 B7
Saundby DN22 52 B7
Saxilby with Ingleby LN1 66 D2
Scotter DN21 29 B3
Sturton Le Steeple DN22 52 B3
West Rasen LN8 57 A7
Willingham DN21 53 E4
6 Winthorpe NG24 104 B7
Wiseton DN10 39 A1
Gainsthorpe Rd E
DN21 30 D4
Gainsthorpe Rd W
DN21 30 C4
Gallamore Ct 5 LN8 57 C8
Gallamore La 6 LN8 57 C8
Galletly Cl PE10 213 D6
Galley Ct HU9 181 C6
Gallions Cl 2 PE4 221 B1
Galway Cl 2 PE11 214 A5
Gamlyn Cl 1 PE11 214 D2
Gannet Cl 8 NG31 210 E2
Gannocks Cl PE2 229 F5
Gannocks The PE2 229 F5
Ganton Sch HU10 179 A7
Ganton Way HU10 178 F8
Garbutt Pl DN35 193 A4
Garden Dr DN36 195 C7
Garden End Rd PE1 226 B6
Garden St 5 Brigg DN20 196 C3
Grimsby DN31 191 D7
Gardeners Wlk PE21 208 D2
Gardenfield LN6 200 B3
Gardenia Dr DN17 184 F1
Garfield Cl LN1 201 D8
Garfield St DN21 197 C5
Garfit's La PE21 208 D1
Garibaldi St
8 Grimsby DN32 189 B1
5 Grimsby DN32 191 F8
Garmston St 8 LN1 234 B3
Garner St DN32 191 E6
Garner's La PE34 161 A4
Garnet Gr 6 HU3 180 A4
Garnett St DN35 192 D8
Garnsgate Rd PE12 216 A5
Garrick Cl LN5 205 C3
Garrick La 4 DN36 195 C7
Garrison Rd HU9 181 C6
Garth La DN31 191 D8
Garth Specl Sch The
PE11 214 E5
Garthorpe Rd DN17 7 C4
Garthway 8 DN36 195 D2
Garton Gr
3 Grimsby DN32 192 A5
3 Kingston upon Hull
HU5 179 C7
Garton St PE1 226 A5
Gartree Sch LN4 207 B5
Gas House La 16 PE12 160 E4
Gas La
7 Navenby/Wellingore
LN5 107 A8
Stamford PE9 219 C5
5 Thorney PE6 176 A3
Gas St 2 Horncastle LN9 199 C3
19 Stamford PE9 219 C5
Gascoigne 3 PE4 220 E5
Gashouse La 3 DN9 28 A3
Gate La DN33 191 D1
Gate Way DN31 188 E2
Gatehouse Rd DN19 11 F7
Gateroom La PE22 114 E3
Gatewood La DN7 14 E1
Gatherums The DN35 192 E5
Gatram Rd PE24 90 D6
Gaunt St LN5 234 A1
Gauntlet Dro PE20 134 F6
Gauntlet Rd
3 Bicker PE20 135 A4
Grimoldby LN11 62 B6
Gautry La DN9 28 B4
Gayle Rd LN4 110 E8
Gaysfield Rd 6 PE21 126 C1
Gayton Cl Lincoln LN2 202 A7
Skegness PE25 206 C2
Gayton Ct PE3 225 C5
Gayton Rd DN35 193 A3
Gazeley Gdns PE7 231 B2
Gedney Church End Prim Sch
PE12 159 D7
Gedney Cl DN37 190 C8
Gedney Hill CE (Controlled)
Prim Sch PE12 168 D2
Gedney Hill Gate PE12 168 F7
Gedney Rd PE12 216 A6
Gee St HU3 180 C5
Gelder Beck Rd DN17 29 D6
Gelder's La PE12 158 A1
Gelston Rd NG32 119 A4
Gemsbok Cl 3 HU4 179 D2
Geneva Ave LN2 202 B6
Geneva St PE1 226 A3
George Ave
Gedney PE12 148 F4
4 Keadby DN17 17 D5
Skegness PE25 206 B3
George Butler Cl 23
DN37 23 F1
George Farmer Tech Coll
PE12 215 D3
George Mews 2 LN7 33 B4
George St
2 Barton-upon-Humber
DN18 10 F8
5 Boston PE21 208 E4
Bourne PE10 213 D5
Broughton DN20 19 D3
Cleethorpes DN35 192 F5
Gainsborough DN21 197 B6
Grantham NG31 211 B4
Grimsby DN31 191 D7
Helpringham NG34 133 D7
5 Keadby DN17 17 D5
Kingston upon Hull HU1 180 F6
11 Kirton in Lindsey DN21 30 B1
Lincoln LN5 234 C1
Louth LN11 198 B5
Mablethorpe/Sutton on Sea
LN12 64 B3
7 Market Rasen LN8 57 D8
Peterborough PE2 230 F8
Scunthorpe DN15 183 A4
Sleaford NG34 212 C3
George Yd 5 HU1 181 A6
Georgette Gdns 7
PE11 214 B5
Georgian Ct PE3 225 E1
Georgina Ct 27 DN18 10 E8
Gerald's Cl LN2 202 B5
German's La PE34 161 D2
Gerrard Mews LN4 203 D1
Gershwin Ave HU4 179 B4
Gertrude St DN32 191 E5
Gervase St DN15 183 A3
Gibbeson St 6 LN5 205 E8
Gibbet La LN8 57 A5
Gibraltar Hill LN1 234 A3
Gibraltar La 2 DN37 23 F1
Gibraltar Point National
Nature Reserve*
PE24 103 E2
Gibraltar Rd
Croft PE24 103 D1
5 Hemswell Cliff DN21 55 A8
Mablethorpe/Sutton on Sea
LN12 64 B4
Gibson Cl Branston LN4 81 E2
1 Sleaford NG34 212 B6
Gibson Gn LN6 92 E5
Gibson La HU14 2 E4
Gibson Pl 5 PE25 206 A5
Gibson Rd 2 DN7 26 A8
Gibsons Gdn 2 LN11 50 F7
Giddings Cl PE2 229 F4
Gilberts Gr 4 PE25 206 D8
Gilbey Rd DN31 188 D1
Gildale PE4 221 B4
Gildenburgh Ave PE1 226 D5
Gilder Way PE21 209 F2
Gildesburgh Rd LN4 203 B1
Giles Sch The PE22 114 A1
Giles St DN35 192 E6
Gillatts Cl 1 DN20 196 F7
Gillett St HU3 180 B4
Gilliatt St DN15 183 A4
Gilmores La 8 NG24 104 C1
Gilmorton Dr PE1 226 D7
Gilpin St PE1 225 E6
Gimmel's Gate PE12 216 C1
Gipsy Dro
Friskney PE22 114 D7
Langriville PE22 124 F8
Gipsy La Gedney PE12 216 A8
Holton Le Moor LN7 32 C1
Osgodby LN8 45 D3
Owersby LN7 44 F8
Owston Ferry DN9 40 C8
South Kelsey LN7 32 C1
Swineshead PE20 124 A1
Tydd St Mary PE13 160 A2
Wrangle PE22 114 D2
Girdlestone Wlk 2 PE6 166 F1
Girsby La LN8 59 B6
Girton Cl 3 DN16 185 B4
Girton La NG23 78 D1
Girton Way 3 PE9 219 A7
Gisburn Rd HU13 178 F2
Glade The 8 LN12 77 A7
Gladiator Rd LN11 62 B6
Gladstone Dr 1 DN16 183 C1
Gladstone Prim Sch
PE1 225 F5
Gladstone St
Bourne PE10 213 C6
Gainsborough DN21 197 C5
Kingston upon Hull HU3 180 C6
Peterborough PE1 225 F3
Gladstone Terr 3 NG31 211 A5
Glaisdale Gdns NG31 211 B8
Glaisdale Gr HU9 181 F8
Glaisdale Rd 2 DN16 185 D5
Glamis Gdns PE3 225 B2
Glamis Pl LN11 198 B6
Glamis Rd HU13 178 F2
Glanford Gr 12 DN19 11 D8
Glanford Pk (Scunthorpe
United FC) DN15 182 A2
Glanford Rd
Brigg DN20 196 D3
Scunthorpe DN17 184 F3
Glanford Way 1 DN15 182 B3
Glanville Ave DN17 184 F8
Glanville Cres 2 DN17 184 F8
Glasgow St HU3 180 A5
Glastonbury Cl 20 PE6 175 A1
Glatton Dr PE2 231 D6
Gleanings The 5 LN5 107 B8
Glebe Ave PE2 229 E4
Glebe Cl
Burton upon Stather DN15 8 A5
3 Donington on Bain LN11 59 E1
Gorefield PE13 169 E3
Holton le Clay DN36 195 C3
Humberston DN36 36 C8
5 Ingham LN1 54 F2
5 Sibsey PE22 113 B1
1 Skegness PE25 206 A7
Sleaford NG34 212 A2
2 Spalding PE11 214 A4
Glebe Ct PE2 231 B8
Glebe Gdns 2 PE6 175 B8
Glebe Rd Brigg DN20 196 C4
Cleethorpes DN35 192 E6
Grimsby DN33 191 E1
Humberston DN36 36 C7
Peterborough PE2 231 A8
Scunthorpe DN15 183 B4
Thorne/Moorends DN8 15 B8
Wymondham LE14 150 B1
Glebe The
Sturton By Stow LN1 66 D8
Upton DN21 53 D5
Glebe View 1 PE6 217 B6
Glebe Way
Barton-upon-Humber
DN18 11 A8
5 Sutterton PE20 136 A2
Glebe Wlk 3 PE12 167 B8
Gleed Ave PE11 134 E2
Gleed Boys Sch PE11 214 F4
Gleedale LN6 204 F1
Gleeds Girls Gm Sch
PE11 214 F3
Glemsford Rise 2 PE2 230 C7
Glen Ave 4 PE11 145 B1
Glen Cl NG33 153 A1
Glen Cres
7 Essendine PE9 163 D3
Stamford PE9 219 C7
Glen Dr PE21 208 B4
Glen Gdns 2 PE11 145 E3
Glen Hall Rise 10 DN19 11 C8
Glen Rd
Castle Bytham NG33 152 D1
Counthorpe & Creeton
NG33 153 A2
3 Wittering PE8 172 B1
Glen The PE2 231 B7
Glenarm Cres 7 LN5 205 D3
Glenbank Cl LN6 204 F3
Glencoe Cl 2 DN7 14 D4
Glencoe St HU3 179 F6
Glencoe Way PE2 229 D3
Glendale PE2 229 D6
Glendon Cl 5 LN5 205 D3
Gleneagles
Grantham NG31 211 D8
Peterborough PE2 229 F6
10 Waltham DN37 194 C4
Gleneagles Cl 5 PE9 218 E6
Gleneagles Cres 6 DN19 4 E2
Gleneagles Dr
Skegness PE25 206 D6
12 Woodhall Spa LN10 97 C5
Gleneagles Gr 4 LN4 203 D1
Glenfield Rd DN37 190 D8
Glenn Ave 3 PE11 214 C4
Glenrock Pk HU15 2 B6
Glenside NG33 152 E1
Glenside N PE11 156 C8
Glenside S PE11 156 C8
Glentham Cl LN6 205 B3
Glentham Ct 6 LN8 43 F1
Glentham Rd
Bishop Norton LN8 43 D3
5 Gainsborough DN21 53 A8
Glenton St PE1 226 C2
Glentworth Cres 4
PE25 206 D4
Glentworth Rd DN21 53 F4
Glenwood Dr 2 HU4 179 B6
Glenwood Gr LN6 201 D1
Glinton Rd
Helpston PE6 173 C4
Newborough PE6 221 C8
Gloria Way DN37 190 C7
Glossop Rd DN15 182 B2
Gloucester Ave
Grimsby DN34 191 B4
Scunthorpe DN16 185 B7
Gloucester Cl
Skegness PE25 206 B2
1 Sleaford NG34 212 C7
Gloucester Rd
Grantham NG31 210 C5
Peterborough PE2 231 B7
7 Stamford PE9 219 B6
Gloucester St HU4 179 E3
Glover Rd DN17 184 E8
Glovers Ave 8 DN17 17 D4
Glynn Rd LN1 201 E8
Goathland Cl HU3 180 A6
Godber Dr LN4 205 F3
Goddam's La PE12 146 F1
Goddard Cl 37 DN18 10 E8
Goddard Cres 12 PE13 170 D1
Godfrey Ave 6 PE11 145 C6
Godfrey Cl 7 PE6 174 E5
Godfrey Rd 11 DN8 15 A8
Godiva Cl 16 PE6 166 F1
Godiva Cres PE10 213 B5
Godman's La HU10 178 B8
Godnow Rd DN17 16 C6
Godric Sq PE2 230 D6
Godsey Cres 9 PE6 217 C5
Godsey La PE6 217 B6
Godson Ave 1 NG34 122 D3
Godwin Cl PE10 213 B6
Godwin Rd 13 PE13 170 D1
Goffsmill PE3 225 A4
Gold Fen Dike Bank
PE22 114 D2
Gold La LN13 63 A1
Goldcrest Cl
2 Birchwood LN6 200 E1
Scunthorpe DN15 182 D6
Golden Drop 2 PE6 173 C4
Golden Gr PE20 135 C5
Golden Harvest Way 6
PE12 158 B6
Goldenholme La 4 DN22 65 A5
Goldfinch Cl LN6 200 A3
Goldgarth DN32 192 A5
Goldhay Way PE2 229 F2
Goldie La PE2 229 F6
Goldings The 10 DN9 27 D2
Goldsmith Ct 1 LN4 207 A6
Goldsmith Rd NG31 211 D6
Goldsmith Wlk LN2 202 C7
Goldson's La PE22 126 F6
Golf Ct PE12 160 F5
Golf Links Dr HU15 2 B6
Golf Rd LN12 64 A4
Gollands La DN9 27 B2
Gonerby Hill NG31 210 E8
Gonerby Hill Foot CE Prim
Sch NG31 210 E8
Gonerby La NG32 129 A7
Gonerby Rd NG31 210 E8
Goochgate PE12 169 A7
Good La LN1 234 B4
Goodacre PE2 230 A4
Goodens La PE13 170 A5
Goodfellows CE Prim Sch
PE11 156 E3
Goodfellows Rd 7
PE11 156 E3
Goodhand Cl DN18 11 A8
Goodliff Rd NG31 210 E2
Goodman Cl 6 NG31 129 E5
Goodson Cl 3 PE21 209 B4
Goodwin Dr 7 PE24 90 B7
Goodwin La 10 NG24 104 C1
Goodwin Par 1 HU3 180 D5
Goodwin Wlk PE4 221 A4
Goodwood DN17 184 D4
Goodwood Cl LN11 198 A7
Goodwood La 1 DN35 192 F1
Goodwood Rd 8 PE3 224 F3
Goodwood Way LN6 204 C7
Goole Rd DN14 6 C8

Goose Gn 10 PE12 160 E4
Goose La PE23 87 D2
Gooseacre 33 DN17 29 D7
Goosegate La NG32 118 A2
Goose's La PE14 161 A1
Gordon Ave PE2 230 E7
Gordon Boswell Romany Mus* PE12 214 E1
Gordon Fendick Sch The PE13 170 D2
Gordon Field 8 LN8 57 D7
Gordon Gdns 1 DN33 194 F8
Gordon Rd LN1 234 B3
Gordon St
Gainsborough DN21 197 D2
4 Kingston upon Hull HU3 180 B5
Gordon Way PE2 230 C7
Gore La 8 PE11 214 D4
Goredike Bank PE13 169 C2
Gorefield Cty Prim Sch PE13 169 F2
Gorefield Rd PE13 169 F2
Gorehall Dr 10 LN2 68 D7
Goring Pl DN35 192 D7
Gorse Cl 5 Hatfield DN7 14 C3
4 Woodhall Spa LN10 97 E6
Gorse Dro NG34 133 A6
Gorse Hill La
Caythorpe NG32 119 A8
Wellingore LN5 107 C7
Gorse La
Gonerby Hill Foot NG31 211 B1
Great Ponton NG31 139 F8
9 Leasingham NG34 121 B7
Scredington NG34 133 A7
Silk Willoughby NG34 121 C1
Gorse Rd NG31 211 D5
Gorse Rise NG31 211 C5
Gorton Rd HU10 178 E7
Gorton St DN31 189 B2
Gorwick La LN1 66 B6
Gosberton Bank PE11 145 E6
Gosberton Clough & Risegate Prim Sch PE11 144 D4
Gosberton House Specl Sch PE11 145 B6
Gosberton Prim Sch PE11 145 B6
Gosberton Rd PE11 145 C4
Gospel La LN5 106 C3
Gospelgate LN11 198 B5
Gosport Rd 2 DN34 191 A6
Gostwick PE2 229 D5
Gote La PE13 169 E3
Gothic Cl 12 LN6 204 D7
Gouldeby La LN11 72 D6
Goulton St HU3 180 B3
Gover's Dro PE12 159 A2
Gower Rd HU4 179 B3
Gowt Bank PE22 114 C2
Gowts La PE12 159 E3
Goxhill Ave 4 PE11 134 E2
Goxhill Cl 14 LN6 204 D7
Goxhill Gdns 4 DN34 190 F4
Goxhill Gr 13 LN6 204 D7
Goxhill Prim Sch DN19 12 A8
Goxhill Rd DN19 11 E8
Goxhill Sta DN19 11 F8
Grace Ave LN6 204 D3
Grace Cl 4 NG34 212 E3
Grace Cres PE24 77 C3
Grace St LN5 201 F1
Gracefield La NG23 78 A4
Graeme Rd PE5 222 F2
Grafham Cl PE2 231 E4
Grafton Ave PE3 225 C3
Grafton St
Grimsby DN32 189 C1
Lincoln LN2 202 B3
Graham Ave HU4 179 C2
Graham Hill Way 4 PE10 213 E4
Graham Rd PE25 206 B4
Grains Gate LN11 37 E1
Grainsby Ave
Cleethorpes DN35 192 D3
Holton le Clay DN36 195 E1
Grainsby Cl LN6 205 C5
Grainsby La DN36 35 E1
Grainthorpe Sch LN11 50 B7
Graizelound Fields Rd DN9 27 D1
Grammar Sch La DN20 196 C6
Grammar Sch Rd DN20 196 C4
Grammar Sch Rd S 3 DN20 196 C3
Grammar Sch Wlk DN16 185 C4
Grampian Cl 14 NG34 212 B3
Grampian Way
Gonerby Hill Foot NG31 210 D8
2 Grimsby DN33 194 E8
Thorne/Moorends DN8 15 A7
Granary Cl
22 Metheringham LN4 95 C4
5 Waddington LN5 93 F6
Granary Croft 7 DN9 27 D2
Granary La LN4 207 A4
Granary Way LN9 199 A3
Granby Dr 5 NG13 128 A5
Granby Rd LN8 47 B5
Granby St PE1 226 B2
Grand Par PE25 206 D3
Grand Sluice La 1 PE21 208 F6
Granely Cl LN1 201 C6
Grange Ave
18 Barton-upon-Humber DN18 10 E8
Hatfield DN7 14 D4
24 Laceby DN37 23 F1
Misterton DN10 40 A4
Peterborough PE1 226 A6
Scunthorpe DN15 183 A5
Grange Cl 17 Hatfield DN7 14 D4
1 Ingham LN1 54 F2
5 Misterton DN10 40 A5
Grange Cres
Kingston upon Hull HU10 178 E6
Lincoln LN6 205 B3
Peterborough PE2 230 A5
Grange Ct 3 LN5 92 E1
Grange Dr Lincoln LN6 205 B3
Misterton DN10 40 A4
Spalding PE11 214 E4
Stapleford LN6 105 A7
Grange Farm La DN36 195 D6
Grange Field 2 DN20 20 D8
Grange Ind Est DN16 185 E7
Grange Inf & Jun Sch DN34 190 F5
Grange La
Balderton NG24 104 A1
Canwick LN4 81 A4
Covenham St Bartholomew LN11 49 D6
Garthorpe LE14 150 C4
Hough-on-the-Hill NG32 118 E6
2 Ingham LN1 54 F2
Keddington LN11 198 E8
8 Manby LN11 62 C6
Nocton LN4 94 F6
North Cockerington LN11 50 A1
North Kelsey LN7 32 A3
Stixwould & Woodhall LN10 97 B6
Utterby LN11 49 A4
3 Willingham by Stow DN21 53 E3
Grange La Jun Sch DN16 185 D5
Grange La N DN16 185 D7
Grange La S DN16 185 C5
Grange Mdws PE22 113 A1
Grange Paddock 8 NG32 210 A5
Grange Pk 2 Brough HU15 2 C5
17 Kirk Sandall DN3 14 A3
8 Swanland HU14 3 B6
Grange Rd
Bracebridge Heath LN4 205 F2
Gainsborough DN21 41 A1
Garthorpe & Fockerby DN14 7 E8
14 Mablethorpe/Sutton on Sea LN12 77 A7
4 Metheringham LN4 95 D4
Peterborough PE3 225 D4
8 Ruskington NG34 108 D1
Sutton Bridge PE34 161 B4
10 Wisbech PE13 170 C1
Grange St LN4 109 C7
Grange The 1 NG31 211 A4
Grange Wlk
Grimsby DN34 191 A6
6 Misterton DN10 40 A5
Grangehill Rd PE12 169 B6
Gransley Rise PE3 225 C5
Granson Way LN4 203 A2
Grant St
Cleethorpes DN35 192 E7
Grimsby DN31 189 D1
Granta Cres NG31 211 C7
Grantham Ave DN33 191 D1
Grantham Canal Nature Reserve* NG31 210 D1
Grantham Church VA High Sch The NG31 211 E7
Grantham Coll NG31 211 B4
Grantham Cricket Gd NG31 211 B1
Grantham District Hospl NG31 211 A6
Grantham Dr
5 Skegness PE25 206 C4
2 Skegness PE25 206 B3
Grantham Fun Farm The* NG31 210 F4
Grantham House (NT)* NG31 211 B5
Grantham Mus* NG31 211 B4
Grantham Prep Sch The NG31 139 F8
Grantham Rd
Boothby Graffoe LN5 94 A2
Bottesford NG13 128 B5
Bracebridge Heath LN4 205 F2
Carlton Scroop NG32 119 C3
7 Great Gonerby NG31 129 D5
Great Gonerby NG31 210 D8
Harmston LN5 93 F6
Hough-on-the-Hill NG32 119 A4
Ingoldsby NG33 141 C5
Navenby/Wellingore LN5 107 A8
Old Somerby NG33 140 D8
Ropsley & Humby NG33 131 A1
2 Skillington NG33 151 A8
Sleaford NG34 212 B2
Grantham St LN2 234 B2
Grantham Sta NG31 211 A3
Grantham Town FC NG31 210 D3
Granthams The 12 LN2 68 E6
Grantley St NG31 211 A3
Granville Ave
12 Boston PE21 136 D8
Northborough PE6 217 E1
Granville St
Boston PE21 208 D5
Grantham NG31 211 C3
Grimsby DN32 191 F6
1 Kingston upon Hull HU3 180 A6
Peterborough PE1 226 A4
Granville Terr PE12 160 D4
Grasby All Saints CE Prim Sch DN38 32 E7
Grasby Cl 4 DN21 53 A8
Grasby Cres DN37 190 D7
Grasby Rd
Great Limber DN37 22 C3
North Kelsey LN7 32 D5
Scunthorpe DN17 184 E5
Grasby Wold La DN38 21 F1
Grasmere Ave PE24 90 E6
Grasmere Cl 3 DN21 197 E6
Grasmere Gdns PE4 221 B3
Grasmere Gr 5 DN36 192 E1
Grasmere Way LN6 200 D1
Grassdale Pk 2 HU15 2 B5
Grassgate La PE14 170 E3
Grassmoor Cl 2 LN6 93 B8
Gravecoat La PE11 144 E6
Gravel Cswy PE6 166 D1
Gravel Pit Hill DN20 31 D6
Gravel Pit La 1 DN39 22 A6
Gravel Pit Rd
Barton-upon-Humber DN18 3 D1
Scotter DN21 29 C4
Gravel Pits La PE24 102 C8
Gravel Rd
Market Deeping PE6 165 D3
Revesby PE22 99 B4
Gravel Wlk PE1 226 A2
Graveley Cl 4 LN6 204 B6
Gravelhill Dro LN4 109 E7
Gravelholes La DN10 39 F5
Gravelpit La LN9 199 F2
Gray Ct PE1 225 E8
Gray Rd DN17 184 D6
Gray St LN1 234 A4
Grayingham Rd DN21 42 E7
Grayling Cl 2 DN37 190 D7
Graylings The PE21 208 B6
Gray's Ct 4 LN11 198 B6
Gray's Rd 2 LN11 198 B6
Great Casterton CE Prim Sch PE9 171 C8
Great Cl 1 NG33 151 D2
Great Coates Prim Sch DN37 190 E8
Great Coates Rd
Grimsby DN37 190 C8
Healing DN41 23 F5
Great Coates Sta DN37 24 B5
Great Field La 1 HU9 5 E8
Great Grimsby Swimming Pool DN33 191 D4
Great Hale Dro NG34 123 A2
Great N Rd
Balderton NG24 117 C8
Empingham PE9 162 B2
Great Gonerby NG32 129 C6
Long Bennington NG23 117 D2
Tinwell PE9 218 D5
Wansford PE8 222 D1
Great Northern Terr LN5 234 C1
Great Northern Terr Ind Est LN5 234 C1
Great Ponton CE (Aided) Prim Sch NG33 140 A5
Great Steeping Prim Sch PE23 101 E7
Great Thornton St HU3 180 D6
Great Union St HU9 181 A7
Greatford Gdns PE9 164 B3
Greatford Rd
Baston PE6 164 D4
5 Uffington PE9 172 C6
Grebe Cl 2 LN6 204 C1
Greek St HU3 179 F5
Green Acres HU10 178 C6
Green Bank DN8 15 D6
Green Dro
Billinghay LN4 109 F6
Crowland PE6 175 D8
Helpringham NG34 133 F7
Little Hale NG34 134 A7
Thorney PE6 175 F6
Green Dyke PE12 148 D1
Green Farm Cl PE5 223 E2
Green Gate PE22 114 D1
Green Hill DN35 192 D3
Green Hill Rd NG31 210 F5
Green La
Algarkirk PE20 136 B3
Aunsby & Dembleby NG34 132 A4
18 Barrow upon Humber DN19 11 D8
10 Barton-upon-Humber DN18 10 F8
Beckingham LN5 105 C4
Belton DN9 16 D2
Belton & Manthorpe NG32 130 B7
Green La *continued*
Boston PE21 208 E7
Bottesford NG13 128 B5
Bratoft PE24 102 C7
Brigsley DN37 35 D4
Broughton DN20 19 F4
5 Broughton DN20 19 E3
Cherry Willingham LN3 203 D5
Collingham NG23 91 D3
Deeping St Nicholas PE11 166 C8
Dunham-on-Trent NG22 65 B1
Dunston LN4 95 D6
Eagle & Swinethorpe LN6 79 C2
Eaton NG32 138 A2
Gedney PE12 159 A1
Girton NG23 78 C1
Gosberton PE11 145 C7
Grantham NG31 211 D7
Hatfield DN7 14 E1
Hemingby LN9 72 C3
Heydour NG32 131 D5
Hogsthorpe LN13 90 A8
Kingston upon Hull HU13 179 A1
Kirton PE20 135 E6
Lea DN21 52 F5
Leake Commonside PE22 113 F3
Leverington PE13 169 F2
Lincoln LN6 201 D2
Mablethorpe & Sutton LN12 63 F4
Marston NG32 118 D1
Middle Rasen LN8 57 C7
Moulton PE12 146 E1
13 North Kelsey LN7 32 A4
North Somercotes LN11 50 F7
Peterborough PE1 226 A4
Pilham DN21 41 D4
Pinchbeck PE11 145 C2
7 Skegness PE25 103 E4
8 Skegness PE25 103 E4
Skellingthorpe LN6 200 B5
Spalding PE11 214 C3
Stamford PE9 219 B7
Stickney PE22 113 A7
Stixwould & Woodhall LN10 97 B8
Strubby with Woodthorpe LN13 63 B1
Sutterton PE20 136 A2
Swinderby LN6 92 B5
Thimbleby LN9 85 C5
Threekingham NG34 132 E3
Wainfleet St Mary PE24 102 A1
18 Welton LN2 68 D6
Westborough & Dry Doddington NG23 117 F5
Wigtoft PE20 135 E1
Willoughby with Sloothby LN13 89 C5
Witham St Hughs LN6 92 D5
Woodhall Spa LN10 97 C5
Wyberton PE21 136 F8
Yaxley PE7 233 D6
Green La Mid Sch DN8 15 B7
Green Man La LN4 94 F1
Green Man Rd LN5 94 C1
Green Pastures 4 PE12 158 B7
Green Rd
Aswarby & Swarby NG34 131 F7
Newborough PE6 174 F2
Green St 1 NG31 129 D5
Green The
3 Allington NG32 128 F7
8 Brough HU15 2 D6
Castor PE5 223 E2
Cherry Willingham/Reepham LN3 203 F8
1 Coddington NG24 104 D5
Collingham NG23 91 C4
Corby Glen NG33 152 E7
Dunston LN4 95 C5
2 Glinton PE6 220 C8
8 Leasingham NG34 121 B8
5 Mablethorpe/Sutton on Sea LN12 64 A4
8 Minting LN9 84 C8
15 Navenby/Wellingore LN5 107 A7
Peterborough PE4 221 A3
3 Reepham LN3 82 A8
Revesby PE22 99 B4
6 Scothern LN2 68 F4
Scotter DN21 29 C3
Spalding PE11 214 E5
4 Swanland HU14 3 B7
23 Thorne/Moorends DN8 15 A8
11 Thorney PE6 176 A3
Thurlby PE10 164 C7
Welbourn LN5 106 E4
Yaxley PE7 233 E5
Green Wlk PE6 217 A5
Greenacre Cl 7 DN7 14 C2
Greenacres
6 Donington on Bain LN11 59 E1
Peterborough PE4 220 E4
5 Swanland HU14 3 C7
Greenbank Dr LN6 205 A5
Greendyke La PE13 160 A2
Greenfield Cl 13 DN3 14 A3
Greenfield Dr 9 DN20 31 A5
Greenfield La LN13 75 D4
Greenfield Rd
Coningsby LN4 207 D5
3 Sleaford NG34 212 D7
Greenfields
3 Glentham LN8 43 F1
Holbeach PE12 215 F2
22 Nettleham LN2 68 D2
Greenfields La 5 NG34 142 D8
Greenfinch Dr DN35 192 E1
Greengarth DN17 184 F2
Greengate 11 DN9 27 E6
Greengate Ct PE1 226 C4
Greengate La 14 DN19 12 A8
Greengate Rd PE23 88 D3
Greenham PE3 225 A4
Greenhill 8 DN20 19 D3
Greenhill Dr 1 LN8 43 D3
Greenhill Rd DN9 27 C2
Greenhoe Rd DN17 184 D3
Greenlands Ave 10 DN36 195 C6
Greenock Way LN6 204 B7
Greenrigg Gdns 1 PE11 214 D5
Green's Rd 4 DN7 14 C3
Greenstiles La HU14 3 C7
Greenstock La PE13 170 A6
Greenway
7 Barton-upon-Humber DN18 3 F1
Waltham DN37 194 E3
2 Welton/Dunholme LN2 68 C7
Greenway The 1 HU4 179 C6
Greenways 1 HU14 3 A5
Greenwood Cl 1 PE12 215 E2
Greenwood Dr PE21 208 F6
Greenwood's Row 5 NG31 211 A4
Greestone Pl LN2 234 B3
Greestone Strs* LN2 234 B3
Greetham's La DN32 192 C5
Greetwell Cl LN2 202 B5
Greetwell La LN2 202 F8
Greetwell Pl LN2 202 B5
Greetwell Rd LN2 234 C3
Greetwellgate LN2 234 C3
Gregg Hall Cl 2 LN6 205 B4
Gregg Hall Cres LN6 205 B4
Gregg Hall Dr 4 LN6 205 B4
Gregory Cl 1 NG32 139 C7
Gresham St LN1 201 D4
Gresley Ct 11 NG31 210 E2
Gresley Dr Lincoln LN6 201 D1
4 Stamford PE9 219 B4
Gresley Way
Immingham DN40 186 F5
Peterborough PE3 225 C6
Gretton Cl
1 Claypole NG23 117 E8
Peterborough PE2 230 C7
Grevel Cl 6 PE11 214 B5
Grey Friars DN37 190 D7
Grey St
Gainsborough DN21 197 B6
Kingston upon Hull HU2 180 D7
Greyfleet Bank 7 LN11 51 C4
Greyfriars La 9 PE21 208 F4
Greyfriars Rd 11 DN20 19 E3
Greyling Cl 5 LN1 201 E8
Greystone Ave HU5 179 E7
Greystones Rd DN21 197 B7
Gride Bank PE22 126 E8
Gride The PE22 113 E1
Griffins Cl 4 PE6 174 E5
Griffiths Ct PE2 229 E5
Grime St DN31 191 E8
Grimmer's Rd 12 PE13 170 E1
Grimoldby Prim Sch LN11 62 C6
Grimsby Auditorium DN34 190 F8
Grimsby Coll DN34 191 C4
Grimsby Coll Sch of Art & Design DN34 191 B5
Grimsby Docks Sta DN31 189 A1
Grimsby Hospl DN33 191 C2
Grimsby Leisure Ctr DN34 190 F8
Grimsby Maternity Hospl DN33 191 C3
Grimsby Rd
2 Binbrook LN8 47 C5
Brackenborough with Little Grimsby LN11 61 A8
Cleethorpes DN35 192 D8
Fotherby LN11 49 A1
Grimsby DN32 189 D1
Humberston DN36 192 E1
Laceby DN37 190 A2
Louth LN11 198 A6
Swallow LN7 34 B6
Waltham DN37 194 F5
Grimsby Town Sta DN32 191 D7
Grimshaw Rd PE1 226 B6
Grimsthorpe Castle* PE10 153 D5
Grimsthorpe Cl
Grantham NG31 210 E6
12 Market Deeping PE6 217 A5
Grimston Rd 5 HU10 178 F6
Grindell St HU9 181 D8
Gringley Rd DN10 39 E4
Grinter Cl 3 LN6 93 C8
Groose La PE24 115 D8
Grosvenor Ave
Birchwood LN6 200 D2

Grosvenor Ave *continued*
Bourne PE10 213 E4
Grosvenor Cres
Grimsby DN32 191 D6
Louth LN11 198 D7
Grosvenor Ct 3 DN7 14 D8
Grosvenor Mews 2
LN4 203 D1
Grosvenor Rd
9 Billingborough NG34 133 B1
Kirton PE20 136 C6
Louth LN11 198 D7
Skegness PE25 206 C4
Wisbech PE13 170 D1
Grosvenor Sq 17 LN5 107 A7
Grosvenor St (South) 2
DN15 183 A4
Grosvenor St
Grimsby DN32 191 D6
Kingston upon Hull HU3 180 D8
Grosvenor St N DN15 183 A5
Grove Cl 10 PE11 145 C1
Grove Dr 9 LN10 97 D5
Grove End Rd 3 NG31 211 B4
Grove Hill HU13 178 E1
Grove La
Peterborough PE3 225 A2
Waltham DN37 194 E4
Grove Leisure Ctr
NG24 104 B3
Grove Pk 18 DN10 39 F5
Grove Rd 1 Fishlake DN7 14 D8
9 Mablethorpe/Sutton on Sea
LN12 64 C1
Theddlethorpe All Saints
LN12 63 D6
Grove Sch The NG24 104 B3
Grove St
Heckington NG34 122 E2
5 Kirton in Lindsey DN21 30 B1
Newark-on-Trent NG24 104 B3
Peterborough PE2 230 F8
Grove St E 5 PE21 209 A5
Grove St W 4 PE21 209 A5
Grove The
14 Barrow upon Humber
DN19 11 C8
4 Beckingham DN10 40 A1
Edlington with Wispington
LN9 85 B6
6 Gainsborough DN21 53 A5
Grantham NG31 210 E3
Lincoln LN2 234 C4
Market Deeping PE6 217 B5
Morton PE10 154 B6
Newton on Trent LN1 65 D1
4 Spalding PE11 214 C6
4 Welton/Dunholme LN2 68 D6
Grove Wood Rd DN10 39 F5
Grove Wood Terr 17
DN10 39 F5
Grovefield La PE22 126 D1
Grovenor Ct 5 DN35 193 A1
Grundale HU10 178 C6
Grundy La LN3 57 D2
Grundy's La LN9 84 C8
Grunnill Cl 10 PE25 206 A5
Gardens The 3 PE6 166 F1
Guanockgate Rd PE12 169 A2
Guash Way PE9 219 D7
Gubbole's Dro PE11 145 A3
Guernsey Gr DN40 186 C2
Guild Rd PE13 170 E1
Guildford Cl 11 NG31 210 E5
Guildford La LN5 105 F5
Guildford St DN32 192 A8
Guildhall Dr 2 PE11 156 E8
Guildhall Mus* PE21 208 F4
Guildhall Rd HU1 180 F6
Guildhall St
Grantham NG31 211 A4
Lincoln LN1 234 A2
Guilicarr La LN7 31 F4
Guisefield Rd 9 DN9 27 D6
Gulham Rd LN8 44 D5
Gull Bank
Whaplode PE12 167 F5
Wisbech St Mary PE13 177 E3
Gull Dro PE13 177 D3
Gull La PE13 170 A2
Gull Rd PE13 177 F2
Gullymore PE3 224 F8
Gunby Ave LN6 204 F6
Gunby Hall (NT)*
PE23 89 A1
Gunby La PE23 89 A1
Gunby Pl DN35 192 E4
Gunby Rd
Gunby & Stainby NG33 151 A4
Scunthorpe DN17 184 E5
Gunness & Burringham CE
Prim Sch DN17 17 E5
Gunness La
Amcotts DN17 17 F8
Flixborough DN15 182 A7
Gunthorpe Cty Prim Sch
PE4 221 C2
Gunthorpe Rd
Newborough PE6 221 D4
Owston Ferry DN9 40 C8
Peterborough PE4 221 C2
Sutton Bridge PE14 160 E1
1 Walpole PE14 170 F8
Gunthorpe Ridings 2
PE4 221 E2
Gunton's Rd PE6 174 E3
Gurnard Leys PE3 220 E1
Gurnell St DN15 183 A4
Gurth Ave 6 DN3 14 A1
Guthlac Ave 5 PE4 221 B1
Guy's Head Rd
Sutton Bridge PE12 160 F8
Lutton PE12 149 C1
Guys Head Rd PE12 160 E7
Gynewell Gr 4 LN2 202 D7
Gypsy La Newton PE13 170 C4
Whaplode PE12 167 F3

H

Haalam Bank LN12 63 C4
Haarlem Ct 5 PE11 214 A2
Habbanya Rise LN4 95 C7
Habblesthorpe Cl DN22 52 C1
Habblesthorpe Rd
DN22 52 C1
Habrough La DN39 22 B6
Habrough Rd
Immingham DN40 186 A3
South Killingholme DN40 12 E2
Habrough Sta DN40 22 E8
Hacconby Dro
Dunsby PE10 144 A1
Haconby PE10 155 A8
Hacconby La PE10 154 C7
Hack's Dro PE6 164 F6
Hacke Rd 3 PE3 225 D3
Hackness Gr 2 HU5 179 D8
Hackthorn CE (Controlled)
Prim Sch LN2 55 F1
Hackthorn Pl 4 LN2 201 F8
Hackthorn Rd LN2 68 D8
Haddington La LN6 92 F6
Haddon Cl
Birchwood LN6 200 E1
Peterborough PE2 231 E5
Haddon Rd
Peterborough PE3 225 E3
Peterborough PE7 232 C6
Stamford PE9 218 F6
Haddon St HU3 179 F4
Haddon Way PE7 231 B2
Hadfield Rd 7 LN6 205 A5
Hadleigh Dr LN6 204 F5
Hadleigh Gn 7 DN17 17 D4
Hadleigh Rd DN40 186 D3
Hadley Rd
Peterborough PE4 221 B1
Sleaford NG34 212 E6
Hadrian Dr 10 PE6 164 E5
Hadrians Ct PE2 231 B8
Haff Cl 2 PE20 135 C7
Haffenden Rd LN2 202 A6
Hagbeach Dro PE12 168 A5
Hagbeach Gate PE12 158 C6
Hagg Cross Roads
PE23 87 A4
Hagg La 1 DN17 16 E3
Hagnaby Abbey LN13 76 C7
Hagnaby Rd PE23 100 A6
Haig Ave DN16 183 B1
Haigh Ct DN32 191 F5
Haigh St 4 DN35 193 A5
Haile Rd DN36 193 A1
Hainton Ave DN32 191 F8
Hainton Cl DN21 197 E3
Hainton Rd Hainton LN8 58 F3
Lincoln LN6 205 C5
Haith's La 4 DN36 36 B1
Haldane St DN21 197 B5
Hale Cl 4 LN2 202 E7
Hale Hill La DN7 14 E2
Hale House Rd PE10 153 C2
Hale La PE22 112 F1
Hale Rd
Heckington NG34 122 E2
Helpringham NG34 133 E7
Horsington LN10 84 B2
Hales Cl DN16 185 A2
Hales Entry HU9 181 C6
Hales La 6 LN5 107 B8
Haley Cl 6 PE13 170 D2
Half Acre Wood 3 DN17 17 D4
Halfleet PE6 217 A6
Halford Cl 8 NG33 151 D2
Halfpenny Cl 19 LN2 68 D7
Halfway House La LN6 92 C6
Halfway Houses LN6 92 D5
Halifax App DN20 21 A8
Halifax Cl
5 Skegness PE25 206 B5
3 Skellingthorpe LN6 200 A4
Halkon Cl DN17 7 D3
Hall Bank 3 PE13 169 F7
Hall Cl
Heckington NG34 122 E3
Ropsley NG33 131 B1
Hall Ct DN17 7 A3
Hall Dr Canwick LN4 81 A4
Grantham NG31 211 C5
Lincoln LN6 205 C7
Hall End Rd PE22 114 C1
Hall Farm
5 Market Deeping PE6 217 B6
6 Newark-on-Trent
NG24 104 D5
Hall Gate Fleet PE12 159 B6
Holbeach PE12 215 C1
Moulton PE12 157 F5
Wainfleet St Mary PE24 102 C1
Weston PE12 146 B1
Hall Gate Rd PE12 168 E2
Hall Gdns 8 DN15 9 B5
Hall Hill Rd PE12 215 D1
Hall La Algarkirk PE20 136 B3
Benington PE22 126 F5
Branston & Mere LN4 81 D1
Burgh Le Marsh PE24 102 E7
Elsham DN20 20 F7
Fiskerton LN3 82 C7
Frampton PE20 136 E6
Gunby & Stainby NG33 151 B5
Hough-on-the-Hill NG32 118 E7
Lenton Keisby & Osgodby
NG33 141 E3
Moulton PE12 146 D2
Nettleham LN2 68 B2
Peterborough PE4 221 A4
Stainforth DN7 14 A6
Stenigot LN11 72 D7
Stickney PE22 112 F7
Welbourn LN5 106 E4
West Keal PE23 100 C6
Wrangle PE22 114 D1
Hall Leas Dr 2 LN12 64 C1
Hall Mdw 1 DN20 10 C2
Hall Mdw Rd PE6 217 F7
Hall Orch La 2 LN5 106 E5
Hall Pk
Heckington NG34 122 F1
Swanland HU14 3 C7
Hall Pl 7 PE11 214 D4
Hall Rd Haconby PE10 154 D8
Heckington NG34 122 E1
Hough-on-the-Hill NG32 118 E7
Londonthorpe &
Harrowby without NG31 211 F4
Hall Rise 7 DN17 29 D7
Hall St Crowland PE6 166 F1
Kingston upon Hull HU2 180 D7
16 Navenby/Wellingore
LN5 107 A7
Hall Wath LN5 92 E2
Hall Way DN38 21 F5
Hall Wlk 1 HU15 2 D6
Hall Yd
2 Collyweston PE9 171 B1
26 Metheringham LN4 95 C4
Hallam Cl 3 LN13 75 E2
Hallam Gr LN6 205 C7
Hallam's Dro PE20 123 F2
Hallam's La 3 LN4 96 B1
Hallaton Rd PE1 226 D8
Hallbrook Ct 5 DN16 185 A1
Hallcroft 6 DN39 12 A1
Hallcroft Rd 1 DN9 27 D2
Haller St HU9 181 E8
Hallfield Cres NG32 119 C2
Hallfields La PE4 221 C1
Hallgarth DN36 37 B2
Hallgarth Ave DN16 183 B2
Hallgate PE12 159 E8
Halliwell Cl 5 HU9 5 F8
Halls Ct LN4 95 C6
Halls Hill LN11 72 D6
Halls La 6 Keelby DN41 23 A4
9 North Kelsey LN7 32 A4
Hall's Rd DN10 39 D2
Halmer Gate PE11 214 E4
Halmer Gdns PE11 214 F4
Halmer Paddock 6
PE11 214 F5
Haltemprice Leisure Ctr
HU10 178 E7
Haltemprice St HU3 179 F5
Haltoft End Est PE22 126 C3
Halton Cl
5 Birchwood LN6 204 B8
4 Kirton in Lindsey DN21 42 F8
Halton Holegate CE Prim Sch
PE23 101 B7
Halton Pl DN35 192 D4
Halton Rd PE23 101 A8
Halton Way 3 DN33 191 C2
Halyard Croft 8 HU1 180 F5
Halycon Ave 1 HU13 178 E2
Ham La PE2 229 E7
Ham Mere Bird Sanctuary*
PE2 229 E7
Hambleton La LN8 57 E8
Hambleton Rd PE9 218 E4
Hamerton La 1 LN9 199 C3
Hamilton Cl
6 Bourne PE10 213 C7
6 Grimsby DN34 190 D4
Hamilton Gr LN6 200 B3
Hamilton Rd Alford LN13 75 F2
Grantham NG31 211 D6
4 Lincoln LN6 204 D2
Scunthorpe DN17 184 F8
Hamilton St DN32 189 D1
Hamish Wlk 8 DN40 186 B3
Hamling Way HU4 179 D2
Hamlyn Ave HU4 179 E7
Hamlyn Dr HU4 179 E6
Hammerton Rd DN17 184 E4
Hammond Cl PE8 172 C1
Hammond Ct 11 LN12 64 B3
Hamont Rd DN32 192 B7
Hampden Cl 1 LN6 200 A4
Hampden Cres 3 DN7 26 A8
Hampden Way 8 LN5 94 A7
Hampshire St HU4 179 E3
Hampson Gdns 18 DN3 14 A2
Hampstead Pk 7 DN33 191 B2
Hampton Cl
7 Humberston DN35 192 F1
1 Spalding PE11 214 E2
Hampton Hargate Prim Sch
PE7 230 C2
Hampton La PE22 127 B7
Hampton Rd
2 Hatfield DN7 14 C4
Scunthorpe DN16 185 C8
Hampton St LN1 201 D4
Hanbury PE2 229 F3
Hanby La 11 Alford LN13 75 F2
Welton Le Marsh PE23 89 B4
Handel House Prep Sch
DN21 197 D5
Handley St
Heckington NG34 122 E3
8 Sleaford NG34 212 D4
Hands on History Mus*
HU1 180 F6
Hangman's Cnr PE6 175 F5
Hangman's La
Edenham PE10 153 F7
Haconby PE10 154 A7
Hankey St PE1 225 F4
Hankinson's Est PE34 161 D1
Hannah Cres LN6 92 E5
Hannam Bvd PE11 214 A3
Hannath Rd PE13 170 B8
Hanover Ct PE3 225 A8
Hanover Hill DN21 54 F6
Hanover Sq
5 Kingston upon Hull
HU1 180 F6
3 Kingston upon Hull
HU1 181 A6
Hansard Cres 3 LN7 33 B4
Hansard Way 8 PE20 136 C5
Hansards Dr 2 LN8 70 D5
Hanson Dr 2 LN12 76 F8
Hanson Way DN32 192 B8
Hanthorpe Rd PE10 154 B7
Ha'penny Bridge Way
HU9 181 B5
Harbour Way HU9 181 C6
Harby Cl
Grantham NG31 210 E1
Lincoln LN6 205 B3
Harcourt Dr HU9 181 C8
Harden's La LN9 73 F1
Harding Cl
13 Mablethorpe & Sutton
LN12 64 C1
6 Mablethorpe/Sutton on Sea
LN12 76 F8
Harding House Gall*
LN2 234 B3
Hardings La PE23 88 B2
Hardings The 20 LN2 68 D7
Hardiway PE21 209 B5
Hardwick Cl
Louth LN11 198 A7
3 Saxilby with Ingleby LN1 66 C2
Hardwick Ct PE3 225 B2
Hardwick Pl 1 LN2 202 A8
Hardwick Plot La
PE20 124 C1
Hardwick Rd
5 Kirton PE20 136 C5
1 Stamford PE9 218 F6
Hardwick St HU5 180 B8
Hardy Rd DN17 184 D6
Hardy's Animal Farm*
PE25 90 E5
Hardy's Dro PE10 213 F7
Hardy's La PE6 167 D4
Hardy's Rd DN35 192 F4
Hare Cl 9 NG34 122 E2
Hare St DN32 191 F6
Harebell Cl PE1 221 F1
Harecroft Rd PE13 170 C1
Harewood Ave 7 DN3 14 A2
Harewood Cl PE21 209 B5
Harewood Cres
Lincoln LN6 205 A3
Louth LN11 198 B7
Harewood Gdns PE3 225 B2
Harewood Gr 6 DN35 192 F1
Harford Gate PE12 159 D5
Hargate Cl 1 PE12 159 C7
Hargate La PE34 161 E2
Hargate Way PE7 230 D3
Hargon La NG24 104 B7
Hargrave St DN31 188 D1
Hargreaves Way DN15 183 B6
Harland Rd 9 HU15 2 C6
Harlaxton CE Prim Sch
NG32 139 C7
Harlaxton Cl 2 LN6 204 C6
Harlaxton Coll NG32 139 D7
Harlaxton Dr 4 LN6 204 C6
Harlaxton Gdns*
NG32 139 D7
Harlaxton Rd
3 Grantham NG31 210 F3
Grantham NG31 210 E1
Harlech Grange PE3 225 B1
Harlech Way DN32 191 F8
Harlequin Dr
23 Mablethorpe/Sutton on Sea
LN12 64 B3
6 Spalding PE11 214 A5
Harlestone Ct DN34 190 C4
Harley St HU2 180 E8
Harlow St DN31 188 D1
Harlton Cl PE2 231 E5
Harmston Cl LN2 202 A8
Harmston Pk Ave LN5 93 F4
Harmston Rd LN5 93 A5
Harneis Cres DN37 23 F2
Harold St DN32 192 A8
Harold's Bank PE13 169 B2
Harome Gr HU5 179 C7
Harpe Cl 10 PE11 156 E8
Harpenden Cl 15 DN7 14 D3
Harpendon Dr 16 DN7 14 D3
Harpham Rd
Gate Burton DN21 53 A1
Marshchapel DN36 37 B2
Harpswell Cl 7 DN21 53 A8
Harpswell La DN21 42 C1
Harpswell Rd LN2 202 A7
Harrier Ct 3 LN6 204 E8
Harrier Rd 3 DN18 3 F1
Harriet Cl 5 PE12 160 E4
Harrington Ave 4 LN6 205 C8
Harrington Dr 7 PE6 175 C8
Harrington Pl DN16 185 A5
Harrington Rd 7 NG33 151 D2
Harrington St
Bourne PE10 213 D6
Cleethorpes DN35 189 D1
Harrington Way 6 PE6 175 C8
Harris Bvd 18 LN12 64 B3
Harris Cl 11 PE25 206 A5
Harris Rd LN6 205 B6
Harris St
Kingston upon Hull HU3 179 F5
Peterborough PE1 225 F6
Harrison Cl
Horncastle LN9 199 C5
10 Peterborough PE3 224 F3
Winteringham DN15 9 A8
Harrison Pl
Lincoln LN1 234 A4
North Hykeham LN6 204 D5
Harrison St 4 DN31 191 C7
Harrison's Dro PE20 124 B2
Harrison's La PE24 101 F4
Harrolds Cl 3 PE13 170 F1
Harrow Cl
Gainsborough DN21 197 F6
Heighington/Washingborough
LN4 203 C1
Harrow Gdns DN17 184 F4
Harrow Rd
Deeping St Nicholas
PE11 166 C7
6 Mablethorpe/Sutton on Sea
LN12 64 B4
Harrow St
Grantham NG31 211 B3
Kingston upon Hull HU3 180 B4
Harrowby CE (Aided) Inf Sch
NG31 211 C6
Harrowby Cl Digby LN4 108 E5
Grantham NG31 211 C6
Harrowby Cres NG31 211 E1
Harrowby Est NG31 211 D6
Harrowby La
Grantham NG31 211 D6
Londonthorpe &
Harrowby without NG31 130 C3
Harrowby Rd NG31 211 C3
Harrowdyke 6 DN18 10 E8
Harrows The 15 LN2 68 D6
Harrox Rd 3 PE12 157 F7
Harrox Sq 5 PE12 157 F6
Harrys Dream 3 DN20 19 E3
Harston Rd NG32 138 F7
Hart La DN15 9 B5
Hart St DN35 192 C8
Hartford Ct PE2 231 D6
Harthill Dr HU3 180 C5
Hartland Ave 6 LN6 205 A1
Hartley Bridge HU9 181 C6
Hartley St Boston PE21 208 F6
3 Lincoln LN2 202 C3
Hartshead Ave DN15 182 C3
Hartsholme Dr LN6 205 A8
Hartsholme Prim Sch
LN6 204 F7
Hartwell Way PE3 225 B5
Harvard Cl 1 LN4 203 D1
Harvest Ave 34 DN18 10 E8
Harvest Cl
21 Kirk Sandall DN3 14 A2
23 Metheringham LN4 95 C4
Harvest Cres 2 DN37 194 C4
Harvest Rise 2 DN19 11 C8
Harvest Way 3 NG34 212 C2
Harvester Cl 10 DN9 27 E6
Harvester Way
Crowland PE6 175 B8
Peterborough PE1 226 C1
1 Sibsey PE22 113 B1
Harvey Ave
10 Coddington NG24 104 C5
14 Newark-on-Trent NG24 104 C5
Harvey Cl Bourne PE10 213 B4
11 Wittering PE8 172 B1
Harvey Kent Gdns 4
LN3 83 C4
Harvey St 5 LN1 201 D3
Harwich Cl 12 LN5 205 D3
Harwood Ave PE12 215 C1
Harwood Dr 1 HU4 179 B6
Hassall Rd PE25 206 A2
Hassock Hill Dro
PE13 169 D3
Hasthorpe Rd LN13 89 C5
Hastings Dr 4 PE24 102 D2
Hastings Gr HU5 179 E7
Hastings Rd PE4 221 A2
Hatcliffe Cl 2 NG31 211 A8
Hatcliffe Gdns 11 LN2 202 A8
Hatcliffe Cl 8 DN33 191 B3
Hatfield & Stainforth Sta
DN7 14 C5
Hatfield Crookesbroom Prim
Sch DN7 14 C4

Hatfield High Sch DN7 . .14 D3
Hatfield La DN3 . . . . .14 A4
Hatfield Manor Mid Sch
DN7 . . . . .14 E5
Hatfield Rd Hatfield DN7 . .14 F6
Thorne/Moorends DN8 . . . . .15 A7
Hatfield Water Pk*
DN7 . . . . .14 E5
Hathersage Ave LN6 . . . .204 E2
Hatt Cl 2 PE12 . . . . .157 F7
Hatton Cl 3 LN6 . . . . . . .205 A7
Hatton Gr 9 DN33 . . . . .191 B3
Haugh La LN13 . . . . .75 A3
Haugham Pastures
LN11 . . . . .61 E2
Hauser Cl 8 NG34 . . . . . .212 B2
Havelock Dr PE2 . . . . . . .231 E6
Havelock Sch DN32 . . . .192 C6
Havelock St
Kingston upon Hull HU3 . . .180 A4
Spalding PE11 . . . . .214 C3
Havelok Cl 4 LN11 . . . . .198 D4
Haven Ave Brough HU15 . . . .2 B6
Grimsby DN31 . . . . .191 C8
Haven Bank
6 Skidbrooke with
Saltfleet Haven LN11 . . . . . .51 C4
Wildmore LN4 . . . . .111 B2
Haven Cl 7 Blyton DN21 . . .41 C5
9 Fleet PE12 . . . . .159 C7
Haven Ctry Pk* PE21 . . .137 C7
Haven Garth 1 HU15 . . . . . .2 B5
Haven Gdns DN31 . . . . . .188 C1
Haven High Sch The
PE21 . . . . .208 F7
Haven House Rd PE24 . .102 F3
Haven Rd
4 Barton-upon-Humber
DN18 . . . . .3 E1
North Killingholme DN40 . . .13 A6
Haven Side 8 PE24 . . . . .102 D1
Haven The HU9 . . . . .181 B6
Havenhouse Sta PE24 . .102 F2
Haverfield Rd PE11 . . . . .214 D3
Haverholme Cl 10 NG34 . .108 E1
Haverholme Dro PE12 . .159 D5
Haverlands The 3
NG31 . . . . .210 E8
Haverstoe Pl DN35 . . . . .192 C3
Haveswater Cl 1 PE4 . . .221 C2
Hawerby Rd 3 DN37 . . . . .23 F1
Hawker Dr LN11 . . . . . . .198 D4
Hawkins Dr 20 PE13 . . . . .170 E1
Hawkins Gr DN32 . . . . . .192 B6
Hawkins Way 7 DN40 . . . .12 E3
Hawks Way NG34 . . . . . . .212 B3
Hawksdale Cl 3 NG31 . . . .211 A7
Hawkshead Gr LN2 . . . . .202 A8
Hawkshead Way 2 PE4 . .221 C3
Hawksmede Way
LN11 . . . . .198 D8
Hawksmoor Cl 2 LN6 . . .204 D1
Hawksworth St 2
DN21 . . . . .197 D4
Haworth Cl 3 DN15 . . . . .182 D4
Haworth Way PE21 . . . . .208 D7
Haw's La PE11 . . . . .134 F1
Hawthorn Ave
Brigg DN20 . . . . .196 C4
Cherry Willingham LN3 . . . .203 B6
Gainsborough DN21 . . . . . .197 D6
Immingham DN40 . . . . . . .186 E5
Kingston upon Hull HU3 . . .179 F5
Waddington LN5 . . . . .205 C1
Hawthorn Bank PE11 . . .214 B1
Hawthorn Chase
Lincoln LN2 . . . . .202 E7
1 Moulton PE12 . . . . .157 F6
Hawthorn Cl
Beckingham DN10 . . . . .52 A8
Healing DN41 . . . . .23 F6
4 Market Deeping PE6 . . . .217 B6
3 Newborough PE6 . . . . . .174 E5
7 Ruskington NG34 . . . . . .108 E1
Hawthorn Ct 1 HU3 . . . .179 F6
Hawthorn Dr NG34 . . . . .212 D3
Hawthorn Gate 26 DN18 . . .10 F8
Hawthorn Gr DN21 . . . . .197 D5
Hawthorn Rd
Bourne PE10 . . . . .213 C6
Cherry Willingham LN3 . . . .203 B7
4 Old Leake PE22 . . . . . . .114 A1
Peterborough PE1 . . . . . . .226 C6
Skegness PE25 . . . . .206 A2
Yaxley PE7 . . . . .233 F5
Hawthorn Rise 4 DN19 . . .11 C8
Hawthorn Way 4 LN5 . . . .92 F3
Hawthorn Wlk 1 LN1 . . . .66 D7
Hawthorne Ave
Cleethorpes DN35 . . . . . . .192 D8
4 Grimsby DN33 . . . . .194 F8
9 Hatfield DN7 . . . . .14 C2
Louth LN11 . . . . .198 B6
New Waltham DN36 . . . . . .195 B5
4 Scunthorpe DN17 . . . . . .184 F8
8 Wisbech PE13 . . . . .170 D2
Hawthorne Cl
5 Manby LN11 . . . . .62 C6
6 Scopwick Heath LN4 . . .108 A7
20 Winterton DN15 . . . . .9 A5
Wootton DN39 . . . . .11 E2
Hawthorne Cres 3
DN17 . . . . .184 F8
Hawthorne Ct 4 NG31 . .210 D2
Hawthorne Gdns 8
DN19 . . . . .12 A8
Hawthorne Rise HU13 . .178 B3
Hawthorns The 14 LN2 . . .68 D2
Hawthorpe Rd NG33 . . . .141 E1
Hawton Cl 1 DN21 . . . . . .197 E6
Hawton La NG24 . . . . . . .104 A2
Haxey CE Prim Sch
DN9 . . . . .27 D3
Haxey Gate Rd DN10 . . . .39 F7
Haxey Grange 9 DN9 . . . .27 D2
Haxey La DN9 . . . . .27 D1
Haxey Rd DN10 . . . . .39 F6
Hay Gn Rd (North)
PE34 . . . . .161 E2
Hay Gn Rd (South)
PE34 . . . . .161 D1
Hay Gn Rd PE34 . . . . . . .161 E1
Haycroft Ave 8 DN31 . . .191 C8
Haycroft La PE12 . . . . . .159 B7
Haycroft St DN31 . . . . . .191 C7
Haydon Ave PE25 . . . . . .206 A4
Haydon Cl HU10 . . . . . . .178 D8
Haydor Ave LN2 . . . . . . .202 A8
Hayes Yd 4 LN1 . . . . .54 F2
Hayfield Cl
7 Barnby Dun DN3 . . . . . . .14 A4
6 Haxey DN9 . . . . .27 D2
Hayling Mere 4 DN35 . . .192 F1
Haynes Cl 3 DN8 . . . . .15 B7
Haynes Gdns 13 DN8 . . . . .15 B8
Haynes Gn 6 DN8 . . . . . . .15 B8
Haynes Gr 1 DN8 . . . . . . .15 B7
Haynes Rd DN8 . . . . .15 B8
Hays Cl 4 DN36 . . . . . . .195 C2
Hayton Cl 2 DN15 . . . . .9 B5
Hayton Gr HU4 . . . . .179 D4
Haytons La 2 DN15 . . . . . . .9 D1
Haywardsfield 4 PE3 . . .225 A1
Haze La 5 LN6 . . . . .204 C1
Hazel Cl DN17 . . . . .29 C7
Hazel Croft
4 Immingham DN40 . . . . .186 A4
Peterborough PE4 . . . . . . .220 E4
Hazel Dr LN9 . . . . .199 B5
Hazel Gr
4 Bottesford DN16 . . . . . .185 B2
2 Kingston upon Hull
HU3 . . . . .180 D5
Louth LN11 . . . . .198 E4
Sleaford NG34 . . . . .212 D6
Stamford PE9 . . . . .218 D6
Welton/Dunholme LN2 . . . . .68 C6
Hazel Rd 6 DN7 . . . . .14 C5
Hazeland Cl PE10 . . . . . .154 C6
Hazelbarrow Dr HU10 . . .178 F7
Hazelnut Cl 3 PE22 . . . . . .99 A4
Hazelwood Ave LN6 . . . .204 C8
Hazelwood Dr PE10 . . . .213 B6
Hazelwood La PE12 . . . .159 A7
Hazlewood Dr NG31 . . . .210 F7
Headingley Ave 4
DN17 . . . . .184 E3
Headland Way
3 Haconby PE10 . . . . .154 D8
7 Navenby LN5 . . . . .107 B8
Headlands Dr HU13 . . . .178 C2
Headquarters Cres 5
NG34 . . . . .120 C8
Heads La HU13 . . . . .178 C1
Headstead Bank DN22 . . .65 B7
Healey Cl 5 NG23 . . . . . . .91 D4
Healey La LN12 . . . . .63 C4
Healey Rd DN16 . . . . . . .185 C8
Healing Prim Sch DN41 . .23 F5
Healing Rd 5 DN41 . . . . . .23 D6
Healing Sch DN41 . . . . . . .23 F5
Healing Sta DN41 . . . . . . .23 F6
Heapham Cres DN21 . . . .197 F4
Heapham La DN21 . . . . . . .53 F7
Heapham Rd DN21 . . . . .197 E5
Heath Cl 4 LN2 . . . . .68 C7
Heath Farm Cl NG32 . . . .119 F3
Heath Farm Rd NG31 . . .130 C2
Heath La
Ancaster NG32 . . . . .119 F3
Boothby Graffoe LN5 . . . . . .94 B2
Carlton Scroop NG32 . . . . .119 D4
Great Ponton NG33 . . . . . .139 D4
Honington NG32 . . . . .119 C2
Leasingham NG34 . . . . . . .121 C7
Normanton NG32 . . . . .119 F6
Syston NG32 . . . . .130 D8
Welton LN1 . . . . .67 F6
Wilsford NG32 . . . . .120 B1
Heath Rd
Bracebridge Heath LN4 . . .205 F2
Coleby LN5 . . . . .93 F3
Helpston PE6 . . . . .173 C2
15 Navenby LN5 . . . . .107 A8
5 Nettleham LN2 . . . . .68 C2
Scopwick LN4 . . . . .108 B8
Scothern LN2 . . . . .68 D4
Skegness PE25 . . . . .206 B3
Heathcote Rd
Bourne PE10 . . . . .213 E4
Castle Bytham NG33 . . . . .152 D1
Coningsby LN4 . . . . .207 E5
Heather Ave PE1 . . . . . . .226 A8
Heather Cl
1 Boston PE21 . . . . .208 D3
7 Woodhall Spa LN10 . . . . .97 E6
Heather Gr DN16 . . . . . . .185 E5
Heatherdale Cl
6 Grimsby DN33 . . . . .194 E7
Peterborough PE7 . . . . . . .231 C5
Heathfield Ave
Branston LN4 . . . . .81 E2
Spalding PE11 . . . . .214 F2
Heathfield Cl 9 DN3 . . . . .14 A3
Heathfield Ct DN34 . . . . .191 B6
Heathfield Rd NG31 . . . .210 C3
Heathlea 11 LN2 . . . . .68 F4
Heath's Mdw Nature
Reserve* PE24 . . . . .102 C7
Heaton Cl PE3 . . . . .225 B3
Heaton St 1 DN21 . . . . . .197 D4
Hebden Moor Way 8
LN6 . . . . .93 B8
Hebden Rd DN15 . . . . . . .182 C4
Heckdyke La DN10 . . . . . .40 C7
Heckington 8 Sailed
Windmill* NG34 . . . . . .122 E2
Heckington Rd NG34 . . .122 C1
Heckington St Andrews CE
Sch NG34 . . . . .122 E3
Heckington Sta NG34 . . .122 E2
Hedge Field Rd NG32 . . .210 A4
Hedgefield Hurn PE11 . . .144 F4
Hedgehog La PE20 . . . . .124 D4
Hedgelands
Peterborough PE4 . . . . . . .221 A5
3 Wisbech PE13 . . . . .170 D2
Hedgerow Cl 5 DN19 . . . .11 C8
Hedgerow La 1 DN20 . . .196 D3
Hedon Rd HU9 . . . . .181 B6
Heighington Fen LN4 . . . .82 A5
Heighington Rd LN4 . . . . .81 C4
Heimdal Rd DN33 . . . . . .191 C2
Helen Cres 8 DN40 . . . . .186 A4
Helene Gr DN32 . . . . .192 B7
Helenship La DN22 . . . . . .65 A4
Hell La NG33 . . . . .140 C5
Hellyers Ct HU4 . . . . . . .179 D2
Helm Dr HU9 . . . . .181 C6
Helmsdale Gdns PE4 . . .220 F2
Helmsley Ct 1 PE7 . . . . .231 F5
Helmsley Gr HU5 . . . . . . .179 C7
Helmsley Way PE11 . . . . .214 F4
Helpringham Rd
Burton Pedwardine
NG34 . . . . .122 B1
Helpringham NG34 . . . . . .133 C8
Helpringham Sch
NG34 . . . . .133 D7
Helpston Rd
Castor PE5 . . . . .223 D2
Etton PE6 . . . . .220 A8
Helsby Rd LN5 . . . . .205 D4
Helsey La PE24 . . . . .89 F7
Heltwate Specl Sch
PE3 . . . . .225 B7
Hemingby La LN9 . . . . . .199 C6
Hemingby Way LN9 . . . .199 C5
Hemingford Cres PE2 . .231 E6
Hemington Way 1
PE20 . . . . .136 C5
Hemmingway Wlk
HU13 . . . . .178 E3
Hempdyke Rd 5 DN15 . .182 E4
Hemplands The 9 NG23 . .91 D5
Hemswell Ave
4 Kingston upon Hull HU9 . . .5 E8
Lincoln LN6 . . . . .205 A7
Hemswell Dr 4 DN31 . . .190 F8
Hemswell La DN21 . . . . . .42 D1
Hemswell Prim Sch
LN8 . . . . .43 A1
Henderson Ave DN15 . . .182 F4
Henderson Ave Prim Sch
DN15 . . . . .182 F4
Henderson Cres 2
DN15 . . . . .182 F4
Henderson Way DN15 . . . . .9 A5
Heneage Rd DN32 . . . . . .191 F6
Hengist Cl 7 NG34 . . . . .212 B2
Henley Ct
2 Gainsborough DN21 . . .197 C6
Lincoln LN5 . . . . .205 D8
Henley St LN5 . . . . .205 D8
Henlow Cl
6 Birchwood LN6 . . . . . . .204 B8
3 Kirton in Lindsey DN21 . . .42 F8
Henrietta St 2 PE11 . . . .214 C3
Henry Boot Way HU4 . . .179 B1
Henry La LN3 . . . . .83 D4
Henry St Grimsby DN31 . .191 C8
Lincoln LN5 . . . . .201 F1
Peterborough PE1 . . . . . . .226 A4
Scunthorpe DN15 . . . . . . .182 F3
Henshaw PE1 . . . . .226 E6
Henshaw Ave 2 LN12 . . . .77 A7
Henson Cl 5 PE13 . . . . . .170 D2
Henson Dr 18 LN5 . . . . . .107 A8
Herdgate La PE11 . . . . . .145 D2
Hereford Ave DN34 . . . . .191 C5
Hereford Cl 2 NG34 . . . .212 C7
Hereford St HU4 . . . . . . .179 E3
Hereford Tech Sch
DN34 . . . . .191 B5
Hereford Way 8 NG31 . .210 E5
Heren Pl 9 PE11 . . . . . . .214 A2
Hereward Cl 2 PE1 . . . . .226 B2
Hereward Pl DN16 . . . . . .185 E7
Hereward Rd
Peterborough PE1 . . . . . . .226 B2
Spalding PE11 . . . . .214 B4
Hereward St
5 Bourne PE10 . . . . .213 D5
Lincoln LN1 . . . . .234 B4
Hereward Way
21 Crowland PE6 . . . . . . .166 E1
Market Deeping PE6 . . . . .217 E4
Heritage Pk Prim Sch
PE7 . . . . .231 F5
Herlyn Cres 3 PE25 . . . . . .90 E3
Hermes Way NG34 . . . . .212 A3
Hermit St LN5 . . . . .234 B1
Hermitage The 6 PE9 . . .219 A5
Heron Cl Grimsby DN32 . .192 B4
Heron Cl *continued*
8 Scunthorpe DN15 . . . . .182 C6
Skegness PE25 . . . . .103 C8
3 Surfleet PE11 . . . . .145 E3
Heron Holt 3 DN20 . . . . . .19 D4
Heron Pk PE1 . . . . .226 F6
Heron St HU3 . . . . .180 B5
Heron Way
Holton le Clay DN36 . . . . .195 C3
Wyberton PE21 . . . . .136 F8
Heron Wlk LN6 . . . . .204 C1
Heronry Dr PE6 . . . . . . .224 E2
Herons Cl PE9 . . . . .172 F6
Herrick Cl PE1 . . . . .225 E8
Herrick Ct 2 LN4 . . . . . .207 A6
Herrick Rd DN17 . . . . . . .184 D7
Herring La
1 Pinchbeck PE11 . . . . . .145 B1
4 Spalding PE11 . . . . . . .214 D4
Herrington Ave 3 LN2 . . .68 C2
Hersey Rd 16 LN7 . . . . . . .33 B4
Hervey Rd NG34 . . . . . . .212 C2
Hesketh Cres
12 Skegness PE25 . . . . . .103 E4
11 Skegness PE25 . . . . . .103 E4
Hesketh Ct LE15 . . . . . . .162 A8
Hesketh Dr 3 DN3 . . . . . . .14 A2
Hessle Ave PE21 . . . . . . .208 D4
Hessle Ct PE21 . . . . .208 C4
Hessle Dr PE21 . . . . .208 C3
Hessle High Sch
HU13 . . . . .178 C2
Hessle Lower Sch
HU13 . . . . .178 E3
Hessle Mount Sch
HU13 . . . . .178 C3
Hessle Penshurst Prim Sch
HU13 . . . . .178 F3
Hessle Rd HU4 . . . . .179 D3
Hessle Sta HU13 . . . . .3 E4
Hessle View 4 DN18 . . . . .10 E8
Hetley PE2 . . . . .230 A4
Hewde La DN15 . . . . .2 A1
Hewitt's Ave
Humberston DN36 . . . . . .192 C1
New Waltham DN36 . . . . . .195 D8
Hewitt's Cir DN36 . . . . . .192 C2
Hewitts Manor 1 DN35 .192 D2
Hewson Rd
5 Humberston DN36 . . . . . .36 D8
Lincoln LN1 . . . . .201 C4
Hewson St 23 DN17 . . . . . .29 D7
Hewson's La NG23 . . . . . . .91 D3
Hexham Ct 3 PE1 . . . . . .226 D3
Hey St DN35 . . . . .192 F5
Heysham Cl 8 LN5 . . . . .205 D3
Heythrop Rd 3 DN35 . . . .192 E3
Hibaldstow Cl
10 Birchwood LN6 . . . . . .204 C7
9 Grimsby DN34 . . . . .190 F4
Hibaldstow Prim Sch
DN20 . . . . .31 A5
Hibaldstow Rd LN6 . . . . .204 C7
Hickling Cl 15 NG31 . . . . .210 E2
Hickman Cres DN21 . . . .197 C8
Hickman Ct DN21 . . . . . . .197 E4
Hickman Gr 2 DN21 . . . . . .41 B5
Hickman St DN21 . . . . . .197 C4
Hickory Rd Rd 5 LN6 . . .200 C1
Hicks La PE7 . . . . .230 F5
Hide's La
Addlethorpe PE24 . . . . .90 B1
Skegness PE25 . . . . .103 B8
Higgins Cl LN6 . . . . .204 E7
Higgins Rd 5 LN13 . . . . . . .75 E2
High Bridge Rd DN8 . . . . .15 C7
High Broadgate PE13 . . .169 F7
High Bunning La
NG34 . . . . .143 A7
High Burgage DN15 . . . . . . .2 B1
High Cliff Rd DN35 . . . . .193 A6
High Cres PE9 . . . . .171 C8
High Dike
Cranwell & Byard's Leap
NG34 . . . . .120 B8
Easton NG33 . . . . .151 E8
Great Ponton NG33 . . . . . .140 C4
Navenby/Wellingore LN5 . . .94 B1
North Rauceby NG32 . . . . .120 A5
Old Somerby NG33 . . . . . .130 E2
Waddington LN5 . . . . .93 F8
Welby NG31 . . . . .130 E5
Wellingore LN5 . . . . .107 B6
Wilsford NG32 . . . . .119 F1
High Dyke Rd 2 NG34 . .107 C1
High Fen PE11 . . . . .144 B4
High Ferry La PE22 . . . . .113 A1
High Field Rd DN20 . . . .196 F5
High Fields La PE11 . . . .156 E8
High Garth DN17 . . . . . . .184 F2
High Gate
Helpringham NG34 . . . . . .133 D7
Mablethorpe & Sutton
LN12 . . . . .64 C1
Theddlethorpe St Helen
LN12 . . . . .63 D5
High Holme Rd LN11 . . .198 B6
High House Rd DN22 . . . .52 A2
High La Croft PE24 . . . . .102 D6
Mareham on the Hill LN9 . . . .85 F2
High Leas 1 LN2 . . . . .68 D2
High Levels Bank
Belton DN8 . . . . .15 F5
Hatfield DN8 . . . . .15 E5
High Leys Rd DN17 . . . . .184 F3
High Mdw
Grantham NG31 . . . . .210 D4
High Mdw *continued*
Heighington/Washingborough
LN4 . . . . .203 C1
Westborough & Dry Doddington
NG23 . . . . .117 F5
High Mdws
1 Fiskerton LN3 . . . . .82 A7
Kingston upon Hull
HU10 . . . . .178 C8
High or Main Rd PE12 . .215 A2
High Point Ret Pk
DN31 . . . . .189 A1
High Rd
Barrowby NG32 . . . . .210 A5
Elloughton-cum-Brough
HU15 . . . . .2 D7
Gorefield PE13 . . . . .169 F2
Grantham NG31 . . . . .211 C8
Hough-on-the-Hill NG32 . . .119 A5
Londonthorpe &
Harrowby without NG31 . . .130 D4
Moulton PE12 . . . . .158 A7
Newton PE13 . . . . .169 F5
Weston PE12 . . . . .157 C7
Wisbech St Mary PE13 . . . .177 F2
High Ridge Comp Sch
DN15 . . . . .182 E3
High Ridge Sports Hall
DN15 . . . . .182 E3
High Side PE13 . . . . . . .169 D2
High St 8 Alford LN13 . . . . .75 F3
Alvingham LN11 . . . . .49 F2
Barrow upon Humber
DN19 . . . . .11 D8
Barton-upon-Humber DN18 . . .3 E1
Bassingham LN5 . . . . .92 F2
Baumber LN9 . . . . .85 A8
1 Beckingham DN10 . . . . . .52 B8
Belton DN9 . . . . .16 E1
Benniworth LN8 . . . . .71 F8
Bicker PE20 . . . . .135 A4
Binbrook LN8 . . . . .47 C4
Blyton DN21 . . . . .41 C5
Boston PE21 . . . . .208 F3
Bottesford NG13 . . . . .128 A5
Branston LN4 . . . . .81 E2
Brant Broughton LN5 . . . . .105 F4
Broughton DN20 . . . . .19 D3
Burgh le Marsh PE24 . . . . .102 E8
Burringham DN17 . . . . .17 D4
Caistor LN7 . . . . .33 B4
Carlby PE9 . . . . .163 D4
Carlton-le-Moorland LN5 . .105 E8
Castle Bytham NG33 . . . . .152 D1
Castor PE5 . . . . .223 F2
Caythorpe NG32 . . . . .119 B7
Cherry Willingham/Reepham
LN3 . . . . .203 D5
Cleethorpes DN35 . . . . . . .192 E6
Collingham NG23 . . . . .91 D4
3 Collyweston PE9 . . . . . .171 B1
Colsterworth NG33 . . . . . .151 D6
Coningsby LN4 . . . . .207 A4
Corby Glen NG33 . . . . . . .152 E8
Corringham DN21 . . . . .41 E1
9 Crowle DN17 . . . . .16 D7
Donington PE11 . . . . .134 E2
Eagle & Swinethorpe LN6 . . .79 B2
East Ferry DN21 . . . . .28 B2
Eastoft DN17 . . . . .7 A3
3 Easton on the Hill PE9 . .171 D3
Elkington LN11 . . . . .60 E7
Epworth DN9 . . . . .27 D7
Eye PE6 . . . . .175 A1
Faldingworth LN8 . . . . .56 F3
Fillingham DN21 . . . . .54 F4
3 Fiskerton LN3 . . . . .82 A7
Flixborough DN15 . . . . .8 B2
5 Fulbeck NG32 . . . . .106 C1
Fulletby LN9 . . . . .86 B8
Gainsborough DN21 . . . . .197 D3
Garthorpe & Fockerby
DN17 . . . . .7 E5
Gate Burton DN21 . . . . .53 A1
Girton NG23 . . . . .78 C1
Glentham LN8 . . . . .43 F1
Glinton PE6 . . . . .220 C8
Gosberton PE11 . . . . .145 B6
Grainthorpe LN11 . . . . .50 B8
Grantham NG31 . . . . .211 A4
Great Gonerby NG31 . . . . .129 D5
Great Limber DN37 . . . . . . .22 D3
Gringley on the Hill DN10 . . .39 C1
Hagworthingham PE23 . . . . .87 A4
Harby NG23 . . . . .79 C5
Harlaxton NG32 . . . . .139 C7
Harmston LN5 . . . . .93 F5
Hatfield DN7 . . . . .14 C2
Haxey DN9 . . . . .27 C2
16 Heckington NG34 . . . . . .122 E2
Heighington/Washingborough
LN4 . . . . .203 B2
Helpringham NG34 . . . . . .133 D7
Hogsthorpe PE24 . . . . .90 B7
Holbeach PE12 . . . . .215 E2
Horbling NG34 . . . . .133 B2
Horncastle LN9 . . . . .199 B4
Humberside Airport DN39 . .22 A6
Ingham LN1 . . . . .54 F2
2 Ingoldmells PE25 . . . . . . .90 E3
Ketton PE9 . . . . .171 A3
Kexby DN21 . . . . .53 E5
Kingston upon Hull HU1 . . .181 A5
18 Kirton in Lindsey DN21 . . .30 B1
Laceby DN37 . . . . .23 F1

High St *continued*
Leadenham LN5 106 D3
Lincoln LN5 234 A1
2 Little Bytham NG33 163 A8
Long Sutton PE12 216 C4
Luddington & Haldenby DN17 7 C4
18 Mablethorpe/Sutton on Sea LN12 64 B4
Mablethorpe/Sutton on Sea LN12 76 F8
Market Deeping PE6 217 B4
Market Stainton LN8 72 A6
Martin LN4 96 C2
Marton DN21 65 D8
Maxey PE6 217 A1
Messingham DN17 29 D7
Metheringham LN4 95 C4
Misterton DN10 39 F5
5 Morton PE10 154 C7
Moulton PE12 157 F6
12 Navenby/Wellingore LN5 107 A7
Nettleham LN2 68 C2
Nettleton LN7 33 C2
Newton on Trent LN1 65 D1
North Ferriby HU14 3 A5
8 North Kelsey LN7 32 A4
North Scarle LN6 78 E1
North Thoresby DN36 36 A1
Northorpe PE10 164 C7
Osbournby NG34 132 C5
Owston Ferry DN9 28 B3
Peterborough PE2 231 A6
Pointon & Sempringham NG34 143 B7
Redbourne DN21 30 F2
Reepham LN3 203 F8
Rippingale PE10 142 F2
Ropsley NG33 131 B1
Roxby cum Risby DN15 8 E1
Saxilby LN1 66 D2
Scampton LN1 67 C6
Scotton DN21 29 C1
Scunthorpe DN15 183 A3
Sixhills LN8 59 A7
Skegness PE25 206 C3
Skellingthorpe LN6 200 A5
Snitterby DN21 43 D5
South Clifton NG23 78 C5
South Ferriby DN18 10 A7
South Kyme LN4 123 B8
South Witham NG33 151 D2
Spalding PE11 214 E4
7 Spilsby PE23 88 A1
Stamford PE9 219 C5
Staunton NG13 117 A2
Sturton by Stow LN1 66 C7
5 Sutton Bridge PE12 160 F4
Swayfield NG33 152 D5
Swinderby LN6 92 A5
Swineshead PE20 135 B7
Swinstead NG33 153 A5
Upton DN21 53 D5
3 Waddingham DN21 43 D7
Waddington LN5 93 F7
Wainfleet All Saints PE24 102 D1
Walcott LN4 109 D7
Walesby LN8 46 B5
Walkeringham DN10 39 F3
1 Waltham DN37 194 E4
Welbourn LN5 106 E5
West/East Butterwick DN17 17 D1
Willingham by Stow DN21 53 E3
11 Winterton DN15 9 A5
Wootton DN39 11 E2
Wroot DN9 26 D6
High St E DN15 183 C3
High St N 16 NG34 108 E2
High St S 3 NG34 108 E1
High St St Martin's PE9 219 C3
High St W DN21 29 B4
High Thorpe Cres DN35 192 D3
High Thorpe Rd LN3 83 D1
High Wash Dro 2 PE6 166 E1
Higham Way 1 HU15 2 D5
Highbridge La PE11 145 C6
Highbridge Rd LN11 49 F2
Highbury St PE1 226 A5
Highclere Rd PE7 230 D3
Highcliff Gdns DN15 182 E3
Highcliffe 5 LN5 107 A7
Highcliffe Rd NG31 211 B7
Highdales HU10 178 C8
Highfield Ave
4 Immingham DN40 186 B3
4 Lincoln LN6 205 B7
5 Mablethorpe/Sutton on Sea LN12 64 C1
Scunthorpe DN15 182 E3
Highfield Cl
8 Barnby Dun DN3 14 A4
Foston NG32 117 F2
Gainsborough DN21 197 E5
8 North Thoresby DN36 36 B1
Osbournby NG34 132 C5
Highfield Cres
17 Barton-upon-Humber DN18 10 F8
Croxton Kerrial NG32 138 D3
4 Westwoodside DN9 27 B2
Highfield Dr
2 Kirton in Lindsey DN21 30 B1
Stapleford LN6 105 A6
Highfield Gr DN20 196 C5
Highfield La
Halton Holegate PE23 101 B8
Revesby PE22 99 B5
Highfield Rd
7 Donington PE11 134 F2
North Thoresby DN36 36 B1
14 Saxilby LN1 66 D2
Highfield Terr
4 Glentham LN8 43 F1
2 Lincoln LN6 205 A2
Highfields
1 Barrow upon Humber DN19 11 C7
6 Barrowby NG32 210 A5
17 Crowle DN17 16 D8
2 Nettleham LN2 68 D2
Highfields Rise 29 LN4 95 C4
Highfields Sch NG24 104 B3
Highgate 6 DN35 192 F5
Highgate Cl 4 LN12 64 C1
Highgate La
Claxby with Moorby PE22 99 B6
Normanby By Spital LN8 56 B7
Owmby LN8 55 F6
Highgrove
1 Long Sutton PE12 216 B5
4 Messingham DN17 29 D7
Highgrove Cres PE21 209 C6
Highland Tarn DN40 186 B3
Highlands 1 PE9 163 C1
Highlands Way PE9 218 F5
Highlees Prim Sch PE3 225 C6
Highstock La PE12 168 D1
Higson Rd 4 LN1 201 D7
Hilary Gr HU4 179 B2
Hilary Rd DN33 194 F7
Hilda Cl 6 NG34 212 B2
Hilda St 4 Boston PE21 209 A7
Grimsby DN32 189 C1
Hildyard Cl 1 HU10 178 F6
Hildyard St DN32 192 B8
Hiles Ave 6 DN15 9 A5
Hill Abbey LN4 95 D7
Hill Ave NG31 211 B5
Hill Brow HU10 178 B6
Hill Cl PE1 226 D5
Hill Cres DN21 197 F5
Hill Field 3 PE24 102 D2
Hill La PE20 136 B5
Hill Rd DN21 41 E1
Hill Rise 8 Brough HU15 2 C6
Coleby LN5 93 F3
Louth LN11 198 A7
Hill The 4 Saltfleet LN11 51 C4
Skellingthorpe LN6 200 A4
Worlaby DN20 10 E1
Hill Top 1 LN5 93 E5
Hill Top La 1 DN21 41 B5
Hill Top Pl DN34 190 D3
Hill View Cl NG31 210 E3
Hill View Rd 14 NG33 151 D2
Hillary Cl 1 PE9 219 D6
Hillary Rd DN16 185 B5
Hillary Way DN37 190 E8
Hill's Ct 9 NG34 212 D4
Hillcrest NG34 107 C2
Hillcrest Ave
Kingston upon Hull HU13 178 C2
Yaxley PE7 233 E5
Hillcrest Dr 2 DN15 8 A4
Hillcrest Gdns 3 PE20 135 B7
Hillcroft 1 LN4 203 A2
Hillfoot Dr DN17 184 E3
Hillgate PE12 168 C2
Hillgate St PE34 161 F3
Hillingford Way NG31 210 E3
Hillman Cl LN4 205 F3
Hillman Rd HU13 178 F3
Hills Dr 14 DN36 36 D4
Hillside
4 Ancaster NG32 120 A2
Marton DN21 65 E8
Hillside App 5 LN2 202 C3
Hillside Ave
Lincoln LN2 202 C3
7 Mablethorpe/Sutton on Sea LN12 77 A8
Hillside Cl PE9 172 F2
Hillside Cres
Barnetby le Wold DN38 21 B5
3 Grantham NG31 211 D2
Hillside Dr
5 Barton-upon-Humber DN18 10 E8
Grantham NG31 211 D2
Hillside Est NG34 108 F2
Hillside Rd
6 Broughton DN20 19 E4
Glentworth DN21 54 F7
Woolsthorpe By Belvoir NG32 128 D1
Hillstead Cl 13 DN36 36 D4
Hillsyde Ave
12 Misterton DN10 39 F5
2 Misterton DN10 40 A5
Hilltop Ave DN15 182 D5
Hilltop Cl LN6 79 B2
Hillward Cl PE2 230 C6
Hilton Ave DN15 182 B3
Hilton Cl 2 DN9 16 E2
Hilton Ct DN35 193 B1
Hilton's La PE20 136 E1
Hinaidi La LN4 95 C7
Hinchcliffe PE2 229 E2
Hine Ave NG24 104 B4
Hinkler St DN35 192 E5
Hinkley Dr DN40 186 B5
Hipper La PE20 135 D2
Hither Old Gate PE12 158 D6
Hives La LN6 78 E2
Hix Cl PE12 215 C2
Hix's La PE13 160 A1
Hobart Cl 11 LN5 93 E8
Hobart Rd NG31 211 D7
Hobart St HU3 180 D5
Hobb La 4 DN21 29 C3
Hobson Rd 7 HU15 2 C6
Hobson Way DN41 187 E2
Hockland Rd 2 PE13 169 F7
Hockle's Gate PE12 159 B7
Hockney Hole La PE12 158 A7
Hod Fen Dro PE7 233 F2
Hodder Cl 1 NG31 210 F3
Hoddesdon Cres 20 DN7 14 D3
Hodge Ct 3 HU9 181 C7
Hodgetoft La LN13 63 E1
Hodgson Ave PE4 220 E6
Hodgson St HU8 181 A7
Hodgson Way 3 LN12 77 A8
Hodney Rd 5 PE6 175 A1
Hodson Cl LN6 200 B5
Hoekman Dr 3 PE11 214 B2
Hoekman Way PE11 214 B2
Hogens La PE13 170 A5
Hogg La HU10 178 B8
Hoggard La DN14 7 E8
Hog's Gate PE12 158 A6
Hogsthorpe Prim Sch PE24 90 B7
Hogsthorpe Rd LN13 76 F1
Holbeach Dro Gate PE12 168 C4
Holbeach Hospl PE12 215 B5
Holbeach Prim Sch PE12 215 D3
Holbeach Rd
1 Spalding PE12 157 B6
Spalding PE11 214 F6
Holbeach St Marks CE Prim Sch PE12 147 D6
Holbeck Pl 2 DN40 186 B4
Holborn Rd PE11 214 B2
Holborn St HU8 181 B7
Holcroft PE2 230 B3
Holden Dr 8 PE24 102 E7
Holden Way 7 NG31 129 E5
Holdenby Cl 3 LN2 202 E7
Holderness Rd HU9 181 C8
Holdfield PE3 225 B6
Holdich St PE3 225 E2
Holdingham La NG34 121 E7
Hole Gate PE23 101 C8
Holgate La PE4 220 F7
Holgate Pl 13 HU14 3 B7
Holgate Rd DN16 185 D8
Holkham Rd PE2 229 D3
Holland Ave
18 Crowle DN17 16 D8
Peterborough PE4 221 B1
Scunthorpe DN15 182 E4
Holland Cl
8 Bourne PE10 213 C5
10 Market Deeping PE6 217 A6
Holland Dr PE25 206 C1
Holland La PE22 114 F4
Holland Rd
Horbling NG34 133 B3
Spalding PE11 214 E4
Stamford PE9 219 C6
Swaton NG34 133 E3
Holland St HU9 181 D8
Holland Way PE12 215 B2
Holland's Chase PE11 156 A6
Hollengs La 1 LN11 59 E1
Holles St 3 DN32 191 E8
Hollies The PE12 215 E3
Hollin Bridge La DN7 15 A3
Hollingsworth Ave 1 DN40 186 B4
Hollingsworth Cl 5 DN35 192 D2
Hollingsworth La DN9 27 E6
Hollis' Rd NG31 210 F2
Hollowbrook Cl 3 NG34 108 D2
Hollowdyke La NG24 104 C1
Hollowgate Hill DN21 42 E4
Hollowgate La NG23 78 A5
Hollows The 4 LN11 61 F3
Holly Cl
Cherry Willingham/Reepham LN3 203 E5
5 Grantham NG31 211 D2
Horncastle LN9 199 A5
Lincoln LN5 205 D5
2 Newborough PE6 174 E5
Scunthorpe DN16 185 C4
1 Sleaford NG34 212 D2
6 Stallingborough DN41 23 E6
Holly Dr PE10 213 C7
Holly Hill 1 HU15 2 E6
Holly Rd PE25 206 A2
Holly St LN5 205 D5
Holly Tree Cl 9 LN8 57 D7
Holly Way 2 PE6 217 D4
Holly Wlk PE7 230 D3
Hollytree Ave 2 HU5 179 B7
Hollywell Rd (The Rookery) 23 LN13 75 F2
Hollywell Rd LN5 205 D1
Hollywood Dr 8 NG31 210 F7
Holm La NG23 104 F1
Holm Rd DN9 27 B2
Holme Ave DN36 195 C6
Holme Cl Brigg DN20 196 D4
Castor PE5 223 D2
Thorpe on the Hill LN6 92 F8
Holme Dene 1 DN9 27 C2
Holme Dr
Burton-upon-Stather DN15 8 B5
Sudbrooke LN2 68 F2
Holme Gdns 7 DN7 14 C7
Holme Hall Ave DN16 185 B3
Holme La
Grassthorpe NG23 78 A2
Holme DN16 185 E2
Marnham NG23 78 A4
Messingham DN17 29 E8
4 Ruskington NG34 108 E1
Scunthorpe DN16 185 B3
Winthorpe NG24 104 B8
Holme Rd PE7 233 E4
Holme St DN32 191 E7
Holme Valley Prim Sch DN16 185 C3
Holme Wood Ct 5 DN3 14 A1
Holme Wood La
Claxby with Moorby LN9 99 B8
Hameringham LN9 86 B1
Holmes Cl Louth LN11 198 B7
2 Skidbrooke with Saltfleet Haven LN11 51 C4
Holmes Field 6 LN5 92 F3
Holmes La
North Somercotes LN11 38 A1
Roxby cum Risby DN15 9 D5
2 Welton/Dunholme LN2 68 E6
Holmes Rd
Frampton PE20 124 F1
Glinton PE6 220 D7
Horsington LN10 83 F1
Kirton PE20 136 A8
Stickney PE22 113 A7
Stixwould & Woodhall LN10 84 A1
Holmes Way
Horncastle LN9 199 D1
Peterborough PE4 221 D2
Wragby LN8 70 C5
Holmfirth Rd DN15 182 C4
Holstein Dr DN16 185 A2
Holt Cl 10 Lincoln LN6 93 C8
9 Wittering PE8 172 B1
Holt La Horncastle LN9 199 D4
Mareham Le Fen PE22 99 A3
Holt Prim Sch The LN6 200 A3
Holton Ct DN36 195 C1
Holton le Clay Jun Sch DN36 195 E1
Holton Mount DN36 195 C2
Holton Rd Nettleton LN7 33 A2
South Kelsey LN7 32 D1
Tetney DN36 195 F1
Holton-le-Clay Jun Sch DN36 195 D2
Holy Family Prim Sch DN7 14 D7
Holy Well La LN11 49 A4
Holydyke DN18 10 E8
Holyoake Rd DN32 192 C6
Holyroad Dr DN15 182 D7
Holyrood Cl PE20 134 E3
Holyrood Wlk PE11 214 E2
Holywell Cl 1 PE3 225 A1
Holywell Rd PE9 162 E8
Holywell Way PE3 224 F2
Home Beat Dr DN20 19 C3
Home Cl 7 Bourne PE10 213 C7
Bracebridge Heath LN4 205 F3
Kingston upon Hull HU4 179 C5
Home Ct 8 LN5 107 A7
Home Paddock DN37 194 E4
Home Pasture 4 PE4 220 F5
Home Pk 4 NG34 120 F8
Home St DN15 183 B4
Homefarm La NG23 79 A7
Homefield Ave DN33 191 D3
Homers La PE22 126 D4
Homestead Garth 11 DN7 14 D4
Honey Pot La NG33 151 F4
Honeyhill PE4 221 E1
Honeyhill CP Com Sch PE4 221 E1
Honeyhill Rd PE13 169 C2
Honeyholes La LN2 68 D6
Honeysuckle Cl
4 Lincoln LN5 205 C2
14 Mablethorpe & Sutton LN12 76 F8
Honeysuckle Ct
Humberston DN35 192 E1
Peterborough PE2 230 D7
3 Scunthorpe DN16 185 D4
Honeysuckle Pl 19 HU15 2 C5
Honington App 5 LN1 201 D7
Honington Cres LN1 201 D7
Honington Rd 2 NG32 130 B8
Hood Cl NG34 212 A3
Hood Rd DN17 184 D6
Hood St
Kingston upon Hull HU8 181 A8
8 Lincoln LN5 201 F1
Hook's Dro PE13 177 C4
Hooks La LN5 106 E6
Hoop End DN36 36 D4
Hoop La LN8 70 E2
Hoopers Cl 4 NG13 128 A5
Hop Hills La DN7 14 D5
Hope Gdns PE21 208 F6
Hope St
Cleethorpes DN35 193 A5
6 Grimsby DN32 191 F8
Lincoln LN5 201 F1
Hopfield DN20 31 A5
Hopgardens 1 DN21 53 E3
Hopgarth 11 DN9 27 D2
Hopkins Ave DN17 185 A7
Hoplands Rd LN4 207 D5
Hoplands The 4 NG34 212 F4
Hopton St LN9 199 B3
Hopwood Cl HU3 180 D8
Hopyard La
Bassingham LN5 93 B1
Normanton on Trent NG23 78 A3
Horace St PE21 208 E5
Horbling Fen Dro NG34 133 D2
Horbling La PE22 113 A7
Horbury Cl 2 DN15 182 D4
Horkstow Rd DN18 10 E7
Horn The 7 PE25 206 A7
Hornbeam Ave DN16 185 A5
Hornby Dr 20 LN12 77 A7
Horncastle Coll LN9 199 D3
Horncastle Cty Prim Sch LN9 199 C4
Horncastle Hill PE23 87 A1
Horncastle La
Dunholme LN2 68 B5
Grange De Lings LN1 67 F5
Horncastle Rd
Bardney LN3 83 C4
Boston PE21 208 F8
Fishtoft PE21 125 E5
Goulceby LN9 72 D5
Horsington LN10 84 D4
Louth LN11 198 A4
Mareham Le Fen PE22 98 F4
Raithby cum Maltby LN11 60 F2
Roughton LN9 85 C2
Tathwell LN11 73 A8
West Ashby LN9 199 C8
Woodhall Spa LN10 97 F6
Wragby LN8 70 D4
Horne La 3 NG22 65 B1
Horner Cl 1 LN5 205 C2
Hornsby Cres DN15 182 F4
Hornsby Rd NG31 210 E2
Hornsea Par 4 HU9 181 C8
Hornsey Hill Rd DN21 28 D1
Horse Fair Gn 25 DN8 15 A8
Horse Fayre 7 PE11 214 A3
Horse Mkt 24 LN7 33 B4
Horsegate PE6 217 D4
Horsegate Field Rd DN19 5 B2
Horseham's La PE20 135 A5
Horsemoor Dro PE12 159 B1
Horsemoor La LN9 72 C2
Horsepit La 12 PE11 145 C1
Horseshoe Cl 12 NG34 108 D2
Horseshoe La PE20 136 D5
Horseshoe Rd PE11 214 A2
Horseshoe Terr PE13 170 C1
Horseshoe Yd 11 PE6 166 E1
Horsewells St 1 DN10 39 C1
Horstead Ave DN20 196 D5
Horton St LN2 202 C3
Hospital Dro PE12 160 C3
Hospital La PE21 209 A6
Hospital Rd PE12 161 A5
Hotham Dr HU5 179 B8
Hotham Rd HU5 179 A8
Hotham Rd S HU5 179 B8
Hotham St HU9 181 D7
Hotspur Rd DN21 197 C6
Hough La
Carlton Scroop NG32 119 C4
Claypole NG23 117 F7
Hough Rd
Barkston NG32 130 B8
Carlton Scroop NG32 119 A3
Hough-on-the-Hill NG32 118 E7
Hougham Rd
Hougham NG32 118 B4
Westborough & Dry Doddington NG23 117 F5
Houghton Ave PE2 231 F5
Houghton Rd NG31 211 C2
Houlden Way 1 NG34 122 E3
Hounsfield Cl NG24 104 B5
Houps Rd 8 DN8 15 B8
Hourne The HU13 178 E2
House Ct DN16 185 D4
Howard Cl PE34 161 F2
Howard Gr DN32 192 B6
Howard Rd 10 LN4 108 A7
Howard St LN1 201 C4
Howdale La NG32 119 A3
Howden Croft Hill HU15 2 A8
Howe La
Ashby with Scremby PE23 88 C3
Goxhill DN19 11 F8
Howell Fen Dro NG34 122 D5
Howell Rd NG34 122 E3
Howgarth La PE22 114 F5
Howitts Rd 14 NG13 128 A5
Howland PE2 230 A3
Howlett Rd DN35 193 A4
Howsham La 2 DN38 32 D8
Howville Ave 2 DN7 14 F3
Howville Rd 1 DN7 14 F3

Hoylake Dr
1 Immingham DN40 186 D5
Peterborough PE7 231 C5
1 Skegness PE25 206 B5
Hoylake Rd DN17 184 D3
Hubba Cres PE20 135 C6
Hubbard Cl 2 NG34 122 D3
Hubberts Bridge Sta PE20 124 E2
Hubert's Cl PE12 168 C1
Huckles Way PE25 206 B6
Huddleston Rd DN32 192 B7
Hudson Ave DN15 182 E5
Hudson Cl PE23 88 B3
Hudson Dr LN4 207 E6
Hudson Rd 4 PE11 214 C2
Hudson St HU3 180 D8
Hudson Way 12 PE25 206 A5
Hudson's Gdns 5 PE21 209 B4
Huggin Carr Rd DN7 14 F1
Hugh Hill La DN7 14 D6
Hughes Ford Way 20 LN1 66 D2
Hughson Wlk 3 LN2 68 E6
Hulberry Cl 10 DN41 23 A4
Hull & E Riding Mus* HU9 181 A6
Hull Arena* HU1 180 E4
Hull Coll HU3 179 F7
Hull Coll Pk St Ctr HU2 180 D7
Hull High Sch for Girls HU10 178 D5
Hull Maritime Mus* HU1 180 F6
Hull Rd HU13 178 F1
Hull Royal Infmy HU3 180 C6
Hull Sta HU1 180 E6
Hull Trinity House Sch HU1 180 F6
Hull Truck Theatre* HU2 180 D7
Hull's Dro PE6 167 D3
Humber Bank Factories DN41 187 D4
Humber Bank S DN31 189 C2
Humber Bridge Rd DN31 189 C1
Humber Cres
6 Brough HU15 2 C5
Scunthorpe DN17 184 F6
Humber Dock St HU1 180 F5
Humber Rd
Barton-upon-Humber DN18 3 E1
Immingham DN40 186 A8
North Ferriby HU14 3 A4
Humber St
3 Cleethorpes DN35 192 F5
Grimsby DN31 189 C1
Kingston upon Hull HU1 180 F5
Humber Terr DN31 191 C8
Humber View
3 Barton-upon-Humber DN18 10 E8
Kingston upon Hull HU13 178 C2
4 Swanland HU14 3 B6
Humberdale Cl 5 HU14 3 B6
Humberdale Dr HU14 3 C5
Humberside Int Airport DN38 21 F5
Humberston Ave DN36 195 E6
Humberston CE Prim Sch DN36 36 D8
Humberston Comp Sch DN36 36 C8
Humberston Pk Specl Sch DN36 36 C8
Humberston Rd
Cleethorpes DN36 192 C3
Tetney DN36 36 C6
Humberstone Holt 1 LN11 50 F7
Humberstone Rd DN32 192 A6
Humberville Rd DN40 186 D4
Humby Rd NG33 141 B8
Hume Brae 6 DN40 186 B3
Hume St 5 DN31 191 C7
Hun Gate PE11 145 D3
Hunchback La PE13 170 E2
Hund Oak Dr 9 DN7 14 D4
Hundle Houses La LN4 111 D4
Hundlehouse La LN4 111 D4
Hundred Acres La NG24 104 B1
Hundreds La
Gringley on the Hill DN10 39 A5
Little Sutton PE12 216 F1
Hundreds Rd PE6 175 C6
Hungate LN1 234 B2
Hungate Rd NG32 139 A7
Hungerdike Gate PE12 215 A2
Hungry Hill La LN11 62 C5
Hunsley Cres DN32 192 B4
Hunsley Dr 5 DN41 23 E6
Hunstan La PE22 113 F4
Hunston Rd 4 LN10 97 C5
Hunt Lea Ave
Grantham NG31 210 F1
Lincoln LN6 205 C8
Hunt Rd DN16 185 C5
Huntcliff Comp Sch DN21 30 C1
Hunter Ave LN11 62 C6
Hunter Pl LN11 198 B4
Hunter Rd
Brookenby LN8 47 A6
Brough HU15 2 C6
Hunter's Croft 1 DN9 27 D3
Hunter's Dr 5 DN10 39 C1
Hunters Dr 13 LN4 95 C4
Hunters La Baumber LN9 72 A1
Tattershall LN4 207 C5
Hunting Ave PE2 230 F7
Huntingdon Cl 2 PE12 215 E3
Huntingdon Cres 8 DN15 8 B4
Huntingdon St HU4 179 E3
Huntingtower Rd NG31 211 A3
Huntingtower Rd Cty Prim Sch NG31 211 A3
Huntly Gr PE1 226 A4
Huntly Rd PE2 230 E7
Hunts Cl 7 DN20 19 E4
Hunt's Gate PE12 159 E1
Hunts La 4 DN20 30 F5
Huntsgate PE12 159 D4
Huntsman Cl PE21 209 D2
Huntsmans Chase DN36 195 B7
Huntsmans Gate PE3 224 F3
Hurdletree Bank PE12 158 E4
Hurdman Way PE25 90 E3
Hurford Pl DN37 194 D7
Hurle Cres PE21 208 D6
Hurn Bank PE12 147 E2
Hurn Cl
2 Birchwood LN6 204 B8
7 Ruskington NG34 108 D1
Hurn Dro LN4 110 A8
Hurn La PE22 126 A7
Hurn Rd Holbeach PE12 147 E1
Marholm PE6 220 C3
Hurn The
5 Billingborough NG34 133 B1
Digby LN4 108 E6
Hurnbridge Rd LN4 111 A4
Hurst Cres NG32 210 A4
Hurst La DN17 184 E3
Hurst The 5 PE25 206 A6
Hurstlea Dr DN36 193 B1
Hurstwood Cl LN2 202 D8
Hurton's La LN11 49 C6
Hussey Cl 2 NG34 212 E4
Hussey Twr* PE21 209 A4
Husthwaite Rd 18 HU15 2 D5
Hutchinson Gdns 5 PE12 157 E7
Hutchinson Rd 2 DN35 192 E7
Huteson La DN15 8 C8
Hutson Dr LN6 204 F2
Hutt St HU3 180 D7
Huttoft Bank Pit nature Reserve* LN13 77 B6
Huttoft Prim Sch LN13 76 F3
Huttoft Rd 17 LN12 76 F8
Hutton Rd DN31 189 B2
Hyde Gdns PE6 164 F3
Hyde Pk Cl 6 LN6 204 F1
Hyholmes PE3 224 F7
Hykeham Rd LN6 205 B4
Hykeham Sta
Lincoln LN6 204 D3
North Hykeham LN6 204 D4
Hymers Ave HU3 180 B7
Hymers Coll HU3 180 B7
Hyperion St HU9 181 A7
Hythegate PE4 221 B4

I

Ibbott Cl PE2 231 E5
Icehouse Rd HU3 180 D6
Ickworth Rd NG34 212 D3
Ida Rd PE25 206 C3
Idas Cl HU9 181 A5
Iddesleigh Rd 4 LN10 97 D6
Idle Bank Epworth DN9 15 F1
Haxey DN9 26 E2
Misson DN9 26 E1
Ihlee Cl PE4 221 C1
Ilex Cl PE7 230 C3
Iliffe Gate 3 PE4 221 D2
Immingham Bsns Units DN40 186 D3
Immingham Sch DN40 186 C4
Impala Way HU4 179 D2
Imperial Ave DN35 192 C8
Incredible Fantastic Old Toy Show The* LN1 234 B4
Independence Dr 5 PE11 156 F8
Industrial Est DN36 195 F8
Ing Dro PE20 134 F4
Ingelow Ave PE21 208 C6
Ingham Cl LN6 205 B3
Ingham Ct LN4 207 E6
Ingham Hall Gdns PE13 177 D7
Ingham Prim Sch LN1 54 F2
Ingham Rd
Coningsby LN4 207 E6
3 Stow LN1 66 C8
Inghams La 1 DN36 36 D4
Inghams Rd 3 DN36 36 D4
Ingle Ct 2 NG33 151 D7
Ingleby Cres LN2 201 F8
Ingleby Ct 2 PE11 214 F4
Ingleby Rd 14 DN17 29 D7
Ingledew Cl 8 NG34 122 E2
Inglenook Dr 2 DN8 15 B8
Ingleton Ave HU4 179 C6
Inglewood Dr 4 HU4 179 B5
Ingmires 7 HU15 2 D6
Ingoldmells Prim Sch PE25 90 D4
Ingoldmells Rd
Burgh Le Marsh PE24 89 F1
Burgh le Marsh PE24 102 E8
Ingoldsby Prim Sch NG33 141 D5
Ingoldsby Rd NG33 141 B3
Ingram Cres 9 DN7 14 C4
Ingram Gdns 11 DN20 30 E8
Ingram Gr 10 DN7 14 C4
Ingram La NG23 78 A1
Ingram Pl DN35 192 D2
Ingram Rd
Boston PE21 208 D6
Hatfield DN7 14 C3
Ings Bank PE22 126 E7
Ings Dro
Butterwick PE22 126 D7
Leverton PE22 113 E1
Ings La Belchford LN9 73 B2
Brackenborough with Little Grimsby LN11 49 B4
Bratoft PE24 102 C6
Brough HU15 2 C5
Cumberworth LN13 89 E7
Ellerker HU15 1 F8
2 Hibaldstow DN20 31 A5
Horsington LN10 84 D2
1 Kirk Bramwith DN7 14 C7
Leverton PE22 126 F7
Little Steeping PE23 101 E5
North Coates DN36 37 A3
North Ferriby HU14 3 A4
Saltfleetby LN11 62 F8
Scamblesby LN11 73 A4
Skidbrooke with Saltfleet Haven LN11 51 A3
South Cave HU15 1 E7
South Somercotes LN11 50 E3
Walkerith DN21 40 C3
Waltham DN37 194 F4
6 West Ashby LN9 85 E7
West Ashby LN9 199 D8
West Stockwith DN10 40 C6
Winterton DN15 9 D7
Ings Rd Benington PE22 126 D8
Gringley on the Hill DN10 39 B3
Kirton in Lindsey DN21 29 F1
Mablethorpe & Sutton LN12 76 E7
Inhams Cl PE13 177 D5
Inley Dro PE12 169 A8
Inner St NG31 211 B3
Innings The 1 NG34 212 D3
Inns Cl LN6 204 E3
Inverness Rd 14 DN7 14 D4
Iona Cl DN21 197 E6
Iona Dr DN36 36 D8
Ipswich Gdns NG31 210 E5
Irby Cres 9 PE12 158 B7
Irby Ct DN35 192 D3
Irby Pl PE21 208 F5
Irby Rd DN17 184 E5
Irby St PE21 208 E5
Irish Hill LN11 198 A5
Irnham Rd
Corby Glen NG33 141 C1
Stamford PE9 219 C7
Iron Bar Dro PE11 155 F4
Ironestone Cl LN2 202 C5
Ironmonger St 5 PE9 219 C5
Irvine Rd 2 DN16 185 C5
Isaac Newton Prim Sch The NG31 210 F3
Isaac Newton Way NG31 211 F6
Isaac's Hill DN35 192 E6
Isham Rd 1 PE3 225 D4
Isis Ct HU9 181 B5
Island Carr Rd DN20 196 A3
Island Rd DN17 7 E6
Isle Cl 3 DN17 16 D8
Islip Ct 1 LN9 199 D3
Ison Cl 4 NG34 120 E8
Itlings La HU13 178 F1
Itter Cres PE4 221 C1
Itterby Cres DN35 192 C3
Ivanhoe Rd
4 Scunthorpe DN16 183 C1
1 Scunthorpe DN16 185 D8
Ivatt Ct 13 NG31 210 E2
Ivatt Way PE3 225 C6
Ivel Cl 6 LN12 64 B5
Ivel Gr 4 LN12 64 B5
Ivery La PE22 114 D4
Ivesdyke Cl 3 PE13 170 B2
Ivy Cl DN7 14 E4
Ivy Cres PE21 208 D3
Ivy Farm Ct 20 DN41 23 F5
Ivy Gr PE4 221 B2
Ivy La Coningsby LN4 207 F1
Grainthorpe LN11 37 E1
Wainfleet St Mary PE24 115 C8

J

Jack Haws La 3 PE9 172 D4
Jack Hunt Sch PE3 225 B3
Jack Hunt Swimming Pool PE3 225 B3
Jack Row La DN7 14 B8
Jacklin Cl 5 LN11 50 B8
Jacklin Cres 6 LN12 64 A4
Jacklin Dr 3 LN11 51 C4
Jacklin La DN17 7 C3
Jacklins App DN16 185 A3
Jackson Dr 3 PE20 136 C5
Jackson Mews 6 DN40 186 A4
Jackson Rd 1 DN15 182 E3
Jackson St
1 Grimsby DN31 191 C8
Kingston upon Hull HU3 180 D4
Jacksons La 4 PE24 102 E8
Jackson's Pl DN36 192 D1
Jacobean Rd 4 LN6 204 D6
Jacobs Ct 2 PE11 214 C6
Jade Gr 1 HU3 180 A4
Jaguar Dr LN6 204 D1
Jail La PE22 126 F2
James Ave
3 Mablethorpe/Sutton on Sea LN12 64 C2
Skegness PE25 206 B6
James Pl DN39 12 B1
James Rd 1 DN21 55 A8
James St Boston PE21 208 E5
Brigg DN20 196 B3
Grimsby DN31 191 C8
Lincoln LN2 234 B3
Louth LN11 198 C6
James Way 9 DN40 186 B3
Jameson Bridge St 8 LN8 57 D8
Jameson St 2 HU1 180 F6
Jankin La PE34 161 F1
Janton Ct DN36 195 C7
Japan Rd DN21 197 B5
Japonica Hill 3 DN40 186 C3
Jaque's Bank DN8 16 A5
Jarratt Hill La HU15 1 D8
Jarratt St HU1 180 F7
Jarvis Cl LN6 204 F7
Jarvis's Gate PE12 159 C1
Jasmin Cl 9 PE13 170 E1
Jasmin Rd LN6 204 C8
Jasmine Cl PE10 213 B7
Jasmine Ct
2 Goxhill DN19 12 A8
Peterborough PE2 229 E2
Jasmine Way
Immingham DN40 186 C3
Yaxley PE7 233 F6
Jason Rd 5 LN6 205 A5
Javelin Ave 8 LN8 47 B6
Javelin Rd 12 LN11 62 C6
Jefferson Cl 24 PE8 172 B1
Jefferson Dr 23 HU15 2 C6
Jeffery Ave 6 PE13 170 E1
Jeffrey La DN9 16 E1
Jekil's Bank
Holbeach PE12 158 C1
Moulton PE12 167 F8
Whaplode PE12 168 B8
Jekil's Gate PE12 159 A5
Jellicoe Ave LN2 202 D3
Jenkins Cl Louth LN11 198 C8
5 Skegness PE25 206 A7
Jenkins' La PE22 127 A6
Jenner Pl DN35 192 B8
Jenning St HU8 181 A8
Jenny Brough La HU13 178 B3
Jenny Cl HU13 178 B3
Jensen Rd LN4 205 F2
Jericho La DN40 12 D7
Jermyn Mews LN4 203 D1
Jermyn St NG34 212 D4
Jerusalem LN6 79 F5
Jerusalem Rd LN6 200 A4
Jesmond Ave 5 DN17 184 E3
Jessop Cl
Cherry Willingham/Reepham LN3 203 E5
9 Leasingham NG34 121 B8
Jessop Way NG24 104 B5
Jiggle's Gate PE12 158 F1
Jill Gr HU13 178 F1
Job's La LN6 79 C1
Jobson Rd 2 LN9 199 D2
Jock Hedge PE24 102 E6
Joel Sq 8 NG34 107 F1
John Adams Way PE21 208 F4
John Clare Cty Prim Sch The PE6 173 B4
John Coupland Hospl DN21 197 B7
John Eve Way PE6 217 B6
John Fielding Specl Sch PE21 209 A6
John Foster Cl 9 NG31 211 D7
John Harrison CE Prim Sch DN19 11 C8
John Harrison's Cl 3 DN19 11 D8
John Harrox Prim Sch The PE12 157 F7
John Hunt Cty Jun Mix Sch The NG24 104 B2
John Hunt Infants & Nursery Sch NG24 104 B3
John Leggott Coll DN17 184 E8
John Mansfield Sec Sch PE1 226 B8
John Smith Cl LN13 89 A6
John Spendluffe Sch The LN13 75 F2
John St Lincoln LN2 234 C2
13 Market Rasen LN8 57 D8
Scunthorpe DN15 183 B3
John Wake Cl 2 PE6 217 B6
Johnson Ave PE11 214 E2
Johnson Cl 8 Belton DN9 16 E2
3 Skegness PE25 206 A7
Johnson Ct LN4 207 B6
Johnson Dr LN4 205 F4
Johnson Hospl PE11 214 D3
Johnson St DN35 192 B8
Johnson Way 14 PE24 102 E7
Johnson's Dro PE13 177 B6
Johnson's La 7 DN17 16 D7
Johnston's Rd DN7 14 E7
Jolls La LN9 86 C5
Jolly Comm La LN13 77 A3
Jolly Farmer La PE21 126 C3
Jonathan Dr PE25 206 C8
Jonathan Gdns 1 NG34 212 F3
Jonquil Ave DN16 185 D5
Jordan Mews 2 PE1 226 B3
Jordan's Cradge Bank Rd PE11 156 C2
Jorose St 4 PE3 225 A3
Joseph Ogle Cl DN36 195 B7
Joseph Ruston Tech Coll LN6 205 B5
Joseph St DN31 191 C8
Joshua Way 5 DN21 43 D7
Joy Paine Cl PE21 208 C6
Joy's Bank PE12 158 E1
Jubilee Ave
Boston PE21 208 E6
Grantham NG31 211 C5
Jubilee Cl 4 Bardney LN3 83 B4
Cherry Willingham/Reepham LN3 203 E6
1 Hogsthorpe PE24 90 B7
Lincoln LN6 204 F1
Long Sutton PE12 216 C5
Martin LN4 96 C2
8 Morton PE10 154 C7
1 Spalding PE11 214 C4
Jubilee Cres LN11 198 C8
Jubilee Dr
3 Bardney LN3 83 C4
10 Wragby LN8 70 D4
Jubilee Gr NG34 212 C6
Jubilee Par 6 PE24 90 D7
Jubilee Rd LN11 50 E7
Jubilee St
Peterborough PE2 230 F8
2 Ruskington NG34 108 E1
Jubilee Way LN9 199 B4
Jude Gate PE22 114 E3
Judge Cl 3 PE21 209 C4
Judy Cross PE11 145 B8
Julia Rd LN4 203 D1
Julian Cl HU5 179 A7
Julian St DN32 192 A7
Julian's Wlk 8 HU10 178 F6
Julia's Mead 12 PE11 214 B5
Junction Rd 10 DN7 14 C6
Junella Cl HU3 180 A4
Jungle The* DN35 193 B3
Junior Cadets Rd NG34 120 B8
Juniper Cl
1 Flixborough DN15 182 C6
10 Leasingham NG34 121 B7
3 Lincoln LN5 205 C2
Juniper Cres PE3 225 A2
Juniper Dr 18 LN2 68 F4
Juniper Way
Grimsby DN33 191 C2
3 Sleaford NG34 212 D2
Justice Hall La 10 DN17 16 D8
Justice La DN14 7 B8
Jutland Ct 1 DN36 195 D7

K

Karen Ave 12 DN41 23 A4
Katherine Cres PE25 206 D2
Kathleen Ave
Cleethorpes DN35 192 D8
Scunthorpe DN16 185 B5
Kathleen Gr DN32 192 C7
Kaymile Cl 13 DN36 195 C6
Keadby Cl LN6 204 F7
Keal Hill PE23 100 B7
Kealholme Rd DN17 29 D7
Keats Ave
Grantham NG31 211 E6
Scunthorpe DN17 184 D7
Keats Cl Lincoln LN2 202 C7
17 Mablethorpe/Sutton on Sea LN12 77 A7
Keats Dr NG34 121 E4
Keats Gr 2 PE9 218 E5
Keats Way PE1 225 D7
Keb La DN15 9 D2
Keble Cl 4 PE9 219 A7
Keble Ct 1 LN4 207 B5
Keddington Ave LN1 201 E8
Keddington Cres 2 LN11 198 D7
Keddington Rd
Louth LN11 198 C7
Scunthorpe DN17 184 F4
Kedleston Rd PE7 231 F6
Keeble Dr LN4 203 D1
Keel Dr 9 NG13 128 A5
Keelby Prim Sch DN41 23 A5
Keelby Rd
6 Gainsborough DN21 53 A8

Keelby Rd *continued*
Scunthorpe DN17 184 F5
Stallingborough DN41 23 C6
Keeling St 7 LN11 50 F7
Keeper's Way 6 DN9 16 E1
Keepers Cl 2 LN2 68 D7
Keepers Way NG34 212 E3
Keeton Rd PE1 225 E7
Keightley Rd PE12 147 B5
Keith Cres 15 DN37 23 F1
Kelham Rd
9 Great Gonerby NG31 129 E5
2 Great Gonerby NG31 210 E8
Grimsby DN32 192 D6
Kellet Gate PE12 157 B5
Kells Cl 6 LN5 205 D3
Kell's Dro PE20 124 E1
Kelly Cl 14 PE11 156 E8
Kelsey Ave DN15 182 B3
Kelsey La 1 DN17 17 D4
Kelsey Prim Sch LN7 32 A4
Kelsey Rd LN7 32 C2
Kelsey St LN1 234 A2
Kelstern Cl 1 LN6 204 C6
Kelstern Ct 1 DN34 191 A5
Kelstern Rd LN6 204 C6
Kelston Dr 2 HU13 179 A3
Kelthorpe Cl PE9 171 A2
Kemble Cl LN6 204 B8
Kemp Rd
Grimsby DN31 189 C3
3 Swanland HU14 3 B6
Kemp St PE6 166 E1
Kempton Cl 3 PE11 156 E3
Kempton Dr 4 DN7 14 C2
Kempton Rd HU3 179 E6
Kempton Way NG31 210 F4
Kendal Cl 2 PE4 221 D2
Kendal Rd DN40 186 E3
Kendal Way HU5 179 C7
Kendale Rd DN16 185 E8
Kendon Gdns DN8 15 B8
Kendrick Cl PE2 231 D6
Kenford Ct DN36 195 C7
Kenilworth Cl 3 LN1 66 D2
Kenilworth Dr LN6 205 C5
Kenilworth Rd
Cleethorpes DN35 192 D4
Grantham NG31 211 F5
Scunthorpe DN16 183 C1
Kenlan Rd 23 PE13 170 D1
Kenleigh Dr PE21 209 D4
Kenmar Rd 20 DN37 23 F1
Kenmare Cres DN21 197 F2
Kennedy Ave
21 Alford LN13 75 F2
Skegness PE25 206 C2
Kennedy Cl DN20 196 E3
Kennedy Rd
Bracebridge Heath LN4 205 F3
Holbeach PE12 215 C4
Kennel La
Doddington & Whisby LN6 79 E5
Reepham LN3 203 E8
Kennel Wlk LN3 203 F8
Kennels Rd PE6 224 D4
Kenner Cl 4 LN6 205 A6
Kennet Gdns PE4 221 C1
Kenneth Ave
2 Burgh Le Marsh PE24 102 E8
8 Hatfield DN7 14 C2
5 Stainforth DN7 14 C6
Kenneth Campbell Rd 4 DN36 37 C5
Kenneth St 1 LN1 201 F6
Kennington Cl LN2 68 E5
Kennulphs Cl 5 PE6 175 C8
Kensington Cl PE12 215 F3
Kensington Dr 6 PE11 214 B2
Kensington Gdns 3 LN12 64 B3
Kensington Pl DN33 195 A8
Kensington Rd 4 DN15 182 B3
Kent Ave LN12 63 F5
Kent Cl
Kingston upon Hull HU9 181 C7
3 Sutton Bridge PE12 160 E4
Kent Dr 4 DN20 31 A5
Kent Rd
9 Binbrook Tech Pk LN8 47 B6
Leake Commonside PE22 113 F3
Peterborough PE3 225 E2
Kent St Grimsby DN32 189 B1
6 Lincoln LN2 202 C3
Kentmere Pl 4 PE4 221 D2
Kenwardly Rd HU10 178 E8
Kenwick Cl LN11 198 D3
Kenwick Dr NG31 211 D4
Kenwick Gdns LN11 198 D3
Kenwick Hill
Legbourne LN11 198 E1
Raithby cum Maltby LN11 61 C3
Kenwick Pastures LN11 198 D3
Kenwick Rd LN11 198 D2
Kenya Dr DN17 184 F2
Kenyon Cl 8 DN8 15 A8
Kerries Wlk DN17 184 C7
Kerrison View 5 LN2 68 D2
Kerr's Cres NG32 118 D2
Kerry Dr HU10 178 C6
Kerry Pit Way HU10 178 C6
Kesgrave St 1 DN31 189 C1
Kesteven & Grantham Girls Sch NG31 211 B5
Kesteven & Sleaford High Sch NG34 212 D4
Kesteven Agricultural College-Elms Farm NG32 119 E6
Kesteven Cl 1 PE6 217 D4
Kesteven Ct
3 Habrough DN40 22 E8
7 Lincoln LN6 204 D2
Kesteven Dr 7 PE6 217 A6
Kesteven Gr 19 DN17 16 D8
Kesteven Rd PE9 219 C7
Kesteven St
Lincoln LN5 234 B1
1 Sleaford NG34 212 E4
Kesteven Way 7 PE10 213 C5
Kestrel Cl
6 Birchwood LN6 204 D8
2 Sleaford NG34 212 B3
Kestrel Ct NG31 210 F2
Kestrel Dr LN11 198 D8
Kestrel Rd
8 Scopwick Heath LN4 108 A7
Scunthorpe DN17 184 E6
Kestrel Rise LN6 79 B1
Keswick Cl 2 PE4 221 D3
Ketco Ave PE9 171 A4
Ketlock Hill La 1 DN22 52 B1
Kettering Rd
Scunthorpe DN16 183 C2
Wothorpe PE9 219 B2
Kettlebridge La DN40 12 E6
Kettleby La DN20 20 E3
Kettleby View 3 DN20 196 D4
Kettlethorpe Dr 17 HU15 2 D5
Kettlethorpe Rd LN1 65 E3
Kettlewell St DN32 191 E5
Ketton CE Prim Sch PE9 171 A3
Ketton Rd PE9 171 B2
Kew Rd DN35 192 E6
Kexby La DN21 53 C4
Kexby Mill Cl 5 LN6 93 B8
Kexby Rd DN21 54 D6
Key Theatre* PE1 226 B1
Keyholme La DN36 37 D2
Keyworth Dr 10 LN7 33 B4
Khormaksar Dr LN4 95 C7
Kidd La HU15 2 D6
Kiddier Ave DN37 194 D7
Kidgate LN11 198 B5
Kidgate Cty Prim Sch LN11 198 C5
Kilburn Cres 1 LN6 205 A6
Kildare Dr PE3 225 C4
Kilham PE2 229 E2
Killarney Cl NG31 211 E7
Killingholme Prim Sch DN40 12 E3
Killingholme Rd DN40 12 F2
Kiln Hill 4 LN8 59 A7
Kiln La Brigg DN20 196 B3
Fulbeck NG32 106 C1
Immingham DN41 187 C2
Louth LN11 198 B6
Stallingborough DN41 186 F1
Kiln La Ind Est DN41 187 B3
Kiln Yd LN11 198 C5
Kilnwell Rd 12 LN8 57 D8
Kilverstone PE4 220 F6
Kimberley St HU3 180 C7
Kimbolton Ct PE1 225 F3
Kime Cl NG34 142 C8
Kime's La 6 PE22 98 F4
Kinder Ave LN6 205 A2
Kinderley Rd PE13 170 D2
King Charles Cl HU10 178 E7
King Edward Rd
Thorne/Moorends DN8 15 A8
2 Woodhall Spa LN10 97 C6
King Edward St
Belton DN9 16 E2
Grimsby DN31 189 A1
3 Kingston upon Hull HU1 180 F6
Kingston upon Hull HU1 180 E7
Kirton in Lindsey DN21 30 B1
Scunthorpe DN16 183 A1
Sleaford NG34 212 C3
King Edward VI Gram Sch LN11 198 A5
King Edwards Terr 4 HU15 2 B5
King George Ave 1 LN10 97 D6
King George V Ave 1 PE12 215 F3
King George V Stadium DN32 192 B5
King Georges Ct 3 DN7 14 C5
King John Bank
2 Sutton Bridge PE14 170 F8
Walpole PE14 161 A2
King John St NG34 212 C4
King Johns Rd 6 PE20 135 B7
King St 1 Billinghay LN4 109 F5
Boston PE21 208 E4
East Halton DN40 12 D7
Gainsborough DN21 197 D3
15 Goxhill DN19 12 A8
2 Keelby DN41 23 A4
10 Kirton PE20 136 C5
Lincoln LN5 234 A1
20 Mablethorpe/Sutton on Sea LN12 64 B3
Market Rasen LN8 57 D8
King St *continued*
1 Peterborough PE1 226 A2
Scunthorpe DN15 183 B4
18 Sutton Bridge PE12 160 E4
Thorne/Moorends DN8 15 A8
Wainfleet All Saints PE24 102 A2
West Deeping PE6 173 A8
Wilsford NG32 120 A1
Winterton DN15 9 A5
Yarburgh LN11 49 E4
King St La LE14 150 A6
King William Cl 4 PE34 161 F3
Kingerby Beck Mdws Nature Reserve* LN8 44 E5
Kingerby Cl DN21 197 E3
Kingerby Rd DN17 184 E5
Kingfisher Cl
2 Birchwood LN6 204 D8
4 Scunthorpe DN15 182 D5
Yaxley PE7 233 D5
Kingfisher Dr
2 Skegness PE25 206 A7
4 Surfleet PE11 145 E3
Kingfishers PE2 229 D6
King's Ave Boston PE21 209 C3
Brigg DN20 196 D3
King's Cl 15 DN7 14 D4
King's Bench St HU3 180 B5
King's Cres
Boston PE21 209 C3
Swineshead PE20 135 B8
King's Cross Cl 2 HU3 180 C6
King's Cswy DN14 6 E8
King's Delph Dro PE7 231 E2
King's Gdns PE1 226 A5
King's Rd
Barnetby Le Wold DN38 21 B5
Humberston DN35 193 B3
Spalding PE11 214 D5
King's Sch The NG31 211 B5
Kings Arms Yd 2 LN2 234 B2
Kings Ave PE25 206 E8
Kings Cl PE22 112 C8
Kings Croft 1 DN17 16 E6
Kings Ct Louth LN11 198 E7
9 Scawby DN20 30 F8
Kings Dyke Cl PE2 231 E6
Kings Hill 2 NG32 119 B7
Kings Leigh 1 HU3 180 C6
Kings Mews DN35 193 C1
Kings Par DN35 193 A5
Kings Rd
Holbeach PE12 215 F3
Immingham DN40 186 E5
Metheringham LN4 95 C4
Peterborough PE2 231 B6
Stamford PE9 219 B6
Kings Sch PE1 226 A4
Kings Way LN2 68 C7
Kingsbridge Ct 1 PE4 220 E5
Kingscliffe Rd NG31 211 A8
Kingsdale DN17 184 E2
Kingsdown Rd LN6 204 B7
Kingsgate PE12 159 E7
Kingsley Ave PE10 213 B5
Kingsley Cl
4 Barnack PE9 172 D3
6 Brough HU15 2 B5
Kingsley Gr DN33 191 C4
Kingsley Rd
14 Mablethorpe/Sutton on Sea LN12 64 B4
North Hykeham LN6 204 B5
Peterborough PE1 226 C4
Kingsley St LN1 234 A4
Kingsline Cl 1 PE6 176 A3
Kingsport Cl HU3 180 A7
Kingsthorpe Cres PE25 206 C1
Kingston Ave
Grantham NG31 210 E4
Grimsby DN34 191 A6
Kingston upon Hull HU13 178 F1
Kingston Cl 7 DN35 193 A1
Kingston Dr PE2 231 E5
Kingston Lower Sch HU4 179 C4
Kingston Rd
Kingston upon Hull HU10 178 F8
Scunthorpe DN16 185 A7
Kingston Ret Pk HU1 180 E5
Kingston St HU1 180 E5
Kingston Upper Sch HU4 179 C4
Kingston View 20 DN18 10 F8
Kingston Wharf 4 HU1 180 F5
Kingsway Boston PE21 209 B3
Bourne PE10 213 D6
2 Brigg DN20 196 B4
Cleethorpes DN35 193 A5
11 Leverington PE13 170 E1
Lincoln LN5 201 F1
Nettleham LN2 68 C2
Scunthorpe DN15 182 C3
Stainforth DN7 14 C6
Tealby LN8 46 C1
Kingsway Sta DN35 193 B4
Kinloch Way DN40 186 B2
Kinloss Cl 11 LN6 204 C6
Kinnears Wlk PE2 229 F2
Kinoulton Ct 16 NG31 210 E2
Kinsbourne Gn 40 DN7 14 D4
Kintore Dr NG31 211 C4
Kipling Ave 4 DN17 184 D7
Kipling Cl
4 Grantham NG31 211 E6
3 Stamford PE9 218 E5
Kipling Ct PE1 225 E8
Kipling Dr
4 Mablethorpe/Sutton on Sea LN12 77 A7
14 Sleaford NG34 212 F4
Kipling Wlk 1 HU4 179 D2
Kiplington Cl HU3 180 A7
Kippings The 8 PE10 164 C8
Kirby Ct 5 PE11 214 F4
Kirby Wlk 2 PE3 225 C4
Kirk Gate
Waltham DN37 194 E4
6 Whaplode PE12 158 B7
Kirk Rise HU10 178 C7
Kirkby Bank PE23 99 E3
Kirkby Gravel Pit Nature Reserve* LN4 207 A8
Kirkby La LN10 97 E6
Kirkby la Thorpe CE Prim Sch NG34 121 F4
Kirkby Moor Nature Reserve* LN10 98 A5
Kirkby Rd
Ewerby & Evedon NG34 122 B5
Scunthorpe DN17 184 E4
Kirkby St LN5 201 F1
Kirkby Underwood Rd PE10 154 A8
Kirkby-on-Bain CE (Aided) Prim Sch LN10 98 C5
Kirkdale Cl 4 NG34 121 B8
Kirkden Paddocks DN9 16 C2
Kirkgate
Tydd St Giles PE13 169 F7
Tydd St Giles PE13 170 A7
Kirkgate St PE13 170 E1
Kirkham Cl HU13 178 F2
Kirkhouse Gn Rd DN7 14 A8
Kirklands Rd HU5 179 E8
Kirkmeadow PE3 225 A8
Kirkside 6 DN37 194 D4
Kirkstall PE2 230 B3
Kirkstead Bridge LN10 97 B4
Kirkstead Cres DN33 191 B3
Kirkstead Ct 8 LN10 97 D5
Kirkstone House Sch PE6 164 E4
Kirkton Gate PE3 225 A1
Kirkway HU10 178 B7
Kirkwood Cl PE3 225 E2
Kirman Cres 5 DN17 184 F3
Kirmington CE Prim Sch DN39 22 A6
Kirmington Cl 8 LN6 204 C6
Kirmington Gdns 6 DN34 191 A7
Kirmond Rd LN8 47 A4
Kirness Dro LN4 109 C6
Kirton Dro LN4 110 F1
Kirton Holme Rd PE20 124 D1
Kirton La Hatfield DN8 14 E7
2 Long Bennington NG23 117 D4
Stainforth DN7 14 D6
Kirton Lindsey Prim Sch DN21 30 B1
Kirton Lindsey Sta DN21 30 B2
Kirton Rd Blyton DN21 41 D6
Holme DN16 19 B2
Manton DN21 30 A3
Messingham DN17 29 E6
Scawby DN20 30 C8
Scotter DN21 29 D3
Waddingham DN21 43 B7
Kisgate 10 LN1 66 D7
Kishorn Ct DN40 186 B2
Kisimul Sch LN6 92 A6
Kit Cat La PE20 145 F8
Kitty Briggs La NG31 210 E1
Kitwood Cl 4 PE21 209 B4
Kitwood Rd PE21 209 B4
Knaith Hall La DN22 52 E3
Knaith Hill DN21 53 A3
Knarr Fen Rd PE6 176 E2
Kneeland 24 LN2 68 D6
Knight Cl PE6 217 D5
Knight Pl 2 LN5 205 E8
Knight St
Grimsby DN32 192 B6
4 Lincoln LN5 205 E8
2 Pinchbeck PE11 145 B1
Pinchbeck PE11 156 E8
Knight's Ct DN16 185 A3
Knights Cl 5 Belton DN9 16 E2
18 Laceby DN37 23 F1
Leverington PE13 170 B2
Knightsbridge 2 DN36 195 C6
Knightsbridge Rd 41 DN17 29 D7
Knipe Ave PE11 214 C3
Knipton CE Prim Sch NG32 138 C6
Knipton La NG32 138 D6
Knipton Rd NG32 138 B4
Knoll St DN35 192 F6
Knoll The NG31 210 D8
Knolls The NG32 210 B5
Knowle St 2 LN12 64 B3
Kohima Cl 3 PE10 213 E7
Kooreman Ave 19 PE13 170 D1
Kyme Rd Boston PE21 208 D6
Heckington NG34 122 E3

L

La Milesse Way 1 PE20 135 C7
Labour In Vain Dro LN4 110 A6
Labrador Dr 11 DN20 19 E4
Laburnham Ave DN37 194 D4
Laburnham Cl 7 DN37 194 D4
Laburnum Ave
Gainsborough DN21 197 D6
4 Gunness DN15 17 E6
Yaxley PE7 233 F6
Laburnum Cl
3 Bourne PE10 213 C6
Grantham NG31 211 D5
Lincoln LN6 205 A2
7 Wisbech PE13 170 E1
Laburnum Cres LN11 198 E4
Laburnum Ct 2 LN3 82 A8
Laburnum Dr
Cherry Willingham/Reepham LN3 203 D5
Grimsby DN34 190 E7
Ingoldmells PE25 206 D8
3 Kingston upon Hull HU5 179 B7
Morton PE10 154 B7
Laburnum Gr
8 Burton-upon-Stather DN15 8 B5
16 Crowle DN17 16 D7
Peterborough PE1 226 B8
Scunthorpe DN16 185 B7
Spalding PE11 214 F5
Laburnum Rd NG34 107 C2
Laceby Acres Prim Sch DN34 190 D5
Laceby Rd
Grimsby DN34 191 A4
Laceby DN37 190 C3
Scunthorpe DN17 184 E5
Laceby St LN2 202 B3
Lacey Gdns LN11 198 D6
Lacey Gdns Jun Sch LN11 198 D6
Lacey's Cl PE22 126 F6
Lacey's Dr PE22 126 F6
Lacey's La PE22 126 E6
Lacy Cl 21 LN2 68 D2
Ladds Cl 6 PE21 209 C4
Ladd's Mill Cl 7 LN6 93 B8
Lade Bank
Old Leake PE22 113 F5
Wrangle PE22 114 B6
Lady Bower Cl 9 LN6 205 A2
Lady Charlotte Rd PE7 230 D3
Lady Fen La LN13 76 B1
Lady Frances Cres DN35 192 C5
Lady Frances Dr 1 LN8 57 D8
Lady La PE24 102 A2
Lady Lodge Dr PE2 230 A5
Lady Margaret's Ave PE6 217 C5
Lady Matilda's Dr PE25 206 C8
Lady Meers Rd LN3 203 E6
Ladybower Way PE4 221 C3
Ladysmith Rd DN32 191 F7
Ladywell Gate 4 HU15 2 E6
Ladywood Rd PE11 214 E6
Lafford Ct NG34 212 B5
Lafford Dr 2 LN4 109 F6
Lafford High Sch The LN4 109 F6
Laforey Rd DN31 188 A3
Lagonda Cl LN4 205 F1
Lagoon Rd DN17 184 B6
Laing Cl 2 LN3 83 B4
Lake View Rd LN6 205 C6
Lakeside Anderby PE24 77 C3
Peterborough PE4 221 B5
Peterborough PE7 230 C2
Lakeside Dr DN17 184 C5
Lakeside Gr HU4 179 D4
Lakeside Leisure Ctr PE2 230 A5
Lakeside Ret Pk DN16 185 F6
Lakeside Sta DN35 193 B2
Lakeview Cl 3 LN6 204 C1
Lalrgate Pl 8 DN35 192 F1
Lamb Gdns LN2 202 B6
Lamb La
Benington PE22 127 A4
Newport HU15 1 B8
Lambert Ave 12 HU15 2 C6
Lambert Bank
Fleet PE12 158 D1
Holbeach PE12 168 D8
Lambert Mews 5 PE9 219 C4
Lambert Rd
4 Allington NG32 128 F7
Grimsby DN32 191 D6
Lambeth Wlk 3 PE9 219 A6
Lambourn Ct DN35 192 F1
Lambourne Rise DN16 185 A2
Lambourne Way 5 NG34 122 D2
Lammas Leas Rd 4 LN8 57 E7
Lammas Rd PE1 226 A7
Lammin's La 2 PE22 99 A4
Lamport Cl 9 PE6 217 A6
Lampton Gr DN32 191 D6
Lanark St 2 HU5 180 B8
Lancaster App DN40 12 D4

Lancaster Ave
Grimsby DN31 191 B7
Horncastle LN9 199 C5
Skegness PE25 206 A5
Lancaster Cl
3 Great Steeping PE23 101 D7
Long Sutton PE12 216 C4
Stickney PE22 113 A7
6 Waddington LN5 94 A7
Lancaster Ct
14 Welton/Dunholme LN2 68 D7
Yaxley PE7 233 F6
Lancaster Dr
6 Coningsby LN4 207 D4
Long Sutton PE12 216 C4
Moorland Prison DN7 26 A8
6 Scampton Airfield LN1 67 F5
Lancaster Gate DN36 195 C1
Lancaster Gdns 2 NG31 211 D2
Lancaster Gn DN21 54 F8
Lancaster Pl 4 LN5 201 F1
Lancaster Rd
3 Binbrook Tech Pk LN8 47 B6
Gringley on the Hill DN10 39 D1
Scunthorpe DN16 185 A5
10 Stamford PE9 219 B6
Lancaster Way
Market Deeping PE6 217 B7
2 Skellingthorpe LN6 200 A4
Yaxley PE7 233 F6
Lancelot Ct HU9 181 C6
Lancelot Way 7 PE11 214 B3
Lancewood Gdns 3 LN6 204 C8
Lancia Cres LN4 205 F2
Lancing Cl 7 PE4 221 A3
Lancing Way 4 DN33 194 E8
Land Dike LN11 37 A1
Land of Gn Ginger 10 HU1 180 F6
Landeck Ave DN34 191 B6
Landing La HU15 1 A7
Landmere Gr LN6 200 D1
Landor Ave 3 DN17 184 D7
Landsdowne Cl 22 LN12 77 A8
Landsdowne Rd 2 PE25 206 C4
Landseer Ave PE24 90 D8
Lane The
1 Easton on the Hill PE9 171 D3
West Deeping PE6 173 B7
Laneham Rd NG22 65 A1
Laneham St
Rampton DN22 65 A5
Scunthorpe DN15 183 A3
Lanes The 10 DN36 36 D4
Laney Cl LN2 202 C7
Langary Gate Rd PE12 158 E1
Langdale Ave DN33 194 D7
Langdale Cres NG31 211 A8
Langdyke PE1 226 F6
Langer Cl 5 LN6 204 B6
Langford La NG23 91 A2
Langford Rd PE2 231 A7
Langford Wlk 1 HU4 179 B7
Langham Rd PE24 90 B7
Langhole Dro PE11 145 B1
Langholme La DN9 27 B1
Langholme Wood Nature Reserve* DN9 39 D8
Langley* PE3 225 B8
Langley Cl LN11 198 E4
Langley Dr DN16 185 A2
Langley Pl DN35 193 A4
Langley Rd LN6 204 D2
Langrick Rd
Boston PE21 208 C6
Coningsby LN4 98 C1
Holland Fen with Brothertoft PE20 124 E4
Langtoft Prim Sch PE6 164 F3
Langtoft Drain Rd PE6 165 C4
Langtoft Outgang Rd PE11 165 D6
Langton Cl
Grimsby DN33 191 A3
Horncastle LN9 199 A3
Lincoln LN2 202 B7
Langton Dr
Grimsby DN33 191 A3
Horncastle LN9 199 A3
Langton Hill LN9 199 A3
Langton La LN9 85 C4
Langton Rd
Holton le Clay DN36 195 E2
Peterborough PE1 226 D7
Langwith Dr PE12 215 C2
Langwith Gdns PE12 215 C1
Langworth Rd LN2 69 B4
Langworthgate LN2 234 C3
Lansdall Ave 4 DN21 52 F6
Lansdown Link 1 DN35 192 E3
Lansdown Rd 4 DN40 186 B4
Lansdowne Ave
Grimsby DN32 191 D4
Lincoln LN6 205 C5
Lansdowne Dr 21 LN12 77 A8
Lansdowne Rd
8 Navenby/Wellingore LN5 107 A8
Yaxley PE7 233 F6
Lansdowne St HU3 180 C6
Lansdowne Way PE2 230 D7
Laporte Rd DN40 187 C5
Lapwater La PE12 147 C6
Lapwing Cl LN6 200 A3
Larch Ave 16 LN2 68 D2
Larch Cl 8 Bourne PE10 213 C7
2 Grantham NG31 210 D2
Immingham DN40 186 E5
Yaxley PE7 233 F6
Larch Ct 9 DN21 197 E6
Larch Gn NG34 107 D1
Larch Gr
Peterborough PE1 226 C6
8 Scawby DN20 30 F8
Scunthorpe DN16 185 B7
Larch Rd DN35 192 D2
Larch Way 8 NG34 212 D2
Larchmont Cl 10 HU15 2 C6
Larchwood Cres LN6 200 D1
Larden Ave DN33 194 E8
Lark Cl 13 LN8 70 D4
Lark Dr 4 LN5 107 A7
Lark Rise
6 Market Deeping PE6 217 C5
Scotter DN21 29 B3
Larkin Ave LN3 203 D5
Larkspur Ave 6 DN41 23 F5
Larkspur Croft PE21 208 C6
Larkspur Rd LN2 202 D7
Larmour Rd DN37 190 D7
Larne Cl 12 LN5 205 C2
Larne Rd LN5 205 D2
Larners Fields 6 LN1 66 C7
Lashbrook Garth HU4 179 B4
Lastingham 30 HU15 2 C6
Latham Ave PE2 230 C7
Latimer Gdns 12 NG34 122 E3
Laughton Endowed (Aided) DN21 41 C8
Laughton Rd
Blyton DN21 40 F5
Boston PE21 208 D6
Laughton Way LN2 201 F7
Laughton Way N LN2 201 F8
Launde Gdns PE9 218 E4
Launder Terr NG31 211 A3
Laundon Rd NG34 132 E3
Laura Ct 5 PE25 90 E3
Laurel Cl
6 Donington PE11 134 E2
8 Gainsborough DN21 197 E6
Grimsby DN33 191 C2
Kingston upon Hull HU5 179 B7
Lincoln LN5 205 D5
Yaxley PE7 233 D4
Laurel Dr 7 PE6 176 A3
Laurels Cl 1 DN40 22 E8
Laurier St DN35 192 D8
Laurold Ave 1 DN7 15 A3
Lavender Cl
6 Lincoln LN5 205 C2
10 Sleaford NG34 212 D2
Lavender Cres PE1 226 B8
Lavender Dr PE11 214 A2
Lavender Gr DN36 195 B7
Lavender Way
Bourne PE10 213 B7
6 Scunthorpe DN15 183 B3
1 Stamford PE9 218 D7
Lavender Wlk 1 HU5 179 C7
Lavenham Ct PE2 230 C7
Lavenham Gr LN6 205 A4
Lavenham Rd DN33 194 D7
Lavington Grange PE1 226 E6
Law Ct 1 PE11 214 B5
Lawley Cl LN2 203 B8
Lawn Ave
Peterborough PE1 226 A7
Skegness PE25 206 D2
Lawn Cres 1 PE25 206 D2
Lawn La NG33 152 F2
Lawn Wood Nature Reserve* NG33 152 E2
Lawns The
Collingham NG23 91 D5
9 Grimsby DN31 191 C7
Kingston upon Hull HU10 178 D7
18 Wisbech PE13 170 C1
Lawnswood HU13 178 D2
Lawrance Way 10 PE10 164 C8
Lawrence Ave PE7 231 C2
Lawrence Cl 1 LN6 205 B7
Lawrence La 3 NG34 120 C8
Lawrence Rd PE8 172 C1
Lawrence St 3 DN31 191 C8
Lawrence's Dro PE10 164 F8
Law's Cl PE6 174 C5
Lawson Ave
Grimsby DN31 191 B7
Peterborough PE2 231 D6
Lawson Leas 5 NG32 210 A5
Laxton Gdns 7 PE11 156 E8
Laxton Gr DN16 185 A2
Laxton La NG33 152 E7
Laycock Ave 2 DN10 39 C1
Laythorpe Ave PE25 206 D1
Laythorpe Gdns 2 LN4 207 C4
Lea Dr DN32 191 F5
Lea Frances Olive Anderson CE (Aided) Prim Sch DN21 53 A5
Lea Garth 6 DN17 29 D7
Lea Gdns PE3 225 F1
Lea Gr 2 LN3 83 C4
Lea Rd DN21 197 D2
Lea Rd W DN21 197 D1
Lea The NG34 121 B8
Lea View 2 PE9 163 C1
Leaburn Rd DN17 29 D7
Leadenham CE Prim Sch LN5 106 D3
Leading Dro PE7 233 D3
Leafere Way 1 PE13 170 B2
Leagate Rd
Coningsby LN4 207 F6
Langriville PE22 124 F8
Thornton Le Fen PE22 111 F1
Lealand Way PE21 209 A2
Leame Cl HU3 180 A7
Leamington Cl 2 DN16 183 C1
Leamlands La PE12 149 B1
Leas Cl DN37 194 E5
Leas Jun & Inf Sch The DN37 194 E5
Leas Rd NG34 122 F2
Leas The NG32 119 B1
Lease La DN40 12 D6
Leasingham La NG34 108 D1
Leaver Gate PE24 102 B2
Leaves Lake Dro PE11 155 E7
Lebanon Dr 3 PE13 170 E1
Lechler Cl LN2 68 D3
Leconfield Cl 7 LN6 204 C6
Leconfield Rd 16 LN6 204 C7
Ledbury Dr DN36 195 D7
Ledbury Rd PE3 225 C3
Ledham PE2 229 D4
Lee Ave
Heighington/Washingborough LN4 203 D1
Sutterton PE20 136 B2
Lee Fair Gdns 1 DN17 184 F2
Lee Rd Lincoln LN2 234 C4
Yaxley PE7 233 E4
Lee Smith St HU9 181 E7
Lee St LN11 198 B5
Leek Hill 18 DN15 9 A5
Leeming Cl 8 LN6 204 D6
Lees The PE6 217 E5
Lees Wlk HU3 180 A7
Legard Ave DN16 185 B6
Legard Dr HU10 178 F6
Legarde Ave HU4 179 C6
Legbourne Abbey LN11 61 F3
Legbourne Cl 1 LN1 201 D7
Legbourne Rd LN11 198 E3
Leggott Way 8 DN41 23 E6
Legion Cl 8 HU15 2 C5
Legsby Ave DN32 191 E5
Legsby Pl DN32 191 E4
Legsby Prim Sch LN8 58 A4
Legsby Rd LN8 57 E7
Leicester Cl LN4 203 C1
Leicester Gr NG31 210 D5
Leicester St
Kingston upon Hull HU3 180 D8
1 Sleaford NG34 212 D4
Leiden Fields 2 PE11 214 B2
Leighton PE2 230 C4
Leighton CP Sch PE2 230 C4
Leighton Cres 2 LN6 205 B6
Leighton Gr 1 DN33 191 C4
Leighton Wlk 4 PE12 159 D7
Leinsters Cl PE3 225 D3
Leiston Ct 21 PE6 175 A1
Lemon Wong La LN5 106 C3
Lenton Way 2 PE20 136 D6
Lenton's La
Friskney PE22 115 A5
Leverton PE22 126 F6
Leofric Ave PE10 213 B5
Leofric Cl 19 PE6 166 F1
Leonard Cres 2 DN15 182 F3
Leonard St 4 HU3 180 D8
Leopold Cl DN16 185 A6
Lerowe Rd PE13 170 E1
Leslie Manser Prim Sch The LN6 204 B7
Lessingham PE2 229 D4
Lestrange St DN35 192 C7
Lethbridge Rd PE4 221 D2
Lettwell Cres 1 PE25 206 D1
Levels La Blaxton DN9 26 A4
Misson DN10 39 A8
Leven Rd DN16 185 D6
Levens Wlk PE3 225 B3
Leverett Rd PE21 209 B4
Leverington Comm
Gorefield PE13 169 F1
Wisbech PE13 170 A1
Leverington Cty Prim Sch PE13 170 B2
Leverington Rd PE13 170 C1
Levers Cl PE21 209 F5
Leverstock Gn 33 DN7 14 D4
Leverton Rd DN22 52 B1
Levington St 2 DN31 189 C1
Lewes Gdns PE4 221 A3
Lewis Ave 13 LN12 77 A8
Lewis Rd
Cleethorpes DN35 192 D8
Coningsby LN4 207 D4
Lewis St
Gainsborough DN21 197 D3
Lincoln LN5 234 B1
Lexington Dr HU4 179 C5
Leyburn Rd LN6 204 F4
Leyden Cl 6 DN40 186 B4
Leyland Ave DN7 14 E4
Leys Cl NG32 210 B4
Leys Farm Cty Jun Sch DN17 184 F4
Leys La DN15 9 B6
Leys The
Cherry Willingham LN3 203 E6
Peterborough PE3 225 A1
Leytonstone La PE10 213 D2
Liberty La HU1 181 A6
Lichfield Ave
Peterborough PE4 220 F3
Scunthorpe DN17 184 C7
Lichfield Cl NG31 210 E4
Lichfield Rd
Bracebridge Heath LN4 81 A2
Grimsby DN32 192 B6
12 Hatfield DN7 14 D4
Liddell St HU2 180 E7
Lidgard Rd DN36 193 A1
Lidgate Cl PE2 230 C7
Lidgett Cl 10 DN20 30 F8
Lidgett The 7 DN9 27 D6
Lifeboat Ave PE25 206 D1
Lighter-than-air Rd
Cranwell & Byard's Leap NG34 107 C1
2 RAF Cranwell NG34 120 C8
Lighton Ave 4 PE20 136 C5
Lila Dr 1 PE11 145 B7
Lilac Ave DN16 183 C1
Lilac Cl Bourne PE10 213 B6
Wisbech PE13 170 E1
Lilac Rd
9 Elloughton-cum-Brough HU15 2 C5
Peterborough PE1 226 C7
Lilacwood Dr 5 NG31 210 F7
Lilburn Cl 5 NG34 121 B8
Lilburn Dr PE11 214 C6
Lilford Cl 5 LN2 202 E7
Lilford Rd LN2 202 E7
Lilley St 6 NG23 117 D3
Lillicrap Ct 2 LN1 234 B4
Lillys Rd LN2 234 B4
Lilywood Rd 12 DN20 19 D3
Limber Cl 2 DN21 53 A7
Limber Ct 6 DN34 191 A6
Limber Hill LN8 47 D4
Limber Rd
Humberside Airport DN39 22 A6
Swallow LN7 34 A7
Limber Vale DN34 191 A6
Limburg Dr 7 PE11 214 A2
Lime Ave
Scunthorpe DN16 19 A3
Wisbech PE13 170 D1
Lime Cl
Burgh Le Marsh PE24 102 D7
2 Langtoft PE6 164 F3
3 Old Leake PE22 114 A1
RAF Cranwell NG34 107 D1
Lime Cres LN5 205 C1
Lime Ct PE11 214 E3
Lime Gr 2 Boston PE21 209 C2
2 Bottesford NG13 128 A5
Caythorpe NG32 119 C7
Cherry Willingham/Reepham LN3 203 D5
9 Goxhill DN19 12 A8
Grantham NG31 211 C6
Holbeach PE12 215 D3
Holton le Clay DN36 195 D1
Humberston DN36 36 C7
7 Ingoldmells PE25 90 D3
Louth LN11 198 C7
Scunthorpe DN16 185 B7
Lime Kiln Way LN2 202 C4
Lime St Grimsby DN31 191 C8
Kingston upon Hull HU8 181 A8
3 Sutton Bridge PE12 160 F4
Lime Tree Ave
Gainsborough DN21 197 D5
Kingston upon Hull HU13 178 F2
2 Market Deeping PE6 217 A6
20 Metheringham LN4 95 C4
Peterborough PE1 225 F4
Lime Tree Cl
1 Collingham NG23 91 D4
6 Fulbeck NG32 106 C1
6 Lincoln LN6 204 E8
Lime Tree Gr 4 DN8 15 A8
Lime Tree Paddock 2 LN2 68 F4
Limedale View 2 DN3 14 A3
Limelands 2 LN2 234 C3
Limes The
7 Beckingham DN10 40 A1
Castor PE5 223 F1
4 Stallingborough DN41 23 D6
12 Wittering PE8 172 B1
Limetree Ave DN33 191 C3
Limetree Cl
13 Sleaford NG34 212 D2
Yaxley PE7 233 F7
Limetree Wlk 1 NG34 122 E2
Limewalk PE12 216 C6
Linchfield Cl PE6 217 E5
Linchfield Prim Sch PE6 217 D5
Linchfield Rd PE6 217 D6
Lincoln Ass Rm* LN2 234 B3
Lincoln Ave LN6 205 C8
Lincoln Castle* LN1 234 A3
Lincoln Castle Way DN19 4 D2
Lincoln Cath* LN2 234 B3
Lincoln Christs Hospl Sch LN2 202 B6
Lincoln Cl
4 Crowle DN17 16 D7
Grantham NG31 210 D4
5 Market Deeping PE6 217 A6
Lincoln Cres 2 DN21 42 F8
Lincoln Cty Hospl LN2 202 C4
Lincoln Dr
27 Barton-upon-Humber DN18 10 F8
30 Caistor LN7 33 B4
3 Scampton Airfield LN1 67 F5
5 Waddington LN5 94 A7
24 Winterton DN15 9 A5
Lincoln Gate DN36 48 D5
Lincoln Gdns DN16 185 A6
Lincoln Gdns Infants Sch DN16 185 B7
Lincoln Gdns Jun Sch DN16 185 A6
Lincoln Gn
Kingston upon Hull HU4 179 C7
Skegness PE25 206 B5
Lincoln La Boston PE21 208 E5
Holbeach PE12 147 D5
Kettlethorpe LN1 65 F3
Osgodby LN8 44 F2
Thorpe on the Hill LN6 92 E8
Lincoln Minst Prep Sch (Private) LN2 234 C3
Lincoln Minst Prep Sch LN2 234 B3
Lincoln Minst Sch Pre Prep Sch LN2 234 B4
Lincoln Nuffield Hospl The LN2 234 B4
Lincoln Rd
Bassingham LN5 92 F2
10 Binbrook Tech Pk LN8 47 B6
Brant Broughton LN5 105 F5
Brant Broughton & Stragglethorpe LN5 106 A5
Canwick LN4 81 B3
Caythorpe NG32 119 B6
Cleethorpes DN35 192 C5
Deeping Gate PE6 217 C3
Digby LN4 108 D6
Doddington & Whisby LN6 204 A6
Dunholme LN2 68 D6
Dunston LN4 95 B5
Faldingworth LN8 56 F3
Fenton LN1 65 E3
Fiskerton LN3 203 F4
1 Glinton PE6 220 C8
Heighington/Washingborough LN4 203 A2
Holton cum Beckering LN8 70 B7
Honington NG32 119 C2
Horncastle LN9 199 A4
Ingham LN1 54 F2
1 Leasingham NG34 121 B8
3 Leasingham NG34 121 B7
Lincoln LN6 204 F1
Louth LN11 61 B8
Metheringham LN4 95 C4
Middle Rasen LN8 57 B7
Moorland Prison DN7 26 A8
Nettleham LN2 68 B1
Newark-on-Trent NG24 104 A6
Northborough PE6 217 D1
Peterborough PE6 220 D5
Ruskington NG34 108 D2
Saxilby with Ingleby LN1 66 E1
4 Skegness PE25 206 C3
Skegness PE25 206 B4
Skellingthorpe LN6 200 B4
Sleaford NG34 212 B7
Stamford PE9 219 C7
West Barkwith LN8 71 A7
Lincoln Rd Bridge NG24 104 A5
Lincoln Rd Nocton LN4 95 A7
Lincoln Sch of Science & Tech LN5 205 E6
Lincoln St
Gainsborough DN21 197 C5
Kingston upon Hull HU2 180 F8
Lincoln Sta LN5 234 B1
Lincoln Way 1 PE11 214 C5
Lincoln's Ave PE12 168 C2
Lincolnshire Aviation Heritage Ctr* PE23 99 F5
Lincolnshire Coast Light Rly* PE25 90 D1
Lincolnshire Coll of Ag & Hort NG32 119 D7
Lincolnshire Rd Transport Mus* LN6 204 D5
Lincolnshire Showground* LN1 67 E4
Linda Cres LN11 198 B4
Lindale Gdns DN16 185 C7
Linden Cl 16 DN7 14 D4
Linden Ct PE11 214 E5
Linden Dene 1 LN6 204 D1
Linden Dr PE24 102 D7
Linden Rd LN9 199 C4
Linden Rise PE10 213 D7
Linden Terr DN21 197 D3
Linden Way
Boston PE21 209 A7
Pinchbeck PE11 144 D1
Linden Wlk LN11 198 C4
Lindens Cl PE13 177 A3
Lindholme 5 DN21 29 C3
Lindholme Bank Rd DN7 15 B1
Lindholme Rd LN6 204 D5
Lindis Rd PE21 209 C5
Lindisfarne Ave DN36 195 B6

Lindisfarne Rd PE6 ... 175 A1
Lindisfarne Way NG31 ... 210 E5
Lindley St DN16 ... 185 A6
Lindrick Cl 4 NG31 ... 211 D7
Lindrick Rd 6 DN7 ... 14 F3
Lindrick Wlk 5 DN37 ... 194 C4
Lindridge Wlk PE3 ... 225 A2
Lindsey Ave PE6 ... 217 A6
Lindsey Cl
6 Bourne PE10 ... 213 C5
Peterborough PE4 ... 221 B1
Lindsey Ct 12 DN9 ... 27 E6
Lindsey Dr Crowle DN17 ... 16 D8
6 Healing DN41 ... 24 A5
Holton le Clay DN36 ... 195 C2
Lindsey Lower Sch DN35 ... 192 D6
Lindsey Pl HU4 ... 179 D6
Lindsey Rd
Cleethorpes DN35 ... 192 F4
Stamford PE9 ... 219 C6
4 Uffington PE9 ... 172 C6
Lindsey Rise 3 DN33 ... 194 F8
Lindsey St 2 DN16 ... 183 C2
Lindsey Upper Sch DN35 ... 192 D4
Lindsey Way LN11 ... 198 D4
Lindum Ave
3 Immingham DN40 ... 186 B3
Lincoln LN2 ... 234 C3
Lindum Cotts PE13 ... 170 B2
Lindum Gr
Chapel St Leonard PE24 ... 90 E7
2 Crowle DN17 ... 16 C7
Lindum Rd
Cleethorpes DN35 ... 193 A4
Lincoln LN2 ... 234 B3
Lindum Sq 6 PE25 ... 206 B5
Lindum St DN15 ... 183 B3
Lindum Terr LN2 ... 234 C3
Lindum Way 9 PE11 ... 134 F2
Lindum Wlk 1 LN7 ... 32 A4
Linecroft La DN10 ... 40 B4
Ling Garth PE1 ... 226 B8
Ling House La DN7 ... 14 A5
Ling La NG33 ... 152 C5
Ling Moor Prim Sch LN6 ... 204 E3
Linga La LN5 ... 93 A3
Lingfield Cl 6 LN1 ... 66 D3
Linghall La LN4 ... 111 E5
Lings La DN7 ... 14 D3
Lingwood Pk
5 Peterborough PE3 ... 225 A1
Peterborough PE3 ... 230 A8
Link Rd PE1 ... 225 F3
Link The
Bracebridge Heath LN4 ... 205 F4
Kingston upon Hull HU4 ... 179 C5
2 Leasingham NG34 ... 121 B8
Louth LN11 ... 198 E5
2 Navenby/Wellingore LN5 ... 107 A7
Link Way PE11 ... 214 E4
Linkage Com Trust Sch PE23 ... 88 D2
Links Ave 2 LN12 ... 64 B5
Links Cres
8 Skegness PE25 ... 103 E4
4 Skegness PE25 ... 103 E4
Links Rd DN35 ... 193 A3
Linkside PE3 ... 220 F1
Linkway 7 DN7 ... 14 F3
Linley Cl 4 NG23 ... 91 D4
Linley Dr PE21 ... 208 E2
Linnaeus St HU3 ... 180 C6
Linnet PE2 ... 229 D6
Linnet Cl
7 Market Deeping PE6 ... 217 C5
Scunthorpe DN15 ... 182 D6
Linnet Dr PE10 ... 143 A3
Linnet Way 11 NG34 ... 212 B3
Linthorpe Gr HU10 ... 178 E8
Linton 21 HU15 ... 2 C6
Linton Cl PE22 ... 137 E7
Linton Rise 3 DN15 ... 8 A4
Linton St 5 LN5 ... 201 F1
Linwood Ave 5 DN33 ... 194 F8
Linwood Cl
Gainsborough DN21 ... 197 F3
9 Sleaford NG34 ... 212 C6
Linwood Rd
Lissington LN8 ... 57 D3
Martin LN4 ... 96 B3
Liquorpond St 11 PE21 ... 208 F4
Lisburn Cl 7 LN5 ... 205 D2
Lisburn Gr DN33 ... 191 D2
Lisle Marsden CE Prim Sch DN32 ... 191 E4
Lissett Cl 6 LN6 ... 204 B6
Lissington Cl 2 LN2 ... 201 F7
Lissington Rd
Gainsborough DN21 ... 197 E3
Wickenby LN3 ... 57 C1
Lister Rd
Peterborough PE1 ... 225 F7
Scunthorpe DN15 ... 182 C3
Lister St Grimsby DN31 ... 191 B8
Kingston upon Hull HU1 ... 180 E5
Listoft La PE24 ... 89 F7
Litchfield Cl PE7 ... 233 F5
Little Bargate St LN5 ... 205 E8
Little Belt The DN21 ... 197 D7
Little Bytham Rd
Castle Bytham NG33 ... 152 E1

Little Bytham Rd *continued*
Counthorpe & Creeton NG33 ... 153 A2
Little Casterton Rd PE9 ... 218 F8
Little Cl Edenham PE10 ... 153 D5
15 Eye PE6 ... 175 A1
Little Coates Rd DN34 ... 190 E4
Little Comm PE12 ... 215 B7
Little Dog Dro PE12 ... 158 C1
Little Dowgate PE13 ... 170 B1
Little Dro PE20 ... 124 C2
Little Gate La LN4 ... 82 A1
Little George St HU8 ... 181 A8
Little Gonerby CE (Aided) Infant's Sch NG31 ... 211 B5
Little Grimsby La LN11 ... 49 A1
Little Hale Dro NG34 ... 133 F8
Little Hale Rd NG34 ... 122 E1
Little Holme Rd PE34 ... 161 C2
Little John St 4 DN34 ... 191 B7
Little Johns Cl PE3 ... 224 F3
Little La Broomfleet HU15 ... 1 C6
6 Collingham NG23 ... 91 C4
Gringley on the Hill DN10 ... 39 C1
Louth LN11 ... 198 C5
Surfleet PE11 ... 145 B3
5 Welbourn LN5 ... 106 E5
Whaplode PE12 ... 158 A5
Wrawby DN20 ... 196 F6
Little London PE12 ... 216 D6
Little Marsh La PE12 ... 159 B7
Little Mason St 3 HU1 ... 181 A7
Little Merebalk La LN9 ... 86 B2
Little Michael St 2 DN31 ... 191 B7
Little Northfields PE9 ... 172 E4
Little Ramper PE13 ... 170 B4
Little S St 16 LN11 ... 198 B5
Little Side Rd PE20 ... 135 E8
Little Thorpe La LN6 ... 79 F1
Little Wlk DN21 ... 40 B5
Littlebeck Cl HU3 ... 180 A7
Littlebeck Rd 3 DN36 ... 36 C8
Littleborough La DN21 ... 53 A1
Littleborough Rd DN22 ... 52 C2
Littlebury Gdns PE12 ... 215 C2
Littlechild Dr 4 PE13 ... 170 B2
Littlecoates Prim Sch DN31 ... 188 D1
Littlefair Rd 6 HU9 ... 5 D8
Littlefield La
4 Grimsby DN34 ... 191 A6
Marshchapel DN36 ... 37 B2
Littlemeer PE2 ... 229 F4
Littlemoors La PE22 ... 113 A3
Littleport La
6 Sibsey PE22 ... 113 B1
3 Sibsey PE22 ... 113 B1
Littlewood Rd DN8 ... 15 B8
Littleworth Dro
Deeping St Nicholas PE11 ... 156 D1
Heckington NG34 ... 122 F4
Spalding PE11 ... 156 E2
Sutton St Edmund PE12 ... 176 F8
Livermore Gn PE4 ... 220 E6
Liverpool Dr LN6 ... 200 B2
Liverpool St HU3 ... 180 A3
Livesey Rd DN36 ... 48 E6
Lloyds Ave DN17 ... 184 F8
Lobelia Dr 1 DN17 ... 185 A1
Lock Hill 30 DN8 ... 15 A8
Lock La DN8 ... 15 A8
Lock Rd Alvingham LN11 ... 49 F2
North Coates DN36 ... 37 A3
Lockham Gate PE22 ... 114 B2
Lockhill DN31 ... 189 A2
Locking Cl 17 LN6 ... 204 C6
Locking Garth LN11 ... 49 D5
Locks Cl PE6 ... 174 A8
Locksley Christian Sch LN11 ... 62 C6
Locksley Cl
6 Boston PE21 ... 208 E7
4 North Somercotes LN11 ... 50 F7
Locksley Way 5 LN11 ... 50 F7
Lockton Cl 2 PE20 ... 135 B7
Lockton Gr 1 HU5 ... 179 D8
Lockwood Bank DN9 ... 27 E6
Lockwood Cl 12 DN8 ... 15 B8
Lockwood Ct 1 DN15 ... 182 E4
Lockwood St HU2 ... 180 F8
Loder Ave PE3 ... 224 F2
Lodge Ave 22 DN18 ... 10 F8
Lodge Cl 10 Brough HU15 ... 2 C7
Kingston upon Hull HU13 ... 178 F1
6 Welton/Dunholme LN2 ... 68 D7
Lodge Ct 37 DN7 ... 14 D4
Lodge Dr LN6 ... 105 A8
Lodge La
Flixborough DN15 ... 8 B2
Kirk Bramwith DN7 ... 14 A8
Nettleham LN2 ... 68 D1
Upton DN21 ... 53 D5
Lodge Rd Bourne PE10 ... 213 C7
4 Coningsby LN4 ... 207 A5
Scunthorpe DN15 ... 182 C2
Tattershall Thorpe LN10 ... 97 E3
Lodge Way NG31 ... 211 A6
Lodington Ct 5 LN9 ... 199 D3
Loganberry Dr HU4 ... 179 C4
Lomax Dr 2 NG34 ... 212 C6
Lombard St
2 Grimsby DN34 ... 191 A7
Kingston upon Hull HU1 ... 180 E6
Lombardy Dr PE1 ... 226 B8

Lomond Gr DN36 ... 36 C8
Lomond Rd HU5 ... 179 E8
Londesborough St HU3 ... 180 C7
Londesborough Way
19 Metheringham LN4 ... 95 D4
13 Metheringham LN4 ... 95 D4
London Rd
Boston PE21 ... 208 E1
Bracebridge Heath LN4 ... 205 F5
Frampton PE20 ... 136 D7
Grantham NG31 ... 211 B3
Haugham LN11 ... 74 A7
Long Sutton PE12 ... 216 C4
Louth LN11 ... 198 C3
Newark-on-Trent NG24 ... 104 B2
Osbournby NG34 ... 132 C5
Peterborough PE2 ... 226 A1
Sleaford NG34 ... 212 B1
Spalding PE11 ... 214 C2
Tathwell LN11 ... 61 C2
Wansford PE8 ... 222 B2
Yaxley PE7 ... 233 C5
Londonthorpe La NG31 ... 211 E8
Long Acre 1 LN12 ... 64 B4
Long Bennington CE Prim Sch NG23 ... 117 D3
Long Cl La LN3 ... 82 B7
Long Cswy PE1 ... 226 A2
Long Dro Bourne PE10 ... 155 B1
Gosberton PE11 ... 144 B6
Rippingale PE10 ... 143 D3
Thurlby PE10 ... 164 E7
Walcott LN4 ... 109 E8
Wisbech St Mary PE13 ... 177 D4
Long Farm La DN22 ... 52 E2
Long Field Dr 2 DN3 ... 14 A1
Long Field Rd 23 DN3 ... 14 A2
Long Gates LN11 ... 51 A1
Long Hedge La
Greetham with Somersby LN9 ... 86 C5
Swaby LN13 ... 74 E4
Long Hollow NG33 ... 131 C3
Long La
Aubourn Haddington & South Hykeham LN6 ... 93 B7
Barnby in the Willows NG24 ... 104 F4
Fleet PE12 ... 168 B3
Ingham LN1 ... 54 E2
Leadenham LN5 ... 107 A2
Moulton PE12 ... 157 E5
Mumby LN13 ... 76 E2
Redmile NG32 ... 128 A1
2 Westborough & Dry Doddington NG23 ... 117 F3
Willoughton DN21 ... 42 E3
Long Leys Rd LN1 ... 201 C4
Long Pasture 5 PE4 ... 220 F5
Long Rd
1 Scunthorpe DN15 ... 182 F4
Terrington St Clement PE34 ... 161 F5
3 Tydd St Mary PE13 ... 170 C8
Long St 2 Foston NG32 ... 117 F1
Great Gonerby NG31 ... 129 E5
Long Sutton Butterfly Pk* PE12 ... 216 D6
Long Sutton Cty Prim Sch PE12 ... 216 B5
Long Wood La LN4 ... 95 C2
Long Wood Rd DN21 ... 41 A1
Longcliffe Rd NG31 ... 211 A8
Longcroft Dr 1 NG34 ... 107 C1
Longdales Rd LN2 ... 201 F6
Longden St HU3 ... 180 A7
Longdon Cl 6 PE12 ... 160 E4
Longfield Rd DN34 ... 190 E4
Longhead La PE14 ... 170 D3
Longhedge Dro PE20 ... 134 E5
Longhorn Cl DN37 ... 194 B4
Longhurst Gdns PE21 ... 208 D7
Longlands LN13 ... 63 D3
Longleat Dr LN11 ... 198 A7
Longmeadow Rise 18 DN41 ... 23 A4
Longmeadows PE10 ... 154 B7
Longmeadows Dr DN37 ... 23 F2
Longthorpe Cl 3 PE3 ... 225 A2
Longthorpe CP Sch PE3 ... 225 A2
Longthorpe Gn PE3 ... 225 B1
Longthorpe House Mews 11 PE3 ... 224 F2
Longthorpe Parkway PE3 ... 225 C1
Longton Rd
18 Kirk Sandall DN3 ... 14 A3
4 Kirk Sandall DN3 ... 14 A2
Longueville Ct PE2 ... 230 B5
Longwater PE2 ... 230 B6
Lonsdale Cl 20 DN36 ... 36 D8
Lonsdale Gr PE10 ... 213 E6
Lonsdale Pl 3 LN5 ... 201 F1
Lonsdale Rd PE9 ... 218 E5
Lonsdale St 5 HU3 ... 180 A6
Loop La 1 PE12 ... 157 F7
Loosegate Rd PE12 ... 158 A8
Lopham La DN37 ... 34 F8
Lord Dr 4 NG31 ... 129 E5
Lord St
Gainsborough DN21 ... 197 C4
Grimsby DN31 ... 191 B8
4 Sleaford NG34 ... 212 C3
17 Stainforth DN7 ... 14 C6
Lord's La 6 NG33 ... 151 A8

Lords La 19 DN19 ... 11 D8
Lornas Field PE7 ... 230 D2
Lorne St LN5 ... 234 C1
Losecoat Cl 1 PE9 ... 219 D7
Lotus Cl 7 LN5 ... 93 F7
Lough Rd LN9 ... 72 F1
Loughborough Univ of Peterborough PE1 ... 226 A3
Louis Dr HU5 ... 179 B8
Louis St HU3 ... 180 C8
Louisberg Rd DN21 ... 54 F8
Louth Cty Hospl LN11 ... 198 B6
Louth Mus* LN11 ... 198 B5
Louth Playgoers Riverhead Theatre* LN11 ... 198 D7
Louth Rd
East Barkwith LN8 ... 58 E1
Fotherby LN11 ... 49 A3
Grimsby DN33 ... 191 D1
Holton Le Clay DN36 ... 36 A4
1 Holton le Clay DN36 ... 195 D2
2 Holton le Clay DN36 ... 195 D1
Horncastle LN9 ... 199 C5
New Waltham DN36 ... 195 B5
Skidbrooke with Saltfleet Haven LN11 ... 51 C4
2 West Ashby LN9 ... 85 E7
Wragby LN8 ... 70 D5
Lovat Cl HU3 ... 180 D5
Love La
Caythorpe NG32 ... 119 C7
Gainsborough DN21 ... 197 C6
Louth LN11 ... 198 A5
Spalding PE11 ... 214 E3
9 Sutterton PE20 ... 136 A2
Wrangle PE22 ... 114 C4
Loveden Ct DN35 ... 193 A3
Loveden View 6 NG32 ... 119 B7
Lovell Rd DN17 ... 184 E3
Lovell Way PE34 ... 161 F2
Lovers La PE5 ... 222 F2
Love's Hill Castor PE5 ... 223 F1
Peterborough PE5 ... 224 A1
Love's La PE20 ... 135 C8
Loves La LE15 ... 162 A1
Lovett St DN35 ... 189 E1
Low Burgage DN15 ... 2 B1
Low Church Rd 2 LN8 ... 57 C8
Low Comm La HU15 ... 2 D4
Low Cross St 6 DN17 ... 16 D8
Low Deeps La DN10 ... 26 C1
Low Farm Dr NG34 ... 142 C8
Low Field La HU15 ... 2 E5
Low Fields Ave 1 PE11 ... 214 F4
Low Fulney Est PE12 ... 157 C5
Low Garth DN17 ... 184 F2
Low Gate
Friskney PE22 ... 115 A6
Gosberton PE11 ... 145 C7
Marshchapel DN36 ... 37 C1
Moulton PE12 ... 146 C1
Surfleet PE11 ... 145 C3
Tydd St Mary PE13 ... 160 A1
Low Gate La 6 PE20 ... 135 A4
Low Holland La DN22 ... 52 C2
Low La Croft PE24 ... 102 D6
Holbeach PE12 ... 215 F4
Kirk Bramwith DN7 ... 14 A6
Middle Rasen LN8 ... 45 C1
Terrington St Clement PE34 ... 161 E3
Wrangle PE22 ... 114 B3
Low Levels Bank DN8 ... 15 D4
Low Leys Rd 6 DN17 ... 184 E3
Low Mill La PE20 ... 136 E1
Low Moor Rd LN6 ... 204 E5
Low Pk La LN4 ... 81 F4
Low Rd Barrowby NG32 ... 210 A4
Besthorpe NG23 ... 91 C7
Blyborough DN21 ... 42 E6
Croft PE24 ... 102 F5
Crowland PE6 ... 175 A8
Friskney PE22 ... 114 F4
Grantham NG31 ... 211 C8
Harmston LN5 ... 93 D6
Healing DN41 ... 23 F5
Holbeach PE12 ... 147 F2
Marshchapel DN36 ... 37 A1
Osgodby LN8 ... 45 B3
South Kyme LN4 ... 123 B8
Spalding PE11 ... 214 F4
Wainfleet St Mary PE24 ... 102 C1
Walpole Cross Keys PE34 ... 161 D3
Worlaby DN20 ... 20 C8
Wyberton PE21 ... 136 E7
Low St Beckingham DN10 ... 40 A1
Billingborough NG34 ... 133 B1
Collingham NG23 ... 91 C4
Dunham-on-Trent NG22 ... 65 A1
Harby NG23 ... 79 B5
Haxey DN9 ... 27 D2
North Ferriby HU14 ... 3 A4
5 South Ferriby DN18 ... 10 A7
Winterton DN15 ... 9 A5
Low Thorpe Rd LN3 ... 83 D1
Low Toynton Cl LN9 ... 199 D5
Low Toynton Rd LN9 ... 199 D5
Low Wood La LN6 ... 91 F8
Lowbridge La 4 PE11 ... 145 C6
Lowcroft Ave 3 DN9 ... 27 D2
Lowcroft Cl 4 DN9 ... 27 D2
Lower Church Rd LN6 ... 200 B5
Lower High St 9 LN5 ... 93 F7
Lower Kenyon St 10 DN8 ... 15 A8
Lower Rd NG32 ... 119 A5
Lower Spring St 1 DN31 ... 189 A1

Lowerdale 27 HU15 ... 2 C6
Lowfield Cl
4 Barnby Dun DN3 ... 14 A3
31 Kirton in Lindsey DN21 ... 30 B1
Lowfield La
Balderton NG24 ... 104 A1
Belchford LN9 ... 73 C2
Lowfield Rd HU10 ... 178 E5
Lowfields Inf Sch LN5 ... 205 C2
Lowfields Jun Sch LN5 ... 205 C2
Lowfields La
Allington NG32 ... 128 F7
Butterwick PE22 ... 126 E5
Lowfields Rd PE22 ... 126 E6
Lowgate Fleet PE12 ... 159 C8
Kingston upon Hull HU1 ... 181 A6
Lutton PE12 ... 160 A8
Lowgate Ave 7 PE20 ... 135 A4
Lowgate Cres PE12 ... 159 E8
Lowgate Rd
Ashby with Scremby PE23 ... 88 D2
Conisholme LN11 ... 50 C5
Hogsthorpe PE24 ... 90 B8
Lowick Gdns PE3 ... 225 C5
Lowmoor La LN9 ... 85 C3
Lowther Gdns PE4 ... 221 B2
Lowther St HU3 ... 180 A7
Loxley PE4 ... 220 E4
Loxley Gn HU4 ... 179 B7
Loxley Way 6 HU15 ... 2 D5
Loyd St HU10 ... 178 F6
Lucan Cl 18 PE22 ... 113 B1
Lucas Ct 4 DN41 ... 23 F5
Lucerne Cl PE11 ... 214 B6
Lucetta Gdns 9 PE11 ... 214 B5
Lucy Twr St LN1 ... 234 A2
Ludborough Pk DN36 ... 48 E6
Ludborough Rd
13 North Thoresby DN36 ... 36 B1
North Thoresby DN36 ... 48 D8
Ludborough Sta DN36 ... 48 F6
Ludborough Way 6 DN35 ... 192 F3
Luddington & Garthorpe Prim Sch DN17 ... 7 C3
Luddington Rd
Garthorpe & Fockerby DN17 ... 7 E5
1 Peterborough PE4 ... 221 B1
Ludford CE Sch LN8 ... 59 B8
Ludford Cres DN21 ... 197 E3
Ludford Dr 9 LN6 ... 205 A7
Ludford Rd LN8 ... 47 C4
Ludford St DN32 ... 191 E6
Ludgate Cl 2 DN37 ... 194 D4
Ludlow Ave DN34 ... 191 A7
Ludlow Gdns 4 PE11 ... 145 A8
Ludlow Pl DN35 ... 192 E5
Ludney La LN11 ... 50 C6
Luffenham Cl 4 PE9 ... 218 E5
Lulworth Ave HU4 ... 179 A3
Lumley Ave PE25 ... 206 D3
Lumley Cres 3 PE25 ... 206 D4
Lumley Pl 2 LN5 ... 201 F1
Lumley Rd PE25 ... 206 C3
Lunds The HU10 ... 178 C6
Lundy Ct DN40 ... 186 C2
Luneburg Pl 1 DN15 ... 182 C5
Luneburg Way DN15 ... 182 C6
Lunedale Rd DN16 ... 185 D5
Lunn La 5 NG23 ... 91 C4
Lunn's Cres 21 DN18 ... 10 E8
Lupin Rd LN2 ... 202 C8
Lurgan Cl LN5 ... 205 D3
Lusher Way DN21 ... 41 A1
Luton Cl
1 Birchwood LN6 ... 200 B1
1 Birchwood LN6 ... 204 B8
Luton Rd HU5 ... 179 F8
Lutton Bank PE12 ... 148 D1
Lutton Garnsgate PE12 ... 216 A4
Lutton Gate Rd PE12 ... 168 E4
Lutton Gowts PE12 ... 216 D7
Lutton Gr PE3 ... 225 C6
Lutton Lodge La PE12 ... 149 B2
Lych Gate 10 DN20 ... 19 D3
Lydbrook Rd DN16 ... 183 A1
Lydd Cl LN6 ... 204 C6
Lydford Rd DN40 ... 186 D3
Lydia Ct 3 DN40 ... 186 A4
Lygon St DN16 ... 183 B1
Lyle Cl 4 LN12 ... 64 A4
Lyme Wlk 3 PE3 ... 225 C4
Lymington Garth HU4 ... 179 A3
Lymn Bank PE24 ... 102 C4
Lymn Ct 2 NG31 ... 210 E2
Lyn Ellis Cl 2 PE21 ... 209 C4
Lynchwood PE2 ... 229 C5
Lyndale Ave 17 DN3 ... 14 A1
Lyndale Pk PE2 ... 229 C6
Lynden Ave NG31 ... 210 E8
Lyndhurst Ave
3 Grimsby DN33 ... 191 D3
Skegness PE25 ... 206 B5
Lyndhurst Ct 2 PE25 ... 206 B5
Lyndis Wlk PE12 ... 215 E1
Lyndon Bsns Pk LN6 ... 204 B5
Lyndon Cres LN11 ... 198 D8
Lyndon Way
Louth LN11 ... 198 D8
Stamford PE9 ... 218 E5
Lyneham Cl LN6 ... 204 B7
Lynmouth Cl 1 LN6 ... 205 A1
Lynmouth Dr DN17 ... 184 C8

Lynn Rd
Walpole Cross Keys PE34 . . . 161 C3
Walsoken PE13 . . . 170 E2
Lynnwell Cl PE25 . . . 206 A6
Lynton Ave HU4 . . . 179 B3
Lynton Cl 1 DN15 . . . 182 D4
Lynton Prep Sch DN15 . . . 183 A4
Lynton Rd PE1 . . . 225 F6
Lynton Rise DN35 . . . 192 E4
Lynwood Ave HU10 . . . 178 E6
Lyric Cl 1 HU3 . . . 180 C5
Lysaghts Way DN15 . . . 8 C1
Lytham Cl
8 Heighington/Washingborough LN4 . . . 203 D1
Londonthorpe & Harrowby without NG31 . . . 211 E7
Lytham Dr DN37 . . . 194 C3
Lythemere PE2 . . . 230 C4
Lytton St LN2 . . . 234 C2

M

Mablethorpe Com Prim Sch LN12 . . . 64 A4
Mablethorpe Rd
North Coates DN36 . . . 37 A3
Theddlethorpe St Helen LN12 . . . 63 F5
Macaulay Dr
Lincoln LN2 . . . 202 B6
Newark-on-Trent NG24 . . . 104 B3
Macaulay Jun & Inf Sch DN31 . . . 191 B8
Macaulay St DN31 . . . 191 B8
Mace Rd PE2 . . . 231 D5
Machray Pl DN35 . . . 192 D7
Mackender Ct 4 DN16 . . . 185 C6
Mackenzie Pl 5 DN40 . . . 186 B3
Maclure St DN31 . . . 189 B2
Macmillan Ave LN6 . . . 204 C2
Macphail Cres LN1 . . . 66 E2
Maddison La PE23 . . . 88 B3
Madeley St HU3 . . . 180 C4
Madely Cl 3 LN9 . . . 199 D3
Maffit Rd PE5 . . . 223 D3
Magdalen Cl 4 DN16 . . . 185 B4
Magdalen Rd PE24 . . . 102 D2
Magdalene Rd DN34 . . . 190 F5
Magee Rd PE4 . . . 221 B1
Magellan Dr 9 PE23 . . . 101 A8
Magellan Way PE11 . . . 214 C2
Magna Cres 15 NG34 . . . 122 E2
Magna Mile LN8 . . . 59 B8
Magnolia Ave PE3 . . . 225 A2
Magnolia Cl LN4 . . . 81 D2
Magnolia Dr 5 DN36 . . . 195 D1
Magnolia Rd NG34 . . . 212 D2
Magnolia Rise 4 DN40 . . . 186 C3
Magnolia Way DN16 . . . 185 B7
Magpie Cl LN6 . . . 200 A3
Magpie La DN22 . . . 52 C1
Magrath Ct 1 DN20 . . . 196 C3
Maiden Cl 1 DN40 . . . 186 A4
Maiden Ct 19 LN1 . . . 66 D2
Maiden Gr 2 NG34 . . . 212 E3
Maiden La
Hogsthorpe PE24 . . . 90 B7
11 Stamford PE9 . . . 219 C5
Maiden Well La 5 LN5 . . . 107 A8
Maidens Rd 10 PE20 . . . 136 A2
Maidenwell La 11 LN7 . . . 32 A4
Maidment Dr LN1 . . . 201 C7
Maidwell Way DN34 . . . 190 C4
Main App Rd DN16 . . . 183 C3
Main Ave
Bracebridge Heath LN4 . . . 205 F3
Scunthorpe DN17 . . . 184 C6
Main Rd Anwick NG34 . . . 109 B1
Ashby cum Fenby DN37 . . . 35 D3
Barkston NG32 . . . 130 B8
Belchford LN9 . . . 73 A2
Benniworth LN8 . . . 59 B1
Bourne PE10 . . . 154 C5
Carrington PE22 . . . 112 C7
Collyweston PE9 . . . 171 B1
2 Donington on Bain LN11 . . . 59 E1
Dunsby PE10 . . . 143 B2
East Kirkby PE23 . . . 99 F5
Etton PE6 . . . 173 E5
Friskney Eaudike PE22 . . . 115 C6
Gedney PE12 . . . 159 D7
Goulceby LN11 . . . 72 D6
Gunby & Stainby NG33 . . . 151 B5
Haconby PE10 . . . 154 C8
Heighington/Washingborough LN4 . . . 203 B2
Leadenham LN5 . . . 106 D3
Little Hale NG34 . . . 122 E1
Little Steeping PE23 . . . 101 D6
Long Bennington NG23 . . . 117 D3
Nocton LN4 . . . 95 B7
North Willingham LN8 . . . 58 D7
Parson Drove PE13 . . . 177 F8
3 Potterhanworth LN4 . . . 82 B1
Quadring PE11 . . . 134 F1
Saltfleet LN11 . . . 51 C4
Saltfleetby LN11 . . . 51 B1
2 Sibsey PE22 . . . 113 B1
Spilsby PE23 . . . 87 F1
Stickford PE22 . . . 100 B3
Stickney PE22 . . . 113 B5
Tallington PE9 . . . 172 E6
Thurlby PE10 . . . 164 D8
Toynton All Saints PE23 . . . 100 F6
Main Rd *continued*
Tydd St Giles PE13 . . . 170 C8
2 Tydd St Mary PE13 . . . 170 C8
7 Uffington PE9 . . . 172 C6
Utterby LN11 . . . 48 F5
West Keal PE23 . . . 100 C3
Wigtoft PE20 . . . 135 E3
Wisbech St Mary PE13 . . . 177 A2
Withern with Stain LN11 . . . 62 E1
Main Ridge E PE21 . . . 209 A5
Main Ridge W 9 PE21 . . . 209 A5
Main St (Southorpe) PE9 . . . 172 E2
Main St Ailsworth PE5 . . . 223 D2
Ancaster NG32 . . . 119 F3
Ashby De La Launde & Bloxholm LN4 . . . 108 B5
Barlings LN3 . . . 69 C3
Barnack PE9 . . . 172 D3
Barrowby NG32 . . . 210 A5
Baston PE6 . . . 164 E4
4 Bishop Norton LN8 . . . 43 D3
Bonby DN20 . . . 10 C2
Boothby Graffoe LN5 . . . 94 A2
Boothby Pagnell NG33 . . . 140 F5
Bottesford NG13 . . . 128 C4
Broomfleet HU15 . . . 1 C6
Brough HU15 . . . 2 C6
Buckminster NG33 . . . 150 E5
Cadney DN20 . . . 31 E6
Careby Aunby & Holywell PE9 . . . 163 B7
Carlton Scroop NG32 . . . 119 C4
Castor PE5 . . . 223 D3
Claypole NG23 . . . 117 F7
Clipsham LE15 . . . 162 C7
Crowle DN17 . . . 16 E6
Croxton Kerrial NG32 . . . 138 D3
Denton NG32 . . . 139 A7
Doddington & Whisby LN6 . . . 79 D5
Dorrington LN4 . . . 108 E3
Dunham-on-Trent NG22 . . . 65 B1
East/West Stockwith DN10 . . . 40 C5
Edenham PE10 . . . 153 F4
Ellerker HU15 . . . 2 A8
Ewerby & Evedon NG34 . . . 122 C6
Farcet PE7 . . . 231 C2
Fenton NG23 . . . 105 C1
Fishlake DN7 . . . 14 D8
Foston NG32 . . . 117 F1
Fulstow LN11 . . . 49 B8
Gedney PE12 . . . 148 B1
1 Grasby DN38 . . . 32 E7
Greatford PE9 . . . 164 C2
Gunby & Stainby NG33 . . . 151 B4
Hackthorn LN2 . . . 55 E1
Haconby PE10 . . . 154 D8
Hatfield DN7 . . . 14 F3
Honington NG32 . . . 119 C1
Horkstow DN18 . . . 10 A5
Horsington LN10 . . . 84 D3
Hougham NG32 . . . 118 C3
Ingoldsby NG33 . . . 141 D5
Laneham DN22 . . . 65 A3
Mablethorpe & Sutton LN12 . . . 64 B1
Mareham Le Fen PE22 . . . 98 F3
Marston NG32 . . . 118 D2
Newark-on-Trent NG24 . . . 104 C2
Normanby By Spital LN8 . . . 55 F7
North Kyme LN4 . . . 109 F3
North Leverton with Habblesthorpe DN22 . . . 52 B1
North Rauceby NG34 . . . 120 E5
Norton Disney LN6 . . . 92 C2
Osgodby LN8 . . . 45 A3
RAF Cranwell NG34 . . . 120 C8
Ryhall PE9 . . . 163 D1
Scawby DN20 . . . 30 F7
Scopwick LN4 . . . 95 D1
Scothern LN2 . . . 68 F4
Scredington NG34 . . . 132 F7
South Rauceby NG34 . . . 120 E4
South Scarle NG23 . . . 91 E6
Southorpe PE9 . . . 172 E1
Sproxton LE14 . . . 138 F1
Sutton on Trent NG23 . . . 91 A8
Swanland HU14 . . . 3 B7
Syston NG32 . . . 130 A7
Thistleton LE15 . . . 151 C1
Thorney NG23 . . . 78 F7
Thornton Curtis DN39 . . . 11 E5
Thorpe on the Hill LN6 . . . 92 E8
1 Timberland LN4 . . . 96 B1
Torksey LN1 . . . 65 D6
Ufford PE9 . . . 172 F3
Upton DN21 . . . 53 D5
Welby NG32 . . . 130 F5
West Ashby LN9 . . . 85 E7
Westborough & Dry Doddington NG23 . . . 117 E5
Whitton DN15 . . . 1 E3
Wilsford NG32 . . . 120 C2
1 Worlaby DN20 . . . 20 D8
1 Wymondham LE14 . . . 150 C1
Yaxley PE7 . . . 233 E5
Maine Ave DN15 . . . 182 B5
Mainwaring Cl 5 LN2 . . . 68 E6
Mainwaring Rd LN2 . . . 234 C4
Maisdike La PE12 . . . 159 B5
Malborne Way PE2 . . . 230 B4
Malborough Dr 4 LN12 . . . 64 A3
Malborough La LN5 . . . 93 A4
Malcolm Ave NG34 . . . 107 C1
Malcolm Rd DN34 . . . 190 F4
Malcolm Sargent Gm Sch PE9 . . . 218 E5
Maldon Dr HU9 . . . 181 C6
Malham Ave HU4 . . . 179 C6
Malham Cl LN6 . . . 200 C1
Malham Dr LN6 . . . 200 C1
Malim Way 3 NG31 . . . 210 F8
Malkinson Cl
4 West Halton DN15 . . . 8 E7
21 Winterton DN15 . . . 9 A5
12 Winterton DN15 . . . 9 A5
Mallalieu Ct 2 DN15 . . . 182 E4
Mallard Ave
6 Barnby Dun DN3 . . . 14 A4
12 Barnby Dun DN3 . . . 14 A3
Mallard Cl
Birchwood LN6 . . . 200 E1
5 Essendine PE9 . . . 163 D3
19 Healing DN41 . . . 23 F5
Skellingthorpe LN6 . . . 200 A3
Spalding PE11 . . . 214 E2
Mallard Ct
10 Grantham NG31 . . . 210 E2
4 North Hykeham LN6 . . . 204 C1
5 Stamford PE9 . . . 219 B4
Mallard Dr 6 LN7 . . . 33 B4
Mallard Dro PE11 . . . 134 B1
Mallard Mews DN32 . . . 191 E6
Mallard Rd
Low Fulney PE12 . . . 157 C5
Peterborough PE3 . . . 220 E1
3 Scunthorpe DN17 . . . 184 E6
Mallard Way PE25 . . . 103 C7
Mallards Reach 8 PE11 . . . 134 F2
Mallards The 5 PE6 . . . 174 A5
Malling Wlk DN16 . . . 185 B2
Mallory Cl 6 LN6 . . . 204 C7
Mallory Dr 3 PE11 . . . 214 C2
Mallory Rd
1 Ashby De La Launde & Bloxholm LN4 . . . 108 A7
Peterborough PE1 . . . 226 C2
4 Scunthorpe DN16 . . . 185 D5
Mallowfield 2 LN8 . . . 57 B8
Mallows La PE22 . . . 113 C2
Malm St HU3 . . . 180 B6
Malmesbury Dr 3 DN34 . . . 191 C6
Malmsgate La PE20 . . . 135 F6
Malpas Ave 4 DN21 . . . 197 D5
Malt Kiln La 1 LN5 . . . 93 F6
Maltby Ave DN37 . . . 190 C3
Maltby Cl 20 PE8 . . . 172 B1
Maltby Dr PE6 . . . 164 D4
Maltby La 12 DN18 . . . 3 E1
Maltby Rd
Scunthorpe DN17 . . . 184 E5
Skegness PE25 . . . 206 D5
Malten La 8 PE12 . . . 158 B7
Malting La PE11 . . . 134 E2
Maltings La NG31 . . . 210 E7
Maltings The
5 Alford LN13 . . . 75 F3
1 Leasingham NG34 . . . 121 B7
6 Thorney PE6 . . . 176 A3
Wothorpe PE9 . . . 219 C2
Maltkiln La
Brant Broughton LN5 . . . 105 F5
2 Elsham DN20 . . . 20 F7
Maltkiln Rd
Barton-upon-Humber DN18 . . . 3 F1
Fenton LN1 . . . 65 E3
Malton Rd LN6 . . . 204 F3
Malvern Ave
Grimsby DN33 . . . 191 A3
Heighington/Washingborough LN4 . . . 203 D2
Spalding PE11 . . . 214 E6
Malvern Cl 20 Lincoln LN6 . . . 93 C8
15 Lincoln LN6 . . . 93 C8
Lincoln LN5 . . . 205 D4
Sleaford NG34 . . . 212 B2
Spalding PE11 . . . 214 E6
4 Thorne/Moorends DN8 . . . 15 A7
Malvern Dr 5 NG31 . . . 210 E8
Malvern Rd
5 Mablethorpe/Sutton on Sea LN12 . . . 64 B4
Peterborough PE4 . . . 221 C2
Scunthorpe DN17 . . . 184 F7
Manasty Rd PE2 . . . 229 C2
Manby Hall Bsns Pk DN40 . . . 186 D5
Manby Middlegate LN11 . . . 62 D7
Manby Rd
Immingham DN40 . . . 186 C6
Legbourne LN11 . . . 61 E4
Scunthorpe DN17 . . . 184 E4
Manby St LN5 . . . 205 D6
Manchester Rd 11 LN5 . . . 94 A7
Manchester St
Cleethorpes DN35 . . . 192 D8
Kingston upon Hull HU3 . . . 180 A4
Manchester Way
3 Donington PE11 . . . 134 F2
Grantham NG31 . . . 210 C5
Mandalay Dr 1 PE10 . . . 213 E7
Mandela Link 2 DN31 . . . 191 C7
Mandeville PE2 . . . 229 F4
Mandike Rd PE20 . . . 136 C2
Manifold Rd DN16 . . . 185 E5
Manlake Ave DN15 . . . 9 A5
Manley Ct 1 DN9 . . . 27 D6
Manley Gdns
Brigg DN20 . . . 196 B3
4 Cleethorpes DN35 . . . 192 F3
Manley St 4 DN15 . . . 183 B3
Mann La DN9 . . . 16 D2
Mannaberg Way DN15 . . . 183 B6
Manners Cl 3 PE9 . . . 172 C6
Manners Rd NG24 . . . 104 B2
Manners St NG31 . . . 211 A6
Manning Rd PE10 . . . 213 D5
Manor Ave
Grimsby DN32 . . . 191 D6
Peterborough PE2 . . . 231 B7
Manor Cl 6 Bardney LN3 . . . 83 C4
11 Baston PE6 . . . 164 E5
East Kirkby PE23 . . . 99 F4
3 Great Gonerby NG31 . . . 129 E5
11 Keelby DN41 . . . 23 A5
Langtoft PE6 . . . 164 E3
7 Leasingham NG34 . . . 121 B7
Lincoln LN2 . . . 234 B4
14 Metheringham LN4 . . . 95 D4
15 Ruskington NG34 . . . 108 D2
Ryhall PE9 . . . 163 C2
7 Sibsey PE22 . . . 113 B1
2 Spalding PE11 . . . 214 C1
6 Welbourn LN5 . . . 106 E5
13 Wittering PE8 . . . 172 B1
Yaxley PE7 . . . 233 D5
Manor Cliff 1 LN8 . . . 55 F6
Manor Ct
9 Bourne PE10 . . . 213 C5
2 Carlton-le-Moorland LN5 . . . 105 E8
9 Grimsby DN32 . . . 191 D7
17 Nettleham LN2 . . . 68 C2
Nocton LN4 . . . 95 B7
1 Stallingborough DN41 . . . 23 E6
2 Sudbrooke LN2 . . . 68 F3
Manor Ct Rd 7 DN9 . . . 27 E6
Manor Dr 12 Baston PE6 . . . 164 E5
2 Binbrook LN8 . . . 47 C4
3 Bonby DN20 . . . 10 C2
4 Brough HU15 . . . 2 C6
1 Great Gonerby NG31 . . . 129 E5
5 Great Gonerby NG31 . . . 129 D5
Halton Holegate PE23 . . . 101 B7
7 Harlaxton NG32 . . . 139 C7
Holbeach PE12 . . . 215 D3
1 Long Bennington NG23 . . . 117 D3
Peterborough PE6 . . . 221 E3
3 Scawby DN20 . . . 30 E8
2 Sudbrooke LN2 . . . 68 F2
Waltham DN37 . . . 194 E5
7 Wragby LN8 . . . 70 D4
Manor Farm Cl 43 DN17 . . . 29 D6
Manor Farm Dr 3 LN1 . . . 66 D7
Manor Farm La
Castor PE5 . . . 223 E2
3 Essendine PE9 . . . 163 D3
Manor Farm Rd DN17 . . . 184 E6
Manor Gdns
Boston PE21 . . . 209 A4
8 Hatfield DN7 . . . 14 E4
Peterborough PE2 . . . 231 C7
Manor Hill LN11 . . . 60 A1
Manor Hill Cnr PE12 . . . 169 D7
Manor House La NG23 . . . 117 E5
Manor House Mus* LN13 . . . 75 F3
Manor House Rd PE12 . . . 146 F2
Manor House St
1 Fulletby LN9 . . . 86 B8
6 Horncastle LN9 . . . 199 B4
Peterborough PE1 . . . 226 A3
Manor La Aisthorpe LN1 . . . 67 C7
4 Barrow upon Humber DN19 . . . 11 D8
Bourne PE10 . . . 213 C4
Broadholme LN6 . . . 66 D1
5 Carlton-le-Moorland LN5 . . . 105 E8
Goxhill DN19 . . . 11 F8
Hougham NG32 . . . 118 C3
Threekingham NG34 . . . 132 E3
16 Waddington LN5 . . . 93 F7
1 Welton/Dunholme LN2 . . . 68 D6
Wrangle PE22 . . . 114 B2
Manor Leas Cl LN6 . . . 205 B3
Manor Leas Inf Sch LN6 . . . 205 B3
Manor Leas Jun Sch LN6 . . . 205 B3
Manor Paddock 6 NG32 . . . 128 F7
Manor Pk 7 LN11 . . . 61 F3
Manor Pl NG34 . . . 212 C5
Manor Rd
Barrowby NG32 . . . 210 A5
Bottesford NG13 . . . 128 A5
Burton Coggles NG33 . . . 152 C8
Carlby PE9 . . . 163 E4
2 Collingham NG23 . . . 91 D4
Coningsby LN4 . . . 110 E8
1 Crowle DN17 . . . 16 D7
Folksworth PE7 . . . 232 D1
4 Hagworthingham PE23 . . . 87 A4
Hatfield DN7 . . . 14 E4
Heighington/Washingborough LN4 . . . 203 B1
Kingston upon Hull HU5 . . . 179 B8
Kirton PE20 . . . 136 B5
Lincoln LN2 . . . 234 C4
Northorpe DN21 . . . 42 A8
Saxilby LN1 . . . 66 D2
Scunthorpe DN16 . . . 185 B3
Sleaford NG34 . . . 212 B2
5 Stainforth DN7 . . . 14 C7
Stretton LE15 . . . 162 A6
Swanland HU14 . . . 3 B6
Swinderby LN6 . . . 92 A5
Twin Rivers DN14 . . . 7 E7
Manor Rd *continued*
Wansford PE5 . . . 222 F2
Manor Rise LN3 . . . 203 F8
Manor St
7 Heckington NG34 . . . 122 E3
Keelby DN41 . . . 23 A5
8 Kingston upon Hull HU1 . . . 180 F6
Ruskington NG34 . . . 108 D2
Manor Stables Craft Ctr* NG32 . . . 106 C1
Manor Way
Kingston upon Hull HU10 . . . 178 F6
6 Langtoft PE6 . . . 164 F3
Market Deeping PE6 . . . 217 E4
Manrico Dr LN1 . . . 201 C7
Manse Ave LN5 . . . 205 D4
Mansel St
3 Grimsby DN32 . . . 189 D1
Grimsby DN32 . . . 192 B8
Mansell Cl 1 PE11 . . . 214 B3
Mansfield Ct PE1 . . . 226 C5
Mansfield Rd DN15 . . . 182 B2
Mansgate Hill LN7 . . . 33 B3
Mansion Ct Gdns DN8 . . . 15 A8
Manson Cl 11 DN34 . . . 190 D4
Manthorpe Dro PE10 . . . 164 F8
Manthorpe Rd NG31 . . . 211 B7
Mantle Gn PE22 . . . 115 B6
Manton PE3 . . . 225 A3
Manton Ct DN20 . . . 30 F6
Manton La DN20 . . . 30 E6
Manton Rd Lincoln LN2 . . . 201 F7
Manton DN21 . . . 30 B4
Mantree Cross DN21 . . . 41 A8
Maple Ave
15 Crowle DN17 . . . 16 D7
Grimsby DN34 . . . 190 E7
Keelby DN41 . . . 23 A4
Kingston upon Hull HU10 . . . 178 F8
13 Northorpe PE10 . . . 164 C8
4 Scunthorpe DN15 . . . 182 C5
10 Wisbech PE13 . . . 170 D1
Woodhall Spa LN10 . . . 97 C6
Maple Cl Brigg DN20 . . . 196 E3
Gainsborough DN21 . . . 197 B7
9 Keelby DN41 . . . 23 A4
5 Kingston upon Hull HU5 . . . 179 C7
Leasingham NG34 . . . 121 C7
Louth LN11 . . . 198 D7
42 Messingham DN17 . . . 29 D7
Thimbleby LN9 . . . 199 A5
4 Waddington LN5 . . . 93 E8
Maple Ct PE7 . . . 233 F6
Maple Dr
5 Bassingham LN5 . . . 92 F3
1 Sudbrooke LN2 . . . 68 F2
Maple Gdns PE10 . . . 213 D6
Maple Gr 22 Healing DN41 . . . 23 F5
Holbeach PE12 . . . 215 A2
Immingham DN40 . . . 186 C5
New Waltham DN36 . . . 195 B5
Peterborough PE1 . . . 226 C7
3 Scopwick Heath LN4 . . . 108 A7
Spalding PE11 . . . 214 F4
Maple Rd PE21 . . . 209 C2
Maple St LN5 . . . 205 D5
Maple Tree Cl E 2 DN16 . . . 183 A1
Maple Tree Cl W 1 DN16 . . . 183 A1
Maple Tree Way DN16 . . . 183 A1
Maple Way 12 PE11 . . . 134 E2
Maple Wlk PE7 . . . 230 C2
Maples The PE1 . . . 226 F5
Maplewood Ave HU5 . . . 179 B7
Maplewood Cl NG31 . . . 210 F7
March Rd PE13 . . . 177 F1
March St 18 DN21 . . . 30 B1
Marconi Dr PE7 . . . 233 D6
Marcus St DN34 . . . 191 A6
Mardale Gdns PE4 . . . 221 D2
Mareham La
Aswarby & Swarby NG34 . . . 132 E7
Pointon & Sempringham NG34 . . . 142 F7
Sleaford NG34 . . . 212 F2
Threekingham NG34 . . . 132 F3
Mareham le Fen CE (Controlled) Prim Sch PE22 . . . 99 A4
Mareham Rd LN9 . . . 199 D2
Marfleet Ave 4 HU9 . . . 5 D8
Marfleet Cnr 9 DN36 . . . 36 B1
Marfleet La HU9 . . . 5 E8
Marfleet Prim Sch HU9 . . . 5 E8
Margaret Ave 1 DN17 . . . 17 D5
Margaret Dr PE21 . . . 209 B6
Margaret Gr 1 HU13 . . . 178 F1
Margaret Pl DN36 . . . 195 C6
Margaret St
6 Grimsby DN32 . . . 191 F7
Immingham DN40 . . . 186 C3
Margrave La
Garthorpe & Fockerby DN17 . . . 7 E5
Reedness DN14 . . . 6 E7
Marham Cl 4 LN6 . . . 204 B8
Marholm Rd
4 Peterborough PE3 . . . 220 F1
Peterborough PE6 . . . 224 B3

Marholm Rd *continued*
Ufford PE9 172 F2
Marian Ave 22 LN12 64 B3
Marian Rd PE21 208 F7
Marian Way
6 Skegness PE25 206 B3
Waltham DN37 194 B4
Mariette Way PE11 214 B6
Marigold Cl
Lincoln LN2 202 C8
Stamford PE9 218 C6
Marigold Wlk
3 Humberston DN35 192 E1
5 Sleaford NG34 212 F3
Marigolds PE6 217 D5
Marina Rd 19 LN12 64 B3
Marina View 8 DN8 15 A7
Marine Ave
12 Mablethorpe/Sutton on Sea LN12 64 C1
4 Mablethorpe/Sutton on Sea LN12 76 F8
North Ferriby HU14 3 A4
Skegness PE25 206 D1
Marine Ave W 8 LN12 76 F8
Marine Rd PE11 214 E5
Marine Wharf 5 HU1 180 F5
Mariners Arms Flats 2 DN17 17 D6
Mariners Cl HU9 181 C6
Marisco Ct 2 LN12 77 A8
Marjorie Ave LN6 205 D8
Mark Ave
Horncastle LN9 199 A5
Sleaford NG34 212 F4
Mark Rise 1 DN21 41 C5
Market Cl 3 PE24 102 E8
Market Ct 8 DN17 16 D7
Market Deeping Com Prim Sch PE6 217 C6
Market Hall* LN11 198 B5
Market Hill DN15 2 B1
Market La
Old Leake PE22 127 C8
Terrington St Clement PE34 161 E2
Market Pl 3 Alford LN13 75 F2
1 Binbrook LN8 47 C4
21 Boston PE21 208 F5
2 Brigg DN20 196 B3
Coningsby LN4 207 A4
2 Epworth DN9 27 E6
Gainsborough DN21 197 C4
2 Grantham NG31 211 A4
5 Horncastle LN9 199 B4
6 Kingston upon Hull HU1 181 A6
Long Sutton PE12 216 C4
9 Louth LN11 198 B5
10 Market Rasen LN8 57 D8
Owston Ferry DN9 28 B3
4 Sleaford NG34 212 D4
6 Spalding PE11 214 D4
Swineshead PE20 135 B7
4 Wragby LN8 70 D5
Market Rasen CE Prim Sch LN8 57 D7
Market Rasen Race Course LN8 57 F7
Market Rasen Rd
Dunholme LN2 68 E6
Holton cum Beckering LN8 70 B8
Lissington LN3 57 E1
Snarford LN8 56 E1
Welton/Dunholme LN2 68 E6
Market Rasen Sta LN8 57 D7
Market Rasen Way PE12 215 E3
Market Sq 17 PE21 208 F5
Market St
Bottesford NG13 128 A5
Cleethorpes DN35 192 F6
Gainsborough DN21 197 D4
Grimsby DN31 191 D8
Long Sutton PE12 216 C5
3 Sleaford NG34 212 D4
11 Spilsby PE23 88 A1
31 Winterton DN15 9 A5
Market Way PE11 214 C8
Markham Mews DN37 194 F4
Markham Ret Pk PE9 219 E7
Markham Way 2 DN20 196 F7
Markhams Orch DN33 194 F7
Markillie La PE12 160 A3
Marklew Ave DN34 191 B7
Marlborough Ave
2 Haxey DN9 27 D2
Heighington/Washingborough LN4 203 C1
Kingston upon Hull HU13 178 D2
2 Spalding PE11 214 E2
Marlborough Cl
5 Lincoln LN2 202 C8
Yaxley PE7 233 E5
Marlborough Dr 1 DN16 185 B8
Marlborough Rd 11 DN8 15 B7
Marlborough St 11 DN21 197 D3
Marlborough Terr 3 HU2 180 E7
Marlborough Way DN35 192 F1
Marlow Rd DN21 197 E6
Marlowe Dr LN2 202 B6
Marlowe Gr PE4 225 E8
Marlowe Rd DN17 184 D7
Marmaduke St 3 HU3 180 C4
Marmion Dr 7 DN15 9 A5
Marmion Rd
Coningsby LN4 207 E5
4 Scunthorpe DN16 185 C8
Marne Ave PE4 221 A1
Marne Gdns LN1 201 E6
Marne St HU5 180 A8
Marquis Ave DN36 195 D7
Marr La HU15 1 A7
Marratts La NG31 129 D5
Marriotsgate
6 Lutton PE12 160 A8
Lutton PE12 216 C8
Marriott Ct PE1 226 E5
Marris Dr 11 DN15 9 B5
Marsden Dr DN15 182 D3
Marsden Rd DN31 189 D1
Marsh Ave PE21 209 A2
Marsh Dro PE11 146 A5
Marsh La
Algarkirk PE20 146 B8
Barnetby Le Wold DN38 21 B4
Barrow upon Humber DN19 4 C2
Barton-upon-Humber DN18 3 F1
Boston PE21 209 A1
Burgh Le Marsh PE24 102 E7
Carlton-le-Moorland LN5 106 A7
Dunham-on-Trent NG22 65 B1
Grainthorpe LN11 50 C7
Kettlethorpe LN1 65 C2
Middle Rasen LN8 57 B8
Misterton DN10 40 A5
New Holland DN19 4 D2
North Leverton with Habblesthorpe DN22 52 E1
North Somercotes LN11 38 C1
Orby PE24 89 E2
Saundby DN22 52 B7
Skidbrooke with Saltfleet Haven LN11 51 C5
South Cockerington LN11 62 B8
South Killingholme DN40 13 B4
Tattershall LN4 97 D1
Tattershall Thorpe LN4 97 D1
Winteringham DN15 2 A1
Wyberton PE21 136 F8
Marsh Rd 3 Crowle DN17 16 C8
Crowle DN17 16 B7
Gedney PE12 148 C2
Holbeach PE12 215 F8
Kirton PE20 137 A3
Orby PE24 90 B3
Spalding PE12 157 B7
Sutterton PE20 146 A7
Tydd St Mary PE13 160 C1
Walkeringham DN10 40 B3
Walpole PE14 170 F8
Weston PE12 145 F1
Marsh The PE14 170 E8
Marsh Way 3 DN36 37 C5
Marshall Ave
Grimsby DN34 191 B7
Kingston upon Hull HU10 178 E8
Marshall Cl 3 PE21 126 C1
Marshall Way 2 DN21 53 A8
Marshall's Bank PE13 177 D8
Marshall's Way PE7 231 C2
Marsham PE2 229 F3
Marshchapel Cl 2 DN35 192 F3
Marshchapel Prim Sch DN36 37 B2
Marshfield Rd 1 DN16 185 C5
Marshfields Sch PE1 226 D7
Marshland High Sch PE14 170 E4
Marshland St 10 PE34 161 F3
Marshlands Dr PE12 215 F3
Marston La NG32 129 A7
Martin Cl
2 Bottesford DN16 185 B2
Heighington/Washingborough LN4 81 E4
Louth LN11 198 D8
Skellingthorpe LN6 200 A3
Martin Ct PE4 221 A4
Martin Dales Dro 1 LN10 97 B4
Martin N Dro LN4 96 D3
Martin Rd LN4 96 C2
Martin S Dro LN4 96 D3
Martin St LN5 201 F1
Martin Way
Ingoldmells PE25 206 C8
New Waltham DN36 195 B6
Martin's Cl 5 DN19 11 D8
Martins Rd
Crowland PE6 167 E4
Ulceby DN39 12 B1
Martins Way PE2 229 F5
Martins Wlk 11 LN12 77 A8
Martinsbridge PE1 226 F7
Marton Gr
3 Grimsby DN33 191 A3
35 Hatfield DN7 14 D4
Marton Prim Sch DN21 65 E8
Marton Rd
Sturton By Stow LN1 66 B7
Willingham DN21 53 E2
Martyn Rd DN35 192 D7
Marvel St HU9 181 B7
Mary Armyne Rd PE2 230 B5
Mary La LE14 138 B1
Mary St DN15 182 F3
Mary Sumner Way 4 DN15 182 E4
Mary Walsham Cl PE2 231 E5
Marylebone Wlk 6 DN33 191 B2
Masefield Dr 10 LN12 77 A7
Maskew Ave PE1 225 E6
Mason Dr DN17 184 E3
Masonic La 5 PE23 87 F1
Masons Ct 25 DN18 10 E8
Massey Cl
11 Epworth DN9 27 D6
Kingston upon Hull HU3 180 A5
Massey Rd LN2 234 C4
Massey St HU3 180 A4
Mast Dr HU9 181 C6
Master Dike PE12 159 D1
Masterton Cl 6 PE9 219 D7
Masterton Rd PE9 219 C7
Mat Pitts La PE24 102 C1
Mathews St DN35 192 C7
Matilda Rd LN6 201 D1
Matley PE2 229 E5
Matlock Dr
6 Grimsby DN37 190 F8
Lincoln LN6 204 E2
Matmore Cl PE11 214 F3
Matmore Gate PE11 214 F3
Matthew Flinders Way PE21 208 D3
Matthew Humberstone CE Sch DN35 192 C4
Mattimore Dr 6 PE12 215 E2
Maud St 2 PE21 209 A5
Mavis Enderby Cross Roads PE23 87 D1
Mavis Rd 2 DN17 184 E6
Mawford Cl PE12 146 E2
Mawson Gdns 6 PE24 102 E2
Mawthorpe Hill Rd LN13 88 F8
Mawthorpe Mus* LN13 88 F8
Maxey Cl 11 PE6 217 A5
Maxey Rd Maxey PE6 173 C6
Northborough PE6 217 C1
Maxey View PE6 217 C3
Maxham's Gn Rd PE6 173 D3
Maxwell Ave LN6 205 C8
Maxwell Ct DN34 190 D5
Maxwell Dr 1 LN12 64 B3
Maxwell Rd PE2 230 D6
May Cres LN1 201 D4
May Gr HU13 178 D2
May St DN35 192 D8
Mayall Ct 23 LN5 93 F7
Mayfair Ave LN6 205 C7
Mayfair Cres 12 DN37 194 C4
Mayfair Ct DN35 193 A1
Mayfair Dr 4 PE11 214 B1
Mayfair Dr W DN37 190 C8
Mayfair Gdns PE21 209 B7
Mayfield Ave
Gainsborough DN21 197 B7
3 South Killingholme DN40 12 F2
6 Stainforth DN7 14 D6
Mayfield Cl
3 Grimsby DN33 194 D8
13 Pinchbeck PE11 156 E8
Mayfield Cres
Louth LN11 198 D4
3 Middle Rasen LN8 57 C8
Mayfield Dr 1 PE25 90 D3
Mayfield Gr 5 PE25 206 B3
Mayfield Rd PE1 226 A6
Mayfield St HU3 180 C8
Mayflower Ave DN40 186 C3
Mayflower Cl
2 Gainsborough DN21 52 F6
6 South Killingholme DN40 12 E3
Mayflower Dr NG34 122 D2
Mayflower Rd PE21 209 C3
Mayflower Way 7 LN12 64 B3
Mayland Ave HU5 179 A8
Mayner's Dike PE12 169 F8
Mayor's Wlk PE3 225 E3
Maypole House Sch LN13 88 E8
Maypole St DN21 42 D2
May's La PE13 170 A2
Mays La LN1 66 E2
Maysfield Ct 10 DN20 31 A5
Maysfield Dr 6 PE13 170 B2
Maythorpe Cl HU3 180 A7
Maytime Cl 7 PE11 214 A5
Maytree Dr PE12 216 D5
McInnes St 4 LN2 202 C3
McVeigh Ct 13 DN41 23 F5
Meadow The 29 LN7 33 B4
Mead Cl 6 Lincoln LN6 205 A5
Peterborough PE3 220 F1
Mead The 11 Laceby DN37 23 F1
Lincoln LN6 205 A5
Peterborough PE4 221 A1
Mead Wlk HU4 179 C6
Meadenvale PE1 226 F5
Meadow Ave DN39 12 A2
Meadow Bank PE22 126 F6
Meadow Bank Ave 1 LN3 82 B6
Meadow Cl
1 Bourne PE10 213 D5
7 Cherry Willingham/Reepham LN3 82 A8
1 Colsterworth NG33 151 E6
Meadow Cl *continued*
5 Goxhill DN19 5 A1
Lincoln LN6 93 C8
3 Louth LN11 198 C4
2 Manby LN11 62 C6
6 Metheringham LN4 95 D4
2 Pinchbeck PE11 145 C1
4 Scothern LN2 68 F4
Spalding PE11 214 E6
Meadow Croft
3 Kirk Sandall DN3 14 A1
Waltham DN37 194 E5
Meadow Ct
Grimsby DN34 190 E7
15 Hibaldstow DN20 30 F5
Meadow Dr
Barton-upon-Humber DN18 10 F8
4 Binbrook LN8 47 C5
Grimsby DN33 194 D8
2 Healing DN41 24 A5
14 Misterton DN10 39 F5
Meadow Dro PE10 213 F7
Meadow End NG31 211 D2
Meadow Field Rd 6 DN3 14 A3
Meadow Gate PE10 213 D6
Meadow La
Aubourn Haddington & South Hykeham LN6 93 B7
Benniworth LN8 59 B1
Girton NG23 78 C2
Leasingham NG34 121 B7
9 Lincoln LN6 93 C8
Normanton on Trent NG23 78 B3
North Cockerington LN11 50 A1
North Hykeham LN6 93 C8
North Scarle LN6 78 F1
Pointon & Sempringham NG34 143 C6
16 Ryhall PE9 163 C1
Meadow Rd
Dunston LN4 95 C5
Langtoft PE6 217 A8
Newark-on-Trent NG24 104 B2
Newborough PE6 221 B8
Scunthorpe DN17 184 C6
Meadow Rise
5 Barnby Dun DN3 14 A4
Blyton DN21 41 C6
1 Gainsborough DN21 53 A5
7 Saxilby LN1 66 D2
Meadow Vale 4 DN20 30 F8
Meadow View
Humberston DN35 192 F1
Morton PE10 154 D6
Swinderby LN6 92 A5
Meadow Way
Billinghay LN4 109 E6
Bracebridge Heath LN4 81 A1
7 Old Leake PE22 114 A1
6 Welton/Dunholme LN2 68 D6
Meadow Wlk
19 Kirk Sandall DN3 14 A2
6 Swanland HU14 3 B7
Meadowbank 5 DN9 16 E1
Meadowbank Rd HU3 179 E7
Meadowbrook
9 Ancaster NG32 120 A3
4 Ruskington NG34 108 D2
Meadowcroft 7 LN11 59 E1
Meadowdale Cres 3 NG31 211 A8
Meadowfield
4 Middle Rasen LN8 57 C8
Sleaford NG34 212 C5
Meadowgate PE9 172 F5
Meadowgate La 3 PE11 214 A3
Meadowlake Cl LN6 200 D1
Meadows Cl 7 NG23 117 D3
Meadows La
Lincoln LN4 202 E2
Reepham LN3 69 A1
Meadows Rise 1 LE14 150 B1
Meadows The
2 Beckingham DN10 52 B8
Burringham DN17 17 D4
8 Long Bennington NG23 117 D3
Mablethorpe/Sutton on Sea LN12 64 C2
5 Market Deeping PE6 217 C5
Messingham DN17 29 D8
7 Pinchbeck PE11 145 C1
Skegness PE25 206 A4
Westwoodside DN9 27 A2
Meadowsweet 2 PE9 218 C7
Meadway
Cherry Willingham/Reepham LN3 203 E6
11 Market Deeping PE6 217 A6
3 Spalding PE11 214 A4
Meakers Way LN13 76 F3
Meals Gate PE4 221 D2
Measham Dr 4 DN7 14 D7
Mechanic La 9 HU3 180 D5
Meden Ave 12 HU15 2 D5
Medeswell PE2 230 C3
Medforth La PE21 208 E8
Medina Gdns LN12 64 B2
Medium Section Rd DN16 19 A4
Medlam Cl PE22 112 C7
Medlam La PE22 112 D7
Medlam Rd PE21 208 C3
Medlar Dr 4 HU15 2 D5
Medlock Cres 5 PE11 214 F5
Medway 7 LN1 66 D7
Medway Cl 3 PE11 145 C6
Medway Cres LN6 205 B2
Medway Pl 6 DN34 191 A5
Medworth PE2 229 F3
Meeres' La PE20 136 A5
Meering Cl 12 NG23 91 D5
Meering La NG23 91 C7
Meers Bank LN12 64 A6
Meeting House La LN5 105 F5
Meggan Gate PE3 225 A1
Meggitt La DN15 2 A1
Megs La 10 LN5 107 A8
Melbourne Ave 4 DN33 191 D3
Melbourne Dr 4 PE25 206 A4
Melbourne Rd
Birchwood LN6 204 C8
Grantham NG31 211 D7
4 Stamford PE9 219 D6
Melbourne Way 9 LN5 93 E8
Melford Cl PE3 225 A2
Melholme La LN11 50 A2
Mellows Cl
Cherry Willingham/Reepham LN3 203 F8
Peterborough PE1 226 C3
Mellwood View DN9 28 A3
Melrose Cl 9 PE9 218 E6
Melrose Dr PE2 231 A7
Melrose Rd DN21 197 C6
Melrose St HU3 179 F6
Melton Bottom HU14 2 F6
Melton Fields HU14 2 F5
Melton Old Rd HU14 2 E5
Melton Rd
North Ferriby HU14 3 A5
Wrawby DN20 20 F4
Wymondham LE14 150 B1
Melville St LN5 234 B2
Melwood Cl DN9 27 F6
Melwood Hill DN9 27 F6
Melwood View 18 DN9 27 E6
Memorial Hall Dr 9 LN5 107 A7
Menasha Way DN16 185 E7
Mendip Ave
Grimsby DN33 191 C1
25 Lincoln LN6 93 C8
Mendip Cl
6 Gonerby Hill Foot NG31 210 E8
2 Lincoln LN5 205 D3
Spalding PE11 214 B6
Mendip Gr PE4 221 C2
Mendip Rd DN17 184 D8
Menson Dr DN7 14 D4
Mercer Rd DN21 197 B6
Mercer Row LN11 198 B5
Mercia Cl 14 NG34 212 B2
Mercia Dr 3 NG32 120 A2
Mercia Gdns 2 PE10 213 B5
Mercia Gr 4 PE6 164 E5
Mercian Ct PE2 231 D7
Mere Balk La LN9 85 A7
Mere Booth Rd PE22 125 A7
Mere Cres DN16 185 D7
Mere Dro
Old Leake PE22 113 F4
Yaxley PE7 233 F4
Mere La Edenthorpe DN3 14 A1
Heydour NG32 131 D6
Winterton DN15 9 A7
Mere Rd
Branston & Mere LN4 81 E1
Waddington LN5 93 F7
Merebalk La LN9 86 B2
Meredith Ave DN17 184 D6
Meredyke Rd DN17 7 D3
Merelade Gr 4 PE4 220 E5
Meres Leisure Ctr & Swimming Pool NG31 210 D3
Meres Rd NG31 210 C3
Mereway The NG33 141 A5
Meridian Cl 1 PE21 209 D4
Meridian Rd PE21 209 C4
Meridian View LN11 198 B4
Meridian Wlk 2 PE12 215 B2
Merleswen LN2 68 D6
Merlin Dr 2 DN20 21 A8
Merlin Rd
14 Binbrook Tech Pk LN8 47 B6
Scunthorpe DN17 184 E6
Merrick St HU9 181 B7
Merriemeade Dr 4 PE25 206 D1
Merrifield Rd 7 PE24 102 E2
Merryweather Ct 7 DN16 185 B2
Merton Rd DN16 185 A3
Messingham La DN20 30 D8
Messingham Nature Reserve* DN17 29 F6
Messingham Prim Sch DN17 29 D7
Messingham Rd
East Butterwick DN17 28 D8
Scotter DN21 29 C4
Scunthorpe DN17 184 F4
Metheringham Airfield Visitor Ctr* LN4 96 A2
Metheringham Cl 1 LN6 204 D7
Metheringham Fen La LN4 95 E5
Metheringham Heath La LN4 94 E3

Metheringham Prim Sch LN4 95 C4
Metheringham Sta LN4 95 D4
Mewburn PE3 220 E1
Mews The HU3 180 C5
Meynell Ave 3 LN6 205 C8
Meynell St DN21 40 D8
Meynell Wlk PE3 225 B3
Michaelgate LN2 234 B3
Mickle Gate PE3 225 A1
Mid Gate PE22 113 E3
Middle Barn Hill DN20 10 D1
Middle Broad Dro PE13 169 D5
Middle Dro
Gedney PE12 148 C2
Holland Fen with Brothertoft PE21 208 A7
Kirton PE20 124 D2
Newton PE13 169 E4
Middle Fen Dro PE20 134 D4
Middle Fen La LN4 82 C5
Middle Holme La 3 NG23 91 A8
Middle La Amcotts DN17 7 E1
Sturton Le Steeple DN22 52 E3
Thorpe on the Hill LN6 92 F8
Middle Marsh Rd PE12 146 F7
Middle Pasture 3 PE4 220 F5
Middle Rasen Prim Sch LN8 57 B8
Middle Rd
Crowland PE6 166 E1
Newborough PE6 221 E7
Terrington St Clement PE34 161 D4
Tydd St Mary PE13 160 B1
7 Whaplode PE12 158 B7
Middle St Aisthorpe LN1 67 D7
Cammeringham LN1 55 A1
Corringham DN21 41 E2
Croxton Kerrial NG32 138 D4
Dunston LN4 95 C5
Farcet PE7 231 C2
Fillingham DN21 55 A5
Gunby & Stainby NG33 151 B5
5 Lincoln LN6 93 C8
Lincoln LN1 201 D7
7 Metheringham LN4 95 D4
14 North Kelsey LN7 32 A4
5 Potterhanworth LN4 82 B1
Rippingale PE10 142 F2
Scampton LN1 67 D6
Scotton DN21 29 C1
5 Skillington NG33 151 A8
South Carlton LN1 67 D3
Willoughton DN21 42 E3
Middle Thorpe Rd DN35 192 D3
Middlebridge Rd DN10 39 B3
Middlebrook La 1 DN8 15 A7
Middlebrook Rd 4 LN6 205 A5
Middlecott Cl 2 PE21 208 F2
Middlecott Sch The PE20 136 C5
Middlefield PE7 230 D3
Middlefield La
Gainsborough DN21 197 E2
1 Glentham LN8 43 F1
Middlefield Sch of Tech DN21 197 E3
Middlegate LN5 92 F2
Middlegate Cl 12 DN19 11 C8
Middlegate La
Bonby DN20 10 C3
Elsham DN20 21 A7
Orby PE24 89 D2
South Ferriby DN18 10 B7
Middlegate Rd (West) 1 PE20 136 D6
Middlegate Rd PE20 136 C6
Middlegate Rd E PE20 136 D5
Middleham Cl
3 Kingston upon Hull HU9 181 E8
2 Peterborough PE7 231 F5
Middlemarsh Rd PE24 103 A7
Middlemere Bank PE22 126 E7
Middlemore Yd 1 NG31 211 B4
Middleplatt Rd DN40 186 E5
Middlesykes La LN11 62 C7
Middlethorpe Prim Sch DN35 192 D3
Middleton PE3 225 A4
Middleton Cl 9 DN17 29 D7
Middleton Ct HU5 180 B8
Middleton Jun Sch PE3 225 A4
Middleton Rd
Newark NG24 104 B6
Scunthorpe DN16 185 B4
Middleton St HU3 180 C8
Middleton Way NG34 121 C7
Middleton's Field LN2 234 B4
Middletons Rd PE7 233 E5
Midfield Pl 16 DN36 36 D8
Midfield Rd DN36 36 D8
Midfield Way 14 DN41 23 A4
Midgate (East) PE22 113 E1
Midgate PE1 226 A2
Midgley Cl HU3 180 C5
Midholm LN3 203 E5
Midia Cl LN1 201 C7
Midland Ind Est DN16 185 D8
Midland Rd
Peterborough PE3 225 E3
Scunthorpe DN16 183 D1
Midsummer Gdns PE12 216 A4
Midthorpe La 3 LN9 85 E7
Midville Cl 10 LN1 201 E8
Midville La PE22 100 B1
Midville Rd
Midville PE22 113 B7
Toynton All Saints PE23 100 F4
Midway Cl 9 LN2 68 D2
Midway Gr HU4 179 E4
Milcroft Cres DN7 14 D4
Mildenhall Dr LN6 204 B8
Mildmay Rd PE4 225 D8
Mildmay St LN1 234 A4
Mile Dro PE6 173 F5
Mile End Ave 19 DN7 14 D3
Mile La LN12 64 A2
Miles Bank PE11 214 C7
Miles Cross Hill LN13 75 D1
Milestone La PE11 145 C1
Milfoil La 11 PE12 167 B8
Milford Ct Bsns Pk LN11 198 A8
Milking Nook Dro PE10 154 F3
Milking Nook Rd PE6 221 C8
Milkinghill La PE20 135 A5
Mill Bank PE12 159 A5
Mill Baulk Rd 3 DN10 39 F3
Mill Cl 7 Alford LN13 75 F3
Billinghay LN4 109 E5
5 Brigg DN20 196 A3
4 Croft PE24 102 E2
5 Marshchapel DN36 37 C2
Murrow PE13 177 D5
2 North Leverton with Habblesthorpe DN22 52 B1
Waltham DN37 194 E3
26 Wisbech PE13 170 D1
Mill Cres
Peterborough PE2 229 E4
20 Scotter DN21 29 C3
Mill Croft 3 Scawby DN20 30 F8
1 Scunthorpe DN16 185 D7
Mill Ct LN1 234 A4
Mill Dr NG31 211 C2
Mill Dro Bourne PE10 213 E7
Cowbit PE12 157 B2
Crowland PE6 175 A8
Deeping St Nicholas PE11 155 D1
Mill Field 1 LN12 64 C2
Mill Field Cl 6 PE6 173 C4
Mill Field Ct 11 DN3 14 A3
Mill Field Rd
8 Donington PE11 134 E2
Fishlake DN7 14 C8
Scunthorpe DN16 183 E3
Mill Field Terr NG34 212 D5
Mill Garth DN35 192 D3
Mill Gate PE12 158 B1
Mill Gn Rd PE11 214 A7
Mill Hill Ellerker HU15 2 A8
Friskney PE22 114 F6
Gringley on the Hill DN10 39 B1
Nettleham LN2 68 C2
Mill Hill Cres DN35 192 E5
Mill Hill Dr DN16 185 C3
Mill Hill Rd DN7 14 E3
Mill Hill Way LN11 62 A8
Mill House La 1 DN15 9 B5
Mill La Addlethorpe PE25 90 D1
Ashby with Scremby PE23 88 D3
Aubourn Haddington & South Hykeham LN5 92 F5
8 Barrow upon Humber DN19 11 C8
Beesby with Saleby LN13 75 F5
Bicker PE20 135 B4
Billinghay LN4 109 E5
Boston PE21 208 E4
Brant Broughton & Stragglethorpe LN5 105 E5
Bratoft PE24 102 C7
Brigg DN20 196 B2
Brough HU15 2 C6
9 Broughton DN20 19 E3
Burgh on Bain LN8 59 D5
Butterwick PE22 126 E4
Caistor LN7 33 C4
Castor PE5 223 F1
7 Croxton Kerrial NG32 138 D4
Donington PE11 134 F2
Eagle & Swinethorpe LN6 79 C2
East Halton DN40 12 D6
Firsby PE24 102 A7
Fleet PE12 168 C2
Fosdyke PE20 136 D1
Friskney PE22 115 C7
Gainsborough DN21 197 B8
Gorefield PE13 169 E1
Gosberton PE11 145 C6
4 Goxhill DN19 5 A1
Grainthorpe LN11 50 B8
Great Ponton NG33 140 A5
Hackthorn LN2 56 B1
Haxey DN9 27 B2
Heighington/Washingborough LN4 81 E4
Hemingby LN9 72 B1
Heydour NG32 131 B5
Hogsthorpe PE24 90 B7
Holbeach PE12 215 B5
Holton Le Clay DN36 36 B4
Horbling NG34 133 B3
Mill La *continued*
Horncastle LN9 199 B4
Huttoft LN13 76 E4
Immingham DN40 186 A4
8 Keelby DN41 23 A4
5 Ketton PE9 171 A3
Kingston upon Hull HU10 178 C6
Kirton PE20 136 A7
Kirton in Lindsey DN21 30 C1
Legbourne LN11 61 F3
Lincoln LN5 201 E1
Little Steeping PE23 101 C6
Louth LN11 198 B7
Maltby Le Marsh LN13 75 F8
Manby LN11 62 C7
4 Marshchapel DN36 37 C2
Marston NG32 118 D2
Martin LN4 96 C3
Middle Rasen LN8 57 C7
Minting LN8 71 B2
Mumby LN13 76 F1
Newton PE13 169 F5
North Clifton NG23 78 C7
3 North Kelsey LN7 32 A4
Osgodby LN8 45 A3
Owmby LN8 55 E6
Peterborough PE5 228 F7
Pickworth NG34 132 A1
Saltfleetby LN11 51 C1
Saxilby LN1 66 D2
Scamblesby LN11 72 F5
Scawby DN20 30 F8
Skegness PE25 206 A8
Skidbrooke with Saltfleet Haven LN11 51 C4
10 South Ferriby DN18 10 A7
South Somercotes LN11 50 D4
South Witham NG33 151 C1
Sturton By Stow LN1 66 C6
Sutterton PE20 135 F2
19 Sutton Bridge PE12 160 E4
Swineshead PE20 135 A8
Tallington PE9 172 F7
Tetford LN9 73 E1
Thorney PE8 228 B7
Tydd St Mary PE13 160 B1
Wainfleet All Saints PE24 102 C1
Walkeringham DN10 39 F3
Welbourn LN5 106 F4
Welton LN2 68 E8
Welton Le Marsh PE23 89 A3
West Keal PE23 100 B4
West Walton PE14 170 F4
Whaplode PE12 158 B7
Wigsley NG23 78 F4
Wildmore LN4 111 C4
Willoughby with Sloothby LN13 89 C6
Woodhall Spa LN10 97 B5
Wrangle PE22 114 D1
Wrawby DN20 20 E3
Mill La Cl 8 PE24 90 B7
Mill La W HU15 2 B6
Mill Marsh Rd PE12 146 D2
Mill Mere Rd
Corringham DN21 41 D2
5 Waddington LN5 93 F7
Mill Moor Way 3 LN6 204 D1
Mill Pl DN35 192 F6
Mill Race DN36 36 E4
Mill Rd Addlethorpe PE24 90 D2
Boston PE21 209 B3
Claypole NG23 117 E7
Cleethorpes DN35 192 E5
Crowle DN17 16 D8
Donington on Bain LN11 59 E2
Hibaldstow DN20 30 E4
2 Keadby DN17 17 D5
Lincoln LN1 234 A4
Luddington & Haldenby DN17 7 C4
Market Rasen LN8 57 D7
Maxey PE6 173 C7
Swanland HU14 3 A6
Walpole PE14 170 F6
Wisbech St Mary PE13 177 D5
Mill Rise
6 Navenby/Wellingore LN5 107 A7
14 Scothern LN2 68 F4
Swanland HU14 3 A6
Mill Row
Barrowby NG32 129 B3
2 Lincoln LN1 234 A4
Mill St
Kingston upon Hull HU1 180 E6
Ryhall PE9 163 C2
Scamblesby LN11 73 A4
Mill View
Peterborough PE7 229 A5
5 Waltham DN37 194 E4
Mill View Ct 12 LN8 70 D4
Mill View Rd 9 LN8 70 D4
Millard Ave DN7 14 D4
Millard Nook 30 DN7 14 D4
Millbeck Bank HU15 1 E8
Millbeck Dr LN2 202 B8
Millbrook Cl 3 LN6 93 B8
Millbrook Sch DN16 185 B6
Millbrook Way 30 DN18 10 F8
Miller Ave DN32 192 C6
Miller Cl 12 DN8 15 B7
Miller La DN8 15 B7
Miller's Cl PE10 143 A3
Millers Cl
Heighington/Washingborough LN4 81 E4
4 Sleaford NG34 212 C2
Millers Ct LN11 198 C6
Millers Dale 2 LN6 204 F2
Millers' Gate PE22 113 A2
Millers Quay 6 DN20 196 A3
Millers Rd LN5 93 F6
Millers Rest PE12 158 C7
Millers Way
6 Alford LN13 75 F3
6 Heckington NG34 122 E2
Millfield Ave
Grimsby DN33 191 D3
8 Saxilby LN1 66 D2
Millfield Cres NG32 119 B6
Millfield Gdns 6 PE6 166 F1
Millfield La E PE20 136 D7
Millfield La W PE20 136 D7
Millfield Prim Sch LN4 81 F4
Millfield Rd
Bratoft PE24 102 C7
3 Market Deeping PE6 217 A6
21 Metheringham LN4 95 C4
7 Morton PE10 154 C7
South Somercotes LN11 50 F5
Thorne/Moorends DN8 15 A8
Millfield The 1 DN20 31 A5
Millfields
22 Barton-upon-Humber DN18 10 E8
18 Caistor LN7 33 B4
Millfields Way 9 DN19 11 C8
Millgate 10 LN5 107 A7
Millgood Cl LN11 198 D5
Millhill La 12 PE20 135 B7
Millhouse St Rise 5 DN40 186 A4
Millom Way DN32 191 F8
Millport Dr HU4 179 B2
Mills Cl 15 NG23 117 D3
Mills Dr DN7 26 A8
Mills Service Rd DN16 19 A4
Millstone Cl LN9 199 A3
Millstone La 3 PE9 172 D3
Millstream Rd LN4 81 E4
Millthorpe Dro NG34 143 E5
Millthorpe Rd NG34 143 B5
Millview Gdns 3 DN20 20 E3
Millview Rd
11 Heckington NG34 122 E2
Ruskington NG34 108 D2
Milman Rd LN2 202 B4
Milne Gn 4 PE20 135 B7
Milner's La 2 PE23 87 F1
Milnyard Sq PE2 229 C2
Milson Cl
18 Barton-upon-Humber DN18 10 E8
7 Broughton DN20 19 D4
Coningsby LN4 207 D4
Milson Rd 17 DN41 23 A4
Milton Cl 2 DN21 197 E6
Milton Dr PE13 170 B1
Milton Rd
Gainsborough DN21 197 E6
Grimsby DN34 191 B4
Peterborough PE2 231 A7
Scunthorpe DN16 185 B5
Milton St Lincoln LN5 205 E7
Newark-on-Trent NG24 104 A3
Milton Way
Kirkby La Thorpe NG34 121 E4
Peterborough PE3 224 E3
2 Sleaford NG34 212 F3
Mina Cl PE2 231 D4
Minden Pl 4 DN21 55 A8
Minnett's Hill NG32 130 B8
Minnow Cl 1 DN37 190 D7
Minshull Rd DN35 192 F4
Minster Dr
Cherry Willingham/Reepham LN3 203 E7
Louth LN11 198 D4
Minster Rd
16 Misterton DN10 39 F5
Scunthorpe DN15 182 B2
Minster Yd LN2 234 B3
Mint La LN1 234 A2
Mint St LN1 234 A2
Minting Cl 9 LN1 201 E8
Minting La LN9 71 D1
Mirfield Rd
Grimsby DN32 191 F4
Scunthorpe DN15 182 C4
Misson Bank DN9 26 C3
Misterton Cty Prim Sch DN10 39 F4
Mitchel Ave 7 NG24 104 C5
Mitchell Cl
3 Hatfield DN7 14 D5
7 Skellingthorpe LN6 200 A4
Mitchell Dr LN1 201 C6
Mitchell Rd LN4 207 F6
Mitre La 16 PE21 208 F5
Moat House Rd 22 DN21 30 B1
Moat La
Bolingbroke PE23 100 A8
Old Leake PE22 114 B1
3 South Killingholme DN40 12 E3
4 Welbourn LN5 106 E5
Moat Rd Scunthorpe DN15 8 C1
Terrington St Clement PE34 161 F1
Modder St 1 DN16 185 B6
Moggswell La PE2 230 B4
Moira Cl 5 DN7 14 D7
Mole Dro PE12 168 C1
Mollison Ave DN35 192 F5
Mollison Rd HU4 179 A3
Monarch Ave PE2 231 A6
Monce Cl LN2 68 C7
Monckton Way LN2 68 D5
Mondemont Cl 4 PE12 215 E3
Money Bridge La PE11 144 F1
Moneys Yd 7 NG34 212 D4
Monic Ave HU13 178 F2
Monkfield Coll LN5 106 C2
Monkhouse Ct 6 PE11 214 A3
Monks Abbey Prim Sch LN2 202 B4
Monks Ave LN11 198 C6
Monks Cl 4 DN7 14 D5
Monks Dr 22 PE6 175 A1
Monks Dyke Com Coll LN11 198 D5
Monks Dyke Rd LN11 198 D5
Monks Gr PE4 220 E5
Monks House La 5 PE11 214 A4
Monks Manor Dr LN2 202 B4
Monks Mdw 5 PE6 175 B8
Monks Rd Lincoln LN2 234 B2
Scunthorpe DN17 184 F6
8 Swineshead PE20 135 B7
Monks Way LN2 202 C3
Monks Way Ind Est LN2 202 D3
Monks Wlk 4 PE11 214 A4
Monkshouse Prim Sch PE11 214 A3
Monksthorpe La PE23 88 F1
Monkton 2 HU15 2 D6
Monkwood Cl 17 NG23 91 D5
Monmouth La PE12 216 E8
Monmouth St HU4 179 E3
Mons Rd LN1 201 E6
Mons St HU5 180 A8
Monsal Dale LN6 204 F2
Monson CE Prim Sch LN1 67 C3
Monson Ct LN5 201 E1
Monson Pk LN6 200 A4
Monson Rd DN21 42 A8
Monson St LN5 234 A1
Montagu Rd PE4 225 D8
Montague St
Cleethorpes DN35 189 D1
Lincoln LN2 234 C2
Montague Terr 1 LN2 234 C2
Montaigne Cl 3 LN2 202 D7
Montaigne Cres LN2 202 D7
Montaigne Gdn LN2 202 D7
Montbretia Dr 2 DN17 185 A1
Monteith Cres PE21 209 B5
Montgomery Rd
Cleethorpes DN35 192 D5
Skegness PE25 206 A3
Montrose Cl
8 Grantham NG31 211 D7
1 Lincoln LN6 204 E1
10 Stamford PE9 218 E6
Montrose St 7 DN16 183 B2
Monument Rd 5 PE20 135 A4
Monument St PE1 226 A3
Moody La DN31 188 C3
Moon's Gn 3 PE12 157 F6
Moor Bank PE22 113 C3
Moor Closes Nature Reserve* NG32 120 A2
Moor Dike Rd DN7 26 A8
Moor Edges Rd DN8 15 B8
Moor Farm Nature Reserve* LN10 98 A6
Moor Gate PE12 159 A4
Moor Gn HU4 179 B7
Moor La
Ashby De La Launde & Bloxholm LN4 108 C3
Besthorpe NG23 91 D7
Blankney LN4 95 E4
Braceby & Sapperton NG34 131 E1
Branston & Mere LN4 81 F2
Caistor LN7 33 A5
5 Cherry Willingham/Reepham LN3 82 A8
Hatfield DN8 15 D3
Horsington LN10 84 D2
Kirkby on Bain LN10 97 F6
Laneham DN22 65 A3
Leasingham NG34 121 C7
Lincoln LN6 204 E1
Long Bennington NG23 117 C3
Martin LN4 96 A2
North Clifton NG23 78 D6
Potter Hanworth LN4 82 B2
Reepham LN3 69 B1
Roughton LN10 98 B7
South Clifton NG23 78 E5
South Witham NG33 151 B2
Stapleford LN6 105 B8
Thorpe on the Hill LN6 79 E1
Thurlby LN6 92 E4
Wroot DN9 26 C6
Moor Owners Rd DN8 15 D8
Moor Pk 5 NG34 108 D1
Moor Pk Dr 9 LN10 97 C5
Moor Rd
Bottesford DN17 184 C2
15 Collingham NG23 91 D5

Moor Rd *continued*
Crowle DN17 ....16 C8
Newborough PE6 ....174 C5
Owersby LN8 ....45 A5
Snitterby DN21 ....43 D5
Thorne DN8 ....15 C7
Walesby LN8 ....45 E3
Moor Side PE22 ....111 C8
Moor St LN1 ....201 D4
Moorby Cl LN1 ....201 E7
Moore Cl NG23 ....117 F7
Moore's La 1 PE6 ....175 A1
Moorfield Rd 2 PE3 ....225 D3
Moorfields La DN14 ....6 F7
Moorgate Cl PE10 ....154 D7
Moorhouse Rd HU5 ....179 B8
Moorhouses Rd PE22 ....111 F8
Moorings The
Broughton DN20 ....196 A3
Burton LN1 ....200 D7
Moorland Ave
1 Lincoln LN6 ....205 A5
4 Walkeringham DN10 ....39 F3
Moorland Cl
8 Carlton-le-Moorland LN5 ....105 E8
5 Walkeringham DN10 ....39 F3
Moorland Cres 5 LN6 ....205 B6
Moorland Dr DN36 ....195 C7
Moorland Inf Sch LN6 ....205 B7
Moorland Way
5 Epworth DN9 ....27 E6
Lincoln LN6 ....204 F5
Moorlands 9 DN9 ....27 A2
Moorlands The 23 LN4 ....95 D4
Moors Rd DN15 ....182 C3
Moorside PE22 ....98 E3
Moorswood Gate PE12 ....159 D3
Moortown Cl 6 NG31 ....211 D7
Moortown Rd LN7 ....33 A3
Moorwell Bsns Pk DN17 ....184 D3
Moorwell Rd DN17 ....184 E2
Moray Cl 5 PE9 ....218 D6
Morborn Rd PE7 ....230 C2
Morborne Cl PE2 ....231 D6
Morborne La PE7 ....232 D4
Morborne Rd PE7 ....232 C2
Mordaunt Ave DN33 ....194 D7
Morden Cl 12 LN4 ....95 D4
Morecambe Ave DN16 ....185 A4
Moreland Ave 1 LN12 ....77 A8
Morfield Gr 5 DN9 ....27 D6
Morgan Cl PE7 ....233 E6
Morgan Way 5 DN19 ....4 E2
Morgans Cl 2 NG24 ....104 D5
Morkery La
Castle Bytham NG33 ....152 B2
North Witham NG33 ....151 F2
Morley La 10 PE20 ....135 A4
Morley Rd DN17 ....184 F5
Morley St 2 DN21 ....197 C5
Morley Way PE2 ....230 D5
Morley's La NG33 ....152 F7
Morpeth Cl PE2 ....230 C6
Morpeth Rd PE3 ....225 C3
Morpeth St HU3 ....180 D7
Morris Cl 21 LN2 ....68 D6
Morris Ct PE7 ....233 E6
Morris Gdns 3 PE25 ....206 B5
Morris Rd HU3 ....179 E7
Morris St PE1 ....226 B3
Morrison Cl 10 LN12 ....76 F8
Mortal Ash Hill DN16 ....19 C2
Mortimer Dr HU10 ....178 F6
Morton CE (Controlled) Prim Sch PE10 ....154 D7
Morton Cl
Gainsborough DN21 ....197 B8
Immingham DN40 ....186 B5
Morton Dr LN6 ....204 F7
Morton Dro PE10 ....155 A6
Morton La LN6 ....92 C8
Morton N Dro PE10 ....155 B7
Morton Rd
Gainsborough DN21 ....197 C7
Grimsby DN34 ....191 B7
Laughton DN21 ....41 B8
Swinderby LN6 ....92 B7
Morton St HU3 ....180 C8
Morton Terr DN21 ....197 C6
Morton Trentside Prim Sch DN21 ....197 B8
Morton Way LN9 ....199 C1
Morus Cl PE11 ....214 E2
Moss Dr PE25 ....206 C2
Moss Rd Grimsby DN32 ....191 E7
Kirk Bramwith DN7 ....14 A8
Mosscroft La DN7 ....14 F3
Mossdale Cl NG31 ....129 F5
Mossop Dr PE6 ....164 E3
Motherby La LN1 ....234 A2
Moulton Chapel Prim Sch PE12 ....157 F1
Moulton Chapel Rd PE12 ....157 C1
Moulton Cl 1 DN34 ....190 D4
Moulton Gr PE3 ....225 C6
Moulton Marsh Nature Reserve* PE12 ....146 F8
Moulton Mere Bank PE12 ....157 E3
Mount Ave
14 Barton-upon-Humber DN18 ....10 E8
Kingston upon Hull HU13 ....178 D2
10 Winterton DN15 ....9 B5
Mount La
Burton Pedwardine NG34 ....122 A2
Kirkby La Thorpe NG34 ....121 F3
Legsby LN8 ....58 A3
Mount Olivet LN11 ....198 A6
Mount Pleasant
9 Alford LN13 ....75 F2
Binbrook LN8 ....47 B4
1 Holton le Clay DN36 ....195 D1
Kingston upon Hull HU9 ....181 C8
Louth LN11 ....198 C5
8 New Holland DN19 ....4 E2
Peterborough PE2 ....231 C7
6 Wainfleet All Saints PE24 ....102 D2
Waltham DN37 ....194 D5
Mount Pleasant Cl DN21 ....53 B1
Mount Pleasant Rd PE13 ....170 D1
Mount Rd LN4 ....205 F3
Mount Royale Cl DN39 ....12 A1
Mount St
9 Grantham NG31 ....211 A5
Lincoln LN1 ....201 E6
Mount St Inf Sch LN1 ....201 E6
Mount The 15 DN3 ....14 A1
Mount Tumbledown Cl 9 PE12 ....160 E4
Mount View 5 HU14 ....3 A5
Mountbatten Ave
11 Pinchbeck PE11 ....156 E8
Stamford PE9 ....219 A6
Yaxley PE7 ....233 D5
Mountbatten Cl 5 DN16 ....185 B4
Mountbatten Dr 2 PE13 ....170 C1
Mountbatten Way
Bourne PE10 ....213 E7
Peterborough PE3 ....225 B6
Mountsteven Ave PE4 ....221 B1
Mourne Terr 6 LN5 ....205 D2
Mowbray Cl 3 DN9 ....27 D3
Mowbray Ct 23 DN9 ....27 E6
Mowbray Rd
Bretton PE3 ....220 D1
14 Thorne/Moorends DN8 ....15 B7
Mowbray St
Epworth DN9 ....27 E6
Gainsborough DN21 ....197 C6
Moxon's La 13 LN5 ....93 F7
Mrs Mary Kings CE (Controlled) Prim Sch LN4 ....96 B3
Mrs Smith's Cottage* LN5 ....107 B8
Much La LN1 ....234 A2
Muckton Wood Nature Reserve* LN11 ....74 E8
Muirfield
Grantham NG31 ....211 D8
11 Waltham DN37 ....194 C4
Muirfield Cl 6 PE11 ....214 C2
Muirfield Croft DN40 ....186 C4
Muirfield Dr PE25 ....206 D5
Mulberry Ave 3 LN6 ....204 F2
Mulberry Cl
5 North Thoresby DN36 ....36 B1
Sleaford NG34 ....212 D2
Waddington LN5 ....205 C1
Mulberry Ct 6 PE20 ....135 B6
Mulberry Dr 21 DN17 ....16 D7
Mulberry Rd LN8 ....45 E5
Mulberry Way PE11 ....214 E3
Mulgrave St
Kingston upon Hull HU8 ....181 A8
Scunthorpe DN15 ....183 A4
Mull Way DN40 ....186 C2
Multon Ings La PE20 ....136 B7
Mumby Cl 12 DN36 ....36 B1
Mumby Rd LN13 ....76 F2
Mumby's Bridge Rd PE22 ....98 F2
Munton Fields NG33 ....131 A1
Murray St 2 DN31 ....189 B2
Murrow Bank PE13 ....177 D6
Murrow Cty Prim Sch PE13 ....177 D5
Murrow La PE13 ....177 F5
Museum of Lincolnshire Life* LN1 ....234 A4
Musgraves Orch LN2 ....68 E7
Muskham PE3 ....224 F4
Mussons Cl NG33 ....152 E7
Muster Roll La PE21 ....209 A3
Musticott Pl 17 PE13 ....170 E1
Muston La NG13 ....128 B5
Muston Rd NG31 ....210 E2
Muswell Rd PE3 ....225 E4
Mutton La DN10 ....39 F1
Myers Cl NG32 ....120 C1
Myle Cross Jun Sch LN2 ....202 C6
Myrtle Ave PE1 ....226 C7
Myrtle Ct PE1 ....226 C7
Myrtle Gr PE1 ....226 C7
Myrtle Rd 5 DN7 ....14 C4
Myrtle Way 16 HU15 ....2 C5
Myton St HU1 ....180 E6

N

Naam Gr LN1 ....234 A4
Naam Pl LN1 ....234 A4
Nab La DN7 ....14 C8
Nairn Rd PE9 ....218 E6
Nan Sampson Bank DN9 ....26 B4
Nandike Cl 4 HU10 ....178 F6
Nansicles Rd PE2 ....230 D6
Napier Pl PE2 ....229 C6
Napier St LN2 ....234 C2
Narrow Boats The 3 DN20 ....196 A3
Narrow La Belchford LN9 ....73 B2
Kirkby on Bain LN10 ....98 C5
Twin Rivers DN14 ....7 C8
Whaplode PE12 ....158 C4
Naseby Cl 21 Hatfield DN7 ....14 D3
Peterborough PE3 ....225 C5
Naseby Dr DN31 ....191 B8
Nash La 2 LN6 ....204 E1
Nathan Cl PE3 ....225 B2
National Ave HU5 ....179 F8
National CE (Aided) Jun Sch The NG31 ....211 B5
National Fishing Heritage Ctr* DN31 ....191 E8
Natureland Seal Sanctuary* PE25 ....206 E4
Navenby CE Prim Sch LN5 ....107 B8
Navenby La
Ashby De La Launde & Bloxholm LN4 ....107 F6
Bassingham LN5 ....93 A1
Navensby Cl DN31 ....188 A2
Navigation La 28 LN7 ....33 B4
Navigation Way HU9 ....181 C6
Naylors Dr 5 LN8 ....57 B8
Naylor's Row 3 HU9 ....181 B7
Ndola Dr LN9 ....199 C2
Neale Rd 16 LN6 ....93 C8
Neal's Gate PE12 ....158 E2
Neap House Rd
Flixborough DN15 ....182 A7
Gunness DN15 ....17 E6
Neatgangs La DN19 ....5 A3
Neath Rd DN16 ....183 A1
Neaverson Rd 2 PE6 ....220 D7
Needham Dr PE12 ....159 C1
Needham Rd PE10 ....154 C6
Needhams Mdw LN13 ....76 B3
Needles The 8 PE25 ....206 A7
Neile Cl LN2 ....202 D7
Nelson Cl
5 Crowland PE6 ....166 F1
4 Skegness PE25 ....206 A7
Nelson Dr LN4 ....203 B2
Nelson Gdns 31 PE13 ....170 D1
Nelson Rd Fiskerton LN3 ....82 A6
Kingston upon Hull HU5 ....179 B7
5 Mablethorpe/Sutton on Sea LN12 ....64 B3
Nelson St
Gainsborough DN21 ....197 C6
Grimsby DN32 ....189 B1
Kingston upon Hull HU1 ....181 A5
Lincoln LN1 ....201 D3
Nelson Way
9 Boston PE21 ....208 E4
5 Grimsby DN34 ....190 D4
Grimsby DN34 ....190 C5
Nelthorpe Cl 9 DN39 ....12 A1
Nelthorpe St LN5 ....201 E1
Nene Cl
10 Ruskington NG34 ....108 D2
Wansford PE8 ....222 A3
4 Wittering PE8 ....172 B1
Nene Ct
4 Grantham NG31 ....210 E2
3 Spalding PE11 ....214 F5
Nene Mdws 1 PE12 ....160 F4
Nene Par 9 PE13 ....170 C1
Nene Parkway PE3 ....224 F1
Nene Pk 6 LN6 ....204 C1
Nene Rd LN1 ....201 E8
Nene St PE1 ....226 B2
Nene Way PE5 ....222 F2
Nenelands 8 PE12 ....160 F4
Neptune St
Cleethorpes DN35 ....192 E7
Kingston upon Hull HU1 ....180 D4
Neslam Rd NG34 ....143 C7
Ness La DN17 ....7 E6
Netherfield PE12 ....215 B2
Nethergate DN9 ....27 B2
Netherlands Way DN41 ....187 B3
Netherton Rd HU4 ....179 B4
Nettleham CE (Aided) Jun Sch LN2 ....68 C2
Nettleham Cl LN2 ....202 A6
Nettleham Inf Sch LN2 ....68 C2
Nettleham Rd
Lincoln LN2 ....234 C4
Scothern LN2 ....68 E3
Nettleholme 10 DN7 ....14 D4
Nettleton Dr LN6 ....92 E5
Nettleton Prim Sch LN7 ....33 A3
Nettleton Rd LN7 ....33 B3
Neustadt Ct 10 LN2 ....234 B3
Neville Ave PE11 ....214 F4
Neville Cl
5 Keadby with Althorpe DN17 ....17 D4
Neville Cl *continued*
Kingston upon Hull HU3 ....180 D5
Neville Cres 5 DN15 ....9 A5
Neville La DN7 ....14 A8
Neville Rd DN16 ....183 C2
Neville St DN35 ....192 D8
Neville Turner Way 1 DN37 ....194 D4
New Beacon Rd NG31 ....211 C4
New Bridge Rd HU9 ....181 C8
New Bridges Hospl HU9 ....181 D8
New Cartergate 2 DN31 ....191 D7
New Chapel La 8 DN37 ....23 F1
New Cl 3 DN33 ....191 C4
New Clee Sta DN31 ....189 D1
New Cleveland St HU8 ....181 A8
New Cres LN3 ....203 D6
New Cross Rd 3 PE9 ....219 C6
New Cut PE6 ....176 D5
New End Hemingby LN9 ....72 B1
5 Wainfleet All Saints PE24 ....102 D2
New Est
1 Little Bytham NG33 ....163 A8
Swinstead NG33 ....153 A5
New Fen Dike PE12 ....169 A7
New Fen Dro PE12 ....168 B1
New Gdn St 5 HU1 ....180 F7
New George St HU2 ....180 F7
New Gn 3 DN7 ....14 C6
New Hammond Beck Rd
Boston PE21 ....208 A3
Wyberton PE21 ....208 A3
New Haven Terr DN31 ....188 D1
New Hill NG32 ....119 A5
New Holland CE Methodist Prim Sch DN19 ....4 E2
New Holland Rd DN19 ....4 E1
New Holland Sta DN19 ....4 E3
New Ings La DN22 ....52 E3
New Inn La 3 DN7 ....14 C7
New La Girton NG23 ....78 D2
Great Carlton LN11 ....62 E3
Reedness DN14 ....6 E8
Tathwell LN11 ....61 A1
Toynton St Peter PE23 ....101 A5
Wansford PE8 ....222 C1
New Leake Prim Sch PE22 ....113 F7
New Mdw Dro PE7 ....231 D1
New Mill Field Rd DN7 ....14 E3
New Pk Est 1 DN7 ....14 D7
New Rd Blankney LN10 ....96 F5
Brantingham HU15 ....2 C8
Cleethorpes DN35 ....192 F6
Clipsham LE15 ....162 B7
1 Collyweston PE9 ....171 B1
Croft PE24 ....103 C3
Deeping St Nicholas PE6 ....166 D5
5 Easton on the Hill PE9 ....171 D3
9 Eye PE6 ....175 A1
Folksworth PE7 ....232 E6
Laceby DN37 ....35 A8
Langtoft PE6 ....164 F3
Peterborough PE1 ....226 B2
Quadring PE11 ....145 C8
Ryhall PE9 ....163 C1
Scunthorpe DN17 ....184 B6
Silk Willoughby NG34 ....121 A1
Spalding PE11 ....214 D4
Staunton NG13 ....117 B2
Sutton Bridge PE12 ....160 F5
Swinefleet DN14 ....6 C4
Thistleton LE15 ....151 D1
Wainfleet All Saints PE24 ....101 E2
Waltham DN37 ....194 E4
Worlaby DN20 ....10 D1
New River Dro
Cowbit PE12 ....156 F3
3 Spalding PE12 ....214 C1
New River Gate PE12 ....168 D8
New Roman Bank PE34 ....161 D3
New Row
Gonerby Hill Foot NG31 ....210 E7
3 Market Deeping PE6 ....217 D4
8 Messingham DN17 ....29 D7
New St
Aby with Greenfield LN13 ....75 B5
8 Brigg DN20 ....196 C3
Elsham DN20 ....20 E7
1 Gainsborough DN21 ....197 C5
Grantham NG31 ....211 A5
Grimsby DN31 ....191 E7
5 Heckington NG34 ....122 E2
Helpringham NG34 ....133 D7
6 Louth LN11 ....198 B5
Osbournby NG34 ....132 D5
Sleaford NG34 ....212 E4
4 Stamford PE9 ....219 C6
New Town 6 PE9 ....171 D3
New Trent St DN17 ....16 E6
New Waltham Prim Sch DN36 ....195 C7
New Wlk HU14 ....3 A4
New York Prim Sch LN4 ....111 C4
New York Rd LN4 ....110 F6
Newark & Nottinghamshire Agricultural Society's Showground* NG24 ....104 C7
Newark Air Mus* NG24 ....104 D6
Newark Ave PE1 ....226 C6
Newark Hill
Foston NG23 ....117 F1
Great Gonerby NG31 ....129 D6
Newark Hill CP Sch PE1 ....226 D6
Newark Hospl NG24 ....104 A4
Newark La NG32 ....119 C4
Newark N Gate Sta NG24 ....104 A5
Newark Rd
Barnby in the Willows NG24 ....104 E3
Bassingham LN5 ....92 E2
Fenton LN1 ....65 D4
Leadenham LN5 ....106 C3
Lincoln LN6 ....204 F3
Newark-on-Trent NG24 ....104 C5
Norton Disney LN6 ....91 F2
Peterborough PE1 ....226 E2
Stapleford LN6 ....105 B8
Swinderby LN6 ....92 A4
Newark Rd Ind Est PE1 ....226 E4
Newbey Cl PE3 ....225 B3
Newbigg 1 Crowle DN17 ....16 C8
Westwoodside DN9 ....27 B2
Newbolt Ave 2 DN17 ....184 D7
Newbolt Cl 1 LN7 ....33 A3
Newborn Ave DN15 ....182 E4
Newborn Cl PE2 ....231 E5
Newborough Rd PE4 ....174 E1
Newboults La 2 PE9 ....219 A5
Newbridge Hill LN11 ....198 C6
Newbridge La LN11 ....49 E5
Newbury Ave DN37 ....188 A1
Newbury Gr 1 DN34 ....190 E4
Newbury Rd 15 NG24 ....104 C5
Newbury Terr DN37 ....188 A1
Newby Rd DN31 ....191 C7
Newcastle Dr PE2 ....230 D6
Newcastle Rd 4 NG31 ....210 D5
Newcomb Ct 2 NG34 ....212 B7
Newcombe Way PE2 ....229 D2
Newcot La LN4 ....81 F4
Newdike Gate PE12 ....158 C5
Newdown Rd DN17 ....184 D3
Newfield Cl 10 DN3 ....14 A4
Newfield Dr LN4 ....109 F3
Newfield Rd NG34 ....212 C5
Newfields PE13 ....169 D1
Newgate La NG31 ....130 D4
Newgate Rd PE13 ....169 F6
Newgates 3 PE9 ....219 C5
Newhall Rd
13 Kirk Sandall DN3 ....14 A2
10 Kirk Sandall DN3 ....14 A2
Newham La PE22 ....112 A1
Newham Rd 2 PE9 ....219 A7
Newhaven Dr LN5 ....205 D3
Newington Ave HU4 ....179 E5
Newington Prim Sch HU3 ....180 A4
Newington St HU3 ....179 F4
Newland LN1 ....234 A2
Newland Ave DN15 ....182 E2
Newland Dr DN15 ....182 D3
Newland St W 6 LN1 ....234 A2
Newland View 17 DN9 ....27 E6
Newland Wlk DN15 ....182 E3
Newlands DN21 ....197 E5
Newlands Pk DN36 ....193 B1
Newlands Rd
2 Haconby PE10 ....154 D8
Parson Drove PE13 ....177 D7
Surfleet PE11 ....145 F4
Newlyn Cl
4 Kingston upon Hull HU13 ....179 A2
3 New Waltham DN36 ....195 C7
Newman Cl 19 PE8 ....172 B1
Newmarket LN11 ....198 C4
Newmarket Cl PE1 ....226 B6
Newmarket St 2 DN32 ....191 F8
Newnham Cres DN16 ....185 A4
Newport LN2 ....234 B4
Newport Ave NG31 ....210 D4
Newport Cl 4 HU3 ....180 D5
Newport Cres 2 LN5 ....93 F7
Newport Ct 1 LN1 ....234 B4
Newport Dr DN15 ....9 A6
Newport St 8 DN18 ....3 F1
Newsham Dr DN34 ....191 A7
Newsham Garth HU4 ....179 B5
Newsham La DN39 ....22 D8
Newstead Ave
Cherry Willingham/Reepham LN3 ....203 E5
Holton le Clay DN36 ....195 E2
Newstead Cl PE6 ....175 A2
Newstead Rd
Cleethorpes DN35 ....192 E4
2 Mablethorpe/Sutton on Sea LN12 ....64 C3
Ryhall PE9 ....163 D1
Newstead St HU5 ....180 A8
Newton Bar NG34 ....132 A3
Newton Cl
8 Metheringham LN4 ....95 C4
Swinderby LN6 ....92 A5
5 Wragby LN8 ....70 D4
Newton Ct 6 NG33 ....151 E7
Newton La Binbrook LN8 ....47 D5
15 Ruskington NG34 ....108 E2
Newton Marsh La DN36 ....36 F6
Newton Pk 10 NG23 ....117 D3
Newton Rd DN16 ....185 E6
Newton St
5 Grantham NG31 ....211 B4

Newton St continued
3 Kingston upon Hull HU3 ....180 B4
Lincoln LN5 ....234 B1
Newark-on-Trent NG24 ...104 A4
Newton Way
5 Colsterworth NG33 ....151 D7
Sleaford NG34 ....212 D5
Newton-on-Trent CE Sch LN1 ....65 C1
Newtown
8 Spilsby PE23 ....101 A8
Stamford PE9 ....219 D5
Newtown Sq HU9 ....181 E7
Nichol Hill 2 LN11 ....198 B5
Nicholas Ct 28 DN18 ....10 E8
Nicholas Taylor Gdns 1 PE3 ....224 F3
Nicholls Ave PE3 ....225 E3
Nicholson Rd
3 Healing DN41 ....24 A5
Immingham DN40 ....12 E4
Nicholson St 8 DN35 ....192 F5
Nicholson Way 7 DN9 ...27 D7
Nicolette Way 10 PE11 ..214 B5
Nicolgate La DN20 ....196 D4
Nicolson Dr 18 DN18 ....10 F8
Nidd's La PE20 ....136 E4
Nightingale Cl 3 DN15 .182 D5
Nightingale Cres 1 LN6 ....204 E8
Nightingale Ct PE4 ....221 E2
Nightingale Dr PE7 ....233 D6
Nightingales 13 PE6 ....217 C5
Nightleys Rd DN22 ....65 B5
Ninescores La DN9 ....26 B4
Ninth Ave
3 Fixborough Ind Est DN15 ..8 A1
Grantham NG31 ....211 F5
Nipcut Rd PE6 ....175 C2
Nocton Com Sch LN4 ....95 C7
Nocton Dr LN2 ....201 F8
Nocton Fen La LN4 ....83 A1
Nocton Rd
Potter Hanworth LN4 ....95 B8
7 Potterhanworth LN4 ....82 B1
Noel St DN21 ....197 C6
Nook The
Croxton Kerrial NG32 ....138 D3
7 Easton on the Hill PE9 ..171 D3
4 Helpston PE6 ....173 C4
Sproxton LE14 ....150 C7
Nookin The 1 LN5 ....106 E5
Nooking La DN37 ....23 D2
Nooking The DN9 ....27 C3
Nookings Dr 3 DN20 ....31 A5
Norbeck La LN2 ....68 C6
Norburn
2 Peterborough PE3 ....220 F1
Peterborough PE3 ....225 B8
Norfolk Ave DN15 ....8 B4
Norfolk Bank La HU15 ....1 F8
Norfolk Cl 1 LN8 ....47 B6
Norfolk Cres
Bracebridge Heath LN4 ..205 F4
1 Scampton Airfield LN1 ..67 E5
Norfolk La DN35 ....192 E7
Norfolk Pl 4 PE21 ....208 F6
Norfolk Sq 5 PE9 ....219 B6
Norfolk St Boston PE21 ..208 F6
Kingston upon Hull HU2 ..180 E7
Lincoln LN1 ....201 C4
Peterborough PE1 ....225 F4
Norfolk St Ind Est PE21 ....208 F7
Norland Ave HU4 ....179 C6
Norman Ave 5 PE21 ....208 F5
Norman Cl
9 Barton-upon-Humber DN18 ....10 F8
30 Metheringham LN4 ....95 C4
Norman Cres 1 DN17 ....184 F8
Norman Dr 7 DN7 ....14 D3
Norman Mews 3 PE10 ..213 D5
Norman Rd
Grimsby DN34 ....191 B7
Hatfield DN7 ....14 D3
Peterborough PE1 ....226 C4
Norman St 1 LN5 ....234 B1
Normanby Cliff Rd LN8 ..55 D7
Normanby Hall Ctry Pk* DN15 ....8 C3
Normanby Prim Sch LN8 ....55 E7
Normanby Rd
Burton upon Stather DN15 ..8 C3
Nettleton LN7 ....33 B2
3 Owmby LN8 ....55 F6
Scunthorpe DN15 ....183 A5
Stow DN21 ....53 F1
Normanby Rise LN8 ....45 E5
Normandy Rd DN35 ....192 D5
Normanton La NG13 ....128 A6
Normanton Rd
1 Crowland PE6 ....166 F1
Peterborough PE1 ....226 D7
Normanton Rise HU4 ..179 C7
Nornabell St 1 HU8 ....181 C8
Norris Cl 10 NG34 ....122 D3
Norris St LN5 ....201 F1
Norsefield Ave DN37 ..194 E5
North Ave PE10 ....153 D6
North Axholme Comp Sch DN17 ....16 D7
North Bank
Crowland PE6 ....166 E1
Thorney PE6 ....227 D1
North Bank Rd 4 PE1 ..226 D3
North Beck La PE23 ....87 E1
North Bracing PE25 ....206 E3
North Carr La DN20 ....9 F3
North Carr Rd
Misterton DN10 ....39 F7
Scotter DN17 ....28 E5
West Stockwith DN10 ....40 B6
North Church Side 12 HU1 ....180 F6
North Cliff Rd DN21 ....30 C2
North Clifton Sch NG23 ..78 C6
North Coates Rd DN36 ..37 A4
North Cockerington CE Prim Sch LN11 ....50 A1
North Cotes CE (Controlled) Prim Sch DN36 ....37 B3
North Cres 7 NG13 ....128 A5
North Cswy LN4 ....82 D4
North Ct 10 LN2 ....68 C2
North Cty Prim Sch DN21 ....197 B6
North Dales Rd LN4 ....82 A5
North Dr
2 Ancaster NG32 ....120 A3
Balderton NG24 ....104 C1
Kingston upon Hull HU10 ....178 E6
RAF Cranwell NG34 ....107 D1
Swanland HU14 ....3 B7
North Dro Bicker PE20 ..134 E6
Deeping St Nicholas PE11 ....155 F1
Helpringham NG34 ....133 E7
Lutton PE12 ....148 D1
Quadring PE11 ....144 C8
Swaton NG34 ....133 E4
North Eastern Rd DN8 ..15 A8
North Elkington La LN11 ....48 E1
North End 5 Goxhill DN19 .12 A8
South Ferriby DN18 ....10 A8
Wisbech PE13 ....170 C1
North End Cres 9 DN36 ..36 D4
North End La
2 Fulbeck NG32 ....106 C1
Saltfleetby LN11 ....62 F8
South Cockerington LN11 ...50 F1
South Kelsey LN7 ....32 A2
Sturton Le Steeple DN22 ..52 E4
North End Rd 7 DN36 ..36 D4
North Farm Rd DN17 ..184 D3
North Fen Dro PE20 ..134 E4
North Fen Rd
3 Glinton PE6 ....220 C8
Helpringham NG34 ....133 D7
North Field Rd PE6 ....217 B7
North Foreland Dr 3 PE25 ....206 D8
North Forty Foot Bank PE21 ....208 A6
North Gate
Gosberton PE11 ....145 A6
Newark-on-Trent NG24 ..104 A5
Pinchbeck PE11 ....144 E1
Sleaford NG34 ....212 D5
North Halls 1 LN8 ....47 C5
North Heath La NG32 ..106 D1
North Holme 8 DN36 ....36 D4
North Holme Rd LN11 ..198 B7
North Ing Dro PE11 ....134 C4
North Ings La LN13 ....77 A5
North Ings Rd DN7 ....14 E5
North Intake La DN9 ....40 C8
North Kelsey Rd LN7 ....33 A4
North Kesteven Sch LN6 ....204 D1
North Kesteven Sports Ctr LN6 ....204 D1
North Kyme Cty Prim Sch LN4 ....109 E3
North La Coningsby LN4 ..110 E8
Marshchapel DN36 ....37 C2
2 Navenby/Wellingore LN5 ....107 A8
Reepham LN3 ....68 F1
Swaby LN13 ....74 E4
North Leverton CE Sch DN22 ....52 B1
North Leys Rd DN22 ....52 E1
North Lincoln Rd DN16 ....183 F2
North Lincolnshire Coll
Lincoln LN2 ....234 C3
Louth LN11 ....198 D6
North Lincolnshire Mus & Art Gall* DN15 ....183 A2
North Lindsey Coll DN17 ....184 E8
North Marsh Rd DN21 ..197 C6
North Moor Dr 2 DN10 ..39 F3
North Moor La
Martin LN4 ....96 B3
Messingham DN17 ....29 B8
North Moor Rd
Scotter DN17 ....29 C5
Walkeringham DN10 ....39 F3
North Moss La DN41 ....187 B1
North Par
Gainsborough DN21 ....197 F4
Grantham NG31 ....211 A6
Holbeach PE12 ....215 E3
Lincoln LN1 ....234 A3
Scunthorpe DN16 ....185 D6
Skegness PE25 ....206 D3
4 Sleaford NG34 ....212 D7
North Prom DN35 ....192 E7
North Quay DN31 ....189 C3
North Ramper DN21 ....44 A7
North Rd Bourne PE10 ..213 D8
Bratoft PE24 ....102 B8
7 Cranwell NG34 ....107 F1
Gedney Hill PE12 ....168 D4
1 Keadby with Althorpe DN17 ....17 C6
Kingston upon Hull HU4 ..179 E4
Leadenham LN5 ....106 D3
Mablethorpe & Sutton LN12 ....64 B1
Sturton Le Steeple DN22 ..52 B4
Tattershall Thorpe LN4 ....97 F3
Tetford LN9 ....73 F1
Tydd St Mary PE13 ....160 B2
North Scaffold La NG23 ....91 D3
North Scarle Prim Sch LN6 ....78 E2
North Scarle Rd NG23 ..91 F8
North Sea La DN35 ....193 A1
North Shore Rd PE25 ..206 D6
North Somercotes CE (Controlled) Prim Sch LN11 ....50 F7
North St
7 Barrow upon Humber DN19 ....11 D8
1 Barrow upon Humber DN19 ....11 D8
2 Boston PE21 ....208 F6
Bourne PE10 ....213 D5
Caistor LN7 ....33 B4
Cleethorpes DN35 ....192 F6
3 Crowland PE6 ....166 E1
9 Crowle DN17 ....16 D8
Digby LN4 ....108 E6
Folksworth PE7 ....233 A1
Gainsborough DN21 ....197 C5
7 Grantham NG31 ....211 A5
Horncastle LN9 ....199 C4
Kingston upon Hull HU10 ....178 E6
Middle Rasen LN8 ....57 B8
Morton DN21 ....197 C8
8 Nettleham LN2 ....68 C2
Osbournby NG34 ....132 C5
Owston Ferry DN9 ....28 B3
Peterborough PE1 ....226 A2
Roxby cum Risby DN15 ....9 A4
Scunthorpe DN15 ....183 B4
Stamford PE9 ....219 B5
Sturton Le Steeple DN22 ..52 B3
Thimbleby LN9 ....85 B5
West Butterwick DN17 ....17 D1
West/East Butterwick DN17 ....28 D8
Winterton DN15 ....9 B6
North Terr PE1 ....226 E7
North Thoresby Prim Sch DN36 ....36 A1
North Walls HU1 ....181 A6
North Warren Rd DN21 ....197 B6
North Way
6 Lincoln LN6 ....204 D2
Marshchapel DN36 ....37 B2
North Witham Bank LN1 ....234 A2
North Witham Rd NG33 ....151 D3
Northam Cl PE6 ....175 B3
Northampton Rd DN16 ....183 C1
Northborough Cty Prim Sch PE6 ....173 F6
Northcliffe Rd NG31 ....211 A7
Northcroft 4 LN1 ....66 D3
Northcroft La NG23 ....91 C5
North-dale Ct 4 DN21 ..30 B2
Northdale Pk 1 HU14 ....3 B7
Northern Ave DN20 ....196 C5
Northern Rd NG24 ....104 A5
Northern's Cl NG33 ....151 D5
Northey Rd PE6 ....227 C2
Northferry La 2 DN9 ....16 D1
Northfield HU14 ....3 B7
Northfield Ave
Kingston upon Hull HU13 ....178 E3
3 Sudbrooke LN2 ....68 F3
Northfield Cl
1 Scunthorpe DN16 ....185 C6
11 Tetney DN36 ....36 D4
West Butterwick DN17 ....17 D1
Northfield La
Amcotts DN17 ....7 E2
North Clifton NG23 ....78 D7
Thornton Curtis DN39 ....11 D5
Willoughton DN21 ....42 C4
Northfield Rd
Ashby with Scremby PE23 ..88 D1
Kingston upon Hull HU3 ..179 F6
Messingham DN17 ....185 A1
North Leverton with Habblesthorpe DN22 ....52 D1
Peterborough PE1 ....225 F7
4 Ruskington NG34 ....108 E2
Sleaford NG34 ....212 A2
Northfield Rise 1 LN1 ..66 C2
Northfields
Bourne PE10 ....213 D7
Stamford PE9 ....219 C6
Northgate
Kingston upon Hull HU13 ....178 E2
Lincoln LN2 ....234 B4
Louth LN11 ....198 B5
Northgate La LN11 ....62 B7
Northgate Sports Hall NG34 ....212 D5
Northing La LN2 ....68 F5
Northings The 1 NG32 ..210 B4
Northlands Ave 3 DN15 ..9 A5
Northlands La PE22 ....113 A4
Northlands Rd
Glentworth DN21 ....54 E6
Winterton DN15 ....9 A5
Northlands Rd S 10 DN15 ..9 A5
Northminster PE1 ....226 A3
Northmoor Rd DN17 ....6 C1
Northolme
Gainsborough DN21 ....197 D5
Sutton St Edmund PE12 ..168 E5
Northolme Circ 2 HU13 ....178 E2
Northolme Cres
Kingston upon Hull HU13 ....178 E2
4 Scunthorpe DN15 ....182 F3
Northolme Rd HU13 ....178 E2
Northon's La PE12 ....215 C3
Northorpe Cl LN6 ....204 F7
Northorpe La PE10 ....164 C8
Northorpe Rd
Donington PE11 ....134 D3
Halton Holegate PE23 ....101 B8
Scotton DN21 ....29 D1
North's La DN37 ....34 D8
Northside 2 DN9 ....27 C2
Northside La DN22 ....52 C1
Northumberland Ave
13 Scampton Airfield LN1 ..67 E5
6 Stamford PE9 ....219 A6
Northumberland Cl DN34 ....191 B6
Northumbria Rd NG34 ..212 B2
Northway 3 LN11 ....49 B8
Northwood Dr
Hessle HU13 ....178 B3
Sleaford NG34 ....212 C6
Norton Disney Rd LN5 ..92 D1
Norton Gr HU4 ....179 D4
Norton La
Bishop Norton LN8 ....43 C2
Thurlby LN6 ....92 C4
Norton Rd
Peterborough PE1 ....225 F6
Scunthorpe DN16 ....185 B5
Stapleford LN6 ....105 C8
Norton St NG31 ....211 A3
Norwell La NG23 ....91 E1
Norwich Ave DN34 ....191 A4
Norwich Cl
Heighington/Washingborough LN4 ....203 E1
3 Sleaford NG34 ....212 C7
Norwich Dr LN4 ....81 A2
Norwich Rd PE13 ....170 E1
Norwich Way 7 NG31 ..210 E5
Norwood Ave 3 DN15 ..182 F2
Norwood Cl 3 HU10 ....178 E7
Norwood Cty Prim Sch PE4 ....221 C3
Norwood La
Borough Fen PE6 ....174 E1
Peterborough PE4 ....221 F2
Norwood Rd
7 Hatfield DN7 ....14 C5
5 Skegness PE25 ....103 E4
4 Skegness PE25 ....103 E4
Norwood St HU3 ....180 C7
Nostell Rd DN16 ....183 D1
Nottingham Rd 1 NG13 .128 A5
Nottingham Terr 5 LN2 ....234 C3
Nottingham Way PE1 ..226 C6
Nowells La 6 PE10 ....213 D5
Nuffield Cl 6 DN16 ....185 B4
Nunburnholme Ave 5 HU14 ....3 A4
Nunburnholme Pk HU5 ....179 B7
Nuns Rd DN17 ....184 F6
Nunsthorpe Com Sch DN33 ....191 B4
Nunthorpe Cl 36 DN7 ....14 D4
Nursery Cl
4 Barton-upon-Humber DN18 ....3 F1
Peterborough PE1 ....226 A4
10 Saxilby LN1 ....66 D2
Scunthorpe DN17 ....184 F3
Nursery Ct 13 Brough HU15 .2 C5
Sleaford NG34 ....212 D2
Nursery Dr PE13 ....170 E2
Nursery Gdns 7 DN36 ..195 D2
Nursery Gr LN2 ....202 A6
Nursery La
Belvoir NG32 ....138 C6
Peterborough PE1 ....226 D2
Nursery Rd
Boston PE21 ....209 B2
Cranwell & Byard's Leap NG34 ....120 C8
Nursery St 2 LN8 ....57 D7
Nurses La
Skellingthorpe LN6 ....200 A5
4 Wymondham LE14 ....150 C1
Nut La PE22 ....114 C1
Nutfields Gr 7 DN7 ....14 C6
Nutwood View 4 DN16 ..185 D4

O

Oak Ave 13 Brough HU15 ....2 C6
Oak Ave continued
3 Grimsby DN32 ....191 E4
5 Scawby DN20 ....30 F8
11 Welton/Dunholme LN2 ..68 E6
Oak Cl
8 Ingoldmells PE25 ....90 D3
Louth LN11 ....198 E4
14 Sudbrooke LN2 ....68 F2
5 Woodhall Spa LN10 ....97 E6
Oak Cres Boston PE21 ..208 E7
Bourne PE10 ....213 B6
Cherry Willingham/Reepham LN3 ....203 D5
Oak Ct 1 PE11 ....214 E3
Oak Dr HU5 ....179 B7
Oak Gr
3 Barrow upon Humber DN19 ....11 C7
6 Market Deeping PE6 ..217 B6
Oak Hill LN4 ....203 B2
Oak House La PE22 ....126 C4
Oak Rd Glinton PE6 ....220 B8
1 Healing DN41 ....24 A5
Scunthorpe DN16 ....185 B7
Sleaford NG34 ....212 D2
Stamford PE9 ....218 D7
Oak Tree Ave DN21 ....197 F6
Oak Tree Cl
3 Long Bennington NG23 .117 D3
7 Market Rasen LN8 ....57 D7
Oak View
18 Dunholme LN2 ....68 E6
Peterborough PE3 ....224 F2
Oak Way
Cleethorpes DN35 ....192 D2
3 Heckington NG34 ....122 D3
Oakdale Ave
3 Kingston upon Hull HU10 ....178 E8
Peterborough PE2 ....231 D4
Oakdale Cl 4 NG31 ....211 A8
Oakdale CP Sch PE7 ....231 C4
Oakfield 16 LN1 ....66 D2
Oakfield Cl 2 DN20 ....196 E3
Oakfield St LN2 ....202 B3
Oakford Cl DN17 ....184 D8
Oakham Ave 5 LN12 ....64 A3
Oakham Cl NG31 ....210 E6
Oakhurst Cl NG31 ....211 D2
Oakland Ave 39 DN7 ....14 D4
Oakland Cl 3 LN1 ....201 D7
Oakland Way 13 PE11 ..145 C1
Oaklands
3 Beckingham DN10 ....40 A1
8 Collingham NG23 ....91 D4
5 Woodhall Spa LN10 ....97 D5
Oaklands Dr
Kingston upon Hull HU13 ....178 D3
4 Wisbech PE13 ....170 E1
Oaklands Rd DN40 ....186 C5
Oaklands The 6 LN8 ....70 D4
Oakleaf Rd PE1 ....226 C6
Oakleigh DN16 ....185 C3
Oakleigh Dr
Canwick LN1 ....201 C6
Peterborough PE2 ....230 C6
Oakleigh Rd NG31 ....210 C3
Oakley Dr PE11 ....214 E6
Oakley Pl PE12 ....147 F2
Oakroyd Cres 22 PE13 ..170 D1
Oaks La DN10 ....39 F2
Oaks The
15 Nettleham LN2 ....68 D2
1 Scothern LN2 ....68 F3
Oaktree Cl 3 PE11 ....145 B7
Oakwood Ave 4 LN6 ....204 C8
Oakwood Cl HU10 ....179 A7
Oakwood Dr DN37 ....190 C7
Oakwood Glade PE12 ..215 C3
Oakwood Rise 2 DN16 ..185 B4
Oasby Rd NG32 ....131 C7
Oatfield Way NG34 ....122 D2
Oban Cl 7 PE9 ....218 E6
Oban Ct 6 DN40 ....186 C3
Obthorpe La PE10 ....164 C7
Occupation La
Anderby PE24 ....77 C3
Carrington PE22 ....99 C1
6 North Kelsey LN7 ....32 A4
Swanland HU14 ....3 B8
Occupation Rd
Great Gonerby NG32 ....129 C6
Lincoln LN1 ....234 A4
Peterborough PE1 ....225 E6
Ocean Ave PE25 ....206 D1
Ocean Bvd HU9 ....181 B6
Octagon Dr 14 PE13 ....170 C1
Octavia Cl 23 PE13 ....170 E1
Odecroft PE3 ....225 C7
Ogilvy Dr DN17 ....184 F3
O'hanlon Ave DN20 ....196 D3
Old Annandale Rd HU10 ....178 C8
Old Barracks The NG31 ....211 C4
Old Black Dro NG34 ....109 D1
Old Boston Rd LN4 ....207 D3
Old Bowling Gn 4 LN13 ..75 F2
Old Brickkiln La LN5 ....92 F2
Old Brumby St DN16 ....185 A8
Old Carpenter's Yd 1 DN7 ....14 B6
Old Chapel La
2 Burgh le Marsh PE24 ..102 E7

Old Chapel La *continued*
9 Laceby DN37 .... 23 F1
Old Chapel Rd LN6 ..... 200 A4
Old Church La 1 PE23 .. 101 D7
Old Church Rd PE24 ...... 90 D4
Old Clee Infants & Jun Sch
DN32 .... 192 B6
Old Courts Rd 2 DN20 .. 196 C3
Old Crosby DN15 .... 183 A5
Old Dairy 11 DN19 .... 11 D8
Old Epworth Rd (East) 1
DN7 .... 14 F4
Old Farm Ct 4 DN37 .... 194 C4
Old Fen Bank
Wainfleet All Saints
PE24 .... 101 F2
Wainfleet St Mary PE24 ... 102 A1
Old Fen Dike
Gedney PE12 .... 158 F1
Sutton St James PE12 .... 169 B8
Old Fen La
Coningsby LN4 .... 207 E1
Pinchbeck PE11 .... 145 A1
Old Fen Rd PE22 .... 115 A8
Old Fendike Rd PE12 .... 157 B3
Old Field La DN7 .... 14 A5
Old Fleet DN37 .... 190 C6
Old Forge Rd 8 DN10 .... 39 F5
Old Forty Foot Bank
NG34 .... 123 C1
Old Great N Rd
Stamford PE9 .... 218 C8
Thorney PE8 .... 228 B7
Wansford PE8 .... 222 C2
Wothorpe PE9 .... 219 C2
Old Hall Gdns 12 NG24 .. 104 C5
Old Hall La 6 PE11 ...... 145 D2
Old Hall Spinney
NG32 .... 119 C2
Old Hammond Beck Rd
PE21 .... 208 A2
Old Haxey Rd DN10 ...... 39 F6
Old Hill The NG32 .... 138 C6
Old Hundred La PE12 .... 167 F2
Old Inn La PE12 .... 146 E7
Old Ironside Rd DN16 ... 183 D3
Old Knarr Fen Dro
PE6 .... 176 C2
Old La DN14 .... 6 F7
Old Leake Prim Sch
PE22 .... 114 A1
Old Leicester Rd PE8 ... 222 A3
Old Leys La DN21 .... 43 A3
Old Lincoln Rd NG32 .... 119 B7
Old Lynn Rd 2 PE13 .... 170 E1
Old Main Rd
2 Barnetby Le Beck DN37 .. 35 B6
Fosdyke PE20 .... 146 D8
Irby DN37 .... 34 D7
Old Leake PE22 .... 114 B1
Scamblesby LN11 .... 72 F5
Old Mill La
10 Broughton DN20 .... 19 E3
Grimoldby LN11 .... 62 B6
Whitton DN15 .... 1 E3
Wrawby DN20 .... 196 F7
Old Mill Pk LN11 .... 198 C6
Old Mkt Ave
4 Hundleby PE23 .... 87 F1
12 Spilsby PE23 .... 87 F1
Spilsby PE23 .... 100 F8
Old Mkt Pl 5 DN31 ...... 191 D7
Old N Rd PE8 .... 222 A3
Old Orch NG32 .... 210 A5
Old Pl 3 NG34 .... 212 F4
Old Plumtree La 3 DN36 . 36 B1
Old Pond Cl
7 Birchwood LN6 .... 200 D1
Birchwood LN6 .... 204 D8
Old Pond La PE5 .... 223 E2
Old Pond Pl 20 HU14 .... 3 A4
Old Post La NG33 .... 151 D6
Old Post Office La
8 Barnetby le Wold DN38 .. 21 B4
Butterwick PE22 .... 126 E4
4 South Ferriby DN18 ..... 10 A7
Old Rd Grimsby DN37 ... 190 C8
Healing DN37 .... 24 B5
Old Rectory Dr
1 Tallington PE9 .... 172 F7
Wansford PE8 .... 222 A6
Old Rectory Gdns
DN16 .... 185 A6
Old Rectory The* DN9 .... 27 E6
Old Roman Bank
3 Skegness PE25 .... 206 D6
Terrington St Clement
PE34 .... 161 E3
Old S Eau Bank PE12 ... 168 A1
Old Sch CE (Controlled) The
NG32 .... 119 A5
Old Sch Dr 14 DN20 ...... 30 F5
Old Sch La
2 Cranwell NG34 .... 120 F8
Donington on Bain LN11 .... 59 E2
5 Fishtoft PE21 .... 126 C1
2 North Kelsey LN7 .... 32 A4
Scunthorpe DN16 .... 185 B3
Old Sch Mews 12 PE23 ... 88 A1
Old Sch Yd 17 DN21 ...... 30 B1
Old Showfields DN21 ... 197 D6
Old Sluice Rd PE12 ..... 215 B8
Old Smithy Ct 1 LN4 .... 207 D4
Old Sta Yd NG13 .... 128 B6
Old Thorne Rd DN7 .... 14 E4
Old Trent Rd DN21 ...... 197 A5
Old Upper Ings La
DN22 .... 52 D3
Old Vicarage La
12 Lutton PE12 .... 160 A8
Lutton PE12 .... 216 C8
Old Vicarage Pk 2 DN20 .. 30 E8
Old Village St DN15 ...... 17 E6
Old Wainfleet Rd 1
PE25 .... 206 B3
Old Warp La 11 DN18 ..... 10 A7
Old Wharf Rd 9 NG31 ... 211 A4
Old Wood 1 LN6 .... 200 C1
Oldbrook PE3 .... 220 E1
Olde Curiosity Mus*
LN12 .... 64 C3
Oldfield Cl
9 Barnby Dun DN3 .... 14 A4
1 Stainforth DN7 .... 14 B6
Oldfield Cres 16 DN7 ..... 14 C6
Oldfield La PE22 .... 127 C6
Oldfield Rd 20 DN8 .... 15 B7
Oldham Dr 8 PE11 ...... 145 C1
Oldlane Gate DN14 .... 6 D4
Olive Rd PE1 .... 226 C7
Oliver Ct 1 DN31 .... 191 D8
Oliver Quibell Cty Infants Sch
NG24 .... 104 A3
Oliver Rd 16 NG23 ...... 117 D3
Oliver St DN35 .... 192 D8
Olivier Ct HU4 .... 179 E3
Ollard Ave PE13 .... 170 D1
Omega Bvd DN8 .... 14 F8
On Hill 17 HU14 .... 3 B7
Ontario Rd DN17 .... 184 E3
Onyx Gr 2 HU3 .... 180 A4
Oole Rd DN35 .... 192 F6
Oosterbeek Cl 5 PE10 .. 213 E7
Opportune Rd 25 PE13 .. 170 D1
Orangawood Cl 7
NG31 .... 210 F8
Orange Row 3 PE34 ..... 161 F3
Orange Row Rd 1 PE34 .. 161 F3
Orb La DN15 .... 183 A7
Orby Bank PE24 .... 89 D3
Orby Gr DN33 .... 191 A3
Orby Holme Field La
PE24 .... 89 D3
Orby Rd
Addlethorpe PE24 .... 90 B4
Burgh Le Marsh PE24 ...... 89 D1
Orchard Ave 8 DN21 ...... 29 C3
Orchard Cl
4 Barrow upon Humber
DN19 .... 11 C7
23 Barton-upon-Humber
DN18 .... 10 F8
4 Blyton DN21 .... 41 C5
4 Bourne PE10 .... 213 C6
6 Burringham DN17 .... 17 D4
9 Burton-upon-Stather
DN15 .... 8 B5
Cherry Willingham/Reepham
LN3 .... 203 D5
11 Donington PE11 .... 134 F2
4 Gonerby Hill Foot
NG31 .... 210 E8
Great Hale NG34 .... 122 E1
2 Hatfield DN7 .... 14 C3
6 Helpringham NG34 ..... 133 D7
Kingston upon Hull
HU10 .... 178 F7
1 Kirton in Lindsey DN21 .. 30 B2
Louth LN11 .... 198 C7
2 Mablethorpe/Sutton on Sea
LN12 .... 64 A3
4 Market Deeping PE6 ... 217 D4
12 Messingham DN17 ...... 29 D7
25 Metheringham LN4 ...... 95 C4
2 Morton PE10 .... 154 C7
4 Moulton PE12 .... 157 F6
Peterborough PE3 .... 225 D3
9 Pinchbeck PE11 .... 156 E8
8 Scothern LN2 .... 68 F4
5 Scunthorpe DN16 ...... 185 B6
2 Sleaford NG34 .... 212 F4
7 Welton/Dunholme LN2 ... 68 D6
Whaplode PE12 .... 215 A7
Orchard Croft
4 Epworth DN9 .... 27 D7
5 Grimsby DN33 .... 194 E7
Orchard Ct
3 Thorney PE6 .... 175 F3
3 Waltham DN37 .... 194 D4
Orchard Dr
7 Burton-upon-Stather
DN15 .... 8 B5
3 Gunness DN15 .... 17 E6
3 Hatfield DN7 .... 14 C3
12 Heckington NG34 ...... 122 E2
Kingston upon Hull
HU13 .... 178 E1
2 Rampton DN22 .... 65 A5
Winteringham DN15 .... 2 B1
Orchard Garth 16 LN5 .... 93 E8
Orchard Gr
Boston PE21 .... 209 B6
1 Hatfield DN7 .... 14 D5
Misterton DN10 .... 40 A4
Orchard La 12 LN1 .... 66 D2
Orchard Mews PE2 ...... 230 F8
Orchard Pk 4 LN11 .... 62 C6
Orchard Rd
Barnack PE9 .... 172 E3
5 Fiskerton LN3 .... 82 A7
Kingston upon Hull HU4 .. 179 B5
4 Stamford PE9 .... 219 B5
Orchard Sch NG24 .... 104 B3
Orchard St
Boston PE21 .... 208 D6
Lincoln LN1 .... 234 A2
Peterborough PE2 .... 230 F7
2 Spalding PE11 .... 214 D3
22 Thorne/Moorends DN8 .. 15 A8
Orchard The
Market Deeping PE6 ..... 217 B5
New Waltham DN36 ...... 195 C6
Peterborough PE4 .... 221 A3
Washingborough LN4 .... 203 A2
Orchard Way
4 Coningsby LN4 .... 207 C4
5 Cowbit PE12 .... 167 B8
Easton on the Hill PE9 .... 171 C3
1 Mablethorpe/Sutton on Sea
LN12 .... 64 A3
3 Market Rasen LN8 .... 57 E8
6 Nettleham LN2 .... 68 D2
Orchards The
8 Middle Rasen LN8 .... 57 B8
Peterborough PE2 .... 229 F4
Orchid Cl PE7 .... 233 F7
Orchid Rd LN5 .... 205 C2
Orchid Rise DN15 .... 182 F2
Ordoyno Gr 4 NG24 ..... 104 C5
Ore Blending Rd DN16 ... 19 A4
Orford Rd LN8 .... 47 B5
Oribi Cl HU4 .... 179 C2
Oriole Rd DN17 .... 184 E6
Orion Cl 8 HU3 .... 180 B5
Orion Way 4 DN34 ...... 190 D4
Orkney Pl DN40 .... 186 C2
Orme La LN11 .... 198 C6
Orme Rd PE3 .... 225 D4
Ormsby Cl DN35 .... 192 D3
Ormsby Rd DN17 .... 184 E5
Ormsby Ring LN11 .... 74 C1
Orton Ave PE2 .... 230 E7
Orton Brick Works
PE7 .... 233 B8
Orton Longueville Sch
PE2 .... 230 A5
Orton Matley Prim Sch
PE2 .... 229 E5
Orton Mere PE2 .... 230 B7
Orton Parkway PE2 ...... 229 D4
Orton Wistow Prim Sch
PE2 .... 229 C6
Orwell Gr PE4 .... 221 D1
Orwell St DN31 .... 189 C1
Osborn Way 9 NG34 ..... 122 D3
Osborne Cl 3 LN1 .... 201 E6
Osborne Dr DN36 .... 195 D1
Osborne Pk 1 PE13 ..... 170 C2
Osborne Rd
Immingham DN41 .... 187 B2
Wisbech PE13 .... 170 C2
Osborne St
1 Cleethorpes DN35 ..... 192 F6
Grimsby DN31 .... 191 D7
Kingston upon Hull HU1 .. 180 E6
Osbournby Prim Sch
NG34 .... 132 C5
Osbourne Way 7 PE6 ... 217 A5
Ose 3 PE25 .... 206 B6
Oseby La NG34 .... 133 A1
Osgodby Prim Sch LN8 ..... 45 A3
Osgodby Rd LN8 .... 44 E5
Osier Rd PE11 .... 214 E5
Oslear Cres DN35 .... 192 E5
Oslear's La LN11 .... 73 D5
Osprey PE2 .... 229 F2
Osprey Cl 5 NG34 ...... 212 B3
Oster Fen La NG23 ...... 104 F1
Ostler Cl 8 NG31 .... 210 F8
Ostler Dr PE10 .... 213 B4
Ostler's La DN18 .... 10 A5
Oswald Rd DN15 .... 183 A3
Oswin Cl 1 NG34 .... 212 C2
Otby La LN8 .... 46 A3
Ottawa Rd DN17 .... 184 E4
Otter Ave 11 LN1 .... 66 D2
Otterbrook PE2 .... 229 D5
Otterburn St 6 HU3 ..... 180 A5
Otters Cotts LN5 .... 205 D7
Oulton Cl LN6 .... 205 A2
Oundle Cl
Heighington/Washingborough
LN4 .... 203 C1
Scunthorpe DN16 .... 185 C3
Oundle Rd
8 Mablethorpe/Sutton on Sea
LN12 .... 64 C1
Peterborough PE2 .... 229 E6
Our Lady of Good Counsel RC
Prim Sch NG34 .... 212 C5
Our Lady of Lincoln RC
(Aided) Prim Sch
LN2 .... 202 A7
Out Holme La DN36 ...... 36 E3
Outer Circ Dr LN2 ...... 202 C7
Outer Circ Gn LN2 ...... 202 C6
Outer Circ Ind Est
LN2 .... 202 D5
Outer Circ Rd LN2 ...... 202 D5
Outfield PE3 .... 220 E1
Outgang La DN22 .... 65 A6
Outgang The HU15 .... 2 B7
Outgate DN17 .... 16 E7
Oval App LN2 .... 202 B7
Oval The 5 Brough HU15 ... 2 C5
Grimsby DN33 .... 191 C1
5 Hatfield DN7 .... 14 C5
Kingston upon Hull
HU10 .... 178 E8
Lincoln LN2 .... 202 B7
Scopwick LN4 .... 108 B7
Oval The *continued*
2 Scunthorpe DN17 ...... 184 E3
Overcoat La DN22 .... 65 B7
Overgate Rd NG33 ...... 152 D5
Overstone Ct PE3 .... 225 D6
Overton Ave HU10 ...... 178 E8
Overton Cl 4 LN5 .... 107 B8
Overton Ct 9 DN18 .... 3 E1
Overton Rd LN4 .... 207 D4
Overton Way PE2 .... 229 F4
Owen Ave HU13 .... 179 A1
Owen Cl 7 PE9 .... 172 D3
Owe's La LN11 .... 51 A5
Owl End PE7 .... 233 D5
Owmby Cliff Rd LN8 ...... 55 C5
Owmby Hill DN38 .... 32 D8
Owmby La LN7 .... 32 C5
Owmby Rd
4 Searby cum Owmby
DN38 .... 32 D8
Spridlington LN8 .... 55 F3
Owmby Wold La DN38 .... 21 E1
Owston Ferry Rd DN9 ..... 27 F1
Owston Rd DN10 .... 40 B6
Oxburgh Cl
3 Peterborough PE7 ..... 231 F5
1 Wisbech PE13 .... 170 C1
Oxclose PE3 .... 225 A8
Oxcombe Cl DN33 .... 194 D7
Oxcroft Bank
Moulton PE12 .... 157 F1
Whaplode PE12 .... 158 A2
Oxeney Dr 2 LN3 .... 69 C3
Oxford Cl LN4 .... 203 C1
Oxford Ct 1 NG34 .... 212 D7
Oxford Rd
Peterborough PE1 .... 225 F5
6 Stamford PE9 .... 219 A7
Oxford St Boston PE21 .. 208 F3
Cleethorpes DN35 .... 192 F5
Grantham NG31 .... 211 B3
Grimsby DN32 .... 189 B1
Kingston upon Hull HU2 .. 181 A8
2 Lincoln LN5 .... 234 B1
Market Rasen LN8 .... 57 D8
Scunthorpe DN16 .... 185 D6
Oxlands La PE24 .... 102 B7
Oxmarsh La DN19 .... 4 E2
Oxney Rd PE1 .... 226 D5

P

Pacey Cl LN6 .... 92 A6
Packhorse Gdns PE20 .. 135 B6
Packman La HU10 .... 178 B8
Paddington Way PE10 .. 154 D7
Paddock Cl
6 Ancaster NG32 .... 120 A2
Ropsley NG33 .... 131 B1
Paddock Ct 5 DN40 ..... 186 C3
Paddock Gn 3 PE11 ..... 214 D5
Paddock Gr 6 PE21 ..... 208 F4
Paddock La
5 Blyton DN21 .... 41 C5
1 Metheringham LN4 ...... 95 D4
West Butterwick DN17 ..... 17 C1
Paddock Rd NG34 .... 120 C8
Paddock Rise
11 Barrow upon Humber
DN19 .... 11 C8
Ingoldsby NG33 .... 141 C5
Paddock The
3 Barkston NG32 .... 130 B8
2 Burton-upon-Stather
DN15 .... 8 B4
4 Cherry Willingham LN3 . 203 E6
10 Collingham NG23 .... 91 D4
Kingston upon Hull HU4 .. 179 B5
Louth LN11 .... 198 A5
1 Market Deeping PE6 ... 217 A6
4 Morton PE10 .... 154 C7
4 North Ferriby HU14 .... 3 A5
16 Ruskington NG34 ..... 108 D2
Skellingthorpe LN6 ...... 200 A4
5 Sleaford NG34 .... 212 F4
5 Stamford PE9 .... 219 A5
16 Sudbrooke LN2 .... 68 F2
3 Swanland HU14 .... 3 C7
Paddock View PE22 ..... 100 B2
Paddocks The
1 Barnetby Le Beck DN37 .. 35 B6
5 Beckingham DN10 .... 40 A1
6 Bottesford NG13 .... 128 A5
7 Burgh Le Marsh PE24 ... 102 E7
Carlton Scroop NG32 ..... 119 C3
12 Crowle DN17 .... 16 D7
Gedney PE12 .... 159 E7
1 Holbeach PE12 .... 215 E3
Kingston upon Hull
HU10 .... 178 B7
10 Long Bennington NG23 . 117 D4
Newton on Trent LN1 ...... 65 C1
2 Peterborough PE4 ..... 220 E5
Stapleford LN6 .... 105 C8
Swayfield NG33 .... 152 E5
4 Willingham DN21 .... 53 E3
Pademoor Terr DN17 ...... 7 A2
Padholme Rd PE1 .... 226 C3
Padholme Rd E PE1 ..... 226 D3
Padley Rd LN2 .... 202 E6
Padleys La PE23 .... 100 C4
Padmoor La DN21 .... 53 C5
Pado La LN13 .... 74 E4
Pagehall Cl DN33 .... 191 D1
Paignton Ct DN33 .... 194 E6
Pain La PE22 .... 113 E3
Painshall Cl 11 LN2 .... 68 D7
Paisley Prim Sch HU3 .. 180 A6
Paisley St HU3 .... 180 A7
Palace Theatre*
NG24 .... 104 A4
Palma Ct 2 PE24 .... 90 D7
Palmer Ave HU10 .... 178 D8
Palmer Ct 3 NG34 ...... 212 B6
Palmer La 15 DN19 .... 11 D8
Palmer Rd NG32 .... 129 C6
Palmers Rd PE1 .... 226 F5
Palmerston Rd PE2 ..... 230 F7
Palmwood Cl 3 NG31 ... 210 F7
Pamela Rd DN40 .... 186 D4
Pandyke La PE22 .... 113 F3
Panton Cl 6 PE6 .... 217 D5
Panton Rd LN8 .... 71 B8
Papermill La
Ewerby & Evedon NG34 ... 121 E7
Tealby LN8 .... 46 D2
Pape's La PE24 .... 101 F4
Papyrus Rd PE4 .... 220 D3
Parade The LN3 .... 203 E6
Paradise La
5 Fulletby LN9 .... 86 B8
Northborough PE6 .... 173 F6
Paradise Pl 6 DN20 ..... 196 B3
Paragon St HU1 .... 180 E6
Parish Church CE (Aided)
Prim Sch DN21 .... 197 C5
Parishes Sh Ctr The
DN15 .... 183 B3
Parish's La PE22 .... 115 A4
Park Ave
Allington NG32 .... 128 F7
15 Barton-upon-Humber
DN18 .... 10 E8
Billinghay LN4 .... 109 F5
17 Crowle DN17 .... 16 D7
Grimsby DN32 .... 191 E4
Heighington/Washingborough
LN4 .... 203 D2
Kingston upon Hull
HU13 .... 178 E3
Lincoln LN6 .... 204 F7
Louth LN11 .... 198 E6
18 Mablethorpe/Sutton on Sea
LN12 .... 64 B3
Scunthorpe DN17 .... 184 F3
Skegness PE25 .... 206 D4
Sleaford NG34 .... 212 F4
Spalding PE11 .... 214 C5
3 Spilsby PE23 .... 87 F1
Sutterton PE20 .... 136 A2
Park Cl
1 Gosberton PE11 .... 145 B6
Immingham DN40 .... 186 C4
Lea DN21 .... 52 F5
Spalding PE11 .... 214 C5
8 Sudbrooke LN2 .... 68 F2
Thorney PE6 .... 176 B3
7 Westwoodside DN9 ...... 27 A2
Yaxley PE7 .... 233 F5
Park Cres
Heighington/Washingborough
LN4 .... 203 D1
16 Metheringham LN4 ...... 95 D4
Peterborough PE1 .... 226 B5
Sleaford NG34 .... 212 F4
Swinderby LN6 .... 92 B6
Thorne/Moorends DN8 ..... 15 A7
Thorney PE6 .... 176 B3
Park Ct 2 PE12 .... 157 E7
Park Dr Grimsby DN32 ... 191 E5
Market Deeping PE6 ..... 217 A5
6 Westwoodside DN9 ...... 27 A2
Park Est PE6 .... 217 E4
Park Farm Cres PE7 .... 231 F5
Park Farm Rd
Peterborough PE6 .... 224 E5
Scunthorpe DN15 .... 182 F7
Park Farm Way PE7 ..... 231 F6
Park Gate 7 PE21 .... 208 F5
Park Gdns PE12 .... 215 E3
Park Hill
Cherry Willingham/Reepham
LN3 .... 203 E5
28 Kirton in Lindsey DN21 .. 30 B1
Park La 12 Alford LN13 .... 75 F3
Billinghay LN4 .... 109 F5
5 Boston PE21 .... 208 F6
Burton LN1 .... 200 D7
Coningsby LN4 .... 207 C4
Denton NG32 .... 139 A7
2 Donington PE11 .... 134 E2
East Kirkby PE23 .... 99 E5
Ewerby & Evedon NG34 ... 122 B7
Freiston PE22 .... 126 D3
Gorefield PE13 .... 169 F3
Heighington/Washingborough
LN4 .... 203 C2
Holbeach PE12 .... 215 E3
Humberston DN35 .... 192 F1
Leverington PE13 .... 170 A3
Long Sutton PE12 .... 216 C5
Manby LN11 .... 62 C5
Peterborough PE1 .... 226 C4
Pinchbeck PE11 .... 145 D3
Redbourne DN21 .... 30 F3
Saxby All Saints DN20 ..... 10 A3
1 Scawby DN20 .... 30 F8
1 Skillington NG33 ...... 151 A8
Spalding PE11 .... 214 C5
Stamford PE9 .... 219 C4
2 Surfleet PE11 .... 145 D2
Swineshead PE20 .... 135 A7
Westwoodside DN9 .... 27 A2
Wigsley NG23 .... 78 F5
Park La Cl 6 DN7 .... 14 C2

Park La E HU4 179 C6
Park La Rd 11 DN7 14 C2
Park La W HU4 179 C5
Park Rd 11 Alford LN13 75 F3
1 Allington NG32 128 F7
Boston PE21 208 E2
5 Brough HU15 2 E6
Claxby LN8 45 E4
Grantham NG31 211 B5
Holbeach PE12 215 D2
2 Horncastle LN9 199 C4
Long Sutton PE12 216 C5
Mablethorpe/Sutton on Sea LN12 64 C1
Market Deeping PE6 217 D4
Peterborough PE1 226 A3
Spalding PE11 214 C4
Sutton St James PE12 169 D7
Swinstead NG33 153 A5
1 Weston PE12 157 E7
5 Willingham DN21 53 E3
Park Rd E LN12 64 D1
Park Rd W 10 LN12 64 C1
Park Row
Kingston upon Hull HU3 180 D7
Louth LN11 198 E7
Park Springs Rd DN21 197 F2
Park St
Cleethorpes DN35 189 D1
Grimsby DN32 192 B8
Kingston upon Hull HU3 180 D6
Lincoln LN1 234 A2
11 Messingham DN17 29 D7
Peterborough PE2 230 F7
Swinefleet DN14 6 D8
Winterton DN15 9 B5
Park The
Coningsby LN4 207 D5
Lincoln LN1 234 A2
Potter Hanworth LN4 95 B8
Park View
25 Barton-upon-Humber DN18 10 F8
Cleethorpes DN35 192 C8
Crowle DN17 16 D6
Kingston upon Hull HU4 179 E4
6 Mablethorpe/Sutton on Sea LN12 64 C1
10 Messingham DN17 29 D7
15 Northorpe PE10 164 C8
13 Thorne/Moorends DN8 15 A7
Park View Ave LN4 81 D2
Park View Cl 7 DN19 11 C7
Park View Terr DN17 28 C8
Park Wlk
Easton on the Hill PE9 171 D3
Kingston upon Hull HU4 179 B5
Parker Ave LN5 205 D4
Parker Rd
Humberston DN36 36 D8
23 Wittering PE8 172 B1
Parker St DN35 192 F5
Parkers Cl 12 PE24 102 E7
Parkers La DN16 185 C6
Parkes Cl 4 NG24 104 D5
Parkfield Ave 14 HU14 3 A4
Parkfield Dr HU3 179 F6
Parkfield Rd
7 Ruskington NG34 108 E2
18 Ryhall PE9 163 C1
Parkhill Cres 3 DN3 14 A4
Parkhill Rd 2 DN3 14 A4
Parkhill Rise 7 DN15 9 B5
Parkin Rd
7 Cowbit PE12 167 B8
Scunthorpe DN17 184 F4
Parkinson Ave 1 DN15 183 A3
Parkinson's Way 2 LN12 64 C2
Parklands
2 Fleet Hargate PE12 159 C7
6 Mablethorpe/Sutton on Sea LN12 64 B3
1 Mumby LN13 76 F1
4 West/East Butterwick DN17 28 D8
Parklands Cl 13 NG24 104 C5
Parklands Cres 11 HU14 3 A5
Parklands Dr
4 Harlaxton NG32 139 C7
10 North Ferriby HU14 3 A5
Park-lea 6 NG34 108 E2
Parks Cl 4 DN39 12 A1
Parks Rd 3 DN7 14 C4
Parksgate Ave LN6 204 F5
Parkside
17 Nettleham LN2 68 D2
Peterborough PE2 230 B6
Parkside Cres PE11 214 C5
Parkside Dr 18 PE24 90 D7
Parkside The 4 NG33 151 D2
Parkstone Gr 28 DN7 14 D4
Parkway The
Kingston upon Hull HU10 178 E8
Spalding PE11 214 A2
Parkwood Inf & Jun Sch DN17 184 D8
Parkwood Rise 14 DN3 14 A3
Parliament St
5 Brough HU15 2 D6
7 Kingston upon Hull HU1 180 F6
Peterborough PE1 225 F5
Parnell St 3 DN21 197 C5
Parnwell CP Sch PE1 226 F7
Parnwell Way PE1 226 F6
Parris Pl DN35 192 D7
Parry Rd 14 LN12 64 B3
Parslins The PE6 217 F5
Parson Dro
Billinghay LN4 109 F7
Pinchbeck PE11 144 B2
Parson Dro La PE13 170 B2
Parson La LN5 106 C8
Parsonage La PE12 159 F1
Parson's Dro
Holland Fen with Brothertoft PE20 124 A8
Swaton NG34 133 D4
Parson's La PE12 168 B4
Parsons Dr 3 PE21 208 E7
Parsons Halt 1 LN11 198 C6
Parsons La 18 LN13 75 F2
Parthian Ave PE21 136 D8
Partney CE (Aided) Prim Sch PE23 88 B3
Partney Rd PE23 87 C4
Partridge Cl
4 Caistor LN7 33 B4
4 Scunthorpe DN17 184 E6
Yaxley PE7 233 D6
Partridge Dr LN7 33 F2
Partridge Gr PE4 220 E5
Pashley Rd DN8 15 B7
Paston La PE4 221 B1
Paston Parkway PE4 221 C4
Paston Ridings PE4 221 C1
Paston Ridings Cty Jun & Infants' Sch PE4 221 D1
Pasture Ave 9 DN17 17 D4
Pasture Cl
7 Colsterworth NG33 151 E7
Grantham NG31 211 D1
Pasture Dr LN11 198 D4
Pasture Dro PE10 154 F7
Pasture La Amcotts DN17 7 D1
Bassingham LN5 93 B2
Belvoir NG32 138 C6
Garthorpe & Fockerby DN17 7 D6
Market Rasen LN8 57 E8
Northborough PE6 173 F6
Pasture Rd DN21 197 F4
Pasture Rd N DN18 3 F1
Pasture Rd S DN18 4 A1
Pasture St 5 DN32 191 E7
Pasture The PE6 217 C6
Pastures Ct 36 DN17 29 D7
Pastures Rd NG32 210 A5
Pastures The
12 Long Bennington NG23 117 D3
Old Somerby NG33 140 E8
1 Rampton DN22 65 A5
12 Welton LN2 68 D6
Patch Rd LN6 92 D4
Pateley Moor Cl 13 LN6 93 C8
Patman's La PE22 114 E4
Patrick St DN32 191 E5
Patricks Cl 5 LN7 32 A4
Patriot Cl PE11 214 C4
Patten Ave 2 PE24 102 D1
Patterdale Rd
Kingston upon Hull HU5 179 E8
3 Peterborough PE4 221 E2
Paul Cres 4 DN36 36 C8
Paul La 1 DN15 9 D1
Paulette Ct 11 PE11 214 B5
Paul's La LN4 207 C7
Paulsgrove PE2 229 D5
Pavilion Gdns
4 Scunthorpe DN17 182 F2
5 Sleaford NG34 212 D3
Pavilion Way DN36 195 C7
Pawlett Cl PE6 217 D5
Paxton Rd PE2 229 D4
Payne Ave PE13 170 D1
Payne Sch PE13 177 D7
Paynell 23 LN2 68 D6
Paynells PE2 230 A3
Paynesholm PE4 221 E1
Pea Rm Craft Ctr & Heckington Sta Rly Mus* NG34 122 F2
Peace Haven 2 DN37 194 C5
Peach La NG32 128 F6
Peach Tree Cl 5 DN16 185 D4
Peach Tree Ct 5 HU3 180 D5
Peachwood Cl 4 NG31 210 F8
Peacock Ct 5 NG34 212 E3
Peacock St DN17 184 F5
Peacock Way PE3 224 F2
Peacock's Rd PE22 112 B1
Peacocks The 5 NG23 117 D3
Peak Dale LN6 204 E2
Peake Cl PE2 230 F6
Peakirk Rd
Deeping Gate PE6 217 F3
Glinton PE6 220 D8
Northborough PE6 174 A7
Peakirk-cum-Glinton CE Sch PE6 220 C8
Peaks Ave DN36 195 C7
Peaks La Grimsby DN36 191 F2
New Waltham DN36 195 D7
Peaks Parkway
Grimsby DN32 191 E5
New Waltham DN36 192 A1
Pear Tree Cl
4 Epworth DN9 27 D6
4 Waltham DN37 194 D4
Pear Tree Cres 2 PE13 170 B1
Pear Tree La
Covenham St Bartholomew LN11 49 B6
Kirk Bramwith DN7 14 A8
Utterby DN36 48 E5
Pear Tree Rd PE20 136 D5
Pearces La 3 PE10 154 C7
Pearces Rd PE6 227 B5
Pearl Cl 8 PE25 206 C4
Pearl Ct PE12 215 D3
Pearl Leisure Ctr PE5 223 E1
Pearson Pk Prim Sch HU3 180 D8
Pearson Rd DN35 192 F3
Pearson St 5 HU2 180 E7
Peartree Cl 5 LN6 200 D1
Peartree Hill Rd PE12 168 B8
Peartree House Rd PE12 215 F7
Peascliffe Dr NG31 211 A8
Peaseholme HU13 178 C1
Peasgate La
Toynton All Saints PE23 100 F6
Toynton St Peter PE23 101 A7
Peashill La NG32 139 B8
Peat Carr Bank DN9 26 C3
Peatlings La PE13 170 C1
Pebble Cl 4 PE12 160 E4
Peck Ave PE21 208 D4
Peck Hill NG33 131 B1
Peckover Cl 4 PE7 231 F5
Peckover Sch The PE13 170 C1
Peddars Way PE3 225 A2
Pedlar La LN11 62 A7
Pedley La 15 PE13 170 C1
Peel Castle Rd 10 DN8 15 B7
Peel Hill Rd 9 DN8 15 B7
Peel St
Kingston upon Hull HU3 180 D8
Lincoln LN5 201 E1
Peele Sch The PE12 216 D6
Pegasus Gr 6 PE10 213 E7
Pegasus Rd DN20 21 A8
Pelham Ave DN33 191 C1
Pelham Cl
20 Barton-upon-Humber DN18 10 E8
Peterborough PE3 224 F2
7 Sudbrooke LN2 68 F2
Pelham Cres 1 DN41 23 A4
Pelham Dr 1 HU9 181 C7
Pelham Ind Est DN40 186 D6
Pelham Inf Sch DN40 186 D4
Pelham Pl DN33 191 C1
Pelham Rd Claxby LN8 45 D6
Cleethorpes DN35 192 D7
6 Grimsby DN31 191 C7
2 Holton le Clay DN36 195 C2
Immingham DN40 186 B3
1 Skegness PE25 206 C4
Pelham Sq 1 DN35 192 E7
Pelham St LN5 234 B1
Pelham View 3 DN20 30 F5
Pell's Dr 5 PE20 136 D5
Pemberton Dr DN36 195 B6
Pemberton St 1 HU8 181 B7
Pembroke Ave
Peterborough PE2 229 F5
Scunthorpe DN16 185 A3
Pembroke Gr 1 PE6 220 D8
Pembroke Rd
Grimsby DN34 191 A5
Stamford PE9 219 A7
Pen St PE21 209 A5
Pendeen Cl
6 Gainsborough DN21 197 E6
New Waltham DN36 195 C7
Pendine Cres LN6 205 A1
Pendlebury Dr 4 PE6 217 D5
Pendleton PE3 225 B6
Pendred Ave LN6 92 D4
Pendreth Pl DN35 192 D7
Pendula Rd PE13 170 E1
Penfold La 1 LN4 203 C2
Penistone Ct 2 HU9 181 D7
Pennell St LN5 201 E1
Pennine Rd 7 DN8 15 A7
Pennine Way
Gonerby Hill Foot NG31 210 E7
Peterborough PE4 221 B2
Spalding PE11 214 E6
Pennington PE2 229 E3
Pennington St HU8 181 B7
Penny Gdns 6 PE20 136 C5
Penny Hill Rd PE12 215 E3
Penny Toft La PE11 214 B8
Pennycress Cl LN2 202 C8
Pennyfield
16 Pinchbeck PE11 156 E8
Pinchbeck PE11 214 B8
Pennygate PE11 214 A4
Pennyhill Cl PE11 214 E6
Penrose Cl 19 LN6 93 C8
Penshurst Ave HU13 178 F3
Penshurst Rd DN35 192 D4
Penswick Gr 11 NG24 104 C5
Pentelow Cl PE13 177 D5
Pentland Dr 23 LN6 93 C8
Pentlands The 2 PE4 221 C2
Penwald Cl 7 PE6 175 B8
Penway Dr PE11 214 B8
Penwith Dr HU10 178 F7
Penyale 3 PE3 225 A1
Peploe Cres 10 DN19 4 E2
Peploe La 9 DN19 4 E2
Peppercorn Cl
3 Lincoln LN6 201 D1
Peterborough PE1 225 E6
Peppercorn Wlk
12 Grimsby DN32 191 E7
9 Holton le Clay DN36 195 D2
Pepper's La NG34 133 C4
Peppin La LN11 49 A2
Percheron Dr 4 PE11 214 A2
Percival St
Peterborough PE3 225 E2
Scunthorpe DN15 183 A4
Percy St
8 Kingston upon Hull HU2 180 E7
6 Lincoln LN2 202 B3
5 Scunthorpe DN16 183 B2
Peregrine Cl
Kingston upon Hull HU4 179 D2
6 Sleaford NG34 212 B3
Perkin Field 3 PE34 161 F2
Perkins Cl 3 DN37 190 F8
Perkins La PE6 173 C6
Perney Cres 17 LN6 93 C8
Pernys Cl PE7 230 D3
Perrin Ave 6 PE25 206 A5
Perry Rd PE13 170 B2
Perry St HU3 180 A6
Pershore Ave DN34 190 D4
Pershore Way LN6 204 C6
Perth Cl 7 PE25 206 A4
Perth Rd PE9 218 E6
Perth St HU5 179 F8
Perth Way DN40 186 B2
Petchell Way 3 DN32 191 F8
Peter Paine Cl PE22 126 F4
Peter Paine Sports Ctr PE21 208 B5
Peter Seadike La PE11 145 D5
Peterborough Cath* PE1 226 A2
Peterborough Cl 10 NG31 210 E5
Peterborough Coll of Adult Ed PE1 226 B3
Peterborough District PE3 225 E2
Peterborough Dr PE6 224 E2
Peterborough Her Ctr* PE3 225 A1
Peterborough High Sch PE3 225 D2
Peterborough NV Sta PE2 225 F1
Peterborough Rd
Castor PE5 223 E1
19 Collingham NG23 91 D5
23 Eye PE6 175 A1
Langtoft PE6 217 A8
Newborough PE6 174 E4
Peterborough PE7 231 C3
Scunthorpe DN16 185 B7
Wansford PE8 222 A3
Peterborough Regional Coll PE1 226 B5
Peterborough Sta PE3 225 F2
Peterborough Way NG34 212 C7
Petergate 1 PE9 219 B4
Peterhouse Cl 1 PE9 219 B7
Peterhouse Rd DN34 190 F6
Peter's La LN13 63 B2
Petersfield Cl LN6 204 B7
Peterspoint PE12 160 D3
Pethley La NG34 143 A6
Petticoat La 15 PE21 208 F5
Pettit Way 5 PE21 209 C4
Petts Cl 5 PE13 170 E1
Petts La PE12 160 F5
Petuaria Cl HU15 2 B6
Petworth Cl 2 PE6 217 A5
Peveril Ave DN17 184 F8
Peveril Rd PE1 225 F6
Pheasant Cl 5 DN17 184 E6
Pheasant Ct 5 LN7 33 B4
Pheasant Gr PE4 220 E5
Pheasant Way PE7 233 D5
Phelps Pl DN32 192 C5
Phelps St DN35 189 D1
Philip Ave
Cleethorpes DN35 192 D4
Waltham DN37 194 E5
Philip Ct 4 LN6 204 F1
Philip Gr
Cleethorpes DN35 192 D4
Skegness PE25 206 B4
Philips Cres 3 DN15 182 F3
Phillips Ct 6 PE9 219 C4
Phillips La 6 DN37 23 F1
Phoenix Ct DN21 197 F3
Phoenix Parkway DN15 182 E7
Phoenix St 18 DN32 191 D7
Phorpres Cl PE7 230 D3
Phorpres Way PE7 230 E3
Phyllis Ave DN34 191 B7
Piccadilly 4 DN36 195 C6
Piccadilly Way PE10 154 D6
Pick Hill La
Grimoldby LN11 62 C8
South Cockerington LN11 50 C1
Pickards Way PE13 170 C1
Pickathorpe La LN11 50 E6
Pickering Gr 15 DN8 15 A7
Pickering Rd HU4 179 C3
Pickerings The 19 HU14 3 A4
Picksley Cres DN36 195 D1
Pickworth Rd PE9 162 F2
Pickworth's Dro PE10 155 A3
Pidgeon Cote La 20 DN19 12 A8
Pier St 9 HU1 180 F5
Pietermaritz St 4 LN1 201 E8
Pike Dam La PE12 159 A6
Pilgrim Ave DN40 186 D3
Pilgrim Hospl PE21 209 A8
Pilgrim Rd PE21 209 A4
Pilgrim's Cl 5 DN40 12 E3
Pilgrim's Way PE11 214 A4
Pilgrims Way DN40 186 A4
Pilham La DN21 41 C4
Pilley's La PE21 125 F5
Pilmore La PE12 157 B6
Pilots Way HU9 181 B5
Pilton Cl PE4 221 D1
Pimpernel Way 2 DN16 185 D4
Pinchbeck Ave 4 DN16 183 C2
Pinchbeck E CE Prim Sch PE11 156 E8
Pinchbeck Engine Mus* PE11 145 E1
Pinchbeck La PE24 102 F4
Pinchbeck Rd
5 Butterwick PE22 126 E3
Spalding PE11 214 D5
Pinchbeck W CE (Controlled) Prim Sch PE11 156 A8
Pinder La 10 PE11 134 F2
Pine Cl Grimsby DN37 188 A1
Holbeach PE12 215 C3
Lincoln LN1 201 E8
4 Sleaford NG34 212 D3
Stamford PE9 218 D6
7 Waddington LN5 93 E8
Pine Ct 3 DN35 192 D2
Pine Hall Rd DN3 14 A3
Pine Mdws HU10 178 B8
Pine Tree Cl PE1 226 B8
Pine Wlk 5 Brough HU15 2 C6
4 Healing DN41 24 A5
Pinefield Ave 7 DN3 14 A3
Pinefield Rd 3 DN3 14 A3
Pines The DN21 197 F2
Pinetree Ave 11 DN21 29 C3
Pinetree Cl 5 DN20 19 E4
Pinetrees Ct 4 NG34 212 E4
Pinewood Ave PE8 172 B1
Pinewood Cl 5 PE10 213 B5
Pinewood Cres DN33 190 F3
Pinewood Dr NG31 210 F8
Pinewood Gr 2 HU5 179 C7
Pinfold 15 DN9 27 E6
Pinfold Cl
7 Bottesford NG13 128 A6
8 Collingham NG23 91 D5
11 Northorpe PE10 164 C8
Osbournby NG34 132 D5
Pointon & Sempringham NG34 143 B6
Rippingale PE10 142 F2
Pinfold Gdns 4 DN36 195 D1
Pinfold La
11 Bottesford NG13 128 A6
Fishlake DN7 14 D8
Fishtoft PE21 137 C8
Great Steeping PE23 101 E6
Grimsby DN33 191 D1
Halton Holegate PE23 101 C6
3 Holton le Clay DN36 195 D1
Legbourne LN11 61 E3
Marston NG32 118 D2
Minting LN9 71 C1
Pointon & Sempringham NG34 143 B6
8 Ruskington NG34 108 E2
South Rauceby NG34 120 E4
2 Stallingborough DN41 23 D6
Stamford PE9 219 C3
Stickney PE22 113 A6
Swaby LN13 74 E4
Walcott LN4 109 C7
Weston PE12 157 D8
Pinfold Rd
Bourne PE10 213 F5
Castle Bytham NG33 152 D1
Pinfold The LN4 108 D5
Pinfold Way 11 NG34 108 E2
Pingle Cl DN21 197 E4
Pingle La
Bishop Norton LN8 43 D3
Northborough PE6 173 F6
20 Wellingore LN5 107 A7
Pingle The 2 NG34 133 B1
Pingles The 5 PE10 164 C8
Pingley La DN20 196 D2
Pingley Mdw DN20 196 D2
Pinney's Ct 21 DN41 23 F5
Pinnings La DN21 43 D6
Pinstock La 10 PE12 159 C7
Pioneer Way LN6 204 E4
Pipistrelle Ct 4 PE4 221 A3
Pippin Cl LN11 198 C5
Pippin Ct 3 DN15 182 C5
Pippin Dr DN16 185 B2
Pipwell Gate PE12 146 E1
Pit La Gedney PE12 149 A4
Great Ponton NG33 140 B4
Ketton PE9 171 A4
Pitcher Row La PE20 136 B1
Pitman Ave 23 DN18 10 E8
Pitmoor La 8 DN39 12 A1
Pitt La DN10 39 C2
Pitt St HU3 179 F7
Pittneys PE4 221 D1
Pitts Rd LN4 203 C1
Plains La DN8 15 F3
Plane St HU3 180 A5
Plank Dro PE6 175 B8

Plantain Cl 1 DN16 185 D4
Plantation Dr HU14 2 F5
Plantation Rd
Cranwell & Byard's Leap NG34 107 C1
29 Thorne/Moorends DN8 15 A8
Planting Rd NG33 140 B1
Plash Dro PE13 177 F4
Plassey Rd 6 DN21 55 A8
Platform Dr PE12 216 A4
Platt's La NG32 118 B4
Platts La Bucknall LN10 84 B4
Tetford LN9 73 E1
Playgarth Est LN4 108 E4
Playhouse Yd 2 NG34 212 D4
Playing Field La 2 LN8 59 A7
Pleasant Ave LN11 198 D5
Pleasant Pl 6 LN11 198 C6
Pleasure Island Theme Pk* DN35 193 C2
Plimsoll Way HU9 181 B6
Plot La NG23 91 E6
Plough Hill 23 LN7 33 B4
Plough La
1 Cherry Willingham/Reepham LN3 82 A8
Cherry Willingham/Reepham LN3 203 F8
6 Fiskerton LN3 82 A7
6 Newborough PE6 174 E5
Plover Dr 15 HU15 2 C6
Plover Gr LN6 204 E8
Plover Rd 1 PE9 163 D3
Plover Sq 7 LN7 33 B4
Ploverly 2 PE4 221 A5
Plowden Rd HU3 179 F5
Plowright Theatre* DN15 183 A2
Plum Tree Dr 3 DN36 37 C2
Plum Tree Way DN16 183 A1
Plumtree Hill Rd DN7 14 C7
Plumtree La 2 DN36 36 B1
Plymouth Cl 23 DN15 9 A5
Plymouth Rd DN17 182 C1
Poacher's Croft 8 DN9 16 E1
Poachers Brook LN6 200 A5
Poachers Ct 23 LN1 66 D2
Poachers Gate 4 PE11 145 C1
Poachers Hide 2 PE11 145 B7
Poachers La LN2 68 F3
Poachers Mdw 20 LN2 68 D2
Poachers Rest 3 LN2 68 D7
Pocklington Cres 3 NG24 104 B7
Pocklington Rd 24 NG23 91 D5
Pocklington Way 10 NG34 122 E2
Pode La PE22 113 F1
Poffinder Wood Rd DN7 14 E7
Point Rd PE25 90 F3
Pointon Rd NG34 143 B8
Poles Bank DN9 26 E6
Policemans La 2 LN4 203 C2
Pollyplatt La LN1 67 E5
Pollyplatt Prim Sch LN1 67 F5
Polton Cl 3 DN7 14 D7
Polton Toft 2 DN7 14 D7
Polyanthus Dr 4 NG34 212 F3
Pond Cl 19 LN2 68 D6
Pond La 4 PE10 213 E2
Pond Side DN39 11 E3
Pond St
Great Gonerby NG31 129 D5
8 Harlaxton NG32 139 C7
Ponds Way 10 DN18 3 E1
Ponton Ave NG31 211 E2
Ponton Rd NG33 140 D5
Pool Dr DN17 184 F4
Poolbank La HU15 2 E5
Poole's La 8 PE23 87 F1
Pooley Way PE7 233 D6
Pools La 8 PE20 136 A2
Poor Gdn Rd NG34 132 F6
Poor Plat La LN13 62 F3
Pope Way PE1 225 E8
Pope's La
Leverington PE13 170 A2
Terrington St Clement PE34 161 E2
Poplar Ave
Mablethorpe/Sutton on Sea LN12 64 A5
Peterborough PE1 226 C8
Poplar Cl
Anlaby with Anlaby Common HU4 179 A5
Boston PE21 208 D2
Poplar Cres PE10 213 B6
Poplar Ct 5 PE22 114 A1
Poplar Dr Brigg DN20 196 C5
6 Broughton DN20 19 D3
2 Gosberton PE11 145 C6
Humberston DN36 193 B1
Poplar Gdns DN16 185 B7
Poplar Gr
5 Cleethorpes DN35 192 E7
3 Scotter DN21 29 C3
Poplar La DN21 41 D2
Poplar Rd Bucknall LN10 84 A3
Cleethorpes DN35 192 E7
6 Hatfield DN7 14 C4
2 Healing DN41 23 F5
Poplar Rd Bsns Units DN35 192 E7
Poplar St LN5 205 D5
Popple Dro PE13 169 D1
Popple St HU9 181 B6
Popplewell Cl 3 DN9 16 E2
Popplewell Terr 13 DN9 27 E6
Poppy Cl 2 DN15 182 C6
Poppyfield Way DN20 196 B4
Porcher Way PE21 208 C6
Port La PE5 223 E1
Portal Gn 8 PE25 206 A5
Portchester Cl PE2 231 F5
Porter St
Kingston upon Hull HU3 180 E5
Scunthorpe DN15 183 A4
Porter's La 4 PE9 171 D3
Portland Ave
Grimsby DN32 191 E4
Peterborough PE1 225 F7
Portland Dr 6 PE25 206 A7
Portland Manor 2 DN32 191 E4
Portland Pl
Grimsby DN32 191 E4
9 Kingston upon Hull HU2 180 E7
Portland St
Boston PE21 208 E5
Kingston upon Hull HU2 180 D7
Lincoln LN5 234 B1
Portland Terr 5 DN21 197 D3
Portman Cl PE3 225 C4
Portman Rd DN15 182 E6
Portsmouth Cl 1 NG31 210 F5
Post Office Hill NG33 151 B5
Post Office La
Ashby cum Fenby DN37 35 D3
Burton Coggles NG33 152 C8
2 Humberside Airport DN39 22 A6
5 Spilsby PE23 88 A1
3 Sutterton PE20 136 A2
Whitton DN15 1 E3
Posterngate HU1 180 F6
Postland Rd PE6 166 F1
Posts The NG32 129 B3
Pot La PE20 146 E8
Potesgrave Way 8 NG34 122 D3
Pottergate LN2 234 B3
Pottergate Cl 1 LN5 93 F7
Pottergate Rd
Ancaster NG32 120 A3
Caythorpe NG32 119 E7
Fulbeck NG32 106 E1
Normanton NG32 119 E5
Welbourn LN5 106 F4
Potterhanworth CE (Controlled) Prim Sch LN4 82 B1
Potterhanworth Rd
Branston & Mere LN4 82 A1
Heighington LN4 81 F3
Potter Hanworth LN4 95 B8
Potters Cl 2 PE10 213 E4
Potters Way PE1 226 B1
Pottinger Gdns 5 LN7 33 A3
Potts La DN17 16 D7
Poulter Ave PE2 231 D5
Pound Rd LN4 96 C2
Poverty La LN11 61 B2
Powell St PE21 209 C2
Powells Cres DN16 185 B6
Pratt Ave PE4 221 D2
Prebend La LN2 68 C7
Precinct Cres
5 Skegness PE25 103 E4
2 Skegness PE25 103 E4
Precincts The 5 PE6 217 B5
Premier Ct 6 NG31 211 A5
Prenton Cl 8 LN6 205 A5
Prescott Ave 11 HU15 2 C5
Prescott Gr 3 DN7 14 D4
Prestland PE6 217 A6
Preston Dr DN20 196 C4
Preston La 15 DN18 10 F8
Prestwick Cl
2 Birchwood LN6 200 B1
Londonthorpe & Harrowby without NG31 211 E7
Pretoria Rd NG31 210 E7
Pretoria St HU3 179 F5
Pretymen Cres DN36 195 C5
Prial Ave LN6 205 B6
Prial Cl LN6 205 C6
Pride Parkway NG34 212 F7
Pridmore Rd NG33 152 E8
Priestfield Dro 1 PE12 159 D7
Priestgate
3 Barton-upon-Humber DN18 10 F8
4 Peterborough PE1 226 A2
Priestley Cl 7 PE20 136 C5
Priest's House (NT)* PE9 171 C3
Primitive Chapel La 1 DN40 12 F2
Primrose Cl
8 Healing DN41 23 F5
8 Lincoln LN5 205 C2
Morton PE10 154 D6
Peterborough PE1 226 A8
9 Skegness PE25 206 A5
Primrose Cres 4 PE11 156 E8
Primrose Dr
1 Kingston upon Hull HU5 179 C8
Primrose Dr *continued*
Yaxley PE7 233 F7
Primrose La 4 NG34 107 C1
Primrose St DN21 197 D3
Primrose Way
6 Grantham NG31 211 D2
Humberston DN35 192 E1
4 Scunthorpe DN15 182 C6
2 Spalding PE11 214 A2
Stamford PE9 218 C7
Primroses 1 PE6 217 D5
Prince Albert Gdns 2 DN32 189 A1
Prince Alfred Ave 1 PE25 206 D3
Prince Ave 8 PE24 90 D7
Prince Charles Ave 11 LN8 70 D4
Prince Charles Dr 32 DN18 10 F8
Prince George St PE25 206 C3
Prince of Wales Cl 12 PE13 170 D2
Prince Philip Dr DN18 10 F7
Prince St 13 HU1 180 F6
Prince William Dr 8 PE22 126 E3
Prince William Rd 3 LN8 56 D5
Prince's Dock St HU1 180 F6
Prince's Rd DN35 192 E6
Prince's St
Metheringham LN4 95 C4
Peterborough PE1 226 A4
Sutton Bridge PE12 160 E4
Princes Ave HU13 178 E1
Princes Ct 3 PE10 213 D6
Princes Gate PE1 226 B4
Princes Gdns PE1 226 B4
Princes Par PE25 206 D2
Princes Rd
Peterborough PE2 231 A7
1 Stamford PE9 219 C6
Princes St Brigg DN20 196 C3
Holbeach PE12 159 A7
Princess Alexandra Ct 1 DN17 184 F3
Princess Anne Rd PE21 209 C6
Princess Ave DN7 14 C6
Princess Dr
34 Barton-upon-Humber DN18 10 F8
Grantham NG31 211 D7
Princess Margaret Ave 28 LN4 95 C4
Princess Rd PE20 136 C4
Princess Royal Cl 4 LN2 234 C3
Princess Sq LN4 109 E6
Princess St
Boston PE21 208 D5
1 Immingham DN40 186 C3
Lincoln LN5 201 E1
Princess Wlk DN21 197 F4
Pringle Cl LN4 207 D5
Prins Ave PE13 170 D1
Prins Ct 16 PE13 170 D1
Printing Office La 14 DN17 16 D8
Prior St LN5 201 E1
Priors Cl DN36 195 D5
Priors Gate PE4 220 E4
Priory Cl Louth LN11 198 C5
Market Deeping PE6 217 F4
12 Northorpe PE10 164 C8
11 Ruskington NG34 108 E1
12 Swanland HU14 3 B7
Priory Cres
Scunthorpe DN17 185 A6
Ulceby DN39 12 A2
Priory Ct
11 South Witham NG33 151 D2
Stamford PE9 219 D5
Priory Dr 5 LN3 82 B6
Priory Farm Dr 4 HU4 179 D2
Priory Gdns PE7 228 F3
Priory Gr HU4 179 D3
Priory La
6 Barrow upon Humber DN19 11 D8
Dunston LN4 95 D5
Manby LN11 62 C6
Scunthorpe DN17 184 F6
Priory La Inf Sch DN17 184 F6
Priory La Jun Sch DN17 184 E6
Priory Pk HU4 179 B1
Priory Rd Boston PE21 209 F5
Fishtoft PE21 126 C2
Grimsby DN37 190 D6
Louth LN11 198 C6
Peterborough PE3 225 E3
Ruskington NG34 108 E1
Scunthorpe DN17 185 A6
Spalding PE11 214 D3
Stamford PE9 219 D5
Priory Specl Sch The PE11 214 F4
Priory Way
2 Gainsborough DN21 53 A5
Kingston upon Hull HU4 179 A1
Sleaford NG34 212 A2
Private La LN8 55 F7
Proby Cl PE7 233 D5
Procters Dr NG23 78 C1
Proctors Cl 6 PE12 159 C7
Proctors Rd LN2 202 D5
Proctor's Way 6 DN20 31 A5
Promenade
Chapel St Leonards PE24 90 E5
Mablethorpe/Sutton on Sea LN12 64 D1
Prospect Pl
1 Grantham NG31 211 A5
Kingston upon Hull HU9 181 B7
2 Market Rasen LN8 57 E7
Prospect St
Horncastle LN9 199 B5
Kingston upon Hull HU2 180 E7
Prospect Terr 8 DN21 197 D3
Prospero Cl PE2 230 F6
Proudfoot La PE12 159 B6
Providence Cres 17 DN18 10 E8
Providence Pl 3 LN4 207 C4
Provost Rd 11 LN11 62 C6
Prunus Ave HU10 178 F8
Pryme Rd DN16 185 C8
Pryme St HU10 178 F6
Prystie Pl DN35 192 D2
Psalter Rd LN13 88 E6
Puddiners La DN14 6 E7
Pudding Bag La PE9 172 C4
Pudding La
8 Hatfield DN7 14 D4
Pinchbeck PE11 214 E8
Puddingpoke La 8 PE12 160 A8
Pulcroft Rd HU13 178 D2
Pullan Cl 9 LN5 205 D3
Pullman Cl 11 LN4 95 D4
Pullover La PE20 146 E7
Pullover The PE24 90 E7
Pulman St HU3 180 A7
Pulvertoft La 12 PE21 208 F4
Pump Hill DN20 31 D6
Pump La Fenton NG23 105 C1
5 Skidbrooke with Saltfleet Haven LN11 51 C4
Pump Sq 18 PE21 208 F5
Punchbowl La
Boston PE21 208 B7
Holland Fen with Brothertoft PE20 125 B4
Purbeck Rd
5 Grimsby DN33 194 E8
2 Scunthorpe DN17 182 C1
Purcell Cl 1 NG31 211 D6
Puritan Way PE21 208 C7
Puttock Gate PE20 146 D7
Pyecroft PE1 226 B6
Pyewipe Rd DN31 188 E1
Pyhill PE3 225 B7
Pyke Rd LN6 204 D5
Pymoor La PE22 113 B2
Pynder Cl LN4 203 A2
Pyruss Dr HU4 179 B2
Pytchley Wlk DN35 192 E2

Q

Quadring Bank PE11 144 E6
Quadring Cowley & Browns Charity (Controlled) Prim Sch PE11 135 A1
Quadring Rd
Donington PE11 134 F2
Quadring PE11 145 B7
Quaker La
7 Boston PE21 208 F4
Spalding PE11 214 A3
Quantock Cl
7 Kingston upon Hull HU3 180 D5
1 Scunthorpe DN17 184 D8
3 Thorne/Moorends DN8 15 A7
Quantock Ct 9 NG34 212 B3
Quantock Rd DN33 194 E8
Quarry La PE6 173 C7
Quarry Rd LN11 198 C4
Quarryside LN11 198 B4
Quart La DN14 6 D6
Quay La DN14 6 C7
Quayside E 6 PE10 213 E2
Quayside W 7 PE10 213 E2
Quebec Rd
Mablethorpe/Sutton on Sea LN12 64 B4
Scunthorpe DN17 184 E3
Queen Eleanor Com Sch The PE9 219 B7
Queen Eleanor Cty Prim Sch NG23 79 B6
Queen Elizabeth Ave 3 DN18 10 A7
Queen Elizabeth Gram Sch LN9 199 A4
Queen Elizabeth Rd
6 Humberston DN36 36 C8
Lincoln LN1 201 D8
Queen Elizabeth Royal Free Gram Sch PE11 214 D3
Queen Elizabeth St 1 LN8 70 D5
Queen Elizabeth Way 33 DN18 10 F8
Queen Elizabeth's Gram Sch LN13 75 E2
Queen Elizabeth's High Sch DN21 197 C7
Queen Headland La LN5 92 F1
Queen Mary Ave DN35 192 C7
Queen Mary Ave Inf Sch DN32 192 C7
Queen Mary Rd LN1 201 D8
Queen St 5 Bardney LN3 83 C4
6 Bardney LN3 83 B4
Barton-upon-Humber DN18 3 F1
Boston PE21 208 E5
Bottesford NG13 128 A6
6 Brigg DN20 196 C3
4 Collingham NG23 91 D5
Epworth DN9 27 E6
Gainsborough DN21 197 D3
4 Grantham NG31 211 A3
4 Grimsby DN32 191 E8
Horncastle LN9 199 C3
Kingston upon Hull HU1 181 A5
Kirton in Lindsey DN21 30 B1
Lincoln LN5 201 E1
Louth LN11 198 B5
9 Market Rasen LN8 57 D8
2 Peterborough PE1 226 A2
3 Scunthorpe DN16 183 C2
Sleaford NG34 212 C3
6 Spilsby PE23 88 A1
17 Sutton Bridge PE12 160 E4
Thorne/Moorends DN8 15 A8
15 Winterton DN15 9 A5
20 Wisbech PE13 170 D1
Yaxley PE7 233 F6
Queen St Pl 1 LN11 198 C5
Queen's Ave
5 Barton-upon-Humber DN18 3 F1
Market Deeping PE6 217 C6
2 Spalding PE11 157 B6
Queen's Bank PE12 167 C5
Queen's Cres
Lincoln LN1 201 D5
15 Stainforth DN7 14 C6
Queen's Ct 18 DN8 15 A8
Queen's Dr PE25 206 E8
Queen's Dr W PE1 226 A5
Queen's Est PE24 102 C1
Queen's Gate St HU3 180 B5
Queen's Gdns PE1 226 A5
Queen's Par DN35 192 F5
Queen's Rd
9 Barnetby le Wold DN38 21 B4
1 Boston PE21 209 A5
Bourne PE10 213 D6
14 Heckington NG34 122 E2
Newark-on-Trent NG24 104 A5
Queen's View Cres DN16 185 D7
Queen's Wlk PE9 219 A5
Queens Cres DN17 17 D6
Queens Ct 3 LN11 198 D4
Queens Dock Ave 4 HU1 180 F6
Queens Dr Inf Sch PE1 226 A5
Queens Pk Cl 1 LN12 64 C3
Queens Pk Specl Sch LN5 205 E8
Queens Rd
Immingham DN40 187 A4
8 Mablethorpe/Sutton on Sea LN12 77 A8
Peterborough PE2 231 B7
Skegness PE25 206 B4
Spalding PE11 214 F5
Queen's Royal Lancers Mus The* NG32 138 C8
Queens St PE9 219 B6
Queens Wlk PE2 230 F8
Queensbury Way 2 HU14 3 B6
Queensfield
Gainsborough DN21 197 B7
South Kelsey LN7 32 A1
Queensgate Ctr PE1 226 A2
Queensway
Gainsborough DN21 197 F4
1 Grantham NG31 211 E6
Grantham NG31 211 C7
Grimsby DN37 190 F8
1 Ingoldmells PE25 90 E3
Lincoln LN2 202 B5
Long Sutton PE12 216 C6
Louth LN11 198 E5
8 Mablethorpe/Sutton on Sea LN12 64 B4
Pointon & Sempringham NG34 143 B6
2 Potterhanworth LN4 82 B1
10 Ruskington NG34 108 D2
21 Saxilby LN1 66 D2
Scunthorpe DN16 185 C7
Skellingthorpe LN6 200 A3
Sturton By Stow LN1 66 C6
Queenswood Rd DN16 185 C3
Quick La PE12 168 A7
Quilter Ave HU4 179 B5
Quintin Cl LN4 205 F3
Quinton Rd DN32 191 E4
Quorn Cl 7 PE6 174 E4
Quorn Dr 5 LN6 205 C8
Quorn Gdns 1 LN11 198 D4
Quorn Mews 4 DN35 192 E3
Quorum The HU4 179 D3

R

Rabbithill La NG23 78 D3
Race La DN39 11 C3
Racecourse Rd PE9 171 E3

Raceground The
Bourne PE11 ....214 A1
2 Spalding PE11 ....156 E3
Rachel Cl DN21 ....197 C7
Radcliffe Cl 5 PE9 ....219 B5
Radcliffe Rd
7 Healing DN41 ....24 A5
3 Stamford PE9 ....219 B5
3 Stamford PE9 ....219 A5
Radford Cl PE8 ....172 C1
Railway Cl 17 NG33 ....151 D1
Railway La PE12 ....160 E3
Railway Pk Cl 1 LN6 ....201 D1
Railway Pl 4 DN31 ....189 B2
Railway St
Barnetby le Wold DN38 ....21 B4
Grimsby DN32 ....189 B1
Kingston upon Hull HU1 ....180 F5
Railway Terr
3 Grantham NG31 ....211 A3
8 Grimsby DN32 ....191 D7
Railworld Mus* PE3 ....225 F1
Rainsbutt Rd DN17 ....6 C1
Rainton Ct 3 PE11 ....214 F4
Rainwall Ct 2 PE20 ....136 A2
Rainwall's La PE20 ....136 A3
Raithby Ave 20 DN41 ....23 A4
Raithby Cross Roads
PE23 ....87 C2
Raithby Gr 6 DN33 ....191 A3
Raithby Hill PE23 ....87 D1
Raithby Rd PE23 ....87 D1
Rake Bridge Bank DN7 ....14 D2
Raleigh Ct 2 PE11 ....214 C2
Raleigh Dr HU9 ....181 D6
Raleigh Way PE3 ....225 B6
Ralphs La PE20 ....136 C7
Ram Bvd DN15 ....182 E7
Ramper La LN1 ....65 E4
Ramper Rd DN22 ....52 B7
Ramper The 6 PE11 ....156 E3
Rampton Rd DN22 ....65 A4
Ramsay Cl PE25 ....206 C1
Ramsden Ave 8 DN18 ....10 E8
Ramsey Way PE2 ....231 F6
Ramsgate LN11 ....198 C6
Ramsgate Rd LN11 ....198 C6
Ramskir La DN7 ....14 C7
Ranby Rd DN17 ....184 E5
Rand Farm Pk* LN8 ....70 A5
Randall Bank PE12 ....158 A2
Randolph Rd PE20 ....146 D7
Randsfield Ave 20 HU15 ....2 C5
Range Rd NG31 ....211 C5
Rangefield PE2 ....229 E4
Rangell Gate PE12 ....157 B5
Rangoon Way 4 PE10 ....213 E7
Ransom Ct 4 DN39 ....22 A6
Ransome Way 17 HU15 ....2 C6
Ranters Row 8 LN13 ....75 F2
Ranville Cl 11 PE11 ....145 C1
Ranworth Cl 1 PE25 ....206 D7
Ranyard La LN11 ....72 E5
Rase La 5 LN8 ....57 D8
Rasen Cl 3 LN8 ....57 B8
Rasen Ct 2 PE1 ....226 D3
Rasen La LN1 ....234 A4
Rasen Rd Tealby LN8 ....46 B1
Walesby LN8 ....45 F1
Rason's Ct 8 PE21 ....209 A5
Rat Abbey DN15 ....9 C4
Rathkenny Cl PE12 ....215 E2
Rats Pen La LN11 ....62 C1
Ratten Row PE22 ....127 A5
Rauceby CE Sch NG34 ....120 E5
Rauceby Dro NG34 ....120 F3
Rauceby Sta NG34 ....120 F3
Rauceby Terr LN1 ....234 A2
Rauceby Warren Nature Reserve* NG34 ....120 F2
Raven Cl 1 DN20 ....19 D4
Raven St HU9 ....181 D7
Ravencroft La 6 DN10 ....40 A1
Ravendale 31 DN18 ....10 F8
Ravendale Cl
Gonerby Hill Foot NG31 ....211 A8
Holton le Clay DN36 ....195 E1
Ravendale Dr LN2 ....202 A7
Ravendale Rd
Cleethorpes DN35 ....193 A3
Gainsborough DN21 ....197 E3
Ravendale St N 2 DN15 ....183 B3
Ravendale St S 8 DN15 ....183 B3
Ravenhill Cl DN35 ....192 D3
Raven's Bank PE12 ....158 B2
Raven's Dro PE12 ....159 A3
Raven's Gate
Fleet PE12 ....159 A3
Holbeach PE12 ....158 E2
Ravenscar Rd 5 DN37 ....188 A1
Ravensfleet Rd DN21 ....40 C6
Ravensmoor Cl 4 LN6 ....204 E1
Ravensthorpe Prim Sch
PE3 ....225 C7
Rawcliffe Gr HU4 ....179 D5
Rawling Way HU3 ....180 C5
Rawlinson Ave 27 LN7 ....33 B3
Rawnsley Cl 15 LN13 ....75 F2
Rawsons La PE21 ....125 E5
Raybrook Cl 5 PE21 ....208 E7
Raymond Mays Way
PE10 ....213 D2
Raymond Rd DN16 ....185 C7
Rayner Ave PE2 ....231 E5
Raysor's La PE22 ....114 A2
Rayton Cl LN4 ....203 A2
Raywell Cl HU10 ....178 F7
Raywell St HU2 ....180 E7
Reaches The PE6 ....175 C3
Read Way LN4 ....207 D5
Reading Cl LN4 ....203 E1
Reading Gate DN14 ....6 C4
Reading Rm Yd 2 HU14 ....3 A4
Reads La 4 NG33 ....151 D7
Reams Cl 4 PE21 ....209 D4
Reapers Cl 1 PE12 ....215 B2
Reaper's Rise 20 DN9 ....27 E6
Reaper's Way 8 DN9 ....27 D2
Recreation Gd Rd PE9 ....219 B6
Recreation Rd 2 PE10 ....213 D5
Recto Ave DN32 ....191 F5
Rectors Way 6 PE4 ....221 D2
Rectory Cl
1 Barrowby NG32 ....210 A5
7 Binbrook LN8 ....47 C5
2 Fishtoft PE21 ....126 C1
Rectory Gdns
2 Beckingham DN10 ....40 A1
5 Glinton PE6 ....220 C8
Peterborough PE2 ....231 B7
Rectory La
Addlethorpe PE24 ....90 C4
Barrowby NG32 ....210 A5
Bottesford NG13 ....128 A6
Claypole NG23 ....117 F8
Etton PE6 ....173 D5
3 Fulbeck NG32 ....106 C1
Gainsborough DN21 ....52 F5
6 Gedney PE12 ....159 D7
Glinton PE6 ....220 C8
Harlaxton NG32 ....139 C7
Leadenham LN5 ....106 C2
2 Mareham Le Fen PE22 ....98 F4
North Witham NG33 ....151 D4
4 Owmby LN8 ....55 F6
2 Peakirk PE6 ....174 A5
24 Waddington LN5 ....93 F7
Woolsthorpe By Belvoir
NG32 ....138 D8
Rectory Rd
Anderby PE24 ....76 F2
Boston PE21 ....209 B3
Coleby LN5 ....93 F3
Newton PE13 ....170 B5
Ruskington NG34 ....108 D1
Tydd St Mary PE13 ....160 B1
Rectory St
Beckingham LN5 ....105 B4
Epworth DN9 ....27 E6
Red Barn La PE20 ....136 B3
Red Cap La PE21 ....208 E8
Red Cow Dro PE12 ....146 F6
Red Hall* PE10 ....213 D4
Red Hall Dr LN4 ....205 F4
Red Hall Farm La LN4 ....205 F4
Red Hill Nature Reserve*
LN11 ....72 E7
Red La South Ferriby DN18 ....9 F7
Welby NG32 ....130 F5
Red Leas La LN11 ....62 A8
Red Lion St
9 Bicker PE20 ....135 A4
6 Boston PE21 ....208 F5
5 Spalding PE11 ....214 D4
3 Spalding PE11 ....214 D4
8 Stamford PE9 ....219 B5
Red Rd LN8 ....84 B8
Redbourn Cl 2 DN16 ....183 B1
Redbourn E Rd DN16 ....19 A6
Redbourn Way DN16 ....183 B2
Redbourne Dr LN2 ....202 A8
Redbourne Mere DN21 ....30 E2
Redbourne Rd
Grimsby DN33 ....191 B3
Hibaldstow DN20 ....30 F4
Waddingham DN21 ....43 C7
Redbourne St
Kingston upon Hull HU3 ....180 B5
1 Scunthorpe DN16 ....183 C2
Redbridge PE4 ....220 E6
Redcar Cl LN6 ....204 F4
Redcar Gr DN32 ....192 A5
Redcar St HU8 ....181 A8
Redcliff Dr 22 HU14 ....3 A4
Redcliffe Rd NG31 ....211 B7
Redcombe La DN20 ....196 B4
Redcot Gdns PE9 ....219 B6
Redcote Dr LN6 ....204 F4
Redcross St NG31 ....211 B5
Redfern Cl HU3 ....180 D5
Redgate Rd PE13 ....170 C8
Redhall Cl 9 DN3 ....14 A2
Redhill La LN8 ....59 A8
Redland Cres 1 DN8 ....15 B8
Redman Cl DN21 ....197 E5
Redmile Cl
Bourne PE10 ....154 D5
Pinchbeck PE11 ....214 C8
Redmile's La 2 PE9 ....171 A3
Redthorn Way NG23 ....117 F7
Redthorne Cl 2 PE11 ....214 F5
Redwing Cl
Peterborough PE2 ....231 E7
Skellingthorpe LN6 ....200 A3
Redwing Gr 1 LN6 ....204 D8
Redwood Ave 11 NG34 ....212 D2
Redwood Ct DN16 ....185 D3
Redwood Cty Prim Sch
LN5 ....93 E8
Redwood Dr
Cleethorpes DN35 ....192 D2
Waddington LN5 ....205 D1
Reed St 7 HU2 ....180 E7
Reedham La LN4 ....207 F2
Reedings Cl NG32 ....210 B5
Reedings Rd NG32 ....210 B5
Reedmace Cl 8 PE6 ....174 E4
Reedmans Cl 5 PE6 ....164 F3
Reepham PE2 ....229 D4
Reepham CE (Controlled) Prim Sch LN3 ....203 F8
Reepham Rd LN3 ....82 A7
Reet 2 DN31 ....189 B1
Reeves Way PE1 ....226 D5
Refinery Rd DN16 ....183 F2
Reform Pl 2 NG34 ....212 C4
Reform St
9 Crowland PE6 ....166 E1
Kingston upon Hull HU2 ....180 F7
Stamford PE9 ....218 F5
Regal Gdns 2 NG33 ....162 E8
Regency Ct
13 Barton-upon-Humber
DN18 ....3 E1
1 Barton-upon-Humber
DN18 ....10 E8
Regency Gdns NG31 ....211 D5
Regency Way PE3 ....225 E1
Regent Ave LN6 ....200 C1
Regent Cl HU3 ....180 C6
Regent Dr 18 DN17 ....16 D7
Regent Rd LN12 ....64 B4
Regent St PE11 ....214 C3
Regents Cl
6 Collingham NG23 ....91 D4
4 Skegness PE25 ....206 C1
Regents Pk Cl 7 LN6 ....204 F1
Regina Wlk 10 PE24 ....90 D7
Reginald Rd DN15 ....182 F5
Regional Coll PE2 ....230 D6
Reldene Dr HU5 ....179 B7
Rembrandt Way PE11 ....214 B3
Remigius Gr LN2 ....202 C7
Remple Ave 2 DN7 ....15 A3
Remple Comm Rd DN7 ....14 F2
Remple La 3 DN7 ....15 A3
Renault Dr LN4 ....205 F1
Rendel St DN31 ....188 F1
Renew's Dro PE6 ....166 D3
Renfrew Cl 2 LN5 ....205 C2
Renfrew Rd LN5 ....205 C2
Reporto Ave DN32 ....191 F5
Repton Cl LN4 ....203 D1
Repton Dr 2 DN16 ....185 B3
Repton Rd 7 LN12 ....64 B4
Reservation The NG34 ....212 F7
Reservoir Rd PE11 ....145 F4
Reservoir St LN1 ....234 A4
Resolute Cl 6 PE23 ....101 A8
Responso Ave 3 DN32 ....191 F5
Reston Ct DN35 ....193 A3
Reston Gr 4 DN33 ....191 B4
Retief Cl LN1 ....201 D8
Retreat The
Easton on the Hill PE9 ....171 C3
6 Maxey PE6 ....173 C6
Revesby Abbey PE22 ....99 C5
Revesby Ave
Boston PE21 ....208 D4
Grimsby DN34 ....190 F4
Scunthorpe DN16 ....185 A7
Revesby Bank
Carrington PE22 ....99 B1
Revesby PE22 ....112 B8
Revesby Cl
Boston PE21 ....208 D4
Lincoln LN6 ....204 F6
Revesby Cnr 5 PE22 ....99 A4
Revesby Ct DN16 ....185 A8
Revesby Dr PE25 ....206 A4
Revigo Ave DN32 ....191 F5
Revill Cl
5 Claypole NG23 ....117 E8
17 Scotter DN21 ....29 C3
Reynard St 3 PE23 ....88 A1
Reynold's Paddock 2
LN5 ....93 A5
Reynolds Cl HU14 ....2 F5
Reynolds Dr 1 LN6 ....205 B6
Reynolds Gdns 6 PE12 ....157 F7
Reynolds Jun & Inf Sch
DN35 ....192 D7
Reynolds St DN35 ....192 D7
Rhodes Ave 2 NG34 ....212 C3
Rhodes St HU3 ....179 F5
Rialto Ave DN32 ....191 F5
Ribble St 4 HU3 ....180 B4
Riber Cl 2 NG31 ....210 E5
Ribston Cl DN16 ....185 A2
Riby Cl 3 DN21 ....53 A7
Riby Cross Roads DN37 ....23 C3
Riby Ct DN36 ....195 E2
Riby Rd Cabourne LN7 ....33 D6
Keelby DN41 ....23 A4
Scunthorpe DN17 ....184 E5
Stallingborough DN41 ....23 C4
Swallow LN7 ....34 A7
Riby Sq DN31 ....189 B1
Riby St DN31 ....189 B1
Richard St 4 DN31 ....191 C8
Richard Young Cl 4
PE13 ....170 D2
Richards Ave LN6 ....204 F4
Richardson Cl 18 DN36 ....36 D8
Richdale Ave 1 DN21 ....30 B2
Richmond Ave PE4 ....221 A2
Richmond Cl
Caythorpe NG32 ....119 B6
2 Sleaford NG34 ....212 B2
Richmond Ct 1 PE25 ....206 C2
Richmond Dr
Lincoln LN6 ....204 F3
Scunthorpe DN16 ....185 C4
Skegness PE25 ....206 C1
Richmond Prim Sch The
PE25 ....206 C2
Richmond Rd
Cleethorpes DN35 ....192 E5
Gainsborough DN21 ....197 F4
Grimsby DN34 ....191 A6
Kingston upon Hull
HU13 ....178 E2
Lincoln LN1 ....201 D4
Richmond Way PE13 ....170 B2
Riddings Inf Sch
DN17 ....184 E4
Riddings Jun Sch
DN17 ....184 F4
Rider Gdns PE21 ....209 D2
Rides The 7 PE6 ....164 F3
Ridge Cl 14 LN2 ....68 D6
Ridge View
2 Brigg DN20 ....196 D4
Harmston LN5 ....93 F4
Ridge View Rd LN4 ....205 F4
Ridge Way PE2 ....231 B8
Ridgeway 13 LN2 ....68 D2
Ridgeway Rd HU5 ....179 B7
Ridgeway The DN34 ....190 D3
Ridgewell Cl 10 LN6 ....204 D8
Ridgewood Ave 14 DN3 ....14 A1
Ridgewood Dr 5 DN15 ....8 A4
Ridings The
Kingston upon Hull HU5 ....179 A8
Market Rasen LN8 ....57 E7
17 North Ferriby HU14 ....3 A4
Ridley Ave PE25 ....206 D2
Rightwell E PE3 ....225 A5
Rightwell W PE3 ....225 A5
Rigsby Wood Nature Reserve* LN13 ....75 C3
Rigsmoor Cl 2 LN6 ....93 C8
Rileston Pl DN16 ....185 B2
Riley Cl
Bracebridge Heath LN4 ....205 F2
Yaxley PE7 ....233 D6
Rimac Rd LN11 ....51 D2
Rimes La DN22 ....65 A7
Rime's La LN10 ....98 C6
Rimington Rd 4 PE21 ....126 C1
Ring Beck La HU15 ....2 A8
Ring Moor Cl 7 LN4 ....109 F5
Ringers La PE13 ....170 B2
Ringrose St HU3 ....179 F5
Ringstead Rd PE4 ....221 D1
Ringstone Chase PE10 ....142 F1
Ringwood PE3 ....224 F3
Ringwood Cl
4 Birchwood LN6 ....200 D1
1 Scunthorpe DN16 ....185 B4
Rinks La LN5 ....92 E1
Rio Dr NG23 ....91 D5
Ripley Dr LN6 ....205 A3
Riplingham Rd HU10 ....178 A8
Ripon Cl
Grantham NG31 ....210 F5
Peterborough PE4 ....220 F3
Scunthorpe DN17 ....184 C7
Ripon Dr NG34 ....212 C6
Ripon Pl 16 LN12 ....64 B3
Ripon St Grimsby DN31 ....191 C8
Lincoln LN5 ....201 F1
Ripon Way HU9 ....181 C8
Rippingale CE (Controlled) Prim Sch PE10 ....142 F2
Rippingale Rd PE10 ....142 D2
Rippons Dro PE6 ....217 E2
Risby PE3 ....225 B8
Risby Rd DN15 ....9 A1
Rise The
16 Navenby/Wellingore
LN5 ....107 A8
8 North Ferriby HU14 ....3 A5
Scunthorpe DN17 ....184 E3
South Ferriby DN18 ....10 A8
Risedale 26 LN7 ....33 B4
Risegate Rd PE11 ....144 F4
Riseholme PE2 ....229 E3
Riseholme La LN2 ....67 F2
Riseholme Rd
Gainsborough DN21 ....197 F3
Lincoln LN2 ....201 F7
Risewood La NG33 ....130 F1
Riston St HU3 ....180 C5
Rivan Ave DN33 ....194 E7
Rivehall Ave 7 LN2 ....68 D7
Rivelin Cres DN16 ....185 A8
Rivelin Pl DN16 ....185 A8
Rivelin Rd DN16 ....185 A7
Rivendale PE4 ....220 F5
River Bank PE12 ....214 C1
River Gr HU4 ....179 E3
River La Anwick NG34 ....109 B1
Keddington LN11 ....198 E7
Moulton PE12 ....158 A8
Peterborough PE3 ....225 F2
River Mdw DN20 ....196 A2
River Rd
West Burton DN22 ....52 D4
West Walton PE14 ....170 C4
River Terr 4 PE13 ....170 C1
River View 21 DN18 ....10 F8
River Way PE21 ....209 C2
Riverbank Cl PE6 ....217 E3
Riverdale 8 LN2 ....68 D2
Riverdale Rd DN16 ....185 A7
Rivergate
3 Peterborough PE1 ....226 A1
3 Spalding PE11 ....214 D2
Rivergate Sh Ctr PE1 ....226 A1
Riverhead LN11 ....198 D7
Riverhead Rd LN11 ....198 D6
Riverhead Theatre*
DN31 ....191 D8
Rivermead LN6 ....205 C4
Rivermead Cl LN6 ....205 C4
Riverside 2 Brigg DN20 ....196 A3
Grantham NG31 ....211 B4
Market Deeping PE6 ....217 E3
Scotter DN21 ....29 C4
2 Spalding PE11 ....214 B5
Riverside Cl 14 NG13 ....128 A6
Riverside Dr DN35 ....193 C2
Riverside Gdns
Parson Drove PE13 ....177 C7
Peterborough PE3 ....225 D1
Riverside Ind Est
PE21 ....209 A2
Riverside Mead PE2 ....231 B8
Riverside Pk
Grantham NG31 ....211 B6
Spalding PE11 ....214 E2
Riverside Spinney
PE8 ....222 A3
Riverside The NG34 ....212 D4
Riverside Wlk 8 NG13 ....128 A6
Riverton Cl LN1 ....201 D8
Riverview Ave HU14 ....3 A4
Roadwood La NG23 ....78 F8
Robert Ave PE1 ....225 F8
Robert Cl DN40 ....186 B4
Robert Dukeson Ave
NG24 ....104 A6
Robert Manning Sch The
PE10 ....213 E6
Robert Pattinson Sch
LN6 ....204 E2
Robert Rayner Cl PE2 ....230 D6
Robert St DN15 ....183 A3
Robert Tressell Wlk 2
LN2 ....202 C7
Roberta Cl 10 PE25 ....206 A4
Robert's Gr PE25 ....206 D7
Robert's Field Nature Reserve* PE9 ....162 F5
Roberts St DN32 ....192 A8
Robertson Ave 6 NG34 ....121 B8
Robertson Cl 14 LN5 ....93 F7
Robertson Dr NG34 ....212 D5
Robertson Rd
3 Grantham NG31 ....210 F5
Lincoln LN6 ....204 E1
Robey St LN5 ....205 E8
Robin Cl
8 Market Deeping PE6 ....217 C5
12 Sleaford NG34 ....212 B3
Robin Hood Cl PE3 ....224 F2
Robin Hood Cres 13 DN3 ....14 A1
Robin Hood Rd
11 Kirk Sandall DN3 ....14 A1
Skegness PE25 ....206 C3
Robin Hood's Wlk
PE21 ....208 F6
Robinia Dr HU4 ....179 C2
Robins Cl PE2 ....230 E8
Robins Field PE8 ....222 A4
Robins Wood PE8 ....222 A4
Robinson Ave 4 LN13 ....75 E2
Robinson Cl 3 DN15 ....182 E4
Robinson La
Grimsby DN31 ....189 C2
Louth LN11 ....198 C5
Robinson Pl LN5 ....105 F5
Robinson Rd DN40 ....186 F6
Robinson St E 4 DN32 ....191 E7
Robinson's Gr 8 DN20 ....31 A5
Robinson's La 11 DN36 ....36 B1
Robson Rd DN35 ....192 D7
Rochdale Rd DN16 ....185 A5
Rochdale Rd Jun Sch
DN16 ....185 A5
Rochester Ave HU4 ....179 B3
Rochester Cl 1 DN17 ....184 C7
Rochester Ct
2 Bourne PE10 ....213 C7
Humberston DN35 ....193 A1
Rochester Dr
Birchwood LN6 ....200 D2
9 Grantham NG31 ....210 E5
Rochford Cres PE21 ....209 B5
Rochford Twr* PE21 ....209 E5
Rochford Twr La
PE21 ....209 D6
Rock Rd
Peterborough PE1 ....225 F6
Stamford PE9 ....219 B5
Rock The NG32 ....138 B4
Rockingham Cl 8 PE6 ....217 A6
Rockingham Ct 9
DN34 ....190 D4
Rockingham Gr PE4 ....221 A2
Rockingham Rd 4 PE9 ....218 E6
Rod Mill Rd DN16 ....183 E1
Roegate La PE12 ....159 F1
Roeze Cl 14 LN10 ....97 C5
Rogues Alley PE13 ....177 C4
Rokeby Ave HU4 ....179 B5
Rokeby Cl HU4 ....179 B5
Rokeby Pk HU4 ....179 B5
Rokeby Pk Prim Sch
HU4 ....179 B4
Rolleston Cl 3 LN2 ....201 F7
Roman Bank
Bourne PE10 ....213 E4
Holbeach PE12 ....215 D8
Huttoft PE24 ....77 C4
1 Ingoldmells PE25 ....206 D8

Roman Bank *continued*
Moulton PE12 ... 146 E2
Newton PE13 ... 170 B4
6 Skegness PE25 ... 206 C3
Spalding PE11 ... 214 F6
Stamford PE9 ... 219 A5
Roman Cl 9 LN4 ... 95 D4
Roman Dr PE8 ... 222 D2
Roman Pavement LN2 ... 202 C4
Roman Rd PE12 ... 157 D1
Roman Way
7 Ancaster NG32 ... 120 A2
Aubourn Haddington & South Hykeham LN6 ... 93 A8
Horncastle LN9 ... 199 D3
Roman Wharf LN1 ... 201 C3
Romany Gdns PE2 ... 231 D5
Romney Cl 3 LN6 ... 205 B6
Romney Dr LN6 ... 205 B5
Romsey Ct DN34 ... 190 D5
Ronald Cl 3 PE25 ... 206 C4
Rood's La PE12 ... 157 C8
Rookery Ave
2 Grimsby DN33 ... 191 D3
Sleaford NG34 ... 212 B3
Rookery Cl LN11 ... 198 D8
Rookery Croft 14 DN9 ... 27 E6
Rookery La
Ancaster NG32 ... 119 F2
13 Leasingham NG34 ... 121 B7
Lincoln LN6 ... 205 C6
Wildmore LN4 ... 111 E2
Wymondham LE14 ... 150 B1
Rookery Rd
2 Bicker PE20 ... 135 A4
16 Healing DN41 ... 23 F5
Sutton Bridge PE12 ... 160 D7
Rookery The
14 Collingham NG23 ... 91 D5
Peterborough PE2 ... 229 C7
2 Scawby DN20 ... 30 F8
Yaxley PE7 ... 233 D5
Rooklands 10 DN21 ... 29 C3
Rook's La DN10 ... 39 F6
Roosdyke La PE22 ... 137 D7
Rope Wlk Lincoln LN6 ... 234 A1
15 Thorne/Moorends DN8 ... 15 A8
Roper's Bridge La
PE20 ... 136 A4
Roper's Gate
Gedney PE12 ... 159 F8
2 Lutton PE12 ... 160 A8
Roper's La PE12 ... 159 D1
Ropery La 2 DN18 ... 3 E1
Ropery Rd DN21 ... 197 B7
Ropery St
Grimsby DN32 ... 191 F7
Kingston upon Hull HU3 ... 180 D4
Ropewalk 6 LN8 ... 70 D5
Ropewalk Gall* DN18 ... 3 F1
Ropewalk The
1 Caistor LN7 ... 33 B4
8 Colsterworth NG33 ... 151 E6
Ropsley CE (Controlled) Prim Sch NG33 ... 131 A1
Ropsley Rd NG33 ... 140 E8
Rosaire Pl DN33 ... 195 A8
Rosalind Ave DN34 ... 191 B7
Rosamond St 7 HU3 ... 180 B4
Rose Ave PE2 ... 231 C7
Rose Cottage Gdn Ctr & Tropical Forest*
PE11 ... 156 D8
Rose Cottage La LN5 ... 94 A3
Rose Cres PE12 ... 158 D3
Rose Gdns DN40 ... 186 C4
Rose Gr 1 PE25 ... 206 D5
Rose La
Beesby with Saleby LN13 ... 75 F5
Pinchbeck PE11 ... 156 E8
Rose Pl PE21 ... 209 A3
Rose Wlk
Scunthorpe DN15 ... 183 C3
11 Wisbech PE13 ... 170 C1
Roseberry Ave
26 Hatfield DN7 ... 14 D4
Skegness PE25 ... 206 D1
Rosebery Ave
Boston PE21 ... 208 C5
Lincoln LN1 ... 201 D4
Rosedale
Scunthorpe DN17 ... 184 E2
Waltham DN37 ... 194 C5
Rosedale Cl 4 LN6 ... 204 F3
Rosedale Dr NG31 ... 211 B8
Rosedale Gr HU5 ... 179 D7
Rosefields DN21 ... 197 E5
Rosegar Ave PE20 ... 135 F2
Rosegarth St 14 PE21 ... 208 F4
Rosehill Cl 6 LN1 ... 66 D2
Rosehip Rd PE10 ... 154 D6
Roselea Ave 8 LN2 ... 68 D6
Rosemary Ave
Grimsby DN34 ... 190 F6
11 Market Deeping PE6 ... 217 C5
Rosemary Cres NG31 ... 210 E1
Rosemary Gdns PE1 ... 225 F8
Rosemary La LN2 ... 234 B2
Rosemary Rise NG33 ... 141 D5
Rosemary Way DN35 ... 192 E1
Rosemount Dr DN16 ... 185 B6
Rosemount Grange
HU13 ... 178 C3
Rosemount La 6 DN21 ... 43 D7
Roseum Cl LN6 ... 204 E5
Roseveare Ave DN31 ... 191 A7
Roseway 2 DN21 ... 197 D5
Rosewood Cl
2 Birchwood LN6 ... 204 C8
4 Kingston upon Hull HU5 ... 179 B7
Rosewood Dr 5 NG34 ... 212 D2
Rosewood Way 1 DN16 ... 185 B3
Rosey Row 4 HU9 ... 181 C7
Rosina Gr N 2 DN32 ... 192 B6
Rosina Gr S 4 DN32 ... 192 B6
Roslyn Rd HU3 ... 179 E7
Rosmead St HU9 ... 181 D8
Rosper Rd DN40 ... 186 A8
Ross Cl 5 NG24 ... 104 D5
Ross La 6 DN15 ... 9 B5
Ross Rd DN31 ... 189 D1
Rossa Rd LN13 ... 76 D7
Rossall Cl
9 Mablethorpe/Sutton on Sea LN12 ... 77 A7
Scunthorpe DN16 ... 185 C3
Rossetti Ct NG31 ... 211 E5
Rossington Cl 18 LN4 ... 95 C4
Rostrop Rd LN4 ... 95 C7
Rosyth Ave PE2 ... 229 D3
Rothbury Rd DN17 ... 184 F7
Rothwell Ave 10 DN33 ... 191 B3
Rothwell Cl DN21 ... 197 E4
Rothwell Rd
Cabourne LN7 ... 33 C3
4 Lincoln LN2 ... 201 F7
Scunthorpe DN15 ... 182 D4
Rothwell Way PE2 ... 230 C7
Rotten Row
Pinchbeck PE11 ... 156 E8
Theddlethorpe St Helen LN12 ... 63 E5
Rotton Sykes La DN15 ... 1 F2
Roughton Ct 5 LN2 ... 202 A8
Roundhouse Cl PE1 ... 226 D3
Roundway
Grimsby DN34 ... 191 C5
2 Immingham DN40 ... 186 C3
Roundway The HU4 ... 179 C5
Routland Cl 8 LN8 ... 70 D4
Roval Dr DN40 ... 186 A4
Rowan Ave
Peterborough PE1 ... 226 C6
Spalding PE11 ... 214 E5
Rowan Cl
6 Barrow upon Humber DN19 ... 11 C8
16 Keelby DN41 ... 23 A4
10 Wisbech PE13 ... 170 E1
Rowan Cres DN16 ... 185 C3
Rowan Ct 3 Goxhill DN19 ... 12 A8
11 Heighington/Washingborough LN4 ... 203 D1
Rowan Dr 5 Healing DN41 ... 23 F5
Silk Willoughby NG34 ... 121 B2
Rowan Rd Lincoln LN6 ... 204 F3
Waddington LN5 ... 205 D1
Rowan Way
1 Boston PE21 ... 209 A7
Bourne PE10 ... 213 B6
16 Metheringham LN4 ... 95 C4
Rowans The
Holbeach PE12 ... 159 A7
9 Nettleham LN2 ... 68 C2
4 Westwoodside DN9 ... 27 A2
Rowanwood Dr 7 NG31 ... 210 F7
Rowdyke Rd PE21 ... 136 F7
Rowe Ave PE2 ... 230 D7
Rowgate Rd LN11 ... 73 A5
Rowland Ct 1 PE4 ... 220 F5
Rowland Rd 6 DN16 ... 183 B2
Rowlandson St 3 DN31 ... 189 B2
Rowley Rd PE21 ... 209 A4
Rowmills Rd 2 DN16 ... 185 C8
Rowston Cl DN21 ... 197 C6
Rowston St DN35 ... 193 A5
Roxborough Cl LN6 ... 200 E2
Roxburgh Rd PE9 ... 218 F6
Roxburgh St 1 HU5 ... 180 B8
Roxby Cl LN6 ... 204 F6
Roxby Cswy DN15 ... 9 C4
Roxby Rd DN15 ... 8 F4
Roxholm Cl 2 NG34 ... 108 D1
Roxholme Rd NG34 ... 121 B8
Roxton Ave DN41 ... 23 A5
Roxton Hall Dr 15 HU14 ... 3 A5
Royal Air Force Coll The
NG34 ... 120 B8
Royal Arthur Cl 5 PE25 ... 206 C1
Royal Cl 15 PE12 ... 160 E4
Royal Ct DN35 ... 193 B1
Royal Hull Hospitals NHS Trust HU3 ... 180 C6
Royal Oak Ct
18 Heckington NG34 ... 122 E3
19 Louth LN11 ... 198 B5
Royal Oak La 1 LN5 ... 93 A5
Royal St DN31 ... 189 A2
Royal Way PE21 ... 209 F2
Royalty Bank PE22 ... 101 B3
Royce Rd
Peterborough PE1 ... 226 D3
Peterborough PE7 ... 229 A4
2 Spalding PE11 ... 214 F6
Roydon Gr LN6 ... 205 B6
Royle Cl PE2 ... 230 C5
Royston Ave PE2 ... 230 C6
Ruards La DN19 ... 5 A1
Ruckland Ave LN1 ... 201 E7
Rudgard Ave LN3 ... 203 E6
Rudgard La
Lincoln LN1 ... 201 D4
Rudgard La *continued*
Lincoln LN1 ... 234 A3
Rudham Ave 4 DN32 ... 191 E4
Rudkin Dr 5 NG34 ... 212 D6
Rudyard Cl 7 LN12 ... 77 A7
Rudyard Gr PE4 ... 221 C3
Rue De L'yonne 1 NG23 ... 91 D5
Rue De Nozay 3 DN20 ... 19 E4
Rufford Gn 2 LN6 ... 205 C8
Rufford Rd DN35 ... 192 E4
Rugby Rd
4 Mablethorpe/Sutton on Sea LN12 ... 64 B4
Scunthorpe DN16 ... 185 A8
Rugby St 5 HU3 ... 180 B4
Rumbold La 3 PE24 ... 102 D1
Runcorn Garth HU4 ... 179 B3
Runcorn Rd LN6 ... 204 B5
Running Post La PE20 ... 135 B4
Runswick Cl LN6 ... 205 A3
Runswick Rd DN32 ... 192 B6
Rupert Rd 1 DN33 ... 191 D3
Rural Ave PE11 ... 144 D1
Rural Villages Sch Bucknall
LN10 ... 84 B3
Rush Furlong Nature Reserve* DN9 ... 27 E3
Rushcarr La DN17 ... 17 C1
Rushcliffe Rd NG31 ... 211 A7
Rushmere PE2 ... 229 F6
Rushmore Ctry Pk*
LN11 ... 61 F8
Rushton Ave PE4 ... 220 E4
Rushtons Way 12 DN20 ... 30 F5
Rushy Dro PE11 ... 145 C8
Ruskin Ave LN2 ... 202 B6
Ruskin Gn LN2 ... 202 B6
Ruskin Rd 13 LN12 ... 64 B4
Ruskin St
2 Gainsborough DN21 ... 197 D2
Kingston upon Hull HU3 ... 180 B6
Ruskington Sta NG34 ... 108 E1
Russell Ave Lincoln LN6 ... 93 C8
Newark-on-Trent NG24 ... 104 A2
Russell Cl 12 PE6 ... 176 A3
Russell Cres NG34 ... 212 F4
Russell Ct DN35 ... 193 A1
Russell Dr 2 PE12 ... 167 B8
Russell Hill PE8 ... 222 A6
Russell Rd 7 NG34 ... 121 B8
Russell St
Kingston upon Hull HU2 ... 180 E7
Lincoln LN5 ... 205 D6
Peterborough PE1 ... 225 F3
Russell Wlk 2 DN17 ... 29 D7
Russet Cl 2 DN15 ... 182 C5
Rustic La DN21 ... 41 C6
Ruston Rd NG31 ... 211 F7
Rutland Cl 18 NG33 ... 151 D2
Rutland Dr DN36 ... 195 C5
Rutland La 15 NG13 ... 128 A5
Rutland Rd
Kingston upon Hull HU5 ... 179 E8
Scunthorpe DN16 ... 185 D7
Skegness PE25 ... 206 D3
Stamford PE9 ... 219 D7
Rutland St
2 Grimsby DN32 ... 189 D1
Grimsby DN32 ... 192 A8
Rutland Way
Ryhall PE9 ... 163 C1
15 Scampton Airfield LN1 ... 67 E5
Rycroft Ave PE6 ... 217 F5
Rycroft Cl 1 PE6 ... 217 F4
Rycroft St NG31 ... 211 B3
Rydal Ave DN33 ... 194 D7
Rydal Cl LN6 ... 200 D2
Rydal Ct PE4 ... 221 C3
Ryde Ave NG31 ... 210 E4
Rye Cres 3 HU15 ... 2 D5
Rye La LN13 ... 75 D5
Ryecroft 11 LN5 ... 205 D2
Ryedale 6 HU15 ... 2 D6
Ryedale Ave 1 DN15 ... 9 A6
Ryedale Cl NG31 ... 211 B8
Ryefield La PE12 ... 159 B3
Ryhall CE Prim Sch
PE9 ... 163 C1
Ryhall Rd
Great Casterton PE9 ... 171 C8
Stamford PE9 ... 219 D5
Ryland Gdns 10 LN2 ... 68 D6
Ryland Rd LN2 ... 68 E6
Rymac Cres PE25 ... 90 E4
Rymer Pl DN35 ... 193 A4
Ryton Rd PE21 ... 208 B3

S

Sable Cl HU4 ... 179 C2
Sackville Cl DN40 ... 186 D4
Sackville Rd DN40 ... 186 D4
Sackville St 7 DN31 ... 191 C7
Sacred Heart RC Prim Sch
PE3 ... 225 A5
Sacrewell Farm & Ctry Ctr*
PE8 ... 222 C5
Saddle Row NG34 ... 120 B8
Saddleback Rd
Skidbrooke with Saltfleet Haven LN11 ... 51 A3
South Cockerington LN11 ... 50 E1
Saddler Dr PE10 ... 154 C6
Saddler's Cl 11 LN4 ... 95 C4
Saddler's Way 2 DN9 ... 27 D3
Saddlers Cl
Glinton PE6 ... 220 D8
Saddlers Cl *continued*
Osbournby NG34 ... 132 D5
Saddlers Mead 10 PE11 ... 214 A2
Saddlers Way
Fishtoft PE21 ... 209 C2
5 Long Sutton PE12 ... 216 B5
Sadler Cl 9 PE25 ... 206 C1
Sadler Rd LN6 ... 204 B5
Saffrondale HU10 ... 178 E7
Sagefield Cl 5 DN33 ... 194 D8
Sage's La PE4 ... 225 C8
Sailors Wharf HU9 ... 181 C6
Sainsbury Way HU4 ... 179 A1
St Aiden's Rd 5 LN6 ... 204 E2
St Alban's Dr 16 PE6 ... 175 A1
St Albans Ave DN31 ... 191 A8
St Albans Cl
5 Grantham NG31 ... 210 D5
16 Hibaldstow DN20 ... 30 F5
3 Scunthorpe DN17 ... 184 C7
St Andrew's Cl
4 Helpringham NG34 ... 133 D7
Redbourne DN21 ... 30 F3
St Andrew's Cres 6
NG34 ... 121 B7
St Andrew's Dr
1 Burton-upon-Stather DN15 ... 8 B4
Grimsby DN32 ... 192 B4
Lincoln LN6 ... 205 C8
Skegness PE25 ... 206 D5
St Andrew's Gdns LN6 ... 205 C8
St Andrew's Mount
HU10 ... 178 C8
St Andrew's Pl 3 LN5 ... 234 B1
St Andrew's Rd
6 Butterwick PE22 ... 126 E3
Spalding PE11 ... 214 C1
St Andrew's St
8 Heckington NG34 ... 122 E3
16 Kirton in Lindsey DN21 ... 30 B1
4 Lincoln LN5 ... 234 B1
St Andrew's Way
8 Barnby Dun DN3 ... 14 A3
Epworth DN9 ... 27 E7
4 RAF Cranwell NG34 ... 120 C8
St Andrews NG31 ... 211 D7
St Andrews Ave 2
DN17 ... 184 F2
St Andrews CE (Controlled) Prim Sch NG34 ... 121 B7
St Andrews CE Jun Sch
DN40 ... 186 D4
St Andrews CE Prim Sch
LN10 ... 97 C6
St Andrews Cl LN5 ... 201 F1
St Andrews Ct 4 LN4 ... 96 C1
St Andrews Dr 6 LN1 ... 66 C2
St Andrews Gr 33 DN7 ... 14 D4
St Andrews Prim Sch
HU10 ... 178 C7
St Andrews Rd
2 Mablethorpe/Sutton on Sea LN12 ... 64 B4
Northborough PE6 ... 217 E1
St Andrews Wlk 5 LN10 ... 97 C5
St Ann's Ave DN34 ... 191 B6
St Ann's La PE21 ... 208 F3
St Anne's Rd
9 Keelby DN41 ... 23 A5
Lincoln LN2 ... 202 B4
St Anne's Specl Sch
HU15 ... 2 E5
St Anne's St NG31 ... 211 C3
St Anne's Wlk 13 HU15 ... 2 D6
St Annes Ave 8 LN11 ... 50 F7
St Annes CE Prim Sch
NG31 ... 211 C3
St Annes Cl
Lincoln LN2 ... 202 B4
Skegness PE25 ... 206 C6
3 Sleaford NG34 ... 212 C6
8 Spalding PE11 ... 214 C6
St Annes Way PE11 ... 214 C6
St Aubins Cres LN4 ... 81 F4
St Audrey Cl PE2 ... 231 D6
St Augustin Way
NG31 ... 211 A4
St Augustine Ave
DN32 ... 191 E5
St Augustine Cres
DN16 ... 185 B5
St Augustine Webster RC Prim Sch DN15 ... 182 D4
St Augustine's CE Sch
PE13 ... 170 D2
St Augustine's Wlk
PE2 ... 230 E8
St Augustines Jun Sch
PE2 ... 230 F8
St Augustines RC (Aided) Prim Sch PE9 ... 219 C7
St Barbara's Cres 7 DN15 ... 8 B4
St Barnabas CE Prim Sch
DN38 ... 21 B4
St Barnabas Ct 4 HU3 ... 180 C4
St Barnabas Dr 1 HU14 ... 3 C7
St Barnabas Rd DN38 ... 21 B4
St Bartholomew's Cl 4
DN41 ... 23 A4
St Bede's RC Sch
DN16 ... 185 B6
St Bedes RC Sec Sch
PE21 ... 209 B6
St Bee's Dr 19 PE6 ... 175 A1
St Benedict Cl 18 PE6 ... 166 F1
St Benedict's Cl 2 LN6 ... 204 D2
St Benedicts Cl 2 PE6 ... 220 D8
St Benet's Gdns 2 PE6 ... 175 A1
St Bernadettes RC Prim Sch
DN16 ... 185 C6
St Bernard's Cl 13 DN20 ... 19 E4
St Bernards Ave LN11 ... 198 D6
St Bernards Cl LN11 ... 198 E6
St Bernards Specl Sch
LN11 ... 198 E5
St Botolph La PE2 ... 230 C6
St Botolph's Cres 8
LN5 ... 205 E8
St Botolph's Rd DN16 ... 185 C7
St Botolph's Way PE6 ... 176 A2
St Botolphs Cl 2 LN1 ... 66 D3
St Botolphs Infants Sch
LN5 ... 205 D8
St Botolphs Prim Sch
PE2 ... 230 B6
St Botolphs Rd 7 NG34 ... 212 C6
St Catherine's Ct LN5 ... 205 D7
St Catherine's Dr 3 DN7 ... 14 C2
St Catherine's Gr LN5 ... 205 D7
St Catherine's Rd
Grantham NG31 ... 211 B4
Lincoln LN5 ... 205 E7
St Catherines 15 LN5 ... 205 E8
St Catherines Cres
DN16 ... 185 A4
St Catherines Ct DN34 ... 190 F6
St Chad's Rd DN16 ... 185 D7
St Chads Ct 8 LN2 ... 68 E6
St Charles RC Prim Sch
HU2 ... 180 E8
St Christopher's Rd 11
DN36 ... 36 C8
St Christophers Cl 1
NG34 ... 107 F1
St Christophers Specl Sch
LN6 ... 205 B4
St Claire's Ct 6 LN6 ... 204 C8
St Clares Wlk DN20 ... 196 C2
St Clement's 9 PE9 ... 219 A5
St Clement's Ct 3 LN1 ... 234 B4
St Clement's Dr 4 LN3 ... 82 B6
St Clement's Rd
3 Lincoln LN6 ... 204 E2
2 Skegness PE25 ... 206 B4
St Clements Cl LN4 ... 108 E7
St Clements Rd 17
NG34 ... 108 D2
St Clements Way 1
DN36 ... 195 C7
St Crispin's Cl 3 LN6 ... 204 D2
St Crispins Cl 2 DN40 ... 12 E4
St David's Cl 2 LN3 ... 203 E7
St David's Rd LN6 ... 204 D2
St David's Sq PE1 ... 226 D1
St David's St 13 LN8 ... 47 B6
St Davids Cl 2 PE25 ... 206 D6
St Davids Cres DN17 ... 184 E3
St Deny's Cl 2 DN40 ... 12 E3
St Denys Ave NG34 ... 212 B6
St Edith Gate 6 LN11 ... 62 C6
St Edmonds Cl PE24 ... 115 D8
St Edmunds Cl 3 NG31 ... 210 D5
St Edmunds Rd NG34 ... 212 C3
St Edward's Dr 15 LN2 ... 68 F2
St Edwins Cl 18 DN7 ... 14 D4
St Edwins Dr 19 DN7 ... 14 D4
St Faith & St Martin CE (Controlled) Jun Sch
LN1 ... 201 D4
St Faith's St 6 LN1 ... 201 D4
St Faiths CE Inf Sch
LN1 ... 201 D4
St Firmin's Way PE10 ... 164 D7
St Frances Cl PE25 ... 206 B6
St Francis Ave DN31 ... 191 A8
St Francis Ct 5 LN6 ... 204 D2
St Francis Gdns 23 LN12 ... 77 A7
St Francis Gr 1 DN37 ... 23 E1
St Francis Sch LN1 ... 201 E7
St George Ave PE2 ... 231 E6
St George's Ave
6 Hatfield DN7 ... 14 C3
5 Hatfield DN7 ... 14 C2
St George's Cl LN6 ... 204 E2
St George's Coll of Tech
NG34 ... 212 C4
St George's Ct DN21 ... 30 F3
St George's Hill DN21 ... 54 F7
St George's Hospl
LN1 ... 201 C6
St George's Rd
Kingston upon Hull HU3 ... 180 A5
17 Wittering PE8 ... 172 B1
St George's Sq 18 PE9 ... 219 C5
St George's St 6 PE9 ... 219 C5
St Georges Ave 1 PE9 ... 219 D6
St Georges CE Com Prim Sch
DN21 ... 197 F2
St Georges CE Prim Sch
PE9 ... 219 C7
St Georges Cl
4 Cranwell NG34 ... 107 F1
22 Thorne/Moorends DN8 ... 15 B7
St Georges Dr 3 LN10 ... 97 C5
St Georges La LN2 ... 67 F1
St Georges Prim Sch
HU3 ... 180 A6
St Georges Rd 21 DN8 ... 15 B7
St Georges Sch PE1 ... 226 A7
St Gilbert of Sempringham CE Prim Sch NG34 ... 143 B7
St Gilbert's Cl NG34 ... 143 B6
St Gilbert's Rd PE10 ... 213 C6
St Gilberts CE Prim Sch
PE9 ... 219 A5

St Giles' Ave DN33 191 D1
St Giles Ave
Lincoln LN2 234 C4
1 Sleaford NG34 212 F4
St Giles Inf Sch LN2 202 B6
St Guthlac Ave 1 PE6 217 B5
St Guthlac High Sch
PE6 166 F1
St Guthlac's Cl 8 PE6 166 F1
St Guthlac's Way 1
PE21 126 C1
St Helen's Ave LN6 205 B7
St Helenas CE Prim Sch
LN13 89 A7
St Helen's Cl NG31 210 D4
St Helen's Cres DN37 194 D1
St Helen's Dr 14 HU15 2 D6
St Helen's Rd DN20 196 D3
St Helens Ave DN33 191 D3
St Helens Way DN21 42 E2
St Helier's Rd DN35 192 E7
St Hilary's Cl 1 LN6 204 D2
St Hilda's Ave DN34 191 B6
St Huberts Dr PE25 206 B6
St Hugh St LN2 234 C2
St Hugh's Ave DN35 192 E6
St Hugh's Cl 7 LN3 203 E7
St Hugh's Cres DN16 185 C8
St Hugh's Dr
3 Barlings LN3 69 C3
Lincoln LN6 204 E2
St Hugh's Hospl DN32 191 F4
St Hugh's Terr 3 LN1 66 C7
St Hughs CE High Sch
NG31 210 E3
St Hughs RC Prim Sch
LN6 204 B7
St Hughs Sch
Scunthorpe DN16 183 B1
Woodhall Spa LN10 97 D5
St Hybald's Gr 2 DN20 30 F7
St Ives Cres DN34 190 E5
St James Ave
3 Grimsby DN34 191 A6
7 Hatfield DN7 14 C3
Peterborough PE1 225 F7
St James Cl 19 DN17 16 D7
St James' Ct 2 DN34 191 C6
St James Ct 3 DN15 183 A3
St James Rd
Brigg DN20 196 D3
Long Sutton PE12 216 A1
Welton HU14 2 F5
St James Sch DN34 191 C6
St James St HU3 180 D5
St James View LN11 198 B4
St James Way PE12 157 E1
St James's Rd 6 DN20 30 E8
St James's Way 5 PE11 214 D2
St Joan's Dr 5 DN20 30 E8
St John Baptist CE (Aided) Prim Sch PE11 214 C2
St John Fisher RC Gm Sch
PE1 226 C4
St John St 1 PE24 102 D1
St John's Sch LN4 205 F4
St John's Ave
6 Cherry Willingham/Reepham LN3 203 E7
1 Lincoln LN6 204 E2
St John's Cl
11 Leasingham NG34 121 B7
6 Morton PE10 154 C7
6 Ryhall PE9 163 C1
St John's Dr
Corby Glen NG33 152 F7
6 Spalding PE11 214 B3
St John's Rd
Boston PE21 209 A3
Bracebridge Heath LN4 205 F2
9 Humberston DN36 36 C8
Lincoln LN2 201 F6
Scunthorpe DN16 185 C6
Spalding PE11 214 C3
Weston PE12 157 C2
15 Wittering PE8 172 B1
St John's St
3 Holbeach PE12 215 E2
Peterborough PE1 226 B2
Stamford PE9 219 B5
St John's Terr 18 DN21 197 D3
St John's Wlk HU13 178 F2
St Johns Church Sch CE Aided PE2 229 F3
St Johns Cl
2 Baston PE6 164 E5
21 Goxhill DN19 12 A8
Scampton LN1 67 C6
St Johns Prim Sch
PE2 231 C7
St Johns Rd PE2 231 B7
St Joseph Dr HU4 179 C5
St Josephs RC Prim Sch
DN35 192 D4
St Judes Cl PE3 225 C4
St Julian's Wells
HU10 178 D7
St Lamberts Gr 4 PE12 157 D7
St Lawrence CE (Controlled) Prim Sch LN6 200 B4
St Lawrence Rd DN7 14 C4
St Lawrence Specl Sch
LN9 199 D4
St Lawrence St 4 LN9 199 B4
St Lawrence Way 3
PE9 172 F7
St Lawrence's Pl 2
DN16 185 D7
St Lawrence's Rd
DN16 185 D6
St Leodegar's Cl PE20 136 D7
St Leonard Cl PE21 209 A6
St Leonard's Ave
DN31 191 A8
St Leonard's Dr 6 LN10 97 D5
St Leonard's La
1 Lincoln LN2 234 C3
South Cockerington LN11 62 B7
St Leonard's Rd 2 PE13 170 B2
St Leonard's St 8 PE9 219 C5
St Leonards Dr PE24 90 D7
St Luke's Cl
Cherry Willingham/Reepham LN3 203 F7
1 Hatfield DN7 14 C2
St Luke's Cres 8 DN36 36 C8
St Luke's Ct 8 DN32 191 F8
St Luke's St HU3 180 D6
St Lukes CE Prim Sch
LN7 45 B8
St Lukes Sch DN16 185 D7
St Margaret's 6 PE11 145 A8
St Margaret's Ave
PE25 206 A6
St Margaret's Cl
17 Laceby DN37 23 F1
6 Lincoln LN6 205 B4
St Margaret's Cres 6
DN40 22 E8
St Margaret's Dr PE22 113 A2
St Margaret's Gdns
LN6 205 A4
St Margaret's Wlk 5
DN16 185 C6
St Margarets CE (Controlled) Prim Sch LN13 63 A1
St Margarets Pl 2 PE2 230 F6
St Margarets Rd 1 PE2 230 F6
St Mark St
Kingston upon Hull HU8 181 A8
Lincoln LN5 234 A1
St Mark's Ave 3 LN3 203 E7
St Mark's Cl
North Hykeham LN6 204 E3
Skegness PE25 206 B6
St Mark's Ct 3 PE1 226 A3
St Mark's Rd
Holbeach PE12 147 D6
10 Humberston DN36 36 C8
St Mark's Sq
Kingston upon Hull HU3 180 D4
Lincoln LN5 234 A1
St Marks Dr 6 PE6 166 E1
St Marks Rd PE13 169 E3
St Marks St PE1 226 A3
St Martin's Cl
8 Blyton DN21 41 C5
4 Stamford PE9 219 C4
St Martin's Cres
Grimsby DN33 191 C3
7 Scawby DN20 30 E8
St Martin's La LN1 234 B3
St Martin's Pl 5 DN41 23 A4
St Martin's Rd
Newborough PE6 221 F8
4 Scawby DN20 30 E8
1 Wisbech PE13 170 E2
St Martin's St
Lincoln LN2 234 B3
Peterborough PE1 225 F5
St Martin's Way 4
NG32 120 A3
St Martins NG33 152 E1
St Martins Ave 2 HU4 179 E6
St Martins CE Prim Sch
DN9 28 A3
St Martins Cl 2 NG34 107 F1
St Martins Prep Sch
DN32 191 D5
St Mary Cl 12 PE6 166 F1
St Mary's Ave
4 Barnetby le Wold DN38 21 B4
4 Pinchbeck PE11 156 E8
12 Welton/Dunholme LN2 68 D7
Wittering PE8 172 C1
St Mary's Cl
Bainton PE9 172 F5
18 Bottesford NG13 128 A6
2 Brough HU15 2 C7
Farcet PE7 231 C2
Grimsby DN32 192 C6
Peterborough PE1 226 B4
Thorney PE6 176 A2
Wilsford NG32 120 C1
St Mary's Cres
9 Manby LN11 62 C6
5 Stow LN1 66 C8
Swineshead PE20 135 B6
St Mary's Ct 9 DN15 182 C6
St Mary's Dr
8 Hatfield DN7 14 C3
15 Hatfield DN7 14 C2
10 Hatfield DN7 14 C2
2 Hatfield DN7 14 C2
Peterborough PE2 229 F4
St Mary's Gdns
6 Cowbit PE12 167 B8
Long Sutton PE12 216 C5
3 Whaplode PE12 158 B7
St Mary's Hill 17 PE9 219 C5
St Mary's La
4 Barton-upon-Humber DN18 10 F8
Binbrook LN8 47 C4
Claxby LN8 45 E5
Louth LN11 198 A5
St Mary's Mdws 2
PE12 159 D7
St Mary's Pk LN11 198 A6
St Mary's Pl 14 PE9 219 C5
St Mary's Rd
Hatfield DN7 14 C3
2 Lincoln LN6 204 E2
Skegness PE25 206 B6
West Walton PE14 170 E4
St Mary's St Farcet PE7 231 C2
Lincoln LN5 234 A1
12 Stamford PE9 219 C5
St Mary's Way 2 PE22 114 A1
St Marys Cath Prim Sch
NG31 211 C5
St Marys CE (Controlled) Prim Sch
Welton/Dunholme LN2 68 C6
Weston PE12 157 E7
St Marys Cl 5 PE12 157 D7
St Marys Dr 6 NG34 212 C6
St Marys Prep Sch
LN2 234 C3
St Marys RC High Sch
DN33 191 A3
St Marys RC Prim Sch
Brigg DN20 196 C5
Grimsby DN32 191 F8
St Mathews Cl 2 LN6 201 D1
St Matthew St HU3 180 B5
St Matthew's Cl
5 Cherry Willingham/Reepham LN3 203 E7
4 Holbeach PE12 215 D2
St Matthew's Dr 13
PE12 160 E4
St Matthew's Rd 12 DN36 36 C8
St Mawes Cres DN34 191 A7
St Michael Cl 25 LN5 93 F7
St Michael's Ave PE13 170 D1
St Michael's Cl 16 DN8 15 B7
St Michael's Cres 5
DN16 185 C8
St Michael's Ct 22 DN19 12 A8
St Michael's Dr 15 DN8 15 B7
St Michael's Gate PE1 226 F7
St Michael's La
11 Wainfleet St Mary PE24 102 D1
Wainfleet St Mary PE24 115 D8
St Michael's Mount 18
HU14 3 B7
St Michael's Rd
Grimsby DN34 190 D4
3 Louth LN11 198 C5
16 Wittering PE8 172 B1
St Michael's Way 1
NG34 120 C8
St Michaels CE (Controlled) Prim Sch LN11 198 D5
St Michaels Cl 8 LN4 109 F5
St Michaels Terr 7 LN1 234 B3
St Michaels Wlk 8
NG34 212 C6
St Nectan Cl 9 HU3 180 A4
St Nicholas Ave HU4 179 C2
St Nicholas CE (Controlled) Prim Sch PE21 209 B4
St Nicholas CE Prim Sch
DN39 12 A1
St Nicholas Cl
4 Barkston NG32 130 B8
Boston PE21 209 B3
St Nicholas Dr DN37 190 C6
St Nicholas Prim Sch
PE12 160 A8
St Nicholas Rd
Boston PE21 209 B3
Thorne/Moorends DN8 15 A8
St Nicholas St LN1 234 A4
St Nicholas Way 10
PE12 160 A8
St Norberts RC Prim Sch
DN17 16 D7
St Norbett Sch Prim School
PE11 214 C4
St Olaf's Dr DN32 191 D6
St Olave's Dr 17 PE6 175 A1
St Paul Rd DN21 197 B7
St Paul's Ave 4 LN3 203 E7
St Paul's Cl PE13 169 E2
St Paul's Gdns PE10 213 D4
St Paul's La 2 LN1 234 B3
St Paul's Rd
Gainsborough DN21 197 B7
Peterborough PE1 225 F7
Scunthorpe DN16 185 B6
Spalding PE11 214 F5
St Paul's St PE9 219 C5
St Pauls Cl PE24 102 D7
St Pauls Prim Sch
PE11 214 F6
St Pega Cl 17 PE6 166 F1
St Pega's Rd
Glinton PE6 174 A6
Peakirk PE6 220 E8
St Peter & St Paul CE Prim Sch PE24 102 D7
St Peter & St Paul RC High Sch LN6 205 B7
St Peter at Gowts CE (Controlled) Prim Sch
LN5 201 E1
St Peter's Ave
8 Cherry Willingham/Reepham LN3 203 E7
Cleethorpes DN35 192 E6
St Peter's Ave *continued*
Kingston upon Hull HU10 178 E6
Lincoln LN6 204 D2
Scunthorpe DN16 185 B3
St Peter's CE Jun Sch
PE13 170 E1
St Peter's Cl
Burgh le Marsh PE24 102 D8
4 Holton le Clay DN36 195 D2
St Peter's Cres 5 DN36 36 C8
St Peter's Dr 4 LN10 97 D5
St Peter's Gr 14 DN21 29 C3
St Peter's Hill
6 Grantham NG31 211 B4
4 Grantham NG31 211 A4
14 Stamford PE9 219 B5
St Peter's La 4 LN12 64 C2
St Peter's Rd 12 DN21 29 C3
St Peter's Sch DN10 39 B1
St Peter's St PE9 219 B4
St Peter's Way PE6 176 A2
St Peter-in-Eastgate CE (Controlled) Inf Sch
LN2 234 C3
St Peters CE Prim Sch
Cleethorpes DN35 192 F6
Dunston LN4 95 C6
St Peters Cl DN21 40 B5
St Peters Gr 2 DN37 23 E1
St Peters Rd
11 Bourne PE10 213 C5
Peterborough PE1 226 A2
St Polycarp's Dr PE12 168 B3
St Quintins Cl 5 HU9 181 C8
St Rumbold's St LN2 234 B2
St Sebastians CE (Aided) Prim Sch NG31 129 E5
St Simon's Dr 9 LN3 203 E7
St Stephens St HU2 180 D6
St Swithins Cl 1 PE20 135 A4
St Swithuns Sq LN2 234 B2
St Thomas CE (Controlled) Prim Sch PE21 208 F1
St Thomas Ct PE12 216 B5
St Thomas Dr PE21 208 E2
St Thomas Moore RC Prim Sch PE1 226 D4
St Thomas Moore Rd
HU4 179 A4
St Thomas More RC Prim Sch
HU4 179 A4
St Thomas' Rd 13 DN36 36 C8
St Thomas's Rd 2 PE11 214 D2
St Tibba Way 12 PE9 163 C1
St Valentines Way
PE25 206 B6
St Vincent Cl 2 PE25 206 A6
St Vincent's Ave DN15 183 A6
St Vincent's Rd NG31 211 C3
St Wilfrid's Cl 18 LN4 95 D4
Salacon Way 5 DN32 189 C1
Salamander Cl DN31 191 B8
Salem St 5 PE11 145 B6
Salisbury Ave 2 LN8 47 B6
Salisbury Cl
1 Grantham NG31 210 D5
1 Saxilby with Ingleby LN1 66 D2
2 Scunthorpe DN17 184 C7
Salisbury Dr
Canwick LN4 81 A2
8 Waltham DN37 194 D4
Salisbury Rd PE4 220 F3
Salisbury St
Gainsborough DN21 197 C7
Kingston upon Hull HU13 178 D1
Salix App 1 LN6 204 C8
Sallie Bank La LN1 65 D2
Sallows Rd PE1 226 B6
Salmonby Rd DN17 184 E4
Salsbury Ave DN34 191 B6
Saltash Rd HU4 179 A2
Saltburn Gr 5 DN32 192 A5
Saltby Rd
Croxton Kerrial NG32 138 D3
Sproxton LE14 150 C7
Salter Gate LN11 51 A1
Saltergate Lincoln LN2 234 B2
Peterborough PE1 226 E7
Saltergate Rd 28 DN17 29 D7
Salters' La LN11 48 B4
Salters Way 14 PE11 134 E2
Saltersford Gr NG31 211 D1
Saltersford Rd NG31 211 D2
Saltersgate PE1 226 F7
Saltersway NG34 132 F3
Saltfleet La PE11 145 B4
Saltfleet Rd
Saltfleetby LN12 51 D1
Theddlethorpe All Saints LN12 63 E8
Saltfleetby - Theddlethorpe Dunes National Nature Reserve* LN11 51 E3
Saltfleetby CE Prim Sch
LN11 51 A1
Saltford Ave 2 HU9 5 F8
Saltgrounds Rd HU15 2 B5
Salthouse La HU1 181 A6
Saltings The 6 PE34 161 F3
Saltmarsh PE2 230 C4
Saltney Gate PE12 215 A6
Salts Rd PE14 170 F4
Salvesen Rd DN35 189 D1
Salvesen Way HU3 180 A3
Samman Cl HU10 178 D6
Samphire Cl 6 DN36 37 C5
Sampson St DN17 7 A2
Samuel Ave DN32 192 B6
Samworths Cl PE5 223 F2
Sanbeds La DN9 27 B2
Sanctuary Way DN37 190 C6
Sand La Barkston NG32 129 F8
Besthorpe NG23 91 C8
Broadholme LN6 66 D1
4 Broughton DN20 19 D3
Caistor LN7 32 E4
Fenton LN1 65 D3
Great Steeping PE23 101 C7
Hougham NG32 118 C5
Manton DN21 30 A5
Marston NG32 118 E1
Messingham DN17 29 A7
Osgodby LN8 45 B3
Spalford NG23 78 D4
Thorney NG23 79 B8
Torksey LN1 65 E5
Wroot DN9 26 C6
Sand Rd DN17 28 B8
Sandars Rd DN21 53 A8
Sandbeck Ave PE25 206 C2
Sandbeck La DN21 41 B6
Sandcliffe Rd NG31 211 A7
Sanderlings The 6 PE6 174 A5
Sanders Cl Lincoln LN1 201 D8
15 Mablethorpe & Sutton LN12 77 A7
Meering NG23 91 C8
Sanderson Cl 1 DN16 183 B1
Sanderson's Bank
DN10 26 C2
Sandfield Cl DN17 184 D5
Sandfield Dr 3 HU15 2 C5
Sandford PE3 225 B5
Sandford St 8 DN31 188 D1
Sandhill La 1 DN22 52 B3
Sandhill Rd DN14 7 B6
Sandholme La PE20 136 E5
Sandhouse Cres
3 Scunthorpe DN16 183 C1
Scunthorpe DN16 185 C8
Sandhurst Cres 5
NG34 212 B2
Sandhurst Ct 6 LN12 77 A7
Sandhurst Rd 5 LN12 77 A7
Sandilands Cl 22 LN12 77 A7
Sandilands Pit Nature Reserve* LN12 77 A7
Sandlees La NG34 123 B4
Sandlemere Cl 3 HU3 180 A5
Sandon Cl NG31 211 C5
Sandon Rd NG31 211 B5
Sandon Sch NG31 211 C5
Sandown Cl 5 PE11 156 E3
Sandpiper Dr
Kingston upon Hull HU4 179 B1
Peterborough PE2 231 E6
Sandpit Rd 14 PE6 176 A3
Sandra Cres LN4 203 D1
Sandringham Ave 29
PE13 170 D1
Sandringham Cl
5 Stamford PE9 219 B7
3 Whaplode PE12 158 B6
Sandringham Cres
DN17 184 F3
Sandringham Ct 4
PE12 215 F3
Sandringham Dr
Londonthorpe & Harrowby without NG31 211 E5
Louth LN11 198 B7
13 Mablethorpe & Sutton LN12 76 F8
Wragby LN8 70 D4
Sandringham Gdns
PE21 209 C6
Sandringham Rd
Cleethorpes DN35 192 D4
2 Peterborough PE4 225 C8
Sandringham St 2 HU3 180 A6
Sandringham Way 3
PE6 217 A5
Sandringham Wlk 6
PE11 214 D2
Sands Cl 3 DN17 17 D5
Sands Ct 1 HU14 3 A4
Sands La
Brantingham HU15 1 F7
Brough HU15 2 C6
Carlton-le-Moorland LN5 92 E1
Ellerker HU15 2 A6
Scotter DN21 29 B3
2 South Ferriby DN18 10 A7
Sandsfield La DN21 197 D2
Sandtoft Cl LN6 204 D6
Sandtoft Rd
Hatfield DN7 15 A4
Sandtoft DN9 16 B3
Sandwell Dr LN6 200 D1
Sandy Bank PE22 98 C1
Sandy Cl 1 DN36 37 C5
Sandy Gate
Quadring PE11 144 F7
Sutton St James PE12 169 A7
Sandy La Anderby PE24 77 C3
Belchford LN9 73 A2
Candlesby with Gunby PE23 88 F1
Chapel St Leonard PE24 90 E7
Great Steeping PE23 101 D7
Lusby with Winceby PE23 86 F1

Sandy La *continued*
North Willingham LN8 ... 58 C8
Tealby LN8 ... 46 C1
Tydd St Giles PE13 ... 170 A7
5 West Ashby LN9 ... 85 E7
Woodhall Spa LN10 ... 97 E7
Sandyford La PE22 ... 113 E3
Sandygate Cl NG34 ... 133 C1
Sandygate La NG34 ... 133 C2
Saner St HU3 ... 180 B6
Sansford Gn 5 LN6 ... 205 A6
Sapperton PE4 ... 220 F6
Sapphire Cl PE24 ... 89 D2
Sapphire Gr 7 HU3 ... 180 A4
Saracen Cl DN21 ... 197 F2
Sarah Gate PE11 ... 145 B8
Sarge Cl 5 DN36 ... 195 D2
Sargeants Cl 9 PE22 ... 113 B1
Sargent Cl 4 LN4 ... 95 C4
Sargent's Ct 5 PE9 ... 219 A6
Sargon Way 3 DN31 ... 188 A3
Sarthe Cl 5 PE20 ... 135 B7
Sassaby Cl HU4 ... 179 C3
Satinwood Cl 10 LN6 ... 200 C1
Satterley Cl LN6 ... 92 D4
Saunby Gr DN35 ... 192 E7
Saundby Rd DN22 ... 52 B6
Saundergate La PE21 ... 136 D8
Saundergate Pk 11 PE21 ... 136 D8
Saunders St 6 DN31 ... 191 C8
Sausthorpe CE Sch PE23 ... 87 E4
Sausthorpe Rd
Partney PE23 ... 88 A3
Sausthorpe PE23 ... 87 F3
Sausthorpe St 9 LN5 ... 201 F1
Saville Rd PE3 ... 225 D4
Saville St LN5 ... 205 D7
Savory Rd 1 PE13 ... 170 D1
Savoy Ct 7 DN36 ... 195 C6
Sawmill La LN8 ... 70 C5
Saxby Ave PE25 ... 206 D2
Saxby Cliff Rd LN8 ... 55 D4
Saxby Gdns PE1 ... 226 C8
Saxby Gr DN33 ... 191 A3
Saxby Hill DN20 ... 10 B4
Saxby Rd Bonby DN20 ... 10 B2
Scunthorpe DN17 ... 184 E5
Saxilby CE (Controlled) Prim Sch LN1 ... 66 E2
Saxilby Rd Lincoln LN1 ... 201 A7
Skellingthorpe LN6 ... 200 A6
Sturton by Stow LN1 ... 66 D6
Saxilby Sta LN1 ... 66 D2
Saxon Cl
7 Barton-upon-Humber DN18 ... 10 F8
10 Metheringham LN4 ... 95 D4
Spalding PE11 ... 214 F2
Saxon Cres DN35 ... 192 E6
Saxon Ct 2 Blyton DN21 ... 41 C5
Scunthorpe DN16 ... 185 B3
Saxon Rd
8 Barnack PE9 ... 172 D3
Peterborough PE1 ... 226 C3
Saxon St LN1 ... 234 A4
Saxon Way
2 Ancaster NG32 ... 120 A2
Bourne PE10 ... 213 C6
17 Caistor LN7 ... 33 B4
2 Horncastle LN9 ... 199 D3
6 Ingham LN1 ... 54 F2
Kingston upon Hull HU13 ... 178 F1
Saxondale HU4 ... 179 B7
Saxonfield LN7 ... 33 A4
Saxony Way 6 PE11 ... 134 F2
Sayer Ct PE2 ... 229 F2
Scalby Gr HU5 ... 179 D8
Scald Gate PE22 ... 115 B8
Scale La HU1 ... 181 A6
Scalesgate Rd PE12 ... 159 B1
Scalford Dr PE1 ... 226 C8
Scallow La DN17 ... 29 D6
Scalp Rd PE21 ... 137 B7
Scamblesby CE (Controlled) Prim Sch LN11 ... 72 F5
Scamblesby Hill LN9 ... 72 E4
Scampton Airfield LN1 ... 67 E6
Scampton Ave LN6 ... 204 F6
Scampton CE (Controlled) Prim Sch LN1 ... 67 D6
Scampton Cl 4 DN34 ... 191 A5
Scampton Way
Gainsborough DN21 ... 197 E3
Skegness PE25 ... 206 A5
Scandinavian Way DN41 ... 187 B3
Scarborough Bank PE22 ... 100 B1
Scarborough Cl PE10 ... 142 F2
Scarborough St HU3 ... 180 A4
Scarbrough Ave PE25 ... 206 D4
Scarbrough Espl PE25 ... 206 E3
Scargate La LN4 ... 108 F8
Scarle Cl 1 LN6 ... 205 A2
Scarle La LN6 ... 79 B2
Scarrington Cres HU4 ... 179 B6
Scarrow Cl HU3 ... 180 A7
Scartho Jun & Inf Sch DN33 ... 191 D2
Scartho Pk DN33 ... 191 B2
Scartho Rd DN33 ... 191 D2
Scawby Cres LN6 ... 204 F7
Scawby Prim Sch DN20 ... 30 E8
Scawby Rd Brigg DN20 ... 196 A2
Broughton DN20 ... 19 E2
Grimsby DN33 ... 191 A3
Scawby DN20 ... 31 A7
Scunthorpe DN17 ... 184 E5
Schiphol Way DN38 ... 21 E5
Schofield Cl 7 DN19 ... 11 C8
School Cl 1 Maxey PE6 ... 173 C7
Peterborough PE3 ... 225 A5
School Cres
Anwick NG34 ... 109 B1
1 Scothern LN2 ... 68 F4
5 Surfleet PE11 ... 145 E3
School Dr
27 Messingham DN17 ... 29 D7
8 Welton/Dunholme LN2 ... 68 C6
School Hill LE14 ... 150 C7
School House La 6 DN10 ... 39 F3
School Houses 9 DN20 ... 19 E4
School La
Addlethorpe PE24 ... 90 D3
Appleby DN15 ... 9 D1
1 Baston PE6 ... 164 E4
Beckingham LN5 ... 105 B4
8 Bicker PE20 ... 135 A4
Binbrook LN8 ... 47 B5
5 Bonby DN20 ... 10 C2
Boothby Pagnell NG33 ... 140 F5
Buckminster NG33 ... 150 F5
Butterwick PE22 ... 126 E3
Cabourne LN7 ... 33 D5
Canwick LN4 ... 81 A4
Claypole NG23 ... 117 F8
7 Colsterworth NG33 ... 151 D7
1 Coningsby LN4 ... 207 C4
5 Croxton Kerrial NG32 ... 138 D4
4 Donington PE11 ... 134 F2
East Keal PE23 ... 100 E6
Edenham PE10 ... 153 F4
4 Glinton PE6 ... 220 C8
18 Goxhill DN19 ... 12 A8
Grayingham DN21 ... 42 E7
Great Steeping PE23 ... 101 E7
Hainton LN8 ... 58 E3
3 Harmston LN5 ... 93 F5
Heighington/Washingborough LN4 ... 203 C2
5 Helpringham NG34 ... 133 D7
3 Irby DN37 ... 34 D7
1 Irby DN37 ... 34 D7
Kingston upon Hull HU10 ... 178 C8
9 Lincoln LN6 ... 204 F1
5 Lutton PE12 ... 160 A8
Maltby Le Marsh LN13 ... 76 A8
4 Mareham Le Fen PE22 ... 99 A4
Marston NG32 ... 118 D2
3 Maxey PE6 ... 173 C7
1 New Holland DN19 ... 4 E2
North Cockerington LN11 ... 49 F1
3 North Ferriby HU14 ... 3 A4
4 North Kelsey LN7 ... 32 A4
North Scarle LN6 ... 78 E1
North Somercotes LN11 ... 50 F7
Old Leake PE22 ... 114 A1
Old Somerby NG33 ... 140 E8
Raithby PE23 ... 87 D2
Redbourne DN21 ... 30 F3
Ropsley NG33 ... 131 B1
Rothwell LN7 ... 33 E2
1 Scampton Airfield LN1 ... 67 F5
Sedgebrook NG32 ... 128 F4
Silk Willoughby NG34 ... 121 A1
Snitterby DN21 ... 43 D5
South Carlton LN1 ... 67 D3
7 South Ferriby DN18 ... 10 A7
Springthorpe DN21 ... 53 E8
2 Sturton by Stow LN1 ... 66 C7
17 Tetney DN36 ... 36 D4
Thistleton LE15 ... 151 C1
Thorpe on the Hill LN6 ... 92 E8
6 Uffington PE9 ... 172 C6
Walcott LN4 ... 109 C7
3 West/East Butterwick DN17 ... 28 D8
2 Willingham by Stow DN21 ... 53 E3
Wilsford NG32 ... 120 C1
School Rd
1 Barnack PE9 ... 172 D3
Newborough PE6 ... 174 E5
Scunthorpe DN16 ... 185 B6
8 South Killingholme DN40 ... 12 E3
West Walton PE14 ... 170 E4
Winteringham DN15 ... 2 A1
School View 10 NG13 ... 128 A5
School Wlk DN35 ... 192 C5
Schoolhouse La 11 LN11 ... 198 B5
Schooner Ct HU4 ... 179 B3
Schrimshaw Ct 6 PE25 ... 206 C4
Schrimshire's Rd DN22 ... 52 A1
Scoggins Way 4 NG34 ... 122 D3
Scoldall La PE11 ... 145 E4
Scolding Dro PE6 ... 176 E5
Scopwick Pl 3 LN2 ... 201 F8
Scorer St LN5 ... 201 F1
Scotenoon PE2 ... 229 E3
Scotgate PE9 ... 219 A5
Scothern La
Dunholme LN2 ... 68 E5
Stainton By Langworth LN2 ... 69 B4
10 Welton/Dunholme LN2 ... 68 E6
Scothern Rd LN2 ... 68 D3
Scotia Way PE21 ... 209 F2
Scotland La NG33 ... 141 B5
Scotney Dr NG31 ... 211 F5
Scotney St PE1 ... 225 E7
Scott Ave DN17 ... 184 C6
Scott Cl
6 Claypole NG23 ... 117 E8
5 Grimsby DN37 ... 190 F8
Peterborough PE2 ... 231 E6
Scott Gdns LN2 ... 202 C6
Scott St
Gainsborough DN21 ... 197 C5
Kingston upon Hull HU2 ... 180 F7
Scotten Dike Dro PE10 ... 154 E6
Scotter Prim Sch DN21 ... 29 C3
Scotter Rd
Laughton DN21 ... 41 C8
Messingham DN17 ... 29 D5
Scunthorpe DN17 ... 182 C1
Scotter Rd S DN17 ... 184 C3
Scotterthorpe Rd DN21 ... 29 B4
Scottlethorpe PE10 ... 153 E4
Scottlethorpe Rd PE10 ... 153 D3
Scotton Comm Nature Reserve* DN9 ... 27 B1
Scotton Dr 7 LN6 ... 205 A7
Scotton Rd DN21 ... 29 C3
Scott's Cl PE6 ... 164 E3
Scott's Hill 4 NG32 ... 106 C1
Scotts Rd PE6 ... 220 D8
Scrap Bay Rd DN16 ... 19 A3
Scredington Rd
Burton Pedwardine NG34 ... 122 B1
Helpringham NG34 ... 133 C7
Scrivelsby Ct DN35 ... 193 A3
Scrub La Authorpe LN11 ... 75 A8
East Halton DN40 ... 12 E5
Withern with Stain LN11 ... 62 D1
Scullery La NG33 ... 141 A5
Scunthorpe CE Prim Sch DN15 ... 183 A4
Scunthorpe General Hospl DN15 ... 182 E2
Scunthorpe Leisure Ctr DN15 ... 183 B3
Scunthorpe Sh Ctr DN15 ... 183 B4
Scunthorpe Sta DN16 ... 183 A2
Sea Bank Rd PE24 ... 90 E7
Sea Dyke PE22 ... 114 B2
Sea Dyke Way 1 DN36 ... 37 C2
Sea End Rd PE22 ... 127 A4
Sea Front Rd
10 Skegness PE25 ... 103 E4
9 Skegness PE25 ... 103 E4
Sea La Benington PE22 ... 127 B4
Butterwick PE22 ... 126 F3
Friskney PE22 ... 115 C5
Hogsthorpe PE24 ... 90 C7
Huttoft LN13 ... 77 A4
Ingoldmells PE25 ... 90 E3
Leverton PE22 ... 127 B6
Mablethorpe/Sutton on Sea LN12 ... 77 A7
North Coates DN36 ... 37 B4
Old Leake PE22 ... 114 C1
Saltfleet LN11 ... 51 C5
Theddlethorpe St Helen LN12 ... 63 E7
Wrangle PE22 ... 114 E1
Sea Rd Anderby PE24 ... 77 B2
18 Chapel St Leonard PE24 ... 90 D7
Cleethorpes DN35 ... 192 F6
Sea View LN11 ... 51 D3
Sea View Rd PE25 ... 206 D5
Sea View St DN35 ... 192 F5
Seabank Rd 22 PE13 ... 170 E1
Seabrook Dr DN16 ... 185 A2
Seacroft Dr 10 PE25 ... 206 C1
Seacroft Espl PE25 ... 103 E4
Seacroft Rd
Cleethorpes DN35 ... 193 A5
Mablethorpe/Sutton on Sea LN12 ... 64 B3
Seacroft Sq
11 Skegness PE25 ... 103 E4
10 Skegness PE25 ... 103 E4
Seadyke Rd
Kirton PE20 ... 136 E3
Wisbech St Mary PE13 ... 177 F6
Seafield Rd 5 PE13 ... 170 B2
Seaford Rd DN35 ... 193 B1
Seagate Rd PE12 ... 216 D2
Seagull Cl HU4 ... 179 E2
Seaholme Rd LN12 ... 64 B2
Seal Sanctuary & Nature Ctr The* LN12 ... 64 B5
Sealey's La PE13 ... 177 D8
Seamer Gr 1 DN32 ... 192 A5
Searby Hill DN38 ... 32 D8
Searby Rd Lincoln LN2 ... 202 B8
Scunthorpe DN17 ... 184 E4
Searby Wold La DN38 ... 21 E1
Seargeants Cl 1 PE6 ... 174 E4
Searjeant St PE1 ... 225 E5
Seas End Prim Sch PE11 ... 145 D3
Seas End Rd
Moulton PE12 ... 146 D1
Surfleet PE11 ... 145 E3
Seathorne Cres PE25 ... 90 F1
Seathorne Prim Sch PE25 ... 206 D7
Seaton Cl PE7 ... 233 D6
Seaton Gr
Grimsby DN32 ... 192 A5
Seaton Gr *continued*
Kingston upon Hull HU4 ... 179 E5
Seaton Rd
Kingston upon Hull HU13 ... 178 F2
Scunthorpe DN17 ... 184 D8
6 Stamford PE9 ... 219 B4
Seawall La DN36 ... 37 C5
Sebrights Way PE3 ... 224 F3
Second Ave
Fixborough Ind Est DN15 ... 7 F1
Grantham NG31 ... 211 F6
Grimsby DN33 ... 191 B4
5 Scampton Airfield LN1 ... 67 E5
3 Scunthorpe DN17 ... 184 C6
Spalding PE11 ... 214 A4
Second Dro
Crowland PE6 ... 166 E3
Gosberton PE11 ... 144 C3
Peterborough PE1 ... 226 D1
Second Marsh Rd PE14 ... 170 C3
Sedge Cl
6 Barton-upon-Humber DN18 ... 3 F1
Leasingham NG34 ... 121 C7
Sedge Hole Cl Nature Reserve* DN9 ... 27 F2
Sedge Pl 9 PE12 ... 167 B8
Sedgebrook Cl 1 LN2 ... 201 F8
Sedgebrook Rd NG32 ... 128 F6
Sedgemoor Cl 3 LN6 ... 204 E1
Sedgewood Way DN15 ... 182 C6
Seed Cl La 4 DN37 ... 23 F1
Sefton Ave PE13 ... 170 E1
Sefton St 2 HU3 ... 180 B4
Segmere St 3 DN35 ... 193 A5
Segrave Gr HU5 ... 179 D8
Selbourne Rd 5 DN34 ... 190 E4
Selby Cl LN6 ... 205 A3
Selby Rd DN8 ... 14 F8
Selby St HU3 ... 180 A5
Selge Way DN33 ... 190 F3
Selkirk St HU5 ... 180 A8
Sellers Grange PE2 ... 230 B4
Sellwood Gdns LN9 ... 199 B3
Selwyn Ave 16 HU14 ... 3 A4
Selwyn Rd PE9 ... 219 A7
Sempers Cl LN6 ... 92 E8
Sentance Cres PE20 ... 136 C6
Seraphim App Rd DN16 ... 183 E1
Seraphim Rd DN16 ... 183 F1
Serena Rd 5 PE25 ... 206 D2
Serpentine St 1 LN8 ... 57 D7
Serpentine The PE7 ... 230 D3
Service Rd 1 9 DN37 ... 190 E8
Service Rd 2 10 DN37 ... 190 E8
Service Rd 3 7 DN37 ... 190 E8
Service Rd 4 4 DN37 ... 190 E8
Service Rd 5 5 DN37 ... 190 E8
Service Rd 6 6 DN37 ... 190 E8
Service Rd 7 7 DN37 ... 190 F8
Service Rd 8 8 DN37 ... 188 A1
Service Rd 9 7 DN37 ... 188 A1
Service Rd 10 6 DN37 ... 188 A1
Service Rd 12 2 DN37 ... 188 A1
Service Rd 13 4 DN37 ... 188 A1
Service Rd 14 3 DN37 ... 188 A1
Service Rd 15 8 DN37 ... 190 E8
Service Rd 16 DN37 ... 190 E8
Service Rd 17 DN37 ... 190 F8
Service Rd 18 DN37 ... 190 F8
Service Rd 19 8 DN37 ... 190 F8
Service Rd 20 11 DN37 ... 190 E8
Service Rd 21 3 DN37 ... 190 E8
Service Rd 22 2 DN37 ... 190 E8
Service Rd 23 DN37 ... 190 E8
Service Rd 25 1 DN37 ... 190 E8
Service Rd 26 9 DN37 ... 188 A1
Service Rd No 1 5 DN32 ... 189 B1
Service Rd No 2 7 DN32 ... 189 B1
Services Rd DN16 ... 183 E2
Setchfield Pl PE2 ... 230 F7
Setterwood Garth 2 HU10 ... 178 E8
Seven Quay Rd DN40 ... 186 E7
Sevenacres PE2 ... 229 E5
Seventh Ave 3 NG31 ... 211 F6
Severn Cl PE4 ... 221 C1
Severn Rd PE11 ... 214 F5
Severn St LN1 ... 201 C4
Sewell Cl PE6 ... 217 E5
Sewell Rd LN2 ... 234 C3
Sewell's Wlk LN5 ... 201 E1
Sewer La 3 HU1 ... 180 F5
Sewstern La
Allington NG32 ... 128 E7
Long Bennington NG23 ... 117 E1
Sedgebrook NG32 ... 128 D4
Sewstern Rd NG33 ... 151 B4
Seymour Ave LN11 ... 198 C4
Seymour La 14 LN13 ... 75 F2
Seymour Pl PE4 ... 221 F2
Seymour St HU3 ... 179 F5
Sezanne Wlk 10 PE11 ... 214 C6
Shackleton Cl PE6 ... 217 B7
Shaddys Wlk LN13 ... 88 E6
Shaftesbury Ave
Birchwood LN6 ... 200 D2
Grimsby DN34 ... 191 B7
Shaftesbury Mews 6 DN36 ... 195 C6
Shaftesbury Way 2 NG23 ... 91 D5
Shakespeare Ave
Grantham NG31 ... 211 E6
Peterborough PE1 ... 225 F7
4 Scunthorpe DN17 ... 184 C6
Shakespeare Cl 6 HU3 ... 180 D8
Shakespeare St
5 Gainsborough DN21 ... 197 D2
5 Lincoln LN5 ... 205 E8
Shamfields Rd 3 PE23 ... 101 A8
Shamrock Cl PE2 ... 231 C7
Shanklin Dr NG31 ... 210 E4
Shannon Ave LN6 ... 205 A5
Shannon Cl 2 LN6 ... 205 A5
Shannon Rd 8 LN4 ... 207 D4
Shardloes LN4 ... 81 E2
Shardloes Rd 9 PE25 ... 103 E4
Sharma Leas PE4 ... 220 E3
Sharmans Cl 11 LN12 ... 77 A7
Sharpe Cl 35 DN18 ... 10 E8
Sharpe Rd NG31 ... 211 C6
Sharpe's Rd PE6 ... 165 C3
Sharp's Cl PE10 ... 213 B6
Sharp's La PE22 ... 127 A6
Shaw Dr DN33 ... 191 E1
Shaw La PE22 ... 127 B8
Shaw Rd Boston PE21 ... 208 C7
Grantham NG31 ... 210 D2
Gringley on the Hill DN10 ... 39 C2
Shaw St HU9 ... 181 B7
Shaw Way 4 LN2 ... 68 C2
Shawbury Cl 10 LN6 ... 204 C6
Shawfield Cl 10 DN3 ... 14 A3
Shaws La PE12 ... 160 B3
Shays Dr 1 LN6 ... 205 A7
Shearman's Wath
Thimbleby LN9 ... 85 C6
West Ashby LN9 ... 199 A8
Shears Ct DN37 ... 194 F4
Shearwater Cl
3 Birchwood LN6 ... 200 E1
2 Birchwood LN6 ... 204 E8
Louth LN11 ... 198 D8
Shearwater Rd LN6 ... 200 E1
Sheep Cote La DN7 ... 14 D2
Sheep Dip La DN7 ... 14 D4
Sheep Marsh La DN36 ... 37 B3
Sheep Mkt
2 Spalding PE11 ... 214 D4
11 Stamford PE9 ... 219 B5
Sheepdyke La 4 DN20 ... 10 C2
Sheepfold St 10 DN32 ... 191 E7
Sheepgate PE22 ... 127 A6
Sheepwalk
Aubourn Haddington & South Hykeham LN5 ... 92 E5
Peterborough PE4 ... 221 E1
Sheepwash La LN4 ... 81 E4
Sheffield Pk Ave DN15 ... 182 F5
Sheffield St (East) 1 DN15 ... 183 A4
Sheffield St (West) 4 DN15 ... 182 F4
Sheffield St DN15 ... 183 A4
Sheila Cres 4 PE11 ... 214 A3
Sheldrake Rd 1 NG34 ... 212 B3
Shelley Ave
Grantham NG31 ... 211 D6
Grimsby DN33 ... 191 B4
Shelley Cl
3 Mablethorpe/Sutton on Sea LN12 ... 77 A7
12 Stamford PE9 ... 218 E6
Shelley Dr Lincoln LN2 ... 202 B6
7 Sleaford NG34 ... 212 F4
Shelroy Cl DN15 ... 182 C5
Shelton Rd PE2 ... 231 D6
Shenley Cl 11 DN7 ... 14 D3
Shepeau Stow Cty Prim Sch PE12 ... 167 F3
Shepherd's Croft 1 DN9 ... 27 D7
Shepherd's La NG34 ... 133 E7
Shepherds Cl PE4 ... 221 A4
Sheppard's Dro PE6 ... 167 B1
Shepperson's Ave PE11 ... 144 F5
Shepton La NG34 ... 142 A8
Sheraton Cl 15 LN6 ... 204 D7
Sheraton Dr 13 DN36 ... 36 D8
Sherborne Rd PE1 ... 226 D6
Sherbrooke St 2 LN2 ... 202 D4
Sherburn Cres DN15 ... 182 D4
Sherburn St
Cleethorpes DN35 ... 192 F4
Kingston upon Hull HU9 ... 181 D8
Sheridan Cl 1 LN2 ... 202 C7
Sheridan Rd PE1 ... 225 F8
Sheriff Way PE21 ... 208 E7
Sheringham Way PE2 ... 230 C6
Sherwood Ave
Boston PE21 ... 208 E7
Newark-on-Trent NG24 ... 104 A4
4 Peterborough PE2 ... 230 F7
7 Wisbech PE13 ... 170 D1
Sherwood Cl
1 Louth LN11 ... 198 C4
Stamford PE9 ... 218 F5
Sherwood Dr
Kingston upon Hull HU4 ... 179 A7
Spalding PE11 ... 214 D6
Waddington LN5 ... 205 D1
Sherwood Rd
10 Coningsby LN4 ... 207 D4
Grimsby DN34 ... 190 F5
3 Mablethorpe/Sutton on Sea LN12 ... 64 B4
Sherwood Rise 7 NG32 ... 119 B7
Sherwood Vale DN15 ... 182 D3

Shetland Way DN40 186 C2
Shipton Rd DN16 185 C5
Shire Ave PE11 214 A5
Shire Gr PE1 226 C5
Shire La NG23 117 D8
Shiregate 12 LN4 95 C4
Shires Orch 6 NG32 138 D4
Shirley Cres DN16 185 B8
Shivean Gate 5 PE12 157 F7
Shodfriars La 4 PE21 208 F4
Shoe La LN9 72 C5
Shoemaker's La DN21 29 E5
Shoff Dro PE11 134 D1
Shoff Rd PE11 134 D1
Sholt's Gate PE12 158 C7
Shop Hill 7 PE22 98 F4
Shop La LN11 72 D6
Shore Rd
Freiston PE22 126 D2
Garthorpe & Fockerby DN17 7 F5
Short Dro
Gosberton PE11 144 C5
Pointon & Sempringham NG34 143 F4
Thurlby PE10 164 E8
Short Ferry Rd LN3 82 F6
Short Hollow NG33 131 C1
Short La Fotherby LN11 49 A2
Ingham LN1 54 F3
Lincoln LN1 234 A2
1 West Halton DN15 8 E8
3 Wisbech PE13 170 A1
Short St
2 Cleethorpes DN35 192 F6
Kingston upon Hull HU1 180 E6
4 Spalding PE11 214 C4
Short Wheatley La NG23 91 D3
Shortacres Rd PE2 230 F7
Shortfen PE2 230 C4
Shortfield La PE21 209 E8
Shortleys Rd DN22 65 B5
Short's Cnr PE22 112 D3
Shortwood La
Bullington LN8 69 F4
Friesthorpe LN3 57 A2
Shorwell Cl 3 NG31 210 E4
Shotbolt La PE11 214 F8
Shrewsbury Ave PE2 230 D5
Shropshire Rd 9 LN1 67 E5
Shrubberies Nature Reserve The* PE12 216 B5
Shrubwood Cl 3 NG34 122 E2
Shuttlefield La PE20 135 F4
Shuttleworth Ct 12 LN6 93 C8
Sibelius Rd HU4 179 B4
Sibsey Drain Bank PE22 126 A6
Sibsey Free (Controlled) Prim Sch PE22 113 A2
Sibsey La 3 PE21 208 F4
Sibsey Rd Boston PE21 209 B8
Fishtoft PE21 125 F5
Sibthorp St LN5 201 E1
Sibthorpe Dr LN2 68 F2
Sickling Gate Rd PE22 115 B7
Side La DN33 195 A7
Side St 2 NG32 128 F7
Sidebar La NG34 123 C4
Sidings Ct 3 HU15 2 B5
Sidings The
Holbeach PE12 215 D1
Horncastle LN9 199 A3
Lincoln LN6 234 A1
Long Sutton PE12 216 B4
2 Louth LN11 198 C6
23 Mablethorpe/Sutton on Sea LN12 77 A8
Morton PE10 154 D6
8 Moulton PE12 157 F6
9 Ruskington NG34 108 E1
25 Saxilby LN1 66 D2
Sidlaw Gr LN5 205 C2
Sidney Pl DN35 192 B8
Sidney Rd
Grimsby DN34 191 B7
5 Scunthorpe DN17 184 C6
Sidney St
4 Cleethorpes DN35 189 D1
Cleethorpes DN35 192 B8
Grantham NG31 211 A6
Lincoln LN5 205 E8
Sidney Way DN35 192 B8
Signal Rd NG31 211 C5
Signhills Ave DN35 193 A4
Signhills Inf & Jun Sch DN35 193 A4
Silica Cres DN17 184 C5
Silt La PE20 136 E3
Silt Pit La PE21 137 A7
Siltside PE11 144 D4
Silver Birch Rise DN16 185 B3
Silver Hill PE7 230 D3
Silver St Bardney LN3 83 C4
Barnetby le Wold DN38 21 B4
Barrow upon Humber DN19 11 C7
Baumber LN9 72 A1
Benniworth LN8 71 F8
Branston LN4 81 E2
Coningsby LN4 207 C4
Gainsborough DN21 197 C4
Holton le Clay DN36 195 D1
11 Kingston upon Hull HU1 180 F6
Lincoln LN2 234 B2
Silver St *continued*
Minting LN9 84 C8
North Clifton NG23 78 C7
Owston Ferry DN9 28 B2
Peterborough PE2 230 F7
1 Ruskington NG34 108 E1
Stainforth DN7 14 C6
Theddlethorpe St Helen LN12 63 E5
4 Waddingham DN21 43 D7
6 Wainfleet All Saints PE24 102 D1
Winteringham DN15 2 B1
Wisbech PE13 170 D1
5 Wragby LN8 70 D5
Silvergarth DN32 192 B5
Silverines Mdws Nature Reserve* LN11 72 E5
Silver's La PE13 177 E7
Silversides La DN20 196 A2
Silverstone Rd 17 LN6 204 C7
Silvertoft La PE20 136 B8
Silverwood Rd
8 Bottesford NG13 128 A5
Peterborough PE1 225 F5
Silvester Rd PE5 223 E2
Simon Weir La PE20 135 D8
Simons Cl
4 Donington on Bain LN11 59 E1
5 Louth LN11 198 D4
Simon's Gn LN6 205 C6
Simons Pl DN35 192 D7
Simpson Cl 17 DN19 11 D8
Sincil Bank (Lincoln City FC) LN5 201 E1
Sincil Bank LN5 234 B1
Sincil St LN5 234 B2
Sinclair Cl PE21 208 E8
Sinderson Rd DN36 36 D8
Singerfire Rd PE5 223 D2
Sir Francis Hill Prim Sch The LN6 205 C8
Sir Isaac Newton Cl 3 PE12 215 E3
Sir Isaac Newton Dr 3 PE21 208 F1
Sir John Nelthorpe Sch DN20 196 C3
Sir William Robertson High Sch LN5 106 E4
Sirius Cl 3 HU3 180 B5
Siskin Cl PE10 143 A3
Siskin Cres DN16 185 B2
Sitwell St HU8 181 A8
Six House Bank PE11 144 D1
Six Hundreds Dro PE20 123 E3
Sixfields Cl LN6 205 A7
Sixhills La LN8 59 A7
Sixhills Rd LN8 58 D6
Sixhills St DN32 191 E7
Sixth Ave
Fixborough Ind Est DN15 8 A1
2 Grantham NG31 211 F6
Scunthorpe DN17 184 B6
Skaters Way PE4 221 A4
Skayman Fields 7 LN5 105 E8
Skegness & District Hospl PE25 206 B3
Skegness (Ingoldmells) Aerodrome PE25 90 D1
Skegness Gram Sch PE25 206 C4
Skegness Inf Sch PE25 206 C4
Skegness Jun Sch PE25 206 C4
Skegness Motor Racing Stadium PE24 90 A2
Skegness Rd
Burgh Le Marsh PE24 103 A7
Chapel St Leonards PE24 90 D6
Partney PE23 88 B3
5 Wainfleet All Saints PE24 102 E2
Skegness Ret Pk PE25 206 A3
Skegness Sta PE25 206 C3
Skegness Water Leisure Pk* PE25 90 E1
Skeldyke Rd PE20 136 D5
Skellingthorpe Rd LN6 200 D2
Skelton Rd DN17 184 C7
Skerries Cl 5 LN6 205 A1
Skerry La NG13 128 C5
Skillings La HU15 2 C5
Skillington Rd NG33 151 B6
Skinnand La LN5 106 D7
Skinner's La
Middle Rasen LN8 45 C1
South Kyme LN4 110 B1
Skinners La
6 South Ferriby DN18 10 A7
Waltham DN37 194 E4
Skipmarsh La
Leverton PE22 126 E8
Old Leake PE22 113 E1
Skippingdale Rd DN15 182 F6
Skipwith Cres 20 LN4 95 D4
Skipworth Way PE25 206 C8
Skirbeck Dr 15 LN1 66 D2
Skirbeck Rd PE21 209 A3
Skirmore Rd PE22 114 E5
Skirth Rd LN4 109 F6
Skitter Rd DN40 5 D1
Skylark Dr DN16 185 B2
Slack The 4 DN17 16 D8
Slash La LN9 86 D3
Slate Drift 2 PE9 171 C2
Slate Mill Pl NG31 211 B5
Slay Pit Cl 3 DN7 14 F4
Slay Pit La DN7 14 F3
Sleaford Leisure Ctr NG34 212 E4
Sleaford Rd
Ancaster NG32 120 A2
Barnby in the Willows NG24 104 F5
Boston PE21 208 B4
Bracebridge Heath LN4 81 A1
Branston & Mere LN4 81 E1
Coningsby LN4 207 A4
Cranwell NG34 120 F8
East Kirkby PE23 99 E4
Folkingham NG34 142 D8
Heckington NG34 122 D3
Honington NG32 119 C2
Leadenham LN5 106 D2
14 Leasingham NG34 121 B7
Metheringham LN4 95 B4
18 Navenby/Wellingore LN5 107 A7
Newark-on-Trent NG24 104 A5
North Kyme LN4 109 E2
Ruskington NG34 108 E1
Tattershall LN4 110 D7
Walcot Near Folkingham NG34 132 D2
Sleaford Sta NG34 212 D3
Sledge La LN8 59 B8
Sledmere Gr HU4 179 E5
Sleepers Cl 1 PE12 216 B4
Sleights Cl HU3 180 A7
Sleights Dr 2 PE14 170 F1
Sleights La HU15 1 B6
Slessor St 2 LN5 94 A7
Slipe Dro PE11 155 F5
Slipe The PE10 213 F4
Slippery Gowt La PE21 136 F8
Slipway DN35 193 A6
Sloothby High La
Hogsthorpe PE24 90 A6
Willoughby with Sloothby PE24 89 F6
Sluice La DN18 9 E8
Sluice Rd
Holbeach PE12 215 B8
South Ferriby DN18 9 F8
Sutton Bridge PE12 161 A6
Whaplode PE12 147 B4
Small Dro PE12 157 E7
Small Dro La PE11 144 E1
Small End Rd PE22 114 E6
Smalley Rd PE21 209 D4
Smallwood PE3 225 B5
Smeeton Ct 6 NG34 212 D6
Smeeton's La PE20 146 C7
Smith Field 10 DN36 36 B1
Smith St Lincoln LN5 201 E1
Scunthorpe DN15 182 F4
Smithdale Cl 9 PE11 214 C6
Smithfield PE6 176 B3
Smithfield Rd DN16 185 D6
Smithy La
7 Barnetby le Wold DN38 21 B4
Friskney PE22 115 A6
Smooting La 4 LN3 82 A8
Smoothing The LN8 46 C1
Smythe La DN22 52 D1
Snaffer's La PE12 158 C5
Snainton Gr 4 HU5 179 D8
Snaith Ave PE20 146 D7
Snaith Cl 9 LN6 204 B6
Snarford Rd LN3 69 D8
Snelland Rd LN3 69 E8
Snetterton Cl 1 LN6 204 C7
Snipe Dales Ctry Pk* PE23 86 F3
Snitterby Carr La DN21 43 F5
Snitterby Rd DN21 43 D6
Snowberry Gdns 5 LN6 204 C8
Snowden Cl 1 PE6 175 C8
Snowdon Cl 4 LN5 205 D3
Snowdon Rd 3 NG23 91 D4
Snowdonia Ave DN15 182 D7
Snowdrop Cl 10 DN41 23 F5
Snowdrop Pl 8 PE11 214 A5
Sods La PE11 145 D5
Soff La DN19 12 A6
Soke Parkway PE1 221 E1
Soke Rd PE6 174 D5
Solhem Ave 13 PE21 136 D8
Solomon Ct DN35 192 D5
Solway Ave PE21 136 E8
Somerby Cl
8 Moulton PE12 157 F7
3 Stamford PE9 219 B7
Somerby Gr NG31 211 D2
Somerby Hill NG31 211 C2
Somerby Pl NG31 211 E1
Somerby Rd
Gainsborough DN21 197 F5
Ropsley & Humby NG33 141 A8
Scunthorpe DN17 184 D5
Somerby Wold La DN38 21 C1
Somerden Rd HU9 5 F8
Somersby Ave 9 LN12 64 B4
Somersby Cl LN6 205 C4
Somersby Ct 15 LN11 198 B5
Somersby Gn PE21 209 B7
Somersby Gr 2 PE25 206 D1
Somersby St 7 DN31 191 D8
Somersby Way PE21 209 B7
Somerset Dr 4 DN15 8 B4
Somerset St HU3 180 A5
Somerton Dr 3 DN7 14 F3
Somerton Gate La LN5 93 D7
Somerton Rd DN40 186 D3
Somervell Rd DN16 185 C4
Somerville PE4 220 E5
Somerville Cl 15 LN5 93 E8
Somerville Ct 14 LN5 93 E8
Somerville Rd 1 PE9 219 A6
Somes Cl 1 PE9 172 C6
Sonia Crest DN40 186 B4
Sophia Ave DN33 191 C1
Sorbus Ct 5 HU3 180 D6
Sorbus View 4 HU5 179 C7
Sorby Cl PE25 206 E8
Sorrel Cl 3 Binbrook LN8 47 C5
1 Market Deeping PE6 217 D6
4 Stamford PE9 218 D6
Sorrel Dr PE11 214 A5
Sorrel Way DN15 182 C6
Soss La DN10 40 A5
Sour La DN7 14 E8
Soutergate 18 DN18 3 F1
South Airfield Rd NG34 120 C8
South Axholme Com Sch DN9 27 D6
South Bank 3 DN17 17 D6
South Brick Lines NG34 120 B8
South Bridge Rd HU1 181 A5
South Carr Rd DN20 31 A4
South Church Side 14 HU1 180 F6
South Cliff Rd 27 DN21 30 B1
South Cres
11 Bottesford NG13 128 A5
1 Chapel St Leonards PE24 90 D7
South Dale LN7 33 B4
South Dr
5 Balderton NG24 104 C1
4 Stow LN1 66 C8
South Dro Bicker PE20 134 E4
Helpringham NG34 133 E6
Lutton PE12 149 A1
Quadring PE11 144 A8
Spalding PE11 156 E2
South Ella Dr HU10 178 D7
South Ella Way HU10 178 D7
South End Boston PE21 208 F4
Collingham NG23 91 C4
Hogsthorpe PE24 90 B6
Thorne/Moorends DN8 15 A7
South End La DN22 52 E3
South Fen Rd
Bourne PE10 213 F4
Helpringham NG34 133 D6
South Ferriby Prim Sch DN18 10 A7
South Furlong Croft 22 DN9 27 E6
South Gate NG34 212 D4
South Heath La NG32 106 D1
South Holland Ctr* PE11 214 D4
South Humberside Ind Est DN31 188 B2
South Hunsley Sch HU14 2 E5
South Hykeham Cty Prim Sch LN6 93 B7
South Ing Dro PE11 134 E1
South Ings La PE24 90 B5
South Intake La DN9 40 C7
South Kesteven Works NG31 210 F3
South La
Kingston upon Hull HU13 178 E1
Willingham DN21 54 A3
South Leys Sch DN17 184 D4
South Lincs Con Ctr NG31 211 A1
South Marsh Rd
Immingham Power St DN41 187 F1
Stallingborough DN41 23 F7
South Marsh Rd Ind Est DN41 187 F2
South Mkt Pl 7 LN13 75 F2
South Moor Rd DN10 39 F3
South Par Boston PE21 208 C4
11 Caythorpe NG32 119 B7
Grantham NG31 211 B2
6 Grimsby DN31 191 D8
7 Lincoln LN1 201 D4
Peterborough PE3 225 E3
5 Saxilby LN1 66 D2
Skegness PE25 206 D2
South Kyme LN4 123 B8
Spalding PE11 214 C3
Thorne/Moorends DN8 15 A7
South Par Jun Sch DN31 191 D8
South Pk LN5 205 F8
South Pk Ave
Bracebridge Heath LN5 205 F8
Lincoln LN5 201 F1
South Pk Rd DN17 184 D3
South Ramper DN21 44 A5
South Rd Bourne PE10 213 D4
Chapel St Leonard PE24 90 E6
5 Keadby with Althorpe DN17 17 C6
Mablethorpe/Sutton on Sea LN12 64 C1
North Somercotes LN11 50 E7
Sturton Le Steeple DN22 52 C4
South Rd *continued*
Tetford LN9 73 F1
South Ridge Cres 2 DN17 184 F3
South Rise 6 LN8 47 C4
South Scaffold La NG23 91 E3
South Scarle La LN6 78 E1
South Scarle Rd NG23 91 E6
South Sea La DN36 36 D7
South Side DN15 2 A1
South St 17 Alford LN13 75 F2
12 Alford LN13 75 F2
10 Barnetby le Wold DN38 21 B4
Bole DN22 52 C5
Boston PE21 208 F4
Bourne PE10 213 D4
Caistor LN7 33 B4
1 Cleethorpes DN35 193 A5
20 Crowland PE6 166 F1
Horncastle LN9 199 B3
Keelby DN41 23 A5
Louth LN11 198 B5
Morton DN21 197 C8
15 North Kelsey LN7 32 A4
Owston Ferry DN9 28 B2
Peterborough PE1 226 B2
Roxby cum Risby DN15 8 F3
Scamblesby LN11 72 F5
Swineshead PE20 135 B7
West Butterwick DN17 28 D8
17 Winterton DN15 9 A5
South St Mary's Gate 6 DN31 191 D7
South Terr
Boston PE21 208 F3
Louth LN11 198 C4
South View
Broughton DN20 19 D4
Fillingham DN21 54 F4
Holton le Clay DN36 195 E1
Humberston DN36 193 A1
Peterborough PE2 230 F7
South View Ave
Brigg DN20 196 C5
Burringham DN17 17 D4
South View Cl 4 PE25 206 D2
South View La LN11 62 A7
South View Prim Sch PE6 166 E1
South View Rd PE4 225 D8
South Witham Nature Reserve* NG33 151 F2
South Witham Prim Sch NG33 151 D2
South Wood Dr 10 DN8 15 A7
Southburn Ave HU5 179 E7
Southcliffe Rd 19 DN21 29 C3
Southcoates La HU9 181 E8
South-Dale Cl 3 DN21 30 B2
Southdown LN5 205 D1
Southdown Rd PE7 233 F5
Southern Dr HU4 179 C5
Southern La LN6 92 B7
Southern Rd DN40 186 D7
Southern Way DN40 186 C7
Southern Wlk DN33 194 F7
Southfield 7 Belton DN9 16 E1
4 Kingston upon Hull HU13 3 E4
Southfield Ave DN33 194 F7
Southfield Cl
18 Thorne/Moorends DN8 15 B7
Ulceby DN39 12 B1
Southfield Dr
10 Epworth DN9 27 D6
2 Louth LN11 198 C4
21 North Ferriby HU14 3 A4
Southfield La
Fishtoft PE21 137 C8
6 Old Leake PE22 114 A1
Old Leake PE22 127 A8
Willoughton DN21 42 D3
Southfield Pl 7 LN9 199 C3
Southfield Rd
1 Broughton DN20 19 D3
13 Crowle DN17 16 D7
Grimsby DN33 194 F7
Holton le Clay DN36 195 D1
North Kelsey LN7 31 F3
Scunthorpe DN16 185 C5
Thorne/Moorends DN8 15 B7
1 Winterton DN15 8 F5
Southfields
7 Binbrook LN8 47 C4
Bourne PE10 213 D4
3 Sleaford NG34 212 D3
Southfields Ave PE2 231 D5
Southfields Cl 10 PE13 170 D2
Southfields Dr PE2 231 D6
Southgate
Kingston upon Hull HU13 178 E1
12 Pinchbeck PE11 156 E8
Southgate Spinneys 3 NG34 120 E4
Southgate Way PE2 229 C2
Southland Dr 5 LN6 205 B4
Southlands Ave
Gainsborough DN21 197 B8
Louth LN11 198 D3
Peterborough PE1 226 A6
Southlands Dr
Grantham NG31 211 C4
Morton DN21 197 B8

Southlands Gdns DN21 197 B8
Southmoor La
Newton on Trent LN1 78 D8
Snitterby DN21 43 E5
Southmoor Rd
Crowle DN17 16 C8
Newton on Trent LN1 78 D8
Southoe Rd PE7 231 D2
Southorpe La DN21 42 A7
Southorpe Mdw Nature Reserve* PE9 172 D3
Southorpe Paddock Nature Reserve* PE9 172 E1
Southview Leisure Ctr PE25 103 C8
Southwell Ave
3 Kingston upon Hull HU9 5 F8
Peterborough PE4 220 E4
Southwell Cl NG31 210 C5
Southwell Rd
9 Wisbech PE13 170 D1
2 Wisbech PE13 170 D1
Southwell's La 1 LN9 199 C4
Southwold Cres DN33 194 E8
Sovereign Cl
12 Grimsby DN34 190 D4
12 Wisbech PE13 170 C1
Sovereign Pl PE3 225 E2
Sovereign St NG34 142 E4
Sowers La DN15 9 A5
Spa Bldgs LN2 234 B2
Spa Hill 9 DN21 30 B1
Spa Rd Lincoln LN5 234 C2
2 Woodhall Spa LN10 97 D6
Spa St LN2 202 B3
Spafford Cl DN21 65 E8
Spain La 5 PE21 208 F4
Spain Pl PE21 209 A4
Spalding Bulb Mus* PE11 145 C1
Spalding Comm 6 PE11 214 B1
Spalding Dro
Cowbit PE12 157 A3
Spalding PE12 214 E1
Spalding Gate PE12 158 B8
Spalding High Sch For Girls PE11 214 F3
Spalding Parish CE Sch PE11 214 E2
Spalding Prim Sch PE11 214 B5
Spalding Rd
Boston PE21 208 E3
Bourne PE10 213 E5
Deeping St James PE6 165 D1
Gosberton PE11 145 C5
Holbeach PE12 215 A2
Market Deeping PE6 217 E5
Pinchbeck PE11 214 C8
Scunthorpe DN16 185 B8
Wigtoft PE20 135 E1
Spalding Rd Bsns Pk PE10 213 F5
Spalding Sta PE11 214 C4
Spalford La LN6 78 E2
Spalford Rd LN6 78 E3
Spalford Warren Nature Reserve* NG23 78 D2
Spanby Dr 5 LN6 205 A7
Spanning Dr 22 LN13 75 F2
Spark St DN34 191 A7
Spark's La PE12 158 A4
Sparrow La
2 Long Bennington NG23 117 D3
Marnham NG23 78 A5
Newball LN8 69 F2
Sparrowgate Rd PE14 170 F1
Spaw La 5 LN11 198 B6
Spayne Rd PE21 209 A4
Speechley Rd PE7 233 F6
Speechley's Dro PE6 174 F7
Speedwell Cres DN15 182 C6
Speedwell Ct 7 PE6 217 D6
Speight Cl 5 NG24 104 B7
Spence St 10 PE23 87 F1
Spencer Ave
Peterborough PE2 231 D5
Scunthorpe DN15 182 F4
Spencer Cl
3 Long Sutton PE12 216 B5
West Walton PE14 170 E4
Spencer Gdns 7 PE22 126 E3
Spencer St
Grimsby DN31 189 D1
6 Kingston upon Hull HU2 180 E7
9 Lincoln LN5 205 E8
Spendla's La PE12 159 F3
Spendluffe Ave 3 LN13 75 F3
Spennymoor Cl 1 LN6 93 B8
Sperrin Cl 5 LN5 205 D2
Speyer Ave PE11 214 C5
Speyside Ct 1 PE2 229 D4
Spice Ave PE21 136 D8
Spicer's La PE22 127 B5
Spilsby Cl 8 LN6 204 D8
Spilsby Hill PE23 100 B8
Spilsby Prim Sch PE23 88 A1
Spilsby Rd
Boston PE21 209 A6
Eastville PE22 101 A1
High Toynton LN9 86 B4
Horncastle LN9 199 E4
Spilsby Rd *continued*
Scunthorpe DN17 184 E5
Spilsby PE23 101 A8
Thorpe St Peter PE24 102 B4
Spindles The PE10 213 D7
Spindlewood 1 HU15 2 C7
Spinnaker Cl HU9 181 C6
Spinners Cl 3 NG34 212 E3
Spinney Cl
Immingham DN40 186 C4
7 Manby LN11 62 C6
9 Ryhall PE9 163 C1
Spinney Croft Cl 14 HU14 3 A5
Spinney La 10 Ryhall PE9 163 C1
2 Scopwick Heath LN4 108 A7
Spinney The
1 Barnby Dun DN3 14 A3
18 Barrow upon Humber DN19 11 D8
8 Grimsby DN31 191 C7
2 Market Deeping PE6 217 B5
2 Swanland HU14 3 B7
7 Winthorpe NG24 104 B7
Spinney Wlk HU4 179 C6
Spinneys The 5 LN2 68 D7
Spion Kop La PE20 135 E3
Spire View
1 Bottesford NG13 128 A6
1 Kingston upon Hull HU13 178 E1
Sleaford NG34 212 A2
Spire View Rd LN11 198 D5
Spirea App LN6 204 C8
Spirewic Ave PE25 206 D8
Spital Hill
Gainsborough DN21 197 E5
18 Louth LN11 198 B5
Spital La LN8 55 B8
Spital St LN1 234 B4
Spital Terr DN21 197 D4
Spitalgate CE (Controlled) Prim Sch NG31 210 D3
Spitfire Ave LN11 62 B6
Spittal Hill Rd PE22 126 D4
Splash La
Ailsworth PE5 228 E8
Castor PE5 223 E1
Spotfield La PE20 136 C7
Spout Hill HU15 2 C8
Spout Yd 6 LN11 198 B6
Spratt Cl LN9 199 D1
Spratton Ct DN34 190 C4
Spridlington Rd LN8 56 D3
Spriggs Cl NG34 212 C3
Sprignall PE3 224 F4
Spring Bank
5 Binbrook LN8 47 C4
Grimsby DN34 191 A7
Kingston upon Hull HU3 180 D7
Spring Bank W HU5 179 D7
Spring Cl 9 LN2 68 E6
Spring Ct Dunston LN4 95 C5
18 Welton/Dunholme LN2 68 D7
Spring Dr
Balderton NG24 104 C1
Farcet PE7 231 B2
Spring End 3 NG31 129 D5
Spring Gdns
Gainsborough DN21 197 D4
Grantham NG31 211 B2
Long Sutton PE12 216 B4
18 Louth LN11 198 B5
Sleaford NG34 212 C5
Spalding PE11 214 C3
Spring Gdns E HU4 179 B6
Spring Gdns S HU4 179 B5
Spring Gdns W HU4 179 B6
Spring Gr
Kingston upon Hull HU3 180 A7
Terrington St Clement PE34 161 F2
Spring Hill
3 Binbrook LN8 47 C4
Cherry Willingham/Reepham LN3 203 F8
Grantham NG31 211 D3
Lincoln LN1 234 A3
Spring La
Balderton NG24 104 C2
8 Colsterworth NG33 151 D7
4 Folkingham NG34 142 D8
Horbling NG34 133 B2
14 Laceby DN37 23 F1
5 Leasingham NG34 121 B7
4 Wymondham LE14 150 B1
Spring St
Immingham DN40 186 D4
Kingston upon Hull HU2 180 D7
Spalding PE11 214 D3
Spring View 4 LN8 47 C4
Springbank DN20 196 C5
Springbok Cl HU4 179 D2
Springburn St HU3 180 A5
Springdale Cl
2 Kingston upon Hull HU9 5 D8
Kingston upon Hull HU10 178 F8
Springfield PE2 231 A7
Springfield Ave
Brough HU15 2 C6
7 Hatfield DN7 14 E4
Springfield Cl
Gainsborough DN21 197 E4
Lincoln LN2 234 B4
2 Scunthorpe DN16 185 C6
Springfield Est LN4 95 D1
Springfield Prim Sch DN33 194 D7
Springfield Rd
2 Brigg DN20 196 D3
Grantham NG31 211 A2
Grimsby DN33 191 C1
Kingston upon Hull HU3 179 F6
Parson Drove PE13 177 D7
Peterborough PE1 225 F5
6 Ruskington NG34 108 D2
Yaxley PE7 233 F5
Springfield Rise 1 DN20 196 E3
Springfield Way HU10 178 E7
Springfields LN8 46 B1
Springfields Ex Ctr PE12 157 B7
Springhead Ave HU5 179 A7
Springhead Ct HU10 179 A6
Springhead Gdns HU10 179 A7
Springhead La HU5 179 A7
Springhead Prim Sch HU10 178 E7
Springs La DN22 52 A2
Springs Rd DN10 26 C1
Springs Way DN20 196 B3
Springthorpe Rd
Corringham DN21 41 E1
Gainsborough DN21 197 F4
Springville Ave HU13 178 F2
Springway Cres DN34 191 A7
Springwood Cres DN33 194 D7
Sprite La LN4 109 D5
Sproxton Rd
Buckminster NG33 150 D6
Skillington NG33 151 A8
Spruce Cl PE12 215 C4
Spruce La DN39 12 A1
Spurn Ave DN33 194 F8
Spurn Lightship* HU1 180 F5
Spurr The 7 LN5 107 A7
Spyvee St HU8 181 A7
Square The
2 Barnack PE9 172 D3
Barrowby NG32 129 B3
12 Goxhill DN19 12 A8
Kingston upon Hull HU13 178 E1
4 Leasingham NG34 121 B7
5 Ryhall PE9 163 C1
Toynton All Saints PE23 100 F6
Squires Gate PE4 221 D3
Stable La 3 DN18 3 E1
Stacey Cl 2 PE25 90 D3
Stackyard The PE2 229 E5
Stafford Ave NG24 104 A2
Stafford St
3 Boston PE21 208 F6
Kingston upon Hull HU2 180 E8
Staffordshire Cres 6 LN6 204 D7
Stagsden PE2 229 F4
Stagshaw Dr PE2 231 B8
Stain La LN12 63 E3
Stainby Rd
Buckminster NG33 150 F5
Gunby & Stainby NG33 151 C4
Staindale Rd DN16 185 D5
Stainesway LN11 198 E7
Stainfield Rd
Kirkby Underwood PE10 142 D1
Morton PE10 154 B7
Stainforth Inf Sch DN7 14 C6
Stainforth Kirton La Prim Sch DN7 14 C7
Stainforth Moor Rd DN7 15 C3
Stainforth Rd DN7 14 A5
Stainton Ave 1 DN21 43 D7
Stainton Cl 5 DN21 53 A5
Stainton Dr
Grimsby DN33 191 A3
8 Immingham DN40 186 B4
Scunthorpe DN17 184 E4
Stainton Gdns LN1 201 E7
Stainton La LN2 69 B4
Stallebrass Cl PE2 231 E5
Stallingborough CE Prim Sch DN41 23 E6
Stallingborough Rd
Immingham DN40 186 B2
Keelby DN41 23 A5
Stallingborough Sta DN41 23 E6
Stamford & Rutland Hospl PE9 219 D6
Stamford Bsns Pk PE9 219 E6
Stamford Cl 4 PE6 217 B5
Stamford Coll (Spalding FE Centre) PE11 214 D4
Stamford Coll PE9 219 C6
Stamford High Sch PE9 219 C4
Stamford Jun Sch PE9 219 B3
Stamford Leisure Ctr PE9 219 D6
Stamford Lodge Rd PE6 224 C5
Stamford Mus* PE9 219 C5
Stamford Rd
Barnack PE9 172 C4
Buckminster NG33 151 A4
Collyweston PE9 171 C2
Colsterworth NG33 151 E5
Easton on the Hill PE9 219 A1
Stamford Rd *continued*
Essendine PE9 163 D2
Helpston PE6 173 C1
Ketton PE9 218 A2
Marholm PE6 220 A1
Market Deeping PE6 217 A4
Tinwell PE9 218 A6
West Deeping PE9 173 A7
Stamford Ret Pk PE9 219 D6
Stamford Sch PE9 219 C6
Stamford St NG31 211 B2
Stamford Sta PE9 219 C4
Stamfords Art Ctr* PE9 219 C5
Stamp End LN2 234 C2
Stamper St 2 PE3 224 F3
Stan Rowing Ct PE2 231 C7
Standard La LN5 93 A2
Standish Gr PE21 209 B7
Standish La DN40 186 B5
Stanfield Rd 2 DN9 27 D6
Stanford Cl 1 DN37 23 F1
Stanford Jun & Inf Sch DN37 23 E1
Stanford Wlk 4 PE3 225 C4
Stanground Coll PE7 231 C5
Stanground Cty Inf Sch PE2 231 D5
Stanholme La DN36 36 A1
Stanhope Ave
4 Balderton NG24 104 C1
7 Woodhall Spa LN10 97 D6
Stanhope Gdns 1 PE21 209 C4
Stanhope Pl DN35 192 C7
Stanhope Rd LN9 199 C4
Stanhope Terr 3 LN9 199 C4
Stanhurst La DN7 15 A5
Staniland Cty Prim Sch PE21 208 D4
Staniland Rd PE21 208 D3
Staniland Way
1 Humberston DN36 36 D8
Peterborough PE4 221 A5
Staniwell Rise DN17 184 D7
Staniwells Dr 11 DN20 19 D3
Stanley Ave 4 LN12 64 B3
Stanley Cl 2 PE24 102 D2
Stanley Cres LN4 205 F4
Stanley Dr
11 Sutterton PE20 136 A2
Sutton Bridge PE12 160 E4
Stanley Gdns 18 DN7 14 C6
Stanley Pl 1 LN5 201 F1
Stanley Rd
Peterborough PE1 226 A3
Scunthorpe DN15 182 C3
18 Stainforth DN7 14 C6
Stanley St Bourne PE10 213 C6
Gainsborough DN21 197 D2
Grimsby DN32 189 C1
Kingston upon Hull HU3 180 C7
Lincoln LN5 205 D7
1 Stamford PE9 219 C5
Stansted St 5 DN31 188 D1
Stanton Cl PE10 213 E5
Stanton Rd 4 LN12 77 A8
Stanton Sq PE7 230 D2
Stanton St 7 NG31 211 A4
Stanton's Pit Nature Reserve* PE10 163 C8
Stapes Garth 1 LN11 50 B8
Staple La NG24 104 B1
Staple Rd DN40 12 F3
Stapledon Rd PE2 229 D2
Stapleford Ave LN2 201 F8
Stapleford La
Coddington NG24 104 E6
Collingham NG23 91 E1
Staples La 12 LN5 93 F7
Star Carr La DN20 196 D8
Star Cl PE1 226 C3
Star Fen Dro NG34 123 A4
Star La Holbeach PE12 215 C7
4 Stamford PE9 219 C5
Star Lode Dro PE11 144 B1
Star Mews PE1 226 C2
Star Rd PE1 226 C2
Starella Gr HU3 180 A4
Starham Rd LN7 31 C4
Starks La LN8 58 D7
Stather Rd DN15 8 A1
Stathern Rd PE1 226 D7
Stathers Wlk 3 HU10 178 F6
Station App
6 Ancaster NG32 120 A3
Boston PE21 208 E4
11 Donington PE11 134 E2
Louth LN11 198 C6
Station Ave
New Waltham DN36 195 D6
16 South Witham NG33 151 D2
Wisbech St Mary PE13 177 D5
Station Cl 9 NG23 91 D4
Station Ct 7 DN7 14 D4
Station Field LN6 200 B3
Station La
Horncastle LN9 199 A3
Searby cum Owmby DN38 32 D7
Station Rd (West) NG31 211 A3
Station Rd
Ailsworth PE5 223 C1
Alford LN13 75 E2
Algarkirk PE20 146 B8
Bardney LN3 83 B4
Barkston NG32 129 F8
Barlings LN3 69 B3
Barnack PE9 172 E4
Station Rd *continued*
Beckingham DN10 52 B8
1 Billingborough NG34 133 B1
Blyton DN21 41 C5
Bottesford NG13 128 A6
Bourne PE10 155 C3
Branston LN4 81 E2
Brough HU15 2 B5
Burgh Le Marsh PE24 102 C8
Burringham DN17 17 E4
Candlesby with Gunby PE24 89 B1
Careby Aunby & Holywell PE9 163 A8
Castle Bytham NG33 152 D1
6 Cherry Willingham/Reepham LN3 82 A8
Cherry Willingham/Reepham LN3 203 F8
Cleethorpes DN35 192 F7
Collingham NG23 91 D4
Corby Glen NG33 152 D7
Deeping St James PE6 174 B7
Digby LN4 108 E5
Donington on Bain LN11 59 E1
East Halton DN40 12 D7
Epworth DN9 27 D7
6 Essendine PE9 163 D3
Fulstow LN11 49 A7
Garthorpe & Fockerby DN17 7 E6
Gedney Hill PE12 168 C1
Gosberton PE11 145 A5
Grantham NG31 211 B3
Grasby DN38 32 E6
Great Steeping PE23 101 F6
Grimsby DN37 190 C8
Gunness DN15 17 E5
Habrough DN40 12 F1
Halton Holegate PE23 101 B8
Harby NG23 79 B5
Harmston LN5 93 E5
Hatfield DN7 14 D4
Haxey DN9 27 D1
Healing DN41 23 F5
Heckington NG34 122 E2
Heighington LN4 81 E4
Helpringham NG34 133 D7
9 Hibaldstow DN20 30 F5
Holbeach PE12 215 D2
Holton Le Clay DN36 36 B4
Keadby with Althorpe DN17 17 D6
6 Ketton PE9 171 A3
Kingston upon Hull HU13 178 E1
Kirton PE20 124 E1
Kirton in Lindsey DN21 30 B2
Knaith DN21 53 A4
Legbourne LN11 61 E3
Lincoln LN6 204 D3
Little Steeping PE23 101 D5
5 Long Sutton PE12 216 B4
Ludborough DN36 48 E6
16 Mablethorpe & Sutton LN12 76 F8
20 Mablethorpe/Sutton on Sea LN12 64 B4
Metheringham LN4 95 D4
Midville PE22 113 E8
1 Misterton DN10 40 A5
Misterton LN13 89 A6
Morton PE10 154 D6
Moulton PE12 157 F6
Mumby LN13 76 F1
North Kelsey LN7 32 B4
North Thoresby DN36 36 B1
Northorpe PE10 164 C7
Owston Ferry DN9 28 A2
Peterborough PE3 225 F2
Potter Hanworth LN4 82 A1
Ruskington NG34 108 E1
Scawby DN20 30 F7
Scredington NG34 132 F7
Scunthorpe DN15 183 A2
Sibsey PE22 113 C1
Sleaford NG34 212 D3
South Kelsey LN7 32 D2
South Killingholme DN40 13 A5
South Willingham LN8 59 A1
Stallingborough DN41 23 E6
Stamford PE9 219 B4
Stixwould & Woodhall LN10 97 A8
Sturton Le Steeple DN22 52 B3
Surfleet PE11 145 E3
Sutterton PE20 136 A1
Swinderby LN6 92 A6
Swineshead PE20 123 F1
Theddlethorpe All Saints LN12 63 D7
Thorney PE6 176 A3
Thornton Curtis DN39 11 F5
Thorpe on the Hill LN6 79 E1
Thorpe St Peter PE24 102 B3
Timberland LN4 96 B1
Torksey LN1 65 D6
Tydd St Mary PE13 170 C8
Ulceby DN39 12 B1
Waddington LN5 93 F7
Wainfleet All Saints PE24 102 D1
Walkeringham DN10 40 A3
Walpole Cross Keys PE34 161 C2
Waltham LE14 138 A1
Waltham DN36 195 A5
Whitton DN15 1 D3

Station Rd *continued*
Wickenby LN3 57 B1
Woodhall Spa LN10 97 D6
Station St Boston PE21 208 E5
Donington PE11 134 E2
Rippingale PE10 143 A3
1 Spalding PE11 214 D4
Station Terr LN5 106 D3
Staunt Rd PE22 112 E2
Staunton St 3 LN1 201 D3
Staveley Rd 8 LN13 75 E2
Staverton Cres LN6 200 B1
Staverton Rd PE4 220 E3
Staves Ct 5 DN36 36 D4
Staxton Cl PE6 220 A1
Staxton Ct HU9 181 D8
Steadfold La PE9 218 A3
Steadings The DN15 8 B2
Steamer Point Rd LN4 95 C7
Steapas Cl 2 PE23 101 D7
Steep Hill LN2 234 B3
Steepers The 4 LN2 68 D2
Steeping Dr DN40 186 A3
Steeping Rd PE23 101 C6
Stells La PE21 208 F3
Stenigot Cl 3 LN6 204 C6
Stenigot Gr LN6 204 D6
Stenigot Rd 1 LN6 204 D6
Stenner Rd LN4 207 F6
Stennett Ave 1 PE11 156 E2
Stephen Cl 3 DN39 12 A1
Stephen Cres
16 Barton-upon-Humber DN18 10 F8
Grimsby DN34 190 E4
Humberston DN36 36 C8
Stephen Rd NG24 104 A6
Stephen's Way NG34 212 F3
Stephens Way 4 PE6 217 F4
Stephenson Ave
Gonerby Hill Foot NG31 210 F8
Pinchbeck PE11 214 E8
Stephenson Cl
9 Alford LN13 75 E2
4 Boston PE21 208 F1
Yaxley PE7 233 D6
Stephenson Way PE10 213 D7
Stepping Stones Sch PE4 221 B1
Sterling Cres DN37 194 C4
Sterne Ave 9 DN20 19 D3
Stevenson Pl 1 DN35 192 D5
Stevenson's Way 33 DN18 10 E8
Stewton Gdns LN11 198 D4
Stewton La LN11 198 E4
Steyning La PE20 135 A7
Steynings The PE4 221 A3
Stickney CE (Aided) Prim Sch PE22 113 A8
Stickney La PE22 112 D7
Still Cl PE6 217 B5
Still The PE13 170 B1
Stirling Cl 4 DN21 197 E6
Stirling Ct
14 Grantham NG31 210 E2
Heckington NG34 122 D2
Stirling Rd PE9 218 F5
Stirling St
Grimsby DN31 189 D1
Kingston upon Hull HU3 179 F6
Stirling Way
Market Deeping PE6 217 C7
Peterborough PE3 220 E1
4 Skellingthorpe LN6 200 A4
Stixwould Rd LN10 97 C7
Stockbridge Pk 3 HU15 2 C7
Stockbridge Rd HU15 2 C7
Stockhouse La PE11 145 B3
Stockman's Ave 2 PE12 215 F3
Stockmoor La LN8 57 A8
Stocks Hill 4 Belton DN9 16 E1
Castor PE5 223 F1
Stocks La LN8 56 F3
Stockshill Rd DN16 185 C6
Stockwell Gate PE12 215 A4
Stockwell Gr 6 HU9 5 F8
Stockwell Prim Sch HU9 5 F8
Stockwith Mill* PE23 87 B5
Stockwith Rd
Haxey DN9 27 E1
Walkeringham DN10 40 A3
Stokes Dr NG34 212 B6
Stokesay Ct 8 PE3 225 B1
Stone Cl 8 PE10 213 C6
Stone Dr LE15 152 A1
Stone Gate
Cowbit PE12 157 B1
Weston PE12 145 F2
Stone Hill DN7 15 A4
Stone Hill Rd DN7 15 A4
Stone La
Aubourn Haddington & South Hykeham LN5 92 E6
Burringham DN17 17 E4
Peterborough PE1 225 F5
Sutterton PE20 135 F1
6 Waddington LN5 93 F7
Stone Moor Rd 14 LN6 93 B8
Stone Pit La
Skendleby PE23 88 D4
Willingham DN21 53 F8
Stonebow Ctr LN2 234 B2
Stonebridge PE2 230 C5
Stonebridge Lea PE2 230 C5
Stonebridge Rd NG31 211 B4
Stonefield Ave LN2 234 B4
Stonefield Pk LN2 68 C7
Stonegate
Gedney PE12 159 D6
Spalding PE11 214 E3
28 Thorne/Moorends DN8 15 A8
Stonehouse Rd PE7 233 E5
Stonemasons Ct 4 NG31 211 B4
Stonepit La
Marston NG32 118 C2
8 Skillington NG33 151 A8
Stonepit Rd HU15 2 E6
Stones Cl 3 PE24 90 B7
Stone's La PE24 77 C1
Stones La 13 Spilsby PE23 88 A1
West Keal PE23 100 C5
Stones Pl 1 LN6 200 E1
Stonesby Rd LE14 138 E1
Stoney La DN21 54 F7
Stoney Way 15 DN36 36 D4
Stoney Yd LN6 200 A5
Stong's Dro PE11 144 F8
Stool Cl Rd 2 DN9 16 E1
Storbeck Rd 15 PE13 170 D1
Storey's Bar Rd PE6 227 A3
Storey's La PE24 102 E7
Storrington Way PE4 221 A3
Stortford St 7 DN31 188 D1
Story St 11 HU1 180 E7
Stothards La 7 DN19 12 A8
Stoton's Gate PE12 158 E2
Stour Ct 7 NG31 210 E2
Stove Ct LE15 162 A8
Stovin Cres DN15 9 A5
Stow Cl DN37 190 D8
Stow Hill LE14 150 C7
Stow La NG34 133 A1
Stow Pk Rd
Marton DN21 65 E8
Stow LN1 66 B8
Stow Rd
Scunthorpe DN16 185 B7
Sturton By Stow LN1 66 C8
Willingham DN21 53 E2
Wisbech PE13 170 E1
Stowe Rd PE6 164 E2
Stowehill Rd PE4 221 D2
Stowgate Rd PE6 174 A8
Strafford St DN21 197 D2
Stragglethorpe La
Caythorpe NG32 118 E8
Fulbeck NG32 105 E2
Strahane Cl LN5 205 C3
Straight Dro PE7 231 E1
Strait LN2 234 B3
Strand Cl 10 LN12 64 B3
Strand Infants Sch DN32 189 B1
Strand Jun Sch DN32 189 B1
Strand St DN32 189 B1
Strand The 9 LN12 64 B3
Stratford Ave DN34 191 A4
Stratford Dr 5 DN16 183 C1
Stratten Cl 5 NG34 107 C1
Stratton Pk 1 HU14 3 C6
Strawberry Cl 13 PE13 170 C1
Strawberry Hill DN37 194 B4
Strawberry St HU9 181 B7
Stray Gn 12 NG34 108 E2
Strayfleets La PE22 126 D5
Street La
North Kelsey LN7 32 B4
North Leverton with Habblesthorpe DN22 65 A8
Street La Rd DN22 52 C1
Street Life Mus of Transport* HU9 181 A6
Streetway PE21 136 E7
Stretham Way 5 PE10 213 C7
Stretton Cl 4 LN1 66 C7
Stretton Rd LE15 162 B6
Strickland Rd DN17 7 A3
Strickland St HU3 180 C4
Stricklands Dr 4 PE6 175 C8
Strong's Bank PE12 158 F4
Strong's Gate PE12 158 F3
Stroxton La NG33 139 F5
Strubby Airfield LN13 75 E8
Strubby Cl
9 Birchwood LN6 204 D8
Cleethorpes DN35 193 A4
Strugg's Hill La PE20 136 B3
Stuart Cl
Peterborough PE2 231 C6
Scunthorpe DN17 184 F2
Stuart St NG31 211 C3
Stuart Wortley St 1 DN31 189 B2
Stubton Hall Boarding Sch NG23 118 B7
Stubton Rd NG23 117 F7
Studcross DN9 27 D6
Studley St HU8 181 B8
Stukeley Cl Lincoln LN2 202 E6
Peterborough PE2 231 D5
Stukeley Gdns 2 PE12 215 C2
Stukeley Rd PE12 215 D2
Stump Cross Hill NG34 212 C1
Stumpacre PE3 225 A8
Stumpcross La PE20 135 B6
Stumps La PE12 157 B7
Sturdy Hill LN11 62 E4
Sturgate Airfield DN21 53 E6
Sturgate Cl 15 LN6 204 C7
Sturgate Wlk DN21 197 F3
Sturmer Ct 1 DN16 185 B2
Sturrock Ct 12 NG31 210 E2
Sturrock Way PE3 225 C8
Sturton by Stow Prim Sch LN1 66 D8
Sturton CE Prim Sch DN22 52 C2
Sturton Cl 1 LN2 201 F7
Sturton Gr 2 DN33 191 B4
Sturton La DN20 30 E7
Sturton Rd
North Leverton with Habblesthorpe DN22 52 B1
Stow LN1 66 C8
Sturton Way PE12 216 B5
Stutte Cl LN11 198 E3
Styles Croft 6 HU14 3 C6
Subway St HU3 180 B3
Subway The DN16 19 A4
Sudbeck La 17 LN2 68 D6
Sudbrook Rd NG32 119 D4
Sudbrooke Dr LN2 202 A7
Sudbrooke La LN2 68 E2
Sudbrooke Rd LN2 68 F3
Sudbury Cl LN6 205 A5
Sudbury Ct PE7 231 F5
Sudbury Pl LN11 198 B4
Suddle Way 19 DN41 23 A4
Sudthorpe Hill
8 Fulbeck NG32 106 C1
Fulbeck NG32 119 C8
Suffolk Cl PE3 225 B2
Suffolk Rd 10 LN1 67 E5
Suggitt's Ct DN35 192 D8
Suggitt's La DN35 192 D8
Suggitt's Orch DN35 192 D8
Sullivan Rd HU4 179 B4
Summer Hill DN21 197 E5
Summer Lesure La PE12 159 F2
Summerdale 28 DN18 10 E8
Summerfield Ave DN37 194 E5
Summerfield Cl
Waltham DN37 194 E5
16 Wisbech PE13 170 C1
Summerfield Ct 3 NG34 212 D6
Summerfield Dr 4 NG34 212 D6
Summerfield Rd PE1 225 F4
Summerfields PE22 114 B1
Summergangs La DN21 197 D1
Summergates La PE24 102 C7
Summergroves Way HU4 179 B2
Sunbeam Ave LN6 204 D1
Sunbeam Rd HU4 179 D5
Suncastle* PE25 206 E4
Sunderfleet La LN11 51 A5
Sunderland Cl 6 LN6 200 A4
Sunfield Cres LN6 200 D1
Sunfields Cl PE12 157 C3
Sunningdale
Grantham NG31 211 C8
Peterborough PE2 229 E6
8 Waltham DN37 194 C4
Sunningdale Ave
Brigg DN20 196 C5
Spalding PE11 214 C2
Sunningdale Cl
Chapel St Leonard PE24 90 E7
1 Skegness PE25 206 D4
6 Woodhall Spa LN10 97 C5
Sunningdale Cres 2 PE25 206 D4
Sunningdale Dr
Boston PE21 208 C6
Chapel St Leonard PE24 90 E7
4 Immingham DN40 186 D5
Lincoln LN5 205 D8
Skegness PE25 206 D4
Sunningdale Gr LN4 203 D1
Sunningdale Rd
5 Hatfield DN7 14 F3
Kingston upon Hull HU13 178 F2
Scunthorpe DN17 184 D4
Sunny Bank HU3 180 B7
Sunny Bank Gdns DN10 39 C2
Sunny Cnr DN33 191 D1
Sunny Hill 8 DN21 30 B1
Sunnybank 11 DN18 10 E8
Sunnydale Cl 1 PE11 145 D2
Sunnymead PE4 220 E6
Sunway Gr DN16 185 B5
Sunway Inf Sch DN16 185 A5
Surfleet Bank PE11 145 F5
Surfleet Lows Nature Reserve* PE11 145 D3
Surfleet Rd 5 PE11 145 D2
Surfside 5 LN12 77 A8
Surrey Garth HU4 179 B4
Surtees St DN31 189 B2
Sussex Ave PE21 208 B4
Sussex Cl 7 LN8 47 B6
Sussex Gdns 16 LN1 67 E5
Sussex Rd PE9 219 B6
Sussex St DN35 192 B8
Susworth Rd DN17 28 E4
Sutcliffe Ave DN33 191 A3
Sutherland Way PE9 218 F5
Sutterton Dro LN4 110 E1
Suttling Dales La PE22 126 B8
Sutton Cl
Heighington/Washingborough LN4 203 A1
Sutton Cl *continued*
15 Nettleham LN2 68 C2
Sutton Ct 2 PE25 206 C3
Sutton Gate PE12 159 D1
Sutton Mdws PE13 170 C2
Sutton on Sea Prim Sch LN12 76 F8
Sutton Pl 4 DN20 30 F7
Sutton Rd
Beckingham LN5 105 B4
Bilsby LN13 76 C4
16 Kirk Sandall DN3 14 A3
Mablethorpe/Sutton on Sea LN12 64 C2
Newton PE13 170 B6
Sutton St James PE12 159 D2
Terrington St Clement PE34 161 F2
Sutton St James Prim Sch PE12 159 C1
Sutton's La PE6 217 D4
Svenskaby PE2 229 B6
Swaby Cl LN2 202 A8
Swaby Cres 4 PE25 206 B4
Swaby Dr DN35 192 D3
Swaby Valley Nature Reserve* LN13 74 F4
Swadales Cl 11 NG31 129 E5
Swain's Dro PE13 170 C8
Swale Ave PE4 221 C1
Swale Bank PE11 144 D5
Swale Rd 14 HU15 2 D5
Swaledale 10 HU15 2 D6
Swaledale Pl 2 DN16 185 E6
Swales Rd 12 DN36 36 D8
Swallow Ave LN6 200 A3
Swallow Cl
5 Chapel St Leonard PE24 90 D7
4 Gainsborough DN21 53 A7
1 Sleaford NG34 212 C3
Swallow Ct 6 DN9 27 D7
Swallow Dr
3 Claypole NG23 117 E8
15 Healing DN41 23 F5
Louth LN11 198 D8
Swallow Gate Rd LN11 51 B2
Swallow Hill PE10 164 B7
Swallow La
Tydd St Giles PE13 170 B8
Wootton DN39 11 E2
Swallow Wlk 3 PE6 217 D5
Swallowbeck Ave LN6 205 A4
Swallowfield PE4 220 E4
Swallowfield Dr HU4 179 B2
Swallowfields Ct 2 PE25 206 A4
Swallow's Cl NG31 210 E7
Swan Dr
Skegness PE25 103 C7
6 Sturton by Stow LN1 66 D7
Swan Moor Bank PE22 114 C3
Swan St 1 Lincoln LN2 234 B2
Spalding PE11 214 D4
Swanella Gr HU3 180 A4
Swanhill PE8 222 A4
Swanhole La PE22 126 D4
Swanholme Cl LN6 204 E5
Swanland Butts Cl HU10 178 C6
Swanland Cl 25 DN8 15 B7
Swanland Ct 24 DN8 15 B7
Swanland Cty Prim Sch HU14 3 B6
Swanland Dale HU14 3 B8
Swanland Garth 6 HU14 3 A5
Swanland Hill HU14 3 B5
Swanland Rd HU13 178 C2
Swannacks View 3 DN20 30 F7
Swan's La LN5 105 F5
Swanspool PE3 225 B6
Swapcoat La PE12 216 B5
Swarby La NG34 132 A7
Swaton La NG34 133 C3
Swayne Cl LN2 202 D7
Swaythling Cl LN6 204 E5
Sweet Briar Cl 6 DN37 194 C5
Sweet Cl 2 PE6 217 D5
Sweet Dews Gr HU9 181 D8
Sweetbriar 3 PE9 218 C7
Sweetbriar La PE4 220 F6
Sweetlands Way PE11 145 B5
Swen Cl 17 LN2 68 D7
Swift Cl PE6 217 D4
Swift Gdns LN2 202 C7
Swift Rd DN17 184 D6
Swift Way PE10 164 B7
Swiftsure Cres DN34 190 D4
Swin Cl PE20 135 C6
Swinburne La DN17 184 D7
Swinderby Gdns 2 DN34 191 A5
Swinderby Rd
Collingham NG23 91 E4
Eagle & Swinethorpe LN6 79 B1
North Scarle LN6 78 F1
Norton Disney LN6 92 C2
South Scarle NG23 91 F7
Swinderby Sta LN6 92 B7
Swindler's Dro PE12 157 C6
Swine Hill NG32 139 C7
Swine's Mdw Rd PE6 217 D8
Swinefleet Rd DN14 6 B8
Swinegate
Grantham NG31 211 A5
Kingston upon Hull HU13 178 E1
Swineshead Cowleys Foundation CE VC Prim Sch PE20 135 C7
Swineshead Rd
Boston PE21 208 A3
Frampton PE20 124 E1
Swineshead Sta PE20 123 F1
Swingbridge Rd NG31 210 D2
Swinhope Hill LN8 47 C5
Swinhope Rd LN8 47 B6
Swinstead (CE) Prim Sch NG33 153 B5
Swinstead Rd
Corby Glen NG33 152 F7
Counthorpe & Creeton NG33 153 A3
Irnham NG33 141 E1
Swinster La DN40 12 E6
Switchback LN8 47 C2
Swithin Cl HU13 179 A2
Swynford Cl LN1 65 D2
Sybil Rd 18 PE13 170 D1
Sycamore Ave
Grimsby DN33 191 C3
Peterborough PE1 226 C6
Sycamore Cl
1 Barnetby Le Wold DN38 21 B4
4 Birchwood LN6 204 E8
Bourne PE10 213 A5
2 Broughton DN20 19 D3
Cherry Willingham/Reepham LN3 203 D5
Croft PE24 102 E4
Kingston upon Hull HU5 179 C7
5 Scopwick Heath LN4 108 A7
Sycamore Cres 5 LN6 204 E8
Sycamore Ct 3 NG31 210 D2
Sycamore Dr
7 Gainsborough DN21 197 E6
Louth LN11 198 E5
9 Newark-on-Trent NG24 104 C5
Sleaford NG34 212 D6
6 Waddington LN5 93 E8
3 Waddington LN5 93 E8
Sycamore Gr LN4 81 A1
Sycamore La 2 LE14 150 B1
Sycamores The 5 PE11 214 B1
Sydney Dr 3 PE25 206 A4
Sydney Rd PE2 231 D5
Sydney Smith Sch HU10 179 A5
Sydney St PE21 208 D5
Sykemouth Dro PE20 124 C1
Sykes Cl
6 Kingston upon Hull HU10 178 F6
15 Swanland HU14 3 B7
Sykes La Goxhill DN19 5 A2
Saxilby with Ingleby LN1 66 C3
Sykes St 2 HU2 180 F7
Sylvan Ave 5 LN10 97 D6
Sylvden Dr 24 PE13 170 E1
Sylvester St 12 DN21 30 B1
Symmington Cl PE2 230 F8
Sympson Cl LN2 202 E6
Syne Ave 5 PE25 206 D1
Syston Gr LN5 205 D4
Sywell Cl 16 LN6 204 C6

T

Tadman St HU3 180 D4
Taggs Dr 7 PE25 206 A6
Tait Cl PE1 226 C5
Talbot Ave PE2 230 D6
Talbot Cl 4 PE23 101 A8
Talbot Rd
Immingham DN40 186 D3
Skegness PE25 206 C4
Talisman Dr DN16 185 A2
Tall Gables 2 NG22 65 B1
Tall Trees HU13 178 C3
Tallert Way DN33 190 F3
Tallington Dry Ski Ctr* PE9 172 F7
Tamar Ct 5 NG31 210 E2
Tamar Dr 4 DN36 195 D7
Tamar Way 3 LN6 205 A2
Tamarisk Way DN16 185 D5
Tame Ct 4 NG34 212 D5
Tamson Way 5 NG34 212 D5
Tanashi Dori DN17 182 E1
Tanglewood PE4 220 F6
Tanglewood Cedar Falls 3 PE11 214 B1
Tanhouse PE2 230 C5
Tanners' La NG33 152 E8
Tanner's La LN5 234 A1
Tannery La 3 NG34 142 D8
Tansor Garth PE3 225 C5
Tantallon Ct 6 PE3 225 B1
Tapin Cl LN1 201 C6
Tarleton Ave 1 LN10 97 E6
Tarleton Cl 2 DN3 14 A2
Tarran Way PE25 206 B5
Tarrant PE4 220 E6
Tasburgh St DN32 191 F6
Tasman Rd 5 PE23 101 A8
Tathwell CE Sch LN11 61 B2
Tattershall Ave DN34 190 F4
Tattershall Castle (NT)* LN4 207 A4
Tattershall Cl 3 NG31 210 E5

Tattershall Coll Bldgs* LN4 ... 207 A4
Tattershall Dr 10 PE6 ... 217 A5
Tattershall Rd
Billinghay LN4 ... 109 F5
Boston PE21 ... 208 D7
Fishtoft PE21 ... 125 C5
Woodhall Spa LN10 ... 97 D5
Tattershall Sta Gall & Pottery* LN4 ... 110 E7
Tattershall Way LN11 ... 198 A8
Tatwin Dr 8 PE6 ... 175 B8
Taunton Cl 2 NG34 ... 212 D7
Taunton Rd HU4 ... 179 A3
Taunton Way DN33 ... 194 E8
Tavella Ct 1 DN9 ... 27 B2
Tavern Cl LN13 ... 89 A6
Tavern La 6 PE24 ... 90 B7
Taverner Rd PE21 ... 208 D6
Taverners Rd PE1 ... 225 F4
Tavistock Cl 15 PE6 ... 176 A3
Tavistock Rd PE11 ... 214 B2
Tawney St PE21 ... 208 F6
Taylor Cl 6 Belton DN9 ... 16 E2
5 Boston PE21 ... 209 D4
Taylor St DN35 ... 189 D1
Taylor's Ave DN35 ... 192 E4
Taylor's Dro PE12 ... 159 C1
Teal Cl 4 Brigg DN20 ... 196 A3
3 Skegness PE25 ... 206 A6
Teal Gr 10 PE12 ... 167 B8
Teal Pl LN7 ... 33 A4
Teal Rd LN4 ... 110 E8
Tealby Cl 1 DN21 ... 53 A7
Tealby Gr 5 DN33 ... 191 B3
Tealby Rd
Middle Rasen LN8 ... 57 E8
Scunthorpe DN17 ... 184 D5
Tealby Sch LN8 ... 46 D1
Tealby St 11 LN5 ... 205 E8
Teale St DN15 ... 183 A4
Team Gate DN37 ... 190 C6
Teanby Ct 5 PE3 ... 224 F3
Teanby Dr 8 DN15 ... 9 A5
Teasles 6 PE6 ... 217 D6
Tedder Dr
3 Waddington LN5 ... 93 F7
3 Waddington LN5 ... 94 A7
Tedder Prim Sch The LN4 ... 108 B7
Teddy's Farm* LN5 ... 105 C4
Tee La DN15 ... 8 B5
Teesdale Cl LN6 ... 200 C2
Teesdale Rd NG31 ... 211 A7
Telford Dr
Newark NG24 ... 104 B6
Yaxley PE7 ... 233 D6
Temper Rd DN16 ... 185 F8
Temperance Ave 5 DN17 ... 29 D7
Temperance La 2 NG23 ... 91 C4
Temperton's La 5 DN9 ... 28 A3
Tempest St LN2 ... 202 B3
Templar Ct DN16 ... 185 B3
Templars Way 2 NG33 ... 151 D2
Temple Cl 2 Alford LN13 ... 75 E2
4 Belton DN9 ... 16 E2
3 Brough HU15 ... 2 E6
Temple Gdns LN2 ... 234 B3
Temple Grange PE4 ... 220 F6
Temple La DN37 ... 23 E1
Temple Rd
Aslackby & Laughton NG34 ... 142 E5
Welbourn LN5 ... 107 A4
Temple Terr LN11 ... 198 B6
Temple Wlk 2 HU15 ... 2 E6
Templefield Rd DN21 ... 42 D4
Templeman Dr PE9 ... 163 E5
Templemans La DN36 ... 36 A1
Templemeads Cl PE10 ... 154 D6
Temples Ct 3 PE6 ... 173 B4
Templeway Cl 5 NG32 ... 119 B7
Templeway Sq 8 NG32 ... 119 B7
Ten Acre Dro PE11 ... 135 C1
Ten Acre La
Pinchbeck PE11 ... 145 C1
Wyville cum Hungerton NG32 ... 139 B5
Tenens Way PE21 ... 209 A1
Tennyson Ave
Grantham NG31 ... 211 E5
16 Mablethorpe/Sutton on Sea LN12 ... 64 B4
Sleaford NG34 ... 212 D5
4 Thorne/Moorends DN8 ... 15 B8
Tennyson Cl
Benniworth LN8 ... 59 B1
Brigg DN20 ... 196 D2
2 Caistor LN7 ... 33 A3
12 Mablethorpe/Sutton on Sea LN12 ... 77 A7
14 Metheringham LN4 ... 95 C4
Tennyson Dr
Bourne PE10 ... 213 D3
22 Welton/Dunholme LN2 ... 68 D6
Tennyson Gdns 1 LN9 ... 199 D2
Tennyson Gn 3 PE25 ... 206 C2
Tennyson High Sch The LN12 ... 64 C3
Tennyson Rd
Cleethorpes DN35 ... 192 E7
Louth LN11 ... 198 C4
Tennyson Rd *continued*
17 Mablethorpe/Sutton on Sea LN12 ... 64 B4
Peterborough PE1 ... 225 F7
2 Ruskington NG34 ... 108 E2
Scunthorpe DN16 ... 185 D7
Tennyson St
5 Gainsborough DN21 ... 197 D5
Grimsby DN31 ... 191 D8
1 Lincoln LN1 ... 201 D4
Tennyson Way 1 PE9 ... 218 E5
Tensing Rd DN16 ... 185 C5
Tenter La 6 LN5 ... 107 A8
Tentercroft St LN5 ... 234 A1
Tenters The PE12 ... 215 E2
Terrace La PE22 ... 99 C5
Terrace The
Great Ponton NG33 ... 140 A5
10 Spilsby PE23 ... 88 A1
Terrington Pl DN35 ... 192 D4
Terry O'Toole Theatre* LN6 ... 204 D1
Tetford Hill LN9 ... 73 E3
Tetford Prim Sch LN9 ... 73 F1
Tetford Rd LN9 ... 86 A5
Tethering La DN10 ... 39 A2
Tetley Rd DN16 ... 185 C7
Tetley View 3 DN17 ... 16 E6
Tetney Blow Wells Nature Reserve* DN36 ... 36 E3
Tetney Cl 6 LN1 ... 201 E8
Tetney La DN36 ... 195 E2
Tetney Lock Rd DN36 ... 36 E4
Tetney Marshes Nature Reserve* DN36 ... 37 C7
Tetney Prim Sch DN36 ... 36 D4
Tetney Rd DN36 ... 36 C7
Tewkesbury Dr 4 DN34 ... 191 C6
Thacker Bank LN12 ... 63 B7
Thackers Cl PE8 ... 222 A4
Thackers La LN4 ... 81 D2
Thacker's Rd PE22 ... 112 B2
Thackers Way PE6 ... 217 D5
Thames Cl 2 PE24 ... 90 B7
Thames Cres 4 PE24 ... 90 B7
Thames Rd
Grantham NG31 ... 210 E2
Spalding PE11 ... 214 F5
Thames St
Hogsthorpe PE24 ... 90 B7
Louth LN11 ... 198 D6
Thary La PE11 ... 145 E4
Thatchers Wlk PE22 ... 113 B2
Theaker Ave DN21 ... 197 F5
Thealby La DN15 ... 8 E5
Theatre Royal* LN2 ... 234 B2
Theddlethorpe Com Prim Sch LN12 ... 63 D6
Theddlethorpe Rd LN12 ... 63 F4
Theodore Rd DN15 ... 182 E4
Theodore St LN1 ... 234 A4
Theresa Cl 8 PE25 ... 206 A4
Thesiger St
Grimsby DN32 ... 189 B1
Lincoln LN5 ... 201 F1
Thetford Ave 5 PE6 ... 164 E5
Thimbleby Hill LN9 ... 85 C5
Thinholme La DN9 ... 27 A1
Third Ave
1 Fixborough Ind Est DN15 ... 8 A1
Grantham NG31 ... 211 F7
4 Scampton Airfield LN1 ... 67 E5
2 Scunthorpe DN17 ... 184 C6
Spalding PE11 ... 214 A4
Third Dro
Gosberton PE11 ... 144 B4
Moulton PE12 ... 146 F7
Peterborough PE1 ... 226 E2
Third Hill Rd LN4 ... 81 F3
Third La DN37 ... 35 D3
Third Marsh Rd PE14 ... 170 C3
Thirkleby Cres DN32 ... 192 B4
Thirlmere Ave DN33 ... 194 E7
Thirlmere Cl 8 LN6 ... 205 A2
Thirlmere Gdns 3 PE4 ... 221 C3
Thirlmere Way 1 LN6 ... 200 D1
Thirsk Dr LN6 ... 204 F4
Thistle Cl LN2 ... 202 C8
Thistle Dr PE2 ... 231 C7
Thistlemoor Rd PE1 ... 225 E7
Thistleton La LE15 ... 151 D1
Thomas Cl 7 PE3 ... 224 F3
Thomas Cowley Sch The PE11 ... 134 F2
Thomas Gibson Dr 4 LN9 ... 199 D3
Thomas Magnus Sch NG24 ... 104 A4
Thomas Rd DN17 ... 184 F8
Thomas St
Grimsby DN32 ... 191 F7
Kingston upon Hull HU9 ... 181 B7
Lincoln LN2 ... 234 C2
Sleaford NG34 ... 212 D4
Thomas Sumpter Sch DN17 ... 184 E7
Thompson Cl
Skegness PE25 ... 206 C5
3 Spalding PE11 ... 214 C3
Thompson Dr 25 DN7 ... 14 D4
Thompson St 7 DN15 ... 183 B3
Thompsons Gd PE7 ... 230 D3
Thompson's La
Fosdyke PE20 ... 146 E8
Hough-on-the-Hill NG32 ... 119 A5
Thonock Cl LN2 ... 201 F7
Thonock Dr 7 LN1 ... 66 C2
Thonock Rd DN21 ... 197 D8
Thoresby Pl DN35 ... 192 E4
Thoresby Prim Sch HU5 ... 180 B8
Thoresby Rd
Fulstow LN11 ... 49 A8
Scunthorpe DN17 ... 184 D5
Tetney DN36 ... 36 D3
Thoresby St HU5 ... 180 B8
Thoresway Dr LN2 ... 202 A7
Thoresway Gr 5 DN33 ... 191 A3
Thorganby Rd DN35 ... 193 A3
Thorn Bank DN9 ... 26 E4
Thorn La DN19 ... 12 A8
Thorn Leigh 3 HU3 ... 180 C6
Thornbury Rd DN40 ... 186 D3
Thorndales La PE22 ... 113 A5
Thorndike Way DN21 ... 197 E3
Thorndyke Mews 7 DN21 ... 197 D3
Thorne King Edward Fst Sch DN8 ... 15 B8
Thorne N Sta DN8 ... 14 F8
Thorne Rd
Edenthorpe DN3 ... 14 A2
Sandtoft DN8 ... 16 A3
8 Stainforth DN7 ... 14 C7
Thorne S Sta DN8 ... 15 B7
Thorne Swimming Baths DN8 ... 15 B8
Thorne Waste Drain Rd DN8 ... 15 E8
Thorne Way PE20 ... 136 C4
Thorney Heritage Mus* PE6 ... 176 A3
Thorney Rd
2 Crowland PE6 ... 175 C8
Newborough PE6 ... 174 D5
Wisbech St Mary PE13 ... 177 C2
Thorngarth La 9 DN19 ... 11 D8
Thorngate LN5 ... 234 B2
Thornham's Way 8 HU15 ... 2 C7
Thornhill Cres 4 DN17 ... 184 F3
Thornhill Gdns 1 DN34 ... 191 A7
Thornhill La DN22 ... 52 E1
Thornholme Dr DN16 ... 185 A3
Thorniman La PE20 ... 136 E6
Thornleigh Dr PE2 ... 230 C6
Thornmead PE4 ... 221 B4
Thorns La NG32 ... 210 A8
Thornton 20 HU15 ... 2 C6
Thornton Abbey* DN39 ... 12 B5
Thornton Abbey Sta DN39 ... 12 A5
Thornton Ave
Boston PE21 ... 208 D3
Scunthorpe DN16 ... 185 A7
Thornton Cl
3 Heighington/Washingborough LN4 ... 203 A2
Kingston upon Hull HU13 ... 178 D1
Langriville PE22 ... 124 F8
6 Lincoln LN6 ... 205 A7
Peterborough PE4 ... 221 C3
Thornton Cres
Cleethorpes DN35 ... 192 E4
5 Horncastle LN9 ... 199 C2
Thornton Ct DN36 ... 195 D8
Thornton Gdns 21 DN41 ... 23 A4
Thornton Gr 6 DN34 ... 190 E4
Thornton Pl DN40 ... 186 B3
Thornton Rd
Barrow upon Humber DN19 ... 11 D6
7 Collingham NG23 ... 91 D4
Goxhill DN19 ... 11 F6
Owersby LN7 ... 44 E7
South Kelsey LN7 ... 32 A1
Spalding PE11 ... 214 F3
Thornton Curtis DN39 ... 11 E4
Thornton St
Barrow upon Humber DN19 ... 11 C7
6 Gainsborough DN21 ... 197 D3
Thornton Way LN3 ... 203 E6
Thornwell La 2 PE23 ... 87 A4
Thornwick Ave HU10 ... 178 E8
Thornwick Cl 2 HU3 ... 180 C5
Thorold Ave
5 Cranwell NG34 ... 120 E8
Cranwell & Byard's Leap NG34 ... 107 E1
Thorold Gdns 1 NG32 ... 130 B8
Thorold Pl 1 DN3 ... 14 A2
Thorold Rd NG32 ... 210 A4
Thorold St Boston PE21 ... 208 F6
Grimsby DN31 ... 189 C1
Thorold Way LN5 ... 93 F4
Thorolds Charity CE (Aided) Prim Sch NG32 ... 118 D2
Thorolds Way PE5 ... 223 D2
Thorpe Ave
Lincoln LN1 ... 201 D8
Moulton PE12 ... 157 E2
Peterborough PE3 ... 225 C2
Thorpe Bank PE22 ... 101 B3
Thorpe Camp Visitor Ctr* LN4 ... 207 B8
Thorpe Cl 3 NG24 ... 104 D5
Thorpe CP Sch PE3 ... 225 B3
Thorpe Culvert Sta PE24 ... 102 B3
Thorpe Dr NG34 ... 120 E2
Thorpe Dro NG34 ... 120 E3
Thorpe La
Aubourn Haddington & South Hykeham LN6 ... 93 A8
Thorpe La *continued*
Brattleby LN1 ... 67 B7
Eagle & Swinethorpe LN6 ... 79 C1
Tealby LN8 ... 46 B1
Thorpe Lea Rd PE3 ... 225 E2
Thorpe Mdws PE3 ... 225 C2
Thorpe Pk Rd PE3 ... 225 C3
Thorpe Rd
Doddington & Whisby LN6 ... 79 E2
Ewerby & Evedon NG34 ... 122 C6
Peterborough PE3 ... 225 B1
Tattershall LN4 ... 207 C6
Thorpe St Peter Cty Sch PE24 ... 102 B4
Thorpe Tilney Dro
Timberland LN4 ... 97 A1
Walcott LN4 ... 109 C8
Thorpe Wood PE3 ... 224 F1
Thorpehall Rd
16 Kirk Sandall DN3 ... 14 A2
12 Kirk Sandall DN3 ... 14 A2
Thorpe-on-the-Hill CE (Controlled) Prim Sch LN6 ... 92 E8
Thorpes La 3 NG32 ... 138 D4
Thorpe's La PE12 ... 158 B6
Thorseby Cl PE3 ... 225 B3
Threadneedle St 9 PE21 ... 208 F5
Three Bridge La LN11 ... 63 A7
Three Leys La DN22 ... 52 B2
Threekingham Bar NG34 ... 132 D3
Throstlenest PE7 ... 231 C3
Thrumber Marsh La LN13 ... 76 F1
Thrunscoe Infants Sch DN35 ... 192 F5
Thrunscoe Rd 7 DN35 ... 192 F5
Thrush Cl 10 NG34 ... 212 B3
Thurlaston Cl PE3 ... 225 B2
Thurlby Cl 4 LN4 ... 203 A2
Thurlby Com Prim Sch PE10 ... 164 C8
Thurlby Cres LN2 ... 202 B8
Thurlby Fen Nature Reserve* PE10 ... 164 F7
Thurlby Rd
Bassingham LN5 ... 92 F3
Bilsby LN13 ... 76 B3
Gainsborough DN21 ... 197 E4
Thurlow Ct 1 LN2 ... 202 E7
Thurning Ave PE2 ... 231 C6
Thuro Gr PE2 ... 230 A3
Thursfield PE4 ... 221 A4
Thurstan Cl PE10 ... 213 B6
Thurston Gate 2 PE3 ... 225 A1
Thyme Ave 12 PE6 ... 217 C5
Tichbourne Cl 6 HU3 ... 180 C5
Tilbury Prim Sch HU4 ... 179 B3
Tilbury Rd HU4 ... 179 B3
Tilebarn La PE20 ... 134 F7
Tilia Cl
Kingston upon Hull HU4 ... 179 B2
Scunthorpe DN16 ... 185 D4
Tilia Way 5 PE10 ... 213 E2
Till Bridge La
Marton LN1 ... 65 F8
Scampton LN1 ... 67 A6
Stow LN1 ... 66 A8
Tillbridge Rd LN1 ... 66 D7
Tilley Gate LN11 ... 51 B3
Tilney Ave PE21 ... 208 D6
Tilney The 10 PE12 ... 158 B7
Tilton Ct PE1 ... 226 C8
Timber Hill NG33 ... 151 A4
Timberland DN16 ... 185 C4
Timberland Dro LN4 ... 96 E2
Timberland Rd LN4 ... 96 C2
Timberley Dr DN37 ... 190 C7
Timm's La 18 LN5 ... 93 F7
Timms's Dro PE20 ... 134 E8
Timson Ct 5 DN10 ... 52 B8
Tin La PE10 ... 213 C5
Tindale Bank Rd
Haxey DN9 ... 39 C8
West Stockwith DN10 ... 40 A7
Tindall Cl 2 PE13 ... 170 D2
Tindall Way 10 PE24 ... 102 D1
Tinkermere Cl 3 LN2 ... 68 D6
Tinker's Dro PE13 ... 170 D1
Tinker's La Girton NG23 ... 91 C8
2 Waddington LN5 ... 93 F6
Tinkle St LN11 ... 62 C7
Tinsley Cl NG23 ... 117 F7
Tintagel Ct 7 PE3 ... 225 B1
Tintagel Way DN36 ... 195 C7
Tintern Rise 4 PE6 ... 175 A1
Tinwell Rd
Stamford PE9 ... 219 A4
Tinwell PE9 ... 218 D3
Tinwell Rd La PE9 ... 218 F4
Tip La PE24 ... 102 B4
Tirrington PE3 ... 225 A3
Tison Garth HU10 ... 178 F6
Tithe Barn La 9 DN8 ... 15 B8
Tiverton Rd PE3 ... 225 C3
Tiverton St DN35 ... 189 E1
Tobias Gr 4 PE9 ... 218 C7
Tobruk Cl LN1 ... 201 D8
Toby's Hill Nature Reserve* LN11 ... 51 C5
Todd La DN21 ... 41 C4
Todds Cl 1 HU14 ... 3 C6
Todds Ct 26 DN17 ... 29 D7
Todds La 1 DN15 ... 8 A4
Todd's La HU15 ... 2 A8
Todkill's La 7 PE12 ... 160 F4
Toft Cl PE24 ... 115 D8
Toft Field La PE22 ... 114 A3
Toft Hurn 1 PE22 ... 98 F4
Toft La LN8 ... 56 E7
Toft Tunnel Nature Reserve* PE10 ... 154 A1
Toftland PE2 ... 230 C5
Tofts Rd 10 DN18 ... 10 E8
Toletorpe Sq 6 PE9 ... 219 B6
Toll Bar Ave
6 Bottesford NG13 ... 128 A6
New Waltham DN36 ... 195 B6
Toll Bar Rd Croft PE24 ... 103 D3
Grantham NG31 ... 211 C3
Toll Bar Sec Sch DN36 ... 195 A5
Toll House Rd PE2 ... 230 C7
Tollbar Rd
Great Gonerby NG32 ... 129 B8
Marston NG32 ... 118 C1
Tollemach Rd (South) NG31 ... 139 F8
Tollemache Fields 9 NG33 ... 151 D2
Tollemache Rd (North) NG31 ... 139 F8
Tollesby La 34 DN7 ... 14 D4
Tollfield Rd PE21 ... 209 B7
Tollgate
Peterborough PE3 ... 225 A5
Spalding PE11 ... 214 C4
Toll's La PE12 ... 215 E5
Tom La NG34 ... 120 E5
Tom Otter's La LN1 ... 66 B1
Tomline Rd 5 DN41 ... 23 A5
Tomline St 1 DN31 ... 189 B1
Tomlinson Ave 4 DN15 ... 182 E3
Tomlinson Cl 3 LN4 ... 207 A5
Tomlinson Way 5 NG34 ... 108 E2
Tonbridge 1 DN33 ... 194 E8
Toneham La PE6 ... 175 F2
Tonglet Cl 3 PE25 ... 206 C1
Tonnant Way DN34 ... 190 D5
Tooley La PE22 ... 114 C2
Tooley St Boston PE21 ... 209 A3
Gainsborough DN21 ... 197 D3
Toot La PE21 ... 209 D4
Toothill Gdns DN34 ... 190 F6
Top La Goulceby LN11 ... 72 C6
Kirk Bramwith DN7 ... 14 A6
Top Rd
4 Croxton Kerrial NG32 ... 138 D4
Little Cawthorpe LN11 ... 61 E2
Osgodby LN8 ... 45 A2
South Killingholme DN40 ... 12 E3
Thorney NG23 ... 78 F7
Winterton DN15 ... 8 F6
Worlaby DN20 ... 10 D1
Topaz Gr 3 HU3 ... 180 A4
Topham Cres 13 PE6 ... 176 A3
Topmoor Way PE4 ... 221 D1
Topsgate PE12 ... 159 C7
Torbay Dr DN33 ... 194 E6
Torchil Cl HU10 ... 178 C6
Torfrid Cl 14 PE6 ... 166 F1
Torfrida Dr PE10 ... 213 B6
Torgate Ave LN5 ... 92 F2
Torgate La LN5 ... 93 A2
Torkington Gdns 9 PE9 ... 219 B5
Torkington St PE9 ... 219 A5
Torksey Ave LN1 ... 66 C2
Torksey Dr DN33 ... 191 B3
Torksey Ferry Rd DN22 ... 65 B5
Torksey Pl 2 DN33 ... 191 B3
Torksey St
14 Kirton in Lindsey DN21 ... 30 B1
Rampton DN22 ... 65 A5
Tor-o-moor Gdns 2 LN10 ... 97 E6
Tor-o-moor Rd LN10 ... 97 D5
Toronto St 2 LN2 ... 202 C3
Torpel Way 5 PE6 ... 173 C7
Torr St DN21 ... 197 D4
Torrington La
East Barkwith LN8 ... 71 A8
Fleet PE12 ... 159 B5
Legsby LN8 ... 58 C1
Torrington Rd
Lincoln LN2 ... 201 F8
Scunthorpe DN17 ... 184 C8
Torrington St DN32 ... 191 F5
Torskey Castle* LN1 ... 65 D5
Tortoiseshell Wood Nature Reserve* NG33 ... 152 B2
Tossey La LN11 ... 50 B2
Tothby Cl 1 LN13 ... 75 E3
Tothby La LN13 ... 75 E2
Totnes Rd DN33 ... 194 E6
Tottermire La 5 DN9 ... 27 D7
Touthill Cl PE1 ... 226 A2
Tow La 5 NG32 ... 117 F1
Towell Cl PE21 ... 209 B3
Tower Ave
Bracebridge Heath LN4 ... 205 F3
Lincoln LN2 ... 202 D4
Tower Cl
24 Mablethorpe & Sutton LN12 ... 64 B3
Woodhall Spa LN10 ... 97 F7
Tower Cres LN2 ... 202 D4
Tower Dr Lincoln LN2 ... 202 D4
Woodhall Spa LN10 ... 97 F7
Tower Espl PE25 ... 206 D3
Tower Gdns 1 LN2 ... 202 D4

Tower Hill
Kingston upon Hull HU13 178 E1
Westwoodside DN9 27 B2
Tower Hill Dr HU13 178 E1
Tower Hill Mews 2 HU13 178 E1
Tower House La 7 HU12 5 F8
Tower La LN4 94 B4
Tower Rd PE21 209 A5
Tower St 14 Boston PE21 208 F5
Gainsborough DN21 197 D5
Kingston upon Hull HU9 181 A6
Peterborough PE2 230 F8
Tower View
Kingston upon Hull HU10 178 C5
Sleaford NG34 212 B3
Towers The 2 PE25 206 D5
Towler St PE1 226 A3
Town Bridge 22 PE21 208 F5
Town Dam Dro PE11 144 F8
Town Dam La PE11 134 F2
Town Dro PE11 144 F8
Town End NG32 120 B2
Town Farm Cl 1 PE11 156 F8
Town Hall St 9 DN31 191 E7
Town Hill DN20 19 E4
Town Hill Dr DN20 19 E4
Town Rd Sleaford NG34 212 B1
Tetney DN36 36 D4
Town St Cottam DN22 65 B6
Immingham DN40 12 E4
South Somercotes LN11 50 E4
Westborough & Dry Doddington NG23 117 F3
Townfield La 5 PE20 135 C7
Towngate E PE6 217 C7
Towngate W PE6 217 A6
Towning Cl 9 PE6 217 D6
Townley Cl LN9 199 D1
Townsend Cl DN36 193 C1
Townsend Rd 6 PE8 172 B1
Townside DN40 12 D6
Toynton All Saints Prim Sch PE23 100 F6
Toynton Cl 3 LN6 205 B4
Toynton La PE23 101 B6
Toynton Rd DN33 191 B3
Trader Bank
Frithville PE22 125 F8
Sibsey PE22 113 A2
Trafalgar Ave
Grimsby DN34 190 D5
Skegness PE25 206 D1
Trafalgar Ct 2 LN4 203 B2
Trafalgar Pk DN36 195 D7
Trafalgar Pl 3 PE21 208 E4
Trafalgar Sq
Long Sutton PE12 216 B4
4 Sutton on Trent NG23 91 A8
Trafalgar St 5 HU3 180 D7
Trafford Rd
Kingston upon Hull HU10 178 E8
13 Wisbech PE13 170 E1
Trafford St DN15 183 B4
Traffords Way DN20 30 F6
Train Gate 23 DN21 30 B1
Tranby Ave HU13 178 D2
Tranby Dr DN32 192 B4
Tranby La
Anlaby with Anlaby Common HU10 178 B5
Swanland HU14 3 C6
Tranby Mdws Pk HU13 178 C3
Tranby Ride HU10 178 C5
Tranmere Cl HU3 180 B5
Travellers Sch The PE1 226 F6
Travis Ave 16 DN8 15 B8
Travis CE Fst Sch DN7 14 E4
Travis Cl 14 DN8 15 B8
Travis Gr 15 DN8 15 B8
Traviss Cl 2 DN16 185 B8
Treadgold Ave 10 NG31 129 E5
Treading Bank PE13 169 C4
Treasure La LN11 49 F5
Treece Gdns 10 DN18 3 F1
Trehampton Dr 4 DN21 53 A5
Trelawney Cres 2 LN1 201 E8
Tremayne Ave 1 HU15 2 C5
Trenchard Ave 1 NG24 104 C5
Trenchard Cl DN40 186 E5
Trenchard Rd
9 Ashby De La Launde & Bloxholm LN4 108 A7
8 Mablethorpe/Sutton on Sea LN12 64 B3
Trenchard Sq
2 Scampton Airfield LN1 67 F5
1 Waddington LN5 94 A7
Trent La Besthorpe NG23 91 B7
Girton NG23 78 B1
Newton on Trent LN1 65 C1
South Clifton NG23 78 B5
Trent Port Rd DN21 65 D8
Trent Rd
Grantham NG31 210 D2
Keadby with Althorpe DN17 17 D6
Trent Side DN17 7 F1
Trent St
Gainsborough DN21 197 D3
Scunthorpe DN16 183 B2
Trent View
Keadby DN17 17 D5
Trent View *continued*
Marton DN21 65 E8
Trent Wlk 18 HU15 2 D5
Trentholme Dr 37 DN17 29 D7
Trenton Ave HU4 179 B6
Trentside
Gainsborough DN21 197 B8
Keadby with Althorpe DN17 17 C3
Trentvale Prep Sch DN17 17 D6
Tresham Rd PE2 229 D3
Trevitt Cl 1 NG34 212 B7
Trevor Cl 22 DN37 23 F1
Trevose Dr 2 LN6 205 A1
Triangle Dr 9 HU14 3 A4
Triangle The 13 HU14 3 A4
Trienna PE2 230 B5
Trinity Cl
10 Crowland PE6 166 E1
10 Goxhill DN19 12 A8
Trinity Ct 9 DN20 19 D4
Trinity Gr HU13 178 E2
Trinity La LN11 198 D6
Trinity Rd
Cleethorpes DN35 192 E5
Newark-on-Trent NG24 104 A2
Scunthorpe DN16 185 A4
Stamford PE9 219 A6
Wisbech PE13 170 E1
Trinity St Boston PE21 208 E4
Gainsborough DN21 197 D3
3 Grimsby DN31 189 C1
Kingston upon Hull HU3 180 C7
3 Peterborough PE1 226 A2
Trinity Wlk 1 DN18 3 F1
Tritton Rd LN6 201 D2
Trollope St LN5 234 B1
Troon Cl
Grantham NG31 211 D8
7 Heighington/Washingborough LN4 203 D1
11 Stamford PE9 218 E6
Troon Rd DN7 14 D4
Trotters La 2 NG32 139 C7
Troughton Way 10 PE13 170 B2
Troutbeck Cl
6 Lincoln LN2 202 A8
1 Peterborough PE4 221 D3
Troutsdale Gr HU9 181 F8
Truesdale Gdns PE6 164 E3
Trunch La PE24 90 D5
Trundle La 2 DN7 14 D8
Trunkass La DN37 34 D7
Truro Cl
6 Grantham NG31 210 F5
5 Sleaford NG34 212 C7
Truro Dr LN6 204 B8
Truro Way 2 PE11 214 C4
Trusthorpe Rd 3 LN12 64 C1
Tucker's Yd PE2 231 C7
Tuckers Nook PE6 173 C7
Tudor Cl
Northorpe PE10 164 C7
Peterborough PE4 221 C2
4 Sutterton PE20 136 A2
1 Toft Newton LN8 56 D5
Tudor Dr 4 Boston PE21 208 E7
Louth LN11 198 C4
Tudor Pk LN9 199 D4
Tudor Rd LN6 204 D6
Tudor Way PE12 215 D1
Tudworth Field Rd DN7 15 B5
Tudworth Rd DN7 15 A5
Tulip Rd 1 DN15 183 C3
Tulipwood Ave 11 LN6 200 C1
Tumby PE22 207 F8
Tumby La PE22 98 D2
Tumby Rd LN4 207 E6
Tummel Ct DN40 186 B2
Tunnard St
Boston PE21 208 F6
Grimsby DN32 192 B8
Tunnel Bank PE10 213 F3
Tunnel Rd DN20 196 F7
Turbary Rd DN9 27 B6
Turf Moor Rd 4 DN7 15 A3
Turnberry App DN37 194 C4
Turnberry Cl 1 NG31 211 D7
Turnberry Cl 4 LN10 97 C6
Turnbury Cl LN6 204 B7
Turner Ave 3 LN6 205 A6
Turner Cl 2 LN5 107 B8
Turner St
15 Kirton in Lindsey DN21 30 B1
Lincoln LN1 234 A4
Turner's La 17 HU14 3 A5
Turnor Cl 5 NG33 151 E6
Turnor Cres NG31 211 C5
Turnor Rd NG31 211 F4
Turnpike Cl
Great Gonerby NG31 210 D1
14 Wisbech PE13 170 E1
Turnpike Rd PE9 163 C2
Turnpole Cl 2 PE9 219 D7
Turnstone Way PE2 231 D7
Turpin Cl DN21 197 F5
Turves Rd PE6 175 A2
Tut Hole PE23 100 F7
Tuxhill Rd PE34 161 E1
Tweed Cl 3 LN9 199 D2
Twelve Foot Bank LN4 109 F5
Twelvetree Ave PE4 220 E5
Twenty Dro PE10 155 C3
Twenty Foot Bank LN4 110 C6
Twitchell 4 LN1 66 D7
Two Plank La PE11 214 B6
Two Pole Dro PE7 231 F1
Two Sisters Cl 8 PE12 160 E4
Twyford Cl 2 NG33 151 E6
Twyning Pl DN35 192 D7
Tydd Low Rd PE12 160 A3
Tydd Rd PE11 156 C6
Tydd St Giles Sch PE13 169 F6
Tydd St Mary CE (Aided) Prim Sch PE13 160 A1
Tydeman Cl DN16 185 A2
Tye's Dro PE6 165 D2
Tyghes Cl PE6 217 F5
Tyler Ave DN31 191 A7
Tyler Cres 2 PE22 126 E3
Tylers Cl PE24 90 D7
Tyndal Rd NG31 210 F5
Tyne Cl 4 LN6 205 A2
Tyne St HU3 180 B4
Tynedale Ct 5 DN3 14 A2
Tyrrell Pk PE1 226 D2
Tyson Cl NG31 211 C6
Tytton Cl 2 PE21 136 D8
Tytton La E PE21 136 D8
Tytton La W PE21 136 D8

U

Uffington Ave LN6 205 A6
Uffington Rd
2 Barnack PE9 172 D4
Stamford PE9 219 E6
Ulceby Cross LN13 88 B8
Ulceby Rd
Scunthorpe DN17 184 D5
South Killingholme DN39 12 C2
Wootton DN39 11 F3
Ulceby Sta DN39 12 C2
Uldale Cl LN6 200 C2
Uldale Way PE4 221 D2
Ullswater Ave PE4 221 B2
Ullswater Cl 6 LN6 205 A2
Ulster Ave DN33 191 D2
Ulster Rd DN21 197 D6
Ulverston Rd HU4 179 A3
Ulyett La DN17 28 C8
Unicorn Row 10 DN21 30 B1
Union Pl 1 PE21 208 F5
Union Rd Lincoln LN1 234 A3
Thorne/Moorends DN8 15 A8
Union St 2 Boston PE21 208 F5
Grantham NG31 211 A5
Holbeach PE12 159 A7
Louth LN11 198 B6
14 Market Rasen LN8 57 D8
Unity Ave HU13 178 F1
Unity Rd DN32 192 C6
Unity Sq 5 LN2 234 B2
University of Humberside HU1 180 F7
University of Lincoln LN6 234 A2
University of Lincolnshire & Humberside City Ctr Campus HU1 180 E6
Upgate LN11 198 B5
Upland Cl LN9 199 A5
Uplands PE4 221 A5
Uplands Dr NG31 211 D6
Upper Burgess St
1 Grimsby DN31 191 E8
3 Grimsby DN31 191 E7
Upper Cl The 8 LN1 66 D7
Upper Ings La DN22 52 D2
Upper Kenyon St 9 DN8 15 A8
Upper Lindum St LN2 234 C3
Upper Long Leys Rd LN1 234 A4
Upper Row NG22 65 A1
Upper Saxon St LN1 234 A4
Upperthorpe Hill DN9 27 A2
Uppingham Rd 7 LN12 64 C1
Upsall Rd 9 PE22 126 E3
Upton Cl
Peterborough PE3 225 A2
Peterborough PE2 231 E5
Upton Rd DN21 53 B4
Upton Wlk DN21 197 F3
Urban St LN5 205 D6
Uredale Pl DN16 185 E5
Usher Art Gall* LN2 234 B3
Usher Gn 3 Lincoln LN6 205 B7
4 Lincoln LN6 205 B6
Usher Jun Sch The LN6 205 B7
Utgard Way 4 DN33 191 B2
Utterby Dr 1 DN34 191 C5
Utterby Prim Sch DN36 48 D5

V

Vacherie La LN4 109 F3
Valda Vale DN40 186 A4
Vale of Ancholme Sch DN20 196 B4
Vale Rd
Gonerby Hill Foot NG31 210 F8
10 Spilsby PE23 101 A8
Vale The HU10 178 B7
Vale View NG23 117 F5
Valence Rd PE2 229 F4
Valentine Cl
Boston PE21 209 C3
1 Kingston upon Hull HU4 179 A2
Valentine Rd LN6 201 C1
Valiant Rd
6 Coddington NG24 104 C5
Manby LN11 62 C5
Valletta St HU9 5 E8
Valley Dr HU10 178 B7
Valley La
Long Bennington NG23 117 B4
Swaby LN13 74 E4
Valley Rd
Grantham NG31 210 C4
1 Waddington LN5 93 E8
Valley View 8 NG24 104 D5
Valley View Dr DN16 185 A2
Valliant St 7 LN5 94 A7
Vampire Rd LN11 62 C5
Van Gogh Dr 8 PE11 214 B3
Vancouver Cres DN17 184 E4
Vane St HU3 180 D7
Vanessa Dr DN21 197 C7
Vanessa Rd LN11 198 A4
Vanguard Ct 4 NG34 212 A3
Vanwall Dr 8 LN5 93 F7
Varah Cl 39 DN18 10 E8
Varlow Rd 8 LN7 33 B4
Varsity Cl 4 DN7 26 A8
Vasey Cl LN1 66 E2
Vaughan Ave
Bottesford NG13 128 B6
Grimsby DN36 192 B4
Vauxhall Rd
12 Boston PE21 209 A5
Bracebridge Heath LN4 205 F2
Veal St 1 DN31 191 C7
Velden Way 5 LN8 57 D7
Venables Cl 13 PE24 102 E7
Vence Cl 1 PE9 219 A5
Venom Rd LN11 62 C5
Ventnor Ave NG31 210 E4
Venture Way NG31 210 D2
Verdun Cl LN1 201 E7
Vere Rd PE1 225 F7
Vere St LN1 201 F6
Vere Terr DN31 191 C8
Vergette Rd PE6 220 D8
Vergette St PE1 226 B3
Vermont Gr PE3 225 E1
Vernatts Gn PE11 214 C7
Vernon Ave NG31 210 F8
Vernon Rd PE25 206 C4
Vernon St LN5 201 D1
Vicar La 2 HU1 180 F5
Vicarage Ave
4 Wrawby DN20 20 E3
2 Wrawby DN20 196 F6
Vicarage Cl
5 Collingham NG23 91 D5
4 Cowbit PE12 167 B8
Holbeach PE12 158 D1
Vicarage Cres 4 DN15 8 B5
Vicarage Dr LN6 200 B3
Vicarage Dro PE20 134 D5
Vicarage Farm Rd 5 PE1 226 D3
Vicarage Gdns
2 Brough HU15 2 C6
Scunthorpe DN15 182 F2
1 Wrawby DN20 20 E3
Vicarage La
Beckingham DN10 40 B1
Broughton DN20 19 E1
Cadney DN20 31 D6
4 Carlton-le-Moorland LN5 92 E1
3 Carlton-le-Moorland LN5 105 E8
Dunston LN4 95 C6
Elsham DN20 20 F7
Grasby DN38 32 E7
Harmston LN5 93 F5
1 Helpringham NG34 133 D7
1 Immingham DN40 12 E4
3 Kingston upon Hull HU13 178 E1
4 Long Bennington NG23 117 D3
Long Sutton PE12 216 D2
11 Lutton PE12 160 A8
21 Nettleham LN2 68 C2
1 Scawby DN20 30 E8
Scopwick LN4 95 C1
9 Scothern LN2 68 F4
4 Sibsey PE22 113 B1
South Clifton NG23 78 C5
Wainfleet All Saints PE24 102 D1
19 Wellingore LN5 107 A7
Wootton DN39 11 E3
Vicarage Pk 4 DN15 9 D1
Vicarage Rd
3 Heckington NG34 122 E3
Willoughton DN21 42 E4
Wrawby DN20 196 F6
Vicarage Way PE7 233 D5
Vicar's Wlk 6 DN17 16 D7
Viceroy Dr PE11 156 F8
Vickers La 4 LN11 198 B5
Victor Dr 1 LN6 204 C1
Victor St Grimsby DN32 189 C1
Kingston upon Hull HU9 181 C8
Victor Way
Bourne PE10 213 E3
10 Waddington LN5 94 A7
Victoria Ave
1 Hatfield DN7 14 E4
Sleaford NG34 212 C3
1 Woodhall Spa LN10 97 D5
Victoria Bank NG34 133 B1
Victoria Cl
Gainsborough DN21 197 F2
Victoria Cl *continued*
2 Marshchapel DN36 37 C2
2 Stainforth DN7 14 C5
Victoria Ct 5 DN15 8 B5
Victoria Dock Prim Sch HU9 181 B6
Victoria Dr 5 DN18 3 E1
Victoria Gr
Heighington/Washingborough LN4 203 D1
Morton PE10 154 D7
Victoria Pas LN1 234 A3
Victoria Pier* HU1 181 A5
Victoria Pl
8 Boston PE21 208 F4
3 Bourne PE10 213 E4
Peterborough PE1 225 F4
Victoria Rd
Barnetby le Wold DN38 21 B4
10 Keelby DN41 23 A5
Louth LN11 198 C7
Mablethorpe/Sutton on Sea LN12 64 B3
2 Market Rasen LN8 57 E8
Scunthorpe DN16 185 A5
Skegness PE25 206 B3
Stamford PE9 219 B6
Victoria Ret Pk DN31 189 A1
Victoria St
Billingborough NG34 133 B1
3 Billinghay LN4 109 F6
Grantham NG31 211 A2
4 Holbeach PE12 215 E2
Kingston upon Hull HU13 179 A1
Lincoln LN1 234 A3
Peterborough PE1 226 A5
Peterborough PE2 230 F6
10 Spalding PE11 214 D4
3 Wragby LN8 70 D5
Victoria St N DN31 189 A1
Victoria St S 1 DN31 191 E7
Victoria St W
6 Grimsby DN31 191 E7
3 Grimsby DN31 191 D7
Victoria Terr LN1 234 A3
Victoria Way DN31 188 D2
Victory Cl 6 PE12 157 F6
Victory Ct 1 PE11 214 C3
Victory Way
2 Barton-upon-Humber DN18 3 F1
8 Grimsby DN34 190 D4
Viersen Platz PE1 226 A1
Viking Cl 6 Bourne PE10 213 C6
Immingham DN40 186 A4
7 Swineshead PE20 135 B7
11 Waddington LN5 93 F7
Viking Sch The PE25 206 B4
Viking Way
32 Metheringham LN4 95 C3
7 Northorpe PE10 164 C8
Spalding PE11 214 F2
Villa Cl PE12 216 A5
Villa La PE20 135 B7
Village Farm Dr 5 LN1 66 C7
Village St
Burton Coggles NG33 152 C8
Easton NG33 139 F2
Pickworth NG34 142 A8
Sedgebrook NG32 128 F4
Woolsthorpe By Belvoir NG32 128 D1
Village The PE2 230 B5
Ville Rd DN16 185 D6
Vincent Cl 3 HU4 179 A2
Vine Cl 13 NG13 128 A5
Vine Cres 8 PE21 136 D8
Vine Ct 3 NG34 133 B1
Vine Rd
6 Skegness PE25 103 E4
2 Skegness PE25 103 E4
Vine St
Billingborough NG34 133 C1
12 Grantham NG31 211 A5
Lincoln LN2 234 C2
Spalding PE11 214 D4
Stamford PE9 219 C5
Vinegarth 3 DN9 27 E6
Vinehall Rd 3 DN9 27 C2
Vineyard Cl PE1 226 D5
Vineyard Rd PE1 226 B2
Vinters Way PE22 126 E3
Vintners Cl PE3 225 D3
Violet Cl
4 Humberston DN35 192 E1
Morton PE10 154 D6
Virginia Cl 1 PE3 225 A2
Virginia Dr LN11 198 E5
Viscount Rd PE2 231 A6
Viscount Way 6 DN36 36 D8
Vista The 3 PE11 214 D3
Visual Arts Ctr* DN15 183 C3
Vivian Ave DN32 192 B5
Vivian Cl 1 NG31 210 F8
Vixen Cl PE7 233 F6
Voases Cl HU10 178 E6
Voases La HU10 178 E6
Vulcan Cres LN6 204 C2
Vulcan Dr 4 LN1 67 F5
Vulcan St 9 LN5 94 A7
Vulcan Way DN7 15 A1
Vyner Cl 15 LN12 64 B3

W

Waby Cl DN37 190 D7
Waddingham Pl
5 Habrough DN40 22 E8
New Waltham DN36 195 D5
Waddingham Prim Sch DN21 43 D7
Waddingham Rd LN7 31 F1
Waddington Dr 1 DN17 184 E3
Waddington La NG23 91 C7
Waddington Pl 5 DN34 191 A5
Waddingworth Gr LN2 202 A8
Wade Pk Ave PE6 217 C4
Waggoners Way PE10 154 C6
Waggoners Wlk PE22 113 B1
Waggons Way 4 DN7 14 C5
Wainer Cl LN6 204 C5
Wainfleet Magdalen Sec Sch PE24 102 D2
Wainfleet Rd
Boston PE21 209 D7
Croft PE24 102 D7
Firsby PE23 101 F6
Fishtoft PE21 209 D7
Grimsby DN33 191 B3
Irby in the Marsh PE24 102 B6
Skegness PE25 206 A3
Thorpe St Peter PE24 102 C3
Wainfleet Sta PE24 102 D1
Wainman Rd PE2 230 D5
Wainwell Mews 3 LN2 234 C3
Wainwright PE4 220 E5
Waithe La DN37 35 E4
Wake Rd PE1 226 B2
Wake St LN1 234 A4
Wakefield Ave DN21 29 D4
Wakefield Cl NG31 210 C4
Wakerley Dr PE2 230 C7
Wakerley Rd 6 DN21 29 C3
Wakes Cl 1 PE10 213 E4
Walbury Cl 4 LN5 205 D2
Walcot Bar NG34 132 D2
Walcot Cl LN6 204 F6
Walcot La NG34 142 C8
Walcot Rd
Alkborough DN15 8 B8
Ufford PE9 172 F3
Walcot Way 2 PE9 218 E6
Walcott Prim Sch LN4 109 C7
Walcott Rd LN4 109 E6
Walcott St HU3 180 C4
Waldeck St LN1 234 A4
Walden Gdns 1 PE21 208 E4
Waldo Rd LN4 205 F5
Waldorf Rd DN35 193 A1
Walesby Cl DN33 194 D8
Walesby Hill LN8 46 B3
Walesby La LN8 46 B2
Walesby Rd
Market Rasen LN8 57 E8
Middle Rasen LN8 45 E1
Scunthorpe DN17 184 E4
Walford Cl 2 NG13 128 A5
Walford Dr LN6 205 A6
Walgrave PE2 230 B4
Walk La
Humberston DN36 36 C7
4 Irby DN37 34 D7
Langton By Wragby LN8 70 F4
Walker Ave DN33 194 F8
Walker Cl 1 DN15 8 E7
Walker Dr 4 DN15 9 A5
Walker Rd PE6 220 D7
Walker St HU3 180 C5
Walkergate 14 LN11 198 B5
Walkeringham Prim Sch DN10 39 F3
Walkeringham Rd
Beckingham DN10 40 A2
Gringley on the Hill DN10 39 D2
Walkerith Rd
East Stockwith DN21 40 B5
Gainsborough DN21 197 B8
Morton DN21 40 D3
Walker's Cl 5 DN38 21 B4
Walkers Cl 4 NG13 128 B5
Walkers Ct 20 DN17 29 D7
Walkers Way
Barrowby NG32 210 A3
Peterborough PE3 224 F3
Ulceby DN39 12 B2
Walkington Way 18 LN12 77 A7
Walks Rd NG34 120 F1
Walks The 4 PE9 171 B1
Wall St
Gainsborough DN21 197 D3
Grimsby DN34 191 A7
Wallace's Dro PE6 176 D4
Walled Gdn The 5 LN5 93 F5
Waller St HU9 181 C8
Walliker St HU3 180 A6
Wallingfen La HU15 1 B8
Wallis Ave LN6 205 B4
Wallis Rd LN11 198 D5
Wallisgate PE12 158 C7
Walls Ave 5 PE24 102 E7
Wall's La PE25 90 E2
Walmer St 1 LN2 202 C3
Walmsgate DN34 191 B4
Walmsgate Pl 3 DN33 191 B4
Walmsley St HU3 180 D7
Walnut Cl
5 Newborough PE6 174 E4
14 Ruskington NG34 108 E2
2 Waddington LN5 93 E8
Walnut Cres DN35 192 D2
Walnut Dr 1 DN20 30 F7
Walnut Gr 3 NG33 151 E7
Walnut Pl LN5 234 B1
Walnut Rd
3 Bottesford NG13 128 A5
Kirton PE20 136 C6
Walnut Way DN17 29 C7
Walnutgarth 6 NG34 212 F3
Walpole Bank PE14 170 F7
Walsall Garth HU4 179 B4
Walsingham Ct 3 PE13 170 C1
Walsingham Way 13 PE6 175 A1
Waltham Cl 9 LN6 204 C6
Waltham Grange 5 DN35 192 F3
Waltham Mus of Rural Life* DN37 194 D3
Waltham Rd
Barnoldby Le Beck DN37 194 A3
Birchwood LN6 204 B6
Brigsley DN37 194 C1
Croxton Kerrial NG32 138 A4
Grimsby DN33 194 F8
Waltham St 1 HU1 180 F6
Waltham Windmill* DN37 194 E3
Walton Comp Sch PE4 221 A2
Walton Gdns NG31 211 A2
Walton Girls High Sch The NG31 210 F1
Walton Gr DN33 191 C4
Walton Heath Cl 2 NG31 211 D7
Walton Infants Sch PE4 221 A1
Walton Jun Sch Cty PE4 221 A1
Walton Pk PE4 221 A1
Walton Rd
7 Leverington PE13 170 B2
Marholm PE6 220 C1
Wisbech PE13 170 E1
Walton St HU3 180 A7
Walton St Leisure Ctr HU3 180 A6
Walton Way 3 NG32 139 C7
Wandell's View HU15 2 C8
Wansbeck Rd 8 NG34 121 B7
Wansford Rd PE8 222 A3
Wanton La PE34 161 F3
Wanton's Cross Gate PE12 159 D2
Wanton's La PE12 159 E2
Wapping La DN21 65 E8
War Meml Hospl LN9 199 C4
Warbon Ave PE1 225 F7
Ward Cres PE21 209 E4
Ward St DN35 192 C8
Wardall St DN35 192 F6
Wardentree La PE11 157 A8
Wardour Dr NG31 211 F5
Ward's La PE22 114 A3
Wareley Rd PE2 225 F1
Wares Way 5 DN15 182 B3
Wargate Field La PE11 145 C5
Wargate Way PE11 145 B6
Waring St LN9 199 B3
Warley Ave 1 DN16 185 C8
Warley Dr DN16 185 C8
Warley Rd DN16 185 C7
Warneford Rd DN35 192 D8
Warping Way 2 DN15 182 B3
Warren Cl DN21 197 B6
Warren Rd
North Somercotes LN11 51 A6
Scunthorpe DN15 183 B5
5 Thorne/Moorends DN8 15 B7
Wothorpe PE9 219 C1
Warren Way NG31 211 F7
Warrendale 12 DN18 10 E8
Warrenne Cl 21 DN7 14 D4
Warrenne Rd DN7 14 D4
Warth La PE25 206 A5
Warwick Ave DN33 191 A4
Warwick Cl
9 Grantham NG31 210 D5
4 Hatfield DN7 14 F3
2 Saxilby with Ingleby LN1 66 C2
Warwick Dr 24 DN18 10 E8
Warwick Rd
7 Chapel St Leonard PE24 90 D7
Cleethorpes DN35 192 D4
Louth LN11 198 B8
Newark-on-Trent NG24 104 B2
Peterborough PE4 221 A2
Scunthorpe DN16 183 C1
Warwick St HU9 181 B7
Wascana Cl HU4 179 B3
Wasdale Cl 2 LN6 200 C1
Wasdale Gdns 1 PE4 221 E2
Wash Bank PE12 167 A5
Wash Dike La PE22 115 A6
Wash Rd Fosdyke PE20 146 D7
Kirton PE20 136 D4
Washdike Dro PE11 135 C1
Washdike La
Croft PE24 102 E4
Donington PE11 135 A1
Stoke Rochford NG33 140 A3
Toynton St Peter PE23 101 B6
Washdike La *continued*
Wainfleet St Mary PE24 102 C1
Washdike Rd
Algarkirk PE20 136 B1
Kirton PE20 136 A6
Washdyke La
Belton & Manthorpe NG32 130 A6
Boston PE21 208 B7
Cumberworth LN13 89 E8
Elsham DN20 20 D6
2 Glentham LN8 43 F1
Immingham DN40 186 B5
Leasingham NG34 121 B7
Mumby LN13 76 F1
Nettleham LN2 68 B2
Old Leake PE22 113 F4
Osgodby LN8 45 A3
Washdyke Rd 7 NG32 106 C1
Washdyke Ret Pk DN40 186 C4
Washingborough Prim Sch LN4 203 C2
Washingborough Rd
Heighington/Washingborough LN4 81 E4
Lincoln LN4 202 D1
Washinghall La DN17 7 A2
Washington Cl 6 LN4 207 C4
Washington Dr 5 LN8 56 D5
Washington St 4 DN21 197 D2
Washtub La NG23 91 E6
Washway Rd
Fleet PE12 159 B8
Holbeach PE12 215 C6
Moulton PE12 146 F4
Wass La LN8 71 E5
Wassand St HU3 180 C4
Waste Gn La PE20 146 C7
Water Bank DN9 26 E5
Water End
Marholm PE6 220 B1
Peterborough PE7 229 A5
Water Gate
Quadring PE11 145 B8
Sleaford NG34 212 D4
Water La
1 Ancaster NG32 120 A2
Bourne PE10 213 D2
Castle Bytham NG33 152 D1
Castor PE5 223 F1
6 Colsterworth NG33 151 D7
Gunby & Stainby NG33 151 B5
5 Hagworthingham PE23 87 A4
4 Lincoln LN6 93 C8
Lincoln LN1 234 A2
1 Long Bennington NG23 117 D4
12 South Witham NG33 151 D2
4 Spalding PE11 214 D2
Threekingham NG34 132 F3
Thurlby LN5 92 E3
Thurlby PE10 164 C8
2 West Halton DN15 8 E7
Water Mill La PE23 100 F6
Water Mill Rd 2 LN9 199 B4
Water Side DN15 2 B1
Water St PE9 219 C4
Waterbelly La PE20 136 A1
Waterfall Gdns 2 PE6 174 E4
Waterford La LN3 203 D5
Waterfurlong PE9 219 A4
Watergall
1 Peterborough PE3 220 F1
Peterborough PE3 225 A8
Watergall CP Sch PE3 225 B8
Watergate
11 Grantham NG31 211 A5
10 Stamford PE9 219 C5
Waterhouse La HU1 180 E5
Watering Dyke Houses LN2 67 F4
Waterlees Rd PE13 170 D1
Waterloo Cl 1 NG32 119 B7
Waterloo Dr
8 Grimsby DN33 191 B2
Morton PE10 154 D6
Waterloo La LN6 200 B3
Waterloo Paddock LN5 106 D3
Waterloo Rd
Mablethorpe/Sutton on Sea LN12 64 B4
Peterborough PE1 226 A5
Waterloo St
Kingston upon Hull HU2 180 E8
Lincoln LN6 201 D2
4 Market Rasen LN8 57 D8
Waterlow Dr 22 DN15 9 A5
Watermill La 18 LN2 68 C2
Waters Edge DN20 196 A3
Waters' Edge Ctry Pk* DN18 3 F2
Waterside
5 Billinghay LN4 109 F5
3 Ryhall PE9 163 C1
Thorne DN8 14 F8
Waterside Bsns Pk HU13 3 F4
Waterside Cl 10 PE10 213 C7
Waterside Dr 5 DN31 191 D8
Waterside Gdns 5 PE12 215 E2
Waterside N LN5 234 B2
Waterside Rd DN18 3 E2
Waterside S LN5 234 B2
Waterslade Rd PE7 233 C4
Waterton Cl 2 PE6 217 E4
Waterton La DN7 14 D2
Waterwell La NG32 120 C4
Waterworks La PE6 220 B6
Waterworks St
1 Gainsborough DN21 197 D2
Immingham DN40 186 D5
Watery La Asterby LN11 72 F5
Butterwick PE22 126 F3
Goulceby LN11 72 D6
Lissington LN3 57 D1
Little Cawthorpe LN11 61 E2
Mareham Le Fen PE22 98 F4
Swaby LN13 74 E4
4 Welton/Dunholme LN2 68 E6
1 West Ashby LN9 85 E7
Wickenby LN3 70 A8
Watford Ave DN34 190 F4
Watkin St N DN31 188 F1
Watkin St S 2 DN31 188 F1
Watkins La 2 DN22 52 B3
Watling Cl 7 PE10 213 C6
Watson Pk 4 DN10 52 B8
Watsons Croft 5 DN7 14 D6
Watt Cl PE4 221 C2
Watts La LN11 198 C4
Wauldby Cl 4 HU10 178 E7
Wauldby View 2 HU14 3 B7
Waumsley Way 1 LN13 75 E2
Wavell Dr LN2 202 E4
Waveney Cl 1 DN15 8 B5
Waveney Gr PE4 221 C2
Waverley Ave LN6 204 F3
Waverley Gdns
3 Leverington PE13 170 B1
Stamford PE9 218 F6
Waverley Pl 3 PE9 218 F6
Waverley St HU1 180 E5
Waverly Cl PE10 154 D7
Wayet Rd 6 PE11 156 E8
Wayford Cl PE3 225 A2
Wayside Cl
6 Holton le Clay DN36 195 D2
Scunthorpe DN16 185 A3
Wayside Dr DN36 195 C7
Weatherthorn PE2 230 C5
Weaver Rd LN6 204 B5
Weavers Croft 11 DN9 27 A2
Webb Cl 36 DN18 10 E8
Webb St LN5 205 D8
Webster Ave DN15 182 E3
Webster Cl 3 LN6 205 A5
Webster Way NG31 210 E7
Websters Cl PE6 220 D8
Wedgewood Cl 10 LN6 204 D7
Wedgewood Dr 4 PE11 214 B5
Wedgewood Gr 9 LN6 204 D7
Wedgewood Rd LN6 204 D7
Wedland La PE24 102 D3
Weekes Rd DN35 192 F4
Weelsby Ave DN32 191 F4
Weelsby Gr 1 DN32 191 E4
Weelsby Prim Sch DN32 192 A8
Weelsby Rd DN32 191 D5
Weelsby St
4 Grimsby DN31 189 C1
Grimsby DN32 192 A8
Weelsby St S DN32 192 A7
Weelsby View DN36 195 D8
Weelsby Way HU13 178 C2
Weeping Elm Way 6 DN16 185 D4
Weeton Way 5 HU10 178 E7
Wegberg Rd LN4 95 C7
Weir Cl 3 DN9 27 A2
Weir Farm 3 LN2 68 F4
Weir Rd DN9 27 A2
Weir St LN5 205 D8
Weir The HU13 178 E1
Weirs La PE22 126 D4
Wel Fen La NG23 117 E8
Welbeck Dr PE11 214 C5
Welbeck Pl 3 DN34 190 E4
Welbeck Rd DN35 192 C5
Welbeck St HU5 180 B8
Welbeck Way
Louth LN11 198 B6
Peterborough PE2 230 D7
Welbourn CE (Controlled) Prim Sch PE4 221 A4
Welbourn Gdns 9 LN2 202 A8
Welbourn Rd LN5 106 A5
Welbourn Wlk HU4 179 B6
Welbourne PE4 221 A4
Welbourne La PE12 215 C4
Welbourne's Cl 6 NG23 117 D4
Welbourne's La 7 NG23 117 D4
Welby Dr 3 PE11 145 B6
Welby Gdns
Grantham NG31 211 A6
Holbeach PE12 215 B2
Welby St 6 NG31 211 A4
Weldon Rd DN21 42 E1
Welham St NG31 211 B4
Welholme Ave DN32 191 D5
Welholme Jun & Inf Sch DN32 191 F6
Welholme Rd DN32 191 E6
Well High La LN13 75 D1
Well La LN2 234 B3
Well St
5 Bishop Norton LN8 43 D3
Messingham DN17 29 C7
Well Turn LN13 75 F1
Well Vale 2 DN33 194 D8
Well Vale Cl 28 PE24 90 D7
Welland Ave DN34 190 F4
Welland Bank PE6 166 C1
Welland Cl
Peterborough PE1 226 A7
9 Ruskington NG34 108 D2
1 Spalding PE11 214 C2
Welland CP Sch PE1 226 C8
Welland Ct 3 NG31 210 E2
Welland Dr 2 DN15 8 B5
Welland Hospl PE11 214 F6
Welland Mews PE9 219 C4
Welland Rd
Borough Fen PE1 174 E1
Boston PE21 208 B3
Lincoln LN1 201 D8
Peterborough PE1 226 B8
Spalding PE11 214 D3
2 Wittering PE8 172 B1
Welland Way PE6 217 E4
Wellbeck Cl 4 DN20 196 D4
Wellbeck Rd DN34 190 E4
Wellesley Cl 3 LN8 57 D8
Wellesley Way NG34 120 B8
Wellfield Cl 6 NG33 151 D2
Wellgarth DN32 192 B5
Wellhead La LN4 95 B7
Wellingore Rd
5 Lincoln LN2 201 F8
7 Lincoln LN2 202 A8
Wellington Ave 11 LN12 64 B4
Wellington Cl
7 Heckington NG34 122 E2
Skellingthorpe LN6 79 F6
Wellington Dr 1 NG31 211 D2
Wellington La HU3 180 D8
Wellington Rd
Boston PE21 209 B4
Mablethorpe/Sutton on Sea LN12 64 B4
Wellington Sq 12 LN5 94 A7
Wellington St
12 Gainsborough DN21 197 D3
Grimsby DN32 191 F8
Kingston upon Hull HU1 180 F5
Lincoln LN1 201 D4
4 Louth LN11 198 C6
Peterborough PE1 226 B2
7 Scampton Airfield LN1 67 E5
Wellington St Wes HU1 180 E5
Wellington Way
1 Elsham Wold Ind Est DN20 21 A8
Market Deeping PE6 217 B7
1 Skegness PE25 206 A5
Wellington Yd 4 PE23 88 A1
Wellowgate 7 DN32 191 D7
Wells Cl
Grantham NG31 210 C5
Heighington/Washingborough LN4 203 E1
Peterborough PE4 220 F3
Wells Cres DN35 192 E2
Wells Dr 5 LN8 57 E7
Wells La DN22 65 B7
Wells Rd DN37 23 D4
Wells St
1 Grimsby DN31 191 B7
Kingston upon Hull HU3 180 A5
Scunthorpe DN15 183 B4
Wells The 13 LN2 68 D6
Wellsted St HU3 180 C5
Wellsyke La LN10 98 A6
Welmore Rd PE6 220 D8
Welsdale Rd LN11 59 E2
Welton Cl 32 DN18 10 E8
Welton Gdns LN2 201 F8
Welton Low Rd HU15 2 C6
Welton Old Rd HU15 2 E6
Welton Rd Brough HU15 2 C5
Nettleham LN2 68 C3
Welton Wold View 9 HU14 3 B7
Welwyn Cl NG31 210 E1
Wembley Rd LN11 50 F7
Wembley St DN21 197 C4
Wendan Rd 9 DN8 15 A7
Wendover Cl
19 Humberston DN36 36 D8
Messingham DN17 29 D7
Rippingale PE10 142 F2
Wendover Mews PE10 213 E5
Wendover Rd 18 DN17 29 D7
Wendover Rise DN35 192 E5
Wenlock St HU3 180 C7
Wensleydale Cl 1 NG31 211 A8
Wensleydale Rd DN16 185 E6
Wensum Cl 4 PE11 214 F5
Wentworth Cl
Heighington LN4 203 E1
4 Skegness PE25 206 D6
1 Spalding PE11 214 C1
Willerby HU10 178 F8
Wentworth Cres 2 DN19 4 E2
Wentworth Dr
Dunholme LN2 68 E5
Grantham NG31 211 D8
25 Messingham DN17 29 D7
2 Saxilby with Ingleby LN1 66 D2
Wentworth Rd
Grimsby DN34 191 B7
Scunthorpe DN17 184 D2
Wentworth St 1 PE1 226 A1
Wentworth Way
Kingston upon Hull HU9 181 C7
7 Woodhall Spa LN10 97 C5
Wentworths The PE12 216 A4
Werneth Rd DN32 191 F8

Werrington Bridge Rd
PE6 221 B6
Werrington Ctr PE4 220 F4
Werrington Gr PE4 220 F2
Werrington Mews 5
PE4 221 A3
Werrington Parkway
PE6 220 C5
Werrington Pk Ave 2
PE4 221 A3
Werrington Sports Ctr
PE4 220 F4
Werry's La 4 PE10 213 C5
Wesley Ave 5 PE34 161 F3
Wesley Cl 4 Epworth DN9 27 E6
15 Metheringham LN4 95 C4
Sleaford NG34 212 C2
11 Terrington St Clement
PE34 161 F3
2 Winterton DN15 9 A5
Wesley Cres 2 DN35 192 E3
Wesley Ct 8 HU3 180 C5
Wesley Rd Brigg DN20 196 C3
Scunthorpe DN16 185 E7
9 Terrington St Clement
PE34 161 F3
Whaplode PE12 158 C7
Wesley St 19 DN21 30 B1
Wesley Way LN9 199 D3
Wesleyan Rd PE1 226 A7
Wesselow Rd LN4 207 F6
Wessex Cl
Peterborough PE2 231 D7
Sleaford NG34 212 B1
West Acridge DN18 3 E1
West Ave
Cranwell & Byard's Leap
NG34 120 B8
Grantham NG31 210 D3
6 Stainforth DN7 14 C6
West Bank
Crowland PE6 166 E1
Saxilby with Ingleby LN1 66 C2
Stainforth DN7 14 B7
Strubby with Woodthorpe
LN13 63 E2
West Bank Rd PE12 161 A8
West Banks NG34 212 C4
West Bight 1 LN1 234 B3
West Brook La NG23 91 D3
West Butterwick CE Prim Sch
DN17 28 D8
West Coates Rd DN31 188 D2
West Cob Gate PE12 157 F6
West Comm Cres
DN17 184 F8
West Comm Gdns
DN17 184 F7
West Comm La DN17 184 E7
West Comm N Rd DN17 29 A8
West Comm Sports Hall
DN17 184 E8
West Cross St 24 DN21 30 B1
West Ct 14 DN8 15 A7
West Dock Ave HU3 180 B4
West Dock St HU3 180 B3
West Dr Coningsby LN4 110 E8
Sudbrooke LN2 68 F3
West Dro PE12 168 C2
West Dro N PE12 168 C3
West Dro S PE12 168 C1
West Ella Rd
Kingston upon Hull
HU10 178 A7
Swanland HU14 3 C7
West Ella Way HU10 178 C7
West Elloe Ave PE11 214 E6
West End
Burgh le Marsh PE24 102 D8
Garthorpe & Fockerby
DN17 7 E5
Gorefield PE13 169 E3
Harlaxton NG32 139 B7
Hogsthorpe PE24 90 B7
Holbeach PE12 215 D2
Ingham LN1 54 F2
Langtoft PE6 164 E3
7 Spilsby PE23 87 F1
Swanland HU14 3 B6
Walcott LN4 109 C7
Winteringham DN15 2 A1
Yaxley PE7 233 D4
West End Cl 9 NG13 128 A6
West End Cres 9 PE23 87 F1
West End La DN36 37 B1
West End Rd
Boston PE21 136 D8
Epworth DN9 27 C8
2 Habrough DN40 22 E8
Kirton PE20 136 B7
Maxey PE6 217 A1
Ulceby DN39 11 F1
Wyberton PE21 208 B2
West Fen Drain Bank
PE22 112 D1
West Fen La PE22 100 A1
West Field La
1 Swanland HU14 3 B6
Thorpe on the Hill LN6 92 E8
West Gate
9 Ruskington NG34 108 E2
Wainfleet All Saints
PE24 101 E2
Weston PE12 157 D2
West Glanford Leisure Ctr
DN17 184 D3
West Gn
Kingston upon Hull HU10 3 C8
West Gn *continued*
29 Messingham DN17 29 D7
West Gr
7 Colsterworth NG33 151 E6
Kingston upon Hull HU4 179 D4
West Halton La DN15 8 C8
West Hann La DN19 4 C1
West Haven Way
DN40 186 B8
West Hill 1 HU13 3 E4
West La Baumber LN9 72 A1
Girton NG23 78 C1
Haltham LN9 98 C6
7 Keelby DN41 23 A4
Skidbrooke with Saltfleet Haven
LN11 51 A2
5 Winterton DN15 9 B5
West Lea DN33 194 F7
West Leys Pk 7 HU14 3 B6
West Leys Rd HU14 3 B6
West Marsh La
Barrow upon Humber DN19 4 B1
Goxhill DN19 5 A3
West Marsh Rd
Pinchbeck PE11 145 E1
Spalding PE11 214 F6
West Mid Mere Rd
DN40 12 D3
West Mill 1 PE9 171 C2
West Mill Gate 2 LN3 203 E6
West Moor Rd 1 DN10 39 F3
West Par
Kingston upon Hull HU3 180 C7
Lincoln LN1 234 A3
Peterborough PE3 225 D3
Spalding PE11 214 B4
Wisbech PE13 170 C1
West Parklands Dr 9
HU14 3 A5
West Rd
Billingborough NG34 133 B1
Bourne PE10 213 B4
Deeping St Nicholas
PE11 156 D3
Haconby PE10 154 C8
2 Keadby with Althorpe
DN17 17 C6
Pointon & Sempringham
NG34 143 A6
4 Ruskington NG34 108 D1
3 Ruskington NG34 108 D1
2 Tallington PE9 172 F7
Tetford LN9 73 E1
Thorney NG23 78 F8
1 Tydd St Mary PE13 170 C8
West Row 4 PE21 208 E4
West St Alford LN13 75 E2
Barkston NG32 119 A1
Barnetby le Wold DN38 21 B4
Billinghay LN4 109 F6
Boston PE21 208 E4
Bourne PE10 213 C5
Brant Broughton LN5 105 F5
Cleethorpes DN35 192 F6
Clipsham LE15 162 B7
7 Crowland PE6 166 E1
Easton on the Hill PE9 171 C3
Folkingham NG34 142 C8
Gainsborough DN21 197 B8
Hagworthingham PE23 87 A4
Helpston PE6 173 B4
Hibaldstow DN20 30 F5
Horncastle LN9 199 A3
Kingston upon Hull HU1 180 E6
Long Sutton PE12 216 B4
11 Navenby/Wellingore
LN5 107 A7
North Kelsey LN7 32 A4
Osbournby NG34 132 C5
1 Roxby cum Risby DN15 8 F3
Scawby DN20 30 E8
Scunthorpe DN15 183 A3
Stamford PE9 219 A4
Swaton NG34 133 C4
Thorne/Moorends DN8 15 A7
2 Timberland LN4 96 B1
West Halton DN15 8 E7
West/East Butterwick
DN17 28 C8
Winterton DN15 9 A5
West St Gdns 8 PE9 219 A5
West St Mary's Gate 10
DN31 191 D7
West Stonebridge
PE2 230 C5
West Syke La LN1 66 B7
West Terr DN20 196 B3
West Terr St 10 DN17 16 D7
West Town Cty Sch
PE3 225 E3
West View
3 Ancaster NG32 120 A3
5 Bardney LN3 83 B4
Messingham DN17 29 C7
16 North Ferriby HU14 3 A4
Scunthorpe DN17 184 E3
West View Cl 8 DN41 23 A5
West View Cres 24 PE24 90 D7
West Way PE25 206 D7
West Wells La 4 DN10 39 C1
Westbeck 2 NG34 108 D2
Westbeck La DN21 42 C5
Westborough La
NG23 117 D4
Westborough Way
HU4 179 B6
Westbourne Ave 3
HU13 178 E2
Westbourne Dr
22 Crowle DN17 16 D7
6 Glinton PE6 220 C8
Westbourne Gdns 5
PE11 214 D3
Westbourne Gr
6 Grimsby DN33 194 F8
Kingston upon Hull
HU13 178 D2
6 Lincoln LN1 201 D3
Westbourne Pk PE10 213 B5
Westbourne Pl 2 NG31 210 E4
Westbourne St 5 HU3 180 A4
Westbrecks La DN22 65 A7
Westbridge Rd PE21 208 A3
Westbrook Ave 1 PE2 230 F7
Westbrook Pk Cl 2 PE2 230 F7
Westbrook Pk Rd PE2 230 E7
Westbrooke Cl LN6 205 B8
Westbrooke Rd LN6 205 B8
Westburn Ave 4 DN19 4 E2
Westbury Pk 2 DN35 193 A1
Westbury Rd DN35 193 A1
Westby Rd
Bitchfield & Bassingthorpe
NG33 140 F2
Burton Coggles NG33 152 C8
Westcliff Gdns DN17 184 F7
Westcliffe Prim Sch
DN17 184 D6
Westcliffe Rd
Ruskington NG34 108 C2
21 Scotter DN21 29 C3
Westcliffe St LN1 201 D6
Westcombe Sq PE1 226 D4
Westcroft Dr 3 LN1 66 D3
West-dale Cres 2 DN21 30 B2
Westdale Dro PE11 134 C2
Westerdale 5 HU14 3 B7
Westerdale Gr HU9 181 E8
Westerdale Rd
2 Grantham NG31 211 A7
Scunthorpe DN16 185 D5
Westerly Way 1 PE11 214 A5
Western Ave
Brigg DN20 196 C5
Easton on the Hill PE9 171 C3
Holbeach PE12 215 C2
Lincoln LN6 205 C7
Peterborough PE1 226 B7
8 Saxilby LN1 66 C2
Western Cres LN6 205 C8
Western Dr
Balderton NG24 104 C1
11 Barton-upon-Humber
DN18 3 E1
9 RAF Cranwell NG34 120 C8
Western Gn DN15 2 A1
Western Outway
DN34 191 A4
Western Prim Sch
DN34 190 E5
Western Tech Sch The
DN34 190 F5
Westfield App LN2 203 A8
Westfield Ave
Boston PE21 208 D4
Greetwell LN2 203 B8
Grimsby DN33 191 C3
Westfield Cl 8 LN4 95 D4
Westfield Dr
Greetwell LN2 203 A8
22 Messingham DN17 29 D7
1 Pinchbeck PE11 156 E8
3 Skegness PE25 206 B4
11 Swineshead PE20 135 B7
Westfield Garth 2 DN17 16 E6
Westfield Gr DN35 192 D6
Westfield La
Collingham NG23 91 B4
Cumberworth LN13 89 D8
Kirk Bramwith DN7 14 B8
Westfield Pk 11 HU15 2 C6
Westfield Rd
Bardney LN3 83 D1
Barton-upon-Humber DN18 3 C1
Fishlake DN7 14 B8
13 Goxhill DN19 12 A8
6 Hatfield DN7 14 E4
Kingston upon Hull HU4 179 D5
Newton PE13 169 F5
Peterborough PE3 225 E4
Scunthorpe DN17 184 B6
Waltham DN37 194 C4
2 Wisbech PE13 170 E2
Yarburgh LN11 49 D3
Yaxley PE7 233 D5
Westfield Rise HU13 178 D2
Westfield St 4 LN1 201 D3
Westfield Villas 5 DN7 14 E4
Westfield Way PE6 164 E2
Westfields 1 Alford LN13 75 F2
Easton on the Hill PE9 171 C3
Westgate
Grantham NG31 211 A4
Grimsby DN31 188 F1
Kexby DN21 53 E4
Lincoln LN1 234 A3
Louth LN11 198 A5
Peterborough PE1 225 F2
Scotton DN21 29 C1
Sleaford NG34 212 C4
Westgate Jun Sch
LN1 234 A4
Westgate Pk 3 NG34 212 C4
Westgate Pl 7 LN11 198 B5
Westgate Rd DN9 16 D2
Westhall Cl 1 LN5 92 E1
Westhall Rd 16 LN2 68 D7
Westhaven 2 PE9 171 D3
Westhawe PE3 224 F7
Westhill Rd DN34 191 A5
Westholm 2 LN3 203 E5
Westholm Cl LN2 202 D8
Westholme Cl 11 DN15 8 B4
Westholme La DN38 21 C5
Westhorpe Rd PE11 144 F5
Westhouses PE22 112 F5
Westkirke Ave DN33 191 D1
Westlaby La LN3 69 E8
Westland Rd
Kingston upon Hull
HU10 178 B7
5 Westwoodside DN9 27 B2
Westlands Ave
Grimsby DN34 191 C5
4 Tetney DN36 36 D4
Westlands Rd HU5 179 B8
Westlode St PE11 214 D4
Westmere Cty Prim Sch
PE12 160 E4
Westminister Way 2
NG31 210 F5
Westminster Dr
Grimsby DN34 191 C6
14 Hatfield DN7 14 C2
1 Spalding PE11 214 B1
Westminster Gdns 24
PE6 175 A1
Westminster La 6 PE10 213 B5
Westminster Pl PE1 226 F5
Westminster Rd
5 Broughton DN20 19 D4
Lincoln LN6 204 D4
Westmoor La LN1 65 E2
Westmoreland Ave 14
LN1 67 E5
Westmoreland Cl 1 DN9 27 A2
Westmoreland Rd 2
PE12 157 F6
Westoby La DN19 11 C7
Weston Gr DN40 186 B5
Weston Hills CE (VC) Prim Sch PE12 157 D2
Weston Hills Rd PE12 157 B4
Weston Miller Dr 8
PE13 170 D1
Westonville 6 PE9 171 B1
Westover Dr 4 DN15 8 A4
Westport Rd 1 DN35 193 A1
Westrum La DN20 196 D2
Westry Cl
Barrowby NG32 210 A3
1 Leverington PE13 170 F1
Westry Cnr NG32 210 A4
Westside Ave NG31 139 E8
Westside Rd
Cranwell & Byard's Leap
NG34 107 E1
Grimsby DN31 188 F2
Westville Rd PE22 112 B2
Westward Cl 3 DN34 191 C5
Westward Ho 2 DN34 191 C5
Westward House
DN34 191 B5
Westway 18 LN2 68 D2
Westwick Dr LN6 205 B7
Westwick Gdns LN6 205 B6
Westwinds Gdns 19 DN15 9 A5
Westwold Rd 25 LN7 33 B4
Westwood
6 Broughton DN20 19 D4
5 Peterborough PE3 225 C4
Westwood Cl LN6 205 A8
Westwood Dr
Bourne PE10 213 B4
3 Kingston upon Hull
HU4 179 B6
Lincoln LN6 205 A8
Westwood Pk Cl PE3 225 C3
Westwood Pk Rd PE3 225 D2
Westwood Rd 1 DN41 23 F5
Westwoodside CE Prim Sch
DN9 27 B2
Wetherby Cl
3 Bourne PE10 213 C7
6 Market Rasen LN8 57 E7
Wetherby Cres LN6 204 F4
Wetherby Way 1 PE1 226 D3
Wetmoor La LN2 56 C1
Weydike Bank PE12 159 A4
Weyford Rd 4 DN35 193 A1
Weymouth Cl 10 LN5 205 D3
Weymouth Cres DN17 182 C1
Weymouth Way 4 PE1 226 D6
Whale Dro
Holbeach PE12 168 A1
Whaplode PE6 167 E1
Whalebone La NG31 140 B7
Whalley St PE1 226 B3
Whaplode CE Controlled Prim Sch PE12 158 C7
Wharf Rd Crowle DN17 16 D7
Grantham NG31 211 A4
8 Horncastle LN9 199 B4
13 Misterton DN10 39 F5
Stamford PE9 219 C4
Wharf St 20 PE12 160 E4
Wharf The DN36 37 A5
Wharfdale Cl 6 DN15 17 E6
Wharfe La
Kirkby on Bain LN10 98 C5
Tattershall LN4 207 D6
Wharfedale Dr 2 LN6 204 F3
Wharfedale Pl 1 DN16 185 E6
Wharfside Mews 6
NG34 212 D4
Wharncliffe Rd N
DN31 189 B3
Wharncliffe St HU5 180 A8
Wharton Rd DN21 41 A5
Wharton St DN31 191 B7
Whattoff Way PE6 164 D4
Whatton's Cl NG32 128 F5
Wheatfield Cl
5 Barnby Dun DN3 14 A3
Epworth DN9 27 F6
2 Kingston upon Hull
HU4 179 D2
Wheatfield Dr 7 DN37 194 C5
Wheatfield Rd LN6 200 C1
Wheatfields 1 PE12 158 B7
Wheatfield PE6 164 E2
Wheatgrass La NG32 119 B7
Wheatholme La NG23 78 D6
Wheatley Bank PE14 170 F1
Wheatley La
2 Carlton-le-Moorland LN5 92 E1
1 Carlton-le-Moorland
LN5 105 E8
Collingham NG23 91 D2
Wheatley Rd DN22 52 A3
Wheatmere Dro PE12 157 B5
Wheatsheaf Cl
3 Holbeach PE12 215 B2
Sibsey PE22 113 B2
Wheatsheaf La 4 NG23 117 D4
Wheel Yd PE1 226 A2
Wheeldon St 9 DN21 197 D3
Wheeler Cl PE21 209 A4
Wheeler Prim Sch
HU3 179 F5
Wheeler St HU3 179 F6
Wheelwright Cl PE10 154 C6
Wheelwrights Ct
NG34 109 B1
Whelpton Cl 7 LN9 199 D3
Whichcote Rd PE6 174 C7
Whimbrel Way
6 Long Sutton PE12 216 B4
New Waltham DN36 195 D7
Whin Moor La HU15 2 A7
Whins Gate DN17 7 A4
Whipchicken Rd PE6 167 B3
Whisby Ct DN36 195 E2
Whisby Nature Pk*
LN6 79 F1
Whisby Rd LN6 204 A4
Whisby Way LN6 204 C5
Whiston Cl 5 PE4 221 D2
Whiston Way 9 DN18 3 F1
Whitacre PE1 226 E6
Whitby Dr DN32 192 A5
Whitby St HU8 181 B8
White Croft PE3 225 B6
White Cross La 4 PE11 145 D2
White Gate LN9 73 E2
White Hart La 1 NG23 91 C4
White House Cl
29 Hatfield DN7 14 D4
4 Stainforth DN7 14 C7
White House Garth 19
HU14 3 A5
White House La
Boston PE21 209 D3
3 West Halton DN15 8 E8
White House Mews 16
HU14 3 A5
White La Harmston LN5 93 F5
Thorne DN8 15 A8
White Leather Sq
NG34 133 C1
White Row La LN12 64 C1
White St HU3 179 F5
White Wlk HU10 178 C6
Whiteacres 3 PE12 216 B4
Whitebeam Cl HU3 180 D5
Whitebread Rd PE20 136 A7
Whitecross Gate PE20 146 D8
Whitecross La NG34 121 F1
Whitecross St 12 DN18 10 F8
Whitefriargate HU1 180 F6
Whitegate Hill LN7 33 C3
Whitehall 5 PE11 145 C6
Whitehall Cres LN4 205 F4
Whitehall Gr LN1 234 A3
Whitehall Rd 6 DN35 193 A1
Whitehead Cl 5 LN12 64 B5
Whitehorse La 10 PE21 208 F4
Whitehouse Rd 1 NG34 108 E2
Whitemoor La NG23 91 C3
Whitepit Way LN13 74 D4
Whitepost Rd PE6 174 F3
Whites La LN5 92 E2
White's Rd DN35 192 F5
White's Wood La
1 Corringham DN21 53 A8
Gainsborough DN21 197 F4
Whites Wood La Jun Sch
DN21 197 F4
Whitestone Rd DN17 184 C6
Whitethorn Gr 7 LN6 200 C1
Whiteways PE2 229 D6
Whitewell Cl 4 DN21 30 B1
Whitfield Rd DN17 184 D6
Whitgift Cl 21 DN37 23 F1
Whitgift Sec Sch
DN37 190 D8
Whiting Sq PE21 208 F6
Whitley Cl 5 LN6 200 A4

- Whitley St 11 LN1 67 E5
- Whitley Way PE6 217 B7
- Whitman Cl 9 PE9 172 D3
- Whitman Rd DN17 184 C6
- Whitsed Rd 8 PE6 174 E5
- Whitsed St PE1 226 B3
- Whittington PE1 226 E7
- Whittle Cl 2 PE21 208 F1
- Whittlesey Rd
  - Peterborough PE2 231 B7
  - Thorney PE6 175 F1
- Whitton Rd
  - Alkborough DN15 1 C1
  - Whitton DN15 1 E2
- Whitwell PE4 221 E2
- Whitworth Way 12 LN8 57 D7
- Whoofer La DN21 40 E8
- Whyalla Cl 2 LN11 50 B8
- Whyche The LN4 109 E5
- Wicken La PE22 113 F3
- Wicken Way PE3 225 C6
- Wickenby Airport LN3 69 F8
- Wickenby Cl
  - 6 Grimsby DN34 190 F4
  - Lincoln LN6 205 A3
- Wickenby Cres LN1 201 E7
- Wickenby Rd LN3 57 D1
- Wickham Rd DN31 189 C2
- Wicklow Ave DN33 194 E8
- Wide Bargate 8 PE21 208 F5
- Widford Gn 8 DN7 14 D3
- Widow Fen La LN13 76 C3
- Wigford LN5 234 A1
- Wigford Way LN5 234 A2
- Wigg La PE24 90 D8
- Wigmore Dr PE7 231 F5
- Wignal's Gate PE12 215 A2
- Wigsley Cl 7 LN6 204 D6
- Wigsley Rd
  - 6 Birchwood LN6 204 D6
  - Harby NG23 79 B5
  - North Scarle LN6 78 E3
- Wigtoft Bank PE20 135 D1
- Wigtoft Rd PE20 135 F2
- Wike Gate Cl 4 DN8 15 B7
- Wike Gate Gr 2 DN8 15 B7
- Wike Gate Rd DN8 15 B8
- Wilberforce Dr 6 HU1 180 F7
- Wilberforce House* HU1 181 A6
- Wilberforce Rd PE1 225 E7
- Wilberforce St HU3 180 D6
- Wildfowlers Way PE12 148 F4
- Wildlake PE2 230 C5
- Wildmore Cl LN4 111 C6
- Wildmore Cres PE22 114 F6
- Wildshed La PE24 102 D7
- Wiles's La PE20 135 B4
- Wilford Gr PE25 206 C1
- Wilfred Ave NG24 104 B2
- Wilkie Cl DN15 182 C3
- Wilkie Dr NG34 142 C8
- Wilkinson Dr 9 LN8 57 B8
- Wilkinson Rd 7 NG32 117 F1
- Will Row LN12 63 C5
- Willders Garth PE12 215 F2
- Willerby Rd HU5 179 C8
- Willerton Rd 3 LN11 50 F7
- Willesby Rd PE11 214 E5
- Willesden Ave PE4 225 D8
- Willey's La PE24 90 B8
- William Alvey Sch NG34 212 E5
- William Barcroft Jun Sch DN32 192 C7
- William Farr CE Comp Sch LN2 68 D6
- William Gn Cl 9 LN12 76 F8
- William Harrison Sch DN21 197 E2
- William Hildyard CE (Aided) Prim Sch PE6 217 B5
- William Lovell CE Sch PE22 113 A7
- William St
  - Cleethorpes DN35 192 E5
  - 2 Grantham NG31 211 A3
  - Kingston upon Hull HU1 180 E5
  - 24 Saxilby LN1 66 D2
  - 3 Scunthorpe DN16 183 B2
- William Stukeley CE Prim Sch PE12 215 D2
- William Tow Cl 7 LN12 76 F8
- William Way PE25 206 B2
- Williams Cl 1 PE6 174 E5
- Williams Dr DN39 12 B1
- Williamson Ave PE3 225 E3
- Williamson St
  - Kingston upon Hull HU9 181 C7
  - Lincoln LN2 234 B4
- Williamson's Dro LN4 110 A7
- Willing Way DN32 191 F8
- Willingham Ave LN2 201 F8
- Willingham Hill LN8 58 E7
- Willingham La LN8 57 F6
- Willingham Rd
  - East Barkwith LN8 58 E1
  - Fillingham DN21 54 D4
  - Lea DN21 53 A5
  - Market Rasen LN8 57 E7
  - Marton DN21 53 B1
  - Tealby LN8 58 A7
- Willingham St DN32 191 E6
- Willington Rd PE20 136 A7
- Willis Cl LN1 234 A4
- Willonholt PE3 225 C7
- Willoughby Ave 2 PE6 217 C5
- Willoughby Branch Line Nature Reserve* LN13 89 A7
- Willoughby Cl
  - Corby Glen NG33 152 F7
  - Helpringham NG34 133 E7
  - Silk Willoughby NG34 121 B1
- Willoughby Ct PE1 226 E8
- Willoughby Dr 1 PE23 88 A1
- Willoughby Gall The* NG33 152 F8
- Willoughby Gr 5 DN34 190 F4
- Willoughby La
  - Authorpe LN11 74 F8
  - Muckton LN11 62 C1
  - Waddington LN5 205 C1
- Willoughby Rd
  - 16 Alford LN13 75 F2
  - Ancaster NG32 119 E2
  - Aunsby & Dembleby NG34 132 B4
  - Boston PE21 209 A7
  - Bourne PE10 213 E4
  - Cumberworth LN13 89 E8
  - 14 Hibaldstow DN20 31 A5
  - 11 Mablethorpe/Sutton on Sea LN12 64 C1
  - Scunthorpe DN17 184 E5
  - Sleaford NG34 120 F3
  - Stamford PE9 219 C7
- Willoughby Specl Sch PE10 213 D3
- Willoughby St 1 DN21 197 D3
- Willoughton Prim Sch DN21 42 D4
- Willoughton Rd 3 PE25 206 D2
- Willow Ave
  - 5 Misterton DN10 39 F5
  - Peterborough PE1 226 B7
- Willow Cl
  - Gainsborough DN21 197 B7
  - 10 Heckington NG34 122 E3
  - Horncastle LN9 199 A5
  - 6 Laceby DN37 23 E1
  - 17 Saxilby LN1 66 D2
  - Scopwick LN4 95 D1
- Willow Ct
  - Heighington/Washingborough LN4 203 C2
  - 1 Sleaford NG34 212 E3
- Willow Dr
  - 14 Barton-upon-Humber DN18 3 F1
  - 9 Bourne PE10 213 C7
  - 2 Coningsby LN4 207 D4
  - Kingston upon Hull HU10 178 D8
  - Louth LN11 198 C8
  - 35 Messingham DN17 29 D7
- Willow Dro PE6 174 E6
- Willow Gdns 2 DN19 11 D8
- Willow Gr
  - 1 Keadby with Althorpe DN17 17 D6
  - 7 Scawby DN20 30 F8
  - Scunthorpe DN16 185 C7
- Willow Hall La PE6 227 D6
- Willow Holt PE7 230 C3
- Willow La
  - 9 Cranwell NG34 107 F1
  - 3 Cranwell NG34 120 F8
  - Dunston LN4 95 C6
  - 6 Goxhill DN19 5 A1
  - 1 Goxhill DN19 12 A8
  - Grantham NG31 210 F2
  - Ruskington LN4 109 B3
- Willow Rd Lincoln LN6 204 F2
  - Stamford PE9 218 D7
- Willow Row PE11 214 E5
- Willow Row Bank LN11 62 F6
- Willow Wlk PE11 214 E5
- Willowbrook Dr DN20 196 E3
- Willowfield Ave 12 LN2 68 D2
- Willows Cl PE13 160 A1
- Willows La PE22 125 F7
- Willows Prim Sch DN37 190 E8
- Willows The
  - 6 Cranwell NG34 107 F1
  - 5 Crowland PE6 166 E1
  - Glinton PE6 220 D8
  - Kingston upon Hull HU13 178 E4
- Wilmington Dr 18 LN12 77 A8
- Wilsford La NG32 120 A2
- Wilson Cl 8 HU14 3 A4
- Wilson Ct LE15 162 A8
- Wilson St
  - Cleethorpes DN35 192 D8
  - Gainsborough DN21 197 B5
  - Kingston upon Hull HU10 178 E6
  - 4 Kingston upon Hull HU9 181 B7
  - Lincoln LN1 234 A4
- Wilton Ave 14 PE24 90 D7
- Wilton Cl PE3 225 C4
- Wilton Dr PE3 225 C4
- Wilton Rd DN36 192 D1
- Wilton St HU8 181 B8
- Wiltshire Ave DN15 8 B4
- Wiltshire Rd HU4 179 E2
- Wilyman Cl 21 LN12 77 A7
- Wimberley Cl 3 PE12 157 D7
- Wimberley Way
  - 8 Pinchbeck PE11 156 E8
  - 3 South Witham NG33 151 D2
- Wimbishthorpe Cl 3 NG13 128 A6
- Wimborn Ave DN34 191 B6
- Wimborne Dr 2 PE1 226 E7
- Winceby Ave DN31 191 B8
- Winceby Gdns LN9 199 D4
- Winchcombe Ave DN34 190 E4
- Winchelsea Prim Sch The NG34 108 D1
- Winchelsea Rd 14 NG34 108 E1
- Winchester Ave DN33 191 A3
- Winchester Ct 9 LN6 93 B8
- Winchester Dr
  - Bottesford DN16 185 C3
  - Heighington/Washingborough LN4 203 C1
  - 6 Mablethorpe/Sutton on Sea LN12 64 A3
- Winchester Rd
  - Grantham NG31 210 E4
  - 13 Hatfield DN7 14 D4
  - 8 Wainfleet All Saints PE24 102 D2
- Winchester Way
  - Peterborough PE3 225 E1
  - Sleaford NG34 212 C7
- Wincolmlee HU2 181 A7
- Windermere Ave
  - 4 Grimsby DN33 194 E7
  - Lincoln LN6 205 A2
- Windermere Cres DN36 192 E1
- Windermere Rd LN2 202 D8
- Windermere Way PE4 221 C3
- Windgate Way PE8 222 A6
- Windlass Cl 16 DN8 15 A8
- Windlesham Ave DN33 194 D7
- Windmill Cl
  - Holbeach PE12 215 B2
  - 4 Waddington LN5 93 F6
- Windmill Dr
  - Burgh le Marsh PE24 102 D8
  - 13 Heckington NG34 122 E2
- Windmill Gdns 3 PE13 170 E2
- Windmill La
  - 5 Alford LN13 75 F2
  - Gosberton PE11 144 F6
- Windmill St PE1 225 F5
- Windmill View 3 LN1 234 A4
- Windmill Way HU13 178 F1
- Windrush Dr PE4 221 D1
- Windsmoor Rd 15 LN8 47 B6
- Windsor Ave
  - Holbeach PE12 215 F2
  - Kingston upon Hull HU10 178 E7
  - 3 Peterborough PE4 225 C8
- Windsor Bank PE21 209 A3
- Windsor Cl
  - Collingham NG23 91 D4
  - 6 Keelby DN41 23 A5
  - 1 Sleaford NG34 212 B2
  - 4 Stamford PE9 219 B7
  - 6 Sudbrooke LN2 68 F2
- Windsor Cres
  - Boston PE21 209 A4
  - 1 Crowle DN17 16 C7
  - 4 Ingoldmells PE25 90 D3
  - Scunthorpe DN17 184 F2
- Windsor Ct 12 DN7 14 C2
- Windsor Dr 19 Caistor LN7 33 B4
  - Grantham NG31 211 E5
  - Peterborough PE2 231 D6
  - Spalding PE11 214 D2
  - Wisbech PE13 170 D2
- Windsor Gdns PE12 216 C5
- Windsor Gr 1 DN19 5 A1
- Windsor La DN17 16 C7
- Windsor Pk Cl 5 LN6 204 F1
- Windsor Rd
  - Cleethorpes DN35 192 C5
  - Crowle DN17 16 C7
  - Louth LN11 198 B8
  - Yaxley PE7 233 F6
- Windsor Terr 11 PE21 209 A5
- Windsor Way
  - Barnetby le Wold DN38 21 B5
  - Broughton DN20 19 E4
- Wine Hill La LN11 51 B5
- Winfrey Ave PE11 214 D4
- Wing Dr PE21 209 C4
- Wingate Rd DN37 190 D8
- Wingate Way PE10 213 E7
- Wingfield PE2 229 F3
- Winn La 4 LN9 86 B8
- Winn St Lincoln LN2 234 C2
  - 4 Scunthorpe DN16 183 B2
- Winniffe Gdns LN2 202 D7
- Winnowsty La LN2 234 C3
- Winship Cl 4 HU3 180 C5
- Winslow Dr DN40 186 B5
- Winslow Gate PE12 159 B8
- Winslow Gr
  - 3 Grimsby DN34 190 F4
  - 2 Grimsby DN34 190 F4
- Winslow Rd
  - 4 Boston PE21 209 C4
  - Peterborough PE3 225 C3
- Winsover Rd PE11 214 B3
- Winston Ave DN34 191 B6
- Winston Gdns PE21 209 A7
- Winston Rd PE23 100 F8
- Winston Way
  - 5 Brigg DN20 196 D4
  - Farcet PE7 231 C2
- Winterbeck Cl 5 NG13 128 A6
- Wintergold Ave PE11 214 A5
- Winteringham La DN15 8 E8
- Winteringham Prim Sch DN15 2 A1
- Winteringham Rd DN15 9 B6
- Wintern Ct 6 DN21 197 D2
- Winter's La
  - 9 Long Bennington NG23 117 D4
  - Long Sutton PE12 160 A3
- Winterton CE Inf Sch DN15 9 A5
- Winterton Comp Sch DN15 9 A6
- Winterton Cty Jun Sch DN15 9 A5
- Winterton Rd
  - Roxby cum Risby DN15 8 F2
  - Scunthorpe DN15 183 B4
  - Winteringham DN15 9 B8
- Winthorpe Ave PE25 206 D8
- Winthorpe Cl 17 LN6 204 D7
- Winthorpe Gr 16 LN6 204 D7
- Winthorpe Prim Sch NG23 104 C8
- Winthorpe Rd
  - Birchwood LN6 204 D7
  - Grimsby DN33 191 B3
  - 4 Kingston upon Hull HU13 179 A3
  - 8 Newark NG24 104 B7
- Winthorpe Way
  - Ingoldmells PE25 206 D8
  - Skegness PE25 90 E1
- Winton Rd 11 LN5 107 A8
- Wintringham 26 HU15 2 C6
- Wintringham Rd DN32 191 E6
- Wintringham Sec Sch DN32 191 E4
- Winwick Pl PE3 225 C5
- Winyates Prim Sch PE2 230 A3
- Wire Hill La LN8 70 E5
- Wirral Ave 7 DN34 190 F4
- Wisbech Rd
  - Long Sutton PE12 216 E1
  - Thorney PE6 176 A3
  - Walpole PE14 161 C1
  - Walsoken PE14 170 E2
  - Wisbech St Mary PE13 177 A2
- Wiseholme Rd LN6 200 B2
- Wiseman's Gate 1 PE12 157 D7
- Wiske Ave 7 HU15 2 D5
- Wistaria Rd PE13 170 E1
- Wisteria Ave LN4 81 D2
- Wisteria Dr DN41 23 F5
- Wisteria Rd PE7 233 D4
- Wisteria Way
  - Bourne PE10 213 B7
  - Scunthorpe DN16 185 E4
- Wistow Gr HU4 179 D5
- Wistow Way PE2 229 D6
- Witchford Cl 2 LN6 204 B6
- Witchford Rd 3 LN6 204 B6
- Witham HU9 181 B7
- Witham Bank
  - Dogdyke LN4 110 D8
  - Timberland LN10 97 C3
- Witham Bank E 4 PE21 208 E6
- Witham Cl Lincoln LN6 205 D5
  - 11 Ruskington NG34 108 D2
  - Stamford PE9 219 C6
- Witham Ct 2 PE21 208 E6
- Witham Dr 6 DN15 8 B5
- Witham Gdns PE21 208 E6
- Witham Gn PE21 208 E6
- Witham Hall Prep Sch PE10 163 D7
- Witham Pl PE21 208 E5
- Witham Rd
  - Gunby & Stainby NG33 151 C4
  - 5 Long Bennington NG23 117 D4
  - Thistleton LE15 151 C1
  - Woodhall Spa LN10 97 B5
- Witham St 3 PE21 208 F5
- Witham Town PE21 208 E6
- Witham View LN4 203 A2
- Witham Way PE4 221 D1
- Witham/Haven Mouth Nature Reserve* PE22 137 F6
- Withambrook Pk NG31 211 F7
- Withern Rd DN33 191 A3
- Withington St 1 PE12 160 E4
- Wittering Airfield PE8 171 F1
- Wittering Cl 5 LN6 204 D6
- Wittering Rd PE9 172 D3
- Witty St HU3 180 A3
- Wivell Dr 1 DN41 23 A5
- Woad Farm Rd PE21 209 B4
- Woad La Fishtoft PE22 137 C7
  - Grimsby DN31 188 A2
  - Long Sutton PE12 216 E5
- Woburn Ave LN1 201 E6
- Woburn Cl Louth LN11 198 B7
  - 4 Market Deeping PE6 217 A5
  - Peterborough PE3 225 A1
- Woburn Dr
  - Grantham NG31 211 F5
  - Thorney PE6 176 A2
- Woburn Gr 1 LN10 97 C5
- Woburn St HU3 179 F4
- Woffindin Cl 12 NG31 129 E5
- Wold Rd
  - Barrow upon Humber DN19 11 D7
  - Kingston upon Hull HU5 179 C8
  - Worlaby DN20 10 E1
- Wold View
  - 1 Brigg DN20 196 D4
  - 25 Brough HU15 2 C6
  - Caistor LN7 33 C4
  - Fotherby LN11 49 A2
  - Holton le Clay DN36 195 C2
  - 3 Nettleham LN2 68 D2
  - Rothwell LN7 33 F2
- Woldcarr Rd HU3 179 F6
- Wolds Cl 5 DN17 16 D7
- Wolf La PE13 169 F1
- Wolfreton Dr HU10 178 F6
- Wolfreton Garth HU10 178 D8
- Wolfreton La HU10 178 F8
- Wolfreton Rd HU10 178 F7
- Wolfreton Sch HU10 178 C7
- Wolla Bank Nature Reserves* PE24 77 D1
- Wollaston Rd
  - Cleethorpes DN35 192 E6
  - Peterborough PE3 225 C6
- Wolseley Cl PE7 233 D6
- Wolsey Dr 6 DN19 11 C7
- Wolsey Rd NG24 104 A6
- Wolsey Way LN2 202 D8
- Womersley Rd DN31 189 C2
- Wong Gdns NG32 210 A4
- Wong Row 10 NG31 211 A5
- Wong The LN9 199 B3
- Wongs La PE24 102 B7
- Wood Carr La DN9 16 C2
- Wood Cl
  - 14 Barton-upon-Humber DN18 3 E1
  - Grimsby DN33 194 F7
- Wood Dr 4 HU14 3 A4
- Wood End NG33 131 A1
- Wood Hill Rd DN21 29 B3
- Wood La Bardney LN3 83 B4
  - Beckingham DN10 52 A8
  - Croxton Kerrial NG32 138 A6
  - Gringley on the Hill DN10 39 C2
  - 1 Lincoln LN6 93 A8
  - Lincoln LN6 204 A1
  - Little Cawthorpe LN11 61 F2
  - Louth LN11 198 D4
  - Moulton PE12 158 A7
  - Norton Disney LN6 92 B3
  - Quadring PE11 135 C1
  - South Kyme LN4 109 F1
  - South Kyme LN4 123 B8
  - South Scarle NG23 91 F7
  - Sturton Le Steeple DN22 52 A3
  - Thurlby PE10 213 C1
- Wood La Prim Sch PE12 159 B6
- Wood Rd 24 LN13 75 F2
- Wood St 4 DN32 191 F8
- Wood Vale DN16 185 C3
- Wood View
  - Bourne PE10 213 C5
  - 1 Messingham DN17 29 D7
  - 3 Swanland HU14 3 B7
- Wood Way LN11 198 E5
- Woodale Cl 3 DN15 182 C6
- Woodapple Ct 4 DN41 23 E6
- Woodbank
  - Deeping St Nicholas PE11 166 C6
  - Skellingthorpe LN6 200 A5
- Woodbine Ave DN20 196 C4
- Woodbine St PE2 231 A8
- Woodbridge Rd NG34 212 E6
- Woodburn Cl LN1 201 E8
- Woodbyth Rd PE1 226 A6
- Woodclose Rd DN17 184 D6
- Woodcock St HU3 180 A4
- Woodcote Cl PE1 226 A7
- Woodcroft Cl 9 PE6 217 A5
- Woodcroft Rd
  - Marholm PE6 220 A3
  - 4 Saxilby LN1 66 C2
- Wooden Beck Hill DN10 39 E2
- Woodfield 7 PE9 171 B1
- Woodfield Ave LN6 200 C1
- Woodfield Cl
  - 9 Birchwood LN6 200 C1
  - 15 Humberston DN36 36 D8
  - Spalding PE11 214 F2
- Woodfield La HU13 178 C1
- Woodfield Rd
  - Gainsborough DN21 197 F5
  - Peterborough PE3 225 D3
- Woodgarr Ave 4 DN17 17 D6
- Woodgate PE6 173 C4
- Woodgate La
  - Beckingham LN5 105 C4
  - Kingston upon Hull HU5 179 F8
  - Maxey PE6 217 A1
- Woodgate Rd
  - Kingston upon Hull HU5 179 F7
  - Leverington PE13 170 A2
  - Moulton PE12 157 E1
- Woodgates Cl 13 HU14 3 A5
- Woodgates La HU14 3 A6
- Woodgates Mount 3 HU14 3 A5
- Woodhall Cl PE21 208 C5
- Woodhall Cres 9 LN1 66 C2
- Woodhall Dr
  - Lincoln LN2 201 F8

Woodhall Dr *continued*
Waltham DN37 ... 194 C4
Woodhall Rd LN9 ... 85 C3
Woodhall Rise PE4 ... 220 F6
Woodhall Spa Cottage Mus*
LN10 ... 97 D6
Woodhead Cl 4 PE9 ... 219 D7
Woodhill Ave DN21 ... 197 E6
Woodhill Cl 2 HU10 ... 178 E7
Woodhill Rise HU13 ... 178 C2
Woodhouse Gn Rd DN7 ... 14 B8
Woodhouse La
2 Belton DN9 ... 16 E3
Hatfield DN7 ... 14 D2
Holbeach PE12 ... 159 A8
Moulton PE12 ... 146 E1
Woodhouse Rd DN16 ... 185 E8
Woodhouse St HU9 ... 181 D7
Woodhurst Rd PE2 ... 231 D6
Woodland Ave
1 Bourne PE10 ... 213 B5
22 Brough HU15 ... 2 C6
15 Crowle DN17 ... 16 D8
Gainsborough DN21 ... 197 B7
Skellingthorpe LN6 ... 200 B2
Woodland Dr
8 Broughton DN20 ... 19 D4
5 Elsham DN20 ... 20 F7
Grantham NG31 ... 211 F7
Kingston upon Hull
HU10 ... 178 C6
6 Woodhall Spa LN10 ... 97 E6
Woodland End HU4 ... 179 C5
Woodland Lea 2 PE6 ... 173 B4
Woodland Rise LN11 ... 198 A6
Woodland View
2 Barnetby Le Wold DN38 ... 21 B4
Scunthorpe DN15 ... 182 C3
Woodland Way 16 DN9 ... 27 E6
Woodland Wlk 1 DN35 ... 192 E1
Woodlands
Langford NG24 ... 104 B8
Long Sutton PE12 ... 216 D4
5 Louth LN11 ... 198 C6
Woodlands Ave
Immingham DN40 ... 186 C5
15 Keelby DN41 ... 23 A4
6 Spilsby PE23 ... 87 F1
2 Spilsby PE23 ... 88 A1
Woodlands Cl 5 DN19 ... 11 C7
Woodlands Dr
1 Colsterworth NG33 ... 151 E7
Grantham NG31 ... 211 C4
Woodlands La 14 HU15 ... 2 C6
Woodlands Prim Sch
DN33 ... 191 A2
Woodlands Rd HU5 ... 179 B7
Woodlands Rise 7 HU14 ... 3 A5
Woodlands The
3 Market Deeping PE6 ... 217 B5
Peterborough PE1 ... 226 E5
1 Stallingborough DN41 ... 23 D6
Woodman's Ct 4 PE22 ... 98 F4
Woodmill Bank PE12 ... 159 F2
Woodpecker Cl LN6 ... 200 A3
Woodrow Pk DN33 ... 191 D1
Woodrush Rd 6 LN2 ... 202 C8
Woods Cl 14 NG23 ... 117 D3
Wood's La
Kingston upon Hull HU1 ... 180 E5
3 Pinchbeck PE11 ... 145 D2
Woods La 2 DN40 ... 12 F2
Woods Mdw 1 DN20 ... 30 F6
Woods Terr DN21 ... 197 C7
Woodside Boston PE21 ... 208 E1
Branston & Mere LN4 ... 81 D2
Kingston upon Hull
HU13 ... 178 D1
Woodside Ave NG34 ... 212 D6
Woodside Cl 1 PE10 ... 164 C8
Woodside E PE10 ... 164 D8
Woodside Falconry &
Conservation Ctr*
LN3 ... 69 D3
Woodside La DN9 ... 26 D6
Woodside Rd PE20 ... 136 B5
Woodsley Ave DN35 ... 192 E5
Woodstock Rd DN16 ... 183 D1
Woodstock St 4 LN1 ... 201 D4
Woodston Cty Prim Sch
PE2 ... 231 A7
Woodthorpe Ave
PE21 ... 209 C4
Woodvale Ave LN6 ... 204 C6
Woodvale Cl 14 LN6 ... 204 C6
Woodville Gdns E 3
PE21 ... 208 D3
Woodville Gdns W 2
PE21 ... 208 D3
Woodville Rd PE21 ... 208 D4
Woodward's La
Little Sutton PE12 ... 160 B3
Long Sutton PE12 ... 216 F1
Woodyard The 4 NG32 ... 119 B7
Woolcroft Cl 2 PE13 ... 170 A1
Woolfellhill Rd PE6 ... 174 F1
Woolgard PE3 ... 225 A3
Woolley's La
Castle Bytham NG33 ... 152 A4
North Witham NG33 ... 151 F4
Woollin Ave DN17 ... 185 A6
Woolram Wygate
PE11 ... 214 C5
Woolsthorpe La
Belvoir NG32 ... 138 D7
Bottesford NG13 ... 128 C4
Woolsthorpe Manor (NT)*
NG33 ... 151 D7
Woolsthorpe Rd 3
NG33 ... 151 D7
Woolwich Dr 2 HU4 ... 179 B2
Wootton Ave PE2 ... 230 F6
Wootton Rd
Grimsby DN33 ... 191 A3
Wootton DN39 ... 11 F2
Wootton St Andrews CE Prim
Sch DN39 ... 11 E3
Worcester Ave DN34 ... 191 A4
Worcester Cl
11 Birchwood LN6 ... 204 D7
Bracebridge Heath LN4 ... 81 A2
5 Louth LN11 ... 198 C5
Scunthorpe DN16 ... 185 A2
Worcester Cres 4 PE9 ... 219 B6
Worcester Rd
Grantham NG31 ... 210 D4
4 Wisbech PE13 ... 170 D1
Wordsworth Cl
3 Grantham NG31 ... 211 E6
Peterborough PE4 ... 225 E8
Wordsworth Ct 13 NG34 ... 212 F4
Wordsworth Gr PE10 ... 213 D3
Wordsworth Rd DN17 ... 184 D6
Wordsworth St 6 LN2 ... 234 B3
Workhouse La
Algarkirk PE20 ... 136 B1
Hogsthorpe PE24 ... 90 C7
Workington Ave 8 HU4 ... 179 B6
Worlaby Prim Sch
DN20 ... 20 D8
Worlaby Rd DN33 ... 191 B1
World's End Rd PE13 ... 160 A1
Worldwide Way DN41 ... 187 C2
Wormgate PE21 ... 208 F5
Worship St HU2 ... 180 F7
Worsley PE2 ... 230 A4
Worsley Cl
1 Holton le Clay DN36 ... 195 C2
Immingham DN40 ... 186 D4
Worsley Rd DN40 ... 186 D4
Worthington La NG32 ... 128 D1
Wortley St 2 DN16 ... 183 A2
Wortley's La PE21 ... 208 A2
Wothorpe Mews 3 PE9 ... 219 B4
Wothorpe Rd PE9 ... 219 B4
Wragby Prim Sch LN8 ... 70 D5
Wragby Rd Bardney LN3 ... 83 C4
Holton cum Beckering
LN8 ... 70 C7
Lincoln LN2 ... 234 C3
Lissington LN3 ... 57 E2
Reepham LN3 ... 68 F1
Scunthorpe DN17 ... 184 D5
Wragby Rd E
Greetwell LN2 ... 203 A8
Reepham LN3 ... 68 E1
Wragby St 3 DN32 ... 191 F7
Wragholme La LN11 ... 50 A8
Wragholme Rd LN11 ... 50 A8
Wrangle Bank PE22 ... 114 B4
Wrangle Prim Sch
PE22 ... 114 D2
Wrawby CE Prim Sch
DN20 ... 20 E4
Wrawby Rd
Brigg DN20 ... 196 D4
Scunthorpe DN17 ... 184 E5
Wrawby St DN20 ... 196 C3
Wray Cl 9 DN37 ... 194 C5
Wray St 20 DN21 ... 30 B1
Wren Cl
Deeping St Nicholas
PE11 ... 166 B6
11 Healing DN41 ... 23 F5
15 Market Deeping PE6 ... 217 C5
Scunthorpe DN16 ... 185 B2
4 Sleaford NG34 ... 212 B3
Wren Cres DN33 ... 191 B2
Wressle Rd DN20 ... 19 E3
Wright Ave PE2 ... 231 D5
Wright St HU2 ... 180 E7
Wright's Dro PE6 ... 175 B7
Wright's La
Friskney PE22 ... 115 A5
Sutton Bridge PE12 ... 160 E4
Wrights Gdns DN10 ... 40 A3
Wrights La 5 LE14 ... 150 C1
Wrightsway LN2 ... 202 D5
Wroot Rd DN9 ... 26 A3
Wroot Travis Charity Prim
Sch DN9 ... 26 D5
Wroxall Dr NG31 ... 210 E4
Wroxham Ave DN34 ... 190 E5
Wroxham Cl 7 LN6 ... 205 A2
Wrygarth Ave 7 HU15 ... 2 C5
Wulfram Dr NG31 ... 211 E2
Wulfric Sq PE3 ... 225 C8
Wyatt Ave 13 DN20 ... 19 D3
Wyatt Cl LN4 ... 96 B2
Wyatt Rd LN5 ... 205 D7
Wybeck Rd DN15 ... 183 A6
Wybers Way DN37 ... 190 D7
Wybers Wood Jun & Inf Sch
DN37 ... 190 C8
Wybert Cres 6 PE21 ... 136 D8
Wybert La PE21 ... 136 F8
Wyberton Low Rd
3 Boston PE21 ... 208 F2
1 Boston PE21 ... 208 F2
Wyberton Prim Sch
PE21 ... 136 E7
Wyberton Roads PE20 ... 137 A7
Wyberton W Rd PE21 ... 208 C2
Wyche Ave 13 PE6 ... 166 F1
Wycliffe Gr PE4 ... 220 E5
Wydham Pk PE2 ... 229 D6
Wye Pl PE4 ... 221 C1
Wygate Mdws PE11 ... 214 B5
Wygate Pk PE11 ... 214 A5
Wygate Rd PE11 ... 214 B4
Wyggeston Ave 22
NG13 ... 128 A6
Wyggeston Rd 21 NG13 ... 128 A6
Wyke St HU9 ... 181 D7
Wyke The 8 PE11 ... 214 A3
Wykeham La
Burgh on Bain LN8 ... 59 C6
Weston PE12 ... 145 F1
Wykes La PE11 ... 135 A2
Wykes Rd
Donington PE11 ... 135 B1
Yaxley PE7 ... 233 D4
Wylson Cl 5 NG34 ... 120 F8
Wyman Way PE2 ... 229 F5
Wymark View DN33 ... 190 F3
Wymersley Rd HU5 ... 179 A8
Wyndham Cl NG31 ... 211 C5
Wyndham Rd 9 DN36 ... 195 C6
Wyndham St HU3 ... 180 C7
Wynmoor Rd DN17 ... 184 F7
Wyredale Rd DN16 ... 185 D5
Wythes La PE21 ... 126 C2
Wyton Cl 8 LN6 ... 204 B6
Wyvern Cl 16 DN17 ... 16 D8
Wyville Rd
Grantham NG31 ... 210 E1
Little Ponton & Stroxton
NG31 ... 139 E8

Y

Yale Cl LN4 ... 203 D1
Yarborough Cl 3 DN36 ... 195 C2
Yarborough Cres
17 Broughton DN20 ... 19 E4
Lincoln LN1 ... 201 E6
Yarborough Dr 4 DN31 ... 191 D8
Yarborough Leisure Ctr
LN1 ... 201 E7
Yarborough Prim Sch
DN34 ... 190 F7
Yarborough Rd
Boston PE21 ... 136 E8
Brigg DN20 ... 196 D3
Grimsby DN34 ... 190 F6
Keelby DN41 ... 23 A5
1 Lincoln LN1 ... 234 A4
Scunthorpe DN16 ... 19 A4
9 Skegness PE25 ... 206 A6
Yarborough Sch LN1 ... 201 E7
Yarborough Terr LN1 ... 234 A4
Yarburgh Rd LN11 ... 49 E2
Yarde The 2 PE10 ... 213 E2
Yardley Way 2 DN34 ... 190 D4
Yarmouth Ave
Grantham NG31 ... 210 D4
3 Kingston upon Hull
HU4 ... 179 A3
Yarra Rd DN35 ... 192 F6
Yarrow Rd DN34 ... 190 F7
Yarwell Cl PE2 ... 230 D7
Yawling Gate Rd PE22 ... 114 F5
Yaxley Jun Sch PE7 ... 233 E6
Yew Tree Cl 1 PE10 ... 213 C6
Yew Tree Gr 1 PE21 ... 209 C2
Yew Tree Way 2 NG24 ... 104 C5
Yews La 4 DN37 ... 23 E1
Yewtree Dr HU5 ... 179 B7
York Ave Lincoln LN1 ... 201 D4
Scunthorpe DN16 ... 185 B4
York Cl LN4 ... 203 D1
York Gdns
2 Gosberton PE11 ... 145 B6
30 Wisbech PE13 ... 170 D1
York House Rd 6 NG34 ... 120 C8
York Pl DN35 ... 192 C4
York Rd
5 Binbrook Tech Pk LN8 ... 47 B6
Brigg DN20 ... 196 D4
Hatfield DN7 ... 14 D4
Kirton in Lindsey DN21 ... 30 C1
Mablethorpe/Sutton on Sea
LN12 ... 64 D1
Peterborough PE1 ... 225 F6
RAF Cranwell NG34 ... 107 C1
Sleaford NG34 ... 212 C6
9 Stamford PE9 ... 219 B6
Wisbech PE13 ... 170 D1
York Ride 4 PE12 ... 216 B5
York St (Boston United FC)
PE21 ... 209 A5
York St Boston PE21 ... 209 A4
Grimsby DN31 ... 191 C8
York Terr 3 DN10 ... 40 A5
York Way NG31 ... 210 C5
Yorkshireside DN17 ... 7 A3
Youlgrave Ave 6 LN12 ... 77 A8
Young Pl DN35 ... 192 B7
Younger's La PE24 ... 103 A8

Z

Zara Cl PE21 ... 209 C6
Zetland St HU3 ... 180 A5

Notes

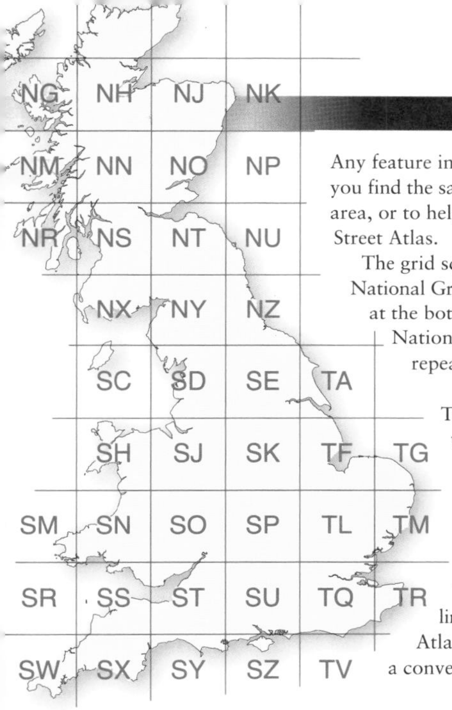

Using the Ordnance Survey National Grid

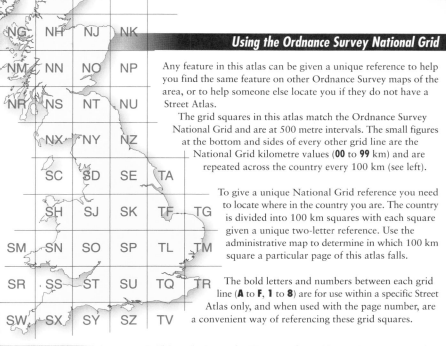

Any feature in this atlas can be given a unique reference to help you find the same feature on other Ordnance Survey maps of the area, or to help someone else locate you if they do not have a Street Atlas.

The grid squares in this atlas match the Ordnance Survey National Grid and are at 500 metre intervals. The small figures at the bottom and sides of every other grid line are the National Grid kilometre values (**00** to **99** km) and are repeated across the country every 100 km (see left).

To give a unique National Grid reference you need to locate where in the country you are. The country is divided into 100 km squares with each square given a unique two-letter reference. Use the administrative map to determine in which 100 km square a particular page of this atlas falls.

The bold letters and numbers between each grid line (**A** to **F**, **1** to **8**) are for use within a specific Street Atlas only, and when used with the page number, are a convenient way of referencing these grid squares.

***Example** The railway bridge over DARLEY GREEN RD in grid square B1*

Step 1: Identify the two-letter reference, in this example the page is in **SP**

Step 2: Identify the 1 km square in which the railway bridge falls. Use the figures in the southwest corner of this square: Eastings **17**, Northings **74**. This gives a unique reference: **SP 17 74**, accurate to 1 km.

Step 3: To give a more precise reference accurate to 100 m you need to estimate how many tenths along and how many tenths up this 1 km square the feature is (to help with this the 1 km square is divided into four 500 m squares). This makes the bridge about **8** tenths along and about **1** tenth up from the southwest corner.

This gives a unique reference: **SP 178 741**, accurate to 100 m.

Eastings (read from left to right along the bottom) come before Northings (read from bottom to top). If you have trouble remembering say to yourself "Along the hall, THEN up the stairs"!

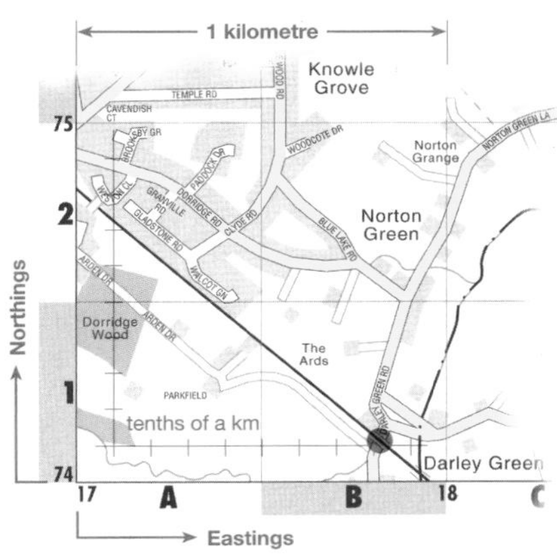

Addresses

Name and Address	Telephone	Page	Grid reference